INVESTMENTS

Principles and Practices

Second Edition

INVESTMENTS

Principles and Practices

Second Edition

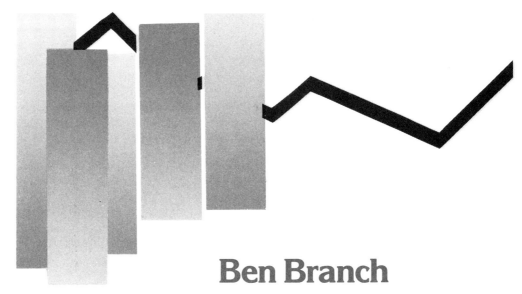

Ben Branch

Professor of Finance
School of Management
University of Massachusetts at Amherst

Longman Financial Services Publishing
a division of Longman Financial Services Institute, Inc.

© 1985, 1989 by Longman Group USA Inc.

Published by Longman Financial Services Publishing, a division of Longman Financial Services Institute, Inc.

Printed in the United States of America
89 90 91 10 9 8 7 6 5 4 3 2

Executive Editor: Richard A. Hagle
Acquisitions Editor: Arnis E. Burvikovs
Development Editor: Margaret M. Maloney
Project Editor: Jack L. Kiburz
Editorial Assistant: Kirsten Benner
Copy Editor: Jean Scott Berry
Proofreader: Loretta Faber
Cover/Internal Design: Edwin Harris
Manager/Composition Services: Gayle Sperando

Library of Congress Cataloging-in-Publication Data

Branch, Ben, 1943–
    Investments: principles and practices.

    Includes bibliographies and indexes.
    1. Investments. I. Title.
HG4521.B6463   1988   332.6'78   88-13521
ISBN 0-88462-717-9

Contents

SECTION FIVE   Mutual Funds, Bonds, and Options   445

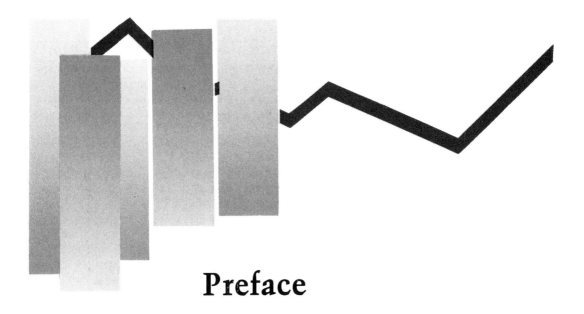

Preface

Investments: Principles and Practices is written for people who want to become successful investors. As a professor of finance I have specialized in teaching and conducting research in investments. I have always concentrated on the practical (i.e., profit-oriented) aspects of the issues.

I myself began investing in stocks on a small scale when I was a college student. Since that beginning, I have continued to be an active investor. Managing several portfolios for my family and myself has put me in a position where I have been able to learn a substantial amount about real world investing. I myself have been involved in and learned from a number of relatively sophisticated investment-related activities: participating in financial reorganizations of troubled firms and contests for control (proxy fights) of takeover candidates, filings of form 13Ds, searches for asset plays for large investors, seeking to protect bondholders by filing a lawsuit to force a firm into bankruptcy, arbitraging different classes of a firm's securities, calling the attention of the financial press to a particularly interesting investment situation (which resulted in an article in *Barron's*), and instructing my broker to become an OTC market maker in particular securities so that I could buy on the bid side and sell on the ask side. This text reflects the knowledge (particularly the practical and usable knowledge) that I have gained as an investor, teacher, and researcher.

Some readers of this book are already active investors. Most others hope eventually to begin an investment plan. This text is designed to help them understand the nature of the securities markets and investment opportunities. It does not offer a get-rich-quick type of approach. Those books that seem to offer simple, easy answers tend to take an extremely simplistic approach. Investing effectively is rarely either easy or simple. Nonetheless, those who seriously study the materials contained herein should find the book to be a useful guide. Practical aspects of investing are stressed. Abstract theoretical issues are introduced only when they are relevant to actual investing.

Topics are approached from a viewpoint that is relevant to the small to medium-sized investor. Such investors usually begin with no more than a few thousand dollars to invest. Much of the material in this book is, however, also relevant to those who manage large portfolios. Indeed, many of my own former students are now doing exactly that.

This book takes a broad view of investing. Both nontraditional topics (life insurance, pensions, estate planning, collectibles, commodities, and real estate) and more traditional finance/investment topics (investment theory, fundamental analysis, market timing, mutual funds, bonds, and option securities) are considered in detail. Readers should, however, realize several relatively discouraging facts of life. First, much of what we know about investing relates to how difficult outperforming the market averages is. Second, many suggested investment techniques do not live up to their advocates' expectations. Third, much of what may be helpful only works some of the time and the advantages offered may only be relatively minor.

Nonetheless, investing is seen by many as a worthwhile "game." Those who are going to play the game may as well play it to win. Whether or not the game is worth playing, it is certainly worth winning. This book should help the reader both learn the rules and learn something about the strategies that are most likely to prove effective.

SOURCES OF INVESTMENT KNOWLEDGE

Our knowledge of investing is drawn largely from two rather separate and somewhat separated sources: academic journals (reflecting the research of professors of finance like myself) and the popular financial press (reflecting the thinking of those in the investment trenches managing portfolios, analyzing securities, or writing about the financial markets). This text's eclectic approach draws extensively from both literatures. Articles appearing in such academic journals as the *Journal of Finance* and *Journal of Financial Economics* are cited (and explained in language that a nonexpert can understand) along with others appearing in such nonacademic sources as *Forbes* or *Barron's*. Not surprisingly, the academic work is generally more reliable. Nonetheless, many interesting issues are only treated in the nonacademic literature. Moreover, that literature provides a fertile source of testable hypotheses that academicians may someday explore. Those who seek to be true experts on investing cannot afford to overlook either literature.

THE ORGANIZATION OF THE CHAPTERS

The text is divided into six sections. The first section (Chapters 1 to 3), on Basic Investment Concepts, introduces and provides an overview to the topic of investing.

Chapter 1 introduces the topic by exploring various generalizable investment characteristics (risk, return, liquidity, marketability, investment tax treatments, etc.). Chapter 2 briefly surveys a variety of different types of investment. Chapter 3 deals with the mechanics, regulation, and economic functions of the securities markets.

Section Two (Chapters 4 to 6) treats various aspects of Investment Theory. Chapter 4 examines investment valuation. Primary emphasis is placed on valuing and forecasting expected income streams. Chapter 5 explores the roles of risk and diversification in investment valuation. Chapter 6 discusses the empirical evidence relating to various predictions of investment valuation.

Section Three (Chapters 7 to 10) deals with Fundamental Analysis: Security Selection. Chapter 7 considers traditional approaches to fundamental analysis including economic, industry, and firm analysis. Accounting statements are covered in Chapter 8, in which the misuse of accounting discretion is given particular attention. Chapter 9 examines a variety of operational and largely ad hoc approaches to security selection. Sources of investment information are explored in Chapter 10.

Section Four (Chapters 11 to 13) deals with Investment Timing. The stock market impacts of the business cycle and inflation are discussed in Chapter 11. Emotional aspects of stock market behavior are considered in Chapter 12. Chapter 13 covers the timing of individual security trades.

Section Five (Chapters 14 to 18) treats various types of investments including Mutual Funds, Bonds, and Options. Mutual funds and other types of investment companies are considered in Chapter 14. Chapter 15 discusses both short- and long-term debt securities. Chapter 16 examines the determinants of debt security yields. Pure option securities including puts, calls, warrants, and rights are discussed in Chapter 17. Convertibles and other types of combination securities are considered in Chapter 18.

Section Six (Chapters 19 to 21) covers three important but often-neglected investment areas: Commodities, Real Estate, and Personal Investing. Chapter 19 deals with commodity futures and related topics such as strategic metals. Real estate and real estate oriented stock are discussed in Chapter 20. Chapter 21 discusses several aspects of personal investing including life insurance, pension planning, and estate planning.

REORDERING THE CHAPTERS AND SKIPPING MATERIAL

The current chapter order represents one logical sequence of investment topics. Some people, however, may prefer to read the chapters in another ordering. For example, Chapters 14 to 20 (on types of investments) are largely self-contained and thus may be taken up in any order. Similarly, Chapter 10 (Investment Information Sources) may be taken up earlier in the fundamental analysis section. Moreover, some readers may prefer to read Chapter 7 (Traditional Approaches to Fundamental Analysis) and Chapter 11 (The Stock Market and the Economy) together. Economic analysis comes up in both chapters.

In addition to reordering the chapters, certain material may be skipped altogether. For example, the appendixes contain technical material much of which may be avoided. Similarly, the chapters on commodities (Chapter 19) and real estate

(Chapter 20) may or may not be skipped. In fact, Chapters 14 to 20 cover in detail the same material that is surveyed briefly in Chapter 2. Thus some readers may prefer to read one or the other but not both treatments. Finally, some people may be particularly interested in such topics as investment selection and timing (Sections Three and Four) and not want to read much of the rest of the book.

The careful reader will notice that this book contains a rather extensive set of citations. These citations document points made in both the academic and the popular literature. Many readers will simply read the text and ignore the notes. They can usually see and understand the relevant point without referring to its source. Such extensive citations do, however, direct the interested reader to the relevant documentation. Some may even use the citations as a source for further readings on some interesting topic. Thus, for example, a student writing a term paper or a professor working on a journal article may use the numerous sources cited herein as a beginning bibliography.

DIFFERENCES IN THIS EDITION

The first edition of this text (entitled *Investments: A Practical Approach*) appeared in 1985. It borrowed freely from my earlier effort (*Fundamentals of Investing*, published by Wiley Hamilton) but was much more than a revision of the earlier text. This second edition is a revision of the 1985 text. It is, however, a very extensive revision, differing from the first edition in a number of important ways. Many of the changes reflect input received from users of the first edition. Others originate with the author or the editor.

One of the most significant changes relates to the way the financial press is brought into the book. I believe that one of the important functions of a text such as this is to familiarize its readers with the kinds of articles and other materials that appear in the financial press. Those who would be serious and successful investors need to know how to get the most use out of the information available in financial newspapers and other periodicals. This familiarization requires a knowledge of the relevant language and the context in which the issues arise.

Relevant economic/finance/investment issues have always been given considerable attention throughout each of the investment books I have written. Here the unique terminology of investing is introduced in the text and defined in an extensive glossary. Still, more attention is required to help readers establish the practice of reading, understanding, and enjoying the financial press. Accordingly, most of the chapters in this edition contain at least one interesting and relevant article from the popular financial press (*The Wall Street Journal, Forbes, Business Week, The New York Times, Barron's*, etc.). Each article is related to topics that are treated in the chapter. These articles should help readers relate the material in the text to material in the financial press, and vice versa.

Another important change is in the treatment of the end-of-chapter questions and problems. The first edition contained both question and problem sets at the end of each chapter. The question sets have now been expanded and updated to reflect the substantive changes made in the text. The problem sets have received considerably more attention. The previous edition's problem sets contained two types of problems. Some of the old problems were self-contained in that sufficient data were provided to work out a single correct answer. Other problems in the form of review projects required that outside real world data be collected. Such review projects do not by their very nature have a single correct answer. Each person is likely to base his or her answer on a different set of data. Since the two types of problems were rather different, mixing them into one set may not have been ideal. Many users and potential users of a text like this one will make extensive use of problem sets. An extensive list of problems that have a single correct answer are essential for such users. Accordingly, the self-contained problems are now separated from the review projects. Extensive sets of both self-contained problems and review projects appear at the end of each chapter. Solutions to a selection of the end-of-chapter problems appear at the end of the book, following the glossary. Additional solutions appear in the *Instructor's Manual.*

A number of additional structural changes have been made. The chapter dealing with personal investing has been moved from the beginning to the end of the book. Those who prefer the earlier ordering are, of course, free to cover Chapter 21 first. Many people, however, indicated that they preferred that personal investing be put at the end where it could be covered last or skipped if time were short. In the first edition Chapter 2 included treatments of both characteristics of investments and types of investments. These two topics are sufficiently important to warrant separate chapters. Accordingly, in the current edition investment characteristics are treated in Chapter 1 and types of investments are treated in Chapter 2. The index has been expanded to include authors and the table of contents has been made much more detailed. The number of citations, while still substantial, has been cut back considerably in this edition. Each footnote, however, tends to contain more separate sources. Thus the number of sources referenced is still quite substantial.

Revising an investment book such as this really drives home the massive changes that have occurred in even the past several years. One of the most dramatic events occurring during the mid- to late-1980s period was the crash of 1987. Completing the revision of this book in 1988 allowed me to assemble some perspective on this (hopefully) once-in-a-lifetime event. As a result, some of the important lessons derived from the October 19, 1987, stock market crash are now woven into various parts of the book. For example, the 1987 crash facilitates the treatment of such important and timely concepts as market efficiency, timing and overreactions, the dividend discount model, program trading, index arbitrage, portfolio insurance, cash settlement, circuit breakers, and the specialist system.

A large number of other new concepts have also been introduced and discussed in this edition. Thus REMICs, resids, MLPs, Americus Trust securities (primes and scores), and securitization; sector, country, and 12b-1 funds; the White Knight and Pac Man defenses; LYONs, yield curve notes, and PIKs; dividend capture; cramdown; parking; asset allocation; flipping; DOT and SuperDOT systems; defeasence; and a host of other topics are now covered. Similarly, a substantial amount of relevant new research has appeared in the academic press. Moreover, many new and revised approaches to investing have been introduced and discussed in the popular finance press. Much of this "new knowledge" has been introduced into the current edition. I have always sought to write as readable and clear a book as I am capable. Thus I have attempted to maintain and, where possible, to improve the clarity and readability of each of the topics covered herein.

ACKNOWLEDGMENTS

This book has been in process for several years. During that time it has gone through a number of drafts and benefited from a wide and diverse set of reviews. Many of the reviewers were anonymous so I can not thank them by name. Nonetheless, everyone who read and commented on the book offered useful ideas.

The following is a partial list of those who were retained by publishers to review the first edition of the book: Seth Anderson, University of Alabama; Donald Chambers, Penn State; Eugene Drzycimski, University of Wisconsin, Oshkosh; Adrian Edwards, Western Michigan; Larry Guin, Murray State; Thomas Johnson, William Rainey Harper College; Carl Schweser, University of Iowa; Harold Stevenson, Arizona State; Peter Williamson, Dartmouth; Randall Woolridge, Penn State; and Howard Van Auken, Iowa State. In addition, several of my past and present University of Massachusetts colleagues read and commented on various chapters: Joseph Finnerty, Joanne Hill, and Thomas Schneeweis.

The current revision also involved a host of reviewers including: Robert Bohn, Golden Gate University; Jerry Boswell, Metropolitan State College; Mary Broske, Oklahoma State University; Patrick Gaughan, Fairleigh Dickinson University; Jamshid Mehran, Indiana University, South Bend; Henry Oppenheimer, University of Rhode Island; Ira Smolowitz, American International College; Philip Swensen, Utah State University; Robert Strong, University of Maine; and George Trivoli, University of South Florida.

A number of people at Longman also deserve acknowledgment: Arnis Burvikovs, Acquisitions Editor–Economics and Finance; Richard Hagle, Executive Editor; Margaret Maloney, Development Editor; Jack Kiburz, Project Editor; Edwin Harris, Art Director; Kirsten Benner, Editorial Assistant; Ivy Lester, original Acquisitions Editor; and Paul Revenko-Jones, interim Acquisitions Editor.

SECTION ONE

Basic Investment Concepts

This beginning section lays the groundwork for a practical approach to investment and money management. The following hypothetical case raises many of the issues that are dealt with in the three chapters of this section.

THE NEWLEYS: A YOUNG COUPLE'S FINANCES

Dick and Jane Newley have decided to take a careful look at their finances. They got married immediately after graduation from college five years ago and now have two children aged 3 and 1½. Dick earns $23,000 per year as a history teacher at Metropolis High School. He expects modest salary increases if he remains a teacher. He may, however, move into school administration, in which case his income should rise somewhat faster. Jane is a CPA with the prestigious accounting firm of Earnest Anderson, earning $34,500 a year. She seems on a fast track and may become a partner in 10 to 15 years. Even junior partners in the firm earn in excess of $200,000.

The Newley's principal assets are a home (estimated market value of $150,000 with a $90,000 mortgage), $25,000 in savings, and a tract of land left to them by Jane's parents. Jane's father was a real estate developer who died three years ago. Her mother, who is in ill health, is supported from a large trust whose principal asset is her father's development firm. The real estate company will be sold and principal of the trust will be divided between Jane and her two brothers upon her mother's death.

Dick's parents are in good health and have relatively modest assets. Dick and Jane both have small amounts of life insurance through their respective employers. They are currently adding about $5,000 per year to their savings.

The Newleys are already relatively well off financially. They have a sufficiently large combined income to meet most of their needs. They have also begun to accumulate some assets (house, savings, etc.). Nonetheless, they believe that a careful examination of their situation will reveal a variety of ways of preparing better for the future. For example, their joint income places the Newleys in a relatively high tax bracket. They would like to reduce that tax burden. Should anything happen to Dick and Jane, they also want to protect their children. Finally,

1

they expect their financial situation to improve over time. Accordingly, they want their personal financial management to grow as their professional careers progress. Consider each of the following questions that relate to their situation:

1. They maintain a balance of about $2,000 in their NOW checking account. Should they switch to a superNOW, Money Market, or Cash Management Account?

2. Their $25,000 in savings is currently in a passbook savings account at their bank. That money serves as an emergency reserve, but they could also borrow against the equity in their house (the excess of its market value over the mortgage is at least $60,000). Thus they are now ready to begin investing the sum now in the savings account for growth and are willing to take some risks. What might they do?

3. Jane's share of her parents' estate will probably exceed $300,000. She would like to learn more about investment opportunities. What are the various types of investment media for her to consider?

4. Dick has been a stamp collector since he was eight. Although he has a large collection, most of his stamps are relatively inexpensive. Thus, the entire collection has only a modest value. He is, however, thinking of becoming more serious and using the hobby as an investment vehicle. Should he? Why or why not?

5. After some thought the Newleys concluded that they should begin investing some of their savings in the stock market. How should they go about selecting a broker? Should they use a discounter or a full service broker?

6. Having selected a brokerage firm, they now would like to buy stock in a company recommended to one of Jane's colleagues. What orders should they give their broker? Should they try to diversify? What about mutual funds?

7. The Newleys have heard about such aspects of stock market trading as short selling, margin trading, the over-the-counter markets and tender offers. What do they need to know about each of these issues?

Although many of these questions do not have single simple answers, the basic issues are dealt with extensively in the first three chapters. Chapter 1 provides an overview of the investment scene including a discussion of generalizable investment characteristics such as return, risk, liquidity, marketability, investment effort, minimum investment size, and tax treatment. A variety of specific investment types are then introduced in Chapter 2: short-term debt securities, long-term debt securities, common stock, preferred stock, pure option securities, convertibles, mutual funds, small firm ownership, venture capital, real estate, commodities, collectibles, noncollectible off-beat investments, and Ponzi schemes. Most of these topics are covered in greater detail in later chapters. The coverage here is designed to give readers a framework in which to evaluate specific investment types.

Chapter 3 explores security market mechanics in considerable detail. The coverage begins with such topics as brokers, investment advisors, stock exchanges, commissions, types of orders, specialists, floor traders, the over-the-counter market, short selling, margin trading, secondary offerings, block trades, and tender offers. Then securities market regulation is examined with principal emphasis placed on the developing central market. The chapter primarily focuses on how security trades of various sizes may be executed. Although often neglected, effective security market execution is an extremely important aspect of successful investing. The chapter concludes with a discussion of the economic role of the securities market. The capital allocation, management allocation, and use in implementing economic policy roles are all considered.

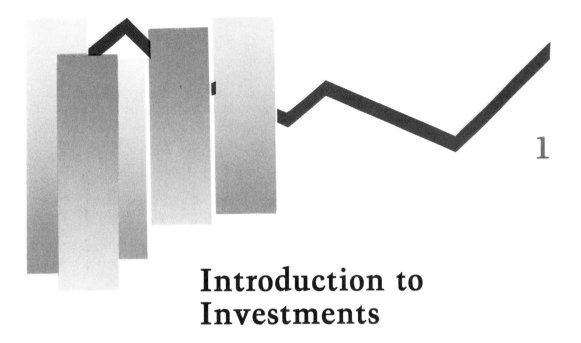

Introduction to Investments

1

Virtually all of us are at least somewhat involved in the management of our own financial situations. Different people take different approaches to their personal finances. A few people focus entirely on their present circumstances. They spend all of their money as soon as it is available and worry about tomorrow when it comes. Children whose allowances burn holes in their pockets are examples of this type of financial (mis)management. Those who never outgrow this tendency are forever facing financial crises. Most people, however, eventually learn to plan for the future. They always keep at least one eye on the longer term aspects of their financial situations.

Effective financial management inevitably involves some investment-like decisions. We decide how much to spend on current consumption, how much to spend on durable goods like a car or stereo (which will provide long-term value), and how much we will save for later. Moreover, most people do periodically put aside some portion of their current income or they have already accumulated, inherited, or been given some money or other types of financial resources. Such individuals need to decide what to do with those assets. Choosing not to spend the money is one decision. Determining what to do with the resulting funds requires a second decision. The available choices are virtually limitless. Each investment opportunity has advantages and disadvantages. Each investor has a unique set of needs, goals, attitudes, and resources that influence the relative attractiveness and suitability of particular investments.

Clearly, those with significant amounts of money to invest need to know something about investing. Such knowledge should help them select and manage their investments intelligently. Even those who do not now have much money to invest may well expect to have more in the future. Thus most of us have good reasons for wanting to learn more about investing.

Investing involves three separate but related processes: selection, implementation, and timing. The beginning investor must decide which investments to purchase, how to go about executing the transactions, and when to do it. Similarly, an investor who manages his or her portfolio encounters the same basic decisions in adding to (buying) and subtracting from (selling) the portfolio over time. For example, investors often seek to convert some of their portfolio to cash. They may need to sell one or more of their investments so that they can either withdraw funds for consumption or obtain the funds required to make another investment. Such an investor will need to go through the same process: decide what, how, and when to sell. This book is designed to help current and prospective investors perform each of these tasks.

Various aspects of investing are explored in this book. The first three chapters (Section I) deal with investment basics: generalizable characteristics of investments, the primary types of investments, and the mechanics of the securities markets. Section II is devoted to the theory of investment valuation. With the foundation laid in the first two sections, Section III examines a number of different approaches to stock evaluation and selection. Section IV discusses the issues involved with market timing. These first four sections focus primarily on stocks. Sections V and VI, in contrast, consider a variety of other types of investments: mutual funds, bonds, options, convertibles, commodities, real estate, life insurance, and retirement plans.

This chapter introduces the characteristics of investments that largely determine their appeal.

THE CHARACTERISTICS OF INVESTMENTS

Many types of investments are available to the investment community. Each one attracts at least some interest from the universe of potential investors. Indeed, many types of investments have been tailor-made to appeal to specific types of investors. Obviously, investors themselves have a diverse array of interests. They range from unsophisticated individual investors with modest resources to huge institutional investors (banks, mutual funds, insurance companies, etc.) with literally billions of dollars to put to work. Individual investors will, for example, differ in such dimensions as: age, wealth level, income level, tax bracket, risk orientation, financial sophistication, access to commission discounts, ability to spend time researching and managing their investments, need for current income, access to relevant investment information, ethical and moral attitudes toward particular investments, and a host of other dimensions. Institutional investors will also differ in many of these same dimensions. Accordingly, each of the very large number of types of investments may appeal to some of the many different types of investors.

Some assets promise nearly certain short- or long-term yields. More risky investments offer less certain but potentially much higher returns. Some investment areas require detailed management whereas others are virtually trouble free. *Liquid* investments can be quickly converted into spendable form at little cost or risk while *marketable* assets can usually be bought and sold in quantity at the current *market price.* That market price, however, may or may not be an attractive price to the current holder. Some investment areas are open to people of modest means while other areas require large minimum commitments. Some investments finance activities to which many people object while other investments are much more innocuous. Finally, investment income may be subject to a variety of different types of tax treatments depending upon how the return is generated. Clearly, investments vary in a number of important dimensions.

We begin this coverage of investment characteristics with a discussion of return. Risk and the risk–return trade-off are then examined. Liquidity, marketability, investment effort, minimum investment size, socially responsible investing, and the differing tax treatments of various investment categories are discussed next. Finally, we explore psychological aspects of investing.

Return

Most people accumulate at least a small amount of what might be called excess funds. Such savings or reserves are not required for immediate consumption and therefore are available for other things. These excess funds can be "spent" in several ways. They can be used to finance some current expenditure such as a new car, vacation, cosmetic surgery or other type of consumption spending. A second possibility would be to let the funds accumulate in a bank (checking) account where they earn little or no interest. Finally, the owner of such funds could consciously "spend" them on one or more investments. Those who choose to invest do so because they expect to earn a satisfactory profit on their investment. Why invest to earn an unsatisfactorily low, break-even, or negative return? Virtually everyone prefers profits to losses on investments and prefers higher profits to lower profits. Investors invest rather than consume currently available funds because they expect that the investment will generate a positive return. Thus by investing some money now they will eventually have more money to spend later.

The profit or return expected on an investment is a key factor in determining its relative attractiveness. Such profits generally take two forms: income and appreciation. Most investments are structured to yield periodic and relatively dependable income payments (such as dividends, interest, or rents). Some investments (such as a savings account) have a value that remains very near to the amount that it initially cost the investor. Many other investments (such as shares of stock) have market values that may either increase or decrease substantially over time.

Clearly, an increase in value adds to the investment's overall return whereas a decrease reduces it. Thus a determination of the profit or return on an investment needs to take in account both periodic payments (income, which may be either positive or zero) and gains or losses (appreciation, which can be either positive or negative) in market value.

While investments are expected to yield a positive return, their actual return may turn out to be very different from the expected level. Indeed, many investments do not produce a positive return even though that was the expectation. This discussion raises the issue of risk, which we shall address shortly. First, however, we need to explore the mechanics of defining and computing returns.

The Holding Period Return.   The overall profitability of an investment is often expressed in the form of a relatively simple concept called the holding period return (HPR). The HPR relates the profit on an investment directly to its beginning value. A concept called the holding period return relative (HPRR) is useful in its own right as well as being helpful in introducing the HPR:

$$\text{HPRR} = \text{Current Value of Investment} \div \text{Initial Value of Investment}$$

Thus the HPRR is the ratio of the current value of the investment (including any payments made during the holding period) relative to its initial cost. The HPR is the profit for the holding period relative to the initial investment. Mathematically the HPR is simply the HPRR less 1. The "1" reflects the initial amount invested. Thus the HPR is the total profit or gain on the investment as a percentage of the amount initially invested. That is:

$$\text{HPRR} - 1.00 = \text{HPR} = \text{Holding Period Profit} \div \text{Initial Value of Investment}$$

Suppose, for example, an investment purchased for $100 is sold for $130 and made no income payments during the holding period. The HPRR would be:

$$\text{HPRR} = \$130/100 = 1.30$$

The HPR itself would be:

$$1.30 - 1.00 = .30, \text{ or } 30\%$$

Alternatively, suppose an investment that cost $1,000 made a payment of $100 during the holding period and was sold for $1,500. The total holding period profit would be the sum of the appreciation of $500 ($1,500 − $1,000) and the income payment of $100. Dividing this sum ($600) by the initial cost ($1,000) is one approach to computing the HPR. Alternatively, one could first compute the HPRR and subtract 1. Thus:

$$\text{HPR} = \$600/\$1,000 = .60, \text{ or } 60\%$$

or:

$$\text{HPRR} = \$1,600/\$1,000 = 1.60$$
$$\text{HPR} = \text{HPRR} - 1.00 = 1.60 - 1.00 = .60, \text{ or } 60\%$$

The holding period return, or HPR, is a convenient concept because it reveals how much more (or less) an investment is worth than when it was initially purchased. A profitable investment will have an HPR that is greater than 1. An investment with an HPR of less than 1 is showing a loss.

The HPR return has one principal drawback. It is not adjusted for the length of time that the investment is held. Thus an HPR of 2 might be considered quite good if the investment has been held for only a relatively short time (two years for example). Alternatively, such an HPR would be very poor if the holding period is very long (20 years, for example).

The Per Period Return.   The per period return (PPR), in contrast, provides a more standardized concept for computing returns. An asset's PPR is defined as the sum of that period's income payments and price appreciation divided by its first-of-period price:

$$PPR = \frac{\text{Per Period Income Payments} + \text{Price Change}}{\text{Beginning Price}}$$

Actually, a one-period return computed by the PPR formula will produce the same value as a one-period return computed by the HPR formula. The two formulas, however, produce different return values when the holding period differs from one standard length holding period. PPRs are generally expressed for standard periods of one year's length. Thus a one-year PPR is the same as an HPR for a one-year holding period. In contrast, a PPR earned for two years would correspond to a different and higher HPR value. Indeed, if the PPR equaled x, the two-year HPRR would be $(1 + x)(1 + x)$, and the HPR would be this value less 1. Such one-year returns are called annual, or annualized, returns. For example, a stock that was bought a year ago for $100 per share, paid a $5 dividend, and now trades for $108 would have the following annual return:

$$(\$5 + \$8)/\$100 = 13\%$$

Obviously returns can also be negative. If the price of the stock in the example had declined by $10, the result would have been:

$$(\$5 - \$10)/\$100 = -5\%$$

These two examples represent simple one-year returns. Clearly, earning a given return for six months will produce a very different result from earning that same return for six years. The longer the investment earns a given PPR, the greater will be its ending value. Accumulating returns over time and earning a return on the return of prior periods is called compounding. An investment's value will grow through the process of compounding.

The Impact of Compounding.   Stated returns, particularly for longer holding periods, generally reflect the impact of compounding. Returns are compounded when an investment earns a return for more than one period. After the first period, such an investment earns a return on both the initial sum invested and on the returns that accumulate from earlier periods.

Consider an investment that yields 10% per year for two years. It earns 10% during the first year. At the end of that first year the investment will show an HPRR of 1.10. Earning another 10% during the second year would generate an HPRR of 1.21 for the two years. This compound value results from earning 10% on the initial principal in the first year, another 10% on principal during the second year, and 10% on the first year's 10% return (.10 × .10 = .01, or 1%). The sum is 10% + 10% + 1% plus the initial investment, or 121% of the original amount. A simpler way of making this computation is to take 110% of 110% (1.10 × 1.10 = 1.21).

One can also work backward from the appreciated value to the interest rate that produced it. Thus an investment that, after one year, was worth 110% of its initial value is said to have yielded a return of 10%. Similarly an investment that appreciated by 21% over a two-year period would be said to have generated a 10% annual return compounded annually.

PPRs are generally stated on an annualized basis with annual compounding. That is, the standard period for stating returns and for computing compound values is generally one year. Returns can, however, be compounded more frequently than once a year. For example, a return might be described as 10% compounded semi-annually. This would imply that the investment is to earn one-half of the annual rate of 10% each six months (5% per six months, or .05). An investment earning this rate of return would appreciate to 121.55% of its initial value after two years: (1.05 × 1.05 × 1.05 × 1.05). Had the return been compounded annually, the compound value after two years would, in contrast, be only 121%. The semiannual compounding increased the compound value by .55% compared with annual compounding. Indeed, the more frequently an investment's returns are compounded, the more rapidly it will grow.

Increasing the frequency of compounding only modestly increases the rate of growth, however. For example, 10% compounded quarterly is equivalent to 10.38% compounded annually. Thus a return of 10.5% compounded annually would be preferable to 10% compounded quarterly. Still, 10% compounded quarterly produces a higher rate of appreciation than 10% compounded annually. The rate of compounding does matter. Accordingly, the complete description of a stated return must include both the PPR return and the frequency of compounding.

Measuring the Mean Return.   Mean returns often need to be computed for two different types of circumstances: an investment (single asset or portfolio) over time and a group of investments over the same time. We may, for example, know the PPRs for each year and wish to know the average return for the entire holding period. Alternatively, we may know the individual returns for the components of a portfolio and wish to compute the portfolio's overall return.

The Mean Return of a Portfolio.   The mean return for a portfolio can properly be represented as the arithmetic average of the returns of the individual components. If equal amounts are invested in each component, the portfolio's overall return is a simple unweighted average of its components. If different amounts are invested in the various investments, a weighted average (with weights equal to the relative amounts invested in each asset) must be computed. Such an arithmetic average return has a very desirable property. If that average return were earned on each investment in the portfolio, the total value of the portfolio would be the same as it was for what was actually earned.

The Mean Return for a Single Investment.   We may also know the returns for a single investment over several periods and wish to compute its mean, or average, return over the entire period. Clearly, if the same per period return were earned in each period, that PPR would also be the mean return. Frequently, however, the investment will produce different PPRs during different periods. An arithmetic average of these returns could be computed by summing the PPRs and dividing by the number of periods. Such an average is simple to compute and reasonably useful when the individual returns are similar. An investment that earned successive returns of 7%, 7.5%, and 8% would grow to a compound value equal to 1.24227 times its initial level. The arithmetic average of these three returns is 7.5%. Had the investment actually earned 7.5% per period for three years, its compound value would be 1.24230. Thus the actual compound value and the value derived from the arithmetic mean return are very similar for this case. When the separate returns vary over a wide range, however, the arithmetic average of returns earned over time presents a relatively unrealistic picture. Ideally, the number reported for the overall return should be one that, if earned every period, would produce the same end-of-period value as has resulted from the separate per period returns actually earned. The arithmetic mean does not have that property.

The following example illustrates just how far off the arithmetic mean can be. Consider an investment of $1,000 that doubles in value (to $2,000) in the first period (a return of 100%) and then falls to half of its value (to $1,000) during the next period (a return of −50%). Such an investment would have the same value at the end of the second period ($1,000) as it had at the start of the first ($1,000). Most people would agree that an investment with the same beginning and ending value would generate a return of 0% over the two periods. Yet if we average +100% and −50%, we obtain +25%. Thus we see that using the arithmetic mean can yield a misleading return figure.

The Geometric Mean Return.   The geometric mean return (GMR), in contrast, is a number that has the desired property. An investment that earns its GMR each period will grow to the same end value as it would from earning the separate returns used to compute that mean. The GMR is obtained by first computing the holding period return relative. The HPRR may be determined in either of two ways. We can simply divide the current value by the initial value. Sometimes, however, we may have access only to the PPRs. In this circumstance, we can form the product of each of the individual HPRRs (1 plus the PPRs) for the entire set of periods. Then the nth root is taken of the result, where n is the number of periods. This result minus 1 is the geometric mean return (GMR):

$$HPR_n = PPR_n + 1.00$$
$$HPRR = HPRR_1 \times HPRR_2 \times \ldots \times HPRR_n$$
$$GMR = \sqrt[n]{HPRR} - 1.00$$

where:

$$PPR_n = \text{PPR for period n}$$
$$HPRR_n = \text{HPRR for period n}$$

Thus in the simple example above:

$$HPRR = 2.00 \times .50 = 1.00$$
$$GMR = \sqrt{1.00} - 1.00 = 0\%$$

This is exactly the result that we would expect for an investment that doubled and then lost half of its value. The value of the investment would be back where it started. Thus a 0% return is consistent with our expectations.

Now let us consider a more complicated example. Suppose an investment generated annual returns of 13%, 17%, 2%, 8%, and 10%. We would like to know its GMR. We would start the process by computing its HPRR:

$$\text{HPRR} = 1.13 \times 1.17 \times 1.02 \times 1.08 \times 1.10 = 1.60$$
$$\text{GMR} = \sqrt[5]{1.60} - 1.00 = 1.10 - 1.00 = .10, \text{ or } 10\%$$

Note that in this relatively straightforward case the arithmetic and geometric means are very similar. Indeed, whenever no negative returns and no very high returns are present, the two means are relatively close to each other.

Risk

In popular usages the term risk refers to the probability of some undesirable and uncertain event. Thus a risky investment is one that might well produce a return substantially less than is expected. Investors may talk of the *downside risk* (that an investment's return will be less than anticipated) perhaps coupled with the *upside potential* (that the return will exceed expectations). No doubt such statements convey information. The element of risk that troubles investors is the possibility of downside fluctuations in price and return. And yet using the term risk in this way is imprecise. Where does the downside risk end and the upside potential begin? What units are used to measure the amount of risk? How is the risk of one investment compared with another?

The more serious experts (e.g., scholars) in finance and economics use the term risk to refer to the dispersion of possible returns. We shall follow their usage and thus relate risk to the likelihood that realized returns will differ from those that were expected. An asset with a wide range of possible returns is considered risky while one with a narrow range of potential returns is considered more secure. For this discussion the reader should think in terms of the range of possible one-period returns. The analysis can, however, be generalized to holding periods of greater length.

The range of returns is generally measured in terms of the distance from the mean or expected (per period) return. An asset's expected return is the average of its possible returns weighted by their respective likelihoods. Thus the probabilities of below-expectation and above-expectation returns balance out. The actual yields of risky assets are often well above or well below the market's expectations. Low-risk assets, in contrast, usually generate returns that are very close to their expected values. The owner of a (relatively risky) asset whose return is expected to be between 2% and 18% bears the "risk" that the actual return could be anywhere within this range. The investor who owns a (relatively secure) asset with a 99+% of earning exactly 7.5% has very little risk to be concerned with.

In subsequent chapters we will explore how the range or dispersion of returns can be measured as well as the role of portfolio formation and diversification in the assessment of risk. For present purposes, however, we shall work with the simplified concept that risk refers to range of possible returns.

The Risk–Return Trade-Off

Although a few people may thrive on risk, most prefer to limit their exposure to unpleasant surprises. The popularity, profitability, and success of the insurance industry illustrates the demand for risk reduction.

Insurance companies are in the business of selling protection from risk. The insurer and the insured in effect wager on the possibility of a significant casualty loss. For most families the loss of their one and only house to a fire or other cause would be catastrophic. The insurance company, in contrast, has insured thousands of houses. Having to pay off on a particular policy (even yours) is for the insurer just part of being in the insurance business. In a given year claims will be filed on only a small portion of the homes covered by the company. The payoff odds on homeowners' insurance must be structured to favor the insurer. That is, the amount that the insurance company pays out in claims in a typical year must be well below the amount collected in premiums. Otherwise no company would want to be in that business. Indeed, a homeowner's insurance premium must exceed the sum of expected benefit claims, administrative costs, and commissions by a sufficiently large profit to keep the insurance company interested in the business. Thus the insurance premium must not only cover the risk of loss but also administrative costs, commissions, and a reasonable profit for the insurer. The insured pays these extra costs to achieve the peace of mind that the protection offers. Because most homes are insured, the risk reduction must be worth the cost for a large fraction of the population. Similar arguments apply to other types of insurance (life, auto, medical, etc.).

Like those who purchase insurance, most investors are willing to sacrifice some potential return if they can thereby obtain a sufficiently large reduction in risk. Accordingly, to be salable, risky assets must offer a high enough expected return to offset their disadvantage in the risk dimension. When an investment offers too low an expected return to justify taking the risk associated with the return expectation, the asset must fall in price until the market views its risk to be in line with its expected return. For example, an asset that is expected to be worth $1,000 in six years will generate an expected return of 12% if it is priced at $500. If, in contrast, that same investment was priced at $335, its expected return would be 22%. In general, the lower the price on any given investment, the higher its expected return will be.

Risky assets, however, do not automatically produce a high expected return. Rather, the market tends to set a price that is appropriate for the expected return and risk level. An appropriate price is not possible for every potential investment, however. For example, a company or partnership proposing to exploit the moon's mineral resources would certainly be risky. With current technology, such a venture would have little chance of yielding a positive return. The expected value of any sum invested would probably be less than the amount invested. Thus no price on such an investment would be likely both to allow sufficient capital to be raised to fund the project and to offer a high enough expected return to compensate investors for the risk. On the other hand, a company organized to mine the nodules on the ocean floor might very well offer a high enough expected return to justify the risk. Thus the nodule company could probably raise capital in spite of its high risks.

The moon company's expected return, in contrast, would probably be too low to offset its risks.

Liquidity

Liquidity relates to the ease of extracting the original commitment from an investment. The most liquid of assets is cash itself. Other types of liquid assets are close to cash but cannot be spent in their present forms. Such assets can, however, be readily converted to cash with relatively little sacrifice for the investor. That is, the owner who wishes to sell can do so at little or no cost, inconvenience, or danger of receiving less than the sum of purchase price and accrued interest. Examples of extremely liquid investments include paper money, coin, and depository account balances. Such "investments" are immediately spendable or at most require a minimum amount of effort to make them so. Bonds with short maturities or the right to be redeemed upon demand are also quite liquid. The more distant the redemption date, however (i.e., the longer until its maturity), the less liquid the investment is considered to be. Thus long-term debt securities and nondebt investments like stocks and real estate (no maturity date) tend to be very illiquid.

Marketability

Marketability refers to the ease or difficulty of buying or selling the asset at its market value. The market value of an investment is the price that a willing buyer and willing seller would reach if neither were under immediate pressure to trade. Investments differ substantially in their degree of marketability. Thus shares in very large firms like Exxon or General Motors are very marketable. They trade nearly continuously at prices that vary little from transaction to transaction. Assets that are exchanged in active high-volume markets generally sell at or very close to the then current market price.

Market prices may, of course, vary appreciably over time. Indeed, a market price may or may not be an attractive price for the investor. One who, for example, bought IBM stock at its 1987 precrash high of 175 might not think the prospect of selling it at its March 1988 market price level of 115 was such a good deal. The advantage of marketable assets is that they will sell easily for their market prices, whatever those prices might be at the time. Such market prices may or may not yield an acceptable profit for the investor, however.

Investments with poor marketability present their owners with another kind of problem. For example, such difficult-to-market assets as a house, rare painting, or other one-of-a-kind investments appear on the market rather infrequently. Potential buyers and sellers of such investments are relatively scarce. Thus their owners must either be patient or be willing to trade at a substantial sacrifice from the theoretical market level. Suppose the owner of a house that should sell for $200,000 (according to current conditions in the local real estate market) is seeking to make a quick sale. He or she might have to accept a sacrifice price of $150,000. To obtain a reasonable price (fair to the seller), the seller would need to be prepared for a potentially significant wait for the right customer to come along.

Although marketable assets tend to be liquid, some exceptions exist. A widely held stock can generally be sold for the current market price (marketable) but that price may vary substantially from the purchase price (illiquid). Conversely, U.S. government savings bonds and low denomination CDs may be cashed in early at face plus reduced interest (liquid) but are not negotiable (unmarketable).

Investment Effort

The selecting and managing of some types of portfolios require little or no special knowledge, facilities, or time commitment. For example, the investor need not be an expert on short-term debt securities to understand the relevant characteristics (risk, expected return, liquidity, marketability, tax treatment, etc.) of Treasury bills and similar securities. Moreover, the certificates of ownership can be conveniently held by a brokerage firm or in a safe deposit box. Those who invest in other assets such as real estate, collectibles, soybean futures, or mink farms need very special knowledge, talent, and/or facilities. Similarly, some types of assets may be maintained with little or no effort (bonds) whereas others require constant management (an apartment complex). Accordingly, would-be investors need to consider carefully the expertise, talent, facilities, and time required to assemble and manage the particular type of investment portfolio effectively.

Minimum Investment Size

Portfolios of some types of investments may be assembled with small sums whereas others require a much larger minimum commitment. Moreover, some investments are so low risk that a portfolio consisting of a single asset is an appropriate holding. For example, a savings account can be opened for as little as $100 and some higher yielding bank certificates are available in $500 units. Most mutual funds will accept initial deposits of $1,000. Many collectibles sell for a few hundred dollars or less. On the other hand, several thousand dollars is generally needed to purchase a single stock or bond position. Such a holding, however, would be very much at the mercies of the market for that particular stock or bond. A reasonably well diversified stock or bond portfolio would require several times as much. A single real estate purchase (to say nothing of a diversified real estate portfolio) is likely to require at least several thousand dollars for just the down payment. Similarly, most brokers will not accept commodity accounts having less than $20,000 to $50,000 in investor capital.

Obviously, the capital requirements of investment areas differ appreciably. Those beginning with relatively small sums are restricted to investments that are available in modest size units. Over time, however, investors may be able to shift into investments that are traded only in larger size units. Thus a beginning investor may start with a savings account and then move into certificates of deposit. Later he or she may buy into a mutual fund and still later begin assembling a portfolio of stocks and/or buy some rental property.

Ethical and Moral Appeal

Investments may also differ substantially in their ethical and moral appeal, particularly to certain groups of investors. Many investors take the attitude that if an activity is legal, it is a proper area in which to seek investment profits. Other investors, however, want their investment dollars associated only with activities of which they personally approve. Accordingly, the perceived social responsibility of the activity is a relevant consideration for many investors. Most investors would probably prefer not to have their investment money help promote what they consider to be objectionable activities. What is socially unacceptable for some, however, is not socially unacceptable for other socially aware investors. Social responsibility is largely in the eye of the beholder. Each investor has his or her own code of what is a comfortable area in which to invest. No doubt many, but by no means all, investors would draw the line at pornography and prostitution even when and where they were allowed by the law. Others would refuse to become slumlords even if all health and safety codes were adhered to and the profit potential were substantial. Still others would object to investments in companies involved with one or more of the following types of products or activities: alcohol, tobacco, armaments, war toys, major pollution, nonunionized employees, unionized employees, South African connections, misleading advertisements, or poor safety records.

TAXES

Investors are able to retain only the after-tax component of their returns. Because not all types of investment income are taxed equivalently, tax considerations are an important factor, particularly for investors in high tax brackets.

To understand how investment income is taxed we need to examine our tax system's basic structure. Total income from wages, salaries, and most other sources are added to compute adjusted gross income. That sum is then reduced by personal exemptions ($2,000 per dependent in 1989) and itemized deductions or the standard deduction. The resulting taxable income is the amount on which one's tax liability is based. The actual tax liability incurred depends upon both taxable income and filing status (joint, individual, etc.). Itemizing is advantageous if allowable deductions exceed the standard deduction. Deductions are allowed for charitable contributions, certain business expenses, some types of interest payments, a portion of high medical expenses, and casualty losses as well as most state and local income and property taxes (but not sales tax).

Tax Treatment of Extra Income

Additions to adjusted gross income almost always increase taxable income. Moreover, extra income is taxed at a higher rate than the average rate on preaddition income. An example should help to clarify this point. Jan Q. Investor's $47,000 per year income is sole support for her family of four. The three dependents (including her husband) and her personal exemption permit her to exclude $8,000

TABLE 1.1 1988 Tax Rate Schedule for Joint Filers

Taxable Income	Tax
$0 to $29,750	15%
$29,750 to $71,900	$4,462 + 28% of amount over $29,750
$71,900 to $145,000	$16,264 + 33% of amount over $71,900
over $145,000	$40,600 + 28% of amount over $145,000 (but the personal exemptions are phased out so that the effective rate remains at 33% until the exemptions are used up)

while deductions of another $6,000 (primarily mortgage interest and property and state income taxes) reduce her taxable income to $33,000. The tax table (Table 1.1) shows that joint filers (Jan and her husband file jointly) with taxable incomes between $29,750 and $71,900 pay (1988 rates) $4,462 plus 28% of the excess over $29,750. This formula yields a tax liability of $5,372 ($4,462 + $910). This amount is equivalent to an average tax on gross income of 11.9% (5,372/47,000) or 16.9% (5,372/33,000) on taxable income. Any additional income would be taxed at the marginal tax rate, however. If Mrs. Investor's income increased to $48,000 without changing deductions, her taxable income would increase to $34,000 and her tax would rise by $280, or 28% of the income increase.

An individual's taxable income results from adding investment income to other forms of income (after subtracting appropriate deductions). Thus we can view investment income as the last increment of income. If the investment income had not been earned, total income would have been reduced by that amount. Taxes would then be reduced by the amount of the investment income not earned times the tax rate of that increment of income. The last increment of income is always taxed at the marginal rate. Thus the marginal rate is the relevant rate to use in assessing most investment decisions.

Different tax brackets apply to the various filing statuses. For example, single filers reach the higher tax brackets at lower levels of income than do joint filers. Although Congress may change the tax rates from time to time, each investor's marginal rate (whatever its current level) remains the relevant rate for most investment decisions.

The relevant tax laws as this is written (1988) are discussed in the section that follows. Tax laws are frequently revised. Most revisions are relatively minor but some, such as the Tax Reform Act of 1986, result in substantial changes. The possibility of tax law changes increases both the complexity and the desirability of tax planning. Serious investors need to stay abreast of the relevant tax laws. They may well want to change their strategy and adjust their portfolio in light of such changes or even in light of expected changes.

Tax Treatment of Investment Income

Whether, and if so how, the income from an investment is taxed can have a major impact on the net return that the investor receives. Accordingly, effective tax planning is an important aspect of both investing and personal finance. The form of investment income determines how it is taxed. Interest income on savings accounts, corporate bonds, and U.S. government bonds is taxed as ordinary income (i.e., like wages and salaries) whereas state and local government bond interest is untaxed at the federal level. After any relevant expenses are deducted, rents, royalties, and most dividends are fully taxed just as is income from wages and salaries. Dividends not covered by current profits are considered "capital distributions." Such distributions are taxed when received but do affect the taxable capital gains or losses on such assets when they are sold.

Capital Gains and Losses

Capital gains and capital losses arise whenever capital assets such as stocks or bonds are bought and sold for different amounts. Normally the taxable gain equals the sale price (minus commissions) less the purchase price (plus commissions). Any capital distributions must, however, be subtracted from the purchase price to determine the basis. The basis is the sum that is subtracted from the sale price to produce the taxable gain.

Suppose 100 shares of the BDC Company are purchased for $25 per share and sold for $35 per share. The taxable gain (ignoring commissions) would normally be $1,000 ($3,500 − $2,500). Prior capital distribution dividends of $500 would, however, reduce the basis from $2,500 to $2,000, increasing the taxable gain to $1,500 ($3,500 − $2,000).

Capital losses are first netted against capital gains. The net gain or loss is added to or subtracted from taxable income. A maximum of $3,000 of income per year may be offset by capital losses. Any excess may be carried over to the next year. Capital gains distributions of mutual funds are taxed in the same way as capital gains.

Under current tax law, capital gains are taxed as ordinary income. Two important points need to be borne in mind, however. First, only realized gains are subject to tax. Thus a profit on a stock or other investment position incurs no tax liability until it is sold. Second, during most of the history of U.S. income tax, long-term capital gains (holding periods of six months or one year) received special tax treatment. For example, in 1986 only 40% of long-term gains were taxed, while in 1987 the maximum tax rate on gains was 28%. Those industries with an interest in the issue (securities, mutual funds, real estate, venture capital, etc.) are sure to put their lobbyists to work seeking restoration of such provisions. Thus long-term capital gains may again receive favorable tax treatment sometime in the future.

The Alternative Minimum Tax

Individuals with large amounts of tax-sheltered income (accelerated depreciation, etc.) may be subject to the alternative minimum tax (AMT). To determine whether the AMT applies, tax liability is first computed in the ordinary way. Then all of the includable tax-sheltered items are added back to adjusted gross income and certain allowable deductions are subtracted. The AMT equals 21% of this sum.

TABLE 1.2 Tax Treatment of Investment Income

Not subject to Federal Income Tax	Capital distributions Interest on state and local bonds
Taxed as Ordinary Income	Dividend and interest income (other than municipal interest) Rents, royalties, and any other investment income payments Capital gains (net of capital losses)

The individual's tax liabilities computed for the two different ways (ordinary and AMT) are then compared. Tax must be paid on the higher of the two figures.

State and Local Taxes

Investment income may also be subject to state and local taxes. U.S. Treasury issues are exempt from state and local taxes. State and local bonds are not taxed within the state that issued them. In contrast, those issued by other jurisdictions are fully taxed in the owner's own state and local residence jurisdiction.

Tax Treatment Summary

The two basic types of investment income for federal tax purposes are:

1. Capital distributions and the interest on state and local government bonds. These are tax free.
2. Dividend and nonmunicipal interest income, net rents, royalties, other investment income, and capital gains. These are taxed as ordinary income.

Table 1.2 illustrates these tax categories.

Implications of Investment Tax Treatment

Those whose incomes put them in high tax brackets will find tax-sheltered investments particularly attractive. Table 1.3 shows the fully taxable yield that is necessary to produce a 10% after-tax return (1988 rates). Regardless of the tax-free rate, however, the basic point remains—a given tax-free yield is worth more to people in higher tax brackets.

Investors are able to retain only the after-tax portion of their returns on investments. Investors focus on the portion of the return that they get to keep. For two investments with the same before-tax return, investors would tend to prefer the one with the higher after-tax return. Accordingly, asset prices generally reflect the way their returns are taxed. If other things such as risk are the same, a tax-

TABLE 1.3   Tax Equivalent Yield (Joint Return 1988 Rates)

Taxable Income	Marginal Tax Bracket	Tax Equivalent Yield (at 10%)
$0–29,749	15%	11.8%
$29,750–71,899	28	13.9
$71,900 and over	33	14.9

free or tax-sheltered payment stream will be priced higher than a payment stream of equal size that is fully taxed. Pricing investments in this way produces a trade-off between before-tax returns and tax treatment. Investments offering a tax-free or tax-sheltered return are priced to offer a lower before-tax return than otherwise equivalent investments whose returns are fully taxed. Thus, for example, the before-tax yields of tax-free bonds are generally well below otherwise equivalent taxable bond returns.

The market-determined trade-off between fully taxed and tax-preferred income reflects the average tax impact on the relevant investors. Different investors, however, face different tax rates. Some investors do not pay taxes on their investment income while others pay taxes at various rates (15%, 28%, and 33% as this is written). A fully taxable return of 10% might be equivalent to an after-tax return of 8.5%, 7.2%, or 6.7% depending upon the tax bracket. State and local income tax levels further complicate the after-tax return comparisons. Thus the after-tax return on a given investment will depend, among other things, on the tax bracket of the particular investor.

Suppose tax-free bonds offer a 7.2% yield while otherwise similar taxable bonds offered 10%. An investor in the 28% tax bracket would earn the same after-tax return on either investment (.72 × 10% = 7.2%). Those in higher brackets will retain more from the tax-free investment whereas those in lower brackets will achieve a higher after-tax return from the taxable investment. Thus tax-sheltered investments will normally offer those in very high tax brackets relatively higher after-tax returns while those in below-average tax brackets will find fully taxed investments more attractive. Table 1.4 lists the principal investment characteristics and high and low examples for each.

TABLE 1.4   Investment Characteristics

High Example	Characteristic	Low Example
Gold Mine	Expected Return	Savings Account
Futures Contract	Risk	Treasury Bill
Money Market Account	Liquidity	Small Business
Actively Traded Stock	Marketability	Collectibles
Real Estate	Investment Effort	Mutual Fund
Commercial Paper	Minimum Investment Size	Savings Bonds
Most Collectibles	Social Responsibility	Pornographic Movies
Municipal Bonds	Favorable Tax Treatment	Corporate Bonds

Do You Have the Emotional Makeup to Play the Market?

Most types of investing involve significant amounts of risk. Those who play to win need to be prepared for the possibility that they may lose. If losses are too painful, investors should avoid risks and stick to safe if unexciting investments. An old saying on Wall Street is, "Always sell down to the sleeping point." For some people the sleeping point is little or no money at risk. Others thrive or at least tolerate relatively large amounts of risk. Each of us needs to determine how we react to bad news about our portfolios. How we react may affect not only how we experience the ups and downs but equally important how we manage our portfolio under pressure.

Rod Fadem, vice president of the Missouri investment firm of I. M. Simon and Co., wrote an article for *Barron's* dealing with this question. He begins with six questions:

1. Do you find yourself jumping at every downtick (every slight price decline)?
2. Do scare headlines make you want to sell at low prices?
3. Do you have a Type A market personality?
4. Are you bothered by losses no matter how little money is involved?
5. Do you have a large ego?
6. Are you bothered when you sell something and then see it rise to a higher price?

Fadem asserts that a "yes" answer to all of these questions is a sure indication that you should avoid risky investments. Four yes answers is a suggestion of trouble. One or two may be OK. Alternatively six "no" answers imply a winning market personality.

Source: Adapted from R. Fadem, "No Emotions, Please," *Barron's*, July 28, 1986, p. 34.

PSYCHOLOGICAL ASPECTS OF INVESTING

Investors need to take account of their own psychological tendencies. Otherwise, such factors may unduly influence their decisions. Investors are subject to all of the shortcomings and biases inherent in human judgment. Individuals who evaluate their own biases and tendencies may be better able to control and perhaps offset those that could otherwise lead them astray. For example, a tendency to invest impulsively could cause the investor to trade too frequently. Overly active trading may be profitable to the broker (in commissions) but is usually rather costly for the investor. Such a tendency might be reduced by taking a day to think over each trade.

Paul Slovic and his coworkers at the Oregon Research Institute have pioneered in the study of human judgment biases and their impacts on investor decisions. His classic work, "Psychological Study of Human Judgment: Implications for Investment Decision Making," synthesizes the investment implications of a number of psychological studies.[1] For example, Slovic observes that the human mind frequently makes random judgmental errors. This trait may be dealt with by programming individual decision processes. The decision maker would use mathematical models of the considerations, weights, and estimates involved to check the logic of the decision. Random human error can cause the unprogrammed approach to yield different results from the programmed approach. The programmed result may or may not be superior to the unprogrammed one, but knowledge of the differences should generally be helpful.

Slovic also reported that people usually react to new information by revising their opinions in the correct direction but more conservatively than is warranted by the new information. On the other hand, people tend to extrapolate from a small nonrandom sample to an unsupportable generalization.

Complex decisions may be divided into a series of smaller subquestions with the judgments on each combined into an answer for the initial major problem. Systematic biases in the smaller decisions may lead to a biased decision on the larger question, however.

Selective recall is one typical human bias. Some events are more easily remembered than others. People also tend to see patterns where none exist and to ascribe causation when they see spurious correlation. The claimed success of many investment chartists may be due to such tendencies.

Individuals also sometimes respond differently to the same question asked in different ways. For example, an individual might simultaneously predict a 10% and $5 price rise on a $40 stock (10% of $40 is $4, not $5). Thus questions should be phrased to elicit the most accurate approach to answering them. If available data are in percentages, for example, a question phrased in percentage terms may elicit a more reliable response.

Apparently the degree of risk aversion is not a universally generalizable characteristic. People may be very risk averse in their investment decisions but much less so in their driving, or vice versa. Moreover decisions made by a group tend to be riskier than individual decisions. Finally people tend to overrate the reliability of their own judgments. A related set of common psychological errors (Table 1.5) was compiled by Pines.[2]

TABLE 1.5 Cognitive Sources of Common Errors in Investor Judgment

Judgmental Bias or Error	Cognitive Source
1. Being bearish at market bottoms and bullish at market tops	Unavailability of a "contrarian," causal scenario
2. Selling winners and holding losers	Inconsistent risk preference and the biasing effects of decision frames
3. Overoptimistic appraisal of a security	Believing that special factors will allow the stock to do better than historical experience would suggest
4. Acting on unreliable "tips"	Experiencing vivid, "personal" information as more memorable than statistical data
5. Indecision and/or inconsistency	Effect of emotion on information availability and probability
6. "It's the 1960s again!"	Selective recall, misleading market metaphors
7. The "sure thing" that wasn't	Overreliance on one available, causal scenario

SUMMARY AND CONCLUSIONS

The expected return and its associated risk are key factors in most investment decisions. Other relevant characteristics include liquidity (the ease of converting the asset into spendable form without a sacrifice of return), marketability (the likelihood of trading at the market price without waiting), effort (the time and expertise required of a serious investor), capital requirements (the minimum sum needed to purchase one unit and/or a diversified portfolio), appeal to socially responsible investors, and tax treatment. Moreover, investments differ appreciably in the way that they are taxed. Some investment returns, such as municipal bond interest and capital distribution dividends, are not taxed. Most other types of investment income are fully taxed. Long-term capital gains have at various times been taxed at lower rates than ordinary income. Currently such gains are fully taxed but only after they have been realized.

REVIEW QUESTIONS

1. Explain what is meant by return and risk. Put your explanation into words that an individual with little or no economic or financial background can understand.

2. Discuss the various return concepts, including holding period return relative, holding period return, compound interest, arithmetic mean return, and geometric mean return.

3. What is meant by the risk–return trade-off? Does it imply that risky investments offer high returns? Explain why or why not.

4. Define and compare liquidity and marketability. Are liquid investments always marketable and vice versa? Explain your answer.

5. Discuss the various aspects of investment effort. Illustrate your discussion with specific examples.

6. Discuss the roles of minimum investment size and ethical and moral appeal in investment selection and portfolio management.

7. Outline the various ways investment income may be taxed.

REVIEW PROBLEMS

1. Compute the HPRR and HPR for each of the following:
   a. an investment in land purchased for $5,000 and sold for $7,000

b. a $3,000 land contract non-interest-bearing note purchased for $1,800 and held until maturity, at which time it is paid off at its face value

c. a building that is held for nine months, during which time it generates $3,500 in rental income (in excess of costs), and then sold for a $30,000 profit. Its original purchase price was $195,000.

2. Compute the annual return for each of the following investments:

a. an investment in 100 shares of stock costing $10 per share, sold one year later for $11 per share during which time a 30-cent per share dividend is received. Ignore commissions in your computations.

b. A $1,000 one-year CD with a stated yield of 7% compounded quarterly. To compute its return determine what an equivalent one-year investment would have to earn if its returns were not compounded.

c. a long-term bond purchased for $890 and sold a year later for $850. The bond pays a coupon of 8% of its face value. The first coupon is payable in the middle of the one-year holding period. To be precise the interest earned on the coupon payments should be computed. Assume the interest on the coupon accrues at the same rate as the bond.

3. Compute the appreciated value of an investment held for two years with a 10% return compounded annually, semiannually, quarterly, and monthly.

4. Compute the arithmetic mean return for equal amounts invested in assets yielding returns of 7.8%, 9.3%, 4.5%, and 11.5%. Now suppose the amounts invested were in the proportions of .2, .3, .4, and .1. What would be the mean return?

5. Compute the geometric mean return (GMR) for an investment with the following per period returns (PPR): 5.6%, 8.9%, 10.0%, 7.7%, and 13.0%. Compare the result with the arithmetic mean.

6. Compute the average and marginal tax rates for the Jan Q. Investor example in the chapter text using current tax rates.

7. Obtain the most recent year's tax forms and compute the tax liability for the following information:

Wages: $29,000
Dividends: $750 (jointly held)
Municipal bond interest: $500
Savings account interest: $500
Long-term gain on stock: $1,200
Insufficient deductions to itemize
Three dependents, married filing jointly

First determine the amount of taxable income; then compute the tax on that income. What is the marginal and average tax rate for this situation?

8. As in Problem 5 compute the tax liability for the following information:

Profit of a sole proprietorship: $60,000
Dividend and interest income (no municipal interest): $3,000

Mortgage interest payments: $9,000
State income taxes: $1,500
Gifts to charity: $800
Two dependents, unmarried head of household

First determine the amount of taxable income; then compute the tax on that income. What is the marginal and average tax rate for this situation?

REVIEW PROJECTS

1. Evaluate your own approach to investing in light of the psychological errors that are frequently made. (If you do not have an investment portfolio per se, refer to your portfolio of longer term consumer assets.) Make a list of pitfalls to which you tend to be subject. What can you do to avoid these pitfalls?

2. Go to a local bank and obtain the rates on the CDs that they offer. Ask how often they compound the stated return. Compute the holding period return and annualized equivalent per period return for each instrument.

3. Compare the returns on the bank CDs of Project 2 with the returns on equivalent maturity Treasury securities.

4. Ask a brokerage firm to recommend three high-quality (AA rating) short (two-year), intermediate (five-year), and long (20-year) municipal bonds. Ask for quotes on these bonds. Compute their yields to maturity and compare them with the yields on otherwise similar Treasury issues.

5. For Project 4 compute the marginal tax brackets that make the after-tax yields equivalent for the taxable and tax-free bonds.

NOTES

1. P. Slovic, "Psychological Study of Human Judgment: Implications for Investment Decision Making," *Journal of Finance*, September 1972, 779–799.

2. H. Pines, "A New Psychological Perspective on Investor Decision Making," *American Association of Individual Investors Journal*, September 1983, 10–21.

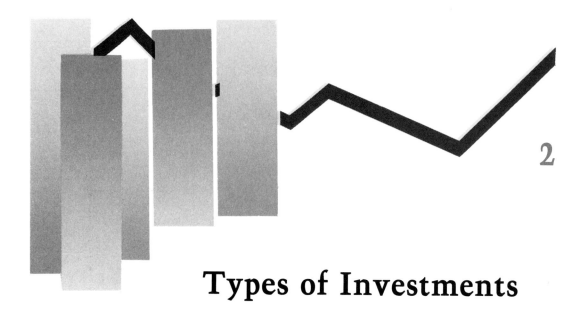

Types of Investments

The preceding chapter laid some necessary groundwork. Accordingly, we can now explore some of the more important types of investments. This discussion treats investments in three (somewhat arbitrary) categories: debt securities, equity investments, and a catchall category that includes real estate, commodities, collectors' items, and other nontraditional investments. Readers should realize that this chapter is designed as an overview. A more detailed discussion of many of these investments is presented later in the book.

DEBT INSTRUMENTS

The first time most of us are introduced to the concept of investing is when a savings account is opened in our name. Such an account is one of the many types of debt instruments. The bank (or other type of financial institution) holding the account can be said to owe the owner the balance in the account. The borrower, in this case the bank, is legally obligated to repay the lender (in this case the depositor) the amounts deposited plus the agreed rate of periodic interest.

The provisions of a savings account illustrate the nature of a debt instrument. The borrower and lender enter into a legally enforceable contract. The lender agrees to provide the borrower with a sum of money for a period of time. The borrower agrees to pay interest at a prespecified rate and repay principal (amount borrowed) according to the terms of the debt instrument (because a savings account principal is to be available to the depositor upon demand). Failure of the borrower to fulfill any of the contract's provisions (such as missing a scheduled interest or principal payment) constitutes a default. If the default itself is not cured, the borrower may undertake appropriate legal action. Such action may eventually result in a seizure of assets (collateral), bankruptcy, and/or liquidation of assets for the borrower.

Equity investments, in contrast, involve a share of ownership in an asset. The holder of an equity instrument (such as stock) has no more than a residual claim on the property of the instrument's issuer. The claims of the issuer's creditors have priority over those of the equity holders.

Short-Term Debt Securities

Debt securities are generally classified according to the length of time until they must be paid off. Those that come due within a year are classified as short term. Short-term securities are available from a relatively large number of issuers. One of the most popular of these types of investments is the savings accounts offered by banks and thrift institutions.

Such accounts are both very liquid and very safe investments. Funds can normally be deposited or withdrawn at any time during office hours and most accounts are guaranteed up to a maximum of $100,000 by a United States government agency. Accordingly, depositors need not spend much time shopping around for a "safe" bank or thrift. Rather they should focus on convenience, service, and return (including premiums). Banks and savings institutions have generally paid similar rates. Compared with other depository institutions, credit unions usually offer a slightly higher government-insured return coupled with valuable borrowing privileges.

Depository institutions were once subject to maximum rate limitations on most of their accounts and certificates. Now, however, they are allowed to pay whatever rates the competitive situation requires.

Money market securities (Treasury bills, for example) have relatively high minimum denominations ($10,000 or more). This characteristic of such securities has prevented many small investors from participating. Money market mutual funds are designed to serve small investors who want access to this market. Money funds pool the resources of many individual small investors. They thereby accumulate relatively large sums to invest in the high-denomination money market securities that would otherwise be unavailable to these small investors. Thus the money funds assemble a diversified portfolio of money market instruments.

After subtracting administrative expenses, money funds yield slightly less than the rates on the money market instruments themselves. If, for example, money market returns are 9%, a $1,000 money fund account would earn about 8.5%. Such a return may compare very favorably to that paid on a savings account. Money fund deposits are readily accessible by check or wire transfer. Because most money funds buy only high-quality short-term securities, they are considered quite safe.

The money market accounts offered by banks compete directly with the money market funds. They offer rates that are competitive with those of the money market funds. These accounts require a $1,000 minimum balance (many banks set their own higher minimums) and allow six withdrawals (three by check) per month.

U.S. government savings bonds also compete for small investors' funds. Their yield is set at 85% of the government bond rate on five-year or longer bonds. They also have a fixed minimum. Thus if the minimum is 6.0% (as it was in 1988 when this was written) and 85% of the five-year government bond rate is 5%, the savings bond would yield its 6.0% minimum. Although they are not really short-term securities, the early-redemption feature of U.S. savings bonds provides an analogous degree of liquidity. Early redemption leads to a yield sacrifice, however. Savings bonds do allow the investor to defer federal income taxes on their return until maturity. Moreover, no state and local income taxes are assessed on interest earned on this or any other type of federal government debt security.

A number of other types of securities also compete in the short-term market. Virtually all of these (Treasury bills, bankers' acceptances, Eurodollar deposits, commercial paper, and short-term municipals) are available only in large denominations. Moreover, unlike savings bonds, they do not provide an early redemption option. The owner must either hold such securities until their maturity or sell them in the marketplace. Such a sale will usually require the payment of a commission to the agent (broker) handling the sale. Moreover, as with any publicly traded security, the sale price may differ somewhat from the purchase price. The prices of such securities, however, seldom differ greatly from their cost. Their maturity and redemption at face value is always relatively close so that short-term debt securities almost always sell for a price that is relatively close to both what was paid for them and their value at redemption.

In summary, short-term debt securities generally offer a very secure (often government-guaranteed) return. Savings accounts are highly liquid whereas savings certificates and money market instruments are somewhat less so, depending on maturity. Marketing these securities is seldom difficult or costly. Indeed, some issuers allow redemption prior to maturity. Little or no time commitment or special expertise is required to purchase or manage portfolios of many types of short-term debt securities. On the other hand, interest income from most of these investments is fully taxable. Moreover, the returns are often below those available on less liquid investments, and only the high-denomination ($10,000–$100,000) securities offer the highest short-term returns.

Bonds and Similar Long-Term Debt Instruments

Bonds are obligations to pay interest periodically and principal at the end of a specified period. The issuer's "guarantee" makes most bonds less risky than most stocks. Corporate bonds are at least as secure as the financial conditions of the issuing company. Similarly, extensive taxing power minimizes the default risk on federal and many state and local government bonds. Not all of the cities and smaller governmental units that issue bonds are in strong financial condition, however.

Bond investors face two types of risk: default and interest rate. An issuer failing to fulfill (defaulting on) its interest and/or principal obligation risks bankruptcy and possibly liquidation. Relatively few bonds default, and those that have were almost always rated as speculative prior to their default. Thus one can largely avoid default risk by investing only in nonspeculative bonds. Even in a default, however, the bondholder will often receive a portion of the promised principal and accrued interest. Moreover, the promised return on a bond tends to rise with its perceived risk.

The possibility of an adverse interest rate move is a major risk facing long-term bond investors. As market interest rates rise, the price of bonds (which yield a fixed dollar amount) decline. A bond with a market price below its purchase price does promise to repay its full face value at maturity. A hold-to-maturity strategy, however, misses out on the higher market yields that become available when rates rise. The gain from a favorable interest rate move, on the other hand, may be limited by the call feature. Callable bonds permit the issuer to repurchase its issues prior to maturity usually for slightly more than their face value.

A bond's vulnerability to interest rate fluctuations varies directly with its maturity. The prices of debt instruments that will soon be redeemed at their face values are unlikely to fluctuate greatly. While shorter term debt instruments are less sensitive to adverse interest rate moves, their yields are often below those on longer term bonds.

Corporate bonds are issued at $1,000 face values (market prices are typically $600 to $1,200). Bond prices are generally quoted in percentages of 100. Thus a bond selling at 90 (points) is priced at $900. Bond commissions are generally set at or about $5 per bond with a $50 minimum (ten bonds). A minimum of five (some would say 15) different companies' bonds is required for effective diversification. Thus a diversified portfolio could easily require $50,000 (five different positions of ten $1,000 bonds each) or more. Such a minimum sum puts serious bond investing beyond the reach of small investors.

In summary, most bonds are riskier and less liquid than most short-term debt securities but are typically less risky and more liquid than most equity instruments. Individual bonds differ substantially in risk, yield, and liquidity, however. Because U.S. government bonds have very low default risks, their yields are almost always below those of similar-maturity corporates. Moreover, corporate bond yields vary appreciably with their respective risks. Short-term bonds are more liquid than longer term issues. Even long-term governments are subject to considerable interest rate risk. Bonds of well-known issuers are generally quite marketable whereas those of small corporations and governmental units often trade in rather thin markets. Inexperienced investors can use bond ratings to help them select bonds matching their own risk preferences. Relatively little time or effort is required to manage most bond portfolios. Table 2.1 lists the principal types of short- and long-term debt securities.

EQUITY INSTRUMENTS

As previously mentioned, equity securities represent partial ownership in an asset such as a corporation. The owners have a residual claim on its assets and earnings. Equity-related assets include publicly traded common stock, preferred stock, options, convertibles, and mutual funds as well as ownership positions in small firms and venture capital investments. Each of these investments represents direct or indirect ownership in a profit-seeking enterprise. Equityholders' claims are junior

TABLE 2.1 Types of Debt Securities

	Short-Term
Securities Available to Small Investors	Deposits in Banks and Thrift Institutions
	Money Market Mutual Funds
	Money Market Accounts
	U.S. Savings Bonds
Money Market Securities (available in large denominations that appeal primarily to large investors):	T-Bills
	Bankers' Acceptances
	Eurodollars
	Commercial Paper
	Short-Term Municipals

Long-Term

Corporate Bonds
Federal Government Notes and Bonds
State and Local Bonds (Municipals)

to those of all debtors but encompass all residual value and income in excess of the claims of the senior securities.

Common Stock

By far the most important type of equity-related security is common stock. Approximately 47 million U.S. investors own stock directly while many more participate indirectly in the stock market. Such vehicles as mutual funds, trust funds, insurance company portfolios, and the invested reserves of pension funds all provide indirect access.

As the residual owners, shareholders are paid dividends out of their firm's profits. The portion of profits not paid out (retained earnings) is reinvested in the company, thereby helping it grow. Growth in sales, assets, and particularly profits should lead to a higher overall value for the firm. The benefit of any appreciation in the firm's value accrues to its owners, the stockholders.

A company's stockholders theoretically control it by electing its board of directors. The board in turn selects upper level management and makes major policy decisions. Most stock ownership groups are, however, widely dispersed and unorganized. Existing management generally fills the resulting power vacuum by nominating and electing friendly slates of directors.

In general, stock returns compare favorably with those of most bonds and depository accounts. On the other hand, returns on particular stocks over particular periods have differed greatly from the average. Furthermore, the returns on most stocks were well below these long-term averages during much of the 1960s and 1970s (see Tables 2.3 and 2.4 later in the chapter). Deciding which stocks to buy and when to trade are quite difficult tasks. Many books have been written on the subject and no doubt many, many more will be written. "Playing" the stock market is and always will be a very challenging "game."

Dividends are not assured and common stock never matures. Thus shareholders are particularly dependent on their firm's future profitability and market acceptance. Investors whose holdings reduce or eliminate their dividends are likely also to see a dramatic decline in the values of their stocks. Bond prices generally fluctuate much less than stock prices. Moreover, their promised interest must be paid regardless of the firm's profit picture. Thus bonds almost always have less downside risk than the stocks of the same or similar-risk firms.

Stocks can be bought and sold effectively in increments of as little as a few thousand dollars. Thus the relatively low minimum cost of a stock portfolio makes stocks relatively accessible to small investors. Commissions, however, are disproportionately high on very small transactions (less than about $1,000 and/or less than 100 shares). The average (median) stockholder's portfolio was worth around $6,200 in 1985.

In summary, common stock offers somewhat higher but more risky expected returns than bonds. Stocks are not very liquid but those of most large and medium-sized firms are quite marketable. Small investors can begin assembling a stock portfolio with relatively modest sums. Informed stock selection requires considerable skill and time, however.

Preferred Stock

Preferred stocks vary greatly in risk but, as a class, tend to be more risky than most types of debt securities. While also a form of ownership, preferred stock is generally less risky than common stock. Common dividends may be paid only after the preferred dividend requirement is satisfied. Unpaid back dividends (arrearage) on cumulative preferred shares must be made up before common dividends may resume. Moreover, in any reorganization of the company the preferred shareholders must be paid the liquidation value of their stock before common stockholders receive anything. While preferred is senior to common, bondholders are assured of interest income and principal payments before preferred stockholders receive any dividends or liquidation payments.

Preferred dividend yields are usually below the average long-term total return (dividend plus capital gains) on common stocks. As relatively fixed income securities, preferreds are subject to the same type of interest rate risk as bonds. Moreover, most preferred shares have relatively little long-term appreciation potential. The preferred of a weak company may, however, be riskier and have a higher expected yield than the common of a stronger company. The prices of preferreds vary inversely with interest rates. While dividends paid to individuals are fully taxed, only 20% of those paid to corporations are subject to federal tax. This special tax treatment is a particularly attractive feature for preferreds when dividends constitute most of the return. Like common, preferred stock is not particularly liquid although it is generally marketable. Assembling a diversified portfolio of preferreds requires a modest amount of time, funds, and effort.

Small Firm Ownership

Most people who invest in companies hold very small stakes in relatively large firms. Others, however, hold a relatively large stake in a small company. The firm may be organized as a sole proprietorship, partnership, or closely held corporation. Those who take an active role in their enterprise are much more involved in the management side of the business than the investment side. This management commitment may cut deeply into the time for other activities. Moreover, joint ownership can lead to troublesome policy disputes, and nonexpert part-time owner–managers may be at a disadvantage relative to specialist–competitors. Finally, valuing and ultimately selling a small business can be especially difficult.

Silent-partner owners have different problems. A suitable manager may be difficult to find. Managers may misuse their positions (legally or illegally) and, unless given a share in the firm's profits, may have less incentive than the owners to operate the business profitably. Moreover, the owners are personally liable for the unpaid debts of a partnership or sole proprietorship, and many creditors require the owners of a small corporation to cosign its loans.

Limited Partnerships and Master Limited Partnerships

Most businesses are organized as partnerships or corporations. The corporate form provides limited liability for owners (shareholders) but its income is first taxed at the corporate level and its shareholders are taxed again on their income (dividends) from the firm.

Unlike that of a corporation, the income of a partnership is taxed only once. Partnership profits, whether distributed or retained by the partnership, are treated for tax purposes as the imputed income of the partners. Partners are, however, individually and collectively liable for all of the partnership's obligations. Limited partnerships provide an alternative way of organizing business enterprises. They combine the benefits of a corporation's limited liability with the single taxation advantage of a partnership. A single general partner, who is usually the organizer, does have unlimited liability. The limited partners, however, are not liable for the partnership's debts and obligations beyond their initial capital contribution. Most limited partnerships do have one major drawback. Because they are relatively small, their ownership units trade in very thin markets. The master limited partnership (MLP) is designed to overcome this drawback. Most MLPs are relatively large (compared to limited partnerships). Their ownership units are designed to trade actively in the same types of markets as stock.

MLPs have generally been organized around oil and gas holdings. Others are designed for real estate. Mesa Limited Partners (oil and gas) is one of the best known of the MLPs. Investing in MLPs involves many of the same advantages and disadvantages as investing in common stock. Note, however, that the stated current yields on MLPs are often inflated and unsustainable. The managers of these MLPs are depleting assets to make what appear to be attractive payouts. Moreover, the tax advantages of MLPs may well be limited by future Congressional action. No doubt if the Treasury begins to lose large amounts of revenue from corporations reorganizing themselves as MLPs, Congress will be asked to act.

Venture Capital

Venture capitalists provide risk capital to otherwise undercapitalized companies that they believe have attractive growth prospects. In exchange, the venture capitalist receives a ground-floor equity position in what may turn out to be a highly lucrative venture. For example, Georges Doriot invested $70,000 of the American Research and Development's (ARD) money into what eventually grew into several hundred million dollars worth of Digital Equipment common stock when Textron acquired ARD in 1972.[1]

Venture capital may be used to help fund both start-up firms and undercapitalized going concerns. Most types of direct venture capital investing are open only to institutions and wealthy individuals. New ventures generally require a minimum of $500,000 or more. Investors of more modest means can, however, participate indirectly through public venture capital funds, venture capital limited partnerships, venture capital clubs, mutual funds that specialize in venturing, small business investment companies (SBICs) geared toward venture capital investing, newly public companies needing venture capital, commercial banks with venture capital components, and private venture capital funds. Regardless of how investors participate, they will find venture capital to be a risky business. Martin and Petty, however, found that publicly traded venture capital companies tended to outperform the average market performance as indicated by the S&P 500.[2] Thus the potential rewards may justify the risk.

Options: Calls, Puts, Warrants, and Rights

Most options give the holder the right to acquire or dispose of an equity-related security. The owner of a call contract has an option to buy something. The call writer sells the call buyer the right (but not the obligation) to purchase an investment asset, such as 100 shares of a particular stock. The contract will specify the price (called the striking price) at which, and the period over which, the call may be exercised. Similarly, a put is a sell-option contract for a particular security, price, quantity, and period. Exercising the option privilege is solely at the owner's (not the seller's) discretion. The option buyer and option writer in effect have a wager on what will happen to the price of the security on which the option is written. For example, the call buyer will earn a profit if the price of the associated asset rises sufficiently. Call writers, in contrast, usually profit if the relevant price does not rise to or much above the exercise level. In that case they can generally earn the option premium without having to deliver the stock or other optioned asset.

Suppose an investor pays $200 for an option to buy 100 shares of stock at 20 ($20 per share). If the stock's price subsequently rises to 30, the investor can exercise the option (buy the stock) at 20 and then immediately turn around and sell that same stock at 30. Such a set of transactions would yield a profit of $800 (before commissions) compared with an initial cost of $200 for the call. A similar profit would be made on $200 invested in a put if the price subsequently fell from 20 to 10. The same $200 could, in contrast, have only purchased 10 shares at 20 producing $100 gain for a 10-point price rise. An adverse stock price move can, however, lead to a total loss for the optionholder. The shareholder's potential loss is, in percentage terms, generally much less.

Standardized option trading began with the 1973 opening of the Chicago Board Option Exchange (CBOE) and soon spread to other exchanges. Options are now listed on a large number of different stocks. Other options are listed on stock indexes and commodities futures contracts. Most options have relatively short lives (nine months or less) and their prices are dominated by random market fluctuations. Accordingly, option trading is largely the preserve of relatively sophisticated investors. It is an investment area that is ill-suited to novice investors.

Warrants and rights are traded in the same markets that trade the stocks that underlie them. Warrants, like calls, permit their owner to purchase a particular stock at a prespecified price over a prespecified period. Unlike calls, warrants are generally exercisable for relatively long periods such as several years. Furthermore, warrants are issued by the company whose stock underlies the warrant. If the warrant is exercised, the issuing company simply creates more shares. In contrast, existing shares are used to satisfy the exercise of a call. Thus warrants are company-issued securities whose exercise results in additional shares and generates cash for the issuer. Calls are contracts between individual investors that do not involve the underlying company.

Rights, like warrants, are company-issued options to buy stock. Rights differ from warrants in two ways. First, rights are issued for very short-run periods. They expire in a few weeks or at most a few months from the time of their issue. Also rights are generally exercisable at a price that is substantially less than the current market price of the stock. The issuer sets a low enough price to make exercise attractive. Thus most rights are exercised while warrant exercise is more uncertain. For example, a right might allow an investor to buy stock at 40 when the market price is 45. Failure to exercise or sell such rights is like throwing away $5 times the number of rights. Rights are normally issued to existing shareholders on the basis of their current holdings. Thus shareholders might receive one right for each 20 shares that they owned.

Option prices tend to move in the same direction as the underlying common stock but with a considerably greater magnitude. As a result, options are generally considered relatively risky securities. On the other hand, option writing may reduce a portfolio's risk.

In summary, most listed options are quite marketable whereas unlisted options are generally traded in thin markets. Most types of option trading are relatively risky. At least as much expertise and time are required for profitable option trading as for trading common stock.

Convertible Bonds

Convertible bonds are debt securities that can be exchanged for stock of the issuing company at a preassigned ratio. While technically a debt instrument, their conversion feature gives convertibles an equity-related component. They tend to trade in sympathy with their underlying stock. Such securities offer a compromise between the relatively assured income of bonds and the speculative appeal of stock. Convertible prices tend to rise with their conversion values but are somewhat insulated from price falls by their values as income securities. Convertibles generally sell for more than their conversion value. Accordingly, direct stock ownership is normally more profitable in a rising market. Moreover, their conversion feature allows convertibles to be sold for lower yields than otherwise-similar nonconvertible bonds. Thus straight bonds are generally more attractive in declining markets.

Convertible bonds tend to be less risky than common stock but somewhat more risky than straight bonds. Their liquidity, marketability, and minimum investment requirements are similar to those of straight bonds. Convertibles require an amount of expertise and time similar to that required by common stocks.

Mutual Funds and Closed-End Investment Companies

Many investors have neither the time nor the inclination to manage and monitor their investments carefully. Such investors can leave most of this work to a mutual fund. The fund's shares represent proportional ownership of its managed investment portfolio. Funds pool the resources of many small investors. Their fundholders' money is used to assemble and manage a diversified portfolio of investments. Funds may invest in a large variety of types of investments. Most funds, however, work with portfolios of debt or equity securities. Mutual funds agree to redeem their shares at their net asset values (NAVs). A fund's NAV equals the market value of its portfolio divided by the number of its outstanding shares.

Some mutual funds (load funds) are sold by agents who receive a fee (typically 8.5% of the purchase price). No-load funds, in contrast, sell and redeem their shares through the mail, thereby eliminating the need for a sales force and load fee. No-load fund portfolios generally offer about the same average risk-adjusted returns on their portfolios as those of load funds.

Mutual funds are classified as open-end investment companies. New shares of such funds will be issued and sold to the public if demand is sufficient. Alternatively, the fund will redeem outstanding shares if its fundholders so request. Closed-end investment companies, in contrast, do not either issue additional shares or redeem them on demand. The number of outstanding shares of such a closed-end fund is established at the founding of the fund and remains relatively constant through time. These shares are usually listed on an exchange, although some are traded off the exchanges in the so-called over-the-counter market. (The operations of exchanges and the over-the-counter market are discussed in the next chapter.) Unlike mutual funds, closed-end share prices can vary substantially from their net asset values.

Unit investment trusts and variable annuities are additional types of pooled portfolio arrangements. Unit investment trusts generally hold unmanaged portfolios. Variable annuities are much like mutual funds but organized and managed by insurance companies.

The investment goals and portfolio compositions of mutual funds differ widely. Portfolios may be made up of low-risk or speculative bonds or stocks, tax-exempt securities, short-term highly liquid securities, combinations of stocks and bonds, and so on. Still other mutual funds invest in such assets as options, commodities, and collectibles. Thus mutual fund investors can choose from a wide array of characteristics. Average mutual fund performance does not differ appreciably from the average market performance, however.

In summary, mutual fund risks, liquidities, and tax treatments vary greatly. One can invest as little as $500 or $1,000 in a mutual fund. Most mutual funds are well diversified and as such are considerably less risky than most individual common stocks or small portfolios consisting of a few different stocks. Individuals

TABLE 2.2 Equity-Related Securities

Direct Ownership of a Company	
Common Stock	Residual ownership of corporations
Preferred Stock	Preferred to common in dividends and liquidation
Small Firm Ownership	May be organized as corporation, partnership, or sole proprietorship
Master Limited Partnerships	Combine the tax advantage of a partnership with the limited liability and ease of trading of a corporation
Venture Capital	Risk capital provided to start-up companies
Options	
Call	Private option-to-buy contract
Put	Private option-to-sell contract
Warrant	Company-issued buy option
Right	Short-term company-issued option to buy
Indirect Equity Ownerships	
Convertible Bonds	Debt securities that may be exchanged for a prespecified amount of stock
Mutual Funds and Closed-End Investment Companies, Unit Investment Trusts, and Variable Annuities	Pooled portfolios of securities and other types of investments

with sufficient funds can, however, assemble their own diversified portfolios. No-load funds are at least as liquid and marketable as individual common stocks. Load funds are costly to trade, however. While mutual funds require less expertise and time commitment than individually managed portfolios, selecting a suitable fund does require some effort. Table 2.2 summarizes the various types of equity-related investments.

OTHER INVESTMENTS

We have already discussed debt and equity securities. Two other important investment types (in dollar value outstanding and traded) remain to be considered: real estate and commodity futures contracts. Other somewhat less important topics discussed in this section include collectibles, noncollectibles, and Ponzi schemes.

The Shift toward Other Investments

Rather poor stock and bond performance during the 1970s heightened interest in other types of investments (Table 2.3). By 1987, however, the relative performances had changed appreciably (Table 2.4). The 1970–1980 rankings differed substantially from those for the period 1980–1985. Similarly, the one-year performance differed markedly for 1986 and 1987. For example, stocks were at the bottom for

TABLE 2.3 Performance of Stocks, Bonds, and Other Types of Investments over a Long Period

One-Year Rankings, 1985 vs. 1984

	This Year (Period Ended June 1, 1985)		Last Year Period Ended June 1, 1984)	
	Return	Rank	Return	Rank
Bonds	42.9%	1	−7.2%	14
Stocks	28.7	2	−1.2	9
Old Masters(a)	13.6	3	14.3	1
U.S. Coins	11.5	4	7.4	3
Treasury Bills	9.5	5	9.4	2
Chinese Ceramics(a)	5.9	6	3.0	6
CPI	3.7	7	4.6	5
Housing	2.5	8	5.5	4
Diamonds	0.0	9	0.0	7
Oil(b)	−4.5	10	−2.4	10
Stamps	−9.6	11	−4.0	13
U.S. Farmland	−10.0	12	−0.7	8
Foreign Exchange	−11.3	13	−3.0	11
Gold	−20.3	14	−4.0	12
Silver	−34.3	15	−25.2	15

a-Source: Sotheby's. b-Reflects revision in oil index.

Compounded Annual Rates of Return

	15 Years	Rank	10 Years	Rank	5 Years	Rank
Oil(a)	19.7%	1	8.0%	9	−5.4%	12
U.S. Coins	17.7	2	20.4	1	0.1	9
Gold	15.5	3	6.9	13	−11.0	14
Chinese Ceramics(b)	14.3	4	17.1	2	1.0	8
Stamps	14.1	5	14.5	3	0.1	10
Diamonds	10.4	6	9.5	7	1.2	7
Old Masters(b)	9.1	7	10.7	4	1.5	6
Treasury Bills	9.1	8	10.0	6	12.0	3
Bonds	8.7	9	9.3	8	13.2	2
Silver	8.7	10	3.5	14	−15.9	15
Stocks	8.5	11	10.4	5	15.2	1
U.S. Farmland	8.5	12	6.9	12	−1.7	11
Housing	8.2	13	7.9	10	4.3	5
CPI	7.1	14	7.3	11	5.7	4
Foreign Exchange	2.0	15	−0.6	15	−7.9	13

a-Reflects revision in oil index. b-Source: Sotheby's. All returns are for the period ended June 1, 1985, based on latest available data.

A Tale of Two Decades

Compound Annual Rates of Return

June 1970 to June 1980	Return	Rank	June 1980 to June 1985	Return	Rank
Oil(a)	34.7%	1	Stocks	15.2%	1
Gold	31.6	2	Bonds	13.2	2
U.S. Coins	27.7	3	Treasury Bills	12.0	3
Silver	23.7	4	CPI	5.7	4
Stamps	21.8	5	Housing	4.3	5
Chinese Ceramics(b)	21.6	6	Old Masters(a)	1.5	6
Diamonds	15.3	7	Diamonds	1.2	7
U.S. Farmland	14.0	8	Chinese Ceramics(a)	1.0	8
Old Masters(b)	13.1	9	U.S. Coins	0.1	9
Housing	10.2	10	Stamps	0.1	10
CPI	7.7	11	U.S. Farmland	−1.7	11
Treasury Bills	7.7	12	Oil(a)	−5.4	12
Foreign Exchange	7.3	13	Foreign Exchange	−7.9	13
Bonds	6.6	14	Gold	−11.0	14
Stocks	6.1	15	Silver	−15.9	15

ªReflects revision in oil index. ªSource: Sotheby's. All returns are for the period ended June 1, 1985, based on latest available data.

Source: R. Schatz, "Soft Assets Lick Hard Assets," *Barron's*, June 17, 1985, p. 30. Reprinted by permission, © Dow Jones & Company, Inc. All rights reserved.

TABLE 2.4   Changes in Relative Performances of Stocks, Bonds, and Other Types of Investments

One-Year Rankings, 1987 vs. 1986				Compounded Annual Rates of Return					
	This Year		Last Year						
	Rank	Return	Rank	Return		15 Years	Rank 10 Years	Rank 5 Years	Rank
Silver	1	39.8%	14	-15.5%	U.S. Coins	18.8%	1 16.3%	1 11.4%	3
Gold	2	29.1	5	9.2	Oil	13.9	2 3.0	13 -11.8	14
Oil	3	27.4	15	-48.8	U.S. Stamps	13.6	3 11.8	3 -1.3	12
Foreign Exchange	4	25.0	.1	35.0	Gold	11.9	4 9.2	8 6.8	7
Stocks	5	20.6	2	34.8	Silver	10.3	5 9.7	6 4.0	9
U.S. Coins	6	10.7	7	7.2	Treasury Bills	9.2	6 10.2	5 8.5	6
Old Masters	7	8.6	10	4.8	Old Masters	9.2	7 9.7	6 9.5	5
Diamonds	8	7.0	6	7.5	Stocks	8.6	8 13.9	2 24.1	1
Housing	9	6.8	8	7.2	Bonds	8.7	9 9.7	7 19.7	2
Chinese Ceramics	10	6.7	12	1.5	Chinese Ceramics	8.3	10 11.3	4 3.4	11
Treasury Bills	11	5.7	9	7.1	Housing	8.2	11 7.4	10 4.8	8
Bonds	12	5.7	3	26.0	Consumer Price Index	6.9	12 6.5	11 3.5	10
Consumer Price Index	**13**	**3.8**	**11**	**1.5**	U.S. Farmland	6.3	13 1.5	14 -7.8	13
U.S. Stamps	14	0.5	4	14.5	Foreign Exchange	4.6	14 4.1	12 6.8	7
U.S. Farmland	15	-7.9	13	-12.2	Diamonds	4.1	15 8.9	9 10.2	4
Years end June 1.									

Source: J. Palmer, "Hard Assets or Soft?", *Barron's*, June 15, 1987, p. 15. Reprinted by permission, © Dow Jones & Company, Inc. All rights reserved.

the 1970–1980 period, at the top for 1980–1985, ranked fifth for 1986, and second in 1987. For the same time periods silver was ranked fourth, 15th, 14th, and first. Clearly, different types of investments have exhibited very different types of returns over time.

Real Estate

Many fortunes have been built from small initial investments in real estate. Real estate investing offers the potential of large percentage profits as well as a number of tax advantages. On the other hand, the life savings of many small investors have been wiped out by the Florida land boom–bust in the 1920s and other less spectacular market collapses.

Real estate investors have good reasons to be cautious. First, the more leverage used to finance real estate purchases, the greater the risk is. Yet one of the primary attractions of real estate is the ability to finance a large percentage of the price. Second, the one-of-a-kind nature of individual real estate investments makes such properties relatively difficult and costly to buy and sell. Having to sell real estate on short notice can result in a substantial sacrifice. Third, determining the value of a prospective real estate investment requires considerable expertise. Fourth, managing improved property is a time-consuming task. Fifth, real estate commissions are considerably higher than those of securities. Thus real estate is more difficult, time consuming and costly to buy and sell. Sixth, most real estate purchases require a relatively large initial investment (down payment). Finally, those who move often or travel frequently may have difficulty properly overseeing their property.

In summary, real estate may offer attractive returns to investors with the required talents, but the securities markets demand less time and expertise and

are generally less risky. The stock of real estate related
:ing compromise, however. Real estate investment trusts
way of participating. Like MLPs, REITs offer the tax
and the limited liabilities and ease of trading of the
e to qualify as REITs, however, they must meet rather
iust derive almost all of their income from real estate
il estate and they must pay out at least 95% of that

Contracts

s represent another major investment area. Commod-
buy and sell contracts for future delivery of a pre-
mmodity—such as so many ounces of silver, bushels
lars worth of T-bills. Standardized commodities con-
ous commodity exchanges. To execute a trade, com-
re required only to deposit between 5% and 15% of
sult, price fluctuations are magnified 8 to 20 times.
d at $100,000 might require a 10% margin ($10,000
icrease in the contract's value (to $120,000) would
less commissions), or 200% of the original $10,000
ontract's price would, however, wipe out the original

iire individuals seeking to open a commodity trading
ly large beginning balance and to have a substantial
ons on commodity trades are only a tiny fraction of

its generally involves outguessing the commodity
ier conditions, government intervention, consumer
iy other factors that may influence the underlying
mand. Thus its risky nature and the need for a very
special understanding of a complex market makes commodity speculation a very
tough challenge for most individual investors. Some traders, however, use the
commodity futures markets to hedge their risks. For example, a farmer might sell
bean futures and in effect tie down a price for his or her expected soybean harvest.
Others may assemble relatively complicated but lower risk combination positions
that depend upon relative price movements (straddles).

In summary, commodity speculation is generally quite risky. Futures contracts
are marketable but illiquid. Substantial expertise, time, and resources are required.
Still, some individual investors find the fast-paced action and potential for rapid
riches (coupled with at least as great a potential for disaster) very appealing.

Collectibles

Although a relatively minor investment medium, collectibles have grown substantially in popularity in recent years. As an indication of their importance, both

TABLE 2.5a   The Sotheby Index, 1975–1983

Category	Weights	1975	1976	1977	1978	1979	1980	1981	1982	1983	1984
Old Master Paintings	17	100	105	131	173	224	255	199	199	217	242
19th Century European Paintings	12	100	99	118	160	215	225	176	183	197	209
Impressionist & Post-Impressionist Paintings	18	100	107	114	133	175	206	239	255	298	317
Modern Paintings (1900–1950)	10	100	105	108	132	178	204	232	245	275	301
American Paintings (1800–pre-WW II)	3	100	129	171	255	315	350	424	459	501	589
Continental Ceramics	3	100	121	154	213	261	336	299	266	272	284
Chinese Ceramics	10	100	159	181	241	353	462	459	460	445	459
English Silver	5	100	89	95	124	165	205	160	183	219	237
Continental Silver	5	100	89	92	113	146	179	143	134	156	161
American Furniture	3	100	109	120	134	150	172	209	213	239	241
Continental Furniture	7	100	104	121	148	197	232	218	234	254	270
English Furniture	7	100	125	156	195	244	256	270	263	309	342
AGGREGATE		100	111	128	164	217	253	244	251	275	295

The figures are based on a year ending September 1975 = 100.

Source: Sotheby Parke Bernet as reported in various issues of *Barron's* © 1984 Sotheby Parke Bernet Inc. Reprinted with permission. (The dates reflected in the Sotheby Index are based on results of auction sales by affiliated companies of the Sotheby Park Bernet Group and other information deemed relevant by Sotheby's. Sotheby's does not warrant the accuracy of the data reflected therein. Nothing in the commentary furnished by Sotheby's nor any of Sotheby's Indices is intended or should be relied upon as investment advice or as a prediction, warranty or guaranty as to future performance or otherwise. All individual prices quoted in this review are aggregate prices, inclusive of the buyer's premium.)

Barron's and *Forbes* now report the Sotheby Index of prices on a variety of types of art, ceramic, silver, and furniture collectibles (Tables 2.5a and 2.5b).

A bewildering assortment of items are now considered collectibles. Investments in such assets are usually relatively illiquid and very speculative. Collectibles are generally sold at a high markup, subject to a substantial fraud risk, and involve all of the uncertainties present in the more traditional types of investing. Nonetheless success stories abound. Investors should enter the collectibles market very slowly (if at all), so that their initial mistakes are made with relatively small sums.

Coins, stamps, art, and antiques have long been of interest to collectors. For almost as long, investors have sought to profit from the price appreciation that must "certainly" follow the "inevitable" growth of the hobby. As prices have risen for established collectibles, many newer hobbies have sprung up to take advantage of the lower prices on what had until recently been thought of as out-of-date junk. Among the more unusual collectibles that have been recently recognized are manhole covers and the insulators off old telephone poles.

New collectible areas seem to go through a relatively predictable cycle. First, everything is very cheap and most collectors are amateur hobbyists. As time passes the hobby becomes more commercial. The entry of professional dealers and serious investors causes prices to rise. For a while all is well as increased interest raises the value of everyone's material. New investors, attracted by the sharp increase in values, drive prices still higher. Eventually, however, the arrival of unscrupulous promoters increases the likelihood of fraud, unconscionable markups, and unfairly graded material. Many unaware novices are taken in by these people. Once they discover what has been done to them, their interest in the hobby is likely to wane.

TABLE 2.5b Sotheby's Art Index, 1982–1988

Sotheby's Art Market Trends

Index sectors	March 1988	One month ago	One year ago	Two years ago	Five years ago	One month % change	One year % change	Two year % change	Five years % change	Five years average annual % change
Old Master paintings	373	373	329	303	212	nil	+ 13.4	+ 23.1	+ 75.9	+ 12.0
19th C. Euro. paintings	333	333	284	249	185	nil	+ 17.3	+ 33.7	+ 80.0	+ 12.5
Impressionist & Post-impressionist art	723	723	521	380	267	nil	+ 38.8	+ 90.3	+ 170.8	+ 22.0
Modern paintings (1900-1950)	757	757	544	364	245	nil	+ 39.2	+ 108.0	+ 209.0	+ 25.3
Contemporary art (1945 onward)	609	609	551	497	342	nil	+ 10.5	+ 22.5	+ 78.1	+ 12.2
American paintings (1800–pre-WWII)	871	871	698	667	452	nil	+ 24.8	+ 30.6	+ 92.7	+ 14.0
Continental ceramics	407	407	320	284	266	nil	+ 27.2	+ 43.3	+ 53.0	+ 8.9
Chinese ceramics	581	581	526	486	440	nil	+ 10.5	+ 19.5	+ 32.0	+ 5.7
English silver	388	388	343	314	209	nil	+ 13.1	+ 23.6	+ 85.8	+ 13.2
Continental silver	220	220	201	181	139	nil	+ 9.5	+ 21.5	+ 58.3	+ 9.6
American furniture	469	469	451	333	239	nil	+ 4.0	+ 40.8	+ 96.2	+ 14.4
French & Continental furniture	324	324	299	273	239	nil	+ 8.4	+ 18.7	+ 35.6	+ 6.3
English furniture	657	657	523	419	282	nil	+ 25.6	+ 56.8	+ 133.0	+ 18.4
Aggregate index*	517	517	420	347	257	nil	+ 23.1	+ 49.7	+ 101.2	+ 15.0

Basis: 1975 = 100 ($).   ©Sotheby's 1988
*Contemporary art was added to the Art Index in September 1987. The aggregate index excludes this category prior to that date.
Sotheby's Art Market Trends reflect subjective analyses and opinions of Sotheby's art experts, based on auction sales and other information deemed relevant. Nothing in Sotheby's Art Market Trends is intended as investment advice or as a prediction or guarantee of future performance or otherwise.

Monthly highlights

Celebrity-linked auctions dominated the international art auction world last month, notably a sale of rock 'n' roll memorabilia in London, the contents of Liberace's numerous homes auctioned in Los Angeles and the extensive collection of Andy Warhol in New York.

Warhol's art collection, over 10,000 diverse items, ranged from serious items to "collectible" cookie jars. An untitled 1967 blackboard painting by Cy Twombly achieved $990,000, and a drawing of Andy Warhol by David Hockney fetched $330,000. A set of two cookie jars and a salt-and-pepper shaker together fetched $23,100. The total reached $25.3 million, nearly double its estimate.

Interest in rock 'n' roll was such that a satellite link was set up between England and Japan to enable collectors assembled in one of Tokyo's leading department stores to bid directly. They acquired 19 lots, of which the top price was $6,800 paid for an original manuscript by Paul McCartney. The Liberace collection met expectations when it raised over $2 million, with all 2,365 lots selling.

As for Old Master paintings, a sale in Paris provided a rare glimpse of corporate buying; a subsidiary of a Milanese bank paid $508,000 (in line with expectations) for a recently discovered Veronese. In Milan a 9-foot-wide painting of the Last Supper attributed to Giovanni Agostino da Lodi sold to a local collector for $664,000, a price all the more significant given that the painting has been a listed national treasure since the beginning of the century and so couldn't leave the country. Had export been possible, the price could have gone even higher.

New York was also the site for English silver auctions. As is frequently the case, dealers acquired the leading pieces. A London dealer bought the top lot, a Charles II silver ewer, for $89,100, over double the estimate.

Source: *Forbes*, May 30, 1988, p. 304. Reprinted by permission, © Forbes Inc.

After those most likely to enter the collectible areas have been attracted, the hobby's growth rate slows. Some collectors become bored and drop out. Higher prices further discourage potential interest. Without growing numbers of hobbyists, prices soften. Some who entered the hobby for its profit potential may try to sell. They soon find that buying interest will only absorb their collections at appreciably lower prices. Declining prices may lead others to sell or stop buying. The area may even experience a temporary panic.

Toy collecting is an example of a relatively young hobby. The nostalgia fad has greatly increased interest in old toys. Model trains of the 1920s and 1930s have long been collected but now even relatively recent windup toys of the 1950s are collectible. Many an attic or cellar contains a gold mine of old toys. No doubt many unaware souls can be persuaded to part with such junk for a song. This too is a common experience for a young hobby. The 1976 bicentennial gave 19th century Americana collecting a big boost. With collectibles from the 18th century garnering ever higher prices, interest inevitably shifted forward—indeed flea markets abound with material from the first half of this century. Thus the pinball machines, juke boxes, and neon signs of the 1960s and 1970s are becoming collectors' items.

Another type of collectible is a subject close to the heart of many people: automobiles. Antique cars have long been collected, though many can remember when such items were available for next to nothing. More recently Classic cars of the 1920s and 1930s and even Milestone cars of the 1940s, 1950s, and 1960s have become collectible. Old cars are an expensive but interesting hobby. World War II aircraft are even more costly to collect.

Numerous other items are now collectibles. For example, popular articles have been written on each of the following: antique furniture, prints, young artists, literary collectibles, porcelain, oriental rugs, photographs, diamonds, Christmas plates, colored gems, old stock certificates, oriental art, antique maps, antique jewelry, autographs, musical instruments, credit cards, record albums, shotguns, tin cans, and even old clothes.

Selling is one of the most difficult aspects of investing in collectibles. Investors may of course use the same outlets to sell as were used to buy but this approach may not always be best. A set of guidelines adapted from a *Business Week* article on the subject is reproduced in Table 2.6.

Noncollectibles

Collectibles constitute one class of nontraditional investments. Additional types include Broadway shows, movies, California vineyards, discos, coal mines, computerized home delivery groceries, racehorses, baseball clubs, freight cars, and the list goes on and on. Some of these investment media may be worth pursuing but others should be avoided entirely. For example, Lloyd's of London takes on partners to bear its insurance risks. While the risk exposure is technically unlimited, the likelihood of losses beyond the initial investment is relatively small. This type of investment may offer those with substantial resources an attractive return. Moreover, only a letter of credit is required to back up the potential loss.

Many others have, however, been taken in by promoters of such "investments" as scotch whiskey and farm co-ops. The scotch whiskey warehouse receipts case

TABLE 2.6 How to Sell What You Have Collected

Item	Percent appreciation 1969–79	Selling advice
Americana (19th century paintings, furniture, folk art)	100 to 150%	Use regional and country auctions, paying a 10% to 25% commission. Breaking up sets can trim 20% or more from the total selling price.
Automobiles (antique and classic)	100 to 200	Use antique car dealers, selling on consignment for a 30% commission. Small pre-1920 cars and cars costing over $20,000 are hard to sell today.
Coins (government issue, collector quality)	200 to 400	Use a numismatic auction house, paying a 15% to 20% commission. Pre-1915 issues sell the best.
Commemorative coins and medals (private issue)	Appreciation in the intrinsic value of the metal but no gain in numismatic value	Try coin dealers, or advertising in newspapers or numismatic publications. But you will seldom get what you paid, and you may have to settle for the "melt" or intrinsic price of the metal.
Diamonds	100 to 400	Use jewelers of established reputation, trying an outright sale first, then consignment. But expect only 40% to 60% of the current retail price.
Fine jewelry	100 to 200	Use a reputable auctioneer, who will charge a 10% to 25% commission. But you will seldom get what you paid.
Prints	100 to 500	Art auctioneers in major cities run special print auctions. The commission is 10% to 25%.
Rare books	50 to 100	Use book auction houses, waiting for a sale fitting your item. The commission is 20%. For highest prices, sell in complete sets.
Rugs	150 to 200	Persian rug market is unsettled because of uncertainty over the supply of new rugs from Iran. Sell at rug auctions, setting a minimum bid 20% below the price you hope to get.
Stamps	250 for pre-1940 issues	Use a stamp dealer-auctioneer, paying 25% of the value for appraisal and 10% to 20% in commission. The market for pre-1940 issues is strong; the market for later issues is weak.
Western art	100 to 200— and more for top names	Use major auction houses, but wait for special sales of Western art. The commission is 20%. Inflated prices of a few years ago have sagged, and profits will be hard to come by.

TABLE 2.6   Continued

Item	Percent appreciation 1969–79	Selling advice
Works of young artists	0 to 500	Use a dealer in contemporary art, selling on consignment, with a 50% commission common. It's a long-shot market, and the work may take a long time to sell, if it sells at all.
Wine	200 and more, depending on vintage	Advertise for a private sale. The major auction is in London. You pay shipping and a 20% commission.

Source: Adapted from "How to Sell What You Have Collected," *Business Week*, June 11, 1979.

illustrates a familiar pattern. Investors are attracted to a potentially legitimate investment medium by a rapid price run-up. Soon, unscrupulous promoters are using (often exaggerated) stories of very attractive returns to push sales at inflated prices. By the time the uninformed investor is ready to sell, the promoters have long since departed for greener pastures. Reselling scotch whiskey warehouse receipts from this side of the Atlantic is not easy even in the best of times. The scenario for strategic metals investing is similar. The "New Farm Co-op" experience is even more distressing. The life savings of many were "invested" and lost because they did not believe that a proposed theme park to be called "Bible City" could be a fraud.

Dozens of similar examples of offbeat investments with disastrous results could be cited. Gross mismanagement, highly inflated prices, and totally unrealistic profit forecasts are all too common. Anyone considering a nontraditional investment outlet should exercise extreme caution. While most traditional investments (securities, real estate, and commodities) are risky, at least the investor has a better idea of past history and a modicum of regulatory protection. All too often investors in offbeat investments have almost no knowledge of the subject—a nearly certain recipe for disaster.

Ponzi Schemes

The Ponzi scheme is not a true investment but it is sold as one. Ponzis are a classic type of investment fraud. Prompters of Ponzi schemes attract purchasers by promising high "yields" that they secretly plan to finance from capital, at least as long as the money holds out. Such schemes are inverted pyramids that need ever larger new "investments" to pay returns on earlier "investments." Eventually not enough new money is brought in and the scheme collapses. Those holding such "investments" are left with little or nothing.

Investments in Perspective

One very offbeat investment area is in groups sponsoring searches for sunken treasures in the sea, as described in an article in *The Wall Street Journal.*

Despite Considerable Risk, Many Investors Sink Cash Into Hunts for Sunken Treasure

By JOSEPH PEREIRA
Staff Reporter of THE WALL STREET JOURNAL

When a friend suggested earlier this year that John Ropes invest in sunken-ship treasure hunts, he scoffed at the idea. "I don't know how anyone in their right mind could get involved in something that risky," Mr. Ropes, a 38-year-old Florida businessman, recalls saying.

A few days later, Mr. Ropes invested more than $25,000 in a limited partnership searching for gold that purportedly sank with the British luxury liner R.M.S. Republic 55 miles off Massachusetts' Nantucket Island in 1909. "Underwater treasure is adventure," he says, explaining why he changed his mind—without even reading the prospectus.

Dreaming of long-lost riches, thousands of investors are putting money into treasure hunts despite overwhelming odds against success. Although tens of millions of dollars have been spent on some 30 treasure hunts off American shores in the past five years, only one has recovered any substantial riches. "It's called gambling, and all the odds are stacked against you," says Charles Harper, associate regional administrator for the Securities and Exchange Commission in Miami. "The treasure hunt is today's siren song."

'No Treasure and No Hunt'

It may also be the latest occupation for some swindlers. "We're looking at blatant frauds where not only is there no treasure,

there is no hunt," says Lawrence Fuchs, Florida's deputy comptroller.

Five salvage companies, which have collected $1,000 to $10,000 from a total of 1,000 investors, are under investigation in Florida, and four more may soon be added to the list, Mr. Fuchs says. In addition, investigators are examining whether salvagers are inflating the values of potential discoveries, adequately informing investors of risks and backing claims with historical research.

Still, many investors are undeterred. "It beats talking about HMOs and malpractice with my colleagues," says Richard Brunelle, a 39-year-old Florida surgeon who has also invested $25,000 in the Republic search. "Besides, I made the 7 o'clock news with Dan Rather," when the salvage efforts were filmed recently.

Interest in treasure hunts has surged since 1985 when salvager Mel Fisher—following 20 years of futility—recovered a trove off Florida's coast that he estimates is worth $400 million. (Its commercial value has yet to be determined). New technology that permits searchers to scan ocean floors and lower robots to probe wrecks have also raised hopes.

Indeed, many salvagers have little trouble finding investors. To raise $5 million to search the wreckage of the S.S. Central America off South Carolina's coast, ocean engineer Thomas Thompson says he only had to approach 120 investors; 106 put money in the venture. The ship, a gold carrier, was destroyed by a hurricane in 1857. Investors put in money even though "they were told that there was only a 10% chance of finding the gold," Mr. Thompson says.

Investors haven't lost interest even though the 1986 tax act has limited the deduction of losses from passive activities such as limited partnerships. (Most treasure hunts are structured as limited partnerships.) Those losses may be deducted only against income from like investments and not from salary income or gains on investments in stocks and bonds.

Finding investors may be easy. But finding treasure isn't. Whether it is because the ships really weren't carrying riches or the salvagers can't find them, there is a litany of failures. The S.S. Central America's treasure hunters, using remote-control cameras, have taken 2,000 photos and hundreds of hours of video film footage, but there's been no sign of gold. Salvagers have spent $2 million looking for $500 million in gold that reportedly went down with the British warship H.M.S. De-Braak off the Delaware coast in 1798. They did find 23,000 artifacts—but no gold.

"From a business point of view we fought the good fight and lost," says John Davidson, chief executive officer of the project. But the group may resume its search if it can find suitable electronic sensors—and more money. "My better business judgment tells me stop," he adds. "But my personal judgment tells me the treasure is down there."

The hunt for $1.6 billion in gold that supposedly sank with the Republic off Nantucket has been similarly discouraging. With money running out, the group might try to raise an additional $250,000 to continue the search for another month. (Republic investors still could get back 60% of their money if the partnership sells the ship and salvage equipment, claims Michael Gerber, chief financial officer for Sub-Ocean Salvors International Inc., which is conducting the search.)

One problem is that deep-sea searches are expensive. Sub-Ocean says daily operations cost $8,000 to $10,000. The process is even costlier in deeper waters; the S.S.

Central America project, probing depths of more than a mile and a half, has cost $2.5 million so far this summer.

In fact, other than Mel Fisher, who is hunting for artifacts from nine vessels, no treasure hunter has recovered significant amounts of gold or silver. And not all of Mr. Fisher's investors shared in the treasure, which comes from the Atocha and the Margarita, sister Spanish vessels that went down off Florida's coast in the 1600s. For the most part, only those who invested in 1985, the year the valuables were found, received some of the treasure.

An Investor's Booty

Mark Hylind, 33, who invested $10,000 in the Atocha in 1985, was lucky. His share: a seven-carat emerald, a 21-ounce gold bar, two silver bars, each weighing 83 pounds, eight silver coins and a silver salt shaker. He says he is having "a million dollars worth of joy, right now," but is wary about redeeming his booty. "I have no idea how much it's worth," he says.

It may not be worth as much as some think, cautions James Williams, editor of Treasure Magazine, a trade publication. "Treasure hunters hype the value of the treasure at the beginning to gain investor interest," Mr. Williams says. "Then the values do a slow descent. They get lower for the IRS, and even lower when it comes time to cash in the loot."

Until now, the exact market value of Mr. Fisher's find is uncertain because government claims to the treasures, which largely have been denied by the courts, have limited their sales. Since February, Treasure Coins Ltd. of New Jersey has sold 80 silver "pieces of eight" from the Atocha; the coins have fetched $350 to $1,250, with most selling in the lower range. A clearer picture of the treasure's value will emerge when more objects are auctioned Sept. 26 in Las Vegas, Nev.

Investors' interest, however, may soon be curtailed by something other than their losses: passage of a bill, currently in Congress, that would make all wrecks in U.S. waters prior to the Civil War government property. Says Charles Taylor, a backer of Mr. Fisher, "Let's face it, we're in this as capitalists, not donors."

Ponzi schemes were named after Charles Ponzi who, in 1919, promised $1.40 in 90 days for each $1 "invested." Ten million dollars was taken in before the fraud was discovered and Ponzi sent to jail. He later died in Brazil in impoverished obscurity. Since Ponzi's time, numerous imitators have appeared, one of the largest of which was an oil hoax that took in over $100 million. Some of the biggest names in the business and entertainment world were purchasers, each apparently believing that the others must have checked it out. More recently a securities firm named J. David cost its "investors" about $125 million. It claimed to be earning "returns" of 30% to 40% per year in foreign currency transactions.

A Ponzi can utilize almost any type of investment medium. A number have involved chain letters applied to whiskey, savings bonds, and gold. Others have used the appeal of oil wells, precious metals, and gemstones. Investors should always be wary of returns that seem unrealistically high. By the time the scheme is revealed, usually almost nothing is left for the "investors."

Various types of other (not debt or equity securities) investments are summarized in Table 2.7.

TABLE 2.7 Investments Other Than Debt or Equity Securities

Real Estate	Huge market with many risks
Commodity Futures	Contracts calling for deferred delivery of some physical commodity
Collectibles	Diverse array of tangible assets
Noncollectibles	Diverse array of investments including Broadway shows, coal mines, race horses, sports clubs, freight cars, etc.
Ponzi Schemes	Frauds which secretly pay out high returns from principal

SUMMARY AND CONCLUSIONS

Generalizing about the various types of investments is difficult. Clearly each type offers advantages and disadvantages. Although an assortment of the more popular investment vehicles have been discussed, the list is by no means complete. Such diverse investments as wildcat oil wells, equipment leases, and currency speculation were not covered.

Very conservative investors may prefer fixed-income investments such as savings accounts, bonds, and preferred stock. Commodities or options may be attractive to more speculative investors. Those with the time and special expertise may find real estate, collectors' items, or small businesses appealing. Investors with limited time, funds, expertise, and willingness to take risks may find common stock and related securities (convertible bonds, convertible preferreds, warrants, mutual funds) an attractive compromise. Investors should, however, carefully consider any investment opportunity before making a commitment. In particular, whenever an unrealistically high return is offered, the investor should be wary of a possible Ponzi scheme.

Avoiding Ponzis and Other Investment Scams

Most investment scams are relatively easy to spot for those who are cautious. The basic rule is that if an offer seems too good to be true, it probably is. *Forbes* offers the following set of rules.

Rules for not getting rooked

Here's some commonsense advice about how to protect yourself from being scammed:

• Never give money to a faceless voice over the telephone—even if you have been impressed by his boss' TV commercials.

• Beware of high-pressure tactics that are aimed at forcing you to commit yourself before you understand the nature of the deal. Look at it this way: If you don't understand it, don't sign it.

• Pass up promises of ''can't miss'' deals or urgent requests to send money immediately because the market is moving so fast that you can't delay. If it sounds too good to be true, it probably is.

• Don't trust someone because of an affiliation, like a club or a religious group. Remember: Business is business.

• When it comes to commodities, the Commodities Futures Trading Commission notes: ''For every dollar made in the commodities markets, there's at least one dollar lost.''

• If it's a new stock issue, demand the prospectus first. Really read it. The con men in the business are betting you won't take the time. The salesmen are likely to tell you that the prospectus is just junk that the regulators force them to file.

• If it doesn't make sense as a business, it doesn't make sense as a tax shelter. Anyhow, if some of the smartest types in the country have been taken here, what chance do you have? Better to pay tax than lose everything.

• Always remember that the salesman gets his, even if you don't get yours. Your interests are simply different from his.

Finally, when you are able to double your money, tax free, in municipal bonds in eight or nine years, why should you reach for rabbit-breeding, diamonds and risky startup stocks?

Source: R. Stern and L Gubernick, ''The Smarter They Are the Harder They Fall,'' *Forbes*, May 20, 1985, p. 41. Reprinted by permission, © Forbes Inc.

REVIEW QUESTIONS

1. Discuss the advantages and disadvantages of the following types of fixed-income securities: savings deposits, savings bonds, money market mutual funds, Treasury bonds, corporate bonds, and municipal bonds. In your

discussion explore the dimensions of risk, return, liquidity, marketability, minimum investment size, investment effort, and moral and ethical appeal. Also note any special tax treatments applied to any of these types of investments.

2. Equity or ownership of part or all of a business may be acquired directly by investing in common or preferred stock. Compare these various types of investments. In your discussion explore the dimensions of risk, return, liquidity, marketability, minimum investment size, investment effort, and moral and ethical appeal. Also note any special tax treatments applied to any of these types of investments.

3. An indirect equity position may be acquired with warrants, options, convertible bonds, and mutual funds. Compare these various types of investments. In your discussion explore the dimensions of risk, return, liquidity, marketability, minimum investment size, investment effort, and moral and ethical appeal. Also note any special tax treatments applied to any of these types of investments.

4. Real estate, commodity futures, a small firm ownership position, and a portfolio of collectors' items offer investment opportunities attractive to certain types of investors. Discuss the characteristics of these instruments that determine their popularity. In your discussion explore the dimensions of risk, return, liquidity, marketability, minimum investment size, investment effort, and moral and ethical appeal. Also note any special tax treatments applied to any of these types of investments.

5. What is a Ponzi scheme? Where did the term originate? How should one seek to spot Ponzi schemes?

6. Compare each of the following ways of organizing a business: corporation, partnership, limited partnership, master limited partnership, and real estate investment trust. What are the advantages and disadvantages of each to individual investors?

REVIEW PROBLEMS

1. What would be the yield on U. S. Savings Bonds under the following circumstances? Assume the guaranteed minimum is 6%.
   a. five-year government bond rate of 7%
   b. five-year government bond rate of 8%
   c. five-year government bond rate of 9%

2. What would be the typical bond commission for each of the following trades?
   a. purchase seven bonds for a per bond price of 70
   b. sell 15 bonds for a per bond price of 105
   c. purchase three bonds for a per bond price of 56

3. Compute the percentage commissions for the dollar figures in Problem 2.

4. Compute the after-tax yield for a preferred stock with a before-tax return (all in the form of dividends) of 7.5% for an individual in the 28% bracket and a corporation in the 36% bracket.

5. Compute the percentage holding period return for an investment in a stock at 20 sold for 30. Assume that call options were bought with a striking price of 20 for 2 and exercised when the stock reached 30, with the resulting stock position then sold. What would be the holding period return?

6. Compute the holding period return for a load fund purchased with a NAV of 10 and sold when the NAV reaches 12. How much would the holding period return be if the fund were no-load?

7. Suppose you invested equal amounts in venture capital opportunities with the following returns: 80%, −25%, −15%, 12%, 105%, −80%, 350%, −100%, and 0%. What would be the overall return from venturing? If these returns were earned over a five-year period, what would be the geometric mean per period (annual) return?

8. Suppose you purchased a futures contract having a value of $150,000 with 10% margin. How much would be required in your margin account? If the value of your position were to rise to $200,000, what would be your position's value, profit in dollars, and profit as a percentage invested? What would be the result if you close out your position after it fell to a value of $100,000? Ignore commissions in your computations.

9. Compute the 1970–1980 holding period and per period geometric mean returns on each of the indexes of the Sotheby Index. Suppose equal amounts were invested in each index. What would be the resulting overall return?

10. According to the airplane game, each player starts as a passenger. Passengers pay the pilot $1,000 to begin their flight. Then each passenger must find two new passengers (each of whom must pay the pilot $1,000) to move up to first class. When these new passengers each find two new passengers themselves (a total of four new passengers), they move to first class and you (the initial new passenger) become a copilot. When these four new passengers find two passengers each (a total of eight), you become the pilot. As each of the current crop of new passengers finds his or her two new passengers you, the pilot, will receive $1,000 payments from each of the plane's 16 new passengers ($16,000). Assume that you live in a community of 50,000 people and 25% have ready access to enough money to play the game. Further, assume that 30% of those with the funds would be receptive and 15% of them are likely to hear about the game before it collapses. How many generations can the game be played before all of the potential players have been used at least once? If a generation takes three days to complete,

how long will the game go on? What type of "investment" does participation in this game sound like?

REVIEW PROJECTS

1. Ask three local banks for their terms on all of their various savings/investment vehicles. Do the same for a local credit union and a savings and loan association. Also ask about rates on U.S. government savings bonds. Make a table of the various alternatives and indicate which offers the most attractive terms for the following:

    a. $500 available for one year
    b. $5,000 available for six months
    c. $20,000 available for three years
    d. $1,000,000 available for three months

    Find comparable rates in the advertisements in *The Wall Street Journal*.

2. Visit a local coin dealer and record the asking prices and description of five high-priced (over $100) coins. Next ask a second coin dealer what he or she would pay for the coins that the first dealer is offering for sale. Compute the percentage markup. Realize that the first coin dealer would probably take less for the coins and that the second dealer would need to see the coins to give a firm offer. Write a report.

3. Try to identify the most unusual area for potential collectibles that you can imagine. Investigate to see if it is actually being collected. Write a report.

NOTES

1. R. Phalon, "Getting a Little Crowded: The Venture Capital Businesses Booming—A Mixed Blessing for Venture Capitalists," *Forbes*, February 15, 1982, 51–52; V. Zonana, "Despite Greater Risks, More Banks Turn to Venture-Capital Business," *The Wall Street Journal*, November 28, 1983, p. 83.

2. J. Martin and J. Petty, "An Analysis of the Performance of Publicly Traded Venture Capital Companies," *Journal of Financial and Quantitative Analysis*, September 1983, 401–410.

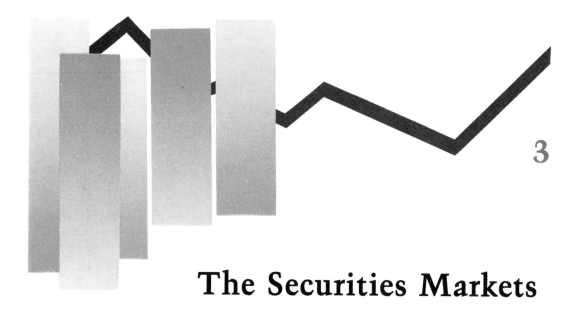

The Securities Markets

This chapter explores the mechanics, regulation, and economic functions of the securities markets. While common stocks are the principal focus, preferred stocks and warrants are traded in virtually identical fashions. Moreover, the listed option, mutual fund, and bond markets have much in common with the stock market. Thus the topics covered in this chapter apply to much of the investment scene.

This chapter deals largely with security market mechanics. First, the basics are covered. The broker's role is explored followed by a discussion of investment managers, exchanges, and the over-the-counter market. Then we examine commissions, bid–ask spreads, and types of orders in the context of how to minimize transactions costs. This is followed by a discussion of short selling and margin trading. Then various specialized institutional arrangements for trading stock are considered: third and fourth markets, new issues, private placements, rights offerings, secondary distributions, block trades, and tender offers.

After market mechanics have been covered in some detail, security market regulation is then discussed. Such regulation is first put in its historical context, and then progress toward a competitive central market is analyzed. The third and final topic of this chapter is the place of the security market in the economy, particularly its capital allocation role. How the security market helps allocate managerial talent and how it helps the Federal Reserve Board implement monetary policy are also considered.

THE MECHANICS OF THE SECURITIES MARKETS

Unlike the purchase of something like a can of beans, buying and selling stocks and bonds frequently involve a variety of relatively complex trading arrangements. For example, brokers, exchanges, limit orders, specialists, margin borrowing, stock certificates, commissions, underwritings, and tenders could each be utilized. Serious investors need to understand these concepts.

The functions of and alternatives to brokers are considered first, followed by a discussion of the exchanges and other markets where securities are traded. Attention next turns to executing transactions with a special focus on methods of minimizing trading costs. Then short selling and margin trading are explored. We end the section on mechanics by examining the various institutional arrangements for handling new issues and large trades.

Brokers and Brokerage Firms

An investor's principal link to the securities market is through his or her broker. The term broker is frequently used to refer to both the individual employee and the employing firm. To minimize such confusion, here the term *broker* will mean the employee, and *brokerage firm* or *brokerage house* will refer to the employer. Brokers and their firms perform a number of functions, the most basic of which is linking investors to the securities markets. Like real estate agents, stock brokers implement their customers' trading instructions. Dealers, in contrast, make markets by advertising a willingness to buy and sell.

In addition to facilitating trades, most full-service brokerage firms engage in a variety of other activities such as offering investment advice, holding customers' securities, sending out periodic statements, lending money on the collateral value of certain securities (margin loans), and acting as investment bankers (marketing new security issues and large blocks of already-outstanding securities called secondary offerings). Many brokerage firms also manage and sell mutual funds, make a market in unlisted securities, sell insurance, offer and manage various types of pension plans, manage some customer accounts individually, provide access to commodity exchanges, deal in government securities, sell tax-sheltered annuities, and so on.

The lines between brokerage and other types of financial firms are quickly eroding. Indeed, many erstwhile nonfinancial firms such as retailers and manufacturers have entered the field, mainly through acquisitions. Such diverse companies as Sears, RCA, Gulf and Western, National Steel, Greyhound, General Electric, and Control Data not to mention American Express, Merrill Lynch, Prudential, Beneficial, and Transamerica now have financial services components. Some of these firms offer an entire array of financial services including checking, credit cards, travelers checks, personal loans, insurance, pension packages, and real estate trading and management as well as the traditional brokerage functions.

What Should Be Expected of a Broker.   Investors need to know what is realistic and what is unrealistic to expect from their brokers. Brokers should implement customers' orders effectively and should quickly correct their own firms' all-too-frequent errors. Brokers also provide customers with investment advice. Most such recommendations are, however, no more useful than the rather unreliable advice of investment analysts. On the other hand, discussing prospective trades with one's broker often provides some perspective.

Many investors, particularly beginning investors, have rather unrealistic expectations. They do not understand why their brokers cannot make them a lot of money in a hurry. They want to know which stocks are going to make a quick and dependable rise. Individuals with such crystal balls would not need to earn their livings as brokers. Brokers usually act as investment counselors, not investment managers. Moreover, an individual broker can only follow a small fraction of the more than ten thousand actively traded U. S. stocks. Thus brokers are often unfamiliar with the issues that interest particular investors. Accordingly, investors should either assume the full responsibility for their portfolio management or hire a mutual fund or investment manager. Indeed, many investors have switched to discount brokers who offer minimal service but low-cost executions.

Although seeking investment miracles from a broker is unrealistic, investors have every right to expect financial soundness and integrity. Even these modest expectations are not always realized, however.

Bankruptcy of Brokerage Firms.   Prior to 1971, customers of failed Big Board firms were compensated by the NYSE through membership assessments. While no failure of a NYSE member ever cost a customer money, by late 1970 the trust fund was exhausted and the solvent NYSE members opposed further assessments. Congress then set up the Security Investors Protection Corporation (SIPC). SIPC protects investor customers against losses that would otherwise result from the failure of their brokerage firm. Customers are not protected against losses due to market fluctuations. SIPC liquidates troubled firms at the SEC's request. Customers are insured up to $500,000, not more than $100,000 of which may be in cash. Any claims above those sums are applied against the firm's available assets. Some brokerage firms have purchased additional insurance.

The SIPC takes as long as several months to complete a liquidation. As a result, many of the bankrupt firm's investors are locked into their portfolio until the liquidation is complete. Furthermore, the securities of bankrupt brokerage firms' margin customers are sold to pay their loans. Such investors must incur commissions on the sale and repurchase (perhaps at higher prices) if they are to restore their positions. The 1981 failure of John Muir again illustrated SIPC's inability to cope quickly with a large failure.[1]

Integrity of Brokerage Houses.   Most brokers and brokerage firms are honest. The exchanges and the Securities and Exchange Commission (SEC) try to monitor their industry closely. Those found guilty of serious wrongdoing soon lose their right to work in the industry. Still, improprieties such as the following are uncovered with some frequency:

1.   Conflicts of interest: Potential conflicts are raised by managing mutual funds, underwriting securities, making a market in some stocks, and advising customers. Most firms do take great pains to avoid even the appearance of a conflict, however.

2. Kickbacks: Order clerks may receive kickbacks to steer over-the-counter (OTC) orders to particular market makers. The cost of paying for the kickback is passed on to the customer in the form of higher prices.

3. Misuse of customer assets: Brokerage firms sometimes use customers' funds and the collateral value of their securities for positioning stocks and operating expenses. As long as the firm remains solvent, the customer may not be harmed but the practice is questionable and dangerous.

4. Embezzlement: Alert customers should quickly detect misappropriation of their assets by carefully monitoring their monthly statements. Because the brokerage firm is responsible for any employee's fraud, the stolen property should be easy to recover, if detected.

5. Improper use of discretionary authority: Sometimes brokers trade without specific customer approval. Customers who give their broker limited or complete money management powers may encourage churning. Brokers who actively buy and sell generate substantial commissions for themselves but few profits for their customers.

Investment Managers

Some investors retain professionals to manage their investments. Individuals with $100,000 or more have long been able to hire a portfolio manager. Many investment advising firms and banks will handle portfolios as small as $10,000, making professional advice available to investors of rather modest means. Accounts of less than $100,000 are generally managed as part of a pool with a pro rata return assigned to each account. Accounts of $100,000 or more may be managed individually.

The risk-adjusted returns of most mutual funds are no higher than those of the market averages. Moreover, the advice of investment analysts is about as likely to be inaccurate as accurate. Investment managers tend to combine the random performance of mutual funds and random accuracy of advice of investment analysts. Furthermore, such advisors charge a management fee of up to 2% (small accounts) compared with fees of 0.5% for most mutual funds. Investors can even hire someone to help select and monitor the manager. No-load mutual funds, however, offer small investors greater diversification, lower management cost, and more specialized attention than do most investment advisors. Those who do decide to use an investment advisor may find the following questions useful in choosing one.

1. How does the firm make its money? Some base their fee on the account's assets. Others charge commissions for the work done, which can prove more costly.

2. Is financial counseling the only service offered? An investor should know in advance if the firm also sells insurance, tax shelters, pension packages, or mutual funds.

3. Is the firm independently owned? If it is owned by a bank or a brokerage house, how independent is it? Does it do its own research, for instance?

4. Will the firm provide at least three reliable business references, such as a top local banker? The investor should not expect an advisor to supply client names, however.

5. What is the firm's track record? Will it list its recent market selections and fully explain its investment philosophy?

6. How many accounts are handled by one portfolio manager? High-quality firms assign each manager no more than 20 to 60 accounts. Some firms hesitate to answer this question, but the investor should press the point.

7. Does the firm use a limited power of attorney? Otherwise, how would it handle a situation requiring quick attention when the owner is unavailable?

8. Will the firm contact clients, if necessary, while they are traveling? If the account is large and service personalized, a conscientious firm should even be willing to phone overseas.

Whether to manage one's own investments, hire an investment manager, or purchase mutual fund shares is an individual decision. The investor should take into account the sum to be invested, time available, and his or her goals. Presumably most of the readers of this book intend to manage their own investments.

TYPES OF SECURITIES MARKETS

Regardless of how the portfolio is managed, securities must be bought and sold. Potential buyers could try to find sellers themselves but relatively few people wish to trade any one stock at a particular time. The need to bring buyers and sellers together efficiently led to centralized facilities (exchanges) for trading stocks, bonds, commodities, and options. Other trading takes place in somewhat less organized over-the-counter markets.

The Stock Exchanges

NYSE-listed companies produce about half of the economy's gross national product. NYSE rules tend to be followed by most other exchanges. Only members can transact business on the exchange and only listed securities may be traded. Large established firms are generally traded on the Big Board. Smaller firms may be listed on the American Stock Exchange (AMEX), which is the second largest in terms of primary listings. Still smaller firms trade on the regional exchanges. Table 3.1 reports NYSE and AMEX listing requirements. Some exchanges permit trading other exchanges' listings, and many stocks are listed on more than one exchange (dual listings).

TABLE 3.1   NYSE and AMEX Listing Requirements

	NYSE	AMEX
Pre-Tax Income Last Year	$2,500,000	$750,000
Pre-Tax Income Last Two Years	$2,000,000	—
Net Income Last Year	—	$400,000
Net Tangible Assets	$16,000,000	$4,000,000
Shares Publicly Held	1,000,000	400,000
Market Value Publicly Held Shares	$16,000,000	$3,000,000
Number of Round Lot Holdings	2,000	1,200

To become listed, a firm meeting the requirements must apply, pay a fee, and not engage in any practice prohibited by the exchange. The exchanges have much less stringent delisting criteria and may defer applying them in specific cases.

The Over-the-Counter Market

Although most large firms are listed on a stock exchange, numerous small publicly owned firms and several hundred NYSE-eligible companies are unlisted. Their stock trades in the over-the-counter market (OTC), an informal network of market makers who offer to buy and sell unlisted securities. Many listed companies are also traded OTC. To trade in the OTC market an investor would have his or her broker ask the brokerage firm's trading department to contact an appropriate OTC dealer.

Until the National Association of Securities Dealers (NASD) set up the National Association of Securities Dealers Automated Quotations System (NASDAQ), OTC stocks were relatively difficult to trade. Now, however, NASD connects the quoting dealers and brokers and reports the best available prices for NASD issues.

NASD securities are listed in one of three categories of OTC quotations. The National Market System (NMS) list contains the largest and most actively traded issues. National Market System newspaper quotations use the same format as that employed for NYSE and AMEX securities. More than 3,000 firms are "listed" on the NMS. Firms with financial characteristics similar to those for AMEX listing appear on the NASDAQ's National List. Fewer than 1,000 firms appear on this list. Another 2,000 or so NASDAQ OTC issues are included on the Supplemental List.

In addition to the NASDAQ's issues, the National Daily Quotation Service reports the bid and ask prices for all actively traded OTC issues (about 6,000 NASDAQ and 22,000 other issues). These price quotations appear daily in the Pink Sheets, copies of which are available at most brokerage firms. Investors wishing a current quotation of a Pink Sheet stock would need to have their brokers call one or more of the firms listed as making a market in the stock for a price. The phone numbers of these firms are listed in the Pink Sheets.

Size of the Stock Markets

In 1987 about 47 billion shares changed hands on the NYSE. NASDAQ volume was about 38 billion and AMEX was 3.5 billion. These numbers are not directly

FIGURE 3.1   Typical Ticker Tape Reading

comparable, however. NYSE share prices average two to three times those of AMEX issues, and the NASDAQ average price is even lower than that for the AMEX. Moreover, the frequency with which a given share is traded varies from market to market. Finally, institutional trading makes up a much larger part of NYSE volume than that of the AMEX or NASDAQ.

Other Securities Markets

Preferred stocks, warrants, and rights are traded on the same exchanges and OTC markets as common stocks. Standardized (price, delivery date, etc.) options are also traded on a number of exchanges. While corporate bonds may be listed on exchanges, most are traded OTC. Moreover, unlike warrants and preferreds, bonds have a different commission structure, and bond trading on an exchange is generally physically separated from equity trading. While some U. S. government bond trading takes place on exchanges, the vast majority of trades are handled by a small number of OTC government bond dealers. Commercial paper, large CDs, municipal bonds, and other money market instruments primarily trade in similar OTC markets. Commodity exchanges differ substantially from the stock market.

The Ticker Tape

Actual transactions for listed securities are reported on the ticker tape. Most brokerage houses display the ticker tape on a large electronic screen in their offices. The ticker tape is also available on a few cable television stations such as those of the Financial News Network (FNN). Each stock has an identifying ticker symbol. For example, the symbol "T" stands for telephone (American Telephone and Telegraph), and "XRX" is Xerox. The volume and price for each transaction appear below the company ticker symbol. A typical ticker tape reading is shown in Figure 3.1. The first entry, C with 6¾ below, reports a single round-lot sale of Chrysler Corporation at $36.75 per share. The second entry, X with by 2s 9 below, indicates a trade of 200 shares (2s) of USX at $29 per share. The entry G, with 2700 7½, reports that 2,700 shares of Greyhound traded at $17.50 each. Those who follow the tape are expected to know the general price range for the stocks they follow. The full number of shares are displayed for trades of 1,000 shares or more. Company names and the corresponding ticker symbols are contained in some investment references such as the *S&P Stock Guide* and most brokerage houses keep booklets with the same information.

TRANSACTIONS COSTS

Investing involves three basic processes:

1. Selection: what to trade, including how to screen a large list for a relatively few candidates for more detailed study

2. Timing: when to trade, including economic and technical analysis of the market's direction

3. Execution: how to trade, especially how to trade cheaply and effectively

Most books and articles on investing deal with what and when to trade. How to trade at the lowest costs is often ignored or only briefly treated. Nevertheless, relevant techniques are not only worthwhile but are also considerably more straightforward to apply than the various approaches to successful timing and selection. The sections that follow deal with the two major costs of executing a trade: commissions (broker fees) and spreads (wholesale/retail markups).

Commissions

Security market commission rates were long fixed by agreement. Indeed the so-called Buttonwood agreement setting up the original New York Stock Exchange in the late 18th century had a rate-fixing clause. In the 1930s the SEC assumed regulatory authority over the rate structure.

Deregulated Rates.   By the late 1960s institutional traders had come to make up a large and growing percentage of stock market volume. These institutional traders began to find various ways around the high fixed commissions. The brokerage industry was forced to respond by making commission setting competitive. Since May 1, 1975, each brokerage firm must set its own schedule rather than agreeing to some common formula.

A hypothetical commission formula based on that of a large retail brokerage firm is illustrated in Table 3.2. If this table is applied to a 200-share trade of a $15 stock, as an example, the commission on the principal value of $3,000 would be $30 plus 1.25% of $3,000 ($37.50). In addition, a lot charge of $8 per round lot, or $16, is applicable. This commission of $83.50 ($30.00 + $37.50 + $16.00) is equivalent to 2.78% of the $3,000 principal. Commissions on trades of this size (a few thousand dollars) average about 2% to 3% of the dollar value of the trade. Commissions on larger transactions are generally less and smaller trades proportionately more.

TABLE 3.2 A Hypothetical Retail Commission Table

Stocks, Rights, and Warrants Selling for More Than $1.00	
Principal Value	Commission
$0–300	11% of principal
$301–800	$9 + 2.75% of principal
$801–2,500	$18 + 1.75% of principal
$2,501–20,000	$30 + 1.25% of principal
$20,001–30,000	$125 + .90% of principal
$30,001–300,000	$210 + .60% of principal
$300,001 and over	$1,300 + .25% of principal

Lot Charges	
Number of Shares	Charge
100 or less	No charge
101–1,000	$8 per lot
1,001 or more	$80 + $5.50 per lot
Maximum commission charge per share	$ 1.00
Minimum commission for principal value exceeding $300	$35.00

Stocks, Rights, and Warrants Selling for Less Than $1.00	
Principal Value	Commission
$0–1,000	11% of principal
$1,001–10,000	$50 + 7% of principal
$10,001 and over	$200 + 5.5% of principal

Discount Commissions. The end of fixed commissions greatly expanded potential competition among brokerage firms. This primarily benefited institutional customers such as mutual funds, insurance companies, and bank trust departments. Although full-service firms are willing to negotiate discounts with their large individual customers, most do not compete openly on a price basis. Small investors will generally find the most attractive rates at discount brokers. Some discounters' rates are a specific percentage below the old fixed rates whereas other schedules are based on the dollar value of the trade, the number of shares traded, or a combination of factors.

Some comparative rates for five retail brokers (Merrill Lynch, Shearson, Bache, Kidder, and Paine Webber) and five discounters (Brown, Citicorp, Fidelity, Quick and Reilly, and Schwab) are given in Table 3.3. Discounts range from 40% to 70% below the average retail rate for larger trades. In addition to executing trades, a few discounters offer services similar to retail houses. Thus investors should shop for the combination of discounts and services (including the quality and quantity of investment information) that best suits their needs.

Spreads

Spreads represent the second major component of transactions costs. OTC dealers and their stock exchange equivalent, the specialist, quote both a *bid price*, at which

TABLE 3.3 Representative Retail and Discount Commissions, 1987

		RETAIL BROKERS					DISCOUNT BROKERS				
		MERRILL LYNCH	SHEARSON LEHMAN	PRUDENTIAL-BACHE	KIDDER PEABODY	PAINE WEBBER	BROWN & CO.	CITICORP BROKERAGE	FIDELITY BROKERAGE	QUICK & REILLY	CHARLES SCHWAB
		SHARE PRICE: $5						**SHARE PRICE: $5**			
Number of Shares	25	$31.25 (25.0%)	$12.50 (10.0%)	$35.00 (28.0%)	$9.45 (7.6%)	$21.25 (17.0%)	$26.00 (20.80%)	$38.00 (30.40%)	$33.00 (26.40%)	$35.00 (28.00%)	$34.00 (27.20%)
	100	$50.00 (10.0%)	$35.00 (7.0%)	$39.25 (7.9%)	$35.63 (7.1%)	$36.00 (7.2%)	$29.00 (5.80%)	$38.00 (7.60%)	$33.00 (6.60%)	$35.00 (7.00%)	$34.00 (6.80%)
	1000	$189.50 (3.8%)	$201.25 (4.0%)	$205.50 (4.1%)	$173.95 (3.5%)	$201.00 (4.0%)	$65.00 (1.30%)	$100.00 (2.00%)	$68.00 (1.36%)	$50.00 (1.00%)	$76.00 (1.52%)
		SHARE PRICE: $20						**SHARE PRICE: $20**			
Number of Shares	25	$50.00 (10.0%)	$35.00 (7.0%)	$39.25 (7.9%)	$19.73 (3.9%)	$36.00 (7.2%)	$26.25 (5.25%)	$38.00 (7.60%)	$33.00 (6.60%)	$35.00 (7.00%)	$34.00 (6.80%)
	100	$71.00 (3.6%)	$57.25 (2.9%)	$63.00 (3.2%)	$63.81 (3.2%)	$59.00 (3.0%)	$30.00 (1.50%)	$38.00 (1.90%)	$46.60 (2.33%)	$35.00 (1.75%)	$51.00 (2.55%)
	1000	$356.00 (1.8%)	$415.75 (2.1%)	$410.50 (2.1%)	$375.15 (1.9%)	$397.00 (2.0%)	$75.00 (0.38%)	$136.00 (0.68%)	$123.00 (0.62%)	$97.62 (0.49%)	$122.00 (0.61%)
		SHARE PRICE: $70						**SHARE PRICE: $70**			
Number of Shares	25	$63.00 (3.6%)	$52.13 (3.0%)	$58.00 (3.3%)	$44.86 (2.6%)	$54.50 (3.1%)	$27.00 (1.54%)	$38.00 (2.17%)	$44.03 (2.52%)	$35.00 (2.00%)	$47.00 (2.69%)
	100	$97.00 (1.4%)	$98.00 (1.4%)	$109.25 (1.6%)	$102.89 (1.5%)	$102.00 (1.5%)	$33.00 (0.47%)	$91.00 (1.30%)	$80.40 (1.15%)	$48.44 (0.69%)	$83.00 (1.19%)
	1000	$680.00 (1.0%)	$730.75 (1.0%)	$764.50 (1.1%)	$690.20 (1.0%)	$740.00 (1.1%)	$105.00 (0.15%)	$211.00 (0.30%)	$182.00 (0.26%)	$179.59 (0.26%)	$204.00 (0.29%)

Scheduled broker commission rates in total dollar amounts (and as a percentage of the overall trade value.)

Source: Adapted from B. Donnelly, "Even at Discount Brokers, Getting the Real Bargains Isn't Automatic," *The Wall Street Journal*, August 24, 1987, p. 25. Reprinted by permission, © Dow Jones & Company, Inc. All rights reserved.

they will buy, and an *asked price*, at which they will sell. The difference, or spread, between the buy and sell prices is the dealer's markup. Spreads tend to represent a smaller percentage of the price for higher priced and more actively traded stocks. OTC spreads average 4% to 5% for actively traded issues but are often much higher for less actively traded issues. To understand how the impact of the spread may be reduced, we need to explore the ways to place purchase and sale orders.

Market and Limit Orders

A customer wishing to trade a security begins by placing an order with his or her broker. Either a market or a limit order is likely to be used. A market order requires an immediate execution at the best available price. Normally this type of order results in a trade at the highest unexercised bid for a sale and at the lowest unexercised ask for a purchase. Sometimes, however, a buy and sell order will arrive simultaneously and be crossed with each other, usually at a price within the bid–ask range. In contrast, customers using limit orders specify the prices at which they are willing to do business. Thus a limit order is only executable at the limit price (or better). A market order ensures a transaction, whereas a limit order transaction must await an acceptable price.

Brokerage firm representatives take their customers' orders to the section of the exchange where stocks are traded (trading stations, or *posts*) and attempt to execute them. For example, a representative may seek to fill a client's limit order to purchase 100 shares of XYZ at 23. If the stock is available at 23 or less, the trade will be executed forthwith. Indeed, the order will be filled at less than 23 if possible. A limit order only stipulates the least favorable price that will be accepted. One would normally enter a limit order at a level that is more favorable to the initiator than the current price, however. Thus the order to buy XYZ at 23 might be entered when the stock was offered at 23¾ (asked) and others were willing to pay 23¼ (bid). After waiting a short time, the representative will leave any unexecuted orders with the specialist who makes a market in that stock.

Stop-Loss and Stop-Limit Orders

Stop orders are designed to limit exposure to an adverse price move. A stop-loss sell order implements a sale at market if the price falls to the prespecified level. Such orders seek to protect the investor from a further fall. Because the stock must be traded immediately after the stop price is reached, the realized price is usually relatively close (but not necessarily identical) to the stop-loss price. A stop-limit order, in contrast, activates a limit order when the market reaches the stop level. Thus when the stop level is reached, a stop-limit order may or may not liquidate the position. The vast majority of stop orders are set to sell a position if the price drops. Buy stop orders, in contrast, are triggered by a price rise. Such an order might be used to protect a short position. Thus a stop-loss buy order at 30 might be placed on a stock trading at 25. As long as the price stays below 30 nothing is done. Once it touches 30, the stock is bought.

One relatively popular use of stop orders is called the crawling stop order strategy. Few individuals use stop orders, but they may find the crawling stop order approach attractive. Using this approach, the investor protects his or her position with a stop order at a price a bit below the current market level. As the price moves up the stop price is also raised. As long as the price of the stock rises or does not fall back very much, the investor continues to hold onto a position whose value is stable or increasing. Profits can compound without great risk of losing them in a market decline. As with any kind of mechanical strategy, however, this approach has its limitations. For example, a modest price pullback may trigger a sale just before a major advance. Moreover, the strategy can only be applied to a stock whose price rises.

Good Till Canceled, Day, Fill-or-Kill, and All-or-Nothing Orders

Because market orders require immediate execution, specifying how long to keep trying to fill the order would not normally be necessary. Limit, stop-loss, and stop-limit orders, in contrast, may be entered either as *good till canceled (GTC)* or as executable for a specified period. An order can be placed to remain on the books for a day or week or some other period or until it is executed, whichever comes first. Day orders are canceled automatically, whereas the broker must remember to cancel other orders on the prespecified day. Fill-or-kill orders must be either executed immediately or canceled.

Commission charges are based on trades of the same security taking place during the same day. If an order to purchase 500 shares is executed in several pieces throughout the same day, the commission will (or should) be computed for a single 500-share trade. If that same trade took several days to be executed, however, the commissions would be computed separately on each day's trade. The total commission on such a stretched-out trade would appreciably exceed that on a single 500-share transaction. A customer who wishes to trade more than one round lot may either allow the order to be filled a bit at a time or stipulate an all-or-nothing order. An all-or-nothing order must trade as a unit incurring a single commission (with any volume discount applying) but can be executed only when sufficient volume is simultaneously available. A regular order might be filled pieces at a time even though insufficient volume existed for a single fill. Moreover, all-or-nothing orders are automatically superseded by any other limit orders at the same price. Thus those who would use all-or-nothing orders need to compare the potentially lower commission with the reduced likelihood of execution.

Versus Purchase Orders

Investors frequently sell only a portion of their holdings of a particular issue. For example, an investor might sell 200 shares from a 1000-share position. Such holdings may themselves have been accumulated over an extended period. Such purchases may well have been at different prices. Obviously the tax implication of the trade will depend heavily upon the price applied to the purchase side of the trade. The higher the cost basis is, the lower the gain or the higher the loss that is reported to IRS. Normally the shares that were purchased earliest are recorded as the ones sold (first in, first out: FIFO). The seller may, however, prefer to utilize a trade with a different purchase price. Identifying securities that were purchased at a later date as the ones that were sold may produce a higher basis (thereby reducing the profit or increasing the loss for tax purposes). Making the order *versus purchases* allows the seller to specify which block of shares is to be sold. Table 3.4 summarizes the various types of orders.

The Specialist

Specialists manage the markets in listed stocks. They do so primarily by quoting bid and asked prices on the securities assigned to them. They maintain an inventory of their assigned stocks and buy and sell for and from that inventory. A given specialist may make markets in a dozen or so securities and a few actively traded securities are handled by more than one specialist. Most securities, however, are handled by a single specialist. Securities that are traded on more than one exchange will have an assigned specialist for each exchange.

Specialists record limit and stop orders in their order books. They are responsible for executing these orders whenever the prespecified limit prices are reached. If the bid dropped from 23¼ to 23⅛, for example, a limit order to buy at 23 would

TABLE 3.4   Types of Orders to Buy and Sell Stock

Principal Types of Orders:

Market Order	Requires an immediate execution at the best available price
Limit Order	Stipulates the minimum (sell) or maximum (buy) price acceptable for a trade to take place
Stop-Loss Order	Requires an immediate trade if the specified price is reached
Stop-Limit Order	Activates a limit order if a specified price is reached

Period for Which an Order Is Executable:

GTC (good till canceled)	Executable until filled or canceled
Day	Executable only during the day the order is placed
Fill-or-Kill	Canceled if not immediately executed

Orders for More Than One Round Lot:

All-or-Nothing	Must be executed as a block
If Not Specified	May be executed in pieces of as small as one round lot

Sales of a Portion of One's Holdings of a Particular Issue:

Versus Purchase	Allows the seller to specify which block of stock within his or her holdings is to be sold
If Not Specified	Identifies as sold the shares that were purchased earliest (FIFO)

still be below all buy orders at 23⅛. Once all orders to buy at 23⅛ are filled, the bid will fall to the next highest unexercised order—in this case 23. Orders at the same price are executed chronologically. For example, a particular order to purchase 100 shares at 23 may be preceded by another buy order at 23 for 500 shares and another 300 shares at 23 may follow. Once the 500 shares at 23 are purchased, our 100-share order will be crossed with any incoming market sell order or limit order to sell at 23 or lower. On the other hand, any offer to pay more than 23 would immediately supersede our order.

Individual specialists are members of specialists firms. Such firms may handle up to 70 or so stocks. Under most types of market conditions these specialists firms perform their jobs effectively. They are supposed to ensure that the markets for each of their stocks is always orderly and well managed. In an orderly and well-managed market, someone is always supposed to be prepared to buy and someone is always supposed to be prepared to sell at prices that are reasonably close to recent levels. Similarly, prices are not supposed to swing too widely from transaction to transaction.

The specialist is expected to fill any temporary gaps by offering to buy and/ or sell as necessary. Specialists are supposed to be net buyers when the public wishes to be net sellers. Under normal circumstances, specialists firms may be managing a few stocks that are under selling pressure while others have more public buyers than sellers. During the October 1987 crash, however, almost all of the public orders were on the sell side. Most of the specialists' capital was quickly committed. Some firms were unable to provide an orderly market as they were hit with more and more sell orders at lower and lower prices. The specialists system is under review to determine what might be done to improve its ability to cope in the event of another such crash.

Floor Traders or Registered Competitive Market Makers (RCMMs)

Specialists, who make markets, and unexecuted limit orders, which represent potential demand and supply, both have a major influence on stock prices. Individuals called *floor traders* or RCMMs also have a modest role in the price formation process. RCMMs own exchange seats and trade for their own account. They benefit from quick access to the market, very low incremental trading costs (coupled with the high fixed cost of exchange membership), and the information available at the center of the action. As recently as the 1960s a substantial fraction of NYSE members were floor traders. Since that time, however, various restrictions have substantially reduced their ranks. By 1982 only 23 were registered and only 10 of them were active on the NYSE.[2] The options and commodity exchanges continue to have many floor traders, however.

TRADING AT THE MOST ATTRACTIVE PRICE

Investors should always seek to trade at the best available price. Why should an investor pay $23\frac{1}{4}$ for a stock that can (with a little effort) be bought at 23? Because future prices are very likely to be both higher and lower, the current level is seldom the best obtainable price. Nonetheless, between 75% and 85% of all transactions utilize market orders that require immediate execution at the current level. Limit orders, in contrast, are structured to take advantage of short-run imbalances in supply and demand. Most buy limit orders are set for execution slightly below the current price. Similarly, sell limit orders normally await somewhat higher prices. While saving a fraction of a point on a single small trade will not make investors rich, enough small savings could easily be the difference between outperforming and underperforming the market.

If limit orders are so useful, why are they not more widely employed? First, brokers may be reluctant to explain their more complicated mechanics to their clients. The broker's commission is certain to be realized when a market order is used. A limit order, in contrast, might not result in a trade and therefore might not generate a commission for the broker. Second, many investors may prefer a certain execution to a possible fraction of a point savings.

Unlike a limit order, a market order can result in an appreciably less favorable price than the investor expects. With a current bid of $23\frac{1}{4}$ and an asked of $23\frac{3}{4}$, for example, a buy market order on 100 shares would normally be executed at the quoted asked of $23\frac{3}{4}$. The price could move above $23\frac{3}{4}$ between the time the quote is obtained and the order reaches the floor, however. Alternatively, the quotation itself could be incorrect. Prices seldom change markedly in the short time required for an order to reach the post, but an eighth or quarter of a point move is not uncommon. A dramatic news event such as an assassination rumor could cause a much greater change. A GTC buy limit order at $23\frac{3}{4}$ would, in contrast, either be executed at the current asked price if it is less than or equal to $23\frac{3}{4}$ or be held for possible later execution. Thus a limit order set at or near the reported market price protects the trader from both a temporary price change and a trade based on an incorrect quote. In ordinary circumstances, however, it is executed at the same

Investments in Perspective

As was mentioned in the text, market orders can be executed at prices that are appreciably worse than the trader expected. Normally the amounts involved are modest, but not always. The sad story that follows illustrates just how badly things can go when they are already going poorly.

TOUGH OPTIONS: AN INVESTOR WHO HEDGED HIMSELF OUT OF A BUNDLE

The morning after Bloody Monday, Martin Cohen, a Westport (Conn.) investor, sought to protect what was left in his $60,000 pension plan. Rather than sell the stocks outright, he decided to buy put options on the Standard & Poor's 100-stock index, which trade on the Chicago Board Options Exchange. The S&P 100, known by the ticker symbol OEX, is the country's most popular option contract. Because puts appreciate in value as prices decline, purchasing them is a prudent way to hedge stocks in a falling market. But instead of buying protection, Cohen wound up wiping out his entire pension plan.

Ironically, the day after the market's 508-point plunge, Cohen's pension plan was in a lot better shape than most. While the Dow Jones industrial average dropped 22.5%, Cohen estimated the retirement account lost 14% of its precrash value. But because the market still looked shaky, Cohen decided to hedge.

An investor buying an OEX put gets the right to sell the underlying index at a predetermined level, called the "strike" price. Cohen wanted the cheapest possible protection, so he targeted "out-of-the-money" puts expiring in November. These are puts with a strike price that is way below the current value of the index and are cheaper than puts with higher strike prices. The underlying S&P 100 index was at 255. Cohen decided to buy the far-out November 190 puts.

NO RELIEF. But on the morning of Oct. 20, Cohen's broker could not find a price for such an option on the screen. The broker was able to get quotes for November 290 puts at 110 (that's $11,000 per option) and November 255 puts at 50. By comparison, Cohen and his broker figured that on the CBOE floor, the November 190 puts would be selling for around 10, or $1,000 each. Cohen entered a "market order" for 20 November 190 puts, which means he directed his broker to buy the puts from a CBOE market-maker, usually an independent trader who trades for his own account, at the prevailing market price.

The order was filled. But instead of 10, Cohen paid 83, or $8,300 per option, for a total of $166,000. Cohen protested

When Martin Cohen tried to guard against further losses after the crash by investing in put options, he lost his entire pension plan to his broker. You don't need fancy options formulas to realize that a 190 put option is worth a lot less than a 255—and the 255s had traded around 50 only minutes before. In Cohen's opinion, the market-maker took advantage of the volatility and confusion, and of the public's inability to get good price information.

Cohen says by the time he learned of the trade, he couldn't sell the options. The stock-index options shut down because many of the underlying stocks were not trading. When the market finally reopened, the puts were worth only 33.

When Cohen refused to pay for the options, his broker's clearing firm, Edward A. Viner & Co., sold the options on Oct. 21 for 8½, or $17,000—a loss of $149,000. To make up the deficit, Cohen says Viner liquidated the pension account and then sold securities in his unrelated accounts. No one at Viner was available for comment. Co-

hen also complained to the CBOE, which is already investigating the day's trading. But even if there were violations of exchange rules, the CBOE can't award damages. That would take a lawsuit or arbitration. Cohen is planning to sue.

"I feel for the guy," says Michael J. Razar, one of the biggest market-makers in the OEX. "But the price is not as outrageous as it sounds." Razar says that the prices of the 255 and 290 puts were not benchmarks for the 190s because by the time the 190s started trading, many of the underlying stocks had stopped trading, and the market was heading south. Options traders also feared the futures would soon shut down and they would be left without anywhere to hedge. In that kind of environment, says Razar, a market-maker is taking a huge risk to sell a put at all. Given that risk, 83 may have been reasonable at the time. "Other market-makers had the opportunity to bid lower, but they didn't," he says. The moral: Caveat emptor, especially in Chicago.

By Jeffrey M. Laderman in New York

Source: J. Laderman, "Tough Options: An Investor Who Hedged Himself Out of a Bundle," *Business Week*, November 30, 1987, p. 133. Reprinted by permission, © McGraw-Hill, Inc.

price as a market order. Thus such an order combines the advantage of a market order's very high probability of being executed with the protection from an unexpectedly adverse price.

Setting the Limit Price

A limit order placed close to the current price (bid for a sell and ask for a buy) incurs little nonexecution risk but is unlikely to result in a better price than a market order. Setting a more favorable limit than the current quote increases both the nonexecution risk and the potential gain from a more attractive price. In a journal article several years ago, I suggested three rules for striking a favorable balance between the probability of execution and the possibility of obtaining a better price.[3]

First, if an imminent development is expected to affect the price, the limit should be set to assure a quick execution. For example, if year-end tax-loss selling temporarily depresses the price, the limit might be set very near or equal to the current level.

Second, when the trade is not dictated by imminent developments, the limit price should be set near the expected forthcoming low for a buy or expected high for a sale. Past trading ranges may help identify the expected highs and lows. For example, suppose a stock has a two-week high and low of 24⅝ and 22½ and a last trade of 23½. It would seem to be trading in a range of a point above and a point below the current price. Thus one might try to buy close to 22½ and sell close to 24½. Setting the limit closer to the current level would reduce the nonexecution risk.

Third, the investor should take advantage of the tendency for prices to cluster at focal points. More trades occur and more prices are quoted at whole numbers than at halves, which are more common than quarters. Quarters, in turn, are more common than eighths. Most investors prefer to think and trade in what they view as round numbers. Their placement of limit orders reflects this preference. More sophisticated investors can place their own limit orders to take advantage of this tendency. The investor should bear in mind that, when several orders are entered at the same price, they are executed on a first-come-first-serve basis. If for example the bid is at 23, each buy order at 23 will be executed in the chronological order in which it was placed. The bid could easily move above 23 before all orders at 23 are filled. The tendency of prices to cluster at round numbers implies that far fewer unexecuted limit orders will be entered at 23⅛ or 22⅞ than at 23. Thus a buy at 23⅛ or sell at 22⅞ is considerably more likely to be executed than an end-of-the-line order at 23. Accordingly, one should normally set limit orders to buy at ⅛ and sell at ⅞. One should generally not change limit orders once they are entered because such changes cause the trader to lose his or her place in line.

An investor wishing to acquire a relatively large block of stock might effectively utilize several limit orders placed at varying prices. Some near the current quote would be very likely to be executed while orders entered further away would produce a lower average price if the stock reaches their level. Only round-lot orders should be used, however. The total commission on below round-lot (odd-lot) orders would generally be too large to justify the price savings.

In summary, investors should generally use limit rather than market orders. In doing so they should refer to past trading ranges and take advantage of the tendency of prices to cluster at round-number values.

OTC Limit Orders.   While properly placed limit orders can help to avoid the spread on a listed stock, most OTC transactions must be executed against a dealer's quote. To buy, the investor must generally pay the dealer's ask and sell at the dealer's bid. The present system does not provide an effective mechanism for matching incoming OTC buy and sell orders. Large investors can get around this constraint by having their own brokerage firm become a market maker. They can then enter their own bid or asked price into the NASDAQ system. Brokerage firms, however, are only likely to accommodate those who have enough trading interest to make their temporarily becoming a market maker in the issue worthwhile.

A relatively modest reform could make OTC limit orders a much more useful device. Market makers could simply substitute superior outside limit orders for their own quotes. As a result spreads would tend to narrow and many outside orders would be crossed against each other. Because spreads on actively traded OTC issues average 4% to 5% or more (compared to 1% to 2% on the NYSE), a significant narrowing of OTC spreads would make OTC stocks appreciably more attractive to trade. OTC market makers could charge for handling limit orders much as specialists receive a fee (floor brokerage) for processing limit orders on an exchange. Moreover, limit orders would reduce the market maker's need for inventories and provide useful information on potential supply and demand. Commission fees would have to be shared with the market maker but a likely increase in OTC activity might offset this loss.

Permitting exchange trading of unlisted OTC stocks might also improve the OTC market's efficiency. The more efficient markets arising from effective OTC limit order mechanics would clearly benefit society and impose no more than modest costs to brokers and market makers. Such a change could come through competitive pressure, SEC action, an antitrust suit, or legislation.

OTC versus Listed Stocks

Listed stocks are generally more marketable than those traded OTC. On the other hand, the local issues that are most familiar to many individual investors are usually unlisted. Furthermore, a disproportionate percentage of the numerous small companies traded OTC may be misvalued. A market tends to be most efficient when the greatest attention is paid to each stock. Actively traded large capitalization companies (AT&T, IBM, GM, Exxon, USX, etc.) are followed by so many analysts that very little relevant information is likely to be overlooked. Thus the prices of their stocks probably closely reflect what publicly available information can reveal about the true underlying values of the stocks. Less actively traded stocks, in contrast, are more likely to be ignored by analysts. Similarly, portfolio managers, business writers, and individual brokers generally pay much more attention to the actively traded issues. As a result, the prices of securities receiving little attention are much freer to stray appreciably from their underlying values.

Jessup and Upson (1973) concluded that average risk-adjusted returns on OTC stocks were significantly below those of NYSE stocks.[4] Senchack and Beedles (1979), in contrast, found that a group of Southwest OTC stocks exhibited higher returns and higher risks than the national markets' stocks.[5] This finding may be more reflective of the 1970s performance of Sun Belt stock than of the entire OTC. Both studies, however, reveal appreciably different returns patterns for OTC and listed stocks. Thus investors should weigh the OTC's poorer marketability and different returns pattern with the potential advantages of greater familiarity and a higher percentage of misvalued situations than for listed stocks.

The Third and Fourth Markets

Most trading and virtually all trades involving individual investors take place on an exchange or in the traditional OTC market for unlisted issues. Institutional investors, in contrast, make significant use of two other markets. OTC trading of listed stocks takes place in the third market, while the fourth market is an informal arrangement for direct trading between institutions. The third market grew up in response to the exchanges' then-fixed commission schedules. The fixed commission rate on a large institutional transaction (over $500,000 for example) could exceed $10,000 for paperwork similar to that of a single round lot. NYSE members could not depart from these rates.

Third market dealers were not bound by exchange-set commissions. Thus they were usually able to charge high-volume institutional traders much less. By the time the exchanges stopped setting commissions, the third market was already established. Third market dealers often offer a more attractive overall price (stock price and commission) than is available on the exchanges. The fourth market provides its institutional participants with an even less costly way of trading. Because the institutions trade directly with each other, no commission is incurred. Those who help put the two sides of the trade together usually receive a finder's fee but it is much less than the commission on a trade of equivalent size.

Dually Traded Securities

Many high-volume stocks trade simultaneously on the NYSE, several regional exchanges, and OTC. Each market's bid and asked prices may differ somewhat. *Arbitragers* seek profits from price disparities. While they do tend to drive the prices on different markets together, frictions permit some disparities. Thus shopping around may be worthwhile for large orders.

MANAGING EQUITIES

Buying on Margin

The Federal Reserve Board allows collateralized margin loans on almost all listed and on many OTC securities. A margin requirement of x% permits marginable stock to be purchased with x% cash and (1 − x%) borrowed funds (initial margin). Thus a 60% margin requirement would allow the purchase of $10,000 worth of stock with as little as $6,000 in cash. The margin requirement has typically been set at between 50% and 90% (1988, 50%).

A margin account is said to have *buying power* based on the equity in the account compared to the amount of margin borrowing that is already outstanding. For example, an investor with $20,000 worth of marginable stocks and no margin debt could, with a 50% margin rate, buy another $20,000 worth of stocks with the account's buying power. On the other hand, an investor with $35,000 in marginable stocks and an outstanding margin balance of $10,000 would be able to purchase another $15,000 worth of stock with the account's buying power. Buying power equals the maximum dollar value of stock or other securities supportable by the account's equity minus the current value of stocks in the account. In the example, an account with an equity of $25,000 ($35,000 − $10,000) could support $50,000 worth of securities including a margin balance of $25,000 ($25,000

in equity and $25,000 in borrowing equals the overall account value of $50,000).
With a current value for the account of $35,000, another $15,000 ($50,000 −
$35,000) in buying power is available.

To be marginable, an OTC stock must have at least 1,200 shareholders and
a market value of $5 million or more. Listed companies are marginable unless
specifically excluded by the SEC. Most brokerage firms will not extend margin
loans on low-priced shares (below $5), however. Moreover, the customer must
have at least $2,000 in equity to open a margin account.

Margin Calls

Margin loans may remain outstanding as long as the borrower's equity position
does not fall below the maintenance margin percentage. Margin borrowers are not
expected to make payments according to any particular schedule. The one time
the borrower may be required to make a payment is when the equity in the account
falls to too low a level. A margin account's equity will rise and fall as the price of
the securities in the account rises and falls.

Margin accounts are not supposed to become in danger of having a larger loan
against them than the value of the securities collateralizing the loan. As long as
the value of the collateral exceeds the amount of the loan by a comfortable cushion,
the outstanding loan is considered to be relatively secure. If the cushion becomes
too small, however, the lender begins to risk a loss on the loan. Should a general
market decline lead to substantial margin account losses for brokerage firms, the
stock market and economy could suffer. Clearly, neither the regulators nor the
brokerage firm industry wants to risk such losses. Accordingly, the Federal Reserve
Board sets a minimum maintenance margin percentage (25% as of this writing).
Most brokerage firms set a somewhat higher figure for their customers. Thirty-five
percent is typical. An investor whose equity falls below this percentage of the value
of his or her portfolio (counting only marginable securities) will receive a margin
call. A margin call may be satisfied in one of three ways: adding more money,
adding more marginal collateral, or selling stock and using the proceeds to reduce
the margin debt. In each case the result must raise the equity percentage above the
margin maintenance minimum.

An example will illustrate the application of these margin percentages: A 50%
margin rate allows $10,000 in marginable stocks to be purchased with $5,000 in
cash and $5,000 in credit. Any fluctuation in the portfolio's value will be reflected
in a change in the equity position (equity equals portfolio value less margin debt).
If the value of such margined stock falls to $7,700 (equity position is $2,700, or
35%), however, the investor will receive a margin call. Unless the loan value is
reduced or additional collateral is deposited, the brokerage firm must sell some of
the borrower's stock. In the example, a $1,000 stock sale would reduce the loan
from $5,000 to $4,000, increasing the equity position to 40% ($2,700/$6,700).

The Leverage of Margin Borrowing

Margin loans are normally used to purchase more stock than could be bought with
cash alone. Such loans tend to magnify both gains and losses. With $5,000 the

TABLE 3.5 Margin Example: $5,000 Available to Invest in Stock Selling for $100 per Share

Stock Price Moves to	Purchase 100 Shares Using 50% Margin		Purchase 50 Shares for Cash	
	Change in Holding's Value	Change Relative to Equity	Change in Holding's Value	Change Relative to Equity
70	−$3,000	−60%	−$1,500	−30%
80	− 2,000	−40%	− 1,070	−20%
90	− 1,000	−20%	− 500	−10%
100	0	0	0	0
110	+ 1,000	+20%	+ 500	+10%
120	+ 2,000	+40%	+ 1,000	+20%
130	+ 3,000	+60%	+ 1,500	+30%

investor could buy 50 shares of a marginable stock outright or (with a 50% margin rate) 100 shares by borrowing the additional $5,000. Table 3.5 illustrates some possible results (neglecting the impact of dividend payments and interest charges) from a cash versus margin purchase. Clearly margin purchases increase both the upside potential and the downside risk.

To examine the impact of margin interest, assume the loan costs 9½%. If a year later the stock illustrated in Table 3.5 had risen to 120, the cash purchase would have appreciated by $1,000 ($20 × 50) compared with a $1,525 gain on the margin purchase ($20 × 100 = $2,000; 9.5% × $5,000 = $475; $2,000 − $475 = $1,525). Should the stock fall to 80, the losses would be $1,000 and $2,475, respectively. Interest costs on the margin position would, however, be at least partially offset by dividend payments. Commissions and taxes also affect the amounts modestly but leave the basic point unaffected. Margin credit tends to magnify both gains and losses. As long as the stock's return exceeds the cost of the loan, leverage will enhance the overall return. Using margin may also have some tax advantages. Interest costs are fully deductible (but only against investment income) as incurred whereas any price appreciation is taxable only when the asset is sold.

Brokerage firms finance some of their margin lending from other customers' credit balances, such as those generated through short sales. A positive balance in a customer's account is called a *credit balance* while a negative one (i.e., a margin loan) is referred to as a *debit balance*. Additional loan funds are obtained from commercial banks at the *broker call-loan rate*. Interest charges on margin loans are based on the exact length of each part of the loan. If, for example, $10,000 is borrowed and then $750 is repaid a week later, interest will be calculated on $10,000 for a week and on $9,250 thereafter. Margin loan interest rates are usually determined by a sliding scale added to the broker call loan rate. Table 3.6 is typical.

Banks generally set their call loan rate below their prime rate (the lowest advertised business rate). Thus margin loan rates are normally no more than 2% above the prime business rate. Relatively favorable interest rates and flexible payment schedules make margin loans an attractive credit source.

Preferreds, warrants, and convertibles are subject to the same margin requirements as common stocks. Margin restrictions also apply to corporate bond pur-

TABLE 3.6 Typical Margin Loan Rates

Net Debit Balance	Call Rate Plus
$ 0– 9,999	2 1/4%
$10,000–29,999	1 3/4%
$30,000–49,999	1 1/4%
$50,000 and over	3/4%

chases although their proportional collateral value is typically higher (35% margin rate in 1988). A 10% margin requirement applies to government bonds.

While brokerage houses specialize in margin loans, banks and other financial intermediaries also accept securities as collateral. If such loans finance other security purchases, the Fed's margin restrictions apply. Otherwise the lender can determine the maximum loan value.

Short Selling

To understand the concept of short selling, consider the following situation. A friend stops by and mentions that he badly needs a particular record for a party that he is having tonight. Unfortunately, he had to work late and all of the record stores are closed. When he sees the needed record in your record rack, he offers to pay double the retail price. That particular record, however, belongs to your roommate who has left for the weekend. You know that your roommate would not mind if you sold his record as long as you replaced it. So you sell the record in the rack and replace it with a new copy before your roommate returns. You made a profit and your roommate still has his record. The new copy of the record is at least as good as the one that was sold. The trade that you made is in effect a short sale. You sold something that you did not own but you had the (implicit) permission of the owner to make the sale and you intended to replace it. Such short sales are not uncommon in the securities markets.

Most stock trades involve the purchase and sale of securities that the seller owned prior to the transaction. Unlike offering to sell the Brooklyn Bridge, however, an investor who sells stock that he or she does not own (short selling) is involved in a perfectly legal practice. The short seller's broker simply sells someone else's shares. The short seller then owes the lender the shorted shares. The customer whose stock is borrowed is as secure as a bank depositor whose funds are loaned. Should the lender wish to sell the loaned stock, the brokerage firm will simply borrow replacement shares from another customer or brokerage firm.

Occasionally a trader will try to use his or her own trades to influence the price of a particular security. For example, someone may try to cause a stock's price to run up by buying large quantities on the market. Alternatively, he or she might try to drive a price down through excessive selling. Traders of course are entitled to buy or sell even in large quantities when the purpose is simply to accumulate or liquidate a position. Any type of effort to manipulate the market, however, is illegal. Thus, for example, using short sales to drive a stock's price down is considered an illegal attempt to manipulate. To forestall such attempts, traders are not allowed to sell short immediately after a negative price change (downtick) in a stock. Thus if the last price changed was a decline, a would-be short seller must wait until the price begins to rise again (two or more successive trades at rising prices, an uptick) before implementing a short sale.

The short seller hopes the price will fall far enough for the stock to be repurchased at a profit. Shorting 100 shares at 50 and then repurchasing them at 35 produces a gross profit of $1,500 (100 × [50 − 35]). This gain would be reduced somewhat by commissions on the short sale and covering (repurchase) transactions. Furthermore, the short seller must pay any dividends accruing on the borrowed stock. Should the stock price increase to 65, however, the seller would incur a loss of $1,500 plus commissions and accrued dividends. Moreover, the short sale proceeds and an additional percentage (margin) of the sale price must be left in a non-interest-bearing account at the brokerage house. Still more margin may be required by an adverse price move.

The short seller may legally remain short indefinitely. The dividend payment and margin deposit requirements make such positions costly to maintain, however. Moreover, stock prices have no ceiling. Thus losses are technically unlimited on a short sale. Clearly, short selling is a relatively risky and sophisticated device. Amateur investors should probably avoid short sales.

As the preceding discussion indicates, the word *short* may be used as a noun, adjective, and verb. To short stock is to sell stock that is not owned with the intention of covering (buying it back) later, hopefully at a profit. The act of executing a short sale may be described as shorting or, in the past tense, as having shorted the stock. To be short or have a short position is to have executed such a trade and not yet covered. Similarly, an investor can be long or have a long position. This is just another way of saying that the investor owns the stock. The word *long* cannot, however, be used in this context as a verb. One would not, for example, say that a trader who purchased a stock had longed it.

Cash Management Accounts

Most brokerage firms offer a flexible type of personal financial management account that combines checking, credit card, money fund, and margin accounts into a single framework. Merrill Lynch, which originated the concept, calls theirs Cash Management Accounts. Other firms offer a similar service under their own trade name.

These types of accounts transfer funds back and forth to minimize interest costs and/or maximize short-term yields. When an account holder writes a large check, his or her checking account is first drained of funds. Then, if necessary, the money fund balance is tapped. If still more funds are needed, a margin loan is extended. Credit card balances are handled in a similar fashion. Alternatively, a large deposit will first be applied to loans and then put into the money fund. Such accounts relieve the investor/money manager of some of the cash management burdens.

Street Name

Margined securities must be left on deposit with the shareholder's brokerage house, and unmargined securities may be. Broker-held securities are generally registered in the *street name* (name of the brokerage house) although the customer retains beneficial ownership. Street name registration offers secure storage and allows securities to be traded without having to reissue the certificates.

Street name registration has a number of disadvantages. Assets held in street name may be tied up during a bankrupt brokerage firm's reorganization. Moreover, dividends and interest on street name securities are sometimes credited to an improper account. The customer must discover and report the error before it is likely to be corrected. Even a properly credited dividend may be retained by the broker in a non-interest-bearing account for a month before being sent to the shareholder. Furthermore, all company reports (annual reports, quarterly reports, proxy materials, class-action suit notices, etc.) for street name securities are sent initially to the brokerage firm. Thus street name holders will receive their company reports only after the brokerage firm has forwarded them. Those who want to be sure of receiving all company mailings may retain a small portion (say 10 shares) of each security in their own names. Clearly, street name registration has both advantages and disadvantages.

The Stock Certificate

In this day of computerized accounting and electronic transfers, using stock certificates to prove ownership is akin to a cash-only payment system. Stock certificates must be issued whenever a stock is registered in an individual's name. Because the certificates require a great deal of paperwork and may be stolen or forged, many experts have advocated substituting computer cards or bookkeeping entries. Individuals might still receive a stock certificate upon request or at least be given some proof of ownership such as a receipt or a bill of sale.

Institutions are involved in a large percentage of securities transactions as either the buyer or seller or both. Many other trades involve individuals who leave the stockholding function to their brokerage firm. With such trades, appropriately safeguarded bookkeeping entries have largely eliminated the need for stock certificates. Stock certificate reissues are minimized by the National Securities Clearing Corporation (NSCC). It records all members' transactions, verifies the consistency of their accounts, and reports net positions daily. NSCC members settle within the clearinghouse rather than between individual brokerage firms. Moreover, the Depository Trust Company (DTC) immobilizes many certificates by holding member firms' securities. Securities traded between members can be handled internally by simply debiting one account and crediting another. As of 1986 over 50% of NYSE stocks and 70% of corporate bonds were held in DTC vaults. While institutional and street name accounts benefit from these facilities, investors with non–street name securities continue to experience all the inconveniences inherent in a stock certificate transfer system.

OTHER TRADING MECHANISMS

The vast majority of security trades take place in modest-sized lots on an exchange or OTC (including the third and fourth markets). Special mechanisms have, however, been devised both for newly issued securities and trades whose size would strain everyday market facilities.

The Primary Market

The primary or new issues market handles initial sales of securities, while subsequent exchange and OTC trading takes place in the secondary market. Some shares of a primary distribution may already be actively traded in the secondary market. Alternatively the issuing firm may have heretofore been privately held (owned by a very few people). A private firm that sells a substantial block of additional shares and thereby creates a more active and diverse ownership is said to *go public*. Normally an *investment banker* (usually also a brokerage firm) is retained to assemble a syndicate to *underwrite* the issue.

Investment bankers facilitate new issue sales of debt and equity by agreeing to buy the securities for resale (underwriting). Together the firm and its investment banker compose a registration statement and a *prospectus* detailing all of the relevant material information. These statements must be filed with the SEC and supplied to every buyer. The investment banker deducts its underwriting fee from the offering price. Approximately 8% of NYSE member revenues come from underwriting fees. The investment-banking syndicate generally guarantees to sell the issue, although the job might be taken on a best-effort basis.

Shelf Registration.   While most primary sales are marketed quickly after their registration, *shelf registration* is permitted by the SEC's Rule 415. Under this authority a firm can file one registration statement for a relatively large block of stock and then sell parts of it over a two-year period. The shelf registration option tends to reduce red tape and (because the stock can be sold directly to institutional investors) often eliminates the underwriting fee.

Private Placements.   New issues are sometimes sold in large lots to a small group of buyers in what is called a *private placement.* Such placements allow start-up firms to demonstrate viability by successfully raising some capital on their own. Additional shares may subsequently be marketed to the public through an underwriter. The private placements are usually sold below the public offering price. In exchange for a favorable price, the initial investors may agree to accept *lettered stock.* Under SEC Rule 144, such securities can only be resold after a reasonable holding period and in a manner that does not disrupt trading markets. Debt issues may also be placed privately, usually to large buyers such as insurance companies.

Rights Offerings.   We have already seen that shares may be bought and sold through an underwriting syndicate, private placement, or the ordinary channels of trade (exchange or OTC). In addition, firms may sell their stock in a rights offering. Indeed a preemptive rights clause, if part of the corporate bylaws, ensures shareholders of the right to maintain their proportional ownership of the company. In a 5% stock sale, stockholders with preemptive rights would have first refusal on one new share for each 20 shares that they owned. Stocks sold through rights offerings are generally priced sufficiently below the market level to make them attractive to exercise before they expire. Normally stockholders may sell their rights for a price that reflects the savings offered. If 20 rights are required to buy one share of a $50 stock at 40, rights will sell for about 50 cents each: $(50 - 40)/20$. While some companies still use rights offerings, many have persuaded shareholders to give up their preemptive rights.

A sale of additional stock through an underwriting or a rights offering inevitably increases shares outstanding. Any stock sale that increases shares outstanding beyond the number authorized must first receive the stockholders' approval. Suppose a company wished to sell 200,000 shares when 400,000 are authorized and 300,000 are already issued. Such a sale would require an additional 100,000-share authorization. Most companies try to maintain a substantial cushion of unissued but authorized shares so that they can issue additional shares as needed.

Indirect Stock Sales: Warrants and Convertibles

Firms often require capital but consider the current stock price too low to undertake a direct sale. Any sale, which immediately increases shares outstanding, dilutes the ownership position of existing shareholders. Accordingly, management may choose to raise the needed funds by selling convertibles or a package of bonds and warrants. With either approach the firm raises the needed funds by initially selling securities that are mainly or exclusively debt but with the potential of becoming equity. Such an indirect sale of similar magnitude causes less dilution because exercise (convert or purchase stock at a prespecified price) becomes attractive only if the stock's price rises above the exercise price. If the exercise does eventually take place, fewer shares will be issued than had the same sum been raised through an immediate stock sale. Clearly, the stock's price must rise above the exercise level or the warrants will not be exercised and the convertibles will not be converted. Thus an indirect stock sale is an uncertain approach to raising equity.

LARGE SECONDARY MARKET TRADES

The vast majority of secondary market trades can be handled comfortably by the specialists or OTC market makers who earn their living positioning the stock. Other institutional arrangements are, however, used to handle trades that would strain the specialist's or market maker's capital resources. Very large amounts of stock usually require a secondary distribution (sale) or tender offer (buy) while intermediate-sized trades may go through a block trader or be handled as a special offering.

Block Trades. Attempting to buy or sell 10,000 shares or more in the ordinary channels might result in a very unfavorable price. Therefore such trades are often handled by a block trader. For a large sell order the block trader first obtains buyer commitments for part or all of the shares. He or she then offers to buy and resell the lot at a bit below the current price, charging commissions to both sides of the trade. To facilitate the transaction the block trader may purchase some of the lot. This facilitating purchase may ultimately have to be sold at a loss. While block traders are usually given the task of selling large quantities of stock, they sometimes are asked to assemble large blocks for single buyers.

Special Offerings.   Special offerings or spot secondaries are also sometimes used to sell relatively large blocks of stock. Brokers who buy the securities for their clients receive a special incentive fee. The exchange must approve the offering, which is then announced on the ticker. It must remain open for at least 15 minutes. The offering price must generally equal or exceed the current bid and not exceed either the last sale price or the current ask.

Secondary Distributions.   Block traders do not want to hold a large position long enough for an adverse price movement to offset their commission profit. Moreover, very large blocks generally require relatively long periods to be sold at reasonable (non-distress-level) prices. Such very large blocks are generally sold in secondary distributions. Such distributions are handled in much the same way as new issues. A syndicate or the original seller directly markets the issue over time at a price somewhat below the preoffering level. The offering price includes a discount to the selling syndicate. No direct commission is charged.

Tender Offers.   Large investors sometimes seek to make a substantial purchase, acquire control, or buy out most of the smaller shareholders (*go private*). A tender offer is generally used for such large purchases. For a limited period the buyer offers to purchase a substantial block of stock, normally at a premium price. The tenderer usually pays an additional fee to brokers who handle their customers' trades. If the offer is oversubscribed and the buyer does not want the excess, stock may be bought on a pro rata basis. If too little is tendered, the buyer may reject all bids or purchase what is offered. Table 3.7 summarizes the various ways stock may be traded.

SECURITY MARKET REGULATION

Because they are "clothed with the public interest," the securities markets are regulated. Investors need to understand the nature and direction of the regulation in order to take maximum advantage of any resulting opportunities. The following section first discusses the historical development and current state of regulation and then considers the emerging central market system.

Historical Background

For many years the securities markets were operated largely in the interests of Big Board members. Typical of a rational monopolist, the NYSE responded to potential competition by seeking to combine with, destroy, or limit the power of the rival

TABLE 3.7 Various Ways of Trading Stock

Initial Stock Sales (Primary Market)

New Issues (Public Sale)	Sold through a syndicate of investment bankers organized to underwrite the issue
New Issue (Private Placement)	Sold to one or a few buyers who may agree to take lettered stock
Rights Offerings	Gives existing shareholders the opportunity to maintain their proportional ownership by purchasing stock from the company at below-market prices
Warrants and Convertibles	Indirect, uncertain, and delayed stock sales depending on exercise by holders

Trading in Already-Issued Stock (Secondary Market)
Small to Moderate Size Blocks

Exchanges	Organized trading in shares of large to medium size firms
OTC	Informal hookup of market makers trading small and medium size companies
Third Market	OTC trading in listed securities
Fourth Market	Direct trading between institutional investors

Large Blocks of Stock

Block Trade	Trades of 10,000 shares or more with the passive side assembled by a block trader
Special Offerings	Offerings pay special incentive commissions to brokers who buy for their customers
Secondary Distributions	Offerings of very large blocks of stock through a syndicate of investment bankers
Tender Offers	Offers to purchase large amounts of stock almost always at a premium over the preoffer market price

exchange. In its first serious threat, the NYSE merged with the Open Board and Government Bond Department (1869). In the late 19th and early 20th centuries, the Consolidated Board (or "Little Board") provided a challenge. After the NYSE responded by forbidding its members to deal with the rival exchange's members, disreputable elements took control. The Consolidated soon withered away. The outdoor traders of the New York Curb Exchange only traded unlisted stocks. When the Curb went indoors (1921) and eventually changed its name to the American Stock Exchange (1953), it did so with NYSE's blessing.

More recent forces have been draining the NYSE of its power and authority. Institutional investors have forced some changes. Commodity exchanges have invaded its presumed turf by listing options and financial futures. The Securities and Exchange Commission, under pressure from the Justice Department's Antitrust Division, has taken a harder line against the Exchange's quasimonopoly position. Finally, competition from the third and fourth markets and the regional and foreign exchanges is being felt over, under, around, and through the exchange's regulations.

Current State of Security Regulation

The exchanges, led by the NYSE, engage in a great deal of self-interest self-regulation. The NYSE maintained three monopolistic rules into the mid-1970s: fixing commissions, prohibiting exchange members from trading listed shares off the exchange, and prohibiting the AMEX from trading NYSE-listed securities. After a long struggle and rearguard action to preserve them, fixed commission rates were ended by SEC order in 1975. While the AMEX no longer automatically delists companies that obtain NYSE listings, only a relative handful of the NYSE's listings are dually traded with the AMEX, and most of the volume in those issues takes place on the NYSE. Thus the two New York exchanges still do not compete head-on. Off-exchange member trading of listed securities is no longer prohibited per se but effective restrictions still discourage such activity.

Some NYSE regulations help both the exchange and its customers. For example, protecting customers from fraud or bankruptcy of member firms inspires public confidence.

Although the SEC has broad powers to oversee the industry, the sympathies of this commission, like those of most regulatory commissions, often lie with the industry. The Antitrust Division may, however, prod the commission when its industry orientation appears to be too cozy. Furthermore, other groups (institutional investors, for example) can sometimes foster reforms.

The SEC has been diligent in protecting investors against fraud, misrepresentation, financial manipulation, and trading on inside information. Full and frank disclosure is also a top priority. Public security offerings must be accompanied by a prospectus that fully discloses all pertinent information. Publicly owned firms must file periodic financial statements with the SEC, the exchanges where they are traded, and their stockholders. Trading by insiders must be reported to the SEC. In spite of the SEC's efforts, however, substantial insider-informed trading continues. Any attempt to manipulate security prices runs afoul of both SEC regulations and the antitrust laws. The SEC has also extended its jurisdiction to many nonstock investments and has pushed for greater corporate disclosure. The major remaining security regulation controversy involves the central market.

THE DEVELOPMENT OF A CENTRAL MARKET

Congress has mandated that all of the exchanges and other securities markets (third and fourth) be fully linked. If and when that mandate is realized, buyers and sellers in all submarkets will be able to trade directly with each other. The more numerous alternatives should move buying and selling prices closer together (narrower spreads), and the greater diversity of reachable markets should allow larger blocks to be absorbed. Not surprisingly, this vision requires a number of difficult changes.

Consolidated Reporting

Until the mid-1970s security trading was highly segmented. To obtain the best available price, each market had to be checked separately and NYSE members could not trade in the third market. Most NYSE brokers simply funneled their orders to the market with the greatest volume. In 1974 consolidated trades began to be reported on a common ticker tape. The financial press initiated consolidated quotation reporting in 1976.

Consolidated reporting without fully consolidated trading is confusing, however. Investors expect a buy limit order to be executed if the subsequent low falls below the limit price. If, however, the limit order is entered on the Big Board, and the low (high) occurs on the third market or another exchange, the trade may not take place. A Composite Limit Order Book (CLOB) and free order flow would allow all orders to be executed in any market where the security is traded. Thus investors would always have access to the best available price regardless of where the order was entered. Not surprisingly, however, NYSE specialists, regional specialists, and third market dealers are each interested in preserving their existing advantages. The various submarkets cannot be linked without exposing the participants to some risks. Such conflicts coupled with the SEC's unwillingness to impose a solution has slowed the pace of reform.

Rule 390

As with the CLOB and market-link controversy, rules barring member off-exchange trading of listed securities have been fiercely defended by the securities profession. NYSE Rule 394, which prohibited such trading, was replaced with Rule 390, which restricts such trading. In 1977 the SEC announced that it intended to require the repeal of Rule 390 by January 1, 1978. That deadline was moved forward a number of times and then seemingly abandoned.

Industry sources argued that if Rule 390 were repealed prior to the complete establishment of a central market, off-exchange markets made by the larger brokerage houses would cause some exchanges to close and others to shrink. According to this argument, brokerage houses too small to make markets for their customers would be unable to obtain competitive prices on the exchanges. Cohen, Maier, Schwartz, and Whitcomb go so far as to advocate concentrating trading on a single exchange.[6] Similar self-serving arguments were used to oppose the end of fixed commissions, which in fact left the overall security trading system largely intact. In any case, the linkup of the various markets could be hastened rather than to continue stalling on the repeal of Rule 390. Easy access to the third and fourth markets should increase competition and lead to more efficient pricing.

The intermarket information system, which facilitates an exchange of price quotations, is a small step toward centralized trading. Congress has, however, mandated that trading on and off the exchanges be unrestricted and orders be allowed to flow freely from market to market. If the industry fails to devise such a system, the SEC could exert more pressure or impose a solution.

THE ECONOMIC FUNCTIONS OF THE SECURITIES MARKETS

Securities markets play an important but not all-important role in the economy. They assist with capital and managerial allocation. They also provide a vehicle for the Fed to transmit monetary policy to the economy. Thus the securities markets have a significant impact on both the short- and long-run economic performance.

Shifting technology, evolving tastes and preferences, and the introduction of new and improved products lead to changes in consumer spending patterns. Increasing demand frequently outstrips existing capacity and bids up prices in some areas. Overcapacity tends to drive prices down elsewhere. Profits increase where demand is strong at the expense of firms with excess capacity. The securities markets tend to react to these shifting spending patterns. Generally more capital is allocated toward firms that appear to have bright prospects and away from firms where the outlook is poorer. Clearly this market-based reallocation of capital is an uncertain process. Let us consider how effectively the task is performed.

Sources and Uses of Funds

Companies need to finance their plant, equipment, and working capital. Funds can be obtained in the form of either debt or equity. Corporate debt sources include bonds, notes, trade credit, bank loans, accrued expenses, and all other firm borrowings. Stock sales and earnings retention (profit after taxes and dividends) are the primary ways of raising equity capital. Retained earnings supply most equity capital for most firms over most time periods. Stock sales generate only a modest portion of total new equity funds. For example, initial public offerings (stock sales of companies going public) amounted to $23.8 billion in 1987 compared with $22.4 billion in 1986. Although 20-plus billion dollars may seem like a substantial sum of money, it represents only a very small fraction of the equity market. Publicly held U. S. equity securities have a combined market value of about $2 trillion.

Corporate bond sales amounted to $318.3 and $281.9 billion in 1986 and 1987, respectively. Thus debt security sales amounted to perhaps 10 times the amount of new capital raised from new stock sales. The stock market's capital availability impact is much greater, however, than the relatively modest amount of capital raised through stock sales might suggest. Most firms try to maintain what they view to be an appropriate balance between debt and equity capital.

On the one hand, debt allows firms to lever their shareholder's equity position. If the gross profits earned with the borrowed funds exceed the cost of the loan, the return attributable to the owners (shareholders) is enhanced. Thus shareholders will benefit from an effective use of debt. On the other hand, firms have several reasons for not seeking to rely too much on debt. First, a borrower firm must make principal and interest payments on its debt or risk legal action that could lead to bankruptcy. Equity is, in contrast, permanent capital supplied by the owners. Thus the issuing company may suspend, reduce, or freeze its payments to shareholders (dividends) without violating any legally enforceable commitment. Second, a high debt ratio tends to increase the interest rate on all of the company's borrowings. Thus, as the firm's debt ratio rises, its interest expense increases as a result of two factors: the greater amount borrowed and the higher cost of the funds borrowed. Third, if the borrowing rate exceeds the return on the additional investment, debt will depress the firm's earnings. The greater the percentage of debt, the greater will be the adverse effect of leverage. Thus even though the target ratio may vary with the industry, the firm, and over time, efforts to stay within the desired debt–equity range still limit borrowing and encourage equity sales.

The Role of the Securities Markets in Allocating Capital Funds

The amount of equity capital that a firm can raise is constrained by the price it can get for its stock. Firms are expected to avoid selling more stock when such sales would adversely affect their existing shareholders. While the long-term impact is very difficult to judge, some attention is given to the effect of stock sales on per share book value (accounting value of equity). Book value is one, admittedly imperfect, measure of the firm's own resources (as opposed to borrowed resources). Per share book value measures the resources attributable to each share. Thus a stock sale that increases per share book tends to raise the amount of resources attributable to each share, whereas a sale that decreases per share book has the opposite effect. The higher a stock's price relative to its per share book value, the easier equity capital is to raise. A high relative share price allows a given sum to be raised with less dilution.

Consider this example. The BCD Company has a total accounting equity value of $5,000,000 and 1,000,000 shares outstanding selling for 10. To raise $1,000,000 (ignoring underwriting costs), it could sell 100,000 shares. The sale would increase shares outstanding by 10%. Its per share book value would rise from $5 ($5,000,000/ 1,000,000) to $5.45 ($6,000,000/1,100,000). Now contrast this situation with that of the CDE Corporation. CDE also has a total accounting equity value of $5,000,000 but its stock sells for $2.50. To raise $1,000,000, CDE would need to sell 400,000 shares. As a result shares outstanding would increase 40% and per share book value would fall to $4.29 ($6,000,000/1,400,000). Many of its shareholders would likely object to a sale of stock at a price below its per share book value.

Thus companies like BCD, with high stock prices relative to book values, can usually raise additional equity more easily than those like CDE, with lower relative stock prices. Moreover, because debt is considered less risky when the capital structure contains proportionately more equity, a high relative stock price indirectly contributes to the success of a debt offering. Thus both debt and equity capital tend to be more available to firms with the greatest perceived potential.

The stock market also has an impact on a firm's ability to retain earnings. Stocks of rapidly growing firms are unlikely to be hurt by a large retention ratio (percentage of earnings not paid out in dividends). Increased per share earnings are generally associated with rapid growth. Rapid growth (particularly rapid growth in profits) tends to raise stock prices sufficiently to offset the foregone dividends. Other firms may maintain a higher payout (percentage of earnings paid as dividends) to compensate for their slower growth, however. Alternatively, companies with otherwise unneeded funds may repurchase and then retire their own stock, thereby channeling funds toward firms with greater potentials.

Allocating Management Talent

The stock market also helps allocate managerial talent. Stock prices of poorly managed firms often do not fully reflect their potentials. Such undervalued situations attract investors who may try to take control, put in more effective managements, and profit from the improved operation. Sometimes the mere threat of a takeover is enough to stimulate better management. Such well-known investors as T. Boone Pickens, Saul Steinberg, Carl Icahn, Irwin Jacobs, the Bass family, Sir James Goldsmith, and a host of others have found these strategies to be very profitable.

Takeover artists frequently utilize a technique called the *leveraged buyout*. The acquisition targets' own asset values are used to finance much of the acquisition costs. Once in control, the acquirer may replace ineffective management and sell company assets in order to increase profitability and generate cash. For example, Mobil Oil's unsuccessful attempts to acquire Conoco (acquired by Du Pont) and Marathon Oil (acquired by U.S. Steel); Texas International's takeover of Continental, Frontier, People, and Eastern Airlines; Icahn's takeover of TWA; Pickens' attempts to acquire Phillips, Gulf, and Unical; Goldsmith's effort to acquire Goodyear; and Bass's move on Disney all envisioned substantial management turnover. Otherwise, why do the targets resist so vigorously?

While takeovers have many motivations, almost all stem at least in part from the acquirer's belief that the acquisition is undervalued relative to its potential. Such potential can best be exploited (even in a friendly takeover) by bringing in fresh ideas, resources, and faces. Thus takeovers and potential takeovers help weed out deadwood and keep managers on their toes. Although such acquisitions are often accomplished through tender offers, proxy fights have become increasingly popular because they are generally cheaper for the raider.

The stock market may also play a significant role in facilitating the hiring of individual managers. Senior level managers are often compensated with a package of benefits including a base salary and pension benefits coupled with possible bonuses and stock options that depend on performance. Because the value of stock option packages tends to increase with the firm's growth potential, the options of promising firms may help attract managerial talent that other firms could only hire with higher salaries.

Criteria for Efficient Capital Allocation

To distribute capital and management talent effectively the stock market needs accurately to reflect each firm's earnings potential. Otherwise funds and talent may flow toward overvalued firms and away from undervalued firms. Moreover, high transactions costs would raise barriers to resource flows.

Friend carefully considered pricing efficiency and transactions costs.[7] He concluded that the stock market has been markedly unsuccessful in forecasting firm performance although its record has improved since the 1920s. He also found that while underwriting fees have declined since the 1920s, commission rates have tended to increase. More recently the end of fixed commissions has reduced trading costs for some while raising them for others. Friend also believed that increased security regulation contributed to improved market performance although he offered no suggestions for facilitating further improvement. Benston, in contrast, contended that the Securities Exchange Act of 1934 did not improve market efficiency. He found no evidence that trading on fraudulent and misleading reports decreased with the act's passage.[8]

OTHER ROLES OF THE MARKET

Consumers' spending is influenced by both their current income and their financial resources. One of the important types of financial assets is holdings of stocks and related assets (common stock mutual funds, pension funds with stockholdings, insurance policies with reserves invested in stocks, etc.). Thus a rising stock market tends to increase investor wealth and spending whereas a declining stock market has the opposite effect. The Federal Reserve Board (Fed) relies on the impact of stock-market-induced wealth effect. That is, when the Fed seeks to influence the economy through changes in monetary policy, it depends upon the stock market to transmit part of the impact to consumers. While the Fed may also adjust the margin rate to encourage spending or discourage speculation, it rarely does so. Figure 3.2 illustrates the relationship between stock prices and consumer spending.

FIGURE 3.2   How Stock Values Move Consumer Spending

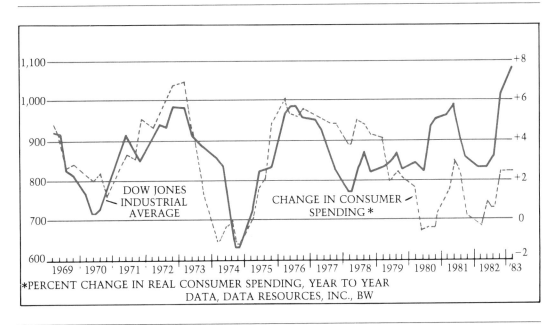

Source: "Wall Street's Big Gift to the Recovery," *Business Week*, May 9, 1983, pp. 126–128. Reprinted with permission of McGraw-Hill, Inc.

SUMMARY AND CONCLUSIONS

This chapter considered the trading mechanics, regulation, and economic functions of the securities markets. A wide array of mechanisms may be used to buy and sell securities. Most trading involves the larger companies listed on an exchange. Smaller companies are generally traded OTC. Newly issued securities may be sold through a rights offering, underwriting syndicate, or private placement. Large blocks of already-issued securities are normally marketed through a block trader, special offering, or in a secondary offering. A tender offer is generally used for a large purchase. Short sales are employed by those seeking to profit from a price decline while margin purchases lever one's equity position. A variety of different types of orders are used in securities trading. Market orders require immediate execution whereas limit orders await an acceptable price. Stop orders offer protection from adverse price moves.

Six stock-trading rules were offered. First, for a large transaction, shop for the best price on the third market, regional exchanges, and principal exchange. Second, use discount brokerage firms to obtain reduced commissions. Third, take careful account of the advantages and disadvantages of the OTC market. To yield a profit an OTC stock's price must rise sufficiently to offset the spread. OTC spreads are usually wider than on listed stocks. Furthermore, many unlisted stocks are not marginable. On the other hand, local OTC stocks may be more familiar to individual investors and more likely to be undervalued. Fourth, limit orders, which offer flexibility and protection from adverse price moves, should generally be used rather than market orders. Fifth, margin credit, a flexible source of funds available at relatively low interest costs, may be used to magnify profit potential. Sixth, if a stock is held in a street name, a portion should be retained in the customer's name to ensure receiving company reports promptly.

As for the development of the central market, reform forces are quite powerful; much progress has been made; opposition to additional reform is intense; further reforms have been recommended and will probably be enacted. The principal unresolved issues involve the consolidation of trading, limit order access, and repeal of off-board trading restrictions. The question is not whether but when these reforms will take place.

The securities markets play an important but not all-important role in allocating capital and managerial talent as well as in facilitating the Fed's implementation of economic policy.

REVIEW QUESTIONS

1. Discuss the expanding functions of brokerage firms and financial services companies. How are commercial banks becoming more like brokerage firms and brokerage firms more like banks? What limits these two types of financial institutions from merging into a single type?

2. Explain the role of SIPC. How does it compare with the FDIC? How might its operations be reformed?

3. Consider the pros, cons, and selection of investment advisors. How do their costs and average performances compare with mutual funds and individually managed portfolios?

4. Compare exchanges with the OTC market. What is the NASD? Discuss the various lists for OTC stocks. From an investor's standpoint, what are the advantages and disadvantages of an exchange listing?

5. Discuss commissions and discount brokers. Who should use a discounter and who should use a retail broker? What levels of discounts are available through discounters? Can a discount be obtained through a retail broker? If so, how and under what circumstances are such discounts available?

6. Explain the various types of orders. Under what circumstances is each appropriate? What are the limitations of each of these types of orders?

7. Discuss Branch's three rules for setting a limit price. Under what circumstances should one ignore these rules and use a market order?

8. Why are limit orders on regional exchanges and the OTC relatively ineffective? Does the investor have any alternatives?

9. How has the NYSE acted in the past to maintain its dominance? Discuss the current attitude toward the NYSE.

10. What forces have led to the decline of the NYSE's power? Are these forces continuing to have an impact? What has been the impact of the October 19, 1987, stock crash on the image of the NYSE and the securities industry in general?

11. In the past how have the exchanges regulated themselves and how has the SEC regulated the industry? Discuss the present regulatory situation.

12. What would the institution of a central market accomplish? What further reforms are required to create a central market for securities?

13. Discuss street name securities, the elimination of the stock certificate, and unlisted trading. What are the roles of the third and fourth markets?

14. How do the securities markets affect a firm's ability to raise funds? How important is the equity market to firms seeking to raise capital? Can most firms rely primarily on debt capital? Why or why not?

15. What role do the securities markets play in allocating management talent? How do raiders enter into this process? What is the role of stock options?

16. What factors are necessary for the securities markets to be able to allocate capital and management talent efficiently? How effectively have the securities markets performed these tasks?

17. How do the securities markets affect the economy? How does the Fed use this relationship? What happened to the economy after the October 19, 1987, stock market crash? How did the Fed respond to the crash?

REVIEW PROBLEMS

1. Using the schedule in Table 3.2, compute the commissions for the following:
   a. 300 shares selling at 21
   b. 5,000 shares selling at 3¾
   c. 50 shares selling at 250

2. Compute the total cost of the trade (commission plus bid–ask spread) for the following OTC trades. Assume that the investor buys at the bid and sells at the ask and pays commissions according to the schedule in Table 3.2.
   a. purchase 500 shares when the quote is 15–15½ and sell when the quote is 19–20
   b. purchase 3,000 shares with a quote of 1–1⅜ and sell when the quote is 1¼–1⅝
   c. purchase 200 shares with a quote of 80–81 and sell when the quote is 105–106

3. Compute the spread, percentage spread, holding period return, and trading costs as a percentage of the initial costs for the quotes and transactions in Problem 2.

4. Using Table 3.2, compute the commission on a single trade of 1,500 shares at $7 per share. Now compute the commission on 15 separate 100-share trades at $7 per share. Compare the two commissions.

5. Assume you purchased XYZ stock in five 300-share blocks at prices of 15, 18, 31, 23, and 40. You then sell 700 shares. What would normally be your basis? What would be the maximum basis? How would you achieve that basis?

6. Compute the percentage gains and losses on margined and unmargined investments assuming the following:

   purchase stock at 100
   hold for a year
   margin rate = 50%
   margin borrowing cost = 10%
   stock sells at the end of year for: 50, 60, 70, 80, 90,
       100, 110, 120, 130, 140, 150, 200

7. Assume the broker call loan rate is 8½% and that the margin loan rates of Table 3.6 apply. Compute the cost of margin for each of the following, using monthly compounding:
   a. $53,000 borrowed for six months
   b. $27,000 borrowed for three months
   c. $7,000 borrowed for ten months.

8. Joe Ann Investor uses $5,000 plus maximum margin (50%) to buy stock in the Up Up Corporation at $10 per share. The stock is a clear winner. It rises to 15 in the first month that she holds it. It then splits three for two and continues rising. When, after another four months, it reaches 20, Joe Ann buys as many more shares as her position allows. It then pays a 25% stock dividend and rises to 30 after another six months. At that point she again increases her holdings to the maximum allowed by her equity. Up Up then goes to 50 a year later. What does Joe Ann's position now look like? How many shares does she own? How much are they worth? How much does she owe in margin? What is her equity position? In this exercise ignore the impact of taxes, dividends, interest, and commissions.

9. Joe Investor uses $50,000 plus maximum margin (50%) to buy stock in the Down Down Corporation at $50 per share. After six months the stock falls to the point where he gets a margin call (35% equity). To satisfy the call he sells enough of his position to bring his equity back up to 50%. Two months later he gets another margin call and repeats the process. When four weeks later he gets the third margin call, he liquidates his position. How much of his original investment is left? In this exercise ignore the impact of taxes, dividends, interest, and commissions.

10. Repeat Questions 8 and 9, bringing in the impact of taxes, interest, dividends, and commissions. Assume both investors are in the 28% tax bracket and incur a margin interest rate of 9%. Up Up pays a quarterly dividend equal to 1% of its price. The first dividend is paid in the second month of the holding. Down Down pays no dividends. Use Table 3.2 to compute commissions.

11. You sell 500 shares of the Loser Corporation short at 50. How much margin must you put up? The stock eventually falls to 30, at which point you cover. What is your gross profit? What is it after commissions (use Table 3.2)? Compute the holding period return relative to the amount put up as margin.

12. The ABC Corporation has 5,000,000 shares outstanding and a total net worth of $60,000,000. If it sells an additional 750,000 shares for a price to buyers (15% flotation costs) of $18 per share, what will happen to its net worth and per share book value?

13. Rework Problem 12 but assume that the stock is sold for $10 per share.

REVIEW PROJECTS

1. Ask two retail and two discount brokers for their rate schedules. From these schedules compute the rates for the following:

    100-share order for stock at 5, 10, 20, 40, and 80
    300-share order for stock at 5, 10, 20, 40, and 80
    1,000-share order for stock at 5, 10, 20, 40, and 80
    2,000-share order for stock at 1, 2, 5, 10, and 50

    Compare the rates and write a report.

2. Select four groups of five OTC stocks: (1) priced under $5 per share, (2) priced at $5 to $15 per share, (3) priced at $15 to $25 per share, and (4) priced at more than $25 per share. Compute the average spread on each and display the results graphically.

3. Ask a broker for a list of five OTC stocks selling for $10 a share or less. Ask for a current bid–ask quote on each. The Pink Sheets should list them. Compute the percentage spread. Do the same thing for five OTC stocks selling for approximately $10 per share. Do the same thing for five NYSE stocks selling for over $50 per share. Such quotes are available from a quotation machine. Write a report.

4. Plot the price of a stock for two weeks. Select a level to place a limit order to buy the stock. Follow the security for two weeks after you have selected a limit order level to see whether you would have bought it and if so how much lower it goes. Now repeat the process for a sell order. Write a report.

5. Select a stock to sell short. Determine how much margin would be required to sell 100 shares. Assuming you maintain the short position for one year, determine the price to which the stock must fall for you to break even. Realize that you must cover commissions on the sale and repurchase, the opportunity cost of foregone interest on the margin deposit (assume 10%), plus any dividends on the shorted stock.

NOTES

1. P. Brimelow, "SIPC Falls Short," *Barron's*, April 19, 1982, p. 12; "Panel Recommends Congress Broaden SIPC's Authority," *The Wall Street Journal*, May 10, 1982, p. 20; M. Brody, "When Brokers Go Bust," *Barron's*, May 16, 1983, pp. 8, 9, 38.

2. J. Pearl, "Smart Money?" *Forbes*, October 11, 1982, 132–137.

3. B. Branch, "The Optimal Price to Trade," *Journal of Financial and Quantitative Analysis*, September 1975, 497–514.

4. P. Jessup and R. Upson, *Returns in Over-the-Counter Stock Markets* (Minneapolis: University of Minnesota Press, 1973).

5. A. Senchack and W. Beedles, "Price Behavior in a Regional Over-the-Counter Securities Market," *The Journal of Financial Research*, Fall 1979, 119–131.

6. K. Cohen, S. Maier, R. Schwartz, and D. Whitcomb, "An Analysis of the Economic Justification for Consolidation in a Secondary Security Market," *Journal of Banking and Finance*, no.6, 1982, 117–136.

7. I. Friend, "The Stock Market and the Economy," *American Economic Review*, May 1972, 212–219.

8. E. G. Benston, "Required Disclosures and the Stock Market: An Evaluation of the Securities Act of 1934," *American Economic Review*, March 1973, 133–135.

SECTION TWO

Investment Theory

Section II explores the theoretical foundation of investment valuation. Much of this material is relatively abstract, but it provides a workable format for evaluating investment opportunities. The following hypothetical case raises many of the issues that are dealt with in this section.

EVALUATING CASH FLOWS: THREE INVESTMENTS

Your grandmother is a smart lady but knows little about investing. She is now considering three different investment ideas that a family friend/broker suggested to her. Since your grandfather recently died leaving her a relatively large sum of money, she is quite at a loss as to her future course. You, a business school major and her favorite grandchild, are the one she asks first for advice.

The first investment is a long-term (20-year) corporate bond in a local electric utility (no nuclear exposure). It has a 12% coupon and currently sells for 95. Its yield to maturity is 1.5% above that of otherwise similar government bonds. The broker says it is quite safe (AA rating).

The second investment is stock in a newly formed company that claims to be close to discovering a practical way of generating electricity from the lightning in thunderstorms. The broker acknowledges that the risks are substantial but claims that this investment offers the potential for spectacular gains. If the technology is successful, it could be supplying 5% of our energy needs by the year 2000. While the firm's founders and managers are keeping most of the stock for themselves, they need risk capital. Accordingly they recently sold stock to outside investors through a new issue (prospectus available). The broker estimates that 100 shares of this stock (now trading for about $10 per share) could be worth one to ten million dollars in 10 to 20 years. Alternatively, it could be worth nothing. The current technological problems may not be overcome and the firm has no other operations. Moreover, because of continuing capital needs, no dividends are likely to be paid for at least 10 years. Indeed, the company is likely to have to sell still more stock over time.

The final investment option is a common stock mutual fund. In the past this fund's price has tended to move in approximately the same pattern as the S&P 500 index. It currently pays a dividend plus capital gains distribution of around

8% and its per share price has tended to rise an average of 6% per year over the past five years. It is part of a family of funds that allow investors to switch into different types of investments without extra charge. The other funds in the family are: (1) money market mutual fund, (2) international fund, (3) tax-free bond fund, (4) long-term government bond fund, (5) social responsibility stock fund, and (6) option fund.

Buying any of these investments will incur commissions. Bond trades will cost $5 per $1,000 face amount of the bonds. The stock is subject to a 3% commission and trades at $10 bid, $10.50 asked. The mutual fund is subject to an 8.5% load, but this is reduced to 6% for purchases over $20,000.

Your job is to explore the pros and cons of each of these investment opportunities, both for your grandmother's specific circumstances and more generally. You should first analyze the projected cash flows of each investment and then relate the expected returns to the risks associated with each. Finally you should recommend a strategy. Realize that you may recommend only one investment or a combination. Also note that as one of her heirs, you have a personal interest in the performance of your grandmother's portfolio.

Once your own analysis is complete, write a report on your findings. Make sure your case in convincing. While your grandmother has confidence in you, she will want to understand clearly not only what you advise but why you have made that particular recommendation. Be sure to explain all of your assumptions and the relevant risks to each investment.

While you would need considerably more information to analyze these investments thoroughly, the descriptions contained herein do illustrate some of the commonly encountered issues in cash flow evaluation. Section II explores the theory of such valuations. Chapter 4 examines the discounted-expected-income-stream approach to valuation. Both stock and bond applications are used to illustrate this method of valuing assets. The chapter ends with a discussion of various approaches to forecasting income streams. Chapter 5 explores risk and portfolio theory's role in investment valuation. Several simplified ways of estimating portfolio risk are given particular attention. Tests of three major implications of portfolio theory are discussed in Chapter 6: (1) Markets are efficient; (2) Discount rates are only related to market risk; and (3) Realized returns are linearly related to risk.

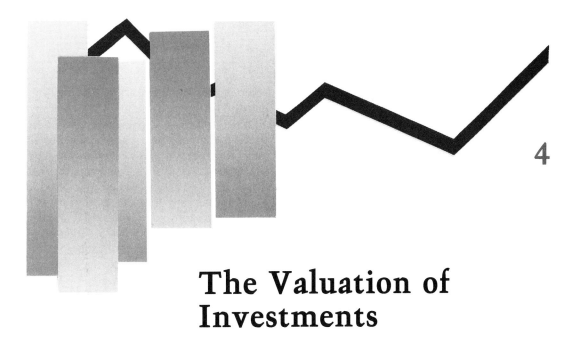

The Valuation of Investments

Most prices (including the prices of investment assets) are established and maintained by market forces. That is, the interplay of supply and demand sets such prices at levels that allow the relevant markets to clear. At the market price all would-be buyers have bought and all would-be sellers have sold. Additional buyers are available at lower prices and more sellers are available at higher prices. Market prices fluctuate as market forces vary over time. That is, market prices change as new buyers (demand) or new sellers (supply) enter or leave. Underlying the determination of the market price is a more complex set of processes. Understanding these processes and the implications of these prices is an important step in any comparative valuation process.

Investments trade largely on the basis of their expected income and price appreciation. Accordingly, we shall examine how such expectations influence market values. First, time value is introduced and its investment valuation role assessed. Both bond and stock valuations are explored in the context of their expected income stream values. The role of risk in establishing the appropriate discount rate is also discussed. The remainder of the chapter deals with various approaches to forecasting income streams of stocks.

TIME VALUE

Time value is crucial to expected income stream valuations. Suppose you were offered the choice of receiving $100 now or $100 a year from now. Which would you choose? Almost everyone would choose to have the money now rather than later. Even those who did not intend to use the money for a year would not want to wait for it. Any funds that are available now but not needed until a year from now can be invested. For example, the funds could earn a year's interest in a government-guaranteed savings account. At 5% the $100 would grow to $105 in a year. Clearly, a sum of money that is available now is worth more than that same sum to be received at a later time. In other words, money has what is called time value. The concept of the time value of money is central to the valuation of investments. Investments pay or are expected to pay a return over time.

To understand how time value enters into investment valuation, consider the value of a commitment to pay $100,000 a year for 20 years. Such a commitment could arise in a number of ways. For example, one could sell a business to a buyer who commits to such a payout. Alternatively, it could arise when a university chair is endowed. The benefactor of a chair must supply the university with enough money to pay the professor's salary and other expenses (secretarial, etc.) until retirement. If the professor is now 45 years old, he or she can be expected to continue to hold the chair for another 20 years. The giver might offer to make a separate payment each year, but few if any universities would be comfortable with such an arrangement. The university would have committed itself to make the payments to the chaired professor until he or she retires. What would happen if the benefactor died, went broke, or changed his or her mind? Because of these uncertainties, the university would expect the chair to be funded up front.

How much would be required to assure the university that it would be able to cover the payments? Although $2,000,000 in payments are promised, the value of the commitment is considerably less. Even at a 5% annual interest rate, a $2,000,000 savings account would yield $100,000 a year forever. If the university could earn 8% on its investments, it could generate a $100,000 payment each year with $1,250,000 (8% of $1,250,000 is $100,000). It could do the job with even less if it used part interest and part principal each year. With this strategy, at the end of 20 years the initial sum would be depleted. On the other hand, if the payments were to be raised each year to offset the impact of inflation, the initial sum would need to be greater. Clearly problems like this one have a number of dimensions. They involve relating current stocks of money to flows of money through time. How much, for example, is a promise to pay X dollars a year for Y years worth in current funds? The answer turns out to be relatively straightforward.

As we have already seen, a current dollar can begin earning interest immediately. Thus, a currently payable dollar should be worth more than a promise to pay an identical sum in the future. How much more should the current dollar be worth? The current value of a future payment depends upon three things: how much is to be received, when it is to be received, and how much of a (time) discount is applied to future values compared to present values. Similarly, the value of a stream of payments to be received over time depends upon the amounts, timings, and time discounts of the payments.

Discounting to Take Account of Time Value

Valuing an expected stream of future payments involves placing a value on each individual expected future payment. That valuation should put each such payment on the same plane as an immediate payment. The current or discounted value of a future sum is often called its *present value*. Once the present value of each expected future payment is determined, the individual present values can be summed. The resulting sum is the present value of the expected future payments. The trade-off between present and future values is called the discount rate. The appropriate discount rate will vary substantially with the specific circumstances of the item to be evaluated and the economic environment. If a present dollar is viewed as equivalent to $1.06 a year from now, the corresponding discount rate is 6%. Using a 6% discount rate, one dollar received today is equivalent to $1.1236 two years hence (1.06 × 1.06 = $1.1236). Similarly, a promise to pay a dollar next year is worth $.944 today (.944 × 1.06 = 1.00). Discounting an asset promising three annual payments of $100 at 6% yields:

$$PV = \frac{\$100}{1.06} + \frac{\$100}{(1.06)^2} + \frac{\$100}{(1.06)^3} = \$267.30$$

where:

$$PV = \text{present value of the income stream}$$

Discounting the first year's payment at 6% is equivalent to dividing it by 1.06. The second year's payment is discounted at 6% twice, which corresponds to dividing it by (1.06 × 1.06) or $(1.06)^2$. Similarly, the third year's payment is divided by 1.06 × 1.06 × 1.06 or $(1.06)^3$.

Valuing an asset (again using a 6% discount rate) yielding successive annual payments of $100, $300, $50, $100, and $300 and a sale price of $1,000 involves a little more complicated arithmetic but the principle is the same:

$$PV = \frac{\$100}{(1.06)} + \frac{\$300}{(1.06)^2} + \frac{\$50}{(1.06)^3} + \frac{\$100}{(1.06)^4} + \frac{\$1,300}{(1.06)^5}$$

or:

$$\$94.34 + \$267.00 + \$41.98 + \$79.21 + \$971.45 = \$1,453.98$$

Note that the sale price and final payment are both discounted by $(1.06)^5$ because both are to be paid five years hence. Present value tables or an electronic calculator with financial functions are often employed to simplify present value computations.

Present Value Applied to Bonds

Let us see how the concept of time value can be applied to the income stream of a bond. The reader will recall that bonds are debt securities that make periodic fixed-level interest (coupon) payments and then return their face value at maturity. Thus, for example, a 10-year 8%, $1,000 bond would promise the following income stream: coupon payments of $40 every six months (half of 8% of $1,000) for 10 years and at the end of 10 years a principal payment of $1,000. An investment promising such an income stream can be valued by the present value formula (Equation 4.1).

$$PV = \frac{CF_1}{(1+r)} + \frac{CF_2}{(1+r)^2} + \cdots \frac{CF_n}{(1+r)^n} \cdots \qquad (4.1)$$

where:

$$CF_i = \text{cash flow received in period i}$$
$$r = \text{appropriate discount rate}$$

We see from the examples that investment assets can be viewed as streams of expected incomes. Clearly, the discount rate plays a central role in the valuation of such expected income streams. A given expected income stream will have a higher computed value, the lower the discount rate is. Similarly, a lower discount rate will increase the value placed on an expected income stream. For example, a $1,000 (face value) bond paying $50 per year and maturing in seven years is, at an 8% discount rate, worth:

$$\text{Present value} = \frac{\$50}{1.08} + \frac{\$50}{(1.08)^2} + \frac{\$50}{(1.08)^3} + \frac{\$50}{(1.08)^4} +$$

$$\frac{\$50}{(1.08)^5} + \frac{\$50}{(1.08)^6} + \frac{\$50}{(1.08)^7} + \frac{\$1,000}{(1.08)^7}$$

$$= \$50 \, (.926 + .857 + .794 + .735 +$$

$$.681 + .630 + .583) + \$1,000 \, (.583)$$

$$= \$843$$

Note that the present value of this bond is less than its $1,000 face value. Indeed, any bond with a coupon rate below the discount rate sells for less than face. In this instance, the promised coupon rate is $50 on $1,000 or 5% (50/1,000 = .05), which is below the assumed discount rate of 8%.

Where a constant amount is to be paid forever, a simpler formula relates the market price to the discount rate.

$$PV = \frac{CF}{r} \qquad (4.2)$$

where:

$$PV = \text{present value of the income stream}$$
$$CF = \text{each period's cash flow}$$
$$r = \text{appropriate discount rate}$$

Thus a perpetual $50 annual payment rate divided by 5% has a present value of $1,000. Put another way, $1,000 invested at 5% can earn $50 per year forever. If the market interest rate changes, the value of the $50 payment stream also changes. Suppose, for example, interest rates rise to 10%. Dividing the $50 per year payment stream by 10% produces a $500 value. A fall in interest rates has the opposite effect. At 4% the $50 payment stream is worth $1,200 ($50/.04). Although Britain has issued some infinite-maturity bonds called Consols, the vast majority of debt obligations promise to repay principal at some future date.

Why Bond Prices Vary from Their Face Values

Most bonds are initially sold for a price close to their par, or face, values. Their coupon rate is generally set to yield a return very close to the market interest rate on such bonds. The subsequent market interest rate and price, however, seldom stay very close to that level. Economic forces invariably cause market interest rates to fluctuate over time. Such market forces also lead to changes in the prices on existing bonds.

A 7% bond will pay $70 per year and return $1,000 of principal at maturity regardless of the future market rates. If otherwise similar newly issued 9% bonds ($90 per year coupon) sell at their face values, the 7% bond must also be priced to return 9%. No one will pay $1,000 for a bond yielding $70 per year when equally safe bonds yielding $90 per year trade for $1,000. Rather than sell for its face value, the 7% coupon bond must offer a yield to maturity (YTM) equivalent to the otherwise similar 9% bond.

The YTM is the discount rate that makes the present value of the coupon and principal payments equal to the market price of the bond. The YTM is analogous to the internal rate of return concept of capital budgeting. Thus a bond whose present value at 9% is $950 will have a 9% YTM if it sells for $950. The YTM can be computed by hand, but most people prefer to use a bond book or financial calculator.

Thus bond prices and, indeed, most security prices move inversely with market interest rates. If interest rates rise, bond prices will decline, and vice versa. The face value of a seasoned bond may bear no more resemblance to its market value than a new sticker price on a car does to the car's later value as a used or antique car.

DETERMINANTS OF THE DISCOUNT RATE

Discount rates clearly play an important role in investment valuations. The appropriate discount rate varies both over time and from investment to investment. We shall now explore some of the factors that influence their determination.

Changing market conditions can affect the general level of interest rates, as we have just seen. Such changes will in turn cause individual bond prices to move up and down as market interest rates move down and up. What causes market rates to change? At times the supply of funds available for borrowing (relative to the demand) is tight while at other times loanable funds are more plentiful. Market interest rates vary inversely with the relative supply of loanable funds. More money in the system looking for borrowers corresponds to lower interest rates, whereas more borrowers looking for money to borrow correspond to higher rates. The state of the economy and the government's economic policy (covered in detail in Chapter 11) play a major role in determining conditions in the credit markets and thus the general level of interest rates. The discount rate applied to a particular expected income stream will vary up and down as general market rates move up and down.

In addition to the generalized impact of the credit markets, a particular asset's appropriate discount rate will vary with several other factors, especially risk. The more certain the expected outcome, the lower the appropriate discount rate is. Because a lower discount rate increases the value of an income stream, low-risk expected income streams are valued more highly than high-risk expected streams of equivalent magnitude. For example, the bonds of very secure companies should be discounted at lower rates than those of less secure companies. Similarly, a stock with a stable or steadily increasing dividend should be evaluated with a lower discount rate (and thus have a higher market price) than an otherwise similar stock whose dividends are expected to be less stable.

Interest Fluctuation and Default Risk

A bond's risk may be decomposed into two categories. The likelihood that the issuer's obligation will not be fulfilled (e.g., bankruptcy or repudiation) is called default risk. Interest fluctuation risk, in contrast, stems from sensitivity to changing market rates.

The government guarantee of savings accounts eliminates their default risk while the ability to withdraw part or all of the account eliminates their interest fluctuation risk. Similarly, short-maturity Treasury bills have very little default or interest fluctuation risk. Indeed, all government-guaranteed investments have minimal default risk. The market trusts the guarantee, the government has extensive taxing power, and the Fed can facilitate its debt sales.

The default risk of municipal and corporate debt securities is always considered greater than that of Treasury issues. How much greater depends on the income-producing and/or liquidation values of the issuers. Some issues with strong financial positions are only slightly more risky than federal government securities, while default is much more likely for others.

Interest fluctuation risks also vary substantially. The prices of longer maturity debt issues and all equity securities are much more sensitive to interest rate shifts than are shorter term debt issues. For example, a one-year bond that will pay $1,000 in principal and $70 in interest is worth about $1,000 if discounted at 7%. Similarly, a long-term bond that has a coupon rate equal to 7% of face will sell for its face value if discounted at 7%. If relevant interest rates move up to 8%, the value of the short-term bond will fall by about $10 to $990 (1% of $1,000 = $10). On the other hand, a long-term 7% bond (that is worth $1,000 when valued with a 7% discount rate) will fall by a much greater amount if long-term rates rise to 8%. In the case of a Consol, the price of the bond would fall from $1,000 by $125 to $875 ($70/.8). A long-term but finite life bond would fall by almost this much. Thus we might well expect higher discount rates for longer term issues. While the so-called term structure of interest rates often has this pattern (higher rates for longer maturities), the relationships are more complex. We shall return to this topic in a later chapter.

The Discount Rate for a Risky Asset

The discount rates applied to risky investments can be viewed as determined by two basic forces. First, general credit conditions determine the general level of interest rates, including the rate for riskless assets. The appropriate rates for risky assets are scaled up from the current market rate on riskless assets. Yields on government bonds are often used to proxy for the riskless rate. A riskless rate of 9% and *risk premium* (inducement required to attract risk-averse investors) of 2% would imply an 11% (9% + 2%) discount rate. Should the riskless rate fall to 7%, the appropriate rate for this risky asset would become 9% (assuming the 2% risk premium remains unchanged). The appropriate rate for discounting any income stream equals the riskless rate plus a specific risk premium associated with the asset's risk.

The Risk Premium. A bond's coupon and principal repayment terms are fixed by the indenture encompassing all of the commitments the company makes to its bondholders. If a bond does default, the trustee (usually a bank identified in the bond's indenture) is obligated to take appropriate legal action to protect the bond-holders' interests. With the income stream commitment fixed in the indenture, the risk premium set by the market is directly observable as the difference between the bond's stated YTM and the riskless rate. For example, a medium-grade corporate bond yielding 11% has a risk premium of 3% when government bonds with similar maturities yield 8%.

Examples of Risk Premiums. Some estimated risk premiums for early 1982, a period of relatively high interest rates and late 1987, a period of lower interest rates, are given in Table 4.1. This table illustrates the wide range in risk premiums (defined here as the difference the yield can take on for a risky security and an otherwise similar risk-free asset). For example, the Public Service of New Hampshire (PSNH) 14½% bonds of 2000 were priced to yield 18.1%, compared with similar maturity Treasury bonds yielding 8.9%. The PSNH bond's risk premium of over 9% reflects the very real threat that the utility will be forced to declare bankruptcy. PSNH is the lead utility (with the largest percentage ownership) in a troubled project to construct a nuclear power facility at Seabrook, New Hampshire. Indeed, shortly after this particular set of quotations was compiled, PSNH did declare bankruptcy. Similarly, the Texas Air 15¾% bonds of 1992 had an 8.2% risk premium. Texas Air was also experiencing major difficulties as its various subsidiary airlines were all having problems reaching their breakeven load factors (the percentage of seats filled on an average flight). Coincidentally one of Texas Air's subsidiaries is Eastern Airlines, whose 17½% bonds of 1998 were priced to yield 18.1% in 1982. Texas Air subsequently acquired Eastern and exchanged its own debt securities (at a discount) for those of Eastern. While investors in Eastern's bonds have as of mid-1988 avoided a default, they continue to hold very risky securities. On the other hand, the AT&T and Citicorp bonds were low-risk instruments in 1982 and remained so in 1987. Their bonds were priced to yield very little more than comparable maturity Treasuries. Thus the market persists in thinking that these issuers are very unlikely to default.

TABLE 4.1 Yields to Maturity for Selected Bonds

January 4, 1982

Issuer	Coupon Rate	Maturity	Price	Yield	Risk Premium
U.S. Treasury	13¼	1991	94⁷⁄₁₆	13.8%	0%
AT&T	13	1990	94	14.1	.3
Citicorp	14⅜	1986	97¼	14.5	.7
Pacific Telephone	15⅛	1988	100	15.0	1.2
Alabama Power	14¾	1995	95	15.5	1.7
Montgomery Ward	16	1986	98¼	16.3	2.5
Georgia Pacific	16.9	1987	97¼	17.3	3.5
Eastern Airlines	17½	1998	96⅞	18.1	4.7

December 30, 1987

Issuer	Coupon Rate	Maturity	Price	Yield	Risk Premium
U.S. Treasury	11¾	2001	121⅝	8.9%	0%
AT&T	8¾	2000	94⅛	9.3	.4
Citicorp	8⅛	2007	83⅝	9.7	.8
Alabama Power	8⅞	2003	89¼	9.9	1.0
Georgia Power	11	2009	100¼	11.0	2.1
GAF	11⅜	1995	94⅜	12.1	3.2
Ramada Inns	11⅝	1999	88⅞	13.1	4.2
Pennzoil	14⅝	1991	101	14.5	5.6
Texas Air	15¾	1992	92	17.1	8.2
Public Service of NH	14½	2000	80	18.1	9.2

ᵃThe risk premium is the yield less riskless yield.
Note: The computed risk premiums are approximations that ignore the impact of differential tax rates and maturity differences.

The risk premium on a debt security, as the term is used here and as it is commonly understood, reflects both the expected loss from default and an additional increment called the pure risk premium. Consider the Georgia Power 11% bonds of 2009. On December 30, 1987, it was priced at 100¼ to yield 11%. This pricing corresponds to a risk premium of 2.1%. Suppose that the market estimates the Georgia Power bond's probability of default to be 1% and the expected loss from a default (if it occurs) to be 50% of the payment stream's present value. The market's actual expectations are not directly observable. These particular numbers may or may not be reasonable estimates. For the sake of the analysis, however, let us use them as if they are accurate estimates of the true market expectations. The corresponding expected loss from default would equal .5% (.01 × .5) of the principal. Subtracting this expected default loss of .5% from the total risk premium of 2.1% leaves a pure risk premium of 1.6%. Thus, according to this analysis, the pure risk premium needed to induce risk-averse investors to purchase this risky security was 1.6%.

While the decomposition of the risk premium into its two components cannot be observed directly, inferences can be drawn from historical default experience.

For the vast majority of bonds (particularly those rated medium risk or better) the default loss has, since the end of World War II, been very much lower than the risk premiums of the various risk classes.[1] Thus either the market does not trust the forecast value of past default experience or expected default losses are a relatively small component of risk premiums.

Other Factors Affecting the Discount Rate

We have already seen that both general credit conditions and the risk of default play a large role in determining the appropriate rate for discounting a bond or other asset's expected income stream. The term structure has also been mentioned. While a more detailed exploration of these issues must wait, a bit more can be said at this juncture. Relations between rates for different maturities (the term structure) are determined by the market. Finally, various special characteristics such as whether or not a particular bond can be called (repurchased by the issuer at a specified price prior to maturity) may affect its price and thus its discount rate.

DETERMINING THE APPROPRIATE DISCOUNT RATE

This exploration of discount rate determinants has only shifted our focus. To ascertain the appropriate rate we must still identify the riskless rate, assess the asset's risk, and estimate the appropriate risk premium. The market rate on government securities approximates the riskless rate. Assessing risk and determining the appropriate risk premium (pure and default) are, however, rather complicated topics requiring more detailed treatment.

Applying Present Values to Stocks: The Dividend Discount Model

Stocks can be valued with the same basic approach as is used for bonds. A share of stock represents fractional ownership of a corporation. Shareholders are able to participate in the firm's performance in two ways. First, most firms pay out a portion of profits to shareholders in the form of dividends. Not all firms pay dividends in a given year but most are expected to do so sooner or later. Second, profits not paid out as dividends (retained earnings) are plowed back into the company. The additional resources acquired with these retained earnings should help increase future earnings and dividends. If all goes according to plan, the firm's growing assets and sales will be accompanied by increases in earnings, dividends, and its stock price. Stockholders can then sit back and enjoy the higher dividends and the rise in the value of their portfolio. Alternatively, they can take advantage of the higher stock price to sell some or all of their shares at a profit. Thus stock market returns may take the form of both dividends and price appreciation.

Obviously, not all stocks experience rising earnings, dividends, and stock prices. Indeed, some companies experience losses, pay no dividends, and their stock's price declines. In extreme cases the company may be forced to declare bankruptcy and thereby leave the shareholders with nothing but some worthless stock certificates and a tax write-off. Nonetheless, those who buy stock expect to receive a return in the form of dividends and/or price appreciation. Thus, in principle, discounting a stock's expected dividend stream and future market value should yield its present value:

$$S_o = \frac{d_1}{(1 + r)} + \frac{d_2}{(1 + r)^2} + \frac{d_3}{(1 + r)^3} + \ldots + \frac{(d_n + S_n)}{(1 + r)^n}$$

where:

$$S_o = \text{present value of share}$$
$$d_t = \text{expected dividend for year t}$$
$$r = \text{appropriate discount rate}$$
$$S_n = \text{expected stock price for year n}$$

Moreover, S_n can be evaluated by discounting subsequent dividends. Note that S_n's value stems entirely from the future dividends that its owners expect to receive. That is:

$$S_n = \frac{(d_n + 1)}{(1 + r)^{(n + 1)}} + \frac{(d_n + 2)}{(1 + r)^{(n + 2)}} + \ldots$$

Thus:

$$S_o = \frac{d_1}{(1 + r)} + \frac{d_2}{(1 + r)^2} + \frac{d_3}{(1 + r)^3} + \ldots + \frac{d_n}{(1 + r)^n} + \ldots \qquad (4.3)$$

Note that Equation 4.3 merely restates Equation 4.1.

The Constant Growth Case.   A much simpler formula applies when dividends can be assumed to grow at a constant rate. Define g as the expected growth rate of initial dividends, d. Thus $d1 = d(1 + g)$. Equation 4.3 then becomes:

$$S_o = \frac{d(1 + g)}{(1 + r)} + \frac{d(1 + g)^2}{(1 + r)^2} + \frac{d(1 + g)^3}{(1 + r)^3} + \ldots + \frac{d(1 + g)^n}{(1 + r)^n} + \ldots$$

This formula reduces to the following:

$$S_o = \frac{d}{(r - g)} \qquad \text{for } g < r \qquad (4.4)$$

Equation 4.4 yields a value for a stock when its dividends are expected to grow at a constant rate g. In other words, the equation says that a stock's price should equal its current dividend rate divided by the difference between its expected growth rate and the appropriate discount rate. According to this formula, the price of a stock rises with both its current dividend rate and its expected growth rate and falls as the discount rate is increased. This relationship (Equation 4.4) is exactly correct when the expected growth rate g is a constant value. It is approximately correct when g represents an average value and each year's actual value is not expected to deviate greatly from that average. This relationship is the basis for the so-called dividend discount model. This model and various modifications provide investment analysts with a tool for evaluating relative stock values.[2] Their advocates claim that such models can be quite helpful in identifying misvalued securities.

The formula holds only for expected growth rates that are below the discount rate. Stocks whose dividends have expected growth rates that are forever above the discount rate would have infinite prices. That nonsensical result would occur because each successive expected dividend would have a higher present value than the one before it. Because the dividend payments would be expected to continue forever, their sum would grow without bound. Clearly, only finite stock prices are observed. Thus we need not concern ourselves with the possibility that long-term expected growth rates might exceed the appropriate discount rate. For short periods companies may grow more rapidly than their market-determined discount rate. Such growth rates are, however, anomalies. In the long run, dividends are expected to grow more slowly than the rate at which they are discounted.

Stock Prices and PE Ratios.   Investors and investment analysts often focus on the price of a stock in relation to its earnings per share. The per share price divided by the per share earnings is called the price earnings or PE ratio. The more optimistically the market views the prospects for particular stock, the more it is prepared to pay relative to current earnings. Thus the stocks of companies with favorable growth opportunities (often called growth stocks) tend to have high PE ratios. Stocks with more mundane potentials have lower PEs. Equation 4.4 can be restated to illustrate the relation between PE and growth:

$$S_o/e = \frac{(d/e)}{(r - g)}$$

or:

$$PE = \frac{p}{(r - g)} \qquad (4.5)$$

where:

$$e = \text{earnings per share}$$
$$PE = S_o/e, \text{ the price earnings ratio}$$
$$p = d/e, \text{ the expected payout ratio}$$

Thus the PE ratio is a function of three variables: the expected growth rate g; the expected payout ratio p (the percentage of earnings that are paid to shareholders); and the discount rate r. It rises with g and p and falls as r is increased.

The Market Price of an Investment

Investment prices implicitly reflect their discounted expected income streams. Very few potential traders explicitly compute discounted expected incomes. Nonetheless, an implicit analysis of future returns prospects and the associated risk is an integral part of the pricing process. The more efficient the market, the more accurately the price will reflect available risk/returns information.

Applying the Dividend Discount Model: An Example

AT&T provides us with a useful opportunity to see how the dividend discount model might be applied. At year-end 1987 AT&T's common stock was priced at 27. Its indicated dividend rate was $1.20 per share per year. Earnings per share (EPS) through the first nine months of 1987 were $1.42. These nine-month earnings extrapolate to a 12-month EPS estimate of about $1.90 (4/3 $\times$ 1.42). (AT&T's actual 1987 EPS turned out to be $1.88 but the market did not know this until several weeks past year-end 1987.) Such estimated earnings correspond to payout of .63 (1.20/1.90). Long-term Treasuries were at this time yielding about 8.9% while AT&T's own bonds were yielding in the range of 9.3% to 10%. AT&T's common stock is by its very nature considerably riskier than its bonds. Thus the risk premium of its common stock should be appreciably higher than that of its bonds. Perhaps a risk premium in the area of 4% would be appropriate for the common. That would imply an appropriate discount rate of 12.9%. AT&T's expected annual EPS of $1.90 implies a PE of 14.2. Applying these numbers to the PE ratio equation yields the following:

$$14.2 = \frac{.63}{(.129 - g)}$$

or:

$$g = .129 - \frac{.63}{14.2} = .085$$

Thus the market at year-end 1987 appeared to be pricing AT&T's common stock at a level that implies an expected growth rate in the range of 8.5%. This result is, however, sensitive to our assumed values for dividends, EPS, and the risk premium.

Suppose, for example, we thought a 3% risk premium were more appropriate than the initial assumption of 4%. That change would imply an expected market growth rate of 7.5%. Alternatively, suppose our annual EPS estimate were changed to $2. This EPS would change the payout to .6 and the PE to 13.5. Curiously, the resulting expected growth rate remains almost unchanged at 8.5%. The impact of the decline in the payout largely offsets the impact of the lower PE. A change in the stock price, however, has a more significant impact. A week earlier AT&T's common had been priced at 29. That implied a PE of 15.3, which in turn implied a market expected growth rate of 8.8%.

These estimated growth rates in the range of 7.5% to 9% may or may not be accurate but they do seem reasonable. The economy generally grows at a rate of about 3% to 4% in real terms (adjusted for inflation), and inflation may add about another 4% to 5%. Thus, in nominal terms, the economy generally grows in the range of 7% to 10%. Presumably, AT&T will grow at approximately the growth rate of the economy. While interesting, none of this analysis has indicated whether AT&T is an attractive investment (underpriced), an unattractive investment (overpriced), or fairly priced. Such a determination requires us to take a further step. We must compare the market's expectations with our own. In other words, we must assess the accuracy of the market price.

The *promised* future income stream of bonds (coupon plus principal) is directly observable. For those who hold onto their bond investments until they mature, the promised return generally differs little from the "expected" future income stream (coupon plus interest less expected default loss). Only if the bond defaults or is called early will the actual return be different from the promise. Similarly, preferred stocks normally have observable promised future income streams (indicated dividends) close to their expected values (expected dividends). Moreover, some preferreds mature and most are callable.

Common stocks, in contrast, do not promise a future income stream or redemption and are not callable. Thus, expected income streams of common stock are much more difficult to observe than those of fixed income securities. While one may use market analysts' forecasts or historical extrapolations to estimate expectations, the market's true expectations may differ. The market does, however, almost always generate a price. In and of itself the price does not reveal the market's income stream expectations. The price is jointly determined by the expected payments and the rate used to discount them. Nonetheless, the price, which is observable, does provide some insight into the market's income stream expectations, which are not observable.

Implications of the Market Price

The market's weighted-average opinion of a particular investment (as reflected by the price that it determines) is, by itself, of little help in investment selection. Market expectations may or may not be accurate. The investment selection process can be viewed largely as a search for assets that the market has improperly valued. In other words, investment analysis generally involves an attempt to understand and find errors in the market's evaluation. Investors can compare their own discounted dividend forecasts with the market's or compare their assessments of the company's growth prospects with the market's expectations. The two approaches are mathematically equivalent. With either, investors identify "undervalued" and "overvalued" securities by contrasting their valuations with the market's. Selections based on such analysis can fail to produce the expected result for a number of reasons:

1. The income stream forecasts can be inaccurate.
2. Even if the income forecasts are on target, errors in the assumed discount rates can account for the apparent difference between the investor's and the market's evaluations.
3. The anticipated earnings increase can be offset by an increase in risk.
4. The investor may sell the asset before the market reevaluates it.
5. The investor may correctly identify undervalued securities whose subsequent revaluations are offset by a general market decline.

Clearly, a security identified as undervalued may not necessarily produce profits for its owners.

If the investor's analysis proves to be both timely and more accurate than the market's analysis, the selections should show superior risk-adjusted returns. Where the market's expectations are essentially correct, the selections will tend neither to outperform nor underperform the market. Frequently, however, both the market's and the investor's analysis are too optimistic and the selections underperform the market. Equally frequently, a general market decline pulls down the prices of even many "undervalued" securities. Investment analysts hope that their evaluations are more accurate than the market's often enough to outweigh the times that they are either too optimistic or the market declines. Because average market performance reflects the weighted-average performance of all participants, however, the average investor/analyst cannot outperform the market average. The stock market is in fact a zero (or constant) sum game. This basic fact illustrates the difficulty of successful investing. Only a minority of stock market participants can outperform the market averages and only a still smaller minority can do so consistently. Nonetheless, most investors continue to try. Investing is a game that may not be worth playing but it is certainly a game worth winning.

FORECASTING THE INCOME STREAM

Evaluating an investment involves forecasting its income stream and assessing the corresponding risk. A more detailed analysis of risk is beyond this chapter's scope. We shall, however, now discuss efforts to forecast the income streams of stocks. Risk will be considered in detail in the next two chapters.

The Relationship Between Dividends and Earnings

Most stock valuation models call for dividend forecasts. In practice, however, earnings per share are usually forecast instead. This substitution of EPS for dividends is at best imperfect. Only for a 100% payout will the value of the expected dividend stream precisely equal the value of that firm's expected earnings stream. Payouts very rarely reach 100%. Thus stock values based on earnings streams are at best only an approximation. The appropriateness of such an approach depends upon the relation between expected dividends and earnings. Earnings are a useful proxy for dividends if they move up and down proportionately together.

Many firms try to maintain a stable, long-term relationship between dividends and earnings (payout).[3] Payouts do, however, tend to vary from firm to firm and over time for the same firm. More specifically they tend to move inversely with growth, risk, and earnings volatility. Thus a company with rapidly growing, volatile, and uncertain earnings tends to pay out a smaller fraction of earnings than a slower growth firm with a more dependable earnings stream. Most mature companies have a relatively high, stable long-run payout ratio, however. Typically, between 50% and 60% of corporate after-tax earnings are paid out as dividends.

The Value of Accurate Earnings Predictions

One extensive study covering the 1962–1963 period found that stocks with above-average earnings growth outperformed Standard & Poor's 500 stock average by

4.3% while stocks with below-average earnings growth underperformed the S&P index by 12%. Similar results have been found for many different samples and time periods.[4] The key question, however, is not whether accurate earnings forecasts would be useful, but how accurate most earnings forecasts are.

Types of Earnings Forecasts

Investment analysts base their earnings predictions on relevant available data (usually public). Management forecasts generally utilize at least some nonpublic information. In addition, annual earnings predictions can be based on already-reported quarterly earnings. Finally, past earnings can be extrapolated mechanically.

Although the short-run relationship between dividends and earnings is variable and uncertain, the longer run relationship is relatively stable and certain. Moreover, dividends are often slow to adjust to a change in profitability. Thus a given year's dividends may not reflect the firm's long-term ability to pay dividends as well as do its earnings. Finally, that portion of profits not paid out as dividends (retained earnings) is plowed back into the company. Hopefully these retained earnings will enhance subsequent growth, profits, and dividends. Accordingly, security evaluation often begins with earnings predictions. Accurate earnings predictions should facilitate similarly reliable dividend forecasts. Such dividend forecasts should, when appropriately discounted, yield meaningful value estimates. The relationship between earnings and stock prices is illustrated in Figure 4.1.

Investments Analysts.   The predictions and recommendations of investment analysts are notoriously uneven. For example, in July 1972, Wertheim & Company said: "Equity Funding's inherently conservative approach to business may be viewed as a strong defensive weapon in the hands of a group of uncommonly able executives aggressively seeking and obtaining a growing share of the financial service market."[5] In April 1973 Equity Funding was exposed in a $2 billion phony insurance scheme. Similarly, Jas. H. Oliphant and Company had been recommending Levitz Furniture since it was 5. After it reached a high of 60½ in 1972, Oliphant recommended Levitz Furniture at 41 and again at 26. The stock fell to 1⅝ in December 1974.

One of the nation's largest brokerage firms, Merrill Lynch, Pierce, Fenner & Smith issued favorable reports on Scientific Controls between March 1, 1968, and

FIGURE 4.1   Earnings, Dividends, and Stock Prices

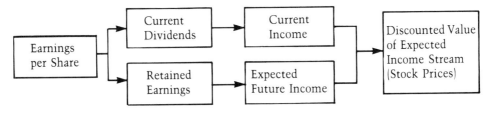

Investments in Perspective

Most recommendations from brokerage houses are not disastrous but merely average. Investors might have done about as well by chance, as the following article from The *Wall Street Journal* illustrates.

Last Summer's Lists of Hot Stock Picks From Brokerage Firms Weren't So Hot

---
YOUR
MONEY
MATTERS

By JOHN R. DORFMAN
Staff Reporter of THE WALL STREET JOURNAL

Popular magazines can tell you the 10 best-looking movie stars or the 10 mistakes that ruin a marriage. Brokerage houses can tell you their 10 favorite stocks.

Timetables vary, but brokerage firms are especially fond of issuing stock lists in the summer. That's partly due to Shearson Lehman Brothers Inc., which has made its list of "Uncommon Values in Common Stocks" a summer tradition for 39 years. The list's long-term track record is impressive: To date, its picks have appreciated 24,981%, compared with 2,044% for the Standard & Poor's 500 index, according to Shearson Lehman.

But a look at five lists issued last summer shows that investors shouldn't expect any special magic. In most cases, investors could have done almost as well by throwing darts at the New York Stock Exchange listings. They would have done considerably better just buying the 30 stocks in the Dow Jones Industrial Average.

Is Big Better?

A backward glance at last summer's lists also shows that the best recommendations don't necessarily come from the biggest and best-known brokerage houses. Piper, Jaffray & Hopwood Inc., a relatively small firm based in Minneapolis,

outdid Shearson and two other big New York firms, as well as Hartford, Conn.-based Advest Inc.

The midyear lists analyzed included 10 stocks each from Shearson, the Merrill Lynch Market Letter and Prudential-Bache Securities. Piper Jaffray's list consisted of 14 stocks; Advest's had eight.

The accompanying table shows the results investors would have achieved by purchasing equal dollar amounts of each list's recommended stocks on Aug. 1, 1986, and holding the shares until July 31, 1987, regardless of any subsequent recommendations. Dividends were included in the analysis; commissions and taxes weren't.

Piper, Prudential-Bache and the Merrill Lynch Market Letter all beat the New York Stock Exchange Composite Index, but not by much. Shearson's highly touted list didn't match the index, and Advest's fell well short of it.

The Minneapolis firm picked four solid winners—Champion International Corp., General Electric Co., Geo. A. Hormel & Co., and NCR—each up between 60% and 70%. Alone among the five firms, it showed a gain on every stock recommended.

John A. Tauer, a managing director in Piper's research department, says the firm looks for undervalued stocks selling for reasonable multiples of earnings per share. Last summer, he says, the firm was emphasizing interest-sensitive stocks. Now, it is emphasizing cyclical and technology stocks.

Both Piper and runner-up Prudential-Bache stressed consumer stocks, reasoning that tax revision, lower gas prices and lower interest rates would enable consumers to spend briskly in 1986-87. Prudential-Bache had the two biggest winners on

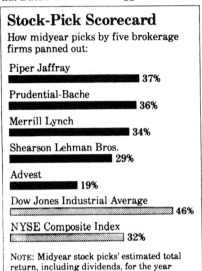

Stock-Pick Scorecard

How midyear picks by five brokerage firms panned out:

Piper Jaffray **37%**

Prudential-Bache **36%**

Merrill Lynch **34%**

Shearson Lehman Bros. **29%**

Advest **19%**

Dow Jones Industrial Average **46%**

NYSE Composite Index **32%**

NOTE: Midyear stock picks' estimated total return, including dividends, for the year ended July 31, 1987. Stock indexes' gains don't reflect dividends.

any of the five lists—Gillette Co. (up 94%) and clothing retailer Merry-Go-Round Enterprises Inc. (up 87%).

Prudential-Bache analysts liked Gillette for its commanding market share in the razor and blade market. But in the end, it was takeover interest from Revlon Group that got the stock into a lather.

Despite its pair of big hits, Prudential-Bache's total return was pulled down by one major loser—Mellon Bank Corp. Bad loans and plunging profits sent Mellon shares reeling downward 30%, contradicting Prudential-Bache's expectation of an "exciting turnaround story."

Anne E. Gregory, publisher of the Merrill Lynch Market Letter, stresses that its stock picks don't constitute official recommendations of parent company Merrill Lynch, Pierce, Fenner & Smith Inc. She says the letter is sold to some 70,000 subscribers, many of whom aren't Merrill Lynch customers.

The letter, Ms. Gregory adds, recommends stocks twice a month, not just once or twice a year. It highlights "midyear

investment ideas" in a special format only for "competitive reasons," she says.

Ms. Gregory maintains a fairer way to evaluate is to use the past 24 issues, not just one, or to focus on Merrill Lynch's more closely watched year-end list of stocks, which she says was up 56.5% since December.

At Shearson, company officials concede that the company's list underperformed the market in 1986-87 and in three of the past four years. Jack Rivkin, Shearson's recently appointed research director, says that even in a year like the past one, the list met its goal, which is "to make money for people." He adds that "to the extent there were mistakes, I think the mistakes were in focusing on some smaller companies." Foreign investors, who have had a big impact on the market, have been concentrating on big-capitalization and well-known companies, he notes.

His aim on this year's list, Mr. Rivkin says, was to shift the focus back to "uncommon values," as opposed to "uncommon companies." Thus, the 1987-88 list includes such household names as McDonald's Corp. and Northwest Airlines.

Big Loser

The performance of the 1986-87 Shearson list was hurt by three stocks that declined—H.F. Ahmanson & Co., Boeing Co., and Nicor Inc.

Advest, which trailed the rest of the group, was hurt by a 32% loss in S.E. Nichols Inc., a regional retailer, and a 26% loss in Shared Medical Systems Corp., a provider of computer systems to hospitals.

Howard Nichol, a vice president and analyst, says that the firm had changed its recommendation on Shared Medical Systems in February when the company indicated its growth targets wouldn't be met. A customer who heeded the change would have gotten out before the price collapsed, and, in fact, would have made money on the stock, he says.

Advest also changed its opinion on S.E. Nichols in October. But that was too late to avert most of the damage, as the price had already slid to less than $7.50 from more than $10 a share in early August.

November 14, 1969—just one week before the firm filed for bankruptcy. An SEC suit alleged that Merrill Lynch either knew or should have known that its recommendation was based on false and misleading information. Merrill Lynch eventually paid $1.6 million to customers who lost money by following the firm's misguided recommendation. Many similarly disastrous recommendations could be cited.

On the other hand, an extensive study by Elton, Gruber, and Grossman found that new buy recommendations outperformed new sell stocks by about 4.5%.[6] Two basic problems with most investment analysts are their tendency to utilize similar approaches and their reluctance to recommended sales. Thus those rare analysts who do not follow the herd and sometimes recommend selling may deserve close attention.

Although not all recommendations and forecasts are disastrous, many are ill-advised. Cragg and Malkiel studied five financial institutions covering 185 companies over the 1962–1963 period. They found the growth rates predicted by analysts highly correlated with past growth but not with the actual growth rates that they were attempting to forecast:

> Evidence has recently accumulated that earnings growth in past periods is not a useful predictor of future earnings growth. The remarkable conclusion of the present study is that careful estimates of the security analysts participating in our survey, the bases of which are not limited to public information, perform only a little better than these past growth rates. Moreover, the market price-earnings ratios themselves were not better than either analysts' forecasts or the past growth rates in forecasting future earnings growth.[7]

Similar conclusions emerged from a series of studies appearing in the early 1970s.[8]

More recently, Richards, Benjamin, and Strawser studied 92 firms over the 1972–1976 period and another 50 for 1969–1972.[9] They reported that security analysts' forecasts had relative absolute errors of 24.1% compared with 28.9% for the best mechanical rule that they tested. Similarly, Brown and Rozeff found that Value Line's 1972–1975 earnings predictions for 50 randomly selected firms were superior to the best forecasts that they could generate by mechanical means.[10] A follow-up study of 11 Value Line analysts' performance for the 1973–1975 period produced equivalent results.[11] Thus the earlier studies emphasized the forecasts' shortcomings and the more recent work stressed their superiority over naive prediction methods. Brown and Rozeff's samples were, however, restricted to a small number of Value Line company forecasts, and the Richards, Benjamin, and Strawser sample included only firms having forecasts for every year from 1972 to 1976. Thus both studies were based on small and possibly biased samples.

Branch and Berkowitz, in contrast, examined a much larger and broader based sample of forecasts that appeared annually in *Business Week* over the 1973–1977 period.[12] They concluded that these earnings forecasts tended to outperform their trend estimates and were significantly more accurate than random chance. The forecasts were, however, biased and except for 1976 explained substantially less than 10% of the interfirm variation in per share earnings changes.

The Branch-Berkowitz findings shed light on the apparent conflict between the first and second generation of earnings forecast papers. According to Brown and Rozeff, "past comparisons of analysts' forecasts are not more accurate than time series forecasts" while their own results "overwhelmingly favor the superiority of analysts over time series models."[13] In fact, however, Cragg and Malkiel (whom they cite as one source of their statement on past research) actually stated that "careful estimates of the security analysts participating in our survey, the bases of which are not limited to public information, perform only a little better than these past growth rates."[14] "Only a little better than" does not translate into "not more accurate than." Thus the two sets of studies largely disagree in emphasis and interpretation while agreeing in substance.

In addition to the level of errors in analysts' forecasts, we would like to know the nature of the errors. Are some situations more likely to lead to large forecast errors? Do analysts learn much from experience? Does a wide range in forecasts indicate anything about the likely error? A study by Elton, Gruber, and Gultekin addresses these types of issues.[15] They reached the following conclusions:

1. Analysts' forecast errors tend to decline monotonically as fiscal year-end approaches.

2. Analysts tended to forecast overall earnings for groups of stocks accurately.

3. Errors in forecasting industry earnings were appreciably less than those for individual companies.

4. Most analysts tend to overestimate the growth in those earnings that they expect to be strong and underestimate the growth that they expect to be weak.

5. Difficulty in forecasting earnings in one year is associated with similar difficulty in the following year.

6. Divergence of earnings forecasts is associated with errors in the forecasts.

Corporate Forecasts.   For a number of years the SEC has encouraged corporations to make their own internal earnings predictions public. Corporate officials have direct access to nonpublic corporate information and special expertise in analyzing expected profit impacts. Thus their estimates should be relatively accurate. Furthermore, stockholders are not likely to forgive a poor forecasting record. Accordingly, managers usually have both the means and the incentive to forecast effectively. In spite of SEC encouragement, however, relatively few corporations have released earnings forecasts for their firms. Moreover, the firms that have disclosed their forecasts tend to have more stable and therefore more predictable earnings streams than those that have not.[16]

Stockholders are thought to utilize announcements of dividend changes to assess management's confidence in future earnings. A dividend increase is interpreted as evidence that management expects earnings to remain at current levels or rise. A dividend reduction or suspension is viewed as indicating a lack of management confidence in the future. Both Pettit and Watts reported that unexpected dividend changes accompany stock price changes.[17] Both authors also found that dividend changes tended to forecast earnings changes. Somewhat more to the point, Copeland and Marioni found executive forecasts superior to naive forecasts (trend extrapolation).[18] Basi, Carey, and Twark reported that management forecasts were slightly more accurate than analyst forecasts whereas Ruland found no significant difference between the two groups.[19] Porter found both that management's ability to forecast depended upon the corporation's past earnings variability and that utilities' earnings were easier to forecast than manufacturers' earnings.[20] Penman reported that both dividend change announcements and managements' earnings forecasts reflected managements' expectations.[21] In a more recent study Penman reported that corporate forecasts of substantial earnings increases coupled with insider purchases around the time of the forecast release were associated with strong subsequent performance.[22]

Quarterly Earnings Extrapolations.   Investors often implicitly extrapolate interim results into annual estimates. If the first quarter's earnings are up by 20%, for example, does this imply the annual earnings are likely to improve by a similar amount? The reliability of such inferences needs to be tested. Green and Segall found almost no relationship. Brown and Niederhoffer, in contrast, reported a very modest relationship between first quarter and annual earnings growth.[23] Apparently year-end adjustments dominate the first quarter results. Boyle and Hogarty did find that firms tend to delay releasing unfavorable earnings.[24] Perhaps their managements were preparing their defenses for the reaction once the poor results are reported. Thus delay in an earnings report may be taken as a forecast of unfavorable results. On the whole, however, quarterly earnings tell us relatively little.

Past Earnings Growth.   We might well expect a high correlation between past and future growth in earnings. Able managements should, according to this line of reasoning, generate consistently above-average performance. Similarly, ineffective managements should tend to produce consistently poor performances. Thus past growth rates should be useful guides to the future. "Not so," said Little in "Higgledy Piggledy Growth."[25] Indeed, Little found very little relation between past and subsequent growth rates.

Little's work was confined to British corporations, but subsequent work with U. S. firms supported his conclusion.[26] Lintner and Glauber did find that firms with the most stable relationship (first quintile) between growth, income, and production showed a significant positive correlation (.40) between successive growth rates.[27] Subsequent work, however, has found somewhat greater association between future earnings growth and more sophisticated extrapolations of past growth.[28] Nonetheless, past growth is of no more than modest help in forecasting future earnings.

An Integrated Forecasting Approach.   The largely unsuccessful results of past forecasting efforts suggest the need for a more comprehensive approach. Although simple extrapolations of past earnings may not produce especially reliable forecasts, perhaps a more insightful use of past earnings data could facilitate superior predictions. Chant, for example, reasons that past business cycle sensitivity of earnings reflects future earnings relationships.[29] That is, earnings may be more accurately forecast when the firms' relations to their economic environments are considered. Preliminary work utilizing leading indicators has produced encouraging results. As yet, however, forecasts based on leading indicators are not publicly available.

Implications for Investment Analysis

Analysts' forecasts are of modest value; corporate forecasts are largely unobtainable and, when available, may not be appreciably more reliable; interim earnings have very little explanatory power; past growth rates are poor forecasters except when the growth rates have been stable; and forecasts based on leading indicators are not publicly available. The relative inaccuracy and/or unavailability of most types of year-ahead earnings predictions suggests that longer term forecasts may be especially unreliable. Year-to-year fluctuations may be smoothed, but the uncertainties of the more distant future tend to compound the inaccuracies of long-term forecasts. Indeed, few analysts even make such forecasts.

The shortcomings of earnings forecasts should be put in perspective. Anyone seeking to analyze investment opportunities encounters substantial difficulties and uncertainties. Success relative to others may lead to satisfactory results even when everyone must rely on rather inaccurate forecasts. Furthermore, other aspects of fundamental analysis may help investors form useful expectations of the future income streams that do not presuppose the accuracy implicit in the present value approach.

SUMMARY AND CONCLUSIONS

The price of an investment represents the market's assessment of the present value of the investment's expected future income stream. Observing the expected income streams and implied discount rates of bonds is relatively straightforward. The expected income streams and discount rates for stocks are, in contrast, appreciably more difficult to observe. Investment analysis seeks to generate superior (to the market's) estimates of the future income stream and appropriate discount rate. Thus investor/analysts compare the present value implied by their estimates of an asset's future income stream and appropriate discount rate with its market price. An undervalued asset is a good buy—particularly if it is more undervalued than the available alternatives. Such an analysis is, however, only as reliable as the inputs on which it is based. The approach may be useful when the estimates are relatively accurate (bonds). For stocks, however, forecasting difficulties make a straightforward application of present value estimates very nearly useless. Valuing assets on the basis of their discounted expected income streams provides a useful framework but identifying undervalued securities requires a much more effective approach.

REVIEW QUESTIONS

1. Explain what is meant by time value. How does the concept enter into investment valuation? Define and distinguish present value and compound value.

2. Explain how a 20-year bond with a $1,000 face value could sell for $600 or $1,200. What would cause such bonds to rise or fall in value?

3. How is an approach based on the present value of the expected future income stream used to value investment assets? How does such an approach compare with the capital budgeting methodology in financial management?

4. Discuss the various components of risk: default, interest fluctuation, pure risk premium. How does each enter into the valuation of debt securities?

5. Discuss how the market's evaluation and our own evaluation may be used to identify misvalued securities. What are some of the errors that can be made in such an approach to investment evaluation?

6. Why do investment analysts concentrate on earnings predictions rather than dividend predictions? Under what circumstances is such an approach warranted?

7. Compare earnings forecasts based on analysts' predictions, current earnings growth, management forecasts, interim earnings, and an integrated approach. Which methods are most accurate and which are least accurate?

REVIEW PROBLEMS

1. Compute the present value for the following income streams:
   a. $50 annually forever discounted at 10%
   b. $200 annually for 20 years discounted at 20%
   c. bond with $150 coupon for 12 years, maturing at $1,070 discounted at 16%
   d. payment stream of
        year 1: $200
        year 2: $300
        year 3: $400
        year 4: $500
     subsequent years: 0
        discounted at 8%

2. Compute the price of a 20-year bond with a 10% coupon when comparable market interest rates are:
   a. 7%
   b. 9%
   c. 10%
   d. 11%
   e. 13%

3. The American Pig Company (ticker symbol PORK) currently pays a dividend of $3.00 per share, which is expected to rise by $.25 per share for

the next five years. The stock currently sells for $36 per share per year, a ratio of 12 times its current dividends. The same ratio of dividends to price is also expected at the end of five years. Compute the present value of PORK's expected income stream for discount rates of 8%, 10%, 12%, 15%, 18%. Repeat the computation for a stable dividend of $3.00.

4. Evaluate the stock of ZYX Corporation using the following information:
   a. Current dividend rate—$1.00
   b. Dividend rate over next five years—$1.10, $1.20, $1.30, $1.40, $1.50
   c. Current market discount rate—16%
   d. Current market price/dividend rate—6.5

5. Repeat the analyses in Problem 4 using discount rates of 10% and 20%.

6. Using the dividend discount model, compute the market price for the following sets of information.
   a. $d = \$1;\ g = 10\%;\ r = 12\%$
   b. $d = \$2;\ g = 11\%;\ r = 12\%$
   c. $d = \$1.50;\ g = 8\%;\ r = 12\%$

7. Assuming a payout of 55%, what would be the PE ratios for Problem 6?

8. Compute the market-implied expected long-term growth rate for the following information:
   a. $PE = \ \ 8;\ p = 40\%;\ r = 12\%$
   b. $PE = 10;\ p = 50\%;\ r = 12\%$
   c. $PE = 15;\ p = 60\%;\ r = 12\%$

9. Suppose that you believe the firm described in Problem 8a will earn $1 and pay a dividend of $.40 next year. In fact, it will earn $1 but only pays out $.25 and continues with that payout ratio. How much lower must its PE ratio fall to be consistent with that dividend assuming the growth rate remains unchanged? Alternatively, how much higher must its expected growth rate be to justify the current PE? Which is more realistic? Explain.

10. Repeat Problem 9, this time assuming that the dividend increases to $.75 and that payout is maintained.

REVIEW PROJECTS

1. Select eight bonds with various yields and make a table similar to Table 4.1. Write a report.

2. Select 10 large companies at random and record the earnings forecast from the previous year's *Business Week* annual year-end investment issue. Compare these forecasts with the actual earnings for that year. What was the average percentage error? Write a report.

3. Update the analysis of AT&T in this chapter.

4. Choose a company that interests you and apply the PE ratio model to it.

NOTES

1. G. Pye, "Gauging the Default Premium," *Financial Analysts Journal*, January/February 1974, 49–52.

2. J. Farrell, "The Dividend Discount Model: A Primer," *Financial Analysts Journal*, November/December 1985, 16–25; P. Estep, "A New Method for Valuing Common Stocks," *Financial Analysts Journal*, November/December 1985, 26–33; B. Fielitz and F. Muller, "A Simplified Approach to Common Stock Valuation," *Financial Analysts Journal*, November/ December 1985, 35–41; D. Rie, "How Trustworthy Is Your Valuation Model?" *Financial Analysts Journal*, November/December 1985, 42–48; R. Michaud, "A Scenario-Dependent Dividend Discount Model: Bridging the Gap between Top-Down Investment Information and Bottom-Up Forecasts," *Financial Analysts Journal*, November/December 1985, 49–59; E. Sorensen and D. Williamson, "Some Evidence on the Value of Dividend Discount Models, *Financial Analysts Journal*, November/December 1985, 60–69.

3. H. Baker, G. Farrelly, and R. Edelman, "A Survey of Management Views on Dividend Policy," *Financial Management*, Autumn 1985, 78–83.

4. M. Kosor and V. Messner, "The Filter Approach and Earning Forecasts—Part One," unpublished manuscript cited in J. Lorie and M. Hamilton, *The Stock Market Theory and Evidence* (Homewood, Ill.: Irwin, 1973), 157. R. Brealey, *An Introduction to Risk and Return from Common Stocks* (Cambridge, Mass.: MIT Press, 1969); H. Latane and D. Tuttle, "An Analysis of Common Stock Price Ratios," *Southern Economic Journal*, January 1967, 343–354; C. Lee and K. Zummalt, "Associations between Alternative Accounting Profitability Measures and Security Returns," *Journal of Financial and Quantitative Analysis*, March 1981, 71–94.

5. M. Connor, "Wall Street Analysts Give Lots of Bad Advice Along with Good," *The Wall Street Journal*, May 25, 1973, p. 1.

6. E. Elton, M. Gruber, and S. Grossman, "Discrete Expectational Data and Portfolio Performance," *Journal of Finance*, July 1986, 699–714.

7. J. Cragg and B. Malkiel, "The Consensus and Accuracy of Some Predictions of the Growth of Corporate Earnings," *Journal of Finance*, March 1969, 67–84.

8. M. Richards, "Analysts' Performance and the Accuracy of Corporate Earnings Forecasts," *Journal of Business*, July 1973, 350–357; E. Elton and J. Gruber, "Earnings Estimates and the Accuracy of Expectational Data," *Management Science*, April 1972, 409–424.

9. M. Richards, T. Benjamin, and R. Strawser, "An Examination of the Accuracy of Earnings Forecasts," *Financial Management*, Fall 1977, 78–86.

10. L. Brown and M. Rozeff, "The Superiority of Analyst Forecasts as Measures of Expectations: Evidence from Earnings," *Journal of Finance*, March 1978, 1–16.

11. L. Brown and M. Rozeff, "Analysts Can Forecast Accurately," *Journal of Portfolio Management*, Spring 1980, 31–35.

12. B. Branch and B. Berkowitz, "The Predictive Accuracy of the *Business Week* Earnings to Forecasts," *Journal of Accounting Auditing and Finance*, Spring 1981, 215–219.

13. Brown and Rozeff, op. cit., 1.

14. Cragg and Malkiel, op. cit., 83.

15. E. Elton, M. Gruber, and M. Gultekin, "Professional Expectations: Accuracy and Diagnosis of Errors," *Journal of Financial and Quantitative Analysis*, December 1984, 351–364.

16. B. Jaggi and P. Grier, "A Comparative Analysis of Forecast Disclosing and Non-Disclosing Firms," *Financial Management*, Summer 1980, 38–46.

17. R. Pettit, "Dividend Announcements, Security Performance, and Capital Market Efficiency," *Journal of Finance*, December 1972, 993–1007; R. Watts, "The Information Content of Dividends," *Journal of Business*, April 1973, 199–211.

18. R. Copeland and R. Marioni, "Executive Forecasts of Earnings per Share versus Forecasts of Naive Models," *Journal of Business*, October 1972, 497–511.

19. B. Basi, K. Carey, and R. Twark, "A Comparison of the Accuracy of Corporate and Security Analysts' Forecasts of Earnings," *The Accounting Review*, April 1976, 244–254; W. Ruland, "The Accuracy of Forecasts by Management and by Financial Analysts," *The Accounting Review*, April 1978, 439–447.

20. G. Porter, "Determinants of the Accuracy of Management Forecasts of Earnings," *Review of Business and Economic Research*, Spring 1982, 1–13.

21. S. Penman, "The Predictive Content of Earnings Forecasts and Dividends," *Journal of Finance*, September 1983, 1181–1199.

22. S. Penman, "A Comparison of the Information Content of Insider Trading and Management Earnings Forecasts," *Journal of Financial and Quantitative Analysis*, March 1985, 1–17.

23. D. Green and J. Segall, "The Prediction Power of First Quarter Earnings Reports," *Journal of Business*, January 1967, 44–55; R. Brown and V. Niederhoffer, "The Prediction Power of Quarterly Earnings," *Journal of Business*, October 1968, 488–497; D. Green and J. Segall, "Brickbats and Strawmen: A Reply to Brown and Niederhoffer," *Journal of Business*, October 1968, 498–502; V. Niederhoffer, "The Predictive Content of First Quarter Earnings Reports," *Journal of Business*, January 1970, 60–62.

24. S. Boyle and T. Hogarty, " 'Good' News vs. 'Bad' News: Another Aspect of the Controversy Between Manager and Owner," *Industrial Organization Review*, vol. 1, 1973, 1–14.

25. I. Little, "Higgledy Piggledy Growth," *Institute of Statistics*, vol. 24, no. 4, November 1962; I. Little and A. Rayman, *Higgledy Piggledy Growth Again* (Oxford: Basil Blackwell, 1966).

26. G. Murphy, "Relative Growth in Earnings Per Share—Past and Future," *Financial Analysts Journal*, November/December 1966, 73–76.

27. J. Lintner and R. Glauber, "Higgledy Piggledy Growth in America?" paper presented to the seminar on the Analysis of Security Prices, University of Chicago, May 1967; "Further Observations on Higgledy Piggledy Growth," presented to same seminar; R. Brealey, "The Character of Earnings Changes," paper presented to the seminar on the Analysis of Security Prices, University of Chicago, May 1967.

28. W. Ruland, "On Choice of Simple Extrapolative Model Forecasts of Annual Earnings," *Financial Management*, Summer 1980, 30–37.

29. P. Chant, "On the Predictability of Corporate Earnings Per Share Behavior," *Journal of Finance*, March 1980, 13–21.

APPENDIX. PRESENT VALUE TABLES

TABLE 4A.1   Present Value of $1

Years hence	1%	2%	4%	6%	8%	10%	12%	14%	15%	16%	18%	20%	22%	24%	25%	26%	28%	30%	35%	40%	45%	50%
1	0.990	0.980	0.962	0.943	0.926	0.909	0.893	0.877	0.870	0.862	0.847	0.833	0.820	0.806	0.800	0.794	0.781	0.769	0.741	0.714	0.690	0.667
2	0.980	0.961	0.925	0.890	0.857	0.806	0.797	0.769	0.756	0.743	0.718	0.694	0.672	0.650	0.640	0.630	0.610	0.592	0.549	0.510	0.476	0.444
3	0.971	0.942	0.889	0.840	0.794	0.751	0.712	0.675	0.658	0.641	0.609	0.579	0.551	0.524	0.512	0.500	0.477	0.455	0.406	0.364	0.328	0.296
4	0.961	0.924	0.855	0.792	0.735	0.683	0.636	0.592	0.572	0.552	0.516	0.482	0.451	0.423	0.410	0.397	0.373	0.350	0.301	0.260	0.226	0.198
5	0.951	0.906	0.822	0.747	0.681	0.621	0.567	0.519	0.497	0.476	0.437	0.402	0.370	0.341	0.328	0.315	0.291	0.269	0.223	0.186	0.156	0.132
6	0.942	0.888	0.790	0.705	0.630	0.564	0.507	0.456	0.432	0.410	0.370	0.335	0.303	0.275	0.262	0.250	0.227	0.207	0.165	0.133	0.108	0.088
7	0.933	0.871	0.760	0.665	0.583	0.513	0.452	0.400	0.376	0.354	0.314	0.279	0.249	0.222	0.210	0.198	0.178	0.159	0.122	0.095	0.074	0.059
8	0.923	0.853	0.731	0.627	0.540	0.467	0.404	0.351	0.327	0.305	0.266	0.233	0.204	0.179	0.168	0.157	0.139	0.123	0.091	0.068	0.051	0.039
9	0.914	0.837	0.703	0.592	0.500	0.424	0.361	0.308	0.284	0.263	0.225	0.194	0.167	0.144	0.134	0.125	0.108	0.094	0.067	0.048	0.035	0.026
10	0.905	0.820	0.676	0.558	0.463	0.386	0.322	0.270	0.247	0.227	0.191	0.162	0.137	0.116	0.107	0.099	0.085	0.073	0.050	0.035	0.024	0.017
11	0.896	0.804	0.650	0.527	0.429	0.350	0.287	0.237	0.215	0.195	0.162	0.135	0.112	0.094	0.086	0.079	0.066	0.056	0.037	0.025	0.017	0.012
12	0.887	0.788	0.625	0.497	0.397	0.319	0.257	0.208	0.187	0.168	0.137	0.112	0.092	0.076	0.069	0.062	0.052	0.043	0.027	0.018	0.012	0.008
13	0.879	0.773	0.601	0.469	0.368	0.290	0.229	0.182	0.163	0.145	0.116	0.093	0.075	0.061	0.055	0.050	0.040	0.033	0.020	0.013	0.008	0.005
14	0.870	0.758	0.577	0.442	0.340	0.263	0.205	0.160	0.141	0.125	0.099	0.078	0.062	0.049	0.044	0.039	0.032	0.025	0.015	0.009	0.006	0.003
15	0.861	0.743	0.555	0.417	0.315	0.239	0.183	0.140	0.123	0.108	0.084	0.065	0.051	0.040	0.035	0.031	0.025	0.020	0.011	0.006	0.004	0.002
16	0.853	0.728	0.534	0.394	0.292	0.218	0.163	0.123	0.107	0.093	0.071	0.054	0.042	0.032	0.028	0.025	0.019	0.015	0.008	0.005	0.003	0.002
17	0.844	0.714	0.513	0.371	0.270	0.198	0.146	0.108	0.093	0.080	0.060	0.045	0.034	0.026	0.023	0.020	0.015	0.012	0.006	0.003	0.002	0.001
18	0.836	0.700	0.494	0.350	0.250	0.180	0.130	0.095	0.081	0.069	0.051	0.038	0.028	0.021	0.018	0.016	0.012	0.009	0.005	0.002	0.001	0.001
19	0.828	0.686	0.475	0.331	0.232	0.164	0.116	0.083	0.070	0.060	0.043	0.031	0.023	0.017	0.014	0.012	0.009	0.007	0.003	0.002	0.001	
20	0.820	0.673	0.456	0.312	0.215	0.149	0.104	0.073	0.061	0.051	0.037	0.026	0.019	0.014	0.012	0.010	0.007	0.005	0.002	0.001	0.001	
21	0.811	0.660	0.439	0.294	0.199	0.135	0.093	0.064	0.053	0.044	0.031	0.022	0.015	0.011	0.009	0.008	0.006	0.004	0.002	0.001		
22	0.803	0.647	0.422	0.278	0.184	0.123	0.083	0.056	0.046	0.038	0.026	0.018	0.013	0.009	0.007	0.006	0.004	0.003	0.001	0.001		
23	0.795	0.634	0.406	0.262	0.170	0.112	0.074	0.049	0.040	0.033	0.022	0.015	0.010	0.007	0.006	0.005	0.003	0.002	0.001			
24	0.788	0.622	0.390	0.247	0.158	0.102	0.066	0.043	0.035	0.028	0.019	0.013	0.008	0.006	0.005	0.004	0.003	0.002	0.001			
25	0.780	0.610	0.375	0.233	0.146	0.092	0.059	0.038	0.030	0.024	0.016	0.010	0.007	0.005	0.004	0.003	0.002	0.001	0.001			
26	0.772	0.598	0.361	0.220	0.135	0.084	0.053	0.033	0.026	0.021	0.014	0.009	0.006	0.004	0.003	0.002	0.002	0.001				
27	0.764	0.586	0.347	0.207	0.125	0.076	0.047	0.029	0.023	0.018	0.011	0.007	0.005	0.003	0.002	0.002	0.001	0.001				
28	0.757	0.574	0.333	0.196	0.116	0.069	0.042	0.026	0.020	0.016	0.010	0.006	0.004	0.002	0.002	0.002	0.001	0.001				
29	0.749	0.563	0.321	0.185	0.107	0.063	0.037	0.022	0.017	0.014	0.008	0.005	0.003	0.002	0.002	0.001	0.001	0.001				
30	0.742	0.552	0.308	0.174	0.099	0.057	0.033	0.020	0.015	0.012	0.007	0.004	0.003	0.002	0.001	0.001	0.001					
40	0.672	0.453	0.208	0.097	0.046	0.022	0.011	0.005	0.004	0.003	0.001	0.001										
50	0.608	0.372	0.141	0.054	0.021	0.009	0.003	0.001	0.001	0.001												

TABLE 4A.2   Present Value of $1 Received Annually for N Years

Years (N)	1%	2%	4%	6%	8%	10%	12%	14%	15%	16%	18%	20%	22%	24%	25%	26%	28%	30%	35%	40%	45%	50%
1	0.990	0.980	0.962	0.943	0.926	0.909	0.893	0.877	0.870	0.862	0.847	0.833	0.820	0.806	0.800	0.794	0.781	0.769	0.741	0.714	0.690	0.667
2	1.970	1.942	1.886	1.833	1.783	1.736	1.690	1.647	1.626	1.605	1.566	1.528	1.492	1.457	1.440	1.424	1.392	1.361	1.289	1.224	1.165	1.111
3	2.941	2.884	2.775	2.673	2.577	2.487	2.402	2.322	2.283	2.246	2.174	2.106	2.042	1.981	1.952	1.923	1.868	1.816	1.696	1.589	1.493	1.407
4	3.902	3.808	3.630	3.465	3.312	3.170	3.037	2.914	2.855	2.798	2.690	2.589	2.494	2.404	2.362	2.320	2.241	2.166	1.997	1.849	1.720	1.605
5	4.853	4.713	4.452	4.212	3.993	3.791	3.605	3.433	3.352	3.274	3.127	2.991	2.864	2.745	2.689	2.635	2.532	2.436	2.220	2.035	1.876	1.737
6	5.795	5.601	5.242	4.917	4.623	4.355	4.111	3.889	3.784	3.685	3.498	3.326	3.167	3.020	2.951	2.885	2.759	2.643	2.385	2.168	1.983	1.824
7	6.728	6.472	6.002	5.582	5.206	4.868	4.564	4.288	4.160	4.039	3.812	3.605	3.416	3.242	3.161	3.083	2.937	2.802	2.508	2.263	2.057	1.883
8	7.652	7.325	6.733	6.210	5.747	5.335	4.968	4.639	4.487	4.344	4.078	3.837	3.619	3.421	3.329	3.241	3.076	2.925	2.598	2.331	2.108	1.922
9	8.566	8.162	7.435	6.802	6.247	5.759	5.328	4.946	4.772	4.607	4.303	4.031	3.786	3.566	3.463	3.366	3.184	3.019	2.665	2.379	2.144	1.948
10	9.471	8.983	8.111	7.360	6.710	6.145	5.650	5.216	5.019	4.833	4.494	4.192	3.923	3.682	3.571	3.465	3.269	3.092	2.715	2.414	2.168	1.965
11	10.368	9.787	8.760	7.887	7.139	6.495	5.988	5.453	5.234	5.029	4.656	4.327	4.035	3.776	3.656	3.544	3.335	3.147	2.752	2.438	2.185	1.977
12	11.255	10.575	9.385	8.384	7.536	6.814	6.194	5.660	5.421	5.197	4.793	4.439	4.127	3.851	3.725	3.606	3.387	3.190	2.779	2.456	2.196	1.985
13	12.134	11.343	9.986	8.853	7.904	7.103	6.424	5.842	5.583	5.342	4.910	4.533	4.203	3.912	3.780	3.656	3.427	3.223	2.799	2.468	2.204	1.990
14	13.004	12.106	10.563	9.295	8.244	7.367	6.628	6.002	5.724	5.468	5.008	4.611	4.265	3.962	3.824	3.695	3.459	3.249	2.814	2.477	2.210	1.993
15	13.865	12.849	11.118	9.712	8.559	7.606	6.811	6.142	5.847	5.575	5.092	4.675	4.315	4.001	3.859	3.726	3.483	3.268	2.825	2.484	2.214	1.995
16	14.718	13.578	11.652	10.106	8.851	7.824	6.974	6.265	5.954	5.669	5.162	4.730	4.357	4.033	3.887	3.751	3.503	3.283	2.834	2.489	2.216	1.997
17	15.562	14.292	12.166	10.477	9.122	8.022	7.120	6.373	6.047	5.749	5.222	4.775	4.391	4.059	3.910	3.771	3.518	3.295	2.840	2.492	2.218	1.998
18	16.398	14.992	12.659	10.828	9.372	8.201	7.250	6.467	6.128	5.818	5.273	4.812	4.419	4.080	3.928	3.786	3.529	3.304	2.844	2.494	2.219	1.999
19	17.226	15.678	13.134	11.158	9.604	8.365	7.366	6.550	6.198	5.877	5.316	4.844	4.442	4.097	3.942	3.799	3.539	3.311	2.848	2.496	2.220	1.999
20	18.046	16.351	13.590	11.470	9.818	8.514	7.469	6.623	6.259	5.929	5.353	4.870	4.460	4.110	3.954	3.808	3.546	3.316	2.850	2.497	2.221	1.999
21	18.857	17.011	14.029	11.764	10.017	8.649	7.562	6.687	6.312	5.973	5.384	4.891	4.476	4.121	3.963	3.816	3.551	3.320	2.852	2.498	2.221	2.000
22	19.660	17.658	14.451	12.042	10.201	8.772	7.645	6.743	6.359	6.011	5.410	4.909	4.488	4.130	3.970	3.822	3.556	3.323	2.853	2.498	2.222	2.000
23	20.456	18.292	14.857	12.303	10.371	8.883	7.718	6.792	6.399	6.044	5.432	4.925	4.499	4.137	3.976	3.827	3.559	3.325	2.854	2.499	2.222	2.000
24	21.243	18.914	15.247	12.550	10.529	8.985	7.784	6.835	6.434	6.073	5.451	4.937	4.507	4.143	3.981	3.831	3.562	3.327	2.855	2.499	2.222	2.000
25	22.023	19.523	15.622	12.783	10.675	9.077	7.843	6.873	6.464	6.097	5.467	4.948	4.514	4.147	3.985	3.834	3.564	3.329	2.856	2.499	2.222	2.000
26	22.795	20.121	15.983	13.003	10.810	9.161	7.896	6.906	6.491	6.118	5.480	4.956	4.520	4.151	3.988	3.837	3.566	3.330	2.856	2.500	2.222	2.000
27	23.560	20.707	16.330	13.211	10.935	9.237	7.943	6.935	6.514	6.136	5.492	4.964	4.524	4.154	3.990	3.839	3.567	3.331	2.856	2.500	2.222	2.000
28	24.316	21.281	16.663	13.406	11.051	9.307	7.984	6.961	6.534	6.152	5.502	4.970	4.528	4.157	3.992	3.840	3.568	3.331	2.857	2.500	2.222	2.000
29	25.066	21.844	16.984	13.591	11.158	9.370	8.022	6.983	6.551	6.166	5.510	4.975	4.531	4.159	3.994	3.841	3.569	3.332	2.857	2.500	2.222	2.000
30	25.808	22.396	17.292	13.765	11.258	9.427	8.055	7.003	6.566	6.177	5.517	4.979	4.534	4.160	3.995	3.842	3.569	3.332	2.857	2.500	2.222	2.000
40	32.835	27.355	19.793	15.046	11.925	9.779	8.244	7.105	6.642	6.234	5.548	4.997	4.544	4.166	3.999	3.846	3.571	3.333	2.857	2.500	2.222	2.000
50	39.196	31.424	21.482	15.762	12.234	9.915	8.304	7.133	6.661	6.246	5.554	4.999	4.545	4.167	4.000	3.846	3.571	3.333	2.857	2.500	2.222	2.000

The Uses of Present Value Tables

Present value tables facilitate a comparison of present and future sums. For example, to determine the value of $150 to be paid 11 years hence discounted at 12%, one could either calculate:

$$\$150 \times (1 + .12)^{11}$$

or look in a present value table for the equivalent of:

$$(1 + .12)^{11}$$

Table 4A.1 shows the expression to be .287. Thus the present value of $150 discounted at 12% for 11 years is:

$$.287 \times \$150 = \$43.05.$$

Turn the problem around. What is the value of $150 growing at 12% per year for 11 years? Now the expression to be evaluated is $150 (1 + .12)^{11} or:

$$\$150(.287) = \$522.65$$

Thus Table 4A.1 may be used both to discount future income and to determine compound values.

A second form for a present value table helps value assets that periodically pay a constant amount for a prespecified time. Table 4A.1 could be used. One would multiply the present value factor for each payment and then sum. Table 4A.2 reduces some of the work. Each of its entries represents the sum of the factors to that point in Table 4A.2. Thus the 4% five-year entry in Table 4A.2 is 4.452, which is the sum of .962, .925, .889, .855, and .822 (rounding accounts for slight differences) from Table 4A.1. A payment of $100 a year for five years discounted at 4% is worth $445.20.

Table 4A.2 may be used to compute a bond's yield to maturity. Suppose a bond has a coupon of 6½%, matures in 16 years, and is currently selling at 85. The yield to maturity may be approximated in various ways. Dividing the coupon rate by the price of $65/$850 = 7.65% provides a crude estimate. This so-called current yield neglects the appreciation from holding the bond to maturity, however. Allocating the straight-line appreciation to the coupon generates a closer approximation. Since the bond matures in 16 years at $150 more than the current price, $9.38 ($150/16) could be added to the coupon for a coupon-plus appreciation of $74.38 per year. Dividing by the $850 price produces an estimate of 8.75%. This return estimate is, however, too high because the end-period appreciation is not discounted to reflect the wait for payment. Calculating the present value of the appreciation factor, subtracting it from the purchase price, and proceeding as before produces a somewhat closer approximation. Discounting the $150 gain ($1,000 − $850 = $150) to be received in 16 years requires the selection of an approximate discount rate, however. The proper rate to discount the appreciation is the rate that makes the entire repayment and income stream equal to the market price. Since this is the rate we are seeking, it must be approximated. Our previous efforts suggest a value between 7.65% and 8.75%. Thus 8% can be taken as an approximation.

The discount factor for 8% for 16 years is .292, so the present value of the appreciation is approximately $43.80 (.292 × $150). Subtracting $43.80 from the $850 purchase price produces $806.80 for cost less present value of appreciation. Dividing this amount into the coupon rate provides a rate estimate of: $65/$806.80 = 8.06%. This value is probably sufficiently close to the 8% estimate to require no further work. If greater accuracy were required, the 8.06% rate could be used to discount the bond's return.

The procedure for determining a bond's rate of return may be summarized as follows:

1. The approximate yield is determined by dividing the coupon by the current price. If the market price is near par, this approximation may be close enough. If par and market differ substantially, further work is required.

2. Using an approximation of the appropriate rate, the difference between market and par is discounted to the present.

3. This present value of the difference between market and par is then applied to the current price.

4. The result is divided into the coupon and this estimate is compared with the rate used to discount the difference between market and par.

5. If the rates are close, no further work is required. If not, the new estimate is used to discount the difference, and the present value is subtracted from the market price.

6. This result is then divided into the coupon.

7. The procedure is repeated until the rates are approximately equal.

An even easier way to find a bond's yield to maturity is to use a computer or financial calculator.

Risk and Modern Portfolio Theory

Most investors have a basic understanding of the risk concept. They generally realize that: (1) risk is related to the confidence placed in return expectations, (2) most investors are willing to accept a lower expected return to obtain a reduction in risk, and (3) the discount rate applied to the valuation of any expected income stream should vary directly with its risk. This chapter expands on that base. We primarily focus on risk's role in investment analysis and portfolio management. First, the definition of risk is explored and then its primary forms (individual and portfolio) are introduced. Next, portfolio risk is analyzed. Finally, a simplified approach to portfolio risk is introduced and analyzed.

A SIMPLE EXAMPLE OF INVESTMENT RISK

Suppose investment A guarantees a return of precisely 5%. Now consider investment B with a 90% chance of a 5% return, a 5% chance of 0% return, and a 5% chance of a 10% return. The expected return of B is 5% [(.90 × .05) + (.05 × .00) + (.05 × .10) = .05], which is the same as that of A. The actual (or realized) return of B is less likely to equal its expected return than is that of A. Thus risk-averting investors would prefer A. Investment A offers an equivalent expected return and lower risk than does investment B. Comparing A to B is very straightforward.

FIGURE 5.1   A Histogram of Possible Returns

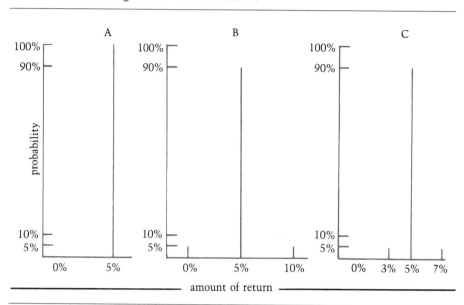

Now consider asset C with a 90% chance of a 5% return, a 5% chance of a 3% return, and a 5% chance of a 7% return. Like A and B, C offers an expected return of 5% [(.90 × .05) + (.05 × .03) + (.05 × .07) = .05]. Because B's actual return is uncertain, risk averters would prefer A. On the other hand, because B's return variation is less than that of B, C seems the less risky asset. That is, the possible returns for B are 0%, 5%, and 10% while they are 3%, 5%, and 7% for C. B's actual return could be 5% above or below its expected value whereas C's can differ only 2% from its mean. Return possibilities such as these are often illustrated graphically. For example, a histogram of investment C's return possibilities is provided in Figure 5.1. Similar histograms could be constructed for investments A and B. The vertical axis in Figure 5.1 reports the probability of each event while the horizontal axis identifies the event (such as the realized return).

THE RISK OF A DISTRIBUTION OF POSSIBLE RETURNS

Although determining the expected value of a distribution of returns is rather straightforward, measuring its risk is more complex. B's return could vary from 0% to 10% compared with 3% to 7% for C. Because its range in possible returns is greater, most people would rate B as riskier. This comparison suggests that a measure of risk could be based on the difference between the maximum and minimum possible returns. Such an approach would capture at least some of the flavor of what people mean when they talk about an investment's risk. The magnitude

FIGURE 5.2   A Probability Distribution of Returns

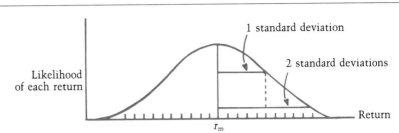

of the range of returns, however, ignores the shape of the distribution between the two extremes.

Rather than use the range of possible returns, a risk measure could be based on the average deviation from the expected return. The simple average deviation from the mean is precisely zero (the negative differences exactly offset the positive differences). The absolute value of the deviation from the mean measures the average distance of the actual return from the expected return. This mean absolute deviation statistic is difficult to work with, however. Thus the deviations are generally first squared (producing nonnegative values) and then averaged. The result is called the *variance*. The variance and its square root, the standard deviation, are frequently employed descriptive statistics. To understand how the variance and more frequently the standard deviation serves as a risk measure, we first need to explore its relationship to probability distributions.

Probability Distributions

Histograms such as Figure 5.1 relate possible discrete events to their likelihoods or frequencies whereas probability distributions are used for continuous phenomena. Figure 5.2, a probability distribution, illustrates the relation between a large number of expected returns and their probabilities. The probabilities rise to a peak at return r_m and decline symmetrically thereafter. With a symmetrical distribution, the probabilities for returns equidistant from r_m are equal. The simple average of such paired returns is r_m. Thus the weighted average of all of these averages must also be r_m.

Figure 5.2 also illustrates one and two standard deviations from the average. For most commonly encountered distributions, the actual value will be within one standard deviation of the mean approximately two-thirds of the time, while about 95% of the time it will be within two standard deviations. Thus the standard deviation of the return distribution is a useful measure of a distribution's spread. It may be used as an index of the degree of confidence (or risk) in the expected return (expected return variability).

A Simple Example. Suppose we had N equally likely returns denoted by R_t where t ranges from 1 to N. The mean or expected return for R_t is given by the formula:

$$E(R) = \sum_{t=1}^{N} R_t/N$$

Similarly, the variance would be:

$$\sigma^2 = \sum_{t=1}^{N} [R_t - E(R_t)]^2/N$$

The standard deviation is, of course, the square root of the variance. For unequal weights the mean and standard deviation computations are a bit more complex. Rather than take the simple (unweighted average) of returns, a weighted average is computed. Thus:

$$E(R) = \sum_{t=1}^{N} P(R_t)R_t$$

where:

$$P(R_t) = \text{probability of return } R_t$$

Similarly:

$$\sigma_r^2 = \sum_{t=0}^{N} P(R_t)[R_t - E(R_t)]^2$$

In a simple example we might have equal probabilities of returns of 0%, 4%, 10%, and 14%:

$$P(R_1) = P(R_2) = P(R_3) = P(R_4) = .25$$

R_1	R_2	R_3	R_4
.00	.04	.10	.14

We begin by computing the average or expected return for this set of possible returns:

$$E(R) = \left(\frac{.00 + .04 + .10 + .14}{4}\right) = \frac{.28}{4} = .07$$

The next step is to form the deviations of each possible return from its expected value:

$$X_t = R_t - E(R);$$

X_1	X_2	X_3	X_4
−.07	−.03	.03	.07

These values are then squared:

$$(X_t)^2 = [R_t - E(R)]^2 \quad ; \quad$$

.0049	.0009	.0009	.0049

The results are then summed and averaged. (Had the probabilities not been equal, a weighted average would have been taken.) The result of this computation is the variance (σ_r^2):

$$\sigma_r^2 = \frac{.0116}{4} = .0029$$

The standard deviation is simply the square root of the variance:

$$\sigma_r = .0029 = .054$$

Thus, investment R has an expected return of 7% and standard deviation of 5.4%. Stated in words, this means that the best guess for R's return is 7%. Two-thirds of the time R should yield between 1.6% and 12.4%. This range of possible returns is relatively large (i.e., risky).

Suppose investment Y had an expected return of 6.5% with a 2% standard deviation. Two-thirds of the time Y's investors could expect to earn between 4.5% and 8.5% compared with 1.6% to 12.4% for R's investors. In spite of its slightly lower expected yield (6.5% versus 7%), many investors might prefer Y to R. Let us now explore why.

RISK AVERSION

Most people are thought to be risk averse. As investors they will always prefer less risk when expected returns are equivalent. Thus, when two investments offer the same expected return, risk-averse investors will choose the investment having the lower risk. The choice becomes more difficult when the riskier asset also offers the higher expected return. The investor's attitude toward the two investments will depend upon the relative differences in expected return and risk. Risk-averse investors are willing to invest in risky assets only if the incentives are sufficient to offset their preference for a more certain return.

The concept of risk aversion can be illustrated with an example. Consider two assets with the same expected return but different risk levels. The riskier asset will have a higher probability of achieving a lower return but also a higher probability of earning a higher return. The probability that its return will be near the mean expectation is correspondingly lower for the riskier asset. Mathematically the upside potential and the downside risk offset. As a result both the higher risk and the lower risk assets have the same expected returns. And yet risk-averse investors will prefer the asset with the more dependable return.

Risk-averse investors dislike the prospect of an unexpectedly low (perhaps negative) return more than they like the possibility of a favorable return of similar magnitude above the mean. For example, if the mean return is 10%, a −10% return (20% below the mean) is viewed as more undesirable than a return of +30% (20% above the mean) is viewed desirable. To avoid the possibility of experiencing the pain of an unexpectedly low return, risk-averse investors prefer assets whose expected returns are more certain.

Individual investor circumstances will differ greatly. Most, but not all, investors are risk averse. As an example, many retired couples depend upon their investments for a substantial fraction of their income. Their own budgeting decisions are relatively simple if they have a dependable source of investment income. Their finances would, in contrast, be much more difficult to plan if their investment income varied substantially from month to month. Similarly, a younger couple saving for a down payment on a house or for their children's college education would much prefer a relatively known rate of return. Such people would have a better idea of how much they need to save if they knew how much they would earn on what they were able to save. No doubt many other circumstances also incline investors toward risk aversion. Such investors do not necessarily prefer safe secure investments no matter what the trade-offs, but they do prefer less risk to more.

Although most investors would prefer investments that contain little or no risk, most investments contain a significant degree of risk. That is, most investments offer the possibility of a wide range of outcomes (possible returns). Such (risky) investments must be priced low enough relative to their prospective payoffs to attract risk-averse investors. In practice this means that a higher discount rate is applied to their expected income streams. Thus, for example, an investment that is expected to be worth $1,000 in five years could now sell for $700, $500, or $300 depending upon its risk. At $700 the market is applying a 7% discount rate whereas $500 corresponds to a 15% rate and $300 implies a rate of 27%. The greater the risk, the lower the current value is and the higher the discount rate applied to the investment.

INDIVIDUAL VERSUS PORTFOLIO RISK

We have already seen that the standard deviation is a useful measure of the risk of an individual investment. The standard deviation of the expected return of an individual asset is an inadequate risk measure, however, if the asset is part of a larger portfolio. For example, an investment with an expected return of 12% and a standard deviation of 3% will on the average earn between 9% and 15% two-thirds of the time and between 6% and 18% for 95% of the time. Such statistics indicate the particular investment's downside risk and upside potential. The standard deviation of the expected return of an individual asset does not, however, reflect the potentially important impact of diversification.

An investor's wealth stems from his or her entire portfolio. If poor performance by some parts of the portfolio tend to be offset by more favorable performance in the rest of the portfolio, the investor's overall wealth position may not suffer. Accordingly, investors should primarily concern themselves with portfolio risk rather than the risks of the portfolio's components. If the values of two investments fluctuate by offsetting amounts, the owner is no poorer or richer than if neither had varied. The return variabilities of a portfolio's components are usually somewhat offsetting. Thus the portfolio's overall return variability is almost always below the average variabilities of the components. Moreover, different assets may contribute disproportionately to a portfolio's total risk. Thus, risk measures of the components of a multiasset portfolio need to reflect their diversification impacts.

TWO-ASSET PORTFOLIO RISK

The simplest type of portfolio contains a single asset, such as stock in one company. Such a portfolio is undiversified. The next simplest portfolio contains two separate assets, such as stock in two different companies. Such a two-asset portfolio begins to take advantage of the risk reduction potential of diversification. The formula for a two-asset portfolio's risk is:

$$\sigma_p^2 = X^2\sigma_x^2 + 2XYC_{xy} + Y^2\sigma_y^2 \qquad (5.1)$$

where:

$$X = \text{portfolio weight of asset x}$$
$$Y = \text{portfolio weight of asset y}$$
$$\sigma_x^2 = \text{variance of asset x}$$
$$\sigma_y^2 = \text{variance of asset y}$$
$$C_{xy} = \text{covariance of asset x with y}$$

For simplicity, the weights X and Y are restricted to the 0–1 range (ruling out short selling and borrowing). The terms $X^2\sigma_x^2$ and $Y^2\sigma_y^2$ are the squares of each component's weight times its respective variance. The remaining term, $2XYC_{xy}$, requires further explanation. The key, and indeed a central aspect of portfolio risk in general, is the covariance C_{xy}.

The Covariance

The covariance is, like the mean and standard deviation, a statistic computed from past values of the relevant variables. It measures the comovement or covariability of two variables. Thus the covariance of two assets' returns is an index of their tendency to move relative to each other. For example, stocks of two similar companies that operate in the same industries would probably tend to move together. On the other hand, stocks of two very different types of companies would probably tend to move largely independently of each other. The former pair of stocks would have a relatively high covariance whereas the latter pair would have a relatively low covariance.

    To understand how the covariance statistic is defined, first consider the difference between asset x's period t return (x_t) and its mean value $(\bar{x})$. Because a mean value is generally located near the center of the distribution, this difference $(x_t - \bar{x})$ should be equally likely to be positive or negative. Now consider the product $(x_t - \bar{x})(y_t - \bar{y})$. When the two asset returns are either both above or both below their means together, the product is positive. The product is negative when one deviation is above its mean and the other below. The covariance is defined as the average of the product $(y_t - \bar{y})(x_t - \bar{x})$ and reflects the relatedness of the assets' returns. An analogous statistic, the correlation coefficient of x and y, is their covariance divided by the product of their standard deviations. The divisor scales the correlation coefficient between a maximum of $+1$ and a minimum of -1. The following discussion will utilize the covariance but it could all be recast in correlation terms with the substitution:

$$\rho_{xy} = C_{xy}/\sigma_x\sigma_y$$

Figure 5.3 helps illustrate the meaning of the covariance. Suppose we are interested in the comovements of assets x and y. We might explore this relation by plotting $(x_t - \bar{x})$ and $(y_t - \bar{y})$ over time. Whenever investments x and y are above their averages together, we would place the observation in the upper right-hand quadrant. When they are simultaneously below their means, the point will plot in the lower left-hand quadrant. Investments that tend to vary together will largely plot in an area concentrated in those two quadrants (Figure 5.3a). Indeed, most asset pairs exhibit this so-called positive covariance. An investment may, however, experience above average returns while another is below average (upper left and lower right quadrants). If the returns move in opposite directions more than they move together, the covariance will be negative (Figure 5.3b). Finally, if the returns move in a totally independent fashion, a zero covariance will result (Figure 5.3c).

Computing a Covariance.   To explore how a covariance of two variables is computed, suppose we have the following five observations on variables x and y:

$$(x_1, y_1) = (1, 3)$$

$$(x_2, y_2) = (2, 7)$$

$$(x_3, y_3) = (3, 8)$$

$$(x_4, y_4) = (4, 10)$$

$$(x_5, y_5) = (5, 12)$$

First we must compute $\bar{x}$ and $\bar{y}$:

$$\bar{x} = \left(\frac{1 + 2 + 3 + 4 + 5}{5}\right) = \frac{15}{5} = 3$$

$$\bar{y} = \left(\frac{3 + 7 + 8 + 10 + 12}{5}\right) = \frac{40}{5} = 8$$

Next we must compute $(x_t - \bar{x})(y_t - \bar{y})$ for each pair of values:

$$(1 - 3)(3 - 8) = -2 \times -5 = 10$$

$$(2 - 3)(7 - 8) = -1 \times -1 = 1$$

$$(3 - 3)(8 - 8) = 0 \times 0 \quad = 0$$

$$(4 - 3)(10 - 8) = 4 \times 2 \quad = 8$$

$$(5-3)(12-8) = 2 \times 4 \quad = 8$$

Finally we obtain the covariance by averaging these values:

$$(10 + 1 + 0 + 8 + 8)/5 = 5.4$$

Note that in this example the x and y values tended to move together, producing a positive covariance. The result is a relationship like that in Figure 5.3a.

FIGURE 5.3 Covariances for Different Types of Relatedness

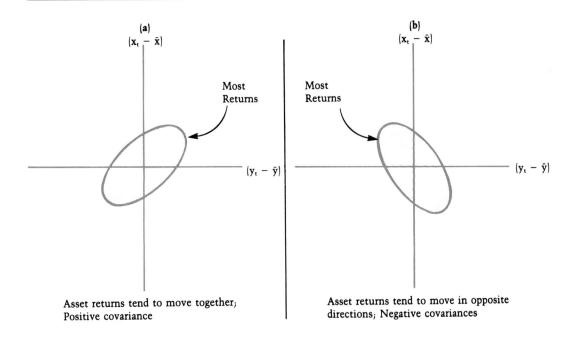

Asset returns tend to move together;
Positive covariance

Asset returns tend to move in opposite
directions; Negative covariances

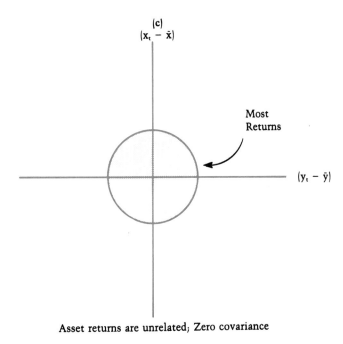

Asset returns are unrelated; Zero covariance

An Example of a Two-Asset Portfolio's Risk. Returning to Equation 5.1, consider a simple example. Suppose x and y have standard deviations of .10 and .15, respectively, and a covariance of .01. We could form a portfolio composed half of x and half of y. If the expected returns of x and y are .09 and .11, the portfolio's expected return would be .10, a weighted average of the component returns. We might think that the portfolio's standard deviation would also be a weighted average of .10 and .15 as well (.125). The formula reveals a different result, however:

$$\sigma_p^2 = X^2\sigma_x^2 + 2XYC_{xy} + Y^2\sigma_y^2$$

$$\sigma_x = .10$$

$$\sigma_y = .15$$

$$X = .5$$

$$Y = .5$$

$$C_{xy} = .01$$

Thus:

$$\sigma_p^2 = (.5)^2(.10)^2 + 2(.5)^2(.01) + (.5)^2(.15)^2$$

$$\sigma_p^2 = .25(.01) + .5(.01) + .25(.0225)$$

$$\sigma_p^2 = 0.013125$$

$$\sigma_p = \sqrt{0.013125} = .115$$

In this case, diversifying the portfolio has clearly reduced the risk below the two components' average risk. The average risk (as measured by the standard deviation of the expected return) of the two components is .125 compared with the portfolio's overall risk of .115. The next section will consider the issue in greater detail.

Two-Asset Portfolio with Equal Weights and Variances

The two-variable portfolio variance depends upon the variance of each asset and the covariance between them. If weights X and Y are equal and variance σ_x^2 and σ_y^2 are equal, Equation 5.1 reduces to:

$$\sigma_p^2 = (1/2)^2 \sigma_x^2 + (1/2)C_{xy} + (1/2)^2 \sigma_y^2$$
$$= (1/4) (\sigma_x^2 + 2C_{xy} + \sigma_y^2) \qquad (5.1a)$$
$$= (1/4) (2\sigma_x^2 + 2C_{xy})$$
$$= (1/2) (\sigma_x^2 + C_{xy})$$

The reader will not be burdened with a proof, but C_{xy} can in this example be no larger than $2\sigma_x^2$ and no smaller than $-\sigma_x^2$. If $C_{xy} = \sigma_x^2$, the two assets' returns x and y move in precise lockstep. Stocks of two firms planning to merge (by exchanging the stock of the target company for a prespecified amount of stock in the acquiring company) might approach this degree of relatedness. In this extreme case:

$$\sigma_p^2 = (1/2) (\sigma_x^2 + \sigma_x^2) = \sigma_x^2 \qquad (5.1b)$$

If $C_{xy} = -\sigma_x^2$, the returns of the two assets always vary inversely by precisely proportional magnitudes. Few, if any, such asset pairs exist, but otherwise-equivalent (underlying stock, maturity, terms to exercise, etc.) puts and calls would come close. As the underlying stock fluctuated, the puts and calls would move in opposite directions.

When:

$$C_{xy} = -\sigma_x^2$$

Equation 5.1a becomes:

$$\sigma_p^2 = (1/2) (\sigma_x^2 - \sigma_x^2) = 0 \qquad (5.1c)$$

When the returns of two risky assets move precisely inversely, portfolio risk can be entirely eliminated by an appropriate choice of weights. A covariance that is at its minimum theoretical value is extremely rare. Indeed, negative covariances are unusual. A covariance at or near zero (the assets' return fluctuations are unrelated) is more likely to be encountered, however. Therefore it is an interesting special case.

$$\sigma_p^2 = (1/4) (2\sigma_x^2 + 0) = \sigma_x^2/2 \qquad (5.1d)$$

Where the assets are unrelated, the portfolio's variance is equal to half of the components' variance. Even a zero covariance of returns is relatively uncommon, however. Most covariances are positive reflecting the tendency of stocks to move together. Thus a typical two-asset portfolio's covariance will lie between zero and $+\sigma_x^2$ (its maximum possible value). As a result, the typical two-asset's portfolio variance will be between $\sigma_x^2/2$ and σ_x^2.

Some Examples.   Suppose:

$$\sigma_x^2 = \sigma_y^2 = .1 \text{ and } C_{xy} = .06$$

Equation 5.1a reveals:

$$\sigma_p^2 = (1/2) (\sigma_x^2 + C_{xy})$$

$$= \frac{(.1 + .06)}{2} = \frac{.16}{2} = .08$$

Now suppose:

$$\sigma_x^2 = \sigma_y^2 = C_{xy} = .1$$

Then from Equation 5.1b we have:

$$\sigma_p^2 = (1/2) (\sigma_x^2 + \sigma_y^2) = \sigma_x^2 = .1$$

If $\sigma_x^2 = .1$ and $C_{xy} = -.1$, then from Equation 5.1c we have:

$$\sigma_p^2 = (1/2) (\sigma_x^2 - \sigma_x^2) = (1/2) (.1 - .1) = 0$$

FIGURE 5.4 Two-Asset Portfolio Variances for Different Values of C_{xy}

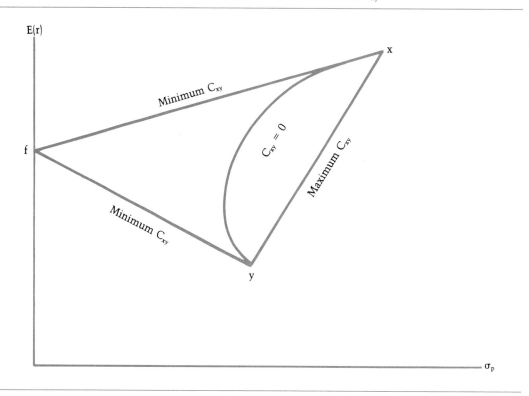

The reader may wish to verify these formulas by computing portfolio risk for the above examples from Equation 5.1:

$$(\sigma_p^2 = X^2\sigma_x^2 + 2XYC_{xy} + Y^2\sigma_y^2).$$

Two-Asset Portfolio with Unequal Weights and Variances

The relationships are similar to those stated when the equal weights and equal component variance assumptions are relaxed. The covariance for a given set of assets will be some specific value. In general, however, it can range from its maximum value (σ_x^2) to its minimum value $(-\sigma_x^2)$. Whenever $C_{xy}\sigma$ is at its maximum, the portfolio variance equals the weighted average variance of the components. If C_{xy} is at its minimum value, an appropriate choice of weights can eliminate the portfolio's variance. If C_{xy} equals zero, the portfolio variance equals one-half the weighted average variance of the components. Figure 5.4 illustrates this relationship. Table 5.1 summarizes the various possibilities for the two-asset case.

When C_{xy} is at its maximum possible value, the expected returns and standard deviations of a portfolio of x and y will be a simple weighted average of individual expected returns and standard deviations of x and y. This risk return relationship

TABLE 5.1 Portfolio Variances for Two-Asset Cases

Case	Portfolio Variance	
General Formula	$X^2\sigma_x^2 + 2XYC_{xy} + Y^2\sigma_y^2$	(Equation 1)
Equal Variances and Weights		
General Case	$1/2\ (\sigma_x^2 + C_{xy})$	(Equation 1a)
Perfectly Related Assets		
$(C_{xy} = \sigma_x^2)$	σ_x^2	(Equation 1b)
Perfectly Inversely-Related Assets		
$(C_{xy} = -\sigma_x^2)$	0	(Equation 1c)
Unrelated Assets		
$(C_{xy} = 0)$	$\sigma_x^2 \div 2$	(Equation 1d)
Normal Case		
$(0 \leqq C_{xy} \leqq \sigma_x^2)$	$\sigma_x^2 \div 2 \leqq \sigma_p^2 \leqq \sigma_x^2$	
Unequal Variances and Weights		
Perfectly Related Assets		
$(C_{xy}$ at maximum value)	$X\sigma_x^2 + Y\sigma_y^2$	
Perfectly Inversely-Related Assets	0 (possible to choose weights to	
$(C_{xy}$ at minimum level)	make variance = 0)	
Unrelated Assets		
$(C_{xy} = 0)$	$1/2\ (X\sigma_x^2 + Y\sigma_y^2)$	
Normal Case		
$0 \leqq C_{xy} \leqq (X\sigma_x^2 + Y\sigma_y^2)$	$1/2\ (X\sigma_x^2 + Y\sigma_y^2) \leqq \sigma_p^2 \leqq (X\sigma_x^2 + Y\sigma_y^2)$	

is illustrated by a straight line from x to y. The relative proportions of x and y will determine where on line xy the portfolio lies. When C_{xy} is at its minimum possible value, the portfolio risk/expected-return levels lie on lines xf–fy. Note that p = 0 at point f. That is, for that particular combination of x and y, the portfolio's risk is totally eliminated. When $C_{xy} = 0$, the portfolios of x and y lie on a curved line connecting x and y that lies partway between that for C_{xy} at its maximum and C_{xy} at its minimum. Indeed, for every other value of C_{xy}, a curved line between x and y represents the possible-risk/expected-return levels. The closer C_{xy} is to its maximum value, the closer the curve approaches line xy.

N-ASSET PORTFOLIO RISK

The N-asset equivalent of Equation 5.1 contains variance and covariance terms for every asset and asset pair in the portfolio. While a thorough analysis of this case is beyond the scope of this book, Figure 5.5 does illustrate the fact that risk declines as the number of portfolio components increases. Note, however, that portfolio risk declines only asymptotically toward the average covariance t of the components. For randomly selected stocks a large portfolio will have about one-third of the risk of a typical one-stock portfolio. Once the diversified portfolio's risk is reduced to this level, it cannot be reduced further by adding still more stocks. As will be discussed more fully in the next chapter, a relatively small number of stocks is sufficient to obtain most of the risk reduction potential of diversification.

FIGURE 5.5 Portfolio Risk Declines as N Increases

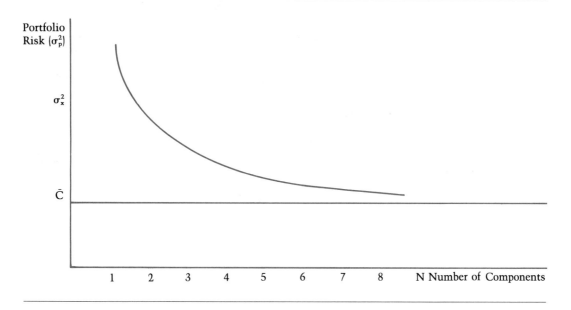

Estimating Variances and Covariances. Covariance and variance statistics can be estimated from past data. That is, a data series for the past returns of a group of investments can be used to compute variance and covariance estimates. Where possible, however, such estimates should also utilize future-oriented information. For example, the stock of a firm whose future environment is expected to be similar to its past is likely to behave much as its historically estimated variance and covariance statistics imply. On the other hand, some firms have recently experienced a major change such as a merger, new product introduction, changed regulatory environment, or large capital infusion. Such firms are more likely to behave differently from their history than are firms that have not had major changes. If the change has tended to increase risk, historically based risk measures should be adjusted upward. For example, when AT&T divested itself of its telephone operating companies, it lost a major and dependable source of revenue. The company became appreciably riskier as a result. Any computations based on predivestiture returns data would be misleading. Similarly, a change that decreased risk should lead to a downward adjustment in the historically based measure.

SIMPLIFYING PORTFOLIO RISK DETERMINATION

We could estimate a portfolio's risk by applying all the relevant weights, variances, and covariances to the N-asset equivalent of Equation 5.1. Possible composition shifts could be assessed by reapplying the formula. Mutual funds and other institutional investors, those best situated to utilize the methodology, rarely evaluate portfolio risk in this way, however. First, the required data [N variances and N(N − 1)/2 covariances] grow exponentially with N. Most institutional investors consider large sets of securities. Thus making and continually updating the required estimates for such large portfolios would be costly and time-consuming. Second, like earnings forecasts, historically based variance and covariance estimates are rather unreliable. Moreover, adjusting them to reflect future-oriented information is an uncertain process at best. Third, several simplified approaches provide risk estimates that are about as reliable as those of Equation 5.1, particularly for a large N.

Using the full form of the portfolio risk equation to assess a portfolio's risk is a relatively difficult task. A portfolio with many components requires as many variance estimates as it has components as well as many times that many covariance estimates. For large N the impacts of the component variances on σ_p^2 are small enough to ignore. Still, a very large number of covariances would need to be estimated. The complete equation requires estimating the covariability of each component return with every other component return. Other approaches simplify the process.

One could, for example, restrict the analysis to the covariability of each component's return with the market as a whole. Such an approach might be appropriate if the influence of the overall market is the primary type of return covariability. Generalizable factors (business cycle, interest rates, energy availability, inflation, war scare, etc.) do tend to affect the market and most firms similarly. Moreover, the impact of these factors on the market and the firms making it up are nonrandom. Thus such influences cannot be diversified away. Random firm-specific and industry-specific influences, in contrast (strikes, weather impacts, competitor moves, etc.), will largely offset each other in a portfolio made up of many different assets.

Estimating Market Covariability: Betas

All methods for portfolio risk assessment depend on the estimated relatedness of the component returns. Thus we need a way of estimating such relatedness. Decomposing return variability into two categories greatly simplifies the analysis of portfolio risk. The return variability of individual assets may be divided into two components: that associated with the general market and that not associated with the general market. To observe an individual security's degree of market relatedness, we may plot its returns, S_{it}, relative to the market M_t (Figure 5.6).

Most securities experience positive returns when the market rises and negative returns when it falls (positive covariance with the market). A line centered through the data would illustrate the average tendency of the security to move with the market (Figure 5.7). The slope of that line, called the beta, measures the degree of proportionality between movements of the security's returns and those of the market. An asset with returns that tend to be proportional to the market will have a beta close to unity. A beta greater than 1 indicates that the asset's returns tend to exceed the market's when the market's return is positive and tend to be lower when the market's return is negative. Similarly, a beta between 0 and 1 implies that the asset's returns tend to fluctuate proportionately less than the market.

FIGURE 5.6 Asset Return versus the Market

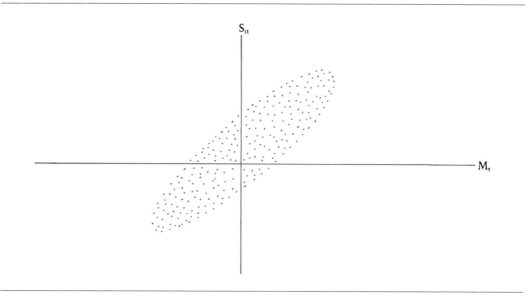

FIGURE 5.7 Regression Line for Fitting α and β

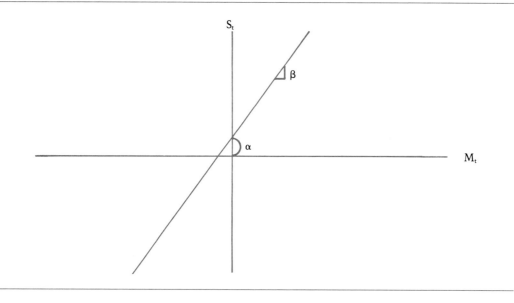

Negative betas reflect a tendency for such assets' returns to move inversely with the market. Table 5.2 summarizes these probabilities.

TABLE 5.2 Expected Asset Returns for Different Betas and Market Returns

Range	Expected Asset Return for Positive Market Return	Expected Asset Return for Negative Market Return
$\beta \geq 1$	above market	below market
$\beta = 1$	market	market
$0 < \beta < 1$	below market	above market
$\beta < 0$	negative	positive

Estimating the Market Model for Stocks

Although a beta may be estimated for any investment, most applications have been to stocks. If future relationships are like the past, a given stock's beta may appropriately be estimated from past data (daily, weekly, or monthly stock and market index returns). The following type of equation is often used in the estimation:

$$S_t = \alpha + \beta M_t + e_t \qquad (5.2)$$

where:

S_t = percentage return of stock for period t

M_t = percentage return of market for period t

β = beta ratio (to be estimated)

α = intercept (to be estimated)

e_t = random error term (to be minimized in estimation process)

The generalized form of Equation 5.2 is called the market model. Each stock's own specific equation is called its *characteristic line*. Separate alphas and betas can be estimated for each relevant stock. The resulting alpha forecasts the stock's return for a 0% market return. Its beta estimate reflects the tendency of the stock's returns to vary with the market. A statistical estimation technique called *regression analysis* is used to determine alpha and beta estimates. The regression of Equation 5.2 is illustrated graphically by a straight line through a scatter diagram of S_{it} and associated M_t values (Figure 5.7). The regression line estimated by ordinary least squares minimizes the squares of the distance of the data points to the regression line. The line's alpha is its intercept and beta its slope coefficient.

The Capital Asset Pricing Model

An alternative formulation of the security return/market return relationship called the capital asset pricing model (CAPM) is often used in more advanced security market work. The CAPM specifies a more specific relationship between security and market returns. Rather than allow the intercept to take on an estimated value (the α) the risk-free return (R_{ft}) is brought explicitly into the model as the intercept:

$$S_t = R_{ft} + \beta(M_t - R_{ft}) + e_t \qquad (5.3)$$

Thus, the CAPM intercept equals the risk-free return and the market return variable $(M_t - R_{ft})$ is measured in deviations from the risk-free rate. Since the expected value of e_t is zero:

$$E(S_t) = R_{ft} + \beta(M_t - R_{ft}) \tag{5.3a}$$

Note that the CAPM model yields some interesting results. If the market return is 0, the stock's expected return becomes $R_{ft} - \beta R_{ft}$. In this circumstance if $\beta = 1$, the stock's expected return is also 0. Thus when the market return is 0, a stock with a β of 1 (the market's β) will also be expected to have a 0 return. More generally if $\beta = 1$, the stock's expected return will equal the market return. That is:

$$E(S_t) = R_{ft} + \beta(M_t - R_{ft}) = R_{ft} + 1(M_t - R_{ft}) = R_{ft} + M_t - R_{ft} = M_t$$

Thus a stock with the same beta as the market will have the same expected return as the market. Such a relationship is probably consistent with what most people would expect.

The market model and CAPM, although conceptually similar, do have some significant differences. CAPM may be derived precisely from theoretical specifications whereas the market model includes the CAPM as a special case: $\alpha = (1 - \beta)R_{ft}$. Because the market model is easier to work with and understand, and more general than the CAPM, we shall use it exclusively. The discussion could be recast in CAPM terms, however.

Market versus Nonmarket Risk

Most investors hold stocks and other investment assets in a portfolio containing a number of different components. Thus the risk of their investments depends upon the joint impacts of their holdings. Return fluctuations peculiar to one security tend to be offset by unrelated return fluctuations of other securities. As a result, the nonmarket component of most assets' risks can be largely eliminated through diversification. About two-thirds of a typical stock's risk stems from nonmarket sources. That leaves about one-third as due to market risk. These market-related return fluctuations cannot be diversified away by simply increasing the size of the portfolio. Dealing with this residual risk requires a more complex approach than simple diversification.

Because a well-diversified portfolio contains little or no nonmarket risk, analysis of its remaining risk is particularly concerned with its market risk or beta. A portfolio's beta equals the components' weighted average betas. Thus the only way to reduce a portfolio's beta is to reduce the average beta of its components. Moreover, the expected returns of individual assets tend to vary inversely with betas. Therefore reducing a portfolio's beta tends to sacrifice its potential return.

Four Approaches to Portfolio Risk Estimation

Now that the simplification facilitated by the market model has been introduced, we can discuss four specific approaches to estimating portfolio risk. Markowitz' classic 1952 article proposed estimating a portfolio's risk from an extensive analysis of each component asset. Such an approach requires estimating a mean return and variance for every asset in the portfolio as well as estimating a covariance for every pair of assets.[1] Many estimates are required even for a relatively small portfolio. Each possible two-security combination in a 100-stock choice set would require 4,950 unique covariance estimates. Indeed, a 1,000-stock universe would call for 501,500 separate estimates. Estimating thousands of such parameters is time-consuming, expensive, and likely to produce unreliable inputs. Accordingly, a number of techniques requiring less information and effort have been developed.

Sharpe's single-index model[2] is much simpler to apply than the full Markowitz model. Each portfolio asset's estimated alpha, beta, and corresponding characteristic line's goodness-of-fit (or R^2) are used to analyze each relevant portfolio's risk. For a 100-stock universe the Markowitz model requires more than 5,000 estimates, whereas Sharpe's model needs only 300. Furthermore, the Sharpe model requires only conditional forecasts (the model implies different return forecasts for each possible market return). Such forecasts tend to be easier to construct and thus may well be more meaningful than the absolute forecasts needed for the full covariance model.

The multi-index model's complexity lies between that of the single-index Sharpe model and the full variance–covariance Markowitz model. This model uses separate indexes for estimating the alphas and betas of related assets such as stocks in the same industry. Then a covariance matrix between the indexes is formed and used in the portfolio risk computation. According to Cohen and Pogue, industry-index/portfolio-risk estimates offer little improvement over the single-index model.[3] Farrell suggests, however, that improved multi-index model results are obtained by grouping stocks on the basis of such characteristics as growth, stability, and so on.[4] A more sophisticated form of the multi-index model called the Arbitrage Pricing Theory (APT) will be introduced in the following chapter.

Sharpe's linear model, the simplest of the four approaches, requires only alpha and beta estimates.[5] If each security represents only a small proportion of the portfolio (less than 5%, for example), the linear model is a close approximation of the single-index model. One significant advantage of the linear model is that it can easily be applied without a computer. Table 5.3 summarizes the four approaches.

TABLE 5.3 Approaches to Portfolio-Risk Estimation

Markowitz's Full Model	Utilizes full complement of estimated returns, variances and covariances for each component
Sharp's Single-Index Model	Only requires α, β and R^2 for each component
Multi-Index Model	Uses separate indexes for groups of stocks to estimate their α and β values
Sharp Linear Model	Only requires α and β for each component

Price Impact of Market and Nonmarket Risk

Note that the linear model computes portfolio risks with only component alphas and betas. The alphas should have average values close to 0 and thus not affect the portfolio's return. As a result alphas should have no impact on portfolio risk and thus can be largely ignored in portfolio work. Moreover, nonmarket risk, which is fully diversifiable, should be irrelevant to those who can diversify effectively. Accordingly, a well-diversified portfolio's risk should depend exclusively on its component's market risks (betas). Furthermore, well-diversified investors (those institutional and other large investors who make up a substantial fraction of the market) may well largely determine market prices. If separating risk into market and nonmarket components and then ignoring the nonmarket portion is justified, an asset's risk would be fully reflected in its beta. Thus, the risk premium contained in market discount rates should be based only on market risk (beta). In other words, nonmarket risk should not affect asset prices.

CHOOSING AN EFFICIENT PORTFOLIO

Thus far we have seen that: (1) a security's total risk can be defined as the standard deviation (or variance) of its expected income stream; (2) total risk can be decomposed into market and nonmarket components; (3) beta may be used to measure market risk; (4) a diversified portfolio's risk is largely a function of its component's beta; and (5) if most market participants can diversify effectively, nonmarket risk should not have an impact on an asset's risk premium. In light of these findings, how should an investor go about assembling a portfolio?

Assume that portfolios may be assembled from a group of risky securities, that short selling and borrowing are not allowed, and that risks and expected returns (for any given market return) may be estimated from historical data. How should these data be used to assemble the most attractive portfolio? In principle, the expected returns and risks could be plotted for every possible combination of securities. Because the number of possible portfolio combinations is infinite, an efficient search requires some shortcuts.

The Market Portfolio

The so-called *market portfolio* offers a useful starting point. The market portfolio includes each investment in the relevant universe of possible investments. Each component is weighted in proportion to its share of the value of that universe. For example, the relevant investment universe might be divided as follows: real estate 40%, stocks 25%, bonds 15%, and other 20%. The market portfolio would then represent each category in these proportions. Moreover, within each category the proportions assignable to each specific asset would be so allocated.

The market portfolio is the appropriate index to apply to the market model. As such, it has a beta of precisely unity. Moreover, the market portfolio, which is fully diversified, contains no nonmarket risk. Finally, if securities have been accurately priced relative to their expected performances, the market portfolio will be efficient in the sense that all other portfolios will offer either a lower expected return, a higher risk, or both. Figure 5.8 illustrates an efficient market portfolio in risk–return space. Portfolio M, the market portfolio, has a beta of 1 and an expected

FIGURE 5.8   An Efficient Market Portfolio

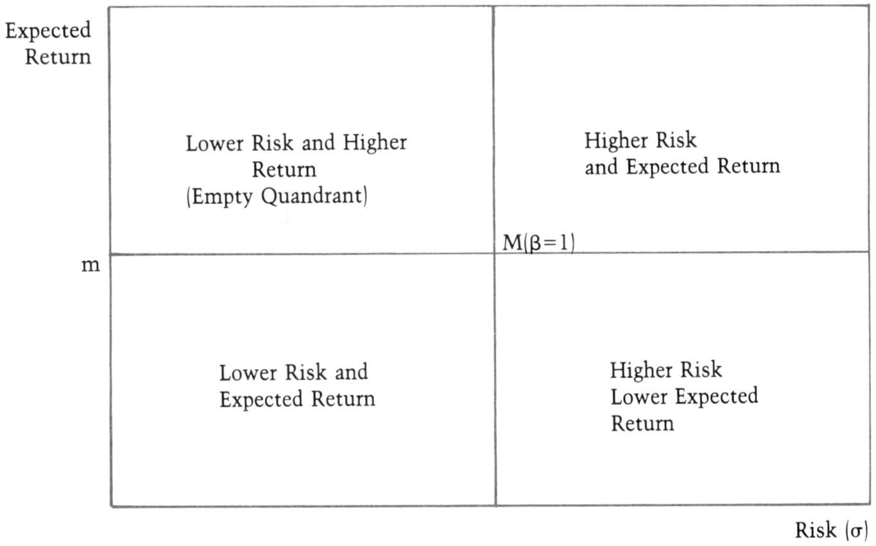

return of m. All portfolios with lower betas also have lower expected returns whereas all portfolios with higher expected returns also have higher betas.

The Efficient Frontier

A given universe of assets contains many portfolios that are efficient. That is, a large number of different portfolios may be constructed to offer the highest expected return for their particular level of risk. Mathematical procedures can identify all such efficient portfolios from any given set of assets. Figure 5.9 illustrates a typical set of efficient portfolios. Drawing a line through each of these efficient portfolios creates a relationship called the *efficient frontier.* All efficient portfolios lie on the efficient frontier. All other feasible portfolios are inefficient. A portfolio is inefficient if a more attractive risk-expected return trade-off is available at the frontier. The concave (bowed downward) shape of the efficient frontier indicates that increasing risk increments must be sacrificed to gain additional expected return increments.

Choosing the Most Attractive Risk–Return Trade-off.   Each efficient portfolio offers the highest expected return for its risk level. Rational risk-averse investors might, depending on their degrees of risk aversion, legitimately choose any efficient portfolio. A very risk-averse investor would select a low risk point while a less risk-averse investor would accept greater risk to achieve a higher expected return. The rational investor should choose a portfolio whose risk-expected return trade-off equals his or her own willingness to trade off expected return for risk.

FIGURE 5.9   The Efficient Frontier (No Lending or Borrowing)

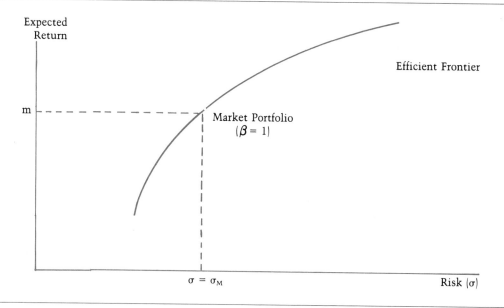

The Efficient Frontier with Lending.   Thus far we have assumed that investors assemble portfolios by purchasing risky securities. Borrowing, selling short, and purchasing a risk-free asset have not been allowed. If one or more of these restrictions is relaxed, however, the efficient frontier takes on a different shape. The effect of lending risklessly (for example, investing in riskless government bonds) is illustrated in Figure 5.10.

Asset F yields a riskless return f that is below the expected market return m. A horizontal line from f to the efficient frontier (fH) contains all portfolios that offer an equal expected return and higher risk than F. Clearly fH is superior to all portfolios below it. Still more attractive risk–return trade-offs are possible with asset F, however. Risk-free return f has a zero covariance with all other returns. Thus the risk of a portfolio containing F equals the weighted average risk of the risky components and its own zero-risk level. Similarly, the portfolio's expected return equals the weighted average of the expected returns of the risky and riskless components. In fact, the risk-expected return combinations of any portfolio that combines F with risky portfolios lie on a straight line between the two portfolios (fA). A derivation of these relationships can be found in more advanced textbooks. Only combinations of F and efficient portfolios (on the old efficient frontier) should be considered. A line from f to a tangency point on the efficient frontier could be found by rotating a ray beginning at f. The risk-expected return combinations along that ray from f to the tangency point are superior to those of any lines below it. Moreover, because fT is tangent to the efficient frontier, no ray (beginning at f) above fT intersects the efficient frontier.

The Efficient Frontier with Borrowing.   Suppose we could borrow at rate f (for example, margin borrowing at the riskless rate) to invest in some efficient portfolio

FIGURE 5.10   The Efficient Frontier with Lending and Borrowing at the
                   Risk-Free Rate

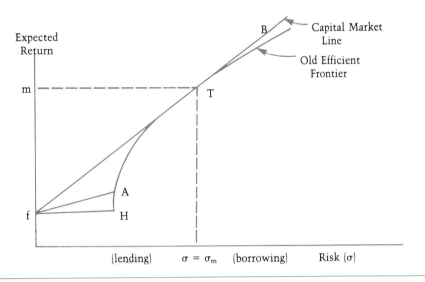

G. In effect, asset F is sold short and the proceeds invested in G. How does allowing such borrowing or short selling affect the efficient frontier? Clearly, the additional funds should only be invested in otherwise efficient portfolios. As with permitting riskless lending, the risks and expected returns of the leveraged portfolio equals a linear combination of the risks and expected returns of its components. With borrowing or short selling, however, the weight on the risky component is greater than unity whereas the riskless component's weight is negative. In fact, financing additional investments (at rate f) in a risky portfolio simply extends the line of risk-expected return combinations of F and the risky portfolio. Again, an infinite number of lines begin at f and pass through the efficient frontier. The one passing through the tangency point (fTB) reflects the most attractive available set of risk-expected return combinations. Accordingly, the efficient frontier, when lending and borrowing are at the riskless rate, is formed by drawing a line from point f through the tangency point T on what would have been the efficient frontier had lending and borrowing not been allowed.

The Capital Market Line. When all marketable assets are considered part of the choice set, the just derived relationship (fTB) is called the capital market line. For the assumptions used to derive it, the capital market line identifies the market's optimal risk-expected return combinations. Thus, one should invest in the tangency portfolio and F in the proportions (either positively or negatively) that produce the desired risk-expected return trade-off. Investors will maximize their expected returns by levering the tangency portfolio to the desired risk level and should, regardless of their risk preferences, hold risky assets in the proportions of the tangency portfolio. Only if the weights are the same as those of the market portfolio will the market clear. Indeed, asset prices would adjust so that investors would hold assets in proportion to their relative market values. If, for example, investors wished to hold too much (relative to supply) of some assets and too little of others, the prices of the former would be bid up and the latter bid down. This process would continue until the prices reached the level at which the quantity demanded precisely equaled the quantity available (the market would clear). Indeed market prices generally adjust up or down to bring supply and demand into balance. Therefore, the market portfolio is the only sustainable tangency portfolio consistent with the stated assumptions.

The capital market line can be expressed in equation form as:

$$E(R_p) = W_f(f) + (1 - W_f) E(R_m) \tag{5.4}$$

where:

$E(R_p)$ = expected return on portfolio
W_f = percentage of portfolio invested in risk-free asset
　　　(negative if investor is a borrower)
f = risk-free return
$E(R_m)$ = expected return of market

The above type of analysis allows us to divide the investment from the financing decision. Investors are assumed to invest in the market portfolio (the investment decision) and choose their desired risk level by levering (lending or borrowing) that portfolio to the desired risk-expected return level (the financing decision). Particularly risk-averse investors will choose risk–return trade-offs lying on the lower portion of the capital market line. More risk-oriented investors will choose a financing level that offers a higher expected return coupled with a higher risk. This division of the investment and financing decision is called the *separation theorem*.

In practical terms the separation theorem or two-mutual-fund theorem implies that investors can achieve optimal efficient diversification with just two assets. Thus an investor who can buy into a governments-only fund (Money Market Mutual fund that buys only T-bills) and a well-diversified common stock mutual fund (including the right to buy on margin) can construct a series of risk-expected/return-efficient portfolios from varying combinations of these two assets. In theory any risk-expected/return combination on the efficient frontier can be reached with these two assets. Moreover, since the two assets already allow the investor to reach the efficient frontier, no other portfolio (even one constructed from a larger number of securities) can produce a more attractive risk-expected/return trade-off.

The Security Market Line.   The security market line extends our analysis to the pricing of individual assets. If individual assets are priced efficiently, their expected returns should be linearly related to their market risk or beta (Figure 5.11). Because

FIGURE 5.11 The Security Market Line

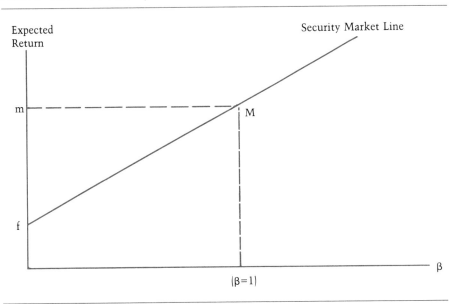

the expected return for a zero-beta asset is the risk-free rate, the equation of the security market line may be expressed as:

$$E(R_i) = f + {}_i[E(R_m) - f]$$

where:

$$E(R_i) = \text{expected return of asset i}$$
$$f = \text{risk-free return}$$
$$E(R_m) = \text{expected return of market}$$

Assumptions. Let us now state explicitly the assumptions that were used to derive the capital market and security market line relationships:

1. Market-equivalent portfolios may be assembled, bought, and sold as easily as any other investment asset. That is, all investment assets are available in very small units; transaction costs (commissions, bid–asked spreads) can be ignored; no individual investor or group of investors can appreciably affect market prices; and no institutional or psychological barriers retard the free flow of investable funds.

2. Investors are rational risk averters who want to maximize their expected return and minimize its standard deviation. Moreover, they are unconcerned with any other properties of expected returns.

3. Differential tax treatments are in the aggregate irrelevant to investment decisions.

TABLE 5.4   Assumptions Used to Derive Capital and Security Market Lines

1. Market equivalent portfolios are easy to assemble.
2. Investors seek to maximize expected return and minimize its standard deviation.
3. Differential tax treatments are irrelevant.
4. Investors have identical asset return expectations.
5. Investors may borrow or lend all they want at the riskless rate.

4.   Investors have access to the same body of public information and analyze it in identical fashions so that they have equivalent asset return expectations.

5.   Investors may borrow and lend without limit at the riskless rate.

Table 5.4 summarizes these assumptions.

If the market behaves at the margin as assumed, the model will precisely explain its actions. This is much too much to ask, however. All models are built on assumptions that depart from reality even at the margin. The best test of a model's value is not the realism of its assumptions but the reliability of its predictions. A model whose assumptions are severely violated may still yield useful predictions. For example, Kepler's model of planetary motion heroically assumes all masses are concentrated in a single point and that the universe is frictionless. Nonetheless, Kepler's model accurately explains planetary motions. In like manner, the security market line might accurately explain asset prices in spite of its unrealistic assumptions. Thus we need to examine the empirical evidence relating to the model's predictions.

SUMMARY AND CONCLUSIONS

The modern portfolio theory discussed in this chapter yields a number of interesting conclusions: An asset's total risk may be defined as the standard deviation of its expected return distribution. Portfolio risk depends crucially on the covariance (covariability between component returns). The market model offers a simplified way of analyzing portfolio risk and expected return. This model assumes that market risk (return variability with the market portfolio) justifies a risk premium whereas nonmarket risk (return variability unrelated to market return variability) is fully diversifiable and therefore irrelevant to asset pricing. The efficient frontier of portfolios each offer the highest expected return for a given risk level. When borrowing and lending at the risk-free rate are allowed, the efficient frontier becomes a straight line. This line stretches from the point of the risk-free rate on the vertical axis through the tangency position at the market portfolio and beyond. This capital market line implies that investors should obtain the highest risk-adjusted expected return for their risk preferences by levering the market portfolio to the desired risk-expected return level. The security market line implies that expected asset returns are a linear function of β. The real world should behave as the model implies if at the margin investors act according to the assumptions used to develop this framework.

REVIEW QUESTIONS

1. How is an asset's risk generally defined in finance? How does this definition compare with the common concept that risk has to do with something undesirable happening?

2. State and explain the formula for two-asset portfolio risk. How does the covariance enter into the picture? What role do the individual variances and weights play? When is risk zero and when is it at a maximum? How does the formula change as the number of assets is increased?

3. Discuss the N-asset portfolio risk case and the full variance–covariance formula.

4. Why is portfolio risk normally analyzed in a simpler fashion than the full variance–covariance approach? Has the increased power of modern computers had an impact on this issue? Explain why or why not.

5. Discuss the three simplified approaches to estimating portfolio risk. What are the advantages and disadvantages of each?

6. Compare the market model and capital asset pricing model. What assumptions underlie the use of each?

7. Define and discuss market and nonmarket risk. How are the two types of risk related to diversification?

8. Discuss the concept of risk. Indicate how risk may be measured and what role it plays in the investment selection process.

9. What is a beta? What is an alpha? How might each be used in investment selection and portfolio management?

10. Define the efficient frontier, first without and then with a riskless lending and borrowing rate. What does the efficient frontier look like with riskless lending but no borrowing? What happens if the two rates differ?

11. What is the capital market line and what does it imply about the cost of raising capital?

12. What is the security market line and what does it imply about the cost of raising capital?

REVIEW PROBLEMS

1. Compute the expected return and standard deviation for the following:
   a. Equally probable returns of: -5%, 0%, 5%, 10%

b. 10% chance of a 0% return
   15% chance of a 5% return
   25% chance of a 10% return
   25% chance of a 15% return
   15% chance of a 20% return
   10% chance of a 25% return
c. 100% chance of a 10% return
   Now plot the risk and expected return for each investment.

2. Compute the portfolio variance for the following:
   a. $X = Y = .5$
      $\sigma_x^2 = \sigma_y^2 = .05$
      $C_{xy} = 0$
   b. $X = .3, Y = .7$
      $\sigma_x^2 = .03, \sigma_y^2 = .05$
      $C_{xy} = .8$
   c. $X = .1, Y = .9$
      $\sigma_x^2 = .08, \sigma_y^2 = .06$
      $C_{xy} = -.05$

3. Compute the covariance estimate for the following observations:

   $(X1, Y1) = (.03, .05)$
   $(X2, Y2) = (.05, .03)$
   $(X3, Y3) = (-.01, -.05)$
   $(X4, Y4) = (.10, .08)$
   $(X5, Y5) = (0, 0)$
   $(X6, Y6) = (.01, -.01)$

4. If $\sigma_x = .05$ and $\sigma_y = .08$, what is the correlation for the covariance estimate of Problem 3?

5. Assuming equal weights, covariances of C, and equal component variances of σ_{xi}^2, compute and illustrate the portfolio risk for N = 3, 5, 10, 15, and 20 components.

6. Use the following data to plot a scatter diagram and draw a characteristic line (using a straight edge to center a line through the dots).

Market Return	Stock Return
9%	9%
3%	2%
5%	6%
−2%	0%
−5%	−8%
12%	14%
−7%	−9%

   From your line-of-sight estimate of the characteristic line, estimate the alpha and beta.

7. For three separate stocks having alphas and betas of .01, .7; .05, 1.1; and −.02, 1.5, respectively, compute their expected returns for market returns of .05, .10, .15, −.05, and −.10.

8. Plot an efficient frontier for the following combinations of portfolio risk return: .03, .10; .05, .11; .06, .14; .07, .16. Now assume a riskless rate of .08 and extend the frontier.

9. Plot the capital market line for the following information:
    a. risk-free rate = 7%; expected return on the market = 14%
    b. risk-free rate = 9%; expected return on the market = 16%
    c. risk-free rate = 5%; expected return on the market = 10%

10. For the capital market lines of Problem 9, what would be the expected returns for efficient portfolios with betas of .7, 1.0, 1.3, and 1.6?

11. For the same information supplied in Problem 9, plot the security market line.

12. For the security market lines of Problem 11, compute the expected returns for assets having betas of .7, 1.0, 1.3, and 1.6. In what sense do these answers differ from those of Problem 11?

REVIEW PROJECTS

1. Select five stocks with published β estimates (Value Line estimates βs for the companies that it covers) and compute your own estimates. Compare the two estimates. Discuss the differences.

2. Identify five mutual funds that publish the average βs of their portfolios. Track the performance of these funds' shares compared to the market. Discuss the differences between their actual performances and the performances implied by their βs.

3. Plot an efficient frontier using the mutual funds from the previous review project (2). Use their prior year performance as the estimate of their expected returns and the six-month Treasury bill rate as the risk-free return.

NOTES

1. H. Markowitz, "Portfolio Selection," *Journal of Finance*, March 1952, 77–91.

2. W. Sharpe, "A Simplified Model for Portfolio Analysis," *Management Science*, January 1963, 277–293.

3. K. Cohen and J. Pogue, "A Compound Evaluation of Alternative Portfolio Selection Models," *Journal of Business*, April 1967, 166–193.

4. J. Farrell, "Analysis of Covariance of Returns to Determine Homogeneous Stock Groupings," *Journal of Business*, April 1974, 186–207.

5. W. Sharpe, "A Linear Programming Algorithm for Mutual Fund Portfolio Selecting," *Management Science*, March 1967, 499–510.

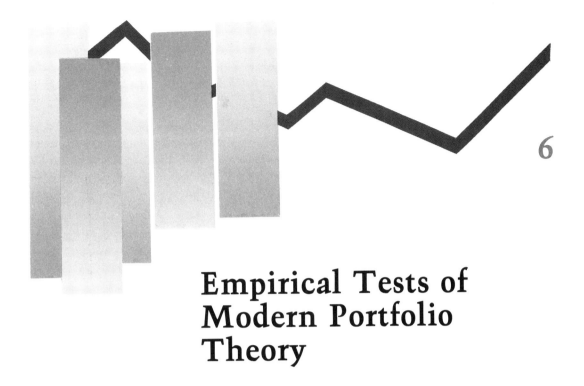

Empirical Tests of Modern Portfolio Theory

Modern Portfolio Theory (MPT) provides an elegant theoretical framework. Most of its features may be derived from a short list of admittedly heroic assumptions. Because a theory is best judged by the accuracy of its predictions, this chapter considers three interesting implications of modern portfolio theory. First, no trading method can consistently generate risk-adjusted returns that exceed those implied by the model (market efficiency). A capital market theory could be derived for inefficient markets, but the resulting market portfolio would not necessarily be efficient and nonmarket risk would not necessarily be irrelevant. Second, nonmarket risk does not affect the discount rate applied to risky assets. Finally, returns tend to vary linearly (the security market line) with (nondiversifiable) market risk. Thus most returns should approximate their corresponding market model-simulated estimates.

TYPES OF INVESTMENT ANALYSIS

To discuss the *efficient market hypothesis* in a meaningful fashion we need a basic understanding of the two primary types of investment analysis. Fundamental analysts forecast returns by analyzing the factors affecting the worth of expected future income streams. Thus fundamental security analysts assess a firm's earnings and dividend prospects by evaluating such factors as its sales, costs, and capital requirements. Fundamental commodity analysts base their futures forecasts on the relevant demand and supply factors. Fundamental real estate analysts generate price and rental value expectations from future construction costs and demand–growth estimates.

Technical analysts, in contrast, concentrate on past price and volume relationships (narrow form) or technical market indicators (broad form). Both types of technical analysts claim to be able to identify evolving investor sentiment but neither possesses a very sound theoretical base. Most technicians are not particularly concerned with a theoretical justification for their method. They are more inclined to argue that results are what ultimately matter. Taken to its logical extreme this position implies that if witchcraft produces attractive returns, investors should follow the advice of talented witches. A wealth of available data facilitates the application of technical analysis to the security and commodity markets. The lack of such data has prevented any extensive application to most nonsecurity investment types such as real estate or collectibles.

THE EFFICIENT MARKET HYPOTHESIS

Market efficiency, or as it was once known the "random walk hypothesis," questions the usefulness of technical analysis and in some versions fundamental analysis as well. Many natural phenomena follow a random walk, or what the physical sciences call Brownian motion. A drunk in the middle of a large field who is as likely to move in one direction as another follows a random walk. Similarly, the next price change of a randomly moving stock is unrelated to past price behavior. Obviously, if prices move randomly, the repeating price patterns that technical analysts claim to observe do not exist.

Price movements need not be precisely random for past price data to be useless. Marginally associated relations between past and future price changes may be either too small or too unreliable to generate gross returns that consistently exceed transaction costs. Indeed commissions, search costs, and bid–ask spreads would generally offset any expected price change of less than two or three percent.

Adjusting Returns for the Impacts of Risk and the Market

Theoretical and empirical studies of market efficiency need to take proper account of the impact of both risk and the market. We have already seen how a tendency toward risk aversion causes investors to expect higher returns on more risky investments. Virtually everyone who studies the securities markets realizes that actual returns generally do increase with risk. Thus any type of study of market performance needs to take account of the impact of risk on expected and actual returns. Similarly, individual security returns tend to be higher when the overall market is strong than when it is weak. Failing to adjust for the impacts of risk and the market could lead to very misleading results. Two standard methods are used to adjust actual returns for these effects: differential returns and risk-adjusted (or abnormal) returns.

Differential Returns.   In some types of studies the impact of risk tends to average out and thus can be ignored. When this is the case, an adjustment that produces what are called differential returns can be performed:

$$D_{it} = R_{it} - M_t$$

where:

D_{it} = Differential return for firm i during period t
R_{it} = Actual return for firm i during period t
M_t = Market return for period t

Risk Adjusted Returns.   When an adjustment is needed for both risk and the market, abnormal or risk adjusted returns are computed:

$$RA_{it} = R_{it} - (\alpha_i + \beta_i M_t)$$

where:

RA_{it} = Risk-adjusted return of firm i during period t
α_i = Estimated alpha for firm i
β_i = Estimated beta for firm i

Thus the appropriate risk adjustment reduces the gross return by the portion of that return that was due to the level of riskiness of the investment. The standard method of risk adjustment subtracts an increment due to market risk as measured by the investment's beta. Virtually all serious securities market research utilizes risk and/or market adjusted returns such as those described.

The Weak Form of the Efficient Market Hypothesis

The random walk or weak form of the efficient market hypothesis implies that knowledge of past price behavior has no value. That is, such knowledge cannot be used to manage a portfolio that outperforms the market on a risk-adjusted basis. The weak form implies that once we know the most recent price quote, we know as much about possible subsequent returns as those who know the full price history up to that point. In other words, prices have no memory and thus do not move in predictable patterns. Weak form adherents argue that, if prices did move in dependable patterns, the reactions of alert market participants would rapidly destroy any resulting profit opportunities. Thus if a particular price pattern was thought to forecast a rise, some market participants might react before most investors could take advantage of the move. Indeed, premature actions by some traders would frequently prevent the full pattern from occurring. Eventually the action of traders who jumped the gun would destroy the value of any recognized patterns.

The Semistrong Form of the Efficient Market Hypothesis

The weak form of the efficient market hypothesis implies that technical analysis is useless, but it does not address the effectiveness of fundamental analysis. The

TABLE 6.1   Forms of the Efficient Market Hypothesis

Weak Form	Future returns are unrelated to past return patterns. (Charting does not work.)
Semistrong Form	Future returns are unrelated to any analysis restricted to public data. (Fundamental analysis does not work.)
Strong Form	Future returns are unrelated to any analysis based on public or nonpublic data. (Inside information is useless.)

semistrong form, in contrast, asserts that the market quickly and correctly evaluates all relevant publicly available technical and fundamental information. Thus, according to this form, market prices should accurately reflect the relevant public information.

If markets are semistrong form efficient, then risk-adjusted returns can exceed those of the market in only two ways. Investments may be affected by unexpected developments. Thus some (lucky) investors may do the right things for the wrong reasons while other (unlucky) investors suffer from unexpectedly unfavorable developments. Second, nonpublic knowledge may facilitate superior analysis. For example, a corporate insider, lender, supplier, or a friend may know and be able to trade profitably (but also illegally) on relevant knowledge prior to its public release.

The Strong Form of the Efficient Market Hypothesis

According to the strong form of the efficient market hypothesis, the market anticipates inside information so effectively that those with such knowledge are rarely able to react quickly enough to use it profitably. Table 6.1 summarizes the various forms of the efficient market hypothesis.

Outperforming the Market

We have seen that the returns generated from applying both technical and fundamental analysis should be judged relative to the returns on the market. If the market is rising, most investment strategies will produce positive returns, while a declining market tends to have the opposite effect. The market return may be used as a benchmark against which to judge the usefulness of a particular type of analysis. To be judged successful, a trading rule or strategy needs to generate returns that after an appropriate adjustment for risk must in the aggregate exceed the market returns of the corresponding periods. Thus the techniques of both technical and fundamental analysis need to be tested against real world data. Such data can be used to generate hypothetical returns for various investment strategies. These hypothetical returns can then be compared with the market's returns for the same period. Normally a stock market index such as the New York Stock Exchange Composite (a weighted average of all NYSE listings) is used to represent the overall market performance. If the technique to be tested leads the investor to assemble a portfolio whose average market risk (average beta) differs appreciably from that of the market's (a beta appreciably different from one), the market return benchmark should be adjusted accordingly. Thus either differential or risk-adjusted returns (or some other similar adjustment) should be used to examine the effectiveness of any strategy based on fundamental or technical analysis. Virtually all academic studies utilize such adjusted returns data. The results and conclusions of those that do not are suspect.

Weak Form Tests.   Technical market influences have been explored empirically in two basic ways. First, the relationship between past and future price changes has been tested for statistical dependence (relatedness) or independence (unrelatedness). Second, filter rules analogous to technical trading rules have been applied to historical data. If past price patterns help forecast future price change, past and future price changes should be related, and technically inspired filter rules should help identify profitable trading opportunities.

Some studies have examined serial correlation (relationship between past and present price changes) while others investigated runs of prices. A *run* is an uninterrupted series of price increases or an uninterrupted series of price decreases. Many different studies have consistently failed to find any important dependences (relation in price changes). Thus past price patterns do not appear to forecast future price movements. Chartists point out that these statistical tests look largely for linear relations and say they are much too crude to capture subtleties. Moreover chartists assert that their "craft" is as much art as science as it depends heavily on judgment, interpretation, and experience; that is, beneath the apparent randomness of stock price movements is a distinct nonrandom pattern that can be discerned from charts. Chartists argue that these patterns are very difficult to quantify by standard statistical methods. Nonetheless, most nonlinear dependencies that they claim to see should show up in the tests as linear approximations. Furthermore, chartists have offered no convincing (to academicians) counterevidence.

A second set of tests has explored technical analysis using what are called *filter rules*. Filter rules mechanically identify supposed buy and sell situations. One such rule flashes a buy signal whenever a stock increases by x%. After an x% decline from a subsequent high, a sell signal is given. Thus a 5% filter would signal to buy whenever a stock rose 5% from the preceding high.

A second type of filter rule, Levy's so-called relative strength criterion, identifies stocks that have recently outperformed the market as buys and underperformed the market as sells. For example, a stock rising 10% when the market rose only 5% would have outperformed the market and thereby exhibited relative strength. Filters attempt to reflect the momentum/resistance-level factors that technical analysts claim to be important. When transactions costs are included, none of these various types of filter rules has been shown to outperform a buy-and-hold strategy.[1]

Semistrong and Strong Form Tests.   General tests of the semistrong and strong form are virtually impossible to devise and perform. Moreover, as Summers has pointed out, existing test procedures are not very powerful in discriminating between efficient and inefficient markets.[2] That is, the market pricing process generates so much noise that prices can stray quite a bit from their intrinsic values without detection by the commonly used tests. Nonetheless, various subhypotheses of the efficient market hypothesis have been examined. Many studies claim to have found specific types of fundamental analysis useful. For example, a number of studies suggest that stocks with low price–earnings ratios, small market capitalizations, low per share prices, or related characteristics tend to outperform the market.[3]

On the other hand, a classic study of the impact of splits on performance found the market to react rather efficiently.[4] That is, prior to the split announcement the stocks tended to outperform the market but after the announcement performance was random. Some academicians suggest that, since institutional investors with all their professional expertise rarely outperform the market on a risk-adjusted basis, individual investors are unlikely to do better. Others claim to see enough examples of market imperfections to convince them that talented investment analysts are able to outperform the market. Even if the market eventually evaluates public information accurately, the nimble investor/analyst may be able to take advantage of lags in the price adjustment process. With so much conflicting evidence, the extent of semistrong form efficiency remains controversial.

Most strong form supporters would concede that insider information is sometimes useful, but they contend that such examples are rare. Several studies, however, have found insider trading to be generally quite profitable. That is, insiders tend to earn above-market returns when they buy and sell the stock of their own companies. Indeed, those who derive signals from the SEC's insider trading reports tend to outperform the market.[5]

The Emerging Consensus on the Market Efficiency Debate

Some continue to hold extreme positions, but the dimensions of the market efficiency debate have narrowed appreciably. Few academicians who have examined the issue now believe that the market is strong-form efficient or always semistrong-form efficient. On the other hand, virtually all serious finance scholars agree that the weak form of the hypothesis is essentially correct. The principal disagreements relate to the importance, extent, and causes of the imperfections of the semistrong form. Thus far, however, little or no theoretical work has been devoted to portfolio models that allow for market imperfections. Such imperfections are largely viewed as departures or exceptions to normal behavior.

Causes of Persistent Market Imperfections

Why, if the market contains many talented rational investors, do imperfections persist? No consensus has yet emerged but informed speculation is possible. A market imperfection exists whenever any group of investors can consistently earn risk-adjusted returns that are above those of the market. Such imperfections can have numerous causes.

Brokers, investment advisors, and the financial press continually pull investors in many directions. Most investors have difficulty discriminating between valid

Investments in Perspective

The central figure in a major inside trading scandal, Ivan Boesky clearly proved that one could trade profitably with such information. He admitted to trading extensively on inside information that he bribed a variety of people in order to obtain. He was sentenced to three years in prison and had to give up $100 million of illegal profits. He was able to obtain relatively lenient treatment for himself by implicating a number of others.

Economics

MARKET THEORY

CAN INVESTORS REALLY BEAT THE MARKET—WITHOUT CHEATING?

THE BOESKY AFFAIR HAS FANNED THE CONTROVERSY OVER 'EFFICIENCY' AND FAIRNESS

As Ivan F. Boesky recently proved, there's one sure-fire way to make money: Know something that virtually no one else does, and act on it first. Of course, you can get in a lot of trouble that way. Still, for law-abiding investors, the key to investing is what you know, and in theory, all investors have access to a wealth of public information. The question is, can anyone really make big money knowing what everyone else knows?

For years, economists argued that the answer was no. The received wisdom was that markets are "efficient"—that is, all available information is fully reflected in stock prices, so there is no way to outguess the market and make supernormal profits. If investors threw darts at stock tables instead of trying to pick winners, they would do neither better nor worse than the market averages, Burton G. Malkiel argued in his 1973 classic, *A Random Walk Down Wall Street.*

BEYOND REASON. In recent years, though, some economists have wondered just how efficient markets really are. They've tracked numerous anomalies that permit some players to make out-

size profits. In some instances, economists are challenging the very underpinnings of the efficient-markets hypothesis by observing excess volatility in stock prices. Obviously, stocks fluctuate in response to new information, and the efficient-markets hypothesis allows for a reasonable amount of volatility. Critics contend, however, that stock prices frequently move beyond the bounds that business and economic events would seem to dictate.

But a great deal more is at stake than whether the individual investor can make big profits in the market, because truly efficient markets have macroeconomic effects. Efficient markets mean not only that no investor can beat the averages but also that the economy's capital resources are being allocated efficiently.

If it were shown, however, that significant market inefficiencies do exist that allow investors to reap big profits, it would follow that capital might be misdirected into less and less productive investments. A company whose stock is bid way up will find its cost of capital lower than it might otherwise have been, and unnecessary investments might result. By contrast, a company whose stock is undervalued will find its cost of capital higher, thus hindering productive investments.

The Boesky case both supports and discredits the efficient-markets theory. It ratifies the concept of randomness because it turns out that Boesky, rather than being a smart stock picker, simply had the edge of inside information, without which he would have done no better than other professional investors. On the other hand, the Boesky affair suggests the game can be rigged often enough to render the market inefficient.

Efficient-markets proponents have long believed that insider trading is too infrequent to affect the market's overall efficiency. But because mergers, takeovers, and restructurings have mushroomed lately, and because Boesky's trades focused on companies going through such changes, some worry that insider buys are more frequent than had been thought. "It's a question of magnitude," says Malkiel, dean of the Yale University School of Organization & Management. "If [insider trading] seems to be more pervasive rather than the exception, then the markets might be perceived to be unfair."

Yet even in a market most people believe to be fair, investors beat the averages at least some of the time, and in a perfectly legal fashion—which suggests that prices somehow aren't right. "Market prices are supposed to be rational and reflect rational expectations," says economist Lawrence H. Summers of Harvard University, "but clearly we've seen movements which exceed the initial fundamentals. Financial markets are volatile, not merely because of real information but also because of changing moods and guesses."

Look at the huge runup in stock prices of takeover or restructuring candidates. "It's hard to believe that the market was right both before and after the takeover," says Summers. Not at all, counters Michael C. Jensen of Harvard University and the University of Rochester. "The market is properly valuing the stock in both instances. Takeovers or in-

ternal changes in management are huge pieces of new information, and they're often accompanied by real changes such as recapitalizations, stock buybacks, and the like." It's only appropriate, says Jensen, that the market respond to this new information positively.

FAD BUYING? The biggest challenge to the efficient-markets theory has been posed by economists who believe that fads and fashions, or "behavioral" aspects of decision-making, have an influence on stock prices. In a study that has aroused much controversy, economist Robert J. Shiller of Yale found that stock prices generally were "excessively volatile" over more than 100 years.

Shiller points out that the Standard & Poor's 500-stock index, adjusted for inflation, rose 85% from 1927 to 1929 and fell 56% from 1973 to 1975—as much as five times the deviation that his statistical model would have predicted for the century of stock price data that he studied. News events and company fundamentals, says Shiller, simply can't explain that volatility. His critics, however, have argued that his work is statistically flawed and exaggerates the volatility.

The idea that there are inefficiencies in the marketplace comes as no surprise to old hands on Wall Street. Investors make it their business to sniff out profit-making opportunities, however short-lived they may be. Indeed, a number of analysts at Wall Street firms are studying these so-called anomalies and creating investment strategies around them.

Fischer Black, a partner at Goldman, Sachs & Co., former Massachusetts Institute of Technology professor, and co-author of the Black-Scholes Option Pricing Model, says that "the forces tending to make markets efficient don't seem to be as strong as they once were." For instance, says Black, index futures have been "persistently different" from where they were supposed to be this year and last, based on such factors as their underlying stock prices.

Other examples abound. A veritable cottage industry has developed in academia to study different instances where stock prices appear to deviate from expectations. There are, for example, studies showing that the stocks of small and growing companies, even adjusted for their greater risk, consistently outperform those of larger companies over time. One study shows that after stocks are split, they experience more volatility than before. Other studies highlight "weekend" or "January" effects, when outsize movements in stock prices seem to occur. All of these effects—and the studies that describe them—apparently chip away at the efficient-markets hypothesis.

'SELF-DESTRUCTIVE.' Despite the contention, most economists maintain that markets are basically efficient, even if they are not purely so. Malkiel, for one, believes that the anomalies don't add up to a lot, mainly because inefficiencies, once discovered, ultimately "self-destruct" as investors race to take advantage of

them. Jensen, while acknowledging that excesses and mistakes sometimes occur, insists that "there's still no better empirically documented proposition in the social sciences anywhere" than the efficient-markets theory. And most would agree with economist David Romer of Princeton University that recent research hasn't invalidated the theory, because "it's still the case that there's no easy way to make money."

To Summers and others who look at how behavior affects the market, the fact that the efficient-markets hypothesis has been difficult to disprove doesn't make it right. Researchers would have to examine an incredible amount of stock price data—Summers estimates 5,000 years' worth—to disprove the theory to the satisfaction of stalwarts.

The debate is not likely to carry on quite that long. Indeed, if the insider trading scandal widens to include far more players than had previously been imagined, economists may have to rethink some of their notions about just how efficient the market is and just how "anomalous" some events are.

By Karen Pennar in New York

The key question: Is insider trading rare— or more pervasive than had been thought?

Source: K. Pennar, "Can Investors Really Beat the Market—Without Cheating?" *Business Week*, December 15, 1986, 82–84. Reprinted by special permission, © 1986, McGraw-Hill, Inc.

and invalid analysis. (Why else do so many newsletters prosper in spite of the random and often conflicting nature of their advice?) Eliminating market imperfections requires that the reaction to an observed mispricing be of sufficient magnitude to force prices back into line. If the transactions of investors acting on valid mispricing evidence are swamped by trading based on incorrect analysis, observable mispricings will persist. Treynor argues that investors are often led into shared errors by their reliance on a common body of information from such sources as published investment research.[6] Thus investors and analysts who erroneously project abnormally high past earnings growth into the future may bid prices up to the point where they pay too much for "growth stocks." Such a process would allow others to outperform the market by avoiding or shortening such issues (contrary opinion). Subsequent growth rates that differ from those expected should lead to price "corrections." Indeed, such scenarios could occur frequently enough for some to profit from their ability to "predict" the resulting price moves. Mispricings will continue as long as trading by those who recognize them is insufficient to bid prices back into line. Moreover, the investors who recognize such misvaluing tendencies have an incentive to keep quiet.

Modern portfolio theory generally assumes that market prices are formed by a homogeneous group of investors analyzing the same sources of information in identical fashions. While market efficiency does not require perfect homogeneity of investor expectations, marginal investors must behave as if they accurately analyze all relevant public information and are unaffected (or identically affected) by such matters as tax status, costs of trading, risk orientation, borrowing power, liquidity preference, familiarity with local markets, and total available funds. In the real world, however, the resources of those who are best positioned to profit may be insufficient to eliminate some mispricings. Because investment analysts and periodicals concentrate on the larger, better known firms, the security prices of many smaller firms may depart from the values that a careful analysis would yield. Such firms generally trade in localized markets, and thus few investors are positioned to observe the mispricings. Other types of mispricings may only be exploited by those who can purchase control. An investor acquiring control of a firm worth more dead than alive could liquidate its assets for more than the firm's value as a going concern. Such takeovers are not usually easy to accomplish. The effort tends to bid up prices and provoke vigorous defensive efforts by those whose interests are threatened. Thus investors with the necessary resources may frequently have inadequate incentives to eliminate the mispricing. Still other imperfections (arbitrage opportunities) may require very quick and low-cost access to several markets. Only if enough investors are able to take advantage of such imperfections will their actions right the price imbalances.

Finally, market efficiency assumes that investors rationally pursue the highest available risk-adjusted returns. In a broader context, however, investors are not merely maximizers of risk-adjusted return but also consumers with many-dimensional utility functions. Thus investors who choose to maximize their total welfares by devoting more resources to leisure time, education, or earning extra income may seem to slight their investment management roles. As a result some apparent imperfections may not be fully exploited because those best positioned to take advantage of them are unaware of or unconcerned with the potential gains. Far from being irrational, such investors are simply maximizing their total utility. Concentrating exclusively on the risk-adjusted return of their portfolios would not be rational. Table 6.2 summarizes these points.

TABLE 6.2 Reasons for Persistent Market Imperfections

- Difficulty in discriminating between valid evidence and useless advice
- Differing investor circumstances: tax status, trading costs, risk orientation, borrowing power, liquidity preferences, wealth level, familiarity with local markets, etc.
- The pursuit by investors of overall utility maximization rather than the maximizing of their portfolios' risk-adjusted return

THE RISK PREMIUM ON NONMARKET RISK

According to modern portfolio theory, the risk premiums applied to the expected returns of individual investments should be solely determined by each asset's market risk. Thus two assets with the same level of market risk should have equal expected returns even if they have very different levels of nonmarket risk. A number of studies have found, however, that risk premiums are also related to nonmarket risk. This apparent conflict between MPT and the evidence has spawned a number of hypotheses.

If, for example, effective diversification were relatively difficult or costly, many investors would diversify incompletely rather than incur the high costs of achieving a fully diversified portfolio. Because nonmarket risk would contribute to overall portfolio risks for such investors, they would consider it relevant. The relative ease of individual investor diversification is therefore explored next.

Practical Diversification

Risk-neutral investors maximize expected returns without regard to risk. While few investors are truly risk neutral, those with adequate financial protection provided by insurance, retirement benefits, appreciable holdings of low-risk investments, and other means may view their remaining portfolio through approximately risk-neutral eyes. Thus some investors may put part of their wealth in less risky assets such as well-diversified mutual funds, preferred stocks, or convertible bonds and manage the remainder for maximum return.

Investors with long time horizons may focus most of their attention on an attempt to maximize their portfolio values 10 or 20 years hence. Such investors may be relatively unconcerned with the interim values of their portfolios. For example, investors may start with small positions in one or two stocks and periodically expand their portfolios' size and diversity. Such investors might initially opt for high-risk securities with high expected return in the hope that the "winners" will eventually make the strategy pay off. Such an approach, however, risks what is called gambler's ruin: a streak of bad luck may wipe out the investor's limited resources even though the chosen strategy might eventually pay off with unlimited resources.

Investors who are neither risk neutral nor have long time horizons may either diversify their own portfolios or let mutual funds or other institutional investors do the job. Efficient portfolio diversification requires purchasing a number of different securities. Although commission and search costs may not be worth the resulting risk reduction for a small portfolio, a rather modest number of stocks may yield substantial diversification. Evans and Archer concluded: "Much of the unsystematic variation (or returns) is reduced by the time the eighth security is added to a portfolio."[7]

Other researchers have also found that effective bond diversification requires few issues.[8] On the other hand, Frankfurter argues that even efficiently diversified portfolios will contain a substantial amount of nonmarket risk.[9] Also, when portfolios are assembled nonrandomly, for example by following brokerage firm recommendations, diversification may be rather difficult. Under such circumstances, Tole shows that eliminating most nonmarket risk requires substantially more than eight to 10 stocks.[10] Beedles, Joy, and Ruland, in contrast, report that conglomerate firms tend to offer greater diversification value than single-industry firms.[11]

One should not conclude, however, that effective diversification is easy or automatic. While risk declines, administrative costs increase appreciably with portfolio size. Furthermore, portfolios whose components are concentrated among firms or industries that are likely to be affected by similar factors (energy companies or GM and Ford) may not be effectively diversified. All firms are affected by economic fluctuations. Industry-specific and firm-specific impacts are, in contrast, averaged over the securities represented in the portfolio. These industry-specific and firm-specific factors are diversified away only if the portfolio itself does not systematically overrepresent certain of these factors.

Consider the investment impact of a breakdown of price discipline by OPEC and other oil-producing nations. A well-diversified portfolio of U.S. stocks would not be greatly affected by such a breakdown. Some of its investments (e.g., the stocks of heavy energy users such as airlines) might be helped while others (e.g., those who sold fossil fuels or serviced the companies in the oil patch) would be hurt. A portfolio with a large representation of Texas banks would, in contrast, be very sensitive to such a development. Most of the banks in the Southwest are very dependent on the health of their local economy, which in turn is very dependent on energy prices. A decline in oil and natural gas prices not only adversely affects the profit outlook for oil companies, but also for local real estate investments, the companies that service the oil industry, and the employees of both the oil companies and the oil service companies. Inevitably the banks in that region will have made extensive loans to local borrowers. The ability of most of these borrowers to service and repay that debt depends upon the health of the local economy.

Diversification difficulty for some might not by itself account for the price effect of nonmarket risk. If small investors' aversion to nonmarket risk caused some securities to be underpriced (vis-à-vis their market risk), large investors could exploit that aversion by constructing well-diversified portfolios of such securities. Indeed, the market might well contain enough such large investors to keep security prices in line with their market risks. Since, however, the empirical evidence points to a nonmarket risk effect, we need to search further.

Additional Reasons for a Nonmarket Risk Effect

Miller and Scholes found that various possible sources of estimation error were unlikely to account for the price effect of nonmarket risks.[12] Their results did suggest two factors: inefficiently estimated betas and a positive correlation between estimated betas and nonmarket risk. If betas are inefficiently estimated, the true effect of market risk will not be fully captured by the beta estimate. If the true beta and the estimate for nonmarket risk are correlated, the nonmarket risk variable may act as a second proxy for market risk.

A second attempt to explain the apparent premium paid for nonmarket risk relates to the borrowing and lending assumption. Black, Jensen, and Scholes reasoned that if investors cannot borrow and lend at the same riskless rate, effective diversification of nonmarket risk may be impossible.[13]

The possibility that returns are not normally distributed provides yet another

FIGURE 6.1 Skew Distributions

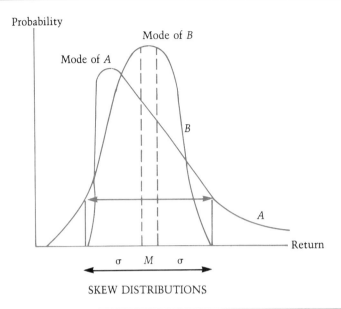

SKEW DISTRIBUTIONS

possible explanation. The mean and variance completely specify the shape of normal distributions. All normal distributions have the same basic shape and differ only in scale. Nonsymmetric or skewed distributions, in contrast, may have identical means and variances and yet have very different shapes. Portfolio theory generally assumes that expected returns are normally distributed. When expected returns are not normally distributed, the model's implications may not apply. For example distributions A and B (Figure 6.1) have the same mean and standard deviation yet offer markedly different return possibilities.

Distribution A's returns have some probability of being very large coupled with almost no chance of being more than one standard deviation below the mean. Distribution B's return could well be more than one standard deviation below but is unlikely to be even one standard deviation above its mean. The mode (point of greatest probability) of B exceeds the mode of A, however. While individual preferences vary, most investors seem to prefer some possibility of a very large gain.[14] McEnally found that stocks with highly variable returns also tended to have highly skewed returns that on average were lower than those of less risky stocks.[15] An investor preference for skewness may cause very high-risk stocks to be priced to offer a lower expected return than less risky stocks. Moreover, Duvall and Quinn found that investors who seek to achieve their desired skewness level must hold too few securities to be fully diversified.[16]

Real world distributions may differ from the normal form in several respects. We have already discussed the degree and direction of skewness. Normal distributions are symmetrical while skewed distributions are not. Another area of potential difference relates to the relative distribution of the probabilities. All normal distributions have the same probability associated with each distance (scaled in standard deviations) from the mean: approximately two-thirds within one standard deviation; 95% within two; and 99% within three. Two other classes of distributions have somewhat different shapes. Compared with the normal, leptokurtic distributions are skinnier and more spread out at the extremes. That is, they are relatively more dense in the peaks and the tails and relatively less dense in the intermediate zones than are normal distributions. Platokurtic distributions, in contrast, are relatively more dense in the intermediate zones.

The distributions of expected returns for any particular asset are not directly observable. No doubt some are close to normal, others highly skewed while still others exhibit lepto- or platokurtosis. We can, however, observe actual return distributions. The longer the holding period, the more nearly actual returns tend to approach the normal.[17] The normal is a reasonably accurate working hypothesis for the monthly returns of both portfolios and individual securities. Daily returns may be somewhat leptokurtic and skewed.[18] Most of the nonnormal behavior, however, occurs at the beginning and end of the trading day.[19]

Assessment: The Price Impact of Nonmarket Risk

To sum up, most empirical studies found that nonmarket risk affected security prices. A variety of factors may contribute to the effect: (1) Evans and Archer's results notwithstanding, most investors' portfolios contain significant amounts of nonmarket risk; (2) errors in estimated betas may be correlated with nonmarket risk contributing to an apparent empirical relationship; (3) investors who are unable to lend and borrow risklessly may find inefficient portfolios the most effective way of achieving their desired risk levels; (4) nonnormal expected return distributions coupled with an investor preference for skewness may further compound the difficulty of assembling efficient portfolios and thus increase the relevance of nonmarket risk.

ESTIMATED BETAS AND SUBSEQUENT PERFORMANCE

Estimated betas are potentially useful statistics. Those who expect the market to move in a particular direction would like to be able to assemble a portfolio that will take full advantage of the expected market move. For example, if the market is expected to rise, the portfolio manager would like to be concentrated in high beta stocks. Alternatively, if a market decline is anticipated, the portfolio manager would prefer to be invested in low beta stocks.

A large number of investment firms seek to service these investors. They sell their lists of beta estimates to investors and portfolio managers. Value Line, for example, publishes estimates for the more than 1700 stocks it analyzes. Similarly, Barr Rosenberg, the "guru" of modern portfolio theory, and Bill Fouse of the Wells Fargo Bank are two among a number in the same business. Betas are normally estimated by regressions of historical security returns on market returns.

Beta estimates are clearly both available and potentially useful. Therefore some idea of their reliability would be quite useful. Investors who would use them as a guide to sensitivity to market moves need to know how well they explain individual security performance. A number of tests have, in fact, been directed at the usefulness and accuracy of beta estimates. One approach is to compare actual returns with those implied by the market model estimates and actual market returns.

A security's performance can be simulated by adding its estimated alpha to the product of its estimated beta and the corresponding period's market return. We may refer to this as the simulated risk-adjusted return. That is:

$$SRAR_{it} = \alpha_i + \beta_i(M_t)$$

where:

$$SRAR_{it} = \text{Simulated risk-adjusted return}$$
$$\alpha_i = \text{Estimated } \alpha \text{ for firm i}$$
$$\beta_i = \text{Estimated } \beta \text{ for firm i}$$

This simulated return is, in fact, the increment that is subtracted from an actual return to produce the corresponding risk-adjusted return. In an efficient market, risk-adjusted returns should have an average value very close to 0. In other words, the actual returns and the simulated risk-adjusted returns should be approximately equal.

The accuracy of any individual security return simulation is related to both random nonmarket influences and the appropriateness of the simulation process. A sufficiently sizable sample, however, should largely eliminate individual random influences and reveal any biases and inefficiencies in the estimation process. Thus a comparison of actual returns with simulated risk-adjusted returns should shed light on the accuracy of estimated betas. Therefore, we shall now consider some properties of estimated betas.

Properties of Beta Estimates

Estimated betas have an average value of 1. Moreover, most beta estimates are relatively close to unity. Less than 10% have values greater than 2 and less than 2% have negative values.[20] Betas estimated from historical data are generally similar to risk estimates based on fundamental analysis (financial ratios, etc.). Individual beta estimates have been found in a number of different tests to be relatively unreliable. Portfolio betas, in contrast, appear to be much more dependable. Thus Farrar found that mutual fund portfolios are usually near both the efficient frontier and the risk–return trade-off indicated in their prospectuses.[21] Growth-oriented funds had high-risk efficient portfolios while more conservative funds were less risky and had lower expected returns. Such funds tended to perform as their betas implied. Moreover, hypothetically constructed portfolios generally performed close to their predicted levels.

Apparently errors inherent in individual company beta estimates are largely offsetting. The inconsistency between actual returns and those implied by individually estimated betas could be due to instability in the underlying betas and/or errors in the estimation process. Does the estimation process introduce systematic errors and if so can an improved process be devised?

Improved Beta Estimates

A number of different phenomena including beta estimates exhibit a tendency for extreme-value estimates to move toward the grand mean (regression toward the mean). For example, individual high and low first month batting averages generally move toward the overall all-player average. Note, however, that this phenomenon describes the behavior of extreme values, not the entire population. Thus batting averages and betas near the mean tend to move randomly away from the mean with sufficient frequency to repopulate the extremes as the prior-period extremes move in. Several estimation techniques called Stein estimators take account of the regression-toward-the-mean phenomena.

Blume suggests adjusting the beta for next year as follows: adjusted beta = .35 + .68 (average unadjusted beta estimate based on data for the past three years.[22] Vasicek has proposed a more sophisticated adjustment.[23] The Vasicek adjustment is a weighted average of the sample's average beta estimate and the unadjusted beta estimate for the individual security. The weights are based on the relative uncertainty of the two estimates. Extensive study of the three beta estimation techniques (unadjusted, Blume adjustment, and Vasicek adjustment) shows the Blume and Vasicek approaches to be clearly superior both in explaining future betas and future security return correlation matrices. On the other hand beta adjustments appear unnecessary for large portfolios. Further efforts to generate more reliable beta estimates include either substituting or combining fundamental factors with historically estimated betas. Although such efforts may have improved the resulting beta estimates, the best estimates are still not especially reliable. Both instability in the underlying betas and a variety of other factors probably contribute to this unreliability.

The Market Index

The market index used in the beta estimating equation may also introduce error into the estimation process. The theoretical model (of MPT) assumes that betas are estimated with an index reflecting all capital assets in proportion to their relative contribution to investor wealth. In practice, however, the NYSE composite or an even less broad index is usually employed. The NYSE index is an acceptable measure of U.S. stock movements. NYSE-listed securities are a large part of the total U.S. stock market and NYSE, AMEX, regional, and OTC stocks all tend to move together. Moreover, option, warrant, and convertible prices also tend to vary with stock prices. Thus the NYSE composite reflects the movements of U.S. stocks relatively well.

The NYSE index's acceptability declines, however, as the relevant universe expands progressively to include U.S. debt securities, real estate, futures contracts, foreign securities, collectibles, precious metals, and so on. Even though many of these assets are influenced by the U.S. equity market, the correlations are relatively weak for most and essentially zero for others.

Investments other than U.S. stocks represent an appreciable part of most investors' total wealth. Accordingly, using only U.S. stocks in the market index may

FIGURE 6.2   Risk and Portfolio Size

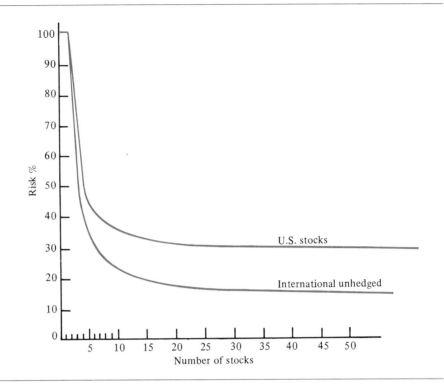

bias the resulting beta estimates. Indexes of varying quality do exist for debt securities, foreign securities, commodities, some collector's items, real estate, and non-NYSE equities.

Ibbotson and Siegel come reasonably close, but no one has yet dared to make all the arbitrary assumptions needed to assemble a complete broad-based market index.[24] Stambaugh has, however, investigated the impact of an expanded index. While his work was restricted to U.S. assets, he did find that the inclusion or exclusion of a particular asset class had relatively little impact.[25]

International Diversification

The stock markets in different countries appear to have a large component of independent variability. That is, a large part of the variability in their returns is unrelated to fluctuations in domestic markets. Thus a strategy of adding foreign securities to a portfolio of domestic securities can be used to reduce the impact of the home country's market cycle. Hill and Schneeweis found that an international portfolio of debt and equity securities offers even greater diversification gains.[26] The risk-reduction potential of international diversification is shown in Figure 6.2.

Investors can diversify internationally in a variety of ways. They can purchase shares in an international mutual fund, a U.S.-based multinational company, a foreign company's stock, or American Depository Receipts (ADRs) representing ownership of such securities. Well over 500 foreign firms are tradable as ADRs. The securities of U.S.-based multinational firms continue to fluctuate with those of other domestic firms but may offer slightly higher risk-adjusted returns.[27] Brokerage houses now pay closer attention to foreign investment opportunities and foreign business news, but data on most foreign firms are still not readily available or easy to interpret. Furthermore, offshore mutual funds are less closely regulated than U.S. funds. Finally, investing in foreign securities exposes the investor to exchange rate and political risk.

Diversification across Types of Investments

Buying international assets is not the only way of diversifying beyond the U.S. stock market. Robichek, Cohn, and Pringle find that nonsecurity assets such as commodities and real estate have considerable diversification appeal.[28] Similarly, McEnally's results suggest that government bonds can be effectively used to diversify a stock portfolio.[29] Thus international stocks and bonds and domestic nonstock assets may all be useful diversification vehicles.

Implications of Modern Portfolio Theory Tests

As a whole, the research presents a relatively discouraging picture for these implications of modern portfolio theory: (1) the markets are not as efficient as MPT assumes; (2) contrary to the theory, nonmarket risk may affect prices; and (3) relative return forecasts based on the market model are unreliable. In view of these shortcomings, why does modern portfolio theory continue to receive so much attention? The answer to this question has three parts.

First, just as the Mandarins of China clung tenaciously to their complicated alphabet made up of thousands of characters, the Mandarins of modern portfolio theory have a huge human capital investment. Not surprisingly, they would prefer to preserve as much of that investment as they reasonably can.

Second, modern portfolio theory offers a useful point of departure. Economists need to understand the competitive model even though very few markets are truly competitive. Similarly, most physicists are quite familiar with the properties of a frictionless world and perfect gas. These idealized models yield interesting insights and testable predictions. A particular nonidealized effect may be observed in the difference between the model forecast and the actual event. Finance theorists and empiricists are therefore expected to know the implications of modern portfolio theory even if the real world often behaves differently.

Third, while the model's predictions are not uniformly accurate, some of the evidence is approximately consistent, and insights provided by the theory may be useful:

1. Individual inefficiencies notwithstanding, the market appears to be relatively efficient.

2. Although market prices may take nonmarket risk into account, the rational investor may be able to profit from the observed price effects.

3. Some inaccuracies in relative-return forecasts based on the market model may result from inadequate estimation techniques and data errors rather than shortcomings of the model.

Moreover, the beta estimates for diversified portfolios are relatively reliable. Thus, until a demonstrably superior theory is devised, the standard form of modern portfolio theory will continue to provide the foundation for the study of finance.

ARBITRAGE PRICING THEORY

For all its shortcomings, modern portfolio theory has only one meaningful competitor: the arbitrage pricing theory (APT). This model expands the number of return-generating factors from traditional portfolio theory's one (the market index) to several.[30] APT was introduced by Ross in 1976. It begins with the idea that returns vary from the expected because of unanticipated changes in various basic economic forces. Like MPT, APT assumes that when other things are held equal, investors seek to construct portfolios that are expected to produce the highest returns. MPT assumes that investors assemble their portfolios so as to maximize a utility function that takes account of only two variables: risk and return. In other words, MPT investors maximize return subject to the impact of market risk. APT, in contrast, assumes that investors seek to maximize expected return subject to simultaneously seeking to minimize the portfolio's sensitivity to unexpected changes in economic variables: industrial production, interest rates, unemployment rates, inflation rates, balance of payments, exchange rates, energy prices, and so on. In other words, MPT focuses exclusively on market risk whereas APT sees risk as a multidimensional force emanating from a variety of economic factors. According to APT, investors would substitute securities in their portfolio whenever the expected return could increase without increasing sensitivity to unanticipated changes in economy-wide factors.

MPT can in fact be viewed as a special case of APT in which only one economic factor, market risk, is relevant. The general form of APT is considerably more complex than is the standard form of MPT, however. The important question in comparing the two approaches to explaining investment market prices is this: Does the greater complexity of APT add to our understanding of markets and our ability to explain real world prices?

The initial tests of APT failed to demonstrate clear superiority over the more standard MPT.[31] Nonetheless, the APT model has continued to generate much interest. More recent empirical work, however, continues to be mixed. Some studies are relatively favorable.[32] The results of others are inconsistent with APT.[33] Such results do not necessarily imply that standard MPT is preferable. No doubt work will continue toward a more satisfactory model of asset pricing. For now, however, the standard version of MPT seems likely to remain the basis for comparison.

SUMMARY AND CONCLUSIONS

We have explored predictions of modern portfolio theory dealing with market efficiency, nonmarket risk, and the properties of estimated betas. Much of the evidence conflicts with the theory's predictions: Various inefficiencies are observed; nonmarket risk does appear to affect prices; and the relationship for securities between market risk and expected return is not demonstrably linear. A number of real world violations of the model's assumptions were considered. Too few investors may be appropriately situated to eliminate some mispricings; different investors borrow and lend at differing rates; return distributions may be nonnormal; some investors may be concerned with skewness; most empirical work with the market portfolio utilizes an index that excludes everything but U.S. equity securities; and imperfections such as taxes and transactions costs influence market prices.

In spite of the drawbacks, MPT continues to be studied and utilized. Most researchers have a substantial human capital stake in the theory; the current model seems appreciably ahead of whatever is in second place (APT); it offers a useful point of departure; and it fits some aspects of the real world reasonably well. APT, the primary alternative to MPT, has generated a great deal of interest but has yet to demonstrate that its much greater complexity yields superior results.

REVIEW QUESTIONS

1. Compare the two principal types of investment analysis. Which is most popular with most investors?

2. Discuss the three forms of the efficient market hypothesis. What do each imply about the types of investment analysis? Summarize the relevant evidence on each.

3. Discuss the possible causes of persisting market imperfections.

4. Compare the theoretical price impact of nonmarket risk with real world experience. Discuss the possible explanations for the apparent inconsistency.

5. Discuss the practical approaches to diversification. How do foreign securities markets enter into this issue?

6. What does portfolio theory usually assume for return distributions? How are actual returns generally distributed on a daily basis and on a longer term basis? How do most investors seem to react to skewness?

7. How are betas estimated? What problems arise? How may betas be adjusted? What problems remain?

8. What is the impact of international diversification? How might a portfolio be diversified internationally and what are the advantages and disadvantages of each of these methods?

9.   Summarize the problems of MPT. What alternatives exist to MPT?

10.   Why, in spite of its shortcomings, is MPT still studied?

11.   Compare MPT with APT.

REVIEW PROBLEMS

1.   For the following series of prices test the effectiveness of a 5% filter rule: 51, 51¼, 52, 51½, 50⅞, 49, 48¼, 49, 50½, 52, 52¾, 53, 53⅞, 55, 57, 56½, 57⅞, 58½, 60, 62, 61½, 59, 57, 58½, 59. Ignore the impact of commissions.

2.   Repeat Problem 1 using a 3% filter.

3.   Repeat Problem 1 using a commission rate of 3% per trade.

4.   Plot the following histogram of possible returns: less than 5%, .05; 5%–10%, .10, 10%–15%, .25; 15%–20%, .20; 20%–25%, .15; 25%–30%, .10; 30%–35%, .8; 35%–40%, .5; 40%–100%, .2. Compute the mean and standard deviation. What type of distribution is this an example of?

5.   Find and plot a normal distribution having the same mean and standard deviation as that of Problem 4. Compare the two plots.

6.   Compute Blume-adjusted betas for each of the following unadjusted betas: 1.34, .57, .78, 1.20, 1.47, 1.73, .45, 1.44, .89, .95, 1.80, 1.11, .69, .87, 1.15.

7.   Using first the Blume-adjusted and then unadjusted betas of Problem 6, compute portfolio betas for portfolios composed as follows:

   a. equal weights of all components
   b. equal weights for all components with betas above the mean beta value
   c. equal weights for all components with betas below the mean beta value

8.   Discuss the results of Problem 7. How do the adjusted and unadjusted betas differ? Why? Under what circumstances are adjusted portfolio betas likely to differ substantially from unadjusted betas? When are they likely not to differ greatly?

9.   A diversified portfolio of stocks is expected to generate a return of 15% with a beta of 1. A diversified portfolio of long-term bonds offers an expected return of 11% and has a beta of .3. A diversified portfolio of short-term debt securities has an expected return of 8% and a beta of .1. How can you combine investments in these choices to:

   a. maximize expected return?
   b. minimize risk?
   c. provide a maximum beta of .5 and a maximum return for that beta level?

10. Suppose in Problem 9 that you also have the option of investing in a diversified international portfolio with an expected return of 14% and beta of .3. How would this change the answers to Problem 9?

REVIEW PROJECTS

1. Interview three brokers and three serious investors on market efficiency. What form or forms of investment analysis do they utilize? What has been their experience? Ask them for counter examples of market efficiency if they assert the market is inefficient. Write a report.

2. Survey the investors that you know. Ask each about his or her tax status, cost of trading, risk orientation, borrowing power, liquidity preference, familiarity with local markets, and portfolio size. Also ask each one how long he or she has been an investor and what his or her average return (preferably relative to the market) has been. Look for patterns. For example, do the more risk-oriented investors report higher returns? Write a report.

3. Construct a list of five investment opportunities. Describe each so that a reader would conclude that they have equivalent expected returns and market risk levels. Give one positive skewness and one negative skewness symmetrical distributions for the others. Now ask a sample of potential investors to choose the investments that they find most and least attractive. Write a report.

4. Plot monthly returns on 10 stocks for six months. Obtain beta estimates for these stocks from Value Line or some other source and compute their expected returns with the market index (use NYSE Composite). Correlate expected returns with actual returns. Repeat the process using the Dow Jones Industrial Average and S&P 500. Write a report.

5. Identify five major foreign companies and study their investment attractiveness. Explore how to go about buying their stocks and following their performances. Repeat the process for five U.S. mutual funds that invest in foreign stocks. Write a report.

6. Construct a list of five hypothetical companies and describe their return possibilities. They should correspond to the following types:

   a. low risk, low expected return
   b. moderate risk, moderate expected return
   c. high risk, high expected return
   d. moderate risk, moderate expected return, positive skewness
   e. high risk, high expected return, positive skewness

Now choose 10 people at random and ask them to rank the investment opportunities. Write a report.

NOTES

1. R. Levy, "Random Walks: Reality or Myth," *Financial Analysts Journal*, November/December 1967, 69–77. E. Cama and M. Blume, "Filter Rules and Stock Market Trading," *Journal of Business*, January 1966, 226–241; M. Jensen and G. Benington, "Random Walks and Technical Theories: Some Additional Evidence," *Journal of Finance*, May 1970, 469–482.

2. L. Summers, "Does the Stock Market Rationally Reflect Fundamental Values?" *Journal of Finance*, July 1986, 591–602.

3. S. Basu, "The Investment Performance of Common Stocks in Relation to Their Price Earnings Ratios: A Test of the Efficient Market Hypothesis," *Journal of Finance*, June 1977, 665–682; H. Oppenheimer and G. Schlarbaum, "Investing with Ben Graham, A Test of the Efficient Market Hypothesis," *Journal of Financial and Quantitative Analysis*, September 1981, 341–360; G. Smith, "A Simple Model for Estimating Intrinsic Value," *Journal of Portfolio Management*, Summer 1982, 46–49.

4. E. Fama, L. Fisher, M. Jensen, and R. Roll, "The Adjustment of Stock Prices to New Information," *International Economic Review*, February 1969, 1–21.

5. J. Finnerty, "Insiders and Market Efficiency," *Journal of Finance*, September 1976, 1141–1148; J. Jaffe, "Special Information and Insider Trading," *Journal of Business*, July 1974, 410–428.

6. J. Treynor, "Market Efficiency and the Bean Jar Experiment," *Financial Analysts Journal*, May/June 1987, 50–53.

7. J. Evans and S. Archer, "Diversification and the Reduction of Dispersion," *Journal of Finance*, December 1968, 761–767.

8. R. McEnally and C. Boardman, "Aspects of Corporate Bond Portfolio Diversification," *Journal of Financial Research*, Spring 1979, 27–36.

9. G. Frankfurter, "Efficient Portfolios and Non-Systematic Risks," *Financial Review*, Fall 1981, 1–11.

10. T. Tole, "You Can't Diversify Without Diversifying," *Journal of Portfolio Management*, Winter 1982, 5–11.

11. W. Beedles, O. Joy, and W. Ruland, "Conglomeration and Diversification," *Financial Review*, Winter 1981, 1–13.

12. M. Miller and M. Scholes, "Rates of Return in Relation to Risk: A Reexamination of Some Recent Findings" in *Studies in the Theory of Capital Markets*, ed. M. Jensen (New York: Praeger, 1972).

13. F. Black, M. Jensen, and M. Scholes, "The Capital Asset Pricing Model: Some Empirical Tests," in *Studies in the Theory of Capital Markets*, ed. M. Jensen (New York, Praeger, 1972), 79–121.

14. G. Barone-Adesi, "Arbitrage Equilibrium with Skewed Asset Returns," *Journal of Financial and Quantitative Analysis*, September 1985, 299–313.

15. R. McEnally, "A Note on the Return Behavior of High Risk Common Stocks," *Journal of Finance*, March 1974, 199–202.

16. R. Duvall and J. Quinn, "Skewness Preference in Stable Markets," *Journal of Financial Research*, Fall 1981, 249–264; A. Kane, "Skewness Preference and Portfolio Choice," *Journal*

of *Financial and Quantitative Analysis*, March 1982, 15–25; R. Sears and G. Trennepohl, "Diversification and Skewness in Option Portfolios," *Journal of Financial Research*, Fall 1983, 199–213.

17. E. Fama, *Foundations of Finance* (New York: Basic Books, 1976).

18. J. Rozelle and B. Fielitz, "Skewness in Common Stock Returns," *Financial Review*, Fall 1980, 1–23.

19. R. Wood, T. McInish, and J. Ord, "An Investigation of Transactions Data for NYSE Stocks," *Journal of Finance*, July 1985, 723–741.

20. R. A. Levy, "On the Short-Term Stationarity of Beta Coefficients," *Financial Analysts Journal*, November/December 1971, 55–62.

21. D. Farrar, *The Investment Decision Under Uncertainty* (Englewood Cliffs, N.J.: Prentice-Hall, 1965); T. Bos and P. Newbold, "An Empirical Investigation of the Possibility of Stochastic Systematic Risk in the Market Model," *Journal of Business*, January 1984, 35–42.

22. M. E. Blume, "On the Assessment of Risk," *Journal of Finance*, March 1971, 1–10.

23. O. Vasicek, "A Note on Using Cross-Sectional Information in Bayesian Estimation of Security Betas," *Journal of Finance*, December 1973, 1233–1239.

24. R. Ibbotson and L. Siegel, "The World Market Wealth Portfolio," *Journal of Portfolio Management*, Winter 1983, 5–17.

25. R. Stambaugh, "On the Exclusion of Assets from Tests of the Two-Parameter Models," Journal of Financial Economics, November 1982, 237–269.

26. J. Hill and T. Schneeweis, "Efficient International Diversification of Equities and Fixed Income Securities," *Journal of Financial Research*, Winter 1983, 333–344; M. Adler, "Global Fixed-Income Portfolio Management," *Financial Analysts Journal*, September/October 1983, 41.

27. B. Jacquillat and B. Solnik, "Multinationals Are Poor Tools for Diversification," *Journal of Portfolio Management*, Winter 1978, 8–11; H. Brewer, "Investor Benefits from Corporate International Diversification," *Journal of Financial and Quantitative Analysis*, March 1981, 113–126; V. Errunza and L. Senbet, "The Effect of International Operations on the Market Value of the Firm: Theory and Evidence," *Journal of Finance*, May 1981, 401–418.

28. A. Robichek, R. Cohn, and J. Pringle, "Returns of Alternative Investment Media and Implications for Portfolio Construction," *Journal of Business*, July 1972, 427–443.

29. R. McEnally, "Some Portfolio-Relevant Risk Characteristics of Long-Term Marketable Securities," *Journal of Financial and Quantitative Analysis*, September 1973, 565–585; W. Sharpe, "Bonds Versus Stocks: Some Lessons from Capital Market Theory," *Financial Analysts Journal*, November/December 1973, 74–80.

30. S. Ross, "The Arbitrage Theory of Capital Asset Pricing," Journal of Economic Theory, 1976, 341–360.

31. M. Reinganum, "The Arbitrage Pricing Theory: Some Empirical Results," *Journal of Finance*, May 1981, 313–322. Also see J. Shanken, "The Arbitrage Pricing Theory: Is It Testable?" *Journal of Finance*, December 1982, 1129–1140; R. Folger, "Common Sense on CAPM, APT and Correlated Residuals," *Journal of Portfolio Management*, Summer 1982, 20–29; N. Chen, "Some Empirical Tests of the Theory of Arbitrage Pricing," *Journal of Finance*, December 1983, 1393–1414; P. Dhrymes, I. Friend, and N. Gultekin, "A Critical Reexamination of the Empirical Evidence on the Arbitrage Pricing Theory," *Journal of Finance*, June 1984, 323–346; R. Roll and S. Ross, "A Critical Reexamination of the Empirical Evidence on the Arbitrage Pricing Theory: A Reply," *Journal of Finance*, June 1984, 347–350.

32. N. Gultekin and R. Rolalski, "Government Bond Returns, Measurement of Interest Rate Risk, and the Arbitrage Pricing Theory," *Journal of Finance*, March 1985, 43–61; P. Dhrymes, I. Friend, M. Gultekin, and N. Gultekin, "New Tests of the APT and Their Implications," *Journal of Finance*, July 1985, 659–675; D. Cho, C. Eun, and L. Senbet, "International

Arbitrage Pricing Theory: An Empirical Investigation," *Journal of Finance*, June 1986, 313–329.

33. D. Cho, "On Testing the Arbitrage Pricing Theory: Inter-Battery Factor Analysis," *Journal of Finance*, December 1984, 1485–1502; P. Dybvig and S Ross, "Yes, The APT Is Testable," *Journal of Finance*, September 1986, 1173–1188; M. Grinblatt and S. Titman, "The Relation between Mean-Variance Efficiency and Arbitrage Pricing," *Journal of Business*, January 1987, 97–112.

SECTION THREE

Fundamental Analysis: Security Selection

Most investors utilize fundamental analysis to evaluate and select investments. This section explores various approaches to fundamental analysis/stock selection. Particular attention is given to what is practical and potentially usable. In a sense this section and Section IV on investment timing are the heart of the book. The following case illustrates many of the issues that are encountered in fundamental analysis.

DEMONSTRATING YOUR SKILLS AS AN INVESTMENT ANALYST

You are given a golden opportunity but you must show that you are worthy of it. A small midwestern brokerage firm is looking for a junior securities analyst. Although the firm's starting salaries do not reach New York levels, management is willing to consider applicants who have had no direct securities market experience. They are looking for a person with a keen mind and sufficient background to begin producing meaningful analyses immediately. Your school's placement director has identified you as one of the top finance majors in this year's graduating class.

Each applicant has been asked to demonstrate his or her analytical skills by completing the following assignment: Analyze two firms from the 30 companies of the Dow Jones Industrial Average and two smaller (AMEX or OTC) issues. Each candidate must write an extensive report on each selected company's investment potential. You and the other candidates are to conduct relevant economic, industry, and company analyses for each firm. Examine each company's financial statements for its strengths and weaknesses, hidden assets, accounting gimmicks, and future potential. Obtain as much background material as you can to back up your analysis. Assemble a file of your sources. Come up with an investment recommendation on each company.

This section covers the topics that are needed to complete such an assignment. Chapter 7 takes up traditional methods of the fundamentalists, beginning with economic analysis. Then industry analysis is explored. Specific approaches to both economic and industry analysis are discussed. Most of the chapter, however, deals with company analysis. Scale economies, competitive position, and management quality are each considered, and the analysis of financial strengths and weaknesses is stressed.

Chapter 8 explores accounting discretion and the problems caused by its abuse. Examples of misleading accounting are discussed along with methods for spotting accounting gimmickry. Chapter 9 considers a variety of operational approaches to fundamental analysis: Forbes lists, low PE stocks, small and neglected firms, R&D intensive firms, takeover candidates, bankruptcy stocks, contrary opinion, specialized advisory services, and management-oriented firms. This is followed by a discussion of PE ratio models. Finally, Chapter 10 explores investment information sources. Company-issued reports, business and investor-oriented periodicals, systematic coverage of companies, and investor-oriented computer data and manipulative systems are all discussed.

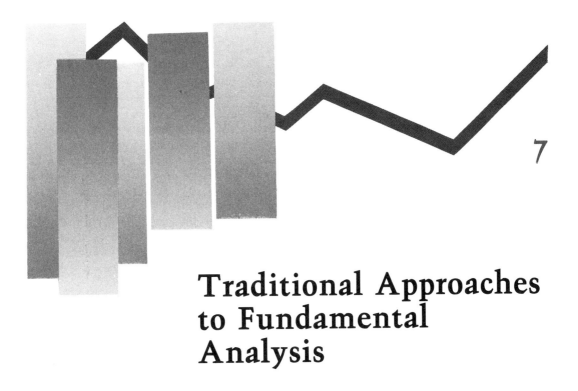

Traditional Approaches to Fundamental Analysis

We have already seen how the value of an investment can be estimated by discounting its expected income stream. Both the theory and the evidence supporting such an approach to valuations are unimpeachable. Unfortunately, the estimates of the required inputs are generally unreliable. Thus most practical fundamental analysis deals with more qualitative factors. Although explicit income stream forecasts can be generated by any type of investment analysis, most analysts do not go that far. This chapter surveys the issues that are typically treated in the fundamental analysis section of traditional investment courses. We first discuss economic analysis. Industry analysis and how it relates to investment selection is explored next. Specific approaches to economic and industry analysis are discussed. Then company analysis is considered. We give particular attention to the evaluation of a company's competitive position, management quality, financial situation, and profitability. Finally, the relevance of such analysis to the market price and the efficient market hypothesis is examined.

AN OVERVIEW OF FUNDAMENTAL ANALYSIS

Fundamental analysis is traditionally divided into three subcategories: (1) economic analysis, (2) industry analysis, and (3) company analysis. Economic analysis seeks to evaluate the current economic setting and its effect on industry and firm

181

fundamentals. Industry analysis assesses the outlook for particular industries, whereas company analysis examines a firm's relative strengths and weaknesses within its industry or industries.

These three subcategories correspond to the three principal influences on stock performances. Clearly each is important. According to Brown and Ball, about 30% to 40% of a firm's annual earnings variability can be ascribed to economy-wide influences.[1] Another 10% to 15% result from factors that are specific to the industry. Thus about half of the variability must be accounted for by firm specific factors. Similarly, the stock market's aggregate moves appear to account for between a third and a half of the returns of an individual stock, and industry factors account for about 10%. Thus in terms of both firm profits and stock returns (dividends plus price changes) market/economy and firm-specific factors are the dominant influences. Industry factors account for only about 10% of the variability.

ECONOMIC ANALYSIS

Publicly held firms make up a large part of the economy. Profit rates, a major determinant of share prices, are closely tied to the nation's economic health. When the economy is depressed (as in a recession), most firms operate well below their capacities. Companies can meet a short-run downturn in the economy by laying off workers, reducing raw material orders, working down inventories, and reducing expansion and modernization spending. They are, however, unlikely to scrap fixed plant and equipment and can do little to reduce property taxes and interest payments to meet a temporary decline in the demand for their output. As sales decline these so-called fixed costs absorb a larger proportion of revenues, thereby squeezing profits. For example, in the 1982 recession John Deere's sales fell by 14% while its profits declined by 97%. At the same time, many of its competitors (International Harvester, Allis-Chalmers, and Massey-Ferguson) were losing money and, in International Harvester's case, threatened with bankruptcy.

The general tendency for profits to drop more than economic activity in a recession is illustrated in Table 7.1. During these recessions personal consumption generally increased (an average of 4.76%), employment dropped modestly (−.92%), while profits fell appreciably (−17.8%). Rapidly growing GNP, in contrast, leads to above-average employment, sales, and profit increases. Although investors generally fare better in booms than recessions, the relationships are complex. The economy's primary stock price impact relates to its effect on expected income streams. The dividend decisions made by corporate managements tend to reflect long-term (not annual) earnings trends. Investors do, however, expect that earnings increases will eventually lead to higher dividends. Thus an earnings increase is still a favorable sign even if the dividend response is slow. If profitably employed, retained earnings should produce still higher earnings. Eventually these higher earnings should lead to both increased dividends and a higher stock price. Similarly, losses or reduced earnings are likely to lead to reduced dividends and stock prices. Figure 7.1 illustrates these linkages.

We see that causation runs from the economy to companies and then to stocks. That is, the state of the economy affects the performance of individual companies.

TABLE 7.1 Percentage Changes in Economic Activity for Postwar Recessions

Recession	Change in Civilian Nonfarm Employment	Change in Personal Consumption Expenditures	Change in Profits
1948–1949	− .66%	+ .01%	−18.4%
1953–1954	−2.47	+ 3.16	− 1.8
1957–1958	−1.91	+ 1.27	−22.3
1960–1961	− .9	− .64	−12.2
1970–1971	+ .08	+ 8.27	−11.4
1973–1975	+ .71	+12.60	−34.2
1979–1980	− .83	+ 6.38	−17.8
1981–1982	−1.40	+ 7.05	−24.3
Average	− .92	+ 4.76	−17.8

Source: Economic data obtained from the Economic Report of the President for various years.

FIGURE 7.1 Links Between the Stock Market and the Economy

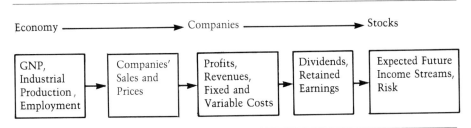

Company performance, in turn, is the major determinant of the stock price. Economic activity is reflected in such data as GNP, industrial production, and the employment (or unemployment) rate. The level of economic activity has a major impact on the sales and prices of individual companies. Their sales revenues coupled with their costs then determine profits. A portion of these profits is paid out in the form of dividends and the remainder is retained earnings. Dividends provide immediate income to investors while retained earnings are used to finance the resources needed to produce future growth. Thus current profitability coupled with an understanding of its relationship to costs and revenues may be used to formulate a guide to the company's expected future income stream and level of risk.

Relations Between the Stock Market and the Economic Outlook

Because economic activity has a major impact on company sales, profits, and dividends, the investment community pays close attention to the business cycle. According to conventional Wall Street wisdom, stock values reflect the expected status of the economy six months hence. Indeed, the National Bureau of Economic Research rates the stock market as the most reliable leading indicator of economic activity. The economy generally moves in the same direction for much longer than six months, with the result that the economy and the stock market often move together. They may, however, move in opposite directions just before a turning point in the business cycle. At still other times the market may incorrectly forecast business behavior and move perversely until its mistake is realized. According to Paul Samuelson (whom many would call the premier economist of the post-Keynesian period), the stock market has predicted nine of the past five recessions.

Not all market moves are related to changes in the economic outlook. What might be termed emotional factors sometimes influence the market. For example, unfavorable news such as the fall of France in 1940, President Eisenhower's heart attack in 1955, the Cambodian invasion in 1970, the Watergate disclosures of 1973–1974, the energy crises of 1974 and 1978, and the Iranian hostage crisis of 1980 were shocks to the stock market. Such noneconomic influences are superimposed on the basic stock market–economy relationship.

Forecasting Economic Performance

Accurate business cycle forecasts might well facilitate profitable investment decisions. Only economic forecasts that are superior to the view of the market (six months ahead) offer any real advantage. Thus an ability to foresee a business downturn one year in advance might afford six months' prior notice of a market move. Accurately forecasting economic behavior is very difficult, however. Indeed, the market itself would probably anticipate the economic outlook by more than the traditionally assumed six months if more reliable forecasts were available.

The various methods of predicting economic activity are taken up in Chapter 11 (the first of three chapters on market timing). Such a forecast can be employed to anticipate how the industries and companies of interest are likely to perform. That is, past relationships among economy, industry, and company could be analyzed to determine how sensitive particular investments are to such matters as the general level of economic activity, interest rates, inflation, exchange rates, and so on. Then investors could use that economic forecast to assess the likely profit–dividend performance of an investment. Finally, this estimated performance could be compared with the market's view as reflected in its price.

Investors should keep in mind that investment values are relative. To demonstrate this point, suppose that the economic outlook is quite favorable for a particular firm. This outlook will make the firm's stock an attractive investment only if its price does not already reflect the favorable outlook. Similarly, a very poor economic outlook may so depress the market that many stocks are underpriced relative to their potentials.

A Specific Approach to Economic Analysis

Investment analysts do economic analysis when they use their knowledge of the economic environment to assess the outlook of the stock market. One approach to this task begins with the basic valuation models. The reader will recall the dividend discount model and the PE ratio model that were introduced in Chapter

4. We have already seen that the price of a stock or other investment equals the present value of its expected income stream. Where the growth rate of that income stream can be approximated by a constant defined as g, the (dividend discount) valuation formula may be expressed as:

$$P = d/(r - g) \tag{7.1}$$

where:

P = stock price
d = anticipated dividend rate over forthcoming year
g = expected long-term growth rate for dividends
r = the appropriate discount rate for dividends

Most investors prefer to relate stock prices to per share earnings (PE ratio). Thus a more usable form for this relationship brings in the expected earnings per share for next year e, anticipated long-term payout ratio, p and the PE ratio:

$$PE = p/(r - g) \tag{7.2}$$

Both equations will generate relatively accurate valuations when reliable long-term average values for p, r, and g are used (assuming that the values for individual years are generally relatively close to these averages). Thus we can, in many circumstances, use the two equations to express the determinants of the price and PE of a stock.

Although Equation 7.2 is expressed in the form of a single share of stock for a single company, the same basic relationship can be applied to the entire stock market. This market is usually represented by a diversified index. For example, the New York Stock Exchange constructs an average of stock prices called the NYSE Composite Index. All stocks traded on the New York Exchange are represented in proportion to the market value of their shares outstanding. The Standard & Poor's 500 Index (S&P 500) is another broad-based index of stock. A number of other popular indexes are also reported in the financial press, as discussed in Chapter 10.

When applied to the market, Equation 7.2 implies that aggregate stock prices relative to aggregate earnings (as reflected by the PE of a broadly based market index) are a function of the overall payout ratio, the expected growth rate for aggregate dividends, and the appropriate discount rate for the stock market.

The level of stock prices is the product of the market's average PE ratio and its average earnings per share (or the corresponding earnings for the index). Using economic analysis to forecast the market can thus be decomposed into two tasks: forecasting the earnings of the market (or an index) and forecasting its corresponding PE ratio.

Forecasting the Market's Earnings. The per share earnings attributable to a market index are computed according to the same principle as the value or price of the index. The individual earnings of each of the component stocks making up the index are assigned the same weights as they have in the index itself. The per share earnings of the index then are the weighted average of the component's earnings.

One logical approach to forecasting the market's earnings is to forecast its sales and expenses and then take the difference. A forecast for sales can be obtained from a prediction of GNP. GNP reflects the sale of final output whereas total corporate sales also includes the sales of intermediate products (for example, the steel that goes into automobiles). The two types of sales numbers (final and intermediate) do tend to move together. Thus aggregate corporate sales bear a close relation to GNP. Moreover, the stocks traded on the NYSE represent a very large percentage of the economy's overall production. Accordingly, sales attributable to the firms represented in the NYSE index are very closely related to total corporate sales. Methods for forecasting GNP are taken up in Chapter 11.

The average ratio of GNP to NYSE index sales can be combined with a GNP forecast to obtain a forecast for the sales attributable to the NYSE index. The next step is to determine what percentage of these sales represents profits and what percentage represents expenses. The most fruitful approach is generally believed to be first to estimate the gross profit margin (income before depreciation and taxes). Then an estimate for the net profit margin (after-tax profit as a percentage of sales) is generated. The earnings of the NYSE index can be forecast as the product of their forecasted sales and estimated net margin. First, however, an estimate for gross margin is needed.

Gross margin is largely a function of two forces: how intensively productive capacity is utilized (capacity utilization) and how efficiently labor is utilized (unit labor costs). The overall state of the economy plays a large role in determining both capacity utilization and unit labor costs.

A strong economy implies a high rate of capacity utilization, which in turn means a large amount of output relative to productive facilities. High capacity utilization tends to produce a high gross profit margin. Sales revenues tend to increase proportionately more than costs as capacity is utilized more intensively. On the other hand, as the economy weakens (and perhaps moves into a recession), capacity utilization declines and profits fall disproportionately.

Unit labor costs reflect the joint impact of two forces: wage rates and labor productivity. Aggregate wage rates almost always go up as time passes. The rate at which they rise depends upon a number of factors:

1. The overall tightness of the labor market. The unemployment rate is a useful measure of labor market tightness.

2. The rate of inflation. Rapidly rising prices lead workers to press for compensatory wage increases.

3. The strength of the economy. Employers are more inclined to grant wage increases when demand for their output is strong.

4. The amount of foreign competition. Strong price competition from imports encourages employers to keep down their own prices and costs, including labor costs.

Long-run productivity is largely responsive to the rate of implemented technological change. Such change is brought about by investments in education and research and development. Although important in the longer run context, such activity is largely ignored by those who are trying to forecast short-run profit and stock market performance. In the short run, labor productivity is mainly responsive to how it is combined with capital using existing up-to-date technology.

Thus we see that the gross margin is principally a function of capacity utilization and unit labor costs (which in turn is largely determined by labor productivity and wage rates). The overall state of the economy, including unemployment and inflation rates, plays a large role in determining these factors. The next step is to forecast the percentage of sales attributable to depreciation and taxes. Depreciation expense bears a relatively stable relation to the amount of depreciable plant and equipment. In a growing economy, plant and equipment typically expand each year by about 7%. Similarly, depreciation on plant and equipment increases each year by about 7%. The actual forecast can be a bit above or below 7% depending upon circumstances for the particular year. Dividing the depreciation forecast by the aggregate sales forecast yields the percentage of sales attributable to depreciation.

When the estimated percentage of sales attributable to depreciation is subtracted from estimated gross margin, we obtain an estimate for before-tax profits as a percentage of sales. Generally, next year's ratio of corporate taxes to before-tax income is rather similar to the current year's ratio. Sometimes, however, tax rates and rules change. At those times the ratio tends to move in the direction indicated by the change. For example, if corporate tax rates go up or allowable deductions go down, the ratio of corporate taxes to profits will rise. Thus we can start with the current ratio and adjust it for the effect of statutory changes. Once the proportion going for taxes is subtracted, what remains is net margin.

The forecasted earnings for the NYSE index may be obtained by multiplying the estimated net margin by the forecasted sales attributed to the index. The final step is forecasting the PE of the market or index.

Forecasting the Market PE.   Many analysts predict the market's earnings and then derive a forecast for the market's price level by applying their earnings forecast to the current market PE ratio. For example, in mid-1987 the NYSE Composite Index stood at about 180 with a PE of about 21 and most recent 12-month earnings of $8.60. If year-ahead earnings are expected to be $10, a PE of 21 would imply an index value of 210. Such a simplistic approach, however, ignores the possibility that the market PE may change. It often does. As luck would have it, the market did change dramatically shortly after the above passage was initially written. The great stock market crash of October 1987 saw the market fall by more than one-third in the space of a few weeks. By late November the NYSE index was down to around 135. That level corresponded to a PE of 16. If the NYSE index does generate 1988 earnings of $10, a PE of 16 would imply a value for the index of around 160. Clearly market forecasts need to explore the factors that may cause the average PE to change.

Recall the determinants of the PE reflected in Equation 7.2:

$$PE = p/(r - g)$$

Thus the market PE ratio is largely a function of p, the payout ratio; r, the appropriate discount rate; and g, the expected growth rate in dividends. The overall market payout ratio has averaged close to or a bit above .5. In a given year the ratio varies up or down mainly in response to the growth in earnings. Dividends tend to adjust to changes in earnings after a lag. Thus if earnings grow rapidly in one year, dividends will not immediately rise in proportion and the payout ratio will fall. The payout ratio is also affected by the inflation rate. More rapid inflation encourages companies to retain more of their profits to offset the higher costs and taxes of operating in an inflationary environment (more on this in Chapter 11).

The long-run growth rate in the economy is around 3% to 4% in real (non-inflationary) terms. While the growth in earnings will vary greatly from year to year, the long-term growth rate will be similar to that of the economy. The growth rate in nominal terms would tend to be increased by the inflation rate. That is, the expected nominal growth rate should approximately equal the long-term real rate plus the expected inflation rate. In periods of rapid inflation, however, the nominal growth in earnings is likely to be somewhat less than the inflation rate plus the long-term real growth rate. Rapid inflation tends to depress the real value of earnings.

The appropriate discount rate is a function of several factors. Suppliers of capital seek a return that will compensate them for both risk and the expected rate of inflation. Thus r should equal the real riskless rate plus a premium for risk and an amount to compensate for the expected inflation. According to many theorists and analysts, market discount rates tend to be set to compensate investors fully for expected inflation. Thus a real riskless rate of 3% and risk premium of 4% would produce a market discount rate of 7% plus the expected inflation rate.

No doubt the causes of the great crash of 1987 will long be debated. One relevant factor, however, was the rise in interest rates. Long-term government bond rates rose from a bit above 7% in mid-1986 to slightly below 9% at the market's August 1987 top to over 10% just before the crash of October. This rise in market interest rates translated into a higher rate for discounting the expected income stream of the stock market. The result was a much lower appropriate level for the market PE. The crash in stock prices brought about that decline.

Inflation plays a role in all three components of the PE equation. A rise in the inflation rate tends to depress p, thereby reducing the PE. That is, the higher the inflation rate, the larger the fraction of reported earnings represent unsustainable profits. For example, profit sources such as sales from inventories carried on the books at long out of date cost levels tend to be greater at high inflation rates. Firms are unlikely to increase their dividend rates when their earnings increases are expected to be temporary. As we have already seen, more rapid inflation encourages companies to retain more of their profits to offset the higher costs and taxes of operating in an inflationary environment.

A rise in the inflation rate also tends to increase both r and g but the greater impact is on r. Thus (r − g) tends to increase as inflation rises, thereby reducing the PE. Overall, an increase in expected inflation tends to decrease the numerator and increase the denominator of our PE ratio equation, thereby tending to lower its overall value.

Interestingly, the inflation outlook appears to have had little or no role in the crash of 1987. Inflation was running at 4% to 5% both before and after the crash. The rise in interest rates was largely due to the government's efforts to deal with the international situation, particularly the large deficit in the balance of trade. That is, the United States was importing far more than it was exporting and running a large payments deficit in the process.

Using Economic Analysis to Forecast the Market: A Summary

One logical approach to forecasting the average level of the stock market is to forecast its earnings and PE multiple. A broad diversified market index such as the NYSE Composite is often used to represent the total market. Forecasting the market's earnings involves the following steps:

1. Make or obtain a forecast for GNP (see Chapter 11) and use the result to derive a forecast for total corporate sales. Use past relationships and this forecasted sales figure to obtain a specific sales forecast for the index.

2. Estimate the gross profit margin on sales. This margin can be estimated from past gross margin data and its relation to capacity utilization, unit labor costs, and the inflation rate.

3. Estimate depreciation expense and the percentage of before-tax profit going to taxes. Past data and the impact of changes in tax rates can be used to form these estimates.

4. Combine the gross margin, depreciation, and tax estimates to obtain a net margin estimate. Multiply net margin by forecasted sales to predict earnings for the index.

Similarly, the market PE multiple is obtained as follows:

1. Estimate the market's overall payout ratio p from past data, the stage of the business cycle, and expected inflation rates.

2. Estimate the aggregate stock market discount rate r as the sum of the real risk-free rate, the market risk premium, and the expected inflation rate. Alternatively, add the appropriate risk premium to the current nominal (no inflation adjustment) riskless rate.

3. Forecast the nominal long-term growth rate in the market's earnings, g. The real long-term growth rate is largely a function of the stage of the business cycle. The nominal rate is the sum of the expected long-term real growth rate and a percentage (close to but probably less than 1) of the expected inflation rate.

4. Apply the values for p, r, and g to Equation 7.2 to obtain the forecasted market PE.

The value for the market index forecast, then, is the product of forecasted earnings and PE of the index. The steps just summarized represent an extremely ambitious approach to assessing the market's outlook. Relatively few market analysts are likely to undertake such an extensive analysis. No doubt some shortcuts are possible. Nonetheless, this type of analysis is one reasonable, logical approach to assessing the outlook for the stock market. The accompanying discussion, "Using the PE Ratio Model to Examine the Crash of 1987," demonstrates how a related type of analysis might have helped anticipate the 1987 stock market crash.

Using the PE Ratio Model to Examine the Crash of 1987

The PE ratio model can be used to examine how the stock market is viewing the future. Transforming the model to solve for the implied growth rate, g yields the following:

$$g = r - p/PE$$

Thus with estimates for r, p, and PE (appropriate discount rate, expected long-term average payout ratio, and PE using expected earnings for next year) we can solve for the implied market expected growth rate in dividends, g.

Data from the stock market crash of 1987 can be used to illustrate how the growth expectations vary. Doing so requires reasonable estimates for the required inputs. Only one of the needed inputs is directly observable: the market price on our index. Everything else must be estimated. Ideally, we should use the market's expectations for the long-term future discount, payout, and earnings data. Presumably, however, current values of these data are reasonably close to the market's expectations. That is, the current long-term riskless interest rate is close to what the market believes to be the appropriate rate for discounting riskless assets. Adding a reasonable amount for the risk premium should produce a relatively accurate value for the appropriate discount rate for stocks.

The current payout ratio should be relatively close to what the market expects to be the long-term average. Similarly, the most recent 12-month earnings figure should be reasonably close to what the market expects for the following year. The market would normally expect next year's earnings to grow by about the long-term growth rate, g. Thus current earnings would generally differ from expected earnings for next year by only a modest scale factor.

Accordingly, our estimate for the appropriate discount rate is scaled up 3% from the current value for the long-term government bond rate. The actual premium could be somewhat different. Any differences would (assuming a relatively constant risk premium for the period of analysis) have similar impacts on each of our estimated discount numbers. The actual payout ratio, p, can be used for the market's long-term estimate. Similarly, the PE computed with the most recent 12-month earnings can be used as a proxy for the market's actual expectation. Although these proxies are imperfect, they are probably reasonably close to the market's actual (unobserved) expectations. Hopefully relying on these estimates will not lead to systematic errors over the time of this analysis.

Our objective is to use market data on PEs, interest rates, and payouts to assess the change in market expectations. Minor errors in estimating the expected payout, discount rate, and next year's expected earnings will have similar effects on our analysis of expectations for each date. Thus any errors in our inputs will have little impact on the observed changes in market expectation.

The following table reports relevant data on the state of the market (using the S&P 500 index) at various dates around the time of the crash of 1987. Using these values produces the implied growth rates reported in the table.

The S&P 500 Around the Time of the 1987 Crash

Date	30-Year Government Bond Rates	S&P 500 Index	PE	Payout Ratio	Implied Growth Expectation
May 30, 1986	7.47%	247.35	16.93	56%	7.17%
December 12, 1986	7.73%	247.35	16.86	56%	7.73%
June 12, 1987	8.75%	301.62	19.66	58%	8.80%
August 21, 1987	8.90%	335.90	22.42	58%	9.31%
October 16, 1987	9.84%	282.70	21.17	64%	9.82%
October 24, 1987[1]	0.13%	248.22	17.92	62%	9.67%
December 31, 1987	8.97%	247.08	15.64	57%	8.33%

These data reveal an interesting picture. Long-term interest rates varied from about 7.5% to over 10% while the market PE ratio varied from under 16 to over 22. The payout ratio was relatively stable in a range around 60%. The implied expected growth rate varied from somewhat over 7% to almost 10%. Clearly the market's growth expectations changed substantially over this period.

Consider first the market situation on May 20 and December 12, 1986. These dates precede the major market rally that began in early 1987. The S&P 500 stood at about 250 on both dates. Long-term government bonds were yielding around 7.5% to 7.75% and the S&P's PE was around 17. These numbers implied an expected long-term growth rate in the range of 7.25% to 7.75%. Such expectations are consistent with recent historical experience of real growth of 3% to 4% and inflation in about that same range or perhaps a bit higher. We expect aggregate dividends to grow at about the same rate as the economy.

By June 12, 1987, the S&P 500 index was up substantially (over 50 points, or 22%) from the end of 1986. At that point the PE had risen to almost 20 while long-term government bonds were yielding 8.75%. Both the PE ratio and interest rates had gone up. Normally the two numbers move in opposite directions. These values for the market's PE and interest rates implied an expected long-term growth rate of 8.8%. This implied expectation was a full point above the growth expectation of just six months earlier. A one-point difference in growth expectations may not seem like a lot. Over a period of years, however, such differences become quite substantial. For example, a sum growing at 8% will double in nine years. A sum compounding at a 9% rate will, in contrast, double in eight years. Thus in this example a 1% difference in the growth rate resulted in a year's difference in the time required to double.

From June to August the market continued to rise. On August 21, 1987 (near the market top), the S&P index stood at 335.90. This was almost 90 points, or 36%, above its 1986 year-end value. The PE exceeded 22. Had interest rates been falling, such a rise might not have been unusual. Interest rates had been continuing to rise, however. At this point the long-term government bond rate was 8.9%. These values combine to produce an implied growth expectation of 9.31%. This expected growth rate was one-half of a percent higher than the already high implied expectation for June 1987.

Stock prices fell some as the crash date approached. The Friday before the crash (the crash itself occurred on Monday, October 19) the S&P 500 had fallen to 282.70. Compared with its August 21 level, this represented a decline of more than 50 points, or about 16%. Nonetheless, the market in retrospect was clearly poised for a further fall. Interest rates had continued their rise (reaching 9.82%) while the S&P's PE remained quite high (21.17) by recent standards. These values implied a growth expectation of 9.82% just before the crash. Such an expectation exceeded the corresponding expectation for mid- to late 1986 by 2% or more. This represents a huge change in expectations. Returning to our earlier example, at 10% a sum will double in seven years (compared to eight years at 9% and nine years at 8%). Thus a 2 point increase in growth expectations implies a two-year difference in the time required for a sum to double. Clearly, the market's growth expectations were very different just before the crash than they had been a year earlier.

A week later (October 24) the S&P had fallen 35 more points (12.6%) and the PE was down to 17.92. The market had actually fallen even more from Friday (October 16) to Monday (October 19) but by the end of that week it had recovered somewhat. Interest rates were, however, still continuing their rise (to 10.13%). As a result, even after the crash the implied growth expectation remained very high by historical standards (9.67%).

As the remainder of the year unfolded, interest rates declined modestly. On December 31, 1987, long-term government yields were a bit under 9% and the S&P's PE was below 16. The S&P index itself was in very nearly the same range that it had been during May and December 1986. The implied growth rate expectation was 8.83%.

In retrospect the market was very overpriced at its August peak and even more overpriced just before the October crash. If the market's growth expectations in late 1986 were realistic, its expectations in mid-1987 clearly were unrealistic. This seems obvious now, but only because everyone has 20-20 hindsight. Economic analysis of the market is not at all easy. Nonetheless, the analysis demonstrated in "Using the PE Ratio Model to Examine the Crash of 1987" could have been helpful in analyzing the overall stock market around the time of the crash. We shall return to this topic in Chapters 11 and 12.

INDUSTRY ANALYSIS

Economic analysis assesses the general environment and its impact on firms and industries. Industry analysis, in contrast, examines the specific environment of the markets in which they compete. Investors might begin a search for attractive investments by either evaluating the component companies of a selected industry or analyzing a particular firm first and then its industry and competitors. With either scenario both company and industry analysis are undertaken. In the discussion that follows, the process is assumed to begin with industry analysis.

Before proceeding, we should establish the relevance of industry analysis to investors. The evidence is rather clear on one point: Individual industries have,

FIGURE 7.2 The Life Cycle of an Industry

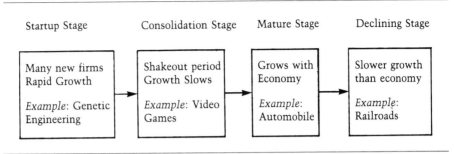

over time, experienced very different investment returns. For example, Latane and Tuttle's extensive study of industry returns found an average market value increase of 500% for the period 1950–1967. The least successful industry (brewing) actually declined while the most successful (office and business equipment) exhibited a 4,000% gain.[2] Thus, over specific periods some industries show much higher returns than others. On the other hand, several studies revealed wide dispersion in the performance of individual firms within particular industries.[3]

Their independent movements notwithstanding, attractively performing industries contain a disproportionate number of profitable investments. Therefore, we would like to know how to identify industries that will show the highest future returns. One possibility might be to select industries with strong recent records. Projecting past industry performance, however, involves uncertainties similar to those of extrapolating past earnings growth. Past growth may imply some momentum but also establishes a higher base. The central issue is whether past growth reflects the industry's stage of development or isolated circumstances. Thus identifying an industry's development stage may help assess its growth prospects.

Stages of Industry Development

Industries are thought typically to pass through several developmental stages (Figure 7.2). Initially many new firms are established (start-up stage) and growth is rapid. A shakeout then reduces the number of firms (consolidation stage). After the adjustment, growth slows to that of the economy (mature stage). Finally, new industries begin to grow at the expense of the existing industry (declining stage). Predicting evolution from one stage to another is not easy. In fact, some industries follow different schemes from this normal one. For example, the solid waste disposal industry experienced modest performance until the ecology movement brought it to life.

A firm moving from one stage to another usually experiences substantial stock price volatility. For example, firms and industries introducing new products or concepts (start-up stage) will eventually see growth slow (mature stage) to the level of replacement demand. Examples have included automobiles in the 1920s; black and white television in the 1950s; bowling equipment in the early 1960s; color television in the mid-1960s; fast food restaurants (McDonald's); retailing concepts (Levitz Furniture); rest homes, mobile homes, campers and motor homes, and camping equipment in the early 1970s; gambling stocks in the early 1980s; and biotechnology in the mid-1980s. Future candidates include personal computers, proprietary hospitals, and genetic engineering. Rapid growth should never be projected beyond a reasonable saturation point. Stock prices usually suffer once the market realizes that growth is slowing.

Some experts deny the validity of the life cycle approach to industry analysis. They note that the Coca-Cola Company has been a successful competitor deriving much of its revenues from a product that has changed relatively little in 100 years. Similarly, a product like baking soda has been around for many years but continues to be popular as new uses are found.

Differential Industry Risk

Although past industry growth offers little guide to the future, several studies have found that individual industries exhibit rather different risk levels. On the other hand, the risks of each industry tended to be relatively stable over time.[4]

A Specific Approach to Industry Analysis

The same basic methodology that was examined in the section on economic analysis can be used to analyze an industry. That is, the market performance of an industry can be forecast from an analysis of its earnings and PE potentials. Such an analysis is easier to perform when the industry is represented by an index. In addition to the broad stock indexes, a number of indexes are compiled for the stocks of individual industries. Data on such indexes and the stocks that make them up allow investors to forecast their earnings and PEs. If no industry index is readily available, a quasi-index can be formed from the stocks of the principal companies making up the industry.

We want to forecast both sales and the profit margins on the sales. The first step in forecasting industry sales is to find one or more economic data series that move closely with the industry's revenues. GNP is a possibility. Personal disposable income might be a better choice for industries that are consumer oriented. In some instances the sales forecast may be based on several variables. For example, many industries are particularly sensitive to interest rates. Others may be very much affected by the strength of the dollar, the cost of energy, or changing demographics. Still others may be very dependent on the level of government spending (e.g., defense) or regulatory action (e.g., telecommunications).

The industry sales forecast should be based on whatever relationships have been established from past experience and an understanding of how the industry is structured. The analyst could either incorporate these factors into an ad hoc forecast or develop an equation that related the explanatory variables to the industry sales. In the latter case, estimates of the future values of these variables would be applied to the equation to generate a forecast for industry sales.

To the extent possible, the gross profit margin for the industry should be estimated from past historical relationships, knowledge of the industry's capacity utilization, and unit labor costs. Industry (as opposed to aggregate) data may or may not be available on these factors. Trade associations and trade publications are potential sources for such data (both historical and expectational).

As with the value for the overall economy, industry depreciation is relatively easy to estimate. The analyst simply adds a percentage to the prior year's depreciation figure. The size of the percentage to be added depends upon the past average value and any factors specific to that year. Thus in a "normal" year we would add the average rate of increase to the prior year's depreciation level. In years when some special factor was expected to have an impact, the added increment would be adjusted to reflect that factor.

Most industries pay taxes at about the same rate as the all-corporation average. Historical data can reveal the past relationship. Recent changes that withdraw or add tax advantages to firms in the industry should be factored into the analysis.

The resulting industry earnings forecast must be scaled to the index value and compared with the most recent historical earnings number. How does the forecast of this industry's percentage change in earnings compare with that for the economy? As a general rule, industries that are expected to grow more rapidly than the average should have higher PEs than the market average PE.

A fuller picture of the industry's prospects can be obtained by examining its current and potential future PE ratio. Equation 7.2 helps us understand the current PE level and forecast the industry's future PE. Past historical experience can give a rather dependable idea of the likely payout ratio, p. Some adjustments may be made in the light of the industry's expected growth and inflation rates.

The appropriate discount rate, r, for the industry will differ from the rate for the overall market by the amount that the two risk premiums differ. The historical relationship between the risk premiums would provide a relatively accurate guide to the difference. Unfortunately, such premiums are not directly observable but must be inferred from other data such as relative PE ratios or direct data on relative risks.

The industry's expected growth rate, g, is related to the overall growth rate of the economy and the specific circumstances of the industry. The rate of growth of the industry's earnings is largely determined by the amount of new capital invested in the industry and the return on new and old invested capital. The amount of new capital is closely related to the industry's retention rate, which is 1 minus its payout rate, p. Return on equity is related to a number of factors such as capacity utilization, leverage, and product prices.

The estimated values for p, r, and g can be applied to the PE equation to forecast the industry's PE. A second approach relates movements in the market's PE ratio to the industry's ratio. Thus expected changes in the market ratio can be applied to the current industry ratio. Both approaches may be used and the results averaged. The product of the industry's forecasted earnings and PE can then be used to forecast the future value of the industry index. The predicted percentage change in the industry index may be used as a guide to whether the industry represents an attractive place to look for investment opportunities.

Using Economic Analysis to Forecast the Industry's Outlook: A Summary

One logical approach to forecasting the average level of the industry's stock prices is to forecast its earnings and PE multiple. An industry index such as one of the S&P industry averages is often used to represent the industry's stock prices. Forecasting the industry's earnings involves the following steps:

1. Make or obtain a forecast for GNP (see Chapter 11), personal disposable income, or some other factor or group of factors that has in the past been highly correlated with industry sales. Use the result to derive a forecast for the industry's sales. Use past relationships and the forecasted sales figure to generate a specific sales forecast for the industry index.

2. Estimate the industry's gross profit margin on sales. This estimated margin can be derived from past gross margin data and its relation to capacity utilization, unit labor costs, and the inflation rate.

3. Estimate depreciation expense and the percentage of before-tax profit going to taxes. Past data and the impact of changes in tax rates can be used to form these estimates.

4. Combine the gross margin, depreciation, and tax estimates to obtain a net margin estimate. Multiply net margin by forecasted sales to obtain forecasted earnings for the index.

Similarly, the industry PE multiple is obtained as follows:

1. Estimate the industry's overall payout ratio, p, from past data, the stage of the business cycle, and expected inflation rates.

2. Estimate the aggregate stock market discount rate, r, as the sum of the real risk-free rate, the market risk premium, and the expected inflation rate. Adjust that figure to reflect the differential risk premium for the industry.

3. Forecast the nominal long-term growth rate in the industry's earnings, g. The real long-term growth rate is largely a function of the stage of the business cycle. The nominal rate is the sum of the expected long-term real growth rate and a percentage (close to but probably less than 1) of the expected inflation rate.

4. Apply the values for p, r, and g to Equation 7.2 to obtain forecasted industry PE. As a second approach, adjust the forecasted market PE to obtain an industry PE forecast using the past relationships. Compare the two industry PE forecasts and perhaps take their average.

The value for the industry index forecast, then, is the product of the index's forecasted earnings and its PE.

Industry Analysis: Assessment

Industry analysis could be discussed in much greater detail. Analysts would like to be able to forecast accurately future levels of industry sales, costs, and profitabilities. Relevant governmental policies should be assessed. The interrelationships with competing, complementary, supplier, and customer industries should all be considered. Such analysis is relatively difficult to perform effectively. Nonetheless, industry analysis is helpful only when it is superior to the market's assessment.

As with economic analysis, investors should bear in mind the relative nature of the process. Although the prospects of individual industries need to be evaluated, the most attractive industries for investment are not necessarily the ones with the brightest profit and growth prospects. Rather, investors seek investments with greater potentials than the market recognizes. Thus an industry with bleak prospects may contain attractive investments if the market is even more pessimistic than is justified by the true outlook.

COMPANY ANALYSIS

Once industry analysis has identified a potentially attractive area for investment, the companies within that industry need to be evaluated. Three important company characteristics are competitive position, management quality, and financial soundness. Each relates to how successful a firm is likely to be within its industry or industries.

Competitive Position

While somewhat more difficult to evaluate than its financial strengths and weaknesses, the company's competitive position is an important performance determinant. How able is the firm to withstand competitive pressures? How vigorous are its rivals? What is the government's attitude? Clearly, these are interesting questions.

A company's ability to compete within its industry depends on how its resources compare to those of its rivals. Scale economies in production, distribution, and advertising generally give larger companies an advantage. On the other hand, difficulties in exercising effective control increase with size. For example, U.S. Steel (now USX) has, since its inception, been described as a lumbering dinosaur too large for effective control. Antitrust vulnerability is yet another disadvantage of size. Every competitive move of high market share companies such as Kodak, IBM, Xerox, General Motors, and AT&T risks antitrust action. Mere size does not constitute an offense, but a company whose own sales represent a very large percentage of its market has difficulty avoiding illegal actions. Kodak, for example, has sought to avoid antitrust suits by sharing new product technology with its competitors. Similarly, IBM's chairman ordered his salespeople not to solicit RCA customers after Sperry Rand bought out RCA's customer base. Antitrust pressure led AT&T to agree to spin off its operating companies. Even when within-market expansion is legal, a dominant firm has little opportunity to grow other than with its industry or by diversifying. For the giants, even diversification-inspired mergers may provoke an antitrust suit. Procter & Gamble's acquisition of Clorox and General Foods' acquisition of S.O.S were both undone by government action. Thus, some companies may be too small to compete effectively, whereas the existing size of others may limit further growth. Within a wide range of viable sizes, however, other factors have greater impacts on differential performance.

Management Quality

A perceptive, aggressive, forward-looking management improves the odds of realizing a company's full potential. Cohen, Zinbarg, and Zeikel list the following as relevant: motivation, R&D activity, willingness to take risks, success in integrating merged firms, effectiveness in delegating authority, information systems, use of a board of directors, relations with financial analysts, and social responsibility.[5] Others have noted that managers who are especially interested in stockholder welfare generally outperform those more concerned with their own well-being.[6] Still other studies imply that highly rated managements generally do not produce high returns for their shareholders but do tend to reduce risk.[7] A broad array of information on managerial quality is probably relevant, but few investor/analysts have the resources to evaluate most of these factors effectively. Past performance is one useful guide although of less help when needed most—when leadership shifts. Investors can normally do little more than read the financial press. A few may contact some managers directly (particularly those of small local companies), however.

Financial Position

An attractive industry environment, strong competitive position, and effective management are all important components of a company's fundamental position. Only companies with adequate financial resources can fully exploit their opportunities, however. Accordingly, much of fundamental analysis involves assessing the company's financial strengths and weaknesses.

Basic Accounting Concepts Used in Fundamental Analysis.   Because accounting data are utilized extensively in financial analysis, we shall briefly review the principal types of financial statements. First, a balance sheet provides an instantaneous picture of a company's resources and obligations. A classified listing of assets appears on the left. Plant and equipment are valued at cost less depreciation whereas most other assets are valued at the lower of either cost less depreciation or market value. Liabilities (both long- and short-term debts) and net worth (the stockholder's residual ownership position) appear on the right. Because net worth equals assets minus liabilities, the two sides of the balance sheet are always equal—hence its name.

The income statement begins with total revenues. Various expenses are then subtracted until only the company's earnings remain. The income statement helps answer questions such as: How much did the company make or lose in the recent

FIGURE 7.3 Types of Accounting Statements

Balance Sheet	Income Statement	Change in Financial Position
Instantaneous picture of resources (assets) and obligations (liabilities)	Revenues less expenses equal earnings	Liquidity/Cash Flow position

period? How much went to its stockholders? How do current earnings compare with past results? Every year the company's net worth will change by that year's retained earnings (profit after taxes less dividends). The income statement and balance sheet are thus connected by changes in net worth.

The change in financial position statement, the third of the principal statements, helps one analyze the company's liquidity/cash flow position. Figure 7.3 summarizes the three types of statements.

Preparing accounting statements necessarily involves many subjective judgments and subjectivity opens up opportunities for abuse. Unfortunately, the temptation may be too great for some managers. Permissible accounting conventions are frequently misused to alter a company's financial appearance. Nevertheless, the vast majority of accounting statements probably reflect a consistent and meaningful financial picture.

Ratio Analysis. Relative magnitudes of financial data are generally more revealing than absolute levels. A company with a bank balance of a million dollars could be very rich or very poor depending upon its overall size. Accordingly, ratios of financial aggregates have long been used to assess the financial positions of various sized companies.

Ratios may be grouped into four categories. Liquidity ratios measure the company's ability to meet its short-run obligations. Debt ratios measure the company's long-run strengths and weaknesses. Finally, profitability and efficiency ratios are designed to reflect the firm's productivity.

Liquidity Ratios. The current ratio is an index of the short-run picture. It is defined as current assets (cash, short-term investments, accounts receivable, prepaid expenses, and inventories) divided by current liabilities (accounts payable notes due in one year and the current portion of long-term debt). According to conventional wisdom, the current ratio should be two or greater. As with all ratios, however, the optimal value varies from company to company, industry to industry, and over time. Stable incomes and reliable sources of short-term credit lessen the need for liquid assets and therefore reduce the optimal current ratio level. Indeed, a high current ratio may indicate that resources are being tied up unnecessarily. A ratio below two is generally less worrisome than a major decline in the ratio.

The quick, or acid test, ratio is defined as liquid assets (current assets less inventories) divided by current liabilities, including interim debt. Therefore inventories, which may be relatively difficult to liquidate, are part of the current ratio's numerator but excluded from the quick ratio. Most analysts recommend a quick ratio of one or more. The appropriate level, however, varies from industry to industry, over time, and with special characteristics of the company.

The inventory turnover ratio equals the cost of goods sold divided by average yearly inventory. The ideal inventory level differs with the industry and in some cases with the season and business cycle. A high turnover suggests brisk sales and well-managed inventories. A very high ratio might indicate inadequate inventories, however. A low turnover, in contrast, reflects idle resources tied up in excess inventories and/or a large obsolete inventory component.

The average collection period (ACP) is the weighted average life of outstanding accounts receivable. It should be compared with the company's stated credit policy. For example, a manufacturer might have a credit policy based upon an expectation of receiving payments within 30 days of billing. If the ACP is close to or longer than 30 days, the firm may have a problem with credit extensions. Perhaps the firm's credit standards are too lax or its collection policy is too loose.

Unless substantial losses or a major adjustment (i.e., a large merger) have clouded the picture, short-run financial pictures of most established companies will be satisfactory. Small, less-experienced companies, in contrast, frequently encounter short-run financial difficulty either because of poor capitalization or poor rates of profit/cash flow.

Debt Ratios.   Debt–equity and times-interest-earned ratios are used to assess the prospects for a company's continued success and stability. Debt–equity ratios (liabilities divided by net worth) vary considerably from industry to industry, company to company, and over time. A public utility with highly predictable earnings, a bank with very liquid assets, or a construction company that undertakes very large projects relative to its equity base may have quite a hefty ratio. This ratio could be as high as 2:1 or even 20:1. Companies with volatile earnings (e.g., automobile manufacturers) may choose to have a much lower target ratio, such as 1:10.

Companies that borrow are generally seeking to increase their profits relative to their net worth (i.e., return on equity). Their debts must be serviced, however, regardless of the returns earned with the borrowed funds. Thus companies that are planning to be heavy borrowers need to be relatively confident that the return that they earn will exceed their borrowing costs. Accordingly, a company with a stable return is better positioned to borrow than one with a similar average but less stable profit rate. Burdensome debt obligations may in difficult times force a company with favorable long-run prospects to liquidate needed assets and, in an extreme case, to file for bankruptcy. Thus, a substantial amount of leverage (high debt–equity ratio) is both potentially profitable and risky. The more secure the company, the greater is the percentage of debt that may be safely accepted.

A company's appropriate debt–equity ratio varies with its earning stability. A comparison of debt–equity ratios over time and within the industry may help assess the adequacy of the current level. A rapid rise in the ratio suggests potential problems. If the increased debt still leaves the firm with a substantial cushion of equity and profitable operations, no concern need be shown. The company may simply be taking advantage of heretofore unused debt capacity. If the firm is experiencing losses or only modest profits, however, its increased reliance on debt suggests possible problems. It may well be taking on additional debt to finance a risky strategy. Such debt may, for example, be designed to finance a program that the borrowing firm hopes will eventually show sufficient profits to finance that additional debt. Such hopes, however, may not be realized. Even if the firm's greater debt is accompanied by increased profits, the investor needs to be cautious. The recent profit growth may not be sustainable. At a minimum, further growth would be difficult to finance if it required a still greater proportion of debt.

Leases complicate accounting statement analysis. Purchasing assets with borrowed funds increases the debt–equity ratio whereas leasing the same assets does not increase debt per se. The long-term obligations are very similar, however, whether the assets are leased or purchased. Thus, debt–equity ratios do not always accurately reflect a company's financial commitments. Investors need to look beyond the debt ratios of companies that lease a large fraction of their operating assets. Companies must show their capitalized long-term lease obligations on their balance sheets. Leases that call for payments of less than 80% of the asset's value need not be capitalized.

The absence of an allowance for unfunded pension liabilities can also distort a corporation's reported financial picture. Rising values on pension fund portfolios are expected to pay a substantial part of the promised benefits. When the portfolio does not produce the expected gains, pension funds may be inadequate to cover pension obligations. Moreover, many pension funds are underfunded by the corporation. Pension reform legislation now requires that many benefits be paid even if the employee leaves well before retirement age (vested benefits) or the company leaves the industry. These unfunded pension liabilities have a high priority claim in any bankruptcy proceeding. Over the next several decades, companies are required to set up reserves to cover such liabilities.

Some financial analysts prefer to use the debt–asset ratio rather than the debt–equity ratio. Assets equal debt plus equity. Thus the two ratios are closely related. They have the same numerator. Moreover, both have equity in the denominator. The debt–equity ratio's denominator is equity whereas the debt–asset ratio's denominator is assets, which are the sum of debt and equity. Therefore the debt–asset ratio's denominator is increased by the same number that appears in each ratio's numerator. The main difference in the two ratios is in their scales. Equity can be either a small or large percentage of assets or something in between. Therefore the debt–equity ratio can vary from a number close to 0 (almost no debt) to a very large number (almost no equity). The debt–asset ratio, in contrast, generally lies between 0 (almost no debt) and 1 (almost no equity). Because the debt–equity ratio varies over a larger range, some analysts prefer it to the debt–asset ratio.

The times-interest-earned ratio (profit before tax and interest payments divided by current interest payments) also reflects a company's debt risk. Unlike the debt–equity ratio, however, it relates the company's interest obligation to its earning power. Obviously, the higher the ratio, the greater is the probability that interest will be paid.

Profitability and Efficiency Ratios.   Five important and related profitability-efficiency ratios are: return on equity (ROE); return on assets (ROA), also sometimes called return on investment (ROI); return on sales (ROS), also sometimes called profit margin; asset turnover; and debt margin. One other efficiency ratio is the average collection period. It reflects how long accounts receivables remain outstanding.

Annual averages are generally used to compute profitability and efficiency ratios. One can of course use a shorter time frame but seasonal influences may distort the results.

$$ROE = \frac{\text{After-Tax Profit}}{\text{Shareholders' Equity}}$$

$$ROA = \frac{\text{Before-Tax Before-Interest Profit}}{\text{Total Assets}}$$

$$ROS = \frac{\text{After-Tax Profits}}{\text{Total Revenues}}$$

$$\text{Asset Turnover} = \frac{\text{Total Revenues}}{\text{Total Assets}}$$

$$\text{Debt Margin} = \frac{\text{Total Assets}}{\text{Shareholders' Equity}}$$

Note that ROE is the product of ROS, asset turnover, and debt margin:

$$ROE = ROS \qquad \times \text{Asset Turnover} \times \text{Debt Margin}$$

$$\frac{\text{After-Tax Profit}}{\text{Shareholders' Equity}} = \frac{\text{After-Tax Profit}}{\text{Total Revenues}} \times \frac{\text{Total Revenues}}{\text{Total Assets}} \times \frac{\text{Total Assets}}{\text{Shareholders' Equity}}$$

Thus one can examine the source of profitability or profit problems by looking at these components of ROE. ROE as a measure of profitability relative to shareholders' equity is a major determinant of share prices. Because its denominator (equity) is smaller and more variable, ROE tends to be more variable than ROA.

ROS is also called the profit margin. ROS tends to vary inversely with turnover. A high turnover operation such as a supermarket tends to have a low profit margin whereas a high margin operation such as a jewelry store tends to have a low turnover.

Profitability and growth prospects are forward-looking concepts. Is the past profit and growth record likely to improve or get worse? An examination of past results helps assess various possible scenarios.

High growth rates resulting primarily from increased debt, higher capacity utilization, accounting changes, cost cutting, or price increases must eventually cease. Earnings forecasts should project a more favorable margin, debt–equity ratio, output–asset ratio, or depreciation rate only if the projected change seems likely.

Other Ratios. In addition to liquidity, debt, profitability, and efficiency ratios, investors may find several other ratios useful. Earnings per share (EPS) are the company's total earnings (less any preferred dividends) divided by the number of shares outstanding. Several different earnings numbers are often reported. Fully diluted EPS gives effect to the exercise and conversion of any outstanding warrants

A Hypothetical Example

Consider a hypothetical group of companies each having a five-year per share earnings growth of about 10%. Firm A's sales and profits have grown proportionately while its assets have remained nearly constant. Firm B's debt has increased from 10% to 40% of its assets. Firm C's profit margin has increased from 10% to 16%. Firm D's assets, sales, and profits have all grown proportionately. Firm E has lengthened the useful life assumption for most of its plant and equipment.

Firm A (little asset growth)	1983	1988
Assets	$10,000,000	$11,000,000
Liabilities	3,000,000	3,000,000
Sales	30,000,000	50,000,000
Profits	3,000,000	5,000,000
Profits Per Share	1.00	1.61
Firm B (increased debt)		
Assets	10,000,000	17,000,000
Liabilities	1,000,000	7,000,000
Sales	30,000,000	50,000,000
Profits	3,000,000	5,000,000
Profits Per Share	1.00	1.61
Firm C (increased margin)		
Assets	10,000,000	10,000,000
Liabilities	3,000,000	3,000,000
Sales	30,000,000	30,000,000
Profits	3,000,000	5,000,000
Profit Per Share	1.00	1.61
Firm D (balanced growth)		
Assets	10,000,000	17,000,000
Liabilities	3,000,000	5,000,000
Sales	30,000,000	51,000,000
Profits	3,000,000	5,000,000
Profit Per Share	1.00	1.61
Firm E (reduced depreciation)		
Assets	10,000,000	10,000,000
Liabilities	3,000,000	
	3,000,000	
Sales	30,000,000	30,000,000
Depreciation	3,000,000	1,000,000
Profits	3,000,000	5,000,000
Profit Per Share	1.00	1.61

Clearly the profits of these companies have grown for different reasons. Increased capacity utilization accounts for most of Firm A's profit growth. Eventually existing capacity is fully utilized. Once that point is reached, expanding capacity further would increase relative costs. Profit growth would suffer in the process. Firm B's profit rise is largely due to increased use of leverage. A further increase in the debt ratio would probably raise both the cost of borrowed funds and the risk to the stockholders. Thus, a sale of additional equity may be required for continued growth. Such a sale would dilute the ownership position of existing shareholders. Firm C has either raised prices or reduced its costs. In either case, opportunities for additional profit increases are probably limited. Increasing prices may encourage greater competition while further cost cutting could reduce quality or increase future costs. Firm E's brightened profit picture is due, at least in part, to more optimistic depreciation assumptions. As with increases in leverage, capacity utilization, and profit margins, the profit-enhancement potential of imaginative accounting is limited. The accountants may soon need to run very fast just to stand still. The growth of Firm D for the next five years may well be like growth in the past. Although other factors could intervene, at least the past growth rate has been balanced and therefore is potentially sustainable.

and convertibles. Earnings figures may include or exclude extraordinary items and the results from noncontinuing operations. Several differing earnings numbers are often reported. As we have already seen, the PE ratio or ratio of the per share market price to EPS is a measure of the relative stock price.

The current annual dividend rate (usually four times the quarterly rate) divided by the price per share is the current yield. The total return reflects both capital gains and dividends. The dividend–payout ratio (r in the PE ratio model) equals dividends per share divided by EPS. A very low payout may indicate a substantial need to finance internal growth, management's desire to expand, or abnormally high current earnings. A very high ratio may suggest few attractive investment opportunities. Cash flow per share is the sum of after-tax profits and depreciation divided by the number of shares outstanding. When reported depreciation is overstated (understated profits) or depreciating assets are not replaced (funds available for other uses), the cash flow per share figure reflects an important source of discretionary funds.

Book value per share equals the company's net worth (after subtracting that attributable to preferred shareholders) divided by its common shares outstanding. A high book value relative to the stock's price may indicate either unrecognized potential or overvalued assets. Railroad book values, for example, are often many times the market price of the stock. Unless the assets can be sold for close to their book values, however, the rails' modest profit rates justify their low stock prices. Alternatively, the per share book value may be much lower than the per share price of the stock, perhaps reflecting some hidden or undervalued assets (patents or real estate valued at historical costs). Because book values that diverge appreciably from stock prices suggest that securities may be misvalued, further analysis could be indicated. Table 7.2 summarizes the various ratios discussed.

TABLE 7.2 Types of Fundamental Ratios

Liquidity Ratios

Current	$\dfrac{\text{Current Assets}}{\text{Current Liabilities}}$
Quick, or Acid, Test	$\dfrac{\text{Current Assets} - \text{Inventories}}{\text{Current Liabilities}}$
Inventory Turnover	$\dfrac{\text{Cost of Goods Sold}}{\text{Average Yearly Inventory}}$

Debt Ratios

Debt–Equity	$\dfrac{\text{Total Debt}}{\text{Shareholders' Equity}}$
Times-Interest-Earned	$\dfrac{\text{Profit Before Tax and Interest Payments}}{\text{Current Interest Payment}}$

Profitability and Efficiency Ratios

Return on Equity (ROE)	$\dfrac{\text{After-Tax Profit}}{\text{Shareholders' Equity}}$
Return on Assets (ROA)	$\dfrac{\text{Before-Tax Before-Interest Profit}}{\text{Total Assets}}$
Return on Sales (ROS)	$\dfrac{\text{After-Tax Profit}}{\text{Total Revenues}}$
Asset Turnover	$\dfrac{\text{Total Revenues}}{\text{Total Assets}}$
Debt Margin (Leverage)	$\dfrac{\text{Total Assets}}{\text{Shareholders' Equity}}$
Average Collection Period	$\dfrac{\text{Accounts Receivables}}{\text{Total Revenues}}$

Other Ratios

Earnings Per Share (EPS)	$\dfrac{\text{Profits After Taxes} - \text{Preferred Dividends}}{\text{Number of Shares}}$
Price–Earnings (PE)	$\dfrac{\text{Price Per Share}}{\text{EPS}}$
Current Yield	$\dfrac{\text{Indicated Annual Dividend}}{\text{Price Per Share}}$
Dividend Payout	$\dfrac{\text{Dividends Per Share}}{\text{EPS}}$
Cash Flow Per Share	$\dfrac{\text{After-Tax Profits} + \text{Depreciation}}{\text{Number of Shares}}$
Book Value Per Share	$\dfrac{\text{Net Worth Attributable to Common Shareholders}}{\text{Number of Shares}}$

Sources of Ratios.   A company's ratios are most effectively analyzed by comparing them with those of similar companies. Thus averages of industry-wide ratios would be helpful. Robert Morris Associates collects data and computes ratios for a large group of industries. Other sources include Dun & Bradstreet and Standard & Poor's. Individual industry ratios may be computed with appropriate data from several similar companies.

A Specific Approach to Company Analysis

The same basic approach that was explored in the discussion of economic and industry analysis can be applied to individual companies. That is, the investor can direct his or her analysis toward forecasting a company's earnings and its PE ratio. The product of these forecasts is then a prediction of its stock price. The discussion that follows assumes that the company analysis is preceded by economic analysis and an analysis of the industry in which the company operates.

First, per share sales are forecast. As a first pass the company's sales can be estimated to grow at the same rate as its industry. In a more refined forecast the company's expected growth rate would be adjusted to reflect individual circumstances. A second type of sales forecast can be generated from economic data. Thus the company's past sales would be related to various economic data such as GNP, interest rates, and unemployment. These economic data are then forecast (see Chapter 11) and the results used to derive a company sales forecast. The analyst could rely on either of these approaches to forecasting sales or could average them. Each forecast can be given equal weight or the one that is considered more reliable can be given greater weight.

Estimating the company's profit margin can also make use of the corresponding industry estimate. Past data will reveal how the company's profit margin has tracked the industry average. The forecast for the change in the industry's margin can then be applied to the current margin for the company. The result is the estimated margin for the company. A second estimate for the company's profit margin can be generated from an analysis of its specific cost situation. Thus trends in labor, raw materials, and other costs can be combined with knowledge of the company's potential product and service prices to produce this second profit margin estimate. These two gross margin estimates can then be averaged (weighted or unweighted) and the result adjusted to take account of estimated depreciation and taxes. Multiplying the estimated net after-tax margin by the sales per share estimate generates an estimate for the earnings per share.

Various approaches can be used to forecast the company's PE. One method examines the historical relation between the company and market PEs. The forecasted change in the market PE can then be applied to the current company PE value. A second PE estimate can be obtained by using the predicted change in the industry PE. Finally, Equation 7.2 [PE = p/(r − g)] can be used to derive a prediction for the company's PE. Values for payout p, appropriate return r, and expected growth g, can be estimated and used to generate the forecast. Forecasted values for these factors can be derived both from the industry estimates and from an analysis of the specifics of the company.

The resulting PE for the company can be averaged with the forecasts obtained from the industry and market forecasts. That average is then multiplied by the per share earnings forecast. The result of this process is a forecast for the company's stock price. Several such forecasts can be obtained by using the different earnings and PE forecasts. Comparing the current price of the stock with the forecasts should indicate whether the stock is appropriately priced. A low current-to-forecast price suggests a buy whereas a high current-to-forecast price suggests a sale.

To summarize, one logical approach to forecasting the average level of a company's stock prices is to forecast its earnings and PE multiple and take the product of the result.

1. The company's sales can be adjusted from the industry's estimated growth rate to reflect individual circumstances. Alternatively, one can make or obtain a forecast for GNP (see Chapter 11), personal disposable income, or some other factor or group of factors that has been correlated with company sales. The result can be used along with past relationships to the company's sales figure to generate a specific sales forecast for the company. The analyst can then use either forecast or an average (weighted or unweighted) of the two.

2. Estimate the gross profit margin on sales. This estimated margin can be derived from past industry margin data or its relation to the company's specific capacity utilization, unit labor costs, and the inflation rate. Again, the two estimates may be averaged.

3. Estimate depreciation expense and the percentage of before-tax profit going to taxes. Past data and the impact of changes in tax rates can be used to form these estimates.

4. Combine the gross margin, depreciation, and tax estimates to obtain a net margin estimate. Multiply net margin by forecasted sales to obtain forecasted company earnings. Divide the result by shares outstanding to derive the per share earnings forecast.

Various approaches can be used to forecast the company's PE:

1. The historical relation between the company and market PEs can be utilized. The forecasted change in the market PE can then be applied to the current company PE value.

2. Predicted change in the industry PE can be applied to the current company PE.

3. Finally, the PE equation (Equation 7.2) can be used to derive a prediction for the company's PE. Thus the company's payout ratio p, appropriate discount rate r, and expected growth rate g, can be forecast from past data, the stage of the business cycle, expected inflation rates, and so on.

These three PE forecasts can then be averaged. The value for the stock price forecast is the product of the company's forecasted earnings and its PE.

Relation of a Firm's Fundamental Position to Its Market Price

Stock prices usually reflect the company's economic and industry environment, competitive position, management quality, and financial strength. Thus a company with a strong balance sheet, market position, profit potential and management team operating in an industry with bright growth prospects is likely to be fully priced and may be overpriced. A weaker company, in contrast, may be underpriced if its prospects are viewed too negatively. Accordingly, stock prices should always be evaluated in relative terms. While stronger firms deserve higher PEs than weaker firms, a strong firm with a high PE may be fully priced whereas a somewhat less strong firm with a low PE may not be.

FUNDAMENTAL ANALYSIS VERSUS MARKET EFFICIENCY

If markets are relatively efficient (semistrong form), the (known) fundamental strengths and weaknesses of companies are already accurately reflected in their market prices. Under these circumstances fundamental analysis is largely a waste of time. On the other hand, if the market sometimes misvalues securities vis-à-vis the available public information, fundamental analysis may be worthwhile. Although the degree of market efficiency is a controversial topic, whatever level is achieved occurs because some market participants analyze fundamentals. That is, fundamental analysts tend to make markets more efficient than they would otherwise be. Indeed, many investors (both large and small) devote considerable amounts of time and money undertaking or buying such research.

If markets are efficient, those who bear the cost of making them so (i.e., those who do or pay for the fundamental analysis) are wasting their resources. The market for fundamental information is inefficient if too much is being spent on it for the benefits received. On the other hand, if such analysis does tend to pay for itself by identifying misvalued securities, the security markets are exhibiting a degree of inefficiency. Thus either the securities market or the market for its analysis is inefficient (or possibly both are inefficient). The two markets cannot both be efficient simultaneously.

APPLYING FUNDAMENTAL ANALYSIS

The preceding discussion might be summed up as follows: Investors should acquire stocks of companies whose industry, financial, competitive, and managerial strengths are not fully appreciated by the market. Although difficult to dispute, such advice is not very operational. Clearly, investors need more practical approaches. The next two chapters, particularly Chapter 9, discuss such approaches.

SUMMARY AND CONCLUSIONS

This chapter explored traditional approaches to economic, industry, and company analysis. Both general and specific approaches were considered. Industries exhibit very different performances but selecting those with the best prospects is quite difficult. Past performance offers very little guidance whereas evaluating the industry's developmental stage may offer some modest help. Company analysis involves assessing a company's relative strengths and weaknesses within its industry or industries. Ideally, a company should be large enough to compete effectively but not so large as to be constrained by the threat of antitrust prosecution. Management quality, another important company characteristic, is especially difficult to judge. Financial statement analysis utilizes a variety of different types of ratios. Liquidity ratios reflect short-run strengths and weaknesses. Debt ratios relate to a company's longer run prospects. Profitability and efficiency ratios reflect current operating effectiveness with an eye toward the future. Various other ratios such as earnings per share, PE, cash flow per share, payout, and book value may be used to provide additional insights.

Although assessing industry and company strengths and weaknesses is one way to search for attractive investments, such an approach is useful only if the analysis uncovers overlooked values. An efficient market has, by definition, no misvalued securities. On the other hand, an efficient market for investment analysis implies that on balance those paying for research receive full value for their costs. The security market and the market for fundamental analysis cannot both be efficient.

REVIEW QUESTIONS

1. Discuss the three principal types of accounting statements. How is each prepared and used?

2. List and analyze the various classes of ratios. In general how should ratios be analyzed? What are the advantages, disadvantages, and alternatives to ratio analysis?

3. When examining the cause of past growth, which factors are likely to be temporary and which capable of producing sustainable growth? What is the relevance to investment analysis?

4. Discuss the impact of a company's competitive position on its investment attractiveness. Consider the saturation effect and potential antitrust problems. How might the antitrust environment vary over time?

5. Discuss the role of management quality in investment analysis. How should an investor seek to assess the quality and orientation of management?

6. Outline how economic analysis can be used to forecast the market's performance.

7. Outline how economic analysis can be used to forecast the industry's performance.

8. Outline how economic analysis can be used to forecast the company's performance.

REVIEW PROBLEMS

1. Assume that the market's dividend payout ratio is .50, the required rate of return is 13%, and the expected growth rate is 9%.
   a. Compute the market PE.
   b. What would happen to the market PE if the payout ratio fell to .45 and all else remained unchanged?
   c. What would happen to the market PE if the growth rate increased by 2% and everything else remained unchanged? Is such a change at all likely? Why or why not?
   d. What would happen if the required rate of return declined to 10% and everything else remained unchanged? Is such a change at all likely? Why or why not?

2. Assume that the market payout ratio is .55 and the required rate of return is .15. What must the expected growth rate be to justify a market PE of 11? Suppose the market PE rose to 20 while the payout and the required rate of return remained unchanged. What would such a PE imply for the increase in the expected growth rate? Could the PE reach a level that could not be explained by a growth rate expectation? Why or why not?

3. Forecast next year's sales per share for the XYZ High Tech Index using the following information: Current GNP of $2.3 trillion is expected to grow by 6%. Current index sales per share are running at an annual rate of $500 and expected to grow by 1.7 times the growth of GNP. If GNP actually falls by 3%, what would the High Tech per share sales be?

4. Continuing Problem 3, estimate per share earnings for the High Tech Index using the following information: Current gross margin is expected to remain constant at 21%. Per share depreciation is running at a rate of $100 and is expected to increase at the same rate as sales. Taxes are expected to equal 33% of before-tax profits.

5. Estimate the PE ratio for the High Tech Index in Problems 3 and 4 using the following information: Current payout ratio of .50 is expected to continue through next year. The required rate of return on the overall market is 13%. The High Tech Index usually is accorded a 2% risk premium above that of the overall market. Growth is expected to continue indefinitely at the rate indicated in Problem 3.

6. Turn ahead to Figure 10.5. Using the data from *Moody's Industrial Manual*, compute all of the ratios listed in Table 7.2 for 1986.

7. Again using the Moody's data provided in Chapter 10, compute the ratios listed in Table 7.2 for the past five years. Plot the results and discuss any trends that you observe.

8. Apply the equation
$$ROE = ROS \times \text{Asset Turnover} \times \text{Total Assets}$$
to Firms A, B, C, D, and E in "A Hypothetical Example."

9. Apply the PE ratio equation to a firm with an expected payout, appropriate discount, and growth rate of .5, .1, and .05, respectively. Suppose the payout ratio declined to half of its prior value while the expected growth rate increased to .07. What would happen to the PE?

10. The Go Go Corporation currently has a payout of .2 and is accorded a risk premium of 3% above the market required rate of return of 15%. It currently sells for 35 with EPS of $1.25. What is the implied growth rate? Suppose EPS grows at a rate of 25% for five years and then declines to a rate of 10%, a rate that is expected to continue. What will the stock then sell for if the payout rises to .4 and the required return for Go Go Corporation declines 16%?

REVIEW PROJECTS

1. Obtain the latest annual reports for a utility company, a manufacturer, and a bank and compute the various ratios discussed in the text. Use Table 7.2 as a guide.

2. Select an industry with a number of companies having differing levels of financial strengths. Now choose one company in the industry that is thought to be strong and another that is thought to be weak. Compute relevant ratios for each and compare. Write a report.

3. Make a list of 20 industries that are frequently mentioned in investment periodicals. Classify each according to its life cycle stage. Ask a fellow student to classify the same group of industries. Compare the two sets of classifications. Write a report.

4. Select three industries and read about them in the financial press. Rank their members according to market share and competitive strength. Write a report.

5. Rank the companies in the industries selected for Problem 4 according to the quality of their managements. Write a report. (Note: This is a nearly impossible assignment even for an expert, but give it a try.)

6. Obtain the year-end issues of *Forbes* and *Business Week* and read their industry analyses. Rank the industries covered in the two periodicals and compare the rankings. Write a report.

7. Assemble a list of 20 large companies. Compute the stock price to per share book value for each and plot it relative to the ROE. Do you see a pattern? If so, try to explain it.

NOTES

1. P. Brown and R. Ball, "Some Preliminary Findings on the Association Between the Earnings of a Firm, Its Industry and the Economy," Empirical Research in Accounting, Selected Studies, 1967, Supplement to vol. 5, *Journal of Accounting Research*, 55–77.

2. H. Latane and D. Tuttle, "Framework for Forming Probability Beliefs," *Financial Analysts Journal*, January/February 1968, 51–61.

3. E. Brigham and S. Pappas, "Rates of Return on Common Stock," *Journal of Business*, July 1969, 302–316; F. Reilly and E. Drzycimski, "Alternative Industry Performance and Risk," *Journal of Financial and Quantitative Analysis*, June 1974, 423–446.

4. Reilly and Drzycimski, op. cit.; M. Blume, "On the Assessment of Risk," *Journal of Finance*, March 1971, 1–10; R. Levy, "On the Short-Term Stationarity of Beta Coefficients," *Financial Analysts Journal*, January/February 1971, 55–62.

5. J. Cohen, F. Zinbarg, and Z. Zeikel, *Investment Analysis and Portfolio Management* (Homewood, Ill.: Irwin, 1973), 324–366.

6. B. Branch, "Corporate Objectives and Market Performance," *Financial Management*, Summer 1973, 24–29; S. Levin and S. Levin, "Ownership and Control of Large Industrial Firms: Some New Evidence," *Review of Business and Economic Research*, Fall 1982, 36–49.

7. M. Clayman, "In Search of Excellence: The Investor's Viewpoint," *Financial Analysts Journal*, May/June 1987, 54–63; W. Simpson and T. Ireland, "Managerial Excellence and Shareholder Returns," *American Association of Individual Investors Journal*, August 1987, 4–11.

8

Misleading Accounting: The Danger and the Potential

Investors pay a great deal of attention to earnings per share (EPS). The actual numbers reported to shareholders are, however, far from precise. They are prepared by company accountants and checked and attested to by auditors whose exercise of discretion can substantially affect what is actually reported. Moreover, the ill-defined boundaries of many accounting procedures lead to both controversy and confusion. Most users expect financial reports (balance sheets, income statements, and changes in financial position statements) to reveal an accurate picture of the company's performance and financial position. No doubt this is also the goal of most of those involved in the preparation of the statements. Nonetheless, an uncritical acceptance of the reported data has at least two potential drawbacks.

First, applying differing accounting techniques to similar facts may properly produce very different reports. For example, Leonard Spacek illustrated how generally accepted accounting procedures could easily be used to report EPS of from $.80 to $1.79.[1] Any given set of actual sales and expenditures by the company can be used to produce and report a relatively wide range of earnings numbers. Accordingly, investors should know whether the reported figures are near the high or the low end of that range.

Second, firms sometimes misuse accounting discretion to generate misleading earnings reports. Overstating earnings one year usually reduces what can legitimately be reported in future years. Those who rely on untrustworthy data may pay too much for a company whose books have been "cooked."

Most accounting statements probably represent an honest effort to reveal rather than conceal. The accounting profession and its Financial Accounting Standards Board (FASB) work hard to establish reasonable rules and procedures to be applied by their member accountants. Nevertheless, the all-too-frequent exceptions to the goal of clear and accurate financial statements warrant careful attention.

Some problems result from a purposeful effort to misuse accounting discretion (with Equity Funding and Saxon Industries as examples). Even conscientiously prepared accounting statements may be misleading, however. Thus a careful and informed reader of the full set of financial statements (including the footnotes) and other public data may discover far more than would be revealed by a cursory glance at key figures such as sales growth and EPS. Such a detailed analysis may either expand upon the initial perception (no surprises) or uncover a very different picture. Market acceptance of misleading financial statements may allow more knowledgeable investors to avoid or short overvalued securities (when overoptimistic accounting numbers are trusted) and buy undervalued securities (when asset values are hidden).

This chapter explores the nature of the accounting problem and how accounting discretion can affect the reported data. Both optimistic and pessimistic accounting assumptions and statements are examined and illustrated with a series of real-world examples. Finally, methods of spotting misleading accounting are discussed.

ACCOUNTING DISCRETION

Generally accepted accounting principles (GAAP) and the pronouncements of the FASB are designed to limit the extent of discretion and thereby enhance the consistency of accounting statements. In spite of the best efforts of the FASB and others, appreciable uncertainty and differences of opinion remain. No doubt most accountants do a fair job under difficult circumstances. Nonetheless, some companies continue to report misleading results. Such companies thereby expose their shareholders to the risk of substantial shocks when a clearer picture emerges.

Abraham Briloff, a pioneer in the analysis of accounting abuse, has in a series of *Barron's* articles (later compiled into several books) reported numerous examples of GAAP being perverted to produce misleading statements.[2] Since Briloff's original disclosures, accounting abuses have received additional attention, but problems persist.

The common practice of keeping more than one set of accounting records illustrates the extensive nature of accounting discretion. A company may properly maintain two sets of books—one for the IRS and one for stockholders. Some companies also keep a third set of books for their own internal use. The IRS books generally utilize every permissible deduction, write-off, and reserve to minimize taxable profits. A more favorable view may appear in the shareholder books. The internal books may be the most realistic but are the least accessible to outsiders.

The Valuation Problem

Valuing assets and liabilities is one of the principal accounting problems. Values must be assigned to inventories, securities, plant, equipment, acquired assets, receivables, and a host of other items. Liabilities such as accrued pension benefits, long-term lease obligations, and pending damage claims also need to be valued. Establishing an accurate value for such money-dominated assets and liabilities as cash, receivables, and payables is generally rather straightforward. Most assets and liabilities, however, are not already denominated in dollars (particularly current dollars). Thus such valuations inevitably involve substantial subjectivity.

Assets are generally valued at their acquisition cost less accumulated depreciation. If available, a ready market quote may be used, especially if it is lower than cost. Because few usable market prices exist for plant and equipment, such assets are almost always valued at historical cost less accumulated depreciation. Even when the secondary market is relatively active (e.g., transportation equipment), historical cost less accumulated depreciation is still generally employed. With rapid inflation, however, replacement costs often exceed historical cost valuations for plant and equipment. The conservative bias of accounting is supposed to reduce the likelihood of unpleasant surprises. Excessive conservatism can, however, be as misleading as excessive optimism.

Exceptions to General Accounting Rules

The many exceptions to accounting practices increase both the complexity of the process and the diversity of possible reported results. For example, one general principle of accounting is that assets should be valued at cost or market, whichever is lower. This principle is not generally applied, however, to the loan and security portfolios of banks, thrift institutions, insurance companies, and other types of financial institutions. These institutions typically hold substantial portfolios of debt instruments that bear fixed interest rates. Thus the true values of their assets will vary inversely with market rates of interest. Nonetheless, these fixed interest assets are generally carried on the books at cost regardless of what happens to market interest rates (and thus regardless of what happens to the market values of these assets). The aggregate market value of marketable securities (but not of loans) is reported alongside the cost figure but not used to compute book values. Even exceptions have exceptions. One primary exception exists to the cost-based valuation rule for fixed interest assets of financial institutions. Portfolio components slated for sale or for which payment is substantially overdue are written down to their estimated sale prices.

Two justifications are offered for permitting financial firms to ignore the valuation impact of interest rate changes. First, many such firms have offsetting liabilities whose values are also affected by changing interest rates. Thus, as interest rates rise, the values of an institution's fixed interest assets will decline, but so will the market values of its fixed rate liabilities. Second, investors and depositors or policyholders will be at least partially protected from the impact of adverse interest fluctuations as long as the institution's cash flow remains adequate. Why, so the argument goes, unnecessarily concern people with a restated balance sheet when the income picture is sound? Moreover, interest rates may eventually move in the opposite direction.

Regardless of the validity of these arguments, investors should not ignore the adverse effect of rising interest rates on the balance sheets of financial institutions.

Similarly, the favorable impact of falling interest rates should not be overlooked. Taking due account of the impact of the net interest fluctuation on asset values reveals a much clearer picture of the firm's current worth than do its unadjusted book values.

Other exceptions allow asset values to be increased to market. A sale and repurchase accomplishes the revaluation by brute force. A new historical cost may also be established with a partial sale. Alternatively, a swap for dissimilar assets may facilitate a revaluation. Such transactions having a legitimate business purpose may be quite proper. The investor should, however, question the desirability of any transaction designed to increase the book valuation. Why must management go to such lengths? Investors are perfectly capable of looking beyond inaccurate book values.

Depreciation

Many assets offer useful service over a number of accounting periods. Expensing their costs either when the items were purchased or when they were taken out of service would be misleading. Allocating and charging off a portion of each asset's cost (depreciation) to each relevant accounting period much more closely matches revenues to expenses. If the depreciation charge accurately estimated the decline in an asset's value due to wear, tear, obsolescence, or other factors, asset book values would approximate market values. Accounting depreciation, however, is primarily an attempt to spread asset costs over their useful lives. As such, it is only tangentially related to the actual decline in asset values.

Depletion and amortization also involve charging off an asset's cost over its useful life. As a general rule, manufactured and otherwise constructed assets are depreciated; mineral resources are depleted; and intangible assets, such as patents, copyrights, and goodwill, are amortized. The periodic depreciation, depletion, and amortization amounts are deducted from revenues in profit determination and from the asset side of the balance sheet to determine net worth. The greater the charges, the lower is reported income, its corresponding tax liability, and the stated value of assets and net worth. Obviously, the rate at which assets are written off affects both financial statement values and after-tax cash flows.

Allowed Depreciation Methods.   With straight-line depreciation, a constant sum is deducted annually over the estimated life of the asset. Thus a 10-year asset that cost $100,000 would be depreciated at $10,000 a year (assuming no salvage value). In contrast, accelerated depreciation increases charge-offs in the early years of the asset's life, thereby postponing tax payments. The tax postponement is very nearly permanent for a rapidly growing firm. Newly acquired depreciable assets of such firms generally more than replace those whose depreciated value is approaching zero. Thus taxes postponed to the current year are more than offset by taxes postponed into the following year, and so on. Even when the postponement is temporary, the effect is like an interest-free term loan from the government. In addition to choosing from among the permitted depreciation methods, some discretion may be exercised in determining an asset's depreciable life. Thus, a firm can affect the amount that it reports as profits by choosing the depreciation method and by setting the depreciable life.

Accounting Abuse with Depreciation: The Leasco Example.   The Leasco case illustrates the misleading results of an inadequate depreciation provision. In 1961 Leasco began offering computer rentals at about 82% of the manufacturer's rental rate. A rental company like Leasco might be somewhat more efficient in lease management than a manufacturer like IBM. Nonetheless, successful companies such as IBM should be difficult to beat at their own game: mainframe computers. Few would expect an 18% savings through greater rental efficiencies.

Subsequent events reveal that the lower rental rates offered by Leasco (the nonmanufacturer) were based largely on an understated depreciation allowance. Regardless of which depreciation method is chosen, the total amount of the charges must eventually equal the acquisition cost less any salvage value. The principal question is, How should the asset's cost be allocated over its useful life? This in turn breaks down into two questions:

1. What is the useful life?

2. At what rate should depreciation be charged at various stages of that useful life?

The useful life estimate is central to the Leasco case.

Forecasting a computer's technological life is much more difficult than estimating its physical life. Technological advances have, historically, been known to reduce the value of existing computers at a rapid rate. Thus the annual rent on new computers should equal a substantial percentage of their purchase prices. For example, a computer might begin with a first-year rent equal to 30% to 40% of the computer's cost and then rent at somewhat lesser rates each year thereafter. The rental company would need rather high initial rents (relative to the purchase cost of its equipment) if it is to recover its investment and show a profit. The rental value of a computer will decline with its rate of technological obsolescence. Thus the rental rate on a computer will decline each year of its life. Depreciation charges should be computed so that they accurately reflect the computer's expected rate of obsolescence.

Leasco's lower depreciation and rental rates for its computers were based on the company's own useful life assumptions. Leasco assumed that its computers' useful lives would exceed the manufacturer's estimates on the same make and model. As a result of its more optimistic useful life estimate, Leasco was able to justify (at least on its own books) a slower rate of depreciation on its computers. This lower depreciation rate in turn allowed the firm to charge lower rental rates and still report profits.

Leasco's unwarranted optimism eventually resulted in large write-offs, however. For all its accounting gimmickry, Leasco lost $7 million on its computer rentals during the seven years from 1962 to 1969. When its 1970 loss of $30.8 million was reported, the firm's stock fell dramatically. Its misleading accounting had come home to roost.

Leasco's shareholders may not have been particularly well served by the firm's early history. One need not, however, shed too many tears for its founder. Saul

Steinberg first burst upon Wall Street as a brash young man in his early 20s. Leasco's initial profit and growth reports inflated the stock's price. Steinberg used his company's high-priced stock to acquire several attractive properties. His effort to take over New York's Chemical Bank did fail, largely because of vigorous establishment opposition. Moreover, the losses from the computer rental operation did eventually surface and depress the stock's price. By then, however, Steinberg had acquired Reliance, a large and profitable insurance company. Reliance's financial strength was more than sufficient to absorb the losses from Leasco's rental operations. Leasco and Reliance were merged. Leasco was later spun off and still later it acquired a substantial block of Reliance. Steinberg and his relatives owned a large share of both firms. More recently, Steinberg and his associates bought out the other shareholders and took both firms private. Steinberg took advantage of each of these financial maneuvers to strengthen his own position. Steinberg is now a very rich man due in no small part to the shareholders who made the mistake of believing his accounting numbers.

Leasco provides but one of many examples of firms whose optimistic depreciation expectations produced unrealistic income reports. Once the investment community is made aware (by a Briloff article in *Barron's*, for example) of the profit overstatement, the stock's price is almost certain to fall. Even if no one discovers the misstatements, the company's accountants will eventually run out of gimmicks. At that point earnings will not keep pace with expectations and the stock's price will decline. Obviously depreciation accounting is one area investors should closely watch.

Kaplan and Roll examined the stock performance of 71 firms that switched back to straight-line reporting to shareholders (while continuing to use accelerated depreciation for the IRS).[3] Such switches increased EPS but had no effect on cash flows and no long-term stock market impacts.

Inventory Valuation

Valuing inventories poses another difficult accounting problem. One-of-a-kind items are generally relatively easy to handle. Unless they remain in inventories for an extended period, historical cost valuations are generally adequate. Most inventories, however, consist of identical units that are frequently added to and subtracted from the warehouse. Such inventories and their corresponding accounting entries for cost of goods sold can more conveniently be valued at some cost per unit multiplied by the relevant number of units. Two principal techniques are used: LIFO and FIFO.

Using LIFO (last in, first out), units removed from the inventories are generally valued at the most recent purchase price. Sometimes all purchases at the most recent price have been accounted for by corresponding sales. When that happens, the next most recent price is used. Thus, just-purchased units will be charged out (cost of goods sold) at the most recent purchase price until the number of units sold exceeds the units purchased at that price. Once the most recently purchased units have been accounted for, the next most recent purchase price will be applied, and so forth.

Using FIFO (first in, first out), the oldest cost figure remaining on the books is applied to items removed from inventories. Thus, inventories are generally valued at relatively recent costs while the figures for cost of goods sold tend to reflect out-of-date prices.

Neither LIFO nor FIFO attempts to match individual physical units with their purchase prices. Thus, a firm may ship the oldest units first, but use LIFO to value them at the most recent invoice cost. Both LIFO and FIFO normally provide a reasonably consistent picture of inventory and cost of goods sold. With rising prices, FIFO will tend to yield a lower value for cost of goods sold, thereby inflating profits and the value of ending inventory. Compared to FIFO, LIFO generally deflates profits, taxes, and ending inventory values.

With relatively stable prices, the choice between LIFO and FIFO will not greatly affect reported earnings. With rapid price changes, the LIFO–FIFO choice does have a larger effect, but the earnings impact may still be modest if inventories are only a small part of total assets. A shift from one method to another can substantially affect reported earnings, however. Thus, until the FASB changed the relevant accounting rules (thereby making such shifts much less attractive), a poorly performing firm could switch from LIFO to FIFO in order to show a substantial one-time earnings increase. Such inventory profits were illusory because more funds are required to replenish inventory at the higher per unit cost. On the other hand, rapid inflation rates have encouraged some firms to shift from FIFO to LIFO and thereby reduce their inventory profits and the resulting taxes.

Sunder studied the market impact of 110 firms switching to LIFO and 22 switches to FIFO.[4] The LIFO switches showed above-market risk-adjusted returns prior to the switch and random returns thereafter, probably because profitable firms tended to make the switch. On the other hand, firms switching to FIFO typically did poorly subsequent to the switch because they were generally unprofitable.

Merger Accounting

When two firms merge, their two balance sheets need to be combined. The consolidated statements should be consistent and allow meaningful comparisons to be made between pre- and postmerger operations. Two different approaches to consolidation are permitted: pooling of interest or purchase accounting. With pooling of interest, the balance sheet values of the acquired firm's assets and liabilities are added to the acquiring company's balance sheet. Their premerger book values are used regardless of the acquiring firm's acquisition cost. In purchase accounting, the acquisition cost (cash or market value of the securities used in the exchange) is allocated among the acquired firm's assets and added to the acquiring firm's balance sheet.

The acquiring firm can report illusory gains by entering the acquired assets on its books at unrealistically low values and then selling them at much higher market values. Reporting profits from sales of acquired assets is perfectly appropriate when the sold assets are valued at their fair share of the acquisition costs. Gains can be overstated by undervaluing the assets to be sold, however.

Such overstatements may occur with pooling-of-interest accounting if the firm's acquisition cost substantially exceeded its book value. With purchase accounting, the acquiring firm may place unrealistically low values on assets to be sold while valuing retained assets more highly. Thus, the "manufacturing" of profits is easier with pooling-of-interest accounting, but purchase accounting may also be abused.

False growth represents another potential problem from mergers. When a firm with a high PE acquires a firm with a lower PE, the acquiring firm's earnings per share tend to go up. The relatively high earnings per share of the acquired firm tend to increase EPS of the combined operation. Thus the surviving firm will appear to show earnings growth because of the way the combined books compare with the preacquisition books of the acquiring firm. Clearly, such "growth" is unlikely to reoccur except through further acquisitions. Eventually, however, a high PE firm acquiring low PE firms will tend to take on the characteristics of its acquisitions (especially the low growth potential that is usually the cause of a low PE). If that happens, the acquiring firm's PE is likely to decline, thereby offsetting the gains from the increasing EPS. Thus investors should be wary of the false growth that may result from mergers. Such false growth has very different implications from internal growth.

Merger Accounting Gimmicks.   Briloff devoted most of three chapters of *Unaccountable Accounting* to the same basic merger accounting theme. An acquired firm's assets are entered on the books at low values and then disposed of at the fair market value. The difference is claimed as income. In a more recent book, *The Truth about Corporate Accounting*, Briloff criticized the allocation of acquisition costs under both types of merger accounting.[5]

When, for example, General Electric acquired Utah International for approximately $2 billion, only UI's $600 million book value was entered on the GE balance sheet. This approach greatly reduced depreciation and inventory costs. As Briloff put it, "$1.4 billion . . . of the cost evaporated—not even leaving the smile like that of the Cheshire cat."[6] In the United Technologies–AMBAC merger (1978), a book value of $122 million was acquired for $220 million. Of the $98 million difference, $87.5 million was allocated to goodwill to be written off over a 25-year period. Two years earlier, United Technologies had acquired Otis Elevator and in the process added $27 million in goodwill to the books. In 1979, UT acquired Mostek for $314 million, of which $214 was goodwill. By year-end 1979, 32.3% of UT's book value was goodwill. Although the going-concern value of a firm often reflects earning potential above the sum of the assets acquired, such large amounts are difficult to justify. Moreover, UT's long-term approach to goodwill write-off seems unwarranted.

More recently, Briloff took a look at accounting at Viacom.[7] According to his analysis, 93% of the 1985 earnings came from highly questionable accounting. Furthermore, goodwill grew from $78 million in 1983 to $811 million in March 1986. Most of this increase resulted from acquisition of MTV and Showtime/The Movie Channel at prices far in excess of book values. Briloff's greatest criticism is of Viacom's decision to write off this goodwill (using straight-line depreciation) over a 40-year period. This very slow write-off had the effect of greatly increasing profits relative to what would have been reported had the write-off been more rapid.

Hong, Kaplan, and Mandelker, who studied the market response to 122 pooling and 37 purchase accounting mergers, found no systematic reaction.[8] Investors do not seem to be fooled by "dirty pooling."

Income Anticipation and Expense Deferral

Income from an installment sale creates yet another accounting problem. The profit might logically be claimed at many different points: when the purchase contract is signed, upon delivery of the product, when a given percentage of the purchase price is received, when a given percentage of the product's production costs has been incurred, upon full payment of the purchase price, or upon completion of the product. Alternatively, the profit may be prorated on the basis of the payment schedule or work fulfillment. Clearly, reported profits can depend substantially on when the profit is recognized.

Similarly, expenses may be recognized in two ways: the cost may be charged off in the year incurred (expensed) or it may be allocated over a period of years (capitalized). Expenses may be appropriately capitalized when the resulting benefits are expected to continue for a number of years. Otherwise, the cost should be expensed. Capitalizing costs that might more appropriately be expensed tends to overstate current earnings.

Income Anticipation Gimmicks. Briloff discussed an income anticipation abuse involving Minnie Pearl Franchises (an affiliate of National General):

> Essentially, I am indicting the company's (and their auditor's) failure to consider the substance of the franchising agreements and instead swallowed the form. Thus, as it turned out, these officers, et. al., participated importantly in forming a corporation, with only a minor capital contribution and with only limited capital resources. These corporations then entered into franchising agreements with Performance Systems whereby (and this presumes the typical franchising arrangement):
> 1. The newly formed franchise is obligated to pay an initial franchise fee—mostly payable in notes (with or without interest).
> 2. For this fee the franchisee receives the right to use the franchiser's name, patents, etc., for an indefinite period (frequently, however, with a right on the part of the franchiser to cancel under certain circumstances); the franchisee was also entitled to assistance in site selection, lease negotiation, equipping the premises, advertising, and in selecting personnel.
> 3. The franchisee was also obligated to pay a royalty based on sales; and was frequently required to purchase inventory and supplies from the franchiser.
> Where then was there an abuse of logic and reality, to say nothing of fairness, in the application of GAAP? Briefly, despite the limited capitalization of the franchises, the franchiser (Minnie Pearl, for example) would pick up as income at the time of the initial franchise agreement the entire amount of the fee—even though, as we have seen, so much of it is in the form of paper generated by the undercapitalized franchisee—with little or no provision for collection and cancellation losses.
> All that the principals in the franchiser operations had to do was to form a corporation with a minimal capital, use some ink and paper to sign up with themselves in behalf of the franchiser, and Presto! Merlin reports income of the franchiser.[9]

Briloff also explored the anticipation of income by National Student Marketing, R. Hoe, Telex, and Memorex. In the case of National Student Marketing and R. Hoe, "fudgeness" in reporting income on the percentage basis caused the overstatement. For Telex and Memorex, inventory was, in effect, valued at retail. Since these abuses came to light, FASB reforms have severely restricted the opportunity to anticipate income through franchise operations.

Land companies are criticized (Boise Cascade, AMREP, and GAC) for claiming as income the entire profit from a land sale when only a small payment is received (as little as 2½% of the purchase price).[10] Another land company, Commonwealth United, offset poor operating results with the profits from an incestuous transaction. On December 31, 1968, Commonwealth purchased 4,000 acres of Hawaiian property for $1,656,800 and resold it for $5,450,000. The purchasing syndicate was composed of three groups: Commonwealth's underwriters (Kleiner and Bell), the controlling stockholder of the underwriter (Shapiro), and a counsel for Commonwealth and the underwriter (Freling). The transaction involved a cash payment of $541,000. Commonwealth had no recourse in the event of a default beyond reclaiming the property. The reported profit of this one transaction represented $.20 of $.98 EPS for 1968. Also, on December 31, 1968, the underwriters purchased an office building from Commonwealth, producing another substantial portion of the company's 1968 profit. Thus Commonwealth and its underwriter spent most of the last day of 1968 "improving" the profit report.[11]

Bernard Cornfeld of Investors Overseas Services (IOS) executed a particularly ingenious income anticipation scheme. A portion of some Canadian Arctic oil and gas land was sold and the per acre price applied to the entire parcel. Ordinarily such a revaluation would be justified by an arm's-length sale of 25% or more. IOS sold less than 10% to King Resources. How independent King and IOS were was unclear, although Arthur Andersen audited both sets of books. This sale allowed IOS to claim $102 million in unrealized appreciation on the Fund of Funds it managed. Then IOS paid itself a management fee of 10% of the profit.

When Robert Vesco acquired IOS from Cornfeld, he revalued the Canadian land, wiping out the profit. Vesco later took $224 million dollars of IOS money with him to Costa Rica, later to the Bahamas, and was last reported to be operating out of Cuba. Cornfeld managed to stay just clear of the law on this side of the Atlantic, but did serve time in a Swiss jail. Because of the efforts of the Canadian liquidators, however, Fund of Funds shareholders may ultimately receive liquidation payments approximately equal to their initial investments. Moreover, much of the projected value is derived from the Arctic oil and gas properties that Cornfeld went to such lengths to revalue: Wonders never cease!

Other Misleading Accounting Examples

Briloff, with his *Barron's* connection, is clearly the best-known authority on misleading accounting. Others have also investigated accounting gimmicks, however. For example, R. Golden, a technology specialist at Edwards and Hanly, estimated that Western Union's bookkeeping maneuvers produced about 80% of the firm's 1972 EPS. These devices included capitalizing interest, pension, and severance pay while flowing through the net benefit of tax credits. The company's purchasing of its own bonds below par and claiming the gain as ordinary income was especially misleading (under FASB reforms the gain is now reported as extraordinary income).

Golden claimed that Western Union's $1.40 annual dividend had been covered by operating income in only one year from 1968 to 1972.[12]

Similar motives may explain a number of exchanges of common for preferred stock or bonds, bonds for common or preferred, straight bonds for convertibles, and so forth. Firms may achieve an extraordinary gain by retiring below-par bonds early, often to offset an extraordinary write-off or write-down.

Without claiming an attempt to mislead, Bowler points out that revised accounting methods for life insurance underwriters permit widely varying reports:

> Under statutory regulations, a company may select from a variety of reserve valuation methods, each with its own assumptions as to interest and mortality rates. The choice of methods is significant, especially to new business. For example, Company A writes a certain policy, reserves of which are based on the net level premium basis (the most stringent) with interest assumed at 3%. It sets aside a reserve of $22.50.
>
> Company B issues a policy identical except that reserves are computed on the commissioners' method, also known as modified preliminary term. It sets aside no reserves during the first year. Did Company B earn $22.50 more than Company A on this piece of business? Both methods are actuarially sound.
>
> And, does Company A have a liability Company B does not? As *Best's* points out, if a typical life insurer were to change its reserve basis from net level premium $3\frac{1}{2}\%$ to modified preliminary term $3\frac{1}{2}\%$, its surplus would double. A change from net level 3% would triple surplus.
>
> The shortcomings, for shareholder purposes, of an accounting system with arbitrary variables such as these is clear. About all that can be said in favor of statutory reserve methods is that they enjoy the sanction of regulatory authorities. Under GAAP, on the other hand, policy reserve assumptions are not subject to official approval. They are made by companies in light of their own experience and judgment.[13]

Clearly, such discretion presents some opportunities for abuse. Table 8.1 summarizes some of the areas in which misleadingly optimistic accounting has occurred in the past.

TABLE 8.1 Past Areas of Misleadingly Optimistic Accounting

- Not adjusting the book values of interest-sensitive assets to changing interest rates
- Overestimating the useful lives of assets, thereby understating their depreciation
- Switching to FIFO inventory accounting
- Undervaluing assets that are acquired through merger and later sold
- Claiming income from franchise sales prior to receipt of cash flow
- Claiming income from nonarm's-length sales when the seller has little recourse if the transaction is later reversed
- Claiming income from installment sales prior to the receipt of revenue
- Choosing an allowed method for insurance reserve that produces the greatest current profit

UNDERVALUED ASSETS

Accounting statements may be as misleadingly conservative as the previous examples were misleadingly optimistic. Because accounting procedures are supposed to lean modestly toward conservatism, a variety of different types of assets are often substantially undervalued: developed real estate, land and mineral resources carried at historical costs, overfunded pension funds, such intangible assets as tax-loss carryforwards, patents, trademarks, copyrights, leaseholdings, government-granted privileges (such as broadcast rights and acreage allotments), and pending damage claims.

Real estate is almost always valued at historical cost, which in inflationary times is usually well below current market values. A number of different types of companies, including railroads, real estate developers, agricultural combines, paper companies, and REITs have major property holdings whose liquidation values often exceed the market values of the stock.

Many oil companies own reserves that may be worth considerably more than either their book or stock market values. A series of large mergers brought particular attention to the oils. The New York Stock Exchange floor was frequently mentioned as the only place left where oil was still available at $5 a barrel (of proven reserves). Even allowing for the extraction costs, this differential is large. In smaller trans-actions proven reserves often sold for $9 or more per barrel. And yet, on the balance sheet, proven reserves may not even be valued at $5 a barrel. Table 8.2 illustrates one view of undervalued oil properties. The values of oil reserves are, however, quite sensitive to the market price of crude oil. Thus the fluctuations in oil prices have had a tremendous impact on oil company breakup values.

TABLE 8.2   Estimated Net Asset Values of Some Oil Stocks

	Stock Price	Net Asset Value*	Current Price/Asset Value
Amerada Hess	$22⅝	$ 35	65%
Amoco	63⅞	97	66
Ashland Oil	54	127	43
Arco	66⅞	122	55
Diamond Shamrock R&M	7½	21	36
Kerr-McGee	30⅜	43	71
Maxus Energy	7⅛	9	79
Murphy Oil	21⅜	48	45
Occidental	23⅝	38	62
Phillips	10¼	26	39
Sun Co.	48¼	62	78
Unocal	25⅜	62	41

*Salomon Brothers estimate.
Source: C. Solomon, "New Round of Oil Mergers May Be at Hand As Mighty Giants Look Over Weaker Firms," *The Wall Street Journal*, December 8, 1987, p. 67.

Tax-Loss Carryforwards

Tax-loss carryforwards are generally reported in a footnote to the financial state-ments. Yet the income tax shelter provided by such carryforwards may be worth a substantial fraction of their dollar amount. A company that has to pay taxes

Investments in Perspective

Articles in *Forbes* often include lists of interesting stocks. The following contains a list and discussion of firms with large carryforwards.

Taxing Matters

Edited by Laura Saunders

First Congress hit tax-loss carryforwards. Then it created a nifty loophole.

Tax-loss two-step

NET OPERATING LOSS carryovers have been pure gold to dealsters and acquisitors, a means of turning losses into cash. Firms with net operating losses can carry them backward up to three years and claim a tax refund. Or they can carry them forward for up to 15 years, sheltering future taxable income.

Used to shelter subsequent profits, the carryforwards are a dealmaker's best friend. Buyers use them to shelter earnings from businesses that are unrelated to the business that generated the losses. Under raider Ronald Perelman, for example, Revlon Group is presumably reducing its taxes on lipstick profits with $400 million of losses left from Pantry Pride's grocery business, which he sold.

It was only natural that Congress would use the 1986 tax reform act to try yet again to restrict dealmakers' use of carryforwards. Under the new law, if stock ownership of a company with accumulated losses changes by more than 50%, the annual deduction for the acquired company's losses is limited to a portion of the firm's value—usually the purchase price—multiplied by a rate published monthly by the IRS. The rate is now 6.41%. Thus, a company bought for $100 million

Carrying forward the carryforwards

Companies with big tax losses could be more attractive than ever. Below, some companies with large carryforwards.

Company	Latest 12-mo revenues ($ mil)	Latest 12-mo EPS	Net operating loss ($ mil)	Net operating loss per share	Recent price
AM International	$819	$0.40	$262	$5.08	7
Bethlehem Steel	4,600	−5.52	1,600	30.71	5
Cigna	16,786	−7.12	1,800	22.90	57
Continental Illinois	627	0.56	625	2.91	5¼
Cook United	224	−3.44	115	11.50	2
Tacoma Boat	108	−1.02	120	10.08	1⅛
Navistar	3,357	−0.14	1,100	10.14	5⅝
Telecommunications Inc	86.3	0.83	243	2.51	25¼
United Cable	203	0.31	106	4.34	27
Wickes	4,101	0.41	450	1.82	4

could generate only $6.41 million a year in tax offsets for the buyer, no matter how large the carryforward.

"The days of paying 25 cents on the dollar for net operating losses are behind us," says Coopers & Lybrand tax expert Thomas Fitzpatrick.

But as Congress closed one loophole, it opened another. The new one will make some companies with net operating losses (see table) even more attractive as merger candidates than they have been in the past.

To understand why, shift gears for a moment. The new law repeals the General Utilities doctrine. That makes it tougher for acquirers to write up assets to get high depreciation deductions. To do so, they must pay tax, at corporate income rates (maximum: 40% next year, 34% in 1988), on the amount of the writeup.

Suppose you pay $100 million for a company with a $50 million carryforward and assets carried at $20 million. Write up the assets to the purchase price, and you owe $32 million in post-General Utilities taxes in 1987.

This is where the new loophole comes in. Buyers can use the full car-

ryforward to offset the taxable write-up of the assets. In our example, the writeup is $80 million, the carryforward $50 million. Throw the latter against the former, and net gain is $30 million. Now the tax on the writeup is only $12 million, and the buyer gets all that extra depreciation.

If there's no income to shelter with that depreciation, that's okay, says Peat Marwick's merger expert Robert Willens. The new company will generate its own operating losses, which can be used without restrictions in the future.

According to Coopers' Fitzpatrick, companies whose takeover values could be enhanced by this technique include cable-TV firms that have accumulated losses from laying cable but are about to make money. Ditto for R&D-heavy high-tech firms that have recently become profitable.

Because the tax-loss two-step is so complicated, competent instructors like Willens and Fitzpatrick will be much sought after as the tax code is reformed. Whatever the new tax code does, it is not going to impoverish the accountants.—**L.S.**

equal to 33% of its profits will save 33 cents on each dollar of tax-loss carryforward that it is able to use. Whether or not the carryforwards can be realized depends on the firm's future earnings potential and/or the possibility of its takeover by a company that can utilize its tax loss. The Tax Reform Act of 1986 greatly restricts the ability of acquired firms to utilize the carryforwards of their acquisitions.

When Liquidation Values Can Be Realized

Firms with potentially undervalued assets have been relatively plentiful in the stock markets of the 1970s and 1980s. Three relevant questions relate to the ease or difficulty facing individual investors who seek to realize the underlying asset values of such potential investments. First, how can such asset values be estimated? Second, how does the market price of the stocks compare with the company's hidden values? Third, if the market price does not accurately reflect the underlying asset values, will it eventually?

Obtaining estimates of the market values of undervalued assets is often rather easy. Among the oil companies, for example, large acquisitions such as the Du Pont takeover of Conoco and the U.S. Steel purchase of Marathon generated a large amount of interest. The result was the publication of extensive lists of estimated breakup values for many of the other potential takeover targets in the oil patch. Interest in oil takeovers eventually waned as the price of oil collapsed. Interest was rekindled when crude oil prices began to show renewed life (Table 8.2). For other industries, lists also appear from time to time of takeover targets with high breakup value.

Estimates of the market values of undervalued assets may serve as a starting point. In other cases, the investor's job is much more difficult. Relevant articles may appear in the financial press or inferences may be drawn from published financial reports. The more difficult the valuation job, the less likely is the market to reflect such values. Thus the most attractive opportunities may be the most difficult to uncover.

Knowing that a company's breakup value appreciably exceeds its market price does not necessarily imply that its stock is undervalued. Often the market's low valuation reflects poor earnings prospects coupled with little likelihood of early liquidation. Unless easily killed, a firm worth more dead than alive will be priced as a going concern rather than a liquidation prospect. An entrenched management with a strong ownership position often stands in the way of any outsiders who might otherwise take over and liquidate the company. Thus small stockholders may have to wait and hope for management to decide to liquidate. If the managers like their positions, the wait may be long. On the other hand, investors who specialize in takeover and liquidation plays such as Carl Icahn, Irwin Jacobs, Ronald Perleman, and Saul Steinberg may eventually help out. Unless the investor has sufficient resources to acquire an influential position, however, he or she must wait for someone else to act.

Predicting when a liquidation might occur is hazardous. The ease of acquiring control is one relevant factor, however. If the liquidation value is appreciably above the market price, if the floating supply of stock (not locked up by those opposed to a liquidation) is a substantial majority of the total, if the acquisition cost is not

Investments in Perspective

Stocks with high breakup values relative to their book and stock price were listed by *Business Week* in 1985, when breakup value first captured the imagination of Wall Street.

Finance
MARKETS & INVESTMENTS

'BREAKUP VALUE' IS WALL STREET'S NEW BUZZWORD

Parker Pen Co. made a rather paltry 32¢ a share last year. No matter. The stock is selling at 18, and Wall Street analysts say the company has a "breakup" value in the mid-20s. General Foods Corp. is selling at 82 right now. True, it earned a solid $7 a share over the past 12 months, and takeover rumors are boosting the price. But its breakup value of about $130 a share is what's really driving the stock, analysts say. "I do think that this is the new way of valuing a company," says Mitchell S. Fromstein, Parker's president.

Breakup value is the new buzzword on Wall Street. It is a measure of the separate prices that the market would place on the parts of a company. And the new hot stocks are those where the sum of the parts amounts to far more than the current stock price. In the go-go years of the 1960s, growth in earnings and cash flow were what lured investors. In the inflation-ridden 1970s, the Street looked for resources in the ground. But now, high breakup value is a new source of glamour on the Street.

Actually, the hard-asset plays of the late 1970s spawned the kind of analysis that has the Street hunting for breakup value. The search for "hidden" assets began in earnest about seven years ago, when canny investors began picking apart inflation-disguised balance sheets.

They noticed that a company's book value—its assets stated at their original cost minus liabilities—was much lower than its inflation-adjusted value, particularly when skyrocketing real estate prices were taken into account.

LARGE REWARDS. During that period, however, earnings could still be expected to spiral upward, helped along by double-digit inflation. But now earnings projections leave investors cold. With inflation on the wane and international competition fierce, profit growth looks sluggish. Raiders such as T. Boone Pickens Jr., Carl C. Icahn, and Ivan F. Boesky have shown how to create value in this environment. In a sense, breakup value is a legacy of the raiders, but it goes far beyond them. Wall Street firms are eager for all investors to get in on the action. So they are attempting to pinpoint a magic number.

Investors who latched onto the idea that the parts of a company could be worth more than the whole have already scored handsomely with Greyhound, Gulf & Western, RCA, ITT, Kidde, Litton, Penn Central, Teledyne, and Whittaker. Greyhound stock, which lay dormant for years, doubled shortly after the company sold off several businesses. "The rewards have been large recently for investors who got in early," says David S. Moore, a conglomerate analyst with

Donaldson, Lufkin & Jenrette Securities Corp. So Wall Street is now fixated on the next crop of companies that may be ready to shed divisions.

There is, of course, no sure-fire way to estimate breakup value. "It's much talked about but little understood," says Moore. The methods for arriving at such a figure are controversial. The easy part is to start with book value, an out-of-favor statistic that basically indicates what assets originally cost. Then an analyst with a critical eye determines the current market value of the real estate. Balance-sheet footnotes are scoured for overfunded pension plans and undervalued inventory.

But then the going gets tough. Analysts screen for companies with units that don't fit in with the core business. There are plenty around. It is considerably more difficult to estimate what other companies would be willing to pay for the misfits and what the slimmed-down company would be worth without them.

PRIME PARTS. For example, Crane Co., an engineering company, acquired Uni-Dynamics Corp., a defense and plastics manufacturer, only four months ago. Mel Schmidt, an analyst with Drexel Burnham Lambert Inc., suspects that Crane wants only some select parts of its acquisition and will soon put much of it back on the block along with other businesses Crane has long owned. This speculation leads some analysts to assign a breakup value to Crane of $55 per

COMPANIES WHOSE BREAKUP VALUE MIGHT LEAD TO SELL-OFFS

Company	Per Share			Main Business	Possible Divestiture
	Breakup value	Book value	Price 6/25/85		
Adams-Russell	$45	$9	$28	Electronics	Cable TV
Colgate-Palmolive	35	17	26	Household & personal care	Health care, industrial
Crane	55	22	35	Engineering, water treatment	Automation devices
Cyclops	80	50	50	Specialty steel	Retailing
Edison Brothers	42	27	36	Women's shoes	Hardware
Fluor	30	21	18	Plant construction	Mining
General Foods	130	40	82	Packaged food	Bakery, food service
General Host	25	17	16	Specialty retailing	Frozen foods
General Instrument	40	20	16	Electronics	Gambling devices
General Mills	95	28	60	Consumer food	Apparel, toys
Hamilton Oil	25	10	16	Oil & gas production	Refining
National Distillers & Chemical	50	30	32	Chemicals	Insurance, liquor
Parker Pen	25	8	18	Writing instruments, temporary help	Writing instruments
Ralston Purina	75	12	45	Livestock feeds	Restaurants
Revlon	55	28	41	Beauty products	Health care

DATA: BW, BASED ON A SURVEY OF SECURITIES ANALYSTS

share, compared with its current price of 35 and book value of $22.

Revlon would have somewhat less of a breakup premium because its health care division, much of which might be sold, has already been recognized on the Street as a hot business in its own right. "We think that if Revlon were broken up, it would be in the low 50s," compared with its current price of 41, says George A. Roche, an analyst with T. Rowe Price Associates Inc.

All this talk about breakup values has not been lost on the management of those companies that Wall Street pulls apart on paper. "In the past, breakup value just wasn't spoken about, and today the analysts do it on just about every company that exists," says Parker's Fromstein, who thinks his own company's stock has been bid up largely on speculation that it will shed its money-losing writing instruments division. Although he isn't tipping his hand on a divestiture, talk about one has been rife for some time, and it seems awfully late in the day to make much money speculating on Parker's eventual breakup.

A FAD? High breakup value is propelling stocks even when divestiture is a remote possibility. Salomon Bros. estimates that publishing and broadcasting companies have extremely high breakup values relative to current share prices. Salomon figures Capital Cities Communications

Inc., which just bought American Broadcasting Cos., has a breakup value of $325 per share, some 50% above its stock price. Washington Post Co. is estimated to have a breakup value of $155, a premium of 30% above its current price and light-years above book value. But virtually all this value is in its core business, and a sale would be tantamount to partial liquidation, because management would have a tough time reinvesting the proceeds at a higher rate of return.

But even so, the market will pay so high a price for hidden assets that companies are willing to sell off parts of their main businesses. That's why Holiday Corp. sold several hotel properties on June 24 at premium prices. "They're using the money to buy back their own shares as opposed to buying somebody else's," says Roche of T. Rowe Price.

Many believe that the search for hidden assets is a fad inspired by the success of the raiders and that in a few years investors will focus once again on earnings and cash flow. "First it was, 'O. K., how's the company doing?'" says Parker's Fromstein. "Now it's, 'Can you guess what the effect will be of a divestiture?' But let me tell you one thing from experience: The way a brokerage firm figures a breakup value isn't always the way it is. And you can lose because it isn't always broken up."

By Stuart Weiss in New York

Source: S. Weiss, "'Breakup Value' Is Wall Street's New Buzzword," *Business Week*, July 8, 1985, 80–81. Reprinted by special permission, © 1985, McGraw-Hill, Inc.

too large for those inclined to take over the firm, and if the firm is in a relatively visible industry, takeover and liquidation are reasonably likely. Otherwise, liquidation may be a more distant prospect. If the profit potential is great enough, however, someone is eventually likely to act. Thus, a strategy of assembling a diversified portfolio of undervalued asset plays may produce enough winners to make it worthwhile. Both Evergreen and Mutual Shares funds have generated substantial returns with such a strategy.[14]

THE EFFECT ON THE MARKET OF DISTORTED ACCOUNTING REPORTS

Accounting statements are by their very nature at least somewhat misleading. Some managers go out of their way to overstate (or understate) the earnings and assets of their companies. In other instances arbitrary accounting rules lead to misleading financial statements in spite of the best efforts of accountants to produce an accurate picture. Yet the market is full of talented analysts seeking to uncover the true story. Do misleading financial reports cause a large number of stocks to be mispriced? Can improved accounting rules reduce the problem? Several recent studies bear on these questions.

The Financial Accounting Standards Board (FASB) has sought to make accounting statements more realistic by a number of its rulings. FASB 33 required companies to provide certain inflation-adjusted data. Similarly, FASB 34 provided for the capitalization of the interest costs incurred for assets that took a significant amount of time to put into service. Both rules sought to foster the production of earnings data that more closely matched true economic earnings (as opposed to the more arbitrary accounting earnings concept).

Beaver and Ryan explored the ability of inflation-adjusted earnings to explain stock prices.[15] They found that historical earnings did a better job. McDonald, Morris, and Nichols examined the market reaction to a switch to capitalizing interest as provided by FASB 34.[16] They found no market impact for the stocks of firms making the shift. Thus both studies seem to imply that the market was already able to look beyond the actual accounting numbers and adjust for the impacts of inflation and interest expense. No doubt many specific examples of the market being temporarily misled by accounting numbers can be cited. The writings of Briloff illustrate the problem. Why else would managers try to mislead? Nonetheless, the market may well be relatively efficient in digesting the true meaning of most accounting statements.

Misleading Accounting and Individual Investors

Work by Briloff and others has had a major impact on the accounting profession. Many reforms have taken place and many others are underway. Future changes will not take place overnight nor will they eliminate the possibility of confusing or misleading financial statements. As the rules become tighter, the methods of those who use them to mislead become more sophisticated. Moreover, the increasingly complex accounting problem for large multinational conglomerates in a period of rapidly fluctuating inflation and exchange rates is bound to magnify the ambiguities. Thus, investors may well be rewarded for reading financial statements carefully and trying to detect accounting abuses before the market does. Waiting for Briloff or someone else to expose an industry's misleading accounting causes the investor to risk losses that could have been avoided by sidestepping the investments. According to Kaplan and Roll, the price of a stock may rise when an inflated earnings announcement is released, but it will usually fall once careful analysis has revealed the overstatement.[17] Emery as well as Kaplan and Roll concluded that the market eventually sees through most efforts to manipulate accounting numbers.[18]

DETECTING ACCOUNTING GIMMICKS

Even talented analysts may be unable to discover a purposeful deception from published data alone. Equity Funding's fraudulent insurance policies and Saxon's bogus inventories probably could not have been exposed without insider help. Even when no outright fraud is intended, detecting the misleading techniques from public documents may still be very difficult.

Accounting statements are summaries containing only those aspects of financial operations that are deemed materially important. Facts that the firm and its auditors consider unimportant may not appear in the statements. Finally, many investors do not have the expertise to uncover the abuses even if the necessary information is available in published records.

To detect potentially misleading accounting procedures, investors should carefully examine published financial statements as an interdependent whole. The various pieces should form a consistent framework. The footnotes, an integral part of the financial statement, are often added at the auditor's request to present a fairer picture.

The statements should also be carefully checked for internal consistency. For example, in the absence of special circumstances, tax payments should approximate the product of the statutory rate times before-tax profits. A lower ratio of taxes to before-tax profits has several possible explanations. The industry may receive special tax treatment; the firm may utilize various tax shelters; or the firm may be reporting different results to the IRS and the stockholders. Providing different reports to the IRS and the stockholders is not necessarily improper but does raise the possibility that the report to the stockholders is too optimistic. The SEC requires firms to explain departures from the statutory rate that are greater than 5%.

In addition to searching for inconsistencies, the investor/analyst should be familiar with the various areas in which misleading accounting has been practiced in the past: understated depreciation, inventory penetration, disposal of merger-acquired assets, anticipation of installment sale income, and repurchase of outstanding securities. Many of the examples described earlier in the chapter are not, however, permitted by current accounting practices. Because newly discovered gimmicks may be the most dangerous, investors should not limit their analysis to areas of past abuses. Table 8.3 summarizes the procedure for detecting accounting abuses.

SUMMARY AND CONCLUSIONS

Accounting involves substantial discretion. The use of this discretion may at times lead to the production of misleading financial statements with or without a conscious effort on the part of the preparer. Valuation involves a number of arbitrary choices in depreciation methods, inventory reporting, merger accounting, and so

TABLE 8.3   Detecting Potentially Misleading Accounting Procedures

1. Examine financial statements as an interdependent whole.
2. Carefully read all footnotes.
3. Check for internal consistency: taxes, depreciation, and so on.
4. Be familiar with past areas of abuse:
   - Understated depreciation
   - Disposal of merger-acquired assets
   - Anticipation of installment sale income
   - Repurchase of outstanding securities
5. Realize that the largest risks may come from new techniques.

on. The timing of income and expense recognition and the purchase of bonds below book value further complicate the picture.

Such income-inflating devices as using unrealistic depreciation estimates, switching inventory methods, anticipating income, manufacturing profits through merger accounting, and reacquiring low-coupon bonds were discussed and illustrated with examples. Next the profit potential created by misleadingly pessimistic accounting statements was considered. Real estate, mineral resources, and tax-loss carryforwards are especially likely to have unrealistically low balance sheet values. The liquidation value/stock price differential may or may not be relevant depending on the prospects for liquidation. Finally, ways of spotting misleading accounting were presented. Statements should be examined as a whole with particular attention given to footnotes, internal consistency, and areas of past abuse.

REVIEW QUESTIONS

1. Why are accounting gimmicks relevant to the stockholder? Discuss some examples of accounting gimmickry.
2. Compare the various methods of depreciating assets. How does the use of each affect reported income?
3. Discuss how the use of LIFO and FIFO affect reported earnings and taxes. How does their use affect reported income?
4. Compare pooling of interest with purchase accounting. How does the use of each affect reported income?
5. Describe the potential abuses available to firms that must allocate income and expenses from installment sales. How does the stock market generally react to the discovery of such abuses?
6. In what way may bond refinancings lead to misleading earnings reports? How does their use affect reported income?

7. Discuss the difficulties of discovering accounting gimmicks. What methods are available and what are their limitations?

REVIEW PROBLEMS

1. The CDF Bank purchased $5 million in 20-year 9% Treasury bonds. A year later these bonds are selling in the market with a yield to maturity of 11%. If they are the only marketable security held by CDF, how will they show up on CDF's financial statements? What impact will they have on the firm's net worth? How would the answer change if the bonds were to be sold?

2. The ACF Corporation is a manufacturer of auto parts. It has annual revenues of $3,000,000, expenses of $2,500,000 (excluding depreciation and taxes), and 500,000 shares outstanding. Its depreciable assets (primarily plant and equipment) have a book value of $2,000,000 and an average useful life of 10 years. Compute total and per share earnings assuming that either straight-line depreciation or depreciation equal to 20% of current book value is used. Assume a 33% tax rate on profit.

3. Recompute Problem 2 for one year later. Sales have increased but ACF had sufficient excess capacity to cover the additional sales. Assume that earnings and expenses have both increased by 10% and that no additional depreciable assets were purchased.

4. Recompute Problem 2 for two years later. Sales have again increased but ACF must invest more in plant and equipment to satisfy the additional demand. Assume that a further 10% increase in revenues and expenses has occurred but that to meet the sales increase another $1,000,000 in assets were bought at the beginning of the year.

5. Compile the results from Problems 2, 3, and 4. Construct brief income statements for each year. Discuss the difference that the method of depreciation makes.

6. The Acquirer Corporation takes over the Acquired Corporation utilizing pooling of interest accounting. Just prior to the merger Acquired reported assets of $150 million and debts of $50 million while Acquirer showed equity of $400 million and debts of $200 million. What would the merged balance sheet show if the purchase of Acquired was accomplished with stock?

7. Using the data in Problem 6, suppose Acquired Corporation was purchased by issuing bonds equal to the book value of its equity. How then would the merged balance sheet look?

8. Again using the data in Problem 6, suppose that purchase accounting was used for the merger and that the purchase by Acquirer utilized stock with a

market value equal to twice the book value of Acquired's total assets. This stock was distributed to Acquired's shareholders and its bondholders. How would the merged firm's balance sheet look? How does this differ from the balance sheet when pooling of interest is used?

9. The ZXV Corporation is a retailer of processors. It has annual revenues of $5,000,000, expenses of $2,000,000 (excluding cost of goods sold), and 1,000,000 shares outstanding. It sold 1,000,000 processors during the year. ZXV began the year with 300,000 processors in inventory at a cost of $2 per unit. It purchased 500,000 units in January for $2.60 per unit and another 500,000 units in February for $2.90 per unit. Assume all sales took place after these purchases and that taxes are charged at a 33% rate. Compute total and per share earnings for both LIFO and FIFO inventory accounting. Also compute ending inventory and cost of goods sold for both inventory accounting methods.

10. Estimate the per share breakup value for the ABC Land Bank. Balance sheet entries for the firm are: cash and marketable securities, $4 million; developed property (primarily shopping centers), $15 million; undeveloped land, $6 million; bank debt, $10 million. The shopping centers were built in 1971 and 1972. They have been depreciated to 60% of their initial cost. Their actual market value approximates their initial cost plus appreciation equal to the inflation rate. The land was acquired in 1967 for $4 million (equivalent to $200 per acre) with real estate taxes and capitalized interest added to arrive at its current book value. Equivalent land now sells for around $1,000 per acre. The land could, however, be developed into half-acre building lots at a cost of $9,000 per lot for construction of roadways (eliminating 10% of the property), utility hookups, grading, and so on.

11. Recalculate the per share breakup value in Problem 10, but now assume that the selling costs of the property would equal 10% of the value, that the sales would take place at a constant rate over three years, that a 12% discount rate is appropriate, and that all profits on sales are subject to a tax of 33%.

REVIEW PROJECTS

1. Obtain a detailed financial statement of a savings and loan association. Using market interest rates on GNMA mortgage passthroughs and government bond quotes as a guide, estimate the value of the S&L's loan and securities portfolio. Compare the values with its book values.

2. Obtain the financial statements of a firm that uses accelerated depreciation and another that uses straight-line depreciation. Estimate what depreciation

would be if each switched to the method used by the other. Use this estimate to show the impact on each firm's reported profits for the most recent year.

3. Find the most recent Briloff article (in *Barron's*) on the misleading accounting of a company or industry. Track the performance of its securities for three months before and three months after the article appeared. Write a report.

4. Search *Barron's* and *Forbes* for a relatively recent listing of companies with liquidation values exceeding the market value of their stocks. Track their subsequent performance relative to the market. How many have been liquidated? How many outperformed the market? How many have been acquired? How many remain "undervalued"? Write a report.

5. Select an industry that is likely to contain many companies with assets whose market values substantially exceed their reported values. Estimate the liquidation values of each company. Construct a hypothetical portfolio of the most undervalued firms. Track their performance relative to the market for the succeeding six months.

NOTES

1. L. Spacek, "Business Sources" in *Stock Market*, eds. J. Lorie and M. Hamilton (Homewood, Ill.: Irwin, 1973), 146.

2. A. Briloff, *Unaccountable Accounting* (New York: Harper & Row, 1972).

3. R. Kaplan and R. Roll, "Investor Evaluation of Accounting Information: Some Empirical Evidence," *The Journal of Business*, April 1972, 225–257.

4. S. Sunder, "Relationship Between Accounting Changes and Stock Prices: Problems of Measurement and Some Empirical Evidence," Empirical Research in Accounting: Selected Studies, 1973, Supplement to vol. 11, *Journal of Accounting Research*, 1–45.

5. A. Briloff, *The Truth About Corporate Accounting* (New York: Harper & Row, 1981).

6. Ibid, p. 93.

7. A. Briloff, "Fine Tuning, A Critical Look at Viacom's Accounting," *Barron's*, July 14, 1986, pp. 15, 30, 33.

8. H. Hong, R. Kaplan, and G. Mandelker, "Pooling vs. Purchase: The Effects of Accounting for Mergers on Stock Prices," *The Accounting Review*, January 1978, 31–47.

9. A. Briloff, 1972, 113–114.

10. Ibid, 163–171.

11. Ibid, 171–180.

12. S. Jacobs, "Heard on the Street," *The Wall Street Journal*, January 24, 1973, 39;"Western Union Corp. Sets Exchange Offer for $75 Million of 5¼% Convertible Debt," *Barron's*, June 25, 1973, 18; and R. Lenzer, "Fair Exchange? More Companies Are Swapping Bonds for Stock," *Barron's*, June 25, 1973; "SEC May Require Telling Holders of Suits Over Firms' Outside Lawyers' Accountants," *The Wall Street Journal*, July 26, 1973, 2; F. Andrews, "Accounting Board Acts to Tighten Rules on 'Profits' When Firms Buy Back Bonds," *The Wall*

Street Journal, February 3, 1975, 13; R. Greene, "Games Companies Play," *Forbes*, August 30, 1982, 43.

13. W. Bowler, "Credibility GAAP, Life Underwriters' Earnings Can't Be Taken At Face Value," *Barron's*, April 29, 1974, 9; A Briloff, "GAAP and the Life Insurance Companies," *Financial Analysts Journal*, March/April 1974, 30–38; W. Dyer, "Life Insurance Accounting Under Fire," *Financial Analysts Journal*, September/October 1974, 42–51.

14. B. Weberman, "Lieber's Love: Owning Takeover Candidates," *Forbes*, September 14, 1981, 234–235; R. Phalon, "Getting a Dollar for 50 Cents," *Forbes*, March 29, 1982, 146–148.

15. W. Beaver and S. Ryan, "How Well Do Statement No. 33 Earnings Explain Stock Returns?" *Financial Analysts Journal*, September/October 1985, 66–70.

16. B. McDonald, M. Morris, and W. Nichols, "Capitalization of Interest Costs: Security Price Reaction to SAFA No. 34 Disclosures," *Review of Business and Economic Research*, Spring 1985, 78–88.

17. Kaplan and Roll, op. cit.

18. J. Emery, "Efficient Capital Markets and the Information Content of Accounting Numbers," *Journal of Financial and Quantitative Analysis*, March 1974, 139–140; Kaplan and Roll, op. cit.

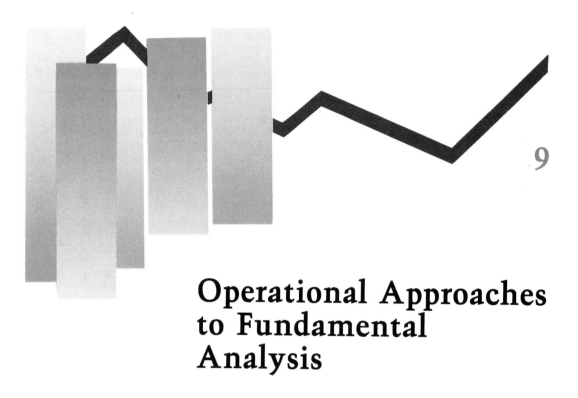

9

Operational Approaches to Fundamental Analysis

Most investments texts devote several chapters to what may be referred to as the standard approach to fundamental analysis. They thoroughly discuss methods of assessing company strengths and weaknesses. They also cover economic, industry, and company analysis in considerable detail. Identifying misvalued securities, however, is quite distinct from analyzing a firm's prospects. Practical investing requires approaches to investment selection that are tangible, relevant, and cost effective. Although a full-blown analysis of the economy, industry, and firm may be useful at times, most investors are unable to undertake such an effort. Even those with the necessary time, skills, and resources for the effort require approaches that allow them to winnow down their lists to the worthwhile prospects. Thus shortcuts are needed to allow the analyst to identify potentially attractive investments on a first-pass basis. That is, investors need methods for screening a long list of stocks and selecting those that deserve closer scrutiny. More detailed analysis may or may not be undertaken on the narrowed down list.

This chapter therefore surveys operational approaches to fundamental analysis. Background information on such approaches has been derived from both the academic journals and the financial press.

First, we consider a variety of narrow fundamental approaches. *Forbes* magazine, *Value Line*, and several other periodicals publish lists of interesting stocks that may well constitute a useful starting point. Similarly, many analysts recommend stocks with low PEs. Others prefer companies with rapid growth records

238

(even if that means paying a high price relative to earnings). Still others concentrate on small firms, low-priced stocks, R&D intensive firms, or potential takeover candidates. Thus groups of stocks may be screened for those with such characteristics. Avoiding firms with appreciable bankruptcy risks and focusing attention on out-of-favor stocks are yet other suggested screening techniques. Additionally, some services offer specialized investment advice and some analysts particularly recommend firms that are stockholder oriented as opposed to management oriented. Each of these characteristics may be used to screen out unattractive stocks and screen in those that may be worth a closer look.

Next, the investment implications of PE models are explored. Such models may help investors identify stocks whose PEs are out of line with those with similar characteristics (risks, growth rates, dividend yields, and so on). Finally, several integrated methods to investment selection are discussed. Such methods are based on a simultaneous analysis of a number of different selection criteria. All of these approaches are designed to start with a relatively long list of stocks and end up with a much shorter list of potentially attractive investments. Note, however, that nothing assures the realization of that goal.

NARROW FUNDAMENTAL ANALYSIS APPROACHES

Forbes and Other Lists

Lists of stocks having something unusual in common appear regularly in *Forbes*. Two examples in the previous chapter were tax-loss carryforwards and high breakup values. The discussion that accompanies the lists generally implies that an appreciable number of the listings are undervalued or otherwise attractive. For example, *Forbes* has since 1952 annually listed firms that sell for a small fraction of the potential values of their underlying assets. The criteria for *loaded laggard* membership varies over time but always includes firms that are underpriced relative to their tangible assets.

The original loaded laggards are now called *net-nets*. The procedure for identifying them is as follows: Start with the firm's current assets and subtract current liabilities. The result, of course, is working capital. The firm's long-term debt is then subtracted from this working capital figure. The remainder is the amount of liquid assets the firm would have after paying off both short- and long-term liabilities. Now divide this amount by the firm's number of shares outstanding. The result is in the per share net (of short-term liabilities) net (of long-term liabilities) liquid assets of the company. If the firm's stock sells for less than this amount, it is called a net-net. Note that the firm's long-term assets do not figure into the analysis. These assets are viewed as a bonus. Net-nets could use their short-term assets (assuming that these assets can be liquidated at their book values) to pay off all liabilities, have enough value to repurchase all shares at their current market price, and still have some short- and all long-term assets left. Some net-nets and loaded laggards will outperform the market. Others, however, will stay on the list for years. Determining which stocks are truly undervalued is up to the investor.

Loaded laggards are compiled only once a year. Most *Forbes* issues, however, contain at least one list of interesting stocks. Examples include: stocks with low

TABLE 9.1   Stock Characteristics Covered in *Value Line* Lists

Timely Stocks I (ranked #1 for next 12-month performance)
Timely Stocks II (ranked #2 for next 12-month performance)
Conservative Stocks I (ranked #1 for safety)
Conservative Stocks II (ranked #2 for safety)
High Yielding Stocks (estimated year-ahead dividends)
High Three- to Five-Year Appreciation Potential
Biggest Free Cash Flow Generators
Best Performing Stocks (past 13 weeks)
Worst Performing Stocks (past 13 weeks)
Widest Discount from Book Value
Lowest PE
Highest PE
Highest Annual Total Returns (three to five years)
Highest Estimated Three- to Five-Year Dividend Yield
Highest Percentage Earned on Capital
Untimely Stocks (ranked #5 for next 12-month performance)
Highest Yielding Nonutility Stocks
High Growth Stocks
Stocks Trading at a Discount from Their Liquidation Values

PEs and high growth rates, former institutional favorites, companies with dividend reinvestment plans, companies that are expected to emerge from bankruptcy with big profit potentials, potential growth companies, stocks disliked by the experts, cash-rich and cash-poor companies, high-yield utilities, stocks that *Forbes* analysts expect to show substantial earnings increases, and emerging growth companies in a difficult market environment.[1]

The prices of most stocks, including those on *Forbes* lists, are likely to be relatively close to their intrinsic values. That is, most stocks are probably priced in a market that processes the public information on them efficiently. Indeed, some lists may just by chance contain a below-average number of undervalued situations. Stocks that appear undervalued by one criterion (such as tangible assets) may be accurately priced relative to a more important criterion (such as prospects for growth or survival). If identifying undervalued stocks were easy, we could all be rich. Nonetheless, *Forbes* and similar lists may very well provide investors with a useful starting point. *Value Line*, for example, compiles weekly lists for each of the characteristics shown in Table 9.1.

Low-PE Stocks versus Growth Stocks

Many lists are based on one of two concepts: PE and growth. Indeed, investment analysts have long debated the relative merits of low-PE and growth stocks. A firm whose profits are expected to grow rapidly will command a high price relative to its current earnings. One with less bright prospects will generally command a lower

PE. The PE ratio equation (introduced in Chapter 4 and discussed again in Chapter 7) illustrates the relation between the PE and expected growth:

$$PE = p/(r - g)$$

where:

p = payout ratio
r = appropriate discount rate (which varies with risk)
g = expected growth rate

Clearly, PEs should differ with the firms' prospects (dividend payout, risk, and expected growth). Growth expectations play a key role. Consider, for example, a company with a payout of .5 and an appropriate discount rate of 13%. An expected growth rate of 5% would correspond to a PE of 6.25. In contrast, if an 8% or 10% growth rate is expected, the corresponding PE would be 10 or 16.7, respectively. If this is put in terms of price per share, a company whose EPS is expected to be $1 next year would be priced at 6¼, 10, or 16⅝ depending upon whether its long-term expected growth rate was 5%, 8%, or 10%. Thus, for a given payout and discount rate, differing growth expectations can have a dramatic impact on how the market prices a stock relative to its earnings.

No one argues with the arithmetic. High growth expectations do justify higher PEs. The debate over low-PE versus growth stock centers on how well the market prices securities relative to their actual potentials. According to such well-known fundamental analysts as Graham and Templeton, the market frequently goes to extremes. These acknowledged experts believe that the market tends to overestimate the growth prospects and underestimate the risks of many stocks (especially the highly touted growth stocks). As a result, the market accords them even higher PEs than their fundamentals warrant. The stocks of less exciting companies, in contrast, may be viewed by the market as having less attractive prospects than they deserve. Stocks that the market views too pessimistically would then end up with unrealistically low PEs. Once the market realizes the true potentials of these stocks, the prices of low-PE stock should rise at a faster rate than the market averages whereas the high-PE stocks should do less well. Those who accept this line of reasoning tend to recommend low-PE stocks. They prefer a portfolio that is heavily weighted toward low-PE stocks and largely avoids stocks with high PEs.

T. Rowe Price and other growth-stock advocates, in contrast, have contended that stocks with rapid growth potentials are attractive investments even at relatively high prices. A high current PE may not seem overpriced relative to future earnings whereas low PEs may accurately reflect poor potentials. The two views (low-PE and growth stock) have alternated in popularity. Although each viewpoint has some merit, the key question is not, Can a high PE be justified? The question is, Are the PEs on many so-called growth stocks justified?

High PEs can decline dramatically. For example, the Dow's composite PE rose from 12.1 on December 31, 1957, to 24.2 on September 29, 1961. It then fell to 16.2 nine months later. Since that time, the multiple has generally stayed under 20 and has often been below 10. In retrospect, the high growth expectations for the soaring 1960s were unrealistic. Moreover, many individual multiples were hit hard during this period. The stock market crash of October 1987 also took place when the Dow was at a relatively high level (21.5). Do these experiences hold any lessons for the future? The arguments need closer scrutiny.

Advocates of growth stock recommend investments in companies with outstanding past records and/or growth potentials. They do not generally seek out stocks with high multiples. They are, however, quite prepared to pay a high price (relative to current earnings) when strong future growth is anticipated. Their arithmetic can appear quite persuasive. Earnings that grow at 20% will double in approximately four years. Should the multiple remain constant, the price will also double over the same four-year period.

Those who advocate stocks with low multiples do not question the arithmetic of growth stock proponents, but rather their implicit assumptions. As some have put it, "Very high multiples often discount not the future but the hereafter." Rapid current growth rates may simply be an anomaly. Such growth rates are extremely unlikely to continue for very many years into the future. One well-known growth stock, IBM, exhibited very rapid growth during the 1950s and into the early 1960s. In many of those years it grew at rates of 20% or more. Some analysts seem quite willing (at least implicitly) to project growth rates such as this far into the future.

Writing in 1963 Malkiel noted that, if IBM were to grow 20% per year from 1960 to 1989, its total revenues would exceed the 1962 gross national product. GNP was $560 billion in 1962. This sum compares with actual IBM sales of $54 billion in 1987, a 5.8% increase over 1986. Clearly IBM's post-1960 growth slowed, as it had to do. Were its sales to have reached $560 billion in 1989, IBM as an economic entity would have represented an intolerably large fraction of the U.S. economy. Its size would, for example, be comparable to the entire U.S. defense industry. No independent-minded national government could allow any single firm to account for such a large part of the country's economy.

Although IBM is a sizable company, many of the other traditional high-multiple stocks such as Xerox, 3M, Kodak, Disney, Avon, and Polaroid are also large. Moreover, even medium-sized firms would grow to a large fraction of the economy if an abnormally high growth rate continued for several decades. If nothing else put a brake on growth, government action such as an antitrust-based divestiture (e.g., AT&T's breakup) probably would.

Almost always, however, the factors that allow a firm or industry to grow rapidly begin to fade before governmental action becomes necessary. When a small entity grows faster than the economy, its overall impact remains relatively small and isolated. In contrast, as a larger entity exhibits an above-average growth rate, it must expand at the clear and identifiable expense of other economic entities. These competitors will fight to maintain their existing shares of the economy. Firms and industries with attractive products and talented managers will eventually find themselves locked in head-to-head combat with other firms and industries whose assets are comparable to their own. Rapid growth is likely for firms that have clear advantages over their rivals. Rapid growth is much less likely when the rivals are comparably equipped to compete.

Malkiel conducted a study of high growth, high multiple stocks. The reasoning just given led him to assume that the growth rates of heretofore high growth companies would eventually decline to about the national average.[2] Such an assumption has an interesting impact on the application of the PE formula. A firm now growing at an above-average rate g^* should be expected eventually to have its growth rate slow to, or perhaps drop below, the economy-wide rate g'. Solving the PE formula with g* would produce a PE that is too high. Similarly, using g' would yield a value for the PE that is too low. In fact, the appropriate g value to use with the formula will lie between g* and g'. The longer the growth rate is expected to remain high, the closer the appropriate value will be to g*. On the other hand, the quicker g* declines to g', the closer the appropriate g value is to g'.

Much of the fluctuation in stock prices reflects a change in the PE ratio. The change in PE ratio in turn reflects changing views within the market regarding the firm's growth potential. Let us therefore examine more closely just how much differing growth expectations can affect PE ratios.

To focus on the impact of growth, assume in the following examples that the payout ratio p is kept at .5 and the appropriate discount rate is 12% for both the economy and individual stocks. An economy-wide growth rate of 7% (3% real and 4% inflation) would produce an average PE of .5/(.12 − .07) = 10. If a particular company's g is 8%, its PE would be 12.5. A g of 9% produces a PE of 16.7 while a g of 10% implies a PE of 25. Should g be as high as 11%, the PE would rise to 50. Thus relatively small changes in the expected growth rate g can have a dramatic impact on the PE ratio. This impact is particularly great when the PE is already relatively large. A more realistic example would take account of the tendency for higher values for g to correspond to lower payouts and greater risk premiums (and thus higher discount rates). Nonetheless, the basic relationship between high expected growth rates and high PEs remains.

Advocates of low PEs note that stock prices rise dramatically when both earnings and multiples increase. Quite possibly a multiple may more easily increase from 5 to 10 than from 10 to 20 and will have an easier time growing from 10 to 20 than from 20 to 40. That is, the market may well become more nervous about the price of a stock as its PE rises. Thus low-PE stocks may well have a better chance of achieving truly outstanding performances than high-PE stocks, which may be more likely to be fully priced already. Suppose, for example, a company selling initially at a PE of 5 experiences per share earnings growth of 20% per year for 10 years. Its earnings will be six times as high as when it started. Such an earnings growth is likely to lead to an increase in the PE multiple. Rapid past growth often leads to expectations of rapid future growth. If the PE of this company doubles, its stock will sell for more than 12 times its earlier price.

The advocates of low multiple stocks further contend that high multiple stocks are particularly vulnerable to disappointing news. For example, suppose a growth stock currently earns $2 per share and sells for 50 (PE of 25). If the following year it only earns $1.50, a continuation of its PE of 25 would correspond to a price of 37.50. On the other hand, if the poor earnings led to lower growth expectations and a lower PE, the price decline would be much steeper. Thus, for example, a fall to a PE of 10 would imply a price of 15. Clearly, disappointing earnings can severely wound a stock that had sold for a high multiple. Certainly such disappointments can happen. We would like to know how often they actually do happen. Do high-PE stocks often perform poorly or are they about as likely to outperform the market as to underperform it? Past history provides some guidance.

One-Decision Stocks and the Nifty Fifty. The early 1970s saw the rise and fall of the *one-decision stock* concept. According to a then-popular view, certain high-quality stocks should, like Manhattan real estate, be bought but not sold. Rapid past growth led many investors to expect above-average performance for the foreseeable future. Institutional investors (mutual funds, pension funds, insurance companies, and banks) scrambled to put away additional shares of 50 or so one-decision companies.

The "foreseeable future" lasted about a year. The one-decision (or top tier) stocks eventually fell dramatically toward the end of the 1974 stock market crash. Avon dropped from a 1973 high of 140 to 19, Disney from 121 to 19, and Polaroid from 143 to 14. Somewhat less dramatically, Xerox fell from 170 to 54 and IBM from 365 to 150. By comparison, the Dow Jones Industrial Average declined from 1051 to 576, about a 47% drop. Clearly, the one-decision stocks fully experienced the ravages of the 1974 decline.

During the nine years that followed the purchase of the "nifty fifty" in 1973, the vast majority failed to regain their "one-decision highs" (Table 9.2). Although most of the companies had done well, their stocks had not. Over that same 1973–1982 period the popular market averages had advanced modestly. The market was at relatively low point in 1982. No doubt these stocks did better in subsequent trading. Nonetheless, their extremely high market prices in 1973 made them very poor investments. Table 9.2 points clearly to the dangers of high-PE stocks. Such demonstrations, however, may or may not reveal an accurate picture. We need to examine what has been learned about PE and performance from academic research.

Relative PE Ratios

How well do low-PE stocks do in general? Several filter tests point to the selection value of low-PE ratio investment strategy.[3] Breen concluded that "low price–earnings multiples, measured either relative to the whole population, or to industry classification, when combined with a control on average past growth in earnings give portfolio performance which in most years exceeds that of randomly selected securities." Latane and Tuttle, using seasonally adjusted data, found that 25 low-PE stocks had a six-month return (ignoring commissions) of 6.6% over the 1962–1965 period compared to 3.5% for 25 high-PE stocks. For unadjusted data the low-PE stocks returned 15.6% compared to 4% for the high-PE group. Similar results were found by a number of other researchers. Levy and Kripotos' study failed to support the hypothesis of low-PE advocates, however.[4] Levy also analyzed the resistance of low-PE stocks to market declines. He concluded that low price-earning stocks are resistant to short-term declines; however, the relative advantage dissipates significantly as the downtrend is prolonged. It also disappears during reversals of six months duration.[5]

Reasons for Conflicting Results.   Several factors may explain the differences in PE-subsequent performance results. First, some researchers employed more than one filter: Breen used earnings growth and Jones examined quarterly earnings reports. Thus their results may not be primarily due to the PE ratio screen. Second, low-PE ratio tests have usually used the Compustat data tapes. Compustat assembles its list of firms based on their size and importance at the end of the period of coverage. Thus the 1988 Compustat tape consists of firms that had reached the

TABLE 9.2 The Nifty Fifty in 1982

Company	P/E ratio 1972	P/E ratio recent	Stock price range since 1972	Stock price recent	Stock price change since 1972	Earnings per share latest 12 months	Earnings per share change since 1972	Return on equity	9-year real return
Amer Hosp Supply	50	12	55⅜–18¾	39¼	–19.9%	$3.08	211.1%	14.5%	–58.5%
AMP	51	15	62½–20⅜	48⅜	13.5	3.75	316.7	24.8	–37.5
Automatic Data Proc	76	15	31¾– 5¼	23¼	1.8	1.55	434.5	17.4	–45.1
Avery Intl	64	10	51½–12¼	22¾	–47.1	2.95	227.8	15.1	–64.6
Avon Products	65	8	139¾–18⅝	29⅞	–78.2	3.66	69.4	27.1	–84.4
Bandag	59	9	43 –10⅛	24	–31.4	2.60	306.3	18.4	–61.1
CR Bard	52	15	42 – 9⅝	30⅝	–18.3	2.04	164.9	13.9	–57.2
Baxter Travenol Labs	78	17	34½–12⅛	33¾	21.1	2.15	451.3	16.2	–41.3
Black & Decker	50	11	42⅜–14¼	14¾	–59.0	1.34	88.7	16.6	–75.9
Burroughs	48	9	126⅜–27⅛	31	–71.5	3.58	52.3	3.8	–82.8
Clorox	41	6	53 – 5½	11	–76.3	1.80	68.2	14.8	–82.1
Coca-Cola	47	8	75 –22¼	31⅜	–57.7	3.58	125.2	21.1	–69.4
Colonial Penn Group	65	14	70 –12⅝	16⅝	–73.9	1.23	–5.4	14.9	–84.8
Damon Corp	53	30	70⅜– 3⅝	7¼	–88.1	d0.13	NM	4.3	–75.8
Digital Equipment	59	12	113¼–15⅛	86½	182.8	7.49	1,398.0	17.2	27.9
Walt Disney	81	14	110¼–15½	48½	–54.1	3.45	167.4	13.3	–75.9
Dr Pepper	62	9	30 – 6½	12⅛	–54.0	1.43	232.6	25.5	–70.4
Eastman Kodak	48	9	151¾–41⅛	71¾	–51.6	7.89	132.7	20.2	–70.3
Jack Eckerd	52	10	31⅞– 6¾	21⅛	–23.9	2.22	335.3	18.1	–51.6
Electronic Data Sys	49	16	32¾– 5⅜	22⅞	–15.3	1.47	177.4	24.7	–40.9
Emery Air Freight	62	8	37½–11⅜	11⅝	–61.0	1.46	175.5	30.6	–72.8
Fluor	48	9	71 – 3⅝	25½	246.7	2.83	1,786.7	26.3	119.0
Hewlett-Packard	61	16	53⅞–11½	40¼	86.1	2.55	628.6	19.2	–13.7
Intl Flavors/Fragrances	75	13	49⅜–16⅝	19⅛	–66.0	1.42	140.7	21.1	–74.7
Johnson & Johnson	61	17	44⅜–20¾	36½	–16.1	2.17	201.4	18.7	–55.3
K mart	54	8	51⅛–15⅛	15⅝	–68.0	1.88	88.0	11.5	–82.5
Eli Lilly	46	11	92½–32⅝	54	–32.2	4.76	157.3	20.3	–58.9
Longs Drug Stores	49	9	42¾–15¼	25¾	–34.4	2.79	236.1	17.4	–60.6
Marion Labs	46	25	57¾–11⅛	24¾	–44.7	0.95	0.0	12.5	–65.2
Marriott	56	11	47 – 5¾	34⅜	6.6	3.21	483.6	22.7	–47.7
Masco	46	11	42¼– 9½	35¾	26.3	3.39	413.6	20.7	–32.2
McDonald's	85	9	77⅜–21¼	59½	–22.0	6.54	595.7	21.1	–59.0
Merck & Co	45	15	103 –46⅝	81	–9.1	5.36	169.3	23.6	–46.2
MGIC Investment*	83	13	97⅞– 6⅛	50	–47.8	4.02	211.6	17.8	–72.1
Minn Mng & Mfg	40	11	91⅝–43	54¾	–36.1	5.74	164.5	21.7	–61.6
Natl Semiconductor	49	19	51½– 4⅛	19⅛	153.0	1.01	381.0	18.1	14.6
NCH	55	7	52¾–12¾	15⅛	–65.2	2.08	136.4	17.8	–81.1
Natomas	61	5	45¾– 3⅞	21	132.3	4.23	2,921.4	28.0	–64.3
Perkin-Elmer	47	15	36⅜– 7⅝	26⅜	37.9	1.76	351.3	18.7	–27.6
Polaroid	90	11	149½–14⅛	19¾	–84.3	1.87	43.8	9.0	–91.1
Ponderosa System	69	8	86¼– 3⅝	12⅛	–85.3	1.45	3.6	4.0	–91.8
Rite Aid	64	10	42½– 1⅞	27¾	–23.7	2.78	308.8	20.4	–57.9
Schering-Plough	50	8	87⅝–24⅞	28¼	–58.8	3.31	129.9	20.8	–76.0
Schlumberger	49	12	87⅛– 6⅜	50⅛	320.6	4.00	1,500.0	35.4	133.7
Simplicity Pattern	53	19	58⅞– 6⅛	9¼	–82.8	0.50	–53.3	8.3	–87.6
Sony	54	13	26⅛– 3½	16½	5.7	1.23	296.8	24.7	–45.6
Standard Brands Paint	52	9	56¾–18⅝	24¼	–55.1	2.79	173.5	16.3	–34.3
Texas Instruments	46	15	150¾–58⅝	78⅞	–13.3	5.38	147.9	19.9	–53.8
Wal-Mart Stores	52	18	43⅞– 1⅞	39¼	355.1	2.14	1,088.9	26.2	138.2
Xerox	48	5	171⅞–37⅜	40¾	–72.7	7.08	124.1	18.1	–84.3

*Baldwin-United merger offer at $52 a share. d: deficit. NM: not meaningful.

Source: Wilshire Associates

Source: M. Barnfather, "What Price Quality," *Forbes*, March 1, 1982, pp. 114–115. Reprinted by permission of *Forbes* Magazine, March 1, 1982. © Forbes Inc., 1982.

threshold for inclusion by 1987. As such, the Compustat sample suffers from what is called *selection bias*. Because only firms that grow to Compustat-size are included, successful firms having low beginning PEs are overrepresented. Omitting a disproportionate share of unsuccessful stocks with low PEs at the beginning of the period overemphasizes the importance of successful stocks that had low PEs at the beginning of the test period. Third, because low-PE stocks tend to be riskier than high-PE stocks, ceteris paribus, their apparently higher returns may simply reflect a reward for risk taking. Fourth, PE analysis relies heavily on the method of comparison. The results of those analysts who first get a "feel" for the data by experimenting with several different comparisons may fit the tested data better than future reality.

The controversy over PE performance died down in the mid-1970s, only to be revived by Basu.[6] To overcome some of the objections to the earlier work, tests were based on portfolios of different PE levels and control groups of corresponding risk level. Performance was measured from a point well after the initial earnings announcements. An extensive period and a large number of stocks were included. The results were uniformly favorable: The lowest PE portfolio outperformed the highest by 7%. Although the issue remained controversial, Basu's results seemed to suggest the usefulness of a low-PE selection strategy.

Combining PE Ratios with Other Factors

Several studies have examined the PE ratio combined with other factors.[7] Bidwell and Riddle found PE ratios and a measure of abnormal quarterly earnings useful screens both separately and together. Similarly Goodman and Peavy reported that the ratio of company to industry PE ratios was significantly related to excess returns. Firms with low relative PEs generally outperformed those with higher PEs. Most of the relevant recent work, however, has examined the relative roles of PEs and firm size.

Firm Size.   Much of the evidence suggests that low-PE stocks tend to be underpriced. Nonetheless, a more basic relationship may be at work. For example, a disproportionate number of low-PE stocks may be the issues of relatively small companies. Suppose that the stocks of relatively small companies tend to outperform the market. Size, not PE, might then be the true factor explaining the apparent effect of a low PE.[8] Indeed, Reinganum found that portfolios selected on both PE and firm size tended to generate abnormal returns (above the risk-adjusted market level). The PE effect largely disappeared, however, when size was controlled. Similarly, Banz found (positive) abnormal returns for small firms going back at least five years. He also reported that most of the difference in returns occurred for firms of relatively small size whereas mean returns for average and large firms differed little. In a study covering the 1931–1979 period, Lustig and Leinbach found significantly positive abnormal returns for small capitalization firms but not for larger firms.

Each author hypothesized that the small firm effect was due to a misspecification of the capital asset pricing model (CAPM). CAPM formed the basis for adjusting returns for risk. Lustig and Leinbach, for example, contend that the

Investments in Perspective

The designation low-PE growth stocks sounds like a contradiction in terms. Yet the basic strategy for having the best of both worlds requires stocks with low PEs and relatively attractive growth prospects. The simple rule of thumb is to seek out stocks whose growth rate is expected to exceed their PE. A *Forbes* article included a list of such stocks.

Statistical Spotlight

Buy a stock, an old rule of thumb has it, if its P/E ratio is less than the growth rate. What stocks meet that criterion?

The price of growth

By Michael Ozanian

HIGH-GROWTH companies are worth a premium. But how much of a premium? Limited Inc., the specialty retailer, with a 69% growth rate in earnings per share over the past five years, is trading at 29 times its recent earnings, compared with the average multiple of 22 for the market. Does that make Limited too expensive?

Philip Morris is 16 times trailing earnings and enjoys a five-year 17% annual growth in earnings per share. Is it a better buy? How about Tyco Laboratories (recent growth, 10%; price-to-earnings multiple, 34)?

There is a simple, mechanical rule for comparing growth to P/E ratios. Like all mechanical rules, it can provide only a first pass at screening for stocks. But there is some arithmetic validity to it.

The rule, as stated by Anne E. Gregory, publisher of the *Merrill Lynch Market Letter*: "Companies that have P/E multiples at substantial discounts to their projected earnings-per-share growth rates are often undervalued."

A refinement of the rule is to add the dividend yield of the stock to the growth rate to get an overall figure akin to a total return. A stock with earnings expanding at 10% annually and paying a 5% dividend is about as good as one expanding earnings at 15% annually and paying no dividend. That's because the owner of the former stock can reinvest the dividend and increase his shares by 5% a year. Assuming no change in the P/Es, either stock will provide a total annual return of about 15%.

A simple mathematical exercise will show why Gregory's formula should work—if a few critical assumptions turn out right. First, assume that the market's average P/E multiple remains at its recent level, near 22. Then, assume that the average stock delivers an annual growth rate of 11.4%, as currently projected in consensus earnings estimates. Add to that growth rate the 2.5% yield on stocks, and the total return on the market would be 14% a year.

The question now is, how long does an expensive stock have to keep up its accelerated growth in order to deliver a total return as good as the market's 14%? Not very long. If a growth stock comes through with anticipated earnings gains for 3 years—after which it levels off and trades at the average multiple of only 22 times earnings—then it's a good buy today if it fits Gregory's criterion. For example, if Limited is able to increase earnings at 29% a year for 3 years, after which it descends to average growth and an average P/E ratio, then it's a buy today at 29 times earnings.

Remarkably, the 3-year rule works for any P/E on the growth stock. A P/E of 100 would be justified if a 100% growth rate were certain to continue for 3 years.

The trouble with this approach, of course, is the assumption that a past growth rate will continue or that a projected one will materialize. That kind of assumption would have worked well in the past for Limited buyers. Limited's stock is up almost 47,000% in the past 13 years. The retailer kept growing and growing and still hasn't stopped—yet. But then there's Subaru of America. For five years, until 1986, it expanded earnings per share at a 33% annual rate. Then it hit a wall—a declining dollar and depressed demands for its import-

Price-to-growth ratio

How much should investors pay to get higher growth? An old rule of thumb says to buy a stock whose price-to-earnings multiple is lower than its growth rate. By that measure, these firms would be buys. They all have trailing P/Es at least one-fifth lower than their four-year earnings growth rate. To eliminate erratic or leveraged highfliers, we also required share earnings of at least $1 over the 12 months, trailing five-year earnings growth rates of at least 10%, and debt-to-equity ratios below 100%. Earnings projections are from Value Line.

		Earnings per share			Price-to-earnings		
Company/*business*	Price	latest 12 months	1987 est	projected growth*	latest 12 months	1987 est	Debt/ equity
Adams-Millis/textiles	11⅝	$1.32	$1.40	15%	8.8	8.3	87%
Atlantic Research/aerospace	24¾	1.91	2.16	19	13.0	11.5	45
Bundy/metal fabricating	27⅞	2.23	2.85†	17	12.5	9.8	43
Circuit City Stores/consumer electronics	35	1.72	2.27	26	20.3	15.4	68
Dillard Dept Stores/retail	46¼	2.44	2.91	24	19.0	15.9	56
Dunkin' Donuts/donut shops	26¼	1.70	1.74	20	15.4	15.1	32
Dynatech/precision instruments	30¼	1.98	2.27	21	15.3	13.3	18
E-Systems/electrical equipment	34¾	1.88	2.07	22	18.5	16.8	18
Fleming Cos/food wholesaling	40¼	1.82	2.73	27	22.1	14.7	57
Florida Rock Inds/building materials	23	2.21	NA	15	10.4	NA	15

*Annual growth to 1990-92. †1988 estimate. NA: not available or not applicable.
Sources: *Institutional Brokers Estimate System (IBES); Value Line Investment Services via Lotus One Source.*

Price-to-growth ratio

Company/*business*	Price	Earnings per share: latest 12 months	Earnings per share: 1987 est	projected growth*	Price-to-earnings: latest 12 months	Price-to-earnings: 1987 est	Debt/ equity
Gotäas-Larson/ocean transport	28¼	$2.27	$2.67	19%	12.4	10.6	97%
Hasbro/toys	22½	1.47	1.83	22	15.3	12.3	22
Heilig-Meyers/home furnishings	26¼	1.36	1.75	25	19.3	15.0	75
House of Fabrics/specialty retail	16¼	1.07	1.33	21	15.2	12.2	14
James River/paper products	32⅛	2.00	2.59	23	16.1	12.4	86
Kaman/aerospace	29¼	1.99	2.10	19	14.7	13.9	90
Magna Intl/auto parts	16⅞	1.78	NA	22	9.5	NA	81
McDonnell Douglas/aerospace, defense	76	6.79	7.95	25	11.2	9.6	27
Pic 'N' Save/specialty retail	22¼	1.06	1.35	28	21.0	16.5	1
Rhodes/home furnishings	17⅞	1.36	1.65	20	13.1	10.8	44
Rockwell Intl/aerospace, defense	26¼	2.31	2.45	15	11.4	10.7	20
Rohr Industries/aerospace	32½	1.81	2.36†	31	18.0	13.8	48
Roper/motors, appliances	28⅛	2.35	3.09	14	12.0	9.1	80
Rose's Stores/retail	14¼	1.19	1.47	29	12.0	9.7	44
Savannah Foods & Inds/food processing	28½	1.71	2.00	31	16.7	14.3	62
A.O. Smith/auto parts	22⅝	2.43	2.45	15	9.3	9.2	30
Tab Products/office equipment	17⅛	1.00	1.37	23	17.1	12.5	2
Telex/computer equipment	67½	5.40	6.36	15	12.5	10.6	38
Toro/power motors	20⅜	1.50	1.79†	19	13.6	11.4	37
Van Dorn/containers	36½	2.10	2.35	23	17.4	15.5	18
Wausau Paper Mills/specialty paper prods	28¾	2.55	2.95†	14	11.3	9.7	47
Western Digital/computer equipment	23⅞	1.78	3.00†	20	13.4	8.0	70
Whirlpool/appliances	36¾	2.63	2.73	19	14.0	13.5	13

*Annual growth to 1990-92 †1988 estimate. NA: not available or not applicable.
Sources: *Institutional Brokers Estimate System* (IBES); *Value Line Investment Services via Lotus One Source*

ed cars. In the most recent quarter Subaru was in the red. The stock is off 70% from its high.

Another hazard: The market as a whole is rather expensive by such historical measures as price to earnings and price to book value. There's no assurance that the market's P/E of 22 will remain through 1991. If stocks go down, growth stocks will probably go down further. They tend to be riskier and suffer the most in bear markets.

The analysis above of Gregory's formula doesn't explicitly allow for risk. If it did, it would demand that the growth stock do much better than the market's hypothetical 14% return. After all, if growth stocks can run into ugly surprises like Subaru's, then the investor should be rewarded with a premium return when the growth does come through.

That said, a case can be made for betting on growth stocks now. The smaller ones have been left behind in this blue-chip-dominated bull market. The average P/E on T. Rowe Price's New Horizons Fund is currently 1.3 times the market's average P/E of 22. That looks expensive, but it's below the fund's relative P/E of more than 2, reached in 1983.

Preston Athey, who manages portfolios of emerging growth stocks for T. Rowe Price, believes strong corporate profits will cause many growth stocks to post big gains. "True growth stocks will do well because we're in an earnings-driven market right now and we're no longer going to get P/E expansion," he says. ■

Source: M. Ozanian, "The Price of Growth," *Forbes*, October 5, 1987, pp. 232–234. Reprinted by permission, © Forbes Inc., 1987.

positive abnormal returns may simply be a reward for the extra effort of analyzing small firms. Roll argued that the apparent abnormal returns of small firm portfolios may be due to underestimating their risks. Reinganum, however, found that underestimates of small firm betas could account for no more than part of the computed excess returns. Similarly, James and Edmister found trading activity (a measure of marketability) to be related to firm size. Trading activity was not, however, the underlying cause of the small firm effect. Still other researchers reported that the magnitude of the small firm effect was reduced but could not be fully explained away when adjustments were made for the impacts of risk premium, tax effects, benchmark error, incorrect assumptions about investor risk aversion, nonsynchronous trading, or earnings yield.

Analyst Neglect.   The abnormal returns of small firms could be due to either of two reasons: (1) superior performance relative to their fundamentals (current profitability, apparent growth potential, current leverage, per share book value, and so on) or (2) underpricing relative to those fundamentals.

The evidence of pervasive scale economies argues against small firms consistently managing their assets more effectively than large firms. On the other hand, most institutional investors prefer to invest in large firms. They can make meaningful investments in large firms without having an undue effect on the stock price. Similarly, analysts tend to concentrate on larger firms and thus draw attention to such stocks. This disproportionate attention of institutions and analysts may well cause the issues of large firms to be overpriced relative to the rest of the market. Indeed, Arbel and Strebel find that stocks that are ignored by analysts (whether large or small) tend to outperform the more closely followed issues.[9] Accordingly, a number of mutual funds such as the Acorn Fund have sought to exploit this small firm/neglected firm effect by assembling portfolios of such companies. Still another factor may be at work.

The Low Price Effect.   The results of several studies imply that stocks with low per share prices tend to generate returns above the market averages.[10] Moreover, this low price effect may well be stronger than (and may even swamp) both the PE and the size effects. Exactly why low-priced stocks seem to perform so well is subject to much debate. Low-priced stocks are generally believed to be more risky than the average stock. Thus their higher average return may reflect greater risk. Still, the returns of such stocks continue to be higher when standard risk adjustment procedures are applied. Perhaps low-priced stocks are even more risky than their estimated betas imply. In particular, they may contain a substantially greater amount of nonmarket, and thus diversifiable, risk. We have already seen that, capital market theory notwithstanding, nonmarket risk is generally accorded a premium. That is, stocks with high levels of nonmarket risks are priced to offer higher expected returns than otherwise similar stocks with lower levels of nonmarket risk.

Second, low-priced stocks are also more expensive to trade. Commissions tend to be set on the basis of both the dollar value and the number of shares traded. A given dollar amount invested in a low-priced stock will correspond to more shares. Thus low-priced stocks typically incur higher commissions as a percentage of the amount invested than equivalent size trades of higher priced stocks. Also the bid–ask spread of low-priced stocks tends to be relatively high. Spreads cannot be less than ⅛ on most stocks. The NYSE, for example, will not allow finer gradations for quotes on stocks priced at one dollar per share or more. One-eighth represents a substantial percentage for a stock priced at 2 or so. Stocks that are more expensive to trade probably need to offer higher expected returns to attract investors.

A third possible factor is the general aversion of many investors, especially institutional investors, to low-priced shares. The perceived quality of a stock is thought to be associated with the level of its per share price. If many investors shun a significant segment of the stock market, that group of stocks may tend to be underpriced. The financial performance of some of the group will eventually lead them to achieve quality status and institutional acceptance. Such stocks will produce attractive returns.

The tendency for low-priced stocks to generate above-market returns thus has a number of possible explanations. Nonetheless, the generally favorable performance of low-priced stocks suggests that investors should at least consider their merits when they seem otherwise attractive. Nonmarket risk can be virtually eliminated by careful diversification. The cost of trading is less important to those who expect to hold for a relatively long time. The higher cost of trading is more than offset by (hopefully) higher returns when the investments are held for a number of years. Perceived quality is irrelevant to a careful, well-diversified investor who is focusing on return.

The Price/R&D Ratio

Long-term stock market favorites such as IBM, Xerox, and Polaroid epitomize the growth potential of technologically derived new products. The popularity of smaller newer high-technology companies such as Apple and Genentech illustrates the market's search for a future Xerox. Because most new technologies require extensive research, Burgen of Dean Witter has suggested using the ratio of stock prices to per share R&D spending as an index of growth potential.[11] Firms have been required to disclose such expenditures since 1974. Burgen claims that relative R&D spending is an excellent first screen when combined with other fundamental factors. Careful statistical analysis is needed to confirm (or disprove) the hypothesized relationship, however.

The R&D/profits relationship for seven manufacturing industries (chemicals, electrical equipment, paper, mechanical equipment, nonferrous metals, petroleum refining, and drugs) were studied by this author. The results indicated a significant causal relationship from R&D to subsequent profit and sales growth. Similar findings have been reported by Scherer, Leonard, and Severn and Laurence.[12] Although consistent with the hypothesis that R&D intensive firms are attractive investments, the studies tested only half of the relationship. Further research is needed to determine whether the market price fully reflects the value of R&D activity. Indeed, Doyle and Navratil reported that the market pays a premium for high R&D intensity.[13]

The Price/Sales Ratio

Ken Fisher, a San Francisco money manager, contends that the ratio of per share price to per share sales provides a more useful guide to misvalued securities than

Investments in Perspective

The evidence cited in support of an investment strategy should always be viewed with considerable caution. What seemed to work well in the past is by no means guaranteed to generate similar results in the future. Those who try to profit from a strategy may destroy its value if their own trading begins to dominate the factors that originally allowed the strategy to succeed. Alternatively, the circumstances that created the past profit opportunities may have changed. An article in *The Wall Street Journal* discussed a variety of seemingly promising stock selection strategies that underperformed the market over the mid-1986 to mid-1987 period. This study of a rather short time period by no means invalidates the techniques. It does, however, illustrate how poorly the strategies may sometimes work.

Recent Market Rally Saw Failure Of Proven Stock-Picking Methods

YOUR
MONEY
MATTERS

By Barbara Donnelly
Special to The Wall Street Journal

During the stock market's terrific run-up of the past year, one might have expected that any sensible stock-picking technique would be a winner.

In fact, it turns out that all of the dozen or so known and respected selection techniques backfired.

"This is so rare that it has never happened in the 19-year history of our back-tests," says Robert Jones, a Goldman, Sachs & Co. analyst who has published a recent study of the phenomenon. The twelve strategies he tested included time-honored approaches to value, yield, momentum, growth, risk and liquidity. Usually, these strategies will show a mixed performance: In any given period, some work and others don't. Over time, each of them has been shown to produce average annual returns that beat the market by 1.3 to 9.3 percentage points.

But the stocks that did well over the 12 months ended in June, Mr. Jones's study shows, flew in the face of accepted investment logic. They were overvalued, large-capitalization stocks with high price-earnings ratios, low growth, low yields and a high degree of analyst coverage.

Indeed, in 10 of the study's 12 models, the worst-ranked issues perversely beat the favorites. In the other two cases, the worst- and best-ranked issues performed about equally, indicating that the strategies failed as a means of differentiation.

'No Common Denominator'

Even in retrospect, Wall Street is finding it hard to fathom why such stocks should ever have outpaced the market. "There's no common denominator to the winners," says Laszlo Birinyi Jr., vice president, equity-market analysis, at Salomon Brothers Inc. His research suggests that ignoring all fundamental valuation considerations, and simply buying and holding stocks that already had gone up the most, would have paid off the best.

Such a strategy would certainly have outdone the 85% of professional money managers who, consultants say, failed to match the performance of the S&P 500 index during the market's latest rally. In less baffling times, the S&P index tends to outperform 60% to 70% of the pros.

What's more, adds Mr. Birinyi, "it's a very thin list of stocks that really impacted the market." For instance, his analysis of which stocks in the S&P 500 made the most

---

How Different Strategies Fared

Performances of a sampling of different strategies for the year ended June 30. Returns for the top 20% of stocks ranked by each model are measured three ways: compared with returns for the Standard & Poor's 500 index for approximately the two decades ended June 30; compared with the S&P 500 index for the year ended June 30; and compared with the stocks ranked in the bottom 20% by each model for the year ended June 30.

	RETURNS		
STRATEGY	HISTORICALLY VS. S&P 500	FOR THE YEAR VS. S&P 500	FOR THE YEAR VS. BOTTOM 20%
Dividend discount model	+7.0%	- 6.8%	-16.3%
Low price-earnings	+4.7	- 8.6	-19.8
Price momentum	+7.6	- 5.0	- 6.7
Historical earnings growth	+4.7	-12.0	-29.3
Low earnings uncertainty	+1.3	- 6.4	-20.5
Low analyst coverage	+7.0	- 1.0	- 3.8
Small capitalization	+9.3	- 1.7	- 2.4

Source: Goldman, Sachs & Co.

---

money for investors shows that the top 10% accounted for roughly 55% of the gains in the first half of 1987.

"It's been a strange market, unequivocally," says Robert D. Arnott, a Salomon Brothers vice president and market strategist. To make sense of it, he explains, it's necessary to look at the factors operating on the market's margins—the real testing ground for the valuation strategies.

Theories abound as to what these factors are that have been driving the market to its record highs. Unfortunately, Wall Street's wise men don't agree on the answers—which would lead one to believe that nobody really knows for sure.

Some analysts believe the problem is that the traditional valuation strategies have simply become too popular to be of much use. "By a year ago, things had gone too far in the other extreme, and high P-E stocks, growth stocks and high-beta stocks (those that are considered risky because of volatility) were actually relative bar-

gains," says Michael Wilcox, a quantitative analyst at Morgan Stanley & Co.

Salomon Brothers' Mr. Arnott goes as far as to say, "I'm skeptical that the stellar past effectiveness of these quantitative models can be repeated even once they recover, because they are so widely used."

Other analysts say the problem was, in part, the strategies' failure to pick up on some key market trends, including the rebound of cyclical stocks and such special situations as restructurings and takeovers. "At the bottom of the cycle, cyclicals have high P-Es (because earnings are so low) . . . and show poor growth—factors which don't appear attractive in the models," says Goldman's Mr. Jones. "Still," he adds, "this isn't enough to account for what's gone on."

The Blue-Chip Factor

Foreign buyers, who tend to focus on name-brand issues, and the jittery investors who have crowded into liquid, large-capitalization blue-chip stocks are also blamed in some quarters for the market's unusual performance. But George Douglas, head of quantitative research at Drexel Burnham Lambert Inc., points out, "Foreign buying may be running at a $50 billion annual pace, but it still accounts for only 1% to 2% of average daily trading volume."

The only thing the analysts do agree on is that the market can't ignore fundamental considerations of value forever. They say stocks are already 30% to 60% overvalued relative to bonds. "It's almost a question of, 'How bad can things get?' " says Mr. Wilcox. He adds, however, that "al-

though the market remains overvalued, the wind is still at its back."

If the strategies regain their effectiveness while the market is still relatively strong, analysts say, it would indicate a broadening and extension of the rally and augur the softening of any eventual downturn. (Such a rebound began to emerge last month after a rough July, but it's too early to tell whether it will persist.)

If, on the other hand, the speculative push continues, Mr. Jones says, "this bull market could end with a bang, not a whimper, and value strategies would come back with a vengeance."

does the PE.[14] A low PE, according to Fisher, implies poor future profit expectations by the market. In contrast, when the price/sales ratio is low, the market expects existing revenues to provide low profits. Most firms' sales tend to be relatively stable over time. Thus a firm that has both a low price/sales ratio and the ability to improve its profit margin will generate quite a substantial per share earnings increase. The trick, according to Fisher, is to identify firms that not only have high sales relative to their stock prices but also are likely to survive and eventually return to profitability. Similarly, he argues that firms with high price/sales ratios are frequently overpriced. Such firms typically have very high margins that may be difficult to maintain. Fisher cites stories of a number of stocks to illustrate his approach. Unfortunately, however, he has not subjected his price/sales ratio screen to systematic analysis of past data.

Takeover Candidates

Buying a stock just before it becomes an acquisition target is one of the few ways of making a quick killing in the stock market. Acquiring firms almost always offer a substantial premium over the preannouncement price of the target firm. Moreover, takeover candidates are sometimes bid up in a competition between would-be suitors (e.g., competition between Texas International and Pan Am for National Airlines and the Dupont/Seagram/Mobil contest for Conoco). Acquisitions have had a major impact on U.S. industrial structure. As the railroads linked the nation's local markets in the last half of the 19th century, the U.S. economy took on a national character. The resulting increase in competition led to the first great merger wave. From the passage of the Sherman Antitrust Act (1890) through the turn of the century, merger activity continued at a breakneck pace. U.S. Steel, General Electric, American Can, American Tobacco, DuPont, Pittsburgh Plate Glass, International Paper, United Fruit, Allis Chalmers, Eastman Kodak, and a host of others were assembled during this period. The promoters of the amalgamations profited handsomely. J. P. Morgan, for example, received $62.5 million (1901 dollars) for putting U.S. Steel together. The stocks of the newly created giants were usually priced to reflect the monopoly power that they had just acquired. The severe recession of 1904 and an antimerger ruling on Northern Securities caused a sharp decline in merger activity.[15] An adverse antitrust climate, weak stock market, and slow economy all tend to inhibit merger activity.

A second major merger wave began during the 1920s and ended with the onset of the 1929 stock market crash and the Great Depression. During this time the great public utility holding companies were assembled; vertical integration efforts increased; and many industries saw the growth of a large "number two" firm (e.g., Bethlehem Steel, Continental Can, and Allied Chemical).

Beginning slowly after World War II, a third merger wave reached a peak in the late 1960s. Relatively strict antitrust enforcement blocked most significant vertical and horizontal mergers. Nonetheless, a number of large firms such as LTV, Litton Industries, IT&T, and Gulf & Western Industries were able to emerge through conglomerate acquisitions. The acquiring company's stock was used in virtually all of the takeovers, often at inflated prices. The depressed stock market of the early 1970s abruptly halted this game. Few rode higher or fell farther than the conglomerates (LTV from 169½ to 7½ and Litton Industries from 94½ to 2¾, for example).

In the mid-1970s a new merger wave slowly began. Unlike previous merger activity, most recent acquirers have used cash or debt securities. The post-1973 depressed stock market discouraged exchanges for the stock of the acquiring company and also made cash acquisitions a cheap way of obtaining needed assets.

Takeover Criteria.   Although the lawyers and investment bankers usually do well, most of the merger profits have been made by those who bought their stock early. Indeed, the shareholders of the acquiring firm almost always earn abnormal returns around the time of the takeover. Unless the investor is an insider (who would be legally barred from acting on nonpublic information), identifying takeover candidates before the acquirers make their move is a difficult task. A *Business Week* article and an analogous approach discussed in *The New York Times* do offer some guidelines. Similarly, Stavrou, a takeover candidate specialist at Evans and Company, compiled his own list.[16] Table 9.3 compares the *Business Week* and Stavrou lists. These two sets of takeover criteria both emphasize the importance of substantial asset values, shareholders with reasons to sell, and recent large stock purchases. *Business Week* also lists prior takeover attempts and an industry with current takeover activity. Stavrou, in contrast, looks for companies with high profit potentials that are currently mismanaged.

Taking a slightly different approach, Wansley, Roenfeldt, and Cooley identified merger candidates solely from balance sheet and income statement information.[17] They found that acquisition candidates tended to be smaller and had higher growth rates than firms that were not taken over. They also had lower ratios of PE, debt to assets, and market value of equity to total asset value. Moreover, a trading strategy of purchasing potential acquisition candidates based on these criteria generated substantial excess returns regardless of whether they were taken over.

TABLE 9.3 Takeover Guidelines

Business Week	Stavrou
1. Low price relative to book value, cash, or current assets	1. High liquidation value
2. Large shareholder ready to sell	2. Large shareholder ready to sell
3. Large recent stock purchase	3. A catalyst such as a large recent stock purchase
4. Previous takeover efforts	4. High market share
5. Industry with takeovers underway	5. Problems correctable by effective management

Source: "The Profit Potential in Spotting Takeovers," *Business Week,* October 24, 1977, 100; C. Stavrou, "Choosing Candidates," *Barron's,* April 5, 1982, 15–28.

Acquiring companies themselves seem to be paying increasing attention to estimated discounted cash flows of acquisition candidates. In essence, the would-be acquirer treats the potential acquisition as a capital budgeting problem and assesses the prospective returns. Thus those with attractive discounted cash flows relative to their cost may be likely acquisitions.

Traders who use similar criteria may bid up many potential takeover candidates, thereby discouraging their acquisition and reducing the profit potential if the takeover proceeds. Still, an otherwise attractive stock may be even more appealing if its takeover is likely.

Raiders, Greenmail, and Risk Arbitrage. Much stock market activity focuses on the possibility of a takeover. A number of investors (often called raiders) are well known for their records of attempted takeovers. Only a relatively small fraction of their takeover attempts actually succeed in wresting control from the existing management. Sometimes the target firm buys back the raider's stock at a premium (greenmail) over the market price. At other times, another buyer is brought into the picture by management (the white knight) or another raider eventually outbids the initial raider. Occasionally the target tries to acquire the raider company (the Pac Man defense).

Regardless of the buyer (white knight, target company, or another raider) the initial raider usually sells out at a nice profit. At still other times the initial raider succeeds in taking control. At that point it may do one of several things. It may, for example, seek to restructure the company in order to extract value for itself and, incidentally, the other shareholders as well. Such restructurings usually take the form of increasing the firm's debt and using the borrowed funds to buy out the public shareholders. In other instances, all shareholders may be paid a substantial sum per share (partial liquidating dividend). Once in control, the raider may seek to sell the firm off a piece at a time or as a package. In rare circumstances the erstwhile raider may settle in and run the acquisition as a going concern (e.g., GAF and TWA). Unless the effort fails outright (no greenmail or change in control), such investors usually find a way of taking more out of their investment than they put in.

Another group of investors called risk arbitragers look for potential and attempted takeovers. They then assess the current stock price relative to the proposed or expected terms of the takeover and the likelihood of a successful acquisition. Depending upon that assessment, they may purchase shares of the target firm in hopes of selling later at a profit. What are the implications of such trading on individual investors?

Several studies bear on the activities of raiders and risk arbitragers.[18] Mikkelson and Ruback found that, when one firm acquired enough stock to file a Form 13d (5% or more), the target's price generally rose, probably in anticipation of a takeover attempt. According to Brown and Raymond, the market price of the stock of a target firm acts as a rather accurate predictor of the probability that the takeover attempt will succeed. The closer it is to the proposed terms of the deal, the more likely is success. Thus the activity of risk arbitragers generally drives the stock price toward the terms of a takeover that is likely to go through but not toward the terms of one that is likely to fail. Similarly, Larcker and Lys found that risk arbitragers are able to generate private information on the probability of takeovers succeeding and then earn substantial returns by trading on that information. Finally, Holderness and Sheehan examined the returns generated by six well-known corporate raiders. They found that such traders not only made profits on their own investments but also generally enhanced the values of the other shareholders in the firms that they targeted.

Avoiding Bankruptcy Candidates

We have already seen that selecting companies that are subsequently acquired may yield attractive returns. Similarly, avoiding or perhaps even shorting companies that are likely to go bankrupt may be a profitable strategy. Altman's model for bankruptcy prediction facilitates such a strategy.[19] His early warning system identifies firms with a high bankruptcy probability. Subsequent work indicates that bankruptcies are relatively predictable events. Moreover, the Altman formula seems about as accurate at forecasting failures as most of the alternatives. Whether one can profit from accurate bankruptcy predictions depends on the stock's pre- and postbankruptcy performance.

Aharony, Jones, and Swary found significantly negative returns for risk-adjusted holding periods up to four years prior to a bankruptcy filing.[20] Similarly, Clark and Weinstein reported that shareholders experienced large losses during the month of a bankruptcy filing with much of the losses concentrated during the three days surrounding the announcement.[21] Taking advantage of such performance depends on having lead time relative to the market.

Using one form of risk adjustment, Altman and Brenner found predictable subsequent negative performance associated with deteriorating financial data, but the relationship disappeared when a second risk adjustment procedure was used.[22] Thus trading signals of bankruptcy prediction models may or may not be helpful. Those who want to try them may find a simplified form of the Altman model useful.[23] It involves the calculation of a Z-score value of creditworthiness and financial viability from the following financial data:

$$\text{Altman Z Score} = 1.2A + 1.4B + 3.3C + 1D + .6E$$

where:

A = working capital/assets
B = retained earnings/assets
C = pretax earnings/assets
D = sales/assets
E = market value of equities/liabilities

A firm scoring less than 1.81 is classified as troubled.

A further refinement of the Altman formula has been developed by a consulting firm called Zeta Services (Hoboken, New Jersey). Although the output of the proprietary model is sold primarily to institutional subscribers, its results sometimes appear in publications such as *Forbes* (Table 9.4). The Relative Financial Strength System of *Value Line* provides similar output to subscribers.

Contrary Opinion: Investing in Troubled Firms

Far from avoiding troubled firms, some investors seek them out. Indeed the so-called *theory of contrary opinion* advises investors to concentrate on issues that are out of favor (and therefore presumably undervalued). The market will eventually return to former favorites that are being neglected, or so the argument goes. Contrarians may contrast their concept with what they despairingly refer to as the *greater-fool theory*. Those who follow fads often bid prices up to unrealistic levels hoping that still greater fools will pay even more.

Like many stock market concepts, contrary opinion investing is easier to discuss in the abstract than to reduce to practice. Those who favor investments in stocks with low PEs or small capitalizations, in stocks neglected by analysts, or stocks with low per share prices are practicing a contrarian approach. Concentrating on currently unprofitable companies is another possible approach. In 1980 *Forbes* put together a list of relatively large money-losing companies. Two years later the magazine published a second list along with a report on the subsequent performance of the companies on the first list (Table 9.5).

The results are rather grim. Of the 90 firms, eight filed for bankruptcy and 15 more remained unprofitable two years later. Overall, the list declined by 8%, which was comparable to the S&P 500's performance over the same period. Dividends were substantially higher for the S&P than the list of unprofitable firms, however. Thus the total return of the troubled firms on the *Forbes* list was below that of the market. Nevertheless, *Forbes* prepared a second list and argued that, if the unprofitable firms can hold their own in a weak economy, they might do well in an up market.

We have already discussed such contrarian approaches as investing in low-PE or low-priced stocks or in stocks of small or neglected firms. Conceptually, the most appealing contrary opinion approach is to target troubled firms that are about

TABLE 9.4   Three Categories of Zetas

Zeta says: watch out

All of these firms have "zetas"—measures of financial strength—in the undesirable range below zero. They all have had sharp deterioration in zeta scores over the past year, a suggestion of financial trouble ahead. Zeta can't predict the future, of course; it can only describe the present state of a balance sheet.

Company/business	Price current	Price 12-month high–low	Zeta year ago	Zeta current	Zeta change	Latest 12 months EPS	Current ratio
Anacomp/computer services	3⅜	4¼– 1⅜	–1.46	–20.54	–19.08	$–4.63	0.83
U.S. Sugar/sugar prods	55	55 –44	8.47	–2.07	–10.54	–2.02	0.95
Offshore Logistics/oilfield svcs	1⅜	6½– 1¼	0.74	–4.42	–5.16	–14.32	0.36
Dynascan/electronics	4¾	6¼– 3¼	3.13	–1.91	–5.05	–2.75	1.38
Texfi Inds/textiles	4⅝	5 – 2	–5.54	–9.83	–4.29	–3.02	1.34
Mayflower/moving, storage	21¾	26¾–10¾	2.85	–0.18	–3.02	2.21	1.30
Kaneb Services/oil & gas prod	9	15½– 8⅜	2.51	–0.31	–2.82	–1.39	1.29
Coleco Inds/toy mfg	15⅛	19⅛– 9⅝	–0.06	–2.84	–2.78	–4.04	1.64
Westmoreland Coal/coal production	16¾	25⅜–15½	2.07	–0.52	–2.59	–6.67	1.53
Bayly/apparel	7¼	10¾– 6⅛	2.47	–0.09	–2.56	0.16	1.71
Eastmet/specialty steel	2⅜	9¼– 1⅞	–0.96	–3.51	–2.55	–4.65	0.79
Bally Mfg/recreation	15⅝	23⅛–11⅛	1.90	–0.58	–2.47	–3.69	1.14
Compo Inds/textiles	8¾	11⅜– 6¾	0.62	–1.78	–2.40	–1.72	1.90
Chris-Craft Inds/broadcasting	51¼	51¼–26⅝	1.72	–0.65	–2.37	–3.39	1.62
Facet Enterprises/auto parts	12⅜	14⅜– 9⅛	–1.89	–4.23	–2.34	1.56	2.86

Sources: Zeta Services Inc.; FORBES.

Zeta says: looking better

These firms all had unfavorable zeta ratings a year ago, and all have enjoyed turnarounds into positive territory. To raise its zeta, a firm has to strengthen its balance sheet—most important, by adding to retained earnings. Chrysler's balance sheet, for example, now shows the benefit of last year's robust earnings.

Company/business	Price current	Price 12-month high–low	Zeta year ago	Zeta current	Zeta change	Latest 12 months EPS	Current ratio
Computer & Comm Tech/computer eq	10⅝	16¾– 8⅜	–4.64	1.56	6.20	$ 1.22	3.25
Becor Western/mining mach	13⅝	15⅞–12	–0.30	2.98	3.28	0.26	1.95
Intl Rectifier/semiconductors	13⅝	17⅝– 9¼	–2.21	0.98	3.19	0.53	2.56
Chrysler/autos	36⅛	38½–23	–2.38	0.52	2.90	12.85	0.97
Hayes-Albion/auto parts	10⅜	13⅞– 8	–1.76	0.53	2.28	1.60	1.55
Brown & Sharpe Mfg/precision inst	21¼	26¾–13	–0.18	1.99	2.17	2.09	3.75
Robbins & Myers/electrical eq	12¾	14½–10½	–1.71	0.36	2.08	–0.20	2.89
Ply-Gem Inds/forest prods	15⅝	16½–10½	–1.06	1.01	2.06	1.20	5.24
Huffy/recreation	10⅝	13⅞– 9⅞	–0.03	1.35	1.38	1.14	2.00
Lehigh Press/printing	26⅞	31⅞–13	–0.21	0.83	1.03	2.66	1.88
Tyson Foods/food processing	19¾	21½– 5⅞	–0.56	0.44	1.01	1.47	1.10

Sources: Zeta Services Inc.; FORBES.

TABLE 9.4   (Continued)

Zetas for the nervy investor						
These firms' zetas put them at the bottom of the 2,300 companies followed by Zeta Services Inc. A few, like Fedders, are recovering dramatically, but these stocks are for the steel-nerved contrarian only.						
Company/business	Price current	12-month high–low	Current zeta	Latest 12 months EPS	Current ratio	
Anacomp/computer svcs	3⅜	4¼– 1⅜	−20.54	$ −4.63	0.83	
Pengo Inds/oilfield svcs	⅝	1⅞– ½	−17.07	−2.60	0.30	
Fedders/air-conditioning	6	6¾– 4¼	−14.00	0.39	1.97	
Adams Res & Energy/oil & gas prod	2⅛	3⅝– 1½	−10.65	0.44	0.96	
Texfi Inds/textiles	4⅝	5 – 2	−9.83	3.02	1.34	
Lamson & Sessions/auto parts	3⅜	4½– 1¾	−8.80	0.02	2.11	
Tosco/refinery	2⅝	4⅛– 1	−8.27	−9.63	1.39	
AM Intl/business equip	4¼	5⅞– 2⅜	−7.27	0.87	1.37	
Western Air Lines/airline	6⅞	7 – 2⅝	−4.98	0.05	0.62	
Tiger Intl/airline	6⅞	10½– 5⅝	−4.81	−4.00	0.95	
Instrument Systems/multicompany	1⅞	2¾– 1⅝	−4.56	0.19	2.52	
Intl Harvester/agricultural eq	8¾	11¼– 5⅛	−4.43	−4.81	0.76	
Offshore Logistics/oilfield svcs	1⅜	6½– 1¼	−4.42	−14.32	0.36	
Wean United/steel machinery	6⅜	12½– 4¼	−4.40	−1.48	1.60	
Pauley Petroleum/oil & gas expl	11⅝	12¾– 5½	−4.34	−0.43	1.02	

Sources: Zeta Services Inc.; FORBES

Source: "Provocative Numbers," *Forbes,* July 1, 1985, pp. 130–131. Reprinted by permission, © Forbes Inc., 1985.

to turn around. In this regard Katz, Lilien, and Nelson examined a trading strategy based on whether, according to a bankruptcy model such as Altman's, a firm was moving toward health or distress.[24] They found that the stocks of firms moving from distress to health exhibited positive abnormal returns. Those of firms moving in the other direction were negative. Thus the changes in a firm's Z scores may offer useful trading signals.

An even more daring contrary approach concentrates on one of the most out-of-favor groups: the bankrupts. Thus a *Barron's* author argued, "Equity Funding, Penn Central, Interstate Stores and Daylin all have sought the shelter of bankruptcy. But like corporate Lazaruses, each has risen from the dead."[25] Although bankrupt companies usually decline severely around the time of their filing, a few eventually come back handsomely. Many are total or near-total losses, however (Table 9.6).

Another contrary approach is to buy shares in a contrary-opinion mutual fund. (Contrafund, for example, rose by 300% from its 1976 founding until 1982, compared with a 150% gain for the S&P 500.) Still others include seeking out liquidation candidates and concentrating on the depressed issues favored by insiders. Greenblatt, Pzena, and Newberg find that stocks selling below their liquidation values generally provide above-average risk-adjusted returns.[26]

TABLE 9.5 Forbes Follow-Up

Ashes and diamonds

Here's what happened to the stock prices of FORBES' first "Red isn't dead" list of 90 moneylosing companies September 1980.

Company	% change in price	Company	% change in price	Company	% change in price
American Airlines	92%	Fotomat	–33%	Roblin Industries	–78%
American Biltrite	5	Gateway Transportation[2]	37	Ronson	–24
American Motors	–40	Gino's[2]	71	Salem Carpet Mills	–25
Arctic Enterprises[1]	–50	Goldblatt Brothers[1]	–89	Sambo's Restaurants[1]	–67
Bibb	45	Great A&P	–10	F&M Schaefer[2]	56
Bobbie Brooks[1]	–66	Hayes-Albion	–35	Seatrain Lines[1]	–96
Braniff Intl[1]	–90	Edward Hines Lumber	6	Sheller-Globe	104
Cagle's	–48	Instrument Systems[4]	–85	Soundesign[2]	172
Champion Home Bldrs	120	Intl Foodservice[2]	–64	Spector Industries[2,5]	–80
Chrysler	–28	Intl Harvester	–89	Standard Products	15
City Stores	–27	Itel[1]	–65	Superscope	–62
Coachmen Inds	35	Keystone Consolidated	4	Susquehanna	–7
Combustion Equipment[1]	–100	KLM	1	Talley Inds	–23
Commonwealth Oil	–92	Laclede Steel	–17	Texfi	–45
Continental Air Lines	–52	M Lowenstein	167	Trans World Corp	8
Culbro	166	Manhattan Industries	89	Tyson	10
Dayton Malleable	–34	CH Masland	–13	UAL	–18
Ehrenreich Photo-Opt[2]	24	Massey-Ferguson	–74	UNC Resources	–66
Elixir Industries[3]	142	McLean Trucking[2]	55	Uniroyal	67
Envirotech[2]	1	McLouth Steel	–79	US Steel	–19
Facet Enterprises	5	Memorex[2]	–10	Valmac Industries	–14
Fedders	–18	Monfort of Colorado	44	Victoria Station	–16
Filmways	–32	National Kinney	–29	Vornado	–34
Firestone	54	Orange-co	0	Ward Foods[2]	22
First Pennsylvania	–39	Ozark Airlines	71	Westmoreland Coal	–24
Fischer & Porter	–37	Pan Am World Airways	–38	White Motor	–95
Fleetwood Enterprises	91	Penn-Dixie Industries	–79	Wilson Freight[2]	–100
Food Fair (Pantry Pride)	65	Raybestos-Manhattan	–47	Winnebago Inds	117
Foodarama	0	Republic Airlines	–49	World Airways	–48
Ford Motor	–19	Robintech	–61	WTC	–7

[1]Company filed for bankruptcy within period 9/80 to present. [2]Company merged or acquired within period 9/80 to present. [3]Company went private. [4]Reverse 1/10 split in 1981. [5]Spector division of TeleCom filed Chapter 11 in 1981.

Source: S. Kichen, "Reds II," *Forbes*, July 19, 1982, pp. 102–103. Reprinted by permission of *Forbes* Magazine, July 19, 1982. ©Forbes Inc., 1982.

Specialized Advisory Services

A variety of investment services sell very specialized advice. For example, O'Glove (*Quality of Earnings Report*) carefully analyzes published financial statements to forewarn his clients of bad news. Similarly Crary (at Bear Stearns and Co.) advises clients on the likely outcomes of relevant court cases. Charles E. Simion and Company in Washington monitors SEC filings of specific companies. Finally, Vogel (at Moore & Schley), Monroe (at Cameron & Co.), and several others use their own stock valuation formulas to identify potentially misvalued securities. Indeed, many specialized and a host of generalized advisory services offer investment advice and forecasts. No doubt some advisory services are well worth their cost. Identifying those services may be about as difficult as selecting the misvalued securities themselves, however.

TABLE 9.6   Bankrupts' Performances

| | | Stock price | | |
Company	Bankruptcy filing date	near filing	recent	% change
Allied Artists	4/4/79	1 3/4	1/4	−86%
Allied Supermarkets	11/6/78	5/8	1 1/16	70
Capehart	2/16/79	3/8	0	−100
City Stores	7/30/79	2 1/4	3 1/2	56
Commonwealth Oil Refining	7/23/79	10 1/4	5/8	−94
EC Ernst	12/4/78	4	1 1/4	−69
Inforex[1]	10/24/79	1 7/8	1/4	−87
Interlee (FDI)[2]	12/4/78	7 1/2	3/4	−90
Lafayette Radio Electronics[1]	1/4/80	7/8	1 1/16	21
Mansfield Tire & Rubber	10/2/79	3/4	0	−100
National Shoes	12/12/80	1 3/4	2 1/2	43
Pantry Pride (Food Fair)[2]	10/3/78	2 7/8	4 1/8	43
Penn-Dixie Industries	4/7/80	2 3/8	1 1/2	−37
Piedmont Industries	2/22/79	1 1/4	1/4	−80
Richton Int	3/18/80	1 1/4	1 1/2	20
Sam Solomon	8/21/80	3 3/4	1 1/4	−67
Tenna	12/5/79	1 3/8	0	−100
Triton Gr (Chase Man M&R Tr)[2]	2/22/79	7/8	7/16	−50
The Upson Co	6/25/80	1 1/8	1/2	−56
West Chemical Products	1/22/79	4 3/8	6 1/2	49
White Motor	9/4/80	5 3/8	1/4	−95
Wilson Freight	7/23/80	2	1/4	−88

[1]Acquired. [2]Former name.

Source: S. Kichen and A. Field, "Of Risks and Rat Holes," *Forbes*, March 1, 1982, pp. 134–136. Reprinted by permission of *Forbes* Magazine, March 1, 1982. © Forbes Inc., 1982.

Managerial Objectives

Another approach to identifying misvalued securities focuses on the objectives of their managers. From the time of Adam Smith (circa 1776) until the 1920s, most economists believed that firms were largely motivated by the interests of their owners. With the rise of large publicly owned corporations, however, the managerial and ownership functions became increasingly separated. In 1929, of the 200 largest nonfinancial firms 88 were *management controlled*: no discernible group owned 20% or more of the stock and no smaller block showed any evidence of control.[27] By 1963, the number had increased to 169; only five were controlled by a majority ownership group.[28] The absence of identifiable ownership groups would seem to increase managers' discretion. Do managers have any reasons to sacrifice stockholder interests, and if so how far can they go before jeopardizing their own positions?

Baumol contends that managerial salaries and prestige are more closely related to sales than to profits, and managers might therefore sacrifice income for growth.[29] The empire-building motives of many managers may reinforce this tendency. A high preference for security can also conflict with the profit-maximizing goal. On the other hand, by doing less well than they might, managers widen the gap between the actual and potential market values of their firms. The wider that gap, the greater is the risk of takeover bids, proxy fights, and bankruptcy, all of which jeopardize the jobs of the current managers. Outsiders, however, often have difficulty assessing managerial performance. Thus stockholder interests may be sacrificed appreciably before management's position is threatened.

Even if managers' personal investments in their firms influence their behavior, the potential for conflicting or independent interest exists. Particularly blatant types of abuse include corporate officials overpaying themselves, trading on inside information, disposing of corporate assets at bargain prices to friends or relatives, and favoring certain suppliers.

Upper level managers generally set the firm's compensation policy. Thus they are well positioned to overpay themselves. A probable example was a proposal to give 50 high-level Security Pacific Corporation officials $18 million worth of stock over a 10-year period with no established distribution guidelines.[30] Other likely abuses of power included trading on inside information by Penn Central, Equity Funding, and Texas Gulf Sulphur officials. In another example, two Armour traffic officials in the 1930s directed Armour shipments to rails using specialized gears manufactured by a firm in which they owned stock. The gear manufacturer's market share grew from 1% to 35% before the FTC stepped in.[31]

Emphasizing growth at the expense of profits may be less blatant but more damaging to stockholders. Thus excessive sales promotion, setting low margins, and especially acquiring firms at inflated prices can harm current stockholders. Organizational slack is another potential problem. When not under competitive pressure, firms may allow costs to increase and overall efficiency to decline. Moreover, managers may use the corporation to promote their own social and political goals. Some social and political activity may improve the firm's public image or legal climate, but other actions may reflect the manager's own particular preferences.

Although the impact of these abuses may not be measured directly, the performance of management-oriented firms can be compared with stockholder-oriented firms. In a study of management-controlled versus owner-controlled firms, Monsen, Chiu, and Cooley concluded:

> The net income to net worth ratio was 75 percent higher for owner-controlled firms than management-controlled ones over the twelve year period. This result indicates that the owner-controlled firms provide a much better return on the original investment, and suggests a better managerial capital structure and more efficient allocation of owners' resources.[32]

Similarly, Masson found that "firms with executives whose financial rewards more closely paralleled stockholders' interests performed better in the stock market over the post-war period."[33] In a study that incorporated a survey of 50 years of merger work and some original research of his own, Hogarty stated:

> No one who has undertaken a major empirical study of mergers has concluded that mergers are profitable, i.e., profitable in the sense of being "more profitable" than alternative forms of investment. A host of researchers, working at different points in time and utilizing different analytic techniques and data, have but one

major difference: whether mergers have a neutral or negative impact on profitability.[34]

More recent studies have found that merger activity resulted in increased risk and little or no gain to stockholders of the acquiring firm (while the target firm's shareholders profit handsomely). Thus, either many corporate officials frequently misjudge merger opportunities, or merger activity has often been motivated by managerial interests. Neither of these explanations is very favorable to the managers of firms that engage in extensive merger activity.

Palmer examined the interaction of monopoly power and owner control, finding that "among firms with a high degree of monopoly power, management-controlled firms do report significantly lower profit rates than owner-controlled firms."[35] On the other hand, Kamerschen found no significant difference in profitability between manager- and owner-controlled firms among Larner's sample of the 200 largest nonfinancial corporations.[36]

The relevant evidence on this subject may be summarized as follows: Managers often substitute their own interests for those of the stockholders. Thus firms managed in the interest of stockholders generally tend in some sense to outperform management-oriented firms. Only the Masson study and more recent work by Levin and Levin suggests a direct link between stock market performance and manager orientation.[37] The other cited articles indicated a relationship between a firm's internal performance and management interest that the stock price may have already discounted. Thus manager orientation by itself may or may not be a particularly valuable selection criterion. Nonetheless, a knowledge of management orientation may be useful when the market price is slow to reflect the superior performance produced by a stockholder-oriented management.

Accurately predicting when a firm's managers are about to become more stockholder-oriented may be an especially worthwhile strategy. Management's new orientation should eventually increase earnings. Thus purchasing the stock before these results become obvious could be particularly profitable. Moreover, those who avoid management-oriented companies may thereby sidestep some losers.

To apply these recommendations one must first identify management's goals. One clue is provided by management statements such as the president's letter in the annual report. If growth is emphasized and profits are played down, the implications are obvious. Similarly, corporate officials can be asked to discuss goals at the annual meeting or elsewhere. Previous merger activity and management's compensation packages and portfolio composition may provide additional insight. Periodic efforts to reduce costs demonstrate that excessive organizational slack is not tolerated. A low payout ratio coupled with below-average growth suggests that management may be particularly concerned with its own interests. Management-oriented officials will vigorously oppose takeover bids or try to negotiate guarantees of their own positions. Stockholder-oriented managers will, in contrast, seek the best terms for the shareholders, confident that their past performance will protect their jobs.

Encouraging a shift toward stockholder orientation is clearly in the interest of shareholders. Accordingly, shareholders might well find it in their interest to prefer the dissidents in a proxy fight. A large prodissident vote is likely to make existing management more stockholder oriented. Asking pointed questions of man-

TABLE 9.7 Summary of Narrow Fundamental Analysis Approaches

- *Forbes* and similar lists provide an interesting start in the search for undervalued securities.
- Various studies suggest that stocks with the following characteristics may outperform the market:
    Low PE
    Small capitalization
    Neglect by investment analysts
    Low per share price
- R&D-intensive firms may be identified from their ratio of price to R&D spending.
- Takeover candidates usually do well, but anticipating the targets is difficult.
- Altman's formula may help avoid firms with a high risk of bankruptcy.
- Contrarians advocate buying out-of-favor stocks.
- Specialized advisory services offer specific types of investment advice.
- Stockholder-oriented firms may outperform those with a managerial orientation.

agement-oriented managers either by letter or at annual meetings may also signal potential stockholder dissatisfaction. Finally, a thwarted takeover bid or a new compensation scheme that ties salaries more closely to profits or stock performance may favorably affect managerial goals. Table 9.7 summarizes narrow fundamental approaches.

MODELS WITH INVESTMENT APPLICATIONS

Profitability Models

A company's future stock price performance will be determined largely by its future financial performance, especially its profit rate. A number of industrial organization models relate profitability to various underlying factors. We have already seen that the earnings prediction efforts of investment analysts are largely ad hoc and time series oriented. Profitability models, in contrast, are fitted to cross-sectional data and possess some theoretical underpinnings. In spite of the relevance of profit determinants to investments, the finance profession has largely ignored the literature. Because much of investment analysis assesses potential earnings growth, risk of failure, or probability of success, characteristics associated with profitability might well help to judge a company's long-run potential.

Most of the research on profit determinants has explored possible relationships one or a few at a time. Studies of the relation of profits to company size, type of control, seller concentration, market share, buyer concentration, entry barriers, diversifications, multimarket contacts, risk, product image, advertising, capital intensity, research intensity, and leverage have produced interesting findings but relatively few generalizable investment implications. The efforts of two consulting groups to derive strategic planning profitability models are potentially far more useful.

The Boston Consulting Group. Bruce Henderson of the Boston Consulting Group (BCG) asserted that business units (components of firms serving distinct

FIGURE 9.1 The BCG Growth–Share Matrix

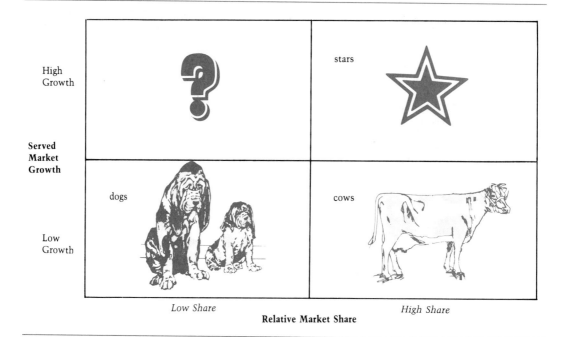

markets) may usefully be grouped into four categories of cash flow generator–absorbers, resulting in the growth–share matrix shown in Figure 9.1. The high-growth stars are expected to be net cash absorbers whereas the cash cows generate excess cash flows. BCG suggests using some of the cow's revenue to maintain its dominant market position through investment and R&D. Additional sums can be devoted to the promising question marks. Most of the dogs should be liquidated.

Although the BCG approach is designed to assist corporate managers, an implicit message applies to investors. Well-situated companies vis-à-vis the growth–share matrix are likely to produce more attractive profit performance than less well-positioned companies. Stocks that do not reflect such potentials are probably misvalued.

The Strategic Planning Institute. The Strategic Planning Institute (SPI) uses a more detailed approach to business profitability than does BCG. Also known as PIMS (profit impact of marketing strategies), SPI grew out of General Electric. Unlike BCG, the SPI models are based on a statistical analysis of real economic data. SPI has about 200 participating companies (a substantial percentage of which are among the Fortune 500). These members supply funding and detailed product line information on about 3,000 business units. This database was specifically assembled for structure/strategy/performance analysis. It has been used to build a number of models of product line performance. By far the best known and most widely utilized of these is SPI's Par ROI model.

TABLE 9.8   The Strategic Planning Institute's Key Determinants of Profitability

	Effect on ROI
Competitive-Position Factors	
Market share	+
Relative share	+
Relative product quality	+
Market-Attractiveness Factors	
Growth in served market	+
Fixed capital intensity	−
Marketing intensity	−
Purchase amount by immediate customers	−
Joint Competitive-Position and Market-Attractiveness Factors	
Investment/Sales	−
Investment/Value added	−
Capacity utilization	+
Value added/employee	+

The Par ROI model incorporates factors explaining approximately 70% of the ROI (return on investment or profit as a percentage of assets employed) variation across SPI businesses. Estimated from the SPI four-year cross-sectional database, the Par equation is designed to capture the steady-state determinants of ROI. The variables of the equation were selected for their consistency with economic theory and the beliefs of knowledgeable businessmen, statistical significance, and controllability by management. Table 9.8 lists 11 key profitability factors in the Par equation.

Competitive position factors (market share, relative market share, and relative product quality) measure strengths and weaknesses of a business within its served market. Market share reflects scale economies while relative market share (this business's share relative to its top three competitors) examines share effects from a different perspective. A 10% to 20% market share is much more impressive if no one else has as much (e.g., Exxon) than if it puts the business in third place (e.g., Chrysler). The relative quality of products has a large impact on customer loyalty, repeat sales, relative price, and vulnerability to price competition.

Market attractiveness variables include growth in the served market, fixed capital intensity, marketing intensity, and purchase amount by immediate customers. Such environmental factors affect the ease or difficulty of competing in a particular market. Operating successfully is easier in an expanding than in a declining market. Everyone can share in the growth rather than fight for the leftovers. Growth has only a modest ROI impact in rapid growth situations. Net book value of plant and equipment tends to reflect recent costs and thus be closer to replacement values. On the other hand, a technology requiring a high percentage of fixed (as opposed to working) capital limits flexibility.

Similarly, selling is costly in a market characterized by high marketing intensity. In addition to the accounting aspects of the relationship (marketing is a large cost component), marketing-intensive industries frequently experience fierce competitive struggles. Combining a high marketing level with a relatively low selling price is an especially damaging strategy. Moreover, customers who typically place large orders (high purchase amount by immediate customers) usually possess greater buying power and price sensitivity. Having such customers tends to increase the difficulty of maintaining a high margin.

The joint competitive position and market attractiveness factors include investment/sales, investment/value added, capacity utilization, and value added/employee. They reflect both the within-market competitive position of the business and the served-market environment. For example, investment intensity (a weighted average of investment/sales and investment/value added) is affected both by how much output the business generates from its investment (its own efficiency) and by the technical nature of industry production. Similarly, capacity utilization and value added/employee are affected by both the efficiency of the individual business and by the technical and cyclical nature of the industry. Clearly, high levels of capacity utilization and value added to investment (capital productivity) and value added per employee (worker productivity) contribute to business unit success. At high operating levels, fixed costs are spread over a large output, usually reducing unit costs. Productivity and profitability go together. Businesses with heavy investment per employee tend to have high levels of value added per employee. But those that are unable to raise value added in proportion to increased investment suffer both low productivity and low profitability.

ROIs that depart from the model values tend to move back toward their Pars, indicating that Par behaves as an equilibrium.[38] SPI has also constructed other strategic planning models including those for cash flow, market share, and start-up businesses. SPI members use the Par ROI equation to establish benchmarks, evaluate performance, set strategy, and estimate the potentials of acquisition candidates.

Only SPI members can utilize its proprietary models and database directly. Moreover, much of the needed data are nonpublic and indeed are not even assembled by most companies that are not members of SPI. Accordingly, the model is difficult to apply directly to investment decision making. Many aspects of the model are in the public domain, however.

Estimating the relative levels of the key factors in Table 9.8 helps to evaluate long-run profit potentials. Thus a low-profit company with a high investment intensity, low market share, low capacity utilization, high marketing intensity, and low product quality may be unable to improve its profitability without strengthening its strategic position. Alternatively, an equally unprofitable company that is appreciably stronger in most of these dimensions may more easily raise its profits.

The BCG approach emphasizes growth and market share whereas that of SPI utilizes a much broader array of profit determinants. Both assume that laws of the marketplace help one understand profitability relations. Clearly, any superior insights into the profit prospects of investment candidates gained through these models should be helpful. As yet, no empirical work tests the validity of such an approach.

PE Ratio Models

Efforts to predict profits are based on the (eminently reasonable) presumption that the market price will eventually reflect profitability changes. Attempts to establish equilibrium PE ratios for particular stocks are more direct. An effective PE ratio model could be used to generate "normal" values for the PE of a particular firm. Departures from that level could be used to predict the movement of actual PEs toward their model values. PEs can change for two primary reasons. First, they can migrate toward their estimated equilibrium PE values. Second, those equilibrium values can themselves change. Depending upon the relative strength of the two forces, knowledge of the equilibrium estimates could help identify misvalued securities. Accordingly, a number of researchers have estimated equations of the "normal" or "predicted" PE ratio. A "normal" PE less than the actual ratio suggests the stock is overpriced. A "normal" PE above the actual PE has the opposite implications. Whitbeck and Kisor's use of this technique is illustrative.[39]

$$\text{Theoretical PE} = 8.2 + 1.5A + 6.7B - .2C$$

where:

A = growth rate
B = payout ratio
C = standard deviation around the trend line price

Relevant data were then used to calculate a theoretical PE for each sample company. For four different dates, the authors found that stocks with a market to theoretical PE ratio of .85 outperformed the S&P 500 index. At the same time, stocks that had a ratio of 1.15 or more underperformed the same S&P 500. The Whitbeck-Kisor model was applied with Bank of New York forecasts. Thus its success depended largely on the accuracy of their analysts. In contrast, the Bower model, which utilized historical data rather than forecasts, was unable to identify misvalued securities.[40] Clearly, expectational variables play an important role in explaining PE ratios.

Very little work has been published on theoretical PE ratio models since the early 1970s. The computed model parameters were fit to data from one period. They generally failed to hold up over subsequent periods. This instability suggests that the underlying equilibrium values for the PE ratio models may change too rapidly for a dependable tendency to move toward the estimated values to emerge.

INTEGRATED APPROACHES TO FUNDAMENTAL ANALYSIS

The narrow selection criteria and the profitability and PE ratio model methodologies concentrate on one or a few variables. Several other approaches integrate a variety of factors. Those of Graham and Templeton are particularly noteworthy.

The Benjamin Graham Approach

Benjamin Graham coauthored the investment text that dominated the market from the 1930s to the 1950s, and he was a frequently quoted authority on investments. Graham advocated investment in financially strong companies with low prices relative to their underlying values. In the last years of his life (he died in 1976) Ben Graham and Dr. James B. Rea listed a set of 10 simple criteria for identifying undervalued stocks.[41] These criteria can be grouped into three categories: low price, strong finances, and growing earnings. Specifically Graham and Rea suggested selecting securities with:

1. An earnings to price yield of at least twice the AAA bond yield. Thus, if AAA bonds yield 10%, EPS should equal at least 20% of the stock's price (PE of 5 or less).

2. A PE ratio no higher than 40% of its five-year high.

3. A dividend yield of at least two-thirds of the AAA bond yield.

4. A stock price below two-thirds of tangible per share book value.

5. A stock price less than two-thirds of net quick liquidation value (current assets less total debt).

6. Total debt less than tangible book value.

7. Current ratio of two or more.

8. Total debt no greater than twice the net liquidation value.

9. Compound 10-year annual earnings growth of at least 7%.

10. Two or fewer annual earnings declines of 5% or more in the preceding 10 years.

Very few stocks ever meet all of these criteria. Those qualifying in seven or more are said to have a high *reward-to-risk ratio*. Graham and Rea particularly stress criteria 1, 3, 5, and 6 (a stock price that is low relative to earnings, dividends, and book value as well as debt that is low relative to book value). They contended that individual high reward-to-risk stocks may not necessarily perform well, but a diversified group of 30 or so such securities should produce handsome returns.

Rea's own work covering the 1925–1975 period supports their conclusion as does research by Robert Fargo, a financial consultant based in San Francisco. Moreover, several Graham-oriented money managers have produced impressive performances. Finally, several studies meeting the more exacting standards of academicians are also supportive.[42] Oppenheimer found that Ben Graham stocks generally did particularly well each January, while Oppenheimer and Schlarbaun reported that over the 1956–1975 period Ben Graham types of stocks returned 3% to 3½% more than the market portfolio. Oppenheimer reported still further evidence supporting the Graham approach in a 1984 article.

Graham and Rea also suggested that investors should sell a stock whenever any of the following occurred:

1. It appreciated by 50% or more.

2. It had been held for more than two years.

3. Its dividend is eliminated.

4. Its earnings drop sufficiently to make it overpriced by 50% or more relative to criterion 1 (too high a PE ratio).

On the other hand, a stock that would still be bought on the basis of the original criteria should be held. Little or no research (other than that implicit in Rea's own work) supports the value of these selling rules, however.

Templeton's Approach

If results are any indication of the value of an investment strategy, John Marks Templeton's growth fund deserves careful scrutiny. Unlike Graham and Rea, Templeton has not reduced his approach to a series of simple rules. Still its major elements may be established from the published record:[43]

1. Templeton advocates a world view to investing. U.S. stocks are only one component. At any one time stocks are cheaper in some countries than others.

2. Like Graham and a host of others, Templeton prefers a low price relative to current earnings, asset values, and dividend yields.

3. Unlike Graham he believes that extensive diversification with risky stocks can produce an acceptable portfolio risk.

4. He suggests selling when the market is particularly optimistic and buying when it is particularly pessimistic (who does not?).

5. He tries to assess emerging socioeconomic trends and their likely investment impact. For example, in 1977 he saw a growing economic role for government with an especially adverse impact on the visible and therefore more vulnerable large firms. Similarly, he saw continued high inflation rates and thus advocated investments where the returns are most likely to move up with the price level.

Like Graham, Templeton seeks conservatively priced stocks that are out of favor. In addition, he tries to assess the future. Will the country offer a favorable investment climate? Is the company well situated for forthcoming economic trends? Compared to Graham, Templeton is less concerned with individual risks: A low current ratio or high debt ratio would not necessarily bother him.

SUMMARY AND CONCLUSIONS

Investment analysts have suggested a wide array of fundamental approaches. One useful starting point is offered by *Forbes* lists. Low-PE stocks may tend to be undervalued, but small firms ignored by the investment analysts seem to be a better bet to outperform the market on a risk-adjusted basis. Low per share price may be an even better criterion. A high R&D intensity may be a modest plus whereas an unrecognized takeover candidate could handsomely reward a timely purchase. Bankruptcy candidates and other depressed issues may be misvalued (contrary opinion) although relevant evidence is scarce. In certain circumstances specialized advisory services and knowledge of manager orientation may help investors. The investment value of PE ratio models seems limited. Of the fundamental approaches considered, the integrated methods of Graham and Templeton seem to show the greatest promise. The available, admittedly limited, evidence does point to their usefulness. Perhaps combining the components of small firm, stockholder orientation, and SPI profit potential with the basic Graham–Templeton framework would prove even more promising.

REVIEW QUESTIONS

1. How should one use the *Forbes* list approach to investment selection? Where other than in *Forbes* are investors able to find or produce lists of interesting stocks?

2. Summarize past empirical work relating the PE ratio to subsequent returns. What are the investment implications of this evidence?

3. Discuss the evidence on the small firm effect, neglected firm effect, and low price effect. What are the investment implications of this evidence?

4. Discuss the use of information on R&D intensity in investment selection.

5. List and analyze the various criteria for identifying takeover candidates. Why would an investor want to be able to identify them?

6. Discuss the principal components of the Altman bankruptcy warning formula. How would an investor apply this model to investment selection?

7. List and discuss the functions of several specialized investment advisory services.

8. What is meant by the separation of ownership and control? Who first noticed this trend? What is its relevance to the investor?

9. In what ways may manager and stockholder goals differ? What is the relevance of these differences to investors?

10. Review the empirical evidence relating to manager-controlled versus owner-controlled firms. What are the implications for investors?

11. Compare the three types of profitability models discussed in this chapter: academic, BCG, and SPI. What are the investment implications of these models?

12. Discuss the two basic types of PE ratio models and compare the relevant evidence on their values.

13. Compare the Graham and the Templeton approaches.

REVIEW PROBLEMS

1. The GRO Company has a PE of 25 and EPS of $1.00. Asset Play has a PE of 8 and EPS of $1.00. If in the next five years GRO's PE falls to 20 while its EPS increases at 10% per year, what will its stock sell for? Similarly, if in the next five years Asset Play's PE increases to 15 and its EPS grows at a 10% rate, what will its stock sell for? Ignoring the impacts of dividends, taxes, and commissions, what are the rates of return for investments in GRO and Asset Play?

2. Using the starting values given in Problem 1, assume that the EPS for both GRO and Asset Play has grown at a 5% rate (annual) for five years. If GRO's and Asset Play's PEs fall to 12 and 6, respectively, what will the stocks sell for?

3. Using the starting values given in Problem 1, assume that GRO's payout is .3 and its appropriate discount rate is 13%. What is its expected growth rate? Suppose Asset Play's payout is .5 and appropriate discount rate is 12%. What is its implied expected growth rate?

4. Apply the cash flow takeover approach to the following situation: The Cash Cow Corporation currently generates a net cash flow after all expenses of $3 million. This cash flow is expected to grow at a rate of 5%. If the appropriate discount rate is 12%, how much is Cash Cow worth?

5. Suppose the Cash Cow Corporation described in Problem 4 has one million outstanding shares and the stock currently sells for 10. How would you proceed if you had the resources to finance a takeover?

6. Compute Altman Z-score values for each of the following companies:

Company	Working Capital	Retained Earnings	Pretax Earnings	Per Share Price	Number of Shares	Assets	Liabilities	Sales
A	2,000	30,000	5,000	10	1,000	100,000	60,000	100,000
B	1,000	10,000	0	5	500	50,000	40,000	60,000
C	3,000	10,000	−15,000	3	8,000	400,000	370,000	450,000
D	20,000	100,000	15,000	25	20,000	900,000	500,000	1,000,000

All data except those pertaining to shares are in thousands of dollars.

7. Compute the EPSs and PEs for each of the companies listed in Problem 6. Assume a tax rate of 33%.

8. Plot the locations on the growth–share matrix for each of the following business units:

Unit	Growth	Relative Market Share
a	5%	.3
b	9	.5
c	3	.8

d	12	.9
e	14	1.3
f	2	.15
g	4	1.6
h	6	.8
i	10	.55

Using the median values for growth and relative share, classify the business units as stars, cows, question marks, or dogs. What would BCG advise the company that owns this portfolio of business units?

9. Use the Whitbeck and Kisor PE ratio model to compute theoretical PE values for each of the three companies for which data are provided (growth rate, payout ratio, and standard deviation around the trend line of price):

Company	Data
A	10, .50, 2
B	8, .45, 3.5
C	13, .40, 4.5

10. For the companies in Problem 9, suppose the required rate of return (in percentages) equals 10 plus the standard deviation around the trend line of price. Compute the theoretical PE ratio for each of the companies. How and why do they differ from the Whitbeck and Kisor values?

REVIEW PROJECTS

1. Choose a *Forbes* list at random and follow the performances of the stocks for six months. Write a report.

2. Choose five low-PE and five high-PE stocks that are touted for their growth prospects and follow their performance for six months. Write a report.

3. Identify a list of stocks with rumored takeovers and a second list with takeover efforts under way. Follow their performance for six weeks after the rumor or announcement. Write a report.

4. Using the takeover criteria lists of *Business Week* and Stavrou, identify 10 potential takeover candidates. Follow their stocks over a period of one year. How many were actually taken over? How would an investor in these stocks have done? How would buyers of the others have done? Write a report.

5. Using the Altman bankruptcy model, identify five companies with substantial bankruptcy risks. Follow them over 12 months. How many filed for bankruptcy? What was the experience of investors in the group? Write a report.

6. Refer to Table 9.5. Look up the stock price of each listed company on May 17, 1982. How many of these companies have now gone bankrupt? What are the current prices of the stocks of those that survived? What has been the return on a portfolio of these stocks?

7. Refer to Table 9.5. Repeat Project 6 but use July 19, 1982 as the starting date.

8. Refer to Table 9.6. Repeat Project 6 but use March 1, 1982 as the starting date.

9. Select 10 companies and analyze them in light of the BCG and PIMS strategic planning criteria. Follow their performance over 12 months. Write a report.

10. Using the Whitbeck-Kisor relative PE ratio formula (adjust the intercept to current S&P level), identify five stocks whose PEs are too high and five that are too low. Follow their subsequent performance for 12 months. Write a report.

11. Identify 10 stocks that approximately meet the Graham criteria. Follow their subsequent performance for 12 months. Write a report.

NOTES

1. S. Kichen, "Loaded Laggards," *Forbes*, July 21, 1980, 76–77; S. Kichen, "A Dash of 20-10-10," *Forbes*, July 20, 1981, 110; "The Nifty Fifty Revisited," *Forbes*, December 15, 1977, 72–73; "Compound Your Holdings," *Forbes*, April 1, 1977, 22–23; R. Flaherty and S. Gilbarg, "Bargains in Bankruptcy," *Forbes*, February 4, 1980, 101–102; G. Smith, "Many Are Called and a Few Are Chosen," *Forbes*, November 12, 1979, 203–216; "How to Play Against the Experts and Win," *Forbes*, November 26, 1979, 122–127; B. Weberman, "Rich Is Better," *Forbes*, December 10, 1979, 92–96; "Risks That Come with 12%," *Forbes*, November 26, 1979; "Act III," *Forbes*, April 28, 1980, 110–111; S. Kichen, "The Stock Market's Flea Market," *Forbes*, October 26, 1981, 210–217.

2. B. Malkiel, "Equity Yields: Growth and the Structure of Share Prices," *American Economic Review*, December 1963, 120–127.

3. W. Breen, "Low Price Earnings Ratios and Industry Relations," *Financial Analysts Journal*, July/August, 1968, 120–127; H. Latane and D. Tuttle, "E/P Ratios, Changes in Earnings in Forecasting Future Prices," *Financial Analysts Journal*, January/February 1969, 117–120.

4. R. Levy and S. Kripotos, "Earnings Growth, P/E's, and Relative Price Strength," *Financial Analysts Journal*, November/December 1969, 60, 62, 64–65.

5. R. Levy, "A Note on the Safety of Low P/E Stocks," *Financial Analysts Journal*, January/February 1973, 57.

6. S. Basu, "The Information Content of Price-Earnings Ratios," *Financial Management*, Summer 1975, 53–64; "Investment Performance of Common Stocks in Relation to Their Price Earnings Ratios: A Test of the Efficient Market Hypothesis," *Journal of Finance*, June 1977, 663–682.

7. C. Bidwell and J. Riddle, "Market Inefficiencies: Opportunities for Profits," *Journal of Accounting, Auditing, and Finance*, Spring 1981, 192–214; D. Goodman and J. Peavy,

"Industry Relative Price-Earnings Ratios as Indicators of Investment Returns," *Financial Analysts Journal*, July/August 1983, 60–66.

8. M. Reinganum, "Misspecification of Capital Asset Pricing," *Journal of Financial Economics*, March 1981, 19–46; M. Reinganum, "Abnormal Returns in Small Firm Portfolios," *Financial Analysts Journal*, March/April 1981, 52–57; M. Reinganum; "Portfolio Strategies Based on Market Capitalization," *Journal of Portfolio Management*, Winter 1983, 29–36; R. Banz, "The Relationship Between Return and Market Value of Common Stocks," *Journal of Financial Economics*, March 1981, 3–18; I. Lustig and P. Leinbach, "The Small Firm Effect," *Financial Analysts Journal*, May/June 1983, 46–49; R. Roll, "A Possible Explanation of the Small Firm Effect," *Journal of Finance*, September 1981, 879–888; M. Reinganum, "A Direct Test of Roll's Conjecture on the Firm Size Effect," *Journal of Finance*, March 1982, 27–36; C. James and K. Edmister, "The Relation Between Common Stock Returns, Trading Activity and Market Value," *Journal of Finance*, September 1983, 1075–1086; K.Chan, N. Chen, and D. Hsieh, "An Exploratory Investigation of the Firm Size Effect," *Journal of Financial Economics*, September 1985, 451–471; J. Booth and R. Smith, "An Examination of the Small-Firm Effect on the Basis of Skewness Preference," *Journal of Financial Research*, Spring 1987, 77–86; J. Booth and R. Smith, "The Application of Errors-in-Variables Methodology to Capital Market Research: Evidence on the Small-Firm Effect," *Journal of Financial and Quantitative Analysis*, December 1985, 501–515; T. Cook and M. Rozeff, "Size and Earnings/Price Ratio Anomalies: One Effect or Two?" *Journal of Financial and Quantitative Analysis*, December 1984, 449–466.

9. A. Arbel and P. Strebel, "The Neglected and Small Firm Effect," Financial Review, November 1982, 201–218; discussed in G. Putka, "Choosing Stocks That Few Analysts Followed Proved Good Strategy in the 1970s, Study Shows," *The Wall Street Journal*, June 3, 1982, 49; A. Arbel and P. Strebel, "Pay Attention to Neglected Firms!" *Journal of Portfolio Management*, Winter 1983, 37–42; A. Arbel and P. Strebel, "Giraffes, Institutions and Neglected Institutions," *Financial Analysts Journal*, May/June 1983, 57–63; M. Hulbert, "Newsletter Stock Picks: The Fewer the Better?" *American Association of Individual Investors Journal*, January 1984, 16–19; B. Donnelly, "In the Shadows: Neglected Stocks Offer Opportunities for Individuals," *The Wall Street Journal*, December 11, 1986, 35.

10. M. Blume and F. Husic "Price, Beta, and Exchange Listing," *Journal of Finance*, March 1973, 283–299; R. Edmister and J. Green, "Performance of Super-Low-Priced Stocks," *Journal of Portfolio Management*, Fall 1980, 36–41. W. Kross, "The Size Effect Is Primarily a Price Effect," *The Journal of Financial Research*, Fall 1985, 169–179; W. Baldwin, "Cheap-Cheap," *Forbes*, October 6, 1986, 200; P. Elgers, C. Callahan, and E. Strock, "The Effect of Earnings Yields Upon the Association Between Unexpected Earnings and Security Returns: A Re-examination," *The Accounting Review*, October 1987, 763–773.

11. "Using R&D as a Guide to Corporate Profits," *Business Week*, May 29, 1978, 75.

12. B. Branch, "Research and Development Activity: A Distributed Lag Analysis, *Journal of Political Economy*, September–October 1974, 999–1011; B. Branch, "Research and Development and Its Relation to Sales Growth," *Journal of Economics and Business*, Winter 1973, 107–111; F. Scherer, "Corporate Investment Output, Profit and Growth," *Journal of Political Economy*, June 1965, 190–197; W. Leonard, "Research and Development in Industrial Growth," *Journal of Political Economy*, March/April 1971, 232–256; A. Severn and M. Laurence, "Direct Investment Research Intensity and Profitability," *Journal of Financial and Quantitative Analysis*, March 1974, 181–193.

13. J. Doyle and F. Navratil, "The Effects of Expectations on Industrial R&D Activity: Evidence Bond on the Efficient Market Hypothesis," *Nebraska Journal of Economics and Business*, Autumn 1981, 17–32.

14. L. Minard, "The Case Against Price/Earnings Ratios," *Forbes*, January 13, 1984, 172–176; S. Kichen, "A New Way to Spot Bargains," *Forbes*, March 12, 1984, 202–208; K. Fisher, "Price-Sales Ratios: A New Tool for Measuring Stock Popularity," *American Association of Individual Investors Journal*, June 1984, 13–17.

15. *U.S. v. Northern Securities Company* 120 Fed. 721 (April 1903), 193 U.S. 197 (March 1904).

16. "The Profit Potential in Spotting Takeovers," *Business Week*, October 24, 1977, 100; V. Vartan, "A Way to Spot a Takeover Target," *The New York Times*, November 15, 1981, 14F; C. Stavrou, "Choosing Candidates," *Barron's*, April 5, 1982, 15–28.

17. J. Wansley, R. Roenfeldt, and P. Cooley, "Abnormal Returns from Merger Profiles," *Journal of Quantitative and Financial Analysis*, June 1983, 149–162.

18. W. Mikkelson and R. Ruback, "An Empirical Analysis of the Interfirm Equity Investment Process," *Journal of Financial Economics*, December 1985, 323–354; K. Brown and M. Raymond, "Risk Arbitrage and the Prediction of Successful Corporate Takeovers," *Financial Management*, Autumn 1986, 54–63; D. Larcker and T. Lys, "An Empirical Analysis of the Incentives to Engage in Costly Information Acquisition, The Case of Risk Arbitrage," *Journal of Financial Economics*, March 1987, 111–126; C. Holderness and D. Sheehan, "Raiders or Saviors? The Evidence on Six Controversial Investors," *Journal of Financial Economics*, December 1985, 555–580.

19. E. Altman, "Financial Ratios, Discriminant Analysis and the Prediction of Corporate Bankruptcy," *Journal of Finance*, September 1968, 589–609; I. Dambolena and S. Khoury, "Ratio Stability and Corporate Failure," *Journal of Finance*, September 1980, 1017–1026; H. Frydman, E. Altman, and D. Kao, "Introducing Recursive Partitioning for Financial Classification: The Case of Financial Distress," *Journal of Finance*, March 1985, 269–291; M. Ramaswami, "Stock Market Perception of Industrial Firm Bankruptcy," *Financial Review*, May 1972, 267–279; R. Collins, "An Empirical Comparison of Bankruptcy Prediction Models," *Financial Management*, Summer 1980, 52–57; E. Altman and J. Spivack, "Predicting Bankruptcy: The Value Line Relative Financial Strength System vs. The Zeta Bankruptcy Classification Approach," *Financial Analysts Journal*, November/December 1983, 60–67.

20. J. Aharony, C. Jones, and I. Swary, "An Analysis of Risk and Return Characteristics of Corporate Bankruptcy Using Capital Market Data," *Journal of Finance*, September 1980, 1001–1016.

21. T. Clark and M. Weinstein, "The Behavior of the Common Stock of Bankrupt Firms," *Journal of Finance*, May 1983, 489–504.

22. E. Altman and M. Brenner, "Information Effects and Stock Market Response to Signs of Firm Deterioration," *Journal of Financial and Quantitative Analysis*, March 1981, 35–52.

23. R. Metz, "Avoiding the Stock of Risky Companies," *The New York Times*, November 18, 1976, 62.

24. S. Katz, S. Lilien, and B. Nelson, "Stock Market Behavior Around Bankruptcy Model Distress and Recovery Predictions," *Financial Analysts Journal*, January/February 1985, 70–74.

25. S. Kulp, "Life After Bankruptcy," *Barron's*, February 8, 1982, 8.

26. J. Greenblatt, Pzena, and Newberg, "How the Small Investor Can Beat the Market," *Journal of Portfolio Management*, Summer 1981, 48–52.

27. A. Berle and G. Means, *The Modern Corporation and Private Property* (New York: Macmillan, 1932).

28. R. Larner, "Ownership and Control in the 200 Largest Nonfinancial Corporations, 1929 and 1963," *American Economic Review*, September 1966, 777–787; R. Larner, *Management Control & the Large Corporation* (New York: Dunellen, 1970).

29. W. Baumol, *Business Behavior, Value and Growth* (New York: Harcourt Brace & World, 1967).

30. R. Metz, "Incentive Plan Under Question," *The New York Times*, March 7, 1973, 56.

31. *In re Waugh Equipment Company et. al.*, 15 F.T.C. 232, 242–243 (1931).

32. R. Monsen, J. Chiu, and D. Cooley, "The Effect of Separation of Ownership and Control on the Performance of the Large Firm," *Quarterly Journal of Economics*, August 1968, 442.

33. R. Masson, "Executive Motivations, Earning and Consequent Equity Performance," *Journal of Political Economy*, November/December 1971, 1278.

34. T. Hogarty, "Profits from Merger, the Evidence of Fifty Years, Conglomerate Mergers and Acquisitions: Opinion and Analysis," *St. John's Law Review*, Spring 1970, 389.

35. J. Palmer, "The Profit-Performance Effects of the Separation of Ownership from Control in Large U.S. Industrial Corporations," *Bell Journal of Economics and Management Science*, Spring 1973, 293.

36. Larner, op. cit.; D. R. Kamerschen, "The Influence of Ownership and Control on Profit Rates," *American Economic Review*, June 1968, 432–447.

37. S. Levin and S. Levin, "Ownership and Control of Large Industrial Firms: Some New Evidence," *Review of Business and Economic Research*, Fall 1982, 37–49.

38. B. Branch, "The Laws of the Marketplace and ROI Dynamics," *Financial Management*, Summer 1980, 58–65.

39. S. Whitbeck and M. Kisor, Jr., "A Tool in Investment Decision Making," *Financial Analysts Journal*, May/June 1963, 58.

40. R. Bower and D. Bower, "Risk and the Valuation of Common Stock," *Journal of Political Economy*, May/June 1969, 349.

41. B. Graham and D. Dodd, with C. Tatham, *Security Analysis* (New York: McGraw-Hill, 1951); R. Murray, "Graham and Dodd: A Durable Discipline," *Financial Analysts Journal*, September/October 1984, 18–23; P. Blustein, "Ben Graham's Last Will and Testament," *Forbes*, August 1, 1977, 43–45.

42. H. Oppenheimer, "Excess January Profits: Theory and Further Empirical Evidence," paper presented to the October 1979 Financial Management Association Meetings; H. Oppenheimer and G. Schlarbaum, "Investing with Ben Graham: An Ex Ante Test of the Efficient Market Hypothesis," *Journal of Financial and Quantitative Analysis*, September 1981, 341–360; H. Oppenheimer, "A Test of Ben Graham's Stock Selection Criteria," *Financial Analysts Journal*, September/October 1984, 68–74.

43. R. Flaherty, "John Marks Templeton: Serving God and Hunting Bargains," *Forbes*, May 15, 1977, 72–79.

44. L. Millard, "John Templeton: Why Common Stocks are a Girl's Best Friend," *Forbes*, November 27, 1978, 45–52; D. Rotbart, "Pioneer in World-Wide Investing Still Believes Emerging Markets Offer Best Opportunities," *The Wall Street Journal*, March 25, 1985, 55.

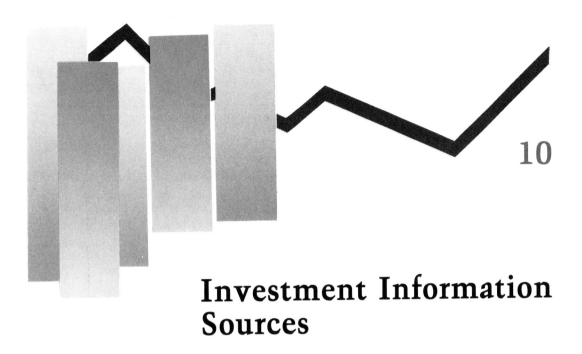

Investment Information Sources

Effective investment analysis requires access to and the evaluation of significant amounts of relevant information. Various types of knowledge may be derived from a diverse set of sources. Investors who seek to review all of the relevant information must, however, know where to look. They often must do a substantial amount of digging to obtain a sufficient quantity of data to make a meaningful assessment. Furthermore, the more difficult information is to obtain, the less likely it is to be widely known. Obscure bits of information, even if publicly available, may not be fully reflected in the market price. Lack of a clear understanding of an investment's fundamentals may well cause the market to misvalue it. Finding misvaluations is what fundamental analysis is all about. Thus serious investors need to become experts at finding and assessing the relevant public information on their prospective investments. Accordingly, successful investment analysis often involves an appreciable amount of detective work. This chapter is designed to assist in such a search.

No one knows more about a particular company than the company itself. Thus the company's own reports deserve careful scrutiny. Up-to-date trading information may be found in the stock market quotations that appear in most daily newspapers. Even more timely information is available from electronic quotations. A number of stock indexes (also reported in most daily newspapers) are designed to reflect trends in the market and various submarkets. Generalized business and investment periodicals contain a substantial amount of ad hoc information. Several

TABLE 10.1 Principal Company-Issued Reports and the Nature of Their Contents

Report	Contents
Annual Report	Financial statements, letter from the CEO, auditor's report, management analysis
10K	Annual report containing detailed financial data, required by the SEC and the listing exchange, if any of the firm's securities are listed
Quarterly Report	Unaudited quarterly financial statements, letter from the CEO
10Q	Quarterly report containing detailed financial data, required by the SEC and the listing exchange, if any of the firm's securities are listed
Prospectus	All relevant facts relating to a proposed action
Proxy Statement	All relevant information relating to any item requiring a shareholder vote
8K	Information on major developments
Press Releases	Descriptive material on newsworthy events

advisory services systematically cover groups of companies. Finally, computer-based information sources facilitate serious statistical analysis.

COMPANY REPORTS

Company-issued reports often include particularly relevant investment information (Table 10.1). Annual and quarterly reports contain the basic financial statements, a letter from the chief executive officer, and a variety of additional descriptive information. The annual report also contains the auditor's statement and a section devoted to management discussion and analysis by management. This section usually offers some worthwhile commentary. More detailed financial data are included in the 10K and 10Q forms. These forms must be submitted to the SEC and listing exchange (if any of the firm's securities are listed). The 10K is the counterpart to the annual report and the 10Q is the quarterly equivalent.

Shareholders of record automatically receive annual and quarterly reports as they are issued. Serious investors should also obtain copies of the more detailed 10Ks and 10Qs. The company must honor shareholder requests for its 10Ks and will usually send 10Qs as well. Copies can also be bought from firms advertising this service in *The Wall Street Journal* and elsewhere. Moreover, many brokerage firms have access to a large number of such reports, which they will copy for their customers. The SEC is yet another source of 10Ks and 10Qs. They will supply them for a copying charge. The Washington Document Service (450 Fifth Street NW Washington, DC 20001, 202-628-5200) will not only supply copies of specifically requested documents but with their Watch service will also monitor particular companies, industries, and situations for their clients. Any time a relevant document is filed, the Watch service informs the client and offers to make and send a copy.

Prospectuses are required whenever the firm makes any other major financial move requiring shareholder approval or notification. For example, a prospectus should be available if the firm publicly sells or repurchases a nontrivial amount of its securities, proposes a significant acquisition or divestiture, or begins a dividend reinvestment plan. The preparers of the prospectus (the firm's lawyers, accountants, and management) are legally obligated to reveal all relevant and material information regarding the proposal. Most prospectuses are therefore quite detailed. Including information that is not required is safer for the preparer than excluding information that a court might later determine should have been revealed.

Proxy materials also contain interesting information about the company. Public companies must hold annual shareholder meetings. Special meetings may also be called from time to time. Such meetings provide the vehicle for electing directors, approving auditors, and acting on a number of other matters requiring stockholder approval such as increasing the authorized number of shares or changing the firm's legal form. Accordingly, a proxy (ballot) accompanied by relevant information on the issues (proxy statement) must be distributed to the shareholders. Proxy statements typically contain the following types of information: names and holdings of the firm's principal shareholders (over 5% of outstanding shares), biographical information and stockholdings in the company of nominees to the board of directors, information on committees of the board, and executive and director compensation as well as information relating to any issue to be voted on. As with a prospectus, the preparers of a proxy statement are liable for any damages resulting from incomplete disclosure.

Both prospectuses and proxy statements must be sent to each of the firm's shareholders. Similarly, a purchaser of an initial offering must be given a prospectus. Brokerage houses generally receive copies of both types of documents for their street name holdings. Most companies will send copies of their prospectuses and proxy statements to anyone who requests them.

Whenever some significant new development occurs that is not reflected in the earlier filings of the firm, it may file an 8K report on the matter. For example, if the firm wins or loses a major court suit or buys or sells a substantial property, it is likely to file an 8K.

Press releases often report additional bits of company information. Unlike the official reports just described, no stringent standards or set forms apply to press releases. Companies issue press releases to disclose newsworthy information relevant to their operations. Until such information is made public, knowledgeable insiders are legally barred from trading the stock. Some press releases are automatically sent to shareholders. Others are usually available upon request. Parts of company press releases generally find their way into some newspapers (such as *The Wall Street Journal*) and appear on the Dow Jones teletype. The fuller story may, however, be obtained only from the complete release.

REPORTS OF LARGE STOCKHOLDERS

Owners of 5% or more of the stock of a public company are required to file a 13D report with the SEC, listing exchange, and the company itself. The document must reveal the extent of their holdings, purpose (investment, takeover, etc.), source of their funds, and any relevant agreements (such as those with other investors). The 13D must be amended whenever a material change requires an update of the prior

Investments in Perspective

Financial reports sometimes conceal as much as they reveal, as discussed in Chapter 8. The same might be said of the annual reports in which they appear. A useful discussion of how to get the most information out of company reports appeared in *Business Week*.

Personal Business

EDITED BY DONALD H. DUNN, BRADLEY HITCHINGS, IRENE PAVE, TROY SEGAL

Investing

READING BETWEEN THE LINES OF AN ANNUAL REPORT

'To our shareholders.'' An innocent enough beginning, but what follows those three words can try the patience of the most savvy investor. Sure, reading a corporate annual report is easy—but extracting the most value from the experience is something else again.

At the beginning there is a "message from the chairman" that doesn't always give a brutally frank version of the year's events. Ignore it for now. Part of the challenge is learning how to translate this verbiage—as we've done in the accompanying illustrations on these pages.

In their quest for higher earnings, more companies are resorting to accounting changes, pension-plan terminations, and other controversial techniques. "There are lots of tricks to make things less obvious in annual reports," observes Douglas W. Kurz, a partner at accountants Coopers & Lybrand.

You needn't be an accountant to do a solid analysis of a company's report. With the tips that follow, you can sift out enough facts to decide whether a company is a good or a shaky investment.

REVEALING GLANCE. A general rule: Look at the back pages of the report first. That's where you find the opinion of the independent auditor that the company hires. Even a glance can be revealing. "Generally the auditor's statement is two paragraphs. Anything longer can be significant," notes Norman Strauss, regional director at accountants Ernst & Whinney in New York. So if the statement's long, better take time to read it.

It's possible that an extra paragraph or two may simply be a note that the company has changed its accounting practices in some minor way. But the additional material also may focus on serious stuff. In Texaco's 1985 annual report, for instance, the auditors at Arthur Andersen added a paragraph mentioning the $11.1 billion judgment against the company in a suit brought by Pennzoil. It noted that the "ultimate outcome of this litigation is not presently determinable." Andersen could endorse the financial statement only "subject to the effect...of such adjustments, if any, that might have been required had the outcome of the litigation-...been known." (It still isn't, although one Texas court has shaved $2 billion from the judgment.)

That kind of cautionary note—or "qualified opinion"—rarely tells the observant stockholder anything that's terribly surprising. Indeed, the initial Pennzoil judgment was old news when the annual report came out. But to skip the auditor's statement risks overlooking a bombshell. At least, it can confirm earlier hints of trouble.

Next, look for the section labeled "Management Discussion and Analysis of Financial Condition and Results of Operations." Undoubtedly, management does a considerable amount of discussing and analyzing throughout the report. But this section has to meet standards set by the Securities & Exchange Commission and the Financial Accounting Standards Board. "The audi-

tors review it to make sure that it's factually consistent with the financial statement," notes Kurz.

STRAIGHT TALK. You can expect the section to present a reasonably straightforward analysis of the company's operations. Let's say that the report says earnings went up, and you wonder why. In U.S. Shoe's 1985 annual report, for instance, readers learned that the company's specialty retailing operations were "dramatically ahead of last year's depressed results." Note that word "depressed." It's significant. If the prior year hadn't been so weak, 1985 wouldn't have looked so good.

For more details, turn to the footnotes to the report. Among them, you'll find a breakdown of the company's lines of business, and how much each unit contributes to sales and earnings. You can also learn if the company has been making heavy use of tax benefits. The new tax law wipes out many such provisions, including the investment tax credit for equipment purchases, so the future might not be as bright.

The footnotes also indicate the health of the company's pension plan. If it's underfunded, coming up with the money to meet future pension liabilities could be a strain. But if the plan is overfunded, the company may be able to terminate the plan and institute a new one, shifting the excess into its own coffers. As an example, knowledgeable readers of the 1985 annual report of U.S. Steel (now USX) were pleased to see that the company's pension plan held 26% more assets—about $2 billion—than would be required to pay its pensioners in the future. Exactly how much the pension plan is overfunded is a matter of controversy, but the footnote was an indication that the amount may be considerable, and could be a possible source of future cash for the corporation.

Your next step: Examine the report's income statement and balance sheet. The income statement tells you how the company has been doing recently. It shows revenues, costs, and earnings for the past three years. Here you can see if the company has been able to sustain or increase the market for its products and services, and you can also gauge the company's ability to control its costs. Further down is the proverbial "bottom line"—earnings per share based on the average number of common shares outstanding during the year. If the company has issued bonds convertible into stock, or if executives have a lot of stock options yet to be exercised, the statement will show the earnings per share "fully diluted"—as if all the potential shares were in existence.

If earnings per share have been increasing steadily, stockholders have reason to be happy. But don't rejoice if the statement shows that significant income has been derived from one-time events, such as selling off the corporate headquarters. Similarly, don't be too apprehensive if the company's earnings have been penalized during the year by the cost of shutting down facilities. Earnings may benefit in the long run.

RIPE FOR RAIDS? Then there's the balance sheet, a snapshot of the company's capital structure. It shows the assets, liabilities, and the common shareholders' equity in the company at the end of the year. That's the same as net worth, or book value: the amount that the common stockholders would get, at least in theory, if the company were liquidated. The balance sheet also tells you how much cash the company has on hand. Too little, and it may have trouble expanding; too much, and it may tempt a raider to move in—which could be bad for management but good for the stock's price. You'll also see the degree to which the company relies on borrowed funds to finance its operations. A heavy debt isn't always bad, if the company's rate of return on its assets is above the cost of borrowing.

With the balance sheet and earnings statement before you, pull out your calculator. Divide common shareholder equity by the number of shares outstanding to get book value per share. If the company's shares are selling at book value or less, they may be a bargain. Generally, shares sell well above book value.

To measure how well the company is using its resources, divide net income by the company's assets, taking the year's average instead of the yearend figure. What you get is the percentage return on assets. And divide net income by average equity to see how well the company is doing for its stockholders. Is there adequate cash? You can find out by dividing the current assets by current liabilities. That's the current ratio.

By deriving these ratios for

the previous and current years, you can tell if the company's financial position is improving or worsening. It also helps to compare your results with the numbers prevailing in the particular industry. A profit margin, of course, is the difference between the price a company gets for its products and the cost of producing them. But retailers commonly have margins as low as 1% or 2%, while 15% isn't unusual among newspaper publishers. To find average ratios, turn to Dun & Bradstreet's annual compendium of 14 key business ratios for all major industries, available at most public libraries. And BUSINESS WEEK's annual ranking of the top 1000 companies, appearing in April, will handily allow you to compare the profitability of the nation's largest companies. A worthwhile reference:

Understanding Financial Statements, part of the Investor Information Kit available for $4.00 from the New York Stock Exchange, 11 Wall St., New York, N.Y. 10005.

Have you mused over the earnings statement and balance sheet? And crunched numbers to your heart's content? Now, finally, you can read what the chairman has to say (or, more precisely, what the chairman's public relations person has to say). You may get some valuable insight into the company's condition. But don't count on it. If the chairman's words jibe with your analysis of the data in the annual report, you will feel more confident as an investor. If not, you may be happier owning stock in a company where rhetoric matches results.

Gary Weiss

Source: Gary Weiss, "Reading between the Lines of an Annual Report," *Business Week*, March 23, 1987, 164–165. Reprinted by special permission, © 1987, McGraw-Hill, Inc.

filing. Because the holdings and intentions of large shareholders often affect share values, 13D filings are another useful information source. For example, when a particular shareholder owns 12% of the stock, intends to purchase more, and seeks an acquirer for the company, the possibility of a takeover is substantially increased.

The SEC will supply copies of 13Ds upon written request and a stated willingness to pay the copying charge. The company involved may or may not send such filings to those who ask. Most brokerage houses have access to these reports and will make copies for their customers upon request. These and other SEC filings are also available "on line" through Disclosure (a data access service) but the access fees are often substantial. Finally, the person making a 13D filing will usually send a copy if asked. Such individuals normally desire good relations with other shareholders.

TRADING INFORMATION

Newspaper Quotations

Stock market quotations appear in most daily newspapers. These quotations report relevant price and volume data plus certain other items. NYSE stock quotations

FIGURE 10.1a   *The Wall Street Journal* Stock Quotation for May 6, 1988

NEW YORK STOCK EXCHANGE
COMPOSITE TRANSACTIONS

Friday, May 6, 1988

Quotations include trades on the Midwest, Pacific, Philadelphia, Boston and Cincinnati stock exchanges and reported by the National Association of Securities Dealers and Instinet

52 Weeks High	Low	Stock	Div.	Yld %	P-E Ratio	Sales 100s	High	Low	Close	Net Chg.	52 Weeks High	Low	Stock	Div.	Yld %	P-E Ratio	Sales 100s	High	Low	Close	Net Chg.
17⅜	6¾	Anthm s			...	19	42	12¾	12½	12½	...	30⅜	14¾	CntryTl	.88	3.0	15	150	29⅞	29⅜	29¾	+ ¼
14⅞	7¾	Anthony	.44b	3.3	8	7	13⅝	13½	13½	...	21⅞	16¼	Cenvill	2.20	11.9	9	15	18¾	18⅜	18½	...
29⅞	20½	Aon Cp s	1.28	5.6	10	1199	23½	22⅞	23	− ¼	44⅝	23¼	Chmpln	.80	2.4	8	3321	34½	33⅝	34	+ ⅛
12½	6⅝	Apache	.28	3.4	...	82	8⅛	8⅛	8⅛	+ ⅛	16⅜	7⅞	ChamSp	.15e	1.3	24	559	12	11⅞	11⅞	+ ¼
8⅜	2¾	ApcP un	.70	24.3	...	684	3	2⅞	2⅞	...	6⅛	1¾	ChartC	.02e	.5	6	97	4⅜	4¼	4¼	− ⅛
91¼	72	ApPw pf	8.12	9.8	...	z100	83	83	83	− ⅝	46¼	19⅜	Chase	2.16	8.8	...	1038	24⅝	24⅜	24½	+ ¼
36	17¼	ApplBk			...	7	25	29⅛	29	29	...	55	45	Chase pf	5.25	10.7	...	12	49½	49¼	49¼	− ¼
20⅞	8½	ApplM s			...	16	681	16¾	16½	16⅝	+ ¼	53⅜	42	Chse pf	4.68e	9.8	...	20	47⅝	47⅝	47⅝	+ 1⅛
27¾	17½	ArchDn	.10b	.4	12	4216	23	22⅝	22¾	− ¼	53¼	37⅞	Chse pf	4.20e	9.9	...	743	43	42¼	42⅜	+ ⅜
38¾	17	ArcoCh	.60e	1.8	...	1363	33	32⅝	33	− ⅛	15¼	3⅞	Chaus			...	14	254	4¼	4⅛	4⅛	...
39	16¾	Aristec	.80	2.5	6	11766	33⅜	32	32⅜	+ ¼	25⅞	11¼	Chelsea	.72	3.8	32	9	19⅛	18⅞	18⅞	− ½
23¾	8⅛	ArkBst	.36	1.5	16	3183	23¾	23¼	23½	+ ⅛	44⅝	25¼	Chemed	1.72	5.1	14	394	34	33¾	34	− ¼
26½	15⅝	Arkla	1.08	5.6	19	1276	19½	18⅞	19⅛	+ ⅛	47⅛	20	ChmBnk	2.72	11.1	...	1180	24⅝	24¼	24½	+ ¼
59	34½	Arkla pf	3.00	7.2	...	3	42	41¾	41¾	− ½	8	2⅝	ChBk B	.76e	22.5	...	907	3⅜	3¼	3⅜	...
15	7⅜	Armada			...	4	11¾	11¾	11¾	− ¼	12¼	7½	ChBk pfC	.89e	10.6	...	2392	8½	8⅜	8⅜	...
14¾	7⅛	Armco			...	22	2531	11	10⅝	10⅝	...	53	40	ChBk pf	4.68e	11.0	...	308	42¾	42½	42½	...

in *The Wall Street Journal* are illustrated in Figure 10.1a. The two columns at the left give the high and low prices for the most recent 52-week period, followed by an abbreviation of the company name. If no symbol follows the company name, the security listed is common stock. An additional symbol designates a security other than common stock. The possibilities include *pf* for preferred, *wt* for warrants, *rt* for rights, *un* for units, and *wi* for when issued. The reader should already be familiar with some of them, but perhaps not with units and when-issued trading. When more than one security is traded as a single entity, the combination is called a unit. For example, a unit could consist of a combination of one share and two warrants. A security will trade when issued if the trade is conditional upon subsequent issuance. The issuance of the when-issued security is authorized but the security itself has not actually been issued. Normally the issuance will take place as planned on a prespecified subsequent date. The settlement (transfer of payment) of such trades occurs when and if the subject security is issued. If for some unanticipated reason the security is not issued, the when-issued transactions are reversed.

The stock quotation then indicates dividend rate and the percentage yield. For preferred shares the indicated rate is usually fixed by the terms stated in the prospectus when the stock was issued. For common stock the indicated rate may be raised or lowered by the firm's directors depending upon their assessment of business conditions. The percentage yield is obtained by dividing the indicated rate by the most recent stock price. Only cash dividends are used in computing the percentage yield.

Next appears the stock's PE; the most recent daily sales volume in units of 100 shares; and the daily high, low, and closing prices. Most securities without an

FIGURE 10.1b *Barron's* Stock Quotation for May 6, 1988

NEW YORK STOCK EXCHANGE COMPOSITE LIST

These composite stock quotations include trades on the Midwest, Pacific, Philadelphia, Boston and Cincinnati stock exchanges, as reported by the National Association of Securities Dealers and Instinet.

52-Weeks High	52-Weeks Low	Name and Dividend	Sales 100s	Yield Pct.	P/E Ratio	Week's High	Week's Low	Last	Net Chg.		EARNINGS Interim or Fiscal Year	EARNINGS Year ago	DIVIDENDS Latest divs.	DIVIDENDS Record date	DIVIDENDS Payment date
		A-B-C													
25⅝	14	AAR s .36	x1169	1.5	20	24¾	23¾	23¾	− 1⅛		Feb9m.93	.72	q.09	5-9	6-3
12⅛	8¾	ACM GI n1.09e	x2361	9.4	...	11¾	11½	11⅝	+ ¼	✚	....	....	.10½	5-12-88	5-26-88
12⅛	10¾	ACM GS n1.26	2735	11.1	...	11½	11¼	11⅜	− ⅛		....	....	.10½	4-28-88	5-12-88
27	10½	AGS s	1742	...	14	18⅜	17¼	18	+ ½		Mar3m.39	.27	....	....	....
7⅞	3⅛	AMCA	154	...	...	3⅜	d 3⅛	3¼	− ⅛		Mar3mDef	Def	.25	9-4-87	9-30-87
...	...	AMCA rt	...	...	...	...	...	...	...		....	....	....	....	....
8⅝	3¼	AM Intl	1504	...	...	4	3¾	3¾	− ¼		Jan6mD.01	Nil	Y	....	10-30-84
29⅜	17	AM Int pf 2	130	10.8	...	19	18¼	18½	...		....	....	q.50	5-1	5-15
65½	26¾	AMR	22476	...	11	45¾	43½	44½	+ 1⅜		Mar3m1.12	.34	Y	....	2-15-80
27¼	24⅞	ANR pf 2.67	11	10.1	...	26⅜	26¼	26⅜	+ ⅛	✚	....	....	q.66¾	5-16	6-1
24¼	19	ANR pf 2.12	557	8.9	...	u24¼	23⅜	23¾	+ ½	✚	....	....	q.53	5-16	6-1
12¼	6⅜	ARX	x673	...	11	8⅞	8¼	8⅜	+ ½		Mar9m.45	.60	S10%	5-11-88	5-25-88
72⅞	40⅛	ASA 3	2704	7.0	...	44⅝	42¾	43	− 1⅝		Sep9mNil	Nil	.75	2-19-88	2-26-88
22⅜	9½	AVX	1833	...	13	18¼	17½	17½	− ½		Apr13w.43	.26	Y	....	9-3-85
66⅜	40	AbtLab 1.20	23899	2.7	15	46½	44	44¼	− 1⅜		Mar3m.76	.62	q.30	4-15	5-15
28	15⅜	Abitibi g 1	171	...	...	17¾	17⅜	17⅜	− ⅜		Mar3m.61	.29	q.25	4-15	4-29
16¾	8½	AcmeC .40	442	3.4	...	12⅛	11¾	11¾	− ½		Mar6mDef	1.25	q.10	4-29	5-13
10½	6⅝	AcmeE .32b	32	4.5	19	7⅜	7	7⅛	...		Jan26w.29	.07	q.08	5-2	6-6
20	14⅛	AdaEx 3.05e	782	19.8	...	15⅞	15⅜	15⅜	− ⅛		....	....	.12	5-16-88	6-1-88
19¼	6⅞	AdamMI .24	5339	1.5	13	18⅝	16¼	16¼	− 2⅜	✚	Apr13w.18	.22	q.06	5-17	5-31

Source: *Barron's*, May 9, 1988. Reprinted with permission.

entry in the PE column have incurred recent losses; warrants and preferred stocks also do not report a PE. The last column reports the net change in price from the previous close.

Barron's, a major investment periodical, provides a more complete stock quotation (Figure 10.1b). Many of the columns are the same as in *The Wall Street Journal*: the yearly high and low, name of the company, dividend rate and yield, PE ratio, and sales. Because *Barron's* is published on a weekly basis, it also reports high, low, and last sales for the week and net change figures. The quotations also include additional dividend and earnings information. The first entry of the earnings columns contains the most recent earnings report. Depending upon the time that has elapsed since the end of the most recent fiscal year, earnings for three, six, nine, or 12 months may be reported. This entry is followed by the previous year's comparable number. The dividend columns begin with the amount of the latest quarterly declaration followed by the stock of record and payment dates. Dividends are sent on the payment date to the owners as of the day of record.

FIGURE 10.2a Regional Stock Quotations

OTHER MARKETS

Selected Stocks; Dually Listed Issues Excluded

Friday, May 6, 1988

Pacific Exchange

Sales	Stock	High	Low	Close	Chg.
6900	AlaskGld	1	1	1	.....
1400	AFn pfF	15⅞	15⅞	15⅞	.....
500	AFin Ent	20	20	20	+ ¼
39200	AmPac	3¾	3	3¼	− ¼
1500	BigSky	7-16	7-16	7-16	− 1-16
5700	CanSoPt g	5¼	5⅛	5⅛	.....
2600	CapCit wt	75⅜	72	74	− ¾
2000	ChiefCnMin	7¼	7⅛	7¼	− ⅛
100	vjCwthO	1-16	1-16	1-16	.....
200	CrystO	4⅝	4⅝	4⅝	− ⅛
12500	CryO pfA	⅛	⅛	⅛	.....
200	Frawley	5⅞	5⅝	5⅝	− ⅛
600	Imreg	14¾	14⅝	14⅝	.....
3000	vjKaiS pfB	3-32	3-32	3-32	+ 1-64
300	MagelPt	2¾	2¾	2¾	.....
24200	NVF	3-16	5-32	5-32	+ 1-32
7900	OKC LP un	5¼	5⅛	5⅛	.....
200	PalmBb pf	5⅞	5⅞	5⅞	.....
1700	Pengo	5-16	9-32	9-32	− 1-32
17800	PE Cp	⅛	3-32	3-32	.....
1000	PopeRs	25½	25	25½	+ ¾
8400	vjPSNH wt	⅝	9-16	⅝	.....

Source: *The Wall Street Journal*, May 9, 1988. Reprinted by permission, © Dow Jones & Company, Inc. All rights reserved.

FIGURE 10.2b Foreign Securities Quotations

FOREIGN SECURITIES

Unless noted, all issues are American Depositary Receipts, or ADRs, representing ownership of securities physically deposited abroad. Quotes are in U.S. dollars. n-Not ADR. Explanatory notes on Over-the-Counter page.

Friday, May 6, 1988

stock & div	sales 100s	bid	asked	net chg.
GREAT BRITAIN				
Burmah Oil .23b	110	43½	43¾	+ ⅝
Rank Organ	147	13⅝	13¾	+ ⅛
JAPAN				
Fuji Photo .05d	93	67	67⅜	− ¼
Japan Airlines	3	244½	246	− ¼
NissanMotr .07b	207	15⅝	15¾	− ⅛
Toyota Motor	521	38⅜	38⅝	− ¼
MEXICO				
TeleDeMex 6k	19195	5-32	3-16	...
SOUTH AFRICA				
AngloA Gold	125	7⅞	8 3-16	− ⅛
AngAm SAf .23b	57	16	16½	− ¼
BlyvoorGld .80b	47	5⅛	5¼	...
BuffelstnG 2.96b	118	17¼	17¾	..

Source: *The Wall Street Journal*, May 9, 1988. Reprinted by permission, © Dow Jones & Company, Inc. All rights reserved.

FIGURE 10.2c Foreign Market Quotations

FOREIGN MARKETS

TOKYO
(in yen)

Friday, May 6, 1988

	Sat. Close	Prev. Close
ANA	1900	1900
Aiwa	830	830
Ajinomoto	3580	3620
Alps Elec	1890	1890
Amada Co	1360	1400
Ando Elec	4310	4380
Anritsu	2730	2750
Asahi Chem	1140	1150
Asahi Glass	2080	2100
Bank of Tokyo	1570	1570
Bk of Yokohama	1690	1680
Banyu Pharm	1640	1630
Bridgestone	1450	1450
Brother Ind	793	791
C. Itoh	840	839
CSK	5700	5650
Canon Inc	1330	1320
Canon Sales	3760	3790
Casio Computer	1320	1310
Chubu Pwr	2970	2940

Source: *The Wall Street Journal*, May 9, 1988. Reprinted by permission, © Dow Jones & Company, Inc. All rights reserved.

FIGURE 10.2d OTC National Stock Quotations

NASDAQ BID AND ASKED QUOTATIONS

Stock & Div	Sales 100s	Bid	Asked	Net Chg.
AdelphiaCm A	9	17½	17¾	...
Advatex Assc	14	2½	2¾	...
AFN Inc	40	11-16	⅞	...
Airsensors	442	1⅝	1¾	− 1-16
AJRossLog ut	10	3⅛	3 5-16	− 1-16
AlliedSc .44	2	43	48	...
Ameribanc	65	15⅜	15½	+ ⅛
AmAircrft s	918	2 5-16	2⅜	...
AmBancp .50	10	22	23½	...
Am ConsltgCp	25	4½	5	...
AmCont'l pf	3	19½	20¾	...
Amerihost P	2950	3-32	⅛	...
ARecreatn .12	12	8	8¼	...
Am W Air deb	3	46¼	48	+ ¼
Andrews Grp	457	6⅝	6¾	+ ¼
APCO Argent	2	7	7¾	...
Arden ItlKitch	9	1⅜	1⅞	...
Artistic Grtg	40	2⅜	2½	...
Asea AB .92b	75	59¼	59⅝	+ ⅛

Source: *The Wall Street Journal*, May 9, 1988. Reprinted by permission, © Dow Jones & Company, Inc. All rights reserved.

The formats for the AMEX and NASDAQ National Market quotations are identical to those for the NYSE in most newspapers. Stock quotations for regional and foreign exchanges and for OTC National and Supplemental listings are less complete, however. They are shown in examples from *The Wall Street Journal* (Figure 10.2a through Figure 10.2e).

FIGURE 10.2e   OTC Supplemental Stock Quotations

ADDITIONAL NASDAQ QUOTES

	Bid	Asked
ACS Enterprise	19-32	11-16
Action Staffing	7/8	1
Admar Grp Inc	3/8	7-16
AdvDisplay Tec	25-32	27-32
AdvPrdctsTc A	1/2	5/8
AdvPrdctsTc C	7-16	1/2
AdvMedical Pr	1-32	3-32
AdvnNMR Syst	5 1/8	5 3/8
AdvNMRSys wt	5 1/8	5 3/8
Advanced Prod	1 3/4	2
Aerosonic Corp	1 3/8	1 7-16
AFP Imaging	1 3/8	1 7-16
Agouron Pharm	13 1/2	14 1/4
AJ Ross Logist	1 3/8	1 1/2
Alaska Apollo	17-32	19-32
Alaska Bancrp	1 1/4	1 1/2
Alcide Corp	4 7/8	5
Alcide Corp wt	1 1/8	1 3/8
Alfa Interntl	4 1/2	4 7/8
AllAm Semicon	2 3/8	2 1/2
Alfa IntlCp wt	2 1/2	3

Source: *The Wall Street Journal*, May 9, 1988, p. 37. Reprinted by permission, © Dow Jones & Company, Inc. All rights reserved.

Explanatory Notes.   Many newspaper quotations include footnotes. They alert the reader to additional information relating to the company or its quotation. For example, a note may indicate that a price is a yearly high or yearly low or that the company is in bankruptcy. Letters are used to key notes to quotations (see Figure 10.3).

NASDAQ's Fifth Letter.   Most OTC issues traded on the NASDAQ system have ticker symbols of four letters. A fifth letter is added to signify a special status for the security. Often these letters come and go as the status of the issue changes. Fifth letters frequently convey important information. Moreover, an investor seeking a quote on an OTC issue that seems to have disappeared should check to see whether it is continuing to trade under a new five-letter ticker symbol. The principal fifth letter symbols and their meanings are listed in Table 10.2.

Electronic Quotations

Although most stock market investors are content to follow the prices of their securities in the newspapers, some use electronic quotations for more frequent and up-to-date reports. Thus Trans-Lux Corp. (110 Richards Ave., Norwalk, CT 06854) offers a ticker tape service (each day's complete trading record for the NYSE and/ or AMEX) and a service that reports sales of up to 100 stocks or futures contracts in real time (no delay in reporting). Both Quotron (1 Battery Place Plaza, New York, NY 10004) and Bunker Ramo Information Systems (35 Nutmeg Drive, Trumbull, CT 06609) provide real-time access to the stock market ticker tape plus the ability to obtain last, bid, and ask quotes on specified stocks and options

FIGURE 10.3   Explanatory Notes for Stock Quotations in *The Wall Street Journal*

EXPLANATORY NOTES

(For New York and American Exchange listed issues)

Sales figures are unofficial.

PE ratios are based on primary per share earnings as reported by the companies for the most recent four quarters. Extraordinary items generally are excluded.

The 52-Week High and Low columns show the highest and the lowest price of the stock in consolidated trading during the preceding 52 weeks plus the current week, but not the current trading day. The 52-week high and low columns are adjusted to reflect stock payouts of 10 percent or more.

u–Indicates a new 52-week high. d–Indicates a new 52-week low.

g–Dividend or earnings in Canadian money. Stock trades in U.S. dollars. No yield or PE shown unless stated in U.S. money. n–New issue in the past 52 weeks. The high-low range begins with the start of trading and does not cover the entire 52 week period. pp–Holder owes installment(s) of purchase price. s–Split or stock dividend of 25 per cent or more in the past 52 weeks. The high-low range is adjusted from the old stock. Dividend begins with the date of split or stock dividend. v–Trading halted on primary market.

Unless otherwise noted, rates of dividends in the foregoing table are annual disbursements based on the last quarterly or semi-annual declaration. Special or extra dividends or payments not designated as regular are identified in the following footnotes.

a–Also extra or extras. b–Annual rate plus stock dividend. c–Liquidating dividend. e–Declared or paid in preceding 12 months. i–Declared or paid after stock dividend or·split up. j–Paid this year, dividend omitted, deferred or no action taken at last dividend meeting. k–Declared or paid this year, an accumulative issue with dividends in arrears. r–Declared or paid in preceding 12 months plus stock dividend. t–Paid in stock in preceding 12 months, estimated cash value on ex-dividend or ex-distribution date.

x–Ex-dividend or ex-rights. y–Ex-dividend and sales in full. z–Sales in full.

pf–Preferred. rt–Rights. un–Units. wd–When distributed. wi–When issued. wt–Warrants. ww–With warrants. xw–Without warrants.

vj–In bankruptcy or receivership or being reorganized under the Bankruptcy Act, or securities assumed by such companies.

much like a stock exchange quotation machine. All of these services involve payments for installation and monthly service as well as additional fees to the relevant exchanges.

A less expensive system is now available to those within 50 miles of most large cities. Telenet America Inc. (Wythe St., Alexandria, VA 22314) offers a Pocket Quote machine about the size of a hand-held calculator. It will display the high, low, and last prices for any NYSE or AMEX stock on a 15-minute delay basis. The machine will also flash whenever news appears on any of up to 20 preselected stocks.

Perhaps the least expensive source of electronic stock market data is the Financial News Network. It provides a continuous real-time stock ticker moving across the edge of the television screen. FNN information, unlike that from other sources, is passive. The subscriber cannot obtain quotations on particular securities from FNN. They must wait for the security of interest to trade and be reported on the tape. Most investors do not have time to sit and watch for their stock to trade.

TABLE 10.2   The Fifth Letter in a NASDAQ Ticker Symbol

Letter	Meaning
Q	Firm has filed for bankruptcy
J	Firm has both voting and nonvoting shares and these shares are voting
K	Firm has both voting and nonvoting shares and these shares are nonvoting
E	Firm has not filed a required SEC form but has been granted an exception
C	Firm no longer meets NASD listing requirements
V	Firm has recently issued additional shares or paid a stock dividend
D	Firm has recently reduced shares outstanding as through a reverse split
Y	Foreign stock traded as an ADR
F	Foreign stock (usually Canadian) not traded as an ADR
S	Shares of beneficial interest (not stock), usually for a REIT
Z	Not common stock; usually limited partnership or ownership units of closed-end investment companies

Taking electronic quotations a step further, several services will watch for major price moves on a selection of stocks and flag the movers (Roscokrantz, Ehrenkrantz, Lyon & Ross, Hicksville, New York; and Window on Wall Street, Bristol Financial Systems, Wilton, Connecticut). Such services require access to a personal computer, computer software, and incur a monthly fee.

Another category of electronic quotations utilizes the personal computer. For example, Dow Jones News/Retrieval, Quotdial™, Dialog, Charles Schwab, S&P, and CompuServe offer an extensive array of on-line computer investor services including stock quotations. Dowphone provides quotes for subscribers with nothing more than touch-tone phones.

Standard and Poor's Stock Guide

The monthly *Standard & Poor's Stock Guide* reports considerably more data than the newspaper stock quotations. A very large number of common and preferred stocks and warrants are included. Typical pages from the S&P guide are shown in Figure 10.4. A security is covered in a single line across two pages. Consider AAR Corp. Coverage begins with the company's ticker tape symbol (AIR) followed by the company name and the market or markets (NY and MW) on which it is traded. The S&P guide rates many of the securities from A+ to C based on the stability and consistency of earnings growth for eight years. AAR is rated B+. An NR rating (as for A & W Brands) indicates that no ranking has been made. Such an entry usually occurs because of insufficient data. The security's par value (1 cent) follows the ranking. The number of institutions (95) and their holdings (9,824,000 shares) takes up the next two columns. Then the firm's business is briefly described (markets aviation parts/service). Past price ranges (1971–1985: 1¼ to 11⅞; 1986: 11⅜ to 17¾; 1987: 14¾ to 25¾); monthly sales volume (5851 round lots); and recent high, low, and last prices (20, 15¾, 16⅝) appear next. They are followed by the dividend yield (2.2%) and PE ratio (16).

The first column of the right-hand page relates to the historical reliability of the firm's dividend. It reports the initial year of the current string of continuous

FIGURE 10.4 Standard and Poor's Stock Guide

8 A &-Adv

Standard & Poor's Corporation

¶S&P 500 ●Options Index	Ticker Symbol	Name of Issue (Call Price of Pfd. Stocks)	Market	Com. Rank. & Pfd. Rating	Par Val.	Inst. Hold Cos	Inst. Hold Shs. (000)	Principal Business	Price Range 1971-85 High	1971-85 Low	1986 High	1986 Low	1987 High	1987 Low	Nov. Sales in 100s	November, 1987 Last Sale Or Bid High	Low	Last	%Div. Yield	P-E Ratio
1	SODA	**A & W Brands**	OTC	NR	1¢	38	3585	Mfr soft drink concentrate	...	...	...	...	16⅝	6¼	3701	10	8	8¾B	...	d
2	AIR	**AAR Corp**	NY,M	B+	1	95	9824	Mkts aviation parts/service	11⅞	1¼	17¾	11⅜	25¾	14¾	5851	20	15¾	16⅝	2.2	16
3	AARN	**Aaron Brothers Art**	OTC	NR	1¢	11	552	Retail:art supplies,frames	...	...	6¼	5¾	15	5¼	830	8¼	6¾	7½B	...	7
4	ARON	**Aaron Rents**	OTC	B+	1	23	1183	Rents & sells furniture	25¾	10⅜	20	14	17¾	7	3484	8¾	7	7B	1.4	9
¶ 5●[1]	ABT	**Abbott Laboratories**	NY,B,C,M,P,Ph	A+	No	734	112385	Diversified health care prod	36	1⅞	55	31⅞	67	40	79611	50⅞	42½	43⅛	2.3	15
6	AB	**ABI Amer Businessphones**	AS	NR	1¢	...	...	Mkts tel interconnect sys	9	5¾	7½	3¾	13½	4¼	575	8	6½	6¾	...	8
7	ABD	**Abiomed**	AS	NR	1¢	1	44	Medical equip/cardiac sys	...	...	...	...	15¼	5¾	434	7⅞	6⅜	6⅜	...	d
8	ABY	**Abitibi-Price**	NY,To,P	B	No	31	1488	Newsprint,pulp,paper prods	21	2¼	28⅝	15⅛	28	15⅜	1748	18⅛	16⅝	17¾	◆2.6	11
9	AGO	**ABM Gold Corp Cl'A'**	AS	NR	No	14	1422	Explor,dvlp gold properties	...	...	...	...	10⅞	4¾	8297	8½	5⅛	6¾	...	75
10	ACAJC	**Aca Joe**	OTC	C	10¢	11	1221	Operate/license apparel strs	10⅛	⅛	8¼	1⅝	3⅜	⅜	20646	¾	⅜	⅜B	...	d
11	ACIG	**Academy Insur Gr**	OTC	C	10¢	15	2624	Accident,health,life insur	17¼	¼	3¾	2	3⅝	1¾	132150	2¾	1⅞	2¾B	...	14
12	ACLE	**Acceleration Corp**	OTC	B–	10¢	15	889	Insurance:credit life/disab	16⅝	2	15½	7⅜	12⅝	4¾	2086	6⅞	4¾	5B	s...	8
13	ACET	**Aceto Corp**	OTC	B+	1¢	17	909	Mfrs & dstr chemicals	16⅞	⅝	19	15⅜	18¾	10½	1335	12½	10¾	11¾B	s1.2	11
14	ACG	**ACM Govt Income Fund**	NY,M	NR	1¢	...	...	Closed-end investment co	...	...	...	...	12	8¾	13792	11¾	10¾	11½	11.0	...
¶ 15	AMT	**Acme-Cleveland**	NY,M	B-	1	64	3897	Mfr automatic mach tools	35⅝	7	14⅞	9	16¾	8½	4707	11½	8½	9½	4.2	13
16	ACE	**Acme Electric**	NY	B	1	16	1077	Pwr conv eq: transformers	11¼	⅜	8⅞	5⅞	10½	6⅛	234	7¾	7	7⅛	s4.5	25
17	ACL	**Acme Precision Prod**	AS	B–	1	2	60	Mfr precision cutt'g tools	12¼	¾	6⅝	2½	6⅜	2	201	3	2⅛	2¼	...	d
18	ACME	**Acme Steel**	OTC	NR	1	32	1860	Produce iron&steel products	...	...	10¾	8	17⅞	9⅛	1071	13½	11	12¾B	...	d
19	ACU	**Acme United**	AS	B	2½	11	1291	Medic eq:shears,scissors	19½	1⅜	12⅛	6⅜	9¼	6	258	6⅞	6	6⅛	0.7	d
20	AXXN	**Action Auto Rental**	OTC	NR	1¢	14	648	Insur replacem't auto rental	...	...	...	...	19½	8	3523	13½	8	9B	...	17
21	ACX	**Action Indus**	AS,B	B–	10¢	19	1864	Merchandising programs	18¼	½	15⅞	7¾	9⅞	3¼	2113	4¾	3¼	3⅝	...	d
22	AVSN	**Activision Inc**	OTC	NR	No	13	2105	Mfr home video game softw	12⅝	⅝	1¾	1	3	¾	9737	1¾	1⅛	1¼B	...	d
23	ACTM	**Actmedia Inc**	OTC	NR	1¢	51	5380	Shop'g cart advert'g displays	16¾	6½	21¾	15½	28	11¾	12767	15¼	12¼	12¼B	...	24
24	ATN	**Acton Corp**	AS,B,Ph	C	33⅓¢	10	159	Owner,operator CATV systems	94¾	1⅜	16¼	6¼	26½	11¼	348	15¼	11⅝	14⅜	...	5
25	WS	**Wrrt(Pur 0.34524 com at$38.15)**	AS	...	...	2		mfr,dstr electronic tel eqp	6½	⅛	⅝	⅛	2⅛	⅛	55	¾	⅝	⅝B	...	...
26	ACSN	**Acuson Corp**	OTC	NR	No	65	5323	Medical ultrasound imaging	...	...	13¼	7½	23¼	10¼	20689	15½	13¼	14B	...	22
27	ADAC	**ADAC Laboratories**	OTC	C	No	16	1611	Nuclear medicine comput sys	27⅜	1	1⅞	½	2⅞	1⅛	7033	2	1¼	1⅝B	...	26
28	ADGE	**Adage Inc**	OTC	B–	10¢	18	2586	Computer graphics term sys	28⅛	⅛	7¼	1⅞	3¾	⅞	4435	1½	1	1⅛B	...	d
29	ADX	**Adams Express**	NY,B,M,P	NR	1	20	254	Closed-end investment co	19⅝	7	23⅞	17½	23¼	15⅜	4710	19⅞	15⅜	15⅜	5.3	...
30	ALL	**Adams-Millis**	NY,B,M,Ph	A–	No	31	3033	Hosiery & yarn products	11⅜	⅞	16¹¹⁄₁₆	9¹³⁄₁₆	19½	7¾	1742	10⅝	8¼	8¼	2.9	6
31	AE	**Adams Res & Energy**	AS,B	C	10¢	5	460	Oil dstr:transp:coal:o&g	35¼	1½	2⅞	1¼	4⅛	1½	475	2⅛	1⅝	1¾	...	13
32	AAR	**Adams-Russell[59]**	AS,B,M	↓B	50¢	36	3285	Owns/operates CATV systems	30⅞	⅛	43	18⅜	43	20⅞	3938	42⅜	37¾	42⅜	...	...
33	AEI	**Adams-Russell Electr**	AS	NR	1¢	29	2657	Mfr defense electronic prod	...	...	21½	14	18¾	6⅛	2556	10⅞	8¾	9¾	...	49
34	ADPT	**Adaptec Inc**	OTC	NR	No	39	3231	Mfr computer data flow sys	...	...	13¼	8⅝	20¾	4⅝	8674	7⅜	4⅝	5¼B	...	7
35	ADCT	**ADC Telecommunications**	OTC	B	20¢	36	5238	Telecommunications equip	10	⅛	14½	8¾	20½	11¾	7180	16½	12¾	13½B	...	13
36	ADDR	**Addington Resources**	OTC	NR	No	26	1021	Mining,mkt bituminous coal	...	...	...	...	31¾	14½	1167	19½	15½	15½B	...	9
37	ADSNB	**Addison-Wesley Pub[63]**	OTC	B+	No	26	851	Pub textbooks, prof, ref books	36½	3¾	42	32½	61¼	36¾	498	44½	37¼	44½B	2.2	13
38	ADIA	**Adia Services**	OTC	NR	25¢	38	1511	Temporary personnel service	12⅞	6¼	16¾	10¼	32¼	12½	5322	18	12½	13B	0.8	13
39	JPAC	**ADMAC Inc[66]**	OTC	NR	1¢	8	354	Indl/ming cutg,drill sys	13¼	10¼	15¼	2	3⅝	½	1745	1⅛	½	⅝B	...	d
40	ADB	**Adobe Resources**	NY,P	NR	1¢	45	7703	Oil & gas exploration,devel-	12⅜	10⅝	12⅝	5¼	11⅞	4⅝	13015	5⅞	4⅝	5⅛	...	d
41	Pr A	**$1.84cm Cv Pfd([67]21.16)**	NY	BB–	20	11	514	opment,production	17⅞	14⅝	18⅜	13¾	20½	16¼	332	17½	16½	17¼	10.7	...
42	Pr B	**12% cm Pfd([68]21.60)**	NY	BB–	20	4	251		18	15¼	20¼	16⅜	21⅞	17½	327	21¼	18⅞	20	12.0	...
43	ADBE	**Adobe Systems**	OTC	NR	No	70	3438	Print,graphic software sys	...	...	13¼	5½	56	12¾	20834	27½	20½	24¼B	...	37
44	ADVC	**Advance Circuits**	OTC	↓C	10¢	14	930	Mfr printed circuit boards	11⅝	...	12¼	2	6¾	2¼	9438	4	2⅜	2¾B	...	d
45	AROS	**Advance Ross**	OTC	B–	10¢	8	210	Metal fabric'n:mineral prop	11⅜	⅝	6⅝	5⅛	9	5⅛	534	6¾	6	6¼B	...	5

Uniform Footnote Explanations—See Page 1. Other: [1]Ph:Cycle 2. [51]Fiscal Jul,'84 & prior. [52]□$0.08,'83. [53]□$0.21,'84. [54]1 Beltran Corp wrrt. [55]©$2.34,'87. [56]©$2.62,'87. [57]©$3.73,'86. [58]△$0.28,'83. [59]Cablevision Systems plans acq,$43.075. [60]Dstr of wrrt. [61]Stk dstr of Adams-Russell Electronics Co. [62]△$0.51,'83. [63]Cl'B'. [64]Fiscal Nov'85 & prior. [65]13 Mo Dec,'86. [66]Flow Systems plans acq,0.46 com. [67]Fr 11-1-90,scale to $20 in'97. [68]Fr 11-1-90,scale to $20 in'98.

Common and Preferred Stocks

A &-Adv 9

Splits ◆ Index	Dividends Cash Divs. Ea. Yr. Since	Latest Payment Per$	Date	Ex. Div.	Total $ So Far 1987	Ind. Rate	Paid 1986	Financial Position Mil-$ Cash& Equiv.	Curr. Assets	Curr. Liab.	Balance Sheet Date	Capitalization Lg Trm Debt Mil-$	Shs. 000 Pfd.	Com.	Earnings $ Per Shr. Years End	1983	1984	1985	1986	1987	Last 12 Mos.	Interim Earnings Period	$ Per Shr. 1986	1987	Index
1	...	None Since Public			...	Nil	...	4.22	18.0	15.1	6-30-87	69.4	1800	8300	Dc	...	d0.75	•0.11	pd0.39	...	d0.25	9 Mo Sep	pNil	0.14	1
2◆	1973	Q0.09	11-30-87	11-5	0.34	0.36	0.293	5.68	169.	75.0	8-31-87	17.8	...	15816	My	0.31	0.43	0.67	0.85	P1.00	1.07	3 Mo Aug	0.22	0.29	2
3	...	None Since Public			...	Nil	...	0.64	19.4	11.9	4-30-87	5.40	...	2766	Ja	...	...	p0.08	0.85	...	1.05	9 Mo Oct	0.30	0.50	3
4◆	1986	S0.05	1-4-88	12-1	0.10	0.10	...	Equity per shr $7.99			9-30-87	29.9	...	4914	Mr	0.92	1.13	1.08	0.91	...	0.75	6 Mo Sep	0.59	0.43	4
5◆	1926	Q0.25	11-16-87	10-8	0.96	1.00	0.80½	470.	2008	1373	9-30-87	285	...	227553	Dc	1.43	1.67	1.94	2.32	E2.80	2.64	9 Mo Sep	1.62	1.94	5
6	...	None Since Public			...	Nil	...	1.40	11.2	3.90	6-30-87	2.65	...	1651	Je	0.09	0.56	0.80	0.34	0.67	0.81	3 Mo Sep	0.06	0.20	6
7	...	None Since Public			...	Nil	...	2.43	3.45	1.39	3-31-87	...	...	★4651	Mr	0.03	[51]0.02	d0.19	0.02	...	d0.06	6 Mo Sep	0.03	d0.05	7
8◆	1949	gQ0.15	10-30-87	10-8	g0.60	0.60	g0.60	...	779.	355.	j6-30-87	★539	5201	69247	Dc	0.48	□1.02	1.42	□1.50	...	1.62	9 Mo Sep	1.11	1.23	8
9	...	None Since Public			...	Nil	...	54.0	55.0	1.23	p6-30-87	...	...	‡13300	Dc	0.55	1.03	0.06	d0.15	...	0.09	9 Mo Sep	d0.13	0.11	9
10	...	2% Stk	7-27-79	6-25	...	Nil	...	2.02	9.12	19.2	8-1-87	0.76	...	18643	Ja	d0.60	d0.56	0.07	d0.84	...	d0.79	6 Mo Jul	d0.21	d0.16	10
11◆	...	5% Stk	7-15-85	6-24	...	Nil	...	Equity per shr $1.06			9-30-87	1.15	...	70834	Dc	△1.03	△d0.79	△d2.85	△d0.31	...	0.19	9 Mo Sep	△d0.47	•0.03	11
12◆	...	5% Stk	12-19-86	11-24	...	Stk	5% Stk	Equity per shr $8.00			12-31-86	20.1	.5	5165	Dc	•△0.55	△•0.59	•△0.54	△0.48	...	0.62	3 Mo Mar	△Nil	△0.14	12
13◆	1985	s0.07	1-4-88	12-15	s0.067	0.14½	s0.126	26.9	62.4	14.3	6-30-87	7.25	260	3291	Je	0.94	1.27	1.35	1.37	1.02	1.05	3 Mo Sep	0.14	0.17	13
14	1987	0.10½	11-27-87	11-6	0.21	1.26	...	Net Asset Val $11.34			11-20-87	...	...	★43509	Dc	...	...	...	...	...	...				14
15	1936	Q0.10	11-13-87	10-26	0.40	0.40	0.40	13.6	86.9	44.9	6-30-87	10.0	161	6279	Sp	■d7.39	d2.11	■d1.90	d2.04	P•0.71	0.71				15
16◆	1939	Q0.08	12-7-87	11-3	s0.316	0.32	s0.300	0.35	30.3	8.43	10-2-87	12.3	...	4257	Je	■0.03	0.54	0.63	0.45	0.16	0.29	3 Mo Sep	0.04	0.17	16
17	...	0.10	12-15-58	11-24	...	Nil	...	0.42	18.8	21.0	6-30-87	5.46	...	984	Sp	□[52]0.25	▲■0.17	d2.07	•2.97	...	d2.31	9 Mo Jun	▲2.64	d2.64	17
18	...	None Paid			...	Nil	...	5.81	80.4	56.3	6-28-87	9.50	...	5819	Dc	...	1.74	d0.24	■d3.66	...	d0.76	9 Mo Sep	d1.97	•0.93	18
19◆	1947	0.04	12-10-87	11-6	0.12	0.04	0.32	0.27	23.4	4.36	6-27-87	7.59	...	3173	Dc	1.03	0.63	0.38	d0.14	...	d0.14	9 Mo Sep	0.10	0.10	19
20	...	None Since Public			...	Nil	...	Equity per shr $2.68			6-30-87	p29.4	...	★5453	Dc	...	...	0.09	0.41	...	0.54	9 Mo Sep	0.24	0.37	20
21◆	1986	0.06	6-15-87	5-26	0.06	Nil	0.12	1.79	91.9	56.4	9-26-87	29.1	...	5495	Je	▲1.28	□[53]0.44	0.92	1.01	d1.37	d1.35	3 Mo Sep	0.03	△0.05	21
22	...	None Since Public			...	Nil	...	9.75	24.4	8.22	6-27-87	1.87	...	36324	Mr	d0.56	d0.32	■d0.17	d0.42	...	d0.31	6 Mo Sep	d0.08	•0.03	22
23◆	...	None Since Public			...	Nil	...	19.0	46.7	20.7	9-6-87	...	...	11744	Dc	•0.15	0.23	0.34	0.42	...	0.52	36 Wk Sep	0.24	0.34	23
24◆	...	5% Stk	7-15-82	6-25	...	Nil	...	0.44	2.16	12.4	6-30-87	...	...	1183	Dc	d5.35	d10.45	d11.15	△d4.70	...	2.90	6 Mo Jun	△d1.66	△5.94	24
25	...	[54]Wrrt	4-1-82	4-2	...	Nil	...	Check terms/trad'g in detail				...	...	641	Dc	...	...	...	...	...	...	Wrrts expire 6-1-89			25
26	...	None Since Public			...	Nil	...	30.3	62.5	15.9	6-27-87	0.35	...	22251	Dc	d0.38	d0.04	•0.10	•0.40	...	0.64	9 Mo Sep	•0.25	0.49	26
27	...	None Since Public			...	Nil	...	4.11	25.4	20.9	6-28-87	2.91	2910	21984	Sp	0.51	d3.51	d3.13	d1.77	P•0.06	0.06				27
28◆	...	None Since Public			...	Nil	...	2.02	33.4	13.3	9-26-87	3.92	...	8376	Mr	0.92	0.33	d1.12	d1.32	...	d0.97	6 Mo Sep	d0.90	d0.55	28
29	1936	[55]0.35	12-21-87	11-17	[56]1.10	0.82	[57]0.72	Net Asset Val $15.68			11-27-87	...	...	24005	Dc	§19.27	§17.96	§20.54	§19.51	...	...				29
30◆	1977	Q0.06	11-30-87	11-10	0.24	0.24	0.21	2.23	75.0	29.0	9-27-87	42.0	...	4685	Dc	[58]△0.77	1.25	1.15	1.28	...	1.30	9 Mo Sep	0.81	0.83	30
31	...	0.10	8-15-78	7-10	...	Nil	...	0.92	7.04	7.21	9-30-87	4.99	34	6958	Dc	•0.59	•0.39	□0.25	•0.11	...	0.13	9 Mo Sep	•0.09	•0.11	31
32	1977	[60]...	6-3-87	5-20	[60]...	Nil	h[61]0.08	3.44	5.38	14.9	6-28-87	57.7	...	6838	Sp	△[62]1.10	1.28	p0.14	0.73	P0.01	0.01				32
33	...	None Since Public			...	Nil	...	3.77	70.3	13.9	6-28-87	23.8	...	6211	Sp	...	...	p1.36	1.06	P0.20	0.20				33
34	...	None Since Public			...	Nil	...	17.2	35.5	4.28	9-25-87	...	...	7510	Mr	d0.55	d0.04	•0.41	•0.79	...	0.79	6 Mo Sep	•0.35	0.35	34
35◆	...	None Since Public			...	Nil	...	23.5	63.4	18.4	7-31-87	3.22	...	12965	Oc	□0.33	△■0.25	0.61	0.93	...	1.04	9 Mo Jul	0.70	0.81	35
36	...	None Since Public			...	Nil	...	1.45	22.7	32.0	6-30-87	73.9	...	★5855	Dc	pd0.27	•p0.08	•p1.31	p1.49	...	1.75	9 Mo Sep	p1.35	p1.61	36
37	1956	Q0.25	1-4-88	11-24	0.92½	1.00	0.62½	6.42	99.0	39.1	9-30-87	32.5	...	‡2591	Dc	2.26	□2.77	[64]2.63	[64]3.12	...	E3.37	9 Mo Sep	3.26	3.51	37
38◆	1984	Q0.02½	12-18-87	11-30	0.10	0.10	0.08	43.3	89.0	32.2	9-30-87	13.6	...	†11209	Dc	0.31	0.60	0.62	0.76	...	1.02	9 Mo Sep	0.58	0.84	38
39	...	None Since Public			...	Nil	...	0.98	11.6	8.45	7-31-87	4.07	400	4950	Ap	...	...	•0.08	0.20	d2.85	d2.88	3 Mo Jul	d0.07	d0.10	39
40	...	None Since Public			...	Nil	...	10.7	41.8	30.6	9-30-87	2.17	9055	29833	Dc	...	pd0.21	pd10.14	d3.03	...	d1.01	9 Mo Sep	d1.99	•0.03	40
41	1986	Q0.46	11-16-87	10-20	1.84	1.84	1.932	Cv into 0.9 com				...	4159	...	Dc	...	...	...	bd1.34	...	...				41
42	1986	Q0.60	11-16-87	10-20	2.40	2.40	2.52	...	...	...		...	4896	...	Dc	...	...	...	bd1.34	...	...				42
43◆	...	None Since Public			...	Nil	...	13.4	18.7	3.68	8-31-87	...	...	10195	Nv	d0.29	0.01	0.06	0.38	...	0.66	9 Mo Aug	0.28	0.56	43
44	...	None Since Public			...	Nil	...	1.23	17.7	10.6	8-29-87	10.2	125	4393	Au	d0.03	0.70	1.16	d0.80	△d0.18	d0.18				44
45	...	h...	11-27-64		...	Nil	...	11.4	15.2	4.48	9-30-87	...	26	2143	Dc	d0.17	0.34	0.23	0.23	...	1.25	9 Mo Sep	0.02	1.04	45

◆ **Stock Splits & Divs By Line Reference Index** [2]3-for-2,'86,'87. [4]3-for-2,'83. [5]2-for-1,'86. [8]3-for-1,'85;1986 & prior prices in Canadian $. [11]2-for-1,'83:Adj for 5%,'85. [12]Adj for 5%,'86. [13]4-for-3,'83:3-for-2,'85:Adj to 4%,'87. [16]10%,'84:Adj to 5%,'87. [19]4-for-3,'83. [21]3-for-1,'83. [23]3-for-2,'85,'87. [24]10%,'83:1-for-5 REVERSE,'87. [28]2-for-1,'83. [30]2-for-1,'86. [35]3-for-2,'83,'86,'87 [38]2-for-1,'86. [43]2-for-1,'87.

Source: *Standard & Poor's Stock Guide*. Reprinted with permission.

dividends (1973). Relevant information on the current dividend situation appears next (Q0.09). If the most recent payment was quarterly, a Q will precede the amount. Then the payment date (11-30-87) and ex-dividend date (11-5) are reported. Dividends are paid to stockholders who own the stock on the day of record. The day after the day of record is called the ex-dividend date. Those who buy on or after the ex-dividend date do not receive the dividend for the period just ended.

These figures are followed by the total per share amount paid in the current year (0.34), the total indicated rate (0.36), and the amount paid in the previous year (0.293). Next, financial position data are provided including: the most recent balance sheet amounts for cash and equivalents (5.68), current assets (169), current liabilities (75.0) and the balance sheet date (8-31-87). Long-term debt amounts (17.8) and the number of preferred (none) and common shares (15816) then appear. Cash, assets, and debt are all in millions of dollars, and share numbers are reported in thousands. Finally, the fiscal year end (May) and annual EPS data are reported for five years (1983, 1984, 1985, 1986, 1987: 0.31, 0.43, 0.67, 0.85, p1.00, respectively) and for the last 12 months (1.07). The final columns report interim earnings for a year ago and most recently (3-month, August: 0.22 and 0.29).

Additional information is included on warrants and preferred stock. Item 25 in the Stock Guide concerns warrants for Acton Corporation. Under the name of the stock appears Wrrt (Pur 0.34524 com at $38.15). Thus the security may be used to purchase 0.34524 shares of the common stock at 38.15 per share. Continuing across, we see under interim earnings that the warrant expires on 6/1/89.

The S&P Stock Guide packs a substantial amount of relevant investor information into a very small space. It is a handy reference that retail brokerage houses will often supply to their customers upon request.

STOCK MARKET INDEXES

Most investors are interested in both the price changes for their own stocks and the overall moves of the market. A number of different indexes reflect market movements. Although all market indexes are based on the average prices of a sample of securities, the samples and averaging processes differ.

The Dow Jones Industrial Average

The simplest and best known of the stock indexes is the Dow Jones Industrial Average (DJIA). The Dow is an unweighted average of the market prices of 30 major ("blue chip") industrial firms. Composition changes are relatively rare. The

TABLE 10.3   Stock Index Correlations[a]

	DJIA	S&P 400	S&P 500	NYSE Composite	AMEX Index	NASDAQ Industrials
S&P 400	.895					
S&P 500	.916	.894				
NYSE Composite	.923	.897	.920			
AMEX Index	.716	.695	.727	.752		
NASDAQ Industrials	.678	.660	.682	.704	.675	
NASDAQ Composite	.794	.772	.800	.829	.788	.785

[a]Correlation coefficients between daily percentage of price changes for alternative market indicator series, January 4, 1972 to December 31, 1979 (2,019 observations).
Source: Investments by Frank K. Reilly. Copyright 1982, Holt, Rinehart, and Winston, Inc.
Reprinted by permission.

prices of the 30 stocks are summed and then divided by a number called the divisor. The divisor is adjusted to maintain comparability whenever a DJIA firm is split. Small stock dividends do not lead to a change in the divisor, however. Moreover, the more rapid growth of the firms that tend to split biases the average downward. Its problems notwithstanding, the Dow remains the most widely followed market index. When people speak of the "market" they usually have the DJIA in mind. Dow Jones, Inc., also computes averages for utilities, transportation companies, and a composite sample. The industrial average, however, receives by far the most attention.

Other Stock Market Averages

Most other stock market averages are weighted to reflect the relative value of their components. Thus, the Standard & Poor's 500 Stock Index is a composite average of the share prices of 500 major corporations weighted according to the relative values of their outstanding shares. S&P also computes indexes of 400 industrials, 40 utilities, 40 finance firms, and 20 transportation firms. The NYSE Composite Index is a value-weighted average of all stocks listed on the Big Board. Similarly, the AMEX Index is a value-weighted average of AMEX stocks and the NASDAQ Index is a value-weighted index of all domestic NASD listed OTC stocks. Finally, the Wilshire 5000 weights stocks in all three markets. Aside from the Dow, the only other unweighted (or, more accurately, price weighted) index of consequence is the Value Line Composite Index.

Relations Between the Indexes

Because stocks are generally affected by similar forces and because most of the indexes tend to have a common component, the indexes should move together. Table 10.3 reports correlations between some of the major averages.[1] Although the various indexes do tend to move together, they also reflect somewhat different market segments. In particular, the DJIA is representative of the larger, more established blue-chip stocks whereas the NYSE index and the S&P 500 are broader based. The AMEX and NASDAQ indexes reflect the pricing of more speculative issues. The Value Line index is a better measure of small capitalization stocks.

THE FINANCIAL AND BUSINESS PRESS

A large number of publications cater to investors and business people. Most of them offer both factual news and opinions that investors may use to stay abreast of current developments. Because these published opinions are as subject to error as those of the investment advisory services, investors should take the advice into account but not rely on it.

Business and Investment Periodicals

First and foremost among sources of current business news is *The Wall Street Journal* (WSJ), which is published five days a week. Most serious investors try to keep up with the relevant business news in the WSJ or the financial sections of major newspapers (*The New York Times*, for example). *The Wall Street Journal Index* is an excellent source for citations in the WSJ. Both the WSJ and *Barron's* are published by Dow Jones, Inc., a long-time leader of the financial press. *Barron's* appears weekly and is more investor oriented than the WSJ. *Investor's Daily*, a relatively recent competitor in the national business newspaper field, stresses tables and statistics. It seems to have achieved a modest degree of success.

Business Week (published weekly by McGraw-Hill) appeals principally to business people, but it contains some useful investment information. For example, McGraw-Hill annually surveys and forecasts business fixed investment (new spending on long-term plant and equipment). Also, the end-of-the-year issue contains an analysis of the investment climate. Another well-known business periodical is *Fortune*, which appears monthly. Compared to *Business Week* it contains fewer articles, but they tend to go into greater detail.

Forbes (published twice monthly) is largely investor oriented. In addition to the lists (discussed in Chapter 9), *Forbes* contains articles on specific companies and other relevant investment subjects. Investor-oriented magazines with a smaller readership than *Forbes* include *Financial World*, *Finance*, and the *Magazine of Wall Street*. Periodicals more oriented to general business and money management include *Money* and *Fact*. Periodicals focusing on small and start-up businesses include *Entrepreneur*, *Inc.*, and *Venturing*.

Financial Analysts Journal and *Journal of Portfolio Management* publish serious work on investment theory and concepts. The typical article, although not easy reading, is intelligible to nonacademicians. The same cannot be said for articles in the more academic journals devoted to finance and economics such as *American Economic Review* or *Journal of Finance*. On the other hand, the *American Association of Individual Investors Journal* is specifically written for serious but amateur investors.

Systematic Coverage of Companies

Most of the financial press covers companies in a very unsystematic fashion. Thus those seeking information on particular companies may wait a long time before finding an article in one of the periodicals. Several publications, however, do periodically report on a list of firms. Thus they serve as handy references. *Moody's Industrial Manual* (published annually) contains a great deal of financial information on the past history of a large number of firms. More up-to-date information on a smaller group of firms is available quarterly in *Value Line*, in Standard & Poor's Stock Reports, and directly from some brokerage firms.

A Moody's report on CBS is reproduced in Figure 10.5. Moody's coverage is quite extensive. First the capital structure is outlined, including a list of securities. This is followed by a brief history of the firm, a discussion of the business and products, and a list of subsidiaries. Under the general heading of management is a list of managers and directors, the name of the auditor, identity of the shareholder relations officer, dates of director meetings and the annual meetings, the number of stockholders and of employees, and the address of the general office. This is followed by annual income statements for the past three years and change of financial position statements for the past two years. A balance sheet for the most recent four years is also included. Extensive notes accompany these financial statements. Next comes a set of financial and operating information such as per share data and financial and operation rates. A brief description of the firm's debt and equity securities appears at the end.

Coverage will vary from firm to firm, although the example in Figure 10.5 is typical for a company the size of CBS. In addition to the Industrial Manual, similar Moody's manuals are published for other types of firms. Most publicly held companies of any consequence are included.

Moody's coverage is quite extensive. The information, however, is largely descriptive and dated. Standard & Poor's publishes a set of manuals very similar to Moody's as well as the more investor-oriented *Standard NYSE Stock Reports*. Figure 10.6 gives an example of such a report.

The S&P report begins with a line containing information on the primary market where the stock is traded (NYSE) and its ticker symbol (CBS). The same line also includes a notation that options on the company's stock are traded on the CBOE on the February cycle and that CBS stock is in the S&P 500 index. The next block of data reports a recent stock price (152½) and the date of the quote (May 9, 1988); price range for the current year (170¼ – 149); PE ratio (22); dividend rate (3.00); current yield (2.0%); S&P ranking (A−); and estimated beta (1.00). The next two blocks contain a summary and discussion of the current outlook for the company. This material is accompanied by a seven-year chart of the company's stock price action. The most recent four years of quarterly sales revenues and common share earnings are reported next. A brief analysis of important recent developments is then presented. Annual per share data based on the income statement and balance sheets for 10 years are then reported. Finally, the firm's business summary, dividends, and capitalization are given.

Compared with Moody's, the material is briefer, more analytical, up-to-date, and investor oriented. Most listed companies and the major OTC-traded companies are covered by S&P reports. S&P also publishes a reference book called the *Stock*

FIGURE 10.5 The CBS Report from *Moody's Industrial Manual*

CBS INC.

CAPITAL STRUCTURE

LONG TERM DEBT

Issue	Rating	Amount Outstanding	Times Charges Earned 1986	Times Charges Earned 1985	Interest Dates	Call Price	Price Range 1986	Price Range 1985
1. Debenture 7.85s, due 2001	**A3**	$37,460,000			F&A 1	[3]102.83	94½-87	77½-65
2. 14½% notes, due 1992	**A3**	55,389,000			J&D 15	[5]100	108-108	
3. 11⅜% notes, due 1992	**A3**	82,160,000			Dec. 20	[9]100.50	109½-103¼	......
4. 10⅞% Euro sterling notes, due 1994	**A3**	[4]52,720,000	2.52	2.67	Dec. 20	[6]100.50	[4]109¼-91	......
5. 10⅞% sr. notes, due 1995	**A3**	399,915,900			F&A 1	[7]100	112¾-102	105¼-96⅞
6. Conv. sub. euro deb, 5s, 2002	**Baa1**	[8]400,000,000			......	......	[8]	[8] ....
7. Medium Term Notes	[2]	112,225,000			M&N 15	......	[2]	[2] ....
8. Other debt	[2]	2,700,000			......	......	[2]	[2] ....

CAPITAL STOCK

Issue	Par Value	Rating	Shares Outstanding	Earned per Sh. 1986	Earned per Sh. 1985	Divs. per Sh. 1986	Divs. per Sh. 1985	Call Price	Price Range 1986	Price Range 1985
1. $1 conv. pref. ser. A	$1.00	......	35,116	......	......	$1.00	$1.00	43.50	99½-85	85¼-52½
2. $1 conv. pref. ser. B	1.00	......	1,250,000	......	......	10.00	4.16667	100	[2]	[2] ....
3. Common	2.50	......	23,528,127	[1]$7.54	[1]$6.89	3.00	3.00	......	15½-110	126¼-70⅞

[1]As reported by company on average shares outstanding based on continuing operations. [2]Privately placed. [3]Subject to change, see text. [4]Defeased on Feb. 12, 1986. [5]Beginning June 15, 1989. [6]Commencing Dec. 20, 1992. [7]Beginning Aug. 1, 1992. [8]Issued March 1987. [9]Commencing Dec. 20, 1990.

HISTORY

Incorporated in New York Jan. 27, 1927 as United Independent Broadcasters, Inc.; name subsequently changed to Columbia Broadcasting System, Inc.; present title adopted on Apr. 18, 1974.

In Dec. 1938, acquired an 80% interest and in Feb. 1939, remaining 20% interest in American Recording Corp. (now CBS Records).

In June 1951, Hytron Radio & Electronics Corp. was merged in exchange for 310,272 class A shares and 310,272 class B shares. These properties were operated as CBS Electronics Division until 1961 when sold on discontinuance of operations.

In 1964, purchased 80% of the New York Yankees Inc. for $11,200,000 and received an option with respect to the remaining 20%. Early in 1965, an additional 10% interest was purchased under the option agreement and in Sept. 1966, the remaining 10% was acquired. Interest in Yankees sold in Mar. 1973 for $10,000,000 cash.

In Jan. 1965, Fender guitar and amplifier companies, Santa Ana, Calif., manufacturer of electric guitars, and V.C. Squier, Battle Creek, Mich., manufacturer of strings for stringed instruments, were purchased for $13,000,000. (Sold in 1985).

In Sept. 1965, acquired Electro Music Inc., Pasadena, Cal., makers of speaker systems for electric organs (sold in 1980).

In Apr. 1966, acquired Rogers Drums, Inc., makers of drums. (Sold in 1985).

In July 1966, acquired business and substantially all assets of Creative Playthings, Inc. and its wholly-owned subsidiary Learning Center, Inc. in exchange for 300,490 common shares of CBS.

Also in 1970, acquired Business Methods Institute, Chicago (sold in 1974), Kansas City (Mo.) Business College, Inc. and Vale Technical Institute, Inc., Blairsville, Pa. (both schools sold in 1979). In Oct. 1970, acquired 49% interest in Klingbeil Co., Columbus, O. (interest sold in 1979).

In Aug., 1971, acquired X-acto, Inc., maker of precision knives and tools for hobbyists. (In 1981, sold for cash substantially all assets and business of its X-acto and House of Miniatures operations, except that which relates to its Terre Haute fulfillment operations.)

In Oct. 1971, acquired Tuna Fish Music, Inc. for 75,000 com. shs.

In 1971, acquired Popular Library, Inc., Bond Publishing Co. and Parkhurst Publishing Co. (Sold in 1982).

In Jan. 1972, acquired Pacific Electronics, Inc., for $5,110,000 plus an additional amount dependent on future earnings. (Sold in 1983).

In Feb. 1972, acquired Brown Institute of Minneapolis, a broadcasting school, and Thompson Institute of Harrisburg, Pa., a business school (both schools sold in 1979).

In Apr. 1972, acquired Steinway & Sons for 375,000 com. shs. (sold in 1985).

In Dec. 1972, acquired World Tennis, Inc., publisher of World Tennis magazine, Houston, Tex., for cash. (Sold in 1985).

In Feb. 1973, acquired Sea Publications, Inc., publisher of Sea magazine, Long Beach, Cal., for com. shs. (sold in 1980).

In Sept. 1973, acquired Gulbransen Industries, Inc., an organ manufacturer, for cash (sold in

In June 1982, acquired Blackhawk Cable Communications Co. (sold in 1985).

In Aug. 1982, acquired Ideal Toy Corp. (sold in 1985).

In Jan. 1983, acquired the music publishing business of United Artists Corp. and MGM/UA Entertainment Co., Inc.

In May 1983, acquired TransMedia Inc., a medical communications company.

In Feb. 1985, Co. purchased the business and assets of the Ziff-Davis Publishing Co.'s consumer magazine publishing operations. The purchase price is $362,500,000 in cash. Co. also will assume the purchased magazines' subscription liabilities.

In July 1985 Co. purchased five radio stations from Taft Broadcasting Company. These newly acquired stations include KLTR (FM) Houston; WLTT (FM) Washington D.C.; KTXQ (FM) Dallas/Ft. Worth; and WSUN and WYNF (FM), Tampa/St. Petersburg.

In June 1985 Co. acquired 50% interest in Winterland Productions, a privately-held San Francisco-based Corp., engaged primarily in design, printing and marketing of merchandise for music and entertainment industries. Will be managed by CBS/Records Group.

In Feb. 1986 Co. announced purchase of a half interest in Mainstream Communications (MCC). Mason Best Co., a Texas-based banking firm owns the other half. Mainstream Data is developing a point-to-multipoint data transmission system which will enable clients to transmit digital information rapidly and economically to a number of

FIGURE 10.5 (Continued)

In Jan. 1967, acquired Bailey Films, Inc., and Film Associates of California, both producers and distributors of educational films and filmstrips (substantially all the properties and assets of BFA were sold in 1981).

In Aug. 1967, acquired 49% interest in Television Signal Corp., a CATV system in San Francisco; additional 32% acquired Aug. 7, 1969 bringing CBS ownership to 81% (spun-off in 1971 as part of Viacom International Inc.).

In Sept. 1966, acquired 10.8% Holt, Rinehart and Winston, Inc., and in April 1967, signed merger agreement which provided for issuance of one share of new convertible preference and ½ common share for each of 3,267,153 outstanding shares of Holt. Shareholders of both companies approved merger plan June 29, 1967 and merger became effective Aug. 1, 1967. Holt operated as a wholly-owned subsidiary within CBS/Publishing Group (formerly CBS/Holt Group, which was formed in August 1967). Holt, Rinehart merged into Co. Dec. 31, 1974, and became unit of CBS Educational Publishing Division. (in 1985 the Holt General Book Unit of Holt, Rinehart and Winston was sold).

In Feb. 1967, acquired Republic Corp.'s 70 acre North Hollywood, Cal., studio and equipment for $9,500,000.

In Dec. 1968, acquired substantially all assets and properties and assumed certain liabilities of W.B. Saunders Co., Philadelphia, Pa., publisher of medical reference books, college texts and medical periodicals, in exchange for 1,092,857 common shares.

In Dec. 1968, acquired assets of Discount Records companies, operators of full catalog retail record shops principally at college campuses. (In Mar. 1976, Disro Records, Inc., subsidiary, sold substantially all of its business, assets and properties, including merchandise inventory.)

In Apr. 1969, acquired Clear View Cable Systems, Inc. and Marin Cable Television Inc., operators of CATV systems in Calif. for 51,510 common shares (spun-off in 1971 as part of Viacom International Inc.).

In May 1969, acquired Tele-Vue Systems, Inc., a CATV system operator in California and Washington, for 346,424 common shares plus 79,868 additional shares dependent on future earnings (spun-off in 1971 as part of Viacom International Inc.).

In Nov. 1969, acquired business and assets of Soundcraft division of Reeves Industries, Inc., a manufacturer of high-quality audio-magnetic tape and related products.

In Dec. 1969, acquired National Handcraft Institute, Inc. (dissolved in 1981).

Early in 1970 acquired Franklin School of Science and Arts, Philadelphia, Pa., a paramedical school (sold in 1975).

1985).

In Mar. 1974, Co. and Memorex Corp. sold their joint interest in CMX Systems for cash.

In May 1974, acquired Movie Book Club, Inc., for cash (sold in 1978).

In May 1975, sold the assets and business of the Professional Products Department of its CBS Laboratories Division to Thomson-CSF, a French electronics company, and transferred broadcasting and audio recording research activities of CBS Laboratories to a new CBS Technology Center.

In June 1975, sold the high-technology governmental and industrial contract business of CBS Laboratories to EPSCO, Incorporated of Westwood, Mass., and donated to the New York Institute of Technology of Old Westbury, N.Y., its contract business involving ultrasonic imaging, for medical diagnosis as well as research activities involving new technology in the field of real-time image displays.

In Aug. 1976, acquired Frank Music Corp. for cash (sold in 1979).

In Dec. 1976, acquired from PepsiCo, Inc. assets of Wonder Products Co. for cash.

In Dec. 1976, acquired that part of assets of Praeger Publishers, Inc. involving scholarly monographs, primarily in the social sciences, and college textbooks for cash (sold in 1986).

In Jan. 1977, acquired Fawcett Publications, Inc. for cash (Fawcett magazine subscription fulfillment operation closed and Fawcett paperback book operations were sold in 1981).

In May 1977, acquired The Gemeinhardt Corp., Elkhart, Ind., and its subsidiary K.G. Gemeinhardt Co., a manufacturer of flutes and piccolos, for cash (sold in 1985).

In May 1977, acquired GTO Records Limited, a record company based in the U.K., for cash.

In Aug. 1977, acquired Lyon & Healy, Inc., a manufacturer of harps, for cash (sold in 1985).

In Oct. 1977, acquired Rodgers Organ Company for cash (sold in 1985).

In Dec. 1977, acquired an 80% interest in Doin Editeurs, a medical and science publisher in France, for cash (sold in 1981).

In Aug. 1978, acquired Gabriel Industries, Inc., a manufacturer of toys, for cash.

In Nov. 1979, acquired Audio magazine for cash.

In Jan. 1980, acquired the national newspaper magazine Family Weekly for cash (sold in 1985).

In Feb. 1980, acquired American Photographer magazine for cash.

In Apr. 1982 acquired Cuisine magazine from Cuisine Magazine, Inc. (In 1984 Co. announced it would cease publication of Cuisine and sell subscription list to Conde Nast, Inc.)

In May 1982 acquired Cassell, Ltd.

remote printers or computers. Data transmission linking publishers with their customers or linking head offices with their field offices and stores are two examples of market needs which Mainstream Data will be well positioned to meet.

In Feb. 1986 Co. announced the sale of Winston-Seabury Press, publishers of religious material and part of the CBS Educational and Publishing Division, to Harper & Row Publishers.

On May 16, 1986, Co. sold KMOX-TV to Viacom International Inc. for a cash purchase price of $122.5 million.

In June 1986 CBS Magazines acquired Automobile Quarterly, a quarterly periodical published in hardcover format and sold exclusively by subscription.

On Nov. 10, 1986, Co. sold its music publishing business to SBK Entertainment World, Inc. Included in the sale was CBS Catalogue Partnership, April Music Ltd., Blackwood Music Inc., Music Theatre International and CBS Songs International.

In Dec. 1986, Co. sold it's Educational and Professional Publishing division to Harcourt Brace Jovanovich, Inc. for $500,000,000. The properties involved in the transaction consist, principally of the Holt, Rinehart and Winston, Inc. and W.B. Saunders school, college and professional publishing businesses.

In 1986 CBS Magazines acquired Leisure Time Electronics.

Spin Off: On June 29, 1970, Co. announced plans to combine its domestic cable television and program syndication operations into an independent new co., stock of which would be distributed to Co. shareholders. Decision to spin off Co.'s cable operations came after FCC announced new regulations barring major broadcasting networks from the cable television field and prohibiting joint ownership of cable TV operations and over-the-air TV stations within same community.

On Nov. 11, 1970, Co. announced a tax-free distribution on Dec. 31 of stock of new co., Viacom International Inc., to Co. shareholders on basis of one sh. of Viacom for each 7 Co. com. shs. held of record Dec. 17, 1970.

Distribution was made June 4, 1971. For description of Viacom International Inc. see alphabetical index.

Joint Ventures:

In 1982, formed CBS/FOX Co. as a joint venture with Twentieth Century-Fox Video, Inc.; CBS Software; and discontinued operations of the CBS Cable and Specialty Stores divisions.

In July 1983 Co. and the Sony Corporation formed the Digital Audio Disc Corporation, a new

FIGURE 10.5 (Continued)

subsidiary of CBS-Sony, a record company equally owned by Co. and Sony. Digital Audio, which will be based in Terre Haute, Inc. and which will be started up at a cost of about $21,000,000, is expected to begin producing compact disks, the first commercially produced digital audiodisks, in the later part of 1984. It will function as a custom pressing plant to manufacture compact disks for Co. and other record companies. In 1985 Digital Audio Disc Corporation stock was sold by CBS-Sony to Sony America.

Also in 1983, Co., CPI Film Holdings, Inc. and HBO Film Holdings Inc. formed Tri-Star Pictures, a new venture which is engaged in the production, acquisition and distribution of theatrical motion pictures. Equity financing of the new venture will be contributed equally by the partners, as required. The management of this new film studio is separate from the managements of the three companies and reports to a committee representing the owners. This venture is accounted for on the equity basis. (sold in 1985).

In April 1983, BRS, a division of the Information Technology Group of Thyssen-Bornemisza, and W.B. Saunders, a unit of CBS Educational and Professional Publishing signed a joint venture agreement to provide online medical information services to physicians and other health professionals via computers or terminals.

Interest Sale: In Feb. 1984, Co. and Rainbow Program Enterprises acquired from Washington Post Co. part of its ownership interest in four SportsChannel ventures. As a result of the sale, each company now owns one-third of/SportsChannel Associates (New York), SportsChannel Prism Associates (Philadelphia), SportsChannel Chicago Associates, and one-sixth of SportsChannel New England.

BUSINESS AND PRODUCTS

CBS Inc. conducts its operations domestically and abroad, either directly or through subsidiaries and joint ventures.

The operations of CBS are classified into the CBS/Broadcast Group, the CBS/Records Group, the CBS Magazines Division and "Other"; "Other" consists of various activities not directly associated with the two operating Groups of the Magazines Division, i.e., The CBS/FOX Company, tax benefit leases, various development projects and other miscellaneous activities.

CBS/BROADCAST GROUP consists of seven divisions, whose operations constitute the Broadcast segment of CBS's business.

SportsChannel Chicago Associates (a Chicago-based network); and a 16.5 percent interest in the SportsChannel New England Limited Partnership (a Boston-based network).

Rainbow: In January 1985 CBS acquired fifty percent interests in The Rainbow Service Co. which produces the Bravo and American Movie Classics cable program services, and in Rainbow Programming Services Co., which markets and distributes those services; all of said interests were sold in January 1987.

CBS CableConnect was discontinued during the fourth quarter of 1986. It had sold local cable commercial availabilities in Chicago to local, regional and national advertisers.

CBS/RECORDS GROUP consists of three divisions.

CBS Records Division produces and acquires master recordings and manufactures and distributes phonograph records and tapes in United States for the CBS/Records Group (under the "Columbia," "Epic," "Portrait," "CBS Masterworks" and other labels) and others.

Subsidiaries, joint ventures and licensees under the jurisdiction of the **CBS Records International Division** manufacture and distribute phonograph records and tapes in foreign countries.

Columbia House Division sells phonograph records, tapes and other products at retail on a mail-order basis through the Columbia Record and Tape Club and videotapes through the CBS/Records Group.

CBS Songs Division which was engaged in music publishing, principally through subsidiary corporations, and through CBS Catalogue Partnership (a limited partnership in which CBS was the general partner and had a 50% partnership interest) and its subsidiary corporations, both domestically and in foriegn countries was sold in Nov. 1986.

CBS owns 50% of the common stock and 100% of the preferred stock of Winterland Conscessions Co. ("Winterland") which is engagaed primarily in the design, printing and marketing of apparel for the concert and entertainment industries. In certain circumstances CBS has the obligation to purchase the remaining 50% of the common stock for a price related to winterland's earnings during the three years ending May 31, 1988.

CBS MAGAZINE DIVISION

CBS Magazines Division publishes magazines, including Field & Stream, Road & Track, Cycle World, Woman's Day, Home Mechanix, Audio,

CBS Magazines Division has offices in New York, NY, Greenwich, CT, Chicago, Ill. and Newport Beach, CA.

All foregoing real estate properties are owned by CBS or a wholly-owned subsidiary of CBS, except: radio studios and offices in St. Louis, MO (leases expire December 31, 1992), Boston, MA (lease expires December 31, 2006) and San Francisco, CA (lease expires December 31, 1995), Dallas, TX (lease expires September 30, 1989) and Houston, TX. (lease expires March 1, 1994). CBS Records Division has office space in Los Angeles, CA (lease expires January 31, 1992). CBS Records International Division leases warehouse space in Germany (lease expires January 31, 1990) and office, studio and manufacturing space in Australia (lease expire May 23, 1989 and September 30, 1990) and warehouse space in Italy (leease expires August 31, 1992). Columbia House Division leases its offices in New York, NY (leases expire April 30, 1988). CBS Magazines Division leases its offices in New York, NY (leases expire June 30, 1991 and January 31, 1988) Newport Beach, CA (lease expires May 14, 1990) and Chicago, IL (lease expires September 30, 1995).

CBS owns or leases other real properties, domestic and foreign, used in connection with its broadcasting, manufacturing, publishing and other activities.

CBS leases offices at CBS/MTM Studios in North Hollywood, CA on a month-to-month basis.

SUBSIDIARIES

Company is an operating and holding company. As of Mar. 20, 1987, company or a subsidiary of company held 100% voting power (except as noted) in the following active subsidiaries.

Aspenfair Music Inc. (California)
Beverlyfax Music Inc. (California)
Cadisco Inc. (New York)
CBS/Australia Pty. Limited (Australia)
CBS Productions Pty. Limited (Australia)
CBS Records Australia Limited (Australia)
CBS Songs Australia Pty. Limited (Australia)
Entertainment Distributors Co. Pty. Limited (Australia) (50%)
Music Publishing Co. of Australia Pty. Limited (Australia) (50%)
CBS Broadcast International of Canada Limited (Canada)
CBS Columbia C.A. (Venezuela)
CBS Columbia A.G. (Switzerland)
CBS Disques/Grammofoonplaten S.A./.N.V (Belgium)
CBS Grammofoonplaten B.V. (Holland)

FIGURE 10.5 (Continued)

CBS Television Network Division distributes a comprehensive schedule of news and public affairs broadcasts, entertainment and sports programming and feature films to more than 212 independently owned and four CBS Owned television stations in 47 states and the District of Columbia and to certain overseas and foreign affiliated stations.

CBS Entertainment Division produces and otherwise acquires entertainment series and other programs, and acquires feature films, for distribution by the CBS Television Network for broadcast.

CBS Sports Division produces and otherwise acquires sports programs for distribution by the CBS Television Network for broadcast.

CBS News Division operates a worldwide news organization which produces regularly scheduled news and public affairs broadcasts and special reports for the CBS Television and Radio Networks.

CBS Television Stations Division operates and serves as sales representative for four CBS Owned television stations (located in New York, Chicago, Los Angeles, and Philadelphia).

CBS Radio Division operates the seven CBS Owned AM and 11 CBS Owned FM radio stations (located in New York, Chicago, Los Angeles, Philadelphia, St. Louis, San Francisco, Houston, Washington, D.C., Dallas/Ft. Worth, Tampa/St. Petersburg and Boston), serves as sales representative for the CBS Owned radio stations and approximately 25 independently owned radio stations, and three independently owned radio networks, and operates the CBS Radio Network which consists of the six CBS Owned AM stations and approximately 410 independently owned AM and FM stations in the United States. A second radio network service "CBS RADIORADIO" provides programming services to seven of the CBS Owned FM Stations and approximately 160 independently owned stations.

CBS Operations and Engineering Division is responsible for all television program production (film and tape) activities of the CBS/Broadcast Group at all domestic production facilities, as well as for all engineering and engineering development operations, satellite and terrestrial systems engineering and network transmission.

Other activities within the CBS/Broadcast Group are briefly described in the following paragraphs:

CBS Broadcast International engages in the worldwide sale and distribution of news and public affairs broadcasts, sports and entertainment programming and feature films to broadcast and other media (including cable, airlines and home video).

SportsChannel: CBS owns the following interests in four regional pay cable networks and various management agreements: a 33 percent interest in SportsChannel Associates (a New York-based network); one-third interest in SportsChannel Prism Associates (a Philadelphia-based network) and

American Photographer, Backpacker, Boating, Car and Driver, Cycle, Flying, Modern Bride, Popular Photography, Skiing, Stereo Review, Automobile Quarterly, and Leisure Time Electronics, Yachting and Skiing Trade News. The division is engaged in magazine newsstand distribution through CBS Magazine Marketing.

OTHER ACTIVITIES

CBS/FOX Company, a partnership in which CBS and a wholly-owned subsidiary of Twentieth Century-Fox Film Corporation each owns a 50% interest, is engaged in the manufacture and marketing of prerecorded videotapes of feature films, television programs, music videos and other products. CBS owns a 50% interest in Mainstream Communications Corp., which in turn owns significant minority interests in Mainstream Data, Ltd., a limited partnership which is developing a point-to-multipoint data transmission system.

Revenues & Profits Before Taxes By Operating Group (in millions of dollars):

	1986	1985
Revenues		
Broadcast Group	2,817.2	2,785.4
Records Group	1,489.4	1,229.7
Magazines	407.2	407.1
Other	41.6	32.6
Elim. of Intergroup Revenues	(1.7)	(2.8)
Total	4,753.7	4,755.6
Operating Profits		
Broadcast Group	228.6	373.8
Records Group	192.1	89.7
Magazines	10.6	4.6
Other	(4.7)	7.7
Total	426.6	475.8

PROPERTIES

The principal executive offices of CBS are in its headquarters building at 51 West 52nd Street, New York, NY 10019.

Major CBS television and radio facilities are located at CBS Broadcast Center in New York, NY; CBS Television City and Columbia Square in Los Angeles, CA; and in Chicago, IL; Philadelphia, PA; St. Louis, MO; Boston, MA; San Francisco, CA; and Washington, D.C.; Dallas and Houston, TX.

CBS Records Division's principal manufacturing plants are located in Pitman, NJ; and Carrollton, GA.

CBS Records International Division has office, manufacturing and warehousing facilities in various parts of the world, the larger ones being in Great Britain, Brazil, Canada, Mexico, Argentina, Italy, the Netherlands, Colombia, Australia and Spain; and has offices and warehouses in France and Germany.

Columbia House Division has a warehouse and offices in Terre Haute and Bloomington, IN.

CBS Songs Holland B.V. (Holland)
CBS Records A.B. (Sweden)
CBS Records ApS (Denmark)
CBS Grammofonselskabs Distributions Centralen A/S (Denmark) (25%)
CBS Records A/S (Norway)
CBS Records Inc. (Baar) (Switzerland)
CBS Records Ltd. (Israel)
CBS Schallplatten G.m.b.H. (Germany)
Discos CBS, S.A. (Spain)
Funckler B.V. (Holland)
Industria de Discos Centroamericana, S.A. (Costa Rica)
Distribuidora Salvadorena de Discos, S.A. (El Salvador)
Distribuidora Panamena de Discos, S.A. (Panama)
Distribuidora Guatemalteca de Discos, S.A. (Guatemala)
CBS/Columbia Internacional, S.A. (Mexico)
CBS Dischi S.p.A. (Italy)
CBS Discos del Peru S.A. (Peru)
CBS Epic (Thailand) Limited (Thailand) (60%)
CBS FMX Stero Inc. (New York)
CBS/FOX Company, The [General Partnership] (New York) (50%)
CBS/FOX VIDEO (Holdings) Ltd. (England)
CBS/FOX VIDEO Limited (England)
CBS/FOX VIDEO (Germany) G.m.b.H. (Germany)
CBS/FOX VIDEO (South Pacific) Pty Ltd. (Australia)
CBS/FOX VIDEO (Canada) Ltd. (Canada)
CBS/FOX VIDEO (Espanola) S.A. (Spain) (90%)
CBS/FOX VIDEO French Film Licensing Corp. (New York)
CBS/FOX VIDEO (France) S.A. (France) (99%)
CBS/FOX VIDEO International S.A.R.L. (France) (99%)
CBS/FOX VIDEO (New Zealand) Limited (New Zealand) (99.99%)
CBS/FOX VIDEO (Far East) K.K. (Japan)
CBS/FOX VIDEO Ltd. (India) Limited (India) (40%)
CBS International S.A. (France)
CBS Disques S.A. (France) (86.62%)
Gilda, S.A.R.L. (France) (25.0%)
CBS Electronics Ltd. (Greece) (95.0%)
CBS Music and Video Enterprises Ltd. (Greece) (95%)
CBS/MTM Company [General Partnership] (California) (50%)
CBS Music (Thailand) Limited (Thailand) (60%)
CBS Nigeria Limited (Nigeria) (60%)
CBS Overseas Inc. (New York)
CBS (Portugal) Musica y Discos Ltd. (Portugal)
CBS Records Canada, Inc. (Canada)
CBS Music Products Inc. (Canada)
CBS Records Chile Ltda. (Chile) (98%)
CBS Records International Ltd. (England)
CBS Records (Kenya) Limited (Kenya) (70%)

FIGURE 10.5   (Continued)

1086

MOODY'S INDUSTRIAL MANUAL

CBS Records (Malaysia) Sdn. Bhd. (Malaysia)
CBS Records OY (Finland) (33.3%)
PEC Musiikkituku OY (Finland) (33.3%)
CBS Shallplattengesellschaft m.b.H. (Austria)
Music Service Center Gesellschaft m.b.H. (Austria) (33.3%)
CBS Singapore (Pte.) Ltd. (Singapore)
CBS/SONY Group Inc. (Japan) (50%)
April Music Inc. (Japan)
CBS/SONY Inc. (Japan)
CBS/SONY California, Inc. (Calif.)
CBS/SONY Family Club, Inc. (Japan)
CBS/SONY Hong Kong Limited (Hong Kong) (51%)
CBS/Sony Publishing Inc. (Japan)
CBS/SONY Records Inc. (Japan)
EPIC/SONY, Inc. (Japan)
Japan Record Distribution System, Inc. (Japan) (50%)
Music Plaza, Inc. (Japan)
SD Hokkaido Inc. (Japan)
SD Kansai Inc. (Japan)
CBS United Kingdom Limited (England)
Diski CBS AEBE (Greece)
CBS Urban Renewal Corporation (New Jersey)
CJG Productions, Inc. (New York)
Columbia Television, Inc. (New York)
Discos CBS Industria e Comercio Ltda. (Brazil)
Discos CBS International de Puerto Rico Inc. (Puerto Rico)
Discos CBS S.A.I.C.F. (Argentina)
Discos CBS, S.A. (Colombia)
Filmvision Inc. (New York)
Houston Motion Picture Entertainment, Inc. (Texas)
Mainstream Communications Corp. (Del.) (70.0%)
Maindata, Inc. (Del.) (70.0%)
SportsChannel Chicago Inc. (New York)
SportsChannel Chicago Associates [General Partnership] (New York) (33.3%)
Sportscene New England Inc. (New York)
Cablevision Programming New England Corp. (New York) (33.3%)
Sportscene New York Inc. (New York)
SportsChannel Associates [General Partnership] (New York) (33.3%)
Sportscene Prism Inc. (New York)
SportsChannel Prism Associates [General Partnership] (New York) (33.3%)
Vista Marketing Inc. (New York)

Winterland Concessions Company (Calif.) (50.0%)
Winterland Productions, Ltd. (Calif.)

MANAGEMENT

Officers

W.S. Paley, Chmn.
L.A. Tisch, Pres. & Chief Exec. Off.
G.F. Jankowski, Vice-Pres. (& Pres. CBS/Broadcast Group)
W.R. Yetnikoff, Vice-Pres. (& Pres. CBS/Records Group)
H.P. MacCowatt, Senior Vice-Pres., Admin.
F.J. Meyer, Senior Vice-Pres., Fin.
J.F. Sirmons, Senior Vice-Pres., Ind. Rel.
J.G. Blowers, Vice-Pres. Inv. Rel.
Louis Dorfsman, Vice-Pres., Creative Dir., Adv. & Design
L.B. Glasberg, Vice-Pres. & Gen. Auditor
P.W. Keegan, Vice-Pres. & Contr.
D.S. McCoy, Vice-Pres., Technology
L.J. Rauchenberger, Jr., Vice-Pres. & Treas.
P.J. Schementi, Vice-Pres. Mgt. Inform. Syst.
Joan Showalter, Vice-Pres., Personnel
Nathan Snyder, Vice-Pres., Acquis.
George Vradenburg III, Vice-Pres. & Gen. Counsel
Marilyn Walsh, Vice-Pres. & Dir. of Taxes
C.T. Bates, Sec.

Directors

(Showing Principal Corporate Affiliations)

Laurence A. Tisch, Pres. & Chief Exec. Off., CBS Inc.; Chmn. & Chief Exec. Off., Loews Corp.; Dir., Bulova Watch Co., Inc., Automatic Data Processing, Inc., R.H. Macy & Co., Inc. and Petrie Stores Corp.

William S. Paley, Chmn., CBS Inc.; Partner, Whitcom Investment Co.

Michel C. Bergerac, Private Investor; Dir., Manufacturers Hanover Corp. & Sybron Corp.

Harold Brown, Chmn. of the Foreign Policy Institute, The Johns Hopkins University; Dir., International Business Machines Corp., AMAX Inc., Philip Morris Inc., Cummins Engine Co., Inc. & Synergen, Inc.

Walter Cronkite, Special Correspondent, CBS News.

Roswell L. Gilpatric, Retired Presiding Partner, Cravath, Swaine & Moore, Attorneys.

James R. Houghton, Chmn. & Chief Exec. Off., Corning Glass Works; Dir., Dow Corning Corp., Metropolitan Life Insurance Co. & J.P. Morgan & Co., Inc.

Newton N. Minow, Partner, Sidley & Austin, Attorneys; Dir., Chicago Pacific Corp., Foote Cone & Belding Communications, Inc., Aetna Casualty and Surety Co., Illinois and Aetna Life Insurance Co. Illinois, & Encyclopaedia Britannica Inc.

Henry B. Schacht, Chmn. & Chief Exec. Off., Cummins Engine Co., Inc.; Dir., American Telephone and Telegraph Co., & The Chase Manhattan Bank, N.A.

Edson W. Spencer, Chmn. & Chief Exec. Off., Honeywell.

Franklin A. Thomas, Pres., The Ford Foundation; Dir., Allied Stores Corp., Aluminum Co. of America, Citibank, N.A./Citicorp, Cummins Engine Co., Inc. and New York Life Insurance Co.

Marietta Tree, Dir., Llewelyn-Davies, Sahni, Inc., architectural and city planning; Pan Am Corp. Lend Lease Corp. (Ltd.) Australia and International Income Property Inc.

James D. Wolfensohn, Pres., James D. Wolfensohn Inc., Advisory & Investment firm; Dir., Timeplex, Inc.; Chmn., Carnegie Hall Corp.

Auditors: Coopers & Lybrand.

Shareholder Relations: J. Garrett Blowers, Vice-Pres., Investor Relations. Tel: (212) 975-6075.

Director Meetings: (in 1986) Each month except Aug.

Annual Meeting: Third Wednesday in May.

No. of Stockholders: Dec. 31, 1986, preferred Series A, 403; common, 17,939.

No. of Employees: Dec. 31, 1986, (approx.) 18,300.

Office: 51 W. 52' St., New York, NY 10019. Tel: (212)975-4321.

FIGURE 10.5   (Continued)

INCOME ACCOUNTS

COMPARATIVE CONSOLIDATED INCOME ACCOUNTS, YEARS ENDED DEC 31
(in thousands of dollars)

	1986	⑤1985	②⑤1984
Revenues:			
Net sales:			
Broadcasting	2,807,500	2,777,800	2,714,500
Products	1,838,800	1,598,200	1,549,200
Interest & other income	107,400	76,000	88,400
Total revenues	4,753,700	4,452,000	4,352,100
Expenses:			
①Cost of sales:			
Broadcasting	2,243,300	2,082,700	1,988,100
Products	1,016,300	897,700	875,900
①Selling, general & admin. exp.	1,068,700	1,052,000	938,500
④Unusual items	16,100	(30,000)	49,300
Interest & other expenses	124,700	115,400	……
Total expenses	4,469,100	4,117,800	3,851,800
Income from cont. oper. before inc. taxes	284,600	334,200	500,300
Income taxes	94,800	142,000	224,600
Income from contin. oper.	189,800	192,200	275,700
Discontinued operations:			
Gain from jt. vent. sale of stk.	13,800	2,100	(36,800)
Gain (loss) from operations, net	185,600	(34,600)	(43,100)
Gain (loss) on disposals, net	(14,100)	(132,300)	16,600
③Extraord. items	……	……	……
Net income	375,100	27,400	212,400
Retained earnings, begin. of year	251,400	1,309,300	1,181,700
Accret. of preference B stk.	12,500	200	100
Preference dividends	70,600	5,200	84,700
Common dividends	……	79,800	……
Retire. of com. stk. repurch.	……	936,800	……
Reclass. to com. stk. subj. to redempt.	……	63,400	……
Retained earnings, end of year	543,200	251,400	1,309,300
SUPPLEMENTARY P. & L. DATA			
Taxes, other than income	……	76,100	70,500
Royalties	398,500	322,823	358,193
Advertising costs	244,764	224,430	183,978
Depreciation & amortization	107,726	105,328	59,911

①Includes related portions of items shown under "Supplementary p. & l. data" below statement.
②Restated for the discontinuance of the toys, theatrical films and home computer software operations.
③1986, loss on extinguishment of debt.
1984 gain on sale of land net of taxes.
④Relating to asset disposition and expense reduction programs due to tender offer.
⑤Restated for the discontinuance of it's educational and professional publishing operations.

Consolidated Statement of Changes in Financial Position (in millions):

	1986	⑤1985
Funds provided by operations:		
Inc. from cont. oper.	$189.8	$192.2
Items not affecting funds:		
Deprec. and amortiz.	107.7	105.4
Def. inc. taxes	12.8	54.8
Share of undistrib. inc. in companies accounted for under the equity method	(21.6)	(16.2)
Funds prov. by cont. oper.	288.7	336.2
Funds prov. by (used for) discont. oper. excl., items not affecting funds	224.4	(121.7)
	513.1	214.5
Net change in working capital excl. cash and debt	181.2	221.4
	(83.3)	(85.1)
Div. to shareholders		
Funds prov. by (used for) investment:		
(Incr.) decr. in property, plant and equip.	(82.6)	(113.6)
Capital expenditures	63.0	82.5
Invest. in joint ventures and other	95.6	(36.0)
(Incr.) decr. in excess of the cost over the fair value of net assets of businesses acq.	12.9	(362.7)
Incr. in other net assets	263.2	(100.2)
Increase (decrease) due to:		
Iss. of Series B pref. stock	352.1	(530.0)
Retire. of repurch. com. stock	……	123.2
		(962.9)

FIGURE 10.5 (Continued)

MOODY'S INDUSTRIAL MANUAL 1087

	1986	1985
Foreign currency fluctuations and other changes	33.5	
Incr. (decr.) in lg.-tm. debt	583.5	(323.5)
Extinguishment of debt ..	14.1	(14.1)
Incr. (decr.) in cash and cash equival. before fin. activities:	(558.5)	845.3
Funds provided by (used for) financing activities:	996.6	(1,004.8)
Incr. (decr.) in sht.-tm. debt	(220.9)	261.8
Net incr. (decr.) in cash and cash equivalents	438.1	(159.5)
Cash and cash equivalents at beg. of year	120.1	279.6
Cash and cash equivalents at end of year	558.2	120.1

[1]Restated.

BALANCE SHEETS

COMPARATIVE CONSOLIDATED BALANCE SHEETS, AS OF DEC. 31

(in thousands of dollars)

	1986	1985	1984	1983
ASSETS				
Cash & cash items	41,700	75,800	13,976	24,150
Short-term market secur. (cost & accr. int.)	516,500	44,300	265,661	18,698
Notes & accounts receivable, net	789,700	785,000	849,787	829,604
[1]Inventories	117,300	173,300	290,503	295,338
Program rights & feature film productions	465,800	483,900	461,998	490,861
Recoverable income tax		130,900		
Prepaid expenses & other	132,400	142,900	143,979	150,885
Total current assets	2,063,400	1,836,100	2,025,904	1,809,536
Property, plant & equipment:				
Land	26,000	27,600	31,395	44,959
Buildings	288,200	304,000	333,568	315,926
Machinery & equipment	578,000	620,400	596,917	573,450
Leasehold improvements	38,200	53,000	51,851	49,402
Total	930,400	1,005,000	1,013,731	983,737
Less: Accumulated depreciation	424,000	445,700	414,405	372,877
Net property plant and equipment account	506,400	559,300	599,326	610,860
Investments	178,900	252,900	200,745	163,806
Excess costs of acquisitions over fair value	397,300	420,800	66,979	68,198
Other intangibles	41,600	70,900	25,749	30,442
Other assets	182,700	368,700	343,060	307,000
Total	3,370,300	3,508,700	3,261,763	2,989,842
LIABILITIES				
Accounts payable	166,200	228,900	174,597	172,228
Accrued royalties	235,800	240,600	252,497	230,108
Accr. salaries, wages & benefits	105,700	130,500	99,985	124,173
Liab. for talent & program rights	264,500	278,700	253,235	247,368
Commercial paper		109,600		64,787
Other current debt	56,600	167,900	15,659	10,682
Income taxes	34,700	14,600	37,416	88,380
Other	436,100	379,400	263,946	198,476
Total current liabilities	1,299,600	1,550,200	1,097,335	1,136,202
Long-term debt	630,800	954,300	370,780	232,507
Other liabilities	248,800	173,800	146,742	110,158
Deferred income taxes	196,000	160,700	93,968	70,514
Com. stk. subj. to redempt.	65,200	65,200		
Ser. B pref. stk. ($1)	123,400	123,200		
Convertible preference, ser. A (par $1)	[6]	[6]	59	67
Common stock ($2.50)	59,900	59,800	76,604	76,597
[3]Additional paid-in capital	230,900	226,900	286,419	286,641
Foreign currency fluctuations	21,400	(7,200)	(68,144)	(51,410)
Retained earnings	543,200	251,400	1,309,300	1,181,689
Total stockholders' equity	855,400	530,900	1,604,238	1,493,584
[4]Less: Treasury stock	48,900	49,600	51,300	53,123
Net stockholders' equity	806,500	481,300	1,552,938	1,440,461
Total	3,370,300	3,508,700	3,261,763	2,989,842
Net current assets	763,800	285,900	928,569	673,334

FIGURE 10.5   (Continued)

[1]At lower of cost (principally based on average cost) or market.
1986: Finished goods, $69,300,000; work in process, $4,400,000; raw materials, $39,200,000; supplies, $4,400,000; total, $117,300,000.

[3]Principal capital surplus changes follow:
1986: After debiting $.1 due to the conversion of Ser. A preference stock and crediting $4.0 for the exercise of stock options and $.1 miscellaneous, net.
1985: After debiting $58.3 due to the retirement of common stock repurchased, reclassification of $4.0 to common stock subject to redemption and $.8 excess of cost of treasury stock over par value of preference stock exchanged on conversion and crediting $3.4 for the exercise of stock options and $.2 miscellaneous, net.
1984: After debiting $327,000 excess of cost of treasury stock over par value of preference stock exchanged on conversion and crediting $105,000 miscellaneous, net.
1983: After debiting $891,000 excess of cost of treasury stock over par value of preference stock exchanged on conversion and debiting $165,000 miscellaneous, net.

[4]Represented by common shares (at cost): 1986, 866,800; 1985, 885,997; 1984, 924,028; 1983, 962,605.
[6]Amounted to $35,000.

Notes To Consolidated Financial Statements
(1) PRINCIPLES OF CONSOLIDATION. The consolidated financial statements include the accounts of the Company, its domestic subsidiaries and substantially all of its foreign subsidiaries. Those foreign subsidiaries that are not consolidated are not significant and are carried at cost. Investments in 20%-50% owned companies are generally carried on the equity basis. Other investments are generally carried at cost. All significant intercompany transactions have been excluded from the consolidated financial statements. The financial statements of most foreign subsidiaries are as of a date one or two months prior to the date of the consolidated financial statements in order to be available for inclusion in the consolidation.
(2) REVENUE RECOGNITION. The Company's practice is to record revenues from sales of products when shipped and services when performed. Allowances for estimated returns are provided based upon prior experience.
(3) INCOME TAXES. The Company recognizes the tax effects of transactions in the year such transactions enter into the determination of net income regardless of when they are recognized for income tax purposes. Deferred income taxes are provided for accelerated tax depreciation, capitalization of interest and for other timing differences. Investment tax credits are applied as a reduction of the current tax provision.
(4) INVENTORIES. Inventories are stated at the lower of cost (principally based on average cost) or market value.
(5) PROGRAMS FOR TELEVISION BROADCAST. Costs incurred in connection with the production of or purchase of rights to programs to be broadcast on television within one year are classified as current assets, representing the principal portion of the balance sheet caption "Program rights and feature film productions." The noncurrent portion is included as a part of the balance sheet caption "Other program rights and feature film productions." The program costs are charged to expense as the respective programs are broadcast.
(6) PROPERTY, PLANT AND EQUIPMENT. Land, buildings and equipment are stated at cost. Depreciation is computed principally using the straight-line method over the estimated useful lives of the assets. Major improvements to existing plant and equipment are capitalized. Expenditures for maintenance and repairs which do not extend the life of the assets are charged to expense as incurred. The cost of properties retired or otherwise disposed of and any related accumulated depreciation are generally removed from the accounts and the resulting gain or loss is reflected in income currently.
(7) INTANGIBLES. The excess of the cost over the fair value at the date of acquisition of net assets of businesses and investments acquired subsequent to October 31, 1970 is being amortized over a period of 40 years on a straight-line basis; amounts applicable to businesses and investments acquired on or prior to that date are not being amortized. The costs of other intangible assets are being amortized over their respective economic lives.

STATISTICAL RECORD

	1986	[2]1985	[2]1984	1983
Earned per share — common:				
[3]On average shares:				
Continuing operations	$7.54	$6.89	$9.28	$6.76
Discontinued operations	8.48	d6.08	d2.69	d0.45
Extraordinary item	d0.60	.....	0.56	.....
Net income	$15.42	$0.81	$7.15	$6.31
Divs. paid per sh.— preference A	$1.00	$1.00	$1.00	$1.00
Preference B	$10.00	$4.17		
common	$3.00	$3.00	$2.85	$2.80
Price Range — preference	99 1/2-85	85 1/2-52 1/2	58 1/2-44 1/4	53 1/2-39 3/8
— common	151 1/2-110	126 1/4-70 7/8	87 3/4-61 1/2	81 3/4-55
Net tangible assets per common share	$15.55	.....	$49.05	$44.99
[1]Times charges earned:				
Before income taxes	3.28	3.90	11.15	.....
After income taxes	2.52	2.67	6.59	.....

FIGURE 10.5   (Continued)

1088

MOODY'S INDUSTRIAL MANUAL

	1986	③1985	③1984	1983
③On average shares:				
Price Range — deb. 7.85s, 2001	94½-87	77½-65	66½-60⅛	85⅞-70
— 14½% notes, 1992	108-108			104¼-104¼
— 11⅜% notes, 1992	109½-103¼			
— 10⅞% notes, 1994	109¼-91			
— 10⅞% sr. notes, 1995	112¾-102	105¼-96⅞		
Net tangible assets $1,000 l. term debt	$2,474	$1,941	$4,938	$6,771
Net curr. assets per $1,000 l. term debt	$1.21	$0.30	$2,504	$2,896
Number of shares — preference A				
— Preference B	35,116	38,026	58,922	67,384
Number of shares outstanding — common	1,250,000	1,250,000		
At year end	23,528,127	23,448,681	29,717,639	29,676,152
Average weighted	23,506,000	27,123,000	28,708,000	29,665,000
Financial & Operating Ratios				
Current Assets ÷ Current Liabilities	1.59	1.18	1.85	1.59
% cash & securities to current assets	27.05	6.54	13.80	2.37
% inventories to current assets	5.68	9.44	14.34	16.32
% net current assets to net worth	94.71	59.40	59.79	46.74
% property depreciated	45.57	44.35	40.88	37.90
% annual depr. to gross property	11.58	10.45	5.92	5.75
Capitalization:				
Long term debt	34.62	53.47	18.38	13.34
Deferred inc. taxes	10.76	9.00	4.66	4.04
% preferred stock	6.77	6.90		0.01
% common stock & surplus	44.27	19.72	76.76	82.61
Sales ÷ Inventories	39.61	25.25	14.68	
Sales ÷ Receivables	5.88	5.57	5.02	
% sales to net property	917.52	730.19	711.42	
% sales to total assets	137.86	124.72	130.71	
% net income to total assets	11.13	0.78	6.51	
% net income to net worth	20.59	5.69	13.67	
Analysis of Operations:	%	%	%	%
Gross sales, less returns, allow., etc.	100.00	100.00	100.00	
Cost of sales	70.15	68.11	67.17	
Selling, general, etc., expenses	23.00	24.04	22.01	
Balance	6.13	7.64	11.73	
Interest and Other income	2.31	1.74	2.07	
Total	8.44	9.38	13.80	
Interest paid				
Other expense	2.68	2.64	1.16	
Balance	5.76	7.74	12.64	
Income taxes	2.04	3.24	5.27	
Unusual items	0.35	(0.09)		
Inc. from cont. oper.	4.08	4.39	6.47	
Discont. oper.	4.29	3.77	1.87	
Extraord. item	(0.30)		0.36	
Net income	8.07	0.59	4.67	

①On income from continuing operations. ②Restated. ③As reported by Co. on aver. shares.

②Restated.

FIGURE 10.5 (Continued)

LONG TERM DEBT

1. CBS Inc. (Columbia Broadcasting System, Inc.) sinking fund debenture 7.85s, due 2001:

Rating — A3

AUTH.—$50,000,000 outstg. Dec. 31, 1986, $37,460,000.
DATED—Aug. 1, 1971. DUE—Aug. 1, 2001.
INTEREST—F&A1 by mail to holders of record on 15th day prior to interest date.
TRUSTEE—Chemical Bank. NYC.
DENOMINATION—Fully registered, $1,000 and any authorized multiple thereof. Transferable and may be combined or split up without service charge.
CALLABLE—As a whole or in part on at least 30 days' notice to each July 31, as follows:

1987 ....103.14	1988 ....102.83	1989 ....102.51	
1990 ....102.20	1991 ....101.88	1992 ....101.57	
1993 ....101.26	1994 ....100.94	1995 ....100.63	
1996 ....100.31	1997–2001..100.00		

Also callable for Sinking Fund (see below).
SINKING FUND—Annually prior to each Aug. 1, to 2000, to retire debs., cash (or debs.) in amount of $2,500,000; plus similar optional payments. Payments calculated to retire 95% of issue prior to maturity.
SECURITY—Not secured. Co. or any restricted subsidiary may not create any lien on its property without equally and ratably securing the debs. (except certain permitted encumbrances such as purchase money mortgages, existing liens, liens in connection with Govt. contracts, etc.) unless after giving effect thereto aggregate of all such secured indebtedness, plus all attributable debt of Co. and restricted subsidiaries in respect to sale and leaseback transactions would not exceed 10% of consolidated net worth.
SALE & LEASEBACK RESTRICTIONS—Co. or any restricted subsidiary may not lease any real property in the United States for a period in excess of 3 years any such property that has been owned for more than 6 months and which has been or is to be sold to such lender or investor unless (1) the property can be mortgaged in an amount equal to debt occuring in such transaction without equally securing the debs., or (2) Co. within 6 months applies to retirement of debs. an amount equal to either net proceeds of such sale or fair market value of such property, whichever is greater.
LISTED—On New York Stock Exchange.
INDENTURE MODIFICATION—Indenture may be modified, except as provided, with consent of 66⅔% of debs.
PURPOSE—Proceeds to repay notes outstg. under revolving credit agreement.
OFFERED—($50,000,000) at 100 (proceeds to Co., 99.125) on July 15, 1971 thru First Boston Corp. and associates. Proceeds to repay notes outstg. on bank line of credit.

2. CBS Inc. 14½% notes due 1992:

Rating — A3

AUTH.—$150,000,000; outstg. Dec. 31, 1986, $55,389,000.
DATED—June 15, 1982. DUE—June 15, 1992.

INTEREST—J&D 15 to holders registered J&D 1.
TRUSTEE—Chase Manhattan Bank N.A.
DENOMINATION—Fully registered, $1,000 and any multiple thereof. Transferable and exchangeable without service charge.
CALLABLE—As a whole or in part on or after June 15, 1989 on at least 30 days' but not more than 60 days' notice at 100 together with accrued interest to the date fixed for redemption.
SECURITY—Not secured. The notes will rank pari passu with Co.'s 7.85% debs. due 2001 now outstg. Co. will not, and will not permit any restricted subsidiary to, incur, issue, assume, guarantee or suffer to exist any indebtedness for borrowed money secured by a mortgage, pledge or other lien on any of its or their tangible property, or on any shares of stock or indebtedness of a restricted subsidiary, without providing that the notes shall be secured equally and ratably with such secured indebtedness, unless after giving effect thereto the aggregate amount of all such secured in-debtedness plus all attributable debt of Co. and its restricted subsidiaries in respect of sale and leaseback transactions, but excluding any sale and leaseback transactions the proceeds of which are applied to the retirement of funded debt, would not exceed 10% of consolidated net worth.
The foregoing restriction does not apply to (1) Mortgages existing on the date of the indenture, (2) Mortgages on property of, or on any shares of stock or indebtedness of, any corporation existing at the time such corporation becomes a subsidiary, (3) Mortgages on property of any corporation existing at the time such corporation is merged into or consolidated with, or at the time of any sale, lease, or other disposition of all or substantially all its assets to, Co. or a restricted subsidiary, (4) mortgages on property existing at the time of acquisition thereof and purchase money mortgages, (5) Mortgages to secure all or part of the cost of repairing, altering, constructing, improving or developing such property as is, in the opinion of Co.'s Board of Directors, substantially unimproved and (6) Mortgages in favor of Co. or a restricted subsidiary; and will not apply to any extension, renewal or replacement of any mortgage referred to in the foregoing clauses (1) through (6).
The mortgage of any tangible property in favor of governmental bodies to secure progress or advance payments is not deemed to create indebtedness secured by a mortgage.
SALE AND LEASEBACK—Co. will not, and will not permit any restricted subsidiary to, enter into any arrangement with any bank, insurance company or other lender or investor providing for the leasing by Co. or such restricted subsidiary for more than six months and which has been or is to be sold or transferred by Co. for such restricted subsidiary to such lender or investor unless (1) Co. or such restricted subsidiary could mortgage such property in an amount equal to the attributable debt with respect to such Sale and Leaseback Transaction without equally and ratably securing

the notes or (2) Co., within six months, applies to the retirement of the notes or funded debt of Co. ranking on a parity therewith an amount equal to the greater of (i) the net proceeds of the sale of the real property leased pursuant to such arrangement or (ii) the fair market value of the real property so leased.
INDENTURE MODIFICATION—Indenture may be modified, except as provided, with consent of a majority of notes outstg.
RIGHTS ON DEFAULT—Trustee, or 25% of notes outstg., may declare principal due and payable (30 days' grace for payment of interest).
PURPOSE—Proceeds were applied to retire certain commercial paper borrowings.
OFFERED—($150,000,000) at 99.375 plus accrued interest (proceeds to Co., 98.700) on June 11, 1982 thru Morgan Stanley & Co., Inc., Lazard Freres & Co. and associates.

3. CBS Inc., 11⅜% notes due 1992

Rating — A3

AUTH.—$100,000,000; outstg. Dec. 31, 1986 $82,160,000.
DATED—Dec. 7, 1984 DUE—Dec. 20, 1992.
INTEREST—Annually Dec. 20.
CALLABLE—As a whole or in part on or after Dec. 20, 1990 at 100.50 together with accrued interest to date of fixed redemption.
OFFERED—($100,000,000) on Dec. 3 1984 thru underwriters led by Swiss Bank Corp. International, Morgan Stanley International and S.G. Warburg & Co. Ltd.

4. CBS Inc. 10⅞% (Euro Sterling) notes due 1994:

Rating — A3

AUTH.—£40,000,000 ($59,320,000) outstg. Dec 31, 1986, £35,550,000 ($52,720,650).
DATED—Dec. 7, 1984 DUE—Dec. 20, 1994.
INTEREST—Annually Dec. 20.
CALLABLE—As a whole or in part on or after Dec. 20, 1992 at 100.50 together with accrued interest in date of fixed redemption.
SECURITY—Issue defeased on Feb. 12, 1986 with U.S. Treasury Securities.
OFFERED—£40,000,000 ($46,680,000) on Dec. 3, 1984 thru a group headed by Swiss Bank Corp. International, Morgan Stanley International and S.W. Warburg & Co. Ltd.

5. CBS Inc. 10⅞% senior notes due 1995:

Rating — A3

AUTH.—$399,915,000; outstanding Dec. 31, 1986, $399,915,900.
DATED—Aug. 1, 1985 DUE—Aug. 1, 1995
INTEREST—F&A1 by mail to holders of record on the 15th day of the month preceeding the interest date.
TRUSTEE—Chase Manhattan Bank, N.A.
DENOMINATION—Full Registered, denomination of $1,000 and any multiple thereof, denominations of less than $1,000 may be issued in denominations of $100 and multiples thereof, up to $900.
CALLABLE—As a whole or in part not less than 30, or more than 60 days notice, at any time after

FIGURE 10.5   (Continued)

MOODY'S INDUSTRIAL MANUAL

1089

August 1, 1992, at 100 plus accrued and unpaid interest to redemption date.

SECURITY — Unsecured Notes will rank pari passu with all other unsecured and unsubordinated debt.

LISTED — On New York Stock Exchange

INDENTURE MODIFICATION — Indenture may be modified, except as provided, with consent of holders of not less than 66⅔% of the Notes.

RIGHTS ON DEFAULT — Trustee, or 25% of Notes outstanding, may declare entire principal due and payable immediately.

PURPOSE — To repurchase common stock.

6. CBS, Inc., Convertible Subordinated Eurodebenture 5s, due 2002:

Rating — Baa1

AUTH. — $400,000,000; outstg. Mar. 13, 1987, $400,000,000.

DATED — Mar. 13, 1987.

OTHER DETAILS — Not reported.

7. Medium Term Notes: Outstg., Dec. 31, 1986, $112,225,000 maturities at varying dates in 1987 and 1988. Interest at varying rates payable semiannually on May and Nov. 15.

8. Other Debt: Outstanding, Dec. 31, 1986, $2,700,000 mortgages and other notes payable.

CAPITAL STOCK

1. CBS Inc. $1 convertible series A preference; par $1:

AUTH. — All series, 6,000,000 shs.; this series, 3,300,000 shs.; outstg. Dec. 31, 1986, 35,116 shs.; par $1.

PREFERENCES — Has preference as to assets and divs.

DIVIDEND RIGHTS — Entitled to cum. cash divs. of $1 annually, payable quarterly, Mar. 31, etc.

DIVIDEND RECORD — Initial dividend of 16.4 cents paid Sept. 30, 1967. Regular dividends paid quarterly thereafter.

LIQUIDATION RIGHTS — In any liquidation, entitled to $43.50 a sh. plus divs.

VOTING RIGHTS — Has one vote per sh. with non-cumulative voting for directors except if divs. are in arrears for 6 quarterly payments then pref. voting as a class may elect 2 directors. Consent of 66⅔% of pref. needed to issue prior stock or change terms adversely.

Consent of 50% of pref. needed to increase authorized amount of pref.

CALLABLE — As a whole or in part on at least 30 days' notice at $43.50 a sh.

CONVERTIBLE — Into com. at any time at rate of 6886/10,000ths com. shs. (adj. for 2% stk. div. paid Dec. 1971 and distribution of Viacom stock), for each ser. A pref. held. No adjustment for interest or divs. Cash paid in lieu of fractional shs. Conversion privilege protected against dilution.

PREEMPTIVE RIGHTS — None.

REGISTRAR & TRANSFER AGENT — Morgan Shareholders Service, Trust Co. New York.

PURPOSE — Issued in connection with merger of Co. with Holt, Rinehart & Winston, Inc.

LISTED — On NYSE (Symbol: CBS Pr); also listed on Pacific Stock Exchange.

2. CBS Inc. $10 convertible series B preference; par $1:

AUTH. — All series, 6,000,000 shs.; outstg. this series, Dec. 31, 1986, 1,250,000 shs.; par $1.

PREFERENCE — Has preference as to assets and divs.

DIVIDEND RIGHTS — Entitled to cum. cash divs. of $10 annually, payable quarterly Mar. 31, etc.

DIVIDEND RECORD — Initial dividend of $1.666667 paid Sept. 30, 1985. Regular dividends paid quarterly thereafter.

LIQUIDATION RIGHTS — In liquidation entitled to $100 per sh. plus accrued and unpaid divs.

CALLABLE — Subject to mandatory redemption on Aug. 1, 1995.

CONVERTIBLE — Into common stock at the rate of 0.6915 common shs. for each ser. B pref.

TRANSFER AGENT & REGISTRAR — CBS Inc.

3. CBS Inc. common; par $2.50:

AUTH. — 100,000,000 shares outstanding, Dec. 31, 1986, 23,528,127 shares; in treasury, 866,800 shares; reserved for conversion of preference, 888,556 shares; reserved for options 531,688 shs.; par $2.50.

As of Feb. 28, 1987, Loews Corp. owned 5,856,921 shs. (24.84%) and W.S. Paley owned 1,914,525 shs. (8.12%).

Par changed from no par to $5 Feb. 14, 1934, by 5-for-1 split; changed from $5 to $2.50 June 4, 1937, by 2-for-1 split; $2.50 par shares split 3-for-1 Apr. 27, 1955 and 2-for-1 Jan. 8, 1964.

Note: Previously outstanding class A and B shares designated share for share as a single class of common shares Dec. 23, 1958.

PREEMPTIVE RIGHTS — None.

DIVIDENDS PAID —

On no par shares:

①1931 .... $3.00   1932-33 .... $4.00

On $5 par shares:

①1934 ...... 2.75   1935 ...... 2.60   1936 ...... $3.30
1937 ...... 1.30

On $2.50 par shares:

1937	1.30	1938	1.25	1939	1.50
1940-41	2.00	1942	1.50	1943-45	1.80
1946	2.30	1947	2.10	1948	2.00
1949	1.40	1950-52	1.60	1953	1.85
①1954	1.90	1955	0.50		

On $2.50 par shares after 3-for-1 split:

①1955	0.60	①1956	0.90	①1957-58	1.00
①1959	1.25	①1960-62	1.40	①1963	1.50

On $2.50 par shares after 2-for-1 split:

①1964	1.05	①1965	1.20	①1966	1.25
①②1967-71	1.40	1972	1.41½	1973-74	1.46
1975	1.51	1976	1.74½	1977	2.10
1978	2.45	1979	2.65	1980-83	2.80
1984	2.85	1985-86	3.00	③1987	1.50

①Also stock dividends: 1931, 15%; 1934, 50%; 1954, 1955 and 1956, 2%; 1957-1963, 3%; 1964-70, 2%; 1971, 4% (2% Jan. 15 and 2% Dec. 24).

②On June 4, 1971 paid one share of Viacom International Inc. for each 7 Co. shares held of record Dec. 17, 1970.

③To June 12.

Dividends payable quarterly Mar. 12, etc. to stock of record about Feb. 25.

DIVIDEND REINVESTMENT PLAN — Co. offers its holders of common stock opportunity to buy additional shares of common stock through automatic investment of CBS dividends and through voluntary cash payments in any amount not less than $10.

Under the Plan, dividends will be promptly invested in purchase of additional shares of CBS common stock at then prevailing market price. Cost to participants is current market price plus a proportionate share of brokerage commission paid by bank plus bank's service charge.

REGISTRAR, TRANSFER AND DIVIDEND DISBURSING AGENT — Morgan Shareholder Services Trust Co., New York.

OFFERED — (1,650,000 shs.) at $58½ per sh. on Dec. 31, 1982 thru Morgan Stanley & Co. and Lazard Freres & Co. and associates. Proceeds to retire certain commercial paper borrowings.

LISTED — On NYSE (Symbol: CBS); also listed on Pacific Stock Exchange. Unlisted trading on Boston, Midwest, and Philadelphia Stock Exchanges.

Repurchase of Common Shares: On Aug. 1, 1985, Co. repurchased 6.365 million com. shs. for $254,900,000 cash and $699,900,000 in 10⅝% senior notes due 1995.

Market Encyclopedia, which contains brief reports on the stocks making up the S&P 500 index.

With about 100,000 subscribers, the circulation of *The Value Line* is several times the size of the next largest similar periodical (*Standard & Poor's Outlook*). Figure 10.7 illustrates a *Value Line* report. The coverage includes a chart of book value, cash flow, and relative strength. Insider and institutional trading decisions are reported in boxes at the top. Some income and balance sheet data are reported along with a projection for the next fiscal year and three to five years hence. *Value Line* tables include rates of return and earnings; capital structure; and quarterly sales, earnings, and dividends for recent years. Projections are given for the next 12 months. Three boxes contain (1) a description of business, (2) an analysis of the firm's position and prospects, and (3) ratings of the firm's performance, safety, and its beta ratio.

The computer-based timeliness ratings for stock selection are the most famous statistics from *Value Line.* The 1,700 stocks are grouped as follows: 100 (I); 300 (II); 900 (III); 300 (IV); and 100 (V). Group I selections (ignoring commissions) have appreciated by 1,528% over the 1965–1985 period compared with only 134% for the NYSE Composite (Figure 10.8). Even the well-known efficient market proponent Fisher Black acknowledges the past success of *Value Line.*[2] More recently, Holloway found that, although it could not be relied on to make after-commission trading profits, a buy and hold strategy based on the *Value Line* selections did produce above-market risk-adjusted returns.[3]

The *Value Line* coverage is clearly investor oriented. The reports contain a great deal of analysis and prediction, although many interesting firms are not covered. On the other hand, separate services are offered for options, convertibles, and new issues.

The Unlisted Market Guide

Taking up where the larger publications leave off, Scot Emerich has introduced the *Unlisted Market Guide.* It covers several hundred OTC companies and has a format quite similar to that of S&P. To be covered in the guide a firm must pay a $750 annual fee. Subscribers are charged $195 per year. Charging for inclusion may lead the guide to have divided loyalties.

Brokerage House Reports

Most full-service brokerage houses either originate or purchase research reports to distribute to their customers. The number of firms covered varies directly with the size of the brokerage house. Large companies are much more likely to be included. The reports may or may not be updated periodically and often are issued as part of an industry survey. In a study of the recommendations of one large national brokerage firm over a seven-year period, Stanley, Lewellen, and Schlarbaum found that "the firm's investment recommendations were generally timely, and conveyed information that would have permitted its customers to earn moderately above-average portfolio returns."[4]

FIGURE 10.6 The CBS Report from *Standard and Poor's Stock Reports*

CBS Inc. 406

NYSE Symbol CBS   Options on CBOE (Feb-May-Aug-Nov)   In S&P 500

Price	Range	P-E Ratio	Dividend	Yield	S&P Ranking	Beta
May 9'88 152½	1988 170¼-149	22	3.00	2.0%	A-	1.00

Summary

CBS operates one of the three nationwide TV networks, operates two radio networks, and owns four TV and 18 radio stations in major U.S. cities. A major restructuring program was completed with the January, 1988 sale of the records division to Sony Corp. for $2 billion; the magazine division was sold to a management-led group in October, 1987 for $650 million; and the educational and professional publishing business and music publishing operations were sold in December, 1986.

Current Outlook

Earnings from continuing operations for 1988 are estimated at about $10.50 a share, versus 1987's $5.21.

The $0.75 quarterly dividend is likely to be raised within the next few quarters.

Broadcasting revenues are likely to rise only modestly in 1988, reflecting the absence of Super Bowl revenues, lackluster advertising demand and pricing pressures. Margins will be squeezed by the small rise in revenues and by higher programming costs. Sharply higher interest income and a lower effective tax rate will contribute to a strong rise in net income.

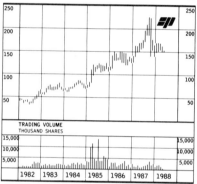

[6]Net Sales (Million $)

Quarter:	1988	1987	1986	1985
Mar.	696	730	1,167	1,101
Jun.	---	714	1,166	1,190
Sep.	---	546	1,017	1,118
Dec.	---	773	1,404	1,347
	---	2,762	4,754	4,756

Net sales from continuing operations for the three months ended March 31, 1988 declined 4.7%, year to year. Operating profit fell 23%. After other items, including a $61 million positive swing in interest income (net), income from continuing operations climbed to $1.73 a share from $0.20.

Common Share Earnings ($)

Quarter:	1988	1987	1986	1985
Mar.	1.73	0.20	0.86	0.89
Jun.	E3.50	2.95	4.77	3.08
Sep.	E2.37	1.27	0.30	1.06
Dec.	E2.90	0.86	1.61	2.23
	E10.50	5.21	7.54	7.27

Important Developments

Jan. '88—CBS completed a major restructuring with the sale of its records division to Sony Corp. for $2.0 billion. Net proceeds from the sale of $866.6 million ($35.34 a share) were posted in the March, 1988 quarter.

Oct. '87—CBS completed the sale of its magazine division to a management-led group for $650 million in cash. The division was accounted for as a discontinued operation through the third quarter, and a net gain from the sale of about $177 million (about $7.00 a share) was recognized in the fourth quarter. Earlier, CBS agreed to sell its interests in various SportsChannel partnerships to Cablevision Systems.

Next earnings report expected in mid-July.

Per Share Data ($)

Yr. End Dec. 31	1987	1986	[4]1985	[4]1984	1983	[3]1982	1981	1980	1979	1978
Book Value[1]	49.72	[5]15.49	[5]d0.59	49.05	45.12	41.21	40.33	37.57	35.10	30.82
Earnings[2]	5.21	7.54	7.27	8.24	6.31	5.35	6.82	6.92	7.21	7.15
Dividends	3.00	3.00	3.00	2.85	2.80	2.80	2.80	2.80	2.65	2.45
Payout Ratio	58%	40%	36%	35%	44%	52%	41%	40%	37%	34%
Prices—High	226¼	151½	126¼	87¾	81¾	67	61¼	55¾	56¾	64¾
Low	127½	110	70⅞	61½	55	33⅜	46	42½	44⅛	43¼
P/E Ratio—	43-24	20-15	17-10	11-7	13-9	13-6	9-7	8-6	8-6	9-6

Data as orig. reptd. 1. Excl. intangibles. 2. Bef. results of disc. opers. of +12.54 in 1987, +8.48 in 1986, -6.46 in 1985, -1.65 in 1984, -1.34 in 1982, -0.95 in 1981; and spec. item(s) of -0.01 in 1987, -0.60 in 1986, +0.56 in 1984. 3. Reflects accounting change. 4. Reflects merger or acquisition. 5. Excl. com. stk. subject to red. 6. Revenues prior to 1987. d-Deficit. E-Estimated.

May 17, 1988
Copyright © 1988 Standard & Poor's Corp. All Rights Reserved

Standard & Poor's Corp.
25 Broadway, NY, NY 10004

FIGURE 10.6 (Continued)

406

CBS Inc.

Income Data (Million $)

Year Ended Dec. 31	Revs.	Oper. Inc.	% Oper. Inc. of Revs.	Cap. Exp.	Depr.	Int. Exp.	⁴Net Bef. Taxes	Eff. Tax Rate	⁵Net Inc.	% Net Inc. of Revs.
²1987	2,762	267	9.6%	34	63	93	218	37.6%	³136	4.9%
²1986	4,646	426	9.2%	83	108	107	285	33.3%	190	4.1%
¹1985	4,677	516	11.0%	114	135	107	354	42.8%	203	4.3%
⁶1984	4,831	516	10.7%	111	97	44	451	45.7%	245	5.1%
1983	4,458	398	8.9%	102	97	48	326	42.7%	³187	4.2%
¹1982	4,052	309	7.6%	131	81	54	233	35.7%	150	3.7%
²1981	4,027	360	8.9%	122	73	61	324	41.2%	³190	4.7%
1980	3,963	380	9.6%	108	69	59	348	44.5%	193	4.9%
1979	3,670	400	10.9%	122	57	³ 29	371	46.0%	201	5.5%
1978	3,242	409	12.6%	98	50	10	386	48.6%	198	6.1%

Balance Sheet Data (Million $)

Dec. 31	Cash	Current Assets	Current Liab.	Ratio	Total Assets	Ret. on Assets	Long Term Debt	Common Equity	Total Cap.	% LT Debt of Cap.	Ret. on Equity
1987	1,498	2,280	674	3.4	3,910	3.7%	964	1,264	2,583	37.3%	11.5%
1986	558	2,063	1,300	1.6	3,370	5.5%	631	803	1,822	34.6%	27.7%
1985	120	1,836	1,550	1.2	3,509	6.7%	954	478	1,785	53.5%	23.2%
1984	280	2,026	1,097	1.8	3,262	7.8%	371	1,550	2,018	18.4%	16.4%
1983	43	1,810	1,136	1.6	2,990	6.6%	233	1,438	1,743	13.3%	13.5%
1982	28	1,622	940	1.7	2,683	5.7%	238	1,331	1,650	14.4%	11.3%
1981	28	1,512	789	1.9	2,426	8.0%	223	1,242	1,554	14.3%	15.7%
1980	103	1,526	753	2.0	2,301	8.6%	217	1,182	1,486	14.6%	17.1%
1979	140	1,528	881	1.7	2,180	10.1%	104	1,066	1,238	8.4%	20.0%
1978	51	1,258	633	2.0	1,780	12.0%	105	934	1,086	9.6%	22.8%

Data as orig. reptd. **1.** Excl. disc. opers. and reflects acctg. change. **2.** Excl. disc. opers. **3.** Reflects acctg. change. **4.** Incl. equity in earns. of nonconsol. subs. **5.** Bef. results of disc. opers. in 1987, 1986, 1985, 1984, 1982, 1981, and spec item(s) in 1987, 1986, 1984. **6.** Excl. disc. opers. and reflects merger or acquisition.

Business Summary

This major U.S. broadcaster completed a major reorganization with the January, 1988 sale of its records division and the October, 1987 sale of its magazines division. Current operations consist almost entirely of the CBS/Broadcast Group. The group includes four owned TV stations in New York (WCBS-TV), Chicago (WBBM-TV), Los Angeles (KCBS-TV), and Philadelphia (WCAU-TV); seven owned AM and 11 FM radio stations in New York (WCBS-AM & FM), Chicago (WBBM-AM & FM), Dallas/Fort Worth (KTXQ-FM), Los Angeles (KNX-AM & FM), San Francisco (KCBS-AM & KRQR-FM), Philadelphia (WCAU-AM & FM), Boston (WMRQ-FM), Houston (KLTR-FM), Washington, D.C. (WLTT-FM), St. Louis (DMOX-AM & KHTR-FM), and Tampa/St. Petersburg (WSUN-AM & WYNF-FM).

The CBS Television Network division distributes programming and feature films to 215 independently owned TV stations in 47 states and the District of Columbia, and to certain overseas and foreign affiliated stations. The CBS Radio division operates the owned radio stations and serves as broadcast sales representative for owned radio stations, 38 independently owned stations, and three independent radio networks. Two CBS radio networks provide programming to 556 independently owned AM and FM radio stations in the U.S. Other divisions produce or otherwise acquire entertainment, news and sports programming for distribution.

Dividend Data

Dividends have been paid since 1931. A dividend reinvestment plan is available.

Amt. of Divd. $	Date Decl.	Ex-divd. Date	Stock of Record	Payment Date
0.75	May 13	May 20	May 27	Jun. 12'87
0.75	Jul. 8	Aug. 20	Aug. 26	Sep. 12'87
0.75	Nov. 11	Nov. 19	Nov. 25	Dec. 12'87
0.75	Feb. 10	Feb. 18	Feb. 24	Mar. 12'88

Capitalization

Long Term Debt: $963,600,000.

$10 Series B Pref. Stk.: 1,250,000 shs. ($1 par); ea. conv. into 0.6915 com. sh.

Common Stock: 23,690,982 shs. ($2.50 par). Loews Corp. owns 24.9%. Institutions hold approximately 72%. Shareholders of record: 19,250.

Office—51 W. 52nd St., NYC 10019. **Tel**—(212) 975-4321. **Chrmn**—W. S. Paley. **Pres & CEO**—L. A. Tisch. **Secy**—C. T. Bates. **VP-Treas**—L. J. Rauchenberger. **Dirs**—M. C. Bergerac, H. Brown, W. Cronkite, R. L. Gilpatric, J. R. Houghton, N. N. Minow, W. S. Paley, H. B. Schacht, F. A. Thomas, L. A. Tisch, M. Tree, J. D. Wolfensohn. **Transfer Agent & Registrar**—Morgan Shareholder Services Trust Co., NYC. **Incorporated** in New York in 1927. **Empl**—16,900.

Information has been obtained from sources believed to be reliable, but its accuracy and completeness are not guaranteed. William H. Donald

Source: Standard & Poor's Corporation, *Standard & Poor's Stock Reports*, March 8, 1988. Reprinted by permission.

FIGURE 10.7   The CBS Report from *Value Line*

CBS INC. NYSE-CBS

RECENT PRICE	164	
P/E RATIO	15.1	(Trailing: 18.6 / Median: 9.0)
RELATIVE P/E RATIO	1.19	
DIV'D YLD	1.8%	
VALUE LINE	371	

TIMELINESS 4 — Below Average (Relative Price Performance Next 12 Mos.)
SAFETY 3 — Average (Scale: 1 Highest to 5 Lowest)
BETA 1.05 (1.00 = Market)

Target Price Range 1990 | 1991 | 1992

Price scale: 320 / 240 / 200 / 160 / 128 / 96 / 80 / 64 / 48 / 40 / 32 / 24 / 16 / 12

1990-92 PROJECTIONS

	Price	Gain	Ann'l Total Return
High	425	(+160%)	28%
Low	285	(+75%)	16%

Legend: 14.0 x "Cash Flow" p sh · Relative Price Strength · Bold figures are Value Line estimates · Options Trade On CBO

Statistical Array (per share data)

	1972	1973	1974	1975	1976	1977	1978	1979	1980	1981	1982	1983	1984	1985	1986	1987	1988	90-92E
Revenues per sh	49.56	55.36	61.86	68.34	78.52	100.65	116.86	131.82	142.13	144.12	136.71	150.23	162.58	199.45	202.04	116.05	120.85	172.75
"Cash Flow" per sh	3.98	4.36	4.87	5.54	6.93	8.06	8.92	9.25	9.40	8.46	7.79	9.57	11.51	14.17	12.10	7.50	13.90	23.85
Earnings per sh	2.88	3.27	3.80	4.30	5.75	6.50	7.15	7.21	6.92	5.86	5.35	6.31	8.24	7.27	7.54	5.21	11.40	19.75
Div'ds Decl'd per sh	1.42	1.46	1.46	1.51	1.75	2.10	2.45	2.65	2.80	2.80	2.80	2.80	2.85	3.00	3.00	3.00	3.00	3.50
Cap'l Spending per sh	1.22	.92	1.01	1.14	1.62	2.32	3.55	4.37	3.87	4.38	4.43	3.42	3.74	4.84	3.51	2.10	2.10	2.50
Book Value per sh	14.26	15.81	18.47	21.39	25.42	28.86	33.66	38.28	42.41	44.44	44.89	48.44	52.17	23.31	37.05	54.05	63.40	78.10
Common Shs Outst'g	28.31	28.09	28.31	28.37	28.41	27.58	27.74	27.84	27.88	27.94	29.64	29.68	29.72	23.45	23.53	23.80	24.00	20.00
Avg Ann'l P/E Ratio	18.8	10.6	8.7	10.5	9.7	8.5	7.4	6.9	7.1	9.1	8.5	10.7	9.0	14.6	17.6	32.7		18.0
Relative P/E Ratio	1.29	1.05	1.22	1.40	1.24	1.11	1.01	1.00	.94	1.11	.94	.84	.90	1.19	1.19	2.07		1.50
Avg Ann'l Div'd Yield	2.6%	4.2%	4.4%	3.3%	3.1%	3.8%	4.6%	5.3%	5.7%	5.3%	6.2%	4.1%	3.8%	2.8%	2.3%	1.8%		1.0%

© VALUE LINE, INC.

Financial Array

	1978	1979	1980	1981	1982	1983	1984	1985	1986	1987	1988	90-92E
Revenues ($mill)	3241.6	3670.4	3962.9	4027.0	4052.3	4458.4	4831.5	4676.8	4753.7	2762.0	2900	3455
Operating Margin	12.6%	10.9%	9.6%	8.9%	7.6%	8.9%	10.7%	11.0%	11.2%	9.5%	10.5%	11.5%
Depreciation ($mill)	49.5	57.0	69.3	72.7	80.9	97.0	97.3	134.9	107.7	55.0	60.0	85.0
Net Profit ($mill)	198.1	200.7	193.0	163.8	150.0	187.2	245.0	202.6	189.8	136.0	285	410
Income Tax Rate	48.6%	46.0%	44.5%	41.2%	35.7%	42.7%	45.7%	42.8%	33.3%	37.6%	38.0%	38.0%
Net Profit Margin	6.1%	5.5%	4.9%	4.1%	3.7%	4.2%	5.1%	4.3%	4.0%	4.9%	9.8%	11.9%
Working Cap'l ($mill)	624.4	647.1	773.1	723.0	682.2	673.3	922.1	285.9	763.8	1760	2500	2060
Long-Term Debt ($mill)	104.5	104.3	217.2	222.6	238.0	232.5	364.3	954.3	630.8	550	550	Nil
Net Worth ($mill)	944.6	1074.5	1190.2	1246.8	1334.6	1440.5	1552.9	669.7	995.1	1410	1640	1690
% Earned Total Cap'l	19.3%	17.4%	14.5%	12.0%	10.5%	11.9%	13.8%	14.8%	14.7%	8.5%	14.0%	24.0%
% Earned Net Worth	21.0%	18.7%	16.2%	13.1%	13.0%	13.0%	15.8%	30.3%	19.1%	9.5%	17.5%	24.0%
% Retained to Comm Eq	13.9%	11.9%	9.7%	6.9%	5.4%	7.2%	10.3%	21.5%	12.2%	4.0%	13.0%	21.0%
% All Div'ds to Net Prof	34%	37%	41%	48%	52%	44%	35%	42%	44%	62%	30%	20%

Price High/Low range:

High	40.4	54.0	61.0	62.3	64.8	56.8	55.8	61.3	67.0	81.8	87.8	126.3	151.5	226.3	170.3
Low	25.0	28.9	46.8	46.4	43.3	44.1	42.5	46.0	33.4	55.0	61.5	70.9	110.0	127.5	149.0

Percent shares traded: 12.0 / 8.0 / 4.0

Insider Decisions

1987 — months: D J F M A M J J A S O N D J F

	to Buy	Options	to Sell

Institutional Decisions

	4Q86	1Q87	2Q87	3Q87	4Q87
to Buy	68	57	66	77	81
to Sell	68	77	73	86	79
Hld's(000)	15024	16339	17204	16868	17449

Capital Structure as of 9/30/87

Total Debt $1071.0 mill. Due in 5 Yrs $130.6 mill.
LT Debt $965.9 mill. LT Interest $120.0 mill.
(LT interest earned: 3.7x; total interest coverage: 3.6x) (50% of Cap'l)

Leases, Uncapitalized Annual rentals $48.5 mill.

Pension Liability None in '86 vs. None in '85

Pfd Stock $123.5 mill. Pfd Div'd $12.7 mill.
Incl. 1.25 mill. shs. $10.00 cum. Series B pfd. shs., conv. into .69 shs. com. each, redeemable at $100 a sh. (1% of Cap'l)

Common Stock 23,633,540 shs. (49% of Cap'l)
(24.4 mill. fully diluted shs.)
as of 10/30/87

FIGURE 10.7 (Continued)

CURRENT POSITION ($MILL.)	1985	1986	9/30/87
Cash Assets	120.1	558.2	763.3
Receivables	785.0	789.7	692.0
Inventory(Avg Cst)	173.3	117.3	143.0
Other	757.7	598.2	592.9
Current Assets	1836.1	2063.4	2191.2
Accts Payable	228.9	166.2	117.6
Debt Due	277.5	56.6	105.1
Other	1043.8	1076.8	972.8
Current Liab.	1550.2	1299.6	1195.5

ANNUAL RATES of change (per sh)	Past 10 Yrs	Past 5 Yrs	Est'd '84-'86 to '90-'92
Revenues	10.5%	6.0%	-1.5%
"Cash Flow"	8.0%	7.0%	11.0%
Earnings	5.0%	3.0%	17.0%
Dividends	6.5%	1.5%	3.0%
Book Value	5.5%	-2.0%	13.0%

Cal-endar	QUARTERLY REVENUES ($ mill.)			Full Year
	Mar. 31	June 30	Sept. 30	Dec. 31	
1984	1128.3	1170.7	1145.1	1387.4	4831.5
1985	1083.8	1170.8	1100.0	1322.2	4676.8
1986	1198.9	1217.2	1150.2	1187.4	4753.7
1987					2762.0
1988	760	580	760	800	2900

Cal-endar	EARNINGS PER SHARE			Full Year
	Mar. 31	June 30	Sept. 30	Dec. 31	
1984	1.38	2.98	1.66	2.22	8.24
1985	.89	3.08	1.06	2.24	7.27
1986	.86	4.77	.30	1.61	7.54
1987					5.21
1988	2.50	4.60	2.40	1.90	11.40

Cal-endar	QUARTERLY DIVIDENDS PAID			Full Year
	Mar. 31	June 30	Sept. 30	Dec. 31	
1984	.70	.70	.70	.75	2.85
1985	.75	.75	.75	.75	3.00
1986	.75	.75	.75	.75	3.00
1987	.75	.75	.75	.75	3.00
1988	.75				

BUSINESS: CBS Inc. operates a radio and a TV network, owns 18 radio and 4 TV stations. CBS-TV Network accounts for about 45% of rev. Owns world's largest record company. Publishes magazines (*Field & Stream, Woman's Day*), makes prerecorded videocassettes. Sold music and text pub. ops., 1986. Disc. toys, theatrical films, 1985. Broadcasting: 60% of revs.; 57% of op. inc.

('86). Foreign ops.: 13% of revs., 29% of op. inc. Has about 18,300 employees, 18,000 shareholders. Wage costs: about 25% of sales. '86 deprec. rate: 11.6%. Est'd plant age: 4 yrs. William S. Paley controls 8.1% of common; Loews Corp. owns 24.9%. Chairman: W.S. Paley. C.E.O.: L.A. Tisch. Inc.: NY. Address: 51 West 52nd St., New York, NY 10019. Tel.: 212-975-4321.

Our expectation that share net in 1988 will rise to $11.40 from $5.21 last year isn't nearly as aggressive as it looks. The 1987 results were restated to eliminate all operating profits from the divested publishing and record operations. No allowance is made for the fact that interest income would have been earned on the cash received from the divestitures. Hence the '87 figure isn't representative of the earnings that CBS can really generate. Our 1988 estimate, of course, includes this considerable interest income.

There are a lot of cross currents affecting network television. First, there's the economy. Our best guess is that there will be no recession, but that the consumer sector will be a laggard. That suggests bad news for ad spending. But 1988 has the Olympics and a presidential election; in the past, these events have spurred advertising and, that seems to be happening again. 1989 will be a much tougher call. Macroeconomic considerations alone might suggest a mediocre year, but in the recent past, advertisers have found that less expensive promotional programs aren't nearly as effective at building consumer brand

awareness as are ad campaigns. As to viewership, networks continue to lose ground to cable, but new ratings measurement techniques distort year-to-year comparisons, making it hard to evaluate how troublesome this really is right now. In the ratings, CBS isn't great. It's a weak number two, not much higher than last place ABC, in prime time, where it has some old shows and a lot of new ones, many of which aren't catching on (some, however, have received critical acclaim and deserve patience).

At present, the earnings-driven timeliness rank is unfavorable. But, we think CBS has about $95 a share in cash, following the early '88 sale of the record division. So, investors, in effect, are paying about $70 a share for the broadcast. business. Measured against our $6.00-a-share '88 estimate of broadcasting profits (excluding interest income), that's a P/E ratio of 11.7, which is below the market multiple. Concerns about how CBS will use the cash (purchases of TV stations and/or a special dividend are possible) are preventing Wall Street from getting more excited about the special situation angle.   *Marc H. Gerstein*

Company's Financial Strength	B + +
Stock's Price Stability	70
Price Growth Persistence	55
Earnings Predictability	75

(A) Based on average shares outstanding. Next earnings report due mid-May. Excl. gain (loss) on discontinued operations: '82, ($1.34); '84, ($1.65); '85, ($6.46). '86, 51¢; '87, $12.53. Excl. extraordinary gain (loss): '84, 56¢; '86, $7.88. (B) Next dividend meet-ing about May 15. Goes ex about May 5. Approx. dividend payment dates: 12th of Mar., plan available. (C) Incl. intangible assets. In '86: $438.9 mill., $18.65/sh. (D) In millions. (E) '87 results restated. Qtr'l figures not yet avail. ■ Dividend reinvestment plan available. (C) Incl. intangible assets. In '86: $438.9 mill., $18.65/sh. (D) In millions. (E) '87 results restated. Qtr'l figures not yet avail.

Factual material is obtained from sources believed to be reliable, but the publisher is not responsible for any errors or omissions contained herein.

Source: *The Value Line Investment Survey*, April 1, 1988, 371. © 1988 Value Line Investment Survey; used by permission of Value Line, Inc.

FIGURE 10.8   Record of *Value Line* Ratings for Timeliness (Five Groups of Stock) Compared with the DJIA and the NYSE Composite

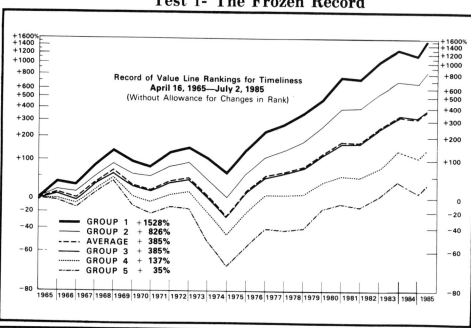

Test 1- The Frozen Record

Record of Value Line Rankings For Timeliness (Without Allowance for Changes In Rank)
April 16, 1965—July 2, 1985

Group	1965*	1966	1967	1968	1969	1970	1971	1972	1973	1974	1975	1976
1	+33.6%	− 3.1%	+39.2%	+31.2%	−17.7%	− 8.9%	+26.5%	+10.1%	−17.1%	−23.1%	+51.6%	+35.3%
2	+18.9	− 6.0	+31.9	+26.3	−16.3	− 4.0	+17.4	+ 7.5	−26.2	−27.8	+53.0	+36.3
3	+ 8.9	− 9.7	+30.1	+21.4	−20.7	− 5.5	+12.2	+ 6.2	−27.0	−28.5	+52.9	+33.8
4	+ 0.8	− 7.2	+25.1	+25.1	−26.8	−11.7	+14.2	+ 3.2	−29.1	−33.6	+48.4	+36.1
5	− 1.2	−12.4	+28.4	+25.9	−35.7	−13.1	+10.5	+ 2.9	−43.1	−36.8	+42.1	+38.2
Avg	+10.1	− 7.9	+29.9	+24.6	−22.1	− 7.5	+14.9	+ 5.5	−27.7	−29.6	+51.2	+35.1

Group	1977	1978	1979	1980	1981	1982	1983	1984	1985**	1965 through 1985**
1	+15.8%	+19.8%	+25.6%	+50.2%	− 1.9%	+33.7%	+25.2%	− 8.6%	+28.4%	+1528%
2	+12.7	+16.1	+30.8	+37.4	+ 0.7	+29.0	+22.2	− 0.1	+18.4	+ 826
3	+ 5.2	+ 9.2	+27.6	+20.8	+ 2.7	+25.5	+26.7	− 1.6	+15.1	+ 385
4	− 0.2	+ 2.4	+23.1	+13.2	− 0.9	+18.5	+35.2	−12.3	+12.5	+ 137
5	− 2.8	+ 4.0	+39.9	+ 8.4	− 4.2	+19.9	+30.0	−17.1	+13.3	+ 35
Avg	+ 5.8	+ 9.6	+28.0	+23.4	+ 0.9	+25.0	+27.5	− 4.7	+16.0	+ 385

Dow Jones Industrials + 46%
N.Y. Stock Exchange Composite + 134%

* April through December
** First half

Investments in Perspective

How do the stock picks of brokerage firms do? No doubt the answer varies from year to year and broker to broker. A rather favorable picture was painted in an article in *The Wall Street Journal*.

Rating the Brokers on Their Stock Picks

Seven of 10 Beat S&P 500 In First Quarter

YOUR
MONEY
MATTERS

By John R. Dorfman
Staff Reporter of The Wall Street Journal

Some brokerage-firm customers were in a better position than others to gain from the surge in small-company stock prices during the first quarter.

A.G. Edwards & Sons Inc. and Merrill Lynch & Co. both tended to recommend stocks of small companies, while others, such as Drexel Burnham Lambert Inc. and Thomson McKinnon Securities Inc., emphasized shares of big companies. Investors who followed the firms' recommendations benefited—or suffered—accordingly.

A study of brokerage houses' stock-picking prowess by Zacks Investment Research Inc. of Chicago shows that the issues selected by Edwards gained an estimated 15.1% in the first quarter. Next best was a 14.1% gain for Merrill Lynch's rec-

ommended stocks. The smallest gains were the 2.9% notched by Thomson McKinnon and 3% for Drexel Burnham.

The study, conducted quarterly by Zacks for The Wall Street Journal, estimates the value of brokerage-house stock recommendations to individual investors. The strong first-quarter showing by Edwards enabled it to wrest the 12-month lead from Thomson McKinnon, which excelled in the first running of the study, published earlier this year.

Slim Gain Leads the Pack

Stocks selected by St. Louis-based Edwards, the only non-New York firm among the 10 large brokerage houses studied, gained an estimated 0.3% for the 12 months, according to the Zacks tally. Slim though it is, the gain looks good in a period that included October's historic stock crash. Buying the other nine houses' favorite stocks, Zacks figures, would have led to losses ranging from 2.4% (for Shearson Lehman Hutton Inc.) to 15.0% (for Prudential-Bache Securities Inc.).

The stocks recommended by seven of the 10 houses last quarter outperformed the Standard & Poor's 500-stock index, which contains the stocks of relatively large companies. And stocks selected by eight of the firms outperformed the Dow Jones Industrial Average, whose 30 stocks all have large market capitalization.

Because small stocks did so well in the

first quarter, however, none of the firms' recommended lists was able to beat the 16.9% jump in the "Zacks Universe" average. That's the average of the approximately 3,000 stocks followed by the 10 brokerage houses; because the stocks are weighted equally and most are relatively small, it amounts to a small-stock index.

Usefulness to Investors

Some firms have criticized the study's methodology, particularly its once-a-month system for pricing recommended stocks. But several investment authorities not associated with the firms say it gives a fair measure of the usefulness of the recommendations to individual investors.

The study measures stock-picking ability only. It doesn't consider another important type of advice: asset allocation, which is the apportioning of an investor's assets among stocks, bonds, cash and other alternatives. The brokerage houses that do best in stock-picking don't always do best in asset allocation, and vice versa.

Here's a firm-by-firm rundown of how the brokerage houses have done and what they expect:

DEAN WITTER: "I'm not looking to knock the cover off the ball," says Manny Korman, Dean Witter Reynolds Inc.'s research director, "because I'm unwilling to accept the risk that would entail." He anticipates a volatile market, with the industrial average oscillating between 1800 and 2100 for the next several months. In that climate, he favors chemical stocks and defensive issues, such as food, beverage and tobacco stocks. "Sometimes," he says, "the tortoise wins the race."

This particular tortoise was in the middle of the pack for the past 12 months and the latest quarter. For the full 21 months covered by the Zacks study, however, it brings up the rear.

DREXEL BURNHAM: The typical company on Drexel's "Priority Selection List," according to the Zacks analysis, has a market value of $5.6 billion. That's about the size of Xerox Corp., one of the largest 100 U.S. corporations in market value. As a result, Drexel missed the action in small stocks, eking out a meager 3% gain in the first quarter and dropping to ninth from fifth in the 12-month rankings.

Drexel's picks generated no fireworks, either on the winning or losing side. Only two of its recommended stocks gained more than 25% during the 12 months: Mobil Corp., up 32%, and General Public Utilities Corp., up 29%. Drexel research director Arthur Kirsch points out that the firm's "Priority Selection List" deliberately sticks to about 35 big stocks suitable for most investors; individual Drexel analysts also recommend other, smaller stocks, however.

A.G. EDWARDS: The firm, which has led the three-month results for the past two quarters, recommended the smallest stocks overall of any house in the study—with an average market value of $692 million, as of March 1. But Terry Dessent, director of research, is reluctant to attribute the firm's stock-picking success to the size of the stocks. He thinks the firm's emphasis on stocks that appear to be undervalued is the reason its recommendations have been performing so well.

The firm's picks do outscore most competitors on some common measures of value. For instance, its favorites had the highest average dividend yield (3.3%) and the lowest price-to-book-value ratio (2.38). In addition, their price-earnings ratio (11.8) was among the three lowest. Other firms use similar value measures, however, and didn't do nearly so well.

Edwards doesn't have a recommended list as such. Zacks judges the firm on the basis of the stocks its analysts say to "buy" or "accumulate."

Four of Edwards's recommended stocks—Elgin National Industries Inc., Union Special Machine Corp., Murray Ohio Manufacturing Co. and Acme Steel Co.—got a boost from takeovers or takeover rumors. "We don't recommend stocks on that basis," Mr. Dessent says. But he suggests that value-oriented stocks often attract takeover bids.

KIDDER PEABODY: Losses in such stocks as Consolidated Stores Corp., Texas Air Corp. and Catalyst Energy Corp. held Kidder Peabody & Co. to eighth place in the 12-month ranking. Longer term, Kidder moved up to fifth, partly because of a change in how it was judged.

Kidder used to publish two separate

How the Big Brokerage Houses' Favorite Stocks Performed

Estimated performance of stocks recommended by major securities firms in periods ending March 31, 1988, and biggest gainers and losers for each firm during the 12 months ended March 31

	12 MONTHS	3 MONTHS	21 MONTHS	BIGGEST GAIN		BIGGEST LOSS	
A.G. Edwards	0.3%	15.1%	8.2%	Walbro	+ 68%	Outboard Marine	–50%
Shearson Lehman Hutton	– 2.4	11.8	16.6	Britoil	+140	Eagle Picher	–38
Merrill Lynch	– 5.0	14.1	10.3	Gillette	+ 90	Lear Petroleum	–75
Thomson McKinnon	– 8.1	2.9	20.3	Squibb	+ 34	Digital Equip.	–35
Dean Witter	– 9.2	10.2	0.8	Sterling Drug	+ 56	Circuit City	–48
PaineWebber	–11.1	9.1	6.4	Inland Steel	+ 90	Hadson	–56
Smith Barney	–11.9	5.2	5.4	Dresser Inds.	+ 47	Limited	–51
Kidder Peabody	–13.2	8.4	7.5	Amer. Cablsys A	+ 40	Consol. Stores	–77
Drexel Burnham	–13.8	3.0	1.3	Mobil	+ 32	Home Federal SD	–40
Prudential-Bache	–15.0	10.0	7.4	Jim Walter	+ 51	Env. Treat & Tec.	–64

Comparison yardsticks:				
Dow Jones Industrial Av.	–10.7%	3.5%	11.4%	NOTE: All figures include dividends; individual investors' results will vary
S&P 500-stock index	– 8.5%	5.7%	7.8%	*Average of approximately 3,000 stocks followed by the 10 brokerage firms
Average stock*	– 9.0%	16.9%	2.8%	Source: Zacks Investment Research Inc.

lists of recommended stocks—a basic list and a high-risk list. Last fall, however, it discontinued the high-risk list and transferred some stocks from it to the basic list. In its previous analysis, Zacks judged Kidder on both lists combined. This time results were recalculated to reflect only the basic list, which Kidder says better reflects the advice customers were given by the firm's registered representatives before the high-risk list was dropped.

R. Joseph Fuchs, appointed Kidder's director of research earlier this year, says he expects a "muddle-through environment" with "treacherous" volatility for the next few months. His list now is tilted toward energy, "predictable growth," and selected manufacturing stocks.

MERRILL LYNCH: Because there's no recommended list at Merrill, Zacks's evaluation is based on the stocks given a No. 1 rating for the "intermediate term," or up to a year, by Merrill's securities analysts. The individual analysts must be doing something right, since Merrill was among the top three finishers in each period.

Partly because it follows so many stocks, Merrill had more big winners and big losers than any other firm. Gillette Co., Beecham PLC, Alberto Culver Co., Koppers Inc. and Compaq Computer Corp. all

gained more than 80% during the 12 months. Lear Petroleum Corp., Safecard Services Inc., Texas Air Corp., Boys Markets Inc. and Matrix Science Corp. all lost more than 60%.

"Our breadth of focus," says Andrew Melnick, research director, allows Merrill to "find companies that others might not find, at a reasonably early stage."

PAINEWEBBER: Though it was in the middle of the pack overall for every time period, PaineWebber Inc. also generated a lot of ups and downs for people who went along with its picks. Inland Steel Industries Inc., for example, rose 90% in the past year, and E-II Holdings Inc. rose 82%. But Hadson Corp. dropped 56% and Deb Shops Inc. fell 55%.

Margo Alexander, PaineWebber's director of research, says the firm has made a special effort lately to give customers timely advice on takeover situations, such as Sterling Drug Corp. and Federated Department Stores Inc. But because takeovers are "fast-moving situations," she says, that advice typically doesn't show up on the recommended list.

PRUDENTIAL-BACHE: Despite a respectable showing last quarter, Prudential-Bache dropped to the bottom of the 12-

month rankings—a far cry from its third-place finish in the first run of the Zacks study. The key to the big drop was the first quarter of 1987. Back then, the firm had chalked up a scorching 35.4% gain—by far the best quarterly gain any firm has achieved in the study. But that quarter isn't part of the most recent 12 months, during which Prudential-Bache suffered nasty losses in such stocks as Environmental Treatment & Technology Corp., Xyvision Inc., QMS Inc., Fur Vault Inc. and Matrix Science Corp.

"I'm not satisfied with the performance, but I'm pleased that we have bounced back in the first quarter," says Michael Culp, director of research. "Probably we were early in focusing on small-cap names. The small-caps (companies with small market value) really got crushed in October."

SHEARSON LEHMAN HUTTON: "What you don't see on the list" often is as important as what you do see, says Jack Rivkin, Shearson's director of research. "We have underweighted retailing (stocks) since last July. I think that's helped us." Indeed, Shearson—along with Drexel Burnham and Thomson McKinnon—was relatively successful at avoiding major losers. But, unlike those two firms, it also came up with some blockbuster winners. In Britoil PLC, up 140%, and Stanadyne Inc., up 104%, it boasted the only two picks that doubled during the past 12 months. (Both were takeover situations.) Thus, Shearson managed to come in second or third in every time period.

Mr. Rivkin favors stocks that are expected to show major growth in earnings. Currently, he likes capital-goods stocks, such as Clark Equipment Co. and Deere & Co. He continues to avoid consumer stocks, figuring that consumers will be "fairly tame" in spending for a year or more.

SMITH BARNEY: New to the survey is Smith Barney, Harris Upham & Co., replacing E.F. Hutton, which was swallowed by Shearson. Smith Barney didn't enter the pool with a big splash, though. It was eighth for the recent quarter and seventh for both the 12-month and 21-month periods. Retail stocks such as Limited Inc. (down 51%) and Liz Claiborne Inc. (down 41%) proved to be poor bets, as did Marion Labs Inc. (down 42%) and Prime Computer Inc. (down 42%)

D. Larry Smith, director of research, says the Zacks study gives an incomplete picture because it ignores advice on which sectors to emphasize. For example, he says Smith Barney recommends a heavy weighting on energy, but doesn't necessarily have many energy stocks on its list; investors are expected to put more money into those stocks than others. (Over the past 12 months, most of Smith Barney's recommended energy issues have been flat. For the full 21 months covered by the study, however, Smith Barney scored gains of 47% in Royal Dutch Petroleum Corp. and 22% in Amoco Corp.)

THOMSON MCKINNON: Thomson publishes several different recommended lists, some of which are specialized; Zacks judges it on the more general "Long-Term Investment" list. The firm's research director, Harry Zisson, recently pulled Digital Equipment Corp. and General Electric Co. (both losers over the past 12 months) off that list, but it's still heavy with large-company stocks. Despite last quarter's puny 2.9% return, Mr. Zisson believes the "blue-chip sector is still the place" to be. He expects the market to be "institutionally dominated," and thinks stock prices will be volatile but show little if any net gain during 1988.

How the Study Tracked Firms' Recommendations

The study of brokerage firms' stock-picking ability, developed jointly by Zacks Investment Research Inc. and The Wall Street Journal, assumes a hypothetical investor with certain peculiar characteristics: intense devotion to brokerage recommendations and a clockwork once-a-month investment pattern.

The investor owns equal amounts of every stock strongly recommended by a particular brokerage house, and no other stocks. Once a month, the investor rebalances the portfolio to include any new recommended stocks and to drop any that are no longer recommended in the highest degree (even if they are still called a "hold," or a weak buy). Then the investor waits a month, regardless of market conditions and new advice, before readjusting the portfolio.

The study covers the 10 U.S. brokerage firms with the largest number of registered representatives. Dividends are included in the performance measurement. No commissions are assessed, mainly to make the results more comparable with stock-market averages.

The brokerage houses are given an opportunity to check the accuracy of Zacks's data about the stocks they picked and the prices at the end of each month. This time around, nine of the 10 firms did so; Smith Barney said it didn't have time to check the data.

Source: J. Dorfman, "Rating the Brokers on Their Stock Picks," *The Wall Street Journal*, May 4, 1988, 25. Reprinted by permission, © Dow Jones & Company, Inc. All rights reserved.

Advisory Services Newsletters

A host of investment services publish newsletters dealing with stock market timing and stock selection. Among the better known names in the field are Joseph Granville (whose panic sell messages phoned across the country led to a 24-point drop in the Dow on January 7, 1981), Martin Zweig (editor of the *Zweig Forecaster* and frequent panelist on the Public Television Program "Wall Street Week"), and Robert Prechter (of the "Elliot Wave Theory"). Much of this advice is of a very mediocre quality. Some advisory services may possibly be better than others, however. *Hulbert Financial Digest* tracks and evaluates advisory services' recommendations. If past results are any indicator, it should help investors sort out the wheat from the chaff. Investors may subscribe directly to Hulbert's (409 First Street S.E., Washington, DC 20003, 800-227-1617).

Industry Periodicals

Some publications cover particular industries. For example, *Brewers Digest*, which is published monthly (Siebel Publishing Company, Chicago, IL 60646), reports on the beer industry. Trade publications such as this may contain articles relevant to potential investors, although the industry's managers are the primary readers. Some other trade periodicals, however, specialize in the stocks of particular industries. For example, *Audits Realty Stock Review* (Audit Investment Research, 230 Park Avenue, New York, New York 10017) covers REITs and other real estate companies.

COMPUTER-BASED INFORMATION SOURCES

The computer has in the past 20 years become an omnipresent reminder of our changing technology. Its use in investment analysis is, if anything, greater than its role in most other areas. Virtually all serious empirical research utilizes the computer to manipulate data in statistically meaningful ways.

Researchers utilize a number of computer-based data sources. A number of these services were mentioned in the discussion of electronic data sources. They provide stock quotes and in many cases will also supply a variety of financial information. Such services are primarily designed for individual and perhaps institutional investors.

Another group of data sources is designed almost entirely for serious (scholarly) research. The best known of this type of financial data banks is the COMPUSTAT service sold by a Denver subsidiary of Standard and Poor's (Investors Management Services, Box 23a, Denver, CO 80201). The primary tape contains security information listed annually for the past 20 years for each of about 4,650 companies. A second tape contains quarterly data. Specialized tapes exist for various groups of companies such as OTC companies, Canadian firms, public utilities, and banks. Most companies with substantial investor interest are included. COMPUSTAT data were long suited only to those with access to a mainframe computer system. More recently, however, it has become available on compact disks with a built-in menu-driven access system.

Also distributed through Standard & Poor's are the ISL tapes from Investors Data Corporation (122 E. 42nd St., New York, NY 10017) and the CRISP tapes from the Center for Research in Securities Prices at the University of Chicago (Graduate School of Business, Chicago, IL 60637). The ISL tapes contain daily high, low, close, and volume figures for NYSE and AMEX stocks. The CRISP tapes contain monthly price and dividend data for the NYSE from 1926 forward as well as daily NYSE stock price data from 1960 to the present.

The Value Line database (Value Line Inc., 711 Third Avenue, New York, NY 10017) contains annual and quarterly data for 1,600 companies beginning in 1963 (annual coverage back to 1954) plus estimated earnings and dividends for the next year. Value Line data are available on floppy disks on a monthly subscription basis.

Finally, the Media General Databank (Data General Financial Services, Box 26991, Richmond, VA 23261) includes current price, volume, and financial data on 2,000 major corporations. These databases appear to be generally but not uniformly accurate.[5]

Investment Software

Programs that utilize input from these databases can screen the data banks for certain characteristics and/or perform numerous manipulations of the available data. Some of them are marketed primarily to institutions. Others are available to people connected with an academic institution. The growth of personal computers will undoubtedly make computer analyses much more accessible to many individual investors. Indeed, a large number of investor-oriented programs have been designed to perform either fundamental or technical analysis.

The fundamental analysis packages are largely designed to sort through a large database to find firms whose characteristics meet certain criteria. For example, the investor may set acceptable ranges for PE, past growth, dividend yield, debt/equity, beta, and so on. The program will then screen for stocks meeting the specified criteria. One example of these types of programs is Stockpak II from S&P. The service offers updated information (monthly floppy disks) on 4,600 stocks and works with 75 specified criteria. The user can construct additional criteria if desired. Another example is Value/Screen Plus from Value Line, which is a condensed version of the *Investment Survey*. Subscribers receive monthly floppy disks containing information on 1,600 stocks. They may work with 37 screening and 10 portfolio management variables. Finally, the Evaluation Form is offered by the National Association of Investment Clubs. The user supplies his or her own information. The program then computes about 50 values and recommends whether to buy, hold, or sell the stock.

Technical analysis programs rely heavily on current market data to analyze and forecast the market for particular securities. Most of these services require an on-line data source, a graphics card, and a color monitor. The Technician (by Computer Asset Management) tracks and graphs 70 technical market indicators. MetaStock (also by Computer Asset Management) allows the user to plot data for up to four years and display up to 36 charts on a single screen. Finally, CompuTrac/PC is a particularly extensive "toolbag of technical analysis tools."

Additional software packages are available for commodities, bonds, options, and real estate. Before purchasing a software package and data service, the investor might wish to refer to one of the publications that reviews computer investment programs: *Financial and Investment Software Review* (quarterly), $45 per year, Box 6, Riverdale, NY 10471; *Wall Street Computer Review* (monthly), $139 per year, Dealer's Digest Inc., 150 Broadway, New York, NY 10038; and *Computerized Investing* (bimonthly), $44 per year, American Association of Individual Investors, 612 N. Michigan Avenue, Chicago, IL 60611.

The ultimate in computerized investing allows the investor to trade securities directly in the marketplace. A program of Instinet in New York affords direct access to the floor of Pacific Stock Exchange. That is, one can dial into the network and first obtain a quote and then execute a trade for any security traded on the Pacific.

Investment Implications of the Computer

Because the computer and computer-based data sources play a large and growing role in investment analysis, investors should be aware of their availability. Those simply wishing to apply the results of such research may find the computer useful but not essential. Mutual funds and other institutions in the best positions to utilize computers have not produced particularly impressive performances with or without them.

INVESTOR ASSOCIATIONS

Three associations are designed to assist small investors. The National Association of Investment Clubs (Box 220, Royal Oak, MI 48068) helps groups of small investors establish investment clubs and provides a vehicle for investment clubs to communicate with each other. The association now has 5,000 clubs representing

90,000 members. For $25 per club plus $6 per member investors can obtain the association's assistance in establishing a club.

The American Association of Individual Investors (612 North Michigan Avenue, Chicago, IL 60611) offers a wide variety of services for its $48 annual membership: a journal of investment theory and practice that appears 10 times a year; an investor's guide to no-load mutual funds; local chapter membership (where available) in a number of metropolitan areas; a series of home computer programs for investors; a tax-planning guide; as well as access to a number of seminars, a variety of home study materials, and a bimonthly publication on computerized investing (optional for extra cost).

United Shareholders of America ($50 per year membership, USA, 1667 K Street, Suite 770, Washington, DC 20006) is primarily designed to represent and fight for shareholder rights. Organized and promoted by T. Boone Pickens, this association is concerned with such issues as uniform securities laws from state to state, one share/one vote, confidential proxy voting, equal access to the proxy system by both management and nonmanagement groups, and restrictions on such potential management abuses as the paying of greenmail or the instituting of golden parachutes and poison pills.

At the other end of the spectrum, the Investment Company Institute (1775 K Street, Washington, DC 20006) services mutual funds and other institutional investors. The institute publishes a periodical called the *Mutual Funds Forum*. Similarly, the No Load Mutual Fund Association promotes the concept of no-load mutual funds.

BUSINESS NEWS PROGRAMS

Television's only nationwide business news program during the 1970s was "Wall Street Week" (WSW). Hosted by Louis Rukeyser and a rotating series of panelists (including Martin Zweig), the program has continued to draw a substantial audience. The Public Broadcasting System (PBS) program combines a format of moderator commentary, panelist discussion, viewer questions, and guest interviews.

The growth of cable systems and the "narrow casting" approach to programming led to the introduction of a rash of new business programs in the early 1980s. For example, on Friday nights "Wall Street Week" is now accompanied on PBS by "Nightly Business Report," which appears five days a week. This half-hour program is devoted to business and particularly stock market news. It ends with a segment by one of its 10 regular commentators. "Insider Business Today," a third PBS offering, is a weekly interview program.

The Cable News Network (CNN) originates a number of business news programs. "Moneyline," with a heavy concentration of economic and market information, appears daily. "Business Morning" and "Business Day" both appear in the early morning of each weekday. Among other features is their report on market conditions around the world, especially those in Tokyo and London (where the markets open before New York's and often influence their opening price levels). "Moneyweek" is a weekly compilation of some of the "Moneyline" stories. "Your Money" appears weekly and is devoted to financial management issues of interest to small investors and household managers. Finally, "Inside Business" and "Pinnacle" provide in-depth looks at corporate leaders.

The Financial News Network offers 12 hours of programs daily. Its FNN Final provides an hour of business and financial news. "Moneytalk" is a call-in show for viewer questions. FNN also runs the stock market ticker tape across the top of its screen while the market is open. Other business-oriented programs include "Wall Street Journal Report," which is produced weekly by Dow Jones and broadcast by Independent Network News; "Biz Net News Today," which is produced daily by the U.S. Chamber of Commerce and broadcast by the Modern Satellite Network; "Business Times," which the Entertainment and Sports Network offers as a daily briefing for top executives; and finally "Moneyworks," which is an interview program produced by Mintzer. As with other types of television programming, new shows are introduced and others are canceled. Thus this discussion may be somewhat out of date by the time the reader sees it.

SOURCES OF INVESTMENT IDEAS

Readers are advised to follow up their reading of this chapter by examining some of the relevant periodicals in the library. The financial press is constantly suggesting interesting investment situations. Brokers also recommend investments as part of their "service." Friends, neighbors, relatives, and local business people sometimes have ideas worth considering. Investors may turn up some ideas at work or even in the supermarket. For example, a product encountered in the course of business or shopping may seem interesting enough to warrant checking out the manufacturer or distributor. *Forbes*, *Value Line*, and some other periodicals frequently list stocks with particular characteristics in common (very low PE ratios, large cash positions, etc.). These may serve as useful beginning points. Investors interested in a particular industry can begin with the *Value Line* sample.

The search for ideas may even begin with an examination of the entire list of NYSE, AMEX, or the national OTC securities. For example, if one believes that a significant number of warrants, convertible bonds, or high-yield bonds are likely to be underpriced, a quick check through the most recent edition of *The Wall Street Journal* will provide a list to investigate. Warrants are identified by *wt* after their name, convertibles by *cv*, and high-yield bonds have high numbers in the yield column. A quicker approach is available to those with a computer, software, and a data source. In any case, once a preliminary list of potential investments is assembled, the investor/analyst can begin the more serious evaluation of fundamentals.

SUMMARY AND CONCLUSIONS

An individual following a particular stock should refer to company-prepared documents such as 10Ks, 10Qs, prospectuses, proxy materials, press releases, and annual and quarterly reports. The 13D filings report large ownership positions. Stock quotations and indexes contain price and other information on individual securities and the market. Business news is covered in publications such as *The*

Wall Street Journal and *Business Week*, whereas *Barron's* and *Forbes* offer more investor-oriented coverage. Investors seeking information about specific firms may wish to consult *Moody's Industrial Manual*, the *Standard and Poor's Stock Reports*, *Value Line Investment Survey*, or brokerage house reports. Tapes containing financial information for many firms for a number of years are very nearly essential for serious statistical analysis. A variety of investment-related computer software is available to those with personal computers.

REVIEW QUESTIONS

1. Discuss the types of information available in corporate reports. Which are most complete and which are likely to be most up-to-date?

2. Compare quotations for the same company from *Barron's* and *The Wall Street Journal*. What additional information is contained in the *Standard & Poor's Stock Guide*?

3. Discuss the various stock market indexes. How do they differ? Which index is the best indicator for blue chip stocks and which is considered a better indicator of small capitalization stocks?

4. Compare the coverage in *Moody's Manuals*, the *Standard & Poor's Stock Reports*, and *Value Line Investment Survey*. What are the trade-offs to consider in deciding which to use? Which is most current? Which is most complete? Which is most oriented toward the investor?

5. Discuss the computer's role in investments. How does it enter in data access, investment analysis, trading execution, and so on?

REVIEW PROBLEMS

1. For the entries in Figures 10.1a and 10.1b, use the latest dividend declaration to compute the indicated rate. Compare the result with that reported in the quotation. Do any discrepancies appear? If so what might account for them?

2. Again for the entries Figures 10.1a and 10.1b, use the indicated dividend rate to compute the percentage yield. Compare the result with the reported percentage yield. Do any discrepancies appear? If so, what might account for them?

3. Make a list of the information reported for a NYSE listed stock in *The Wall Street Journal*. What additional information is available in a *Barron's* quote?

4. Continuing with Problem 3, what is left out in the OTC National list? The OTC Supplemental list? The Regional quotes?

5. Use Figure 10.3 to make a classified listing of the information that may be shown with explanatory notes.

6. Construct a table of the various broad-based stock market indexes. In your table indicate the number of stocks included, the method of weighting them, the nature of the stocks used, and the interpretation placed on the index.

REVIEW PROJECTS

1. Select a company and obtain each of its various reports (see Table 10.1 for a list). Read and analyze each report. Analyze the company on the basis of these reports.

2. Compare the coverage in your local newspaper with *The Wall Street Journal* quotations in Figures 10.1a and 10.1b and Figures 10.2a through 10.2e.

3. Compute the daily percentage change in each of the following market indexes for 10 days: S&P 500, Value Line, Dow Jones Industrials, NYSE, AMEX, and Wilshire 5000. Repeat for monthly changes over the past year. Compare the performances.

4. For the same company as was selected in Project 1, obtain current reports in *Value Line, Moody's, S&P*, and from a brokerage house. Read and analyze each report. Write your own report on the company. Compare it with the one you wrote for Project 1 based only on company-issued data.

5. Read through several recent issues of *Forbes* and identify a list of 10 companies that the magazine has featured favorably. Now consult *Value Line, Moody's*, and *S&P* on each. Finally, obtain company reports on each. Evaluate each company on the basis of each set of reports.

6. Write for literature from the various vendors of investment-related computer software and data sources. Analyze the materials and write a report.

7. Sketch the type of features that would be desirable to have in a computer investing software package.

NOTES

1. F. Reilly, *Investments* (Hinsdale, Ill.: Dryden Press, 1982).

2. F. Black, "Yes Virginia, There Is Hope: A Test of the Value Line Ranking System," *Financial Analysts Journal*, September 1973, 10.

3. C. Holloway, "A Note on Testing an Aggressive Investment Strategy Using Value Line Ranks," *Journal of Finance*, June 1981, 711–720.

4. R. Stanley, W. Lewellen, and G. Schlarbaum, "Further Evidence on the Value of Professional Investment Research," *Journal of Financial Research*, Spring 1981, 1–10.

5. B. Rosenberg and M. Houglet, "Error Rates in CRISP and Compustat Data Bases and Their Implications," *Journal of Finance*, September 1974, 1303–1310; R. Bennin, "Error Rates on CRISP and Compustat: A Second Look," *Journal of Finance*, December 1980, 1267–1271; R. McElreath and C. Wiggins, "Using the COMPUSTAT Topics in Financial Research Problems and Solutions," *Financial Analysts Journal*, January/February 1984, 71–76.

SECTION FOUR

Investment Timing

Selecting attractive investments is only one part of an effective investment program. Investors also want to take advantage of (or at least minimize the damage from) the market's ups and downs. This section explores market timing in three separate chapters. The following case illustrates some of the issues to be examined.

STARTING A NEWSLETTER

You and a friend in the brokerage industry have decided to start an investment newsletter. Your friend plans to quit her job and you will be passing up a job offer in banking to pursue this option. Your friend will be in charge of marketing whereas your primary job will be to write the articles. Because start-up costs (principally advertising) are expected to be quite heavy, you must find some backers. Another friend has assembled a list of potential investors. They are sure to want to see some evidence of your potential. You have agreed to put together a sample of what your newsletter will contain. Accordingly, you must write a sample letter. The proposed sample is to contain three sections. First, you will analyze the current and antic-ipated state of the economy and its likely impact on stock prices. Second, you will assess the market's tone and emotional state. Finally, you will recommend some specific stocks that you expect to make short-term moves. Your letter will be in your potential backers' hands for several weeks before they decide what to do, and they will have an opportunity to compare your forecast with the market's actual performance.

The three sections of your proposed newsletter correspond to the three chapters of this section. Chapter 11 deals with relations between the stock market and the economy. Business cycle–stock market relations are explored first. Various ways of forecasting economic activity are examined. Much of the attention is focused on relations between monetary policy and stock market movements. The remainder of Chapter 11 discusses relations between the stock market and the inflation rate. Noneconomic factors that may be used to forecast stock market activity are ex-plored in Chapter 12. Specifically, the following approaches to timing the market are discussed: percentage changes from previous highs, market PEs, market PEs relative to interest rates, recession patterns, election year cycles, official pronouncements, discount rate changes, company share repurchases, and various technical market indicators. Finally, Chapter 13 examines various methods of timing individual security trades. Chart reading is briefly considered along with anxious trader effects, adjustment lags, and speculative bubbles.

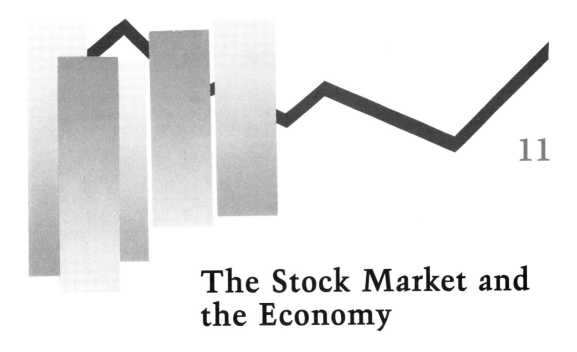

The Stock Market and the Economy

While not necessarily the key to short-term trading profits, understanding stock market–economy relationships may help investors avoid some unprofitable moves. Thus under normal circumstances a falling stock price might encourage investors to buy. If the investor realized that a changed economic outlook had greatly altered profit expectations, however, the decision might be different. Moreover, a solid understanding of stock market–economy relationships, coupled with an ability to forecast the economy's future, may indeed facilitate profitable trading. Accordingly, this chapter is designed to assist investors in understanding such relationships.

First, various ways of forecasting economic activity are considered. This discussion includes econometric models, leading indicators and investor-constructed forecasts. To help investors understand how to formulate a forecast, the economic impact of fiscal and monetary policies are also examined. Then we explore the empirical relations between stock performance and economic policy giving particular emphasis to monetary policy. The remainder of the chapter discusses theoretical arguments and empirical evidence on the impact of inflation on returns.

FORECASTING ECONOMIC PERFORMANCE

The theoretical relations between the stock market and the economy were discussed in Chapter 7. We saw that the business cycle had a major effect on a firm's profits, dividends, and stock price. An expanding economy causes sales to rise, inventory levels to decline, working hours to expand, income to increase, and thus corporate profits and dividends to rise. This economic expansion is also generally accompanied by a strong stock market. On the other hand, a weak economy tends to affect the stock market adversely. Thus knowledge of the direction of the economy should help investors anticipate stock market moves. Accordingly, we shall now consider how to forecast economic activity.

Econometric Models

A number of econometricians have made a business out of forecasting economic activity. Their forecasts are generated by applying the latest economic information and expectations to their own models. Individuals may subscribe directly to such services but the cost would be substantial. Articles based on their predictions frequently appear in the financial press, however, enabling investors to learn about the forecasters' viewpoints for a minimal cost. Economic forecasts may not be especially useful, in any case.

Econometric forecasts of the economy have several noteworthy limitations. First, the predictions are made periodically and thus do not reflect interim developments. Second, stock prices themselves may already incorporate the relevant information. Third, forecasters' past records are far from perfect although they may be improving. Figure 11.1 illustrates their recent performance.

Leading Indicators

Leading indicators are designed to forecast economic activity. In this regard the National Bureau of Economic Research (NBER) and the Commerce Department have identified 12 monthly data series that tend to lead the business cycle: stock prices, average work week, average unemployment claims, inflation-adjusted new consumer goods orders, vendor performance (companies receiving slower deliveries), net business formation, inflation-adjusted contracts for plant and equipment, new building permits, inflation-adjusted change in inventories on hand and on order, change in the prices of sensitive material, change in business and consumer debt, and inflation-adjusted M2. (M2 includes currency and checkable deposits in the hands of the public plus savings and small time deposits, repurchase agreements, and money market deposit accounts.) The list of leading indicators is revised from time to time.

Heathcotte and Apilado studied the profitability of a trading strategy based on the 11 nonstock components of the leading indicators.[1] They found that such a strategy could outperform a buy and hold strategy. Simonson, however, criticized the work as lacking a firm theoretical foundation and relying on filter rules based on hindsight.[2] More recently, research by Wertheim and Company and Geoffrey Moore found leading indicators quite accurate at forecasting economic turns but offering about the same amount of lead time as the stock market itself.[3] Thus by the time the leading indicators forecast an economic turn the stock market would already have made a turn of its own.

FIGURE 11.1 10-Year History of Blue Chip Consensus Forecasts of Year-over-Year Percentage Changes in Real GNP vs. BEA Actuals

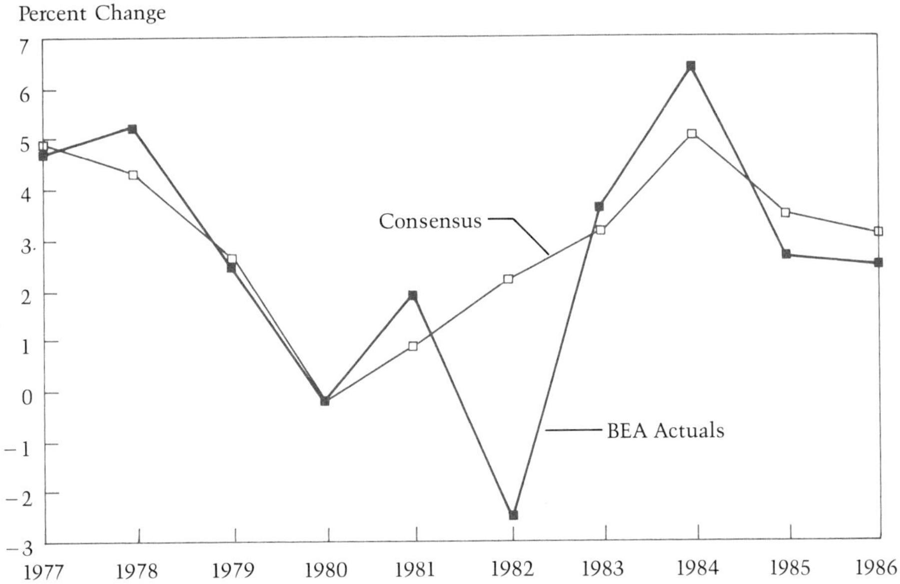

Percent Change

Source: Jim Eggert, "Consensus Forecasting—A Ten-Year Report Card," *Challenge*, July/August, 1987, 59–62. Reprinted by permission of publisher, M.E. Sharpe, Inc., 80 Business Park Drive, Armonk, NY 10504.

The *Business Week* Leading Index (BWLI) appears in the Financial Figures of the Week section. This index provides an alternative to the NBER/Commerce Department index. Geoffrey Moore devised both the original NBER/Commerce Department index and the newer BWLI. Indeed, the BWLI appears to outperform his earlier creation. The BWLI is based on seven data series (initial unemployment claims, bond yields, money growth, stock prices, real estate loans, business failures, and materials prices). The index appears to give rather accurate advance warning of economic downturns but less advance notice of upturns.

Investor-Constructed Forecasts

Both leading indicators and econometric forecasts appear to have relatively limited value in stock timing. Nonetheless, homemade economic predictions might, if timely and accurate, facilitate more profitable performance for stock traders. Many investors seem inclined to make such forecasts. Like the weather, almost everyone has an opinion on the economy. These opinions might as well be based on an accurate understanding of how the economy operates. Moreover, as Malabre argues, understanding economics sufficiently to formulate a forecast is not especially difficult.[4]

Most investors probably prefer not to attempt the implied precision of a point forecast of GNP, unemployment, and inflation. They may, however, be more inclined to estimate the direction and perhaps the general magnitude of the changes in each. That is, few individuals would feel comfortable forecasting an increase in GNP of precisely 4.8% but many might be more capable of correctly predicting greater growth than last year's 3.4%. Indeed, just being relatively confident in a prediction that the economy is likely to be headed for (1) a recession, (2) continued rapid growth, or (3) a pause should help in investment timing. Professional forecasts are usually no more reliable than such directional predictions.

Serious efforts to predict economic activity should take account of the important role played by the government's economic policy. Government spending and taxing policy (fiscal policy) and any activity affecting interest rates and the money supply (monetary policy) have important economic impacts.

Fiscal Policy

Government spending affects the economy in several ways. First, when the economy has room to expand, increased government expenditures call forth additional production. Thus starting a new public works project will put people to work producing the structure and the required inputs (cement, steel, etc.). These newly employed workers will spend most of their income on consumer goods and services, thereby creating demands that put others to work. This multiplier process increases employment and production. At each stage, however, a portion of the extra income is saved, taxed, or spent on imported goods. These so-called leakages reduce the multiplier's power. Moreover, the additional spending forces the government to increase its borrowing or taxes, thereby crowding out other borrowers and/or reducing other disposable incomes. Thus proportionately less goes to each succeeding round. In fact, leakages are so pervasive that the GNP typically increases by only about twice the amount of the government spending increase.

The effect of a tax decrease is similar to a government spending increase. Lower tax rates and reduced withholdings increase after-tax income causing spending to rise. This spending increase in turn leads to additional production, jobs, and income, which cause further increases. Thus either a government spending increase or a tax decrease stimulates the economy whereas a government spending decrease or a tax increase restrains the economy. A spending change, however, has a greater economic impact than a tax change of equivalent size. The full amount of the spending change affects GNP whereas a portion of the tax change affects savings.

Stimulative fiscal policy is normally applied when the economy has sufficient room to absorb the resulting increase in spending. When the economy is already operating near its capacity, however, stimulative economic policy can have little or no impact on output or employment. Under these circumstances the principal effect of stimulation is to increase prices. As we shall soon see, inflation is not a plus for either the economy or the stock market.

Monetary Policy: The Fed's Tools

The Federal Reserve System (Fed) has primary authority over our nation's monetary policy. Its ability to influence the economy stems from its power over credit conditions. By largely determining the rate at which the money supply expands or contracts, the Fed exercises virtual control over the supply and cost (interest rate) of credit.

The money supply itself consists of all cash and coin in circulation outside banks plus all depository accounts on which checklike instruments may be drawn (M1). Most of M1 is held in the form of bank deposits. Federally chartered banks and state banks with Fed memberships are required to maintain reserves with the Fed. These reserves must be equal to a predetermined percentage of their deposits. This percentage is called the reserve requirement.

The Fed can cause the money supply to expand or contract by reducing or increasing the reserve requirement. If the reserve requirement is decreased, banks need less reserves to support their existing deposits and thus may increase their loans. An increase in the reverse requirement has the reverse effect.

Banks grant loans by making a deposit to the borrower's account. Thus the money that is loaned is initially retained in an account at the lending bank. Eventually, however, the borrower begins to spend the money. Checks written against such loan-created deposits will in turn be deposited into the accounts of the person or firms receiving the payments. In this way the money flows largely into other bank accounts. Some of the funds will remain with the bank that made the loan while a much larger fraction will move into accounts of other components of the banking system. A relatively small portion of the loan money may go into additional cash holdings. Thus most of the new money resulting from granting the loan ends up as deposits somewhere in the banking system. The corresponding increase in deposits throughout the banking system creates additional lending power. When this lending power is utilized, more deposits and still more lending power results.

By the time the process is complete, the money supply will have expanded by several times the amount of the initial increase in deposits. Loans outstanding will increase by a comparable amount. The ratio between the initial increase in reserves and the resulting money supply increase is called the *money multiplier*. Any reserves freed by reducing the reserve requirement will eventually be utilized to increase both the money supply and loans outstanding by a multiple of the freed-up reserves.

Changing reserve requirements tends to disrupt the financial markets more than is desirable. Accordingly, the Fed generally prefers to exercise its influence over the banking system through what are called open market operations. Such operations utilize the Fed's substantial portfolio of government bonds. Its management of this portfolio has a major effect on the banking system.

The Fed's portfolio management requires the buying and selling of substantial amounts of government bonds. When it is a buyer, the Fed pays for the bonds with drafts (checks) that increase the recipient banks' reserves. These increased reserves allow a multiple increase in deposits and loans. Similarly, when the Fed sells government securities, reserves are reduced, thereby forcing deposits and loans to contract. The Fed buys and sells Treasury securities daily and thereby pumps in or takes out a targeted amount of reserves. The change in reserves then affects the aggregate money supply Many Wall Street analysts carefully monitor the Fed's open market moves and changes in the money supply.

TABLE 11.1   The Fed's Principal Policy Tools

Reserve Requirement	Increasing (decreasing) the ratio reduces (raises) the amount of money that can be supported by a given reserve base.
Open Market Operations	Fed purchases (sales) of government securities increase (decrease) the reserves available to support the money supply.
Discount Loans	Increasing (decreasing) the discount rate and decreasing (increasing) its willingness to grant discount loans tightens (eases) monetary policy.

The Fed also loans reserves (discount loans) to member banks. The Fed stresses that discounting is a privilege, not a right. It extends such loans only on a short-term basis (as a safety valve) and only to applicants that it views as not abusing this borrowing privilege. The Fed makes discounting more or less attractive by adjusting its interest rate on and its willingness to grant such loans.

Compared with the Fed's other tools, discounting plays a relatively minor role. It is used principally to signal changes in other Fed policy. The stock market generally reacts strongly to changes in the discount rate. Such changes are viewed as unmistakable evidence of a policy shift (either in direction or magnitude). In addition to the *discount window* depository institutions having a temporary shortage of reserves may borrow from others with a temporary excess in the so-called Federal Funds market. Table 11.1 lists the Fed's principal policy tools.

The Economic Impact of Monetary Policy

How does an increase in deposits and loans affect the economy? The supply of money in the form of transactions balances (e.g., checking deposits) and the corresponding amount of outstanding loans of the banking system play a key role in the economy. An increase in the supply of money and loans outstanding tends to reduce interest rates (at least in the short run). The increased supply and lower cost (interest rate) of loanable funds encourages many people to spend more on consumption. Similarly, businesses are encouraged to invest more in such things as plant and equipment. These additional expenditures tend to create more income and jobs and stimulate even more spending. A reduction in deposits and loans, in contrast, tends to reduce spending and income.

As with fiscal policy, stimulatory monetary policy tends to increase real (non-inflationary) output when the economy has slack resources and to increase the prices when bottlenecks appear. Thus stimulative monetary policy is usually favorable to the economy and stock market. That is, such stimulation is likely to increase demand for goods and services and thereby increase profits. Additionally, an increase in the availability of loanable funds may reduce interest rates. As we shall soon see, a decline in interest rates is particularly bullish (favorable) for stock prices. When the economy is already operating near its capacity, however, further stimulation is inflationary. Such inflationary pressures are bearish (unfavorable) for both the economy and the stock market. Such inflation is all too likely to cause economic policy to turn restrictive and thereby throw the economy into a recession.

Monetary and Fiscal Policy: Some Qualifications

As we have seen, the economy may be stimulated by increased government spending, lower taxes, and an increase in the money supply and may be restrained by the reverse processes. Now some qualifications are introduced.

First, changes in tax rates and government spending (fiscal policy) or in the reserve requirement, discount rate, and open market policy (monetary policy) take time for their effects to work their way through the economy. As a result, changes in the direction of government monetary and fiscal policy generally precede changes in the direction of economic activity. Thus knowledge of these changes can be used to help forecast economic behavior.

Second, monetary and fiscal policy are both subject to political pressures. Their degree of sensitivity differs, however. Monetary policy is formulated by the Federal Reserve Board's Governors and its Open Market Committee. Members are appointed by the President for long staggered terms. Furthermore, the Fed is not dependent on Congressional appropriations. Its own interest income is more than adequate to cover its operating expenses. Thus the Fed is generally able to pursue a relatively independent monetary policy. Fiscal policy, on the other hand, is formulated jointly by Congress and the President, and many diverse interest groups more directly affect the decision-making process. As a result, short-term pressures increase the difficulty of implementing long-run fiscal policies.

Third, the stock market also monitors and reacts to its perceptions of the direction of economic policy. Thus to obtain an advantage relative to the market's own economic assessment, investors need to have a superior understanding of economic policy–economy–stock market relationships. In other words, investors need to be able to outguess the market in its forecast for the economy's future. Any economic forecasts should be based on an assessment of the likely direction for economic policy. That direction is very likely to be related to the objectives of the policymakers. Accordingly, would-be forecasters of the economy need to know (and understand the nature of) what goals the policymakers are pursuing.

Goals of Monetary and Fiscal Policy

The primary economic goals of monetary and fiscal policymakers are full employment and price stability. Most people have a general idea of what is meant by full employment and price stability. Nonetheless, the concepts are sufficiently complex and confusing to warrant some discussion.

Price stability is the absence of either a rising (inflation) or falling (deflation) trend in overall prices. Inflation is a general rise in the price level. Thus, for example, a 6% annual inflation rate implies that $1.06 is required to buy the same diverse market basket of goods and services as could be acquired a year earlier for $1. Deflation, in contrast, is a general fall in the price level. During most of our history actual and potential inflation has been much more of a problem than the possibility of deflation.

Full employment could be defined as 100% of the labor force having a job. Realistically, however, some people (not necessarily the same people) will always be unemployed. Thus full employment is generally defined as corresponding to an acceptable level of unemployment. What that acceptable level is will be discussed later in this chapter. The unemployment rate itself is defined as the percentage of the labor force that is out of work. The labor force consists of those who are employed or actively seeking employment. Extensive government statistics are compiled on both employment and inflation.

While not generally viewed as important as price stability and full employment, our relationship to the international economy has taken on increasing importance. Thus, as the world economy has grown more interdependent, such matters as the value of the dollar (exchange rates) and imports relative to exports (balance of trade) and international capital flows (which may take the form of foreigners investing in U.S. securities) have become increasingly important to economic policymakers.

Additional economic goals and concerns include: economic growth, rising productivity, an increasing standard of living, environmental protection, energy independence, economic freedom, economic opportunity, consumer protection, and product safety. Policies designed to achieve some of these goals frequently conflict with other goals, however.

Virtually everyone agrees that price stability and full employment are desirable. Policies to reduce unemployment may, however, accelerate inflation because of what might be termed the *capacity effect*. Stimulating the economy depletes the reservoir of unemployed workers, resources, and excess capacity. Eventually those bidding for an inadequate supply of inputs will force prices to rise. Some stimulation may be administered to a slack economy before bottlenecks accelerate the inflation rate, however.

The international situation adds a further complication. Defending the value of the dollar and seeking to attract capital to help finance both the budget and the trade deficit may require relatively restrictive monetary policy. Such a policy would tend to raise U.S. interest rates relative to rates abroad. High interest rates will, however, reduce domestic economic activity. Thus policymakers may at times have to choose between doing what is best for the domestic economy and what is best internationally.

Some degree of unemployment is inevitable. People change jobs (frictional unemployment), work at seasonal jobs (seasonal unemployment), or are unemployed because of location, background, or training (structural unemployment). Moreover, increasing numbers are employed in unreported underground economy jobs. These various classes of unemployed and unreported employeds create an almost irreducible floor for reported unemployment. The height of this floor, however, changes as the economy evolves (Figure 11.2).

Similarly, the recent history of inflation rates (Figure 11.3) and performance relative to unemployment may provide clues to its future behavior. Figure 11.4 illustrates the inflation–unemployment trade-off. In the early 1960s unemployment was relatively high and the inflation rate relatively low. Stimulative economic policy (first the Kennedy tax cut and then the Vietnam War) tended to reduce

FIGURE 11.2 Unemployment and the Economic Cycle

Percent Unemployment

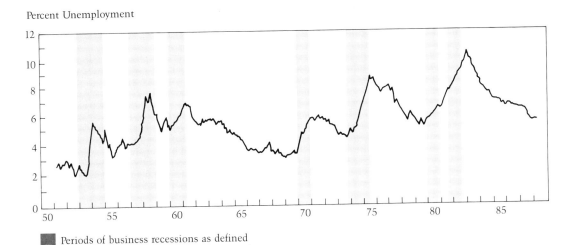

Periods of business recessions as defined
by National Bureau of Economic Research

Source: National Bureau of Economic Research.

unemployment and, once the economy reached its capacity, also tended to increase the inflation rate. Once inflation got out of hand, the rate spiraled upward and unemployment also rose. In the late 1960s and early 1980s we had very high unemployment coupled with a high inflation rate. More restrictive economic policy led to still higher unemployment but some fall in the inflation rate. By late 1987 the unemployment rate was declining and inflation seemed to be rising somewhat.

Predicting a Shift in Economic Policy

Whether economic policy is more likely to be expansionary or contractionary depends largely on how policymakers view the relative importance of unemployment and inflation. Although the trade-offs are quite complex, some guidelines may be helpful.

Most economists once thought that 4% unemployment represented full employment. Those occasions when unemployment dipped below 4% (in the 1966–1969 period) were followed by accelerating inflation. Since 1975, however, unemployment has remained above 4% while inflationary pressures have generally continued. Most policymakers now believe that reported unemployment of 5% or even 6% is acceptable (full employment). Unemployment above 7% or 8% is still a major concern, however. Stimulatory monetary and fiscal policy becomes more likely with every 0.1% rise toward 8%. Once begun, stimulation usually continues until inflation becomes a more pressing problem or unemployment is reduced to the 5% to 6% range.

FIGURE 11.3 Change in the Consumer Price Index

Percent Change

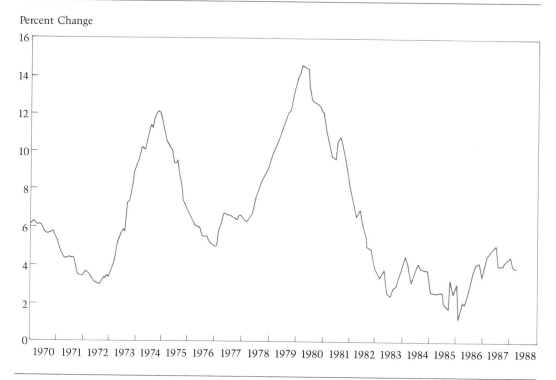

Source: Department of Labor.

In the 1950s and 1960s a 3% inflation rate was generally considered to be a problem. Double-digit inflation of the 1970s and early 1980s made policymakers long for such creeping inflation. Indeed, a 4% to 5% inflation rate may have become marginally acceptable.

The desire to reduce inflation further has not been abandoned, but must be balanced with other goals in the post-1974 environment. After experiencing 10% to 14% inflation, both the public and the policymakers seem to be reasonably willing to settle for restraining inflation to half that rate. The acceptability of a given inflation rate depends greatly on recent experience, however. Thus if inflation can be kept in the mid-single digits for a time, policymakers may seek a rate in the low single digits.

When policymakers consider both inflation and unemployment rates to be too high, economic policy is especially difficult to forecast. Under these circumstances the relevant question is, Which problem is to be given greater attention? Other things being equal, higher inflation and lower unemployment increase the likelihood of contractionary economic policy. Economic policy is quite likely to be restrictive when inflation is a problem and unemployment is below 7%. On the other hand, with 7.5% unemployment and a marginally unacceptable inflation rate, stimulation is likely.

FIGURE 11.4   Inflation and Unemployment Rates

Inflation (Percent)[1]

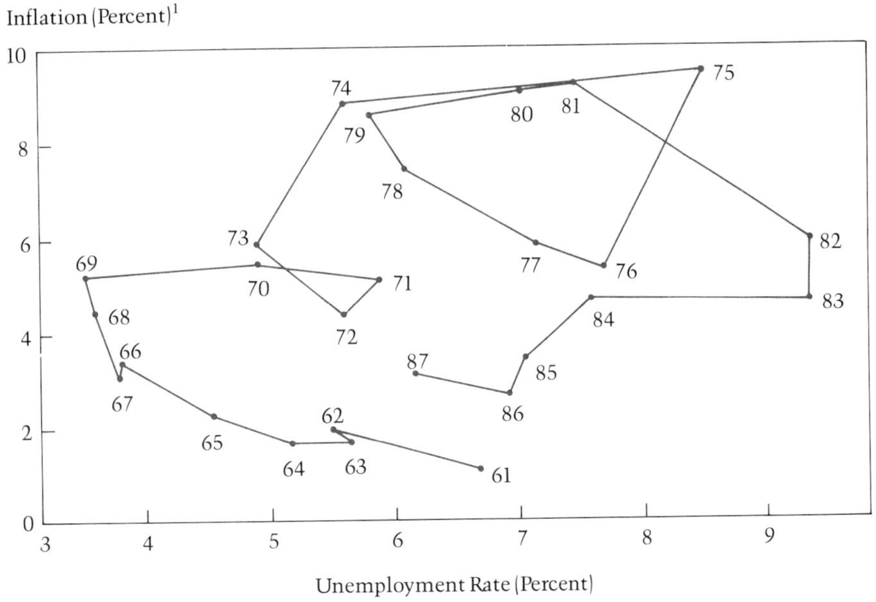

Source: Department of Commerce and Department of Labor.

The international situation adds another factor to the decision matrix. A weak dollar and large trade deficit (U.S. exports less imports) will incline policymakers toward a more restrictive economic policy. That is, those who determine the direction of economic policy may at times find themselves constrained by the status of the United States within the international economy. They may be reluctant to stimulate the U.S. economy too much and thereby risk making the trade deficit worse and the dollar weaker. The constraint is not absolute, however. When the health of the domestic economy is seriously threatened, that threat usually takes precedence over any concerns about the international situation. These policymakers (who may eventually face U.S. voters during an election) would prefer a weak dollar to a weak economy.

Forecasts for the direction in economic policy should be based on up-to-date knowledge of what levels of unemployment and inflation are acceptable. For example, in 1987 and 1988 most economic policymakers would have been quite pleased with unemployment below 6% and inflation below 4%. Twenty years earlier, however, the targets were around 4% for unemployment and 2% for inflation. No doubt the acceptable (or tolerable) unemployment and inflation levels will continue to vary.

Economic policymakers also take note of the direction of change in important economic statistics such as the inflation and unemployment rates as well as the U.S. condition within the international economy (strength of the dollar, balance of trade, balance of payments, creditworthiness of loans to the Third World, etc.). For example, fiscal and monetary authorities tend to be more concerned, other things being equal, with a rising than a constant inflation rate. On the other hand, a falling inflation rate, even if still at a relatively high level, may increase the likelihood of stimulative actions. Similarly, the longer inflation has persisted at an unacceptably high level, the greater is the probability of restraint. Policymakers are also more concerned with a given unemployment rate if that rate is also rising or has persisted too long at too high a level. Similarly, a problem in the international area (weak dollar, trade deficit, etc.) becomes more serious the longer it persists and/or if it seems to be getting worse rather than better. Problems in the international area that appear to be improving will have less effect on how economic policymakers pursue their other goals.

The composition of the overall unemployment rate also provides clues to likely future monetary and fiscal policy. Unemployment rates are reported for various subgroups. The so-called *central unemployment rate* for males between the ages of 25 and 54 may be viewed as particularly relevant to policymakers. The central rate is usually well below the global rate. For a given overall rate, the lower the central rate, the less likely is economic policy to be stimulating. When the central rate is low, further stimulation tends to be especially inflationary. Furthermore, the central group's political pressures are generally more effective than those of other labor force components.

The administration, Congress, and the Fed usually attempt to coordinate the monetary and fiscal policy actions that they take. Nevertheless, differences can occur in the implementation of these policies. Stimulus is politically more acceptable than restraint. Both Congress and the administration are reluctant to take politically unpopular actions. Thus the Fed must sometimes make the initial restrictive move. However, the Fed itself is not immune to political pressures. Like the Supreme Court the Fed does "follow the election returns." Indeed, the Fed's chairman is often called to answer pointed questions before Congressional committees. The chairman is also ever mindful that the legislation under which the Fed operates can be changed. Moreover, the President can fill Fed vacancies with people that he or she expects to pursue policies similar to the administration's.

The unemployment–inflation trade-off also has important political ramifications. All administrations seek low unemployment and stable prices. The more liberal the administration, however, the greater is its desire to reduce unemployment. Conservative administrations, in contrast, focus more on the problem of inflation. Thus the Truman and Kennedy–Johnson administrations sought low unemployment and tolerated increased inflation whereas the Eisenhower, Nixon, and Ford administrations generally sought to reduce inflation at the cost of higher unemployment rates. The Carter administration had the worst of both worlds but became increasingly concerned with inflation as time went by. Volcker, who was chairman of the Fed's Board of Governors while both Carter and Reagan were president, devoted himself to fighting the inflation problem. The Reagan administration's overriding concern with inflation abated only when unemployment reached double digits and inflation declined dramatically. The decline in inflation during the 1980s is thought to be largely the result of relatively restrictive monetary

TABLE 11.2 Factors Affecting the Likelihood of a Shift in Monetary and Fiscal Policy

A shift toward greater stimulation is more likely if:	A shift toward greater restrictiveness is more likely if:
Unemployment is far above its goal	Unemployment is near its goal
Inflation rate is near its goal	Inflation rate is far above its goal
Unemployment is increasing	Unemployment is decreasing
Inflation is decreasing	Inflation is increasing
The dollar is strong	The dollar is weak
The trade deficit is small	The trade deficit is large
Substantial amounts of capital are flowing into the United States	Foreign capital is threatening to withdraw or slow its flow into the United States
Administration is liberal	Administration is conservative
Presidential election is approaching	Presidential election is far off

policy under Volcker's chairmanship. Table 11.2 summarizes the factors affecting shifts in economic policy.

THE PARTICULAR ATTENTION THAT THE STOCK MARKET PAYS TO MONETARY POLICY

Stock market analysts pay particular attention to monetary (as opposed to fiscal) policy for several reasons. First, monetary policy has differential industry effects. Second, monetary policy is usually easier (although not necessarily easy) to track and perhaps easier to predict. The Fed's weekly monetary data releases are intensively analyzed by the financial press. Moreover, monetary policy can shift emphasis more quickly than can fiscal policy. Thus Fed action may have to shoulder the entire macroeconomic adjustment burden when political pressures inhibit discretionary fiscal policy. Third, an influential group of economists (called monetarists, many of them are associated with the University of Chicago) assert that money drives the economy while fiscal policy plays a more modest role. Fourth, monetary policy not only affects the stock market through its economic impact but also has a more direct effect through its influence on interest rates. Each of these matters will be considered in greater detail.

The Disproportionate Impact of Monetary Policy

Monetary policy works by rationing credit. Restrictive monetary policy not only raises interest rates (at least in the short run) but limits loans to stronger credit risks and influences the allocation of funds among the financial intermediaries.

Savings and loan associations and mutual savings banks (thrifts) may be particularly hard hit when money is tight. This sort of restrictive monetary policy causes depositors to move toward higher yield investments such as money funds (disintermediation). Investors inevitably seek out the highest available risk-adjusted rates. The money funds will offer relatively high levels of returns whenever they can earn high rates on the money market instruments that they invest in. At such times the thrifts must offer competitive rates or lose deposits.

The thrifts have historically maintained a large percentage of their portfolios in long-term fixed rate mortgages. Thus, in effect, a large fraction of their deposits have been used to fund mortgage lending. Moreover, much of this has been at fixed rates. The thrifts' deposits, in contrast, have tended to be available to their depositors upon demand or represented by CDs with relatively short terms. This type of situation implies an imbalance between the maturity structure of their assets (long term) and of their liabilities (short term). The result of this imbalance has been to make the thrifts vulnerable to rising interest rates. As interest rates rise the costs of funds tend to go up while the rates that the thrifts earn on existing fixed rate mortgage loans remain constant. The larger the proportion of their assets tied up in fixed rate loans, the more vulnerable the thrifts are to rising interest rates. Having experienced the adverse effects a number of times, the thrifts have sought to limit their exposure.

Over time a shift to adjustable rate mortgages (ARMs) as well as the use of various instruments for hedging interest rate risks (financial futures and options, interest rate swaps, etc.) has reduced this vulnerability. Nonetheless, many thrifts (particularly the smaller ones) remain vulnerable to adverse interest rate moves. The move to deregulate rates has helped offset the loss of accounts but has done little to reduce the resulting profit squeeze. This disintermediation process not only depresses the earnings of the thrifts, but also reduces the availability of mortgage money from which much of their business is derived.

The sensitivity of the thrifts to high interest rates and to the adverse impact of disintermediation increases the vulnerability to tight money of the real estate, construction, building materials, and major appliance industries. Other industries that are heavily levered, such as public utilities, as well as auto and farm machinery manufacturers, the bulk of whose purchases are financed, are also particularly sensitive to monetary policy. Thus tight money differentially affects various types of companies and their stocks.

The Relative Ease of Tracking Monetary Policy

The financial press pays close attention to any news relating to Fed policy. Even the Fed, however, has some difficulty tracking and controlling short-run monetary aggregates. Nonetheless, monetary policy is easier to follow than the lengthy and uncertain path of authorizations, appropriation, and implementation of government expenditures. Tax legislation, the other side of fiscal policy, is equally difficult to follow. Moreover, the greater volatility of monetary policy leads to more signals than is the case with fiscal policy.

Investments in Perspective

Every Thursday at 4:30 P.M. the Fed releases money supply statistics for the week. The numbers are eagerly awaited by the financial community. Each new bit of data is examined for clues to the course of monetary policy and the state of the credit markets. The day after the Fed release, analyses are published in the financial pages of newspapers across the country. The article that follows is typical.

CREDIT MARKETS

Treasury Prices Increase Slightly

Trading Is Cautious Before Deficit Report

By MICHAEL QUINT

Treasury note and bond prices rose slightly yesterday, after trading in a relatively narrow range before the barrage of economic statistics to be announced today.

The closely watched $8\frac{7}{8}$ percent Treasury bonds due in 2017, which serve as a benchmark for other long-term issues, were offered late in the day at 98 18/32, up 7/32d's, to yield 9.01 percent. The $7\frac{7}{8}$ percent two-year notes rose 1/32d, to 100 10/32, yielding 7.70 percent.

"Caution has been the byword in the market the past few days, and everybody is waiting to see how the dollar fares after the trade announcement," one Treasury bond trader said.

Retail Report Has Little Effect

Yesterday's report of a seven-tenths of 1 percent rise in retail sales for December had little effect on trading and provided analysts with little new insight to the pace of economic growth in early 1988. Today's report on the nation's merchandise trade for November is more closely watched than other, more timely data, because it has the potential to cause a quick reaction in foreign exchange markets.

Traders and investors are concerned that even if the deficit falls from the record $17.6 billion reported for October, it will remain large enough to discourage foreign holders of dollars. In that case, they worry that additional declines in the dollar would put upward pressure on interest rates as foreign buyers are deterred and domestic buyers worry about higher inflation.

The alarm that may spread through the credit markets if the dollar weakens might be allayed somewhat, economists said, by the Producer Price Index for December, which could show that inflation is not yet a problem. The price index is expected to be unchanged or to decline slightly for December.

Late in the day the Federal Reserve announced money supply data showing that growth for 1987 was far below, or at the bottom of, the Fed's objectives for the year.

The M-2 money measure rose only $5 billion, to $2,897.1 billion in December, resulting in a growth rate of only 3.4 percent, or well below the Fed's target for 1987. For M-3, the $5.9 billion increase in December, to $3,665.4 billion, resulted in a growth rate that was at the bottom of the Fed's target of 5½ to 8½ percent from the fourth quarter of 1986 to the fourth quarter of 1987.

The basic M-1 money supply measure rose $4 billion, to $756 billion in the week ended Jan. 4, but for the month of December its average level was still $3.7 billion below November. After growing at an average rate of more than 13 percent during 1985 and 1986, M-1 growth slowed dramatically, to only 3.1 percent in the last 12 months and 1.7 percent in the last six months.

Key Rates
In percent

	Yesterday	Previous Day	Year Ago
PRIME RATE	8.75	8.75	7.50
DISCOUNT RATE	6.00	6.00	5.50
FEDERAL FUNDS	6.83	6.72	6.01
3-MO. TREAS. BILLS	5.86	5.78	5.36
6-MO. TREAS. BILLS	6.27	6.28	5.40
7-YR. TREAS. NOTES	8.65	8.67	6.91
30-YR. TREAS. BONDS	9.04	9.04	7.39
TELEPHONE BONDS	9.94	10.00	8.66
MUNICIPAL BONDS*	8.38	8.40	7.10

* Municipal Bond Index, The Bond Buyer
Salomon Brothers estimates for Treasury's bellwether bonds, notes and bills at about 4:30 P.M.

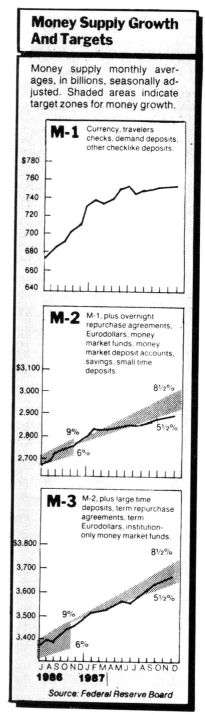

Money Supply Growth And Targets

Money supply monthly averages, in billions, seasonally adjusted. Shaded areas indicate target zones for money growth.

M-1 Currency, travelers checks, demand deposits, other checklike deposits.

M-2 M-1, plus overnight repurchase agreements, Eurodollars, money market funds, money market deposit accounts, savings, small time deposits.

M-3 M-2, plus large time deposits, term repurchase agreements, term Eurodollars, institution-only money market funds.

J A S O N D J F M A M J J A S O N D
1986   1987

Source: Federal Reserve Board

"The slow growth has been a development that raises eyebrows, but we know that money supply growth has not been a dominant consideration at the Federal Reserve," said Robert Ried, president of an economic consulting firm in Westport, Conn.

Economists said Fed officials had been tolerant of slower-than-targeted money supply growth last year because it followed two years of rapid money expansion, and because economic growth was solid. After inflation, the economy is expected to have grown at slightly less than 3 percent last year, about the same as the projected 2½ percent to 3 percent projected by Federal Reserve officials in February 1987.

"I think the Fed's tolerance of slow money supply growth has been correct," noted Lawrence Kudlow, chief economist at Bear, Stearns & Company. "If the economy turns softer, commodity prices weaken and the dollar stabilizes, the Fed may try to ease policy and stimulate faster money supply growth, but all those developments are still in the distance,

and I don't expect any near-term change in the Fed's policy."

In the Treasury bill market, some traders were surprised when the Federal Reserve sold $2 billion of bills for a customer account, and by late afternoon, three-month bills were about 5.86 percent, up one-tenth of a percentage point from early in the day. The sales were a surprise because securities dealers expected the Fed to purchase bills for other central banks that have recently bought dollars in the foreign exchange market.

Analysts hypothesized that the bill sales might have been arranged for Taiwan, which has been selling dollars recently to support its currency. As of last September, Taiwan held about $9.2 billion of Treasury bills.

Elsewhere in the bill market, the Treasury sold a new one-year issue at an average rate of 6.67 percent, down from 6.74 percent at the previous auction four weeks ago.

In the preferred stock market, Puget Sound Power and Light offered $100 million of auction-rate preferred stock through underwriters led by Salomon Brothers. Initial dividend rates were set at 6 percent to March 11, or 6.1 percent through April 8.

Unlike most issues of auction-rate preferred stock, whose dividend yield is adjusted every 49 days, Puget Sound will have the option of extending the dividend rate for periods of 13, 26 or 52 weeks.

Following are the results of yesterday's auction of new one-year Treasury bills:

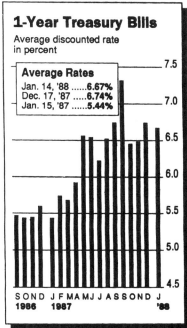

1-Year Treasury Bills

Average discounted rate in percent

Average Rates

Jan. 14, '88	**6.67%**
Dec. 17, '87	**6.74%**
Jan. 15, '87	**5.44%**

S O N D J F M A M J J A S S O N D J
1986   1987   '88

The New York Times/Jan. 15, 1988

(000 omitted in dollar figures)	
Average Price	93.256
Discounted Rate	6.67%
Coupon Yield	7.14%
High Price	93.246
Discounted Rate	6.68%
Coupon Yield	7.16%
Low Price	93.327
Discounted Rate	6.60%
Coupon Yield	7.07%
Accepted at low price	85%
Total applied for	$22,755,530
Accepted	$9,253,430
N.Y. applied for	$20,386,740
N.Y. accepted	$8,606,340
Noncompetitive	$647,160

The one-year bills mature Jan. 19, 1989.

Federal Reserve All data in millions of dollars	Latest Week	Previous Week	Year Ago
Monetary Aggregates			
M-1*as of Jan 4	$756,000	R $752,000	$749,300
Adj. Mon.Base (St.Louis Fed) *(1/13)	269,800	R 267,600	256,800
Reserve Position, Eight New York Banks Daily averages for two weeks ended Jan 13			
Excess (Deficit) Reserves (Incl. carryover)	(48)	(1)	(56)
Borrowings at Federal Reserve	1,024	0	0
Net Federal Funds Purchases	13,653	R 8,895	29,244
Basic Reserve Surplus (Deficit)	(14,725)	R(8,896)	(29,138)
Federal Reserve Credit Daily averages, week ended Jan 13			
Gov'ts. and Agencies Held Outright	227,131	R 226,824	208,222
Gov'ts. and Agencies Under Repurchase	758	4,069	2,874
Float	2,719	1,206	767
Other Assets	15,526	16,144	16,888
Other Factors Affecting Reserves Daily averages, week ended Jan 13			
Gold Stock	11,076	11,078	11,084
Special Drawing Rights	5,018	5,018	5,018
Currency in Circulation	227,825	229,911	208,808
Treasury Deposits	3,871	5,031	4,306
Other Items			
Gov't. Securities Held by Fed for Foreign accounts as of Jan 13	204,386	201,499	163,606
Business Loans, National**, Dec 28	278,156	R 276,264	286,391
Commercial Paper, National, Jan 6	356,652	R 357,512	332,063
Ten New York Banks, Balance Sheet Items Wednesday, Jan 6			
Loans and Leases, Adjusted	175,085	R 172,799	174,924
Business Loans**	59,575	R 58,879	67,488
Treasury and Agency Securities	14,997	R 14,810	13,748
Tax-Exempt Securities	13,351	R 13,422	14,050
Demand Deposits	62,984	R 64,239	61,687
Nontransaction Balances	102,675	R 102,446	98,873
Time Deposits Larger than $100,000	37,226	R 37,578	35,635

R Revised. *Seasonally adjusted   **Excluding acceptances. N.A. Not available.

Source: M. Quint, "Treasury Prices Increase Slightly," *The New York Times*, January 15, 1988, p. D11.
© 1988 by The New York Times Company. Reprinted by permission.

Monetarists versus Fiscalists

Since Keynes published his *General Theory of Employment, Interest, and Money* in 1936, the monetarists have debated with those who emphasize the importance of fiscal policy (fiscalists). While the fiscalists dominated economic thinking throughout the 1940s and 1950s, by the early 1960s the debate was again in full

FIGURE 11.5   Links Between Monetary Policy and the Stock Market

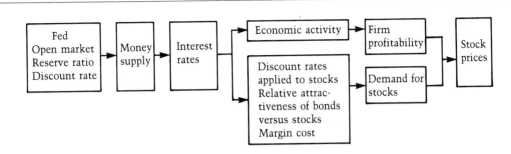

swing. The dispute continues although the issues may be narrowing. During much of the post-1936 period the fiscalists were far more influential in and out of government. Since the late sixties, however, both groups have had substantial influence. Most economists now agree that both monetary and fiscal policy affect the economy but disagree on their relative importance.

Unless monetary and fiscal policy are working at cross purposes, both economic schools expect the same direction (if not the same magnitude) of impact. Moreover, conflicts between monetary and fiscal policy (one stimulating and the other restraining) are usually quite short run. Such conflicts usually arise because monetary policy is leading and fiscal policy will soon follow. Therefore investors, who are principally concerned with direction rather than magnitude, need not assess the relative merits of the monetarists' and fiscalists' arguments.

The Direct Effect of Monetary Policy on the Stock Market

Monetary policy indirectly influences the stock market through its effect on the economy and on corporate profits. Moreover, the impact of monetary policy on interest rates directly affects the stock market in three related ways. First, stock prices reflect the present value of their expected future income streams. Thus interest rates influence the rate at which the expected incomes of stocks are discounted. Second, investors find bonds relatively more attractive as yields to maturity increase. As a result, some investors will shift from stocks to bonds when interest rates rise and in the other direction when they fall. Finally, higher interest rates mean increased borrowing costs for margin investors. Such investors will require a higher expected return to justify the greater cost of financing their margin purchases. Thus rising interest rates should depress stock prices: they imply a higher discount rate, more attractive returns for bonds, and increased costs for margin debt. Falling interest rates have the opposite effect. Figure 11.5 illustrates the linkages between monetary policy and stock prices.

Early Empirical Research on Money–Stock Market Relationships

While everyone agrees that monetary policy affects the stock market, the dependability and the time frame of the relationship are highly controversial. Beryl Sprinkel (then with the Harris Trust and Savings Bank of Chicago, more recently Assistant Secretary of the Treasury and then Chairman of Reagan's Council of Economic Advisors) wrote two books on the money–stock price relationship.[5] Sprinkel argued that monetary policy shifts tended to lead stock price changes and thus generate useful timing signals. Sprinkel offered only visual, impressionistic, and relatively simplistic evidence, however.

In a more sophisticated (i.e., econometric) test, Homa and Jaffee estimated a constant lag relationship between the money supply and a stock price index.[6] Using it to signal a switch between stocks and Treasury bills produced a higher after-commission return (8.6%) than did a buy and hold strategy (7.6%). Thus their work implied that money supply data might be useful in formulating stock timing strategy. Several other researchers reached similar conclusions. Malkiel and Quandt, in contrast, reported that when a revised and extended money supply data series was employed, a buy and hold strategy outperformed a switching strategy based on monetary signals. Moreover, a model using economic variables related to corporate profits and sales (e.g., interest rates) outperformed predictions based solely on the money supply.[7]

More Recent Studies of Money–Stock Market Relations

Two subsequent studies sought to resolve the conflicts raised by the earlier work. First, Rozeff identified various methodological flaws in the studies favorable to the hypothesis that money supply leads stock price movements. In his own study he corrected these flaws. He concluded: "Stock prices do not lag behind growth rates of the money supply, nor would we expect them to do so in an efficient market."[8]

In perhaps the most extensive study of the issue, Rogalski and Vinso noted several shortcomings in all the prior literature (including Rozeff).[9] They specifically noted that prior work failed to remove serial correlation and did not properly account for release lags and frequent revisions of monetary statistics. Their conclusions were, however, virtually identical to those of Rozeff: "Information concerning the actual rate of growth of the money supply is incorporated into stock returns as purported by various monetary portfolio theorists. . . . The stock market is efficient with respect to monetary information."[10] In still more recent studies, Davidson and Froyen and Mitchell and Stansell reached similar conclusions.[11]

Interpretation of the Evidence. No subsequent work has seriously challenged the Rozeff and the Rogalski and Vinso conclusions that timing strategy based on a monetary signal is ineffective. Still, a number of issues remain unsettled. For example, many investors believe that monetary policy yields useful signals. Thus knowledge of the trading patterns of these investors might help explain some day-to-day market movements. Second, monetary signals may still help investors trade stocks that are especially sensitive to interest rate–money supply moves. Third, most of the tests have considered monetary signals only in isolation. Possibly money supply data incorporated into a well-specified economic model (containing interest, unemployment, and inflation rates, for example) would yield more positive results. Finally, virtually all prior work has tested relations between actual (as opposed to anticipated) money supply changes and stock market performance.

Clearly, stock prices and money supply changes are related but the lags seem to be short or nonexistent. Sorensen tested the timing value of predicted money supply changes. Utilizing Barro's[12] money growth rate equation he found stock prices related to anticipated but not unanticipated changes in the money supply. Sorensen concluded that "the potential ability of some analysts to form superior expectations of future money, and act on those expectations, may be the force which drives what has long been accepted as a direct relationship between money and stock prices."[13] More recently, Hardouvelis as well as Pearce and Roley found that the market tended to react to the unanticipated component of economic news.[14]

An Integrated Approach. Basing trading decisions on actual monetary policy changes seems unlikely to outperform a buy and hold strategy. Accurately predicting monetary policy changes, supplementing the analysis with knowledge of other economic influences, and concentrating on interest-sensitive securities might prove more effective. Forecasted fiscal policy changes and other factors having a short-run economic impact might also be considered. In particular, consumer spending and business spending for fixed plant, equipment, and construction often have substantial and sometimes unexpected economic effects. The Survey Research Center of the University of Michigan periodically surveys and reports on consumer sentiments. Similarly, McGraw-Hill surveys and reports business capital expenditure plans (in the November issue of *Business Week*), as does the Commerce Department (in the December *Survey of Consumer Sentiments*). Finally, the Conference Board compiles quarterly capital appropriation statistics (reported in *Manufacturing Industrial Statistics*). These forecasts are widely reported in the press.

The impact of differing economic conditions on particular firms and industries might also be considered. Banking, construction-related companies, and other interest-sensitive firms are especially vulnerable to tight money.[15] Moreover, postponable-expenditure industries (e.g., autos and consumer durables) are typically depressed by recessions, whereas other industries (e.g., utilities and beer) suffer only slightly. Few industries are truly recession proof (their own claims notwithstanding), but vulnerability to the economic climate does vary. Recession-sensitive (e.g., smokestack) companies may be poor performers just before a downturn, whereas they generally rally just before an upturn.

These suggestions may seem logical, but relatively little empirical research has thus far been directed toward resolving the issues. Success in using an understanding of economy–stock market relations will depend upon investors' astuteness vis-à-vis the market consensus. If the market consensus is based on effective analysis, few investors are likely to do better. If market analysts frequently err avoidably, however, those with superior analytical abilities should profit. Clearly further research is needed.

THE INFLATION–STOCK MARKET RELATION

The stock market appears to be influenced by two different aspects of the economy: the business cycle and the inflation rate. Having already explored the impact of the business cycle, we now turn to inflation and its effect on the stock market.

Some people may see inflation as a purely monetary phenomenon. According to this view, inflation affects prices but little else. Those who accept this line of reasoning expect investors to seek to maximize their expected risk-adjusted return without regard to the inflation rate. In their view, most investors believe that inflation will reduce the real (after-inflation) return of anything that they invest in. Thus such investors will choose their investments and manage their portfolios without taking account of the potential impact of inflation.

Most people, however, see inflation as more than a simple monetary phenomenon. Thus the inflation rate is thought to have an impact that goes well beyond simply affecting the price level. These people believe that inflation plays an important role in the determination of the level of economic activity and can have rather different effects on the various components of the economy. As a result, more sophisticated investors are believed to consider the differential inflation protection of various types of investments. These investors' propensities to spend (particularly on durables) may be affected by what they expect their real returns to be. In addition, different investments may offer varying degrees of long-term inflation protection. Thus the appeal of some assets may depend on the expected long-term inflation rate. Finally, investors who are able to anticipate changes in the inflation rate may be able to shift profitably between more and less inflation-resistant investments.

The Wall Street View of Stocks as an Inflation Hedge

Until the 1970s most analysts thought that the stock market offered substantial inflation protection. Stockbrokers and mutual fund salespeople argued that equity returns would tend to keep up with inflation better than would the returns on fixed income securities (bonds). Early thought often confused two rather different inflation hedge concepts. According to one view, the market value of an inflation hedge should rise with the general price level. Thus the real return of a perfect inflation hedge should be independent of price changes. A perfect inflation hedge yielding 4% with stable prices would return 4% plus x% for an inflation rate of x%.

Although few analysts ever claimed that stocks offered complete protection from inflation, many believed that if consumer prices changed by x%, average stocks would yield:

$$a\% + bx\%$$

where:

$$a = \text{a constant value}$$
$$b = \text{some positive number less than unity}$$

Thus if:

$$a = 3$$
$$b = .7$$

then an inflation rate of 5% would imply a nominal (no adjustment for inflation) return of:

$$3\% + (.7 \times 5\%) = 6.5\%$$

Such a nominal return corresponds to a real return of:

$$6.5\% - 5\% = 1.5\%$$

A real return of 1.5% is positive but less than the real return would be at lower inflation rates. Thus this type of behavior relative to the inflation rate would imply that stocks acted as a partial hedge against inflation.

A second form of the inflation hedge concept takes a much longer range perspective. According to this viewpoint, average long-run stock returns will generally exceed the rise in the general price level. In particular short-run periods, nominal returns may be below the inflation rate. Eventually, however, nominal rates will catch up with and exceed the increase in the price level. Thus long-term real returns tend, according to this view, to be positive. If markets behave as this perspective implies, the real value of capital would tend to be preserved in spite of the inflation rate. This form of the inflation hedge concept is less strong because it allows for the possibility that the market will be affected adversely (if temporarily) by high and/or rising inflation rates. In spite of the experience in the 1970s with rapid inflation and poor stock market performance, the view persists that stocks somehow still protect investors from inflation.

The Theoretical Underpinnings of the Stock Market–Inflation Hedge Hypothesis

To provide effective short- or long-run inflation protection, companies must increase their profits (as measured in nominal terms). In periods of rising prices their own costs are almost certain to be increasing. Thus about the only way that such firms might be able to defend their profitability is by raising prices. The ability of stocks to withstand the adverse impact of an inflationary environment is very dependent upon the underlying company's ability to maintain its profitability. Stocks represent ownership of real assets. The replacement value of these assets and their ability to generate income may well rise with the price level. Thus, if firms are able to raise their prices sufficiently, the real (inflation adjusted) value of dividends and share prices may keep pace with price level increases. A number of considerations limit the ability of firms to raise prices by enough to preserve investment values, however.

To illustrate, various aspects of our tax system tend to penalize investment income at high inflation rates. First, the IRS requires that companies use historical costs in computing their profits. As a result, they must pay taxes on sums (statutory profits) that reflect the difference between the historical cost and the replacement value of inventory, plant, and equipment. A company that produces a widget for $1 and sells it for $2 must report a profit of $1 ($2 less $1) even if the next widget will cost $1.5 to produce. A high inflation rate increases these kinds of differences and the tax on profits. As a result, the real after-tax component of reported profits tends to fall as prices increase.

Second, inflation tends to push investors into higher marginal tax brackets, further increasing the penalty. This was a severe problem when our tax system had 11 brackets with a top rate of 50% or even higher. The reduced number of tax brackets and lower maximum rate under the Tax Reform Act of 1986 reduces but does not eliminate this effect.

Third, individuals must pay taxes on sums (dividends and capital gains) that often contain a substantial inflation component. Thus, even if the before-tax return rose point for point with the inflation rate, the after-tax return would not. For example, a one-third tax rate applied to a 3% nominal return and zero inflation (a 3% real return before taxes) provides a 2% after-tax real return. A 6% nominal return with a 3% inflation rate produces a real after-tax return of only 1%. A 9% nominal return and 6% inflation rate would yield a real after-tax return of 0%. For nominal returns above 9%, a 3% before-tax real return corresponds to a negative real after-tax return. The use of leverage makes the relationship considerably more complex, however. If the interest cost of the loan is deductible and below the return on the investment, investors can effectively use leverage to enhance their after-tax, after-inflation return. The cost of borrowing, however, tends to rise with the inflation rate.

Other considerations also increase the difficulty of offsetting inflation's adverse effect. We might suspect that cost and price increases of x% would (neglecting tax effects) approximately maintain the firm's financial position. In fact, however, higher prices and costs generally require a contemporaneous and disproportionate increase in capital to support inventories, accounts receivables, and new plant and equipment. Any increased revenues derived from higher prices come in more slowly. Moreover, if higher inflation rates are associated with higher interest rates, both the amount and the cost of financing tends to increase with inflation. Thus, to offset the effect of taxes on nominal profits and to finance the increased capital requirements at higher interest rates, prices must be raised proportionally more than the direct cost increase. To offset the increased retained earnings requirement (needed to support the additional borrowings) and the investor's inflation-imposed tax burden, prices must rise still more.

Many firms are unable to raise prices sufficiently to recapture their increased production costs, however, to say nothing of increasing them sufficiently to offset tax and financing effects. The more rapid the inflation, the greater is the likelihood of some governmental action designed to reduce demand-side pressures. Such action might take the form of fiscal and monetary restraint, jawboning, price controls, or guidelines. Supply-side efforts to increase efficiency and competition through regulatory reform are also possible. To the extent that these various policies succeed in restraining price increases (even if only in the short run), profits may also be reduced. Moreover, competition from substitutes (whose costs may be more stable) may also limit the ability of firms to raise their prices.

Fourth, international competition tends to hold some prices down, depending on the interplay of such factors as domestic versus international inflation rates, changes in exchange rates, tariffs and import quotas, and the pricing responses of foreign competition. Similar considerations influence the ability of domestic exporters to pass their higher costs on internationally. Thus both governmental pressure and foreign competition constrain the opportunities of many firms to raise

TABLE 11.3 Inflation's Adverse Stock Market Impact

Tax Impact	Cost Impact	Price Impact
Corporate taxes are applied to historical cost plant, equipment, and inventories.	Greater capital is needed for new plant and equipment, accounts receivable, and inventories.	Resistance to price increases. Government exerts pressure to restrain prices.
Investors are pushed into higher tax brackets.	Higher interest costs are incurred on borrowings.	Competition from substitutes increases.
Individual taxes are applied to nominal dividend and interest income.	Revenues come in more slowly.	International competition increases.

their prices sufficiently to offset inflation's negative effect. Table 11.3 summarizes the various adverse stock market impacts of inflation.

Finally, two highly regarded economists, Modigliani and Cohn, argue that investors made two basic errors in pricing securities in the presence of inflation.[16] First, investors are said to capitalize equity earnings incorrectly by comparing the current cash earnings of equity with the nominal rather than real bond returns. Bond returns are fixed until maturity whereas profits and dividends attributable to stocks tend to rise over time. Focusing on the returns on stocks as if they are expected to be constant rather than rise will cause investors to underprice them. Second, the authors contend that investors have failed to take proper account of the impact of inflation on the real value of corporate debt. Over time inflation tends to reduce the real value of outstanding debt. Thus corporations with substantial amounts of debt outstanding will in times of rapid inflation in effect see that debt decline (at least in real terms). According to Modigliani and Cohn, these two alleged mispricing effects reduced the S&P 500 Stock Index by 50% in 1977. Writing in 1982, however, Cagan asserted that the market seemed to be as underpriced as it was alleged to be in 1977.[17] A low point for stocks, however, came in 1982. The market more than tripled over the next five years. Perhaps the market was mispricing and later realized its error. On the other hand, the crash of 1987 indicates that the market can also be mispriced on the upside.

In summary, stocks may for a variety of reasons perform less well during periods of rapid inflation. Taxes tend to reduce a company's real after-tax profits because they are applied to noninflation-adjusted, before-tax profits. Taxes may also reduce the real investment return because they are applied to the nominal returns paid to investors. Some of the higher costs caused by inflation may not be quickly recaptured even if prices are raised proportionally with costs. Cost increases may not always be passed on because of government pressure, competition from substitutes, or international competition. Finally, in an inflationary environment the stock market itself may not price securities correctly.

All of these considerations illustrate the difficulty that companies (and their stocks) have in fully offsetting inflationary impacts. Nonetheless, stocks need to provide a positive expected real return if their issuers (firms) are to continue to attract capital. The capital markets are supposed to assure the availability of sufficient capital for consumer-identified expansion candidates. That is, as consumers demand more of certain types of goods and services, the market needs to provide the suppliers of these goods and services with the capital that they need to serve their customers. Investors have little incentive to invest when they expect to lose money in the process. Thus firms that wish to attract capital need to be able to offer positive expected returns. If new investments yield positive real returns, the shares of firms owning equivalent existing capacity should be bid up to their replacement values. This process may not take place quickly, completely, or for all industries. It should on balance, however, operate to provide the economy with adequate expansion and modernization capital.

Normally an industry whose capacity is outstripped by its demand will be able to raise additional capital. If initially the expected return is too low to attract more capital, firms in the industry will not be able to satisfy the demand for their product at current price levels. Thus they will need to raise prices, thereby increasing the return on their existing capital. A higher return on existing capital coupled with the prospect of a reasonable return on new investments should make new capital easier to raise. Eventually this process should ensure that an appreciable fraction of real returns are at an acceptable level.

Taken together, these various considerations suggest that two opposing forces may be at work. First, the short-run inflation-adjustment process of the stock market may be painful for investors. Second, however, a functioning capitalist system must offer a reasonable expectation of positive, long-run, real after-tax returns even in an inflationary environment.

Empirical Studies of Inflation–Stock Market Relations

Alchian and Kessel conducted the first serious research on the inflation impact of the stock market. They reported that in inflationary environments net monetary debtor corporations experienced an increase in their equity value greater than that of net monetary creditors.[18] Net monetary debtors have a disproportionate percentage of liabilities with nominal values that are independent of price changes (such as loans, bonds outstanding, and accounts payable). Net monetary creditors, in contrast, have a disproportionate percentage of assets with nominal values that are independent of price changes (such as money, time deposits, and bonds). Subsequently, Reilly, Johnson, and Smith found that the average real returns on several well-known stock indexes were negative or below the indexes' long-term average return in each of five periods of rapid inflation.[19] Two of the periods began during expansions and ended during recessions; two began during peacetime and ended during war; and one straddled the 1966 credit crunch. Noninflationary factors may therefore have contributed to the poor performance. In a third study, Keran found that inflationary expectations depressed stock prices (as measured by Standard & Poor's 500), which is inconsistent with an inflation hedge theory.[20]

Cagan, on the other hand, found that U.S. stock prices increased by 3% more annually than wholesale prices from 1871 to 1971.[21] Moreover, British and French stock prices outperformed the annual inflation rate (before adding dividends) by 1.3% and .1%, respectively, over similar periods. The degree of outperformance varied inversely with the inflation rates of three countries, however. Moreover, a typical group of German stocks purchased in 1914 would have lost three-fourths of their value by the end of the hyper-inflation in 1924. Similarly, Branch reported that the stocks of those countries with the highest inflation rates tended to rise faster than those of countries with lower rates.[22]

In an update of their earlier study, Reilly, Smith, and Johnson reported in 1975 that the inflation protection of the stock market depended on the direction of the inflation rate.[23] Thus stocks may perform better with a constant or declining rate than with a rising rate. Similarly, Jaffee and Mandelker in 1976 and Nelson in the same year concluded that, once the market adjusted to anticipated inflation, it generally provided an acceptable expected real return.[24] Unanticipated inflation rate rises typically had a negative effect, however. Unlike other researchers, Bodie defined the hedge value of common stocks in terms of their ability to reduce the real return variability of a portfolio of one-year T-bills.[25] According to Bodie, only a short position in stocks would have reduced inflation risk. Unlike Albian and Kessel, Hong found no inflation-induced transfer from creditor to debtor companies but he did find a differential tax-induced transfer from business to government.[26] A more recent study by Fama challenged all previous work in the area. Specifically, Fama claimed: "The negative stock return–inflation relations are induced by negative relations between inflation and real activity which in turn are explained by a combination of money demand and the quantity theory of money."[27]

Both Fama's theoretical model and his empirical tests seem to support his contention that the observed simple stock market–inflation relation results from the proxy effects of an underspecified model. Similarly, Geske and Roll developed and tested a model that seeks to explain the negative relation between stock returns and inflation. According to their model, the negative relation results from rational investors realizing the adverse impact of inflation on future economic policy.[28] A number of empirical studies support the Geske/Roll findings.[29]

Finally, Hendershott used a theoretical model to test four separate inflation-related hypotheses designed to explain the post-1960s stock price decline: (1) tax-law impacts on real share values; (2) Modigliani-Cohn inflation-induced valuation errors; (3) increased uncertainty leading to a higher risk premium; and (4) biases in the tax laws, valuation errors, and risk premium impacts on real after-tax debt yields.[30] The first three explanations were not by themselves consistent with Hendershott's model and the observed historical behavior. An increase in the risk premium coupled with the tax bias did, however, seem to fit the observed decline in real after-tax debt yields and real share values.

Assessment of the Evidence

Overall, the relevant empirical work suggests that stocks tend to provide long-term inflation protection and possibly some short-term protection from anticipated inflation. For investors to know that stock price rises may eventually offset inflation is small comfort, however, if they must sell before the market rebounds. If, as much of the research suggests, unexpected inflation rate rises depress stock prices, the real value of investments falls both with the rise in the price level and with the decline in the position's nominal value. Some investors may be able to ride out such market declines but others will not.

THE INFLATION PROTECTION OF OTHER INVESTMENTS

The preceding discussion implies that stocks are not particularly effective inflation hedges; but perhaps some types of nonstock investments provide more dependable inflation protection. Stock-related securities such as common stock mutual funds, convertible bonds, preferreds, and options probably behave much like stocks. Thus we expect inflation to affect them in much the same way that it affects stocks. Debt securities, commodities, real estate, and collectibles, in contrast, may offer different levels of inflation protection. Several different studies found that the returns on fixed income securities tended to compensate for anticipated but not for unanticipated inflation.[31] This conclusion, while similar to that reached in a number of stock market–inflation studies, has a very different implication. Unlike stocks, debt securities mature. An inflation rate rise that depresses security prices locks in stock investors whereas bond principal may be reinvested at maturity.

To illustrate, an investor might purchase bonds yielding 10% in an 8% inflation environment. If inflation then rises to 12%, equivalent debt yields might increase to 14% shortly thereafter. With short maturities, such a rise in the unanticipated inflation rate will cause only a modest return loss. Soon the investor's bonds will mature and the resulting principal can then be reinvested at the new higher market rates. The principal of a bond with even longer maturity will eventually become available for reinvestment.

That debt securities, particularly short-term debt securities, seem to provide a degree of current inflation protection leads us to wonder about their long-run performance. For the 1926–1974 period, Ibbotson and Sinquefield found an average inflation-adjusted return of 6.1%, 1.4%, 1.0%, and 0.0% for common stocks, long-term corporates, long-term government bonds, and Treasury bills, respectively.[32] Thus the securities that offer the greatest short-run protection (bills) yielded the least return, and vice versa.

Bodie and Rosansky reported that for 1950 to 1976 commodity futures prices tended to move inversely with stock prices and to do best during periods of rapid inflation.[33] The commodity markets are rather far afield for most security market investors, however. The degree of inflation protection that the futures markets may provide is likely to be accompanied by a very uncertain level of returns. Thus investors seeking to reduce the risk that inflation imposes might well end up with greater total risk by investing in commodities.

Real estate might well provide substantial inflation protection. Replacement costs of developed property vary with labor and material costs (correlated with consumer prices). Thus real estate construction costs should rise with consumer prices. These increased construction costs should eventually affect real estate values although demand considerations may have a greater short-term effect. Fama and Schwert, in fact, find that real estate offers a complete hedge against both expected and unexpected inflation.[34] More recently Folger, Granito, and Smith reached similar conclusions.[35] Since real estate has its own set of drawbacks (e.g., illiquidity), its inflation protection history is not in itself sufficient justification for investing in real estate.

The same underlying factors that cause consumer prices to rise may increase the prices of collectibles. That is, higher money incomes chasing a fixed quantity of collectibles should bid prices up more rapidly when the inflation rate is higher.

Collectors' items have generally done well in the recent inflationary environment. Whether this performance is because of, or in spite of, the high inflation rate requires further study.

Although stocks in the aggregate offer little or no inflation protection, Bernard and Frecka find that certain stock portfolios have provided significant inflation hedges.[36] Selecting stocks on the basis of their 1969–1974 performance, they were able to form portfolios that effectively hedged against the 1974–1979 inflation.

SUMMARY AND CONCLUSIONS

Investors who want to understand and/or forecast the market's behavior need to understand how the economy and the stock market are related. Both monetary and fiscal policy have a substantial economic impact. Economic policy generally seeks to maintain price stability and full employment. Stimulation is designed to reduce unemployment whereas restraint is applied when inflation is the primary concern. Which is the overriding goal depends on a variety of considerations including the relative severity of unemployment and inflation and the judgments of policymakers. Understanding the likely reactions of government should help investors to forecast economic activity and perhaps stock market performance.

Investment analysts pay particular attention to relations between monetary policy and the stock market. Monetary policy affects the stock market both indirectly through its economic effect and directly via its interest rate effect. Some earlier work seemed to find monetary signals helpful, but most careful and comprehensive recent studies have found no usable lag between changes in monetary policy and changes in stock prices. Trading on predicted monetary policy changes may well be profitable, however.

Inflation–stock market relations were also considered. According to pre-1970 Wall Street wisdom, companies could offset the impact of inflation by raising prices. Tax effects, government anti-inflation pressure, and international competition often make implementing the necessary price rises difficult, however. Still, to allocate capital properly, the market must offer the prospect of a positive real after-tax return.

Some empirical research suggests that in the short run unanticipated rises in inflation have been associated with adverse stock market performance. In the longer run, however, average market returns may exceed the inflation rate. Debt securities, particularly short-term debt securities, seemed to provide more effective protection from the adverse inflation impacts, but their long-term return only marginally exceeded the inflation rate. Both commodities and real estate offer intriguing inflation protection but present security market investors with a variety of other problems.

REVIEW QUESTIONS

1. Trace the relationship between the economy and the stock market. Indicate each of the links.

2. Discuss the uses and limitations of econometric and leading indicator forecasts of economic activity. How might they be used in stock market analysis? What are their limitations?

3. Explain how fiscal policy operates through taxes and government spending. How does the government seek to stimulate the economy through fiscal policy? How does it seek to restrain the economy through fiscal policy?

4. Discuss the Fed's three principal tools and how they are used to affect the economy? Which is most and which is least powerful? Which is most often used by the Fed? Which is used primarily as a signal?

5. Discuss how investors can go about predicting changes in fiscal and monetary policy. What are the relative roles of inflation, unemployment, and the international economy? What role do politics, elections, and ideology play?

6. Why do stock analysts generally give so much attention to monetary (as opposed to fiscal) policy? Should an analysis of fiscal policy play any role in investment analysis? Explain why or why not. If the answer is yes, explain how.

7. Why might investors think that stock prices adjust for the adverse impact of inflation on investment returns? What factors may retard this adjustment? What are the implications for investors?

8. Summarize the findings of past work linking inflation and stock price performance. What are the implications for investors?

9. How do bonds, real estate, and commodities behave relative to inflation? What are the implications for investors?

REVIEW PROBLEMS

1. If the government decides to spend $1 billion on a space probe to Pluto, how would that affect the economy for each of the following assumptions?
   a. Spending on food stamps is reduced by $1 billion.
   b. Spending on military aid to Third World countries is reduced by $1 billion.
   c. Taxes on beer are increased by $1 billion.
   d. Taxes on profits from corporate takeovers are increased by $1 billion.
   e. One billion dollars is raised through the sale of government savings bonds to U.S. citizens.
   f. One billion dollars is raised through the sale of six-month Treasury bills to Japanese investors.

2. If the government embarks on a 10-year program to land an American on Mars, how would that affect the economy for the following methods of financing the venture? Assume that the project will cost (in real terms) $30 billion per year.
   a. Government assets (lands, loans, gold holdings, farm surpluses, Amtrak, the Postal Service, national parks, surplus armaments, etc.) are sold each year to raise the needed sum.
   b. Welfare and Social Security programs are reduced by an amount equivalent to the Mars spending.
   c. A nonaggression pact with the Soviets allows Congress to reduce military spending by enough to finance the Mars program.
   d. A national sales tax is instituted to raise the needed sum.
   e. Personal income taxes are increased to raise the needed sum.
   f. The additional spending is financed by selling long-term government bonds in the open market.
   g. The additional spending is financed by selling 270-day Treasury bills to the Fed. The Fed agrees to roll its holdings forward as its portfolio matures.

3. Unemployment is at 5.6%, having declined slowly from a bit above 6% a year ago. Inflation has been running at about 4% for the past six months. How is economic policy likely to shift for each of the following new developments? Explain your answer.
   a. A conservative Republican is elected President defeating an incumbent who is a liberal Democrat.
   b. The trade deficit increases by 20% and the dollar plunges on international exchanges.
   c. The U.S. stock market crashes, losing 500 points on the Dow in a single day and falling by 45% in a seven-week period.
   d. A military coup in the Soviet Union restores the Whites (those who opposed the Reds) to power. They renounce all interest in a military confrontation with the United States. Peace breaks out all over the world. Military budgets are slashed by 50%.

4. Unemployment is at 7.2%, having risen rapidly from 5.8% six months earlier. Inflation is running at a 5% rate, having declined from double digits in the past year. Government bond rates range from 7.5% (short term) to 10.5% (long term). A large trade deficit continues to trouble international exchange markets and the dollar remains a weak currency. How is economic policy likely to shift for each of the following new developments?
   a. A liberal Democrat is elected President defeating a conservative Republican incumbent.
   b. A mammoth oil strike in Lake Michigan promises to make the United States independent in energy. Such independence is expected virtually to eliminate the U.S. trade deficit.
   c. After repeated provocations the United States launches simultaneous invasions of Nicaragua and Cuba. Although the "war" is over quickly, the cost of the occupation threatens to add $25 billion to next year's budget deficit.

d. A peace coalition is victorious in the Israeli election; a Mideast peace treaty results. OPEC falls apart and the price of oil plunges to below $10 per barrel.

5. How would the stock market be expected to react to each of the following developments?

   a. The Fed, fearing that a recession is threatening, lowers the discount rate and expands the money supply. Long-term interest rates fall by over 200 basis points.

   b. Congress finally gets serious about reducing the budget deficit and raises taxes across the board by $100 billion. The Fed cushions the blow by expanding the money supply. Interest rates fall dramatically while GNP continues to grow.

   c. The Third World countries form a debtors' cartel and offer to negotiate. When the bargaining gets nowhere, they announce a total moratorium on interest and principal payments. The creditor nations respond by cutting off all credit.

6. In a stable price environment investments A, B, C, D, E, and F are expected to earn 3%, 5%, 2%, 6%, and 7%, respectively. If they are all perfect inflation hedges, what will be their nominal and real expected returns for inflation rates of 2%, 4%, 6%, and 10%?

7. Compute after-tax real and nominal expected returns for the information supplied in Problem 6. Assume that the tax rate on nominal returns is 30%.

8. Recompute Problem 7, except assume that the investments are only partial inflation hedges. The degree of inflation protection for each investment is of the form a% + bx% where x is the expected inflation rate and b can take on values of .3, .5, .7, or .9. (Note students already have the needed information to determine the values of a.)

9. The TUV Corporation is currently selling its product for $40 per unit. Its annual sales amount to 500,000 units. Last year it earned a profit of $2 million. Because of inflationary pressures, its variable costs will increase by $5 (from $20) per unit. If it absorbs the higher inputs costs (keeping the per unit price unchanged), it can expand sales by 20% with existing capacity. Alternatively, it can raise the price to cover the increased variable costs but will lose 20% of its unit sales. What is the profit impact of each alternative?

10. Your investment alternatives are stocks, short-term bonds, long-term bonds, and real estate. You expect their returns to follow the following pattern:

    Stocks: 8%
    Short-term bonds: 3% + inflation rate
    Long-term bonds: 5% + .3 (inflation rate)
    Real estate: 1% + 1.2 (inflation rate)

    You have the following inflation expectations (inflation rate, probability): 2%, .1; 4%, .3; 6%, .4; 8%, .2. What is your optimal strategy for maximizing your expected real return? How can you best ensure yourself of the greatest expected real return with no possibility of receiving less than a 2% real return?

REVIEW PROJECTS

1. Obtain a number of economic forecasts for the most recently completed year and compare them with that year's actual result. Write a report.

2. Update Figures 11.2, 11.3, and 11.4 and comment on the implications of the newer data vis-à-vis politically acceptable levels of unemployment and inflation.

3. Analyze the current state of the economy. Forecast GNP, unemployment, and inflation for next year. Write a report explaining your forecast. Read it a year later.

4. Assess the current state and forecast the future direction of monetary and fiscal policy. Review fiscal and monetary policy six months later. Explain why your forecast erred, if it did. Repeat the process for the succeeding six months.

5. Assemble a list of five interest-sensitive stocks. Plot their performance relative to a series of interest rates. Write a report.

6. Assemble a list of 15 stocks and group them into three categories: those best able to pass costs along, those least able to pass costs along, and those with an average ability to pass costs along. Plot their monthly returns and the monthly inflation rates over three years. Write a report.

NOTES

1. B. Heathcotte and V. Apilado, "The Predictive Content of Some Leading Economic Indicators for Future Stock Prices," *Journal of Financial and Quantitative Analysis*, March 1974, 247–258.

2. D. Simonson, "Comment: The Predictive Content of Some Leading Economic Indicators for Future Stock Prices," *Journal of Financial and Quantitative Analysis*, March 1974, 259–261.

3. W. McConnell, *Investment Manager's Review*, Wertheim & Company, Inc., March 23, 1981, 10; G. Moore, *Business Cycles, Inflation and Forecasting*, National Bureau of Economic Research Studies in Business Cycles No. 240 (Cambridge, Mass.: Ballinger Publishing, 1980).

4. A. Malabre, "How to Become Your Own Economist: Facts That Count Are Easy to Get and Understand," *The Wall Street Journal*, March 21, 1977, p. 36.

5. B. Sprinkel, *Money and Markets: A Monetarist's View* (Homewood, Ill.: Irwin, 1971); B. Sprinkel, *Money and Stock Prices* (Homewood, Ill.: Irwin, 1964).

6. K. Homa and D. Jaffee, "The Supply of Money and Common Stock Prices," *Journal of Finance*, December 1971, 1045–1066.

7. B. Malkiel and R. Quandt, "Selected Economic Indicators and Forecasts of Stock Prices," Finance Resource Center (Research memorandum #9, Princeton University, 1971); J. Pesando, "The Supply of Money and Common Stock Prices: Further Observations on the Econometric Evidence," *Journal of Finance*, June 1974, 909–922; B. Malkiel and R. Quandt, "The Supply of Money and Common Stock Prices: Comment," *Journal of Finance*, September 1972, 921–926; R. Cooper, "Efficient Capital Markets and the Quantity Theory of Money," *Journal of Finance*, June 1974, 887–908; M. Hamberger and L. Kochin, "Money and Stock Prices: The Channels of Influence," *Journal of Finance*, May 1972, 231, 249; M. Keran, "Expectations, Money and the Stock Market," *Federal Reserve Bank of St. Louis Review*, January 1971, 16–31; F. Reilly and J. Lewis, *Monetary Variables and Stock Prices*, Working Paper #38 (Lawrence, Kans.: University of Kansas, March 1971); J. Rudolph, "The Money Supply and Common Stock Prices," *Financial Analysts Journal*, March/April 1972, 19–25; M. Gupta, "Money Supply and Stock Prices: A Probabilistic Approach," *Journal of Financial and Quantitative Analysis*, January 1974, 57–68.

8. M. Rozeff, "Money and Stock Prices' Market Efficiency and the Lag in Effect of Monetary Policy," *Journal of Financial Economics*, September 1974, 301.

9. R. Rogalski and J. Vinso, "Stock Returns, Money Supply and the Direction of Causality," *Journal of Finance*, September 1977, 1017–1030.

10. Ibid., 1027–1028.

11. L. Davidson and R. Froyen, "Monetary Policy and Stock Returns: Are Stock Markets Efficient?" *Federal Reserve Bank of St. Louis Review*, March 1982, 3–12; C. Mitchell and S. Stansell, "Stock Yields, Bond Yields, and the Money Supply: A Study of the Causal Relationships," *Review of Business and Economic Research*, Winter 1982, 46–54.

12. R. Barro, "Rational Expectations and the Role of Monetary Policy," *Journal of Monetary Economics*, January 1976, 1–32; R. Barro, "Unanticipated Money Growth and Unemployment in the United States," *American Economic Review*, March 1977, 101–115; R. Barro, "Unanticipated Money, Output, and the Price Level in the United States," *Journal of Political Economy*, August 1977, 549–580.

13. E. Sorensen, "Rational Expectations and the Impact of Money upon Stock Prices," *Journal of Financial and Quantitative Analysis*, December 1982, 649–662.

14. G. Hardouvelis, "Reserves Announcements and Interest Rates: Does Monetary Policy Matter?" *Journal of Finance*, June 1987, 407–422; D. Pearce and V. Roley, "Stock Prices and Economic News," *Journal of Business*, January 1985, 47–67.

15. J. Booth and D. Officer, "Expectations, Interest Rates, and Commercial Bank Stocks," *Journal of Financial Research*, Spring 1985, 51–58.

16. F. Modigliani and R. Cohn, "Inflation, Rational Valuation and the Market," *Financial Analysts Journal*, March/April 1979, 24–44.

17. P. Cagan, *Stock Prices Reflect the Adjustment of Earnings for Inflation*, NYU Monograph Series in Finance and Economics (New York: New York University, 1982).

18. A. Alchian and R. Kessel, "Redistribution of Wealth through Inflation," *Science*, September 4, 1959, p. 538.

19. F. Reilly, G. Johnson, and R. Smith, "Inflation, Inflation Hedge, and Common Stocks," *Financial Analysts Journal*, January/February 1970, 104–110.

20. M. Keran, "Expectations, Money and the Stock Market," *Federal Reserve Bank of St. Louis Review*, January 1971, 16–31.

21. A. Malabre, "The Outlook," *The Wall Street Journal*, December 17, 1974, p. 1; P. Cagan, "Common Stock Values and Inflation: The Historical Record of Many Countries," *National Bureau Report Supplement*, March 1974, 1–10.

22. B. Branch, "Common Stock Performance and Inflation: An International Comparison," *Journal of Business*, January 1974, 48–52.

23. F. Reilly, R. Smith, and G. Johnson, "A Correction and Update Regarding Individual Common Stocks as Inflation Hedges," *Journal of Financial and Quantitative Analysis*, December 1975, 871–880.

24. J. Jaffee and G. Mandelker, "The 'Fisher Effect' for Risky Assets: An Empirical Investigation," *Journal of Finance*, May 1976, 447–458; C. Nelson, "Inflation and Rates of Return on Common Stocks," *Journal of Finance*, May 1976, 471–482; J. Ang, J. Chua, and A. Desai, "Evidence That the Stock Market Adjusts Fully for Expected Inflation," *The Journal of Financial Research*, Fall 1979, 97–109; S. Moosa, "Inflation and Common Stock Prices," *Journal of Financial Research*, Fall 1980, 115–128; C. Chu and D. Whitford, "Stock Market Returns and Inflationary Expectations: Additional Evidence for 1975–1979," *Journal of Financial Research*, Fall 1982, 261–271.

25. Z. Bodie, "Common Stocks as a Hedge against Inflation," *Journal of Finance*, May 1976, 459–470.

26. H. Hong, "Inflation and Market Value of the Firm: Theory and Tests," *Journal of Finance*, September 1977, 1031–1048.

27. E. Fama, "Stock Returns, Real Activity, Inflation and Money," *American Economic Review*, September 1981, 545–565.

28. R. Geske and R. Roll, "The Fiscal and Monetary Linkage Between Stock Returns and Inflation," *Journal of Finance*, March 1983, 1–34.

29. B. Solnik, "The Relation Between Stock Prices and Inflationary Expectations: The International Evidence," *Journal of Finance*, March 1983, 35–48; N. Gultekin, "Stock Market Returns and Inflation: Evidence From Other Countries," *Journal of Finance*, March 1983, 49–66; N. Gultekin, "Stock Market Returns and Inflation Forecasts," June 1983, 663–673; C. James, S. Koreisha, and M. Partch, "A VARMA Analysis of the Causal Relations Among Stock Returns, Real Output, and Nominal Interest Rates," *Journal of Finance*, December 1985, 1375–1384; G. Kaul, "Stock Returns and Inflation," *Journal of Financial Economics*, June 1987, 253–276.

30. P. Hendershott, "The Decline in Aggregate Share Values Taxation: Valuation Errors, Risk, and Profitability," *American Economic Review*, December 1981, 909–922; R. Pindyck, "Risk, Inflation and the Stock Market," *American Economic Review*, June 1984, 335–351.

31. J. Jaffee and G. Mandelker, "Inflation and the Holding Period Returns on Bonds," *Journal of Financial and Quantitative Analysis*, December 1979, 959–979; M. Levi and J. Makin, "Fisher, Phillips, Friedman and the Measured Impact of Inflation and Interest," *Journal of Finance*, March 1979, 35–52; Y. Yun, "The Effects of Inflation and Income Taxes on Interest Rates; Some New Evidence," *Journal of Financial and Quantitative Analysis*," December 1984, 425–448.

32. R. Ibbotson and R. Sinquefield, "Stocks, Bonds, Bills and Inflation: Year by Year Historical Returns (1926–1974)," *Journal of Business*, January 1976, 11–47.

33. Z. Bodie and V. Rosansky, "Risk and Return in Commodities Futures," *Financial Analysts Journal*, May/June 1980, 27–40; Z. Bodie, "Commodity Futures as a Hedge Against Inflation," *Journal of Portfolio Management*, Spring 1983, 12–17.

34. E. Fama and W. Schwert, "Asset Returns and Inflation," *Journal of Financial Economics*, November 1977, 115–146.

35. H. Folger, M. Granito, and L. Smith, "A Theoretical Analysis of Real Estate Returns," *Journal of Finance*, July 1985, 711–721.

36. V. Bernard and J. Frecka, "Evidences of the Existence of Common Stock Inflation Hedges," *Journal of Financial Research*, Winter 1983, 301–312.

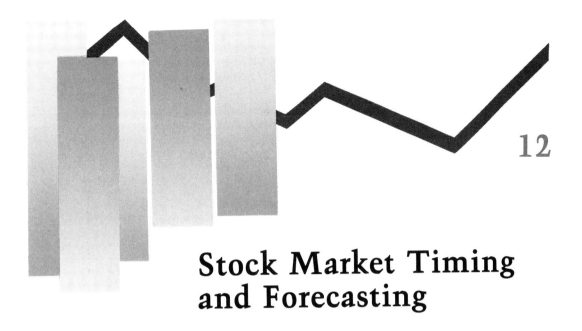

Stock Market Timing and Forecasting

We have already seen that the stock market responds to economic forces (business cycle, money supply, inflation, interest rates, and so on). Does the market also respond to noneconomic forces and/or respond differently to economic information depending on its mood or frame of mind? In particular, does the market sometimes respond to new information (both economic and noneconomic) optimistically and at other times pessimistically?

A truly efficient market is affected only by news that has or is expected to have an impact on the underlying fundamentals. Thus only forces that can affect income expectations should affect market prices. Moreover, new information having the same basic impact on fundamentals should be given the same interpretation regardless of the "mood" of the market. Such a viewpoint would seem to rule out most if not all noneconomic influences. Surely an efficient market would not be described as emotional or moody. And yet most people who follow it would probably say that the market does respond to a variety of noneconomic factors. Moreover, they would probably assert that it responds differently to economic news depending on its emotional state. Sometimes the market may view the economic glass as half full and at other times as half empty.

Indeed, stock prices often appear to swing between extremes of optimism and pessimism. In the crash of 1987 the Dow Jones Industrial Average dropped 508 points (23%) in a single day. That crash followed a very bullish market in which the Dow rose 350% from the 1982 low (777) to the August 25, 1987 high (2738).

365

From this 1987 high the Dow fell to a low of 1738 on October 19. This corresponds to a fall of 36% in seven weeks. These dramatic market moves clearly illustrate how market moods can appear to shift. Analysts might be able to explain the seven weeks' decline of 36% as a response to significant changes in the economic environment. Interest rates had risen substantially and the trade and budget deficits seemed to be getting worse. On the other hand, the 23% fall over the October 16–19 weekend is difficult to explain in efficient market terms. Many observers would agree that the crash was an example of a market in a state of panic. Efficient markets do not panic.

Regardless of how the market's swings are viewed, anyone who bought at or near the 1982 low (when the mood seemed very pessimistic) and sold at or near the August 1987 high (when optimism seemed to run rampant) would have done very well indeed. Similarly, the October 1987 low may also prove to have been an attractive time to buy. Time will tell.

Everyone has relatively accurate hindsight. Buy low and sell high is great advice but useful only if the investor can identify market tops and bottoms as they are happening. Thus we would like to know whether the market tops correspond to favorable moods for the market and bottoms to unfavorable ones. If so, can such moods be identified on a contemporaneous basis and can knowledge of these moods be used profitably? That is the subject of this chapter.

We first consider the stock market's tendency to overreact and then discuss efforts to recognize such overreactions while they are underway. Reliable timing devices are sought in declines from previous highs, market PE ratios and their relation to interest and inflation rates, behavior during recessions, the election year cycle, official pronouncements, margin rate changes, company stock repurchases, Dow Theory, and investment advisors.

Various technical indicators (data series or combinations of data series that are purported to forecast market turns) are discussed in some detail. Specifically, short-interest, odd-lot trading; premiums and discounts on closed-end investment companies; specialist short selling; mutual fund cash positions; secondary distributions; the Barron's Confidence Index, floor trader activity, and the Treasury bill rate are all explored in the context of several relevant empirical studies.

We then examine additional market indicators: the short-term trading index, urgent selling index, January indicator, advisors' sentiments indicator, and advances–declines. Finally, Monday–Friday price patterns are discussed.

STOCK MARKET OVERREACTION

When he was asked to predict stock market performance, J. P. Morgan replied, "It will continue to fluctuate." Anyone who has followed stocks understands the irony of this statement. The market's direction may be difficult to predict, but its continued volatility is not. Stock prices often change dramatically. Specific stock groups frequently go through fads. A stock may rise on a rumor that the firm is entering the nursing home industry (or gambling, motor homes, or genetic engineering) and later that same industry may be an anathema to the market. News sometimes has almost no impact while at other times the market is looking for an excuse to move. To attribute such gyrations to a careful analysis of new information (market efficiency) seems questionable at best. Indeed, stock prices frequently change without any obvious pertinent new information entering the picture.

We have already noted that most investors believe that the market has an emotional side. Still, some supporting evidence would be helpful. In this regard Malkiel examined the implications of growth stock pricing in the early 1960s.[1] From the December 1961 peak to the June 1962 trough, the Standard & Poor's 425 Industrial Average declined 28.5% while an index of high-quality growth stocks (constructed by Malkiel) fell by 52.2%. Malkiel was interested in determining the current growth rate needed to justify the market price. Very high growth rates must eventually decline, as we have already noted in our discussion of the dividend discount model. Malkiel assumed that growth rates would eventually decline to the overall growth rate of the economy. He then computed how many years of abnormal growth were required to justify the PEs of growth stocks. From December 1961 to June 1962 the average PE of Malkiel's sample declined from 62.9 to 24.9. Over that same period the average required years of abnormal growth fell from 6 to 2½. Changes in the earning prospects of these companies seemed unlikely to have caused such drastic reevaluations.

Shiller undertook a more sophisticated study of a similar phenomenon. He found that if real stock prices and dividends are stationary stochastic processes, stock price volatility is inconsistent with market efficiency.[2] Specifically, changes in real dividends are far too modest to account for the historical pattern of real stock price changes in an efficient market. Several others have reached a similar conclusion in more recent studies.[3] Many popular writers have also asserted that the market has become especially volatile as the role of institutions has grown.

Attempts to Identify Overreactions While They Are Happening

Baylis and Bhirud followed up on Malkiel's work by suggesting that investors use as an investment tool the number of years of above-average growth needed to justify current multiples, which they called the *gamma factor*.[4] Suppose, for example, the market has an average PE of 15 and its earnings are expected to grow at 7% per year. How many years would a firm with an above-market PE have to continue to grow at its current rate to justify its PE ratio? The price that the market set for the stock supplies the answer to that problem. The gamma factor represents how long the market expects the rapid growth to continue. More specifically, it is the number of years of rapid growth in earnings that, when coupled with growth equal to the market average thereafter, would equate the present value of the stock with its market price.

Baylis and Bhirud noted that the gamma factor for the favorite growth stock among institutions increased markedly over the 1967–1973 period. Accordingly, in 1973 they wondered if the market was overreacting. A number of others expressed similar opinions. Soon thereafter these so-called top tier stocks followed the rest of the market into a deep depression. Whether by superior insight, luck, or an ability to influence the market with their forecasts (self-fulfilling prophesies), a number of analysts thus correctly identified this particular emotional peak. At any particular time, however, some analysts will be predicting a decline while others will be forecasting a rise. Thus someone will always have correctly forecast the future. Such forecasters may exhibit no more skill than the person who picks a winning lottery number.

Joseph Granville is an interesting example of an analyst who was "hot" for a while and then turned very "cold." He flashed a sell signal to his subscribers when the Dow hit a four-year high of 1004.69 on January 6, 1981. The Dow fell 23.80 points the next day on record volume. While it did reach a high of 1024.05 in late April 1981, the subsequent trend was clearly down (reaching a low of 776.92 on August 12, 1982). Granville had also called an earlier market bottom when he turned bullish on April 21, 1980, with the Dow at 759.13. The Dow climbed 30.72 the following day beginning the advance that led to the four-year high of January 6, 1981.

Baesel, Shows, and Thorp examined Granville's six market timing signals over the period from December 1978 to January 1981. They were found to be significantly better (statistically) than chance.[5] These impressive Granville forecasts contrast sharply with his relatively poor prior and subsequent timing record (Granville was a bear throughout the post-1982 bull market) and his record in selecting individual stocks. Moreover, the publicity of Granville's initial successes gave him considerable market influence. Thus rather than predicting, Granville may have caused the January 1981 sell-off. Some analysts will always be predicting an up market and others predicting a fall, some will be correct just by chance. Quite possibly Granville's success in the early 1980s was nothing more than a lucky streak.

More Evidence on Overreactions

A study in *The Wall Street Journal* of reactions to 15 dramatic news events also suggests a tendency for the market to overreact. Most of these events, listed in Table 12.1, made headlines but had no lasting market impact. Table 12.2, which reports the annual performance of S&P's 500 average, further illustrates the market's volatility. Annual price changes varied from +45% in 1954 to −27.1% in 1974. Only four of 38 annual moves are within 3% of the overall average (8.8%). Clearly, stock prices fluctuate greatly from year to year. For example, the 14% decline in 1957 was followed by a 38% gain in 1958, and the 27% decline in 1974 was succeeded by a 29% rise. Fluctuations such as these reflect the market's tendency to react vigorously to short-term factors.

Table 12.2 reports only year-end price changes. Thus it understates the extent of the market's fluctuations. The long-term upward trend revealed in the table tends to mask considerable within-year movement. For example, the index recorded a low of 34.58 in January 1955 and a high of 46.41 in November of the same year (a difference of 34%). In 1975 the index varied from 62.28 to 79.80 (a 22% difference). Looking at the mean index value for all of the years suggests an upward trend. Noting the differences between highs and lows of the same and succeeding years reveals substantial short-term variability, however. Moreover, most individual stocks and portfolios experience considerably greater return variability from year to year.

TABLE 12.1 News Events and Stock Market Reactions as Measured by the Dow Jones Industrial Average

		Close Trading Day Before	Same Day Close	Close Trading Day After	3 Trading Days Later	21 Calendar Days Later
Korean war*	6-24-50	224.35	213.94	212.07	206.72	197.63
Eisenhower heart attack	9-24-55	487.45	445.56	465.93	468.68	416.13
Egypt seizes Suez Canal*	7-26-56	514.13	515.85	512.30	517.81	517.19
Hungarian revolt*	10-23-56	485.27	485.05	482.67	486.06	486.69
Sputnik I	10-4-57	465.82	461.70	452.42	451.40	435.15
U-2 shot down*	5-1-60	601.70	599.61	607.73	608.32	623.66
Berlin Wall erected*	8-12-61	722.61	718.93	716.18	721.84	718.72
Cuban missile crisis*	10-22-62	573.29	568.60	558.06	570.86	624.41
John Kennedy assassinated	11-22-63	732.65	711.49	743.52	750.52	760.17
Dominican Republic invasion*	4-28-65	918.16	918.86	918.71	922.11	932.12
Israel-Arab war*	6-5-67	863.31	847.77	862.71	873.20	872.11
U.S.S. Pueblo seized*	1-23-68	871.71	864.77	862.23	865.06	831.77
Soviets invaded Czechoslovakia*	8-20-68	887.66	888.67	888.30	896.13	919.38
Cambodian invasion*	4-30-70	737.39	736.07	733.63	709.74	665.25
U.S. mines North Vietnam harbors*	5-9-72	937.84	925.12	931.07	941.83	971.18

*International political (war-related) events.

*International political (war-related) events.
Source: D. Dorfman, "Heard on the Street," *The Wall Street Journal*, May 18, 1972. Reprinted by permission, © Dow Jones & Company, Inc. All rights reserved.

This review of stock market performance illustrates the pervasive time series variability of the market. An unemotional market reacting only to relevant newly public information should be less volatile. The observed volatility does not in and of itself prove that the market overreacts. It does, however, at least raise the possibility that a mood-based market timing strategy might be effective. This leads into the next topic: How can market extremes be identified—or can they?

BUY CHEAP AND SELL DEAR: WHEN ARE STOCKS CHEAP?

Buying and selling at the appropriate times is at least as important as identifying misvalued securities. The relatively unspectacular performance of most mutual funds illustrates the difficulty of anticipating major market moves. Treynor and Mazuy, for example, found that none of the 57 mutual funds studied was able to anticipate market moves successfully.[6] Still, the rewards from accurate timing encourage us to search for any shred of useful evidence.

We should begin by lowering our sights a bit. No one should expect to be able to identify the market's tops or bottoms consistently. Some investors may succeed in developing a feel for when stocks are too high or too low but even this level of predictability may be expecting too much. After the 1929 crash, stocks initially rebounded and then turned down again. Once they started down the second time, they continued to sink lower and lower as what seemed like bargain

TABLE 12.2   Annual Performance of Standard & Poor's 500 Stocks

Year	Difference Between Index Value at Year-End and at End of Previous Year	Year	Difference Between Index Value at Year-End and at End of Previous Year
1950	+15.0%	1969	−11.4%
1951	+16.3	1970	+ 0.1
1952	+11.8	1971	+10.8
1953	− 6.6	1972	+18.2
1954	+45.0	1973	−21.1
1955	+26.4	1974	−27.1
1956	+ 2.6	1975	+29.0
1957	−14.3	1976	+19.2
1958	+38.1	1977	−13.0
1959	+ 8.5	1978	+ 1.1
1960	− 3.0	1979	+12.3
1961	+23.1	1980	+25.9
1962	−11.8	1981	− 9.7
1963	18.9	1982	+14.7
1964	13.0	1983	+17.3
1965	9.1	1984	+ 1.4
1966	−13.1	1985	+26.3
1967	+20.1	1986	+14.6
1968	+ 7.7	1987	+ 2.0

prices were later shown to be extremely expensive (Table 12.3). A similar if somewhat shorter run phenomenon occurred during the market decline of 1973–1974.

While declining markets may continue their decline for some time, they do eventually reverse their trend. Investors would like to buy when the market has completed most of its downward movement but has not yet risen much above its low. If the precise bottom is not usually identifiable ex ante, perhaps buying can at least be concentrated in depressed periods. Such a strategy requires some idea of when stocks are near their cyclical lows.

Declines from a Previous High

Investment analysts continually compare average stock prices with their prior levels. They reason that evidence of the market's past trading ranges can be used to forecast the future. Accordingly, some recent market cycles will now be explored. Because the Dow Jones Industrial Averages comprise by far the most closely watched index, we shall use the Dow to track some of the market's history. Table 12.4 reports the major declines in the Dow since 1919. Purchases near these bottoms were generally superior to purchases at most other times. The problem, however, is to identify when the market is near a low.

The post-1960 experience is revealing. In the 1961–1962 crash, the Dow fell from 734 to 535, whereas the 1966 decline was from 995 to 744. In the 1968–1970 period the Dow declined from 985 to a 1970 low of 631. In 1971 the market fell from a high of 950 to a low of 797. The Dow declined from a peak of 1051

TABLE 12.3 1929 Crash and Recovery

| | CLOSING PRICES | | | | |
	Sept. 3, 1929	Nov. 13, 1929	July 8, 1931	July 8, 1932	July 8, 1933
Dow Jones Industrials	381.17	198.69	143.83	41.22	105.15
Dow Jones Railroads	189.11	128.07	81.21	13.23	55.67
AT&T	302 1/2	207	177 3/8	72 1/8	132
Anaconda	130 7/8	70 1/2	25 3/4	4	21 1/4
Bethlehem Steel	136 3/4	79 1/4	48 1/8	8 3/8	47 5/8
DuPont	215	90	86	22 3/8	80 3/4
Erie Railroad	90 3/4	42 3/4	22 7/8	3	20 1/8
General Motors	71 3/4	36 1/8	37 3/8	7 3/4	32 1/2
IBM	241 3/4	112 1/2	147	54 1/2	139
ITT	147 1/8	53 1/2	32 3/8	3 7/8	19 1/2
Montgomery Ward	134 3/8	49 7/8	19 1/2	4 3/8	27 3/4
Radio Corp. (RCA)	98 1/8	28 3/4	17	3 5/8	12
Sears	171	81 3/8	55 1/8	10 1/4	44 1/8
U.S. Steel	257 5/8	151 1/2	96 1/8	21 1/2	65 1/4
Warner Brothers	60 1/2	30 1/4	7 1/4	5/8	6 3/4
Westinghouse	285 7/8	105	67	15 7/8	54 5/8
Zenith	45 1/2	10 1/8	2 3/4	1/2	2 1/4

Source: G. Gilmar, "A Day to Remember: When the Worst Bear Market Ever Came to No End," *Barron's*, July 5, 1982, p. 22. Reprinted by permission, © Dow Jones & Company, Inc. All rights reserved.

TABLE 12.4 Major Declines in the Dow Jones Industrial Average

Year	High	Low	Down
1987	2722.42	1738.74	36%
1983–1984	1287.20	1086.57	16
1981–1982	1024.05	776.92	24
1976–1978	1014.79	742.12	27
1973–1974	1051.71	577.60	45
1971	950.82	797.97	16
1968–1970	985.21	631.16	36
1966	995.15	744.32	25
1961–1962	734.91	535.76	27
1960	685.47	566.05	17
1957	520.77	419.79	19
1948–1949	193.16	161.60	16
1946	212.50	163.12	23
1939–1942	155.92	92.92	40
1937–1938	194.40	98.95	49
1929–1932	381.17	41.22	89
1919–1921	119.62	63.90	46

in 1973 to a low of 577 in December 1974. The 1976–1978 drop was from 1014 to 742. In 1981–1982 the Dow declined from 1024 to 776. In 1983–1984 the Dow declined from 1287 to 1086. Finally, in 1987 the Dow declined from 2722 to 1738. In percentage terms these declines were 27%, 25%, 36%, 16%, 45%, 27%, 24%, 16%, and 36%. An investor who bought when the market was off 15% would have been near the low twice and far above it six times. Those who bought when the market had declined 25% would have missed three bottoms, been close three times, and have bought much too soon three times. An investor waiting for a 35% drop might buy stocks only once a decade. Apparently past trading patterns provide very little timing insight.

The Market PE Ratio as a Signal

The market average PE ratio is a measure of its relative price. As such it might be used to identify the market's tops and bottoms. The Dow PE rose from 12.1 in 1957 to 24.2 in 1961. A PE this high was seen only once during the post-World War II period. It was clearly overdone. In retrospect the subsequent fall to 16.2 might have been expected. In 1966 the ratio rose to 18.1 only to fall to 13.5 in the same year. The ratio fell from 16.9 to 11.7 in 1969–1970, and in 1971 it fell from 17.3 to 16.2. In 1973–1974 the ratio fell from 16.5 to 6.1. It rose somewhat from that low but ended the decade at 8. It stayed within the 6 to 9 range during the 1980–1981 period but exploded in 1982–1983, reflecting large losses by some of the component firms. It also reached high ground as the market ran up in 1987.

This fluctuating market PE experience illustrates the unreliability of a multiple-based timing strategy. Holmes' composite PE average of 14 for all NYSE stocks (1871–1971) provides a very rough guide at best.[7] Perhaps from an historical perspective, a PE on the Dow of 10 or less is below average. From 1954–1973 the PE did not go lower than 9. In 1949 and 1951 the ratio was around 7 and since 1974 has often been even lower. The low multiple value of 6 to 7 during 1974 and again in 1976–1981 was largely due to concern over high interest rates and rapid inflation. The ratio was above 13 in the 1930s, and until 1947 it was usually above 10. The 1934 multiple of almost 90 and the multiple of over 110 in late 1982 reflected abnormally low aggregated earnings. That is, large losses by a few firms (Chrysler, International Harvester, etc.) offset the earnings of most of the other firms. Thus little or no pattern is revealed. Determining when the market PE is in unsustainably high territory is equally difficult. As the multiple rises close to or above 18, a reversal seems increasingly likely. The market has turned down on many occasions when the Dow's multiple was well below 18, however. In 1987, in contrast, the Dow's PE reached 18 in January with the Dow itself around 2100. The Dow continued to rise, eventually reaching its 2722 peak. At that level the Dow's PE stood at 21.5. Thus investors who sold when the PE reached 18 would have missed most of the 1987 rise. Still, they would have been out of the market for the crash.

Clearly, the market multiple has been an undependable basis for timing decisions. What seems like a very high (or low) multiple in one economic climate may be quite justified in another. Perhaps multiple analysis could usefully be combined with some knowledge of the prevailing conditions and expectations.

The Gray Approach: PE Ratios Relative to Interest Rates

Market interest rates form the basis for discounting the expected income streams of investments. Similarly, PE ratios indicate how much the market is willing to pay for a dollar of current earnings. A PE of 10 indicates that the market is willing to pay $10 for a dollar of current earnings. Similarly, a PE of 5 or 20 indicates that the market will pay $5 or $20 for a dollar of current earnings. The more the market will pay for a dollar of current earnings, the lower is the rate at which it is discounting a firm's expected future earnings stream (or the more optimistic it is about the future growth in earnings). Thus, in a sense, PEs also reflect a discounting of expected income. High PEs imply a low discount rate and low PEs imply a high discount rate for stocks.

From this perspective we should be able to see why Gray bases his approach on the proposition that interest rates and stock multiples (PEs) are related.[8] According to Gray, high interest rates should correspond to a stock market that is willing to pay only a relatively low multiple for current earnings (a low PE). Similarly, low interest rates should be consistent with high PEs in the stock market.

Gray develops the relationship between PEs and market interest rates mathematically. His basic formula is based on two relationships:

1. A stock's total return is equal to its dividend yield (D/P) plus its appreciation rate (g).

2. The dividend yield equals the stock's earning/price ratio (E/P) times its payout ratio (D/E).

Total return is in fact defined as the sum of dividend return (D/P) and price appreciation (g). Thus his first proposition is little more than the definition of total return. Similarly, the product of the earnings/price ratio (E/P) and the payout ratio (D/E) is the ratio of dividends to stock price (D/P). Moreover, the ratio of dividends to the stock price is in fact the dividend yield. Again, the proposition is little more than an extension of a definition. Gray uses the following equation to express the relationship:

$$r = \left(\frac{D}{E}\right)\left(\frac{E}{P}\right) + g$$

where:

r = return on stock
D = dividend per share
E = earnings per share
P = price per share
g = long-term growth rate in price per share (assumed to average 5%)

Note that:

D/E = payout ratio (assumed to average 55%)
E/P = earnings–price ratio
$(D/E) \times (E/P) = D/P$ (which is the dividend yield)

This equation is in fact mathematically equivalent to the PE ratio equation that we have worked with in past chapters. (Demonstrating this relationship is left as an exercise for the reader.) The equation itself only expresses the return on a stock (or the stock market) as the sum of its dividend and price appreciation. Note, however, that the model does illustrate the relationship between r and the PE ratio. The model shows r to be determined by three variables: D/E, E/P, and g. According to Gray, both g (the long-term appreciation rate) and D/E (the payout ratio) can be treated as approximately constant (not varying by enough to matter over time). Thus virtually all of the variability in r is thought to stem from variability in E/P. The E/P ratio is simply 1/PE (the reciprocal of PE). Thus r should vary inversely and almost exclusively with variations in the PE ratio.

The relationship of a variable r to a stock is almost identical to the relationship of yield to a bond. They are the returns (or, in a future-oriented context, expected returns) on the two types of investments. Clearly, the returns offered by these two types of investments should be related. If bonds on the average offer high expected returns (as, for example, measured by the AA utility bond yield), stocks should also on the average be priced to offer high expected returns (as, for example, measured by the returns on the S&P 500), and vice versa.

Not surprisingly, Gray found that the AA utility bond yield tended to vary with r. He also found that, the higher the AA utility yield, the lower the spread is between r (which he calls the "common stock sustainable return") and bond yields. The past behavior of this spread may be a guide for the future. Thus this spread is first regressed on the yield to estimate the historical relation. Then the deviations from the values predicted by the regression are plotted over time.

These deviations provide an indication of the degree and direction of any tendency for stocks to be mispriced relative to bonds. If bond yields are high relative to their historical relationship to common stock sustainable returns (r), then stocks may well be overpriced relative to bonds.

Gray suggests using a spread greater than .2% below or above its predicted value as a buy or sell signal. Thus the investor would first observe the actual r value from the market price of stocks relative to earnings. Then the spread between this r and the value expected from the level of current interest rates (and the historical relationship between the two variables) would be determined. If the spread is greater than a positive .2%, stocks are underpriced relative to bonds, according to Gray. Similarly, a spread of less than −.2% would indicate that stocks were, again according to Gray, overpriced relative to bonds. When stocks are thought to be underpriced the model would generate a sell signal; a buy signal would emerge when the model indicated they were overpriced.

During the test period examined by Gray the (ex post) predictions from his methodology were generally correct, at least directionally. The reliability of Gray's and similar devices should be assessed cautiously, however. Many trading rules would have generated abnormal returns if they had been applied over the test period. Some trading strategies, however, will seem to work once, just by chance (particularly if the data are "mined"). A rule derived from analysis for one period and tested successfully over a second period is, in contrast, much more likely to reflect a continuing relationship.

Gray did not test his approach on a second period nor did he take account of commissions and other trading costs. A predictor (such as Gray's) that seems correct

Investments in Perspective

The Gray approach boils down to the idea that interest rates and PEs should be in line with each other. A similar approach suggests that, when interest rates and market PEs get too far out of line, the market may be about to make a major move to bring them back in line. The 1987 crash was certainly consistent with that scenario, as described in a *Forbes* article shortly after the crash.

Picking up the Pieces

Most investors paid little attention when bond and stock yields got out of sync. They paid for their inattention.

Back in sync?

By Edwin A. Finn Jr.

WHY DID THE stock market crash? A better way to ask the question: How did stock prices get so inflated in the first place? The answer—now—is only too obvious: The prices got out of touch with reality.

It used to be simple. As interest rates rose, the stock market declined. And vice versa. It went more or less like clockwork for six decades: lower interest rates, higher stock prices; higher interest rates, lower stock prices. Then came 1987. A major divergence was occurring. Interest rates had been rising rather fast since January, and Treasury bonds actually crossed the 9% yield figure. But the stock market didn't fall; instead it took off. *(See inset on chart.)* The two markets were completely out of sync.

For nearly 60 years yields on long-term Treasury bonds have done a mating dance with the stock market, represented below by the price/earnings ratios of the 30 stocks in the Dow Jones industrial average. As yields rise, P/E ratios should fall. But this year the P/E signals were screaming that something was wrong. Unfortunately, most of us ignored those signals.

It's fashionable to blame foreign buying and selling for the inflated prices and for the severity of the drop. But the weight of Japanese money shouldn't be overestimated. Of the $200 billion in U.S. stocks owned by foreigners at the end of August, Western Europeans held about 60%, the Canadians 16%, and Japanese about 7%. Overall, the foreigners own only about 7% of all U.S. equities.

In short, the foreigners were simply following the trend. They may have contributed to the upside momentum and the downside, but they didn't cause it. To a large degree, they were simply sucked in by the excitement.

"Too much analysis from 1985 to 1987 compared one stock to another, or one stock market to another," says Roger Brinner, chief economist at Data Resources Inc. "Fundamental analysis would have shown that bonds were a better value."

Now that the stock market is down by a third and interest rates are dropping again, is that a buy signal for the stock market? Are the two markets back in sync? Almost.

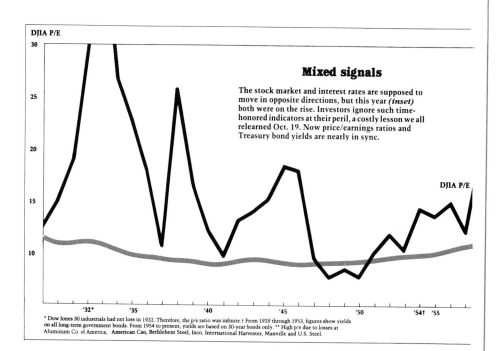

Mixed signals

The stock market and interest rates are supposed to move in opposite directions, but this year *(inset)* both were on the rise. Investors ignore such time-honored indicators at their peril, a costly lesson we all relearned Oct. 19. Now price/earnings ratios and Treasury bond yields are nearly in sync.

DJIA P/E

* Dow Jones 30 industrials had net loss in 1932. Therefore, the p/e ratio was infinite.† From 1929 through 1953, figures show yields on all long-term government bonds. From 1954 to present, yields are based on 30-year bonds only. ** High p/e due to losses at Aluminum Co. of America, American Can, Bethlehem Steel, Inco, International Harvester, Manville and U.S. Steel.

Brinner's study of P/E ratios and bond yields indicates the Dow should fall no lower than 1650. This assumes economic growth of about 1% over the next 12 months.

Comments by Federal Reserve Chairman Alan Greenspan suggest he will likely move to avert an outright recession by cutting rates as needed. But Greenspan doesn't have a free hand. If he drops interest rates too fast, the dollar will fall further, and foreign investors could stampede out of U.S. securities. A falling dollar would threaten to speed up inflation, forcing Greenspan to raise the cost of money again. Says one economist, "Greenspan's really in a box."

Stocks are a bargain compared with two months ago. But compared with two years ago, they are not. Are they a bargain compared with bonds or cash? The answer is not clear and won't be for some time. But meantime, FORBES has detected an interesting gap in perception. See below.

Generation gap

Wonder why there wasn't more gloom and despair after Black Monday? Why people took it so calmly, more like a sporting event than a financial disaster? The answer seems to be that—professionals aside—many individuals thought of the crash more as a buying opportunity than as the worst market crash in history.

"The institutions were nervous, and I was nervous, but our customers were calm," said Fred Jinsler of discount broker Quick & Reilly in Miami. Of Jinsler's orders 70% were buys after Oct. 19. "We had people reactivating accounts that hadn't traded in a couple of years."

"The small investor was buying like crazy, eight buys to one sell," said David Pratt of Piper Jaffray & Hopwood in Minneapolis.

"They sensed a bargain, and that surprised me," said Scottie Mills of Merrill Lynch in San Diego. "They were overwhelmingly buy orders the last three days, eight buys to two sells."

"It was all euphoria buying after Monday. I didn't take one sell order Wednesday morning before opening," said a Charlotte, N.C. broker.

There were some sellers among individual accounts, and this showed an interesting pattern. It was an age gap. Younger, less-experienced investors panicked and ran. Older, grayer heads snapped at bargains. "If the account was more than five years old, I knew they were going to buy," said Joan Curran of Quick & Reilly in Washington, D.C. "Newer accounts would sell."

"Old-timers knew to take advantage of quality," said George Griffin of PaineWebber in Chicago. Other brokers repeated the refrain: Younger investors were selling, older ones buying in the early stages of the collapse.

What do we make of all this? Can it be that these were buyers who missed much of the past year's rise and grabbed at a chance to get back in? Or were they truly getting bargains? Are older heads wiser? We don't know; we're just reporting what we learned.—**Christie Brown**

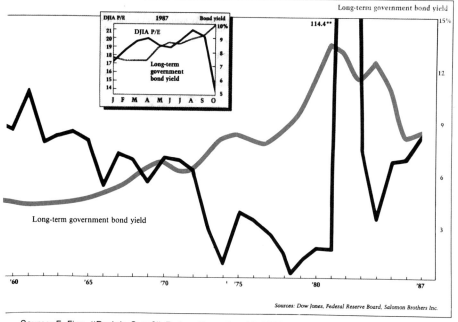

Sources: Dow Jones, Federal Reserve Board, Salomon Brothers Inc.

Source: E. Finn, "Back in Sync?" *Forbes*, November 16, 1987, pp. 34–35. Reprinted by permission, © Forbes Inc.

directionally may not be sufficiently reliable or predict moves of great enough magnitudes to overcome the extra trading costs. Moreover, to be fair, trading rules should be examined in a way that uses only information when it would have been available. That is, tests should not be structured in a way that allows the technique to be tested to take advantage of hindsight. In real-world applications investors do not have the benefit of hindsight.

Because Gray's study and most of the other work discussed here fail to take any of these precautions, the results are only suggestive. Nonetheless, the 1987 stock crash did occur after market PEs had seemed to get far out of line with interest rates. At its August 1987 peak the Dow's PE reached a high of 21.5. The 30-year Treasury yield was as high as 10.41% on October 16, 1987. On that Friday

FIGURE 12.1   PEs and Inflation

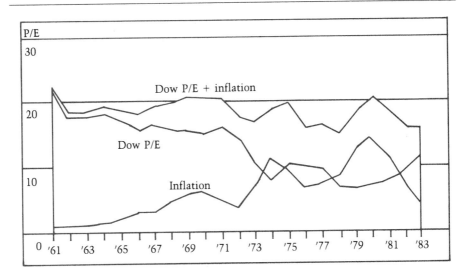

Source: S. Kichen, "The Rate of 20," *Forbes*, July 20, 1983. Reprinted by permission, © Forbes Inc.

before the Monday market crash the PE on the Dow still stood at 17.8. In retrospect, these two numbers were far out of line with each other. Either bond prices were too low (interest rates were too high) or PEs (and thus stock prices) were too high. Investors who believed in the Gray approach to market timing would have taken this inconsistency between the PE and interest rates as a clear signal to sell stocks.

PE Ratios Relative to Inflation Rates

Miller, the chief investment officer of Donaldson, Lufkin, and Jenrette, advocates a trading strategy based on the relation of stock prices to inflation rates.[9] Specifically, he asserts that the PE ratio of the Dow Jones Industrial Average added to the inflation rate tends to move up or down toward 20. Inflation tends to reduce the real return on stocks. Thus PEs tend to decline with rises in the inflation rate, and vice versa. Figure 12.1 seems to support Miller's view. As the sum rises toward 20 it becomes more likely to decline. Note, however, that the actual average of the sum is 18.5, not 20. Moreover, like Gray, Miller has not carefully tested his approach. Still, like the Gray approach, the Rule of 20 would have given a warning before the October 1987 crash.

In 1986 and 1987 inflation was running at about a 4% rate. The PE on the Dow stood at 14.9 on September 30, 1986. Thus the sum, about 19, would have been in line with the 18.5 average. By December 31, 1986, the market PE was up to 16.4, putting the sum over 20. By then the Rule of 20 would have given a warning or perhaps a modest sell signal. An investor who acted on such a signal would have got out of the market ahead of the crash but also ahead of a major further rise. The Dow went from 1896 at year-end 1986 to an August 1987 high of 2722. This represents a rise of 43%. The Rule of 20 would have begun to flash a stronger sell as the year went on. On March 31, 1987 the Dow PE reached 18.9, producing a sum of close to 23. The PE stood at 19.2 and the sum at over 24 on September 30, 1987. By then the market high had passed but the Dow still stood at 2596. The crash and resulting low of 1738 was less than three weeks away. At its low for the year the Dow PE stood at 13.8 for a sum of 17.8, which was only a bit below the long-term average of 18.5. Thus even after the crash the Rule of 20 would not really have given a clear buy signal.

Market Behavior during Recession

Stock market performance during recessions and the subsequent recoveries may follow a predictable pattern. Cullity examined seven postwar economic contractions (1949, 1954, 1958, 1961, 1963, 1967, and 1970), five of which were official recessions as defined by the National Bureau of Economic Research (NBER).[10] The 1963 and 1967 contractions were unofficial mild pauses. Two important conclusions emerged from Cullity's study. First, a pattern of rising markets during recessions is revealed (Figure 12.2). Second, stock price advances tend to be more vigorous after severe than after mild contractions. Somewhat more recently Malabre contended that the market usually turns up when the economy is still deep in a recession and goes nowhere in the subsequent recovery.[11] Similarly Piccini, who studied thirteen 20th century business cycles, found that "investors can often sell stocks without penalty as much as eight months before an expansion peaks and begin repurchasing six months after a recession has begun."[12] Buying after the economic recovery begins does not require a forecast. The beginning of a recovery is generally observable within a few months of the bottom. Selling before an economic peak, in contrast, assumes an ability to predict the tops of economic cycles. Thus Piccini's findings are only modestly helpful to those who cannot forecast the economy's direction.

The Election-Year Cycle

An interesting four-year stock cycle has been observed. Administrations frequently stimulate the economy in presidential election years and then put on the brakes following the voting. As a result "since 1948, the economy has peaked seven months, on average, after Presidential Election Day and sunk to its low 11 months later."[13] Indeed "over the 1961–78 period, stocks returned an average 21.7 percent in the year beginning two years prior to a presidential election, 15 percent in the year of the election, 3.6 percent in the year immediately following and −15.2 percent in the second following year."[14] Thus, if this pattern persists, investors should expect market lows 1½ to 2 years after a presidential election and highs about six months after.

Riley and Laksetich studied a variety of Wall Street election-year stock cycle folklore. They found that positive short-run performance generally followed the election of a Republican and negative performance followed the election of a

FIGURE 12.2   Stock Recovery Patterns After Recessions

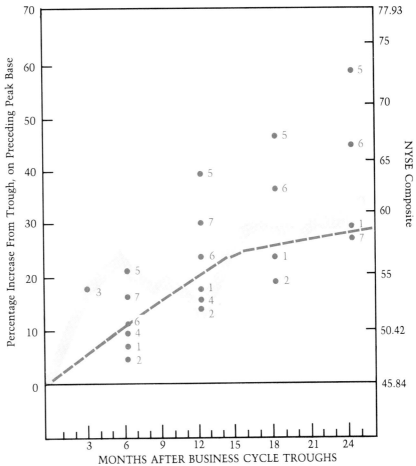

Arabic numerals identify recovery periods arranged according to the severity
of the preceding recessions, beginning with the mildest. The periods start
with business cycle troughs as follows: 1, January 1963; 2, June 1967;
3, November 1970; 4, February 1961; 5, August 1954; 6, October 1949;
7, April 1958.
■■■ Median of previous recoveries that followed mild or moderate
recessions. The unbroken line indicates present expansion.

Source: J. Cullity, "Stock Price Recoveries Following Recessions: A Second Look," *Financial Analysts
Journal*, January/February 1974, 47. Reprinted with permission.

Democrat.[15] They also reported that the market generally rose after the election
outcome was known but fell after an incumbent lost. They even found that "rules
triggered by a Republican victory and/or the anticipation of such victory, consistently earned positive returns."[16]

Official Pronouncements and Company Stock Repurchases

Government officials (President, Secretary of the Treasury, Chairman of the Council of Economic Advisors, Chairman of the Federal Reserve System, and others) sometimes comment publicly on the level of the stock market. Such pronouncements may either reflect nonpublic information about future economic policy or they may be designed to bolster the stock market for political purposes. As with everyone else's advice, investors should listen to but not necessarily rely on the opinions of government officials.

Another bit of evidence on the state of the market relates to companies repurchasing their own stock. Before about 1960 many repurchases were to facilitate acquisitions, stock dividends, and conversions. More recent purchases, however, are viewed primarily as an effective use of cash. Companies often repurchase their stock at bargain prices although they may not pick the bottom.[17]

Dow Theory

Dow Theory is one of the oldest approaches to market timing. Its originator, Charles Dow, was also the founder and first editor of *The Wall Street Journal*. He hypothesized that the market moves in identifiable trends. These trends are revealed by the relations between two indexes of market performance. Specifically, he asserted that a continuing trend may be identified by looking first for a new high in an index defined as primary (such as the Dow Jones Industrial Average) and then seeking confirmation from a second high (such as the Dow Jones Transportation Average). Thus if the Industrials reaches a new high followed quickly by a new high for the Transports, the up trend is said to be intact. In a study of the 1971–1980 period, Glickstein and Wubbels found the technique to have produced useful timing signals.[18]

Table 12.5 summarizes market timing approaches.

Market Forecasters

Rather than try to identify market tops and bottoms, many investors rely on professionals who make their living forecasting the market. To depend on investment managers and stock market analysts has a number of drawbacks. They include unimpressive past records, substantial fees, and even the problem of deciding which professional to use. Similar difficulties confront investors who rely on market timing experts. Nonetheless, such services are a significant part of the investment scene.

Stock market forecasters utilize a variety of techniques. One well-known market forecaster with a reasonably successful recent record is Francis Kelly, chairman of Dean Witter's investment policy committee. Kelly describes himself as a fundamentalist and bases his forecasts on share prices relative to future prospects. He is also a contrarian who is happiest when no one agrees with him.

We have already mentioned the rise and fall of one of the better known forecasters, Joseph Granville. Robert Prechter is in a sense his logical successor. His methodology seems equally obscure and his record equally hot, at least initially.

Investments in Perspective

An article on a Dow Theory sell signal was published in the October 19, 1987, edition of *Barron's*, which appeared on the newsstands on October 17. It reported that on October 15 the Dow Transports closed below their September 21 level, and this confirmed the Industrials' new low of October 9. Thus Dow Theory did give a very timely signal just before the October 19 crash.

Is the Big Bad Bear Back?
Yes, Says a Dow Theorist, and Here's Why

By RICHARD RUSSELL

ON Oct. 15, the Dow Jones Transportation Average broke the Sept. 21 closing low of 1005.80. This penetration confirmed the previous break (on Oct. 9) by the Dow Jones Industrial Average below its own Sept. 21 low of 2492.82. Taken together, these averages' moves below preceding important lows signal the existence of a primary bear market.

In view of the above, the following should be borne in mind:

• The Dow theory, although it has been in use since the turn of the century, makes no claim to infallability.

• It is a tenet of the Dow theory (and one that has withstood the test of time) that neither the duration nor the extent of a primary movement can be predicted.

• The primary trend cannot be manipulated by the President, the Congress, the Treasury, the Federal Reserve Board, or any person or body of people. Once in force, the primary trend will continue until the best (in a bull market) or the worst (in a bear market) is fully reflected in the price structure.

A study of history does indicate a few rough benchmarks worth mentioning. Most bear markets have wiped out half or more of the gains of the preceding bull market. The greater the bull market, the better the odds that a severe bear market will follow.

This writer believes that the great bull market began in December 1974 at 577.60 on the Dow. The bull stopped charging in August 1987 at 2722.42, for a total gain of 2145 points. Half of the total equals 1073 points. If the current bear market performs to average expectations, it should come as no surprise to see a final bear market bottom below 2000.

Every turn in the tide in Wall Street history has come in the face of massive skepticism and doubt. Certainly, this one is no exception. However, history will note that conditions in August 1987 were classically ripe for the emergence of a bear market. "To know values," wrote Charles H. Dow, "is to know the meaning of the market." Values during mid-1987 were as thin and strained as any seen in the century. By August 1987, the yield on the Dow was down to a miniscule 2.61%, one of the lowest levels ever seen in a major advance.

Despite what most investors may think, the Dow theory places its greatest emphasis on values. And the best gauge of values has always been the yield on the Dow. All bull market tops have been associated with average Dow yields around 3% or less. Conversely, all bear market bottoms have been associated with average yields of 6% or better. Thus, the yield cycle may again be of great use in identifying the ultimate bear market bottom, as well as the birth of the next bull market. ∎

Richard Russell publishes Dow Theory Letters from La Jolla, Calif.

TABLE 12.5 Market Timing Approaches

Declines from a Previous High	Market's previous declines exhibit no consistent pattern.
Market PE Ratio	Movements in the market PE are an undependable basis for investment timing.
Gray Approach	Market PEs relative to interest rates may offer useful timing signals.
Rule of 20	The market PE plus the inflation rate may tend toward an average value of 18.5.
Behavior during Recessions	Market tends to turn up early in a recession.
Election-Year Cycle	Market tends to peak shortly after a presidential election.
Official Pronouncements	Administration officials may occasionally make statements that are useful to investors.
Company Stock Repurchases	Large stock repurchases by many firms may signal that a market bottom is near.
Dow Theory	An uptrend is confirmed when a high in the primary index (i.e., DJIA) is soon followed by a high in the secondary index (i.e., DJTA); downtrends are confirmed by the reverse order (DJTA high followed by DJIA).

Prechter bases his analysis on something called the Elliot Wave theory. According to the Elliot principle, stock prices are a barometer of the national mood. That mood moves in predictable waves between optimism and pessimism. The waves are said to unfold in specific sequences. Each wave contains a smaller series of waves. Long waves can last for more than a hundred years whereas the shortest waves can be over in an hour. According to Prechter's view in mid-1987, the market was in the fifth wave of the Grand Supercycle. Prechter expected this Supercycle to reach a Dow index high of 3686 in 1988. That top was expected to be followed by a crash worse than 1929, a depression, and a major war. In fact, the relevant bull market ended in 1987 and topped out about 1000 points below the peak that Prechter had forecast.

TABLE 12.6 Market Timing Letters Recommended by *Money* Magazine

Letter	Author	Frequency	Annual Cost	Address
Zweig Forecaster	Martin Zweig	Every three weeks	$195	747 Third Avenue New York, N.Y. 10017
Professional Tape Reader	Stan Weinstein	Twice a month	$250	Box 2407 Hollywood, Fla. 33022
Lowery's New York Stock Exchange Market Trend Analysis	Paul Desmond	Weekly	$200	Royal Palm Way Palm Beach, Fla. 33480
Granville Market Letter	Joseph Granville	Weekly	$250	Drawer 0 Holly Hill, Fla. 32017
Market Logic	Norman Fosback	Twice a month	$95	3471 N. Federal Highway Fort Lauderdale, Fla. 33306

Martin Zweig is one of the best-known forecasters. A frequent panelist on "Wall Street Week," he publishes a newsletter that has more than 8,000 subscribers. Zweig is best described as an eclectic technician. He relies heavily on his own assessment of Fed policy and various technical market indicators. His advice is often very short term. Those who follow Zweig do a lot of trading but have, according to Connelly, tended to make money.[19] Zweig topped advisor ratings in *Hulbert* in both 1981 and 1982. He did not do nearly as well in 1983, 1984, or 1985. He did, however, have one of the best overall performances over the 1980–1987 period. He also anticipated the 1987 crash, making the announcement of his forecast on "Wall Street Week."

Paul Desmond, president of *Lowery's Reports*, continues a technical advisory service that began in 1938. The Lowery method attempts to detect supply (selling power) and demand (buying power) through changes in price and trading volume.

Robert Farrell, vice president and manager of market analysis for Merrill Lynch, considers himself a market psychologist. He tries to track the behavior of institutional investors and advocates trading against their emotional reactions.

With 10,000 subscribers for his *Professional Tape Reader*, Stan Weinstein has one of the widest followings. His recommendations are based largely on his readings of 47 technical indicators.

Trial subscriptions are available for most of the market timing letters listed in Table 12.6, although this author does not recommend any of them. Investors who wish to know what market forecasters are saying may subscribe directly to some of the letters or read articles reporting analysts' opinions in the popular press. Others may prefer to assess the data that the forecasters use. Most of these analysts make at least some use of technical market indicators.

TECHNICAL MARKET INDICATORS

Thus far we have examined market forecasts based on relative declines in the Dow, market multiples, market multiples relative to interest and inflation rates, historical relationships during recessions, election-year cycles, official pronouncements, share repurchases, Dow Theory, and market analysts' opinions. Technical market indicators are also used to predict market moves. Specifically, many analysts claim to see timing signals in the behavior of certain data series or combinations of data series such as short interest, odd-lot behavior, specialist short selling, and a host of other factors.

Short Interest

As the reader will recall, short sellers sell borrowed stock that they hope later to replace at a profit. At one time they were thought to be sophisticated traders able to anticipate market turns. Thus an increase in short interest (uncovered short sales) was said to forecast a market decline, and vice versa. Others, in contrast, argue that short interest reflects potential demand from covering short traders. According to this view, a rise in short interest forecasts a market rally.

Several studies found that short interest was largely unrelated to market rises and falls. Although some technicians claim that the short interest ratio (number of shares sold short/volume) is a useful indicator, Kerrigan showed that the apparent value of the indicator was due principally to fluctuations in its denominator (volume).[20]

Odd-Lot Activity

According to some analysts, small (odd-lot) traders tend to buy at tops and sell at bottoms. Thus when odd-lotters are buying on balance, the market may be poised for a fall; and when small investors are largely selling, the market may be ready to turn up. Raihall and Jepson attempted to refine the indicator by taking account of the relative prices of odd-lot trades and noting that buy–sell ratios for odd-lotters should be related to past values of the ratios rather than unity.[21] Even with these refinements their results were inconclusive. Gup did find a significant relationship for the 1955–1970 period, however.[22]

Odd-Lot–Short Ratio

According to a related hypothesis, odd-lot short sellers are particularly unsophisticated investors. Thus when odd-lot short sales are high, the market may be near bottom, and vice versa.

Zweig devised an odd-lot index that he claims is more sophisticated than other indicators of odd-lot short sales. He reasoned that when optimism runs rampant, investors eventually exhaust their buying power and stocks are likely to fall. At other times, very pessimistic investors have sold most of their stock so that a modest demand increase can push prices up. The problem then is to measure this investor sentiment:

> Traditionally, odd-lot short selling activity has been measured by the Odd-Lot Short Ratio, which is calculated by dividing odd-lot short sales over some time

period by total odd-lot sales. One difficulty, however, with the ratio is that both numerator and denominator show degrees of pessimism. An alternative might be to use odd-lot purchases in the denominator. This ratio would better record the differences in expectations between bullish investors (odd-lot purchasers) and bearish speculators (odd-lot short sellers).

Again, this ratio has not been entirely satisfactory because of cyclical swings in the balance between O.L. purchases and O.L. sales. For example, in most periods, purchases by odd-lotters exceed sales, but in the past three years the reverse has prevailed for all save a single day. In order to adjust for such cyclical tendencies in O.L. behavior, we have calculated relative O.L. purchases and sales in the denominator. The resulting fraction is called the Total Odd-Lot Short Ratio (TOLSR). Furthermore, in order to smooth out daily aberrations, the TOLSR is computed on the basis of a 10-day moving average.[23]

Zweig's analysis of TOLSR performance for 1947 through 1973 seemed to suggest some value for the index. More recently, however, the indicator has not given particularly useful signals.

Specialists' Short Selling

According to Kent, specialists are especially sophisticated investors having access to nonpublic trading intentions information (their limit order book) and positioned to react quickly to any emerging developments.[24] Because their profits are largely derived from trading their assigned stocks, much of their success depends on effectively managing their inventory. Specialists generally sell short when they expect a price decline and buy when their expectations are positive. Reilly and Whitford, however, failed to find value in following their short selling activity.[25]

Wertheim and Company, which has closely followed short selling by specialists, once said that a ratio below 47% was bullish and above 59% bearish. Since 1976, however, Wertheim has changed their bullish and bearish signals to 40% and 46%, respectively.[26]

Mutual Fund Cash Position

When cash positions (potential buying power) of equity mutual funds become a large percentage of their total assets, the market may have some upside potential. Figure 12.3 illustrates the historical relationship. The market peaks seem to be closely related to troughs in mutual fund cash (1976, 1981, 1983). Similarly, the market bottoms of 1974, 1978, 1980, and 1982 occurred at high points for mutual fund cash. Ranson and Shipman argue, however, that fluctuations in the ratio come largely from variations in the denominator (total assets) rather than differing amounts of funds waiting on the sidelines.[27] According to Cheney and Veit, mutual funds do attempt to time their trading to take advantage of market swings. They do not, however, succeed in successfully altering the composition of their portfolios over the market cycles.[28]

FIGURE 12.3 Mutual Fund Cash versus the Dow

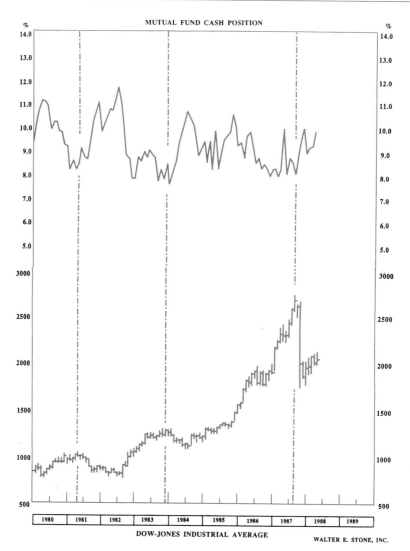

Basic This index shows the month-end cash position of member funds of the Investment Company Institute expressed as a percent of net assets. It provides some measure of the psychology of institutional investors and also the cash they have available for investment. Prior to 1970, the cash position fluctuated in a rough range between 5.0% near market highs and 7.0% near market lows. During the 1970s, there was a definite change in these limits and after reaching a high of 13.5% in 1974 and a low of 5.4% in 1976, the cash position has generally fluctuated between 8.0% near market highs and 10.0% to 11.0% near market lows. As a result, we now classify the cash position as favorable if it moves above 10.0% and unfavorable if it declines below 8.0%.

Current The funds' combined cash position at the end of March was $38.2 billion—up $1.3 billion from the end of February. During the same period, the net assets of the funds declined 1.4%. As a result of these changes, the ratio of the cash position to net assets increased from 9.2% to 9.7%. Since this is still below the 10.0% level, we would continue to classify this series as neutral. However, the Cash Ratio has been increasing on market strength since December and this is very favorable action.

Watch A further advance in the Mutual Fund Cash Ratio above 10.0% would be very favorable.

Source: Walter E. Stone, Inc., *Long-Term Technical Trends*, Boston, Mass., June 1988, 31–32. Used with permission.

TABLE 12.7 Technical Market Indicators

Total Odd-Lot–Short Ratio	When odd-lot short sales are abnormally high (low), the market is said to be near a bottom (top).
Specialist Short Selling	High (low) specialist short selling is thought to forecast a market decline (rise).
Mutual Fund Cash Position	Mutual fund cash is an indication of potential future demand for stocks.
Barron's Confidence Index	Ratio of high-grade to average grade bond yields reflects confidence of "smart" investors.

The Barron's Confidence Index

The Barron's Confidence Index is the ratio of 10 high-grade corporate bond rates relative to the more speculative Dow Jones Bond Index rates. A high value for the ratio indicates that high-grade yields are relatively close to the yields on more speculative issues. At such times the market is unwilling to pay much of a premium for quality. Alternatively, a low ratio implies a substantial premium on quality. The ratio appears in *Barron's* Market Laboratory section. This section is a source of many of the underlying data used to compute market indicators. The users of the Confidence Index believe that "smart money" will move toward quality bonds when the outlook is unfavorable and toward speculative bonds when the outlook is favorable. According to Ring, the index predicted peaks reasonably well but was less accurate in predicting troughs.[29]

As with most of the indicators discussed thus far, the evidence is suggestive but not conclusive. Even in forecasting tops the results are not especially encouraging. A lead varying from one to 14 months is quite undependable.

Table 12.7 summarizes the discussion of these technical market indicators.

Treasury Bill Rate

The borrowing and lending market may also affect the rates used to discount the expected income streams of stock. One index of such conditions is the interest rate on 90-day Treasury bills.

Technical Indicator Studies

Branch Study.   Past work suggested that subsequent market movements were related to odd-lot short selling, specialist and floor trader activity, premiums and discounts on closed-end investment companies, mutual fund cash positions, secondary stock sales, interest rates, and Barron's Confidence Index. Most early research examined each indicator separately using past market behavior to set arbitrary buy and sell signals. These signals were then tested in an ad hoc fashion. The signal was judged successful if the market eventually moved in the forecasted direction. A more definitive test would examine the indicators simultaneously and constrain the investigator from using hindsight to call an eventual market move a success. Multiple regression analysis permits such a test. Accordingly, this author examined the predictive power of the market indicators mentioned in the beginning of this paragraph for the 1960–1974 time period.[30] Separate tests were performed on data for the 1960–1967 and 1968–1974 periods. While most of the variables tested did have the expected signs, many of the coefficients were insignificant. Dropping the insignificant variables revealed four consistently significant indicators: Confidence Index, mutual fund cash position, specialists' short selling, and the 90-day Treasury bill rate. These variables had the expected signs and the relationships persisted over both periods.

Daigler–Fielitz, Van Landingham, and Branch–Schneeweis Studies. More recently Daigler and Fielitz and Van Landingham tested a number of daily market indicators (indicators on which daily data are available).[31] Using multiple discriminate analysis, Daigler and Fielitz were able to develop three trading rules that showed profit potential on a before-commission basis but failed to cover trading costs. Van Landingham's results were similar. Although more sophisticated statistically than my earlier study, the concentration of the Daigler–Fielitz and Van Landingham studies on daily indicators and daily price movements restricts their generalizability. Most market indicators are designed to call market turns rather than short-term moves. Joined by Schneeweis, this author again looked at the predictability of market indicators.[32] With more recent data we examined the performance of several types of market indicators: short selling, odd lot, and mutual fund. We found that the market did a rather effective job of forecasting the indicators, but not vice versa.

Assessment of the Technical Indicator Studies. A careful, long-term study of market indicators is clearly needed to resolve the current controversy. My initial study failed to test actual trading rules or take account of commissions, whereas both the Daigler–Fielitz and the Van Landingham studies analyzed only relatively short-term moves. Nonetheless, these three studies seemed to find some predictive value in technical market indicators. Even forecast methods that fail to produce above-commission excess returns can help time trades that will be made anyway. On the other hand, the more recent Branch–Schneeweis study found little or no use for the indicators studied.

Although the various studies suggest that technical indicators may have some value, the relationships may or may not persist. If, for example, the market pays careful attention to these relations, knowledge of them would become valueless. On the other hand, many indicators have long been touted without losing their followers.

MORE MARKET INDICATORS

Subsequent to the publication of my initial article, market indicator articles appeared in the financial press (*Barron's, The Wall Street Journal,* etc.) with some frequency. Discussing a few of the more interesting indicators is instructive.

Advance–Decline Patterns

The market's strength may be gauged by the ratio of the number of stocks advancing to the number declining. Philippatos and Nawrocki found a tendency for past ratios to persist.[33] That is, if a particular day has many declines relative to the historical average, the next day's declines are likely to lie somewhere between the last day's results and the average. Similar findings for the London and Amsterdam stock exchanges were cited in their study.

Short-Term Trading Index

The short-term trading index is derived from the advance decline ratio. According to Turov, the short-term trading index has a relatively accurate forecasting record. Turov defines the index, which attempts to measure the degree to which volume is concentrated in declining and advancing stocks, as follows: "The number of advancing stocks is divided by the number of declining ones: that equals A. The volume of advancing stock is divided by the volume of declining ones: that equals B. The short-term trading index is A divided by B."[34]

The indicator is available on most stock quotation machines. A little manipulation reveals that the index is the average volume of declining stocks relative to the average volume of advancing stocks. The lower the ratio, the greater is the volume in advancing stocks. According to Turov, the ratio is generally between .70 and 1.30. He contends that a low ratio (high volume in advancing stocks) is a sell signal and a high ratio is a buy signal. Turov suggests .90 in a bear market and .80 in a bull market as a sell signal. The figures for buying are 1.45 and 1.30, respectively. The investor would need to be able to distinguish bull and bear markets to use these thresholds. Turov's article, which appeared in December 1974, correctly called a major market bottom.

Eight years later Zweig studied and, in the process, refined the indicator. Using a 10-day smoothed value (which he called the TRIN) and testing over the 1964–1982 period, Zweig found the (impressive) results reported in Table 12.8. To be accepted in the academic community a study such as this one should be subjected to the professional review that publication in an academic journal implies.

Zweig's Double-Barreled Indicator Approach

Zweig continually tries to improve his set of indicators. In the process he refines some old indicators and introduces some new ones. He more recently has been putting a great deal of faith in a combination of two concepts: Don't fight the tape and don't fight the Fed. His two primary indicators are based on Fed policy and the ratio of advances to declines.

When the Fed lowers either the discount rate or the reserve requirement, Zweig's Fed indicator registers a positive sign. Initial moves are particularly bullish, as are two favorable moves within a few months. Zweig's preferred indicator of market momentum is the 10-day ratio of advances to declines. This indicator is the same as the short-term trading index except that it is not weighted by volume

TABLE 12.8   Zweig's Tests of the Short-Term Trading Index: TRIN versus S&P 500, 10-Day Smoothed Value, 1964 to 1982

TRIN vs. S&P 500, 10-Day Smoothed
1964 to 1982

TRIN Range	S & P Performance		Probability of Up Market
	Period	% Change	
Above 1.5	1 Month Later	+4.97%	63%
0.7 to 1.5	1 Month Later	+0.22%	54%
Under 0.1	1 Month Later	+0.17%	73%
Above 1.5	3 Months Later	+6.55%	78%
0.7 to 1.5	3 Months Later	+0.67%	55%
Under 0.7	3 Months Later	+0.35%	73%
Above 1.5	6 Months Later	+20.07%	96%
0.7 to 1.5	6 Months Later	+1.49%	55%
Under 0.7	6 Months Later	−1.62%	30%
Above 1.5	1 Year Later	+29.99%	96%
0.7 to 1.5	1 Year Later	+3.13%	62%
Under 0.7	1 Year Later	−8.58%	17%

TRIN 10-Day Simple Average 1.5 or Greater
1964 to 1982

Date	3 Months Later		1 Year Later	
	Dow	ZUPI	Dow	ZUPI
09/07/66	+4.0%	+6.3%	+16.9%	+43.6%
10/06/66*	+4.1%	+10.9%	+19.6%	+47.9%
05/04/70	+1.5%	−11.3%	+31.2%	+29.2%
09/30/74	−0.8%	−3.6%	+38.2%	+32.1%
11/19/74*	+21.1%	+27.1%	+39.6%	+39.0%
03/24/80	+14.6%	+20.0%	+31.2%	+47.2%
Avg./Pd.:	+8.0%	+8.4%	+28.2%	+37.8%
$10,000 =	$14,667	$14,993	$28,733	$39,091
Annualized				
Return	+35.9%	+38.3%	+28.2%	+37.8%
Months:	15	15	51	51

ZUPI = Zweig Unweighted Price Index.
*Repeat signal in 1966 includes the one-month return on the first signal (measure is for 4, 7, and 13 months). Repeat signal in 1974 includes two-month returns on the first signal (measure is for 5, 8, and 14 months).
Source: M. Zweig, "Hardy Trader's Tool," *Barron's*, May 4, 1982, pp. 34, 35, 53, 61. Reprinted by permission, © Dow Jones & Company, Inc. All rights reserved.

of advancing verses declining issues. A value of two or greater is taken as a strongly bullish signal.

Zweig is particularly bullish when both the Fed and the advance decline indicators are flashing buy. Zweig's results for these "double-barreled buys" are reported in Table 12.9. Note that when he published the data, the most recent

TABLE 12.9 Zweig's Double-Barreled Indicator

BARRON'S

TABLE 3
Double-Barreled Buys vs. S&P 500: 1926 to 1985

| Date of Buy | _____% Change in S&P 500_____ | | | | |
	1 Month	3 Months	6 Months	12 Months	18 Months
7/21/32	+49.7%	+35.0%	+40.6%	+85.5%*	+85.0%*
5/26/33	+16.4%	+20.8%	+ 7.5%	+ 4.4%	+ 1.9%
4/16/38	− 5.1%	+14.1%	+25.0%	+ 4.1%	+20.0%
9/14/42	+10.3%	+10.2%	+29.4%	+39.1%	+42.9%
7/13/49	+ 3.7%	+ 8.1%	+12.8%	+12.9%	+42.8%
2/15/54	+ 2.0%	+10.6%	+18.0%	+41.7%	+61.9%
1/24/58	− 2.5%	+ 3.4%	+11.8%	+34.3%	+43.0%
12/ 4/70	+ 1.9%	+ 9.5%	+13.2%	+ 8.5%	+22.7%
1/10/75	+ 7.9%	+15.4%	+30.6%	+30.8%	+44.6%
8/23/82	+ 6.6%	+14.5%	+26.4%	+40.2%	+32.9%
1/23/85	?	?	?	?	?
$10,000 becomes:	$22,047	$36,677	$67,984	$119,557	$252,005
Return/Period=	+ 8.2%	+13.9%	+21.1%	+28.7%	+40.0%

*12-and 18-month returns for 1932 buy signal are cut off on 5/26/33 in order to avoid overlap with the latter signal.

TABLE 4
Double-Barreled Buys vs. Zweig Index: 1926 to 1985

| Date of Buy | _____% Change in Zweig Index_____ | | | | |
	1 Month	3 Months	6 Months	12 Months	18 Months
7/21/32	+64.3%	+54.5%	+39.6%	+189.6%*	+189.6%*
5/26/33	+27.1%	+31.2%	+ 4.3%+	+ 48.9%	+ 22.4%
4/16/38	− 2.6%	+28.8%	+37.9%	+ 10.3%	+ 49.8%
9/14/42	+12.5%	+12.3%	+57.4%	+ 77.1%	+ 96.1%
7/13/49	+ 5.7%	+12.5%	+20.2%	+ 18.5%	+ 58.3%
2/15/54	+ .8%	+ 5.5%	+19.2%	+ 44.2%	+ 49.3%
1/24/58	− 1.4%	+ 4.4%	+15.4%	+ 48.9%	+ 58.2%
12/ 4/70	+ 4.8%	+19.8%	+21.8%	+ 7.6%	+ 19.6%
1/10/75	+12.1%	+18.2%	+38.9%	+ 34.6%	+ 59.6%
8/23/82	+ 8.1%	+24.2%	+38.4%	+ 57.1%	+ 47.1%
1/23/85	?	?	?	?	?
$10,000 becomes:	$32,158	$63,894	$122,352	$411,141	$1,093,184
Return/Period=	+12.4%	+20.4%	+28.5%	+ 46.2%	+ 62.9%

*12-and 18-month returns for 1932 buy signal are cut off on 5/26/33 in order to avoid overlap with the latter signal.

Source: M. Zweig, "The Fed and the Tape," *Barron's*, February 4, 1985, pp. 24, 25, and 27. Reprinted with permission, © Dow Jones & Company, Inc. All rights reserved.

signal was too recent to report results. Using the Dow (rather than Zweig's own market index, which is not readily available) to track the 1/23/85 signal reveals the following percentage change in the Dow over 1, 3, 6, 12, and 18 months: 3%, 9%, 9%, 48%, and 44%.

Urgent Selling

Introduced by James Alphier, a market analyst and portfolio manager, the urgent selling indicator is based on the market's performance over the past 15 trading days.[35] A period of urgent selling occurs when any broad market average closed lower four times more often than it closed higher including at least 12 down days. According to Alphier, after a period of urgent selling two out of three times the next 20% move will be up. Over the 1885–1978 period, 62 instances of urgent selling occurred. The next 20% move was up for 41 of these and down for only 21.

Although interesting, this indicator does have its shortcomings. First, signals occur only about once every year and a half. Thus long periods can pass without a signal. Second, because the signal is judged successful if the market eventually moves up 20% before it moves down by that amount, investors might wait a long time for such a "success." Third, the indicator has not been reexamined on more recent data. Thus it may have worked only over the test period.

The January Indicator

The January indicator is a rather simplistic tool that receives a good bit of attention at the first of each year: A market that rises in January is expected to rise during the year, and vice versa. While conceding its apparently high success rate (24 of 29 correct up market calls over the 1934–1976 period), Madrick and others have pointed out a number of flaws.[36] Because the market generally rises both in January and for the year, the success of the January indicator may easily be overstated. Several other months seem to do about as well. Moreover, an investor who followed a straightforward buy and hold strategy would have a higher valued portfolio (even ignoring transaction costs) over the 1952–1976 period than one who had used the January indicator as a trading signal.

The Advisors' Sentiments Indicator

One of the most intriguing of the new wave of market indicators is that based on the investment analysts themselves. A contrary opinion approach would expect the market to peak when advisor sentiment was most bullish and reach a bottom when sentiment was most bearish. Utilizing an index compiled by Cohen, of Investor's Intelligence Inc., Boland found that over the January 1978–August 1980 period the Dow tended to reach a peak just after investment advisors were most bullish and a bottom just after they become most bearish.[37] Figure 12.4 illustrates

FIGURE 12.4   The Advisors' Sentiments Indicator

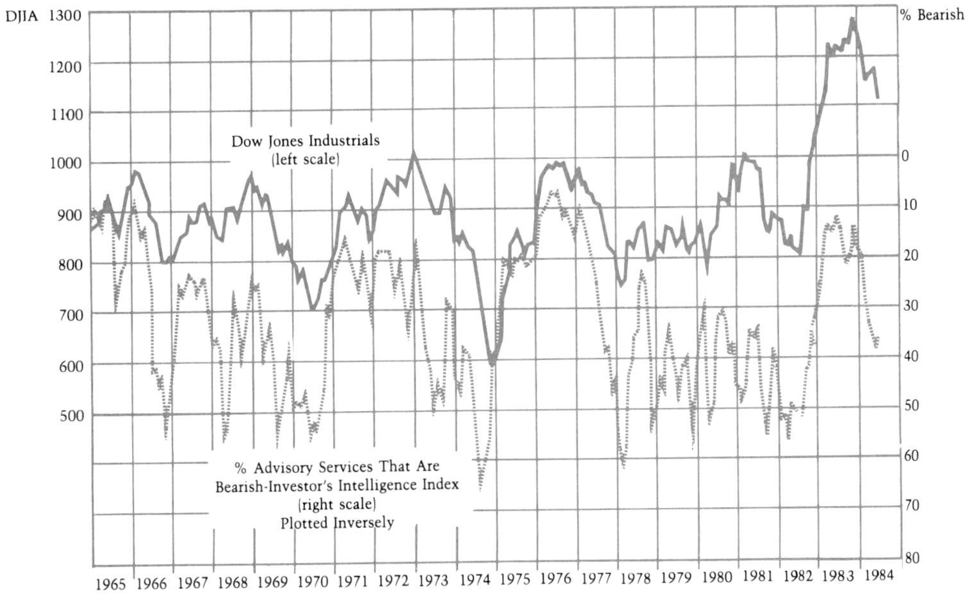

Source: *Investment Strategy Highlights*, Goldman Sachs & Co., June 1984.

the 1963–1984 behavior of the advisors' sentiment index relative to the market. The two series do seem to move together.

Daily Indicators

Most indicators are designed to predict intermediate or long-term market trends. Day-to-day moves are not nearly as interesting to most people because of the high trading costs relative to the typically modest day-to-day moves. Nonetheless, those who trade at little cost (specialists, floor traders, recipients of institutional discounts, etc.) or those who will trade anyway might as well take advantage of any predictable daily price moves. The advance–decline and Monday–Friday price patterns represent two approaches to forecasting such short-term moves.

Monday–Friday and Monthly Price Patterns

Unusual price behavior has been found for Mondays and Fridays. Cross reported that the Standard & Poor's Composite Average rose on 62.0% of the Fridays and on only 39.5% of the Mondays during the 1953–1970 period.[38] These differences were statistically significant. The market was consistently more likely to be up on Friday than on Monday for each of the 18 years of the sample. After a decline on

Friday, the chances of a rise on Monday were only 24%. If Friday had shown an increase, the chances of an increase on Monday were about 50%. The frequent practice of withholding unpleasant economic news until the market's Friday close may account for the phenomenon.

Cross's original study ended with 1970. Subsequent work has refined and extended the analysis. French, who studied the 1953–1977 S&P 500, found positive returns for Tuesday, Wednesday, Thursday, and Friday and negative returns for Monday during each of five five-year subperiods.[39] Similarly, Gibbons and Hess found Monday mean Treasury bill and stock returns low or even negative.[40]

These day-of-the-week price effects suggest that, if no overriding considerations intervene, investors might as well sell on Friday and wait until late in the day on Monday to buy. The Monday after a Friday decline may offer somewhat more attractive buying opportunities.

Ariel finds that returns tend to be highest in the first half of each month.[41] Penman followed this result with a further study of stock market seasonality.[42] He found that the market tended to be particularly strong in the first half of the first month of quarters 2, 3, and 4. This result appears to be due to a tendency for good earnings reports to be issued at that time whereas poor reports are released later.

Whimsical Indicators

Most indicators represent serious attempts to gauge market sentiment. A few, however, may be fun but not really intended to guide investors. Their originators sought only to entertain readers and poke some fun at technical analysts.

Perhaps the best known of these whimsical indicators is based on the hemline. According to this indicator stock prices rise and fall with women's skirt lengths. Hemlines were high in the 1920s and low in the 1930s, seemingly confirming the signal. Another of these indicators is based on who wins the Super Bowl. Whenever a team from the old American Football League wins, the stock market is supposed to go down, whereas a win by a member of the premerger National Football League forecasts a decline for the year. An expansion team win does not give a signal. The record of this indicator since the Super Bowl started is impressive. Only one or two errors have been registered, depending upon which index is used. Finally we have the Billy Martin indicator. Whenever the New York Yankees announce that they have rehired Billy Martin as manager, the market declines. The most recent time for this announcement was October 19, 1987.

Although interesting and perhaps somewhat curious, the records of these whimsical indicators really only point up the difficulty of identifying true indicators of market sentiment. With a large enough search one can always find or devise an indicator that seems to have called the market moves well. Some set of data can almost always be approximated by an appropriate manipulation of another set of data. Such common comovements in the past are, however, no assurance that a true causative relationship is at work. The rooster that always crows before sunrise does not cause the daylight.

Table 12.10 summarizes the additional market indicators discussed in this section of the chapter.

TABLE 12.10 Additional Market Indicators

Advance–Decline Patterns	Past advance–decline patterns tend to persist.
Short-Term Trading Index	High (low) relative volume of advancing stocks is a sell (buy) signal.
Double-Barreled Indicator	A combination of expansive Fed policy and strong market momentum (10-day advance declines over two) is extremely bullish.
Urgent Selling	When at least 12 of the last 15 days have been down, the market is said to be approaching a bottom.
January Indicator	January performance is said to forecast the year but the evidence is unimpressive.
Advisors' Sentiments	Investment advisory sentiment is said to be a contrary indicator.
Monday–Friday Price Pattern	Market tends to rise on Fridays and fall on Mondays.
Monthly Pattern	Market tends to rise in the first half of each month with much of that tendency concentrated in the months of April, July, and October.

ASSET ALLOCATION

Market timers in their most extreme form seek to be totally in the market when it is going up and totally out when it is going down. Others, however, seek a compromise. An increasingly popular timing strategy called asset allocation has recently emerged. The concept has been around for many years but its name and popularity are relatively new. Asset allocators seek to vary their commitment to various types of investments based on the outlook for those investments. For example, an asset allocator may divide his or her portfolio into several components in some way such as the following:

1. Money funds for very low risk and high liquidity

2. Long-term high-grade bonds for moderate risk

3. Junk bonds for speculative appeal in the debt market

4. Blue chip stocks for low risk equity market participation

5. Growth and/or secondary stocks for greater speculation in equities

6. Stock options for short-run speculation in equities

7. Developed real estate for income and inflation protection

8. Undeveloped land for long-term growth

9. Gold, silver, and gemstones for participation in the tangibles market

10. Art, antiques, and other collectibles for alternative tangibles

Few if any asset allocators would seek to be invested in all of these categories but they would plan always to be in several. Most would stick to stocks and bonds.

Regardless of which asset categories are chosen, the asset allocator would vary the percentages invested based on his or her assessment of the investment outlook.

To illustrate, a neutral outlook might imply the following allocations: 20% in money funds, 30% in long bonds, 30% in blue chips, and 20% in growth and secondary stocks. A more conservative stance would imply 50% in money funds, 20% in long bonds, 20% in blue chips, and 10% in growth and secondary stocks. An extremely bearish outlook might imply 80% in money funds and 20% in gold. Alternatively, a more aggressive strategy would move toward greater percentages in growth stocks, secondary stocks, and options.

The goal of the asset allocators is to hedge risks without having to move totally in or out of the market. In this way, they hope to derive some profit from whatever the market does without leaving themselves too vulnerable to an adverse move.

SUMMARY AND CONCLUSIONS

The evidence reveals an emotional side to the market. Many efforts to identify market tops and bottoms have been proposed but none contain a magic formula. The distribution of percentage declines from previous peaks appears to be approximately random. The market PE ratio is almost useless in isolation but, when PE ratios are low relative to their past relationship to interest and inflation rates, a market rise may be likely. Similarly, when PEs are high relative to their past relationship to interest rates, a fall seems probable. Stocks generally rise early in a recession and move sideways (no trend) during most of the recovery period. The election-year cycle provides an interesting approach to market timing. Official pronouncements, discount rate changes, stock repurchases, and Dow Theory may occasionally be helpful. A large number of analysts sell newsletters that attempt to forecast market trends (and make money for the analysts). Some have reasonably accurate records.

Technical market indicators dealt with in this chapter include short interest, odd lot, specialists' short selling, mutual fund cash positions, Barron's Confidence Index, and the Treasury bill rate. My own study found four of these to be reasonably reliable in a multiple regression context: specialists' short selling, mutual fund cash position, Barron's Confidence Index, and the Treasury bill rate. Studies by Daigler and Fielitz and by Van Landingham, however, failed to establish the likelihood of generating after-commission trading profits from timing signals derived from daily market indicators. Moreover, my more recent joint study with Schneeweis found the market to be a better predictor of the indicators than vice versa. Of the indicators not considered in the Branch study, the advisors' sentiments index appeared most promising. In conclusion, the market's emotional volatility seems to be very difficult but perhaps not impossible to predict. Clearly this area needs much more study.

REVIEW QUESTIONS

1. Does the stock market overreact? Explain why or why not. What does the October 19, 1987, crash imply about market efficiency and the market's propensity to overreact?

2. Describe and discuss the relevance of the market's major contractions since 1960. Do any patterns emerge? Why or why not? What is the relevance of the market's patterns or lack of patterns?

3. Discuss the usefulness of market average PE ratios in forecasting the market's direction. What has been the market's average PE? How much has the PE varied from this average over time?

4. What is the Gray approach? On what propositions is it based? What is the evidence on its value? How reliable is that evidence? How should the approach be tested further?

5. How does the market generally perform during recessions? What are the implications for investors?

6. Discuss the election-year cycle. Do the economy and the market follow an election-related cycle? If so, why? What are the investment implications?

7. Assess the forecasting value of official pronouncements, discount rate changes, and corporate stock repurchases. How often are these types of signals generated?

8. What common disadvantages do investment managers, stock analysts, and market forecasters have? How are individual investors able to overcome these disadvantages? How likely are they to do so?

9. Discuss the relevance of short interest and odd-lot behavior in market timing. What is the theory and what is the evidence?

10. Identify the hypothesized relationships for the following indicators: specialists' short selling, mutual fund cash, secondary distributions, and the Barron's Confidence Index.

11. Summarize and compare the Branch, Daigler–Fielitz, Van Landingham and Branch–Schneeweis studies. What are the implications for investors?

12. Identify the hypothesized relationships for the following indicators: short-term trading, urgent selling, January, advisors' sentiments, advance–decline, and Monday–Friday.

REVIEW PROBLEMS

1. Refer to quarterly Dow Jones Industrial Averages in Table 12A.3 in the Appendix to this chapter. Test the results of the following strategies: 1. Buy and hold over entire period with dividends reinvested annually; 2. Buy in 1971 and sell the following year and then repurchase the following year and so on; 3. Start 1971 invested and then use a filter rule to decide when to trade. Sell whenever the market rises by 10%. Repurchase whenever it rises by 10%. Assume trades cost 3% in commissions. Assume that funds not invested in the market earn 5%.

2. Compute the gamma factor for the following circumstance: Market PE and growth rate are 10% and 5%, respectively; Stock A has a PE and current growth rate of 15% and 14%; Stock B has a PE and current growth rate of 30% and 25% respectively.

3. Using the data in Problem 2, recompute the gamma factors for stocks A and B if the market PE falls to 8. Now suppose their prices adjust to the fall in the market PE. How much must their prices decline if their gamma factors fall by the same percentage amount as the market average's PE?

4. Refer to Table 12.1. Compute the percentage change in the index for each event from the value one day prior to the news event to the event day, next day, three days later, and 21 days later. Compute the averages of each of these percentage changes. What would be the results for a strategy of selling on the day of the news and buying back 21 days later? What would be the results if you bought on the day of the event and sold 21 days later? Assume that trades incurred a 3% commission charge.

5. Continue with the question in Problem 1. Test the results for a trading rule of buying when the PE on the Dow is below 9 and selling when it is above 18. Repeat the test using below 12 as a buy and above 16 as a sell.

6. Show the mathematical equivalence between Gray's equation and the PE equation discussed in Chapters 4, 7, and 9.

7. To apply the Rule of 20 assume a sell signal is given when the sum of the inflation rate and market PE exceed 20 by more than 1 whereas a buy signal occurs when the sum is below 20 by more than 1. For inflation rates of 3%, 5%, 7%, 9%, and 12%, what PEs would generate buy and sell signals? For PEs of 6, 9, 12, 15, and 18, what levels of inflation would lead to buy or sell signals?

8. Repeat Problem 7 but this time use 18.5 as the average sum for the inflation rate and the market PE. Now use deviations from the average of 1.5 and 2 for the signals. What corresponding levels of PE and inflation would result in buy and sell signals for the circumstances of Problem 7?

9. Refer to Table 12A.2 in the appendix. Identify the buy and sell signals that Dow Theory gave. Compare a buy and hold with a Dow Theory based trading strategy. Assume commissions of 3%, dividends accrue at the rate of 3%, and uninvested sums earn 5%.

10. Compute both the odd-lot–short ratio and the TOLSR for the following information: 10-day totals, odd-lot sales of 1.3 million; odd-lot purchases of 1.6 million; odd-lot–short sales of .07 million. Now recompute the ratios for odd-lot short sales of .24 million.

11. Compute the Barron's Confidence Index for the following values for high-grade and average-grade bond rates: 5.67%, 6.01%; 7.89%, 8.85%; 9.50%, 11.78%; and 10.34%, 13.89%.

REVIEW PROJECTS

1. Identify five stocks that traditionally have high PEs and are touted for their growth prospects. Track the performances of these stocks over the most recent major up and down moves in the market. Compare their performances with those of market averages.

2. Identify five major news events occurring over the past year or two. Track the market's reaction for 30 days after each event. Write a report.

3. Track the performances of a list of major stocks over the most recent market slide and recovery. (See Table 12.4 for an example.) Describe the result.

4. Plot market PE ratios (e.g., S&P 500) and AAA bond rates monthly for the past five years. Do you see any useful trading rules? Recommend a trading strategy. Now go back another five years and apply it. Would you have made money? Discuss your results in a report.

5. Plot the performance of the stock market relative to the unemployment rate, inflation rate, and prime rate for the past two business cycles. Do you see any exploitable patterns? Formulate a trading strategy and test it over two other business cycles. Would it have made money? Describe your experience in a report.

6. Plot market performance around the time of the most recent presidential election. Is any pattern apparent? Formulate a trading rule and apply it to a prior presidential election period. Would you have made money? Describe your results in a report.

7. Obtain trial subscriptions to five market timing letters and compare each forecast with subsequent performance. Identify the letters with the best and the worst records for the period you studied. Get a friend to obtain a second trial subscription to these two letters and again compare their performance with the market. Write a report.

8. Select five market indicators that can be computed from the data in *Barron's* Market Laboratory section. Compute the indicators weekly for 12 weeks and compare their signals with actual market performance. Choose the two with the best and the two with the worst records and follow them for another twelve weeks. Write a report.

9. Track the Monday–Friday pattern for the past year on both the NYSE and the AMEX. Write a report.

NOTES

1. B. Malkiel, "Equity Yields, Growth, and the Structure of Share Prices," *American Economic Review*, December 1965, 1004–1031.

2. K. Shiller, "The Use of Volatility Measures in Assessing Market Efficiency," *Journal of Finance*, May 1981, 291–303; T. Marsh and R. Merton, "Dividend Behavior for the Aggregate Stock Market," *Journal of Business*, January 1987, 1–40.

3. N. Mankiw, D. Romer, and M. Shapiro, "An Unbiased Reexamination of Stock Market Volatility," *Journal of Finance*, July 1985, 677–689; W. De Bondt and R. Thaler, "Does the Stock Market Overreact?" *Journal of Finance*, July 1986, 793–808.

4. R. Baylis and S. Bhirud, "Growth Stock Analysis: A New Approach," *Financial Analysts Journal*, July/August 1973, 63–72.

5. J. Baesel, G. Shows, and E. Thorp, "Can Joe Granville Time the Market?" *The Journal of Portfolio Management*, Spring 1982, 5–9.

6. J. Treynor and K. Mazuy, "Can Mutual Funds Outguess the Market?" *Harvard Business Review*, July/August 1966, 131–136; F. Fabozzi and J. Francis, "Mutual Funds' Systematic Risk for Bull and Bear Markets," *Journal of Finance*, December 1979, 1243–1250; E. Theodore and J. Cheney, "Are Mutual Funds Market Timers?" *Journal of Portfolio Management*, Winter 1982, 35–42.

7. J. Holmes, "100 Years of Common Stock Investing," *Financial Analysts Journal*, November/December 1974, 38–44.

8. W. Gray, "The Application of Discount Rates in Forecasting; Returns for Stocks and Bonds," *Financial Analysts Journal*, May/June 1974, 53–61; W. Gray, "Developing a Long-Term Outlook for the U.S. Economy and Stock Market," *Financial Analysts Journal*, July/August 1979, 29–39.

9. S. Kichen, "The Rule of 20," *Forbes*, June 20, 1983, 31.

10. J. Cullity, "Stock Price Recoveries Following Recessions: A Second Look," *Financial Analysts Journal*, January/February 1974, 45–58.

11. A. Malabre, "Following the Script: Gain in Share Prices in Midst of Recession Adheres to Pattern," *The Wall Street Journal*, April 18, 1975, p. 1; A. Malabre, "Shifting Stocks: Today's Zigzag Market Is Typical of Periods of Business Expansion," *The Wall Street Journal*, September 29, 1975, p. 1; A. Malabre, "Just as the Economy May Be Recovering, Share Prices Wobble," *The Wall Street Journal*, February 3, 1981, pp. 1, 22.

12. R. Piccini, "Stock Market Behavior Around Business Cycle Peaks," *Financial Analysts Journal*, July/August 1980, 55–57.

13. C. Rolo, "Anticipating Major Ups and Downs," *Money*, June 1982, 44–50.

14. F. Allvine and D. O'Neill, "Stock Market Returns and the Presidential Election Cycle," *Financial Analysts Journal*, September/October 1980, 47–56; V. Vartan, "Stocks in an Election Year," *The New York Times*, December 29, 1983, pp. D1, D5.

15. W. Riley and W. Laksetich, "The Market Prefers Republicans: Myth or Reality?" *Journal of Financial and Quantitative Analysis*, September 1980, 541–560.

16. Ibid., 557.

17. H. Baker, P. Gallagher, and K. Morgan, "Management's View of Stock Repurchase Programs," *Journal of Financial Research*, Fall 1981, 233–248; A. Merjos, "Corporations Have Been Canny Buyers of Their Own Stock," *Barron's*, May 28, 1973, pp. 9, 15; A. Merjos, "Good on the Rebound: Company Stock Buy-Backs Work Only in Rising Markets," *Barron's*, March 15, 1982, 28–30.

18. D. Glickstein and R. Wubbels, "Dow Theory Is Alive and Well!" *Journal of Portfolio Management*, Spring 1983, 28–35.

19. J. Connelly, "Seven Forecasters With Foresight," *Money*, June 1982, 54–58.

20. R. Cole, "Tracking the Short Interest Reports," *The New York Times*, March 28, 1982, p. 14F; C. Comer, "Bullish Indicator, The Short Interest Is Signaling Higher Share Prices," *Barron's*, November 21, 1983, p. 26; R. Russell, "Bearish is Bullish, Analyzing the Stunning Series of Short Interest Ratios," *Barron's*, December 26, 1983, p. 34; T. Kerrigan, "Behavior of the Short Interest Ratio," *Financial Analysts Journal*, November/December 1974, 4549.

21. D. Raihall and J. Jepson, "The Application of Odd Lot Buy Singles to Dividend Stocks," *Mississippi Valley Journal of Business and Economics*, Winter 1972-73, 19–30.

22. B. Gup, "A Note on Stock Market Indicators and Pricing," *Journal of Financial and Quantitative Analysis*, September 1973, 673–682.

23. M. Zweig, "Stalking the Bear: A New Odd Lot Indicator Has Just Turned Bullish," *Barron's*, July 3, 1973, 11.

24. W. Kent, *The Smart Money* (Garden City, N.Y.: Doubleday, 1972).

25. F. Reilly and D. Whitford, "A Test of the Specialists' Short Sale Ratio," *Journal of Portfolio Management*, Winter 1982, 12–19.

26. *Investment Manager's Review* (Wirtheim and Company, March 23, 1981), 19.

27. D. Ranson and W. Shipman, "Institutional Buying Power and the Stock Market," *Financial Analysts Journal*, September/October 1981, 62–69.

28. J. Cheney and T. Veit, "Evidence of Shifts in Portfolio Asset Composition as a Market Timing Tool," *Financial Review*, February 1983, 56–78.

29. J. Ring, "Confidence Index, It Works Better at Tops than at Bottoms," *Barron's*, March 25, 1974, p. 11.

30. B. Branch, "The Predictive Power of Market Indicators," *Journal of Financial and Quantitative Analysis*, June 1976, 269–286.

31. R. Daigler and B. Fielitz, "A Multiple Discriminant Analysis of Technical Indicators on the New York Stock Exchange," *Journal of Financial Research*, Fall 1981, 169–182; M. Van Landingham, "The Day Trader: Some Additional Evidence," *Journal of Financial and Quantitative Analysis*, June 1980, 341–356.

32. B. Branch and T. Schneeweis, "Market Movements and Technical Market Indicators," *Mid-Atlantic Journal of Business*, Summer 1986, 31–41.

33. G. Philippatos and D. Nawrocki, "The Information Inaccuracy of Stock Market Forecasts: Some New Evidence of Dependence on the New York Stock Exchange," *Journal of Financial and Quantitative Analysis*, June 1973, 443–458.

34. D. Turov, "Buy Signal? A New Technical Indicator Is Flashing One," *Barron's*, December 9, 1974, p. 11.

35. J. Alphier, "Urgent Selling," *Barron's*, February 26, 1979, 11–22.

36. J. Madrick, "Shooting Holes in the January Indicator," *Business Week*, January 31, 1977, 71; M. Hulbert, "The January Indicator: Case Against It Still Stands," *American Association of Individual Investors Journal*, January 1987, 20–22.

37. J. Boland, "Stock Market Seers? Investment Advisors Are Usually Wrong at Turning Points," *Barron's*, September 1, 1980, 11–14.

38. F. Cross, "The Behavior of Stock Prices on Fridays and Mondays," *Financial Analysts Journal*, November/December 1973, 67–69; A. Merrill, *The Behavior of Prices on Wall Street* (Chautauqua, N.Y., Analysis Press, 1966); B. Branch, "Explaining Nonrandom Behavior of Stock Prices," *Financial Analysts Journal*, March/April 1974, 10.

39. K. French, "Stock Returns and the Weekend Effect," *Journal of Financial Economics*, March 1980, 55–70; M. Smirlock and L. Starks, "Day-of-the-Week and Intraday Effects in Stock Returns," *Journal of Financial Economics*, September 1986, 197–210.

40. M. Gibbons and P. Hess, "Day of the Week Effects and Asset Returns," *Journal of Business*, October 1981, 579–596.

41. R. Ariel, "A Monthly Effect in Stock Returns," *Journal of Financial Economics*, March 1987, 161–174.

42. S. Penman, "The Distribution of Earnings News over Time and Seasonalities in Aggregate Stock Returns," *Journal of Financial Economics*, June 1987, 199–228.

APPENDIX. STOCK TABLES

TABLE 12A.1   Standard & Poor's 500 Stock Composite Index (1941–1943 = 10): Annual Data

	DAILY CLOSING PRICES			EARNS. PER SHARE $	DIVS. PER SHARE $	BOOK VALUE* PER SHARE $	PE RATIO Last	DIVIDEND YIELD		
Year	High	Low	Last					High	Low	Last
1987	336.77	223.92	247.08	15.84	8.81	N.A.	15.6	3.9	2.6	3.6
1986	254.00	203.49	242.17	16.24	8.40	124.53	14.9	4.2	3.8	4.0
1985	212.02	163.68	211.28	16.30	8.07	125.89	13.0	4.9	3.8	4.3
1984	170.41	147.62	167.24	16.64	7.53	123.28	9.6	4.8	4.4	4.5
1983	172.65	138.34	164.93	14.07	7.09	130.00	11.7	5.1	4.1	4.3
1982	143.10	103.75	140.64	12.65	6.87	123.00	11.1	6.2	4.8	4.9
1981	138.10	112.80	122.60	15.24	6.63	117.20	8.1	5.8	4.7	5.4
1980	140.30	98.22	135.80	14.86	6.16	108.30	9.2	6.3	4.5	4.7
1979	111.30	96.13	107.90	14.86	5.65	18.71	7.3	5.9	5.2	5.6
1978	107.00	86.90	96.11	12.33	5.07	89.72	7.8	5.7	9.9	5.1
1977	107.00	90.71	95.10	10.89	4.69	82.21	8.7	5.2	3.9	5.1
1976	107.80	90.90	107.50	9.91	4.05	72.26	10.8	4.2	3.6	3.9
1975	95.61	70.04	90.19	7.96	3.08	70.84	11.3	5.3	3.9	4.1
1974	99.80	62.28	69.94	9.25	3.66	67.81	7.6	5.8	3.5	5.3
1973	120.24	92.16	97.55	8.16	3.38	62.84	12.0	3.7	2.6	3.4
1972	119.12	101.67	118.05	6.42	3.15	58.34	18.5	2.6	3.1	2.7
1971	104.77	90.16	102.09	5.70	3.07	55.28	17.9	2.9	3.4	3.0
1970	93.46	69.29	92.15	5.13	3.14	52.65	18.0	3.4	4.5	3.4
1969	106.16	89.20	92.06	5.78	3.16	51.70	15.9	3.0	3.5	3.4
1968	108.37	87.72	103.86	5.76	3.07	50.21	18.0	2.8	3.5	3.4
1967	97.59	80.38	96.47	5.33	2.92	47.78	18.1	3.0	3.6	3.0
1966	94.06	73.20	80.33	5.55	2.87	45.51	14.5	3.1	3.9	3.6
1965	92.63	81.60	92.43	5.19	2.72	43.50	17.8	2.9	3.3	2.9
1964	86.28	75.43	84.75	4.55	2.50	40.23	18.6	2.9	3.3	2.9
1963	75.02	62.69	75.02	4.02	2.28	38.17	18.7	3.0	3.6	3.0
1962	71.13	52.32	63.10	3.67	2.13	36.37	17.2	3.0	4.1	3.4
1961	72.64	57.57	71.55	3.19	2.02	34.87	22.4	2.8	3.5	2.8
1960	60.39	52.30	58.11	3.27	1.95	33.74	17.8	3.2	3.7	3.4
1959	60.71	53.58	59.89	3.39	1.84	32.26	17.7	3.0	3.4	3.1
1958	55.21	40.33	55.21	2.89	1.75	30.65	19.1	3.2	4.3	3.2
1957	49.13	38.98	39.99	3.37	1.79	29.44	11.9	3.6	4.6	4.5
1956	49.74	43.11	46.67	3.41	1.74	26.53	13.7	3.5	4.0	3.7
1955	46.41	34.58	45.48	3.62	1.64	25.09	12.6	3.5	4.7	3.6
1954	35.98	24.80	35.98	2.77	1.54	22.01	13.0	4.3	6.2	4.3
1953	26.66	22.71	24.81	2.51	1.45	20.76	9.9	5.4	6.4	5.8
1952	26.59	23.09	26.57	2.40	1.41	20.15	11.1	5.3	6.1	5.3
1951	23.85	20.69	23.77	2.44	1.41	18.66	9.7	5.9	6.8	5.9
1950	20.43	16.65	20.41	2.84	1.47	16.77	7.2	7.2	8.8	7.2
1949	16.79	13.55	16.76	2.32	1.14	15.17	7.2	6.8	8.4	6.8
1948	17.06	13.84	15.20	2.29	0.93	14.53	6.6	5.5	6.7	6.1
1947	16.20	13.71	15.30	1.61	0.84	12.49	9.5	5.2	6.1	5.5

*S&P 400   Source: Reprinted by permission of Standard & Poor's Corporation.

TABLE 12A.2 Yearly Highs and Lows of Dow Jones Averages

	INDUSTRIALS		TRANSPORTATION		UTILITIES	
	High	Low	High	Low	High	Low
1987	2722.42	1738.74	1101.16	660.00	209.82	160.98
1986	1955.57	1502.29	866.74	686.97	219.15	169.47
1985	1553.10	1184.16	723.31	553.03	174.96	146.54
1984	1286.64	1086.90	612.63	444.03	149.93	122.25
1983	1284.65	1027.04	590.04	434.24	140.08	119.51
1982	1070.55	776.92	455.69	292.12	122.83	103.22
1981	1029.05	824.01	447.38	335.48	117.81	101.28
1980	1000.17	759.13	381.08	233.69	117.34	96.05
1979	897.61	796.67	271.77	205.78	109.78	98.24
1978	907.74	742.12	261.49	199.31	110.98	96.35
1977	899.75	800.85	264.64	199.60	118.67	104.97
1976	1014.79	858.71	237.03	175.69	108.67	84.52
1975	881.81	633.04	174.57	146.47	87.07	72.02
1974	891.66	577.60	202.45	125.93	95.09	57.95
1973	1051.70	788.31	228.10	151.97	120.72	84.42
1972	1036.27	889.15	275.71	212.24	124.14	105.05
1971	950.82	797.97	248.33	169.70	128.39	108.03
1970*	842.00	631.16	183.31	116.69	121.84	95.86
1969	968.85	769.93	279.88	169.03	139.95	106.31
1968	985.21	825.13	279.48	214.58	141.30	119.79
1967	943.08	786.41	274.49	205.16	140.43	120.97
1966	995.15	744.32	271.72	184.34	152.39	118.96
1965	969.28	840.59	249.55	187.29	163.32	149.84
1964	891.71	766.08	224.91	178.81	155.71	137.30
1963	767.21	646.79	179.46	142.03	144.37	129.19
1962	726.01	535.76	149.83	114.86	130.85	103.11
1961	734.91	610.25	152.92	131.06	135.90	99.75
1960	685.47	566.05	160.43	123.37	100.07	85.02
1959	679.36	574.46	173.56	146.65	94.70	85.05
1958	583.65	436.89	157.91	99.89	91.00	68.94
1957	520.77	419.79	157.67	95.67	74.61	62.10
1956	521.05	462.35	181.23	150.44	71.17	63.03
1955	488.40	388.20	167.83	137.84	66.68	61.39
1954	404.39	279.87	146.23	94.84	62.47	52.22
1953	293.79	255.49	122.21	90.56	53.88	47.87
1952	292.00	256.35	112.53	82.03	52.64	47.53
1951	276.37	238.99	90.08	72.39	47.22	41.47
1950	235.47	196.81	77.89	51.24	44.26	37.40
1949	200.52	161.60	54.29	41.03	41.31	33.36
1948	193.16	165.39	64.95	48.13	36.04	31.65
1947	186.85	163.21	53.42	41.16	37.55	32.28
1946	212.50	163.12	68.31	44.69	43.74	33.20
1945	195.82	151.35	64.89	47.03	39.15	26.15
1944	152.53	134.22	48.40	33.45	26.37	21.74
1943	145.82	119.26	38.30	27.59	22.30	14.69

TABLE 12A.2 Continued

	INDUSTRIALS		TRANSPORTATION		UTILITIES	
	High	Low	High	Low	High	Low
1942	119.71	92.92	29.28	23.31	14.94	10.58
1941	133.59	106.34	30.88	24.25	20.65	13.51
1940	152.80	111.84	32.67	22.14	26.45	18.03
1939	155.92	121.44	35.90	24.14	27.10	20.71
1938**	158.41	98.95	33.98	19.00	25.19	15.14
1937	194.40	113.64	64.46	28.91	37.54	19.65
1936	184.90	143.11	59.89	40.66	36.08	28.63
1935	148.44	96.71	41.84	27.31	29.78	14.46
1934	110.74	85.51	52.97	33.19	31.03	16.83
1933	108.67	50.16	56.53	23.43	37.73	19.33
1932	88.78	41.22	41.30	13.23	36.11	16.53
1931	194.36	73.79	111.58	31.42	73.40	30.55
1930	294.07	157.51	157.94	91.65	108.62	55.14
1929	381.17	198.69	189.11	128.07	144.61	64.72
1928***	300.00	191.33	152.70	132.60	—	—
1927	202.40	152.73	144.82	119.29	—	—
1926	166.64	135.20	123.33	102.41	—	—
1925	159.39	115.00	112.93	92.98	—	—

    * Jan. 2, 1970 Transportation Average replaced Railroad Average.
   ** From June 2, 1938, the Utility Average was based on 15 stocks instead of 20 as formerly.
 *** On March 7, 1928, the list of rails was increased to 20 from 12.

TABLE 12A.3 Dow Jones Industrial Average: Earnings, P/E, and Quarterly Dividends

		DOW JONES INDUSTRIAL AVERAGE				
	Quarter Ended	Clos. Avg.	Qtrly Earns	12-Mth. Earns	P/E Ratio	Qtrly Divs.
1988	Mar. 31	1988.06	47.03	144.45	13.8	18.52
1987	Dec. 31	1938.83	16.54	133.05	14.6	17.67
	Sept. 30	2596.28	44.77	137.99	18.8	18.05
	June 30	2418.53	36.11	126.23	19.2	18.11
	Mar. 31	2304.69	35.63	126.49	18.2	17.37
1986	Dec. 31	1895.15	21.48	115.59	16.4	17.01
	Sept. 30	1767.58	33.01	118.80	14.9	16.79
	June 30	1892.72	36.37	103.39	18.3	16.94
	Mar. 31	1818.61	24.73	96.43	18.9	16.22
						67.04
1985	Dec. 31	1546.67	24.69	96.11	16.1	17.19
	Sept. 30	1328.63	17.60	90.78	14.6	15.02
	June 28	1335.46	29.41	102.26	13.1	14.95
	Mar. 29	1266.78	24.41	107.87	11.7	14.87
						62.03
1984	Dec. 31	1211.57	19.36	113.58	10.7	16.99
	Sept. 28	1206.71	29.08	108.11	11.2	14.72
	June 29	1132.40	35.02	102.07	11.1	14.98
	Mar. 30	1164.89	30.12	87.38	13.3	19.94
						60.63

TABLE 12A.3 Continued

	Quarter Ended	Clos. Avg.	Qtrly Earns	12-Mth. Earns	P/E Ratio	Qtrly Divs.
1983	Dec. 30	1258.64	13.89	72.45	17.4	14.77
	Sept. 30	1233.13	23.04	56.12	30.0	13.98
	June 30	1221.96	20.33	11.59	105.4	13.70
	Mar. 31	1130.03	15.19	9.52	118.7	13.88
			72.45			56.33
1982	Dec. 31	1046.54	d2.44	9.14	114.4	13.03
	Sept. 30	896.25	d21.49	35.15	25.5	13.44
	June 30	811.93	18.26	79.90	11.2	13.75
	Mar. 31	822.77	14.82	97.13	8.5	13.92
			9.15			54.14
1981	Dec. 31	875.00	23.56	113.71	6.9	13.73
	Sept. 30	849.98	23.26	123.32	6.9	13.73
	June 30	976.88	35.49	128.91	7.6	14.19
	Mar. 31	1003.87	31.40	123.60	8.1	13.86
			113.71			56.22
1980	Dec. 31	963.99	33.17	121.86	7.9	14.40
	Sept. 30	932.42	28.85	111.58	8.4	13.53
	June 30	867.92	30.18	116.40	7.5	13.20
	Mar. 31	785.75	29.66	120.77	6.5	13.23
			121.86			54.36
1979	Dec. 31	838.74	22.89	124.46	6.7	13.87
	Sept. 28	878.67	33.67	136.26	6.4	12.51
	June 29	841.98	34.55	128.99	6.5	12.49
	Mar. 30	862.18	33.35	124.10	6.9	12.11
			124.46			50.98
1978	Dec. 29	805.01	34.69	112.79	7.1	14.34
	Sept. 29	865.82	26.40	101.59	8.5	11.41
	June 30	818.95	29.66	91.37	9.0	11.62
	Mar. 31	757.36	22.04	89.23	8.5	11.15
			112.79			48.52
1977	Dec. 30	831.17	23.49	89.10	9.3	13.24
	Sept. 30	847.11	16.18	89.86	9.4	10.73
	June 30	916.30	27.52	97.18	9.4	11.41
	Mar. 31	919.13	21.91	95.51	9.6	10.46
			89.10			45.84
1976	Dec. 31	1004.65	24.25	96.72	10.4	12.13
	Sept. 30	990.19	23.50	95.81	10.3	9.85
	June 30	1002.78	25.85	90.68	11.1	10.19
	Mar. 31	999.45	23.12	81.87	12.2	9.23
			96.72			41.40
1975	Dec. 31	852.41	23.34	75.66	11.3	9.63
	Sept. 30	793.88	18.37	75.47	10.5	9.05
	June 30	878.99	17.04	83.83	10.5	8.97
	Mar. 31	768.15	16.91	93.47	8.2	9.81
			75.66			37.46

TABLE 12A.3 Continued

	Quarter Ended	Clos. Avg.	Qtrly Earns	12-Mth. Earns	P/E Ratio	Qtrly Divs.
1974	Dec. 31	616.24	23.15	99.04	6.2	10.45
	Sept. 30	607.87	26.73	99.73	6.1	9.43
	June 28	802.41	26.68	93.26	8.6	8.87
	Mar. 29	846.68	22.48	89.46	9.5	8.97
			99.04			37.72
1973	Dec. 31	850.86	23.84	86.17	9.9	10.62
	Sept. 28	947.10	20.26	82.09	11.5	8.36
	June 29	891.71	22.88	77.56	11.5	8.27
	Mar. 30	951.01	19.19	71.98	13.2	8.08
			86.17			35.33
1972	Dec. 29	1020.02	19.76	67.11	15.2	8.99
	Sept. 29	953.27	15.73	62.15	15.3	7.76
	June 30	929.03	17.30	58.87	15.8	7.87
	Mar. 30	940.70	14.32	56.76	16.6	7.65
			67.11			32.27
1971	Dec. 31	890.20	14.80	55.09	16.2	7.85
	Sept. 30	887.19	12.45	53.43	16.6	7.51
	June 30	891.14	15.19	53.45	16.7	7.80
	Mar. 31	904.37	12.65	52.36	17.3	7.70
			55.09			30.86

Timing Individual Security Trades

13

Investment timing involves two important processes: (1) anticipating market trends and (2) formulating reliable expectations for price changes relative to those trends. This chapter explores the latter topic (generalizable factors that may affect individual security prices).

We first consider the theoretical arguments and empirical evidence on technical analysis as practiced by the chart readers. Then a variety of specialized price dependencies (tendencies for prices to behave in a particular fashion) are discussed. These specialized dependencies include the impact of block trades, secondary distributions, intraday dependencies, tax loss trading, announcements of earnings and dividend changes, announcements in *The Wall Street Journal*, brokers' sell recommendations, bond rating changes, pollution disclosures, corporate crime disclosures, "Wall Street Week" recommendations, trading suspensions, option expirations, option listings, insider trading reports, splits, reverse splits, stock dividends, tender offers, mergers, liquidations, stock repurchases, rights offerings, equity sales, forced conversion, debt for equity exchanges, divestitures, voluntary spin-offs, and additions and deletions to the S&P 500 Index. Finally, we examine the timing issues related to cross-correlations, volume-effects, brokerage share prices, dividend reinvestment plans, dollar averaging and a trading strategy called "cut your profits and let your losses run."

TECHNICAL ANALYSIS

Technical analysts seek to time their stock trades by assessing the psychological state of the market. Technical market indicators (which we explored in Chapter 12) are used to take the emotional temperature of the overall market. A second type of tool, charts, is used to assess the market's mood toward specific stocks. Although controversial, chart reading is still widely practiced. Accordingly, no treatment of investment timing would be complete without some discussion of the technical approach.

Types of Charts

Chartists utilize two basic types of charts. The bar chart is used to show the daily price range, closing price, and daily volume. The basic format of the bar chart may be supplemented with a moving average line (for example, the average stock price for the past 50 days) as well a relative strength line. The relative strength line plots the ratio of the stock's price to that of the S&P 500 average.

Point and figure charts are the second way that chartists diagram stock movements. These charts have no time dimension. The vertical axis measures the stock price. To construct the chart a threshold level of price movement is determined. One point (dollar per share) is the typical threshold. Every time the stock of interest moves past a whole number level, a mark is recorded. If the move is upward, an X is entered; a downward move calls for an O. As the price rises Xs are stacked one on top of another. When the price direction changes, an O is entered in the next column. Additional Os are added below as the stock price falls. Point and figure charts provide a compact presentation of price movements. A typical point and figure chart is shown in Figure 13.1a, a typical bar chart in Figure 13.1b.

Major Premises of the Chartist's Approach

Chart readers may illustrate price/volume patterns with either bar or point and figure charts. These patterns are said to reveal future demand and supply relations by reflecting evolving market psychology. Much of chartism is based upon one very basic premise: stock prices follow trends. That is, chartists believe that stock prices often behave as if they have a degree of momentum. This momentum is expected to carry the price along in its current direction until some new force causes a change in direction.

A second tenet of chartists is the belief that volume goes with the trend. Thus in a major uptrend volume will increase as the price rises and decrease when the price declines. In a major downtrend, in contrast, volume will increase as the price declines and increase when the price rises.

The third major premise of the chartist's approach hypothesizes the existence of resistance and support levels. A resistance level emerges as a significant number of investors look to get out when a certain price level is reached. The number of shares offered is thought to increase dramatically as such a resistance level is

FIGURE 13.1a Typical Point and Figure Chart

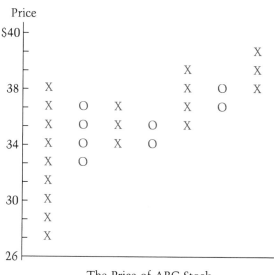

The Price of ABC Stock

approached. Similarly, a support price may exist at about the level that the most recent rise began. Those who missed the first move may be waiting for a second chance to buy if the stock drops back down to that level.

Chartists' Interpretations of Price Patterns

Technical analysts seek to identify favorable buying and selling opportunities from repeating price patterns. These patterns include chart formations such as triangles, coils, rectangles, flags, pennants, gaps, line-and-saucer formations, and V-formations. Perhaps the best known pattern is the *head and shoulders formation*, shown in Figure 13.2. It is a classic pattern of chartists. Lerro and Swayne have explained this pattern as follows:

> It has a remarkable resemblance to the human form. A closer inspection of the configuration reveals the following stages of development:
> *Left Shoulder.* The shoulder builds up as a result of a strong rally, accompanied by significant volume. Thereafter, a profit-taking reaction occurs which forms the right leg. Volume is noticeably reduced on the downward slope.
> *Head.* Rising prices and increased volume initiate the left leg of the head pattern followed by a contraction, on reduced volume, which extends to the neckline. Observe that the head extends well above the left shoulder.
> *Right Shoulder.* Another price rally produces the left leg of this shoulder and finally the rally breaks up and the prices slide downward. Volume action is quite different than in the left shoulder and head formation. More often than not, volume is decidedly smaller than under the left shoulder and head. The right

FIGURE 13.1b Typical Bar Chart

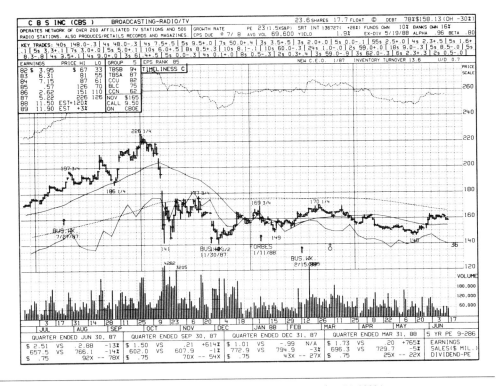

Source: Courtesy Daily Graphs and Long Term Values, P.O. Box 24933, Los Angeles, CA 90024.

shoulder tends to be equal in height with the left shoulder; it is always well below the head.

The unwary trader who unfortunately bought late usually has an opportunity to redeem himself when a brief minor rally pulls price back to the neckline. There is no guarantee that such an event will always occur, but, as a rule, a continued downtrend is normally followed by a slight recovery. Once the throw back is completed, prices tend to head down into a strong retreat. High volume is apparent in this latter phase representing an obvious reversal pattern."[1]

According to the chartists, this pattern forecasts a major decline. The inverted head and shoulders formation is said to give a buy signal. Numerous books discuss many such configurations with more published every year.

Chart Reading and Market Efficiency

The reader should recall the weak form of the efficient market hypothesis from Chapter 4. That hypothesis implies that past market behavior contains no useful investment timing information. That is, investors' efforts to find hidden values should, according to efficient market adherents, cause stock prices to reflect all

Investments in Perspective

Many investors follow the stock market by watching the ticker tape. They may or may not believe in the value of charting but they do believe that the price action of a stock may be telling an interesting story. An article from *The Wall Street Journal* illustrates how some tape watchers operate.

'Tape Watchers' Offer Some Tips For Stock Picks

YOUR
MONEY
MATTERS

By Ed Leefeldt
Special to The Wall Street Journal

Ask stock-market professionals how they decide what to buy and what to sell and when, and chances are they'll say they "watch the tape."

The tape. That's the running list—once punched out on ticker tape but now almost always displayed electronically—that shows all transactions on the New York Stock Exchange as they take place or, at most, within minutes. (There is also a tape for American Stock Exchange transactions, but when the market pros speak of *the tape,* they generally mean the one that lists trades on the New York exchange.)

Arbitragers and traders say that watching the tape, usually on a computer screen, is the single most accurate way to get a feel for the market or for a particular stock. To them, the tape has an almost mystical significance. They say things like, "I bought it off the tape"; "Don't fight the tape"; and, "The tape doesn't lie."

But even small investors can learn a lot from studying the tape in their broker's office and applying some of the tape watchers' tricks to what they read in the newspaper.

Looking for 'Fingerprints'

The first thing, says Eugene Peroni, a veteran market watcher with Bateman Eichler, Hill Richards Inc., is to learn the trading patterns of stock. "Every stock has a fingerprint," he says. "That fingerprint is the way it normally trades—say, within a range of two to three points and on a daily volume of 10,000 shares. When a stock breaks out of its range for several weeks, it's time to start wondering what's happening."

Frequently stocks run up because of rumors of a takeover, leveraged buyout or restructuring. Mr. Peroni suggests that investors look for significant "uptick" volume — heavier-than-usual trading and a steady rise in price—for several weeks before the rumor surfaced. Such activity can indicate that insiders are buying the stock and that the rumor has some credence.

Charles Lewis, a market analyst at Shearson Lehman Brothers Inc., keeps his eye on the stocks that gain or lose the most in percentage terms, as well as the daily lists of most-actives and those setting new highs or new lows. He also watches for signs of "reach"—someone willing to pay 50 cents or more a share above the going rate to buy at least 100,000 shares at a clip. While information about such block-trading activity isn't readily available to those who can't watch the tape all the time, small investors can ask their brokers once in awhile. Brokers will probably cooperate if commissions are in the offing.

Avoiding Attention

Tape watchers say that stocks being accumulated by big investors tend to trade in a particular pattern. "They'll go out and buy some and then pull back," says Trude Latimer of Evans & Co. "It's very rare that they're relentless. They don't want to attract attention."

This pattern becomes obvious to the pros after several weeks, however, as the stock goes up on heavy volume, down on light volume and then repeats the process. Spotting this pattern is easier on a chart. Several professional charting services are available, but expensive. Doing it oneself is more economical, but can get time-consuming if an investor is following more than a few stocks.

Often, the first hint of a big change in a stock's fortunes comes in the options market. Joseph Berland, chairman of Gaines, Berland Inc., says he checks the list of most-active stock options each day for new entries.

Making Money Fast

Options are the right, not the obligation, to buy (a call) or sell (a put) 100 shares of the underlying stock at a specified price for a certain period. Options appeal to many stock-market players because they can make a lot of money fast if they guess right; if they guess wrong, their losses are limited because options cost only a fraction of the stock itself.

Finally, the pros caution that although the tape may not lie, it doesn't always mean what it seems. Looking at the tape action in Texas Oil & Gas Corp. last September, for example, Mr. Peroni decided that a takeover was in the wind. Others reached the same conclusion.

And they were right. But anyone who bought Texas Oil shares when they soared to $21.625 each in the speculative frenzy that followed would have been sadly disappointed. The company sold out to U.S. Steel Corp. for $18 a share.

Source: E. Leefeldt, " 'Tape Watchers' Offer Some Tips for Stock Picks," *The Wall Street Journal*, January 31, 1986, p. 23. Reprinted by permission, © Dow Jones & Company, Inc. All rights reserved.

FIGURE 13.2 Head and Shoulders Formation

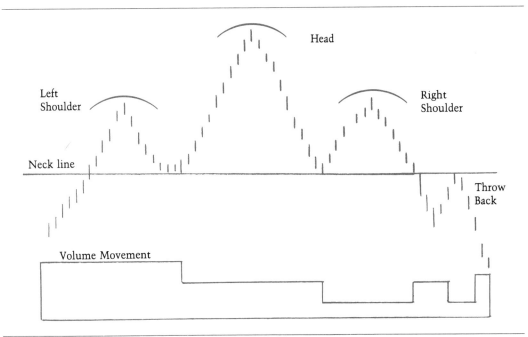

Source: A. Lerro and C. Swayne, *Selection of Securities: Technical Analysis of Stock Market Prices* (Morristown, N.J.: General Learning Press, 1970). Reprinted by permission of the author.

relevant public information accurately and quickly (including any information implicit in past price patterns). Thus, Samuelson showed that a stock price will follow a random walk if its "present price is set at the expected discounted value of its future dividends; where the future dividends are supposed to be random variables generated according to any general (but known) stochastic process."[2] Indeed, if many traders recognized repeating patterns, their rapid reaction would cause an almost immediate change to the predicted level. Eventually some investors' efforts to react to partial patterns would probably eliminate most repeating patterns.

On the other hand, technical analysts assert that their system, while not infallible, does provide useful signals. Why else, they might ask, do so many investors continue to pay for and follow their advice? Why indeed? Why do otherwise intelligent people go to astrologers and fortune tellers?

The efficient market proponents respond that some successes may be due to combining other information with charts and giving credit to the charts alone. Other technicians may simply have been lucky. Just as enough monkeys and enough typewriters will produce *King Lear*, enough analysts and enough market turns will reveal some very high "success" rates. The relevant question is, Do such successes repeat themselves? Hearing from the winners (who are likely to be vocal) but not from losers (who are unlikely to advertise their failures) gives a distorted view. For example, a *Business Week* story featured a technical analyst who correctly called a declining market the day after the market hit its peak January 1, 1973. This analyst continued to forecast a decline at least up to August 31, 1974, when the market itself was still declining.[3] *The Wall Street Journal* featured another successful analyst a few years later.[4] We have already seen how Joe Granville called several market turns. Indeed, at any stage of the market cycle some analysts are likely to have a sufficiently impressive record to justify an article touting their "wisdom."

Such track records are impressive, but one cannot help wondering how many other technical analysts made disastrous forecasts during similar periods. At any particular time some analyst is going to have the best recent record. Someone must be first in any such comparison. The more important question is, Do such records help us identify talented forecasters or those who just happened to have made relatively accurate forecasts for that period? For example, after correctly calling a couple of turns, Granville totally missed the very strong market upturn that began in August 1982. His forecasts continued to be very wide of the mark until 1987, when he again had some successes. Similarly, Prechter had an impressive record until he missed calling the crash of 1987.

Evidence such as that cited in Chapter 6 suggests that past price behavior contains little or no generally useful information. Any generalized time series dependencies exhibited by past price behavior appear to be too weak to offset the impact of transaction costs. A closer look suggests that the issues may not be quite so simple, however.

SPECIALIZED DEPENDENCIES

Smidt argues that researchers should be expected to find certain types of specialized time series return dependencies.[5] First, the large orders of anxious traders may cause short-run price reactions that, when dissipated, produce a price reversal. Second, lags in reaction to new information may lead to short-run price trends. Third, excessive speculation may cause speculative bubbles followed by major declines.

Anxious Trader Effects

Block trades, secondary offerings, intraday dependencies and tax-loss trading may lead to temporary supply–demand imbalances. Initially the price may be disturbed away from its intrinsic value level. Later, as the anxious trader effects dissipate, the price may move back toward its prior level.

Block Trades and Secondary Offerings.   As was discussed in Chapter 3, block trades are transactions involving 10,000 or more shares arranged off the exchange. Grier and Albien examined a strategy of buying stocks whose prices are depressed by block trades.[6] Most block trades do not depress prices by enough to permit after-commission trading profits on the typical rebound. Those with the greatest price declines did offer the most attractive trading prospects. For the first decile of trades ranked by size of open-to-block-price decline, profits from buying at the block price and selling at the close only slightly exceeded commissions. Specialists and floor traders, who incur much lower trading costs could, and probably do, profit substantially, however.

A subsequent study by Dann, Mayers, and Raab found that block trades with large (greater than 4.56%) open-to-block-price declines have by the close generally risen by more than enough to cover transactions costs.[7] Five minutes after the block trade, however, the price recovery had usually progressed too far to afford after-commission profits. Indeed, within 15 minutes most prices had fully recovered. As a practical matter only specialists and floor traders are positioned to react within these time frames. One advisory service (Xerox's Auto Ex division) does report trading interest of major institutions and brokerage houses. The system was designed to facilitate institutional block trades but can be used to forecast such trades (for a fee of $1,000 a month).

Several researchers found price declines associated with large secondary distributions on the day of the sale and subsequently.[8] They also found that secondary distributions of corporate insiders, investment companies, and mutual funds were followed by appreciably greater price changes than when the sellers were banks, insurance companies, estates, trusts, or individuals. Quite possibly corporate insiders, investment companies, and mutual funds are more likely to have based their decision to sell on fundamental grounds, whereas banks, insurance companies, and others may have simply needed liquidity. These secondary distribution results do not exhibit any anxious trader effects per se. Perhaps data on daily closing prices are too crude to reveal them.

General Intraday Dependencies: Specialists and Limit Orders.   Granger and Morgenstern persuasively argue that stock prices closely resemble a random walk for daily movements. They did, however, find temporary intraday barriers to price movements and nonrandom overnight (close to next day's open) price changes.[9]

The authors ascribed these patterns to the interaction of specialists' trading and publicly placed limit orders. Specialists are charged with keeping an orderly market (i.e., avoiding excessive volatility) in their assigned stocks. They rely on a combination of limit orders and buying and selling with their own inventory to keep their markets orderly.

Limit orders tend to collect at even values (whole numbers, halves as opposed to quarters, quarters as opposed to eighths, etc.). A collection of such limit orders at even values may act as temporary barriers to price movements. Once the market has executed a stack of whole-number limit orders, only a few orders may restrict further movement. Continued buying (selling) activity may lead to a rather rapid price increase (decrease) until a new barrier is encountered. For example, buying pressure may move a price from 18⅝ to 18⅞. Once 19 is penetrated, continued buying could quickly propel the price to 19⅞, with 20 becoming the next barrier.

Granger and Morgenstern found overnight and overday price fluctuations of similar magnitude. Because the former involve much lower volume, smaller price fluctuations might well have been expected to occur overnight than overday. Perhaps the specialists are influencing the overnight price swings. Accumulated overnight orders and the specialists' own account are used to set the opening price. Price swings trigger limit orders on which specialists are paid a fee. The more limit orders that are executed, the larger will be the specialists' fee income from this source. Accordingly, Granger and Morgenstern concluded that a fluctuating overnight price is often profitable for the specialists. Lacking the necessary data on specialists' dealings, however, they were unable to prove their suspicions.

Niederhoffer and Osborne also found unmistakable evidence of nonrandom behavior in transaction sign reversals.[10] After a positive (negative) price change, the next nonzero price change has a 3 to 1 chance of being a decline (increase). This nonrandom transaction price behavior is caused by the interaction of market orders with the bid–asked spread. Market orders to buy are immediately executed at the current asked price. A subsequent order to sell will produce a reversal whereas a buy will leave the price at the asked. Indeed, this intraday price behavior indicates that the last trade price (the quote the broker usually gives) is not the best index of the market price. For example, a last trade in XYZ at 23⅝ could be associated with any of the following:

a) Bid 23⅝ Ask 23⅞

b) Bid 23⅜ Ask 23⅝

c) Bid 23½ Ask 23¾

Indeed, in rare instances the market may even have moved away from the last reported price:

d) Bid 23⅞ Ask 24½

e) Bid 23⅛ Ask 23⅜

Thus, those interested in making a trade should always request complete quotes. Such quotations would include the current bid and asked prices rather than only the price of the previous trade. Complete knowledge of the current quote is particularly relevant to those who want to place limit orders. Indeed, traders should usually also ask for a size (number of shares sought at the bid and available at the ask). For example, a large bid and small offer may well indicate that buying pressure is present and may ultimately lead to a higher price for the stock.

Tax-Loss Trading.   Yet another area of possible anxious trader impacts involves year-end selling to establish a tax loss. Their methodologies differ somewhat, but separate studies by a host of different researchers suggest that tax-loss trading has dramatically affected some year-end stock prices.[11] For example, Branch and Ryan studied the first-of-the-year returns over the 1965–1978 period. We found average four-week price moves relative to the market of 6.67% and 14.75% for NYSE and AMEX year-end lows, respectively. Similarly, McEnally found that stocks, which fell by the greatest percentage over the preceding 12 months, were most likely to rise after the first of the year. Such findings suggest (assuming the observed relations persist) that investors should sell tax-loss candidates well before year-end. Similarly, the year-end may be an attractive time to purchase stocks that are under tax-loss selling pressure.

More recent work has refined our knowledge on this subject.[12] For example, Branch and Chang reported that tax-loss trading did not have a similar price pattern in the 1979–1982 period. We did find that stocks that declined by the largest amounts in December were most likely to rise in January. Moreover, a number of studies found that most of the turn-of-the-year effect occurs at the small-firm level. Still other research indicates that stocks with low per share prices are particularly prone to tax loss pressure at year-end.

Assessment of Anxious Trader Effects.   The evidence for anxious trader effects seems relatively persuasive. Block trading and tax-loss trading have both tended to depress prices temporarily, with a reversal generally following. Secondary offerings are also associated with modest price declines. Intraday price dependencies related to specialist trading and limit order activity also reveal some anxious trader effects. With the possible exceptions of the tax-loss results, however, the magnitudes of the dependencies appear to be too small to permit after-transactions cost trading profits. On the other hand, those who intend to trade anyway might as well take advantage of whatever forecasting value these relationships may offer. Table 13.1 summarizes anxious trader effects.

Adjustment Lags

Adjustment lags are another category of specialized dependencies. Specifically, prices may take time to react to such factors as earnings announcements, dividend changes, ex-dividend dates, announcements in *The Wall Street Journal*, brokers sell recommendations, bond rating changes, pollution disclosures, corporate crime disclosures, "Wall Street Week" recommendations, trading suspensions, option expirations, option listings, insider trading reports, splits, stock dividends, tenders, mergers, liquidations, share repurchases, rights offerings, equity sales, debt for equity swaps, forced conversions, divestitures, voluntary spin-offs, and additions and

TABLE 13.1 Anxious Trader Effects

Block Trades	Prices tend to decline with block trade and regain most of the loss by day's end.
Large Secondary Distributions	Prices show modest declines on day of and following a secondary distribution.
Intraday Dependencies	Incoming market orders cause prices to bounce between bid and ask.
Overnight Price Changes	Volatility may result from specialists' seeking to trigger limit orders.
Tax-Loss Trading	Issues under year-end tax selling pressure may rise at the first of the year; small-firm and low-priced issues are particularly likely to be affected in this way.

deletions to the S&P 500 index. Moreover, cross-correlations and volume effects may also be used to identify adjustments in process.

Earnings and Dividend Announcements. Earnings and dividend announcements have been the subject of a number of studies.[13] Prices may not adjust instantly to earnings and dividend announcements, but the lags appear to be quite short. The reactions appear to be faster for firms with listed options. Those without listed options take longer to react to quarterly earnings announcements. Moreover, several studies found a relatively slow market reaction to unexpected earnings changes.

Several different studies have focused on dividends.[14] These studies have generally found that dividend increases often result in substantial reactions that are usually completed by the day of the announcement or soon thereafter. Favorable dividend announcements tend to be made in a timely fashion whereas delayed announcements are associated with dividend omissions or reductions.

Ex-Dividend Behavior and Dividend Capture Strategies. Ex-dividend price reactions also appear to be predictable to an extent. Dividends are paid to stockholders of record on a prespecified date. Dividends on purchases made the day after the ex-dividend date go to the prior owner. Several researchers report that the price of the stock tends to fall by a bit less than the amount of the dividend on the ex-dividend date.[15] The relationship was far from exact, however. Similarly, call option prices tend to fall on the ex-dividend day of the underlying stock.

The predictability of ex-dividend price reactions has led several authors to suggest what have come to be called *dividend capture trading strategies.* Under the Tax Reform Act of 1986 eighty percent of intracorporate dividends are untaxed. This fact led Joehnk, Bowlin, and Petty to advocate buying preferred shares just before the day of record and selling quickly thereafter.[16] Indeed, both preferred and common stock may form the basis for a dividend capture. U.S. investors must, however, own the shares for at least 46 days to qualify for the special tax treatment. Nonetheless, a large fraction of overall stock trading volume is often the result of dividend captures. Japanese investors have been particularly active in capturing the dividends.

The Wall Street Journal **Announcements and Brokers' Sell Recommendations.** Morse examined price and volume effects for various types of announcements in

The Wall Street Journal (earnings and dividend announcements, large product sales, earnings forecasts, acquisitions, stock splits, and labor strikes) for 50 companies over the 11 trading days surrounding the announcement. He found a significant price effect the day before the announcement appeared (which was usually the same day as it was reported on the Dow Jones News ticker) as well as on the day the story appeared.[17] In most cases the excess returns were in the expected direction. Moreover, volume was also usually high at the time of the announcement.

Similarly, Bidwell and Kolb found that brokers' sell recommendations had a negative short-run impact on security returns.[18] Such abnormal returns could be exploited profitably, however, only by those who incur low transactions costs and have prior warnings of the recommendations. On the other hand, stocks depressed by the sell recommendations tended to generate subsequent above-normal returns.

Bond Rating Changes, Pollution Disclosures, and Corporate Crime Disclosures. Several researchers examined the stock price reaction to bond rating changes.[19] They reported an appreciable downgrade effect but an insignificant effect for upgrades. Jaggi and Freedman found significant investor reaction to firms disclosing the extent of their intention to spend money on pollution control.[20] Firms that made such disclosures generally experienced superior investor reaction compared with nondisclosing firms in the same industries. Only monthly data were examined. Accordingly, the timing of the reactions was not explored closely enough to determine if trading profits were possible. Strachan, Smith, and Beedles found a significant market reaction to disclosures of allegations of illegal corporate behavior. Virtually all of this reaction occurs at the time of the announcement.[21]

"Wall Street Week" Recommendations and Trading Suspensions. In a particularly ingenious study, Fosback explored the market reaction for 200 stocks recommended by guests of the public television program "Wall Street Week" from December 1980 to April 1982.[22] On the average, the stocks rose .4% two weeks before the show; .8% the week before; 2.1% the day after, and then fell 3.2% over the next month and a half. Fosback concluded that most WSW guests were unable to select winners, but that the market does pay attention to the program.

Schwartz's study of market behavior during and following trading suspensions implied a relatively efficient pricing process.[23] The specialists' "indications" of reopening ranges almost always contained the actual reopening price, and postsuspension price movements seemed approximately random.

Option Expirations and Option Listings. Two additional events with possible associated price dependencies involve options.[24] Specifically, Officer and Trennepohl found a modest but statistically significant tendency for the price of the underlying stock to be depressed two days prior to option expirations. The price effects were too small to yield trading profits after taking account of the impacts of taxes, transactions costs, and search costs. Strong and Andrew, in contrast, found a tendency for stocks with specialists' traded options (AMEX listed) to move toward their nearest strike in the two days prior to expiration. They reasoned that these specialists were hedging their option positions.

TABLE 13.2 Insider Trading Reports

Securities and Exchange Commission Monthly Report on Insider Trades (Washington, D.C., $70 a year)

Consensus of Insiders, Perry Wysong (Box 10247, Fort Lauderdale, Fla. 33334; weekly, $247 a year)

Insider Indicator, J. Michael Reid (2230 N.E. Brazee St., Portland, Ore. 97212; semimonthly, $145 a year)

The Insiders, Norman Fosback (3471 N. Federal Highway, Fort Lauderdale, Fla. 33306; semimonthly, $49 a year)

The Insiders' Chronicle, William Mehlman (Box 9662, Arlington, Va. 22209; 50 issues a year, $325 a year)

The Insiders Edge Highlights Report, Richard Horowitz (122 Spanish Village, Suite 644, Dallas, Tex. 75248; monthly, $79 a year)

Branch and Finnerty found that initial call option listings were associated with stock price increases. The magnitude, however, was generally too small to be exploited profitably after allowing for transactions costs. Whiteside, Dukes, and Dunne, in contrast, found little or no impact of option listing on either the price or volume of the underlying shares trades.

Insider Trading.   Inside information appears often to facilitate a relatively accurate stock evaluation. Noninsiders must generally wait until the information is publicly released, but traders can observe insiders' trading decisions and act accordingly. Zweig surveyed five academic studies of insider trading signals that all reached similar conclusions: Signals based on significant insider trading allowed investors to outperform the market by a substantial margin.[25] Thus, insider trading appears to be one market signal whose value is well supported by careful academic analysis. According to Nunn, Madden, and Gambola, the inside trades of CEOs and directors are a better predictor of subsequent performance than those of vice presidents and beneficial owners.[26] Apparently CEOs and directors have better access to information. Trivoli finds even more favorable results from joint use of financial ratios and insider trading data.[27]

Insiders must report their trades to the SEC. Thus investors could consult the SEC's records to determine their actions on a particular stock. Moreover, some investment services report SEC insider trading data to subscribers (Table 13.2). Certain periodicals including *Barron's* and *Value Line* report on insider trades. Finally, insider trading activity is sometimes discussed in the financial press, at least on an ad hoc basis.

Stock Splits, Reverse Splits, and Stock Dividends.   Corporate managers and the investors in their firms are believed to prefer per share prices of some normal range ($20 to $60, for example).[28] Very low-priced stocks are considered too speculative and high-priced stocks are costly to purchase in round lots. Accordingly, stock distributions are used to reduce the per share prices of high-priced stocks whereas reverse stock splits may be employed for very low-priced issues. Postsplit shares usually incur proportionately higher commission charges and bid–ask spreads. Thus splits generally increase trading costs. Moreover, stock distributions incur a number of costs: officers' time, printing stock certificates, handling fractional shares, revising the stockholder ledger, communicating with shareholders, transfer taxes, and listing fees.

Because the price of a stock usually rises prior to a split or stock dividend announcement, investors might trade on prior knowledge or accurate forecasts of splits.[29] The former strategy is illegal; the success rate of the latter is untested. On the other hand, several researchers found significant negative price performance associated with reverse splits around the time of the proposal, approval, and ex-split dates.[30]

Three further stock distribution studies reveal additional relationships.[31] First, Nichols and Brown examined earnings and the effects of split announcement over time. They found no indication that the market was becoming more efficient. Second, Nichols reported that, for small stock distributions, a positive impact in the announcement month was followed by a negative adjustment over the succeeding three months. Finally, Woolridge found that investors interpret stock dividends as signals from management on the firm's future. The larger the dividend, the greater is the market reaction.

Tender Offers, Mergers, and Liquidations.   Tender offers, mergers, and liquidations may present investors with still other attractive trading opportunities. Stockholders usually profit when their stock is tendered for and/or merged into another company. The offering price almost always exceeds the previous level. Moreover, a variety of different types of people may benefit from such transactions. For example, those who put the deals together are always well rewarded, as are the target firms' advisors. Even the acquired firms' managers are usually well compensated (the so-called golden parachute) when they are forced to leave. Those who know of planned mergers before the announcement may (illegally) trade on that knowledge. Large investors may buy a sizable position in a company and then try either to force takeover from the inside or to get the company to pay a premium to repurchase their shares (greenmail). The company's own assets are often used as collateral to finance the full takeover (a leveraged buyout, or LBO).

Yet another ploy is to acquire a large position in an undervalued company and then have the company buy out most or all of the small public shareholders. Taking a company private in this way not only buys out most shareholders at depressed prices but also eliminates much of the stockholder relations cost. Finally, a company whose assets are worth more than the market price of its shares may be bought as a liquidation prospect.

While these various maneuvers may yield handsome returns, traders need either inside information of planned takeovers (and a willingness to break the law) or the resources to influence the relevant firms. The only realistic strategy for small investors is to try to anticipate forthcoming acquisitions. They can then be in the right place at the right time when the target company is put "in play." Moreover, once a takeover looks like a success, tendering is almost always advisable. Small holdings of subsidiaries usually have little speculative appeal.

Share Repurchases, Equity Sales, Forced Conversions, Exchanges, and Voluntary Spin-offs.   Earnings retention and minor debt decisions continually alter capital structures. Some actions, however, have more substantial impacts. A number

Investments in Perspective

For every merger that actually occurs perhaps 10 are rumored. Stock prices are often influenced by such rumors. Once the true situation is known, the stock will react appropriately. If the stock is truly a target, the announcement will tend to move the price toward the level of the offer. If the rumor is incorrect, the stock will probably give back most of the price rise brought about by the rumor. Some investors will already own the stock of a company that is rumored to be a takeover target. They would like to know whether to hold for the anticipated event or to sell now before the rumor turns out to be merely unfounded speculation. Those who are contemplating buying do not want to be swept up by information that turns out to be false. Clearly, those with an interest in the situation would like to know how to assess a takeover rumor. An article from *The Wall Street Journal* offers some pointers.

Here's How Stock-Market Experts Decide Which Rumors to Act On

YOUR
MONEY
MATTERS

By GEORGE ANDERS
Staff Reporter of THE WALL STREET JOURNAL

NEW YORK—Rodney Berens figures he hears 20 takeover rumors a day, most of which "are garbage." But as the head of stock trading for Morgan, Stanley & Co., he has learned to pick out the credible ones. That gives Mr. Berens a big edge over most other stock-market partici-pants.

Individual investors—who hear their share of takeover rumors from brokers, friends and business associates—may benefit from studying the filtering techniques that pros such as Mr. Berens use. There's no sure-fire, legal way to find tomorrow's acquisition targets. But there are systematic approaches that investors can use.

Some methods are extremely straight-forward, such as calling the companies mentioned in a rumor. (The pros can learn a lot from a seemingly routine company response.) Other methods are outright wily. A New York arbitrager, for example, routinely checks prep-school records to see if the companies' top executives went to school together. If so, he reasons, they may be more inclined to a merger.

Rumor chasers, of course, are driven by the lure of huge profits if they can anticipate takeovers. Those fortunate enough to buy stock in RCA Corp., General Foods Corp. or Union Carbide Corp. before recent bids could have earned 20% or more within weeks, for example. Profits in options were even larger. But for every accurate rumor, there can be a dozen unfounded ones. And buying on bad rumors often brings heavy losses.

The following are some lines of inquiry that top traders, arbitragers and portfolio managers—some of whom asked that their names be withheld—recommend for sizing up takeover rumors:

Does a merger make sense? That's the most important question to Ronald Gottesmann, an arbitrager at Oppenheimer & Co. He checks public statements by both companies on whether they're interested in mergers or takeovers. He asks research analysts if the two industries fit. And he reviews balance sheets to see if the rumored target company has cash pools or undervalued assets that might attract a suitor.

"It sounds obvious, but you can eliminate a lot of the rumors on that criterion alone," Mr. Gottesmann says. "Your source will always insist it's true, but you have to make your own judgment."

What do the companies say? Not even big-time investors can phone company chairmen every time they want to test a rumor. But pros such as Kenneth Heebner, a portfolio manager at Loomis Sayles & Co. in Boston, have learned to watch for nuances when they deal with investor-relations departments. (These departments also handle questions from small shareholders.)

"Even if they just give you the party line," a defensive tone can signal problems, Mr. Heebner says. A "no comment" after months of saying "no" may be significant. And a competitor might know something even if a target company isn't talking. But Mr. Heebner cautions that unless one regularly talks with a company, it's hard to know the usual response.

A further tip comes from Ignatius Teichberg, a stockbroker who runs his own firm. Mr. Teichberg says he will toss out a possible merger price and see how the target company responds. "If I ask them, 'Would you agree to a merger at $16 a share?' and they say, 'That's too low,' then I know they are willing to negotiate," he explains.

But don't jump to conclusions when companies try to laugh off rumors. One arbitrager says that last month he asked Occidental Petroleum Corp. about rumors that it would bid for MidCon Corp. "Their guy just started laughing, which made me think it was nonsense," the arbitrager recalled. A week later, Occidental bid $3 billion for MidCon.

Are trading patterns revealing? Wall Street's pros say a pickup in volume coupled with a slight rise in price for the target company can be a good sign. Often, options trading can lead the way. But signals can get confusing. The vast majority of volume flurries aren't followed by takeover bids. And even though traders distrust huge flurries in volume ("It means I'm the last guy to hear the rumor," explains one trader), there have been cases, such as RCA Corp.'s, in which a stampede of buying was followed the next day by a merger accord.

Are takeover specialists involved? By watching incoming orders, Wall Street's trading desks know when leading arbitragers are buying. Individual customers seldom get that information, but they or their brokers can check shareholder filings at the Securities and Exchange Commission. Any new holder of 5% or more is required to file with the SEC, and most such filings are reported in the business press.

Just because name players are buying a stock doesn't mean a takeover is inevitable. But Wall Street's pros regard such buying as one more variable to be fitted into their calculations.

Is there a social fit? Arbitragers aren't kidding when they ask who plays golf together or went to school together. For example, it was hockey that first brought Chicago's Pritzker family together with Masonite Corp. a few years ago. (Pritzker ended up buying 10% of Masonite.) Some Pritzker children skated with kids of a top Masonite official, and when the fathers met, they started talking about business. "These sorts of hidden links lie behind a lot of deals," says a takeover speculator.

How detailed is the rumor? The more specific, the easier a rumor is to check. "If the rumor names price, terms and investment banks, that's a lot more to work with than one with just the company's name," says Morgan Stanley's Mr. Berens. But takeover speculators are wary of rumors that specify the exact price in an unfriendly takeover. That's because a hostile-takeover price normally isn't set until the last moment, and any rumored figure is likely to be fiction.

How would a takeover be funded? "The last year or so, acquirers have gone outside a lot more to raise money," says a New York arbitrager. "That means investment banks and commercial banks are getting involved earlier." It also means Wall Street hears more leaks about the raising of money for acquisitions. Small investors can't confirm or disprove such rumors. But they can be alert for times that companies publicly announce they are raising money for acquisitions.

Do takeover patterns apply? Acquisitions have been concentrated lately in broadcasting, chemicals and defense companies. So arbitragers and traders keep a keen ear for talk of more consolidation in those industries. Energy stocks continue to provide grounds for takeover rumors. "But I wouldn't waste a lot of time tracking down a steel rumor," says one trader.

Are stocks "restricted"? When big investment banks take on a merger client, they are supposed to avoid trading in that stock. (A conflict-of-interest principle is at stake.) Thus, some investment bank's top traders get a secret "restricted" list of these stocks. Trouble is, even if the traders keep mum, the mere fact that the firm suddenly stops trading in a stock is enough

to start whispers.

"It's a sensitive issue," says a top Wall Street trader. He acknowledges that merger leaks can occur this way, despite the firm's best precautions. Yet small investors may be hard-pressed to learn about "restricted" lists, and even if they do, not every stock that goes on such a list will be taken over, arbitragers caution.

Despite all these tactics, Wall Street's pros say it's risky to trade on takeover rumors. "When I hear a rumor, I'm nervous about being short or long on the stock," says Morgan Stanley's Mr. Berens. "My main concern is to avoid being caught." And such long-term investors as MacKay Shields Financial Corp. advise looking for stocks that would be worth owning anyway, even without a takeover.

There's one final technique that would be a clincher if it could be done: tracking a rumor to its source. But "most rumors arrive third-hand, or 10th-hand," says a veteran arbitrager. "If your source really knows anything, he won't say. And if he claims to have a high-level source, he's probably bluffing. The usual rules of logic don't apply."

of different types of change can appreciably alter the number of shares outstanding and/or the firm's debt ratio. Such actions can dramatically affect the shareholders' expected income streams and risks. Moreover, capital structure changes that affect the relative amounts of dividend and interest payments have important tax implications. Thus the market may well react to such events as share repurchases (which decrease outstanding shares) as well as rights offerings and forced conversions (both of which increase outstanding shares).

Masulis found the following market reactions to capital structure changes:

1. Changes affecting expected taxes and/or the relative values of stocks versus bonds were associated with significant security price moves in the predicted directions.

2. Different classes of securityholders were often affected differentially by the shift.

3. Shareholders were generally adversely affected by a decrease in leverage.[32]

Both Vermaelen and Dann reported that firms use share repurchases to signal their belief that their stocks are undervalued.[33] They also found that common shareholders usually benefit from such repurchases. Bondholders, on the other hand, do not seem to be either helped or hurt by the repurchases. Market reaction occurs within one day of the announcement, however.

On the other hand, Bradley and Wakeman find that stock repurchases designed to remove potential takeover threats tend to lower the values of the affected firm's stock.[34] Similarly, Dann and DeAngelo find that standstill agreements (agreements between management and large shareholders that limit these shareholders' options by, for example, agreeing not to increase their ownership position or seek to gain control of the firm for a specific period) also tend to harm nonparticipating shareholders.[35] Finally, Dodd and Warner find that proxy contests generally enhance stock prices temporarily.[36] The stock's price usually falls once the day of record for voting passes, however.

Share repurchases decrease shares outstanding and tend to increase per share prices, while rights offerings and other types of equity sales have the opposite effect. White and Lusztig reported that investors generally react negatively to a rights offering on the announcement day. Moreover, they report that the market has not regained any of the lost ground by the fifth day after the announcement.[37] Similarly, several researchers found a negative market reaction to the announcement and implementation of equity sales (including the sale of convertibles).[38] On the other hand, management requests to increase authorized shares had little or no impact whereas equity carve-outs (partial sale of a subsidiary) and announcements of capital expenditures had generally positive impacts.[39]

Like sales of equity, voluntary exchanges of equity for debt and forced conversions of convertible debentures and convertible preferreds increase shares outstanding and reduce leverage. Thus such exchanges and conversions tend to lower both per share earnings and risk. Calling convertibles will force conversion only if the stock price has appreciated sufficiently. Thus the conversion value must exceed the call price by a substantial amount or owners will not convert.

A number of researchers have examined the impact of both voluntary and forced conversions of debt for equity.[40] Not surprisingly, Alexander and Stover find that forced conversions are generally preceded by a strongly positive abnormal return. More surprisingly, however, such forced conversion announcements are also associated with subsequent negative abnormal returns for a period of up to 12 months. Similarly, the announcement of swap of stock for debt is generally associated with negative stock price performance. Subsequent performance is related to the purpose of the swap. If, for example, the swap is part of a refunding operation, subsequent performance is generally favorable. Finally, swaps of preferreds for common stock and reversions of excess assets (from pension funds to the corporation) tend to have a favorable market impact.

A spin-off occurs when a parent company gives its stockholders shares in what had heretofore been a subsidiary of the parent firm. Clearly such distributions create no new tangible assets. The divestiture may increase the investment's value if separating the parent from the former subsidiary enhances its freedom to operate effectively. Miles and Rosenfeld studied 55 spin-offs. They found that most such events were associated with abnormal returns prior to the announcement but random thereafter.[41] Similarly, a number of other studies found that divestitures tended to have a significantly favorable impact on the seller as well as a modestly favorable impact on the buyer.[42]

Additions to the S&P 500 Index.   Standard & Poor's 500 Stock Index is widely followed by the market. It is viewed as a much broader based index than the Dow Jones Industrial Average. As such, the S&P 500 is the index on which many other financial instruments are based. For example, stock index futures, options on index futures, and indexed mutual funds all utilize the S&P 500. Stocks are added to and deleted from the index in order to preserve or enhance its representativeness. The announcement that a stock is to be added to the index tends to cause it to rise whereas a deletion has the opposite tendency.[43]

Cross-Correlation and Volume Effects.   Investment analysts have often asserted that particular stock groups tend to lead other groups (i.e., interest-sensitive stocks tend to lead the market; high-risk stocks are hit first and hardest in an economic downturn; low-PE stocks hold up best in a down market; etc.). The existence of such lead–lag relationships could facilitate useful market forecasting. An efficient market, however, should not exhibit such leads and lags. While academicians have not yet tested specific lead–lag hypotheses, work by Hawawini and others bear on the generalized lead–lag phenomenon.[44] Apparently some securities do tend to lead while others lag. Whether such lead and lag relationships can be profitably exploited remains to be seen, however. Quite possibly any significant effort to trade the stocks that were lagging the market might very quickly eliminate their lagging behavior.

Morse's price–volume relationships study provides a final bit of information on adjustment lags.[45] He hypothesized the existence of investors with information not yet fully impounded into the market price. He further suggested that such investors would have an incentive to trade on one side of the market until the price has fully adjusted. His results confirm that expectation. Price trends are frequently accompanied by abnormally high volume. On the other hand, Smirlock and Starks find that volume tends to be higher on upticks than downticks.[46]

Assessment of Adjustment Lags.   The market appears to adjust quickly to most new information. Reactions generally occur within a day or so of the following types of announcements: earnings reports, dividend changes, bond rating changes, reports in *The Wall Street Journal*, mentions on "Wall Street Week," allegations of corporate crimes, option listings, stock dividends, share repurchases, and rights offerings. Stock price adjustments actually tend to precede the announcement or event for splits, tender offers, mergers, option expirations, and voluntary spin-offs. Thus trading on such relationships would normally require prior knowledge or accurate forecasts. On the other hand, revisions of earnings forecasts, insider trading signals, forced conversions, and possibly ex-dividend date reactions may produce usable price relations (i.e., those that take place over a long enough period to be exploited by nonmembers of the listing exchange). Table 13.3 summarizes adjustment lags.

Speculative Bubbles

Some analysts contend that the market all too frequently gets carried away with itself, only to reverse its direction when faced with reality. Indeed Malkiel goes so

TABLE 13.3 Adjustment Lags

Earnings Announcements	Market reacts quickly to earnings news.
Dividend Announcements	Market reacts quickly to dividend news.
Ex-Dividend Date	Stock price tends to fall by somewhat less than the amount of the payment on ex-dividend date.
The Wall Street Journal Announcements	Significant price effects are seen the day before and the day that significant stories appear in *The Wall Street Journal.*
Brokers' Sell Recommendations	Sell recommendations tend to depress price, with a reversal generally following.
Bond Rating Changes	Price reaction is appreciable for downgrades but not for upgrades.
Pollution Disclosures	Disclosing firms tend to do better than nondisclosures in subsequent market trading.
Alleged Corporate Crime	Market reacts quickly to news of alleged illegal activity.
"Wall Street Week" Recommendations	Recommended stocks tend to rise the Monday after the show and decline over the next six weeks.
Trading Suspensions	Specialists' reopening range indications almost always contain the actual reopening price.
Option Expirations	The price of the underlying stock tends to be depressed two days before option expirations.
Option Listings	Stock prices may increase modestly upon an initial call listing.
Insider Trading	Reports of insider trades appear to provide profitable trading signals.
Stock Splits and Dividends	Stock prices usually rise prior to but not after a split announcement.
Reverse Splits	Stock prices generally decline after reverse splits.
Tender Offers	Holders usually profit from tender offers but anticipating such offers is difficult.
Share Repurchases	Share repurchases often indicate that management believes the stock is undervalued.
Rights Offerings and Equity Sales	Shareholders generally react negatively to announcements of rights offerings and equity sales.
Forced Conversions and Debt for Equity Exchanges	Strong positive performances generally precede forced conversion and debt for equity exchange announcements, with negative performances afterward.
Voluntary Spin-offs and Divestitures	Performances are positive prior to announcements, followed by random performances afterward.
Additions to the S&P 500	Stocks tend to rise when they are added to the S&P 500 Index and fall when they are deleted.
Cross-Correlations	Some securities tend to lead while others tend to lag the market.
Price–Volume Effects	Price trends are frequently accompanied by abnormally high volume.

far as to argue that investors should seek out stocks for which a subsequent positive overreaction is likely:

> I have stressed the importance of psychological elements in stock price determination. Individual and institutional investors are not computers that calculate warranted price–earnings multiples and print out buy and sell decisions. They

are emotional human beings driven by greed, gambling instinct, hope, and fear in their stock market decisions. This is why successful investing demands both intellectual and psychological acuteness.

Stocks that produce "good vibes" in the minds of investors can sell at premium multiples for long periods even if the growth rate is only average. Those not so blessed may sell at low multiples for long periods even if their growth rate is above average. To be sure, if a growth rate appears to be established, the stock is almost certain to attract some type of following. The market is not irrational. But stocks are like people—What stimulates one may leave another cold, and the multiple improvement may be smaller and slower to be realized if the story never catches on.

So my advice is to ask yourself whether the story about our stock is one that is likely to catch the fancy of the crowd. Is it a story on which investors can build castles in the air—but castles in the air that really rest on a firm foundation?[47]

Stocks with a story certainly do attract the attention of Wall Street. Although general tests for speculative bubbles would be virtually impossible, market reactions to new issues and new listings do provide possible examples.

The New Issue Market.   New issues are initial public offerings (IPO) of stocks in heretofore privately held companies. The prices of such issues often rise dramatically in the immediate postsale period. Such trends might be exploited by buying at issue and selling quickly thereafter. The supplies of the most attractive new issues are rationed, however. Thus only the underwriting brokers' best customers may be able to buy such issues at the offering. The after-market performance of new issues also deserves our attention.

A number of studies covering various periods reached the same conclusion: New issues generally produced abnormal short-run returns followed by below-market returns for somewhat longer holding periods.[48] For example, Reilly examined the performance of 53 new issues over the 1963–1965 period. One week after the initial sale the average new issue gained 9.9% but was up only 8.7% by the fourth week. The Dow in comparison gained 3% and 5% over these periods. Even more impressively Ibbotson found a risk-adjusted excess return of 11.4% in the month of issue. Logue pointed out that, in the absence of vigorous competition, underwriters would have an incentive to underprice. Similarly, Baron showed that investment bankers who are better informed than their clients have an incentive to underprice new issues. Because the underpricing will be passed along to the issuer, the sale will be made easier and buyers happier at little cost to the underwriters. Thus, if future new issue performance is to be like the past, investors should generally follow a strategy of realizing gains soon after the initial purchase.

A number of researchers found that issues handled by nonprestigious underwriters tended to show greater appreciation than those of more prestigious firms.[49] In addition, Neuberger and Hammond found that secondary offerings of already issued securities tended to appreciate less than new issues. Nelson argued, however, that the underpricing tendency occurred during periods when the public was enamored with new issues. Moreover, new issues are typically quite risky. For example, an SEC study of the 960 firms going public between 1952 and 1962 found that 37% had failed by 1963 while only 34% were showing profit.[50] Perhaps underwriters initially price securities closer to their risk-adjusted intrinsic values than does the market.

Much of the research on new issues was conducted in the early 1970s on data from the new issue boom of the late 1960s. With the relatively depressed market that followed, both new issues and new issue studies went into decline. By late 1980, however, the new issue market, particularly that for energy and high technology companies, had taken off again. Much of the action was in the Denver OTC market, where a familiar pattern emerged: strong immediate postoffering returns followed by weaker subsequent performance. The most publicized example of these new issues was Genentech. It went public at 35 only to rise to 89 in the immediate after-market. The prior year's profit amounted to $.02 per share. At its high this company with an unproven genetic engineering technology had a market value of two-thirds of a billion dollars. Investors were again paying a high price for hope and a promise. By the spring of 1982, the Genentech price was below its original issue level and had touched as low as 25. Similarly, the Denver Penny market, which had been the center of much of the new issue hysteria, had declined dramatically.

One of the hottest new issues of 1986 was Home Shopping Network (HSN). HSN was offered at $18 per share and the first after-market trade was in the 40s. It quickly rose to the 80s and kept going. It split three times (one share became six), eventually reaching a high of 47 (equivalent to 282 on a presplit basis) in early 1987. At its peak HSN had a greater market capitalization than CBS. Ultimately reality set in and by early 1988 the stock had dropped back to around 5 (equivalent to 30 on a presplit basis).

Two somewhat more recent studies add to our knowledge of new issue performance.[51] Downes and Heinkel reported that new issues tended to do well when their entrepreneurs' confidence is reflected in their own large ownership positions. Alternatively, dividend policy was unrelated to the subsequent performance on new issues. Hess and Frost found no significant price effects from the new issues of seasoned securities.

Those who want to play the new issues game may find the following publications helpful:

- *New Issues*, Norman Fosback, editor, 3471 North Federal Highway, Fort Lauderdale, Fla. 33306
- *Emerging and Special Situations*, Robert Natale, editor, Standard & Poor's, 25 Broadway, New York, N.Y. 10004
- *Going Public, The IPO Reporter*, 150 Broadway, New York, N.Y. 10038

New Listings.   Several studies indicate that newly listed stocks typically exhibit a price pattern similar to that of new issues.[52] When an OTC stock gains a listing or when an AMEX stock is listed on the NYSE, its price tends to rise and then to fall back to the previous level. Goulet contends that the firm and its insiders sometimes utilize the postlisting period to sell stock. Accordingly, both the number of shares outstanding and the number publicly held tend to increase. This increased supply is likely to depress the price of the newly listed stock. Thus the short-term price run-up associated with a new listing or listing on a more prestigious exchange may offer an attractive selling opportunity. The price is more likely to decline thereafter.

TABLE 13.4   Speculative Bubbles

Story Stocks	Market often gets carried away with stocks having an attractive story.
New Issues	New issues generally appreciate in the immediate after-market followed by a subsequent decline.
New Listings	Prices tend to rise prior to listing and subsequently decline to previous level.

Assessment of Speculative Bubbles.   The performance of new issues, and new listings is consistent with the existence of speculative bubbles. The price rises of both new issues and newly listed issues tend to be followed by a reversal. The percentage moves of new issue prices (from offer to immediate after-market) may be large enough to yield abnormal after-commission returns. On the other hand, the difficulty of buying an issue at its initial offering price may substantially reduce the profit potential. The related price effects are generally too small for a new listing based trading strategy to cover transactions costs. Table 13.4 summarizes the discussion of speculative bubbles.

Overall Assessment of Special Situations Dependencies

All three of Smidt's hypothesized special situation price dependencies receive some support from the relevant academic research. The vast majority of the documented dependencies do not, however, provide profit opportunities for most investors. These dependencies either occur and are over with too quickly for non-exchange members to profit or the magnitudes of the average price effects are too small to be exploited by those who must pay commissions (even at a modest discount).

On the other hand, a few of the dependencies seem sufficiently large and long lasting to yield abnormal returns, even to outsiders (non-exchange members). Specifically tax-loss candidates, insider trading and new issues all may offer exploitable price trends. Moreover, those who have already decided to trade may be able to take advantage of other more modest price effects. Note, however, that the reported results reflect historical average relationships. Even if such relations continue, a large portfolio must be managed over a relatively long period to generate results close to the average.

OTHER MARKET TIMING ISSUES

Certain timing topics do not fit neatly into any of Smidt's categories. Nonetheless, some of these topics deserve to be considered. Accordingly, market moves and brokerage shares, dividend reinvestment plans, "cut your profits and let your losses run," and dollar averaging, are now discussed outside the Smidt context.

Market Moves and Brokerage Share Performance

Brokerage houses and investment banks (often the same firm is both) were long organized as partnerships or closely held corporations. Most, however, have now gone public. Their stocks reveal interesting trading patterns. Stock market volume seems to vary directly with the market averages. Brokerage profits are highly dependent on stock market volume. Thus such profits tend to be particularly strong when the market is rising and weak when it is falling. As a result, the amplitude of brokerage stock price movements tends to exceed that of the overall market. Thus those who think they can call market turns may find brokerage house stocks useful trading vehicles. On the other hand, the relationship between stock volume, brokerage profits, and brokerage share prices did not in the late 1980s follow past patterns. Again, we find that as a pattern begins to be noticed it is particularly likely to stop working.

Dividend Reinvestment Plans

Deciding whether or not to participate in a dividend reinvestment plan raises another timing issue. Since Allegheny Power started the practice in 1968, many nonfinancial firms have begun allowing their stockholders to reinvest their dividends directly into the company's stock. Prior to that time a number of financial corporations had such plans. In October 1973 at least 264 nonfinancial firms offered reinvestment programs. By year-end 1980 the number had risen to over 1,102. The numbers have continued to rise throughout the 1980s.

These plans may acquire either existing or newly issued stock. The first plans to be established relied on existing stock purchases. Typically, the corporation sends the dividends of participating stockholders to the managing bank's trust department. This bank maintains an account for each shareholder. The managing bank purchases stock on the open market. Each participant is credited with his or her shares less brokerage fees and administrative costs. Many plans also permit additional stock purchases for cash. Large round-lot purchases by the plan tend to reduce brokerage fees.

In 1969 American Telephone & Telegraph became the first company to sell newly issued stock through a reinvestment plan. Then in 1975 AT&T started the practice of offering a 5% discount on the exchanged stock. By 1980 at least 110 companies gave discounts on their dividend reinvestments. Public utilities offered many of these plans. Firms selling newly issued shares charge no brokerage fees on the transactions.

A number of investment advisors have called attention to the cash purchase option of dividend reinvestment plans. According to Sumie Kinoshita, editor of the *Directory of Companies Offering Dividend Reinvestment Plans* (Evergreen Enterprises, Laurel, Maryland), more than 900 companies now offer their shareholders the right to purchase additional shares directly from the company. Such optional purchases incur no brokerage charges if the plan uses newly issued shares or very modest brokerage charges if existing shares are bought. If, in contrast, small amounts of stock are purchased through a brokerage firm, the commissions are likely to be hefty relative to the amount of money involved. Most dividend reinvestment plans limit optional cash purchases to $3,000 to $5,000 per month. A few such as Coca-Cola, Exxon, and General Electric permit $50,000 to $100,000 per year.

A couple of organizations will assist investors who wish to participate in these plans. For a $15 fee Vita Nelson, editor of *Moneypaper* (Larchmont, New York) will help subscribers start their own plans. Similarly, the National Association of Investment Clubs (NAIC, Royal Oak, Michigan) offers the same service for a fee of $5. Both services will sell participants a single share of any of a selection of stocks without a brokerage fee. They will then see to it that the purchaser receives the forms for that company's dividend reinvestment plan. The NAIC plan includes 40 companies whereas the *Moneypaper* program involves 300.

Dividend reinvestment plans have a number of advantages. From the firm's standpoint, the plans: (1) add to stockholder goodwill, (2) increase demand for the firm's stock, (3) save some dividend-related expenses, and (4) encourage small stockholders to increase ownership. In addition, plans involving new share purchases: (1) reduce the firm's debt–equity ratio; (2) provide a regular source of equity capital; and (3) permit new equity to be sold without incurring underwriting fees or other flotation costs. In addition, the plans have several direct benefits to stockholders:

1. Brokerage costs are reduced or in some cases eliminated.
2. Dollar averaging is encouraged.
3. Dividend payments are immediately reinvested.
4. Some plans offer a discount.
5. The program provides a form of forced savings.

The plans also have a number of disadvantages:

1. Stockholder diversification may be adversely affected.
2. The liquidity of stockholders is reduced.
3. New share issues may cause some dilution.
4. Individual participation may be reduced.

A number of empirical studies have examined the impacts of these plans.[53] Pettway and Malone found that firms with such plans tended to have higher payout ratios and lower PE ratios, earnings growth, and debt–equity ratios. Thus such firms were generally less risky than those not offering plans. Pettway also reported that the stocks of firms introducing reinvestment plans usually rose in the short term. A more recent study, however, failed to confirm this tendency.

To sum up, reinvestment plan participation reduces flexibility but reduces or avoids commissions on stock purchases and in some circumstances allows investors to acquire stock at a discount. For most investors, however, the amounts involved in reinvestment plan participation are small and participation reduces the opportunity to invest dividend payments elsewhere.

A Strategy Called "Cut Your Profits and Let Your Losses Run"

The timing strategies discussed thus far have all been subjected to at least a cursory look at some evidence. Numerous trading strategies are, in contrast, offered without a shred of supporting evidence. One example of such gratuitous advice is that recommended by Jeremy Grantham, a founder of Batterymarch Financial Management. His advice is a convolution of the well-known Wall Street principle that one should sell losers and stay with winners. Grantham, in contrast, advises investors to ride their losers until they become winners.

The British-born Harvard MBA in effect believes that whatever goes up is likely eventually to come down, and vice versa.[54] That is, high-priced highly profitable firms are likely to attract competitors, which erodes their profits, while poorly performing firms will tend to become more profitable as their competition drifts away. He offers no supporting evidence for this theory. Nonetheless, according to Grantham, investors should sell their strong performers and use the proceeds to double up on the poorly performing holdings.

The proposal is an intriguing twist on the theory of contrary opinion. Like so many proposed trading strategies, however, this one has not been rigorously (or even casually) tested by any competent (or even incompetent) academician. Investors have to accept or reject such advice totally on faith.

Dollar Averaging

Most investors have little confidence in their ability to forecast market and/or individual security movements. They may prefer to use a strategy called dollar averaging.[55] Such investors would invest a fixed dollar amount per period and thereby buy more shares when prices are low than when they are high. In a purported refinement Emory recommends that, after a portfolio has shown a profit for a time, the owner should sell some components to realize a tax loss. When the portfolio begins to show losses, the reserve accumulated from past selling should be used to add to the portfolio. In this way the investor hopes to buy when the market is depressed and sell when it is high.

Similarly, Lichell suggests a systematic investment plan involving stocks and savings accounts. The investor puts aside a set amount each month. The percentage going into stocks is determined by the previous price performance. When the market price is below the investor's average cost, the percentage committed to stocks is increased, and vice versa. This approach is designed to produce a maximum gain in a fluctuating market that does eventually rise.

Finally, Sloane discusses dollar cost averaging applied to selling. He advises investors with a mutual fund redemption plan to sell a fixed number of shares per period rather than constant dollar value. The goal is to sell more shares at higher prices. Tomlinson notes, however, that periodic fixed-amount purchases perform poorly if the bulk of the transactions take place at prices that are higher than end period levels. This would, in fact, have happened to investors over a number of different 10-year periods. Similarly, Baldwin points out that no arbitrary timing system can substitute for careful analysis.

SUMMARY AND CONCLUSIONS

We began this survey of individual security timing devices by examining technical analysis. We found little value in the chart reader's magic. On the other hand, some specialized dependencies may well be profitably employed in trading decisions. Following Smidt, we explored special dependencies associated with anxious trader effects, lags in reaction to new information, and speculative bubbles.

Anxious trader effects were observed in the market's reaction to block trades, tax-loss selling, secondary offerings, and intraday interactions of the bid–ask spread with the specialist's quotes. Any adjustment lags were very quick for announcements of earnings, dividend changes, bond rating changes, stories in *The Wall Street Journal*, option listings, share repurchases, and rights offerings. Moreover, the market tended to anticipate splits, tender offers, mergers, and voluntary spin-offs. On the other hand, insider trading signals, forced conversion, and ex-dividend date reactions may produce exploitable patterns. Finally, the price effects of new issues and new listings seemed to reflect a speculative bubble phenomenon. Overall, tax-loss candidates, insider trading, and new issues seem to have offered the most exploitable price trends. The usefulness of most of the other observed dependencies is largely limited to selecting the best times to make a particular trade.

The tendency of brokerage shares to magnify market moves makes them interesting trading vehicles, at least for those with forecasting ability. Because many companies offer dividend reinvestment plans, their investors need to know the pros and cons of participation. "Cut your profits and let your losses run" was included as an example of totally unsubstantiated investment timing advice. Dollar averaging provides an alternative to trying to time individual purchases.

REVIEW QUESTIONS

1. Compare the positions of chartists and those who subscribe to the random walk hypothesis. What is the role of the market efficiency concept in this discussion? What form of the efficient market hypothesis is most relevant to this discussion?

2. Discuss the three types of situations that Smidt believes are likely to lead to specialized time series dependencies in stock prices. What evidence relates to these hypothesized dependencies? What useful trading insights, if any, emerge from this discussion?

3. How do specialists and limit orders affect intraday and overnight stock prices? How can investors interpret and take advantage of this process?

4. Why should traders always ask for a price quote that includes both the bid and ask as well as the last price? What other information might be sought when a quote is obtained? What is the value to the trader of having this information?

5. How do new issues and newly listed stock prices typically perform? Explore both the short and the longer run performance.

6. How might one use tax-loss trading, merger, tender offer, and liquidation relationships in stock market timing? Which show the greatest profit potential?

7. How have brokerage stock prices tended to fluctuate with the stock market? What has been the more recent experience?

8. Discuss and analyze the impacts of stock splits, stock dividends, and reinvestment plans. What are the relevances of these matters to investors?

9. Discuss dollar average buying and selling. What types of market performance are favorable to dollar averagers and what types are unfavorable?

REVIEW PROBLEMS

1. Plot a point and figure chart and a bar chart for the Dow Jones Industrial Average quarterly closes as reported in Table 12A.3.

2. Repeat the assignment in Problem 1 for Dow Jones annual averages for the Industrials, Transportation, and Utilities (Table 12A.2).

3. As treasurer of the Cash Rich Corporation you now manage a portfolio containing $50 million invested in short-term government bonds. A stockbroker approaches you with a dividend capture proposal. What is he talking about? What parameters would you consider in deciding whether to use his strategy?

4. A stockbroker friend approaches you with a proposal to invest in a new issue that he is peddling. The concept sounds attractive but the price seems high relative to the company's fundamentals. What factors would you consider in deciding whether or not to participate? What trading strategies are available should you decide to play?

5. You see on the Dow Jones News ticker that the High Priced Stock Corporation is about to split its stock five for one. High Priced's stock currently sells for 150. Should you rush to buy its stock before the split occurs? Explain why or why not.

6. You hear a rumor that the Asset Play Corporation is likely to be taken over. After a careful look you agree that it is vulnerable but by now its stock has risen 25% from the level a week before you heard the rumor (the market rose 3% over the same period). What factors would you consider in deciding whether to act on your expectation of a takeover?

7. Compute the end-period value of investing $1,000,000 per quarter in the DJIA (Table 12A.3) for the 1971–1975; 1976–1980; 1981–1985; and 1971–1985 periods. Ignore the impact of commissions, dividends, and taxes.

8. Repeat the assignment in Problem 7 for Dow Jones annual averages for the Industrials, Transportation, and Utilities (Table 12A.2).

9. Assuming that you could have the present value of $1,000,000 per quarter at the outset of each five-year period (using a 9% discount rate), compute the buy and hold results for Problem 7 and compare them with the dollar averaging results of the initial problem.

10. Assuming that you could have the present value of $1,000,000 per year at the outset (using a 9% discount rate), compute the buy and hold results for Problem 8 and compare them with the dollar averaging results of the initial problem.

REVIEW PROJECTS

1. Identify the large block trades for a recent week from *Barron's* Market Laboratory section. Collect data on the stocks' highs and lows for the week before, during, and after the trade. Compute the average price variability for each week. Do the same for a matched set of companies. Write a report.

2. Call the nearest stock exchange and ask to have a specialist call you after trading hours so that you can interview him or her for a class project. Ask the specialist how he or she sets the bid and ask and thus the spread. Ask about limit orders and limit order book. Keep a record of all that is said. Write a report.

3. Assemble a list of stocks that reach lows near year-end and have fallen a great deal from their earlier levels. Track their performance after year-end. Write a report.

4. Assemble a list of 10 stocks and follow them for a year. Track their performances around each earnings announcement, dividend announcement, and ex-dividend date. Write a report.

5. Assemble a list of 10 stock split and reverse split announcements in *The Wall Street Journal*. Track their performances for three months before and three months after the split announcements. Write a report.

6. Assemble a list of 10 tender offers. Plot performances from two weeks before the announcements to the time when the tender offers are complete or withdrawn. Write a report.

7. Assemble a list of 10 rights offerings. Plot the performances of the underlying stocks for a period of two weeks before the announcements until the offers are complete. Write a report.

8. Assemble a list of five stocks that fit Malkiel's "Castles in the Air" criteria. Plot their performances for six months. Write a report.

9. Assemble a list of 10 stocks that were new issues six months ago. Plot their performances from then until now. Write a report.

10. Assemble a list of five stocks that have recently been listed on the NYSE. Track their performances for six weeks before and six weeks after their listings. Write a report.

11. Assemble a list of five large brokerage stocks. Plot their performances relative to the NYSE average over a two-year period (by months). Formulate a trading rule and test it over the preceding two years. Write a report.

NOTES

1. A. Lerro and C. Swayne, *Selection of Securities: Technical Analysis of Stock Market Prices* (Morristown, N.J.: General Learning Press, 1970), 30–31.

2. P. Samuelson, "Proof that Properly Discounted Present Values of Assets Vibrate Randomly," *Bell Journal of Economics and Management Science*, Autumn 1973, 369–374.

3. "The Technical Analysts Who Called It Right," *Business Week*, August 31, 1974, 54–55.

4. J. Laing, "The Technician: Don Hahn Calls Turns of Market with Help of Graphs, Psychology," *The Wall Street Journal*, December 23, 1977, p. 1.

5. S. Smidt, "A New Look at the Random Walk Hypothesis," *Journal of Financial and Quantitative Analysis*, September 1968, 235–262.

6. P. Grier and P. Albien, "Nonrandom Price Changes in Association with Trading in Large Blocks," *Journal of Business*, July 1973, 425–433.

7. L. Dann, D. Mayers, and R. Raab, "Trading Rules, Large Blocks and the Speed of Adjustment," *Journal of Financial Economics*, January 1977, 3–22.

8. M. Scholes, "The Market for Securities: Substitution versus Price Pressure and the Effects of Information on Share Prices," *Journal of Business*, April 1979, 170–211; W. Mikkelson and M. Partch, "Stock Price Effects and Costs of Secondary Distributions," *Journal of Financial Economics*, June 1985, 165–194.

9. W. Granger and O. Morgenstern, *Predictability of Stock Market Prices* (Lexington, Mass.: Heath, 1970).

10. V. Niederhoffer and M. Osborne, "Market-Making and Reversal on the Stock Exchange," *Journal of American Statistical Association*, December 1966, 897–917.

11. R. McEnally, "Stock Price Changes Induced by Tax Switching," *Review of Business and Economic Research*, Fall 1976, 47–54; E. Dyl, "Capital Gains Taxation and Year-End Stock Market Behavior," *Journal of Finance*, March 1977, 165–175; B. Branch, "A Tax Loss Trading Rule," *Journal of Business*, April 1977, 198–207; B. Branch and C. Ryan, "Tax Loss Trading: An Inefficiency Too Large to Ignore," *The Financial Review*, Winter 1980, 20–29; R. Roll, "Vas ist Das?" *Journal of Portfolio Management*, Winter 1983, 18–28; D. Givoly and A. Ovadia, "Year-End Tax-Induced Sales and Stock Market Seasonality," *Journal of Finance*, March 1983, 171–816; W. Bondt and R. Thaler, "Further Evidence on Investor Overreaction and Stock Market Seasonality," *Journal of Finance*, July 1987, 557–581.

12. B. Branch and K. Chang, "Tax-Loss Trading, Is the Game Over or Have the Rules Changed?" *Financial Review*, Fall 1984, 55–70; Roll, op. cit.; Givoly and Ovadia, op. cit.; D. Keim, "Six Related Anomalies and Stock Return Seasonality, Further Empirical Evidence," *Journal of Financial Economics*, June 1983, 13–32; J. Lakonishok and S. Smidt, "Volume and the Turn of the Year Behavior," *Journal of Financial Economics*, September 1984, 435–455; M. Blume and R. Stambaugh, "Bias in Computed Returns: An Application to the Size Effect,"

Journal of Financial Economics, November 1983, 387–404; Blume and Stambaugh, op. cit.; W. Kross, "The Size Effect Is Primarily a Price Effect," *Journal of Financial Research*, Fall 1985, 169–179; B. Branch and K. Chang, "Low Priced Stocks and the January Effect," unpublished working paper.

13. J. Ashley, "Share Prices and Changes in Earnings and Dividends: Some Empirical Results," *Journal of Political Economy*, 1962, 82–85; C. Jones, "Economic Trends and Investment Selection," *Financial Analysts Journal*, March/April 1973, 79–83; J. Patell and M. Wolfson, "The Intraday Speed of Adjustment of Stock Prices to Earnings and Dividend Announcements," *Journal of Financial Economics*, June 1984, 223–252; R. Jennings and L. Starks, "Earnings Announcements, Stock Price Adjustment, and the Existence of Option Markets," *Journal of Finance*, March 1986, 107–125; H. Latane and L. Jones, "Standardized Unexpected Earnings—A Progress Report," *Journal of Finance*, December 1977, 1457–1467; D. Joy, R. Litzenberger, and R. McEnally, "The Adjustment of Stock Prices to Announcement of Unanticipated Change in Quarterly Earnings," *Journal of Accounting Research*, Autumn 1977, 207–224; R. Rendleman, C. Jones, and H. Latane, "Empirical Anomalies Based on Unexpected Earnings and the Importance of Risk Adjustments," *Journal of Financial Economics*, November 1982, 219–288; M. Richards and J. Martin, "Revisions in Earnings Forecasting: How Much Response?" *Journal of Portfolio Management*, Summer 1979, 47–52.

14. C. Kwan, "Efficient Market Tests of the Information Content of Dividend Announcements: Critique and Extension," *Journal of Financial and Quantitative Analysis*, June 1981, 193–206; J. Aharony and I. Swary, "Quarterly Dividend and Earnings Announcements and Stockholders Returns: An Empirical Analysis," *Journal of Finance*, March 1980, 1–12; R. Pettit, "Dividend Announcements, Security Performance and Capital Market Efficiency," *Journal of Finance*, December 1972, 1006; R. Watts, "The Information Content of Dividends," *Journal of Business*, April 1973, 191–211; A. Divecha and D. Morse, "Market Responses to Dividend Increases and Changes in Payout Ratios," *Journal of Financial and Quantitative Analysis*, June 1983, 163–174; G. Benesh, A. Keown, and J. Pinkerton, "An Examination of Market Reaction to Substantial Shifts in Dividend Policy," *Journal of Financial Research*, Summer 1984, 131–142; K. Eades, P. Hess, and E. Kim, "Market Rationality and Dividend Announcements," *Journal of Financial Economics*, December 1985, 581–604; A. Kalay and U. Loewenstein, "The Information Content of the Timing of Dividend Announcements," *Journal of Financial Economics*, July 1986, 373–389.

15. J. Campbell and W. Bernek, "Stock Price Behavior on Ex-Dividend Date," *Journal of Finance*, December 1955, 425–429; A. Kalay, "The Ex-Dividend Day Behavior of Stock Prices: A Reexamination of the Clientele Effect," *Journal of Finance*, September 1982, 1059–1070; A. Kalay and M. Subrahmanyam, "The Ex-Dividend Day Behavior of Option Prices," *Journal of Business*, January 1984, 113–128.

16. M. Joehnk, O. Bowlin, and J. Petty, "Preferred Dividend Rolls: A Viable Strategy for Corporate Money Managing?" *Financial Management*, Summer 1980, 78–87; J. Finnerty, "The Behavior of Electric Utility Common Stock Prices Near the Ex-Dividend Date," *Financial Management*, Winter 1981, 59–68.

17. D. Morse, "*The Wall Street Journal* Announcements and the Securities Markets," *Financial Analysts Journal*, March/April 1982, 69–76.

18. C. Bidwell and R. Kolb, "The Impact and Value of Broker Sell Recommendations," *Financial Review*, Fall 1980, 58–68.

19. P. Griffin and A. Sanvicente, "Common Stock Returns and Rating Changes: A Methodological Comparison," *Journal of Finance*, March 1982, 103–120; J. Wansley and T. Clauretie, "The Impact of Creditwatch Placement on Equity Returns and Bond Prices," *Journal of Financial Research*, Spring 1985, 31–42; R. Holthausen and R. Leftwich, "The Effect of Bond Rating Changes on Common Stock Prices," *Journal of Financial Economics*, September 1986, 57–90; J. Glascock, W. Davidson, and G. Henderson, "Announcement Effects of Moody's Bond Rating Changes on Equity Returns," *Quarterly Journal of Business and Economics*," Summer 1987, 67–78.

20. B. Jaggi and M. Freedman, "An Analysis of the Information Content of Pollution Disclosures," *Financial Review*, September 1982, 142–152.

21. J. Strachan, D. Smith, and W. Beedles, "The Price Reaction to (Alleged) Corporate Crime," *Financial Review*, May 1983, 121–132.

22. J. Scholl, "Before and After: What Happens to Stocks Recommended on 'Wall Street Week'?" *Barron's*, October 25, 1982, 32–33.

23. A. Schwartz, "The Adjustment of Individual Stock Prices During Periods of Unusual Disequilibria," *Financial Review*, November 1982, 228–239.

24. D. Officer and G. Trennepohl, "Price Behavior of Corporate Equities Near Options Expiration Dates," *Financial Management*, Summer 1981, 75–80; R. Strong and W. Andrew, "Further Evidence of the Influence of Option Expiration on the Underlying Common Stock," *Journal of Business Research*, August 1987, 289–302; B. Branch and J. Finnerty, "The Impact of Option Listing on the Price and Volume of the Underlying Stock," *Financial Review*, Spring 1982, 1–15; M. Whiteside, W. Dukes, and P. Dunne, "Short Term Impact of Option Trading on Underlying Securities," *Journal of Financial Research*, Winter 1983, 313–322.

25. M. Zweig, "Canny Insiders," *Barron's*, January 21, 1976, p. 5.

26. K. Nunn, G. Madden, and M. Gombola, "Are Some Insiders More 'Inside' Than Others?" *Journal of Portfolio Management*, Spring 1983, 18–22.

27. G. Trivoli, "How to Profit from Insider Trading Information," *Journal of Portfolio Management*, Summer 1980, 51–56.

28. J. Lakonishok and B. Levy, "Stock Splits and Stock Dividends: Why, Who and When," *Journal of Finance*, September 1987, 915–932.

29. E. Fama, L. Fisher, M. Jensen, and R. Roll, "The Adjustment of Stock Prices to New Information," *International Economic Review*, February 1969, 1–21; F. Reilly and E. Drzycimski, "Short-Run Profits from Stock Splits," *Financial Management*, Summer 1981, 64–74; M. Grinblatt, R. Masulis, and S. Titman, "The Valuation Effects of Stock Splits and Stock Dividends," *Journal of Financial Economics*, December 1984, 461–490.

30. J. Woolridge and D. Chambers, "Reverse Splits and Shareholder Wealth," *Financial Management*, Autumn 1983, 5–15; Grinblatt et al., ibid; A. Dravid, "A Note on the Behavior of Stock Returns around Ex-Dates of Stock Distributions," *Journal of Finance*, March 1987, 163–180.

31. W. Nichols and S. Brown, "Assimilating Earnings and Split Information," *Journal of Financial Economics*, September 1981, 309–316; W. Nichols, "Security Price Reaction to Occasional Small Stock Dividends," *Financial Review*, Winter 1981, 54–62; J. Woolridge, "Stock Dividends As Signals," *Journal of Financial Research*, Spring 1983, 1–12.

32. R. Masulis, "The Effects of Capital Structure Change on Security Prices," *Journal of Financial Economics*, June 1980, 139–178.

33. T. Vermaelen, "Common Stock Repurchases and Market Signaling: An Empirical Study," *Journal of Financial Economics*, June 1981, 139–184; L. Dann, "Common Stock Repurchasing: An Analysis of Returns to Bondholding and Stockholders," *Journal of Financial Economics*, June 1981, 113–138.

34. M. Bradley and L. Wakeman, "The Wealth Effects of Targeted Share Repurchases," *Journal of Financial Economics*, April 1983, 301–328.

35. L. Dann and H. DeAngelo, "Standstill Agreements, Privately Negotiated Stock Repurchases and the Market for Corporate Control," *Journal of Financial Economics*, April 1983, 275–300.

36. P. Dodd and J. Warner, "On Corporate Governance: A Study of Proxy Contests," *Journal of Financial Economics*, April 1983, 401–438.

37. R. White and P. Lusztig, "The Price Effects of Rights Offerings," *Journal of Financial and Quantitative Analysis*, March 1980, 23–40.

38. P. Asquith and D. Mullins, "Equity Issues and Offering Dilution," *Journal of Financial Economics*, January/February 1986, 61–89; R. Kolondy and D. Suheler, "Changes in Capital Structure, New Equity Issues, and Scale Effects," *Journal of Financial Research*, Summer 1985, 127–136; J. McConnell and C. Muscarella, "Corporate Capital Expenditure Decisions and the Market Value of the Firm," *Journal of Financial Economics*, September 1985, 399–422.

39. S. Bhagat, J. Brickley, and R. Lease, "The Authorization of Additional Common Stock: An Empirical Investigation," *Financial Management*, Autumn 1986, 45–53; K. Schipper and A. Smity, "A Comparison of Equity Carve-outs and Seasoned Equity Offerings," *Journal of Financial Economics*, January/February 1986, 153–186; R. Masulis and A. Korwar, "Seasoned Equity Offerings," *Journal of Financial Economics*, January/February 1986, 91–118; L. Dann and W. Mikkelson, "Convertible Debt Issuance, Capital Structure Change and Financing-Related Information," *Journal of Financial Economics*, June 1984, 157–186; B. Eckbo, "Valuation Effects of Corporate Debt Offerings," *Journal of Financial Economics*, January/February 1986, 119–151.

40. G. Alexander and R. Stover, "The Effect of Forced Conversions on Common Stock Prices," *Financial Management*, Spring 1980, 39–45; J. Finnerty, "Stock-for-Debt Swaps and Shareholder Returns," *Financial Management*, Autumn 1985, 5–17; R. Rogers and J. Owers, "Equity for Debt Exchanges and Stockholder Wealth," *Financial Management*, Autumn 1985, 18–26; J. Peavy and J. Scott, "The Effect of Stock for Debt Swaps on Security Returns," *Financial Review*, November 1985, 303–327; M. Pineger and R. Lease, "The Impact of Preferred-for-Common Exchange Offers on Firm Value," *Journal of Finance*, September 1986, 795–814; M. Alderson and K. Chen, "Excess Asset Reversions and Shareholder Wealth," *Journal of Finance*, March 1986, 225–241.

41. J. Miles and J. Rosenfeld, "The Effect of Voluntary Spin-off Announcements on Shareholder Wealth," *Journal of Finance*, December 1983 1519–1528.

42. J. Rosenfeld, "Additional Evidence on the Relation Between Divestiture Announcements and Shareholder Wealth," *Journal of Finance*, December 1984, 1437–1448; A. Klein, "The Timing and Substance of Divestiture Announcements: Individual, Simultaneous and Cumulative Effects," *Journal of Finance*, July 1986, 685–697; J. Zaima and D. Heath, "The Wealth Effects of Voluntary Selloffs: Implications for Divesting and Acquiring Firms," *Journal of Financial Research*, Fall 1985, 227–236; P. Jain, "The Effect of Voluntary Sell-off Announcements on Shareholder Wealth," *Journal of Finance*, March 1986, 209–224.

43. A. Shleifer, "Do Demand Curves for Stocks Slope Down?" *Journal of Finance*, July 1986, 579–590; L. Harris and E. Gurel, "Price Volume Effects Associated with Changes in the S&P 500 List: New Evidence for the Existence of Price Pressure," *Journal of Finance*, September 1986, 815–829; C. Lamoureux and J. Wansley, "Market Effects of Changes in the Standard & Poor's 500 Index," *Financial Review*, February 1987, 53–69.

44. G. Hawawini and A. Vora, "Evidence of International Systematic Risk in the Price Movements of NYSE and AMEX Common Stocks," *Journal of Financial and Quantitative Analysis*, June 1980, 331–340; G. Hawawini, "The Intertemporal Cross Price Behavior of Common Stocks: Evidence and Implications," *Journal of Financial Research*, Summer 1980, 153–167; T. McInish and R. Wood, "Intertemporal Differences in Movements of Minute-to-Minute Stock Returns," *Financial Review*, November 1984, 359–371.

45. D. Morse, "Asymmetrical Information in Securities Markets and Trading Volume," *Journal of Financial and Quantitative Analysis*, December 1980, 1129–1148.

46. M. Smirlock and L. Starks, "A Further Examination of Stock Price Changes and Transaction Volume," Journal of Financial Research, Fall 1985, 217–225.

47. B. Malkiel, *A Random Walk Down Wall Street* (New York: W.W. Norton, 1978), 273.

48. F. Reilly, "Further Evidence on Short-Run Results for New Issues Investors," *Journal of Financial and Quantitative Analysis*, January 1973, 83–90; R. Ibbotson, "Price Performance of Common Stock New Issues," *Journal of Financial Economics*, September 1975, 235–272; D. Logue, "On the Pricing of Unseasoned Equity Issues, 1965–1969," *Journal of Financial*

and Quantitative Analysis, January 1973, 91–104; D. Baron, "A Model of the Demand for Investment Banking Advising and Distribution Services for New Issues," *Journal of Finance*, September 1982, 955–996.

49. B. Neuberger and C. Hammond, "A Study of Underwriters' Experience with Unseasoned New Issues," *Journal of Financial and Quantitative Analysis*, March 1974, 165–177; D. Logue and J. Lindvall, "The Behavior of Investment Bankers: An Econometric Investigation," *Journal of Finance*, March 1974, 203–215; B. Newberger and C. La Chapelle, "Unseasoned New Issue Price Performance on Three Tiers: 1975–1980," *Financial Management*, Autumn 1983, 23–28; R. Beatty and J. Ritter, "Investment Banking, Reputation, and the Underpricing of Initial Public Offering," *Journal of Financial Economics*, January/February 1986, 213–232; E. Nelson, "Comment: 'A Study of Underwriters' Experience with Unseasoned New Issues'," *Journal of Financial and Quantitative Analysis*, March 1974, 179–180.

50. U.S. Securities and Exchange Commission, *1963 Special Study of Securities Markets* (Washington: Government Printing Office, 1963), 551.

51. D. Downes and R. Heinkel, "Signaling and the Valuation of Unseasoned New Issues," *Journal of Finance*, March 1982, 1–10; A. Hess and P. Frost, "Tests for Price Effects of New Issues of Seasoned Securities," *Journal of Finance*, March 1982, 11–26.

52. R. Furst, "Does Listing Increase the Market Price of Common Shares?" *Journal of Business*, April 1970, 174–180; J. Van Horne, "New Listings and Their Price Behavior," *Journal of Finance*, September 1970, 783–794; F. Fabozzi, "Does Listing on the AMEX Increase the Value of Equity?" *Financial Management*, Spring 1981, 43–50; S. Kichen and J. Schriber, "The Big Board Is a Roller Coaster," *Forbes*, August 31, 1982, 162–165; J. McConnell and G. Sawyer, "A Trading Strategy for New Listings on the NYSE," *Financial Analyst Journal*, January/February 1984, 34–38; C. Barry and S. Brown, "Differential Information and the Small Firm Effect," *Journal of Financial Economics*, June 1984, 283–284; T. Grammatikos and G. Papaioannou, "Market Reaction to NYSE Listings: Tests of the Marketability Gains Hypothesis," *Journal of Financial Research*, Fall 1985, 215–227; G. Sanger and J. McConnell, "Stock Exchange Listings, Firm Value, and Security Market Efficiency: The Impact of NASDAQ," *Journal of Financial and Quantitative Analysis*, March 1985, 1–25; J. McConnell and G. Sanger, "The Puzzle in Post-Listing Common Stock Returns," *Journal of Finance*, March 1987, 119–140; W. Goulet, "Price Changes, Managerial Actions and Insider Trading at the Time of Listing," *Financial Management*, Spring 1974, 30–36; *Business Week*, "Now the Best Investment May Be Your Broker," *Business Week*, June 20, 1983, 166–167.

53. R. Pettway and R. Malone, "Automatic Dividend Reinvestment Plans and Nonfinancial Corporations," *Financial Management*, Winter 1973, 11–18; R. Pettway, "Automatic Dividend Reinvestment Plans, Valuation, and Dividend Policy," unpublished working paper; P. Peterson, D. Peterson, and N. Moore, "The Adoption of New-Issue Dividend Reinvestment Plans and Shareholder Wealth," *Financial Review*, May 1987, 221–232; R. Hansen, J. Pinkerton, and A. Keown, "On Dividend Reinvestment Plans: The Adoption Decision and Stockholder Wealth Effects," *Review of Business and Economic Research*, Spring 1985, 1–10.

54. "The Man Who Loves Dogs," *Forbes*, December 11, 1978, 87–90.

55. E. Emory, *When to Sell Stocks* (Homewood, Ill.: Dow Jones-Irwin, 1973); R. Lichell, *Superpower Investing* (Lynnbrook, N.Y.: Farnsworth, 1974); L. Sloane, "Cost Averaging in Reverse," *The New York Times*, May 7, 1983, p. 30; L. Tomlinson, "Overrated Technique: Dollar Cost Averaging Has Failed to Pay Off," *Barron's*, October 20, 1975, pp. 5–11; W. Baldwin, "All Coins Have Two Sides," *Forbes*, May 23, 1983, pp. 188–189; W. Baldwin, "The Dollar-Cost Sure Thing," *Forbes*, August 15, 1983, 114–115.

SECTION FIVE

Mutual Funds, Bonds, and Options

The first four sections of this book deal largely with stock market investing. Common stocks are an important type of investment. The universe of investable assets is, however, much broader. Indeed, a variety of significant investment types are related to but distinct from common stocks. These investments are the topics of this section: mutual funds, bonds, and options. These particular types of investment have grown in relative importance in the past several years. The following case illustrates many of the issues that you will encounter in this section.

PASSING THE CFA EXAM

You have been working as a broker in a middle-sized brokerage firm for two years. Your client list has grown and the firm seems happy with your work. Nonetheless, you want to move up on as fast a track as is reasonably possible. One component of your advancement strategy is to become a Chartered Financial Analyst (CFA). Accordingly, you signed up for the CFA course and exam. Through your work as a stockbroker you have become quite familiar with stocks. You expect no trouble with that part of the exam. You know, however, that mutual funds, bonds, and options will also be covered on the exam. Moreover, your own clients have been asking you more and more questions about these investment types. You feel that now is the time to diversify your securities market knowledge.

The chapters of this section provide an extensive background on these non-stock investment types. Chapter 14 discusses mutual funds and other types of pooled portfolios. The types, organizational structures, performance, and advantages of such investments are considered. Chapters 15 and 16 cover fixed income securities. Chapter 15 examines the characteristics and types of both short- and long-term debt securities. Various factors that affect yields are considered in Chapter 16. Specifically, default risk, term structure, duration, the coupon effect, and a variety of specialized characteristic effects on yields are discussed.

Chapter 17 explores the nature of and various ways of trading pure option securities including puts, calls, warrants, and rights. Chapter 18 takes up convertibles and other types of combination securities as well as hedging and arbitraging, trades that often involve combination securities.

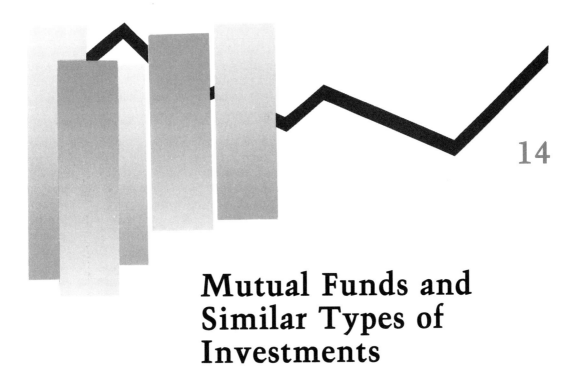

Mutual Funds and Similar Types of Investments

Mutual funds and similar types of investments are designed for people who want "professionals" to manage some of their wealth. These pooled portfolio arrangements combine resources from many investors into a single investment medium. The average risk-adjusted performance of pooled portfolios is generally no better than that of the market averages. Nevertheless, they appeal to many investors because they provide convenience, diversification, record keeping, safekeeping of securities, and portfolio management.

We begin this chapter by discussing the various types of pooled portfolio arrangements. Next the funds' organizational structures, sales fees, asset compositions, and investment priorities (income, growth, liquidity, capital preservation, tax preference) are explored. A listing of some sources of information on mutual funds follows. We then examine fund performance, giving particular attention to the difficulty funds have in outperforming the market. Finally, various criteria for selecting funds are explored.

DIFFERING WAYS OF ORGANIZING FUNDS

Mutual funds and similar investments assemble and maintain pooled portfolios primarily for individual investors who have neither the resources nor the time to manage a portfolio of their own effectively. The ownership of these pooled portfolios is subdivided into shares or units. Each such ownership unit represents ownership of a fraction of the pooled portfolio. Each share of a fund with ten million outstanding shares represents ownership of one ten-millionth of the fund's portfolio.

Suppose that fund's portfolio has a market value of $100,000,000. Each share would in effect represent $10 worth of the portfolio. That is, one ten-millionth of a $100-million portfolio is $10. A share's pro rata ownership of the portfolio is called its net asset value (NAV). If the value of the portfolio rose to $110,000,000, NAV would increase to $11 (assuming that the number of shares outstanding did not change). Gains and losses in mutual fund investments largely stem from increases and decreases in the NAVs. Funds also distribute dividend and capital gains to their shareholders. These distributions reflect the shareholder's pro rata share of the portfolio's dividends and realized capital gains.

The vast majority of pooled portfolio investments are organized as mutual funds. Mutual funds differ from other types of pooled portfolio investments in that they are open ended. Indeed, another name for mutual fund is open-end investment company. Mutual funds are open ended in the sense that they maintain a continuous market for their shares. That is, the company that manages the fund stands willing to buy and to sell shares on demand.

Selling Fees on Mutual Funds

Mutual funds are sold in two basic fashions. The shares of no-load funds are generally sold directly to the fund's investors. The fund charges no sales fee on such transactions. Load funds, in contrast, sell their shares through an agent such as a stockbroker or mutual fund salesperson.

Load Funds.   Purchasers of load funds generally incur substantial sales fees. These fees range from 8.5% of the amount invested on relatively small acquisitions (under $10,000) to 1% on very large purchases (over $1 million). This sales fee is subtracted from the gross amount invested. The standard $850 fee on a $10,000 load fund purchase leaves only $9,150 for investment. A fee of 8.5% on the gross investment is equivalent to 9.3% on the net investment. Such a sales fee compares unfavorably with the 2% to 3% average commission on direct stock acquisitions. Suppose a load fund has a NAV of $20 per share. What would one who paid an 8.5% load pay per share? The formula for computing the load is:

$$P_l = NAV/(1 - l)$$

where:

$$P_l = \text{price after load}$$
$$NAV = \text{net asset value per share}$$
$$l = \text{load percentage}$$

In this example, NAV $= 20$ and $l = .085$. Accordingly:

$$P_l = NAV/(1 - l) = 20/(.915) = 21.86$$

Thus for an NAV of 20 and a standard load of 8.5%, the investor would pay $21.86 per share, or $1.86 above the NAV of $20 per share.

Front-End Loading.   Investors are sometimes persuaded to sign up for a plan to purchase mutual fund shares periodically over an extended period. For example, an individual might agree to invest $2,000 per year for the next 10 years. Perhaps the money is to be earmarked for a child's college education. The agent who sells such a plan is rewarded with an incentive commission based on the total amount of the planned purchase. Under so-called *front-end loading*, the purchaser pays much of this commission in the initial year of the plan. Not infrequently, however, the investor decides to cancel the plan before all of the planned purchases have been made. The fees charged on front-end loaded purchase agreements can be particularly costly to buyers who subsequently cancel.

Under the Securities Amendments Act of 1970 purchasers have 45 days to cancel and thereby receive a full refund. The front-end load is not allowed to exceed 50% of the initial year's payment. Cancellation within a year reduces the load to 15% of the dollar amount of the purchase. Thus an investor who initially invested $1,000, waited a year, and then canceled would have paid an initial sales fee of $500. The amount actually invested in the fund's portfolio ($500 out of the $1,000) would have to double (to $1,000) before the investment's value would even be back to the amount that was initially invested. An investor who canceled before the end of the first year (so that the fee would be reduced to 15%, or $150) or made more than one payment (so that the load was spread over a larger purchase) would not do quite as poorly. Even so, separate yearly purchases are less expensive.

To illustrate, a 10-year plan to invest $1,000 annually would incur a commission of $500 in the first year and a total of $850 over the life of the plan. That commission would be reduced to $150 if the plan were canceled within a year. A straight 8.5% commission on a $1,000 purchase would, in contrast, incur only an $85 sales fee. Additional $1,000 purchases would incur additional $85 commissions in subsequent years. The $85 commissions would stop at the same time that the purchases stopped.

In addition to incurring a higher total commission charge if the plan is canceled, front-end loading reduces the amount that is invested in the earlier years of the plan. Under the normal circumstances of a rising market, having less invested in the early years of the plan means a lower overall return for the participant in the plan. Front-end loading is attractive to the agent but has no advantages for the investor.

12b-1 Funds.   The so-called 12b-1 plan is a relatively new approach to selling mutual funds. With this plan the selling agent is paid a commission at the time of sale but the buyer is not initially charged a fee. A percentage of asset value (up to 1.25%) is subtracted each year to compensate the fund for its selling expenses. Thus the fund in effect advances the fee to the agent and recaptures the sum from the buyer over time (including an implicit interest charge).

Investors who redeem their 12b-1 shares before the full amount of the selling cost is recouped will generally be charged a substantial exit (redemption) fee. Thus 12b-1 funds are structured to cost very nearly the same percentage fee to buy and sell as regular load funds. Indeed, those who hold their shares for long enough may end up paying more in selling fees than if they had purchased a load fund. Moreover, such funds do highlight themselves as 12b-1 funds. Technically they are no-load funds because no initial selling fee is charged. Investors must carefully read the fund's prospectus to determine if a 12b-1 fee is charged. Note, however, that *The Wall Street Journal* quotations now identify funds with a distribution (12b-1) charge.

What the Selling Fees Buy.   The investment performances (portfolios) of no-load, load, and 12b-1 funds tend to be quite similar on the average. From the investor's standpoint the principal difference between these types of funds is that those who purchase no-load funds do not incur an agent or sales fee. They do bear the overall selling expenses that the fund incurs. The pure (not 12b-1) no-load funds, however, have no agents to compensate. Thus their selling expenses are relatively modest. Instead of paying a load or 12b-1 fee equivalent to 8.5% of the amount invested, a no-load fund investor might incur selling expenses of a fraction of one percent per year.

The investor who buys through an agent of course has access to the "service" that the agent provides. Agents may advise their clients regarding the risks, potential returns, tax consequences, and other relevant characteristics of the funds they are able to offer through the company or companies that they represent. Mutual fund agents know the relevant features of their product, but most investors can find suitable no-load funds themselves with a bit of research. The fee of $85 per $1,000 invested on load funds provides a good reason for most investors to prefer a no-load fund.

Many investors already have a broker or financial planner to go to for other (non-mutual-fund) business. This person may be approached for a limited amount of assistance regarding an investment in a no-load fund. Investors should, of course, realize that such a broker or financial planner will not be directly compensated through his or her mutual fund purchases. Accordingly, investors may not want to rely too much on such advisors. Alternatively, they may believe that their advisors have been sufficiently compensated through other business that they as clients have given them to justify asking for a reasonable amount of "free" advice.

Prospectuses for no-load funds may be obtained by responding to advertisements in the financial press or writing to the funds listed in such guides as *Weisenberger's Investment Companies* (an annual publication available in most libraries). Several directories are devoted exclusively to no-load funds. Published annually, they list various types of funds, along with their services, minimum investment amounts, addresses, and telephone numbers. One such guide is available for $2 from the No-Load Mutual Fund Association, 11 Penn Plaza, Room 2204, New York, NY 10001. The *Handbook for No-Load Fund Investors*, $24, from P.O. Box 283, Hastings-on-Hudson, NY 10706 is more comprehensive. Finally, *The Individual Investor's Guide to No-Load Mutual Funds* is available to all members of the American Association of Individual Investors (membership fee of $48 per year, 612 N. Michigan Avenue, Chicago, IL 60611).

Open-End and Closed-End Investment Companies

Mutual funds are one of a broader class of investment vehicles called an investment company. We have already noted that mutual funds are called open-end investment companies. Thus the number of outstanding shares of a mutual fund increases or decreases with new sales and/or redemptions.

If mutual funds are open-end investment companies, the natural question to ask is, What are closed-end investment companies? Again, the answer has to do with their attitude toward the sale of additional shares. The number of closed-end investment company shares outstanding almost always remains constant. Closed-end funds are established at a particular time with a set number of outstanding shares. Thereafter the number of available shares will rarely if ever change.

Unlike the purchase of a mutual fund, the buyer of shares in a closed-end fund does not automatically receive a prospectus when he or she considers a purchase. Investors buy and sell their shares in the open market much as with any other corporation. Thus their share prices are determined by supply and demand. The shares may sell for a premium or, more commonly, at a discount from their NAV.

Boudreau suggests that the divergence of per share prices from their NAVs reflects differences in expected future performance.[1] Malkiel's in-depth empirical study ascribed part of the discount to unrealized appreciation, capital gains distributions policy, and letter and foreign stock investments.[2] Most of the discounts, however, seemed to result from the lack of broker incentives (their fee for selling a load fund is much higher than their commission on a closed-end fund). Leonard and Noble, in contrast, argue that the discounts and premiums are related to uncertain future risk levels and the difficulty of forcing a liquidation.[3]

Richards, Fraser, and Groth found that over the 1970–1976 period deep-discount funds generally outperformed the market.[4] Anderson's update through 1984 obtained similar results.[5] Large shareholders sometimes force closed-end funds to convert to open end. Such conversions tend to be quite profitable for the fund-holders.[6]

Consider for example, a 10,000,000 share closed-end fund with a per share NAV and market price of $10.00 and $7.50, respectively. Such a fund might offer a tempting target. Although a takeover effort would probably drive the price up, perhaps 3,000,000 shares could be purchased over time at an average cost of $8.50. If the remaining stock is widely dispersed, 30% of the outstanding shares should be sufficient for control. The new control group could quickly convert to an open-ended fund. By offering to buy back shares at their NAV, the fund would immediately make each holder's shares worth the $10 NAV (assuming no price change while the takeover was under way). Relatively large resources are required to force such a reorganization, but small fundholders will also profit.

Investment Company Quotations

The closed-end fund quotation shown in Figure 14.1 was taken from *The Wall Street Journal*. Similar quotations appear in *The New York Times*, *Barron's*, and elsewhere. Funds are grouped into three categories: diversified common stock funds, closed-end bond funds, and specialized equity and convertible funds. *Investment company quotations* contain the following information:

1. Name of fund

FIGURE 14.1 Closed-End Quotation

Publicly Traded Funds

Friday, January 15, 1988

Unaudited net asset values of publicly traded investment shares, formerly listed as Closed End Funds, as of Friday. Also shown is the closing listed market price of each fund's shares, with the percentage difference between the net asset value and the stock price.

DIVERSIFIED COMMON STOCK FUNDS

	N.A. Value	Stk Price	% Diff.
AdmExp	16.24	15⅞	- 2.2
Baker	49.03	35½	-27.5
Blue Ch Val	6.96	5¾	-17.4
Clemente-Gl(b)	7.59	5¾	-24.2
Eqty Guard(b)	8.67	7⅞	- 9.2
Gemii Cap	n.a.	n.a.	n.a.
Gemii Inc	n.a.	n.a.	n.a.
GenAln	16.96	14	-17.5
GlobalGr Cap	n.a.	n.a.	n.a.
GlobalGr Inc	n.a.	n.a.	n.a.
GSO Trust	9.25	9⅜	+ 1.4
Lehman	13.62	11⅝	-14.6
Libty A-Star	8.11	6¾	-16.8
NiagSh	14.48	12¼	-15.4
NchAp GrEq	7.34	6	-18.3
QuestFValCap	9.40	6½	-30.9
QuestFValinc	11.64	9⅜	-19.5
Royce Value	8.19	7⅛	-13.0
Schafer Valu	8.04	6⅝	-17.6
Source	36.43	33½	- 8.0
Tri-Cont	23.88	21⅝	- 9.4
Worldwd Val	16.35	12½	-23.5
Zweig Fn	9.55	9⅛	- 4.4

BOND FUND

	N.A. Value	Stk Price	% Diff.
ACM Gov	11.18	11¾	+ 5.0
CIM High	9.53	10	+ 4.9
Hi Yld Inc	9.37	9¾	+ 4.1
MFS Govinc	9.48	10⅜	+ 9.4
MFS I&O	9.76	10½	+ 7.6
MFS Multi	9.18	10⅛	+ 10.3
MFS Muni	8.97	9⅛	+ 1.7
Muni Ins	9.64	9⅞	+ 2.4

SPECIALIZED & CONVERTIBLE FUNDS

	N.A. Value	Stk Price	% Diff.
AmCap(a)	21.97	23¾	+ 8.1
ASA(b)(c)	72.69	49⅝	-31.7
Asia Pac	n.a.	n.a.	n.a.
Bancrt	22.18	21	- 5.3
BGR Prec Mtls(b)(e)	n.a.	n.a.	n.a.
Castle	21.85	20⅞	- 4.4

	N.A. Value	Stk Price	% Diff.
CenFd Canada(b)	6.65	5¾	-13.5
CentS	11.22	9⅜	-16.4
Claremt	48.14	44⅝	- 7.3
Couns Tndm C	6.61	4½	-31.9
Cypress Fd	8.88	6⅝	-25.4
DufPh Util	7.83	8¾	+ 11.7
Ellswth Cv	8.05	7	-13.0
EmgMed	n.a.	n.a.	n.a.
Engex	11.73	8¼	-30.3
Fin New C	16.23	13¾	-15.2
1stAustralia	n.a.	n.a.	n.a.
Fst Fn Fd	6.64	6⅛	- 7.8
France Fd(b)	10.49	8⅞	-15.4
Gabelli E		9.55	8 -16.2
Germany	6.59	6⅝	0.0
H&Q Health	7.59	6¼	-17.7
Helvetia Fd	11.33	10¼	- 9.3
Hopper Sol	n.a.	n.a.	n.a.
Italy Fd(b)	9.70	7¼	-25.2
Korea Fd	35.85	60	+67.3
Malays Fd	7.60	6⅞	- 9.4
CNV Hldg Cap	8.73	4⅜	-50.0
CNV Hldg Inc	9.44	11	+ 17.0
Mexico(b)	4.25	3¾	-11.8
MG SmCap	7.51	6⅛	-18.4
Pete&Res	24.71	23⅛	- 6.4
PilReg	8.29	6⅝	-20.1
Prg Inc	8.78	8⅞	+ 1.0
Reg FinIShs	7.03	5⅞	-16.4
Scandinavia	8.19	6¾	-17.6
ScudderN Asia	10.62	7⅜	-30.5
Taiwan Fd(a)(b)	17.76	29⅝	+ 66.8
TCW CvtSec(b)	7.88	6⅞	-12.8
Tmpl Emrg M(b)	7.61	6⅞	- 9.6
UTD Kgdm Fd	10.63	8⅜	-21.2
Z-Seven(d)	15.64	16½	+ 5.5

(a) Ex-Dividend.
(b) As of Thursday's close.
(c) Translated at Commercial Rand exchange rate.
(d) N.A.V. reflects $1.16 a share for taxes.
(e) In Canadian dollars.
n.a. - Not available.

Source: *The Wall Street Journal*, January 15, 1988. Reprinted by permission, © Dow Jones & Company, Inc. All rights reserved.

2. Market where traded

3. NAV

4. Stock price

5. Premium and discount of stock price relative to NAV

The closed-end quotations may be compared with *The Wall Street Journal* mutual fund quotation in Figure 14.2. Similar quotes appear in *The New York*

FIGURE 14.2 Mutual Fund Quotation

MUTUAL FUNDS

Friday, May 20, 1988
Price ranges for investment companies, as quoted by the National Association of Securities Dealers. NAV stands for net asset value per share; the offering includes net asset value plus maximum sales charge, if any.

	NAV	Offer NAV Price Chg.
AAL CapG	p8.15	8.56+ .01
AAL Incm	p9.53	10.01− .02
AARP Invest Program:		
Cap Grw	21.67	N.L.+ .04
Gen Bnd	14.65	N.L. ...
Ginnie M	15.00	N.L.+ .01
Gro Inc	20.12	N.L.+ .04
TxFr Bd	15.54	N.L. ...
TxF Shrt	15.36	N.L. ...
ABT Funds: ABT Funds:		...
Emrg Gr	p7.59	7.97+ .01
Growth I	p9.64	10.12+ .01
Sec Inc	p8.50	8.92 ...
Util Inc	p12.98	13.63+ .02
AcornFd r	36.37	N.L.+ .11
Addsn Cp	p13.55	13.97+ .01
Adtek Fd	9.31	N.L. ...
Advnt Gv	p9.42	9.84 ...
Advest Advantage:		
Govt r	p8.73	N.L. ...
Growth r	p10.84	N.L.− .03
Income r	p9.44	N.L.+ .01
Specl r	p8.76	N.L.+ .01
Afuture Fd	9.40	N.L.+ .01

	NAV	Offer NAV Price Chg.
Composite Group:		
Bond Stk	p9.67	10.07 ...
Growth	p10.22	10.65− .01
Income	p8.95	9.32+ .01
NW Pt	p13.47	14.03+ .02
Tax Ex	p7.12	7.42+ .01
US Gov	p .99	1.03 ...
Value	p10.38	10.81 ...
Conn Mutual:		
Govt	10.25	10.93 ...
Growth	10.01	10.68 ...
Totl Ret	11.18	11.93 ...
CommonSense Trust:		
Govt	10.98	11.77− .02
Grwth	10.01	10.94+ .02
Gro Inc	9.83	10.74+ .01
Concord In	6.85	7.14 ...
Concrd TE	6.87	7.16 ...
Coun MB	9.61	N.L.+ .01
Continental Equities:		
Equity r	p8.98	9.21+ .01
OptInc r	p8.32	8.53+ .01
US Gov r	p9.01	9.24− .01
Copley F	10.44	N.L.+ .03

	NAV	Offer NAV Price Chg.
SelMD r	7.14	7.29 ...
SelMetl r	12.87	13.13+ .06
SelPap r	11.29	11.52+ .06
SelPrp r	9.77	9.97+ .05
SelReg r	8.89	9.07+ .02
SelRetl r	11.08	11.31− .01
SelSL r	8.34	8.51− .02
SelSoft r	13.60	13.88 ...
SelTec r	17.35	17.70− .02
SelTele r	16.34	16.67+ .09
SelUtil r	24.47	24.97+ .04
Fidelity Plymouth Fds:		
AggInc r	p9.63	10.03− .02
Glob Nat	p10.67	11.11+ .02

	NAV	Offer NAV Price Chg.
IDS Int	p8.49	8.93+ .02
IDS Mgt	p7.22	7.60+ .01
IDS MN	p4.78	5.03+ .01
IDS Mutl	p11.46	12.06+ .03
IDS NY	p4.60	4.84+ .01
IDS ND	p7.63	8.03+ .02
IDS Prec	p7.04	7.41+ .07
IDS Prog	p6.12	6.44+ .01
IDS Selct	p8.36	8.80+ .01
IDS Stck	p16.88	17.77+ .05
IDS Tax	p3.90	4.10 ...
IDS Ag r	p8.78	8.78+ .02
IDS Eq r	p7.14	7.14+ .01
IDS Inc r	p5.61	5.61+ .01

Times and most major newspapers. The offer price reflects the load if any. No-load funds sell at their NAVs. Funds that assess distribution fees (12b-1 funds) are identified with the letter *p* immediately preceding the NAV. Similarly, those that charge a redemption fee are denoted with the letter *r* following their name. Many fund groups such as the American Express Funds or the Dreyfus Group are managed by the same management company. The management companies offer an array of separate funds that appeal to the needs and goals of different investors.

Redemption of Funds

Most mutual funds are set up to facilitate relatively easy redemption at their NAV. Normally investors can call (toll free) or write for a partial or full redemption and receive a speedy reply. Most funds also have an automatic withdrawal plan. Such a plan can be structured to provide a monthly income for the fundholder. Thus the investor can have a sum periodically withdrawn from the fund as long as the remaining balance is sufficient to cover the withdrawal. Some funds do charge a redemption fee. Investors can, however, normally switch funds within the same group (family of funds) without incurring a load or redemption fee or even having to deal with very much paperwork. Most funds do limit the number of switches per year and charge a modest fee such as $5 per exchange. Some investors try to profit from market swings by switching between a group's stock and money market funds.

Unit Investment Trusts and Variable Annuities

Unit investment trusts are similar to but distinct from mutual funds and other investment companies. Units of such trusts, like mutual fund shares, represent part ownership of a common portfolio but, unlike mutual funds, unit trust portfolios are unmanaged. The absence of portfolio management expenses tends to enhance the return. Such trusts are typically set up and marketed by a brokerage firm that receives an underwriting fee from the proceeds of the sale. Once assembled, most debt security portfolios can appropriately be left unmanaged until they mature. The secondary market for the ownership units of such trusts is relatively inactive. Thus unit trusts are costly to trade prior to maturity whereas mutual funds are easy to redeem. Because few investors would want to hold an unmanaged equity security portfolio, most unit trust portfolios are composed of debt securities.

Some insurance companies sell investments called variable annuities. These annuities have much in common with mutual funds, closed-end investment companies, and unit investment trusts.[7] Each of these investment types represents pooled portfolios of assets owned by a group of investors. Unlike the other types of pooled portfolio investments, variable annuities generate a tax-deferred return. Moreover, no tax liability is incurred when funds are shifted from one annuity to another (such as from a stock to a money market annuity). On the other hand, withdrawals prior to age 59½ incur a 10% federal income tax penalty. Expenses and fees tend to be higher with annuities. Thus the annuity investor obtains some tax advantages but has less flexibility than a mutual fund investor.

Other Types of Pooled Portfolios: Operating Companies, Partnerships, and Blind Pools

Several other types of pooled portfolios are available to the investor. For example, some operating companies hold such large portfolios of stock that they are in effect investment companies in all but name. Among the better known of these firms are Alleghany Corporation and Berkshire Hathaway. Alleghany was once a holding company for the New York Central Railroad. More recently it has become a major stockholder in American Express and a number of other companies. Similarly, Berkshire Hathaway was once in textiles but now is primarily an owner of stocks. Its CEO, Warren Buffett, is highly respected for his adroit portfolio management.

Most pooled portfolios are organized as corporations either as investment companies (open-ended or closed-end) or possibly as an operating company. They may also be organized as partnerships.

Perhaps the most risky pooled portfolio device is the *blind pool*. With a blind pool the investor agrees to finance a venture whose precise purposes are to be revealed later. The prospective investor will, however, be told the pool's general purpose (such as to finance a program of risk arbitrage). Most people who invest in blind pools do so on the basis of their faith in the investor or group of investors that they are bankrolling. In some instances the investors are given a clue such as the intended industry or investment approach. At other times the investors are truly blind. Blind pools may be organized as shares of stock (usually of a closed-end fund), limited partnership interests, or debt securities (often to be used in as yet undisclosed takeover attempts). Somewhat surprisingly, many people are quite willing to buy these pigs in a poke.

The Taxation of Pooled Portfolio Investments

The general principle of pooled portfolio taxation is that the investor is to be taxed as if he or she owned a portion of the pooled portfolio directly. The issue is, however, more complicated than it might seem. When shares are bought and later sold the difference is indeed a taxable gain. Under the Tax Reform Act of 1986 such a gain is taxed as ordinary income. Funds also generate their own income when they receive and distribute dividends or interest on their portfolio. Similarly, taxable income for the investor is the result when the funds realize and distribute capital gains on their own portfolios. To qualify as a regulated investment company under Subchapter M of the Internal Revenue Code the fund must distribute at least 90% of its gross income (dividends, interest, and capital gains). Failure to make the minimum distributions on a timely basis subjects the fund to a nonde-ductible 4% excise tax. Accordingly, virtually all funds comply with the income distribution requirements. The investor is liable for income taxes on such distri-butions. Moreover, the timing and amounts of such distributions may not always be easy to predict. Thus both the amount and the timing of the distributions are often a surprise. Sometimes the surprise is unpleasant, particularly for an investor who already has a substantial amount of taxable income.

A particularly controversial provision of the 1986 act deals with the taxation of the fund management expenses. Prior to the 1986 act, such expenses were deducted from the income reported to the fundholders. The 1986 tax reform in effect made the income that had been sheltered by such expenses taxable to most investors. That is, even though only net income is distributed to the fundholder, the gross amount of income is taxable to the fundholder.

The newer law classifies the expenses of managing investments (whether the portfolio is managed by the investor or a portfolio manager) as a miscellaneous deduction. Only the portion of such expenses exceeding 2% of the taxpayer's adjusted gross income (AGI) is deductible. Thus those who do not itemize auto-matically lose the deduction. Similarly, those whose total miscellaneous deductions fall below 2% of AGI receive no tax benefit. Even those who do reach the 2% threshold can deduct only a portion of their miscellaneous expenses. Thus investors whose miscellaneous expenses total 3% of their AGI can deduct only expenses equal to 1% of the AGI.

Table 14.1 illustrates the various types of funds by organizational structure.

DIFFERING TYPES OF MUTUAL FUND PORTFOLIOS

Most mutual fund portfolios consist of stocks and/or bonds (including money market securities and long-term debt securities). Mutual funds can, however, be set up to manage almost any type of investable asset including commodities, op-tions, coins, art, and precious metals.

Bond Funds and Balanced Funds

Bond funds are available in a host of different types. Money market funds hold short-term debt security portfolios. Several categories of long-term bond funds

TABLE 14.1 Pooled Portfolio Types of Funds by Organizational Structure

Type	Characteristics
	Principal Types
Mutual Funds	Open-ended; price based on NAV
Load Funds	Sold through salesperson for a commission
No-Load Funds	Sold directly without a commission
12b-1 Funds	Sales fee assessed over time; penalty charged for early redemption
Closed-End Investment Companies	Corporation owning a managed portfolio; stock traded on an exchange or OTC, usually at a discount from NAV
Unit Investment Trusts	Unmanaged; self-liquidating; largely for debt securities
Variable Annuities	Mutual fund type of instrument sold by insurance companies
	Unusual Ways of Organizing Pooled Portfolios
Operating Companies	A few erstwhile operating companies hold such large portfolios that their performances are more closely related to that of their security holdings than that of their operations.
Partnerships	Some mutual funds have chosen the partnership form because of its greater flexibility and/or tax advantages.
Blind Pools	Investors bankroll enterprises whose purposes will later be revealed; such pools are sometimes involved in takeover financing.

manage portfolios of corporates, governments, or municipals. These broad categories are divided into subcategories such as high-risk corporates and intermediate-term governments. Balanced fund portfolios combine common stocks with bonds and preferred stock and tend to have slightly riskier portfolios with somewhat higher expected yields than comparable-maturity bond funds. The remainder of the chapter will deal with equity (common stock) mutual funds. Other types of funds will be discussed in subsequent chapters.

Common Stock Funds: Their Differing Goals

Common stock funds may be classified into a number of categories reflecting their managers' stated goals. Such funds differ principally in their risk orientation. Performance or "go-go" funds (a type that was popular in the late 1960s and early 1970s) are exceptionally risk oriented. Growth funds emphasize appreciation potential and often accept considerable risk. Income funds concentrate on high-dividend, low-risk stocks with modest growth potentials. Middle-of-the-road funds tend to place a somewhat higher premium on stability than growth funds but less than the income funds. A fund's risk orientation may be determined from its prospectus. *Standard & Poor's Stock Guide* and a number of other sources contain extensive fund classifications.

Specialized Types of Common Stock Funds

Specialized common stock funds include those that invest in specific industries (Chemical Fund), types of companies (Technology Fund), or regions (Northeast

TABLE 14.2 Types of Common Stock Funds

Type	Characteristics
General Categories	
Performance Funds	Exceptionally risk oriented
Growth Funds	Emphasizes price appreciation
Middle-of-the-Road Funds	Seeks a balance between price appreciation and stability
Income Funds	Assembles a low-risk, high-yield portfolio
Specialized Categories	
Industry Funds	Swap Funds
Special Types of Companies	Regional Specialization
Index Funds	International Funds
Country Funds	Socially Responsible Funds
Dual Funds	Penny Funds

Fund). These types of mutual funds are sometimes called sector funds. They come in a variety of categories.

Hedge funds attempt to take advantage of market downswings by shorting some stocks while establishing long positions in others. International funds participate in some foreign markets. Country funds assemble diversified portfolios from the stocks of a single country. Dual funds assign their portfolio's capital gains to half of the shareholders while accruing dividends to the other half. Share selections depend principally on the preferences and tax status of the investor. Swap funds permit purchases with stock of other companies. Index funds are managed to duplicate the performance of some stock index such as the S&P 500. Socially responsible funds restrict their portfolio to companies not involved in activities that they consider objectionable (polluters, war materials, South Africa, tobacco, alcohol, etc.). Penny funds concentrate on low-priced stocks ($1 per share or less).

Table 14.2 outlines the primary categories of stock funds.

Recent Trends

Like many other areas of investments, the investment company industry has experienced a number of changes over the past several years. One of the most noteworthy of these is the huge proliferation of new funds. More than 2,000 different funds are now active and available to the investor. Many of these new funds are very specialized sector funds. Fidelity Select Portfolios has even established what amounts to its own little stock market. Investors can invest in one of Fidelity's sector funds and then switch from sector to sector by making a phone call and paying a modest fee ($10). Thus they can use Fidelity to try to catch the trends in the market without incurring the substantial commission costs that would otherwise be involved. No doubt many more try this strategy than succeed.

Another recent trend is the move of some funds to change from corporations to limited partnerships. Indeed, a number of existing mutual funds have converted to the partnership form to gain some flexibility and tax advantages. Such a shift allows interest on federal government bonds to escape the state corporate tax that could otherwise be assessed on corporate income. Furthermore, as partnerships the funds are not as restricted in their short-term trading activity. Fundholders in such partnership funds become limited partners with the management firm taking on the general partnership. Some such partnerships have been organized to participate in leveraged buyouts. In still another recent change mutual funds can, since 1980, be bought on margin, used as collateral for loans and sold short, much like other types of securities.

In a recycling of an earlier concept, funds of funds invest fundholders' money in other mutual funds. Such funds claim to shift their portfolio around so as to catch the best performing funds of the moment. Generally, however, they only end up adding an extra layer of expenses on their customers' backs.

Finally, a number of new closed-end funds have recently been established, often with a well-known name (e.g., Zweig) associated. Most such funds were marketed with a great deal of hoopla and then promptly fell in price. Initially, at least, few if any were able to outperform the market return after allowing for flotation costs and the discount in price relative to their NAV.

Mutual Fund Information Sources

The most comprehensive mutual fund information source is *Investment Companies*, published by Arthur Weisenberger Services. This annual publication covers over 500 funds with a page-long description on each fund's history, objectives, special services, advisors, sales charges, and 10-year performance. Every three months Weisenberger also publishes *Management Results*, which updates the long-term performance of over 400 funds; *Current Performance and Dividend Record* provides a monthly update of the short-run performance.

United Business Service Company publishes *United Mutual Fund Selection* twice a month. Each issue contains articles on mutual funds, and the first issue of each month reports changes in NAV for the covered funds. *Forbes* examines mutual funds in one of its two August issues. Recent and 10-year returns are reported along with sales charges and expense ratios. Standard & Poor's surveys about 400 funds in the monthly *S&P Stock Guide*. Each issue contains data on goals, type, size, NAV, distributions, prices, and yields. *Barron's* covers mutual fund performance quarterly. Figure 14.3 is taken from the *S&P Stock Guide*.

Several newsletters advise investors on when to switch between a common stock and a money market fund to catch the market turns. This category includes *Telephone Switch* (Huntington Beach, Calif.); *Switch Fund* (Gaithersburg, Md.); *Prime Investment Alert* (Portland, Maine); and *Systems and Forecasts* (Great Neck, N.Y.). Most of these funds offer their subscribers a taped telephone advisory (not toll free) as well as a newsletter. Newsletters that concentrate on fund selection and performance include *No Load Fund X* (San Francisco); *Growth Fund Guide* (Rapid City, S.D.); *No Load Fund Investor* (Hastings, N.Y.); *United Mutual Fund Selector* (Boston); and *The Mutual Fund Letter* (Chicago). Finally, the *Mutual Funds Forum*, published by Investment Company Institute, 1775 K Street N.W., Washington, DC 20006, publishes articles of general interest to the industry.

FIGURE 14.3 Mutual Funds in the *S&P Stock Guide*

Fund	Year Formed	Prin. Obj.	Type	Sept. 30, 1987 Total Net Assets (Mil.$)	Cash & Equiv (Mil.$)	See Foot-notes	Net Assets per Share % Change from Previous Dec. 31 At: 1983	1984	1985	1986	Dec. 31 1987	Nov. 30 Unit	Min. Unit	Max. Sales Chg. %	Distributions per Share from Invest. Income 1986	1987	Security Profits 1986	1987	$10,000 Invested 12-31-81 Now Worth	PRICE REC. 1987 High	Low	NAV Per Sh NAV Per Shr.	Offer Price	% Yield From Inv. Inc.
USAA Tax Ex.Inter.Term.... *'82	I		TF,BD	323.0	18.0	ʃ†	+ 9.5	+ 8.4	+15.8	+12.9		1.8	$3,000	None	0.912	0.622				12.58	10.87	11.50	11.50	7.9
USAA Tax Ex.High Yield... *'82	I		TF,BD	793.0	36.0	ʃ†	+11.2	+ 9.8	+18.9	+16.7		6.3	$3,000	None	1.07	0.745	0.085			14.15	11.10	12.18	12.18	8.8
Value Line Fund........... '49	GI	C	268.3	34.2	......	− 0.8	−14.8	+34.4	+16.8		4.2	$250	None	0.24	0.24	1.75	0.176	15,418	19.16	12.93	13.65	13.65	1.8
Value L. Lev. Growth Inv. '72	G	L	424.2	14.9	......	+ 8.0	− 9.2	+27.0	+23.1		6.0	$250	None	0.34	0.146	2.60	0.216	17,668	31.03	19.33	21.05	21.05	1.6
Van Kamp.M.Ins.Tax Free. *'84	I	TF	494.7	5.6	*ʃ†			+18.1	+19.2		2.5	$1,500	4.9	1.24	1.021	0.108			18.32	15.28	16.48	17.33	7.2
Van Kamp.M.Tax Fr HI Inc *'85	I	TF	331.9	10.8	ʃ†			+21.1	+ 0.5			$1,500	4.9	1.359	1.076				17.18	15.14	15.78	16.59	8.2
Van Kampen M.U.S.Govt. ..*'84	I	GB	4774.2	322.9	³			+20.8	+15.5		1.4	$1,500	4.9	1.846	1.17	0.354	0.212			16.81	13.92	14.95	15.72	11.7
Vanguard Fxd.Inc.Sec.																								
GNMA........................*'80	I	G	2015.6	(13.5)	......	+ 9.1	+12.8	+19.4	+11.1		3.7	$3,000	None	0.994	0.372		0.006	20,280	10.17	8.64	9.30	9.30	10.7
Invest.Gr.Bonds ....'73	I	BD	511.6	15.1	¹	+ 6.5	+12.9	+20.5	+13.5		6.0	$3,000	None	0.885	0.324		0.123	19,508	8.91	7.18	7.76	7.76	11.4
Vanguard Index Trust.......'76	SP	1136.6	4.2	......	+21.2	+ 6.0	+30.7	+18.2		2.1	$1,500	None	0.89	0.54	2.02	......	23,705	33.93	22.58	23.22	23.22	3.8
Vanguard Mun.Short Term. '76	I	TF	973.1	516.0	*ʃ†	+ 4.9	+ 6.6	+ 6.3	+ 7.2		0.0	$3,000	None	0.868	0.321	0.01	......		15.55	15.06	15.12	15.12	5.7
Vanguard Mun.Intermed....'76	I	TF	816.0	95.0	*ʃ†	+ 6.4	+ 9.1	+16.0	+15.8		4.1	$3,000	None	0.875	0.349	0.02	......	19,441	12.64	10.75	11.44	11.44	7.6
Vanguard Mun.Long Term...'76	I	TF	544.3	62.7	*ʃ†	+ 9.2	+ 8.0	+19.2	+18.8		9.0	$3,000	None	0.839	0.334	0.19	......	20,792	11.40	9.19	9.78	9.78	8.6
Vanguard World Fund:																								
Intl.Growth Ptfl. ....'85	G	INTL	645.5	14.0	⁷			+25.8	+55.7	+ 5.2		$1,500	None	0.07	0.11	0.80	1.82		14.68	8.67	9.91	9.91	0.7
U.S.Growth Ptfl. ....'85	G	C	176.7	13.9	⁸			+17.6	+ 7.3		3.3	$1,500	None	0.28		1.94	3.57		13.13	6.19	6.41	6.41	4.4
Washington Mutual Inv. '52	IG	C	3170.0	117.0	......		+25.3	+ 6.8	+29.7	+22.0		3.3	$250	8.5	0.51	0.52	0.66	0.44	26,967	15.12	10.77	10.93	11.95	4.3
Wellesley Income.......... '68	I	FL	532.1	29.3			+18.2	+15.7	+26.4	+18.0		3.4	$1,500	None	1.33	0.84	0.47		23,999	17.19	13.79	14.88	14.88	8.9
Wellington .... '28	GIR	B	1575.2	22.6			+23.1	+10.2	+27.7	+18.1		2.5	$1,500	None	0.94	0.54	0.34		24,594	19.04	14.31	14.92	14.92	6.3
Windsor .... '58	GI	C	5893.6	783.3	⁹		+29.6	+18.7	+26.8	+19.8	4.1	n/a	None	0.85	0.30	2.59	......	27,050	18.21	13.08	13.08	13.08	6.5
Windsor II .... *'85	GI	C	1702.2	153.3						+21.3	5.9	$1,500	None	0.43	0.20	0.52			15.95	10.72	11.46	11.46	3.8

Stock Splits & Divs. (figures adjusted): ¹Rated ''AAAf'' by S&P. ²Rated''AAAf''by S & P. ³Was Westminster Bd. Inv. Gr.. ⁴Was Warwick Municipal. ⁵Was Warwick Intermediate. ⁶Was Warwick Long Term. ⁷Formed Oct'85 from break-up of Ivest. Perf.is from Oct'85. ⁸Formed Oct'85 from break-up of Ivest. Perf.is from Oct'85. *Now closed to new investors.

EXPLANATION OF COLUMN HEADINGS AND FOOTNOTES

Fund-Year Formed: Title of fund and year originated or * initially offered to public.

Principal Objective: G—Growth; I—Income; R—Return on Capital; S—Stability; E—Objectives treated equally; P—Preservation of Capital, in order of importance.

Type: B—Balanced; BD—Bond; C—Com; CV—Cv Bond & Pfd; FL—Flexible; GB—Lg term gov't,GNMA,etc; GL—Global; H—Hedge; INTL—Int'l; L—Leverage; PM—Precious Metals; O—Options; SP—Specialized; TF—Tax Free; ST—Short term investors.

Total Net Assets: Total assets at market value less current liabilities (includes cash/equiv.).

Cash & Equivalent: Cash and receivables plus U. S. Govt securs., short-term commercial paper and short-term municipal and corporate bonds and notes, less current liabilities.

IRA & Keogh: All funds have plans available except where noted as follows: ʃ—No IRA plan available †—No Keogh plan available.

Net Assets per Share % Change: Represents NAV (net asset value) at end of period plus capital gains and dividends distributed during the period, less NAV at beginning of period; divided by NAV at beginning of period, all on a per share basis & excl. sales charge.

Minimum Unit: Minimum initial purchase of shares (exclusive of contractual plans);usually lower for retirement plans.

Maximum Sales Charge %: A charge, covering costs and commissions, added to net asset value in computing the offering price. Represents a percentage of the offering price. (E.R.F.—Early Redemption Fee).

Distributions: Dividends from net investment income and distributions from security profits to record holders in years indicated.

$10,000 Invested 12-31-81 Now Worth: Shows the results of a $10,000 investment assuming that all dividends and capital gains are reinvested at year end. Calculations are based on NAV and exclude any sales charge. Mutual funds formed during 1982 are included from the date of formation.

Price Record: Ranges are based on net asset value per share.

% Yield From Investment Income: Dividends from investment income in 1986 divided by current offering price.

§ —Fund not presently offered.

—1987 prices and NAV % change at end of month.

n/a: Not available.

Source: *Standard & Poor's Stock Guide*, December 1987, p. 256.

MUTUAL FUND PERFORMANCE

The remainder of this chapter considers fund performance relative to their goals, the market, their potential, and individual investor performance as well as the predicting of their future performance.

Fund Performance Relative to Their Goals

Funds usually behave in a manner that is consistent with their stated objectives. That is, funds that advertise themselves as being aggressive assemble risky portfolios and generally achieve somewhat above-average long-term returns. Funds that claim to be less risk oriented usually do assemble portfolios of more stable stocks and generate lower but more secure returns. Ang and Chua also found a high random component in mutual fund performance, however.[8]

Mutual Fund and Other Institutional Investor Performance

According to many different studies, the average risk-adjusted performance of mutual funds rarely outperforms that of the market. Mains undertook what emerged as a relatively favorable study of mutual fund performance. After correcting some earlier researchers' errors, he reported that mutual funds did tend to outperform the market before, but not after, making adjustments for their expenses.[9] Similarly, Shawky found that average fund performances were substantially better in the 1970s than before, but that their average returns still only approximated that of the NYSE Index.[10] Chang and Lewellen report that fund performance was also below that of the market when the Arbitrage Pricing Model (rather than CAPM) was used to set the benchmark.[11] In 1986, for example, the average stock mutual fund gained 13% compared with 19% for the S&P 500 and 27% for the Dow. Moreover, a variety of studies have found that many mutual funds attempt to time the market but rarely succeed in doing so.[12]

The available information suggests that the risk-adjusted performance of other institutional investors is no better than that of mutual funds. For example, Schlarbaum found that the 1958–1967 performance of 20 property liability insurance company portfolios was significantly below the market's average.[13] Similarly, Bogle and Twardowski reported that, among institutional investors, mutual funds did best, followed by investment counselors; insurance companies with banks had the poorest relative record.[14] Long-term performance for the various types of institutional investors was relatively similar, however.

While most mutual funds do not earn abnormal risk-adjusted returns, outperforming a relatively efficient market is difficult. Still, mutual funds do have the resources to hire the best talent, collect the most useful information, and analyze it with the most sophisticated techniques. Furthermore, their large size should facilitate operational efficiency—especially when securities are bought in quantities qualifying for commission discounts. Why then, with all these advantages, do the funds so rarely outperform the market?

Why Mutual Funds Rarely Outperform the Market. Outperforming the average would be difficult for any group of investors who make up a large part of the average. Institutions hold approximately 40% of the total value of U.S. stocks with a still higher percentage of the larger listed issues making up most of the market indexes.

Each type of institutional investor (investment companies, insurance companies, pension funds, college endowments, foundations, and bank trust departments) has access to similar managerial talent, sources of information, and types of analysis. Furthermore, private investment managers, individuals with large sums to invest, and nonfinancial corporations with large stock portfolios all have equivalent advantages. Thus mutual funds must compete with other similarly positioned institutional and noninstitutional investors.

Because their abilities and resources are comparable, the various categories of institutional investors should generate similar average performances. Moreover, still other investors may have an advantage over most institutional investors. For example, companies appear to be particularly adept at choosing attractive times to purchase their own stock.[15] Indeed, corporate officials sometimes take advantage of the firm's stock repurchase decision to sell their own holdings. Insider sales may often signal a price decline.[16] While institutions sometimes trade on inside information, insiders have better access and may more effectively conceal their activities. Those who use inside information to generate excess returns do so at the expense of the remainder of the market. Thus some noninstitutional and corporate investors have advantages that allow them to time their trades and select their investments at least as well as, and often better than, mutual funds. Moreover, many small to moderate-sized investors are at least as sophisticated as the large institutions.

Unsophisticated investors with small to moderate-sized portfolios make up the remainder of the market. The average performance of the market represents the weighted average performances of the portfolios of the various subgroups making up the market. The average large investor (institutional or otherwise) can outperform the market only at the expense of these less sophisticated investors. This is a difficult task for several reasons. Unsophisticated small investors are a relatively small part of the market. Thus a substantial amount of small investor underperformance (vis-à-vis the market) is required to permit any appreciable overperformance by the remainder. Small investor performance may, however, be largely random and thus similar to the market as a whole. Finally, mutual funds themselves have a number of disadvantages that tend to lower their return by more than any likely advantage they may have vis-à-vis unsophisticated investors.

Mutual Fund Disadvantages.   Owners' returns will exceed the market return only if a mutual fund's portfolio outperforms the market by more than the management fees. Such fees average about 0.5% per year. Furthermore, load fund owners incur both the sales fee on purchases of the fund's shares and the commissions the fund pays when it trades. Investors who acquire stock directly or through no-load funds will, in contrast, pay commissions only on the stocks purchased. Quantity discounts on large institutional trades (which are also available to no-load funds) reduce but do not eliminate the double-commission disadvantage of load funds.

Second, funds, particularly those with large portfolios, often adversely affect the market prices of the stocks that they trade. Sizable purchases tend to be above the most recent market price and large sales below it. About 20% of institutional trading is in blocks of 10,000 shares or more. Radcliff reported that sellers may have to give price concessions of up to 12% on such trades. Similarly, the *Institutional Investor Survey* suggests average concessions of 1% to 3%.[17] Moreover, Kraus and Stoll found a tendency for prices to fall after institutional purchases and rise after institutional sales.[18] In an extensive study of trading costs for one institutional investor (Bankers Trust Company), Condon found average price concessions of .92% on purchases and .18% on sales.[19] Finally, Loeb found that trading costs varied directly with market capitalization and inversely with block size, both of which adversely affect large investors such as mutual funds.[20]

Small investors, in contrast, can generally purchase up to several round lots (or even more for an actively traded stock) with little price effect. Funds sometimes attempt to counteract this problem (as well as the control problem) by assigning portions of their portfolio to several managerial groups. Such subdividing may reduce but is unlikely to eliminate the adverse price effects of their large trades. Furthermore, managing costs may be increased by subdividing.

Third, large institutions are vulnerable to certain management abuses that have the effect of reducing their returns. For example, some managers may churn their accounts, producing commissions for their broker friends but reducing the fund's return. A high turnover rate may represent window-dressing dumping of "losers" before quarterly reporting, frustration with past failures, a conspiracy to milk the fund through commission payments, or a sincere belief that active trading may increase the fund's return. Fund returns are often reduced by rapid turnover, however.

Fund managers may also be taken in by false claims designed to support a declining stock. Prebankruptcy rumors and trading in Equity Funding and Penn Central Railroad provide examples of managers seeking to prop up the stock while they unload. Small investors may also be adversely affected by such activities, although the institutional investors are, because of their size, the most likely targets for the tempting fruit of supposedly inside information. Finally, some managers such as Robert Vesco of Investors Overseas Services have purposely defrauded their fund's owners.

Fourth, institutional investors typically restrict their analysis to a small percentage of traded stocks. Institutions frequently focus on as little as 25 to as many as 300 companies compared with about 5,000 listed securities and at least 20,000 traded OTC. Institutional holdings are clearly concentrated among the larger firms. The attention paid to this small segment of the market greatly reduces the likelihood of finding undervalued situations. Other stocks may remain misvalued because much of the market ignores them.

Table 14.3 summarizes this discussion of why mutual fund performance is often no better than the market averages.

TABLE 14.3 Why Average Mutual Fund Performance Is Usually No Better than the Market Averages

- Institutional investors such as mutual funds constitute a large part of the market.
- Some other types of large investors (such as wealthy individuals and large corporations) have advantages similar to those of the institutions.
- Some investors such as corporate insiders have even greater advantages than institutional investors.
- Unsophisticated small investors make up only a small part of the market.
- Mutual funds have a number of disadvantages relative to many other types of investors:
  1. Management fees, expenses, and loads for load funds reduce their returns.
  2. Large investors such as mutual funds usually adversely affect the market when they trade.
  3. Institutions are vulnerable to management abuses that reduce their returns.
  4. Institutions usually restrict their analysis to a small percentage of traded stocks.

Mutual Fund versus Individual Performance

We have seen that institutions, including mutual funds, do not generally outperform the market. Comparable evidence on individual investor performance is limited. The average small investor's risk-adjusted return could be inferior to those of both the market and the average mutual fund. Investors who trade in small lots generally pay full (undiscounted) commissions. Furthermore, their small portfolios are unlikely to be well diversified.

Predicting Fund Performance

Many money managers have sought to equal the market's performance. They do so by assembling a portfolio of stocks having characteristics like the S&P 500 (index fund). Other investors have wondered if some especially well-managed funds might consistently outperform the market. To test this proposition Williamson ranked the risk-adjusted returns of a sample of 180 firms and found no significant correlation between the 1961–1965 and 1966–1970 rankings. The funds tended to persist in the top 20% and 40%. The compositions of the bottom 20% and 40% were essentially random, however. Rudolph suggests that management turnover may help explain why past performance does not appear to provide a particularly useful prediction of future fund performance.[21] Williamson also found the availability of net new money was uncorrelated with past or future performance.[22]

Elsewhere I investigated turnover, size, and load's effect on subsequent return.[23] Turnover appeared to increase costs and reduce returns. Large funds tended to have lower returns than small funds, perhaps because of the greater adverse price effects of their typically larger trades and the more restricted sample of stocks available to go into their portfolios. That load fund returns are inferior to those of no-load funds is not surprising. The load is largely a dead-weight cost. Although the selection of a small, low-turnover, no-load fund may produce returns above those of the average fund, more than 80% of the return variation was left unexplained by the Branch model. Moreover, in earlier work Friend, Blume, and Crockett found that return tended to increase with turnover and was unrelated to size.[24] Investors themselves seem to be largely uninfluenced by most of the criteria discussed here. Size, marketing effort, and prior performance do appear to affect investor choice, however.[25]

Reasons for Buying Funds

If funds do not generally outperform random selection and if accurately predicting future fund performance is very difficult, should individuals invest in mutual funds? In other words, should they pay for professional management that does not increase the risk-adjusted expected return? Levy and Sarnat make such a case.[26] They contend that mutual funds spread risks effectively (provide instant diversification with a single investment); provide safekeeping for the securities, accurate record keeping, and portfolio management; and obtain discount commissions. Funds have generally offered relatively attractive expected returns (compared to the returns offered on the instruments available at banks, thrifts, and insurance companies), a large variety of risk-expected return trade-offs, and an opportunity to spread risk more efficiently than small investors can do on their own.

Mutual Funds and the Small Investor

Where does this leave small investors? Those who choose to have a fund manage their investments should expect no better than average performance (relative to the stock market). Investors who believe that they can outperform the market may

How should an individual proceed who wants to invest in a mutual fund? An article in *The Wall Street Journal* has attempted to answer that question.

Demystifying the Prospectus: Questions Investors Should Ask in Evaluating Funds

MUTUAL FUNDS
MANAGED INVESTING

By Pamela Sebastian
Staff Reporter of The Wall Street Journal

Mutual fund prospectuses have been called the "junk mail of the affluent" and a lot worse.

"A prospectus is a classic example of information overkill," says Edward D. McCarthy, a financial planner in Cranston, R.I. He reads at least four or five mutual-fund prospectuses a week to help size up potentially good investments for his clients. It's necessary, he says, but it can be tedious—and even intimidating—for the uninitiated.

Many mutual funds have paid off handsomely in recent years because of dazzling securities markets, even if investors did only scant homework on the funds beforehand. But as the bull market in stocks and bonds shows signs of age, financial planners say the "shotgun approach" to fund selection is less likely to work. At the same time, investors have more possibilities than ever to chose from—more than 1,580 stock and bond funds, triple the number in 1982.

Market professionals say investors will find it easier to sort out mutual-fund prospectuses if they familiarize themselves with some basic sections and terms. They say it shouldn't take more than 10 or 15 minutes to pluck the vital information from these documents. The following questions can provide a starting point and

perhaps help an investor get through prospectuses more easily.

DO GOALS MATCH?

Financial planners say fund investors sometimes miss an obvious first step in choosing a fund: making certain that the fund's goals, as outlined in the investment objective and policy section, match the needs of the investor. "It's amazing the number of shareholders who shouldn't buy a capital appreciation fund, for instance, because they can't take the risk," but who make such an investment anyway because they want the aggressive growth potential, says Robert Wadsworth, a New York City consultant.

Another mismatching of goals can occur when investors choose certain government-bond funds because they offer limited check-writing privileges and perhaps look similar to interest-paying checking accounts. The recent drop in bond prices, however, has cut the value of many of those funds, bringing home the fact that both principal and interest are at risk.

HOW LONG'S ITS LEASH?

After determining the objectives wanted in a fund, investors should check the prospectus to see if the fund is kept on a tight leash regarding its investment strategy. "I want to know if a fund is using leverage," says Karen Spero, a financial planner in Cincinnati. Leverage, simply put, involves using borrowed money to increase a fund's exposure to the securities markets, and it can amplify gains—or losses. Taking a different and more common tack, many funds are starting to use futures or options as a way to hedge against portfolio declines. This also must be spelled out in the prospectus.

A stock fund may also have the option to swing heavily into Treasury bills or other highly liquid "cash" investments, to capitalize on rising interest rates that can penalize stocks. Again, an investor should know if the fund can use cash to support performance and that the fund isn't forever set in stocks.

There isn't necessarily anything wrong with such strategies, Ms. Spero notes, but they can indicate it is a more aggressive—and riskier—investment. "As soon as I see too much game playing, I'm not comfortable," she says.

WHAT'S THE TRACK RECORD?

To appraise a fund's performance, financial planners say the simplest way is to follow the net asset value—the fund equivalent of per-share earnings—in the 10-year financial table. Many investors buy funds based on rankings that boast a fund is No. 1 in its category, or tops for a specific quarter. But the bottom line is a fund's track record over several years and over different market cycles. That history, plus the fund's payout record, gives a good snapshot of performance.

Newer funds obviously don't have such track records. In some cases, however, a new fund will tout the previous record of the fund manager, particularly when the manager's identity is the fund's most marketable aspect. A new fund also may allude to the reputation of its parent or its sector, as did the Morgan Grenfell Small-Cap Fund, a closed-end stock fund brought out last spring by one of Britain's biggest money managers. While such factors may help attract new investors, the prospectuses routinely carry the caveat that such reputations don't guarantee the same results on a new fund.

In most cases, however, prospectuses provide scant information about the individual actually running the fund—although financial planners say that such information is often helpful and that con-

tinuity in mutual-fund management can be a positive sign. When the manager isn't identified in the prospectus, investors can turn to the fund's annual report and annual meeting proxy for more information about the individual. Those documents may also have information on the fund's outside directors, who are supposed to monitor its operations, and on the fund's investment advisers if it uses an outside investment-management firm.

Financial planners often measure a stock fund's performance by comparing its record with the Standard & Poor's 500-stock index, and funds often include that comparison in the prospectus. For bond funds, there isn't as clear a bench mark. Returns will vary greatly, depending on the average maturity of the bonds in the portfolio and whether the fund invests in top-rated, lower-yielding bonds or more speculative, higher-yielding ones. Many bond fund managers, however, rate their performance against the Shearson Lehman U.S. government and corporate bond index.

HOW DO THE FEES WORK?

Investors, of course, should carefully examine the fees that may be involved in a fund, especially since the charges have become more complex in recent years. Until a few years ago the fund world was divided into two clear groups: load funds, sold by brokers, with an 8.5% upfront sales charge, and no-load funds, sold by direct marketers, without any sales charge.

Lately, though, charges have become much less obvious. The so-called 12b-1 fee, for example, is tagged onto some no-load funds to help defray marketing and distribution costs. This change has jig-sawed fund pricing. Often used in combination with a "low-load" upfront sales charge of just a few percentage points, the fee becomes an important source of broker commissions.

Such fees, which can range from 0.25% to 1%, can be listed under "distribution"—pages away from other charges. In a recent prospectus for a new fund from American Funds Group, the tag "12b-1" isn't mentioned at all in explaining "distribution expenditures'' of as much as 0.30% annually.

In addition, many so-called no-load funds have a small upfront charge. For instance, several such funds from Fidelity Investments actually carry 2% or 3% loads, including the giant Magellan Fund.

Some funds levy a so-called sliding scale back-end load, or "contingent deferred sales charge." Such funds charge only a small upfront fee, or no fee at all, when the product is sold; to encourage investors to leave their assets in the fund, however, a fee is charged if the investor leaves before a certain length of time. The earlier the investor tries to get out of the fund, the higher the exit fee. As a result, new fund investors end up taking a big hit to buy their way out of a declining market.

For load funds, financial planners recommend that investors make sure that loads aren't charged on reinvested dividends; only a handful of funds do that sort of double dipping. Dividends should be reinvested at net asset value, the planners say.

Concerned that costs are scattered throughout a prospectus, regulators are working on a controversial proposal that would gather all fees, sales charges and other expenses in a single table in the prospectus to show how the combined costs affect a theoretical investment over time.

WHAT'S THE EXPENSE RATIO?

Investors also should examine the fund's operating expenses. The key to that is the expense ratio, a line item in the 10-year per-share table. The expense ratio measures a fund's costs as a percentage of assets. An expense ratio of 1% is considered average; money-market expense ratios are currently averaging about 0.75%. The single biggest component of the ratio is the fund's advisory fee, currently averaging about 0.6% of assets.

In general, bond-fund managers try to keep expenses on the low end of the range to help keep their yields up.

ARE THERE WARNING SIGNS?

Financial planners say investors should watch for certain red flags. Sometimes, these danger signs actually *look* like flags. Fluttering out of a prospectus packet or arriving under separate cover, a "supplement to the prospectus" can be as small as 7-by-3-inches. Although it may look insignificant, it can contain vital information, such as a change in the price structure of the fund—the addition of a 12b-1 plan, for instance, or a refiguring of the sales charge. It may also tell investors of an incentive bonus offered to brokers. If the supplement says the fund distributor "will reallow to dealers the full amount of the sales charge," it means the fund company is giving up its share of the load during a kickoff promotion period to provide the bonuses for brokers.

Another eyebrow raiser is the mention of pending lawsuits or regulatory reviews. Funds must disclose any "meaningful" litigation pending against them or any review by a governmental agency. Investors should contact the fund for details when such items are cited.

Financial planners also urge investors to place special emphasis on the standard disclaimers that every prospectus carries, usually under the section on the investment objective. These clauses emphasize the basic risk involved.

In an introductory adult education class that Mr. McCarthy teaches, he requires each student to find the basic disclaimer in a prospectus and read it out loud. Mr. McCarthy calls this the "How can I lose money" clause. He says that when read aloud, such standard warnings as "This fund will invest in unseasoned securities which may or may not have a proven track record" take on more meaning and emphasize the basic risk that is involved.

Go Beyond the Prospectus To Get Even More Details

By a WALL STREET JOURNAL *Staff Reporter*

Investors who want to know more about a fund should request the "statement of additional information." This document can add meaningful detail to the snapshot provided by the prospectus.

For example, an investor reading the prospectus for T. Rowe Price New Era Fund, would get the essentials, including a concise history of the 18-year-old fund, which picks growth stocks to try to outpace inflation, with a leaning toward natural-resource companies. The prospectus also includes notes on its ability to use futures contracts and on its restrictions against investing too heavily in any one stock or industry.

The fund's statement of additional information goes into several pages of detailed explanations of how futures and options work. It also features a table comparing the fund's track record with several market bench marks.

But even investors who do all the homework and request all the documents shouldn't feel too complacent. The financial statements must be updated every year, so new prospectuses are issued annually. Sometimes only the per-share data table changes, but often other revisions are included.

Source: P. Sebastian, "Demystifying the Prospectus: Questions Investors Should Ask in Evaluating Funds," *The Wall Street Journal*, September 18, 1987, pp. 31, 47. Reprinted by permission, © Dow Jones & Company, Inc. All rights reserved.

---

appropriately manage their entire portfolios. Relatively modest resources (e.g., $10,000) may be sufficient to construct a well-diversified portfolio. Moreover, investors who are not especially risk averse may properly choose to manage even very small portfolios. Risk averters of modest means with little confidence in their investment skills and investors with limited time for investment management may well wish to have a mutual fund manage part or all of their wealth. Investors in mutual funds will find relatively few reliable selection guidelines. Clearly, investors should prefer a no-load fund with a risk level corresponding to their preferences. Also, a small, low-turnover fund with favorable past performance may generate a bit better performance than the average fund.

SUMMARY AND CONCLUSIONS

This chapter has considered various aspects of mutual funds and related investments. First, the types of funds were explored. Funds differ on the basis of their organizational structure, selling fee structure (load, no-load, and 12b-1), types of portfolios, and risk orientations. Their performance was discussed next. Mutual funds and similar types of investors generally fail to outperform the market for a variety of reasons: professionally managed portfolios are a large part of the total market, their expenses reduce their net returns, they affect the market when they trade, they are subject to various management abuses, and they are often restricted to relatively few companies. The difficulties involved in predicting mutual fund performance were considered. Small, no-load, low-turnover funds with favorable past performance may (or may not) outperform the averages. Finally, reasons for buying mutual funds in spite of their poor performance were examined. They offer a convenient and relatively cost-effective way of diversifying. Investors who do not wish to manage their portfolios may well prefer to let a mutual fund handle their investment decisions.

REVIEW QUESTIONS

1. Discuss the relative costs of load funds, 12b-1 funds, no-load funds, and front-end loading. How do the quotations differ for these various types of funds?

2. Compare the organizational structures of mutual funds, closed-end funds, and unit investment trusts. What is the relevance of these structures to the investor?

3. List the kinds of assets owned by the various types of mutual funds or other types of pooled portfolio investments. How many relevant types of investments can you list that do not have a corresponding pooled portfolio vehicle for participation? Why would some investors prefer an alternative to direct investment?

4. Describe the various types of risk orientations of common stock funds. Also describe the various specialized types of common stock funds. What is meant by a sector fund? How do families of funds facilitate switching from one type of fund to another?

5. In general how do mutual funds perform relative to the market? How does their performance compare with other institutional investors and individual investors as a group?

6. Why do most mutual funds rarely outperform the market? What advantages and disadvantages do mutual funds have relative to other types of investors?

7. What factors may be used to predict individual mutual fund performance? To what degree, if any, may individual mutual fund performance be predicted? What suggested forecasting approaches appear to have little or no reliability?

8. Make a case for purchasing mutual funds in spite of their relatively poor risk-adjusted return history. What types of investors are most likely to find mutual funds most attractive and what types least attractive?

REVIEW PROBLEMS

1. Suppose that you have $10,000 to invest in a mutual fund. A friend who has just gone to work selling mutual funds offers to sell you shares from one of his funds at the standard load. What would the load amount to? How much would be left for investment? Suppose you know about a no-load fund with no redemption fee that is expected to generate an average return of 8% per year for the next three years. How much must your friend's fund earn to match the performance expected from the no-load fund?

2. Compare the yearly performance of an investment of $3,000 per year for five years in each of the following:
    a. A no-load mutual fund
    b. A load mutual fund with standard fees assessed each year
    c. A front-end load plan assessing the maximum commission in the first year and the remainder in the second

    Assume that each fund generates a return on its net asset value of 11% per year.

3. Continue Problem 2 as follows: Assume that the no-load fund does generate an 11% return. How high must the load fund's annual return be for it to equal the end of period value of the no-load fund? How high must the front-end load plan be to equal the end of period value of the no-load fund?

4. The $$$ Mutual Fund has a portfolio valued at $650,000,000 and 30,000,000 shares outstanding. What is its NAV? Suppose over the next 12 months the fund's portfolio value increases to $800,000,000 and shares outstanding increase by 2,000,000. What is the percentage increase in the NAV?

5. Assume that the $$$ Mutual Fund in Problem 4 is a load fund that charges the standard fee and paid a distribution of $.70 per share over the past year. What would the one-year return be for an investor in the $$$ Fund?

6. The %%% Closed-End Investment Company (%CEIC) sells for 25 with a NAV of 33. Compute the percentage discount. Suppose 10,000,000 shares are outstanding and the P. Boom Pekans Group proceed to take over %CEIC. The Pekans Group pays an average of 28 for 33% of the stock and then converts it to an open-end fund. If the effort takes six months and the NAV is then at 35, what is their gross profit? Suppose legal costs amount to $500,000 and commissions are 2% of trading costs; what is their net return? Assume that %CEIC pays no dividend or other distribution.

7. Continuing with Problem 6, a rough rule of thumb is that an investment management contract is worth about 1% of the money under management. This is an approximation of the present value of the net management fees expected from the business. If the Pekans Group sells their ownership

position and their management contract (for 1% of %CEIC's NAV) when the share price reaches 40, what will they receive? If that occurs two years after their initial investment, what is the annualized return on their investment?

8. The Scupper Group maintains an extensive list of no-load sector funds. The 1990 results for five of the group's funds are reproduced below:

Fund Name	12/31/90 NAV	Dividends	Capital Distributions	12/31/90 NAV
Good Good	14.29	.53	.74	13.01
Bond Bond	12.89	1.12	.47	11.98
Go Go	7.01	.03	.26	13.08
Chip Chip	16.67	.89	.78	17.56
Cash Cash	10.00	.68	.00	10.00

Compute the holding period return for each fund. The market index return for 1990 was 22%. How do these various funds compare? What else should be considered in making the comparison? From the information supplied how would you classify each of these funds?

9. One year's results can be misleading. A better gauge of the potential performance of a fund may be obtained from an analysis of its performance over several years. Consider the following:

Fund Holding Period Return

Year	Good Good	Bond Bond	Go Go	Chip Chip	Cash Cash	Market Index
1983	10.5	8.8	17.7	13.5	6.8	12.5
1984	− 8.5	6.0	−21.6	− 3.5	8.4	− 5.3
1985	15.7	11.4	31.4	23.5	7.3	18.9
1986	14.3	9.6	23.4	17.5	5.3	16.2
1987	−21.3	−9.1	−32.7	−14.5	11.5	−20.2
1988	12.2	10.3	53.4	31.4	7.9	24.3
1989	9.0	11.5	−12.3	16.3	7.1	14.5

Compute the mean return and standard deviation of each of the five funds using results reported for the seven years. Now compute the deviations from the market index returns for each year for each fund. Compute the means and standard deviations for these means. Compare the two sets of means and standard deviations. What do they tell you? How would you use these data to assess the funds? What other information would be useful in your assessment? Now add the returns for 1990 (Problem 8). Repeat the problem. How do the results change?

10. Sharp introduced a means of evaluating portfolio performance that relates return to risk. Specifically, the "Sharp Measure" evaluates reward relative to risk as the ratio of the excess return to the standard deviation of that return. Compute the reward to risk for each of the funds of Problem 9. Subtract the market index from each gross return to obtain the fund's

excess return for each year. Take the average value of these ratios for each fund. Compute these averages with and without the 1990 returns.

11. Treynor suggested measuring reward to risk with the β rather than the standard deviation as the risk index ("Treynor Measure"). Compute the Treynor Measure of the funds of Problem 9 for the following βs: Good Good, 1.1; Bond Bond, .6; Go Go, 1.3; Chip Chip, .9; Cash Cash, .2. Compare the rankings for the two measures of reward to risk. Do this problem both with and without the 1990 results.

REVIEW PROJECTS

1. Update Table 14.2 by going to the library and obtaining recent data on the number and asset size of the various types of mutual funds. Compare the most recent numbers with those in the table.

2. Compare the coverage of mutual funds in each of the sources discussed in the text. Write a report.

3. Assemble a list of five load and five no-load funds having similar objectives. Plot their annual performances for the past five years. Compare the returns to investors in the two groups. Write a report.

4. Assemble a list of five closed-end investment companies and plot their performances and premium/discounts for the past six months. Devise a trading rule. Test it over the next preceding six months. Write a report.

5. Write for five no-load mutual fund information packages and study them carefully. Then invite a mutual fund salesperson to give you his or her sales pitch. Be sure to inform the agent that this is all part of a class project. When the agent finishes the presentation, ask what portion of the load goes to the seller. Write a report.

NOTES

1. K. Boudreau, "Discounts and Premiums on Closed-End Market Funds: A Study in Valuation," *Journal of Finance*, May 1973, 525–528.

2. B. Malkiel, "The Valuation of Closed-End Investment-Company Shares," *Journal of Finance*, June 1977, 847–859.

3. D. Leonard and N. Noble, "Estimation of Time-Varying Systematic Risk and Investment Performance: Closed-End Investment Companies," *Journal of Financial Research*, Summer 1981, 109–120.

4. R. Richards, D. Fraser, and J. Groth, "Winning Strategies for Closed-End Funds," *Journal of Portfolio Management*, Fall 1980, 50–55.

5. S. Anderson, "An Analysis of Tracking Strategies for Closed-End Equity Funds," *Quarterly Journal of Business and Economics*, Winter 1987, 3–19.

6. G. Brauer, " 'Open-Ending' Closed-End Funds," *Journal of Financial Economics*, December 1984, 491–508; J. Brickley and J. Schalheim, "Lifting the Lid on Closed End Investment Companies: A Case of Abnormal Returns," *Journal of Financial and Quantitative Analysis*, March 1985, 107–118.

7. G. Daily, "Variable Annuities: A Product Update," *American Association of Individual Investors Journal*, March 1987, 25–38.

8. J. Ang and J. Chua, "Mutual Funds: Different Strokes for Different Folks?" *Journal of Portfolio Management*, Winter 1982, 43–50.

9. N. Mains, "Risk, the Pricing of Capital Assets, and the Evaluation of Investment Portfolios: Comment," *Journal of Business*, July 1977, 371–384.

10. H. Shawky, "An Update on Mutual Funds: Better Grades," *Journal of Portfolio Management*, Winter 1982, 29–34.

11. E. Chang and W. Lewellen, "An Arbitrage Pricing Approach to Evaluating Mutual Fund Performance," *Journal of Financial Research*, Spring 1985, 15–30.

12. M. Ferri, D. Obenhelman, and R. Roenfeldt, "Market Timing and Mutual Fund Portfolio Composition," *Journal of Financial Research*, Summer 1984, 143–150; R. Merton, "On Market Timing and Investment Performance," *Journal of Business*, July 1981, 363–406.

13. G. Schlarbaum, "The Investment Performance of the Common Stock Portfolio of Property-Liability Insurance Companies," *Journal of Financial and Quantitative Analysis*, January 1974, 89–106; R. Henriksson, "Market Timing and Mutual Fund Performance: An Empirical Investigation," *Journal of Business*, January 1984, 73–96.

14. J. Bogle and J. Twardowski, "Institutional Investment Performance Compared," *Financial Analysts Journal*, January/February 1980, 33–41.

15. A. Merjos, "Taking the Long View: Corporations Have Been Canny Buyers of Their Own Stock," *Barron's*, May 24, 1973, p. 9.

16. J. Kwitney, "As Firms Repurchase Stock, Some Insiders Unload Part of Theirs," *The Wall Street Journal*, June 20, 1974, p. 1; M. Zweig, "Multiple Inside Sales, They're a Useful Guide to What a Stock May Do," *Barron's*, December 17, 1973, 9–21; D. Petty, "An Analysis of Corporate Insider Trading Activity," *Journal of Economics and Business*, Fall 1973, 19–24; J. Jaffee, "Special Information and Insider Trading," *Journal of Business*, July 1974, 410–428.

17. D. Radcliff, "Liquidity Costs and Block Trading," *Financial Analysts Journal*, July/August 1973, 73–80; U.S. Securities and Exchange Commission, *Institutional Investors Study Report*, no. 6, 1971, 81–94.

18. A. Kraus and H. Stoll, "Price Impacts of Block Trading on the New York Stock Exchange," *Journal of Finance*, June 1972, 569–588; A. Kraus and H. Stoll, "Parallel Trading by Institutional Investors," *Journal of Financial and Quantitative Analysis*, December 1972, 2109–2138; M. Scholes, "The Market for Securities: Substitute versus Price Pressures and the Effects of Information on Share Prices," *Journal of Business*, April 1972, 179–211.

19. K. Condon, "Measuring Equity Transaction Costs," *Financial Analysts Journal*, September/October 1981, 57–61.

20. T. Loeb, "Trading Cost: The Critical Look Between Investment Information and Results," *Financial Analysts Journal*, May/June 1983, 39–45.

21. B. Rudolph, "Know the Men Behind the Numbers," *Forbes*, June 6, 1983, 194–196.

22. J. Williamson, "Measuring and Forecasting of Mutual Fund Performance: Choosing an Investment Strategy," *Financial Analysts Journal*, November/December 1972, 78–84.

23. B. Branch, *Fundamentals of Investing* (Santa Barbara, Calif.: Wiley/Hamilton, 1976), 205–206.

24. I. Friend, M. Blume, and J. Crockett, *Mutual Funds and Other Institutional Investors* (New York: McGraw-Hill, 1970).

25. W. Woerheide, "Investor Response to Suggested Criteria for the Selection of Mutual Funds," *Journal of Financial and Quantitative Analysis*, March 1982, 129–138.

26. H. Levy and S. Sarnat, "Investment Performance in an Imperfect Securities Market and the Case for Mutual Funds," *Financial Analysts Journal*, March/April 1972, 77–81.

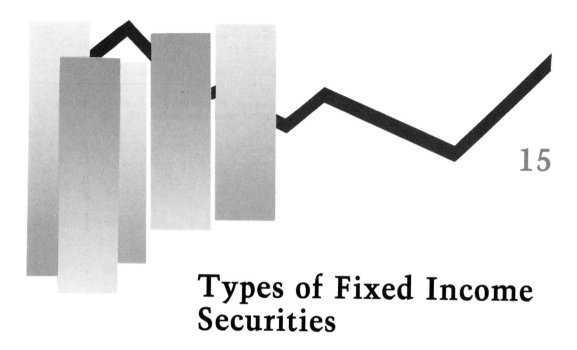

Types of Fixed Income Securities

Fixed income securities provide the principal investment alternative to common stocks. The same brokers and similar markets are used to trade them and many companies issue both types of securities. Their similarities notwithstanding, many stock market investors largely ignore the bond markets. Such neglect was understandable when bond yields averaged 4% to 5%, and the stock market's long post–World War II rally was underway, but times have changed. Far from being a mundane backwater, fixed income securities are made very competitive with common stocks by their diversity and high yields. Their volatility, attention, number of types, ways of participating, and small investor involvement have all increased in recent years. Bonds may not belong in every portfolio, but all serious investors should at least consider investing in them.

This chapter explores the characteristics of the various types of short- and long-term debt instruments along with the mutual funds that invest in such securities. We first consider money market and other short-term securities: large CDs, T-bills, acceptances, commercial paper, Eurodollars, federal funds, repurchase agreements, discount loans, money funds, short-term unit trusts, and low-denomination, bank-issued securities. Then various long-term securities are discussed including governments, agencies, mortgage-related securities, municipals, corporates, long-term bank CDs, income bonds, floating-rate notes, zero-coupon bonds, yield curve notes, Eurobonds, insurance company assembled debt, private placements, and preferred stock.

TYPES OF DEBT SECURITIES

The federal government, state and local governments, corporations, foreign governments, and international organizations all issue fixed income securities. Most debt securities promise to pay a fixed periodic coupon amount and return their face value at a prespecified time. They vary in a number of ways including length to maturity, coupon rate, type of collateral, convertibility, tax treatment, and restrictions placed on the borrower.

Debt instruments largely compete with other similar-maturity instruments. Securities maturing in a year or less are considered short term. High-quality, short-term debt obligations trade in what is called the money market.

The Money Market and Other Short-Term Debt Securities

Money market instruments are highly liquid, quite marketable, and very secure. The principal money market instruments are large bank CDs, Treasury bills, commercial paper, bankers' acceptances, and Eurodollar deposits. Very short-term lending and borrowing in the federal funds market, repurchase agreements, and the Fed's discount window round out this market. In addition, money market mutual funds, short-term unit investment trusts, short-term municipals, and certain securities and accounts of banks and other financial institutions also compete in the short end of the debt security market.

Large CDs.   The interest rates on bank and thrift-issued negotiable CDs of $100,000 and above usually exceed the rates payable on smaller balances. About 25 New York-based CD dealers handle most secondary market trading. CDs are subject to the same government guarantee up to $100,000 as other bank and thrift institution issues. Most of the principal of very high-denomination CDs ($1,000,000 or more) is uninsured, but most CDs are considered quite safe. Those issued by troubled banks may be risky, however. *Moody's* now rates the quality of some CDs. Troubled banks generally have difficulty selling uninsured CDs even at high interest rates. Most CDs have short-term maturities.

Their relatively high minimum denomination puts large CDs beyond the range of small investors. Funds for one large CD may be assembled from several investors, however. Moreover, many banks will lend individuals the funds needed to reach the minimum. Typically the loan rate slightly exceeds the CD rate but the holding's net yield may still be relatively attractive. Other types of securities and accounts offered by banks have, however, greatly reduced the need for small investors to find ways of purchasing large CDs.

Treasury Bills and Other Short-Term Governments.   Short-term U.S. government securities (governments) make up one of the money market's largest segments. This market consists of bills and other securities maturing within a year. T-bills are issued at a discount and mature at par (face value) whereas other governments are sold initially near par and pay a semiannual coupon.

Most short-term governments are issued in $10,000 minimum denominations. Short-term governments are frequently offered for sale (original offerings) and possess excellent (OTC) marketability, very low perceived risk, and competitive yields. Moreover, governments are not subject to state and local taxes. This feature would appreciably increase their relative after-tax yield. A number of non-Treasury government agencies also issue short-term securities.

T-bills can be bought through a broker or bank for a commission of $20 to $50 per $10,000. A direct purchase from the nearest Federal Reserve Bank can be made for the cost of a first-class stamp. A buyer simply writes a letter stating a desire to purchase 13-week or 26-week bills at the noncompetitive (average of competitive) bid for the next weekly auction. The buyer would indicate the amount desired ($10,000 minimum and $5,000 multiples thereafter) and enclose a certified or official bank check for the bill's face value. A refund for the discount on the security will be sent immediately after the next auction. Investors in T-bills can either have the face value automatically reinvested at the next offering or have it sent to them at maturity.

A Treasury securities quotation for January 18, 1988, is illustrated in Table 15.2. The first entry was to mature on January 21, 1988. A seller could sell the security prior to maturity at a price yielding 6.01% whereas a purchaser would receive a 5.74% return. These yield differences reflect the impact of buying at the ask and selling at the bid. Note that the final column in the Treasury bill quote reports the return on a coupon-equivalent basis as opposed to the discount basis used in the bid/asked columns. The appendix to Chapter 15 discusses the relationship between coupon and discount yields. Also note that the bond and note price quotations are in parts of 100 and then in thirty-seconds of a point. Thus the February 1988 notes with a coupon rate of $10\frac{1}{8}\%$ were priced at 100.6 bid and 100.9 ask. These prices correspond to $100\frac{6}{32}$ to $100\frac{9}{32}$ for a spread of $\frac{3}{32}$.

Commercial Paper.   Commercial paper is usually issued by large corporations with solid credit ratings to finance their short-term needs. The paper is secured only by the issuer's good name. The issuer does, however, usually have a backup line of credit at a bank. Such a credit line is available to repay the commercial paper issue if sale of new paper is not possible in the existing market environment. Commercial paper issuers are generally able to pay slightly less than bank rates (the prime rate) on their borrowings. They will incur a fee on their backup credit lines. Even adding in this fee, the commercial paper issuer's borrowing costs are typically below the alternative cost of bank borrowings. Similarly, eliminating the intermediary's (i.e., the bank's) compensation allows those who issue commercial paper to pay investors a slightly higher rate than they would get by buying a bank's CDs.

Commercial paper is rated, but as a practical matter only high-grade issues are salable. Paper is marketed in round lots of $250,000 and is seldom available in smaller than $100,000 denominations. Some paper is registered; most is payable to the bearer.

Bankers' Acceptances.   A banker's acceptance involves an obligation to pay a certain amount at a prespecified time. Once the obligation is accepted (guaranteed) by a bank, it becomes an *acceptance*. The acceptance is a contingent liability of the bank. As such, the bank is required to redeem it whether or not the issuer funds the redemption. With this possibility in mind banks are inclined to check out carefully the credit standing of the issuers of these obligations.

Acceptances usually arise in the course of foreign trade although they may also result from domestic trade. First Boston Corporation describes a hypothetical acceptance as follows:

> Creation and Life of an Acceptance: Consider a coffee processor in the United States who wishes to finance the importation of Colombian coffee on an acceptance basis. The American importer, after negotiating with the exporter in Colombia, arranges with his/her American commercial banker for the issuance of an irrevocable letter of credit in favor of the exporter. The letter of credit specifies the details of the shipment and states that the Colombian exporter may draw a time draft for a certain amount on the American bank. In order for the acceptance to be eligible for discount by the Federal Reserve, the period of time specified, based on the estimated number of days required to liquidate the transaction, may be a maximum of 180 days. The Colombian exporter, in conformity with the terms of the letter of credit, draws a draft with his local bank, receiving immediate payment. The Colombian bank then forwards the draft and the shipping documents conveying title to the coffee to the United States for presentation to the bank that issued the letter of credit. This bank stamps the draft "accepted"— the American bank has accepted an obligation to pay the draft at maturity. An acceptance has been created.
>
> The new acceptance is either returned to the Colombian bank or sold to an acceptance dealer and the proceeds credited to the account of the Colombian bank. The shipping documents are released to the American importer to process and sell the coffee. The proceeds of the coffee sales are deposited by the importer at the accepting bank in time to honor the acceptance. At maturity, the acceptance is presented for payment by its owner and the transaction is completed.[1]

Once created, the acceptance trades like other money market securities. Acceptances are available in a wide variety of denominations and maturity dates. A small number of dealers buy and sell acceptances quoting spreads of about ¼ of 1%. Acceptances, like most money market securities, can be purchased through a stock broker.

Eurodollar Deposits.   Eurodollar deposits are dollar-denominated liabilities of banks located in Europe or anywhere else outside the United States. Most Eurodollars are held as fixed-rate time deposits of $250,000 to $5,000,000 with maturities of from one day to several years.

Eurodollar yields are quite competitive with other money market rates. Indeed, they typically offer a bit more than other components of the money market. On the other hand, Eurodollar deposits of U.S. investors may occasionally be difficult to repatriate. Moreover, disputes between borrower and lender must be settled without reliance on the protections of the U.S. legal system. Finally, the issuing bank's depositors are rarely as protected by insurance and government regulation as those of U.S. banks. Many issuers are subsidiaries of U.S. banks and others are large institutions with long histories of sound operations. Thus risks in the Eurodollar market should not be overrated. Defaults have been very rare in the post–World War II period.

Federal Funds, Repurchase Agreements, and Discount Loans.   Banks and other types of financial institutions also participate in several very active short-term debt markets. The federal funds market arose to facilitate overnight bank borrowing and lending of excess reserves. Subsequently other financial institutions and even some foreign banks and government security dealers entered the market. This federal funds market in fact encompasses all unsecured overnight loans in immediately available reserve-free funds.

Repurchase agreements (repos) are sales of securities with guaranteed repurchase at a prespecified price and date (often one day later). The relation between the purchase and sales prices establishes the instrument's return. For example, a guaranteed resale in six months at 5% above the purchase price would generate a 10% return. Payment is generally required to be in immediately available reserve-free funds transferred between financial institutions. Many banks and other depository institutions now offer retail repos that pay unregulated interest rates on investments below $100,000. These arrangements had been considered quite safe, but the default of Drysdale Government Securities illustrated their potential risk.[2]

Discount loans, another part of the money market, are extended by the Fed to member banks and certain other institutions. Such loans are designed to cure a short-term reserve deficiency. The Fed often signals monetary policy shifts with changes in the rate charged on such loans (discount rate).

Except for retail repos, this part of the money market is almost exclusively restricted to depository institutions such as commercial banks and savings and loan associations. Most money market instruments are available only to those investors with sufficient resources to purchase at least one (high-denomination) unit.

Money Market Mutual Funds.   Interest rate ceilings on many bank savings instruments coupled with generally higher money market rates led to the development of money market mutual funds and short-term unit investment trusts. The money funds invest resources from many small investors in a large portfolio of money market securities. Most funds set a $1,000 minimum account size. The net income of the portfolio is distributed to the fund's owners and may be paid monthly or reinvested.

The returns paid to small investors are generally about one-half of a percentage point below the prevailing rates in the market. Because such money market funds concentrate on very liquid short-term instruments, adverse interest moves are unlikely to affect the fund's share prices significantly. Most money market instruments (CDs, T-bills, etc.) must be sold at the prevailing market price less commissions in discrete and relatively large units. Money market funds can, in contrast, be redeemed in whole or in part on very short notice without a redemption charge. Most funds permit several types of redemption: The fundholder can write or call toll free for an immediate check-mailing or wire transfer into the fundholder's bank account. Most funds also permit checks of $500 or more to be written on the account. Use of this feature allows the investor's funds to earn interest until the check clears.

Individual money funds have somewhat different risk, return, and marketing characteristics. Some invest only in Treasury bills whereas other portfolios contain slightly riskier money market investments. Some funds hold only very short-term instruments. Others are willing to incur the somewhat reduced liquidity of slightly longer maturities. Still others vary their average maturity on the basis of their interest rate expectations. Some short-term municipal funds offer (lower) tax-free yields. Thus different types of money funds appeal to various types of investors.

Most money funds of a given class (general, governments-only, or municipal) offer very similar risks and returns, but they do differ somewhat. Two groups, William Donoghue and the Institute for Econometrics, now rate the safety and performance of the money funds. Standard & Poor's also rates funds that agree to pay a fee for the service. Most funds see little value in the rating services, however.

Short-Term Unit Investment Trusts.   Short-term unit investment trusts offer many of the same advantages as money funds: low-risk, low-denomination investment and money market yields. On the other hand, the money funds are managed and continuous whereas the unmanaged unit trusts mature. Furthermore, the expenses of the unit trusts are appreciably below those of the money market funds, but trusts are less convenient than the money funds. Units must be held until maturity (generally six months) or sold in a relatively inactive secondary market. Because short-term unit trusts invest in longer term securities than most money funds, they are somewhat less liquid.

Unlike the money funds, unit trust yields are established when they are purchased. If, for example, market rates move up subsequently, the trustholder continues to earn the rate originally promised. He or she must wait until maturity to reinvest at the higher rate available in the market. On the other hand, if interest rates decline, the holder will receive an above-market rate until the trust matures. The principal advantage of unit trusts, compared with money funds, is a lower expense ratio and thus, other things being equal, a higher yield. They are, however, less convenient for investors and more exposed to interest-fluctuation risk than most money funds.

Low-Denomination Short-Term Securities of Banks and Other Intermediaries. In the past several years banks and other financial intermediaries have been permitted to offer a variety of low-denomination securities. The relevant regulations have and will no doubt continue to change. Banks and thrifts continued to offer traditional passbook-type savings accounts that allow immediate withdrawals and generally pay about 5½%. Money market rates have, however, usually been above the passbook rates.

Beginning in 1982 banks and other deposit institutions were allowed to offer an account that competes directly with the money funds. The so-called money market accounts have a $1,000 minimum (many banks require $2,500) and are restricted to six withdrawals per month, only three of which may be by check. The rates paid on these accounts are not regulated. Thus the depository institutions can compete for funds by offering whatever yields they like. Banks also sell term certificates of deposit with a variety of maturities. Rates on these instruments are also unregulated.

The response to money market accounts was quite favorable. Unlike Treasury bills, bank and thrift institution certificates and accounts are subject to state and local income taxes. Thus the after-tax yield on T-bills is generally higher than the yield on equivalent depository institution certificates.

While most debt securities may be sold prior to maturity, small denomination CDs are generally nontransferable. Holders can redeem them before maturity at the issuing bank, but up to 90 days' interest is sacrificed. Alternatively, holders may borrow up to the amount represented by the investment using the CD as collateral. Thus before redeeming a CD early, the holder should compare the interest sacrifice with the net cost of such a loan.

As with all debt securities other than municipals, CD interest income is fully taxable at the federal level. On the other hand, the risk of loss through bankruptcy is virtually nil. The FDIC or, in the case of S&Ls, the FSLIC guarantees the security up to $100,000. Thus small short-term CDs appeal to safety-oriented investors.

Money Market Rates.   The rates on CDs, bankers' acceptances, and commercial paper tend to move together. Treasury bills generally offer a slightly lower yield because of their somewhat greater security and marketability. Eurodollar rates tend to exceed other money market rates by a modest increment, reflecting their modestly greater risk. Figure 15.1 is typical of money rate quotations in *The Wall Street Journal*. The interpretation of this figure should be largely self-explanatory. The general range of rates is reported for an extensive series of different markets. For example, federal funds (explained earlier) traded in a range of 6¾% to 7¼%. Near the close the bid price was at around 7%.

Implication of the Money Market for Individual Investors

The market for short-term debt instruments has grown dramatically in recent years. Some individuals may buy money market securities directly, but their large denominations ($10,000 for Treasury bills, $100,000 for CDs, $250,000 for commercial paper) put the market out of reach for investors of modest means. Money funds, short-term unit trusts, and banks' money certificates and money market accounts do, however, offer a viable alternative for those desiring a highly liquid low-risk instrument. Table 15.1 lists the market's various components.

Long-Term Debt Instruments

A wide variety of types of long-term debt securities are also available to investors. Most such securities fall into three categories: government bonds (including agencies), municipals, and traditional corporate bonds. Other categories include mortgage loans and mortgage-related securities, bank CDs, bond funds, income bonds, floating-rate notes, zero-coupon bonds, Eurobonds, insurance company debt securities, and private placements. Preferred stock also competes for the investments that might otherwise go into long-term debt securities.

Treasury Notes and Bonds.   The U.S. Treasury Department issues short (T-bills), intermediate, and long-term debt instruments. Typical bond and note quotations are contained in Table 15.2. The original issue rate appears first, followed by the maturity date. Notes are denoted with an *n* following the maturity date, while the others are bonds that were originally issued for longer than 10 years. The bid and asked prices appear next, followed by the change in the bid and the yield.

FIGURE 15.1 Money Market Rate Report in *The Wall Street Journal*

MONEY RATES

Friday, January 15, 1988

The key U.S. and foreign annual interest rates below are a guide to general levels but don't always represent actual transactions.

PRIME RATE: 8¾%. The base rate on corporate loans at large U.S. money center commercial banks.

FEDERAL FUNDS: 7¼% high, 6¾% low, 6⅞% near closing bid, 7% offered. Reserves traded among commercial banks for overnight use in amounts of $1 million or more. Source: Fulton Prebon (U.S.A.) Inc.

DISCOUNT RATE: 6%. The charge on loans to depository institutions by the New York Federal Reserve Bank.

CALL MONEY: 8% to 8¼%. The charge on loans to brokers on stock exchange collateral.

COMMERCIAL PAPER placed directly by General Motors Acceptance Corp.: 6.70% 30 to 59 days; 6.775% 60 to 89 days; 6.85% 90 to 119 days; 6.90% 120 to 270 days.

COMMERCIAL PAPER: High-grade unsecured notes sold through dealers by major corporations in multiples of $1,000: 6.75% 30 days; 6.80% 60 days; 6.875% 90 days.

CERTIFICATES OF DEPOSIT: 6.06% one month; 6.15% two months; 6.24% three months; 6.47% six months; 6.90% one year. Average negotiable rates paid by major New York banks on primary new issues of negotiable C.D.s, usually on amounts of $1 million and more. The minimum unit is $100,000. Typical rates in the secondary market: 6.80% one month; 6.90% three months; 7.15% six months.

BANKERS ACCEPTANCES: 6.66% 30 days; 6.67% 60 days; 6.73% 90 days; 6.78% 120 days; 6.80% 150 days; 6.81% 180 days. Negotiable, bank-backed business credit instruments typically financing an import order.

LONDON LATE EURODOLLARS: 7 1/16% to 6 15/16% one month; 7 1/16% to 6 15/16% two months; 7¼% to 7⅛% three months; 7 5/16% to 7 3/16% four months; 7⅜% to 7¼% five months; 7⅜% to 7¼% six months.

LONDON INTERBANK OFFERED RATES (LIBOR): 7 5/16% three months; 7½% six months; 7 15/16% one year. The average of interbank offered rates for dollar deposits in the London market based on quotations at five major banks.

FOREIGN PRIME RATES: Canada 9.75%; Germany 6.25%; Japan 3.375%; Switzerland 5%; Britain 9%. These rate indications aren't directly comparable; lending practices vary widely by location. Source: Morgan Guaranty Trust Co.

TREASURY BILLS: Results of the Monday, January 11, 1988, auction of short-term U.S. government bills, sold at a discount from face value in units of $10,000 to $1 million: 5.85% 13 weeks; 6.33% 26 weeks.

FEDERAL HOME LOAN MORTGAGE CORP. (Freddie Mac): Posted yields on 30-year mortgage commitments for delivery within 30 days. 10.18%, standard conventional fixed-rate mortgages; 8.625%, 2% rate capped one-year adjustable rate mortgages.

FEDERAL NATIONAL MORTGAGE ASSOCIATION (Fannie Mae): Posted yields on 30 year mortgage commitments for delivery within 30 days (priced at par). 10.10%, standard conventional fixed rate-mortgages; 8.45%, 6/2 rate capped one-year adjustable rate mortgages.

MERRILL LYNCH READY ASSETS TRUST: 7.07%. Annualized average rate of return after expenses for the past 30 days; not a forecast of future returns.

Source: *The Wall Street Journal*, January 18, 1988, p. 25. Reprinted with permission, © Dow Jones & Company, Inc. All rights reserved.

Governments may either be bearer (payable to bearer) or registered (payable only to the registered owner). Unlike bearer bonds, lost or stolen registered securities will be replaced by the issuer. Bearer bonds appeal to those who would like to conceal their income and/or wealth. Since mid-1983 all newly issued governments must be registered.

TABLE 15.1   Short-Term Debt Securities

Money Market

Type	Issuer	Minimum Denomination
Large CDs	Banks and thrifts	$100,000
Treasury Bills	U.S. Treasury	$ 10,000
Acceptances	Foreign companies, but bank-guaranteed	varies
Commercial Paper	Secure corporations	$250,000
Eurodollars	Foreign-based banks	$250,000

Intra-Institutional Market

Type	Institutions Involved
Federal Funds	Loans between Fed members
Repurchase Agreements	Sale and guaranteed buy-back of securities by banks and other depository institutions
Discount Loans	Loans from Fed to Fed members

Small Investor Market

Type	Term	Minimum Denomination
Money Funds	On demand	$1,000, but many banks require $2,500
Short-Term Unit Trusts	Six months	$1,000
Low-Denomination Bank CDs	Varies	Varies
Money Market Accounts	Limited to six withdrawals per month	$1,000

Governments are generally traded in an over-the-counter market composed of about two dozen dealers. Most of these dealers are New York investment or commercial bankers. Governments are also traded on the NYSE. Finally, the Treasury conducts an active original-issue market for governments. Banks and others may bid for newly issued bills or bonds.

Because of the very large volume and active trading in government debt, spreads are generally quite modest. On short-term issues, $1/32$ to $4/32$ (par of 100) is common. A spread of $1/32$ on $10,000 bonds amounts to only $3.125, while $4/32$ is only $12.50. These spreads correspond to .03125% to .125%. Longer term, less active issues may have somewhat higher spreads. Governments may be bought through stockbrokers, commercial banks (for a fee), or directly through the Treasury auctions.

The federal government's securities will continue to be considered secure as long as the government is willing and able to raise sufficient tax revenues to finance the debt. Because of their lower risk, governments generally yield less than highly rated corporate securities. Governments are not subject to state and local income taxes, however.

Flower Bonds.   Certain U.S government bonds issued prior to March 1973 may be used at their face value to pay estate taxes. Most of these bonds carry rather

TABLE 15.2 Treasury Securities Quotations for January 18, 1988

Treasury Bills, Bonds and Notes

Prices in 32d of a point, bill yields in basis points.

TREASURY BILLS

Date	Bid	Ask	Chg.	Yield
-1988-				
Jan 21	6.01	5.74	+0.03	5.84
Jan 28	5.81	5.54	+0.03	5.64
Feb 4	5.81	5.69	—0.02	5.80
Feb 11	5.61	5.49	+0.05	5.60
Feb 18	5.65	5.53	—0.17	5.65
Feb 25	5.63	5.51	—0.02	5.63
Mar 3	5.75	5.68	....	5.82
Mar 10	5.77	5.70	—0.02	5.84
Mar 17	5.82	5.75	....	5.90
Mar 24	5.86	5.79	—0.01	5.95
Mar .31	5.81	5.74	—0.04	5.90
Apr 7	5.85	5.78	—0.01	5.95
Apr 14	5.89	5.85	+0.01	6.03
Apr 21	5.90	5.83	....	6.02
Apr 28	5.90	5.83	—0.08	6.02
May 5	5.99	5.92	+0.01	6.13
May 12	6.06	5.99	—0.05	6.21
May 19	6.12	6.05	—0.02	6.28
May 26	6.08	6.01	....	6.24
Jun 2	6.14	6.07	....	6.31
Jun 9	6.18	6.11	....	6.37
Jun 16	6.19	6.12	—0.01	6.38
Jun 23	6.21	6.14	—0.01	6.41
Jun 30	6.19	6.12	....	6.40
Jul 7	6.27	6.20	....	6.49
Jul 14	6.25	6.21	....	6.51
Aug 4	6.38	6.31	—0.01	6.63
Sep 1	6.41	6.34	—0.01	6.67
Sep 29	6.48	6.41	....	6.76
Oct 27	6.52	6.45	....	6.82
Nov 25	6.58	6.51	+0.01	6.91
Dec 22	6.57	6.50	—0.01	6.93
-9Jan 19	6.54	6.50	....	6.95

Source— Bloomberg L.P.

BONDS & NOTES

Source—Bloomberg L.P.

Date	Rate	Bid	Ask	Chg.	Yield
Jan 88 p	8⅛	99.31	100.2	....	5.98
Feb 88 n	10⅛	100.6	100.9	....	6.01
Feb 88 p	10⅜	100.6	100.9	....	6.25
Feb 88 p	8	100.3	100.6	....	6.13
Mar 88 n	12	100.31	101.2	....	6.30
Mar 88 p	7⅛	100.1	100.4	— .1	6.34
Apr 88 p	6⅝	99.30	100.1	....	6.42
Apr 88 n	13¼	101.16	101.20	....	6.10
May 88 n	8¼	100.14	100.17	....	6.47
May 88 p	7⅛	100.3	100.6	....	6.53
May 88 n	9⅞	100.30	101.1	....	6.49
May 88 p	10	100.31	101.2	....	6.51
Jun 88 p	7	100.4	100.7	+ .1	6.47
Jun 88 n	13⅝	103	103.3	....	6.47
Jul 88 p	6⅝	99.26	99.29	....	6.80
Jul 88 n	14	103.16	103.19	+ .1	6.41
Aug 88 p	6⅛	99.14	99.18	....	6.85
Aug 88 p	9½	101.11	101.15	....	6.83
Aug 88 n	10½	101.29	102.1	+ .1	6.81
Sep 88 p	6⅜	99.16	99.20	....	6.92
Sep 88 p	11⅜	102.26	102.30	....	6.95
Oct 88 n	15⅜	106.2	106.6	....	6.60
Oct 88 p	6⅜	99.12	99.16	....	7.03
Nov 88 p	6¼	99.6	99.10	....	7.07
Nov 88 n	8¾	101.6	101.10	....	7.06
Nov 88 p	8⅝	101.3	101.7	....	7.05
Nov 88 n	11¾	103.17	103.21	....	7.06
Dec 88 p	10⅝	102.31	103.3	....	7.18
Dec 88 p	6¼	99.1	99.5	— .1	7.18
Jan 89 p	6⅛	98.27	98.31	....	7.18
Jan 89 n	14⅝	107.4	107.8	....	6.91
Feb 89 p	8	100.21	100.25	....	7.22
Feb 89 p	6¼	98.26	98.30	....	7.25
Feb 89 n	11⅜	104.1	104.5	....	7.27
Mar 89 p	11¼	104.9	104.13	— .1	7.32
Mar 89 p	6⅜	98.26	98.30	....	7.31
Apr 89 p	7⅛	99.20	99.24	+ .2	7.32
Apr 89 n	14⅜	108.2	108.6	....	7.31
May 89 p	6⅞	99.8	99.12	....	7.37
May 89 n	9¼	102.9	102.15	— .1	7.24

BONDS & NOTES

Date	Rate	Bid	Ask	Chg	Yield
May 89 n	8	100.21	100.25	— .1	7.38
May 89 n	11¾	105.10	105.14	....	7.34
Jun 89 p	7⅜	99.26	99.30	....	7.42
Jun 89 p	9⅝	102.28	103	....	7.40
Jul 89 p	7⅝	100.3	100.7	....	7.47
Jul 89 n	14½	109.25	109.29	....	7.35
Aug 89 p	7¾	100.7	100.11	....	7.51
Aug 89 p	6⅝	98.20	98.24	— .1	7.48
Aug 89 n	13⅞	109.9	109.13	+ .5	7.42
Sep 89 k	8½	101.12	101.16	+ .1	7.53
Sep 89 p	9⅜	102.22	102.26	....	7.56
Oct 89 n	11⅞	106.30	107.2	....	7.45
Oct 89 p	7⅞	100.15	100.19	....	7.50
Nov 89 p	6⅜	97.31	98.3	+ .1	7.51
Nov 89 n	10¾	105.10	105.14	....	7.49
Nov 89 p	12¾	108.20	108.24	....	7.50
Nov 89 p	7¾	100.6	100.10	....	7.56
Dec 89 p	7⅞	100.14	100.18	....	7.56
Dec 89 p	8⅜	101.11	101.15	+ .2	7.55
Jan 90 n	10½	105.5	105.9	— .1	7.59
Feb 90	3½	92.24	93.10	....	7.02
Feb 90 k	6½	97.26	97.30	+ .3	7.59
Feb 90 p	11	106.7	106.11	....	7.63
Mar 90 p	7¼	99.4	99.8	+ .3	7.62
Apr 90 n	10½	105.20	105.24	....	7.64
May 90 k	7⅞	100.10	100.14	+ .3	7.66
May 90	8¼	102.5	102.15	+ .1	7.07
May 90 p	11⅜	107.18	107.22	+ .1	7.68
Jun 90 p	7¼	98.29	99.1	....	7.69
Jul 90 n	10¾	106.20	106.24	— .4	7.72
Aug 90 k	7⅞	100.7	100.11	....	7.72
Aug 90 p	9⅞	104.24	104.28	+ .2	7.74
Aug 90 n	10¾	106.25	106.29	+ .1	7.73
Sep 90 p	6¾	97.16	97.20	+ .1	7.74
Oct 90 n	11½	108.29	109.1	+ .3	7.76
Nov 90 p	8	100.14	100.18	....	7.77
Nov 90 n	9⅝	104.13	104.17	....	7.80
Nov 90 n	13	112.26	112.30	— .1	7.79
Dec 90 p	6⅝	96.27	96.31	....	7.79
Jan 91 n	11¾	110.4	110.8	....	7.84
Feb 91 k	9⅛	103.9	103.13	— .1	7.85
Mar 91 p	6¾	96.23	96.27	— .1	7.88
Apr 91 n	12⅜	112.13	112.17	....	7.90
May 91 p	8⅛	100.21	100.25	+ .1	7.85
May 91 n	14½	118.27	118.31	....	7.89
Jun 91 n	7⅞	99.26	99.30	+ .1	7.89
Jul 91 n	13¾	117.17	117.21	+ .2	7.86
Aug 91 p	7½	98.22	98.26	+ .2	7.88
Aug 91 n	14⅞	121.7	121.11	+ .2	7.90
Sep 91 k	9⅛	103.18	103.22	+ .1	7.95
Oct 91 p	12¼	113.14	113.18	+ .2	7.97
Nov 91 p	6½	95.4	95.8	+ .3	7.96
Nov 91 n	14¼	120.17	120.21	+ .2	7.88
Dec 91 k	8¼	100.25	100.29	+ .2	7.98
Jan 92 p	11⅝	111.30	112.2	+ .2	8.03
Feb 92 p	6⅝	95.5	95.9	+ .1	8.00
Feb 92 n	14⅝	122.18	122.22	+ .2	7.99
Apr 92 k	11¾	112.25	112.29	+ .2	8.08
May 92 k	6⅝	94.23	94.27	— .2	8.06
May 92 n	13¾	120.4	120.8	+ .2	8.09
Jul 92 p	10⅜	108.9	108.13	+ .2	8.10
Aug 87-92	4¼	92.26	93.12	+ .3	5.92
Aug 92	7¼	97.4	97.8	+ .2	7.98
Aug 92 p	8¼	100.13	100.17	+ .2	8.10
Oct 92 p	9¾	106.1	106.5	+ .2	8.15
Nov 92 p	8⅜	100.26	100.30	+ .3	8.12
Nov 92 n	10½	109.4	109.8	+ .2	8.14
Jan 93 p	8¾	102.4	102.8	+ .2	8.19
Feb 88-93	4	92.27	93.13	+ .3	5.51
Feb 93	6¾	94.7	94.25	+ .3	8.02
Feb 93	7⅞	98.23	98.27	+ .2	8.16
Feb 93 p	8¼	100.13	100.17	+ .2	8.11
Feb 93 n	10⅞	110.18	110.22	+ .2	8.25
Apr 93 p	7⅜	96.10	96.14	+ .2	8.22
May 93 n	10⅛	107.20	107.24	+ .2	8.29
Jul 93 p	7¼	95.12	95.16	+ .4	8.29
Aug 88-93	7½	96.9	96.15	+ .1	8.30
Aug 93	8⅝	101.22	101.30	+ .3	8.18
Aug 93 n	11⅞	115.14	115.18	+ .2	8.32
Oct 93 p	7⅛	94.18	94.22	+ .2	8.30

BONDS & NOTES

Date	Rate	Bid	Ask	Chg	Yield
Nov 93	8⅝	101.29	102.3	— .5	8.16
Nov 93 n	11¾	115.12	115.16	+ .1	8.33
Jan 94 p	7	93.21	93.25	— .5	8.34
Feb 94	9	103.8	103.12	+ .1	8.28
Apr 94 p	7	93.13	93.17	....	8.35
May 89-94	4⅛	93.6	93.24	+ .4	5.30
May 94 p	13⅛	123	123.4	+ .4	8.34
Jul 94 p	8	98.4	98.8	+ .4	8.35
Aug 94	8¾	102.17	102.21	+ .4	8.22
Aug 94 p	12⅝	120.27	120.31	+ .4	8.40
Oct 94	9½	105.12	105.16	+ .6	8.41
Nov 94	10⅛	108.22	108.26	+ .4	8.40
Nov 94 p	11⅝	116.7	116.11	+ .4	8.42
Jan 95 p	8⅝	101.2	101.6	+ .4	8.40
Feb 95	3	92.29	93.15	+ .4	4.07
Feb 95	10½	110.18	110.22	+ .4	8.46
Feb 95 p	11¼	114.11	114.15	+ .3	8.48
May 95	10⅜	110.3	110.7	+ .6	8.47
May 95 p	11¼	114.22	114.26	+ .6	8.49
May 95	12⅝	122.13	122.17	+ .6	8.43
Aug 95 p	10½	110.24	110.28	+ .6	8.52
Nov 95 p	9½	105.9	105.13	+ .5	8.53
Nov 95	11½	116.26	116.30	+ .7	8.49
Feb 96 p	8⅞	101.21	101.25	....	8.56
May 96 p	7⅜	92.18	92.22	+ .2	8.62
Aug 97 k	8⅝	99.23	99.27	+ .2	8.65
Nov 96 p	7¼	91.15	91.19	+ .2	8.63
May 97 k	8½	98.28	99	— .2	8.66
Nov 97	8⅞	101.23	101.27	+ .2	8.59
May 93-98	7	89.7	89.11	+ .2	8.57
Nov 98	3½	92.26	93.12	—1.21	4.27
May 94-99	8½	98.20	98.24	+ .4	8.67
Feb 95-00	7⅞	93.18	93.22	— .3	8.73
Aug 95-00	8⅜	97.6	97.10	— .15	8.73
Feb 01	11¾	122.20	122.26	— .14	8.78
May 01	13⅛	133.16	133.22	— .10	8.78
Aug 96-01	8	94.14	94.20	— .2	8.68
Aug 01	13⅜	135.24	135.30	— .6	8.79
Nov 01	15¾	154.24	154.30	— .2	8.80
Feb 02	14¼	143.4	143.10	— .2	8.82
Nov 02	11⅝	122.6	122.12	— .8	8.88
Feb 03	10¾	115.4	115.10	— .10	8.89
May 03	10¾	115.4	115.10	— .10	8.90
Aug 03	11⅛	118.6	118.12	— .4	8.92
Nov 03	11⅞	124.16	124.22	— .6	8.93
May 04	12⅜	129.14	129.20	— .2	8.90
Aug 04	13¾	141.16	141.22	+ .4	8.89
Nov 04 k	11⅝	123	123.6	....	8.93
May 00-05	8¼	94.26	95	+ .2	8.82
May 05 k	12	126.15	126.21	— .3	8.94
Aug 05 k	10¾	115.22	115.28	+ .2	8.94
Feb 06 k	9⅜	104.19	104.25	— .6	8.84
Feb 02-07	7⅝	88.22	88.28	— .10	8.84
Nov 02-07	7⅞	90.23	90.29	— .11	8.85
Aug 03-08	8⅜	95.8	95.14	— .4	8.86
Nov 03-08	8¾	98.18	98.24	+ .2	8.88
May 04-09	9⅛	101.28	102.2	....	8.88
Nov 04-09	10⅜	112.12	112.18	+ .6	8.92
Feb 05-10	11¾	124.14	124.20	+ .8	8.91
May 05-10	10	109.12	109.18	....	8.90
Nov 05-10	12¾	133.24	133.30	+ .16	8.91
May 06-11	13⅞	144.20	144.26	+ .30	8.88
Nov 06-11	14	146.10	146.16	+ .30	8.87
Nov 07-12	10⅜	112.26	113	— .4	8.96
Aug 08-13	12	128.18	128.24	+ .10	8.92
May 09-14	13¼	141.8	141.14	+ .30	8.88
Aug 09-14k	12½	134.20	134.24	+ .27	8.86
Nov 09-14k	11¾	127.22	127.28	+ .24	8.84
Feb 15k	11¼	125.4	125.10	+ .20	8.78
Aug 15k	10⅝	119.18	119.24	+ .20	8.72
Nov 15k	9⅞	110.24	110.30	+ .2	8.81
Feb 16k	9¼	104.16	104.22	+ .7	8.80
May 16k	7¼	83.23	83.29	+ .3	8.80
Nov 16k	7½	86.11	86.17	+ .3	8.79
May 17k	8¾	99.15	99.21	+ .4	8.78
Aug 17k	8⅞	101	101.6	+ .2	8.76

k—Non U. S. citizen exempt from withholding taxes. n—Treasury note. p—Treasury note and non U. S. citizen exempt from withholding taxes.

Source: *The New York Times*, January 19, 1988, p. D16.

low coupon rates. Accordingly, they generally sell for a substantial discount from their face value. Thus a bond selling for $750 may be worth $1,000 toward an estate tax liability. To be used for estate tax purposes, however, these bonds (called flower bonds) must be part of the estate prior to the owner's death.

For those with likely estate tax liabilities, ownership of flowers is comparable to owning a combination of a bond and a life insurance policy. Because of their value in estate settlement coupled with their relatively limited supply, the yields to stated maturity of flower bonds are generally well below otherwise-equivalent governments. Thus only those expecting to die relatively soon will find flowers attractive. The shorter one's life expectancy, the more attractive flowers become.

Agency Securities. In addition to the Treasury several other government agencies issue debt obligations. These include the Federal Intermediate Credit Banks; the Banks for Cooperatives; the Federal Land Banks, which supply farm credit; and the Federal Home Loan Bank System, which supplies mortgage credit.

Like Treasury issues those of the Federal Home Loan Bank System and those of the sponsored farm credit agencies are not subject to state and local taxes. Securities of the Federal National Mortgage Association (FNMA) and the Government National Mortgage Association (GNMA) are taxed at the state and local level, however. Agency securities generally bear a slightly higher interest rate than Treasury issues of comparable maturity. Somewhat lower marketability accounts for part of the yield differential. Because the trading volumes of most agency issues are less than those of Treasury issues, the market is narrower and spreads wider. The greater trading costs of agency issues lead investors to demand a higher return. Moreover, the wide assortment of agency issues is a bit confusing for many relatively unsophisticated investors. An investment's degree of marketability concerns only those who may need to sell prior to maturity. Holding for a substantial period spreads the buying and selling costs over several years. Moreover, taking time to learn about agencies is a small price to pay for a significantly higher return. Table 15.3 contains a typical agency quotation from *The New York Times*. Its format is essentially identical to that used by *The Wall Street Journal* and many other newspapers.

As with Treasury bonds and notes, the prices of agency issues are quoted in parts of 100 and then thirty-seconds of a point. Thus the first entry in the Federal National Mortgage quote is for a bond maturing in February 1988. It has a coupon rate of 10.3% and is priced at 100.8 bid (100 8/32) and 100.11 ask (100 11/32).

Mortgage Loans and Mortgage-Related Securities. Many agency and some types of nonagency securities either are backed by or represent ownership in a pool (portfolio) of mortgage loans. The vast majority of outstanding mortgage debt is collateralized by a first claim (first mortgage) on developed real estate such as single family homes, apartments, or commercial property. Most such mortgage loans require a minimum initial down payment of 20% to 25%. These mortgages are generally amortized with level monthly payments over an extended period (20 to 30 years is typical). Thus the amount owed usually declines over time. Moreover, the property securing the mortgage loan usually appreciates. As a result the ratio of collateral value to mortgage debt remaining tends to rise as time passes. Accordingly, first mortgages are usually rather low- and declining-risk investments.

TABLE 15.3 Agency Quotation from *The New York Times*

Government Agency Bonds

Prices in 32d of a point.

FEDERAL NATIONAL MTGS

Date		Rate	Bid	Ask	Chg.	Yield
Feb	88	10.30	100.8	100.11	...	4.20
Feb	88	10¾	100.8	100.11	...	4.62
Feb	88	14.40	100.16	100.21	...	2.94
Mar	88	10.40	100.16	100.19	...	5.95
Apr	88	10.45	100.25	100.29	...	6.24
May	88	10½	101.3	101.6	...	6.44
Jun	88	10½	101.14	101.18	...	6.34
Aug	88	9.40	101.9	101.13	...	6.78
Aug	88	16⅜	105.10	105.20	...	5.96
Sep	88	8.55	100.25	100.31	...	6.97
Sep	88	13.20	103.27	103.31	...	6.79
Oct	88	9½	101.21	101.24	...	6.95
Oct	88	12¾	104.1	104.5	...	6.74
Nov	88	8.95	101.9	101.13	...	7.11
Nov	88	11	102.30	103.2	...	7.01
Nov	88	11.70	103.17	103.21	...	6.94
Dec	88	11¼	103.12	103.16	...	7.13
Dec	88	11¾	103.26	103.30	...	7.12
Jan	89	11.10	103.16	103.20	...	7.18
Feb	89	11.60	104.5	104.11	...	7.25
Mar	89	12.10	104.27	105.5	...	7.29
Apr	89	7.55	99.31	100.5	...	7.40
Jun	89	9.30	101.31	102.5	...	7.63
Jun	89	9½	102.7	102.13	...	7.64
Jul	89	8	100.7	100.17	...	7.61
Aug	89	10.05	103.3	103.13	...	7.68
Aug	89	13⅛	107.21	107.27	...	7.68
Oct	89	12.10	106.27	107.1	...	7.65
Oct	89	12¾	107.29	108.3	...	7.63
Nov	89	9.85	103.5	103.15	...	7.74
Nov	89	11.80	106.13	106.19	...	7.80
Dec	89	11.30	105.21	105.31	...	7.84
Dec	89	6½	97.19	97.25	...	7.78
Jan	90	11.45	106.5	106.15	...	7.85
Feb	90	11.05	105.29	106.7	...	7.73
Mar	90	8.65	101.15	101.21	...	7.79
Apr	90	7.35	98.21	98.31	...	7.86
May	90	10.30	104.29	105.3	...	7.83
May	90	11.15	106.17	106.27	...	7.84
Jul	90	9.85	103.23	104.1	...	8.02
Sep	90	10	104.9	104.19	...	8.03
Oct	90	10.15	104.27	105.1	...	8.05
Nov	90	7	97.11	97.17	...	7.99
Nov	90	10.90	106.19	106.29	...	8.10
Dec	90	8.40	100.21	100.25	...	8.08
Dec	90	11.80	108.23	109.1	...	8.22
Jan	91	8¾	101.3	101.13	...	8.21
Jan	91	8⅜	100.15	100.19	...	8.13
Feb	91	6.90	96.15	96.21	...	8.15
Mar	91	12	110.3	110.13	+ .2	8.17
Mar	91	12½	111.5	111.23	+ .2	8.20
Apr	91	7.20	97.1	97.7	+ .2	8.19
May	91	7.45	97.19	97.29	...	8.18
Jun	91	8.55	100.23	101.1	+ .2	8.19
Jul	91	7.65	98.7	98.13	+ .4	8.18
Aug	91	8.70	101.7	101.13	+ .2	8.23
Aug	91	8.40	100.13	100.17	+ .2	8.22
Sep	91	7	95.21	95.31	...	8.30
Oct	91	7.80	98.9	98.19	...	8.24
Oct	91	7⅜	96.25	97.3	...	8.29
Nov	91	9.55	103.25	103.31	...	8.30
Dec	91	11¾	110.25	111.3	...	8.35
Jan	92	8½	100.15	100.19	...	8.32
Mar	92	7	95.5	95.15	+ .2	8.31
Apr	92	12	112.15	112.25	+ .2	8.34
May	92	8.45	99.27	100.1	+ .2	8.44
Jun	92	7.05	95.3	95.13	+ .2	8.32
Jun	92	10⅛	106.1	106.7	+ .2	8.40
Jul	92	8.45	99.27	100.1	+ .2	8.44
Oct	92	10.60	107.21	107.31	+ .2	8.51
Dec	92	9⅞	105.3	105.13	+ .2	8.50
Jan	93	10.90	108.27	109.5	+ .2	8.60
Mar	93	7.90	97.9	97.19	...	8.48
Mar	93	10.95	109.20	109.26	...	8.55
Apr	93	7.55	96.2	96.8	...	8.45
Apr	93	10⅞	109.10	109.16	...	8.58
May	93	10¾	108.27	109.1	...	8.59
Nov	93	7¾	96.2	96.8	...	8.58
Dec	93	7⅜	93.30	94.4	...	8.67
Apr	94	7.65	94.18	94.24	...	8.76
Aug	94	8.90	100.10	100.16	...	8.80
Oct	94	10.10	106.7	106.11	...	8.82
Nov	94	9¼	101.27	101.31	...	8.85
Jan	95	9	100.27	100.31	...	8.81
Jan	95	11.95	115.15	115.25	...	8.87
Feb	95	11½	113.14	113.20	...	8.86
May	95	11.70	114.11	114.21	...	8.92
Jun	95	11.15	111.21	111.27	...	8.92
Sep	95	10½	107.25	108.3	...	9.01
Nov	95	10.60	108.15	108.25	...	9.00
Jan	96	9.20	100.23	101.1	...	9.02
Feb	96	7	87.23	88.1	...	9.13
Feb	96	9.35	101.11	101.21	...	9.05
Jun	96	8¾	97.29	98.7	...	9.05
Jul	96	8	93.23	93.29	...	9.04
Aug	96	8.15	94.9	94.15	...	9.09
Dec	96	7.70	91.15	91.21	...	9.09
Jan	97	7.60	90.29	91.3	...	9.07
Jun	97	9.20	100.15	100.21	...	9.09
Jul	97	8.95	98.29	99.3	...	9.09
Sep	97	9.55	102.21	102.27	+ .2	9.10
Nov	97	9.55	102.25	102.29	+ .4	9.09
Dec	97	7.10	86.19	86.29	...	9.14
Dec	97	9.55	102.25	102.29	+ .4	9.10
Dec	97	9.80	102.15	102.21	...	9.12
Dec	13	12.35	114.19	114.29	...	9.03
Mar	14	12.65	116.11	116.21	...	9.05
Jul	14	0	9.16	9.26	...	8.97
Dec	15	10.35	108.19	108.29	+ .4	9.44
Mar	16	8.20	87.19	87.29	+ .4	9.43
Oct	19	0	6.14	6.24	...	8.68

Source— Bloomberg L.P.

FEDERAL HOME LOAN

Date		Rate	Bid	Ask	Chg.	Yield
Jan	88	10⅝	100.2	100.5	...	4.75
Jan	88	8.45	100.1	100.4	...	0.91
Mar	88	10.20	100.19	100.22	...	6.21
Mar	88	11.90	100.28	101	...	6.15
Apr	88	10.15	100.26	100.29	...	6.54
Apr	88	10⅜	100.27	100.31	...	6.52
May	88	7⅜	100.3	100.7	...	6.66
May	88	10.15	101.2	101.6	...	6.58
Jun	88	7¼	100.4	100.7	...	6.71
Jun	88	8.80	100.23	100.29	...	6.64
Jun	88	10.80	101.23	101.26	...	6.51
Jul	88	9.15	101.3	101.6	...	6.77
Jul	88	6.90	99.30	100.1	...	6.83
Aug	88	6.35	99.14	99.20	...	6.98
Aug	88	7.15	100	100.3	...	6.97
Aug	88	11⅝	102.19	102.23	...	6.89
Aug	88	9.45	101.11	101.15	...	6.89
Sep	88	8	100.18	100.22	...	6.93
Oct	88	6.35	99.11	99.17	...	6.97
Oct	88	8.90	101.9	101.13	...	6.96
Oct	88	11.40	103.3	103.7	...	6.98
Oct	88	9.55	101.25	101.29	...	6.93
Nov	88	8.90	101.14	101.17	...	6.99
Nov	88	14.20	105.22	105.26	...	7.01
Nov	88	7½	100.15	100.18	...	6.79
Dec	88	10.70	103.2	103.6	...	7.12
Dec	88	7.80	100.13	100.17	...	7.20
Jan	89	7.40	100.7	100.11	...	7.04
Jan	89	11⅜	103.25	103.31	...	7.25
Feb	89	6½	99.5	99.11	...	7.12
Feb	89	8.30	100.29	101.3	...	7.24
Feb	89	10.80	103.17	103.23	...	7.22
Feb	89	15.10	106.27	108.5	...	7.27
Mar	89	7.45	99.31	100.5	+ .2	7.30
Apr	89	6.90	99.1	99.11	...	7.44
Apr	89	7⅜	99.25	99.31	+ .2	7.39
Apr	89	14¼	107.21	107.31	...	7.51
May	89	7.40	99.25	99.31	...	7.41
May	89	10.20	103.7	103.13	...	7.48
Jun	89	7.70	100.1	100.5	...	7.58
Jul	89	7	98.23	99.1	...	7.69
Jul	89	14⅛	108.25	109.3	...	7.66
Sep	89	6¾	98.9	98.19	...	7.65
Sep	89	12½	107.3	107.13	...	7.71
Sep	89	14.55	110.13	110.23	...	7.62
Oct	89	9.35	102.13	102.17	...	7.78
Nov	89	6.60	97.25	97.31	...	7.79
Nov	89	11.55	105.27	106.5	...	7.90
Nov	89	8⅛	100.12	100.16	...	7.82
Dec	89	6.55	97.19	97.25	...	7.80
Dec	89	8¼	100.21	100.25	...	7.80
Jan	90	11.20	105.23	106.1	...	7.90
Jan	90	6.55	97.13	97.19	...	7.86
Mar	90	6.70	97.21	97.27	...	7.78
Mar	90	11.90	107.23	108.1	...	7.82
Apr	90	7.05	98.5	98.11	...	7.85
May	90	8¼	100.19	100.25	...	7.87
Jun	90	7¾	99.7	99.17	...	7.96
Jun	90	9½	102.31	103.9	...	7.98
Jul	90	9¾	103.15	103.25	...	8.06
Jul	90	7.80	99.11	99.15	...	8.04
Aug	90	8.10	99.29	100.3	...	8.05
Sep	990	8⅞	101.23	101.29	...	8.06
Sep	90	12½	110.5	110.15	...	8.07
Sep	90	10.30	104.31	105.9	...	8.06
Oct	90	7.05	97.15	97.21	...	8.00
Nov	90	8.40	100.19	100.25	...	8.08
Nov	90	13.70	113.19	113.29	...	8.13
Dec	90	10.90	106.15	106.25	...	8.25
Dec	90	8.70	101.9	101.19	...	8.08
Jan	91	8.30	100.11	100.15	...	8.12
Jan	91	9.10	102.9	102.19	...	8.11
Feb	91	7.10	96.31	97.5	+ .2	8.15
Feb	91	11⅞	109.19	109.29	+ .2	8.19
Mar	91	7¾	98.15	98.25	+ .2	8.19
Apr	91	7.35	97.11	97.21	...	8.18
May	91	7⅞	98.19	98.29	...	8.25
Jul	91	7½	97.13	97.23	...	8.26
Aug	91	7.20	96.21	96.27	...	8.23
Aug	91	11.10	108.9	108.19	...	8.29
Sep	91	7.40	96.29	97.7	...	8.29
Sep	91	11¾	110.15	110.25	...	8.29
Oct	91	9.95	105.1	105.7	...	8.30
Nov	91	7.15	95.29	96.7	...	8.31
Dec	91	7	95.11	95.21	...	8.31
Dec	91	11.40	109.9	109.19	...	8.48
Jan	92	7	95.1	95.11	...	8.39
Feb	92	11.45	109.23	110.1	+ .2	8.50
Mar	92	7.10	95.9	95.19	+ .2	8.37
Apr	92	8.15	98.27	99.1	+ .2	8.42
Apr	92	11.70	110.29	111.7	+ .2	8.50
May	92	8.60	100.9	100.19	+ .2	8.43
Jun	92	8.40	99.19	99.29	+ .2	8.42
Jul	92	8⅜	99.7	99.17	+ .2	8.50
Aug	92	8.60	100.13	100.23	+ .2	8.40
Aug	92	10.35	106.21	106.31	+ .2	8.48
Oct	92	10.85	108.21	108.31	+ .2	8.52
Nov	92	11.10	109.19	109.29	+ .2	8.56
Nov	92	8.80	100.31	101.3	+ .2	8.52
Dec	92	9.05	101.23	101.27	+ .2	8.58
Jan	93	10.70	108.1	108.11	...	8.62
Jan	93	9½	103.9	103.19	+ .2	8.60
Mar	93	10.80	108.26	109	...	8.60
Apr	93	7.55	95.24	95.30	...	8.52
May	93	8⅛	98.5	98.11	...	8.51
May	93	10¾	108.28	109.6	...	8.57
Jul	93	7¾	96.4	96.10	...	8.60
Jul	93	11.70	112.24	112.30	...	8.70
Aug	93	7.45	94.20	94.30	...	8.61
Aug	93	11.95	113.22	114	...	8.73
Sep	93	7.95	96.30	97.4	...	8.60
Oct	93	7⅞	96.19	96.25	...	8.59
Nov	93	7⅜	94.6	94.16	...	8.59
Dec	93	7⅜	94.1	94.7	...	8.64
Dec	93	12.15	115.7	115.17	...	8.74
Jan	94	7.30	93.16	93.22	...	8.67
Feb	94	7.45	93.31	94.9	...	8.67
Feb	94	12	115.1	115.11	...	8.70
Jun	95	10	105.5	105.15	...	8.97
Jul	95	10.30	106.31	107.5	...	8.97
Mar	96	8.10	94.7	94.13	...	9.08
Apr	96	7¾	92.5	92.11	...	9.08
Apr	94	8½	99.2	99.8	...	8.65
May	96	8¼	94.31	95.5	...	9.09
Jun	96	8¼	94.29	95.3	...	9.09
Jul	96	8	93.14	93.20	...	9.09
Aug	96	7.70	91.21	91.27	...	9.08
Sep	96	8¼	94.25	94.31	...	9.10
Feb	97	7⅞	91.31	92.9	...	9.14
Mar	97	7.65	90.27	91.1	...	9.11
Aug	97	9.20	100.27	101.5	...	9.01

Source— Bloomberg L.P.

FEDERAL FARM CREDIT

Date		Rate	Bid	Ask	Chg.	Yield
Jan	88	9.45	100	100.3	...	2.58
Jan	88	8.20	99.31	100.2	...	3.56
Feb	88	7.10	100	100.3	...	4.15
Feb	88	6.85	99.31	100.2	...	4.90
Mar	88	6.80	99.31	100.2	...	6.20
Mar	88	10.90	100.15	100.18	...	5.80
Mar	88	7.20	100	100.3	...	6.22
Mar	88	11.35	100.15	100.19	...	5.97
Apr	88	7.90	100.4	100.7	...	6.63
Apr	88	7⅜	100	100.4	...	6.72
Apr	88	10¼	100.24	100.27	...	6.69
Apr	88	12.65	101.12	101.16	...	6.42
May	88	7⅜	100.1	100.4	...	6.82
Jun	88	7.20	100	100.3	...	6.87
Jun	88	8	100.9	100.12	...	6.88
Jul	88	7.60	100.5	100.9	...	6.93
Jul	88	11½	102.2	102.8	...	6.87
Jul	88	11.70	102.4	102.11	...	6.88
Sep	88	12⅞	103.12	103.16	...	6.95
Oct	88	11½	103	103.4	...	7.13
Dec	88	7½	100.2	100.5	...	7.29
Jan	89	8¾	101.6	101.10	...	7.38
Jan	89	11.65	103.30	104.4	...	7.34
Jan	89	13.05	105.9	105.15	...	7.34
Apr	89	12½	105.17	105.23	...	7.60
Jun	89	7.35	99.9	99.15	...	7.76
Jul	89	13.70	108.5	108.11	...	7.71
Sep	89	7¾	99.17	99.23	...	7.93
Oct	89	10.60	104.1	104.7	...	7.97
Oct	89	15.65	111.31	112.9	...	8.01
Oct	89	12.45	106.31	107.5	...	7.99
Jan	90	10.95	104.29	105.7	...	8.08
Jan	90	11.15	105.9	105.19	...	8.08
Feb	90	10.85	104.25	105.3	...	8.08
Apr	90	11.35	106.9	106.19	...	8.08
Jun	90	14.10	112.11	112.21	...	8.10
Jul	90	9.55	102.25	103.3	...	8.16
Jul	90	10.40	104.21	104.31	...	8.17
Sep	90	12½	109.23	110.1	...	8.17
Oct	90	10.60	105.11	105.21	...	8.25
Apr	91	7.55	97.19	97.29	...	8.29
Apr	91	14.10	115.29	116.7	...	8.30
Jul	91	9.10	102.5	102.15	...	8.27
Jul	91	14.70	118.25	119.3	...	8.31
Oct	91	10.60	106.25	107.3	...	8.35
Dec	91	13.65	116.25	116.31	...	8.41
Jan	92	11½	109.25	110.3	...	8.47
Jan	92	15.20	122.3	122.13	...	8.48
Jul	92	13¾	118.29	119.7	+ .2	8.52
Jan	93	10.65	107.17	107.27	+ .2	8.68
Oct	93	11.80	113.8	113.18	...	8.74
Mar	94	12.35	115.22	115.28	...	8.92
Apr	94	14¼	124.18	124.28	...	8.96
Sep	94	13	119.13	119.23	...	8.98
Dec	94	11.45	112.14	112.20	...	8.94
Oct	97	11.90	116.11	116.21	...	9.26

Source— Bloomberg L.P.

FEDERAL LAND BANK

Date		Rate	Bid	Ask	Chg.	Yield
Jan	88	7.85	99.31	100.2	...	3.22
Jan	90	8.20	100.5	100.15	...	7.94
Apr	91	7.95	98.23	99.1	...	8.29
Oct	96	7.95	92.7	92.17	...	9.21
Jan	97	7.35	88.22	89	...	9.17

Source— Bloomberg L.P.

STUDENT LOAN MKTG.

Date		Rate	Bid	Ask	Chg.	Yield
May	88	9⅝	100.28	101	...	6.61
Jul	88	11.70	102.7	102.11	...	6.44
Jul	89	7.90	99.29	100.7	...	7.74
Sep	89	12.85	107.11	107.29	...	7.55
Sep	89	13.15	107.27	108.13	...	7.52
Feb	90	10.90	105.25	105.31	...	7.77
Aug	90	6.95	97.1	97.11	...	8.10
Sep	90	7.90	99.5	99.15	...	8.11
Dec	90	8.45	100.19	100.23	...	8.16
Aug	91	5.60	91.15	91.25	...	8.33
Aug	91	8	98.29	99.7	...	8.26
Jun	92	8¼	98.19	99.5	+ .2	8.48
Sep	92	9¼	102.3	102.13	+ .2	8.21
Dec	92	8.80	100.23	101.1	+ .2	8.53
Apr	93	10½	108.6	108.12	...	8.49
May	93	7.35	94.26	95.4	...	8.51
Sep	95	0	53.8	53.26	...	9.35
Dec	96	7¾	91.17	91.23	...	9.12
Jan	97	7⅝	90.31	91.5	...	9.08
Sep	97	9½	101.9	101.27	...	9.12
May	14	0	8.19	8.29	...	9.40
Oct	22	0	5.18	5.28	...	8.34

Source— Bloomberg L.P.

WORLD BANK BONDS

Date		Rate	Bid	Ask	Chg.	Yield
Mar	88	10⅜	100.11	100.27	...	7.50
May	88	10	100.22	101.6	...	7.54
Dec	88	15	106	106.16	...	7.84
Oct	89	11	104.3	104.8	...	8.38
Feb	90	4½	93.31	94.15	+ .1	7.79
Jul	91	5⅜	91.1	91.17	+ .2	8.44
Nov	91	16⅝	124.10	124.22	...	8.87
Dec	91	15⅛	120.16	121	+ .2	8.78
Apr	92	5⅜	88.19	89.3	+ .2	8.68
Jun	92	14¾	120.11	120.24	...	8.98
Sep	92	13⅜	117.4	117.18	...	8.99
Mar	93	10.90	108.16	108.28	+ .13	8.80
May	93	10⅜	106.17	106.29	+ .14	8.80
Sep	93	5⅞	85.1	85.17	+ .3	9.37
Mar	94	6½	87.13	87.29	— .1	9.23
Oct	94	6⅜	86	86.16	...	9.23
Dec	94	11⅝	113.20	114.6	+ .18	8.93
Aug	95	8⅜	96.8	97	— .1	9.33
Aug	96	8⅛	91.16	92.8	...	9.61
Dec	00	9.35	98.23	99.16	+ .6	9.52
Jul	01	8.85	95.4	95.28	+ .5	9.50
Dec	01	8⅜	91.25	92.17	+ .7	9.45
May	02	8¼	91.4	92.4	— .11	9.39
Aug	02	8.35	91.13	92.5	+ .7	9.45
Oct	02	12⅜	119.1	120.1	— .12	9.89

Source— Bloomberg L.P.

GNMA ISSUES

Rate	Bid	Ask	Chg.	Yield
8.00	89.14	89.18	+ .3	9.67
8.50	92.10	92.14	— .3	9.75
9.00	95.8	95.12	+ .2	9.82
9.50	98.8	98.12	+ .2	9.88
10.00	101.4	101.8	— .1	9.96
10.50	104	104.4	+ .5	10.04
11.00	106.2	106.6	+ .1	10.23
11.50	108	108.4	+ .5	10.44
12.00	109	109.4	— .1	10.79
12.50	109.25	109.29	— .1	11.16
13.00	110.20	110.24	...	11.52
13.50	111.20	111.28	...	11.83
14.00	112.4	112.10	+ .4	12.25
15.00	114.12	114.16	+ .4	12.86

Source— Bloomberg L.P.

INTER-AMERICAN BANK

Date		Rate	Bid	Ask	Chg.	Yield
Aug	92	14⅝	121.4	121.20	— .8	8.85
Dec	94	11⅝	112.12	112.28	— .24	9.15
Dec	96	7½	89.16	90	— .12	9.25
Oct	97	9½	103.8	103.20	...	8.65
Mar	11	8½	89.20	90.12	...	9.60

Source— Bear Stearns

Source: *The New York Times*, January 19, 1988, p. D18.

Even in a default and distress sale of the property, the mortgage holder is likely to recover a high percentage of the outstanding debt.

Financial intermediaries such as banks, savings and loan associations, and insurance companies write the vast majority of mortgages. Some mortgages are guaranteed by the federal government through the Veterans Administration (VA) or the Federal Housing Administration (FHA), which adds further protection. Several federal agencies and some other groups promote mortgage lending by purchasing mortgage loans from the originator.

Virtually all actively traded mortgage-related securities are issued by two federal agencies, one former federal agency, and a handful of large banks. The oldest and largest of these is the Federal National Mortgage Association (FNMA). FNMA began as a federal agency designed to channel funds to the mortgage market. It purchases mortgages from original mortgage lenders (mortgage bankers, commercial banks, S&Ls, and savings banks) with the proceeds of its own debt security sales. Its bonds have fixed coupons and maturities and trade in a secondary market much like other bonds.

In 1968 FNMA was separated into two parts, one of which (the current FNMA), became a publicly traded profit-oriented corporation. The other part of the old FNMA became the Government National Mortgage Association (GNMA). GNMA continues to promote mortgage lending on a nonprofit basis. It guarantees the timely payment of principal and interest on securities issued by private mortgage institutions and backed by pools of government-insured or government-guaranteed mortgages. Furthermore, the pools contain only FHA- and VA-guaranteed mortgages. Thus GNMA passthroughs are very secure debt instruments.

The principal drawbacks of passthroughs are a relatively high minimum denomination ($25,000, but may be bought in $5,000 units thereafter) and an uncertain amortization rate. Passthrough owners literally own a part of a mortgage pool. They receive monthly interest and amortization payments (less a small service fee to GNMA and the financial institution that administers the mortgage).

Mortgages written for specific periods are sometimes prepaid. As a result a mortgage pool's expected maturity can be well under or well above the 12-year average that is usually assumed. In spite of these drawbacks, GNMA's relatively high secure yields make them quite attractive.

The GNMA is an agency under the Housing and Urban Development Department. The Federal Home Loan Mortgage Association (Freddie Mac) also sells mortgage-related securities. Freddie Mac is an adjunct of the Federal Home Loan Bank Board that regulates the Savings and Loan industry. Freddie Mac purchases conventional (not government-insured) mortgages, pools them, and sells participations that have much in common with GNMA passthroughs. Freddie Mac participations trade in $100,000 minimum denominations. Substantial collateral generally underlies the mortgages and Freddie Mac guarantees them, and thus participations are also considered quite safe.

Encouraged by the success of FNMA, GNMA, and Freddie Mac, several large banks now package and market their own mortgage pools. These pools offer somewhat higher yields and are a bit more risky than the agency securities. While not government-guaranteed, these private passthroughs are backed by the underlying mortgage collateral and most have a partial guarantee from a private insurer. For example, defaults equal to the first 5% of principal on Bank of America's passthroughs are insured by the Mortgage Guaranty Insurance Corporation (MGIC). Because defaults rarely exceed 5% of principal, such insurance offers considerable protection.

Some depository institutions also sell mortgage-backed bonds. Such securities are, however, just another type of corporate bond that happens to have mortgages as collateral. Finally, some mutual funds manage mortgage portfolios, thereby allowing small investors relatively easy access to the mortgage market.

Securitization

The various categories of mortgage-related securities are an example of a broader phenomenon called securitization. Securitization involves taking an asset that heretofore was not easily traded in a secondary market and structuring a security or group of securities from it. The goal of the process is to convert an asset with poor marketability into one with much greater market acceptance. If the effort is successful, the institution doing the converting will be able to acquire the poorly marketable asset for appreciably less than the corresponding securitized assets can be sold for. The difference less the cost of the conversion represents the fee or profit paid for the conversion. Looked at from another perspective, securitization allows an institution to turn over its capital much more frequently than is possible with the more traditional buy and hold approach to the intermediation process. Thus a bank that is only able to make and service loans equal to a fraction of its deposit base can securitize, earn an origination fee, and earn a service fee on a multiple of its deposit base.

Most of the activity in securitization has been based on real estate first mortgage loans. More recently, however, a variety of other types of assets have been securitized. For example, auto loans, credit card loans, second mortgages, sovereign loans to Third World countries, student loans, and a variety of other types of loans are or are suggested as the basis for security creation. Moreover, real estate mortgages themselves are coming in for further securitization, as discussed in the following section.

CMOs and REMICs.   A basic feature of mortgages and traditional mortgage passthroughs is their uncertain rate of repayment. When the underlying property is sold or refinanced, the original debt instrument is generally paid off. The borrower may also have the option of prepaying part of principal. Thus a typical 25- or 30-year mortgage may on the average actually be paid back in 12 years. The rate of prepayments will, however, vary with a number of factors including market interest rates compared to the stated rate on the mortgage, the amount of mobility and the divorce rate in the community, inflation, the stage of the business cycle, the economic conditions in the area originating the mortgages, and so on.

Many investors prefer a more certain payback than is provided by the typical mortgage. The Collateralized Mortgage Obligation (CMO) was devised to deal with this problem. CMOs are multiclass passthrough securities. They offer a potentially improved way of securitization of mortgage loans.

Owners of the various classes of CMO securities are paid out at different but defined rates. Thus one class might receive payments equivalent to a one-year bond, a second class equivalent to a five-year bond, and a third like a ten-year bond. The CMO issuer would be left with the residual cash flow, which might itself be sold as another security. In this way the uncertain cash flows of a pool of mortgages are restructured into a series of bond-like predictable cash flows and a residual. Virtually all of the uncertainty of the payment timing is impounded into the residual security.

Because of the market's general preference for predictable payment rates, the total value of a mortgage pool subdivided into CMOs can be substantially higher than as a single class passthrough. Unfortunately, CMOs have some disadvantageous tax aspects. The Tax Reform Act of 1986 addressed these problems by allowing the issuance of Real Estate Mortgage Investment Conduits (REMICs). REMICs possess most of the advantages of CMOs without the tax problems. They are fast becoming a popular investment vehicle.

Direct Mortgage Investment.   Individuals can also participate directly in the mortgage market. High interest rates and rapidly rising housing prices have led more and more property owners into seller financing. Individual investors can extend collateralized loans much like those originated by financial intermediaries. All that is required is a legal document setting forth the rights and obligations of the borrower and lender. The mortgage may be a first mortgage or it may be junior to some other obligations.

The mortgage agreement contains the borrower's pledge to pay principal and interest at a prespecified rate. Normally the mortgage payment is set to amortize the loan. Some types of mortgages are interest only or only partially amortized. Thus the periodic payments do not pay off the loan over its life. The remaining balance is called the balloon. It is payable in a lump sum at the loan's maturity.

If any of the mortgage payments is not made promptly, the lender has the right to demand that the default provisions of the mortgage contract be enforced. Ultimately a failure to make the required payments allows the lender to seize and dispose of the collateral for the debt owed. The proceeds would first be used to repay the loan and collection expenses. The lender would still have a claim against the borrower for any remaining deficit.

Unlike "firsts," most second mortgages are written for relatively short periods (e.g., five years) and require principal repayment at maturity (the balloon). With a second mortgage, the lender generally has the right, if not repaid, to assume the borrower's position. Thus the second mortgage holder may make up back payments and, when the first mortgage is paid off, take full possession of the property. Alternatively, the second mortgage holder can sell or let his or her interest lapse.

Second mortgages are usually written for an appreciable fraction of the asset's remaining value (after subtracting the first mortgage), and those who need to use them are often overextended. Moreover, second mortgage holders are frequently asked to extend the repayment dates when the mortgagee cannot pay the balloon. Thus such instruments are often quite risky and generally trade in a relatively thin secondary market.

Mortgage Investment Assessment

The advantages and disadvantages of indirect mortgage ownership are, in general, similar to those of bonds. Nonetheless, the various passthroughs and participations offer a less certain maturity and payout rate than do most bonds. Direct mortgage participations (especially seconds if priced competitively) usually bear a high interest rate reflecting the greater risk and trouble involved. Clearly, potential investors should approach direct mortgage lending cautiously.

State and Local Government Debt Obligations

The debt security markets also contain a large number of state and local government securities called municipals. The issuing agency may be as well known as the state of New York or the New York Port Authority, or as obscure as a small rural Alabama water district. Obviously, the adequacy of the tax bases of these units varies enormously. In 1975, for example, New York City was forced to halt the direct sale of its debt obligations. First New York State and then the federal government had to step in to help avoid a default. Cleveland actually did default. In 1983 the Washington Public Power System (WPPS) defaulted on $2.25 billion of its bonds.

As these examples clearly indicate, investors should carefully evaluate the financial resources of the issuing municipal unit. Many of these bonds are rated by Standard & Poor's and Moody's investor services, but effective municipal investing involves substantial individual monitoring. Many of the newer issues are guaranteed by one of several companies. Treynor contends that the primary determinant of municipal bond quality is the unit's ability to pay as measured by its taxable property.[3]

Municipal bond interest is not subject to federal income tax or state and local tax in the state of issue. Capital gains on municipal holdings are taxable, however. The tax advantage of municipals allows issuers to offer lower before-tax returns than otherwise-similar taxable bonds. The relative after-tax return depends on the individual's tax bracket and the differential yields.

Obviously, tax-free income becomes more attractive to those in higher tax brackets. Those with marginal tax rates of 28% or more will often find their after-tax return on municipals above that of similar-risk taxable bonds. Below 28%, taxable bonds tend to offer the higher after-tax yield. One should evaluate the situation on an individual basis, however, because relative interest rates vary over time and with maturity.

Comparing after-tax returns is quite straightforward. First the investor determines his or her marginal rate. For example, a joint taxable income of $25,000 in 1988 would have been taxed at a 15% rate. Thus 15% was the marginal tax rate. On January 18, 1988, the New York State Dormitory Authority 8.125% bonds maturing in 2017 were offered at 101, which corresponded to a before- and after-tax yield of 8.03%. AT&T 8.80% bonds maturing in 2005 were selling for 94½ for a before-tax yield of 9.3%. These two low-risk securities both have relatively distant maturities. The after-tax return on taxable bonds is:

$$\text{Before-Tax Return} \times (1 - \text{Marginal Tax Rate})$$

In this case:

$$9.3\% \ (1 - .15) = 7.91\%$$

Municipal bond insurance has become increasingly popular in the past several years. The pros and cons of investing in insured issues have been discussed in *The Wall Street Journal*.

Insured Municipal Bonds Offer Investors Slightly Lower Yields but Greater Safety

YOUR
MONEY
MATTERS

By Elaine Johnson
Staff Reporter of The Wall Street Journal

In the industry they call it "sleep insurance."

And in the vast majority of cases, that's exactly what municipal-bond insurance is: a comforting but usually superfluous guarantee to bondholders that the timely payment of principal and interest will continue uninterrupted in the unlikely event of a default.

Apparently, millions of investors like a good night's sleep. They have been snapping up insured bonds at an increasingly rapid clip since the first municipal-bond insurer, Ambac Indemnity Corp., opened for business 15 years ago. Some 25% of all new long-term issues—about $50 billion—were insured in 1985, compared with 3% or only $1.4 billion in 1980. Meanwhile, more than half of the unit investment trusts sold in 1985, some $7.9 billion worth, were insured—a 27% increase from the $6.2 billion in insured trusts sold a year earlier.

The swift growth of insured bonds, coupled with the recent downgrading of $6 billion of tax-exempt debt backed by one insurer, has led some industry analysts to raise questions about municipal-bond insurance. Concerns range from whether the insurance is superfluous on higher-quality bonds to whether underwriters have the cash reserves to respond, if necessary, to a string of defaults.

Riskier Credits

"Ten years ago, I would have agreed much more that it's sleep insurance than I do now," says Frederick T. Croft, first vice president of American Portfolio Advisory Service Inc. and a former executive at Ambac. But Mr. Croft says he's now concerned by insurers' willingness "to insure increasingly risky credits."

Issuers request and pay for the insurance. But bondholders ultimately pay the cost by accepting lower yields—usually one-tenth to one-half of a percentage point—on insured bonds than on comparable uninsured bonds.

Still, insurers say it's well worth the price, particularly since municipal bond yields are relatively high. Deciding whether to take insurance is "a no-brainer," says Robert A. Meyer, president of Bond Investors Guaranty. Insurers also say they carefully choose what they insure. Steven D. Schrager, a senior vice president at L.F. Rothschild, Unterberg, Towbin who is working on an analysis of the industry, says he's "relatively impressed by the staffs and capabilities of insurers. They have strong analytical staffs and the understanding of what is and isn't credit quality."

Each of the major municipal-bond insurers—Financial Guaranty Insurance Co., Municipal Bond Insurance Association, Ambac and Bond Investors Guaranty—is rated triple-A by either Standard & Poor's Corp., or both S&P and Moody's Investors Service Inc. In turn, their insurance bestows a triple-A rating on the issues they back.

Issuers have learned that the triple-A backing of insurance both lowers their interest costs and makes their bonds more attractive to buyers who may be confused by the increasingly sophisticated market. "Insurance is a very quick and cost-effective way of bringing huge amounts to the marketplace," says John R. Butler, president and chief executive of Municipal Bond Insurance Association, or MBIA.

> **I**NVESTORS should be aware that if the insurer's rating slips, so do the ratings of all the issues the company has insured.

However, an insured triple-A bond actually trades closer to the price of a double-A, than it does to a bond which is rated triple-A without insurance, experts say. Also, triple-As backed by insurance aren't all created equal, Mr. Croft notes. Bonds backed by MBIA have slightly lower yields, meaning investors consider them less risky than others. Yields on bonds backed by FGIC and Ambac are five to 10 basis points higher. A basis point is one-hundredth of a percentage point.

Investors should also be aware that if the insurer's rating slips, so do the ratings of all the issues the company has insured. That's exactly what happened to some $6 billion of tax-exempt debt backed by Industrial Indemnity Co. after Standard & Poor's recently downgraded the company's parent, Crum & Forster (which is a unit of Xerox Corp.) to double-A from triple-A.

Mr. Schrager suggests that investors check the underlying credit of the bond,

that is, what it would be rated without insurance. In the vast majority of cases, he says, most insured bonds would have a single-A rating, which is still well within what Moody's and S&P consider investment grade. That fact is what leads some analysts to suggest that insurance isn't worth even its small price.

On the other hand, the increasing competition among insurers is prompting some to insure riskier issues, for example, certain housing and hospital bonds. In response, the year-old Bond Investors Guaranty, has staked out a niche as an insurer that will back only bonds that are better than triple-B quality, the lowest investment-grade rating.

To date, only Ambac has admitted to paying claims, including claims on some $23.5 million of defaulted Washington Public Power Supply System 4 and 5 bonds. While it's hard to predict the level of future claims, even insurers note there isn't much room for error. "You can't have enough capital to offset poor underwriting because you can't charge enough. A company can't afford a lot of mistakes," says H. Russell Fraser, president and chief executive of Ambac.

One of the hottest debates in the industry is whether mono-line or multi-line insurers are more secure.

Mono-line companies, such as FGIC, Ambac and BIG, are formed by one-time capital contributions from their parent companies. After that, they depend on revenue generated from a single line of insurance and other contracts to maintain their dedicated cash reserves. Multi-line companies, such as MBIA, are formed as an association of member insurance companies that are committed to backing a percentage of the bond insurer's obligations. The cash reserves that back municipal bonds also back the other lines of insurance—life, property and casualty—underwritten by the member companies.

Multi vs. Mono

Mr. Butler, of MBIA, maintains "there's more strength in a multi-line because it has a greater distribution of risk." Investors seem to agree, since yields on MBIA-backed bonds are lower than on others. But some insurance regulators in New York and elsewhere prefer the mono-line structure because it is easier to monitor.

They also want to avoid any chance that a failing bond-insurance company could become a drag on the more traditional lines of its parents.

Both rating agencies have developed models for assessing an insurer's ability to pay claims in a national economic Depression. So far, insurers have passed muster. The agencies also consider other risks, including the types of issues underwritten and their geographic diversity. Other fac-tors considered are the insurer's capital, the quality of their investment portfolios and their reinsurance policies.

Experts suggest that investors use some of the same criteria in examining insurers. Mr. Schrager notes that insurers' annual reports "provide a fairly good breakdown on these points. Insurers are also fairly open about sharing underwriting cri-teria."

Thus, for an investor in the 15% tax bracket, the after-tax return on the AT&T bond was slightly lower than the Dormitory Authority bond. With a marginal tax rate of 28%, however, the after-tax return on AT&T would be 6.70%, which is lower than that of the municipal bond.

As of this writing taxable investment income may be taxed at the federal level at one of three rates: 15%, 28%, and 33%. Thus the after-tax return on a taxable bond would equal 85%, 72%, and 67% of the taxable income, respectively. A 10% taxable return would, therefore, be equivalent to an 8.5%, 7.2%, and 6.7% tax-free return for an investor in the 15%, 28%, and 33% tax brackets, respectively.

State and local income taxes, if applicable, further complicate the comparison between taxable and tax-free bonds. The presence of such taxes can appreciably enhance tax-free returns, however. For example, a New York City resident escapes federal, state, and city income taxes on any interest income from bonds issued by New York municipal units.

Municipal Bond Funds.   A rather large sum would be required to spread the risks of a municipal bond portfolio effectively. A reasonable degree of diversification would not be achieved with less than five separate bond issues, each from a different governmental jurisdiction. Ideally one would not want to purchase such bonds in smaller than 10-bond units. Five-bond units would be possible, although the per bond commission would be higher. Thus a minimum of 25 to 50 bonds would be required for a diversified portfolio. Such a portfolio would cost $25,000 to $50,000. Sums of this magnitude put diversified municipal bond portfolios out of reach of most investors, even many with high enough incomes to put them in the upper tax brackets.

Fortunately, investors having relatively limited resources have an alternative to assembling their own bond portfolios. Municipal bond funds assemble and manage well-diversified portfolios. Such funds appeal to investors with moderate means who seek tax-exempt income. Many fund's portfolios are, however, weighted toward high-risk securities. Prospective investors may have to do a substantial amount of digging through the prospectus to determine the fund's average risk level.

Like the money market mutual funds, municipal bond funds compete with unit investment trusts that assemble and hold portfolios of municipals. The comparisons are relatively similar. The risk-adjusted yields of municipal unit trusts are somewhat higher, but the units are somewhat less convenient to own than municipal bond funds. A number of funds invest only in the securities of a single state. Thus their residents can take full advantage of the tax-free status of the income at the federal, state, and local levels.

Corporate Debt Obligations

Corporations constitute the third principal category of bond issuers (in addition to governments and municipals). Both convertible and nonconvertible corporate instruments, like government bonds, bear interest and mature. In addition, convertibles (which will not be discussed further here) may at the owner's option be exchanged at some fixed rate for stocks of the issuing corporation. Now consider the corporate bond quotation shown in Table 15.4. It was taken from *The New York Times* but follows the same format as that of *The Wall Street Journal* and many other newspapers.

Corporate bond quotations read much like stock quotations. The first column contains the issuing company's name followed by the bond's coupon rate and the maturity date. For example, the third quote begins with AlaP 9s2000, which indicates that the Alabama Power Company pays 9% on its face value and matures in 2000. The current yield (9.2%) follows. It is the coupon rate divided by the price. Next comes the number of bonds traded during that day. Finally, the high, low, and closing prices and the net change are reported. Corporate bonds are usually sold in units with $1,000 face value while quotations are given in parts of 100. Thus the AlaP quotation of 97½ corresponds to $975 per bond. A bond trading for less than 100 is selling at a discount from its face or par value. One selling for more than 100 is trading at a premium.

Most bond trades involve both the price of the bond and an adjustment for accrued interest. The buyer pays and the seller receives a sum to reflect the portion of interest that has already been earned but not yet paid. Thus a bond that is quoted at 93 would initially cost the buyer $930 principal plus the prorated amount of accrued but unpaid interest. If the bond has a 10% coupon and made its last coupon payment three months ago, unpaid interest would have accrued as follows:

$$\$25 = 3/12 \times .10 \times \$1,000$$

As with dividends on stock, interest is paid to the one who holds the bond on the day of record. When the issuer makes the coupon payment, the new owner will receive and get to keep the entire amount for that period.

A relatively small number of bonds are traded flat. Typically bonds that are in default or whose interest payments are considered very uncertain trade flat. Such bonds are traded without any adjustment for the impact of accrued interest. If such bonds do make their interest payments, they make the payments to the holder of record on the record date. Thus the owner of such bonds on the day of record receives all of that period's interest payments regardless of length of ownership. In the stock quotations, bonds that trade flat have an *f* following the abbreviation for their name.

TABLE 15.4 New York Stock Exchange Bond Quotation

New York Stock Exchange Bond Trading

MONDAY, JAN. 18, 1988

Bonds	Current Yield	Sales in $1,000	High	Low	Last	Net Chge.
	A	B	C		D	
Advst 9s08	cv	8	85	83½	84¾	− ¼
AirbF 7½11	cv	71	78	78	78	...
AlaP 9s2000	9.2	9	97½	95¾	97½	+ 3½
AlaP 7¾s02	9.1	10	85⅛	85⅛	85⅛	+ 1⅞
AlaP 8¾07	9.7	1	90⅜	90⅜	90⅜	+ ⅝
AlaP 9½08	10.0	1	94⅝	94⅝	94⅝	− ⅜
AlaP 9⅝08	10.2	10	94¾	94¾	94¾	− 1¾
AlaP 12⅝10	12.0	97	105⅞	105	105⅛	− ⅝
AlskH 17¾91	15.2	4	119	117	117	− 1
AlskH 15¼92	14.1	7	108	106	108	+ 2
AlskH 11¾92	11.4	5	103	103	103	+ ½
Allgl 10¾99	18.7	121	58	56½	57⅜	+ ⅞
Allgl 10.4s02	17.4	139	59⅞	57	59⅞	+ 5⅞
Allgl 9s89	11.3	30	81	80	80	...
AlldC zr92	...	13	65¾	65⅛	65¾	...
AlldC zr2000	...	5	31⅞	31⅞	31⅞	+ 1⅞
AldC dc6s88	6.1	99	98 23/32	98⅛	98⅛	...
AlldC zr97	...	20	41½	41½	41½	+ 1½
AlldC zr05	...	255	18⅛	18	18	+ ⅛
AMAX 8½96	9.6	4	88½	88½	88½	+ 2½
AMAX 9⅜00	11.2	1	84	84	84	+ ⅛
ACeM 6¾91	cv	6	54	54	54	− ½
ACyan 7⅜01	8.8	6	84⅛	84⅛	84⅛	+ 1⅝
AExC 7.8s92	8.0	20	97¼	97¼	97¼	...
AHoist 5½93	cv	5	77	77	77	+ 1½
AmMed 9½01	cv	39	88	87½	88	+ 1
AmMed 8¼08	cv	16	76	75½	75¾	+ ¼
ATT 3⅞s90	4.2	23	93	93	93	+ ⅛
ATT 3⅞90r	4.1	1	94⅛	94⅛	94⅛	...
ATT 8¾00	9.1	61	96½	96	96¼	...
ATT 7s01	8.4	43	82⅞	82⅝	82⅞	+ ¼
ATT 7⅛03	8.7	27	81¾	81¾	81¾	+ ⅝
ATT 8.80s05	9.3	84	95	93½	94½	+ ⅞
ATT 8⅝s07	9.3	84	92½	91⅛	92½	+ 1⅛
ATT 8⅝26	9.6	161	90	89	89½	...
Ames 10s95	10.9	2	92⅛	92⅛	92⅛	− 2⅞
Amoco 6s91	6.3	10	95	95	95	+ 1⅛
Amoco 9.2s04	9.5	3	96⅞	96⅞	96⅞	+ ¼
Amoco 14s91	13.7	55	102½	102½	102½	− ⅛
Amoco 7⅞96	8.4	5	94	94	94	+ 1

	U.S. Gov't. Bonds	Other Dom. Bonds	Foreign Bonds	Total All Bonds
Today's Sales...	$	a$ 23,830,000	$ 30,000	$ 23,860,000
Friday............		a 33,011,000	129,000	33,140,000
Year to Date.....		a 319,050,000	580,000	319,630,000
1987 Yr. to Date		a$ 479,263,000	$ 1,219,000	$ 481,484,000

a—Includes International Bank Bonds

BOND ISSUES TRADED

	Issues	Advances	Declines	New Highs	New Lows
Jan. 18................	664	375	164	12	13
Jan. 15................	709	457	145	5	16
Jan. 14................	662	290	241	4	10

Bond Tables Explained

Bonds, interest-bearing debt certificates, are quoted in percentage of the par or face value of the bond, represented as 100. The name of the issuing company is followed by the original coupon or interest rate and the last two digits of the year of maturity.

Current yield represents the annual percentage return to the purchaser at the current price. The **High, Low,** and **Last** columns refer to the bond's price during the day, and **Net Chge.** is the difference between the day's closing price and the previous daily closing price. The majority of bonds and all municipal, or tax exempt bonds, are not listed on exchanges; rather, they are traded over the counter.

Other footnotes: **cv**-Bond is convertible into stock under specified conditions. **cf**-Certificates. **dc**-Deep discount issue. **ec**-European currency units. **f**-Dealt in flat— traded without accrued interest. **m**-Matured bonds. **rp**-Reduced principal. **st**-Stamped. **ww**-With warrants. **x**-Ex interest. **xw**-Without warrants. **vi**-In bankruptcy or receivership or being reorganized under the Bankruptcy Act, or securities assumed by such companies. **zr**-Zero coupon issue.

Source: *The New York Times*, January 19, 1988, p. D17. © 1988 by The New York Times Company, Inc. Reprinted with permission.

Many corporate bonds are listed on an exchange, but most of the trading takes place in a very active OTC market. Investors wishing to buy or sell a large dollar value of bonds should obtain several quotations to see which market maker offers the best price. In addition to NYSE listings, small amounts of bonds are also traded on some other exchanges including the AMEX.

High-Risk Corporates. Bonds were once thought of as very secure low-risk investments. More recently, however, many bonds are viewed as very risky and thus bear commensurate yields. One observer reports that 93% of low-rated issues have paid off and that substantial-yield premiums of such issues tend to offset their default risks. Indeed, junk bond speculators have often done quite well.[4] Table 15.5 illustrates some mid-1982 yield differentials. Mid-1982 was a period of relatively high rates. Risk premiums also tended to be high at that time. For comparison, some rates for January 18, 1988, are also shown.

TABLE 15.5   Differential Bond Yields

May 19, 1982

Company	Coupon	Maturity	Price	Current Yield
Very Secure:				
AT&T	13¼	1991	96¼	13.7
GE Credit	13⅝	1991	97	14.0
Risky:				
Eastern Airlines	17½	1998	92⅞	18.8
Rapid American	11	2005	57⅝	18.9
World Airlines	11¼	1994	52⅞	22.3
Very Risky:				
International Harvester	9	2004	28½	31.6
In Default:				
Braniff	10	1986	32½	30.8 (if paid)

January 18, 1988

Company	Coupon	Maturity	Price	Current Yield
Very Secure:				
AT&T	8⅝	2026	89½	9.6
General Motors	8⅝	2005	91½	9.4
Risky:				
Beth Steel	8⅜	2001	74½	11.3
Commonwealth Edison	11¾	2015	103½	11.4
Very Risky:				
Texas Air	15¾	1992	94½	16.7
Resorts International	11⅜	2013	62	18.3
In Default:				
LTV	8¾	2004	25	35.0 (if paid)

Clearly, these substantial indicated yield differentials reflect appreciable differences in risk. Indeed, the higher the "promised" yield, the greater the default risk is likely to be. Although junk bonds are ill-suited to the needs of cautious investors, many risk-oriented investors are attracted to them. Risk and potential returns can be as great as with many stocks. Indeed, a risky firm's bonds sometime offer a more attractive way of speculating than does its stock. The bond investor only needs the troubled firm to avoid bankruptcy or to maintain a substantial value in a reorganization. The stockholder's return, in contrast, may not be attractive unless the firm becomes relatively profitable. A study by Chandy and Cherry strikes a cautious note for would-be investors in junk bonds, however.[5] The authors found that, while the average realized yields on junk bonds generally exceeded that for high-grade bonds, volatility was proportionally even greater. Moreover, in periods of rising interest rates investment grade bonds offered both less volatile yields and higher realized returns.

While always an important investment goal, diversification is crucial for junk bond portfolios. A defaulting issue may eventually pay off but the wait can be long and tedious. Having a diversified portfolio substantially dilutes the impact of a single default. Such risk spreading is especially advisable for junk bond investors. Junk bond funds provide small investors with an effective diversification vehicle. In fact, the growth of such funds has encouraged some firms with relatively low credit ratings to return to the market.

Corporate Bond Funds.   Corporate bond funds have existed for many years. With the stock market depressed and interest rates at historic highs, bond fund yields became increasingly attractive in the early 1970s. The very high interest environment of the early 1980s further enhanced their yields and attractiveness. Markets are of course always changing. Later in the 1980s interest rates fell making bonds and bond funds somewhat less attractive.

As with other types of securities, bond funds may be load or no-load, open-end or closed-end, and managed or unmanaged (unit trusts). As with stock funds most investors will find the no-load type of fund a generally preferable way of buying into a bond portfolio. Most closed-end funds sell at a discount from their NAV. Both open-end and closed-end bond funds have similar advantages and drawbacks vis-à-vis direct bond ownership, as do common stock mutual funds relative to investor-assembled stock portfolios. The bond funds offer diversification, convenience, and low-denomination purchase. On the other hand, the expenses incurred in marketing and managing the funds reduce their yields somewhat. As with other types of funds, unmanaged funds have lower expenses. Thus more of the portfolio's yields flow through to the unit holders.

OTHER TYPES OF DEBT INSTRUMENTS

We have already discussed the most important types of debt instruments: money market, governments, municipals, and traditional corporates. A number of other types of debt security also bear mentioning. Long-term CDs, income bonds, floating-rate notes, zero-coupon bonds, and yield curve notes have unusual interest provisions. In addition, Eurobonds, insurance company debt instruments, private placements, and even preferred stock have characteristics similar to other long-term debt instruments.

Long-Term Certificates of Deposit.   We have already seen that commercial banks and other financial intermediaries offer a number of different types of short-term instruments. They also sell a variety of longer term debt instruments. As a practical matter large CDs seldom have maturities of longer than a year. Banks and other deposit institutions, however, are also permitted to pay unregulated rates on low-denomination CDs. Most banks offer a variety of such instruments. Some offer special rates for IRA and Keogh accounts.

Income Bonds.   Most bonds must either pay the agreed-upon sums (coupon rate) or go into default. Income bonds, in contrast, pay interest only if the issuer earns it. Passed coupons may or may not accumulate. Bonds with large unpaid arrearage may offer attractive speculations. Specific indenture provisions indicate when earned income is sufficient to require an interest payment.

Most income bonds originate in a reorganization exchange. Some, however, are sold initially as income bonds. Income bonds offer issuers about as much flexibility to withhold payments as does preferred stock. In addition, the issuer has the right to deduct the (interest) payments from taxable income. Nonetheless, income bonds are much rarer than preferred stock. McConnell and Schlarbaum, who studied the issue, were unable to explain their relative scarcity satisfactorily.[6]

Floating-Rate Notes.   In 1974, Citicorp introduced a novel type of variable rate security. Soon thereafter several other corporations offered their own floating-rate notes. For example, Citicorp has an outstanding issue that matures in 2004. Its coupon is adjusted every six months to yield approximately 1% over the six-month Treasury bill rate. The floating-rate feature of such bonds generally causes their price to remain relatively close to their par values. The bonds are structured so that their yield adjusts to market conditions. Thus their price can stay relatively constant as interest rates fluctuate. The more distant maturity of most "floaters" does, however, make them more risky to hold (greater default risk) than otherwise similar short-maturity debt instruments.[7]

New issues of floating-rate notes have varied substantially over the past few years. In 1984 about $40 billion were issued including $10 billion from U.S. issuers. The student loan programs in Kansas, Kentucky, and Minnesota have issued intermediate-term notes with tax-free interest pegged at approximately 70% of the T-bill rate. Similarly, the Student Loan Marketing Association (Sallie Mae, a government-chartered but privately owned corporation) has sold notes backed by government-guaranteed student loans whose interest rates are adjusted weekly to .75% above the 91-day T-bill rate. Floating-rate issues are also relatively common in the international market, especially in Asia. Moreover, a few companies have issued floating-rate preferreds.

Zero-Coupon and Other Types of Original Issue Discount Bonds.   Most bonds' coupon rates are initially set so that they will be priced close to their face, or par, value. Original issue discount bonds are sold for appreciably less than their value at maturity (par). These bonds have either a zero-coupon rate or a coupon rate that is well below the market rate. As a result, such bonds initially sell for a market price that is substantially below their face value.

Bonds that do not pay a coupon are called zero-coupon bonds, or zeros. The return on such securities is derived from the difference between their purchase price and maturity value. Treasury bills and certain other securities such as U.S. Savings Bonds have long been sold on a discount basis. For example, a one-year T-bill might be priced at 93. This means that a bill with a $10,000 face value would initially cost $9,300 and pay an additional $700 ($10,000 − $9,300) at maturity. More recently a number of long-term corporate zeros have been issued.

Zero-coupon bonds may also be created from some types of coupon bonds. The coupons are simply separated from the principal portion and the two components sold separately. Most bonds pay interest to the registered owner, but some have attached coupons that may be clipped and sold to an investor seeking periodic income. The bond without its coupons attached is called a strip bond.

Merrill Lynch has created yet another type of zero-coupon security that it calls Treasury Investment Growth Receipts (Tigers). A pool of U.S. government securities is purchased and used to guarantee the issue. Like other zero-coupons, Tigers pay no coupon, but mature at face value and are sold at a discount. Other brokerage firms offer similar instruments also bearing feline names (Cats, Lions, Cougars, etc.).

These various categories of zeros have precisely identifiable maturity values. This feature has an appeal for IRA and Keogh accounts. Investors in zeros know at the outset exactly what the compounded value will be at maturity. The end-period value of funds invested in coupon-yielding bonds, in contrast, is not nearly so certain. The actual compounded value of such a portfolio will depend upon the rate earned on the reinvested coupon payments.

The uncertainty associated with the return on reinvested coupon payments is called reinvestment risk. Because of their lack of reinvestment risk and because of their relative scarcity, zero-coupon bonds have tended to sell for somewhat lower yields than equivalent-risk coupon bonds.[8]

Like other long-term bonds, long-term zero-coupon bonds lock both the buyer and the issuer into a long-term rate. If rates go up after the purchase, the buyer will end up receiving a below-market return. The issuer, in contrast, will pay an above-market rate if market interest rates decline after the issue is sold. Moreover, for a given change in interest rates, the prices of zeros change proportionately more than do those of coupon bonds. Owners of coupon bonds are at least able to reinvest their coupon income at higher rates when market interest rates rise. Owners of zeros receive no coupon payments and thus have no inpayments to reinvest.

Not only do zeros pay no coupons; they impose an annual tax liability on their owners (assuming the investors are subject to the income tax). Original issue discount bonds (including zeros) are taxed in an interesting, if complicated, fashion. To determine a zero's tax liability one first needs to determine the relevant amount of imputed interest. This is the amount that the government assumes is earned but not received each year. The imputed interest rate is computed as if the bond made annual coupon payments equal to its yield-to-maturity rate computed at the time of its purchase. Thus a zero-coupon bond that was sold to yield 10% would be treated for tax purposes as if it did in fact yield 10% each year. The issuer is allowed to deduct the imputed interest cost each year while the owner incurs an equivalent tax liability. As a result the issuer obtains an early tax deduction while the owner must pay out taxes prior to receipt of the associated income.

The tax computation on coupon-paying original issue discount bonds is even more complex. The owner is, of course, liable for taxes on the coupon payments. In addition, taxes are assessed on the appropriate imputed interest as the bond moves closer to maturity. The basis on both types of original issue discount bonds is increased each year by the amount of the accumulated imputed interest. Thus the basis on an original issue discount bond would equal the initial purchase cost plus the sum of the imputed interest amounts.

Yield Curve Notes.   Among the recent entries on new financial instruments is the yield curve note, first issued in 1986. Such securities pay a coupon rate that varies inversely with short-term market rates. For example, the coupon on such a note might be determined by the following formula:

$$\text{Coupon} = 16\% - (\text{Three-month T-bill Rate})$$

A T-bill rate of 6% would produce a 10% coupon while a 9% T-bill rate would correspond to a 7% coupon. Thus the holder of yield curve notes will benefit from lower market rates in two ways. Low market rates imply a higher coupon and a lower rate for discounting that coupon. On the other hand, high market rates have two adverse effects on the yield curve noteholder. Yield curve notes are designed to fluctuate in price inversely with other types of debt instruments. Their prices rise as market rates rise and decline as market rates decline. Moreover, such notes are expected to fluctuate with approximately twice the amplitude of otherwise similar debt securities.[9]

Most yield curve notes have been issued by financial institutions. They can use the notes to reduce their exposure to the impact of market interest rate fluctuations. Having yield curve notes in their capital structure will tend to offset fluctuations in the value of their portfolio of fixed interest assets. For example, as interest rates rise, the value of their fixed rate assets will decline but so will the interest obligation on their yield curve notes.

Investors can use these notes in at least two ways. First, they can speculate on the future direction of interest rates. If, for example, they think interest rates are likely to rise, investors can speculate by buying yield curve notes. Normally the price of a debt security will decline when market rates rise. As we have already seen, yield curve note prices move in the same direction as market interest rates. Second, investors can use the notes to hedge the rest of their own portfolio against adverse interest rate moves. For example, an investor with a money market account will suffer a loss in income as market rates decline. The addition of yield curve notes would tend to stabilize the investor's income.

Eurobonds.   Eurodollars are dollar-denominated accounts held by individuals, firms, or governments domiciled outside the United States. Eurobonds, in contrast, are denominated either in dollars or in some other currency but traded internationally. U.S. and foreign bonds, in contrast, are traded in only one country. The Eurobond issuer benefits from the wider distribution and the absence of restrictions and taxes that are placed on national bonds. Eurobond buyers may obtain greater diversification than from U.S. bonds alone. Moreover, bonds denominated in a foreign currency offer investors an opportunity to speculate against the dollar.

One of the most attractive features of Eurobonds (at least for some investors) is the ease with which they allow investors to evade taxes.[10] Two features of Eurobonds facilitate such activity. Unlike domestic bonds, no withholding is applied to Eurobond interest and principal payments. Moreover, such bonds are issued in bearer (unregistered) form. Without either registration or withholding, Eurobond owners find that taxes are relatively easy to evade. As a result Eurobonds appeal to investors wishing to evade taxes. Because of this appeal, Eurobonds tend to yield less than similar risk domestic bonds.

Most Eurobonds are issued by multinational corporations, governments, and international organizations and most are denominated in dollars or marks. By mid-1984 over $210 billion were outstanding. They may take on any of the forms of regular bonds: straight bonds, convertibles, floating-rate notes, zero-coupon bonds, and so on.

Insurance Company Debt Assemblies.   Two types of insurance company-assembled debt instruments are designed for investors with fixed incomes. Investors seeking a tax-deferred yield may find single-premium (one initial payment) deferred-annuity contracts attractive. The invested funds generate interest that accumulates, while taxes may be deferred until the retiree begins withdrawals (which must not begin prior to age 59½). Such issues are only as secure as the issuer, however. If the issuer encounters financial difficulties, the annuities may not pay off as promised.

A second type of insurance company issue, the guaranteed interest contract (GIC), promises a high interest rate over the security's life as well as the opportunity to earn the same or a higher guaranteed rate on additions. These plans are principally designed for pension funds, but individual investors can also participate. Investors with sufficient resources to assemble their own diversified bond portfolios may not need either type of issue. The instruments do appeal to those with more limited resources, however.

Private Placements.   Approximately one-third of the debt instruments sold are placed privately to a few large buyers (often insurance companies) and publicly announced in the financial press. Such announcements are generally referred to as "tombstones" because of the large white spaces and small amount of lettering. Even if the large size (tens of millions of dollars) of typical private placements rules out direct purchases, individuals may participate indirectly through one of the closed-end funds that specialize in such investments.

Private placements generally yield 1/2% to 1% more than equivalent-risk bonds but lack marketability. Private placements offer issuers greater flexibility. They can be tailored for specific buyers and do not require a prospectus. Moreover, the underwriting cost savings largely offset their somewhat higher coupon. Finally, the relatively small number of owners makes terms easier to renegotiate when need be.

Preferred Stock.   While preferred stock is a type of equity security, it has much in common with debt instruments. The issuer is not required to declare preferred dividends. Payment is required, however, if common dividends are to be paid. Moreover, most preferreds are cumulative, which means that accumulated dividends (unpaid) must be made up before the common dividend can resume. Thus the preferred dividends of many companies are almost as dependable as their bond interest. The preferreds of a weak company may, however, be almost as risky as its common. Some preferreds (participating) may receive an extra dividend payment if earnings or common dividends are high enough.

Preferred stockholders are residual claimants only one step ahead of common stockholders. Unless the creditor's claims are fully satisfied, nothing will be left for either class of stockholders. Unlike corporate interest payments, preferred dividends paid by domestic corporations (incorporated in the United States) to domestic corporations are 70% tax free. That is, only 30% of dividends that one domestic corporation receives from another is taxable. This tax preference is available only to holders who retain ownership of the preferred for at least 46 days. For a corporation in the 34% tax bracket, a 9% preferred yield is equivalent to an after-tax yield of 7.98%. A fully taxable yield of 12.1% would, in contrast, be needed to generate 7.98% after taxes.

Preferreds have become very popular with corporate investors—particularly banks and insurance companies. Because their tax advantage is available only to corporations, most individual investors will not find preferreds attractive.

IMPLICATIONS OF THE LONG-TERM BOND MARKET FOR THE INVESTOR

As with the market's short end, investors may choose from a large number of long-term debt security types. Governments and agencies offer very secure yields. Municipal coupons are tax sheltered. Corporates and municipals can be bought in a wide array of risk and return categories. Specialized types have coupons that vary with earnings or market rates. Still others pay no coupon but mature for substantially more than their issue price. The various types are summarized in Table 15.6.

SUMMARY AND CONCLUSIONS

Security market investors should at a minimum consider the wide variety of risks, returns, marketabilities, liquidities, and tax treatments offered by the bond market. A well-diversified portfolio containing both equity and debt securities is likely to be less risky than a well-diversified portfolio of stocks or bonds alone. Investors should have little difficulty finding issues bearing risks corresponding to their own preferences.

The money market provides relatively attractive short-term rates on high quality securities such as T-bills, commercial paper, large bank CDs, bankers' acceptances, and Eurodollar loans. Small investors can participate in this market through money market mutual funds, short-term unit investment trusts, and the money market certificates and accounts of commercial banks and thrift institutions. Larger investors can assemble their own money market portfolios.

Treasury and federal agency securities make up a large part of the long-term debt security market. Most such issues are untaxed at the state and local level. The agencies tend to offer slightly higher yields but are somewhat less marketable than Treasury issues. A large part of the agency security market is mortgage related. The various bonds, passthroughs, and participations of FNMA, GNMA, Freddie Mac, and the large bank pools offer high, safe, monthly income combined with a somewhat uncertain maturity.

State and local issues, whose interest payments are untaxed at the federal level, form another major segment of the debt security market. Most municipals offer relatively low before-tax yields. Such securities primarily appeal to those in high tax brackets. Municipal bond funds and municipal unit investment trusts provide small investors various ways to enter this market.

TABLE 15.6   Long-Term Debt Securities

Issue Type	Characteristic
Primary Types	
Treasury Notes and Bonds	Lowest risk category
Agency Issues	Slightly higher risks and yields than Treasuries
Mortgage-Related Securities	
FNMA	Mortgage-backed (VA and FHA)
GNMA	Mortgage passthroughs (VA and FHA)
Freddie Mac	Conventional mortgages with Freddie Mac guarantee
Bank Issued	Conventional mortgages, often with a private guarantee
Direct Mortgage, Seller Financing	Risk varies, seconds are usually quite risky
Municipals	Tax-free, risk varies
Municipal Bond Funds	Diversified, may be open- or closed-end
Corporates	Vary greatly in risks and yields
Corporate Bond Fund	Diversified, may be open- or closed-end
Junk Bond Fund	High-risk portfolio
Specialized Types	
Long-Term CDs	Limited variety
Income Bonds	Interest paid only if earned
Floating-Rate Notes	Coupon varies with market rates
Zero-Coupon	Sold at a discount, pays no coupon
Yield Curve Notes	Coupon rate varies inversely with short-term market rates
Eurobonds	Traded internationally
Private Placements	Large and flexible
Preferred Stock	80% tax-sheltered to domestic corporations
Insurance Company Debt	
Single-Premium	Taxes may be deferred until maturity
GIC	Allows additions at high yield

Corporate securities vary greatly in risk. Some high-risk issues offer very high yields. Corporate bond funds (including high-risk bond funds) and closed-end bond funds permit small investors to own part of a diversified debt security portfolio.

Other types of debt securities include income bonds, floating-rate notes, zero-coupon bonds, Eurobonds, insurance company-assembled debt securities, privately placed issues, and preferred stock (an equity asset priced primarily on its stated yield). Each of these securities appeals to specialized segments of the marketplace.

Thus the debt security market offers a wide array of risk–return tradeoffs, maturities, and tax treatments. Moreover, in the past few years a variety of new instruments have improved the access of small investors to these markets. A number of mutual funds and short-term unit trusts facilitate investing in money market, municipal, corporate, high-risk corporate, and various other more specialized types of debt securities. Access is therefore no longer restricted by the difficulty of diversifying across a variety of high-denomination securities.

REVIEW QUESTIONS

1. Discuss each of the various classes of money market securities. What is the relevance of these securities to small investors? What limits the participation of small investors in the market?

2. Discuss the types of short-term debt securities that are available to the small investor. What are the advantages and disadvantages of such investments for individual investors?

3. Describe the three principal types of bonds by issuer. How do they differ? In what ways are they similar?

4. Discuss the relation between Treasury and agency securities. How do they differ (if they do differ) in such matters as tax status, marketability, guarantee, and risk?

5. Compare the various types of mortgage and mortgage-related securities. What is meant by securitization? What is the advantage to the issuer and to the marketplace of the securitization of assets?

6. What types of long-term debt securities can banks sell? How has that list expanded? What has been the role of deregulation in the proliferation of bank issued securities?

7. Explain how to compare municipal bond yields with those of other types of debt issues. How does the market react to nominal versus tax-adjusted yields?

8. Discuss income bonds, floating-rate notes, and zero-coupon bonds. What are the advantages and disadvantages of each?

9. Discuss Eurobonds, insurance company debt instruments, private placements, and preferred stocks. What is the relevance of such securities to individual investors?

10. Describe the various types of mutual funds, unit trusts, and closed-end funds that participate in the short- and long-term bond markets. What do these type of investments offer the individual investor? How do such investments compare with direct management of an otherwise similar portfolio of debt securities?

REVIEW PROBLEMS

1. Compute the discount yield for a one-year T-bill priced at 95.

2. Compute the discount yield for a 180-day T-bill priced at 97.31.

3. Compute the simple interest yield for the T-bill in Problem 2.

4. Compute the coupon-equivalent yield for a 75-day T-bill priced at 98.4.

5. Refer to Figure 15.1 and Table 15.1. Construct a table of money market rates. In your table include rates for Treasury bills, commercial paper, CDs, bankers' acceptances and Eurodollars for maturities of 30, 60, 90, 180, 270, and 360 days when available. Use the maturities closest to these when exact maturities are unavailable. Which rates are highest? Which are lowest? Explain. How do these rates compare with the rate on Merrill Lynch Ready Assets Trust (a money market mutual fund)?

6. Refer to Figure 15.1. Note the prime rates reported abroad compared with the prime rate for the United States. These rates clearly differ substantially. Explain why.

7. Compare the rates on Treasury bonds in Table 15.1 and equivalent maturity agency issues in Table 15.3. Specifically, construct a table containing yields for 1, 2, 3, 5, 7, 10, 15, and 20 year governments (as of the date of the tables). In succeeding columns add in the yields for FNMA, Federal Home Loan, Federal Farm Credit, and Student Loan securities. How do the rates differ? Explain why they differ.

8. The GNMA passthroughs are quoted in the bottom left-hand column of Table 15.3. Separate quotes are listed for different mortgage rates that range from 8% to 15%. Since the GNMAs all have the same government guarantee and similar stated maturities, explain why the quoted rates range from 9.79% to 12.86%. Optional: Assuming a 12-year average maturity, what do the stated yields correspond to in yields to maturity? What do the actual quotes imply for the market assumed average maturity for the different coupons? Do they differ? Explain why or why not.
The following quotes correspond to pricing for tax-exempt municipal bonds on the same day (January 18, 1988) as Tables 15.1, 15.3 and Table 15.4.

TAX-EXEMPT BONDS

Monday, Jan. 18, 1988

Here are representative current prices for several active tax-exempt revenue and refunding bonds, based on large institutional trades. Changes are rounded to the nearest one-eighth. Yield is to maturity.

Issue	Coupon	Mat.	Price	Chg.	Bid Yld.
Brazos Rvr Auth Tex Pcr	9.875	10-01-17	104¾	+ ⅜	9.39
Cal Pub Works Board	6.625	09-01-09	87¼	+ ½	7.85
Calif PCR Pac G&E	8.750	01-01-07	102⅞	+ ⅜	8.45
Calif. PCR Pac. G&E	8.875	01-01-10	103	+ ⅛	8.57
Camden Cty,NJ Util Auth	8.250	12-01-17	103½	+ ⅜	7.94
Cuyahoga County Ohio	8.125	11-15-14	99	+ ½	8.22
Fla Bd Ed Cap Out Ser C	7.125	06-01-17	91⅜	+ ⅞	7.88
Ga Muni Electric Auth	8.375	01-01-20	100⅞	+ ⅜	8.30
Grand Rv Dam Auth Okla	7.000	06-01-06	87⅞	+ ⅜	8.29
Grand Rvr Dam Auth Okla	7.000	06-01-10	86½	+ ½	8.33
Harris Co Hlth Fac Tex	9.000	10-01-17	103⅞	+ ⅜	8.63
Houston Texas	8.125	12-01-17	99⅝	+ ¾	8.15
Ind. Office Bldg Comm.-n	8.750	07-01-12	104⅛	+ ⅜	8.35
Intermntn Pwr Rev Utah	8.625	07-01-21	103⅝	+ ½	8.30
Intrmtn Pwr Agcy Utah	7.000	07-01-15	89⅛	+ ¼	7.98
Jacksonville El Auth Ref	7.250	10-01-19	90⅝	+ ½	8.08
Los Ang Ca Wastewtr Sys	8.125	11-01-17	101⅝	+ ¼	7.98
Lower Colo Riv Auth Tex	7.000	01-01-09	87¼	+ ¼	8.28

MTA N.Y.	8.500	07-01-17	103¼	+ ½	8.20
N.H. Turnpike Sys Rev	8.375	11-01-17	101⅞	+ ¼	8.20
NC Eastrn Muni Pwr Agcy	7.250	01-01-21	88⅜	+ ⅝	8.29
NC Estrn MPA Rev Ser87A	7.500	01-01-15	91½	+ ⅜	8.30
NJ Hlth Care Fac At Cty	8.375	08-01-20	101⅞	+ ¼	8.20
NYC MAC	6.750	07-01-06	88	+ ½	7.99
NYC MAC	6.900	07-01-07	89¼	....	7.98
NYS Dorm Auth	8.125	07-01-17	101	+ ¼	8.03
NYS Energy Res Dev	7.125	03-15-22	86¼	+ ⅜	8.35
NYS Med Care Fac.	8.300	02-15-22	102⅛	+ ⅜	8.12
NYS Med Care Ser 1987A	8.875	08-15-07	105¾	+ ⅛	8.28
NYS Power Auth GenPur	7.000	01-01-16	89⅝	+ ½	7.93
Ocean Cnty NJ Util Auth	6.750	01-01-13	88⅜	+ ⅛	7.81
Orange County Calif	8.125	07-01-16	97⅝	+ ½	8.34
Palm Beach Sch Dist Fla	7.875	08-01-07	100⅛	+ ⅜	7.87
Piedmont Mun Pwr Rev	7.250	01-01-22	88⅜	+ ¼	8.28
Platte Rv Pwr Auth Colo	6.875	06-01-16	87⅛	+ ¾	8.03
Puerto Rico Bldgs Auth	7.875	07-01-16	97⅛	+ ⅝	8.14
Salt Rv Agr Impr & PO	8.250	01-01-28	101¼	+ ¼	8.15
Texas Muni Pwr Agency	7.250	09-01-06	88⅜	+ ½	8.49
Trib Br Tun Auth Ser K	8.250	01-01-17	102¼	+ ⅛	8.05
Trib Brdg & Tun Auth NY	8.125	01-01-12	101¾	+ ¼	7.96

n-New listing. Source: The Bond Buyer, New York

9. Compute the before- and after-tax yield to maturity of the California PCR Pacific G&E 8¾ of 2001. Now refer to Table 15.1 and find the quote for the Treasury 11¾ bonds of 2001. What is its tax-equivalent yield for investors in the 15%, 28%, and 33% tax brackets? What marginal tax rate would make the tax-equivalent yields for the two bonds equal? How do the yields of the two bonds compare? Explain. How do state and local income taxes affect these comparisons?

10. Compute the before- and after-tax yields to maturity for the New York City Municipal Assistance Corporation 6.75% bonds of 2001. Do the same computation for the AT&T 7% bonds of 2001 (Table 15.4). Use marginal tax rates of 15%, 28%, and 33%. What marginal tax rate would make the tax-equivalent yields for the two bonds equal? How do the yields of the two bonds compare? Explain. How do state and local income taxes affect these comparisons? Recompute the after-tax yield assuming a state tax rate of 5% and 10%.

REVIEW PROJECTS

1. Using the formulas in Appendix A and the quotations in Table 15.1 (or a more current quote if desired) compute the actual bid and ask prices for a sample of five T-bills. Now compute the coupon equivalent yields for the issues. Compare the two sets of yields.

2. Make a list of the various money market instruments and track their yields weekly for eight weeks. Which yields are generally highest? How do the yield spreads vary over time? Write a report.

3. Make a list of five money market mutual funds and five short-term unit trusts. Compare their performances over four six-month cycles. (You will have to identify a new list of unit trusts each time.) Write a report.

4. Ask five or more local banks and other depository institutions what their current rates are on money market accounts. Compare these rates with those paid by money market mutual funds.

5. Compare the rates on 10 Treasury issues with similar maturity and coupon agencies.

6. Make a list of the various mortgage-backed and mortgage-related securities. Plot their rates monthly for twelve months. Which offers the highest yields? How does the market vary over time? Write a report.

7. Choose five municipal issues of differing investment quality and plot their rates monthly over two years. Compare the plot with a similar plot for Treasuries and corporates. Write a report.

8. Assemble a list of five bond funds and five long-term unit trusts. Compare their yields. Write a report.

9. Update Table 15.5 with the most recent price quotes. How would an investor in each of these bonds have done?

10. Identify five companies in financial trouble and obtain copies of successive credit agreements. Examine the progression. Assess the relative damage to the bankers and bondholders. Write a report.

11. Assemble a portfolio of five high-risk bonds and five high-quality bonds. Track the portfolio for one year. Compare the returns. Write a report.

12. Assemble a list of five preferred stocks and track their performance relative to portfolios of the underlying common and debentures of the same companies. Compare the returns. Write a report.

13. Select three corporate bonds of varying maturities and three comparable municipal bonds. Compute the marginal tax bracket at which each pair of bonds offers equivalent after-tax returns.

14. Select five T-bills and five U.S. notes with comparable maturities from Table 15.1 (or current quotes if you prefer). Convert the T-bills' discount yields to coupon-equivalent returns and compare the two sets of returns.

NOTES

1. *Handbook of Securities of the United States Government and Federal Agencies* (New York: First Boston Corporation, 1972), 11.

2. T. Carrington and G. Anders, "Drysdale's Default Shows Danger of Intricate Financing Agreements," *The Wall Street Journal*, May 20, 1982, 29; P. Phalon, "Repos and Regrets," *Forbes*, September 13, 1982, 32.

3. J. Treynor, "On the Quality of Municipal Bonds," *Financial Analysts Journal*, May/June 1982, 25–31.

4. S. White, "Not for Widows, Orphans: But Speculative Opportunities Abound in Junk Bonds," *Barron's*, March 8, 1976, 9.

5. P. Chandy and R. Cherry, "The Realized Yield Behavior of Junk Bonds," *Review of Business and Economic Research*, Winter 1983, 40–50.

6. J. McConnell and G. Schlarbaum, "Returns and Prices of Income Bonds 1956–76 (Does Money Have an Odor?)," *Journal of Business*, January 1981, 33–64.

7. K. Ramaswamy and S. Sundaresan, "The Valuation of Floating-Rate Instruments," *Journal of Financial Economics*, December 1986, 251–273.

8. A. Kalotay, "An Analysis of Original Issue Discount Bonds," *Financial Management*, Autumn 1984, 29–38.

9. J. Ogden, "An Analysis of Yield Curve Notes," *Journal of Finance*, March 1987, 99–110.

10. J. Finnerty and K. Nunn, "Comparative Yield Spreads on U.S. Corporate Bonds and Eurobonds," *Financial Analysts Journal*, July/August 1985, 68–73.

APPENDIX. THE MATHEMATICS OF YIELDS

The term yield is often used as if its meaning were unambiguous, but it can actually be taken to mean a number of different things. For example, the current yield reported in the newspaper quotation is simply the coupon rate divided by the current price. Thus an 11% coupon on a bond quoted at 85 would have a current yield of:

$$\text{Current Yield} = 110/850 = 12.94\%$$

Such a computation does not, however, take account of the discount or premium from par. A more complex concept, the yield to maturity does consider the impacts of premiums or discounts. To compute the yield to maturity one would solve for the rate that would make the present value of the income payments equal the price of the bond.

Since some bonds are likely to be called before maturity, the yield to earliest call is often computed for such issues. The computation is similar to that for the yield to maturity except the earliest call date and the call price are used rather than the maturity date and face values.

Those who sell their investment prior to maturity may compute yet another yield: the holding period or realized yield. This is the rate that makes the present value of the payments and sale price equal the purchase price.

Most yields, especially long-term yields, are quoted in coupon-equivalent terms. Short-term yields, in contrast, are often stated in what is called the discount basis. The two yields are computed differently and can produce rather different numbers. Coupon-equivalent yields assume that interest payments take place semiannually and are based on a 365-day year. Discount yields, in contrast, work with a 360-day year and assume that the interest is deducted at the outset. As a result, stated discount-basis yields are somewhat below the coupon-equivalent yield computed for the same security.

The formula for a discount-basis yield of a one-year security is:

$$d = D/F \qquad \text{(15A.1)}$$

where:

$$d = \text{discount-basis yield}$$
$$F = \text{face value}$$
$$D = \text{discount in face value}$$

Thus a $1,000 face value one-year bond selling for $900 would be priced at a $100 discount and offer a discount yield of 10% ($100/$1,000).

A slightly more complicated formula is required for maturities of less than one year:

$$d = (D/F)(360/M) \qquad \text{(15A.2)}$$

where:

$$M = \text{number of days to maturity}$$

Accordingly, the yield for a Treasury bill with 250 days until maturity selling for $9,500 would be computed as follows:

$$\$500/\$10,000 \times 360/250 = 7.20\%$$

We can compute the simple-interest yield from the discount-basis yield with the following formula:

$$i = (365\ d)/(360 - dM) \qquad \text{(15A.3)}$$

where:

$$i = \text{simple-interest yield}$$

Applying formula 15A.3 to our previous example produces:

$$i = 365\ (.072)/[360 - (.072)(250)] = 7.68\%$$

Thus we see that the simple-interest yield (7.68%) appreciably exceeds the discount-basis yield (7.20%) for this security. Table 15A.1 illustrates the differential in the two yields.

The simple-interest yield approximates but does not equal the coupon-equivalent yield. The two yields differ because the simple-interest formula assumes that the interest payments are received at maturity whereas the coupon-equivalent yield takes account of semiannual interest payments. When a security has less than six months to run, the two rates are equivalent. For longer maturity instruments, however, the following formula is employed to compute the coupon-equivalent yield on a security that is priced on a discount basis.

$$r = \frac{\dfrac{2\,M}{365} + 2\sqrt{\left(\dfrac{M}{365}\right)^2 - \left(\dfrac{2\,M}{365} - 1\right)\left(1 - \dfrac{1}{p}\right)}}{\dfrac{2\,M}{365} - 1}$$

TABLE 15A.1   Comparisons at Different Rates and Maturities Between Rates of Discount and the Equivalent Simple Interest Rates on the Basis of a 365-Day Year

Rate of Discount	Equivalent Simple Interest		
	30-Day Maturity	182-Day Maturity	364-Day Maturity
4%	4.07%	4.14%	4.23%
6	6.11	6.27	6.48
8	8.17	8.45	8.82
10	10.22	10.68	11.27
12	12.29	12.95	13.84
14	14.36	15.28	16.53
16	16.44	17.65	19.35

where:

$$r = \text{coupon-equivalent yield}$$
$$p = \text{price as a percentage of face}$$

Thus a six-month Treasury bill selling at \$9,506.53 with 190 days to run would be handled as follows:

$$r = \frac{\dfrac{2(190)}{365} + 2\sqrt{\left(\dfrac{190}{365}\right)^2 - \left(\dfrac{2(190)}{365} - 1\right)\left(1 - \dfrac{1}{.950635}\right)}}{\dfrac{2(190)}{365} - 1} = 9.95\%$$

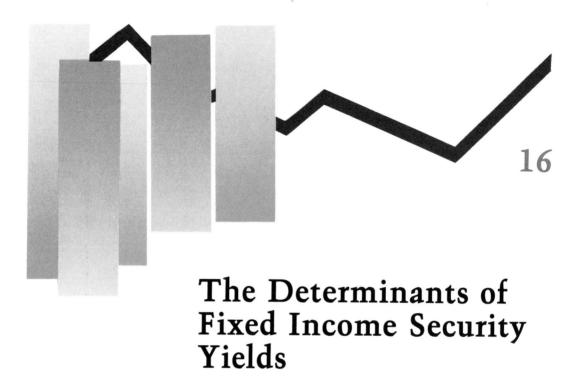

16

The Determinants of Fixed Income Security Yields

The prices of all investments (including debt securities) are affected by the *general* level of interest rates. That general level is in turn related to such factors as the supply and demand for credit, the economy's strengths and weaknesses, inflationary expectations, and energy prices. The *relative* discount rate applied to an individual debt security's promised income stream will vary with a number of other characteristics.

This chapter explores the impacts of a variety of factors that affect individual debt security yields. Default risk, a primary determinant of yields, is given considerable attention. Near-default workouts, Chapter XI and Chapter X bankruptcy proceedings, and bond rating are each considered. We also explore the impacts of term structure, duration, coupon-effect, seasoning, marketability, call protection, sinking fund provisions, me-first rules, usability, industrial classification, condition of collateral, and listing status. The chapter ends with a discussion of bond portfolio management and the relative performance of bonds and stocks.

DEFAULT RISK

No one wants to buy bonds in what seems at the time to be a secure company only to have it subsequently get into financial difficulty. The market prices of such

510

bonds will certainly adjust (downward) to reflect their increased risk. If the problems are not corrected, the issuer may ultimately default. Defaulting bonds may eventually pay part or all of their principal and accrued interest. Alternatively, its owners may be left with nothing more than a tax write-off.

Some investors achieve high yields from diversified portfolios of bonds in or near default. Such a strategy is, however, risky, difficult, and trying. Most bond investors prefer simply to collect their principal and interest when it is due and not have to worry about defaults. Such investors should avoid unduly risky bonds while simultaneously seeking to maximize the return for their desired risk level. Distinguishing safe from unsafe bonds and determining the appropriate risk premium for bonds having particular default risks is a difficult task, however. The issuer's promises to the bondholders is one place to start.

Indenture Provisions

Bond indentures contain a number of provisions. The most important of these provisions relate to each issue's interest and maturity obligations. The borrower agrees to a specified coupon payment until maturity when principal is to be returned. The indenture will also contain a number of other provisions. For example, some debt obligations are backed by specific collateral. The indenture for such a security will specify the nature of the collateral obligation. The provision will typically state that the issuer agrees to maintain any pledged assets or acceptable substitutes in good repair.

The equipment trust certificates of railroads and other transportation companies constitute a major portion of the collateralized corporate bond market. Even weak companies can issue relatively low risk (and therefore low-yielding) equipment trust certificates. The collateral's quality protects owners of equipment trust certificates should the issuer default. For example, the bankrupt Penn Central Railroad continued to pay interest on its equipment trust certificates to maintain control over its rolling stock.

Most corporate bonds called debentures are not backed by any specific collateral. Rather, such debentures are backed by "the full faith and credit" of the issuer. In most instances the issuing firm has a strong enough credit rating not to need to specify any collateral to back up its debt issue. In other cases the issuer may not have any usable collateral. Debentures generally have the same standing as the firm's other general creditors. Thus in a bankruptcy filing debentureholders and other general creditors would be treated equivalently.

In addition to interest, principal, collateral, and liquidation requirements, a bond's indenture may provide for subordination to other debts, a sinking fund, and call privileges as well as dividend and certain other restrictions. Subordination to other debts provides that this debt issue will not receive any liquidation payments until the claims of other specified debt issues are fully satisfied. Sinking funds require that a portion of the issue be retired periodically. To meet this provision bonds may be bought in the open market, they may be called, or funds may be set aside in an escrow account for the issue's eventual retirement.

A call privilege permits the issuer to redeem the securities before maturity at a prespecified price. The call price normally exceeds the bond's face value by an amount that declines as maturity is approached. For example, 10 years before

TABLE 16.1   Indenture Provisions

Provision	Nature of Provision
Principal and Maturity	Specifies amount and timing of principal payment
Coupon	Specifies amount and timing of each coupon payment
Collateral (equipment trust certificate or other collateralized bond)	Identifies pledged collateral and specifies obligation of issuer to maintain collateral's value
Full Faith and Credit (debenture)	Backs bond with the "good name" of the issuer
Subordination	Gives liquidation priority to other specified debt issues
Sinking Fund	Provides for periodic redemption and retirement over the life of the bond issue
Call Provisions Schedule	Specifies length of no-call protection and of call premiums payable over life of the bond
Dividend Restrictions	Restrict dividend payments, based on earnings and amount of equity capital
Current Ratio Minimum	Requires that the ratio of current assets to current liabilities not fall below a specified minimum
Me-First Rule	Restricts the amount of additional (nonsubordinated) debt that may be issued
Trustee	Specifies the institution responsible for enforcing the indenture provisions
Grace Period	Specifies the maximum period that firm has to cure a default without incurring the risk of a bankruptcy filing

maturity, the bond might be called at 105 with the call premium declining by .5 per year thereafter.

Falling interest rates encourage issuers to call and refinance their debt at lower rates. The no-call feature of some bonds prohibits calls for part or all of the bond's life, however. Investors should be wary of call rights. High-coupon bonds often trade for substantial premiums over face. An early call for such a bond would cost the bondholder the difference between the precall market price and the call price. Thus a bond selling for 115 that is called for 105 would cost the investor $100 per bond.

Restrictions on dividend payments are designed to preserve the firm's capital. A firm that pays out too much in dividends could conceivably threaten the bondholder's interests. Thus dividends might be limited to a certain percentage of profits unless and until the firm's net worth exceeds some specific level. A minimum current ratio may be set and *me-first* rules may restrict the future borrowing level. All of these features are designed to protect the creditors. A trustee, usually a bank, is charged with enforcing each indenture provision. Table 16.1 summarizes the typical indenture provisions. Since the value of these provisions to the bondholder depends on how they are enforced, we need to consider what usually happens in a default.

Defaults and Near-Defaults

Firms rarely fail to pay required interest and principal when they have a choice. Sometimes, however, they have no choice. Indeed, the 1980s have seen a large number of financially troubled firms: Braniff, Chrysler, AM International, International Harvester, Saxon Industries, Wicks, Mego, Manville, World Airways, LTV, Bethlehem Steel, A. H. Robins, Texas Air, Pan Am, Continental Illinois Bank, Continental Airlines, First City Bank, First Republic Bank, Texaco, and so on. The experiences of these firms has heightened interest in the default issue.

A firm is in technical default whenever any of the indenture provisions of its bonds are violated. Similarly, a violation of any of the terms of its other debt agreements constitutes a technical default. Many defaults, however, involve relatively minor matters. For example, if the working capital ratio fell below the stipulated minimum, the firm would technically be in default of the relevant debenture provision. Rarely if ever would a default in such a matter in and of itself lead to a bankruptcy filing. The trustee may grant a waiver for the violation or the matter may be quickly cured.

Informal Reorganizations.   Even a failure to pay stipulated interest and principal will not automatically force a bankruptcy proceeding. A late payment may quickly rectify the default. The indenture usually provides a grace period for curing such a default. Even after the expiration of the grace period, the trustee may not immediately institute legal proceedings. Indeed, most defaults do not lead to bankruptcy filings and most bankruptcies do not lead to liquidations. Rather, defaults (and indeed many near-defaults) usually result in a formal or informal reorganization that stops short of a long and costly liquidation.

When a few large creditors (such as banks who have extended substantial loans) can be identified, the troubled borrower may seek concessions that will give it a reasonable chance of avoiding a bankruptcy filing. Big lenders have an important stake in their creditors' survival. An interesting oversimplification of the borrower–lender relationship is seen in the following two sentences:

- A borrower who owes $10 and cannot pay is in trouble.
- A borrower who owes a million dollars and cannot pay puts the lender in trouble.

The weakness of a troubled borrower is in fact a strength in any negotiations with the lender. Accordingly, lenders with large exposures are likely to be asked to accept a payment stretch-out, interest rate reduction, swap of debt for equity or tangible assets, reduction in loan principal, and a change or waiver of certain default provisions. Lenders often agree to such restructurings in the hopes of eventually recovering more than they would in a formal bankruptcy.

Because obtaining concessions from all of the numerous bondholders would be difficult, they are only rarely asked to make them. Accordingly, the bondholders obtain the benefit of the large lenders' concessions without making any corresponding sacrifice. If the effort fails, the bondholders still retain their priority in formal bankruptcy proceedings.

Bankruptcy Filings.   The reorganization of a financially troubled company is not always possible. The alternative is usually a bankruptcy filing. Bankruptcy proceedings may begin with a petition from a creditor, creditor group, trustee, or the firm itself. The firm may choose to file under Chapter XI, which allows time to propose an arrangement with a majority of its creditors (numerically and by dollar amount). Once a majority agree and the court approves, the agreement may be

TABLE 16.2 Absolute Priority of Claims in Bankruptcy and Liquidation
Proceedings

1. Expenses incurred in administering bankrupt estate (legal fees, operating expenses, debt obligations issued after bankruptcy)
2. Wages and salaries up to $600 per employee earned within six months of filing for bankruptcy
3. Federal, state, and local taxes
4. Secured creditors up to the value of pledged collateral with the remaining claims moved to the unsecured level
5. Unsecured creditors
   • Subordinated unsecured creditors
6. Preferred stockholders
7. Common stockholders

imposed on the rest of the creditors. The formal name for these types of majority imposed agreements is *cramdown*. Such cramdowns can only be applied to unsecured creditors. Secured creditors retain their full rights in Chapter XI reorganizations.

An unsuccessful Chapter XI reorganization effort usually leads to Chapter X proceedings. Other cases may begin as Chapter X bankruptcies. In either instance the process is slower, more costly, and may result in the firm's liquidation. When a defaulting firm is thought to be worth more dead than alive, its assets may be sold and the proceeds distributed according to the absolute priority of claims (Table 16.2).

Under the absolute priority of claims principle, the valid claims of each priority class are fully satisfied before the next class receives anything. The marginal priority group receives proportional compensation. Thus if the firm's recoverable value exceeds the legitimate claims of categories 1, 2, 3, and 4 but does not fully cover category 5's additional claims, the unsecured creditors would receive a fraction of their claims while the higher classes would be fully compensated. Priority classes 6 and 7 would receive nothing unless all of the valid claims of 5 were fully satisfied or unless the bankruptcy involved fraud.

Companies generally emerge from bankruptcy after a careful review of their financial and competitive situation. The process is designed to preserve the potentially profitable elements of their businesses in a recapitalized form. Unproductive assets are liquidated. The bankruptcy trustee and courts seek to preserve as much value as is possible for distribution to the creditors. They also try to minimize the risk that the firm will have to return to court protection or have to seek additional lender concessions. Many troubled firms would be financially viable if their debt load were sufficiently reduced. Thus a major objective of most bankruptcy proceedings is to reduce the company's debt load. Bankrupt firms generally have little or no excess cash to distribute to creditors. As a result, most creditors are prevailed upon to accept lower priority securities of the reorganized firm. Senior creditors may receive debentures or preferred shares whereas junior creditors could be given common stock and warrants. The distribution of these securities is governed by the absolute priority of claims principle.

Several factors, however, limit the applicability of the absolute priority of claims principle. The going-concern value of a firm going through a bankruptcy process is quite subjective. The securities to be issued by the reorganized firm will not have an established market price until it emerges from bankruptcy. Thus the relevant values are rather uncertain when (in the course of the bankruptcy proceeding) the securities distribution is being set. Not surprisingly the ability of these securities to satisfy claims is often subject to dispute.

Generally, the lower priority claimants will argue for a higher overall valuation for the company and its securities. In this way they seek to increase the estimated value of the securities that are available for distribution to their priority class. The greater the overall estimated value of the firm, the greater is the proportion of that estimated value that is available to satisfy the lower priority claimants. Suppose for example the high priority claimants have claims of $95,000,000 and the company's value is estimated at $100,000,000. The high priority claimants would be awarded securities representing 95% of the firm's value. Only 5% would be available to the lower priority claimants. Now suppose that the lower priority claimants are able to get the estimated value raised to $110,000,000. At that valuation the higher priority claimants would receive about 86% (95/110) of the firm's value. The lower priority claimants would, in contrast, see their share rise to about 14% (15/110). Clearly, the lower priority claimants would prefer the higher valuation estimate. The higher priority claimants, in contrast, will argue for a more conservative valuation. They want to restrict or concentrate the distribution of the securities to the senior claimants. Unless the low-priority claimants are given something, however, they may use various legal maneuvers to delay and tie up the proceedings. As a result most informal workouts and reorganizations ultimately allocate lesser priority claimants somewhat more than the absolute priority of claims principle requires. In practice, unsecured and subordinated creditors can generally make enough noise to obtain some share of the assets even when senior creditors' claims exceed the firm's remaining asset value.

The reduced debt burden generally permits the reorganized firm to remain solvent. New equity holders may have a long wait before receiving any common or preferred dividend payments, however.

Bond Ratings

The best way to avoid the uncertainty and potential losses from a default and possible bankruptcy is to invest in low-risk bonds. Such a strategy requires a method for assessing the risk level. Bond ratings provide just such a risk assessment. The default risks of both municipal and corporate bonds are rated by several rating services. The best known services are Standard & Poor's and Moody's. Fitch Investors Service and Duff and Phelps Inc. are also bond rating investor services. Each service's ratings is based on its evaluation of the firm's financial position and earnings prospects. Table 16.3 describes the primary rating categories of the two principal agencies. Pluses and minuses are used to discriminate within a rating category.

The agencies do not release their specific rating formulas or analysis, but a number of academic studies do, however, reveal a rather predictable pattern. Ratings tend to rise with profitability, size, and earnings coverage. They decrease with earnings volatility leverage and pension obligations; they vary with industry

TABLE 16.3 Bond Rating Categories

	Moody's	Standard & Poor's	Definition
Highest Grade	Aaa	AAA	An extremely strong capacity to pay principal and interest
High Grade	Aa	AA	A strong capacity to pay principal and interest but lower protection margins than Aaa and AAA
Medium Grade	A	A	Many favorable investment attributes but may be vulnerable to adverse economic conditions
Minimum Investment Grade	Baa	BBB	Generally adequate capacity to pay interest and principal coupled with a significant vulnerability to adverse economic conditions
Speculative	Ba	BB	Have only moderate protection during both good and bad times
Very Speculative	B	B	Generally lack characteristics of other desirable investments. Interest and principal payments over any long period of time are not safe.
Default or Near Default	Caa	CCC	Poor quality issues in danger of default
	Ca	CC	Highly speculative issues that are often in default
	C		The lowest rated class of bonds
		C	Income bonds on which no interest is being paid
		D	Issues in default with principal and/or interest payments in arrears

Adapted from: *Bond Guide* (New York: Standard & Poor's Corporation, monthly); *Bond Record* (New York: Moody's Investor Services, monthly).

classification. Ratings sometimes differ between the rating agencies. Such differences usually reflect a close call on fundamentals. Moody's tends to be the more conservative of the two primary rating agencies. Several researchers have examined the impact of split ratings. They have found that the market price and yield of such issues is much more closely related to the lower than the higher ratings.[1]

For issues of the same company a subordinate issue will usually receive a lower rating than a more senior security of the same issuer. The rating agencies follow the fortunes of issues over time, but rating changes occur relatively infrequently and often take place long after the underlying fundamentals change. Accordingly, several services (including S&P's Creditwatch) now offer more up-to-date analyses including a prediction of rating changes. Moreover, many brokerage firms are paying increasing attention to bond analysis.

Investors can use financial ratios and bankruptcy-prediction models to perform their own bond analysis. Such an examination would probably include an analysis of the level and trend in a variety of financial ratios: current, quick, debt–equity, return on equity, times-interest-earned, and other relevant ratios. These ratios would be compared with industry and national averages in an effort to reveal current deficiencies and/or significant long-term risks. Clearly, high debt–equity ratios and low times-interest-earned percentages are not reassuring. Unfortunately, such analysis can only provide part of the story. Bondholders should also be interested in the firm's future prospects. For example, a seemingly shaky current financial position may be offset by an upcoming product introduction. Alternatively, a firm with a solid financial position may be trapped in an industry that is slowly being eliminated by a changing technology.

Bond Ratings and Performance

How well do bonds of the various risk classes perform? Bonds in the top four rating categories (Aaa, Aa, A, or Baa) are considered investment grade. Bonds with ratings below investment grade are referred to as junk bonds. According to Pye, no bonds that Moody's rated investment grade defaulted in the 1950s or 1960s.[2] A small number of railroad bonds rated Ba or less did default, however. The experience of the 1920s and 1930s is rather different to be sure, but Pye argued that major firms seldom go bankrupt except during major depressions. Moreover, economists and government officials now know how to avoid such depressions.

Subsequent to the Pye article, however, several large firms did go under: W.T. Grant, Franklin National Bank, Penn Central, Braniff, AM International, Penn Square Bank, Continental Airlines, and Manville (with close calls for International Harvester and Continental Illinois Bank). Moreover, government bailouts were required to save Lockheed and Chrysler. Clearly, large firms are not immune to bankruptcy.

Pye also found that, at least down to Baa, differences in default risk could not justify the return differentials. That is, even after subtracting default losses, investors achieve a significantly higher return with Baa than with Aaa issues. In the 1920s and 1930s, on the other hand, the average yield differences accurately reflected default experience. Pye reasons that the substantial premium returns on less highly rated issues result from investors' risk aversion. With default experience as low as it has been, the slight additional safety margins of highly rated issues may not be worth the interest sacrifice. In other words, short of a major depression, A (or perhaps even Baa) rated bonds are probably safe enough for most investors. The additional safety of investments in Aaa and Aa bonds is rarely worth the yield sacrifice.

The issues are less clear for lower rated bonds. The realized (after default loss) yield experience of below-Baa bonds is of considerable interest in light of the growing numbers of such issues. West notes that below-Baa bonds usually command risk premiums above what would be expected on the basis of traditional ratio analysis (leverage, profitability, etc.).[3] Since many institutional investors are not permitted to own below-Baa bonds, such securities may well offer superior risk-adjusted yields. Thus diversified portfolios of medium- to high-risk bonds might outperform similarly diversified high-quality bond portfolios. Diversification across industries would spread the default risk, and the higher indicated yield might more than offset any default losses. McConnell and Schlarbaum, however, found that at least one subcategory of high-risk bonds appears to be efficiently priced.[4] Income bonds with interrupted interest payments tend to offer yields that, while high, are commensurate with their risks. More recent and more extensive studies by Altman and Nammacher and by Fons find that the yield premium on junk bonds has substantially exceeded the loss from default.[5] Such results, however, are derived from studies covering relatively prosperous times. Experience during severe recessions might be quite different.

Investments in Perspective

A number of studies have examined the impact and value of bond ratings. The following article from *The Wall Street Journal* discusses the implications of some of these studies.

Value of Bond Ratings Questioned By a Growing Number of Studies

YOUR
MONEY
MATTERS

By Alexandra Peers
Staff Reporter of The Wall Street Journal

Investors put a lot of faith in bond ratings. But a growing body of research indicates that ratings provide an incomplete and often outdated guide to credit quality.

The studies note that ratings do provide one valuable service: distinguishing between investment-grade bonds and low-rated "junk" bonds. Beyond that, however, the research:

● Questions the significance of the assorted letter grades or notches separating one investment-grade bond from another.

● Finds that there is less correlation than might be expected between ratings and the likelihood of default.

● Indicates that ratings don't tell investors much about other measures of risk like volatility and market performance.

"Ratings provide information, albeit with a lag, to investors who don't have the resources to investigate a firm," says Jerome Fons, an economist at the Federal Reserve Bank of Cleveland. "But there are questions about (their) usefulness."

Paying for Safety

For investors, the implications are significant. With yield differences between ratings grades amounting to as much as half a percentage point, the perception of greater safety can be expensive. The investor who opts for a triple-A bond rather than a single-A may earn a return of 7.35% rather than 8.35%.

Deciding whether to sacrifice yield for safety has become increasingly important this year as bond prices—including those of top-rated bonds—have slumped. Meanwhile, a federal investigation into possible violations involving some 100 municipal bond issues has also focused investor attention on bond ratings; several of the issues under scrutiny received the top rating of triple-A.

The two companies with the lion's share of the ratings business are Standard & Poor's Corp. and Moody's Investors Service Inc. Together, they have evaluated more than 92% of the $260 billion of corporate and municipal bonds issued so far this year, according to Securities Data Co., a New York research firm. Both companies bill issuers from $1,000 to $50,000, depending upon the size and complexity of the issues.

Ratings are based on the financial strength and flexibility of the issuer, on its management's expertise and on either the economic outlook for the municipality or the industrial outlook for the company, says Leo O'Neill, head of S&P's debt-rating division. Investment-grade ratings range from triple-A down to triple-B-minus (at S&P) or Baa3 (at Moody's). Junk bonds—typically issued by troubled municipalities or heavily indebted companies to repay bank loans, buy out shareholders or finance takeovers—are rated double-B-plus (at S&P) or Ba1 (at Moody's) and below. In general, the higher the rating, the cheaper it is for the issuer to sell bonds.

The two companies defend the usefulness of their services, arguing that they don't pretend to answer all questions about a bond—only the likelihood of default. Edward Kerman, a managing director at Moody's, says the ratings offer "an independent arbiter's assessment of relative risk." S&P's Mr. O'Neill acknowledges that there isn't a "huge, wide differential" between top-rated, triple-A bonds and debt that is rated single-A. But he adds that triple-A bonds are "the creme de la creme," which investors will be happy they have "in periods of economic stress."

Much of the research on bond ratings has been spurred by the growth of the $146 billion junk-bond market, which itself challenged the ratings system. The studies do show that junk bonds are riskier.

According to Edward Altman, a professor of finance at New York University and a consultant to Merrill Lynch & Co., corporate bonds had an average annual default rate of 0.14% through 1986 compared with 1.67% for junk bonds. Moreover, he adds, of the $14.2 billion of rated corporate bonds that have gone into default since 1970, about 70% were rated as junk debt at the time of sale.

But studies also indicate that a well-diversified portfolio of junk debt or a mutual fund that includes junk bonds isn't significantly riskier—and may actually be less risky—than an investment-grade bonds portfolio, says Marshall Blume, a professor of finance at the University of Pennsylvania's Wharton School. The reason: Lower-rated debt tends to move up or down in price in line with the issuer's fortunes, avoiding the larger day-to-day swings in the bond market.

Studies also indicate that investors are well compensated for the added risk of junk bonds. Given past default rates, the yield premium on corporate junk debt should be about one percentage point, says Jonathan Kolatch, director of corporate bond research for Goldman, Sachs & Co. Instead, the premium is hovering at about

Assigning Grades

Total value of corporate and municipal bonds sold between Jan. 1 and Sept. 15, in billions of dollars:

	S&P	MOODY'S
Investment grade		
AAA	$80.81	$49.78
AA/Aa	50.39	32.29
A	44.76	53.09
BBB/Baa	19.69	22.53
"Junk" ratings		
BB/Ba	$ 5.41	$ 4.29
B	17.77	22.12
CCC/Caa	.68	.24

Source: Securities Data Co.

2.25 percentage points, he says.

In one study that compared the Salomon Brothers Inc. "high-yield" bond index with a universe of triple-A-rated debt, Mr. Fons of the Cleveland Federal Reserve Bank found that default rates implied by the yields on the junk bonds exceeded actual default rates. The promised return "appears to sufficiently compensate—almost overcompensate—holders for the loss they can experience," he says.

Most research into bond credit ratings has been done with corporate debt. But institutional investors in municipals think the same criticisms of ratings apply to their market.

"There's been numerous examples of the rating agencies' failure to warn investors of potential problems," says Robert Dennis, president of Massachusetts Financial Services Inc.'s managed municipal bond trust. "During all the major crises in the market, the rating agencies caught on after the fact."

A Record Default

Perhaps the best-known incident involved the record $2.25 billion of bonds sold in the late 1970s and early 1980s for two nuclear power plants built by the Washington Public Power Supply System. The ratings firms assigned the debt single-A-plus and single-A1 ratings, indicating a strong capacity to pay interest and principal.

In May of 1981, analysts at Merrill Lynch Capital Markets Inc. and Drexel Burnham Lambert Inc. predicted the power plants would never be built. The ratings agencies downgraded the debt soon after, but it remained investment-grade. It wasn't until seven months later, when the power plants were canceled, that Moody's and S&P assigned the debt junk status. The bonds went into default in June 1982, the biggest default in the history of the municipal market.

Discussing the rating agencies' timeliness, Mr. Kerman of Moody's says only that his agency "reviews and updates ratings periodically" to insure their "accuracy and currency."

The risk that a bond might be downgraded is also an important consideration for investors. And a top rating doesn't guarantee that a bond won't be affected. Indeed, most triple-A debt has two chances of being downgraded. That's because such bonds usually have a "security blanket" of insurance or a letter of credit from a bank that backs the debt. Since there are two parts to many triple-A credit ratings—the issuer and the guarantor—either can be downgraded.

But bond ratings don't indicate whether debt might be downgraded. Since a move by S&P or Moody's to downgrade a bond can erode its price, the two companies "can't act until facts are conclusive," says Richard Ciccarone, senior research analyst of Van Kampen Merritt Inc., an Illinois municipal-bond firm.

Adds Mary Stearns Broske, a professor of finance at Oklahoma State University who conducted a 25-month study of corporate bonds: "Ratings aren't predictors of the future likelihood of bonds to default or an indicator of the way they perform in the market."

Investors can turn elsewhere. Many securities firms analyze bond credits and make their reports available to investors. Such research, says Mr. Ciccarone, "is often able to signal changes and trends before the rating agencies."

Source: A. Peers, "Value of Bond Ratings Questioned by a Growing Number of Studies," *The Wall Street Journal*, September 16, 1987, p. 37. Reprinted by permission, © Dow Jones & Company, Inc. All rights reserved.

THE TERM STRUCTURE OF INTEREST RATES

Its length to maturity is one of three major determinants of a debt security's yield to maturity. (General credit conditions and default risk are the other two.) Yields to maturity tend to vary systematically with length to maturity. This relationship can be illustrated with a yield curve. This curve emerges when yield is plotted versus term to maturity for issues with otherwise-similar characteristics (risk, coupon, call feature, etc.). The yield curve reveals a pattern that at various times rises, falls, does not vary, or rises and then falls (Figure 16.1).

Before discussing the various hypothesized explanations for yield curve shapes, let us review the relationship between an expected income stream's price and its discount rate. The reader may wish to return to Chapter 4 for a more detailed treatment. While all bond prices move inversely with market rates, interest rate sensitivity increases with maturity.

Consider a 100-year bond with a $100 "coupon rate." For such a far-off maturity the simplified formula

$$Price = Coupon/Discount\ Rate$$

is a very close approximation. Accordingly, when corresponding market rates are

FIGURE 16.1   Types of Yield Curves

A Rising Yield Curve: Yields are
low on short-term issues and rise
on long maturities, flattening out
at the extremes.

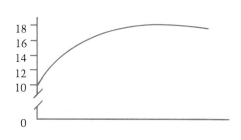

A Declining Yield Curve: High
short-term yields decline as
maturity lengthens.

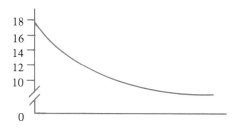

A Flat Yield Curve: Approximately
equal yields on short-term and
long-term issues.

A Humped Yield Curve: Intermediate-
term yields are above those on short-
term issues. Long-term rates decline
to levels below those for short-term
and then level out.

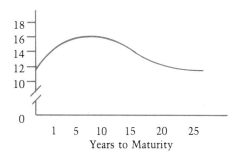

10%, this bond will sell for $1,000 ($100/.10). Should market rates on equivalent-risk issues rise to 11%, this bond's price will fall to $909 ($100/.11). On the other hand, a 9% market rate would price the bond at $1,111 ($100/.09). Since most investors are risk averse, the possibility of an interest rate rise and the consequent capital loss generally causes the greater concern. Furthermore, a bond's call feature limits its upside potential.

Both short- and long-term bond prices respond to changes in market rates. The imminent return of principal limits the interest rate sensitivity of short-term issues, however. For example, a one-year issue with a $100 coupon rate should sell for $1,000 when interest rates are 10%. If rates rise to 20%, the issue must be priced to offer a 20% return. A one-year 10% coupon note selling at $916 would yield about 20% by providing $100 in interest and $84 in capital gains (184/916 = .20). A very long-term bond with an equivalent $100 coupon would, in contrast, need to fall to about $500 ($100/.20). We see that a doubling of interest rates would cause the price of the very long-term bond to fall by nearly half its previous value while the price of the shorter term issue would decline by much less. Thus in a sense short-term issues are less risky to investors than are longer term securities.

Borrowers, on the other hand, may prefer the security of a fixed long-term rate and thus find distant-maturity issues less risky for them. Some investors may also prefer longer term issues as they offer an assured long-term rate. Clearly, the relative risk of a particular maturity depends upon one's perspective (investment horizon, timing of cash needs, etc.)

Term Structure Hypotheses

The segmented markets, preferred habitat, liquidity preference and unbiased expectations hypotheses are all designed to explain the various shapes of the yield curve. The segmented markets hypothesis asserts that supply and demand within each market segment determine interest rates for that maturity class. According to this hypothesis, the yield curve simply reflects the supply and demand for each maturity class for that particular time frame. Some investors are thought generally to prefer to lend short, whereas many borrowers prefer to borrow long term. Thus rates are often lower for short maturities.

A related but somewhat less restrictive form of the segmented markets hypothesis is called the preferred habitat hypothesis. According to this form borrowers and lenders prefer certain maturities. They can only be induced to other maturities by more attractive rates. As with the segmented markets hypothesis, preferred habitat assumes that investors prefer the short end and borrowers prefer the long end of the market.

The liquidity preference hypothesis assumes that markets are not segmented per se but that some lenders (especially commercial banks with their short-term capital sources) generally prefer to lend short. Similarly many borrowers are thought to prefer to borrow long. Thus a rising yield curve is generally needed to compensate lenders for their greater time commitment.

The unbiased expectations hypothesis asserts that long rates reflect the market's expectation of current and future short rates. Thus the one-year rate is simply the geometric average of the current six-month rate and the expected rate six months hence. Suppose that the 12-month rate is Y%. The unbiased expectations hypothesis asserts that current rates have embedded within them the market's anticipated six-month rate six months from now. That anticipation is in fact the rate necessary when coupled with the current six-month rate to yield a 12-month return of Y%.

Consider, for example, six-month and 12-month yields of 8% and 9%, respectively. Taken together such yields imply a specific value for the expected six-month yield for a security whose life begins in six months. Thus the rate for the second six months will cause an investment that yields 8% for the first six months to generate an overall 12-month return of 9%.

An (annualized) 8% return that is earned for six months corresponds to a return relative of 1.04. A 9% return that is earned for 12 months corresponds to a return relative of 1.09. Thus we first seek the return relative for the second six months that will produce the appropriate 12-month return relative. Once we obtain the return relative, the corresponding annualized return is easy to compute. The appropriate formula is:

$$1.04 \times ? = 1.09$$

Solving for ? yields:

$$? = 1.09/1.04 = 1.048$$

A yield of 1.048 for six months corresponds to a 12-month return relative of 1.096. This in turn corresponds to an annualized return of 9.6%. Thus the implied yield for the second six months is 9.6%. In other words, an investment that earns 8% in the first six months must earn 9.6% in the second six months to produce an overall 12-month return of 9%.

The unbiased expectations hypothesis asserts that the market signals its expectations for future interest rates by the rates it establishes for debt securities of various maturities. According to this view, potential arbitrage activity always drives the yield curve into the shape appropriate for that set of expectations.

If long rates seem too high vis-à-vis expected future short rates, some short horizon investors will move toward longer term issues while some longer horizon lenders will switch toward shorter term borrowing. Such activity should quickly drive rates into the appropriate relation. All three hypotheses recognize the existence of such arbitraging activity but only the unbiased expectations hypothesis asserts its overriding power. Table 16.4 summarizes the four term structure hypotheses.

TABLE 16.4 Term Structure Hypotheses

Segmented Markets	Yields reflect supply and demand for each maturity class.
Preferred Habitat	Investors and borrowers can be induced out of their preferred maturity structures only by more attractive rates.
Liquidity Preference	Lenders generally prefer to lend short and borrowers prefer to borrow long, tending to produce an upward sloping yield curve.
Unbiased Expectations	Long rates reflect the market's expectation of current and future short rates.

Each hypothesis explains the various yield curve shapes slightly differently and has somewhat different implications. According to liquidity preference, yield curves are typically rising because, on balance, lenders prefer the short end and borrowers the long end. Segmented markets and preferred habitat are also consistent with a tendency for yield curves to rise. Lenders may be relatively more numerous at the short end.

The unbiased expectations hypothesis, in contrast, asserts that yield curves only rise when interest rates themselves are expected to increase. A constant yield curve indicates neutral expectations. A falling yield curve reflects an expectation that rates will fall. Such an expectation causes borrowers (bond issuers) to rely on short-term financing until the expected fall occurs. Accordingly, borrowers anticipating a decline in interest rates tend to shift demand from the long- to the short-term market. As a result short rates tend to be bid up relative to long rates. Lender expectations have a similar effect. Lenders (bond buyers) want to profit from the expected interest rate decline by owning long-term bonds. Falling rates would cause their prices to rise relative to shorter term issues. Thus investors who expect rates to fall will tend to favor the longer maturities, thereby pushing downward on long rates and upward on short rates. In summary, when rates are expected to fall, the actions of both lenders and borrowers will tend to twist the yield curve downward, causing short-term rates to exceed long-term rates. The very tight monetary policy in 1974 and again in 1980–1981 created just such circumstances: very high short-term rates with lower long-term rates.

None of the term structure hypotheses has gained overwhelming acceptance or been completely ruled out of contention. On theoretical grounds unbiased expectation is generally favored. Liquidity preference may have a slight edge in explaining the data. Most academicians believe that modern debt markets are not segmented per se but that appreciable numbers of borrowers and lenders may have preferred habitats. From the investor's viewpoint the relative strengths and weaknesses of the hypotheses are less important than an understanding of the empirical relationship between yield and maturity.

The Investment Implications of the Term Structure

Yield curve relationships may provide bond traders with two opportunities. First, securities whose yields are some distance from curves plotted with otherwise-similar issues may well be misvalued. Thus bonds whose yields exceed their respective yield curve values may be underpriced. If their market prices adjust more quickly than the curve itself shifts, the strategy would produce an above-market return. Indeed, Brennan and Schwartz find profit potential in purchasing bonds that are underpriced vis-à-vis their own yield curve model.[6]

A second strategy involves what is called riding the yield curve. A steeply rising yield curve may offer an attractive trading opportunity. Suppose, for example, that one-year T-bills yield 7% compared with 5% on six-month securities. Both the six-month bill and a 12-month bill sold six months later would generate a six-month return. Suppose that six-month T-bills are still yielding 5% six months later. Under that scenario the six-month return on the 12-month bill will be quite a bit higher than 5% and indeed above 7% as well. To yield 5% with six months to go, the 7% one-year T-bill must return approximately 9% in the first six months (1.025 × 1.045 = 1.07). Undertaking a strategy of riding the yield curve does incur the risk of an adverse interest rate move, however. Should six-month rates rise to 10%, the six-month return on the 12-month bill would only be around 3% (1.05 × 1.02 = 1.07). According to Osteryoung, McCarthy, and Roberts, riding the yield curve tended to increase both returns and risks, at least for the test period (1976–1978).[7]

DURATION

Up to this point we have discussed debt securities as if measuring the length of such a security were easy to determine. A 12-year bond is a bond that promises to return principal in 12 years. Not all 12-year bonds are alike, however. Measuring their length by the amount of time remaining before principal is to be repaid may be a bit misleading. The term to maturity does not fully reflect the timing of a debt security's payment stream. The final payment on a debt security is only one of the promised payments. Most debt securities also make periodic coupon payments. Each of these coupon payments may be viewed as a partial maturity of the instrument.

The greater the proportion of the return coming from the coupon, the more of the debt security's promised cash flows will be paid prior to its final maturity. Thus a higher coupon is somewhat akin to a shorter maturity. The owner of such a security will receive a higher proportion of his or her investment paid back prior to the return of principal at maturity.

Bonds with coupons close to market yields sell near par. Others having coupon rates that are very low or very high compared to market rates will be priced far from par. Computed yields to maturity will have somewhat different implications for each such issue.

On the one hand, a high coupon reduces vulnerability to adverse interest rate moves. At least the coupon payment of such a bond can be reinvested as received. On the other hand, high coupon payments cannot, in a period of falling yields, be reinvested at rates as high as the bond's initial yield. Thus for equivalent maturities a high-coupon bond has less interest-fluctuation risk but greater reinvestment risk than one with a lower coupon.

The concept of duration allows the investor to make an appropriate adjustment for different maturities and coupon rates. Duration is defined as the weighted average time to full recovery of principal and interest payments. The weight of each of the promised payments is based on its present value relative to the sum of the present values of the payment stream. That is, each weight equals the present value of that payment divided by the bond's market price. The total of the present values equals the bond's market price. In this way duration captures the impact of differing payback rates. The formula for duration (D) is:

$$D = \frac{\sum_{t=1}^{n} \frac{C_t (t)}{(1 + i)^t}}{\sum_{t=1}^{n} \frac{C_t}{(1 + i)^t}}$$

TABLE 16.5   Duration Computation Example

BOND A

1	2	3	4	5	6
				PV as Proportion	
Year	Cash Flow	PV at 14%	PV of Flow	of Price	1 × 5
1	140	.877	122.78	.12278	.12278
2	140	.769	107.66	.10766	.21532
3	140	.675	94.50	.09450	.28350
4	140	.592	82.88	.08280	.33152
5	1140	.519	591.66	.59166	2.95830
Sum (Market Price of Bond)			999.48	.99948	3.91142

Duration = 3.91 years

BOND B

1	40	.877	35.08	.05348	.05348
2	40	.761	30.44	.04641	.09882
3	40	.675	27.00	.04116	.12348
4	40	.592	23.68	.03610	.13440
5	1040	.519	539.76	.82285	4.11425
Sum (Market Price of Bond)			655.96	1.00000	4.52443

Duration 4.52 years

where:

t = payment period (beginning with period one) of coupon or principal
C_t = payment in period t
i = market yield
n = number of periods to maturity

Now consider the durations of two bonds maturing in five years. Bond A has a 14% coupon whereas bond B has a 4% coupon. Table 16.5 reports the results of computing durations of both bonds using a 14% discount rate.

Thus bond B's lower coupon corresponds to a duration of about a half year longer than that of bond A. For equivalent maturities, the lower the coupon, the longer is the duration. The sensitivity of bond price movements to interest rate changes vary proportionately with duration. Thus a bond's duration reflects its sensitivity to interest rate changes more accurately than does the bond's time to maturity. Duration also provides a better measure of the wait to payoff than does time to maturity.

Immunization

Minimizing the reinvestment risk on a bond portfolio is called immunization. One way for the investor to immunize a portfolio is to buy bonds with durations equal to his or her planning horizon.

For example, suppose Jane R. Nearretirement plans to retire in seven years (her planning horizon). At that time she will use her retirement savings to buy an investment that promises her a lifetime income (annuity). A portfolio of bonds having a seven-year duration minimizes her reinvestment risk. Note, however, that to maintain the desired immunization over time she may have to sell some bonds and buy others. Only zero-coupon bonds' durations decrease as rapidly as their lengths to maturity.

Three methods may be used to immunize a portfolio. Purchasing zero-coupon bonds whose maturities are equal to the planning horizon is by far the easiest approach. Consider, for example, a large pension fund with relatively easily forecasted payment obligations. It could immunize its obligations by purchasing a series of zero-coupon securities that mature at times and in amounts that correspond to the projected net cash outflows. Such a strategy encounters two basic difficulties, however. First, cash outflows can rarely be forecasted very precisely. Second, zero-coupon bonds may not be available in the exact maturities needed. Moreover, the assembled zero coupons (e.g., the Tigers) are priced to generate after-expense profits for the assemblers. Thus their yields tend to be somewhat below otherwise-equivalent coupon issues. Accordingly, most immunization strategies involve some degree of managing (with or without some zero-coupon bonds in the portfolio).

A second immunization method involves assembling and appropriately managing a diversified portfolio of bonds. The portfolio is structured and managed so that its average duration equals the owner's (e.g., pension fund's) planning horizon. Over time the fund would receive payments from several sources. In the case of a pension fund inpayments would be made by the group whose pension assets are being managed. Virtually all bond portfolios will receive coupon and principal payments. Similarly a pension fund would have to make benefit payments out of the fund's portfolio. Moreover, the maturities of the initial portfolio components would grow shorter.

Inevitably the fund would find itself faced with either a cash imbalance (depending on cash inflows versus required cash outflows) and an average duration that differed appreciably from its initial target. The fund might be able use its net cash inflows (assuming they are positive) to purchase bonds that moved the portfolio's duration toward its target. Frequently, however, the natural cash inflows will not provide the fund manager with sufficient flexibility to maintain its targeted duration. When such an imbalance occurs, the manager may have to replace some portfolio components with others whose durations more closely matched the target. Thus bonds purchased 10 years earlier that were now close to maturity might be sold and new, longer term bonds bought with the funds. Such an approach appears to be a relatively effective way of immunizing a bond portfolio.[8]

The third and most sophisticated approach to immunization combines a portfolio of debt securities with interest rate futures positions to achieve the desired duration level. That is, commodity contracts calling for the subsequent delivery of debt instruments such as short- or long-term governments are used to lock in a yield on future cash inflows. As coupon payments are received the funds are immediately reinvested in the debt securities whose delivery was assured through the prior purchase of the interest futures contracts. Chapter 19 discusses these interest futures instruments in greater detail. Basically, an interest futures contract calls for subsequent delivery of a specified amount of a specific type of debt instrument such as government bills or bonds at a preagreed price. The contract carefully delineates the date of delivery and amount of securities to be delivered. It also specifies a restricted list of acceptable delivery instruments and a precise formula for their valuation.

Kolb and Gay have shown how such an interest futures strategy can largely eliminate the need to buy and sell bonds.[9] One simply purchases interest futures contracts in amounts and maturities corresponding to the portfolio's forthcoming coupon payments. Thus the inpayments can be immediately reinvested at known rates by taking delivery of the debt securities promised by the interest futures contracts. Table 16.6 summarizes these methods of immunization.

TABLE 16.6   Methods of Immunization

- Purchasing zero-coupon bonds equal to the planning horizon
- Assembling and managing a bond portfolio with an average duration equal to the planning horizon
- Combining a portfolio of debt securities with interest rate futures positions to achieve the desired duration level

The Coupon Effect

The relative amounts of coupon and price appreciation in the return on a bond also have tax implications. Most bond interest income is fully taxed as received. For bonds originally sold at par, capital gains are only taxed when they are realized. Thus price appreciation income on such bonds is tax preferred. Note, however, that the imputed yield from price appreciation on zero-coupon and original issue discount bonds is taxed as if it were received periodically. Only bonds originally issued at or near par generate a capital gains tax break. Still the market generally contains many low-coupon bonds that were initially sold at par but now are priced at a deep discount. Whenever interest rates rise above some past levels, bonds that were issued in the lower interest environment will sell for a discount from their par. If they are purchased at a deep discount and held to maturity, they will produce a substantial capital gain. Moreover, bonds priced well below par (and therefore below their call price) are much less likely to be called than those trading near or above par.

Accordingly, investors tend to prefer deep-discount bonds to higher coupon issues. The before-tax yields to maturity on low-coupon, deep-discount issues are usually somewhat below yields on otherwise-similar issues trading nearer to par. This relationship is called the coupon effect. When capital gains were taxed at a lower rate than ordinary income, the coupon effect had a much greater impact.

OTHER FACTORS AFFECTING BOND PRICES AND YIELDS

The characteristics already discussed (general interest rate levels, risk of default, maturity–duration, coupon effect, tax status) constitute the principal price/yield determinants of specific bonds. Somewhat less important characteristics include: marketability, seasoning, call protection, sinking fund provisions, me-first rules, usability, industrial classification, condition of collateral, and listing status.

The vast majority of bond trading takes place in high-volume markets with narrow spreads and deep supply and demand. Many lower volume issues, however, trade in thin markets with spreads of five and even 10 points. A quote of 70 bid to 80 asked implies a 14% spread. Unless a limit order can be used to reduce the spread's impact, trading such an issue is extremely costly. Other things being equal, the less marketable the issue, the higher will be the yield required to make the bond attractive to investors.

Seasoned issues are established in the marketplace. They have been traded for at least a few weeks beyond completion of the initial (offering) sale. As with new stock issues, new issues of bonds seem to be priced a bit below equivalent seasoned issues. Several authors, however, contend that the apparent yield differences can be explained by the existence of tax, call provision, and other issuer-specific factors.[10]

Call protection varies appreciably from issue to issue. Some bonds are callable when sold. Many others may not be called for the first five or 10 years of their life. Callable issues that are reasonably likely to be redeemed (high yields) should be evaluated on their yield to earliest call rather than their yield to maturity. In marginal cases both yield figures should be computed and compared. Call protection tends to increase a bond's price, but Van Horne finds that the market tends to overvalue call protection.[11] Thus callable issues may generally be superior investments.

The sinking fund's presence increases demand slightly and reduces the probability that refinancing its debts will burden the issuer. Thus a sinking fund generally adds modestly to the value of a bond.[12] Providing sinking funds in the bond indenture does not appear to reduce the debt issuer's ex-post cost, however.

Me-first rules are designed to protect existing bondholders. Such rules prevent their claims from being weakened by the issuance of additional debt with a priority higher or equivalent to theirs. Brauer finds that such rules significantly enhance the market values of the protected bonds.[13]

Usable bonds can be used at their par values in exercising the firm's outstanding warrants. If such bonds sell for less than par, exercising with them is cheaper than with cash. If the stock price is near or below the point where exercising is attractive, the usability feature may add to the bond's value. The price impact of usability depends primarily on two factors: (1) the relative magnitude of the bond's straight-debt value versus its value in exercising the warrant and (2) the relative supply of usable bonds and warrants outstanding.

Boardman and McEnally, who exhaustively studied the factors that affect bond values, found that (1) industrial and transportation issues tend to command higher prices than otherwise-equivalent utility issues; (2) the status of collateral affects values especially when the issue would otherwise have a low rating; and (3) listing has little or no price impact.[14] Table 16.7 summarizes the various factors affecting bond yields.

ASSEMBLING AND MANAGING A BOND PORTFOLIO

Diversified bond portfolios should be managed to meet their owner's needs. A half dozen different bond issues are usually sufficient to achieve relatively effective

TABLE 16.7   Factors Affecting Bond Yields

General Credit Conditions	Credit conditions affect all yields to one degree or another.
Default Risk	Riskier issues require higher promised yields.
Term Structure	Yields vary with maturity, reflecting expectations for future rates.
Duration	The average wait till payback is calculated using the duration formula.
Coupon Effect	Low-coupon issues offer yields that are partially tax sheltered.
Seasoning	Newly issued bonds may sell at a slight discount to otherwise-equivalent established issues.
Marketability	Actively traded issues tend to be worth more than otherwise-equivalent issues that are less actively traded.
Call Protection	Protection from an early call tends to enhance a bond's value.
Sinking Fund Provisions	Sinking funds increase demand and reduce the risk of refinancing, thereby tending to enhance a bond's value.
Me-First Rules	Bonds protected from the diluting effect of additional firm borrowings are generally worth more than otherwise-equivalent unprotected issues.
Usability	Bonds usable at par to exercise warrants tend to be worth more than otherwise-equivalent issues.
Industrial Classification	Industrial and transportation issues tend to command higher prices than otherwise-equivalent utility issues.
Collateral Status	Well-maintained collateral tends to enhance bond values relatively to less well-maintained collateral.
Listing	Exchange listing appears to have little or no impact on bond yields.

diversification of a portfolio of bonds. Bonds should also be selected to produce the desired level of maturity/duration, default risk/quality rating, coupon/price appreciation, etc. Moreover, bonds are usually part of a larger portfolio that also includes stocks and perhaps some other types of assets. Thus bonds should usually be viewed as providing liquidity, dependable income, and so on in the larger context of the portfolio.

Bond Swaps

Portfolio managers frequently finance a bond purchase with the funds freed up by liquidating another position. Such bond swaps may be designed to increase yield to maturity or current yield, to adjust duration or risk, or to establish a tax loss.

Many swaps are not executed simultaneously. Thus swap traders risk making one side of the swap (say the sell) only to encounter an adverse price move before the other side is accomplished. Moreover, transactions costs absorb some of what would otherwise be the expected benefits of the swap. Nonetheless, a variety of circumstances make swaps attractive. For example, a low-coupon, deep-discount issue might be sold and the proceeds used to purchase a higher coupon issue. The sale would normally generate a tax loss. Presumably the purchased issue is designed to offer a higher yield. On the other hand, the swap would probably increase both the call risk and the reinvestment risk.

TABLE 16.8 Selected Bond Quotations

Issuer	Rating (S&P)	Coupon	Maturity	Price	Current Yield	Yield to Maturity
			December 31, 1981			
AT&T	AAA	3⅞	1990	69½	5.6%	9.4%
AT&T	AAA	10⅜	1990	98⅞	10.5	10.6
AT&T	AAA	8.80	2005	79⅝	11.1	11.3
GMAC	AA+	11⅝	1990	101¾	11.4	11.3
GMAC	AA+	11¾	2000	97	12.1	12.2
			December 31, 1987			
AT&T	AA	3⅞	1990	90⅞	4.3%	8.0%
AT&T	AA	8.80	2005	91½	9.6	9.8
GMAC	AA−	11¾	2000	104½	11.3	11.1

In another type of swap an investor might sell one issue that had been held at a loss and then purchase another very similar issue. Such a pure tax swap establishes a loss while leaving the portfolio's basic character unchanged. In yet another type of swap a bond originally purchased as a long-term issue may have moved much closer to maturity. Swapping it for a longer term bond would restore the desired maturity level and possibly enhance yield as well (if long rates are above short rates). Possible bond swaps are illustrated with the help of the quotes in Table 16.8.

Investors owning the AT&T 3⅞s of 1990 at the end of 1981 could have greatly increased their current yield with a switch to the 10⅜s of 1990 (10.5% versus 5.6%). The yield to maturity would also have risen (10.6% versus 9.4%). To be effective a tax swap requires a switch to a different bond issuer. Thus one holding the AT&T 3⅞s or 10⅜s of 1990 at year-end 1981 could have traded them in for GM Acceptance 11⅝s of 1990. The maturities are similar and the GMAC quality was only slightly below that of AT&T (AA+ versus AAA). Maturity swaps could have been made between either AT&T 1990 issues and the 8.80s of 2005 or between the GMAC 11⅝s of 1990 and the GMAC 11¾s of 2000.

Six years later new prices and yields were obtained for this group of bonds. The changes are interesting. First, two of the bonds are no longer listed. Undoubtedly they were called by the issuer and the outstanding borrowings refinanced at a lower interest rate. Second, the remaining three bonds have all been downgraded. The ratings of the AT&T issues were down to AA (year-end 1987) compared with AAA on the earlier date. The divestiture of AT&T's operating companies had increased their risks. Similarly, the GMAC bond was (year-end 1987) rated AA− compared with AA+ at the earlier date. General Motors' share of the auto market had slipped as had its profitability. Fourth, notwithstanding the ratings downgrades, each of the bonds was priced higher on the later date. Market interest rates had declined.

Similar bond swaps are possible with the more recent bond quotes. For example, the investor could execute a maturity/yield swap between the AT&T 3⅞s and the 8.80s. Tax swaps are possible between the AT&T and GMAC issues.

Other Aspects of Bond Portfolio Management

Managing a bond portfolio effectively can involve much more than the simple types of swaps mentioned above. The investor might, for example, speculate on a bond upgrade by buying an issue that the market views pessimistically. Margin borrowing may be used to magnify potential gains and/or to leverage a high yield. Some bonds may have higher promised long-term yields than the current cost of margin money. Whether such apparently attractive yield spreads should be exploited depends on both the likelihood that they will persist and the default risk of high-yielding issues. If market interest rates rise, the margin borrowing rate will increase and bond prices will decline.

Still more complicated maneuvers involve the use of interest futures and hedges between a company's bond and its other securities. For example, a long position in a company with a high default risk might be hedged with a short position in the firm's stock. If the firm goes bankrupt, the stock could become almost worthless while its bonds might still retain some value in a reorganization or liquidation. If the company survives, the bonds will eventually pay off, although the stock may not do well unless the company prospers. Finally, portfolio managers can trade on the basis of their interest rate forecasts. If interest rates are expected to fall, portfolio maturities should be lengthened. An expected rise should cause the manager to shift toward near-cash securities. Such a strategy assumes that the manager can accurately forecast interest rate changes, however.

Comparison of Yields for Various Securities

Now that the various types of debt securities have been discussed, their past returns may be usefully examined as a clue to future rates (Table 16.9).

The reported rates are not realized returns but yields to maturity for the particular time. For money market instruments, this qualification is of little importance because the price fluctuation impact on realized yields is minor. In other words, the yields to maturity for short-term securities will normally not differ greatly from the actual realized returns. For longer term issues, however, the possible deviation of realized returns and yields to maturity is substantial. Such differences arise when a bond is sold prior to maturity. The investor then realizes a return that reflects both the coupon payments and the difference between purchase and sale price on the security. An investor might, for example, have purchased a long-term (30-year) government bond in 1981 when its yield to maturity was an average of 13.44% and then sold it in 1986 when 20- to 30-year bond yields averaged 7.80% to 7.85%. Over that holding period the market price of the bond rose substantially. As a result the return for the 1981–1986 period would be considerably more than 13.44%. On the other hand, an investor who bought the same bond and holds it until maturity would probably not receive even the 13.44% return. Over much of the holding period the coupon payments would not be reinvested at or near the initial yield.

Comparative rates on preferred and common stocks are also included in the long-term securities data in Table 16.9. Current yield on the current price data are not adjusted for capital gains or losses, however. Because preferreds are primarily income securities, the stated rates may approximate their long-term yields. For common stocks the data are not comparable as dividends constitute only a fraction of their average returns. Failing to allow for capital gains or losses is clearly misleading. On the other hand, any estimated allowance would be arbitrary. Past historical returns may bear little relation to the future while expected returns are unobservable.

Transaction Costs for Bonds

As with stocks, investors in bonds need to be aware of the costs associated with trading such securities. The costs can vary enormously depending upon the nature of the trade. In addition to the basic price of the debt security bond, traders need to be aware of three charges: commissions, spreads, and accrued interest.

Compared to stocks commissions on bond trades tend to be relatively low. A trade of 10 bonds or more will typically incur a commission of $5 per bond. A large trade or large trader is likely to qualify for a discount from this rate. Five dollars per bond amounts to 0.5% of a $1,000 face value. Retail commissions on stock trades, in contrast, average closer to 3%. Thus bonds that sell near to their par values will normally incur rather modest commissions.

Two circumstances in which the commissions may be of concern are very small trades and bonds that sell for a small fraction of their par value. Most brokers have a minimum commission charge that overrides their per bond formula. Thus an investor who purchases three bonds may be charged a $50 commission because $50 is the brokerage firm's minimum. Similarly, a trade involving deep-discount or zero-coupon bonds may incur a relatively high commission in terms of its percentage of the dollar value of the trade. That is, $5 per bond is a much higher percentage of the money involved for a bond trading at 20 (2.50%) than one trading at 95 (0.53%).

Spreads are another important consideration in bond trading. Spreads on actively traded bonds tend to be quite narrow. For example, the spreads on most governments are measured in thirty-seconds. A spread of $3/32$ on a $1,000 bond amounts to $0.9375, which is less than 0.1% of the price. On the other hand, less actively traded issues may have much wider spreads. For example, a small inactively traded corporate bond might be quoted 80–85. A five-point spread on a bond with a bid of 80 corresponds to a spread of 6.25% of the bid price. The spreads can be even wider. For example, an inactively traded deep-discount bond might be quoted 30–40. Such a quote corresponds to a spread of 33% of the bid.

The final matter for bond traders to consider is the accrued interest assessed of the buyer. Between coupon payments bonds may be seen as building up an accrual for the forthcoming interest payment. For example, a bond with an 8% coupon will make a semiannual payment of 4% of its par ($40 on a standard $1,000 face value bond). Midway between coupon payments the bond will have accrued half of the coupon ($20). According to standard trading practice a buyer of the bond at that point would pay the seller the price of the bond plus the amount of accrued interest. When the next coupon is paid, the new owner will keep the entire payment and thereby recoup the accrued amount advanced to the seller. Not all bonds are traded this way but most are. The remainder are traded flat, which

TABLE 16.9 Interest Rates, Money, and Capital Markets

	Instrument	1981	1982	1983	1984	1985	1986	1987				1987, week ending				
								June	July	Aug.	Sept.	Aug. 28	Sept. 4	Sept. 11	Sept. 18	Sept. 25
	MONEY MARKET RATES															
1	Federal funds[1,2]	16.38	12.26	9.09	10.22	8.10	6.80	6.73	6.58	6.73	7.22	6.76	6.85	6.95	7.21	7.26
2	Discount widow borrowing[1,2,3]	13.42	11.02	8.50	8.80	7.69	6.33	5.50	5.50	5.50	5.95	5.50	5.50	5.93	6.00	6.00
	Commercial paper[4,5]															
3	1-month	15.69	11.83	8.87	10.05	7.94	6.62	6.86	6.57	6.62	7.26	6.64	6.87	7.29	7.35	7.34
4	3-month	15.32	11.89	8.88	10.10	7.95	6.49	6.92	6.65	6.71	7.37	6.72	6.96	7.40	7.45	7.44
5	6-month	14.76	11.89	8.89	10.16	8.01	6.39	7.00	6.72	6.81	7.55	6.83	7.12	7.61	7.63	7.62
	Finance paper, directly placed[4,5]															
6	1-month	15.30	11.64	8.80	9.97	7.91	6.58	6.80	6.53	6.56	7.20	6.56	6.75	7.23	7.25	7.32
7	3-month	14.08	11.23	8.70	9.73	7.77	6.38	6.77	6.48	6.49	7.08	6.55	6.68	7.08	7.10	7.27
8	6-month	13.73	11.20	8.69	9.65	7.75	6.31	6.50	6.35	6.34	6.90	6.36	6.43	6.85	6.99	7.09
	Bankers' acceptances[5,6]															
9	3-month	15.32	11.89	8.90	10.14	7.92	6.39	6.83	6.59	6.64	7.31	6.69	6.97	7.31	7.35	7.37
10	6-month	14.66	11.83	8.91	10.19	7.96	6.29	6.91	6.65	6.75	7.48	6.83	7.09	7.51	7.53	7.53
	Certificates of deposit, secondary market															
11	1-month	15.91	12.04	8.96	10.17	7.97	6.61	6.84	6.60	6.63	7.25	6.65	6.86	7.25	7.33	7.35
12	3-month	15.91	23.27	9.07	10.37	8.05	6.52	6.94	6.70	6.75	7.37	6.77	7.00	7.38	7.41	7.43
13	6-month	15.77	12.57	9.27	10.68	8.25	6.51	7.15	6.87	7.02	7.74	7.05	7.31	7.78	7.81	7.79
14	Eurodollar deposits, 3-month[8]	16.79	13.12	9.56	10.73	8.28	6.71	7.11	6.87	6.91	7.51	6.91	7.11	7.40	7.44	7.54
	U.S. Treasury bills[5]															
	Secondary market[9]															
15	3-month	14.03	10.61	8.61	9.52	7.48	5.98	5.67	5.69	6.04	6.40	6.24	6.21	6.39	6.36	6.48
16	6-month	13.80	11.07	8.73	9.76	7.65	6.03	5.99	5.76	6.15	6.64	6.25	6.36	6.53	6.65	6.79
17	1-year	13.14	11.07	8.80	9.92	7.81	6.08	6.35	6.24	6.54	7.11	6.65	6.89	7.16	7.10	7.14
	Auction average[10]															
18	3-month	14.029	10.686	8.63	9.57	7.49	5.97	5.69	5.78	6.00	6.32	6.12	6.19	6.45	6.32	n.a.
19	6-month	13.776	11.084	8.75	9.80	7.66	6.02	5.99	5.86	6.14	6.57	6.16	6.34	6.72	6.64	n.a.
20	1-year	13.159	11.099	8.86	9.91	n.a.	n.a.	6.54	6.22	6.52	6.74	n.a.	n.a.	6.74	n.a.	n.a.
	CAPITAL MARKET RATES															
	U.S. Treasury notes and bonds[11]															
	Constant maturities[12]															
21	1-year	14.78	12.27	9.57	10.89	8.43	6.46	6.80	6.68	7.03	7.67	7.16	7.41	7.72	7.65	7.70
22	2-year	14.56	12.80	10.21	11.65	9.27	6.87	7.57	7.44	7.75	8.34	7.89	8.11	8.39	8.31	8.37
23	3-year	14.44	12.92	10.45	11.89	9.64	7.06	7.82	7.74	8.03	8.67	8.13	8.41	8.70	8.64	8.71
24	5-year	14.24	13.01	10.80	12.24	10.13	7.31	8.02	8.01	8.32	8.94	8.41	8.69	8.96	8.94	8.97
25	7-year	14.06	13.06	11.02	12.40	10.51	7.55	8.27	8.27	8.59	9.26	8.67	9.00	9.29	9.27	9.29
26	10-year	13.91	13.00	11.10	12.44	10.62	7.68	8.40	8.45	8.76	9.42	8.85	9.18	9.43	9.43	9.45
27	20-year	13.72	12.92	11.34	12.48	10.97	7.85	n.a.	n.a.	n.a.	n.a.	n.a.	n.a.	n.a.	n.a.	n.a.
28	30-year	13.44	12.76	11.18	12.39	10.79	7.80	8.57	8.64	8.97	9.59	9.04	9.36	9.60	9.61	9.61

29 Composite[13] Over 10 years (long-term)	12.87	12.23	10.84	11.99	10.75	8.14	8.63	8.70	8.97	9.58	9.04	9.35	9.60	9.61	9.60
State and local notes and bonds Moody's series[14]															
30 Aaa	10.43	10.88	8.80	9.61	8.60	6.95	7.48	7.18	7.24	7.66	7.20	7.45	7.75	7.70	7.75
31 Baa	11.76	12.48	10.17	10.38	9.58	7.76	8.68	8.37	8.31	8.67	8.30	8.60	8.90	8.85	8.35
32 Bond Buyer series[15]	11.33	11.66	9.51	10.10	9.11	7.32	7.79	7.72	7.81	8.26	7.80	8.05	8.38	8.32	8.30
Corporate bonds Seasoned issues[16]															
33 All industries	15.06	14.94	12.78	13.49	12.05	9.71	9.87	9.92	10.24	10.64	10.14	10.32	10.58	10.75	10.74
34 Aaa	14.17	13.79	12.04	12.71	11.37	9.02	9.32	9.42	9.67	10.18	9.70	9.87	10.15	10.28	10.25
35 Aa	14.75	14.41	12.42	13.31	11.82	9.47	9.65	9.64	9.86	10.35	9.86	10.05	10.31	10.44	10.42
36 A	15.29	15.43	13.10	13.74	12.28	9.95	9.98	10.00	10.20	10.72	10.19	10.35	10.64	10.85	10.85
37 Baa	16.04	16.11	13.55	14.19	12.72	10.39	10.52	10.61	10.80	11.31	10.82	11.00	11.23	11.40	11.42
38 A-rated, recently-offered utility bonds[17]	16.63	15.49	12.73	13.81	12.06	9.61	10.05	10.17	10.37	10.84	10.44	10.60	10.86	10.93	11.00
MEMO: Dividend/price ratio[18]															
39 Preferred stocks	12.36	12.53	11.02	11.59	10.49	8.76	8.31	8.25	8.32	8.64	8.38	8.55	8.62	8.67	8.67
40 Common stocks	5.20	5.81	4.40	4.64	4.25	3.48	2.92	2.83	2.69	2.78	2.64	2.75	2.82	2.81	2.77

1. Weekly and monthly figures are averages of all calendar days, where the rate for a weekend or holiday is taken to be the rate prevailing on the preceding business day. The daily rate is the average of the rates on a given day weighted by the volume of transactions at these rates.

2. Weekly figures are averages for statement week ending Wednesday.

3. Rate for the Federal Reserve Bank of New York.

4. Unweighted average of offering rates quoted by at least five dealers (in the case of commercial paper), or finance companies (in the case of finance paper). Before November 1979, maturities for data shown are 30–59 days, 90–119 days, and 120–179 days for commercial paper; and 30–59 days, 90–119 days, and 150–179 days for finance paper.

5. Yields are quoted on a bank-discount basis, rather than in an investment yield basis (which would give a higher figure).

6. Dealer closing offered rates for top-rated banks. Most representative rate (which may be, but need not be, the average of the rates quoted by the dealers).

7. Unweighted average of offered rates quoted by at least five dealers early in the day.

8. Calendar week average. For indication purposes only.

9. Unweighted average of closing bid rates quoted by at least five dealers.

10. Rates are recorded in the week in which bills are issued. Beginning with the Treasury bill auction held on Apr. 18, 1983, bidders were required to state the percentage yield (on a bank discount basis) that they would accept to two decimal places.

Thus, average issuing rates in bill auctions will be reported using two rather than three decimal places.

11. Yields are based on closing bid prices quoted by at least five dealers.

12. Yields adjusted to constant maturities by the U.S. Treasury. That is, yields are read from a yield curve at fixed maturities. Based on only recently issued, actively traded securities.

13. Averages (to maturity or call) for all outstanding bonds neither due nor callable in less than 10 years, including one very low yielding "flower" bond.

14. General obligations based on Thursday figures; Moody's Investors Service.

15. General obligations only, with 20 years to maturity, issued by 20 state and local governmental units of mixed quality. Based on figures for Thursday.

16. Daily figures from Moody's Investors Service. Based on yields to maturity on selected long-term bonds.

17. Compilation of the Federal Reserve. This series is an estimate of the yield on recently-offered, A-rated utility bonds with a 30-year maturity and 5 years of call protection. Weekly data are based on Friday quotations.

18. Standard and Poor's corporate series. Preferred stock ratio based on a sample of ten issues: four public utilities, four industrials, one financial, and one transportation. Common stock ratios on the 50 stocks in the price index.

NOTE: These data also appear in the Board's H.15 (519) and G.13 (415) releases.

Source: *Federal Reserve Bulletin*, May 1984, p. A24 and December 1987.

means no allowance is made for accrued interest. Bonds are likely to trade flat only if they have defaulted on a prior coupon payment or if the amount of the interest payment is uncertain (income bonds and floating rate notes, for example).

Two potential concerns with the accrued interest component of a bond's cost should be borne in mind. First, the buyer earns no interest on the amount of the accrued interest advance. The seller receives his or her share of the coupon payment at settlement while the buyer is not reimbursed until the next coupon is received. Thus the accrued interest is analogous to an interest free loan from the buyer to the seller. Normally the amounts advanced are relatively small so this concern is rarely a major consideration. Moreover, the market price paid for the bond may take the impact of accrued interest into account. The buyer should, however, realize that the cost of the purchase will include this allowance for accrued interest. The trader should be sure of having enough money to cover the full amount due at settlement.

The second concern with the accrued interest advance is potentially more serious. Bonds that default during a given interest payment period leave the new buyer without any coupon payment and with no recourse to reclaim the accrued interest paid to the seller. Accrued interest on bonds is not returned in the event of a default. Once the bond defaults, it will begin to trade flat so that accrued interest will no longer be collected from the buyer. During the payment period when the bond defaults, however, the interest will have been accrued and then lost to an investor who bought at that time. Normally bonds default on their interest payment by failing to make the payment and announcing that they are unable to do so. Thus the default action itself almost always occurs at the end of the coupon payment period. Accordingly, a full coupon payment of accrued interest is potentially lost. Because a default on coupon payment generally causes the bond price to fall, the newer buyer of a quickly defaulting bond typically suffers two losses: the bond price decline and the lost accrued interest.

Bond Returns versus Stock Returns

Many investors at least consider having both bonds and stocks in their portfolios. Thus a comparison of past stock–bond return relationships may well be worthwhile. Bonds are widely believed to offer lower but less risky returns than stocks. Norgaard, for example, found that over the 1926–1969 period average stock returns almost always exceeded average after-tax bond returns.[15] Specifically, the mean return on stocks exceeded that on bonds by about 5.5% so that even when stock returns were appreciably below their means, they were still likely to be above those of bonds. Furthermore, a balanced portfolio of bonds and stocks performed little better than the all-bond portfolio. Thus Norgaard's study implies that a well-diversified portfolio of stocks has generally offered a greater expected return with less risk than a bond or a balanced bond–stock portfolio. Massey and still later Grauer and Hakansson obtained similar results for subsequent periods.[16] Finally, a very comprehensive study by Ibbotson, Carr, and Robinson found that stocks tended to offer higher returns than bonds in most countries over most time periods.[17]

An investor who has a specific time horizon may still prefer the certainty of bonds. Similarly, tax-exempt bonds are attractive to many investors. Finally, high-risk bonds may well offer expected returns similar to those of stocks. Thus the results of Norgaard and others question the general attractiveness of bonds but do not rule out the use of bonds for certain people at certain times.

SUMMARY AND CONCLUSIONS

A variety of factors influence bond yields. General market forces affect both the level and term structure of rates. For a given maturity class and market environment, rates differ primarily with default risk. Informal workouts may reduce the impact of technical defaults and near-defaults while Chapter XI proceedings are less costly than the more formal Chapter X process. Rating agencies assess the default risks of bonds and their issuers' financial strengths.

Various hypotheses attempt to explain the term structure of interest rates. Segmented markets ascribe rates to supply and demand for each maturity class. Liquidity preference asserts that borrowers generally prefer the long end while lenders prefer the short. The unbiased expectations hypothesis holds that the term structure reflects a contiguous set of short-term interest rate expectations. Investors may use the term structure relationship to identify securities that are potentially mispriced. Moreover, some investors may ride a yield curve that is expected to remain approximately stable.

Duration, the weighted average term of the payment stream, is a more accurate measure of repayment timing than is length to maturity. Investors and portfolio managers may utilize the duration concept in a strategy designed to immunize their portfolios from reinvestment risk. Specifically, they may minimize the potentially adverse impacts of being unable to reinvest coupons at attractive rates by assembling a portfolio with durations equal to their planning horizons.

The coupon effect refers to the price impact of the relative proportions of tax-deferred capital gains and immediately taxable coupon income. Low-coupon, deep-discount bonds are generally preferred to otherwise-equivalent issues because a higher percentage of their income is tax deferred. In addition, prices tend to be higher for more marketable, seasoned issues with sinking funds, me-first rules, and call protection. Usable bonds may also command higher prices. Industrial classification, condition of collateral, and listing status may have some minor price impacts.

Managing a bond portfolio can involve a variety of complicated maneuvers such as immunizing, swaps, and hedges. A number of researchers have found that average stock returns generally exceeded average bond returns. This relation may or may not continue.

REVIEW QUESTIONS

1. List and discuss the principal provisions of bond indentures. Which are most important to the bondholder?

2. What is a default? How does it relate to bankruptcy and liquidation? What are technical defaults and how are they generally handled?

3. Describe the various possible outcomes of defaults and near-defaults. Explain the nature of an informal workout. Why are such workouts often preferred to more formal proceedings?

4. What is meant by the absolute priority of claims principle? What is its relevancy to most bankruptcies? How is it generally applied in practice?

5. How do Chapter X and Chapter XI bankruptcies differ? Which is more costly and takes longer to accomplish?

6. Discuss bond ratings and default risks. What are the principal bond rating agencies? What are the principal drawbacks to relying on bond ratings to assess default risks?

7. How does performance vary with bond ratings? Do any categories of bonds typically generate higher after-default returns than other categories?

8. Describe the three proposed explanations for the term structure of interest rates. How would each explain the normal yield curve?

9. What are the implications of the term structure for individual investors? What is meant by riding the yield curve?

10. How do yields vary with duration and the coupon effect? What is immunization? How are they related? Explain the various methods of immunization.

11. Discuss the impacts of marketability, seasoning, call protection, sinking fund provisions, and usability on yields. How important are these considerations?

12. What is involved in managing a bond portfolio? What are bond swaps? What trading costs are involved in buying and selling bonds?

13. How have bond and stock yields compared over time? What are the implications for investors?

REVIEW PROBLEMS

1. After all of its assets were sold, Bankrupt Corporation of America realized $453,000. Its legal liabilities were as follows:

    Secured creditors = $47,000 on assets having a value of $39,000
    Other unsecured creditors = $89,000
    Taxes = $29,000
    Back wages (no more than $600 per employee) incurred within the six-month period of the bankruptcy filing = $35,000

      Other back wages = $23,000
      Operating expenses incurred administering the bankrupt
        estate = $150,000
      Legal fees involved in the bankruptcy filing = $121,000
      Preferred shareholders par value = $150,000
      Number of common shares outstanding = 100,000
    How much would each class receive?

2. Recompute your answer to Problem 1 if BCA's asset sale realized $351,000; $581,000, or $691,000.

3. Refer to Table 15.1. Plot government current yields versus lengths to maturity. Using French curves draw in a yield curve (more or less through the outermost data points). Does the resulting yield curve correspond to the rising, falling, or flat shape? What does the shape imply vis-à-vis the unbiased expectations hypothesis? That is, what does the market expect subsequent interest rates to do?

4. Refer to Table 15.3 and repeat the instructions for Problem 3. This time use FNMA quotes. How do the two yield curves (Treasuries and FNMAs) differ? Explain the differences.

5. Recompute the durations for bonds A and B in Table 16.5 using an appropriate discount rate of 10%. What is the result if the rate is 8%? What can you say about the relative change in durations of high and low coupon bonds as the discount rate changes?

6. Compute the durations for the following bonds:

Bond	Price	Coupon	Length to Maturity
a	93	7.5%	10 years
b	96	8.5%	15 years
c	102	9.5%	20 years

Assume that the next interest payment is due in six months.

7. Using the bond information in Problem 6, assemble at least two immunized bond portfolios for an eight-year time horizon. Which of these portfolios has the highest yield to maturity?

8. Using the information in Problem 6, assemble an immunized bond portfolio with a five-year time horizon for five years hence. (Assume that the bonds sell for par.) Why is this portfolio's composition different from that of Problem 7?

9. Return to Problems 3 and 4. The yield curves were computed using current yield and length to maturity information. Clearly, better measures are available for a bond's yield and length until repayment. First, select representative Treasury bonds for 3, 6, and 9 months and 1, 2, 3, 4, 5, 7, 10, 15, and 20 years. Compute yields to maturity and durations for each of

these bonds. Now plot yield curves in three ways: current yields versus length to maturity; yields to maturity versus length to maturity; and yields to maturity versus duration. Discuss the results. Which curve seems a more realistic representation of the market situation? Explain.

10. Repeat Problem 9, this time using FNMA bonds.

REVIEW PROJECTS

1. Plot the term structure of interest rates using government bonds. Repeat the process for AAA corporates, A corporates, B corporates, AAA municipals, and A municipals. Compare the structures. Write a report.

2. Assemble a list of similar-risk and similar-maturity bonds having varying coupon rates. Plot their current yields to maturity versus maturity. Repeat the process for three prior years. Analyze the relationships. Write a report.

3. For the list assembled for Problem 2 compute each bond's duration. Plot current yields to maturity versus duration. Repeat the process for three prior years. Analyze the relationship. Write a report.

4. Obtain the bond indenture of a troubled firm along with its most recent set of financial statements. Identify as many technical defaults as you can.

5. Obtain a reorganization plan for a firm that has recently come out of bankruptcy. Compare the payouts with those that would have been made under the absolute priority of claims principle.

6. From the S&P Bond Guide select 20 bonds with similar maturities and coupons but different ratings. Plot their yields to maturity versus their ratings.

7. From an S&P Bond Guide published five years ago, select five bond portfolios for each rating class. In each case try to identify bonds with approximately equivalent maturities and coupon rates. Now compute the annual returns on each portfolio up to the present.

8. Assume you have a $100,000,000 portfolio to manage for the next three years. Your incentive compensation depends upon promising as high a return as you can while making sure that you deliver. Obviously you want to immunize the portfolio as best you can. Using current market quotes, compare the return you could promise if you purchased zero-coupon bonds (backed by governments) or bought a portfolio of governments and interest futures contracts for the coupon payments. Compute the end value and the return for each approach and compare the results.

9. Assemble a list of 10 usable bonds and collect data on monthly prices of the bonds, warrants, and underlying stocks for the past year. Plot each of

the price series over time. Compute the cost of exercising with cash and bonds for each time and compare that with the cost of an outright purchase of the stock.

10. Update Table 16.8 to the present time. Now compute the relative attractiveness of the various bond swaps discussed in the chapter.

NOTES

1. R. Billingsley, R. Larmy, M. Marr, and R. Thompson, "Split Ratings and Bond Reoffering Yields," *Financial Management*, Summer 1985, 59–65; L. Perry, "The Effect of Bond Rating Agencies on Bond Rating Models," *Journal of Financial Research*, Summer 1985, 307–315; P. Liu and W. Moore, "The Impact of Split Bond Ratings on Risk Premia," *Financial Review*, February 1987, 71–85.

2. G. Pye, "Gauging the Default Premium," *Financial Analysts Journal*, January/February 1974, 49–52.

3. R. West, "Bond Ratings, Bond Yields and Financial Registration: Some Findings," *Journal of Law and Economics*, April 1973, 159–168.

4. J. McConnell and G. Schlarbaum, "Another Foray into the Backwaters of the Market," *Journal of Portfolio Management*, Fall 1980, 61–65.

5. E. Altman and S. Nammacher, "The Default Rate Experience on High-Yield Corporate Debt," *Financial Analysts Journal*, July/August 1985, 25–37; J. Fons, "The Default Premium and Corporate Bond Experience," *Journal of Finance*, March 1987, 81–90.

6. M. Brennan and E. Schwartz, "Bond Pricing and Market Efficiency," *Financial Analysts Journal*, September/October 1982, 49–56; M. Brannard and E. Schwartz, "An Equilibrium Model of Bond Pricing and a Test of Market Efficiency," *Journal of Financial and Quantitative Analysis*, September 1982, 301–330.

7. J. Osteryoung, D. McCarthy, and G. Roberts, "Riding the Yield Curve with Treasury Bills," *Financial Review*, Fall 1981, 57–66.

8. G. Bierwag, G. Kaufman, and C. Latta, "Bond Portfolio Immunization: Tests of Maturity, One- and Two-Factor Duration Matching Strategies," *Financial Review*, May 1987, 203–219.

9. R. Kolb and G. Gay, "Immunizing Bond Portfolios with Interest Rate Futures," *Financial Management*, Summer 1982, 81–89; G. Gay, R. Kolb, and R. Chiang, "Interest Rate Hedging: An Empirical Test of Alternative Strategies," *Journal of Financial Research*, Fall 1983, 187–197; J. Hillard, "Hedging Interest Rate Risk with Futures Portfolios under Term Structure Effects," December 1984, 1547–1569.

10. J. Martin and R. Richards, "The Seasoning Process for Corporate Bonds," *Financial Management*, Summer 1981, 41–48; W. Fung and A. Rudd, "Pricing New Corporate Bond Issues: An Analysis of Issue Cost and Seasoning Effects," *Journal of Finance*, July 1986, 633–644.

11. J. Van Horne, "Called Bonds: How Does the Investor Fare?" *Journal of Portfolio Management*, Summer 1980, 58–61.

12. A. Kalotay, "Sinking Funds and the Realized Cost of Debt," *Financial Management*, Spring 1982, 43–54; W. Lloyd and C. Edmonds, "The Impact of a Sinking Fund on the Firm's Cost of Debt," *Review of Business and Economic Research*, Spring 1982, 74–82.

13. K. Dunn and C. Spatt, "A Strategic Analysis of Sinking Fund Bonds," *Journal of Financial Economics*, September 1984, 399–424; W. Bareet, A. Heuson, and R. Kolb, "The Differential

Effects of Sinking Funds on Bond Risk Premia," *Journal of Financial Research*, Winter 1986, 303–312; T. Ho and R. Singer, "The Value of Corporate Debt with a Sinking-Fund Provision," *Journal of Business*, July 1984, 315–336.

14. G. Brauer, "Evidence of the Market Value of Me-First Rules," *Financial Management*, Spring 1983, 11–18; M. Brody, "Controversial Issue: A Leveraged Buy-Out Touches Off a Bitter Dispute," *Barron's*, September 19, 1983, 15, 19, 22.

15. C. Boardman and R. McEnally, "Factors Affecting Seasoned Corporate Bond Prices," *Journal of Financial and Quantitative Analysis*, June 1981, 207.

16. R. Norgaard, "An Examination of the Yields of Corporate Bonds and Stocks," *Journal of Finance*, September 1974, 1275–1286.

17. J. Massey, "For the Long Haul: Stocks Invariably Outperform Both Bills and Bonds," *Barron's*, January 31, 1977, 5–7; R. Grauer and N. Hakansson, "Higher Returns, Lower Risk: Historical Returns on Long Run, Actively Managed Portfolios of Stocks, Bonds, Bills, 1936–1978," *Financial Analysts Journal*, March/April 1982, 39–54.

18. R. Ibbotson, R. Carr, and A. Robinson, "International Equity and Bond Returns," *Financial Analysts Journal*, July/August 1982, 61–83.

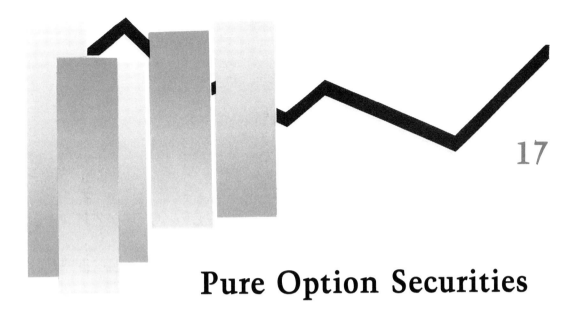

Pure Option Securities

Stocks and bonds and most other types of securities offer their investors a limited set of choices. They can be bought, sold, or held. They may or may not pay dividend or interest income. Stock and bond investors, however, generally have no direct way of turning their securities into anything other than what they already are.

Option securities, in contrast, may be exchanged (with or without additional funds) for some other security or, in the case of puts, permit their owner to sell some other security for a prespecified price. Warrants, rights, calls, and puts are pure options whereas convertible bonds, convertible preferreds, and certain other types of securities are combinations. Combination securities derive value from two sources: the potential worth of their convertibility (the option component) and the income and principal payments that they promise to make (the straight security value). Pure options' values, in contrast, are based solely on what they can do to facilitate a particular purchase or sale. Because option securities constitute an interesting and important component of the investment scene, two chapters of this book are devoted to them.

This chapter concentrates on pure options. We begin with a discussion of puts, calls, and their markets, and special terminology. This is followed by a section on the Americus Trust Securities. Warrants and rights and how they are valued are considered next. Then the leverage potential, quotations, valuation, and performance in various types of markets for options are covered. This is followed by an examination of covered and naked writing, spread trades, tax implications, option mutual funds, institutional participation, and commissions. Appendices A and B explore the Black/Scholes option formula and put–call parity.

WARRANTS, RIGHTS, CALLS, AND PUTS

Warrants, rights, and calls are all options to purchase an asset such as a stock or bond. The option itself will specify a number of matters including the following: the identity of the underlying security, number of units of the security under option, the cost per unit of exercising the option, and the period (almost always limited) over which exercise is allowed. Puts, in contrast, are options to sell a prespecified number of units of a prespecified security at a prespecified price over a prespecified period. A few warrants permit one to purchase or sell bonds or other assets. The vast majority of option securities, however, facilitate the purchase or sale of common stock.

Warrants and rights are issued by the same company as the issuer of the securities underlying the option. The issuing company almost always satisfies warrant and right exercisers by issuing additional units of its securities. Warrants often have lengthy exercise periods (e.g., five years). Rights, in contrast, must generally be exercised within a few weeks of their issue. Companies distribute rights to their shareholders in order to raise equity capital. Rights are usually exercisable at an appreciable discount from the stock's preoffering market price. They normally trade in the secondary market until they expire.

Unlike rights, newly issued warrants are typically exercisable at prices well above those of the underlying securities. Warrants generally trade in the secondary market until their expiration and then are only exercised if doing so is profitable.

Calls and puts represent the private contracts between individual buyers and sellers. Technically the Option Clearing Corporation (set up by the options exchanges) manages the option contracts. Thus each put and call buyer and seller is contracting with the corporation rather than directly. The numbers of buyers and sellers are, however, equal. Thus in effect puts and calls are private contracts between buyer and seller. The Option Clearing Corporation acts as an intermediary between the two principals in an option trade. Unlike the exercise of warrants and rights, put and call exercises do not alter the number of shares outstanding. Call writers (sellers) must stand ready to supply already-issued stock (either from their own portfolios or by an open market purchase). Similarly, a put writer must be prepared to purchase existing shares. Puts and calls are normally written for relatively short periods (nine months is typically the longest available).

Americus Trust Securities

A relatively new type of constructed security has much in common with traditional options. Americus Trust Securities come in two basic categories. In effect, the trust stands ready to divide any of a predetermined list of stocks into two parts: a low-risk and an option component. To create Americus Trust, securities shares of the selected stock are put into a trust. Then two new securities are issued to the owner of each deposited share. The *prime* component entitles the owner to all dividends, voting rights, and up to some prespecified amount of end-period value. The *score* component, in contrast, receives the end value less the portion going to the prime. The trust's organizer receives a small fee for organizing the trust and funneling dividends to the prime holders.

To illustrate, the stock of XYZ Corporation might currently sell for $40 per share. The prime would receive the first $50 of value on a prespecified date such as four years hence. The score would get any value over that amount. Suppose the end-period price of the stock was $80. The prime would receive $50 and all of the interim dividends. The score would receive $30. Thus the score's value depends largely on how much the stock exceeds the value going to the prime. It acts very much like an option with a striking price equal to the value going to the prime and an expiration date equal to the terminal date on the trust.

Option Terminology

Option traders have their own special vocabulary. Several key terms will be defined before they are put to use:

Striking Price (Strike).   Price at which the option is exercisable (sometimes called the exercise price).

Intrinsic Value.   For a call, amount by which stock price exceeds the striking price or zero if the strike is above the market price; for a put, amount by which strike exceeds stock price or zero if below.

Time Value.   Option price less its intrinsic value.

In-the-Money Option.   Option with a positive intrinsic value (striking price below market price for a call, above for a put).

Out-of-the-Money Option.   Option with a zero intrinsic value (striking price above market price for a call, below for a put).

At-the-Money Option.   Option with a zero intrinsic value (striking price equal to market price for a call or a put).

Premium.   Option price (equal to the sum of the intrinsic and time values). Note that some people use premium to refer to the time value. At the option exchanges, however, it is used as defined here.

Warrants and Rights

As pure options, warrants and rights have much in common with calls. The same basic valuation principles and risk–return trade-offs are present with all three types of securities. Each option type has some distinctive characteristics, however.

Rights.   A company that raises capital by offering stock to new buyers dilutes the existing stockholders' interests. For example, a company with 10 shareholders, each having 1,000 shares (10% of the company) might want to sell another 10,000 shares. Offering these shares to the highest bidder might well deny them to the current shareholders and thus dilute their positions. If all of the new stock was bought by outsiders, the existing shareholders would see their interest reduced by half. They had each owned 10% of 10,000, or 1,000, shares each. Now they each own 5% of 20,000 shares.

A rights offering to existing shareholders allows a company to raise additional capital and avoid diluting the current shareholders' positions. Such rights would give to the existing shareholders first refusal on the new stock. The right will specify the terms for the stock purchase (price and time frame). Shareholders wishing to maintain their interest would simply exercise their rights. Most holders of a trivial percentage of a very large company have little or no interest in maintaining their percentage ownership. Thus they may prefer to sell their rights on the open market. Others, however, may take advantage of the offering to increase their investment in the company.

Rights usually allow purchase of new stock at a discount from the current market price. In the terminology of puts and calls, they are in the money. In other words, such rights will have an intrinsic value. If the stock's price then rises further above the strike on the right, the value of the right will also increase. Rights trading is, however, relatively speculative as most rights have a very short lifespan—often only a few weeks.

Usually Issued for Fractional Shares. One right is issued for each outstanding share. Such rights typically give the holder an option on a fraction (say one-quarter) of a share. Thus, the holder of 100 shares of the underlying stock might receive 100 rights, which would entitle him or her to buy 25 shares. As we have seen, rights are generally issued for short exercise periods at striking prices that are far in the money. Accordingly, rights are generally priced very close to their intrinsic values (little or no time value).

Cum-Rights and Ex-Rights. As with dividends, the offering announcements of rights specify a day of record for people owning the stock to receive the rights. Up to that day is the *cum-rights* period. After this date the stock sells *ex-rights*. Setting the record date a few days after the ex-rights date allows time for the company's record keeping. Generally the shares go ex-rights in the marketplace four business days before the record date. The typical timing of a rights offer is shown in Table 17.1.

TABLE 17.1   Typical Timing of a Rights Offering

Date	Day	Event
January 15	Monday	Rights offering announced for shareholders of record on Monday, February 5
January 29	Monday	Last day to buy the shares cum-rights
January 30	Tuesday	Shares go ex-rights
February 5	Monday	Actual record date

Rights Valuation Formulae. The value of the underlying stock depends on whether it is selling cum- or ex-rights. The stock's price will generally drop on the day it goes ex. Subsequent buyers will not receive the rights.

Valuation during the Cum-Rights Period.   Assume that buying 10 shares of XYZ at $40 gives the buyer enough rights to buy one additional share at $38. Accordingly, the buyer can buy 10 + 1 shares of stock for:

$$(10 \times \$40) + (1 \times \$38) = \$438$$

The shares' average price is $438 divided by 11, or $39.82, and the intrinsic value of one right is $40 minus $39.82, or $.18. An owner of 100 shares should be able to sell the rights for $18. Thus the intrinsic value of one right during the cum-rights period is determined by the following formula:

$$\frac{\text{Intrinsic Value of One Right}}{\text{During Cum-Rights Period}} = \frac{\text{Market Price of Stock} - \text{Subscription Price}}{\text{Number of Shares Needed to}} \\ \text{Subscribe to One Share} + \text{One Share}$$

Applying this formula to the above example yields:

$$\text{Intrinsic value} = (\$40 - \$38)/(10 + 1) = \$2.00/11 = \$.18$$

The market value of the right may, however, differ from its intrinsic value. That is, rights' prices may reflect some time value.

Valuation during the Ex-Rights Period.   As a stock goes ex-rights its market value will usually decline slightly (as with the ex-dividend date). The adjusted formula for the intrinsic value becomes:

$$\frac{\text{Intrinsic Value of One Right}}{\text{During Ex-Rights Period}} = \frac{\text{Market Value of Stock} - \text{Subscription Price}}{\text{Number of Shares Needed to}} \\ \text{Subscribe to One Share}$$

If the stock dropped by $.25 to $39.75 when it went ex-rights:

$$\frac{\$39.75 - \$38.00}{10} = \frac{\$1.75}{10} = \$.175$$

How Leverage Works with Rights.   Suppose that the stock rises to $45 after it goes ex-rights, but before the rights expire. The new intrinsic value becomes:

$$(\$45.00 - \$38.00)/10 = \$7.00/10 = \$.70$$

Investors who bought at $.20 (a slight increment over their initial time value) and sold at $.70 would have more than tripled their money in a few weeks. Had the stock dropped below the striking price, however, a total loss would result. Out-of-money rights that are about to expire have very little value. Thus trading rights can be a rather risky short-term speculation.

The Decline of Preemptive Rights.   At one time most corporate charters contained a preemptive rights clause. This clause guaranteed shareholders the opportunity to maintain their proportional ownership. Preemptive rights have been voted out of many corporate charters, however. Companies claim that they need increased flexibility to sell shares in whatever manner seems most attractive at the time of the sale. As a result most new stock issues do not involve rights.

Special Situations and Warrants.   Warrants are often sold in a financing package that also includes bonds. Frequently these bonds may be used at par to exercise the warrant. When the bond's price is below par, exercise becomes more attractive with *usable bonds* (bonds exercisable at their face value as a substitute for cash) than with cash. For example, a warrant may permit the purchase of XYZ stock at 20 when the market price is 15. No one would use cash to exercise at such prices. If usable bonds are selling at 60, however, a bond costing $600 could be used with the appropriate number of warrants to purchase 50 shares of stock having a market value of $750. Clearly, the warrants would have a considerable value in these circumstances.

A takeover threat increases the risk of warrant ownership. For example, Indian Head warrants permitted the holder to purchase stock at 25. Prior to its takeover by the Dutch holding company, Thyssen Bornemisza, Indian Head stock was trading at 22 and the warrants at 5. Thyssen offered 27 for the stock and 2 for the warrants (the difference between the striking price [25] and the purchase price of the stock [27]). The Thyssen action caused the warrant price to fall to 2¼ even though the warrants were not set to expire until 1990. Warrantholders apparently believed that the takeover would leave too thin a market for Indian Head stock to make the warrants attractive. Warrantholders could reject the Thyssen offer, but the warrants' value was greatly reduced by the Dutch company's takeover of Indian Head.

A 1971 Internal Revenue Service ruling encouraged firms to extend the life of warrants that would otherwise expire unexercised. The possibility that a warrant's life may be extended increases the danger to those who sell warrants short. IRS now requires firms to report as profits the sale price of any warrant that expires unexercised. Exercised warrants, in contrast, do not cause the issuer to incur a tax liability.

Finally, warrant-issuing companies occasionally try to ensure that their warrants are exercised by supporting their stock price above the warrant's strike price near expiration. For example, in 1976 Tesovo engaged E. F. Hutton to stabilize (put a floor under) its stock price at $14.50 so that soon-to-expire warrants with a $13.80 strike would be exercised. AT&T engaged Morgan Stanley for a similar operation in 1975.

The Speculative Appeal of Options: Leverage

Options on a large number of units of the underlying security can be bought for relatively small sums. Such an option position greatly magnifies (levers) the upside effect of price moves in that security. For example, Chrysler's common stock experienced the largest rise among NYSE issues in 1982. The stock's price went from just above 3 to slightly above 18 (about a fivefold increase). Its warrants, however, rose from 1⅛ to 10⅛, or an increase of 800%. On the other hand, an option's price can, at worst, fall to zero. Because of this upside leverage and downside loss limitation, in-the-money options are typically priced appreciably above their intrinsic values. Moreover, options with time remaining before expiration and striking prices that are not too far below the stock's market price may also command nontrivial prices. Far out-of-the-money options and any out-of-the-money options near their expirations are, in contrast, usually almost worthless. Consider the following examples.

Option Examples. In 1956 General Tire and Rubber Company stock was selling at 50 while warrants with a 70 striking price and 1959 expiration were trading at 4½. By 1959, the stock price had reached 98½ and the warrant 39. In percentage terms, the warrants had increased 770% compared with a 97% rise in the stock's price. Thus General Tire warrantholders earned eight times the percentage return of the shareholders.

While limited to the initial purchase price, the downside risk of options is still substantial. For example, in 1960 the common of Molybdenum Corporation of America sold for 42, while warrants permitting one to purchase the stock at 30 were available at 16. When the warrants expired in 1963, the stock had fallen to 29. Thus warrantholders experienced a 100% loss at expiration regardless of their purchase price. Stock acquired at 42, in contrast, had lost 31% of its value when the stock reached 29.

In these examples the warrants' striking prices were 70 for General Tire and 30 for Molybdenum. With the stock at 50, General Tire warrants had an intrinsic value of 0. At the later date the intrinsic value was 28½ (98½ − 70). With warrant prices at 4½ and 39, the time values were 4½ and 10½, respectively. With the stock at 42 and warrants at 16, Molybdenum warrants had intrinsic and time values of 12 and 4 respectively. These statistics are summarized in Table 17.2.

These examples clearly illustrate the leverage of warrants. The same principle applies to the other types of options. A given sum of money can purchase far more options than underlying shares. Therefore an upward stock price movement will generally lead to a greater percentage gain for optionholders than for stockholders. If, on the other hand, the stock price is below the striking price as maturity approaches, the options quickly lose their value.

The following hypothetical example further illustrates the relationship between a stock's price and that of its associated option. Suppose a stock selling for 100 has a call (or right or warrant) to buy it at 100 that sells for 10. (Striking price = 100; intrinsic value = 0; and time value and premium = 10.) Figure 17.1 illustrates the relationship between the performance of the stock and call for various near-expiration prices of the stock.

TABLE 17.2. General Tire and Molybdenum Warrants

	General Tire		Molybdenum	
	1956	1959 (near expiration)	1960	1963 (at expiration)
Stock Price	50	98½	42	29
Striking Price	70	70	30	30
Warrant Price	4½	39	16	0
Intrinsic Value	0	28½	12	0
Time Value	4½	10½	4	0

Near expiration, the call should be priced very close to its intrinsic value. For any price below 100 the call will expire worthless and callholders will lose their

FIGURE 17.1 Option and Stock Returns Compared

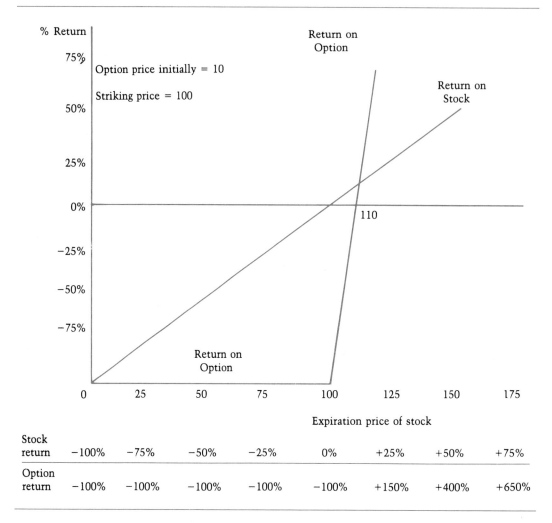

Stock return	−100%	−75%	−50%	−25%	0%	+25%	+50%	+75%
Option return	−100%	−100%	−100%	−100%	−100%	+150%	+400%	+650%

total investment. At a price of 100 to 110 the call's expiration price will be less than its cost. For any stock price above 110 the callholder makes money. Thus at prices below 100 the stockholder experiences a partial loss compared with a total loss for the callholder. At any price between 100 and 110, stockholders will profit while callholders experience losses. The callholder breaks even (ignoring commissions) when the stock price reaches 110.

Callholders' profits rise much faster than those of stockholders as the stock price rises above 110. For prices very slightly above 110, the stockholders' percentage returns are greater, but at somewhat higher prices callholders' percentage returns greatly exceed those of stockholders. At 111, for example, the callholder's return is 10% compared with 11% for the stockholder (ignoring dividends). At 112, however, callholders earn 20% compared with 12% for stockholders.

The gain on the call rises dramatically as the price of the stock increases above the break-even level (110). A price of 120 produces a 20% gain for stockholders while callholders realize a 100% gain. At a stock price of 150, callholders earn 400% compared with 50% for stockholders. Commission and dividend effects have been ignored in the analysis but their net impact would generally be modest.

Note that stockholders and callholders are not in competition with each other. A rising stock price helps both. Only the relative impacts are different.

Options Markets

Actively traded rights and warrants are generally listed on a stock exchange. Most put and call trading takes place on the option exchanges. Unlisted puts and calls and less actively traded warrants and rights are traded over the counter.

Before listed options appeared, all option trading was in the over-the-counter market. OTC options had expiration dates and striking prices that varied greatly. Secondary market trading in OTC options was very haphazard. Virtually all option trading now takes place with listed puts and calls. Such options have standardized striking prices and expire on a consistent, regular basis.

When listed option trading began, expirations were set to occur every three months. Three sets of expiration dates were traded at any particular time. Thus, for example, a company might have options on a January cycle. Its options would be set to expire every three months beginning with January. During various times of the year it would have options expiring in January, April, July, and October. When the nearest expiration was January the other listed options would be April and July. Once the January options expired, a new set of options would be listed for October. Other companies' options were set for February and March cycles. Some companies' options still only expire every three months. Most companies with listed options, however, now have additional expirations that fill in the two nearest months. Consider, for example, a company with a January basic cycle. In early January it would list expirations in January, April, and October. In addition, option expirations would also be listed for February. Thus most companies now have a total of four options expirations. Two are in the nearest two months, and two more distant expirations occur in the next seven-month period. Listed options are set to expire on the third Friday of their month of expiration. Their standardized striking prices and expiration dates facilitate a continuous market in identical securities.

The listed option market experienced spectacular growth throughout the latter half of the 1970s. The four exchanges (CBOE, AMEX, Philadelphia, and Pacific) now list options on a very substantial number of stocks. Option trading in these issues often exceeds that of the underlying shares.

Put and Call Quotations

Typical put and call quotations from *The New York Times* and *Barron's* are shown in Figure 17.2. The system followed by *The New York Times* and most other daily newspapers (including *The Wall Street Journal*) is considerably more compact than

FIGURE 17.2 *Barron's* and *The New York Times* Option Quotations, January 22, 1988

January 25, 1988 **BARRON'S / MARKET WEEK**

OPTIONS TRADING

Chicago Board

Expire date Strike price	Sales	Open Int.	Week's High	Week's Low	Price	Net Chg.	N.Y. Close
Allegis Feb65...	1222	1943	9¼	8½	8⅝	+ ⅝	72½
Allegis Feb65 p	413	1957	1	¾	⅞	− ½	72½
Allegis Feb70...	151	4416	5½	3⅞	4½	......	72½
Allegis Feb70 p	634	2602	2⅛	1⅜	2	− ⅜	72½
Allegis Feb75...	1488	8636	2⅛	1⅛	1⅜	− ⅜	72½
Allegis Feb75 p	115	1368	4	3⅜	3⅝	− 1⅝	72½
Allegis Feb80...	261	4729	⅝	5-16	⅜	− ¼	72½
Allegis Feb85...	236	1679	3-16	⅛	⅛	− ⅛	72½
Allegis May70..	61	198	7¼	6¾	7	......	72½
Allegis May75..	207	279	4½	3⅝	4	− ¼	72½
Allegis May80..	116	526	2⅜	2	2⅛	− ¼	72½
Alcoa Feb40 p..	95	89	1¾	1	1	......	42⅞
Alcoa Feb45....	1558	1845	1⅞	½	1	− ⅞	42⅞
Alcoa Feb50....	54	307	½	¼	¼	− ½	42⅞
Alcoa Feb55 p..	50	49	11⅜	11⅜	11⅜	+ 3⅛	42⅞
Alcoa Mar45...	391	221	2⅝	1¼	1⅞	......	42⅞
Alcoa Mar45 p.	125	13	5½	3⅝	5	......	42⅞
Alcoa Apr40...	323	734	5¼	3⅝	5¼	− ⅞	42⅞
Alcoa Apr45...	152	330	3⅜	2¼	3	− ⅜	42⅞
Alcoa Apr50...	269	889	1½	¾	1	− ½	42⅞
Alcoa Apr55...	64	275	⅝	½	½	......	42⅞
Alcoa Jul50.....	59	58	2½	2	2	− 1	42⅞
Amdahl Feb30..	487	784	4½	1¼	3½	− ¾	32½
Amdahl Feb30 p	55	205	2½	1⅛	1⅛	+ ¼	32½
Amdahl Feb35..	816	1407	1⅝	⅜	1 5-16	− 3-16	32½
Amdahl Feb40..	273	587	½	¼	5-16	− 5-16	32½
Amdahl Feb45..	57	590	3-16	1-16	1-16	− ⅛	32½
Amdahl Mar30.	376	360	5	2½	5	......	32½
Amdahl Mar35.	386	226	3	1⅜	2⅝	......	32½
Amdahl Mar40.	373	79	2	1	1½	......	32½
Amdahl May35	765	654	4⅛	2¾	4	− ½	32½
Amdahl May40	83	345	2½	1½	2½	+ ½	32½
A E P Feb25...	80	606	3	2½	3	+ 1¼	28⅝
A E P Feb30..	286	1590	3-16	1-16	⅛	+ 1-16	28⅝
A E P May30..	434	750	⅜	⅛	⅜	+ 3-16	28⅝
A E P Aug30...	128	90	9-16	⅜	9-16	+ ¼	28⅝
AmGenl Apr30.	178	273	3⅛	2⅜	2⅜	− ⅛	31¼
AmGenl Jul35..	98	120	1¼	1	1¼	− ⅛	31¼

Trading in Stock Options

FRIDAY, JANUARY 22, 1988

Chicago Board Options Exchange

Option & NY Close	Strike Price	Calls-Last Feb	Calls-Last Mar	Calls-Last Apr	Puts-Last Feb	Puts-Last Mar	Puts-Last Apr
Alcoa	40	3½	r	5¼	r	r	2
42⅞	45	1	1⅞	3	3½	r	r
42⅞	50	r	r	1	r	r	r
AmGenl	35	r	r	⅜	r	r	r
AGreet	12½	r	r	r	r	r	½
13⅞	15	⅜	r	¾	r	r	r
13⅞	17½	1/16	s	r	r	s	r
AT&T	25	3	r	3⅞	3/16	⅜	9/16
28⅛	30	5/16	9/16	13/16	2¼	r	2¾
28⅛	35	r	s	3/16	r	s	r
Amrich	80	r	r	r	r	r	1½
88⅜	85	4⅝	r	5⅜	1¼	r	4
88⅜	90	1⅞	2½	3¾	3⅞	r	r
88⅜	95	r	1	r	r	r	r
Apple	45	r	2	r	r	r	r
All R	65	7½	r	r	½	r	r
72⅝	70	3	r	5½	1¾	r	3¼
72⅝	75	1¼	1½	3	r	r	r
72⅝	80	r	s	1½	r	s	r
72⅝	100	s	s	⅛	s	s	r
Avon	22½	r	r	3	r	r	r
24⅝	25	⅝	1	1½	r	r	r
24⅝	30	r	r	¼	r	r	r
BankAm	5	r	r	r	r	⅛	r
8¾	7½	1¼	1½	1⅝	⅛	r	7/16
8¾	10	⅛	5/16	½	r	1¾	1½
8¾	12½	s	s	1/16	s	s	r
8¾	15	s	s	1/16	s	s	r

Sources: *Barron's*, January 25, 1988. Reprinted by permission, *The New York Times*, January 23, 1988,

that followed by *Barron's*. On the other hand, the *Barron's* quotation contains more information.

The left-hand column of *The New York Times* quotation contains the name of the company or an abbreviation. The New York Stock Exchange closing price for the stock appears below the name. For example the *AT&T* abbreviation corresponds to the American Telephone & Telegraph Company. The New York close was 28⅛. The striking price is listed next. AT&T strikes are available at 25, 30, and 35. Then the calls' closing prices are reported for each listed expiration. In the case of AT&T expirations are reported for February, March, and April. AT&T options are on a January cycle. On January 22, however, the January options had already expired. The third Friday of 1988 occurred on January 15. The closing prices are followed by similar quotes for puts. The price is quoted per share although puts and calls trade in 100-share units. Thus one call or put represents an option on 100 shares. An *s* signifies that no option was listed while an *r* indicates none was traded on that day.

The more complete *Barron's* quotation contains the volume, open interest (contracts outstanding), high, low, and change in the price (from the preceding week). *The New York Times* quotation reports only the three closest expirations. *Barron's* also reports trading in the more distant maturity. For example, the AT&T quotes in *The New York Times* only cover the February, March, and April expirations. The *Barron's* quotation also reports information on July expirations.

Striking prices are initially set at levels that are divisible by 5 or 10 (or in some cases 2½) and closest to the current stock price. Thus a stock trading at 43 would typically have options listed at 40 and 45. Similarly, a stock trading at 21 would have options listed at 20 and 22½. Stock prices, however, fluctuate over time. Options with strikes that were near the market price when initially listed will not necessarily remain near the market. As a stock price moves away from the available strikes, trading becomes unattractive in the existing options. For example, a call with a strike of 30 on a stock selling for 50 will be priced too high to offer very much leverage. Similarly, a call with an 80 strike on a stock trading at 60 is very likely to expire worthless. Thus such options have very little speculative appeal. Since stock prices can move quite a bit in a few months, some strikes may differ substantially from the current quote. Accordingly, new strikes are authorized at levels close to the stock's current quote whenever its price changes appreciably. The older strike options continue to be traded but are not replaced with more distant expirations as they expire. For example, in the quotation in Figure 17.2 Chrysler strikes are recorded for prices ranging from 17½ to 50. The stock itself closed at 25¼. Prices are reported for most of the options for strikes of 20, 22½, 25, and 30. Clearly these are the strikes where most of the trading is likely to take place.

Turov's Formula

Turov's formula allows the trader to compute the rate of appreciation in the underlying stock necessary to make the option a more profitable investment than the stock. The relative attractiveness of a warrant or call is related to the price the stock must reach by expiration to generate equal percentage gains on the stock or option. If the stock's price rises above this level, the option will show the greater gain. Otherwise the stock will have a larger gain or lesser loss. This value equals the striking price divided by the stock price minus the current warrant price. Thus:

$$f = e/(s - w)$$

where:

f = appreciation of stock necessary to generate equal gains in the stock and warrant
e = striking price of warrant
s = current price of stock
w = current price of warrant

Turov subsequently revised his formula to take account of dividends.[1] He noted, however, that in practice the impact of the adjustment was minor.

An Example of Turov's Formula.   On November 9, 1983, the Charter Company's stock was trading for 9⅛ while its warrants exercisable at 10 (expiration of 9/1/88) sold for 4⅛. Applying Turov's formula to these data reveals:

$$f = 10/(9⅛ - 4⅛) = {}^{10}\!/_5 = 2$$

Thus if the price of Charter doubled, investments in the stock and warrant would offer equivalent returns. In that instance the stock would trade for 18¼ and the warrant's intrinsic value would rise 8¼, or twice its current market price. Those who expected Charter to appreciate by more than that amount before its warrants expired (1988) would find the warrants to be the more attractive investment. If, however, Charter appreciated by less than this amount, the stock would be the better buy. In April 1988 (five months prior to expiration) Charter was trading at around 4½, putting the warrants far out of the money and likely to expire worthless. An investor who purchased the stock at 9⅛ would be holding at a 50% loss. A warrantholder would be about to experience a total loss.

THE VALUE OF AN OPTION

The valuation of options long intrigued financial theorists. Black and Scholes wrote the classic theoretical option pricing work,[2] following work by Shelton; Samuelson; and Parkinson. Black and Scholes began with the assumption that investors could buy the underlying stock and write calls so as to maintain a fully hedged position. With such a hedge any change in the value of the stock's price would be offset by an equivalent but opposite change in the value of the short position. Suppose that a $1 change in the stock price was known to cause a $.50 change in the call price. Investors could then construct a fully hedged position by writing calls on twice as many shares as are held. Since the investor is short two calls, a $1 increase in the stock price would be matched by a $1 decrease in the value of the call position. Similarly, a $1 decrease in the stock's price would be offset by a $1 increase in the value of the call position. In fact, any small move in the stock's price would be precisely offset by a change in the value of the option position.

As time passes and stock and call prices change, the appropriate hedge ratio (required ratio) will vary. For example, the required ratio of two calls to one share of stock might later change to a ratio of three calls to one share of stock. A fully hedged position may be maintained by adjusting the ratio of shares to calls whenever necessary. Thus if the required ratio changed from two calls per share to three calls per share, the hedger would write an additional call for each share held. The result of this process is what is termed a riskless hedge. The hedge has been designed and managed to insulate the investor from market moves in the underlying stock's price.

In an efficient market an investment in the combined riskless position should earn the riskless interest rate (approximately the rate on short-term governments). Using a model based on the assumptions stated earlier, Black and Scholes were able to develop a call valuation formula that is a function of five variables: Call values increase with time to maturity, interest rates, the price of the underlying stock, and volatility; they decrease as the striking price increases.

The Black/Scholes formula is more than just an interesting theoretical exercise. Active option traders often use programmable calculators to compute Black/Scholes prices. Such traders may follow a strategy of buying undervalued options (vis-à-vis the model) and writing overvalued ones. Investors who become deeply involved in option trading should learn more about the specifics of the Black/Scholes model (see Appendix A at the end of the chapter).[3]

Empirical Studies of the Black/Scholes Model

Not surprisingly the Black/Scholes model led to a host of studies. Much of this work was designed to test the correspondence between Black/Scholes prices and model prices and/or whether apparent price disparities offered profitable trading opportunities. In a study of over 2,000 OTC calls and 3,000 straddle contracts (combination put and call on the same security), Black and Scholes themselves found a significant tendency for low-variance options to be overpriced and high-variance options to be underpriced.[4] When transaction costs were considered, however, the profit potential of a buy high-variance options and sell low-variance options strategy disappeared.

Galai studied initial CBOE option pricing.[5] He found that trading against calls whose prices were out of line with the Black/Scholes formula generally produced profits before allowing for the impact of commissions. Once commissions were considered, however, the trading strategy's profits disappeared. The original Black/Scholes empirical study utilized OTC calls (before the CBOE began) and Galai worked with data for an early period of option trading.

More recent work has produced a variety of results. For example, Gultekin, Rogalski, and Tinic found near-expiration options were often mispriced.[6] Similarly, Trennepohl found that Black/Scholes model prices adjusted for dividends were significantly lower than observed prices.[7] Gleit and Branch reported that a strategy of buying undervalued and writing overvalued options (vis-à-vis Black/Scholes model prices) might be profitable.[8] Bhattacharya, in contrast, found no systematic mispricing of options except for those very close to maturity.[9] Furthermore, Phillips and Smith reported that taking the bid–ask spread into account eliminated most apparent mispricings.[10] Similarly Whaley; MacBeth and Merville; Geske and Roll; and Sterk were able to explain option prices well with more sophisticated versions of the model.[11]

On the other hand, a study by Manaster and Rendleman found that option prices contained information relevant to future movements in the underlying stock's prices.[12] Similarly, Rubinstein reported that the implied volatilities of the underlying stocks tended to rise with the striking prices during some periods and fall during others.[13] Thus the market appeared to be reacting to information other than that incorporated into the standard models.

On balance these results suggest that option pricing is a relatively efficient process. No doubt some mispricings do occur but most seem to be relatively brief and allow profitable trades only for those who can buy and sell at minimum transactions costs.

The key to most successful option trading is effective analysis of the underlying stock's potential. An investor who can somehow identify misvalued stocks may be able to magnify the profit potential with options. Options are short-term wasting assets, however. Even investors who correctly analyze stock values may lose money on the stocks' options unless the market price adjusts before their options expire. All too often the investor may be right on fundamentals but wrong on timing and lose money as a result.

Put–Call Parity

Put–call parity represents another theoretical aspect of option pricing. A put-like position can be created from a call and short position in the stock. Such a *manufactured put* will have the same type of payoff matrix as a put. The loss from a stock price rise is limited by the call while profits from the short position will increase as the stock's price falls. Similarly, a long position in the stock plus a put (manufactured call) has the same kind of payoff as a call. Since a put can be converted into a manufactured call and a call can be converted into a manufactured put, the prices of the two options should be related. Indeed, according to "the law of one price," whenever two assets offer equivalent payoff matrices, their prices must be identical (or within a range permitted by such arbitrage expenses as transactions costs).

Traders normally prefer to buy puts or calls directly, but some people will choose to manufacture puts from calls, or vice versa, when prices get out of line. Moreover, some brokerage firms try to profit from apparent price disparities by taking offsetting positions in the manufactured and nonmanufactured puts and calls (*conversions*). Such arbitrage activity tends to drive the prices back toward their proper parity. Indeed, Klemkosky and Resnick found that the relatively rare departures from put–call parity price relationships seldom persist long enough for traders to profit (even those on the exchange).[14]

As with the Black/Scholes formula, the precise form of the put–call parity formula is a bit too complex to discuss in this treatment. Nonetheless, serious option traders should be aware of its existence. The explicit relationship is presented in Appendix B at the end of the chapter.

In addition to manufacturing calls from puts and puts from calls, investors can manufacture option-like positions with stock and cash. For example, a long stock position coupled with sufficient borrowing is equivalent to a call. While limited by margin restrictions, such a strategy can provide a viable alternative when no listed call is available.

OPTION TRADING STRATEGIES

Option traders have a variety of strategies available to them. The trader could, for example, buy calls outright or engage in combination option trades called spreads. In addition, a trader could write calls on stock that is already owned (covered writing) or write calls on stock that he or she does not own (naked writing). A similar matrix of trades is possible with puts. Still other ways of using options in an investment/trading strategy involve combining positions in pure options with those in other securities such as short positions in the underlying stock or long positions in bonds or convertibles. The discussion that follows will explore some of the various types of trades.

Buying Calls

Many option traders simply purchase individual calls on underlying stock that they hope will rise sufficiently to produce a profit. The hypothetical example summarized in Table 17.3 illustrates the type of outcome desired by an option buyer. This example demonstrates the potential upside leverage of options. A small stock price rise led to a much larger option price increase. The callholder earns 110%—almost 10 times as much as the stockholder. Notice that the time value of the hypothetical call decreased as time advanced and as the option moved deeper into the money. In this instance the value of the option position increased by $275 while the underlying stock position (on an equivalent number of shares) rose by $425. The option investor, however, had to put up only a small fraction of the money required to purchase the stock outright.

TABLE 17.3 Buying Calls in a Rising Market

	XYZ August 35		100 Shares XYZ	
	Price	Cost	Price	Cost
Purchase date value	$2 1/2	$250	$35 1/4	$3,525
Sale date value				
(6 months later)	$5 1/4	$525	$39 1/2	$3,950
Profit		$275		$ 425
Return		110%		12.05%

Although hypothetical, the example is not atypical. Some actual moves over the week of May 28 to June 4, 1982, are reported in Table 17.4. These reported gains may seem very attractive. Optionholders should, however, also expect some

TABLE 17.4. Actual Call Price Changes for May 28 to June 4, 1982

	May 28	June 4	% Change
Esmark—June 45	1	1 5/8	62.5
Esmark Common	45 1/4	46 1/4	2.2
South West Airline—			
September 35	5	7	40
Southwest Common	34	35 7/8	5.5
Whittaker—			
September 20	3 1/4	4 5/8	34.6
Whittaker Common	22 1/4	22 7/8	2.8
Armco, November 20	1/2	3/4	50
Armco Common	16 5/8	17 1/2	5.2

TABLE 17.5 Buying Calls in a Falling Market

	XYZ August 35		100 Shares XYZ	
	Price	Cost	Price	Cost
Purchase date value	$2 1/4	$225	$35	$3,500
Value three months later	$1	$100	$31 1/2	$3,150
Expiration (6 months later)	$0	$0	$31 1/2	$3,150
Loss		$225		$ 350

substantial losses. The example in Table 17.5 (also hypothetical) illustrates the result from holding a long option position in a falling market. Both the stock's price decline and the passage of time reduced the option's price. In this example the optionholder's loss is $225 compared with a $350 loss for a 100-share stock position. In percentage terms, however, the stock price declined by only 10% while the option price fell 100%. These results are hypothetical; those reported in Table 17.6 are actual price changes for the week of January 15 to 22, 1988.

In-the-Money versus Out-of-the-Money Options. Price fluctuations for in-the-money calls (calls whose striking prices are below the market prices of their underlying stock) tend to mirror moves in the stock's prices more fully than do out-of-the-money calls. That is, the price effect is larger dollar for dollar. Moreover, in-the-money calls will retain some value at expiration as long as they stay in the money. An out-of-the-money option, in contrast, will expire worthless unless it moves into the money before expiration.

On the other hand, the higher prices of in-the-money calls reduce the leverage that they offer. Out-of-the-money calls will generally produce a larger gain than in-the-money calls when the underlying stock price increases rapidly, particularly

TABLE 17.6   Actual Call Price Changes for January 15 to 22, 1988

	January 15	January 22	Change
Alcoa, February 50	1½	¾	−50.0%
Common	44⅛	43½	− 1.4
American Home Products, February 80	1⅜	¾	−45.5
Common	74	74¾	1.0
Merrill Lynch, April 30	⅝	⅜	−40.0
Common	22¾	23⅜	2.7
GAF, April 40	7⅜	4¾	−35.6
Common	42¾	42¾	0.0

if it increases to above the call's strike. A slow price rise, in contrast, may be offset by a reduction in the option's time value as it approaches its expiration.

Exercise versus Sale of a Call.   Options that are still some distance from expiration tend to retain a substantial time value. Thus an early exercise of such options is rarely attractive. An investor who wishes to own the stock can usually do so at a lower cost by selling the call and buying the stock outright. A stock that is about to make a substantial payment constitutes an important exception. The callholder loses the right to the dividend once the stock goes ex-dividend. Rather than lose this dividend value, the callholder may choose to exercise or sell the option while its market price still reflects the (cum) dividend payment.

Those who choose to exercise and then sell their stock incur commissions on both the purchase and the sale of the stock. This compares with a single commission incurred by the callholder who simply sells his or her option. Moreover, the option trade involves a much lower dollar value than a trade on a corresponding number of shares of the underlying stock. Commissions are almost always based at least in part on the value of the trade. Thus an option trade involving a particular number of shares generally calls for a considerably smaller commission than the commission on an equivalent number of shares bought or sold outright. On the other hand, the investor wanting to hold the underlying stock would only incur a single commission by exercising. Selling the option and then purchasing the stock would, in contrast, cause the investor to incur two commissions. Clearly, the exercise-or-sell decision requires a careful analysis of the resulting commissions and corresponding stock prices.

Option traders should also consider the impact of time value in exercise-or-sell decisions. As expiration approaches, options may trade at a slight discount from their intrinsic values (negative time values). For example, a soon-to-expire call with a strike of 45 on a stock trading at 46 might sell for ⅞ (⅛ below its intrinsic value). This corresponds to a $12.50 per 100 share discount below the call's intrinsic value. Such a discount represents what option market makers might require to justify an arbitrage trade. The discount must be sufficient to cover the arbitrager's costs of buying the option, exercising, and then selling the underlying stock. Few individual investors could trade that cheaply. Thus they are still generally better off to sell the option unless they want to own the stock. Normally arbitrage trading will keep even very short-term option prices close to their intrinsic values.

TABLE 17.7   Writing Calls in a Rising Market

| | XYZ August 35 | | 100 Shares XYZ | |
	Price	Premium	Price	Cost
Purchase date	$2 1/2	$250	$35 1/4	(owned)
Call exercised	$4 1/2	$450	$39 1/2	$3,950
Proceeds of sale			$35	$3,500
Loss versus selling on open market				$450
Less premium received				$250
Net (opportunity) loss before commission				$200

Call Writing

Every call contract has a buyer on one side and a call writer on the other side. Call writers may write calls under two basically different circumstances. Covered writers write calls on stock that they already own. Naked writers, in contrast, do not own the stock on which they are writing options.

Covered call writing offers stockholders additional income and some downside protection on their investment position. That is, the premium from the calls that they write provides the call writer with income. This income at least partially offsets any potential stock price decline. On the other hand, the writer risks having the stock called away and losing the additional profit on the rising stock price. Thus covered writing reduces both downside risk and upside potential.

Suppose XYZ is now selling at 50 while its calls with a strike of 50 sell for 4. The covered call writer has, for the life of the option, limited further upside potential to $54. The stock could move down to $46 before a loss (relative to an immediate sale at 50) is incurred. At prices below $46 the loss incurred on the stock-call position is still below that of an equivalent pure stock position.

The call writer loses (an opportunity loss) $450 relative to what would have been received by selling the stock in the open market. This loss is partially offset by the initial option sale premium of $250. Thus the net (opportunity) loss amounts to $200, plus commissions. Clearly, the covered writer would have earned more by not writing the call. This example of call writing in a rising market is summarized in Table 17.7.

Covered call writers are concerned with both up and down movements in the underlying stock. A fall in the stock's price reduces the value of their stock position. This loss may be only partially offset by the call premium received. Moreover, a rise in the underlying stock's price exposes them to the risk of exercise. Thus covered call writers may be hurt by either a significant rise or a significant fall in the price of the stock on which they have written options.

Only near-expiration in-the-money options are likely to be exercised. Writers of such options may avoid such exercises by buying identical calls. If the stock price increased between the time the call was written and the time it was repurchased, the covering transaction may incur a loss. That is, the call may have been sold for less than the cost of repurchasing it. Such a loss could be partially offset

TABLE 17.8 Writing Calls in a Declining Market

	XYZ August 35		100 Shares XYZ	
	Price	Premium	Price	Cost
Purchase date	$2 1/4	$225	$35	(owned)
Value three months later	$1	$100	$31 1/2	
Expiration	$0	$0	$31 1/2	(owned)
Paper loss				$350
Less premium received				$225
Net paper loss				$125

TABLE 17.9 Writing Calls in a Stable Market

	XYZ August 35		100 Shares XYZ	
	Price	Premium	Price	Cost
Purchase date	$2 1/4	$225	$35	(owned)
Value three months later	$2	$200	$35	
Expiration	$0	$0	$35	(owned)
Profit or loss				0
Plus premium received				$225
Net positive cash-flow increase				$225

by writing another option at a higher striking price. Once again, however, the writer would be obligated to sell the stock at the new price. The example in Table 17.8 illustrates this point.

The impact of the decline in the price of the underlying stock is partially offset by the premium received on the call sale. As the stock drops to $31½ the value of the stock position declines by $350. The option sale, however, brings in $225 so the net loss is only $125 plus commissions. The writer would have been better off to have sold the stock initially. Less, however, is lost than without writing the option. Presumably, the writer retains the stock and writes another $35 option for a lower premium after the first one expires.

Now consider what happens if the stock price is relatively stable. A stable stock price is particularly attractive for the option writer. Suppose the stock, which costs $35, also pays a $1.50 dividend each six months. The writer would receive $2.25 in call premiums and $1.50 in dividends for a total of $3.75 per share. The position would initially cost the difference between the prices of the stock and of the call ($35 − $2.25 = $32.75). A cash flow of $3.75 on an initial investment of $32.75 (ignoring commissions) is equivalent to a return of about 11.5% on the covered call position. Table 17.9 illustrates this example.

A return of this magnitude over a six-month holding period may well seem quite attractive. Indeed, the writer may try to earn this return every six months by writing a new covered option each time the older option expires. Such a strategy does incur some risks, however. For example, if the stock price rises above the strike, the shares will probably be called away. Similarly, a fall in the price of the underlying stock cuts into the covered writer's potential return.

Research by French and Henderson; Yates and Kopprasch; and particularly Mueller suggests that covered writing tends to yield attractive returns.[15] Indeed, Mueller asserts that a strategy of writing three-month covered calls with striking prices slightly below the stock price also reduces portfolio risk. Thus a well implemented covered writing strategy may offer the advantage of both a higher return and a lower risk than simply holding the same unoptioned portfolio of stocks.

Selling calls on stock that is already owned (covered option writing) is considered to be a fairly conservative procedure. The covered writer of a stock that trades in a relatively narrow range can sell new options each time the old ones expire unexercised. Writers of options that are not exercised could, however, have earned the same amount of premium income without having owned the stock. This observation brings us into the topic of naked writing.

Naked Writing.   Writers of calls on stock that they do not own are said to be naked. Such writers hope that the optioned stock will not rise above the striking price (or at least not rise above the striking price plus their option premium) while the option remains in force.

Suppose the writer writes a $50 call on 100 shares of XYZ stock for $4 per share. If the option expires unexercised, the naked writer gets to keep the entire $400 (less commissions). If the call is exercised, the naked writer is forced to buy 100 shares at the market price (at say $60) and immediately sell them to the optionholder for $50. A naked writer who has to cover usually has to do so at a loss. For this example (option written at $50 and covered when the stock reached 60) the writer would lose $600 ($1,000 − $400) plus commissions on both the purchase and sale of XYZ stock. Alternatively, the naked writer could have covered the in-the-money call by buying back an equivalent position prior to its exercise. Such a maneuver would have avoided most of the commission charges.

The Risks of Naked Writing.   Naked writing is similar to selling short. Both the naked writer and the short seller seek to profit from a price decline and are exposed to potentially unlimited losses (the price of the underlying stock could theoretically rise to any level). Like selling short, naked writing requires a margin deposit that is sufficiently large to insure against a loss in the covering transaction. The potential profit for the naked option writer is limited to the premium received.

One of the potential dangers of naked writing is illustrated in this example. In early 1981 near-expiration calls on AMAX 50s were trading for 50 cents. The AMAX stock was then under 40, and the likelihood of exercise seemed remote. Just before the calls were about to expire, however, Socal offered to acquire AMAX for a price in the 70s. The market value of the AMAX 50s shot up to over 10 dollars. Many option traders who had written AMAX 50s for 50 cents were forced to cover at $10 or more.

A similar dramatic price run-up occurred when Gulf tried to take over Cities Service. Cities Service, which was trading at 42, increased to 53⅛ when Gulf announced its $63 offer. June (1982) calls at 45 (which had only two days until

The Mechanics of Exercise, Assignment, and Settlement

Some relatively complex mechanics come into play when an option is exercised. The following discussion is taken from a pamphlet issued by the Options Clearing Corporation. The pamphlet itself is entitled "Characteristics and Risks of Standardized Options." This pamphlet must be supplied to anyone who wishes to open a brokerage account with the right to trade options. Thus any brokerage firm should be able to supply their customers with a copy.

EXERCISE AND SETTLEMENT

Most buyers and writers of stock options ultimately close out their options positions by an offsetting trade. Investors should nonetheless be familiar with the rules and procedures applicable to exercise. Such an understanding can help an option *holder* determine whether exercise might be more advantageous than a sale. An option *writer* needs to understand exercise procedures because of the possibility of being assigned an exercise.

HOW TO EXERCISE—An American-style option may be exercised at any time until the last trading day before it expires; a European-style option may be exercised only during the established exercise period.

To exercise an option the holder must direct his or her broker to give exercise instructions to Option Clearing Corporation (OCC). To ensure that an option is exercised on a particular day, the holder must direct his broker to exercise before the broker's cut-off time for accepting exercise instructions on that day.

A broker's cut-off time for accepting exercise instructions becomes critical on the last trading day before an option expires. An option that expires unexercised becomes worthless. A holder who intends to exercise an option on the last trading day before expiration must give exercise instructions to his broker before the broker's cut-off time. Investors should determine the applicable cut-off times from their brokers.

In highly unusual circumstances (*e.g.*, where a broker is unable to receive instructions from its customers), a broker may make an exception to its regular cut-off time. However, for an option to be exercised, the broker must pass on its customers' exercise instructions to OCC before expiration. OCC can accept exercise instuctions after expiration only in the unlikely event that OCC is unable to follow its normal procedures for receiving such instructions. With that very limited exception, OCC has no authority to extend the expiration time of any option.

Once an exercise instruction is given to OCC, it cannot ordinarily be revoked.

ASSIGNMENT—OCC assigns exercises in standardized lots (25 contracts or less on the date of this writing). These assignments are made in accordance with established random selection procedures to Clearing Member accounts. A description of OCC's assignment procedures is available from OCC upon request. Assignments are ordinarily made prior to the commencement of trading on the business day following receipt by OCC of the exercise instruction.

Once exercises are assigned by OCC, the broker must in turn assign them to customers maintaining positions as writers of the exercised options. Market rules require that assignment to customers be made either on a random selection basis or on a "first-in, first-out" basis. Brokers must inform their customers which method is used and how it works. Regardless of the method used, writers are subject to the risk each day that some or all of their writing positions may be assigned.

An option writer may not receive notification that an exercise has been assigned to him or her until one or more days following the date of the initial assignment to the broker by OCC. This possibility creates a special risk for writers of American-style and currently exercisable European-style calls (other than for covered writers) when the underlying stock is the subject of a tender offer, exchange offer, or similar event. A writer could fail to purchase the underlying stock on or before the cut-off date for the offer (*i.e.*, the expiration date, or the proration date in the case of an offer for fewer than all outstanding shares). Such a writer may learn after the cut-off date that he or she has been assigned an exercise filed with OCC on or before that date. At that point, neither a regular-way purchase of the underlying stock nor the exercise of an option (*e.g.*, the long leg of a spread) will enable him or her to deliver the stock on the assigned exercise settlement date. But if he or she fails to make timely settlement, he or she may be held liable for the value of the offer (because the nondelivery may in turn have prevented a buyer of the stock from making timely delivery to the offeror). This risk can be avoided only by purchasing the underlying stock on or before the cut-off date for the offer. Some offers require that tendered shares be delivered less than five trading days (the normal settlement time) after the offer's expiration date or proration date. In those cases, call writers must purchase the underlying stock at an earlier point—*i.e.*, at least five trading days before the offeror's delivery deadline—in order to protect themselves.

SETTLEMENT—Settlements between brokers or their agents on exercised stock options are routinely handled through stock clearing corporations.

The regular exercise settlement date for stock options is the fifth business day after exercise. OCC, however, has the authority to postpone settlement when it considers such action to be necessary in the public interest or to meet unusual conditions. Each broker involved in an exercise settles with its own customer.

In certain unusual circumstances, uncovered call writers may not be able to obtain the underlying stock needed to meet their settlement obligations following an exercise. This could happen, for example, in the event of a successful tender offer for all or substantially all of the outstanding shares of an underlying stock or if trading in an underlying stock were enjoined or suspended. In such situations, OCC may impose special exercise settlement procedures. These special procedures, applicable only to calls and only when an assigned writer is unable to obtain the underlying stock, may involve the fixing of cash settlement prices in lieu of delivery of the stock. In such circumstances, OCC might also prohibit the exercise of puts by holders who would be unable to deliver the underlying stock on the exercise settlement date.

When special exercise settlement procedures are imposed, OCC will announce to its Clearing Members how settlements are to be handled. Investors may obtain that information from their brokers.

Source: Options Clearing Corporation.

expiration) rose from ⅛ to 9½. Thus a $1,000 investment multiplied to $76,000 (less commissions). Again some naked writers were severely hurt.

Puts

A put contract enables the holder to sell 100 shares of a specific stock for a set striking price at any time up to a specified expiration date. Putholders profit if the price of the underlying stock declines sufficiently. For example, an investor might purchase an EFG 35 put for 3. If EFG stock falls to a price of 32 (35 − 3) before expiration, the putholder would break even (ignoring the impact of commissions). At a lower price the putholder begins to show a profit. Put writers, in contrast, profit if the stock price does not fall or falls only modestly. In the EFG example, the put writer would break even at the same point (32) as the buyer but would profit if the price stayed above the break-even level. Theoretical put valuation models are very similar to those for calls.

Strategies Using Puts.   Puts can be used in a variety of strategies. For example, a speculator may buy a put in the hopes of profiting from a projected decline in the price of the underlying stock. On the other hand, a speculator who feels that a particular stock's price is set to rise may buy the stock and hedge the position with a put. A decline in the stock's price increases the put's value, thus largely offsetting the loss in the stock. If the stock price rises, the put is allowed to expire unexercised. The payoff matrix of such a strategy is very similar to that for a call position. Indeed, such a strategy is equivalent to manufacturing a put.

Speculators who believe that a stock will be stable or rise may buy the stock and sell a put on it. The cost of the stock is in effect reduced by the put premium. If the stock rises, the trader profits from both the put premium and the price appreciation of the stock. If it falls, however, both positions will show a loss.

Put Terminology.   The Options Clearing Corporation considers a put writer to be covered if and only if he or she also holds a put of the same class with an equal or higher striking price. The term *in the money* implies that the option has a positive intrinsic value. An *out of the money* option has no intrinsic value. The exercise price of an out-of-the-money put is higher than the price of the underlying stock (e.g., the stock is selling at $50 and the striking price of the put is $45).

Manufacturing a Put.   A speculator who believes that a stock's price is about to fall can short the stock and hedge the position with a call. The resulting position is very similar to that of buying a put. In general buying a put incurs lower commissions than buying a call and shorting the stock. When only calls are listed, however, investors who want a put-like position have no alternative to manufacturing it.

Put Buying versus Short Selling.   Various methods are available to those who wish to speculate on the price of a stock going down. For example, rather than hedge a short position with a call, some speculators may simply short the stock. The unhedged short seller, put buyer, and manufactured put buyer all seek to profit

TABLE 17.10 Advantages of Puts Relative to Short Sales

- The risk is limited to the original put investment.
- Puts generally offer greater leverage.
- Puts involve less psychological pressure to cover.
- Puts do not require short dividend payments (but manufactured puts do).
- Put commission costs are lower (but manufactured puts' commissions are not).

from an expected price decline. Buying or manufacturing a put has several advantages vis-à-vis taking an unhedged short position. They are presented in Table 17.10. On the other hand, leverage cuts both ways and time works against the put buyer, as puts eventually expire.

Exercise versus Selling In-the-Money Options.   Optionholders should rarely if ever exercise an option (put or call) whose price reflects a significant element of time value. Most options with more than a few days until expiration will have a positive time value. Thus a put whose expiration is not imminent will almost always be more profitable to sell than to exercise.

Near-expiration puts, in contrast, are likely to be priced at or near their intrinsic values. In this case the sell or exercise question may be a closer call. Nonetheless, as with the sale of near-expiration in-the-money calls, a near-expiration in-the-money put is generally more attractive to sell. The alternative strategy of exercising the put and simultaneously buying the underlying stock is generally inadvisable. Not only is the single put sale transaction simpler to execute, it involves appreciably lower commissions. On the other hand, the putholder may already own the stock and would like to sell it. In this case exercising the near-expiration in-the-money put is usually the most effective way of disposing of the shares. Also, if the put sells for a substantial discount from its intrinsic value, purchasing the stock and exercising the put may be more attractive than selling the put outright.

STRADDLES, STRIPS, AND STRAPS

A straddle is a put and a call on the same stock, with identical striking prices and expiration dates. As with other option writers, straddle writers may be covered or naked. Writing straddles against a stock position is similar to writing a covered call option. Straddle writers have some downside protection and an opportunity to profit if the stock price rises or remains constant. In return for the additional premium, however, the straddle writer undertakes to buy more stock if the put side of the straddle is exercised.

Referring to Figure 17.2 we see that with the stock at 25¼ Chrysler April 25 calls are available for 2⁹⁄₁₆ while the corresponding puts sell for 2¹⁄₁₆. Thus a straddle using these two options would cost the sum of 4⅝ (plus commissions). If the stock were to fall to 20, the put side of the straddle would be worth (intrinsic value) 5, whereas a rise to 30 would give the call side an intrinsic value of 5. Indeed, for any price below 20⅜ or above 29⅝ the straddle would have shown a profit (neglecting commission). The straddle investor is looking for a large move in the stock

TABLE 17.11   Ford Call Prices for June 15, 1984, with Ford Common at 36⅜

Strike	June	September	December
30	47/8	5 7/8	6 1/2
35	1/16	2 1/2	3 5/8
40	1/16	7/8	1 3/4
45	r	3/16	13/16

(either up or down). On the other hand, a straddle writer will make money if the stock stays near the striking price. In the Chrysler example the straddle writer would have come out ahead. Chrysler stock was trading near 25 as the (1987) Aprils approached expiration. Neither the put nor the call side had a significant amount of intrinsic value. The straddle buyer's investment would have been almost totally lost.

In the prelisted option days of the old Put and Call Dealers Association, two other types of put–call combinations were frequently encountered: strips and straps. A strip is a combination of two puts and one call whereas a strap is two calls and a put. With most puts and calls trading separately on the option exchanges, strips, straps and straddles are now only rarely encountered. Many option trades do involve spreads, however.

SPREADS

An option spread is a simultaneous short and long position in options on the same stock that differ either in strike, expiration, or both. Similar types of combination trades may also be constructed from different delivery commodity futures contracts (Chapter 19). The two basic types of option spreads are vertical and horizontal. A vertical spread combines short and long positions of options with different striking prices. A horizontal spread, in contrast, consists of short and long positions for options with different expirations. Spreads can best be illustrated by considering some examples. The constellation of call option prices for Ford on June 15, 1984, given in Table 17.11, is used in the examples that follow.

Vertical Spread Examples. An investor who expected Ford to rise from 36⅜ to 40 or above might have bought the December 35s at 3⅝. Such a purchase would break even (ignoring commissions) if Ford reached 38⅝. Alternatively, the investor could have bought the December 35s at 3⅝ and simultaneously written the December 40s at 1¾ for a net cost (neglecting commissions) of 1⅞ (3⅝ − 1¾). A rise to 40 would produce a gain of 3⅛ (5 − 1⅞) compared with a profit of 1⅝ (5 − 3⅝) if only the long position were taken. Moreover, losses are limited to 1⅞ (compared with 3⅝) on the long position alone. Indeed, for every price up to 41¼ a greater gain is realized on the spread than on the simple long position. Above 41¼, however, the short position limits the gain (i.e., profits are less than those on the long position by itself). Thus compared with only buying the December 35, this spread reduces risk and increases gains for modest price moves.

For larger favorable price moves, however, the gains would be higher on the long call position alone. Indeed, for prices above 4¼ the spread position's profits are lower with the long side alone. Note, however, that even for prices slightly above 41¼ the percentage profit is higher on the spread because the unhedged position requires a higher initial investment (1⅞ on spread versus 3⅝ for the December 35 call alone). Indeed, in the example the stock would have to rise to 44⅝ for the percentage gains to be equivalent. At that level the gain on the call alone has an intrinsic value of 9⅝ (44⅝ − 35), which represents a gain of 6 (9⅝ − 3⅝). This is equivalent to a gain of about 11.5% [6/(3⅝)], which is about the same as that on the spread [3⅛ /(1⅞)].

A vertical spread such as the one just discussed is designed to take advantage of an expected stock price rise. The spread trader could, however, take the opposite set of positions. Such a spread would be designed to profit if the stock's price remains constant or falls. In this instance the spread trader would write the lower strike option and cover it with the purchase of a higher strike option. Thus writing the September 35s while buying the September 40s would initially yield 1⅝ (2½ − ⅞). Should the stock drop below 35 at expiration, the spreader would be able to keep that sum (1⅝) and indeed would show a gain for prices at expiration of as much as 36⅝.

Frankfurter, Stevenson, and Young studied the profitability of a strategy of writing in-the-money calls against out-of-the-money calls. They found that such a strategy would have produced substantial trading profits for the examples that they examined.[16]

A Horizontal Spread Example.   Investors who expected a modest short-run price rise for Ford could have bought the December 40s and sold the September 40s. Such a trade would have a net cost of ⅞ (1¾ − ⅞). If Ford traded at or just below 40 in September, the September 40s would expire worthless. The December 40s, in contrast, would still have three months to run. Such an option would probably be worth about 2. The September 35s with three months until expiration were priced at 2½. At these prices (0 for the September 40s and 2 for the December 40s) the trade would earn around 100%. If the stock goes to 45, however, both the September 40s (the short position) and the December 40s would rise. The difference in the two option prices may either increase or decrease slightly, thereby producing little or no gain or loss.

Alternatively the stock could fall from 36⅜ to say 25, in which case both the September and the December 40s will fall dramatically. With three months to run the Decembers might be worth 3/16. That price would be in line with the September 45s in June, when the stock itself was around nine points below the strike. In this case the initial spread would narrow from ⅞ to 3/16 (11/16). The loss, while not total, is still substantial. Thus the spread trader will not make money under every scenario but losses are limited. With spreads, adverse moves in the short position tend to be offset by favorable moves in the long position, and vice versa.

Other Types of Spreads.   A variety of more complicated types of spreads are also possible to construct. For example each type of spread using call options has a corresponding spread that uses puts. Thus the spread trader can construct both horizontal and vertical spreads with puts. A combination of a call spread and offsetting put spread is called a *box spread*. Box spreads are attractive to undertake when the put and corresponding call spreads are mispriced relative to each other.

A *butterfly spread* involves positions in four contracts. The spreader writes two contracts at one strike price and simultaneously purchases one contract below and one an equal amount above that strike price. The strikes on the two purchased options are equal distances from the two that are sold. For example, the spreader might for a stock trading at 35 write two 35s while buying one 30 and one 40. The combined position has an initial net intrinsic position (degree to which it is in or out of the money) of zero. The two options that were written (the 35s) are at the money, and the low strike option (at 30) is in the money by the same amount that the high strike option (at 40) is out of the money. As the price moves away from 35, the net intrinsic position remains at zero. At a stock price of 40, for example, the option with a strike of 30 has an intrinsic value of 10 while the 40 is now at the money. The two 35s (which the writer is short) have intrinsic values of 5. Thus the net intrinsic position remains at zero ($+10 - 2 \times 5 = 0$). No matter what happens to the price, the butterfly spread position has a net intrinsic position of zero. Thus risk is limited to the relative movements in the time values of the four options.

Normally when the two at-the-money options are written, their time values are substantial. The far in-the-money and far out-of-the-money options will, in contrast, have relatively small time values. Butterfly spreads are designed to make money when the price of the underlying stock stays near the level of the central strike. As the options approach their expirations all of the time values will move toward zero. If the stock's price has not moved much from the central strike, the butterfly spreader will profit as the spreads that he or she is short have higher initial time values than those that he or she is long. If, in contrast, the underlying stock's price moves a substantial distance from the central strike, the butterfly spreader's position will show a smaller profit or possibly a small loss.

A Butterfly Spread Example.   Refer again to the Ford call quotation in Table 17.11. From this we can construct an example of a butterfly spread. One such spread would involve the September 30s, 35s, and 40s. The spreader would write two 35s while buying one 30 and one 40 call. Such a spread would involve purchasing the 30 and 40 calls for 5⅞ and ⅞ while writing two 35s for $2 \times 2½ = 5$. The net cost would be 1¾ (5⅞ + ⅞ − 5) plus commissions. At expiration the position would have a value equal to its intrinsic value. The price of the stock could at that point be within one of several ranges. For example, if Ford stock is then at 40 or above, the combined intrinsic value of the position is zero. That results because the combined long 30 and long 40 calls exactly offset the short two 35s position. Below 30 all options have zero intrinsic values and the position is worthless. For both price ranges (above 40 and below 30) the total sum invested in the butterfly spread (1¾ plus commissions) is lost.

The situation is more complex for prices within the 30 to 40 range. Up to the price of 35, only the 30s have a positive intrinsic value. Thus the position is worth the difference between the stock's price and 30. For example, a stock price of 34 would imply an intrinsic value of the position of 4 compared with a cost of

TABLE 17.12   IBM Call Quotation for January 20, 1988

Strike	February	March	April
105	$8^{1/8}$	$9^{3/4}$	$11^{3/8}$
110	$5^{7/8}$	7	$8^{1/8}$
115	$2^{7/8}$	$4^{5/8}$	6
120	$1^{7/16}$	$2^{15/16}$	4
125	$5/8$	$1^{3/4}$	$2^{13/16}$

$1^{3/4}$ plus commissions. Above 35 the short position in the 35s begins to subtract value from the combined position. Recall that the spreader is short two 35s and long only one of the 30s. Thus for every dollar the stock goes up above 35 (up to 40) the combined position loses one dollar. If for example the stock reaches 37, the combined position's intrinsic value will be 3. The optimal price for the butterfly spreader is at the strike of the middle calls, in this case 35. At that price the 35s and 40s have zero intrinsic value while the 30s have an intrinsic value of 5.

Assembling Spreads

Spreads may be bought and sold as a package or put on one side at a time (legged on). Option market makers normally quote a price that reflects the ask on the long side and the bid on the short side. The investor may use limit orders to "leg on" a somewhat better price on each side. Such a piecemeal approach does incur some risks, however.

To avoid putting up margin, the spread's long side needs to be purchased first. Once the long side is on, the price of the short side could move adversely (down) before the spread is fully established. One would normally close a spread position by covering the short side first (to avoid being short without a hedge).

Regardless of how they are assembled, spreads are relatively complicated trades. They are only briefly explored here. Brokers can, however, supply interested investors with a set of pamphlets from the options exchanges explaining spreads and various other aspects of option trading in much greater detail.

Ratio Writing

Ratio writing takes spread trading to an additional level of complexity. As with spreads, the ratio writer takes offsetting positions in options on the same underlying stocks. Unlike spreads, ratios contain unequal numbers of options in the offsetting positions. Thus the ratio writer is not fully hedged or covered. The risk is greater but so is the potential gain. Consider the IBM call option quotation in Table 17.12.

IBM stock closed at $110^{7/8}$ on January 20, 1988. The investor might believe the stock will rise to around 120 in April. The question is how best to profit from such a move without taking on an excessive amount of risk. Buying the stock outright (with or without margin) would capture a modest profit if the stock does rise to 120. After commissions the return would be around 7% for a three-month holding period. Buying an April 105 or 110 would not offer a much better potential payoff. The 105s and 110s would have intrinsic values of 15 and 10 if the stock reached the 120 target. Such intrinsic values are only a bit above the January 20, 1988, market prices of 11⅜ and 8⅛. A vertical spread between the 110s and 120s would offer a bit better risk/reward ratio. It would cost 4⅛ (8⅛ − 4) and have a potential value at expiration of 10 (120 − 110). Thus the potential profit is 5⅞ (10 − 4⅛) less commissions. Still the investor might hope to do better. Ratio writing can be used to improve the profit potential.

Suppose that instead of writing one 120 call for every 110 call purchased, two of the 120s were written. The net cost of establishing such a position would be ⅛ (8⅛ − 4 × 2) plus commissions. Thus if the stock declines to or below 110, very little is lost. On the other hand, if the stock does reach 120, the gain per position is 9⅞ minus commissions. Depending on commission rates the position should reach a break-even level for an IBM stock price of around 110½. On prices between 110½ and 120 profits are realized with higher profits generated the closer the price gets to 120.

Unlike a spread, however, stock prices near expiration above the higher strike (in this case 120) do have an effect on the position's value. For example, if IBM trades at 125 near expiration, the position's value is reduced by five points by the uncovered short position in the 120. The long–short positions in the 110s and 120s offset. The net effect would be a profit of 4⅞ less commissions for a stock price of 125. Profits continue to erode as the stock price rises. At a price of 129⅞ the ratio position would begin to show a loss. The losses would increase as IBM's stock price rises above 130. In summary, this particular ratio example risks very little should IBM's price fall; breaks even at a price of 110½; incurs increasing profits up to a price of 120; incurs decreasing profits as the price moves from 120 to 129⅞; and incurs losses for prices of 130 and above.

As matters developed this particular ratio position would have proven relatively successful. On April 13, 1988 (two days prior to expiration), IBM closed at 116⅛. The 110s closed at 6¼ while the 120s closed at ¼. Closing the position at these prices would yield net proceeds of 5¾ (6¼ − 2 × ¼). The position cost ⅛ to put on so the net gain (ignoring the impact of commissions) would have been 5⅝. The profit would equal 45 times the initial cost. Commissions would reduce the profit somewhat but this still would have been an attractive result.

Ratio positions can be established with different ratios of short to long positions as well as different strikes and different expirations. Clearly ratio writing is a complicated procedure. It does, however, allow the writer to alter the payoff matrix from that of a standard spread. One final point to consider is the need for a margin deposit on the uncovered portion of the ratio position. In the IBM example the uncovered short position in the 120s would require a margin deposit.

TAX IMPLICATIONS

Option trading involves a number of relevant tax implications. Three of them are:

1. Option profits and losses are treated as capital gains or losses, provided the trader is neither a broker nor a full-time trader (i.e., his or her principal income source is not from trading).

2. The profit or loss on an exercised call is not realized for tax purposes until the stock is sold. Thus the trader can carry over profits to a following year and stretch short-term gains into long-term gains.

3. An option writer whose position is exercised (this problem could have been avoided by covering prior to expiration) will have to sell stock at the striking price. If that stock was purchased at a much lower price the writer will incur a large taxable gain. The writer can avoid realizing such a gain by purchasing the stock on the open market for delivery at the striking price. For example, the writer might have written options at 70 on stock purchased at 40. If the stock's price then rises to $80, the call is sure to be exercised. Delivery of the original stock would cause the writer to realize a profit of $3,000 per 100 shares. If taking additional capital gains this year is unattractive, the investor might well prefer to cover with newly purchased stock.

OPTION MUTUAL FUNDS

Thus far option mutual funds are only a small factor in option trading and no more than a small segment of the mutual fund industry. They do offer investors an additional choice, however. Because option prices are particularly volatile, any mutual fund whose portfolio consisted principally of calls could conceivably lose its entire investment in a down market. Similarly, a put portfolio could be wiped out in a rising market. Accordingly, most recently established funds have chosen more conservative strategies. For example, some funds largely follow a strategy of writing in-the-money covered options on dividend-paying stocks.

A second approach to managing option mutual funds keeps most of the assets in low-risk investments such as Treasury bills. The remainder is used to speculate in options. The covered option type of fund is suited for conservative investors while the fractional option type of investment is more interesting to risk-oriented investors.

INSTITUTIONAL PARTICIPATION IN THE OPTION MARKETS

Option funds continue to be a very minor factor in the option markets. Other institutional investors such as pension funds and bank trust departments have, however, become increasingly active. Such investors can write options against their large stock portfolios. Moreover, the substantial commission discounts available to such institutions makes certain types of combination trades attractive. In particular, conversions (offsetting positions in calls and manufactured calls) can sometimes be structured to yield relatively attractive riskless returns for those who can trade at minimal costs.

BROKERAGE COMMISSIONS ON OPTIONS

Most brokerage firms have a separate commission schedule for options. Like the schedule for stocks, the option schedule is based on the number of units (options) and dollar volume of the trade. Optionholders who exercise their calls will pay a commission on the purchased stock and the writer will pay a selling commission on the called-away stock. Similarly, put traders who exercise also incur commissions on the stock trades. Because the gross profits on option trades, particularly spreads, are often relatively thin, one should pay careful attention to the impact of commissions.

SUMMARY AND CONCLUSIONS

Option securities offer many diverse investment opportunities. Pure options such as warrants, rights, puts, and calls tend to magnify the gains or losses from price changes in the associated stock. The owners of such securities obtain substantial upside potential while their loss exposure is limited to the cost of their positions. Put and call writers, in contrast, take the opposite side of the bet. They have limited profit potential coupled with very substantial risk exposure. Actively traded options are usually listed on an exchange whereas more thinly traded issues trade OTC. According to the Black/Scholes valuation formula, the value of a call should increase with the underlying stock's price and volatility, time to maturity, and the interest rate, and should move inversely with its strike price.

Options seem to be priced relatively efficiently vis-à-vis the theoretical model. Put–call parity relates the price of puts to that of corresponding calls. Options may be bought, sold, or exercised or the option writer may write them against owned stock (covered writing), other options (spreads or ratio positions), or nothing but sufficient assets to cover (naked writing). As with most investments, option securities are generally priced to reflect their potential. Thus to make money with options one generally needs to have a better idea than the market about how the price of the underlying stock is likely to move.

REVIEW QUESTIONS

1. Distinguish between a put and a call option. Explain the rights and obligations of the buyer and the writer for each. Why is the purchase of a call not equivalent to the writing of a put?

2. What kind of option would a bearish speculator buy? Why? What is the relation of such a purchase to a short sale of the same underlying security?

3. What kind of option activity would an investor carry out to protect a profit in a stock he or she owns? How would such a strategy differ from simply selling the position? What are the advantages and disadvantages of the two strategies?

4. What is a straddle? Under what circumstances would one be inclined to buy a straddle? When would one be inclined to write a straddle?

5. What risk does the writer of a naked put take? Can a limit be placed on the potential loss for such a trade? If so, how?

6. What obligation does the writer of a covered call undertake? What are the risks and prospective returns of a covered writing strategy?

7. What type of option trading activity would a bullish speculator carry out? What are the risks and potential returns of such strategies?

8. What type of option trading activity would one who might otherwise be a short seller carry out? What are the risks and potential returns of such strategies?

9. Explain the meaning of the term striking price? How does it relate to intrinsic value, time value, or being in or out of the money?

10. Discuss the various types of spreads. Can spreads utilize both puts and calls? Which spreads are bearish and which are bullish?

11. Distinguish between a warrant and a right. Which is typically the longer term and which is more likely to be out of the money?

12. Rights do/do not lead to dilution (explain). What impact is the announcement of a rights offering likely to have on the price of the underlying stock? What is likely to happen to the underlying stock when it goes ex-rights?

13. Warrants do/do not lead to dilution (explain). What does the sale of warrants and the exercise of warrants typically do to the balance sheet of the issuing company? Will the existing shareholders be helped or hurt?

14. Exercising warrants increases/decreases earnings per share (explain). Similarly, what is the impact of exercising rights on per share earnings in the short and the long run?

REVIEW PROBLEMS

1. Refer to the IBM quotation in Table 17.12. For each entry compute and report the time value and intrinsic value. Which options are in the money and which are out of the money.

2. The ASD Company's stock sells for 32 while six-month options to purchase it at 35 sell for 1⅝. What price must the stock reach within that six months for the option investor to break even? At what end-period price do the stock and option investor earn the same return? What are the percentage gains for each if the stock rises to 40 or 45? How would all of these results change if ASD pays one dividend of $.75 during the six-month period? First assume that no commissions are incurred. Next use the hypothetical

commission schedule of Chapter 3 to compute commissions for the stocks. Use the same table plus 50% for the option commissions.

3. The HiDividend Corporation pays a dividend of $.50 per quarter. Its stock now sells for 25. At-the-money options for three, six, and nine months sell for 1½, 2¼, and 2⅞. Similar options with strikes of 30 sell for ⅜, 1, and 1¼. Compute holding period returns for covered writings for each of these options. Assume first that the stock remains at 25 and then recompute the results if the stock rises to 30 at expiration.

4. The QWE Corporation's stock now sells for 24. Its January 25 calls are priced at 1¾ while the January 30s sell for ⅞. What is the net cost (ignore commissions) of a vertical bull spread with these calls? What is its potential gain? What does that make the risk to reward ratio? If commissions equal 5% of the dollar value of each trade, how would these results differ?

5. Repeat Problem 4 for a vertical bear spread.

6. The ZXC Corporation's stock sells for 47 in March. Its May 50 calls sell for 2 while its August 50s sell for ½. What would a horizontal bull and bear spread using these calls look like? What are the profits and losses on these positions if at the May expiration ZXC sells at 40, 45, 47, 50, 55, or 60? Compute your answer first ignoring commissions and then by assuming a 5% rate.

7. Use the put–call parity relation to compute the theoretical value for a put when the corresponding call sells for 3 and its stock sells for 30, which is also the strike. Assume a risk-free rate of 6%. How would the result change if the risk-free rate changed to 11%?

8. Refer to the IBM quotation in Table 17.12. Compute the payoff matrix for a ratio position involving a short of three April 125s for every one purchase of the 110s. How does this position compare with that for the two to one ratio of the 110s and 120s?

9. XYZ stock is selling ex-rights at $50. The rights entitle the holder to 10 shares at $48. What is their theoretical value? First assume that XYZ stock remains at 50. Then compute the theoretical value assuming that the stock price falls by the amount implied by the dilution.

10. Refer to Figure 17.2. Outline the straddle possibilities using the various Chrysler puts and calls. What are the ranges of profitability for each?

REVIEW PROJECTS

1. Identify a list of five puts and five calls. Compute the time value and intrinsic value for each.

2. Apply Turov's formula to three of the call options in Project 1.

3. Select five put–call combinations and compute their put–call parity values. Compare them with the actual relations. Realize that nonsimultaneous closes, commissions, and bid–ask spread would all work against parity. Explain.

4. Repeat the process from Project 3, this time using the Black-Scholes formula. (You will have to estimate stock variances.)

5. Identify five stocks with high dividend rates and formulate a covered writing strategy for each. Track your performance over time. Write a report.

6. Identify five long-term calls that you would feel least uncomfortable writing naked. Track their performance and assess the results. Write a report.

7. Assemble five vertical spreads and track their performances. Write a report.

8. Assemble five horizontal spreads and track their performances. Write a report.

9. Identify five companies with outstanding warrants and listed calls. Track their performances relative to the common for the life of each call. Write a report.

NOTES

1. D. Turov, "Dividend Paying Stocks and Their Warrants," *Financial Analysts Journal*, March/April 1973, 76–79; D. Turov, "Speculative Security, Warrants, Argues a Fan, Have a Lot Going for Them," *Barron's*, November 28, 1983, 38, 47.

2. J. Shelton, "The Relation of the Price of a Warrant to the Price of Its Associated Stock," *Financial Analysts Journal*, May/June 1967 and July/August 1967, 134–151; P. Samuelson, "Rational Theory of Warrant Prices," *Industrial Management Review*, Spring 1965, 20; P. Samuelson, "Mathematics of Speculation Price," *SIAM Review*, January 1973, 1–42; M. Parkinson, "Empirical Warrant Stock Relationships," *Journal of Business*, October 1972, 563–569; F. Black and M. Scholes, "The Pricing of Option Contracts and Corporate Liabilities," *Journal of Political Economy*, May–June 1973, 637–654.

3. E. Elton and M. Gruber, *Modern Portfolio Theory and Investment Analysis* (New York; John Wiley, 1981), 441–478.

4. F. Black and M. Scholes, "The Valuation of Option Contracts and a Test of Market Efficiency," *Journal of Finance*, May 1972, 399–417.

5. D. Galai, "Tests of Market Efficiency of the Chicago Board Options Exchange," *Journal of Business*, April 1977, 167–197.

6. N. Gultekin, R. Rogalski, and S. Tinic, "Option Pricing Model Estimates: Some Empirical Results," *Financial Management*, Spring 1982, 58–69.

7. G. Trennepohl, "A Comparison of Listed Option Premiums and Black/Scholes Model Prices: 1973–1979," *Journal of Financial Research*, Spring 1981, 11–20.

8. A. Gleit and B. Branch, "The Black/Scholes Model and Stock Price Forecasting," *Financial Review*, Spring 1980, 13–22.

9. M. Bhattacharya, "Empirical Properties of the Black/Scholes Formula under Ideal Conditions," *Journal of Financial and Quantitative Analysis*, December 1980, 1081–1106.

10. S. Phillips and C. Smith, "Trading Costs for Listed Options: The Implications for Market Efficiency," *Journal of Financial Economics*, June 1980, 179–201.

11. R. Whaley, "Valuation of American Call Options on Dividend-Paying Stocks: Empirical Tests," *Journal of Financial Economics*, March 1982, 29–58; J. MacBeth and L. Merville, "Tests of the Black/Scholes and Cox Call Option Valuation Models," *Journal of Finance*, May 1980, 285–300; W. Sterk, "Tests of Two Models for Valuing Call Options and Stocks with Dividends," *Journal of Finance*, December 1982, 1229–1238; W. Sterk, "Comparative Performance of the Black-Scholes and Roll-Geske-Whaley Option Pricing Models," *Journal of Financial and Quantitative Analysis*, September 1983, 345–354; R. Geske and R. Roll, "On Valuing American Call Options with the Black-Scholes European Formula," *Journal of Finance*, June 1984, 443–455; W. Sterk, "Option Pricing Dividends and the In- and Out-of-the-Money Bias," *Financial Management*, Winter 1983, 47–53.

12. S. Manaster and R. Rendleman, "Option Prices as Predictors of Equilibrium Stock Prices," *Journal of Finance*, September 1982, 1043–1057.

13. M. Rubinstein, "Nonparametric Tests of Alternative Option Pricing Models Using All Reported Trades and Quotes on the 30 Most Active CBOE Option Classes from August 23, 1976, through August 31, 1976," *Journal of Finance*, June 1985, 455–480.

14. R. Klemkosky and B. Resnick, "An Ex-ante Analysis of Put–Call Parity," *Journal of Financial Economics*, December 1980, 363–379.

15. D. French and G. Henderson, "Substitute Hedged Option Portfolios: Theory and Evidence," *Journal of Financial Research*, Spring 1981, 21–32; J. Yates and R. Kopprasch, "Writing Covered Call Options: Profits and Risks," *Journal of Portfolio Management*, Fall 1980, 74–79; P. Mueller, "Covered Options: An Alternative Investment Strategy," *Financial Management*, Autumn 1981, 64–71.

16. G. Frankfurter, R. Stevenson, and A. Young, "Option Spreading: Theory and an Illustration," *Journal of Portfolio Management*, Summer 1979, 59–63.

APPENDIX A. THE BLACK/SCHOLES FORMULA

The Black/Scholes formula may be derived precisely given the following assumptions:

1. Frictionless capital markets: no transactions costs or taxes and all information simultaneously and freely available to all investors

2. No short-sale restrictions

3. All asset prices following a continuous stationary stochastic process

4. A constant risk-free rate over time

5. No dividends

6. No early exercise

The resulting formula is:

$$C = S_0 \, N \, (d_1) - \frac{S \times N \, (d_2)}{e^{rt}}$$

$$d_1 = \frac{\ln \, (S_0/S) + (r + 1/2 \, \sigma^2)t}{\sigma\sqrt{t}}$$

$$d_2 = \frac{\ln \, (S_0/S) + (r - 1/2 \, \sigma^2)t}{\sigma\sqrt{t}}$$

where:

C = option value
r = continuously compounded riskless interest rate
S_0 = stock price
S = strike price of option
e = 2.718
t = time to expiration of option as a fraction of a year
σ = the standard deviation of the continuously compounded annual rate of return
$\ln(S_0/S)$ = natural logarithm of S_0/S
$N(d)$ = value of the cumulative normal distribution evaluated at d

APPENDIX B. PUT–CALL PARITY

The formula relating the value of a put to that of a call may be written as:

$$(C_0 - P_0) = \frac{(1 + r_f) \, S_0 - S}{1 + r_f}$$

where:

C_0 = call value
P_0 = put value
r_f = risk-free rate
S_0 = stock price
S = striking price

Convertibles and Other Combination Securities

Several types of securities combine option features with characteristics of other instruments. The two primary types of combination securities are convertible debentures and convertible preferreds. A host of much rarer types include hybrid convertibles, equity notes, LYONs, payment in kind (PIKs, may be either bonds or preferreds), commodity-backed bonds, and stock-indexed bonds. Convertible preferreds and PIK preferreds are equity securities. Convertible debentures, hybrid convertibles, equity notes, LYONs, PIK bonds, commodity-backed bonds, and stock-indexed bonds are all debt securities. Each type of combination security has a close relationship to another type of security or other asset. Most combination securities may be exchanged for a set number of common shares or, in the case of commodity-backed and stock-indexed bonds, their redemption value or coupon rate is indexed to the price of some other asset. PIKs pay their owners a return in the form of more units of the security that is now held. Except for equity notes, conversion of the combination security is at the security owner's option.

This chapter examines the various types of combination securities giving particular attention to convertible debentures. Convertibles' investment appeal, specialized terminology, call risk, and conversion premiums are all addressed. Then we briefly explore convertible preferreds, hybrid convertibles, equity notes, PIKs, LYONs, commodity-backed bonds, and stock-indexed bonds. The chapter ends with a discussion of hedges and arbitrages, trades that often involve pure and combination option securities.

THE APPEAL OF COMBINATION SECURITIES

Combination securities derive value from their current return (preferred dividends or interest) and also as potential common stock or some other asset. If the price of the underlying common stock rises sufficiently, the convertible owner can either acquire stock at a below-market price or sell the combination security at a price that reflects the value of the underlying stock. If the stock's price does not rise sufficiently to make conversion attractive, the owners will still receive income and perhaps eventual redemption on the securities in their roles as preferreds or debentures.

Convertibles do offer an attractive combination of upside potential and downside protection. The convertibility feature does, however, usually come at the cost of reduced interest or dividend income.

Convertible Terminology

As with pure options, a number of specialized terms are encountered with convertibles:

Conversion Ratio.   Number of shares into which the security is convertible.
Conversion Price.   Face value of the security divided by its conversion ratio.
Conversion Value.   Current stock price times the conversion ratio.
Straight-Debt Value.   Market value of an otherwise-equivalent bond lacking a conversion feature.
Conversion Premium.   Bond price less its conversion value.
Premium over Straight-Debt Value.   Bond price less its straight-debt value.

To understand the use of these terms consider a CVD convertible bond. It has a $1,000 face value, 12% coupon, and is convertible into 50 shares of CVD stock (its conversion ratio) any time over the next 20 years. For a $20 a share stock price conversion value of the convertible equals the face value of the bond ($20 × 50 = $1,000). Thus the conversion price is $20 per share. If the stock sells for $15 a share when the bonds are issued, the bond's initial conversion value equals $750. Such bonds will generally trade at a price that more closely reflects their value as bonds (the straight-debt value of their 12% coupon rate). Thus if the market rate on similar-risk long-term bonds is 14%, this bond should sell for at least $860 (12%/14% = .86). It actually should sell for a bit more so that its yield to maturity equals 14%.

Suppose the price of the underlying stock rose sufficiently for the conversion value to approach the straight-debt value of the convertible. In that price environment the bond's price fluctuations would begin behaving more like that of its underlying stock. If, for example, the stock rose to $30 a share, the convertible would have a conversion value of $1,500 (50 × $30). The market price would be at or above the conversion value and would move up and down proportionately with the stock's price. Thus if the stock's price next moved to 31, the conversion value would rise to $1,550 and the bond price would be at least that high.

Conversion and straight-debt values tend to place a floor under the price of convertibles. Because of their "equity kicker," however, they normally yield

TABLE 18.1   Selected Convertible Bond Data for February 1, 1983

Convertible issue	S & P Rating	Conversion Ratio	Stock Price	Conversion Value	Estimated Straight-Debt Value	Market Price
AVCO 5 1/2 93	BB−	18.52	27 5/8	$ 512	$500	$ 670
GELCO 14s 01	BB−	22.13	42 3/8	$ 938	$950	$1,010
GTE 5s 92	BBB	22.98	40 3/4	$ 936	$560	$ 962
Life Mark 11s 02	BB+	30.30	34 7/8	$1,057	$840	$1,215
Ramada Inns 10s 00	B−	129.03	5 3/4	$ 742	$710	$ 960

*Note that the conversion value is almost always below the market price of a convertible. The anomaly revealed here may reflect quotations at different closing times for the convertible and underlying stock, or the bond may have closed at the bid while the stock closed at the asked. Arbitrage profits would of course have been possible if one could have traded at these prices.

appreciably less than otherwise-similar nonconvertibles. Thus a convertible with a 10% coupon would typically command a somewhat higher price than a similar-quality 10% nonconvertible. The difference between the bond's conversion value and market value is known as the conversion premium. The difference between the convertible's market price and straight-debt value is called the premium over the straight-debt value.

Assume the CVD bonds sold for $950 when the stock traded at 15 and similar nonconvertibles were selling for $875. The conversion premium would be $200 ($950 − $750) and the premium over straight-debt value would be $75 ($950 − $875). Table 18.1 contains data on some real world convertibles.

Because convertible bonds are often almost as risky as stocks, the same margin percentage is required: in 1988, 50% versus 30% for straight bonds. Thus $10,000 worth of marginable convertibles could be purchased with $5,000 of investor's equity and $5,000 in margin borrowing. The convertible's coupon payments may offset part or all of the interest cost of a margin purchase. Buying convertibles on margin may be appealing if the (short-term) margin rate is low relative to the (longer term) bond rate. Indeed, low conversion value convertibles often pay relatively high yields and sometimes even return to life.

The Advantages of Convertible Bonds

Convertible bonds offer both a fixed coupon (usually a bit below the market rate on equivalent-risk straight-debt securities) and the possibility of a capital gain. They should not be bought either as income securities (straight bonds almost always offer a higher risk-adjusted yield) or as pure stock plays (the stock itself will usually rise proportionately more in a strong market). Rather, convertibles appeal to investors who find the prospects of the related stock attractive but desire the income and protection of the straight-debt value.

Investing in convertibles has two basic advantages over investments in the underlying common. First, the security's current return is usually higher and certainly more dependable than the corresponding common's dividend yield. Second, their fixed coupons give convertibles considerable resistance to the adverse effect of downward moves in the common's price. Convertible prices do tend to move inversely with interest rates, however. Moreover, they normally yield less than otherwise-similar nonconvertible debentures. Finally the conversion feature will only have value as long as the stock price has a reasonable potential of rising enough for the conversion value to exceed the straight-debt value.

Deep-discount convertibles are often particularly attractive. *Business Week* cited the following example:[1] In the depressed market of August 1974 the Chase Manhattan Bank's 4⅞% bond sold for $630 (a 9% yield), which equaled its estimated straight-debt value. Moreover, the market price exceeded the conversion value by only 10%. A 25% increase in the stock price would lead to a bond price increase of about 18%. A 25% fall in the stock price (assuming interest rates held steady) would, in contrast, probably have produced about a 3% reduction in the bond's price. A substantial decline in the bond's price would require both an increase in interest rates and a fall in the stock's price. Even in this instance, one could simply hold the bond and collect a 9% yield to maturity.

Convertibles' Call Risk

While most debt securities are callable, the call feature is especially relevant to convertible holders. Ingersoll showed that corporations should force conversion whenever the call price is safely below the bond's conversion value.[2] Following such a policy would severely limit convertibles' upside potentials. Thus they may only offer attractive returns (vis-à-vis nonconvertibles) if the conversion value exceeds the call price soon after the security is issued. Moreover, Mikkelson finds that calling to force conversion generally depresses the price of the underlying stock.[3] Most companies, however, do not call their convertibles as quickly as the Ingersoll model predicts.

The Theoretical Value of Convertibles

Because they contain both debt and equity elements, convertibles' theoretical values are relatively difficult to define. Debt values will depend upon the coupon, default risk, maturity date, and other indenture provisions. The value of the conversion feature is affected by the firm's risk and capital structure, dividend policy, calling policy, conversion terms, and the current stock price.

As with call valuation, a convertible's theoretical value should not offer assured arbitrage profits to either buyers or short sellers. Values derived from the Black/Scholes contingent-claim pricing model (used to derive theoretical values for options) have been applied to convertible pricing by Ingersoll; McDaniel; Brennan and Schwartz; and Billingsley, Lamy, and Thompson.[4]

Calculating the price the stock must reach to make investments in convertibles or their associated stocks equivalent is also much more complex than with warrants (Turov's formula, Chapter 17). Both the premium over conversion and the difference between interest and expected dividend income must be considered. Liebowitz has identified three plausible definitions of equivalent return.[5]

The Conversion Premium

As previously mentioned, the conversion premium indicates the amount over the underlying stock value paid for the straight-debt value protection. Not surprisingly, the conversion premium is of considerable interest to investors. Weil, Segall, and Green assembled the following list of potential determinants of the conversion premium.[6]

1. Transactions costs: Bond commissions are generally less (relative to the dollar value of the trade) than those of equivalent-value stock. Thus buying bonds and converting them may result in lower transactions costs than purchasing stock directly.

2. Income differences: The bond's coupon yield is usually greater than the dividend yield on equivalent stock.

3. Antidilution clause: The indenture gives some protection against the diluting effect of additional stock sales or distribution of assets. The specifics of these provisions may affect the premium.

4. Price floors: The convertible's straight-debt value protects holders from stock price falls.

5. Volatility of the underlying stock: As with pure options (Black/Scholes formula), a volatile stock price increases the likelihood of a large payoff.

6. Length to maturity: The longer the life of the conversion option, the more time the stock has to reach an attractive level.

On a priori grounds, Weil, Segall, and Green ruled out antidilution clauses, stock volatility, and length to maturity. They were then left with transaction costs, income differences, and price floors. In their empirical work the income differences variable had the proper sign and was statistically significant. The transaction cost variable had an unexpected negative sign, however. Moreover, the floor variable added little explanatory power and was generally not statistically significant. They believed that the floor variable was unimportant in their equation because it offered relatively little protection. They suggested that similar protection could be obtained with a stop-loss order. Their sample, however, only contained convertibles priced well above their straight-debt values so that the floor was likely to be almost irrelevant. Stop-loss orders liquidate holdings, whereas the convertible's floor reduces the potential loss as the investor waits for the stock to rise again. The floor is more nearly equivalent to a put at the floor level lasting for the bond's expected life. Such a put would probably be quite expensive.

Weil, Segall, and Green's statistical methodology was criticized by Duvel, and Murry questioned their assertion that a stop-loss order provided equivalent protection.[7] Work by Walter and Que and by West and Largay confirmed the importance of the floor variable.[8] In a reply, Weil, Segall, and Green concede this point while demonstrating the relatively modest effect of the floor, especially when the premium over the straight-debt value is large.[9] Thus income differences and floors both affect the conversion premium.

Subsequently, Jennings found the conversion premium to be related to un-diversifiable risk.[10] He also noted that income and transaction cost differences are relevant only if the future conversion value is expected to exceed the future straight-debt value. In addition, he found that bonds whose conversion premiums were below his predicted value tended to appreciate relative to bonds with overvalued conversion premiums.

Convertible Preferreds

While less popular than convertible debentures, convertible preferreds have become much more numerous in the past few years. In 1983 forty-three new issues worth over $3 billion were sold, a tenfold increase over 1982. Much of this increase resulted from various mergers, acquisitions, and leveraged buyouts in which the acquired firm issues new securities rather than purchases with cash.

Convertible preferreds promise (but do not guarantee) to pay a fixed dividend. Like convertible bonds they can be converted into a stated number of common shares within a prespecified period. The convertibility feature may eventually expire at which time the stock becomes a normal fixed-income preferred. As with convertible bonds, convertible preferreds behave more like the underlying stocks when the market price is close to their conversion values and more like straight preferreds when the conversion value is well below the value as a preferred.

The number of common shares that can be obtained by converting is called the conversion ratio. Thus, a preferred convertible into four common shares would have a ratio of 4.00. This conversion ratio may change with time. For example, an issue might be convertible into four shares for the first 10 years after issue, two shares for the next 10 years, and then may become a straight preferred.

A preferred's conversion value is the current price of the common stock multiplied by the conversion ratio. A preferred convertible into four shares of common stock selling at $10 would have a conversion value of $40. A market price of $50 would reflect a conversion premium of $10. The conversion premium is normally expressed as a percentage:

$$\text{Conversion Premium} = \frac{\text{Market Price of Preferred} - \text{Conversion Value}}{\text{Conversion Value}}$$

The conversion premium in the example is:

$$(\$50 - \$40)/\$40 = \$10/\$40 = 25\%$$

Knowing the size of the conversion premium may help an investor determine whether the convertible preferred or the common is the more attractive investment. For example, one might have a choice between a company's 10% convertible preferred selling at $50 and its common stock bearing a 5% dividend yield selling for $20. If the conversion ratio is two and the conversion value is $40, the conversion premium is 25%:

	CVP	Common
Price	$50	$20
Dividend	$5.00	$1
Yield	10%	5%

For the 25% premium, an investor buying the 10% convertible preferred receives a higher current yield (10% versus 5%), a more stable dividend (a characteristic of preferreds), and the option of converting the issue into common. Of course, the higher the conversion premium, the more remote will be the chance of an attractive conversion and the lower the gain even if conversion does become profitable. Moreover, convertible preferreds are exposed to the same kind of call risks and interest rate risks as are convertible bonds.

Hybrid Convertibles

Convertible bonds and preferreds are the primary types of convertible securities, but other types of combination securities also bear mentioning. Unlike traditional convertibles, hybrids (also called exchangeable debentures) are convertible into stock of different companies from those that issue them. For example, in 1980 Textron sold debentures convertible into Textron-owned shares of Allied Chemical (at 66). At about the same time Mesa Petroleum sold a security convertible into General American. Companies with substantial stock portfolios may find hybrids a useful source of funds.

Hybrids are about as attractive to investors as the straight convertibles of the underlying company. The bond's default risk depends on the issuing company's financial position, however. Moreover, the conversion of a regular convertible is a tax-free exchange whereas any profit realized when a hybrid is converted is immediately taxable.

Equity Notes

Equity notes (also called mandatory convertible notes) were developed to meet the capital needs of banks. Such notes are issued as debt instruments that yield a fixed coupon until maturity, when they are automatically converted into common. For example, Manufacturers Hanover Trust (Manny Hanny) sold $100 million in 10-year equity notes in April 1982. Such notes yield 15⅛% and in 1992 must be converted into Manny Hanny shares at a price equal to the 30-day average price prior to maturity with upper and lower limits of 55.55 and 40. Manny Hanny was selling for around 32 when these bonds were issued. In April 1988 the stock was selling for about 25, a long way from the minimum conversion price of 40.

LYONs

One of the most complex of the new instruments is the Liquidity Yield Option Note, or LYON. LYONs differ from ordinary convertibles primarily in being zero-coupon convertibles. In addition, they are callable and redeemable. Making the security even more complicated, both the redemption and call prices escalate through time. The first two of these issues were brought out by Merrill Lynch in 1985.

Investments in Perspective

One of the most recently devised types of combination securities is the payment in kind security (PIK). The following article from *Forbes* describes them and discusses some of their risks and drawbacks.

Forbes

Welcome to the world of pay-in-kind securities, where you can get yields of 50% and more—or maybe nothing. And where even a solid borrower may offer 18%.

PIK 'em with care

By Allan Sloan

THEY USED TO SAY that a 6% rate would draw money from the moon. Boy, have times changed. Not long ago Salomon Brothers and Goldman, Sachs offered 18% to raise money for Southland Corp.'s leveraged buyout—and they couldn't come close to finding enough takers, lunar or terrestrial.

Now, 18% might strike you as a lot of money—but everything is relative. Eighteen percent for what? Salomon and Goldman were trying to sell something called pay-in-kind (PIK) preferred stock, which pays dividends with paper rather than cash. For a PIK preferred, 18% is a low rate. As the

table shows, as of late November only one PIK preferred—the Viacom 15.50, due 2006—had an indicated yield of less than 18% through the end of its PIK period. Viacom—which has the right to pay dividends in stock through mid-1993—is the crème de la crème of PIK preferreds.

The ultimate payoff with a PIK comes only if the issuer survives long enough to make good in cash. The risk is considerable enough to require high yields. How high? Take the troubled Fruehauf leveraged buyout. If Fruehauf survives to make good on its PIK preferred at the end of 1991, a buyer who paid $7.50 for a share this Nov. 18 and kept all the shares re-

PIK and choose

Below, in descending order of yield, are a dozen of the most widely traded pay-in-kind securities. Professionals who deal in these complicated, Byzantine issues figure prospective yields two different ways, both of which are shown in our table. The indicated yields, of course, presume that the company will be able to pay off the PIKs in cash. If you have any doubts about that, look elsewhere.

Security/coupon rate	Price*	Face amount	Years payable in kind†	Indicated yield*— through PIK period	to maturity
Preferred stock					
Fruehauf/14.72%	7½	$25	5	52.6%	29.4%
SPI Holding/16 (Spectradyne LBO)	17⅜	25	5	25.5	20.1
ANAC Holding/15.25 (Revco LBO)	16¼	25	5	25.0	20.5
Supermarkets General/14.08	15¼	25	5	23.9	16.9
Harcourt Brace/12.00	8½	13.50	6	19.9	16.1
Allied Stores/13.25	18½	25	3	19.1	17.4
Viacom/15.50	23⅛	25	6	17.2	16.4
Bonds					
Burlington Holdings/15.25 (Burlington Industries LBO)	$905	1,000	6	17.4	16.4
GACC/14.125 (Taft Broadcasting LBO)	985	1,000	9	16.5	15.8
Harcourt Brace/14.75	945	1,000	5	16.2	15.6
Owens-Illinois/14.5	975	1,000	7	16.2	15.3
GACC/13.25	990	1,000	8	13.8	13.6

*Prices and yield calculations as of Nov. 18˙1987, as provided by brokerage houses.   †From date of issue.

ceived as dividends will have earned more than 50% a year on his money. If the preferred becomes worthless before the PIK period ends, the buyer will have lost not only his principal but four years of dividends as well.

Since the early dividends are in additional pieces of paper, PIK issuers have no problem paying them until the PIK period—typically three to six years from the issue date—expires. By then, the company hopes to be generating enough money to pay in cash or to call the PIK in for redemption.

To illustrate: An owner of a share of the $25 (face value) SPI Holding 16% preferred gets $1 of new SPI 16s every quarter. Those 16s beget other 16s, and so on and so on—the dividends compound, although in paper. SPI has the right to pay with paper rather than cash through Sept. 30, 1992.

PIKs, then, are zero coupon securities. Like zeros, which are issued at a discount from face value and redeemed at face when they come due,

PIKs don't pay cash interest. That's because they are designed to help newly leveraged companies conserve cash in their early years, when things are tight and there isn't likely to be enough in the till to pay interest.

PIK preferreds tend to carry higher yields than even PIK junk bonds because they are junior to them.

The publicly traded PIK is a relatively recent phenomenon. Robert Long, director of high-yield research at First Boston, says the first major PIK bond issue was $1.1 billion of 14.5% paper issued by Safeway Stores as part of the Kohlberg Kravis Roberts leveraged buyout last year. Things went so well that about half the issue was redeemed early, and the rest of the bonds will now pay interest in cash. KKR, like most PIK issuers, kept the right to become cash-paying early.

Safeway redeemed the PIKs early because they were its highest-cost debt. Meanwhile, Safeway securities senior to the redeemed PIK bonds remained outstanding. "They call that 'being Safewayed,'" says First Boston's Long. As a result, the promised yields didn't last very long, this being one of many risks involved in PIKs.

Continues Long: "If you're thinking of buying senior issues, you have to check the covenants very carefully, to see if junior issues can be redeemed ahead of them." If they can be, they will be, because the issuer saves more by redeeming a PIK than by redeeming a regular bond.

Another potential pitfall is figuring out what the yield on PIK issues really is. Dividends or interest are paid based on a PIK's face value, not on its market value. That sounds easy enough, but it's not.

Take the Fruehauf preferred. A share gets quarterly dividends of 92 cents, a total of $3.68—but in Fruehauf preferred, not in cash. Because Fruehauf preferred was selling recently at 30% of face value, the dividend shares had a market value of only $1.104. Thus, the current yield on the issue was only 14.72% ($1.104 divided by the $7.50 market price) rather than the 49.1% ($3.68 divided by $7.50) that appeared in the stock tables of your local paper.

A superhigh yield will prevail only if Fruehauf is able to pay cash dividends on Dec. 31, 1991, when its option to pay in paper expires. At that time the paper presumably will be worth its $25 face value. Anyone paying $7.50 for a share on Nov. 18, keeping all the dividend shares and cashing out at face value the day PIK expires will have earned 52.6% a year.

Assuming all goes well with the underlying, highly leveraged deal.

The most important advice for would-be PIK investors: Know your deal. Do the underlying assets have a good prospect of delivering enough cash flow to make the deal whole a few years down the line? Could the deal withstand a spike in interest rates? Was it done at a reasonable price? What are the fundamental prospects of the business?

Finally, PIK preferreds promise tax problems, according to Robert Willens, a senior vice president at Shearson Lehman Brothers. The potential complexities are endless—figuring out the tax basis of shares received as dividends and later sold involves problems that boggle the mind. That's why accountants were invented. But, of course, if you're good enough to play the PIK game and win, you can make such a high return that you'll be happy to pay your taxes. ■

Source: A. Sloan, "PIK 'em With Care," *Forbes*, December 14, 1987, pp. 32–33. Reprinted by permission, © Forbes Inc., 1987.

TABLE 18.2 Types of Combination Securities

Convertible Bonds	Debt securities that may be exchanged for common stock at a fixed ratio
Convertible Preferreds	Preferred stock that may be exchanged for common stock at a fixed ratio
Hybrid Convertibles	Debt securities of one company convertible into the common of another company
Equity Notes	Debt securities with a mandatory conversion
LYONs	Zero-coupon, convertible, callable, redeemable bonds
Commodity-Backed Bonds	Debt securities whose potential redemption values are related to the market price of some physical commodity such as silver
Stock-Indexed Bonds	Debt securities whose yields are related to stock market volume

Commodity-Backed and Stock-Indexed Bonds

Commodity-backed bonds are debt instruments whose values are potentially related to the price of some physical commodity. For example, in 1980 Sunshine Mining (silver) sold $57.5 million in 8½% bonds whose redemption value was tied to the price of silver. For prices below $20 per ounce the bonds mature at face but at higher prices the bond's redemption value rises proportionately. Thus such bonds allow the owner to speculate on a silver price rise while earning a modest return. The bond's price has moved up and down with variations in both the silver price and market interest rates. When the bonds were issued, silver sold for $14 to $15 per ounce. At year-end 1982 silver was down to $10. Still later silver fell as low as $5. In April of 1988 silver was trading for about $6.50 per ounce, a substantial amount below the $20 price envisioned by the bond.

In 1981 Oppenheimer and Co. marketed a $25 million stock-indexed bond. The coupon rate was indexed to stock trading volume with a maximum of 22% compared with an initial rate of 18%. High stock volume should result in booming business for Oppenheimer. Thus they should be able to pay a higher interest rate when stock market volume is high. Similarly, Salomon issued S&P Subordinated Index Notes or SPEIs whose interest in indexed to the market return. Chase has issued a CD with similar features. An interest rate of 4% is guaranteed with an additional return equal to one-fourth of the rise in the S&P 500. Still other examples include the energy bonds of Petro Lewis and the gold bonds of Refinement International.

Both commodity-backed and stock-indexed bonds were designed to appeal to speculative investors with options that specially positioned issuers can offer. Additional types of innovative combination securities will probably be devised as time passes. Table 18.2 lists the various types of 5combination securities.

HEDGING AND ARBITRAGING

As markets have become more sophisticated, security types more diverse, and takeover activity more widespread, hedging and arbitrage trading has risen markedly. Both brokerage firms and individual investors have got into the act.

Hedging involves taking opposing positions in related assets to profit (or reduce losses) from hoped-for relative price movements. For example, the hedger might buy stocks and short corresponding warrants, or vice versa. Arbitragers, in contrast, simultaneously buy and sell equivalent securities in separate markets, profiting from temporary price differences. Arbitragers will generally take advantage of any appreciable price disparities for securities traded on both the Pacific Stock Exchange and the NYSE or any other combination of exchanges. In addition to their use in debt- and equity-related securities trading, hedging and arbitraging also take place in a wide variety of other markets including those for currencies and commodities. Both hedging and arbitraging may be classified into risk and pure forms.

Hedging

A pure hedge is designed to reduce risk per se. For example, most silver mining companies have relatively stable extraction and processing costs. The risky part of their business stems from the volatility in the market price of silver. The price has, for example, ranged from over $50 to under $5 per ounce in the 1979–1988 period. Establishing a price for its planned production well ahead of time would substantially reduce a silver mining firm's price-fluctuation risk. Hedge trades in the futures market would establish such price well before the silver is ready for sale. Mining companies that hedge each projected output increment largely insulate themselves from subsequent silver spot (immediate delivery) price fluctuations. Similar types of hedge trades may be made by a variety of enterprises. Pure hedging is often advisable whenever establishing a forward price reduces an important business risk. Such pure hedges are incidental to hedgers' main spot-market business.

Risk hedges, in contrast, are designed to yield a relatively likely profit. Rather than reduce the impact of potentially adverse price moves, risk hedgers seek to profit from potentially favorable relative price movements while minimizing their exposure to potentially adverse moves. Put and call spreads and ratio positions are examples of risk hedges.

Arbitraging

Pure arbitragers assume opposite positions on equivalent (or convertible to equivalent) assets when prices in separate markets diverge sufficiently. Pure arbitrage produces a quick certain profit. Risk arbitragers, in contrast, take offsetting positions in potentially equivalent securities. The shares of an acquisition candidate and its proposed acquirer are the primary types of potentially equivalent securities. An exchange for debt or equity securities may or may not be hedged by the arbitrager. A tender for cash does not require the arbitrager to make an offsetting trade, however.

A proposed merger involving an exchange of shares will generally leave the relative prices of the two stocks somewhat out of line with the merger terms. For example, XYZ may offer two of its shares for each share of UVW Corporation. If preoffer prices of XYZ and UVW were 50 and 75, immediate postoffer prices might move to 52 and 85. At these levels the UVW stock would still be underpriced relative to the XYZ offer. Assuming the merger agreement takes effect, the UVW stock is worth 104 (two times the per share price of XYZ). That is, the arbitrager would buy in the ratio of one share of UVW at 85 while shorting two shares of XYZ for a total of 104. The net result would be a gain of 19 (104 − 85) times the number of shares of UVW purchased.

The current price of two shares of XYZ (104) represents a premium of 22.4% over the current market price of one share of UVW (90). That is, $19/85 = 22.4\%$. One can profit from this discount by buying UVW and shorting twice as many XYZ shares. The investment required for the arbitrage would include the amount to be paid for the UVW stock plus the margin percentage required to short the XYZ stock. Normally 50% of the dollar value of the short position would be required for margin. Thus one would need to invest the cost of the UVW shares (85) plus half of the cost of the XYZ (104 × .5 = 52) for a total cost of 137 for each share of UVW purchased. As we have seen, the gross gain (ignoring commissions) on the transaction would in fact be 19. A gain of 19 on an investment of 137 amounts to 13.9%. If the acquisition is completed in six weeks and commissions amount to 5%, the arbitrager would earn an 8.9% profit (13.9% − 5% = 8.9%) in six weeks. This rate of profit is equivalent to 77% per annum. An arbitrager who was able to generate profits at that rate more or less consistently would do well indeed. Such profits, however, depend upon the proposed merger taking place as planned.

In general, when a proposed merger falls through, the acquisition candidate's stock will decline and may decline all the way to its preoffer level. The acquiring company's stock could, in contrast, remain largely unchanged. Thus the arbitrager would be forced to incur a considerable loss to reverse the trade. Suppose, in this example, the merger proposal falls through and the prices return to their premerger proposal levels. The arbitrager who bought UVW at 85 would have to sell at 75 for a loss of 10. The short position in XYZ at 52 would be covered at 50 for a gain of 2. This gain corresponds to 4 (2 × 2) for the two shares shorted per purchased share of UVW.

The net effect of unwinding the failed risk arbitrage trade would be 6 (10 − 4) per share of UVW purchased. This would amount to a loss of 6 relative to an investment of 137, or 4.4%. That loss plus commissions of 5% amounts to a total loss of 9.4%. Clearly the risk arbitrager does not want to be involved in too many takeover plays that are not consummated. The overall profit from a risk arbitrage program should allow for a combination of profitable trades, failed arbitrages, and periods when no suitable trades are available.

Merger proposals can fall through for a number of reasons. Antitrust problems, shareholder opposition, or a management reassessment could block a proposed deal. In other cases a hostile takeover attempt may be derailed by insufficient tenders or the target firm's defensive maneuvers. At still other times a bidding contest or actions of the target firm's management or shareholders may result in an improved offer. In any case many large sophisticated investors have generated substantial profit rates through risk arbitrage. This game is not, however, for the faint of heart.

Most hedge and arbitrage trades are designed to produce relatively modest short-term profits (in percentage terms). Very nimble movements and minimum commissions are needed since profits often depend upon obtaining favorable overall prices in both markets. Few amateur investors have sufficient funds, time, expertise, and courage to undertake serious arbitrage plays. Even professionals have to move quickly when profitable price relationships open up. Hedging is somewhat less demanding than arbitraging. Thus it is more suited to amateur traders. Table 18.3 summarizes the various types of hedges and arbitrages.

TABLE 18.3   The Types of Hedges and Arbitrages

Pure hedging	Reducing the risk of an exposed asset position by making an offsetting trade
Risk hedging	Taking offsetting positions in related assets in the hopes of profiting from relative price moves
Pure arbitraging	Simultaneously buying and selling identical assets on different markets at price differences which guarantee a profit
Risk arbitraging	Taking offsetting positions in the securities of an acquisition candidate and its proposed acquirer at prices that guarantee a profit if the takeover succeeds

REAL WORLD HEDGES: THREE EXAMPLES

During July and August 1974, *Business Week's* Wall Street section discussed three hedge recommendations of independent investment analysts.[11] While *Business Week* did not specifically endorse any of the hedges, the attention that the magazine paid to them suggested the proposals were at least worth considering. While not a scientifically selected sample, these hedge suggestions are typical of the ideas that appear in the financial press from time to time. The outcomes of these particular hedges were examined for those who closed out their positions on either December 16, 1974, or January 24, 1975 (approximately six months after the recommendations were published). The results for other nearby dates were similar.

Northwest Airlines Hedge

The Situation

Investor Jones buys 300 shares of Northwest Airlines at 21¼ a share. The cost of the stock after commissions is $6,472. He can hedge against a price decline of as much as 20% and increase his profits on a rise of up to 18%, if he simultaneously sells 13 six-month call options on the Chicago Board Options Exchange at $150 apiece. Each option entitles the buyer to purchase 100 Northwest shares at $25 a share. The income from the 13 call options after commissions is $1,841.

The Outcome

Possible Result A

The stock is at 25 when the option expires. The option is not exercised, so Jones keeps the $1,841 from the option sale and the value of his stock is up by $1,125.

Possible Result B

The stock is more than 25 when the option expires and Jones is in trouble. He is, in effect, short the 1,000 shares he must buy if the option is exercised, so he loses $1,000 for every $1 the stock climbs over 25. If the stock hits 28, both the income from the option sale and the gain on his stock from 21¼ to 25 (the option price), less commission, are lost.

Possible Result C

The stock falls below 21¼. The option will not be exercised and Jones has the $1,841 from the option sale. Not until the stock falls to 15⅛ will he actually lose money.

Had Northwest's stock price stayed between 15⅛ and 28, the hedger would have made money. The year 1974, however, was a very poor one for the market. Northwest stock closed at 11⅞ on December 16, 1974. This price would have produced an after-commissions loss of $2,989 ($6,472 − $3,483) on the stock position. This loss was only partially covered by the profit on the call short sale. Covering the calls for ¹⁄₁₆ would have produced a profit of $1,760 ($1,841 − $81) leaving a net loss on the transaction of $1,229 ($2,989 − $1,760). On January 24, 1975, the stock had risen to 12⅞, which would have reduced the loss by about $300.

AT&T Hedge

American Telephone warrants are so low—1⅞ at midweek—that it might seem sheer folly to sell them short. But AT&T shares, now below 44, have a long way to go before the warrants, exercisable at 52 until they expire next May, take on any real value. So some speculators are trying an offbeat hedge—shorting the warrants and buying October calls to protect themselves if the warrants rise. As explained by Reynolds Securities' Leroy Gross, the hedge works this way, with commissions figured in:

The speculator shorts 5,000 warrants at 1⅞, for which he receives $8,978. He also buys 50 calls—each on 100 shares—expiring in October. They trade at ⅜, or $37.50 per call, so the hedger puts up $2,157. Gross—whose *Stockbroker's Guide to Put and Call Option Strategies* was recently published by the New York Institute of Finance—outlines three ways the hedger could profit by October.

The shares remain at 45 or below. The calls expire worthless, so the hedger loses $2,157. But the warrants drop to ⅝. The hedger buys warrants for $3,345 to cover the shorts he sold for $8,978, for a gain of $5,634. His net profit is $3,477.

The shares rise to 55. The warrants will trade at 4, Gross figures, so the hedger loses $11,557 covering. But the calls have jumped to 5 ($500), for a profit of $21,039. The net gain: $9,482.

The shares rise only to 50. Gross estimates that the warrants will trade at 1½, for a $1,027 gain, while the calls will be ½ ($50), for a $70 profit—a total gain of $1,097. The danger is that Gross underestimates how much people will pay for warrants with six months to run. Suppose the warrants were to trade at 2½ instead of 1½; the hedger's profit would turn into a $4,000 loss.

By December 16, 1974, the calls had expired worthless while the AT&T warrant traded at ⁹⁄₁₆. Covering the warrant short sale would have cost $2,953. Thus the warrant part of the transaction would have produced a gain of $6,025 ($8,978 − $2,953). The calls cost $2,157 so the net gain on the full hedge would have been $3,868 ($6,025 − $2,157). The hedger was unprotected once the October calls expired, however. On January 24, 1975, the warrants were still trading at 9/16 so the hedger's profit would not have changed by waiting an additional 5½ weeks.

An IBM Tax Hedge

The IBM hedge was designed to convert capital losses into ordinary losses. In September 1973, the IRS ruled that writers must treat the profits on called-away stock as capital gains. The difference in the repurchase (zero if it expires) and selling price of an unexercised call is, however, treated as an ordinary gain or loss. To take advantage of this rule investors were urged to write in-the-money calls—that were very likely to be exercised. The following example was used to illustrate the point.

With IBM common trading at 209 and June 200 calls available at 25, the investor was advised to buy 100 shares of IBM common and write CBOE calls on 200 shares of stock. If the price of IBM stock was higher when the calls expired, the hedger would take an ordinary loss on the calls and realize a long-term gain on the stock. For example, if the stock was at 250 on January 31, 1975, he or she would lose $5,000 on the two calls but make $4,100 on the stock. Someone in the 50% tax bracket would have had a net after-tax gain of $1,475. In other words, the before-tax loss would be $900, but the $5,000 ordinary loss would reduce taxes by $2,500 while the $4,100 gain only would increase taxes by $1,025 for a net tax advantage of $1,475. If the stock's price declined, the tax advantage would disappear but the hedge might still make money. A trader in the 50% bracket would show a profit if the stock stayed between 184 and 269. The hedge did, however, envision investing $20,900 in the stock, which was only offset by the $5,000 received for the calls. Moreover, commissions and foregone return on the funds committed would narrow the profitable trading range somewhat.

On December 16, 1974, IBM closed at 165¼ while the calls sold for 2. Selling the stock would have produced $16,450 after commissions. Covering the calls would have cost $425, producing a net loss of $134 ($4,489 on call − $4,525 on stock). On January 24, 1975, IBM had fallen to 162⅞, while the calls were trading at 1/16, producing a net gain of $112 (−$4,763 on stock + $4,875). Since the calls were not exercised at either date, both the gain and loss would have been short term and thus the hedge failed to yield any tax advantage. Under the Tax Reform Act of 1986 this type of tax hedge could no longer be used effectively.

An Evaluation

The Northwest Airlines hedge lost approximately $1,000 on a $6,500 commitment. The AT&T hedge earned almost $4,000 but incurred considerable risk once the call expired. The IBM hedge failed to produce any tax advantage and essentially broke even. Thus one of the three proposed hedges produced a substantial loss, one broke even, and the one profitable set of trades ceased to be a hedge and became quite risky once the call protection expired. An investor undertaking all three hedges would have earned about $3,000, or about 9% of the $27,000 initial investment. A six-month holding period return of 9% is unspectacular considering the risks. The one profitable trade was the short sale of the AT&T warrants. They fell from 1⅞ to ⁹/₁₆. The short sale would have required a margin deposit of one-half the dollar value of the sale. Thus short sellers had to put up about $1 for each warrant sold for a gain of about $1.25, or 125%. Clearly this single trade was quite profitable whether part of a hedge or not.

Indeed with most hedges, one side makes money while the other side almost always loses. A hedger's net profits or losses depend on the relative sizes of the two sides' profits and losses. When they were recommended, each of the hedges just discussed appeared to those who suggested them to be likely to show profits. If only IBM (then at 209) had stayed between 185 and 269 and if only Northwest Airlines (then at 21¼) had stayed between 15⅛ and 28, the hedges would have generated profits. IBM, however, fell to 165 and Northwest to 11¼ so both hedges lost money. Investors should never underrate the possibility of a particular security's price moving outside a prespecified range over a given period.

SUMMARY AND CONCLUSIONS

Combination securities include convertible bonds, convertible preferreds, hybrid convertibles, equity notes, commodity-backed bonds, and stock-indexed bonds. Each combines a fixed income security with an option (or in the case of the equity note, an obligation) to convert the security to common stock or some other asset. Thus such securities offer some of the upside potential of a stock with the downside protection of a bond or preferred.

Combination securities are priced to reflect their profit and risk characteristics. Thus buyers usually obtain the upside potential at the cost of a lower yield than otherwise-equivalent straight debt or straight preferred securities. Moreover, the call risk further limits the upside potential. Pure and combination option security positions are often combined with each other and/or with nonoption securities to produce hedges and arbitrages. Clearly investors considering investments in some company's common should also weight the pros and cons of taking a position in its other securities.

REVIEW QUESTIONS

1. Discuss the appeal of convertibles. What do investors obtain and what do they sacrifice relative to investors in straight bonds and relative to investors in the underlying stock?

2. Why is call risk particularly relevant to convertibles? Under what circumstances are convertibles particularly likely to be called?

3. Discuss the various factors that affect a convertible's premium over conversion value. How does the premium over conversion value relate to the time value on an option?

4. What are hybrid convertibles and equity notes? How are they different from standard convertible bonds?

5. What are LYONs, PIKs, commodity-backed bonds and stock-indexed bonds? How do they differ from standard convertible bonds?

6. Discuss the two types of hedging and arbitraging. What is the principal risk involved in risk arbitrage?

REVIEW PROBLEMS

1. A convertible preferred selling at $100 may be exchanged for two shares of common, trading at $40. What is the conversion premium?

2. In the example in Problem 1, what should the convertible preferred sell for if the common goes to $60?

3. The SOM Company convertible debentures sell for 105 while its common stock is priced at 4. The convertible's conversion ratio is 200 while its coupon rate is 10%. Its estimated straight-debt value is 90. The stock pays a dividend of $.20 per share per year. The bonds mature in 2007 and are callable at 107. Compute the convertible's conversion price, conversion value, premium over conversion value, premium over straight-debt value, current yield, and yield to maturity. If you purchased the bonds at par and the stock subsequently rose to $5\frac{1}{2}$, what is the minimum profit per bond (ignore the impact of commissions and coupon payments)? Assuming dividend payments are maintained at the current level and the bonds are called to force conversion in five years, what price must the stock have reached for an investment in the stock and the bonds to have produced equivalent percentage profits? (Ignore the impact of commissions.)

4. For the SOM convertibles of Problem 4, what would the price of the bond fall to if the stock price declined to 3? Assume that market interest rates do not change and the premium over conversion value remains at least as great in percentage terms as at the start of Problem 4. Now suppose that the stock price rose to $6\frac{1}{2}$ and the bonds were called. What would the convertibles sell for after the call assuming conversion was still possible?

5. For the convertibles of Table 18.1, compute the premiums over conversion and straight-debt values. Suppose that in each case over the following year the stock rises by 15% and the premium over conversion value drops to zero. What is the percentage return on each stock and its underlying convertible? Assume that the stocks pay no dividends.

6. Redo Problem 5 assuming the underlying stock rises by 5%, 10%, 20%, 30%, and 50%.

7. North South Airlines stock now trades at 21. Its warrants to buy the stock at 25 sell for 3½. These warrants expire in two years. Compute the break-even price points (at warrant expiration) on the stock for a hedge composed of a long position of 1,000 shares and a short of 3,000 warrants. Assume no dividend payments and ignore commissions. What price for the stock results in the maximum profit for the hedge? How would the results change if commissions equaled 2%, NSA paid a dividend of $.25 per share per quarter, and the stock was bought on margin (50%) with an interest cost of 8.5%? Note that the short position in the warrants would require a margin deposit of $2.50 per uncovered warrant.

8. Recompute Problem 7 assuming ratios of long stock to short warrants of 1 to 2 and of 1 to 4.

9. The American Pig Company (ticker symbol PORK) has issued $50,000,000 in bacon bonds. Each bond pays a 7% coupon and matures in 10 years from its date of issue. These bonds may be exchanged for 150 pounds of pork bellies of a prescribed quality and held in warehouses that certify the bellies for delivery in satisfaction of Chicago Mercantile Exchange pork belly contracts. At what price for bellies will the bacon bonds be worth at least par? What price must they reach at maturity to give the bond a yield to maturity of 10%?

10. Suppose the bacon bonds of Problem 9 sell for a 4% discount from the futures market price of pork bellies in the contract calling for delivery in six months. If the broker call loan rate is now 9%, can one arbitrage the bacon bonds against the futures contracts? If so, explain how. If not, explain why not. Assume commissions amount to $5 per bond and $30 per futures market contract. A pork belly contract calls for the delivery of 40,000 pounds. Assume futures contracts in pork bellies call for a deposit of 10% of the value of the contract.

REVIEW PROJECTS

1. Assemble a list of 10 convertible bonds. Compute their conversion value and estimate their straight-debt value from their rating, coupon, and maturity. Plot their market price versus their conversion value and versus their straight-debt value. Now plot the premium over the conversion value versus the premium over the straight-debt value.

2. Assemble a list of five convertibles and compute their conversion premiums.

3. For the list in Project 2, compute the premiums over their straight-debt values.

4. Assemble a list of three recommended hedge trades and track their performances. Write a report.

NOTES

1. "An Opportunity for the Next Bull Market," *Business Week*, August 24, 1974, 45.

2. J. Ingersoll, "An Examination of Corporate Call Policies on Corporate Securities," *Journal of Finance*, 463–478.

3. W. Mikkelson, "Convertible Calls and Security Returns," *Journal of Financial Economics*, September 1981, 237–264.

4. Ingersoll, op. cit; M. Brennan and E. Schwartz, "Analyzing Convertible Bonds," *Journal of Financial and Quantitative Analysis*, November 1980, 907–930; W. McDaniel, "Convertible Bonds in Perfect and Imperfect Markets," *Journal of Financial Research*, Spring 1983, 51–66; R. Billingsley, R. Lamy, and G. Thompson, "Valuation of Primary Issue Convertible Bonds," *Journal of Financial Research*, Fall 1986, 351–260.

5. M. Liebowitz, "Understanding Convertible Securities," *Financial Analysts Journal*, November/December 1974, 57–67.

6. R. Weil, J. Segall, and D. Green, "Premiums on Convertible Bonds," *Journal of Finance*, June 1968, 928–930.

7. D. Duvel, "Premiums on Convertible Bonds: Comment," *Journal of Finance*, September 1970, 923–927; G. Murry, "Premiums on Convertible Bonds: Comment," *Journal of Finance*, September 1970, 928–930.

8. J. Walter and A. Que, "The Valuation of Convertible Bonds," *Journal of Finance*, June 1973, 713–732; R. West and J. Largay, "Premiums on Convertible Bonds: Comment," *Journal of Finance*, December 1972, 1156–1162.

9. R. Weil, J. Segall, and D. Green, "Premiums on Convertible Bonds," *Journal of Finance*, December 1972, 1163–1170.

10. H. Jennings, "An Estimate of Convertible Bond Premiums," *Journal of Financial and Quantitative Analysis*, January 1974, 33–56.

11. "Support Grows for Arbitrage Play," *Business Week*, July 13, 1974, p. 54; "An Offbeat Hedge in AT&T," *Business Week*, July 22, 1974, p. 53; "Abracadabra with Tax Losses," *Business Week*, August 10, 1974, p. 109.

SECTION SIX

Commodities, Real Estate, and Personal Finance

Section Five dealt with mutual funds, bonds, and options. Section Six discusses two more types of investments: commodities and real estate. While somewhat more distantly related to stocks, both of these types of investments have an important place in the economy. The final chapter of this section deals with personal financial management. The following case illustrates some of the issues that are explored in this section.

MAKING PARTNER

You have paid your dues by obtaining a CFA and working as a stockbroker, securities analyst, and newsletter writer. Now you are about to be made partner of a diversified financial services firm. You have considerable background in most aspects of your firm's business, but commodities and real estate are largely foreign to you. Merrill, Shearson, and Jenrette has long been in commodities and has recently acquired Epoch 21 and its nationwide chain of real estate brokerage offices. Because of your highly respected managerial skills, you expect to be given a supervisory role in Epoch 21. Alternatively, you may be moved to the Chicago office with responsibility over the commodity operations. The decision is expected to be taken shortly after you become a partner. You will have very little time to prepare for your expected new assignment. Your bonus will, however, be tied to the performance of your division. Accordingly, you want to learn what you can now. This section should get you started.

Commodities, perhaps the least understood of the major types of investments, are examined in Chapter 19. Futures contracts are defined and their uses discussed. Then we identify the various types of traders and explore the methods of making trading decisions. Finally such topics as specialized commodity investments and strategic metals are examined.

Chapter 20 explores real estate investing in some detail. Real estate's suitability as an investment is considered, along with a series of investment principles and three different approaches to valuing real estate investments. Then various types of real estate are considered including duplexes, apartment buildings, commercial property, undeveloped land, and real estate oriented stock.

Chapter 21 deals with personal finance. Various aspects of short-term debt and asset management, life insurance, pension planning, and estate planning are considered.

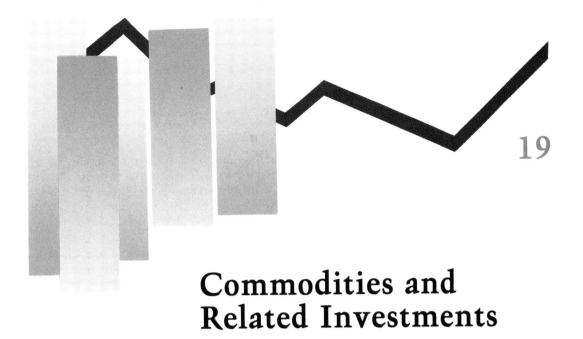

Commodities and Related Investments

Commodities are a bit off the beaten path compared with more traditional investables (stocks, bonds, and real estate). Nonetheless, they are an important investment area. The dollar value of commodity futures contracts traded substantially exceeds that of securities. Moreover, the commodity market's dramatic price swings appeal to many speculators. Finally, futures prices reflect anticipated market conditions in many important consumer goods and services (meat, grain, sugar, silver, lumber, gasoline, interest rates, etc.).

The commodities market challenges even the most skillful of traders. Nonetheless, investors need some understanding of the market to decide intelligently whether to participate. This relatively brief introduction is not designed to equip investors to trade something as complex and risky as commodities. It should, however, provide sufficient background for the interested reader to study the topic in greater depth later if desired.

We begin this chapter by examining the nature, growth, and diversity of commodity futures contracts. The types of professional commodity traders are considered next, followed by a discussion of several large and disruptive individual commodity trades. We then explore various aspects of trading decisions including fundamental and technical analysis. Finally, a variety of specialized commodity types are examined including interest rate and stock market futures commodity options, commodity mutual funds, and such commodity-related investments as gold bullion, gold mining stocks, bullion coins (Krugerrands, etc.), silver coins, and strategic metals.

WHAT IS A COMMODITY?

In spite of the commodity market's size, level of activity, and relevance to the economy, relatively few security market investors understand clearly how and why it works. The word *commodity* is primarily used to refer to deferred-delivery contracts traded on a futures exchange. A commodity futures contract obligates one side (the seller) to deliver a specific quantity of a specific type of asset (wheat, silver, T-bills, etc.) on a prespecified date to a prespecified location or set of locations. The other side (the buyer) promises to pay for the asset upon delivery.

Futures and option contracts are sometimes confused. Both involve subsequent events. An optionholder has a right but not an obligation to buy or sell a specified quantity of some asset at a specified price over a specified time period. The holder of a futures contract, in contrast, has the obligation to accept and pay for a specified quantity of some asset at a specified price at a specified time. Thus those who own options have a right whereas those who own futures have an obligation to do something in the future.

Futures contracts allow those who expect later to have or need that asset to establish a price and quantity ahead of time. Standardizing the contract's terms (grade, quantity, delivery location, and date) facilitates active trading. That is, the same (standardized) contract can be traded by a large number of interested parties.

Futures may be used to hedge spot (i.e., immediate delivery) positions or to speculate on commodity price changes. Rather than make or take physical delivery, most hedgers and speculators eventually close their positions with offsetting trades. Spot and futures market prices that move too far out of line do encourage some traders to make or take delivery, however. Indeed, the threat of such arbitraging activity generally drives spot and near-delivery futures prices together.

Most commodities can be traded with margins (earnest money) of from 5% to 15% of the contract's value. Thus even a small change in the price of a contract can produce a very substantial profit or loss. Margin percentages are generally set just high enough to limit default risk.

The Growth and Functions of Commodity Trading

While organized futures trading is almost as old as organized securities trading, the latter's size and scope have seemed to dwarf the futures. Only a small fraction of those who own stocks and bonds have ever traded commodities. Various factors have, however, contributed to the recent growth of commodity trading. As investors sought alternatives to the generally depressed stock market of the 1970s and early 1980s, and as the inflation rate soared into double digits, many commodity prices rose dramatically. Moreover, the commodity exchanges have devised a variety of intriguing new futures contracts. As a result, commodity trading grew at a time when stockholder numbers declined. Moreover, the value of a seat (membership) on the Chicago Board of Trade (the largest commodity exchange) has frequently exceeded that for the New York Stock Exchange.

Some politicians blame commodity speculators for the high cost of food and other raw materials. Most economists, however, believe that commodity trading has little or no long-run price effect. Large speculators may temporarily be able to drive up the price of any commodity by absorbing enough of the available supply. Almost always, however, they will eventually sell exactly as much as they bought. Thus speculators rarely if ever affect the long-run scarcity of a commodity. Indeed, some argue that speculators' efforts are more likely to be stabilizing than destabilizing. Those rare commodity traders who do take delivery of a substantial amount of the physical commodity often get hurt more than they hurt others (the Hunts). Efforts to corner a market almost never succeed in the long run. Moreover, commodities trading does serve a number of useful functions. For example such trading may facilitate hedging, provide a mechanism for allocating supplies over time, and generate information on future price expectations.

The Different Types of Commodities

Listed futures contracts exist for three basic classes of delivery vehicles: agricultural, mineral, and financial commodities. The principal foods include cattle, hogs, chickens, wheat, oats, corn, soybeans, barley, sugar, potatoes, coffee, and cocoa. The commodity exchanges also trade nonfood agricultural items such as lumber, plywood, cotton, and wool. The minerals traded on futures exchanges include heating oil, copper, zinc, gold, silver, platinum, tin, and lead. Finally, such financial futures as those for Treasury bills, long-term government bonds, CDs, GNMA passthroughs, several stock market indexes, and various currencies have grown increasingly popular.

The prices of all these items are quite volatile, reflecting their underlying supply and demand variability. No legal or theoretical barriers prevent futures trading in rhubarb or peppermint, but interest would probably be insufficient to justify such listings. Commodity exchanges do, however, frequently try to establish futures trading in new commodities. For example, contracts for turkeys, shrimp, apples, and diamonds were tried and failed while live cattle, pork bellies, lumber, plywood, heating oil, and a number of financial futures have been more successful. Many other items such as steel girders, pig iron, scrap aluminum, returnable drink bottles, uranium, milk, butter, coal, cement, cinder blocks, farmland, apartments, shopping centers, tulip bulbs, sulfur, and nails might or might not support futures trading.

Predicting which futures contracts will succeed is quite difficult. Successful contracts have, however, generally possessed most or all of the following characteristics: (1) a relatively competitive spot market, (2) a meaningful standardized contract, (3) storability or its equivalence (a call on production), and (4) sufficient price volatility to attract speculative and hedging interest.

Differences Between Commodities and Securities Markets

The commodities and securities markets differ in a number of important respects. Since futures terms rarely exceed 18 to 24 months, long-term commodities investment is restricted to those willing to take possession and pay storage. Very few traders are prepared to do this and so almost all futures trades are short run. Futures have maximum daily trading limits that prevent prices from moving up or down by more than a set amount. The inability to trade once the price has reached its daily limit may delay a timely coverage of an exposed position. Holding near-delivery futures positions risks having to make or take delivery. Margins are much lower on commodities than on securities; 15% or less is common compared with 50% (1988) for stocks.

Security market short-selling restrictions (short sales must not be on a down-tick) do not apply to the commodities market. Short interest in securities is usually a small fraction of long interest while commodity short positions and long positions are numerically equal. Unpaid commodity margin balances do not incur interest as actual payment only takes place at delivery. The futures market has no specialist system. Certain types of commodity transactions receive commission discounts. No similar discounts apply to securities transactions. Commodity and option positions must be closed with the brokerage firm that handled the initial transaction. Stocks and bonds may, in contrast, use different brokerage firms to buy and sell. Table 19.1 summarizes these differences.

TABLE 19.1   Differences Between Commodities and Stocks

Commodities	Stocks
Limited term	Unlimited term
Maximum daily price moves	No limit on daily price moves
Delivery possible	Never becomes spot
Margins of 5% to 15%	Margins of 50% or more
Long interest equal to short interest	Short interest usually only a small fraction of long interest
No short restrictions	Short sales not permitted on a downtick
No interest charged on unpaid margin	Interest incurred by margin debt
No specialist system	Market making by specialists
Commission discounts on special types of trades	No commission discounts for special trades
Requirement that positions be opened and closed with same brokerage firm	No restriction on opening and closing positions with different firms

Commodity Quotations

Commodity quotations are no more difficult to read than those for stocks and bonds. Figure 19.1 is taken from *The New York Times* and is similar to the format used in *The Wall Street Journal* and a number of other newspapers. Each commodity's heading contains a brief description of the terms of the contract. For example, the first contract listed reads: corn (CBT)—5000 bu.; cents per bu. In order of appearance the heading contains the name of the product on which the contract is written (corn); an abbreviation of the listing exchange (Chicago Board of Trade); the size of a single contract (5,000 bushels); and pricing units (cents per bushel). The individual quotation lists the months in which contracts become due

FIGURE 19.1 Commodity Quotation from *The New York Times*, January 22, 1988

Commodity and Financial Futures

	Friday	Week Ago	Year Ago
WEEK ENDED FRIDAY, JAN. 22, 1988	**238.38**	**236.56**	**212.76**
COMMODITY RESEARCH BUREAU INDEX			

LUMBER (CME)
130,000 bd. ft.; $ per 1,000 bd.ft.

—Season— High Low	High	Low	Close	Chg.	Open Interest
192.90 156.00 Mar	183.80 178.00 180.50			—3.40	3,423
188.30 164.50 May	182.40 177.60 180.10			—1.60	1,554
184.70 165.20 Jul	180.00 177.00 179.20			—.20	737
181.50 164.80 Sep	178.70 176.00 178.30			—.50	376
177.00 161.00 Nov	176.80 173.30 175.00			—.30	68
177.00 160.00 Jan	177.00 173.00 173.50			+.20	16

Fri. to Thurs. sales 6,872.
Total open interest 6,179.

FOODS

COCOA (NYCSCE) 10 tons; $ per ton

—Season— High Low	High	Low	Close	Chg.	Open Interest
2180 1727 Mar	1950 1896 1922			+39	9,474
2160 1750 May	1979 1923 1948			+39	5,518
2200 1786 Jul	2009 1951 1978			+44	3,928
2223 1817 Sep	2029 1974 2000			+39	3,667
2197 1864 Dec	2054 2010 2033			+36	3,582
2088 1883 Mar	2088 2038 2065			+37	1,967
2088 2040 May	2088 2068 2086			+31	364

Fri. to Thurs. sales 21,047.
Total open interest 28,500.

COFFEE (NYCSCE) 37,500 lb. ¢ per lb.

High Low	High	Low	Close	Chg.	Open Interest
178.00 105.00 Mar	131.35 127.55 130.41			+2.75	11,544
150.00 107.00 May	133.80 130.40 132.93			+2.37	5,920
136.10 109.50 Jul	135.95 132.90 135.15			+2.32	2,723
137.85 111.01 Sep	137.85 135.00 137.50			+2.50	1,518
140.50 114.00 Dec	140.50 138.00 140.25			+2.50	601
139.00 131.50 Mar	.... 141.50			+.37	40
139.75 139.75 May	.... 142.00			+1.00	2

Fri. to Thurs. sales 18,522.
Total open interest 11,297.

ORANGE JUICE (NYCTN, CA) 15,000 lb.; ¢ per lb.

High Low	High	Low	Close	Chg.	Open Interest
177.00 119.00 Mar	177.00 168.10 168.65			—6.20	5,015
176.70 119.40 May	176.20 169.50 169.50			—6.00	3,799
178.25 124.00 Jul	176.00 169.20 169.20			—6.20	1,504
177.00 125.50 Sep	173.25 166.50 166.50			—6.50	705
172.75 132.00 Nov	172.50 167.25 165.90			—5.30	327
171.25 132.20 Jan	167.00 165.25 163.10			—5.00	195
164.00 139.50 Mar	.... 161.90			—5.00	28
164.00 139.50 May	.... 161.90			—5.00	....

Fri. to Thurs. sales 7,027.
Total open interest 11,297.

SUGAR, Domestic (NYCSCE) 112,000 lb.; ¢ per lb.

High Low	High	Low	Close	Chg.	Open Interest
21.88 21.30 Mar	21.88 21.73 21.86			+.13	2,141
21.89 20.70 May	21.89 21.78 21.87			+.10	1,495
.... May	.... 21.80			—.03	....
.... May	.... 21.80			—.03	....

Fri. to Thurs. sales 1,305.
Total open interest 8,092

SUGAR, World (NYCSCE) 112,000 lb.; ¢ per lb.

High Low	High	Low	Close	Chg.	Open Interest
10.42 6.39 Mar	10.42 9.43 10.40			+.85	66,763
10.34 6.60 May	10.34 9.34 10.27			+.87	33,542
10.23 6.79 Jul	10.23 9.27 10.20			+.81	11,708
10.23 7.00 Oct	10.23 9.20 10.23			+.93	31,491
.... Jan	.... 10.17			+.82	....
10.23 7.99 Mar	10.23 9.33 10.23			+.78	11,323
10.00 8.28 May	10.00 9.60 10.17			+.71	73

Fri. to Thurs. sales 154,233.
Total open interest 154,900.

GOLD (COMEX) 100 troy oz.; $ per troy oz.

—Season— High Low	High	Low	Close	Chg.	Open Interest
486.80 459.00 Jan	477.00 477.00 477.50			+3.90	1
510.50 371.50 Feb	479.00 475.00 477.80			+3.30	40,515
488.80 477.00 Mar	482.50 477.00 480.20			+3.20	4
514.00 378.00 Apr	484.70 480.50 483.40			+3.10	39,765
523.00 399.00 Jun	490.30 486.60 488.80			+2.90	12,600
527.00 425.00 Aug	496.00 492.50 494.40			+2.60	9,169
533.50 429.00 Oct	500.80 499.00 500.20			+2.20	9,350
546.00 430.80 Dec	508.00 504.00 506.00			+1.80	10,983
549.50 480.00 Feb	513.50 511.00 512.20			+1.50	4,944
550.00 501.00 Apr	522.00 516.50 518.60			+1.20	5,940
570.00 515.00 Jun	528.80 526.00 525.20			+1.00	6,678
575.00 522.00 Aug	534.00 533.00 532.20			+.70	2,357
575.50 539.00 Oct	541.00 539.00 539.40			+.40	1,559

Fri. to Thurs. sales 193,164.
Total open interest 143,865.

SILVER (COMEX) 5,000 troy oz.; ¢ per troy oz.

High Low	High	Low	Close	Chg.	Open Interest
990.0 553.0 Jan	673.0 670.0 677.8			+17.8	5
700.0 650.0 Feb	.... 679.4			+17.0	5
1030.1 530.0 Mar	689.5 667.0 683.0			+17.0	35,358
1041.4 567.0 May	699.0 675.5 692.0			+16.6	15,362
1053.0 580.0 Jul	706.0 685.0 700.8			+16.4	11,179
1064.7 588.0 Sep	706.0 698.0 709.4			+16.4	6,650
1082.9 606.0 Dec	728.0 709.0 723.3			+15.8	5,479
1088.9 711.0 Jan	.... 727.5			+15.6	5
1073.0 658.0 Mar	730.0 730.0 737.7			+15.6	1,311
965.0 725.0 May	.... 747.7			+15.7	344
985.0 715.0 Jul	755.0 751.0 758.5			+15.7	339
820.0 749.0 Sep	767.0 760.0 769.4			+15.9	36

Fri. to Thurs. sales 57,763.
Total open interest 76,073.

SILVER (CBT) 1,000 troy oz.; ¢ per troy oz.

High Low	High	Low	Close	Chg.	Open Interest
720.0 640.0 Jan	680.0 660.0 675.0			+16.0	2
1003.0 569.5 Feb	683.0 663.0 678.0			+16.5	1,405
715.0 665.0 Mar	678.0 665.0 683.0			+16.0	13
1015.0 576.0 Apr	695.0 671.0 698.5			+16.0	4,963
1030.0 600.0 Jun	704.0 683.0 708.0			+16.0	3,348
1040.0 655.0 Aug	715.0 705.0 718.0			+16.0	196
937.0 677.5 Oct	715.0 705.0 718.0			+16.0	41
945.0 680.0 Dec	735.0 713.0 728.0			+16.0	1,023
775.0 710.0 Feb	735.0 724.0 738.0			+16.0	39

Fri. to Thurs. sales 4,596.
Total open interest 11,030.

PALLADIUM (NYM) 100 troy oz.; $ per troy oz.

High Low	High	Low	Close	Chg.	Open Interest
129.00 123.50 Jan	123.50 123.50 123.90			....	....
160.50 103.65 Mar	125.75 120.00 123.80			+.75	3,626
160.50 103.65 Jun	125.00 120.50 124.30			+.50	1,690
142.25 103.65 Sep	123.70 120.00 123.80			+.50	447
139.50 104.50 Dec	.... 123.55			+.50	268

Fri. to Thurs. sales 2,752.
Total open interest 6,031.

PLATINUM (NYM) 50 troy oz.; $ per troy oz.

High Low	High	Low	Close	Chg.	Open Interest
666.00 474.00 Jan	494.00 484.00 491.80			+9.10	209
670.80 484.30 Apr	504.00 489.00 497.40			+7.40	12,644
677.30 492.00 Jul	509.50 498.00 504.70			+7.20	3,410
667.50 500.00 Oct	515.50 506.00 512.20			+6.70	905
646.00 516.00 Jan	522.50 516.00 520.20			+6.70	89
528.00 528.00 Apr	528.00 528.00 528.20			—19.30	1

Fri. to Thurs. sales 22,266.
Total open interest 17,258.

U.S. TREASURY BILLS (IMM) $1 million; pts. of 100%

—Season— High Low	High	Low	Close	Chg.	Open Interest
94.63 91.45 Mar	94.18 93.91 94.13			+.12	17,619
94.40 91.28 Jun	93.91 93.67 93.87			+.11	2,783
94.21 91.15 Sep	93.65 93.42 93.63			+.17	611
94.09 91.17 Dec	93.38 93.13 93.34			+.18	122
93.16 91.26 Mar	93.16 92.93 93.11			+.18	79
92.75 92.12 Jun	92.75 92.67 92.93			+.22	5

Fri. to Thurs. sales 31,492.
Total open interest 21,219.

U.S. TREASURY BONDS (CBT) 8%-$100,000 prin.; pts. and 32d's of 100%

High Low	High	Low	Close	Chg.	Open Interest
100-26 67 Mar	91-24 89-31 91-18			+1-2	250,462
99-23 66-25 Jun	90-26 89-2 90-20			+1-2	36,957
99-12 74-20 Sep	89-30 88-8 89-25			+1-2	7,475
99-2 74-1 Dec	89-2 87-13 89			+1-2	3,242
95-10 73-20 Mar	88-10 86-25 88-9			+1-2	3,180
94-4 73-11 Jun	87-20 86-4 87-20			+1-2	391
93-16 72-26 Sep	87 85-16 87			+1-2	397
92-22 72-18 Dec	86-17 84-27 86-13			+1-2	360
87-9 72-1 Mar	85-28 85-28 85-26			+1-2	50
83-1 75 Jun	 85-8			+1-2	32
81-5 81-1 Sep	 84-23			+1-2	....

Fri. to Thurs. sales 1,364,860.
Total open interest 294,307.

10-YEAR U.S. TREASURY NOTES (CBT) $100,000; pts and 32d's of 100%

High Low	High	Low	Close	Chg.	Open Interest
96-19 84-10 Mar	96-19 95-4 96-13			+31	67,034
95-24 83-30 Jun	95-24 94-16 95-21			+30	10,551
94-5 89-13 Sep	94-3 93-23 94-30			+29	6

Fri. to Thurs. sales 94,685.
Total open interest 77,591.

MUNI BOND INDEX (CBT) 1000x index, pts & 32nds of 100%

High Low	High	Low	Close	Chg.	Open Interest
89-6 71-12 Mar	89-6 88-23			+1-9	11,092
87-10 70-3 Jun	87-10 85-10 87			+1-9	493
85-25 81-2 Sep	85-25 84-4 85-18			+1-9	65

Last index 90-20, up 54.
Fri. to Thurs. sales 29,304.
Total open interest 11,650.

BRITISH POUND (IMM) 25,000 pounds; $ per pound

High Low	High	Low	Close	Chg.	Open Interest
1.8845 1.5360 Mar	1.7950 1.7635 1.7820			+140	28,096
1.8775 1.5320 Jun	1.7850 1.7565 1.7745			+145	2,271
1.8580 1.7400 Sep	1.7720 1.7500 1.7682			+152	22
1.8440 1.7400 Dec	1.7680 1.7580 1.7634			+152	2

Last spot 1.7878, up 128.
Fri. to Thurs. sales 54,933.
Total open interest 30,391.

Investments in Perspective

One interesting possibility for a career would be as a trader in the commodities pits. Not surprisingly, such a career offers substantial risks coupled with the possibility of substantial rewards. The following *Forbes* article discusses some of the pros and cons.

Careers

It takes the nerves of a burglar, the discipline of a Marine, lungs of leather and the grit of a linebacker. It also helps if you're smart. The rewards? Big money, fast. The risks? Big losses, fast.

Life in the pits

By Janet Bamford

TRADING COMMODITIES is not a job for the delicate of mind or body. It is a business where big shoulders come in handy, literally—people regularly get knocked off their feet and sustain scratches, bruises, black eyes and broken bones.

The mental strain is even greater. Traders spend several hours a day shouting across the sunken trading pits. Hearing something wrong can cost a fortune; misjudging the direction of a market can do the same thing.

Small wonder that trading in the pits has always been a game for men and women in their 20s and 30s. These days it is a bigger game than ever. Not only is commodities trading volume way up, but there are a whole host of new exchanges and new vehicles to trade.

Ten years ago the Chicago Board of Trade had 1,400 members trading on the floor. Today it has about 3,300. The Commodity Futures Trading Commission, which registers floor brokers, or those who execute trading orders for customers, reports that in 1980 there were about 4,000 traders registered on all regulated exchanges. There are now 6,400.

Where do they come from? New traders and brokers are made, not born, generally rising from the ranks of clerks and runners. These entry-level jobs aren't particularly lucrative; runners make perhaps $100 or $150 a week. Clerks can make anywhere from $15,000 to $35,000 annually.

But both jobs offer an education in how the markets work. "It used to be that our traders came from clerks who came here just looking for a job and decided that they wanted to make this a career," says Barry Lind, a 24-year veteran of the Chicago Mercantile Exchange trading floor and founder of Lind-Waldock & Co., a discount commodities trading firm.

But nowadays the locals who stumble into an exchange just looking to stay ahead of the rent have lots of competition. "Today, a lot of clerks have planned on coming here, and they are graduates of Ivy League schools," says Lind. "Right now the person who takes my orders has a master's from the University of Chicago, and the previous person graduated from Princeton. It used to be, I would get a guy who graduated from high school and maybe flunked out of college."

The chief lure of the pits has always been the potential to make a great deal of money in a hurry. Both brokers, who execute customer trades in the pits, and traders, who trade for their own ac-count, commonly make $100,000 a year and up. Way up. Stories of high rollers earning a half million or a million dollars in a matter of months aren't unusual.

Besides the money, many young people like the autonomy. "You're only responsible for yourself," says Penelope Miller, a former social worker who has traded in the cattle pits at the Chicago Mercantile Exchange for the last seven years. "If you make a mistake it's yours, and if you do something right it's yours." Traders are affiliated with a clearinghouse but are not usually employed by the house; even brokers who are enjoy a degree of independence unheard of in most corporations.

The risks are also staggering. Traders can see $50,000 of gains evaporate in a day if they guess the market wrong. Brokers, who get paid anywhere from $1.25 or $1.50 to $2 for each trade, are also responsible for mistakes. In a day of heavy volume when trading reaches a fever pitch, errors can get expensive. John Oberman, who trades the S&P's 500 contract at the Chicago Mercantile Exchange, remembers his most expensive outtrade, as such mistakes are called. "We were supposed to have bought 250 contracts and we only bought 15. The market had rallied and we had to cover the mistake. It cost me well into six digits, and that night I called my father, had him come to Chicago, and I moved some assets from one bank to another in his name. I knew if that happened a second day, I was broke, and I thought, 'They'll never get that last little bastion of savings.'"

Many traders spend about a decade on the floor, then graduate to trading out of an office instead of in the pits. "Ten years is a goodly amount of time to trade," says Lind, "and a lot of people become successful and lose some of their hunger. Second, they can't take the grind of being on the floor. So they keep their memberships and go upstairs to the offices and trade from there, calling in orders."

The turnover is pretty brisk. Not every seat sold represents a trader leaving the pits. But last year about 500 seats changed hands at the 3,300-member Chicago Board of Trade. Another 300 were sold on the 2,700-member Mercantile Exchange.

"It's a revolving door," says William Hagerty, a 56-year-old grain trader who has been at the Chicago Board of Trade for 35 years. "If you want to stay, you have to treat it as a business," he says. "It's not a game."

Lee Stern, who is something of a Pete Rose in the trading pits with some 39 years' experience, notes that many of the young traders today are looking for the quick hit and can get burned badly. "You can't overtrade," he says. "Some young traders see the so-called legends trading big and they decide they should, too."

"You have to understand that a lot of trading goes against natural emotion," says Barry Lind. "The primary rule is, if it's going your way stay with it and if it's going against you get the hell out. That's the absolute opposite of a normal reaction."

Two of Stern's sons work in his business with him and have their own memberships at the Chicago Board of Trade. "I try not to have big swings in my trading," says Jeffrey Stern, a 34-year-old University of Michigan M.B.A. who trades financial instruments. "I trade small, maybe ten contracts at a time, because I'm just not comfortable with bigger trades. I've grown up with the markets and have seen what can happen."

Daniel Stern, 32, has been trading grains since he was a junior in college, and he's in the business for the long haul. "I like to make a little money each day rather than try to make a lot at one time. I'm not impressed with someone who has made a million dollars in six months, because if the guy is a screwball he'll lose the million, and he'll probably be out of business before I will."

Would-be traders, after paying their dues as runners and clerks, have to buy or lease a seat on an exchange. Seats in any of the major exchanges don't come cheap. However, several exchanges offer limited memberships at lower costs that permit the holder to trade a few specific contracts. Recently at the Chicago Mercantile Exchange a full seat cost $177,000, while an International Monetary Market seat, which entitles the holder to trade currency and interest rate futures, went for $150,000. A seat on the Index & Options Market traded for $59,000. At the Chicago Board of Trade, in years past full seats have sold for as much as $340,000, but the going rate now is about $220,000. Its limited memberships go for anywhere from $12,000 to $68,000.

At New York's Coffee, Sugar & Cocoa Exchange a full seat costs about $42,000 while an associate seat costs around $8,500.

Leased seats also offer a chance to try trading without making a large capital investment. For instance, an associate seat can be leased at the Chicago Board of Trade that would entitle a trader to work in the bond pit for $500 a month. The Chicago Mercantile Exchange has a similar program. In each case, the exchange requires a trader to keep a minimum balance in his trading account (from $25,000 to $50,000, depending on the exchange) and to be further guaranteed by an exchange member. The precautions are taken lest a beginning trader take a spectacular fall and walk away from his losses.

Many firms will sponsor clerks for membership and help them finance their seats. To start trading for one's own account, traders recommend a beginner have at least $20,000 to $25,000 to cushion the inevitably rough first year or so.

"It's an insecure life," says Penny Miller. "Last year was tough and next year may be, but nothing is secure anyway. Look how many middle managers in big business get canned at age 55. I wouldn't give it up for the world." ■

Source: J. Bamford, "Life in the Pits," *Forbes*, January 27, 1986, pp. 98–99. Reprinted by permission, © Forbes Inc., 1986.

followed by high, low, and settlement prices for that day, along with the change from the previous day's settlement. The remaining columns contain the contract's lifetime highs and lows. Total daily volume and the number of outstanding contracts (open interest) is also included under the price quotation. The format used by The Wall Street Journal is similar but also includes the daily opening price and open interest per contract.

The coffee quotations in Figure 19.1 will serve to illustrate how to read a commodity quotation. Coffee is traded on the Coffee, Cocoa, and Sugar Exchange (CCSE) and a single contract is for 37,500 pounds. Its price is quoted in cents per pound. Contracts expire five times a year in March, May, July, September, and December, with contracts listed for trading up to about 16 months into the future. On January 22, 1988, the March 1988 contract reached a high of 131.35, a low of 127.55, and closed at 130.41. This represented a change of 2.75 from the previous close. This contract has traded as high as 178.00 and as low as 105.00.

THE DIFFERENT TYPES OF COMMODITY TRADERS

A substantial fraction of those who trade commodities are one or another type of professional. For example, large firms in commodity-related industries (mining, baking, meat packing, grain, etc.) often maintain representatives on the relevant exchanges. These particular professionals seek to provide a future supply or market for their company's product. They make it their business to have access to and a detailed understanding of the latest set of information relevant to their particular commodities. For example, they may be following the latest information on crop estimates, cost comparisons, weather reports, information on possible government policy changes, trade figures and the international economy, and a host of other useful data. Access to all of the relevant and available knowledge tends to give such professionals a decided advantage over less-informed traders.

Several additional classes of professional commodity traders bear mentioning. They include scalpers, day traders, position traders, and arbitragers. Like stock exchange floor traders and specialists, these traders usually have seats on the exchange and trade for their own accounts. Scalpers seek to buy at slightly below or sell at slightly above the previous price. They hope to close out their positions within a short time at a modest profit. Scalpers do not plan to maintain their positions for long; an hour is a relatively long time. They are not required or expected to make a market but the scalpers' activity does help keep trading more

TABLE 19.2 Types of Professional Futures Market Traders

Firm Representatives	Hedge needs or outputs of commodity-related firms
Scalpers	Seek to take advantage of very short-run imbalances in supply and demand
Day Traders	Short-run traders who close their positions each day
Position Traders	May hold positions for several days based on fundamental or technical factors
Arbitragers	Seek to exploit departures from expected relative price relationships

orderly. They provide buying or selling interest even when relatively few other traders are available.

Day traders usually close their positions by the end of each day. They trade somewhat less frequently than scalpers but also hope to profit from modest price moves. Unlike scalpers and day traders, position traders seek to profit from fundamental or technical forces that may manifest themselves over several days. Finally, arbitragers try to exploit relative prices that vary from expected relationships. Table 19.2 summarizes these various types.

Disadvantages of Commodity Trading for Amateurs

Professional traders have better access to relevant information, lower cost trading, and/or quicker executions than the vast majority of amateurs. Most small, inexperienced investors should be discouraged by this state of affairs. No one wants to compete in a market in which he or she incurs a significant disadvantage relative to a large part of the market's participants. Moreover, the number of listed commodities is much smaller than the number of actively traded stocks. Thus, each commodity receives proportionately more attention. Presumably such attention leads to relatively well-informed pricing, thereby increasing the difficulty of finding misvalued contracts.

In addition, unlike the securities market, each specific futures contract (such as July wheat) has equal numbers of short and long contracts. If the price declines, the shorts gain what the longs lose, and vice versa. If the professionals make money on balance, the amateurs must lose. Furthermore, both losers and winners must pay commissions. One very out-of-date study of grain trading over the 1924–1932 period sponsored by the Commodity Exchange Authority (CEA) suggested that professionals outperformed the rest of the market.[1]

Hedge Trading Results

One of the interesting questions relating to the futures markets is, Who on balance makes and who loses money? In particular, many people have wondered whether those who hedge generally have to pay for the risk reduction that they obtain.

Hedging is akin to purchasing insurance. Thus those who facilitate hedge trading (speculators) might well be expected to earn a risk premium. Testing this proposition requires identifying those who are seeking to hedge and separating them from those who are speculating. Discriminating between risk takers and hedgers from aggregated data is relatively difficult, however. Dusak hypothesized that most hedgers are short and most speculators are long. Relying on this assumption, she found overall returns of long hedgers in wheat, corn, and soybeans to be very close to zero.[2] She also found these returns to be largely uncorrelated with other investment returns. These results suggest that at least for the three commodities and the time period (1952–1967) tested, returns from long positions were small. The contracts did, however, appear to offer substantial diversifying value. Rockwell's earlier and considerably broader study of 25 markets over an 18-year period reached the following conclusions:[3]

1. Small traders lost slightly more on short positions than they made on long positions.

2. Large speculators profited at the expense of hedgers; the greatest profits were made in large active markets.

3. Hedgers tended to do well in low-volume markets; the profits of large speculators in high-volume markets come mainly from the small speculator.

Thus professionals may well profit at the expense of small traders, and speculators do not seem to receive a risk premium for their risk taking. More recent studies do, however, find evidence of rewards (profits to risk takers) for speculators.[4]

LARGE TRADES AND BIG TRADERS

We have already seen some of the problems faced by small investors. In addition to the difficulties mentioned, large traders can disrupt the markets. These disruptions may well hurt many small speculators. To be on the same side and helped is of course equally possible. Moreover, commodity markets are only infrequently dominated by any single trader or small group of traders. Still large traders pose very real risks for those who would trade commodities.

The Russian Wheat Deal.   The best-known and most massive of the disruptive large trades involved the Russians. In the early 1970s poor weather and an unsuccessful harvest created a major Soviet grain shortage. Apparently unaware of the severity of their problem, the Nixon administration gave the Soviets permission to purchase massive quantities of U.S. wheat and corn. The Russians negotiated shrewdly, separately, and secretly with several of the nation's largest grain dealers. Each dealer, thinking it was the primary Soviet agent, hedged its Russian orders with futures contracts. Their strategy allowed the Soviets to accumulate their entire needs before the price ran up very much.

The massive Russian purchases not only wiped out our long-held grain surpluses but, once their full dimensions were known, threatened to create a severe wheat shortage. Bread prices did not (at that time) reach the feared dollar-a-loaf level but the wheat price did trade in a range not seen before or since. Those who were short wheat while this trade unfolded were substantial losers.

The Russian wheat deal is now ancient history. Rumors of a new buying spree by the Russians, Arabs, or perhaps the Chinese still sweep the exchange floors from time to time, however. A super large trader is needed to have much impact on the grain markets. In other markets smaller but still large traders can also have an impact. The great potato scandal of 1976 involved just such a market.

The Great Potato Default.   While most potatoes are grown in Idaho and nearby states, futures trading has largely been in Maine potato delivery contracts. Since the two types of potatoes compete for the same markets, the New York Mercantile Exchange's Maine potato contract should provide an acceptable vehicle for hedging either type. Most Maine potatoes are grown by relatively small individually motivated farmers. Idaho's, in contrast, are dominated by potato baron J.R. Simplot.

In the mid-1970s Simplot and Taggares (another large factor in the Western potato market) thought that the abundant supply of Idahos would cause the Maine potato price to fall by the time the May 1976 futures contracts became deliverable. Simplot and Taggares ultimately undertook an obligation to deliver 50 million pounds of Maine potatoes. In a competitive market, their abundant stocks of Idahos should have depressed the futures price sufficiently to allow them to close their positions profitably prior to delivery.

They had not, however, counted on the short squeeze that soon ensued. Some of the longs, knowing of the large open interest (numbers of outstanding contracts) in near-delivery contracts, tied up most of the supply of Maine potatoes. By purchasing some potatoes for cash and stranding other stockpiles by renting the available boxcars, these longs prevented Simplot and Taggares from delivering enough potatoes to satisfy their short positions. These longs hoped to force the shorts to bid up the price. Rather than be bullied, Simplot and Taggares chose to default. The shorts were sued for not fulfilling their contracts. The longs were charged with attempting to corner the market. The exchange and the defaulting customers' brokers were each accused of improper surveillance. The Commodity Futures Trading Commission (CFTC) investigated and complained but was itself criticized for allowing the default to develop. The courts took years to sort this matter out. When all was said and done no one emerged a winner.

The Hunts: Silver I.   Simplot and Taggares are big men in Idahos, but they were small potatoes compared to the Hunts (at least before the Hunts' fall). H.L. Hunt, the father of a rather large clan, made quite a lot of money in oil and various other ventures. He supported a number of right-of-center causes and his son Lamar had a major role in establishing the American Football League. Since H.L. Hunt died some years ago, his family, particularly his older sons, have carried on in the best (and worst) Dallas wheeler-dealer tradition. Their substantial resources gave the Hunts an apparent advantage in commodity trading. Among their hobbies were commodities beginning with the letter *S*.

The Hunts began with silver futures. Convinced that the metal was underpriced, Nelson Bunker Hunt and his brothers Herbert and Lamar purchased millions of ounces of futures contracts, which bid up the price. Rumors of large unknown silver buyers propelled the price to still higher levels. Once the shorts compared the number of Hunt-held silver contracts with the amount of qualified physical silver available, they became very nervous. While silver was plentiful, relatively little of the metal was refined to the proper purity, inspected, and deposited in the appropriate warehouses.

The Hunts liquidated their positions by selling some of their contracts at the higher prices then obtaining. They took delivery on some contracts and rolled others forward by selling near-delivery futures and replacing them with more distant-delivery contracts. They made a killing in their first silver venture (but not the second time around, as we shall soon see).

The Hunts: Sugar. After their silver coup the Hunt brothers seemed to stumble onto sugar. A stockbroker friend put them into a small ($1 million) investment in Great Western United (the nation's largest beet sugar refiner) at just about the time sugar futures were moving from under 10 per pound to over 60. Finding the company in a state of disarray, the Hunts had no choice but to buy everyone else out. They next acquired a cane sugar refining capability and negotiated agreements with cane sugar producing countries to swap silver for unrefined cane.

After a big court battle Great Western United acquired a large interest in the Sunshine Mining Company, a major silver producer. Later they recapitalized Great Western United, renamed it Hunt International Resources, and sold its interest in Sunshine Mining for a handsome profit. Some years later, after experiencing a number of reverses, Hunt International Resources was forced to declare bankruptcy.

The Hunts: Soybeans. With silver, sugar and Sunshine Mining already tapped, what commodity is left but soybeans? When their experts predicted a protein shortage (beans are very high in protein), they began their purchases. No unhedged trader or group of traders is permitted to hold more than three million bushels of bean contracts. The Hunts argued that each family member could buy contracts on three million bushels, however. Eventually the family owned contracts on 24 million bushels.

The Hunt contracts amounted to a substantial fraction of the amount left until the next harvest (the carryout). Thus they were positioned to create an artificial shortage. Taking a dim view of this prospect, the CFTC tried to force the Hunts to sell. Claiming that each Hunt acted individually, family members refused to unload. The CFTC revealed the Hunts' trading positions, thereby increasing bean price volatility. The Hunts and CFTC each brought separate suits alleging the other attempted to manipulate prices. While different levels of courts issued various opinions, the matter was left at a draw. The Hunts were told not to do it again but were assessed no penalties. Apparently the Hunts left the bean pits a bit richer than when they entered.

While the Hunts were sure that beans would rise, senior traders at Cook Industries (until then a major commodity trading firm) were equally certain that beans were overpriced. Trading largely against the Hunts, Cook Industries assumed a substantial short position in beans. Losses resulting from persistent high prices eventually forced the firm to liquidate much of its assets. Ironically, soon after Cook covered its short positions, bean prices dropped below the level at which the Hunts began their buying. The Hunts, who were wrong on price direction but right on timing, made money. Cook was right on price direction but wrong on timing and thus lost its shirt.

The Hunts: Silver II.   The latest and most publicized of the Hunts' commodity deals involved a second round with silver. Believing that the sky was the limit they bought large quantities of silver futures contracts in 1979 and into 1980. A group of Arab investors were brought into the Hunts' deal. As prices went up they used the group's paper profits to support additional purchases. Silver ultimately rose from around $8 per ounce to over $50 causing many individuals to sell their silverware for its bullion content. This time the Hunts overreached themselves.

Eventually both the CFTC and the commodity exchanges became alarmed. Very high margin percentages were established for silver and the Hunts were ordered to begin liquidating their positions. The subsequent silver price decline coupled with the illiquidity of the vast majority of the Hunts' assets made their situation precarious. The entire financial market briefly panicked on the rumor that the Hunt empire was about to collapse. Soon, however, a $1 billion bank loan was arranged. The loan was collateralized by Hunt-owned Placid Oil. The Hunts agreed not to speculate in commodities for 10 years and were expected to begin selling their still substantial silver holdings. They eventually did so but not before silver fell as low as $5 per ounce. This deal caused Bunker (whose losses seemed astronomical) to quip that "a billion dollars just doesn't go as far as it used to."

The possibility of events such as these enhances the risk of commodity trading. Those who sleep with elephants, even very nice elephants, are bound to get squashed from time to time. The risks are equally great for those who trade in elephant pits.

TECHNICAL ANALYSIS APPLIED TO COMMODITIES

Chart reading is, if anything, more prevalent in commodity trading than it is for stocks. The short-term nature of futures contracts, coupled with the great difficulty of successfully applying fundamental analysis, encourages traders to seek out other approaches. Indeed, some have gone so far as to program computers to perform technical analysis. Others have sought to make their fortune by teaching technical analysis to potential commodity traders. As always, the buyer should beware.

The same a priori arguments against effective technical stock analysis apply to futures. If the charts provide useful signals, traders who act on the signals should affect their future usefulness. Even if nonrandom price movements are more common in commodities than securities markets, commissions and other trading costs may prevent their successful exploitation. Empirical work in the area is mixed. Some studies found dependencies while other work found none.[5]

FUNDAMENTAL ANALYSIS APPLIED TO COMMODITIES

Fundamental analysts evaluate changes in relevant underlying factors and equilibrium relationships. Such analysts may consider anything that affects the commodity's supply or demand including the weather, input costs, the price of related goods, the potential actions of national and international organizations, and the price relationships among different commodities.

The application of fundamental analysis to commodities trading has been illustrated by Harlow and Teweles. They attempted to predict soybean prices by

FIGURE 19.2 Soybean Supply and Demand

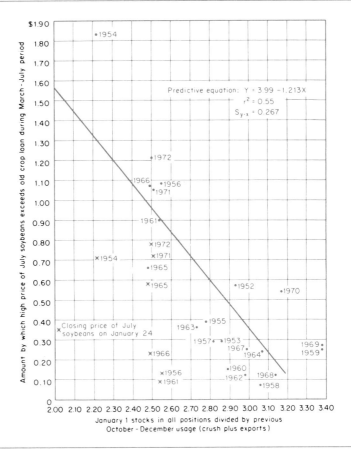

Source: R. Teweles, C. Harlow, and H. Stone, *The Commodities Futures Game*. Reprinted by permission, © 1974, McGraw-Hill, Inc.

analyzing the relevant supply and demand.[6] Exported and crushed soybeans were used as a measure of demand. Stocks in position were used to reflect supply. The ratio of estimated supply to estimated demand is taken as the explanatory variable, x. The difference between the market price and the previous government-guaranteed price is the variable to be explained, y. The relationship between these two variables is estimated by regression analysis (Figure 19.2).

Harlow and Teweles calculated the possible gains from using an x of less than 2.60 as a buy signal. Seven of the 22 years studied had x values below 2.60. January 24 was the first date on which enough information was available to make a decision. Long positions established on that date had at least a 95% chance of showing a profit. The model's profitability was tested with the same data that were used to form the relationship, however. A more convincing test using new data would be an interesting exercise for the reader.

Crop and Weather Forecasts

Agricultural products are the delivery instrument for many of the actively traded commodities including old-line contracts on corn, wheat, and beans as well as some of the newer commodities such as live cattle and pork bellies. Accordingly, a solid understanding of crops, crop forecasts, the weather, and weather forecasts may help in trading such commodities. While knowing what is generally known imparts no advantage, knowing less can be a substantial disadvantage. Only those who obtain the information early (unlikely and probably illegal) or who analyze it in a superior manner (quite difficult at best) are likely to use crop and weather forecasts profitably.

The Basis, Basis Risk, and the Carry

While the possibility of delivery keeps futures and spot prices reasonably close, the difference or basis is usually nonzero and can vary over time. For example on June 12, 1984, corn (No. 2 yellow deliverable in Chicago) traded in the spot market for $3.42½ per bushel. On the Chicago Board of Trade, July delivery contracts traded for $3.46¼ per bushel. Thus the futures contract traded at a 3¾ cents per bushel basis to the spot price.

The risk of an adverse relative price move is called basis risk. Suppose the trader is long spot corn and short a futures contract for July delivery at the prices just given. If basis narrows as delivery approaches, this hedged position will tend to generate a gain regardless of the overall direction of prices. The basis has moved in a favorable direction. For the other side of the contract the basis risk has been adverse.

The size of the basis tends to increase with the distance to delivery. The constellation of futures prices can, however, take on a number of different patterns. With agricultural commodities the pattern will vary with the current and expected future availability of the product vis-à-vis current stocks and expected future harvests. This variation largely reflects the cost of storage (the carry). In the example, spot corn sold for about 4 cents less than contracts calling for delivery a month later. On a $3.43 bushel this represents about 1.2% (14.4% per year), which is probably not too far away from one month's financing and storage cost (the carry). Since carrying a commodity in inventory has a cost, the price usually rises as the distance to deliver is increased. When supplies are short prior to a new harvest, however, the market is sometimes inverted. In such instances the price is lower for the (more distant) deliveries that occur after the next harvest.

Combination Trades

An appreciable portion of commodity trading involves the taking of (offsetting) combination positions on related futures contracts. Just as options are often *spread*, commodity contracts can be used in hedged positions. The spreader might, for example, expect the price of contracts of one delivery month to rise relative to those of another delivery month. He or she would take a long position on the contract that was thought to be relatively underpriced. Simultaneously a short position would be taken on the contract that was thought to be overpriced. A profit would be earned if the price of the long contract rose *relative to* the price of the short contract. Such spreads are designed to eliminate the risk associated with an adverse move in the constellation of prices for a particular physical or related group of physicals. The combination position will show a profit regardless of the *absolute* move in prices as long as the *relative* moves are in the expected direction. Spreads may also involve different exchanges trading futures contracts on similar physicals. For example, one might spread between Chicago and Kansas City wheat and indeed that of the Minneapolis Board of Trade as well.

Crushes and *reverse crushes* are relatively common types of combination trades. They generally utilize the markets for the soybean complex, which consists of futures and spot markets in soybeans, soybean oil, and soybean meal. Most of the soybean crop is processed into soybean oil and meal. A given quantity of beans can be crushed into a predictable quantity of oil and meal at a known cost in a relatively short period. Thus the price relationships between beans, oil, and meal are relatively predictable and well known. If the beans were sufficiently underpriced relative to the oil and meal, a bean trader could actually purchase the beans, have them crushed, and sell the resultant oil and meal for a profit.

In futures terminology, a crush is a trade in which the bean trader buys futures and shorts equivalent amounts of the derivative products. Market forces are expected (although not necessarily depended upon) to drive them back into line with the technological and physical relationships. While the oil and the meal cannot be turned back into beans, market forces should also operate to restore the historical equilibrium when the beans are overpriced relative to their derivative products. A reverse crush would be employed to take advantage of such mispricing.

A similar type of relationship exists for the petroleum complex. Crude oil, gasoline, and heating oil all now have futures contracts. A long crude, short gasoline and heating oil position is called a *crack*. A reverse crack takes opposite positions on the complex.

Combination trades sometimes involve even more distantly related commodities. Since corn and wheat can both be used as feed grains, the prices of the two commodities should influence each other. Why feed corn to cattle when wheat is cheaper (or so the reasoning goes)? Thus when the price of corn rises above the cost of wheat of equivalent food value, some traders will put on a long wheat, short corn spread.

Combination Trade Recommendations.   As an example, two combination trades (a reverse crush and a corn–wheat trade) recommended by Stanley Angrist, *Forbes'* commodity columnist, were examined.[7] The investor was assumed to have entered the trades shortly after the Angrist recommendation appeared in print and covered them near expiration. Angrist advised closing any position once its prices began to move adversely. The results that follow, however, assume that the investor stuck by the original recommendation through thick and thin (perhaps hoping against hope that all would eventually work out).

For the so-called "relatively riskless corn–wheat trade" the investor could have bought the wheat contract in the 2.65½ to 2.66 (per bushel) range. It would have been sold at 2.73½ for a gain of 7¾ cents per bushel. The corn contract would have been shorted at 2.49 to 2.48½ and covered at 2.55 to 2.54½ for a loss of 3½ cents per bushel. The combination traded would have netted a gain (ignoring commissions) of 4½ cents per bushel.

Those who undertook the reverse crush would have paid 141.00 and 18.44 for meal and oil and received 5.23 to 5.22 for beans. Covering would have been at 149.40, 19.95, and 5.56¾ to 5.57, producing a net loss of 24.39 per bushel (plus commissions). Thus the reverse crush would have involved per bushel losses of several times the gain on the "riskless trade." Again, we see that not all hedge trades produce the expected results. Clearly, commodity spreads are not guaranteed to make money.

Commodity Analysts

Fundamental commodity analysis is difficult to apply successfully, but perhaps those who are paid to advise commodity traders generally recommend worthwhile trades. To shed some light on this issue one of the present author's graduate students tested a series of Angrist recommendations. He found that anyone who followed these particular recommendations would have lost money.

After receiving a copy of the student's term paper, Angrist discussed his performance in his *Forbes* column. According to Angrist, about half of his recommendations over the period studied by the student were profitable but the total profits outweighed the losses.[8] He followed this up with further tests of his recommendations. For the last half of 1977 he reported that his recommended trades approximately broke even. Of course, the advice of many other commodity analysts may work out better (or worse) than Angrist's did for 1977. In 1979, for example, Angrist asserted that "traders who followed every recommendation had nothing to complain about as once again I caught hold of a couple of nice winners that more than made up for the dogs."[9] While Angrist still writes for *Forbes*, he has not (at this writing) written a report on his performance for some time.

Diversification with Commodities

Since commodity price volatility (relative to the margin deposit) seems to be largely unrelated to fluctuations in other markets,[10] futures might serve as a useful diversification vehicle. Such diversification is, however, likely to be accompanied by a major increase in nonmarket risk. Thus commodities are probably not an ideal vehicle for diversifying portfolios of other types of investments.

SPECIALIZED COMMODITY MARKETS

Commodity futures have long been traded on agricultural and mineral physicals. The new types of commodity contracts have accounted for much of the market's growth, however. In particular, interest rate, currency, and more recently stock market futures have grabbed the spotlight. While they are as yet still minor factors, commodity options and commodity mutual funds also have substantial potentials.

Finally, a variety of commodity-related investments deserve mentioning. Each of these matters will now be discussed.

Futures on Indexes and Cash Settlement

Traditionally futures contracts have specified delivery of some specific asset. While most contracts may have been closed out with offsetting trades, those few still in force at contract expiration resulted in the long taking and the short making delivery. This same practice continued to be followed with many on the newer financial contracts. For some contracts, however, the delivery instrument did not exist and would be relatively difficult, expensive, or inconvenient to establish. Specifically futures contracts on various market indexes present a potential problem with delivery. The solution was simple. Rather than settling by delivery of a physical asset, index contracts are settled with cash. That is, the buyer and seller determine the difference between the price when they instituted the trade and the index value at contract expiration. The loser pays the winner that difference. Such cash settlements are used with index futures based on stock, bond, and commodity indexes.

Interest Rate Futures

While money lending has gone on about as long as trading in such futures-related items as wheat and gold, no one gave much thought to a debt instruments futures market until the early 1970s. Many individuals and institutions do, however, have a stake in and/or opinion on the future level of interest rates. Just as similar circumstances have long fostered futures trading in other commodities, interest rate futures trading looked like a good bet.

Trading in financial futures began with the Chicago Board of Trade's GNMA futures contracts and the Chicago Mercantile Exchange's T-bill contract. The market subsequently expanded to include long-term Treasury bonds, one- and five-year Treasury notes, municipal bonds, CDs, and Eurodollars. Most of the recent trading has been in notes, bonds, and Eurodollars.

Like all futures contracts, interest rate futures call for delivery of a specific amount of the relevant commodity at the contract's expiration. For example, the Treasury bond contract specifies the delivery of $100,000 face amount of Treasuries priced to yield 8%. Price fluctuations in the contract reflect variations in the expected bond interest rate.

Institutions that plan to borrow at some later time can use interest futures to hedge against adverse interest rate moves. Similarly, financial institutions with future sums to invest may use the market to establish the rate that they will earn on the investment. Finally, those whose expectations differ from the market may speculate in interest rate futures. A number of researchers have explored the productive use of interest futures in hedging and managing interest rate risk.[11]

Interest Futures Examples.   Mortgage bankers can use the interest futures markets to hedge their expected mortgage production. Suppose that on June 1 a banker

TABLE 19.3   Hedging Expected Mortgage Loan Production

Cash Market	Futures Market
June 1	June 1
Commits to originate $10 million in loans based on current FNMA price of 99-24 (yield of 7.989%)	Sells 100 December contracts at prevailing market price of 99-00 (yield of 8.092%)
September 15	September 15
Sells $10 million of GNMA 8s to permanent investors at market of 92-24 (current yield 8.992%)	Buys 100 December contracts at prevailing market price of 92-00 (yield of 9.105%)
Loss: $700,000	Gain: $700,000

expects to originate $10 million in mortgage loans during the next quarter based on the FNMA market. Suppose that the market is at 99-24 (99 and 24/32), which corresponds to a 7.989% yield. To hedge the expected mortgage originations, the banker can sell 100 GNMA December contracts at 99-00 (a yield of 8.092%). One possible result (ignoring transaction costs) from the hedge is illustrated in Table 19.3. The mortgage banker's position was protected. The loss in the cash market caused by an interest rate rise was offset by a gain in the futures market. Had interest rates fallen, the loss in the futures market would largely have been offset by a gain in the cash market.

This example is of a short hedge. The mortgage banker's expected long mortgage position was offset by a sale of futures contracts. A long hedge, in contrast, allows the trader who expects to be short in the future to cover that anticipated need. As an example of a long hedge, consider a money manager who buys $5 million in three-month T-bills. At maturity the manager will need to reinvest the funds. To assure a rate on the funds' rollover he or she could buy December T-bill futures. One possible result from this hedge (again ignoring transaction costs) is illustrated in Table 19.4. As with the short hedge example, the future's market profit has offset the opportunity loss in the spot market. The new T-bill purchase will yield about $25,000 less than the earlier investment but the futures market profit has offset that (opportunity) loss. Had interest rates risen rather than fallen, the future's market loss would have been offset by a spot market gain.

Stock Market Futures

The successful introduction of debt instrument futures spurred interest in equity futures. The Kansas City Board of Trade's (KBT) Value Line stock market index futures contract was followed by the Chicago Mercantile Exchange's (Merc) S&P 500 index and the New York Futures Exchange's (NYFE) NYSE Composite Index. The Chicago Board of Trade's (CBT) effort to list a Dow Jones Industrial type of index was blocked by the opposition of Dow Jones Inc. Their Major Market Index of 20 stocks is, however, designed to track the Dow. Fifteen of its components are Dow stocks.

TABLE 19.4 Hedging for the Reinvestment of Maturing T-Bills

Cash Market		Futures Market	
September 15		September 15	
bought $5 million in T-bills @ 9%		Bought 5 Dec. contracts @ 9% (I.M.M. 91.00)	
Value	$4,886,250	Value	$4,887,500
December 10		December 10	
Sold over $5 million in T-bills @ 7%		Sold (offset) 5 Dec. contracts @ 7% (I.M.M. 93.00)	
Value	$4,911,528	Value	$4,912,500
loss of	$ 25,278	gain of	$ 25,000

The NYFE has also introduced two broad-based index futures: The Russell 2000 and the Russell 3000. The 3000 represents the 3,000 largest capitalization stocks. The 2000 index is for the 2000 smaller capitalization stocks within the group of 3000. Thus the Russell 2000 provides a vehicle for speculating or hedging in relatively small capitalization stocks. These equity contracts offer a variety of ways to speculate or hedge on the stock market's movement. In particular the contracts provide an ideal way for portfolio managers to hedge either their anticipated funds needs or their portfolio against anticipated market reversals.

A Stock Index Futures Example. Suppose a large common stock portfolio manager anticipates a market decline. To liquidate and then later reinvest the portfolio would be costly (spreads, commissions, etc.). The stock index futures market provides a relatively simple way to neutralize the portfolio from market moves. First, the manager would determine his or her portfolio's beta and then use the following formula to determine the number of contracts to short:

$$\frac{\text{Number of Contracts}}{\text{Needed for Hedge}} = \frac{\text{Portfolio Value}}{\text{Contract Value}} \times \text{Weighted Average Beta of Portfolio}$$

Consider a portfolio with a weighted average beta of 1.14 and market value of $20 million. The S&P futures contract value is 500 times the S&P index value.

$$\text{S\&P Futures Contract Value} = 500 \text{ (S\&P Index Value)}$$

In this instance we shall assume the S&P index is 350. Thus a single contract would be worth $175,000 (350 × 500). Accordingly:

$$\frac{\text{Number of Contracts}}{\text{Needed for Hedge}} = (20,000,000/175,000) \times 1.14 = 130$$

Thus selling 130 contracts should approximately neutralize the portfolio from market fluctuations. That is, the fluctuations in the value of 130 contracts should closely approximate those of a $20 million stock portfolio having an average beta of 1.14. If the portfolio's value declines, a short position in the S&P futures contracts should rise by an offsetting amount. Similarly, an increase in the portfolio's value should be offset by a fall in the value of the futures position.

Futures Options

A commodity, or futures, option is an option on a futures contract. As such it is an abstraction on an abstraction. The futures contract is itself a deferred delivery agreement that trades and has a life of its own. An option on such an agreement represents the right but not the obligation to take or make delivery on such a contract. Thus a call on a futures contract is a right to buy such a contract at a prespecified price over a prespecified period. Similarly, a put is an option to sell.

The mechanics of futures options are similar to those for puts and calls on stocks. If the underlying futures price rises sufficiently, the price of the commodity call will also rise. A decline in the futures price will, at worst, only cost the owner the purchase price of the call. The relations are similar for puts except that the holder profits from a price decline and incurs limited risk for an up move. Those who own (or are short) futures contracts outright incur a much greater loss liability. Thus commodity options offer upside leverage and downside protection. A rather hefty premium is required to induce option writers to assume the risks inherent in the contract's sell side.

Listed option trading was prohibited in the United States in the 1930s. Accordingly, traders had to seek a market outside the United States or trade in an over-the-counter market. In either case up-to-date price quotes were difficult to obtain and the market was relatively imperfect. Two major commodity option scandals occurred in the absence of an active U.S. exchange market.

Commodity Option Scams.   In the early 1970s the West Coast firm of Goldstein-Samuelson began selling over-the-counter commodity options. It offered the options at such attractive prices that customers were making a profit on a high percentage of their trades. The net balance in these customers' accounts with Goldstein-Samuelson grew very rapidly. Because the options were underpriced most "investors" made "profits" that encouraged them to purchase new options. In effect Goldstein-Samuelson was operating a Ponzi scheme. By the time the nature of the operation was exposed, losses exceeded $100,000,000.

The Goldstein-Samuelson scandal slowed commodity option trading for several years. Eventually, however, the industry revived by using the London options market. Most of the publicity centered around some very questionable selling tactics employed by fly-by-night commodity option firms. These new option sellers relied upon high-pressure telephone solicitations. They sold options at huge markups. Many relatively uninformed "investors" spent thousands of dollars on these overpriced options. The seller usually claimed to be hedged in the London market. Often, however, no offsetting position was undertaken. Thus many of these options were written naked. Such a strategy proved very profitable to the seller when most of the options expired worthless. When too many option positions showed a profit, the sellers usually disappeared.

Lloyd Carr, the largest of the new-wave commodity options houses, has an instructive history. Operating out of Boston, a man who gave his name as James Carr quickly established a thriving business. The firm maintained boiler rooms with huge banks of telephones. Salespeople were stimulated to ever higher sales by such devices as having their supervisor run down the aisles dressed in a Gorilla costume. Eventually several states began to investigate the numerous complaints. Then CBS's "60 Minutes" broadcast an expose on commodity options firms and Lloyd Carr in particular. Events moved quickly thereafter. Lloyd Carr was prohibited from doing business in several states. "Mr. Carr" was fingerprinted. The firm went bankrupt. "James Carr" was determined to be Alan Abraham, an escapee from a New Jersey prison. Mr. Abraham, who again became a fugitive, was ultimately apprehended in a Florida motel.

Goldstein-Samuelson and Lloyd Carr notwithstanding, the commodity option instrument itself has a legitimate role. Indeed, the commodity exchanges resumed listed commodity options trading in 1982. Currently futures options are listed on a number of agricultural, mineral, and especially financial assets. Both puts and calls are listed. Such trading and the increased flow of information that it generates may well reduce the abuses that have resulted from OTC commodity options trading. A number of pricing models similar to those for stocks have been developed and tested.[12] Figure 19.3 contains a typical futures option quotation.

The abstract nature of futures options makes their quotations somewhat more complex and difficult to interpret than most other types of quotations. Bear in mind that a futures option represents the right to buy or the right to sell a futures contract. Consider the quotation for corn futures options. The options themselves vary in delivery date and strike price. In the case of corn futures options, both puts and calls are listed for the March, May, and July futures contracts. Each of these expirations has options listed for strike prices ranging from 180 to 230.

As an example of how to interpret a futures option quotation, consider the March 200 call priced at 5. This option contract allows the investor to purchase a March futures contract to buy corn at 200 cents per bushel. The investor needs to distinguish the striking price from the price of the option. The strike of 200 refers to the price the owner of the futures contract would pay for corn. The closing price of the option was 5. Thus for 5 cents per bushel the investor could have purchased the right to acquire a March corn futures contract for 200 cents per bushel. An investor who purchased the option and then exercised it would in effect pay 205 (200 + 5) cents per bushel of corn. On the day of this quote the March corn futures contract itself closed for 199 cents per bushel. Thus this particular strike is slightly out of the money. As with options on stocks, commodity options will usually sell for at least their intrinsic values. Thus if the price of the March contract were to rise to 205 before expiration, an investor who paid 5 for the option would just about break even (ignoring trading costs). This buyer's option position would begin to show a profit as the March contract rose above 205.

Program Trading

The advent of stock index futures and options has facilitated the rise of a type of trading that generally utilizes the indexes: program (or programmed) trading. In a

FIGURE 19.3 Futures Options Quotation from *The Wall Street Journal*, January 20, 1988

FUTURES OPTIONS

Wednesday, January 20, 1988.

– AGRICULTURAL –

CORN (CBT) 5,000 bu.; cents per bu.

Strike	Calls—Settle			Puts—Settle		
Price	Mar-c	May-c	Jly-c	Mar-p	May-p	Jly-p
180	19¼	26	30½	¼	1½	2½
190	10¼	18½	23½	1¾	3¼	4¾
200	5	12¼	17½	5¾	7	8½
210	1¾	8	12½	12¾	13	13¼
220	½	5	9¾	....	19	19½
230	¼	3	7	....	....	....

Est. vol. 4,500, Tues vol. 2,832 calls, 1,343 puts
Open interest Tues 23,674 calls, 17,139 puts

SOYBEANS (CBT) 5,000 bu.; cents per bu.

Strike	Calls—Settle			Puts—Settle		
Price	Mar-c	May-c	Jly-c	Mar-p	May-p	Jly-p
575	51¾	63	74	¾	5	9
600	29½	44	56	4½	10½	15
625	14	30	42	14¾	22	225
650	6⅛	19	32	30	35	41
676	2⅝	14	24½	55	52	55
700	1	8	16	....	....	....

Est. vol. 4,500, Tues vol. 2,682 calls, 1,352 puts
Open interest Tues 40,314 calls, 21,349 puts

SOYBEAN MEAL (CBT) 100 tons; $ per ton

Strike	Calls—Settle			Puts—Settle		
Price	Mar-c	May-c	Jly-c	Mar-p	May-p	Jly-p
175	9.40	11.50	....	1.80	6.50	9.00
180	5.75	9.00	11.25	3.00	9.00	11.50
185	3.75	7.00	9.50	5.20	11.80	14.50
190	2.00	5.75	8.00	9.25	15.00	17.75
195	1.10	4.50	7.00	13.25	....	....
200	0.50	2.75	6.00	22.75	....	....

Est. vol. 150, Tues vol. 325 calls, 189 puts
Open interest Tues 4,620 calls, 2,744 puts

SOYBEAN OIL (CBT) 60,000 lbs.; cents per lb.

Strike	Calls—Settle			Puts—Settle		
Price	Mar-c	May-c	Jly-c	Mar-p	May-p	Jly-p
21	1.600	2.150	2.400	.180	....	.600
22	.970	1.500	1.850	.410	.720	1.050
23	.450	1.200	1.350	1.000	1.400	1.500
24	.250	.850	1.150	....	....	....
25	.160	.600	.900	....	....	....
26	....	....	....	....	....	....

Est. vol. 1,000, Tues vol. 762 calls, 170 puts
Open interest Tues 5,329 calls, 3,429 puts

– INDEXES –

MUNICIPAL BOND INDEX (CBT) $100,000; pts. & 64ths of 100%

Strike	Calls—Settle			Puts—Settle		
Price	Mar-c	Jun-c	Sep-c	Mar-p	Jun-p	Sep-p
84	4-42	4-21	....	0-49	2-16	....
86	3-15	....	....	1-20	....	....
88	2-04	2-22	....	2-08	4-07	....
90	1-17	....	....	....	....	....
92	0-46	....	....	....	....	....
94	....	....	....	....	....	....

Est. vol. 58, Tues vol. 0 calls, 46 puts
Open interest Tues; 7,674 calls, 7,928 puts

NYSE COMPOSITE INDEX (NYFE) $500 times premium

Strike	Calls—Settle			Puts—Settle		
Price	Mar-c	Jun-c	....	Mar-p	Jun-p	....
132	10.00	14.00	....	5.40	8.85	....
134	8.80	13.00	....	6.05	9.70	....
136	7.65	11.95	....	6.85	10.60	....
138	6.55	10.05	....	7.70	11.55	....
140	5.55	9.20	....	8.65	12.50	....
142	4.65	8.30	....	9.80	13.50	....

Est. vol. 39, Tues vol. 14 calls, 15 puts
Open interest Tuesday; 613 calls, 222 puts

S&P 500 STOCK INDEX (CME) $500 times premium

Strike	Calls—Settle			Puts—Settle		
Price	Feb-c	Mar-c	Jn-c	Feb-p	Mar-p	Jun-p
235	....	18.50	....	6.50	9.85	16.10
240	....	14.95	22.75	8.20	11.60	18.20
245	8.50	12.05	....	10.25	13.60	20.30
250	6.05	9.40	17.75	12.75	15.90	22.70
255	4.05	7.25	15.55	15.80	18.70	25.30
260	2.50	5.35	13.50	19.20	21.75	....

Est. vol. 3,034; Tues vol. 1,093 calls; 661 puts
Open interest Tues; 11,756 calls; 12,223 puts

– LIVESTOCK –

CATTLE-FEEDER (CME) 44,000 lbs.; cents per lb.

Strike	Calls—Settle			Puts—Settle		
Price	Jan-C	Mar-C	Apr-C	Jan-P	Mar-P	Apr-P
78	4.20	3.35	2.90	0.00	2.00	3.15
80	2.27	2.30	2.05	0.07	2.95	4.25
82	0.75	1.50	1.30	0.50	4.15	....
84	0.10	0.90	0.85	....	....	....
86	0.00	0.52	0.65	....	....	....
88	....	....	....	....	....	....

Est. vol. 502, Tues vol. 506 calls, 195 puts
Open interest Tues; 5,784 calls, 11,017 puts

CATTLE-LIVE (CME) 40,000 lbs.; cents per lb.

Strike	Calls—Settle			Puts—Settle		
Price	Feb-C	Apr-C	Jun-C	Feb-P	Apr-P	Jun-P
64	3.75	5.27	5.35	0.00	0.75	1.25
66	1.85	3.77	4.10	0.10	1.20	1.95
68	0.45	2.60	2.95	0.70	2.00	2.15
70	0.05	1.70	2.10	2.60	3.07	3.85
72	0.00	1.02	1.45	4.55	....	....
74	0.00	0.60	0.95	....	....	....

Est. vol. 2,458, Tues vol. 4,466 calls, 3,310 puts
Open interest Tues; 37,220 calls, 42,632 puts

HOGS—LIVE (CME) 30,000 lbs.; cents per lb.

Strike	Calls—Settle			Puts—Settle		
Price	Feb-C	Apr-C	Jun-C	Feb-P	Apr-P	Jun-P
44	3.87	2.45	5.00	0.00	1.50	1.05
46	1.92	1.50	3.77	0.05	2.42	1.80
48	0.45	0.75	2.85	0.35	....	2.85
50	0.10	0.40	2.00	2.22	....	4.00
52	0.00	....	1.37	....	....	....
54	....	....	....	....	....	....

Est. vol. 673, Tues vol. 320 calls, 171 puts
Open interest Tues; 4,136 calls, 3,985 puts

– METALS –

COPPER (CMX) 25,000 lbs.; cents per lb.

Strike	Calls—Last			Puts—Last		
Price	Mar-C	May-C	Jly-C	Mar-P	May-P	Jly-P
98	10.95	10.95	6.85	4.95	15.50	22.00
100	9.80	10.35	6.40	5.85	16.50	23.45
105	7.40	8.90	5.45	8.40	19.90	27.35
110	5.50	7.50	4.60	11.50	23.50	31.35
115	4.05	6.45	3.85	15.00	27.30	35.45
120	3.00	5.55	....	18.90	31.30	....

Est. vol. 5,400, Tues vol. 2,962 calls, 966 puts
Open interest Tues; 38,958 calls, 15,032 puts

GOLD (CMX) 100 troy ounces; dollars per troy ounce

Strike	Calls—Last			Puts—Last		
Price	Apr-C	Jun-C	Aug-C	Apr-P	Jun-P	Aug-P
440	44.40	51.30	58.00	2.40	4.50	6.40
460	26.60	35.30	42.30	4.40	8.00	10.00
480	11.90	21.30	29.50	9.40	13.50	16.50
500	5.10	13.00	20.80	22.60	24.70	27.10
520	2.40	8.30	14.80	39.90	39.60	40.30
540	1.20	5.40	10.70	57.80	56.20	55.60

Est. vol. 4,500, Tues vol. 2,330 calls, 1,790 puts
Open interest Tues; 40,615 calls, 33,060 puts

SILVER (CMX) 5,000 troy ounces; cents per troy ounce

Strike	Calls—Last			Puts—Last		
Price	Mar-C	May-C	Jly-C	Mar-P	May-P	Jly-P
625	48.5	72.0	89.5	5.0	19.5	27.0
650	30.0	57.0	74.5	11.5	28.0	37.0
675	17.0	44.0	61.5	23.5	41.5	48.5
700	11.5	32.5	52.0	43.0	55.0	64.0
725	8.0	25.5	42.0	64.5	72.0	78.0
750	4.5	21.0	34.0	86.0	92.5	94.5

Est. vol. 1,450, Tues vol. 1,768 calls, 307 puts
Open interest Tues; 33,844 calls, 11,273 puts

– FINANCIAL –

BRITISH POUND (IMM) 25,000 pounds; cents per pound

Strike	Calls—Settle			Puts—Settle		
Price	Feb-c	Mar-c	Apr-c	Feb-p	Mar-p	Apr-p
1750	....	5.50	....	0.55	1.45	....
1775	2.90	3.95	4.45	1.15	2.30	3.45
1800	1.55	2.65	3.25	2.30	3.50	4.75
1825	0.70	1.65	2.35	3.90	5.10	....
1850	0.30	1.05	....	5.95	6.95	....
1875	0.15	0.65	....	8.25	18.95	....

Est. vol. 1,351, Tues vol. 868 calls, 1,478 puts
Open interest Tues; 25,434 calls, 29,416 puts

W. GERMAN MARK (IMM) 125,000 marks, cents per mark

Strike	Calls—Settle			Puts—Settle		
Price	Feb-c	Mar-c	Apr-c	Feb-p	Mar-p	Apr-p
59	1.79	1.09	....	0.17	0.48	0.61
60	1.00	1.40	....	0.39	0.78	0.92
61	0.46	0.88	1.51	0.84	1.26	1.35
62	0.19	0.55	1.08	1.57	1.92	....
63	0.09	0.33	0.75	2.47	2.69	....
64	0.05	0.20	....	3.43	3.54	....

Est. vol. 85,373, Tues vol. 3,468 calls, 8,374 puts
Open interest Tues; 66,581 calls, 77,764 puts

Source: *The Wall Street Journal*, January 21, 1988. Reprinted by permission of *The Wall Street Journal*, Dow Jones Inc., 1988.

Investments in Perspective

Far more people are approached to trade commodities than have the skills and resources to do so successfully. Many ill-equipped "investors" are sucked into futures trading by high-pressure sales pitches. The following article from *The Wall Street Journal* is instructive.

Hot Lines: One Customer's Look At Sales Pitches for Commodities

YOUR
MONEY
MATTERS

By Robert L. Rose
Staff Reporter of The Wall Street Journal

CHICAGO—The financial markets were going wild, and so was my telephone.

"If you are at all serious about investing, this is the time to get in," a young caller named Mark said one recent evening as my dinner cooled.

Charles phoned two days later, and he was no less excited. "We've got all hell breaking loose here," he said. "The currencies are going absolutely wild. . . . The metals have become the major target for making money."

These are heady days for people whose standard of living is tied to telephone selling of commodity futures and options contracts. While these salespeople habitually work the phones, their fingers move faster and pitches grow more insistent when inflation fears jar the markets. And not since 1980 have worries about a new inflationary tide been so widespread.

"The number of calls regarding firms we've never heard of before has increased dramatically over the past few weeks,"

says a spokesman for the Commodity Futures Trading Commission, which fields public inquiries and complaints about commodity-brokerage firms. Despite the fact that few novices make money investing in futures and options (and many lose vast sums), commodity telephone sales seem poised for another boom.

Take Me, I'm Yours

To sample the latest in telephone tactics, I became the willing recipient of some 20 sales pitches for commodity futures and options by dialing toll-free numbers and sending in post-paid cards offered by small or obscure firms. While the array of investment vehicles offered has never been wider, pitchmen's techniques don't change, I found. They still try to evoke a sense of urgency and opportunity by using tactics common for decades, from claims of past windfalls to hints of inside information.

The post-paid cards had simple messages like, "Current levels could be cheap," but the telephone brokers said much more. Some called several times, and talked for as long as there seemed any hope of separating me from my money. They were willing teachers, often telling me to "go get a pencil and paper" so they could explain these complex investments. Most were pushing options, particularly on silver and gold.

A few were refreshingly candid, stating clearly that the investments were risky. When asked, some even admitted they had been in business for only a couple of months or that they actually had clients who lost money.

Others seemed to have less respect for the truth. Here's a sampling of the tactics I endured.

THE HARD SELL: I couldn't see Mark's nose, but it must have been long after his first 30-minute call from Florida.

"What we're dealing with is, the dollar will drop another 8%," he said, explaining why he was bullish on silver. "That's what James Baker says." That might have come as a surprise to the Treasury secretary, who six days earlier was trying to calm the markets by talking up stability for the dollar.

Mark had also found something unheard of in financial markets: unanimity among analysts. It seems all of them were saying silver would go to $12 an ounce by the end of May. (With three trading days to go, the metal is at $7.52 an ounce.)

Charles, meanwhile, had the gold bug. On April 29, he said it was going from $454 to $500 within a week. "A lot of serious money is going to be made," he said.

If serious money has been made, it wasn't from those predictions. Gold finished at about $459 an ounce on May 6, the day by which it was supposed to have hit $500, and closed at about $451 yesterday.

Another salesman, Tim, couldn't understand my hesitation. "Every market is going in our direction," he proclaimed. What's more, he said, calling back 10 minutes later, every one of his firm's clients had made at least 60% on their money since the beginning of the year.

THE LEADING QUESTION: "If you found a way to make a tremendous profit, and could do it on a limited-risk basis, would you want to take advantage of it right now?" one salesman asked.

Or: "The key to making money is timing and leverage, isn't it?" said another.

THE HOT TIP: One salesman promised access to "classified information" on the markets, which turned out to be analysts' published research reports from two little-known Chicago futures firms.

Others were big on the latest news, informing me in one call that the Federal Reserve had "just added money to the system" and in another that banks had just raised the prime rate.

THE GOOD-OLD-BOY ROUTINE: One broker from California, after putting me on hold, said that practically his whole family lives in my Illinois town, and reeled off street names to prove it.

THE HIGH-TECH COME-ON: Many salesmen promised access to "the latest technology," most of it at least two decades old. Two of the most popular: computer screens with "up-to-the-minute prices," and order systems with "direct access to the floor" of the commodity exchanges.

THE OLD AS NEW: One broker was big on stop-loss orders to help control risk. "It costs nothing to do this," he said, talking as though his firm had a patent on the timeworn practice of placing standing orders to close out a position when losses mounted to a certain level. "It's all in the $100 (commission)," he said. "That's why we're so good."

He left it to the risk-disclosure statement mailed to my home later to note the pitfalls: Stop-loss orders, the statement noted, "will not necessarily limit your losses to the intended amounts, since market conditions may make it impossible to execute such orders."

NOTES FROM THE FRONT: The same broker put me on hold early in the phone call. "I'm sorry about that," he said 30 seconds later. "The gold market was just closing. I had to put an order in."

Seconds later, he was at it again, yelling over the sound of traders' shouts and phones ringing in the background: "Hey Warren! Buy one on the close! One!"

THE BIG-SPENDER ROUTINE: Asked about my liquid assets, I told one caller of the $1,000 in my money-market fund. "Lunch money," he sniffed. "Believe it or not, I've spent at least that on lunch, a couple of times."

THE CHANCE-OF-A-LIFETIME LINE: Two salesmen offered to rush new account paperwork via Federal Express. "Any delay at this particular point—while history is being made—would be unwise," said one.

DON'T WORRY, ANY IDIOT CAN DO IT (WITH MY HELP): Most salesmen answered my questions about their track records with anecdotes about customers who made big money on recent trades. One told about an Alabama woman who made $1,275 in options on Japanese yen. What's more, she knew nothing about the investment: "They only know tractor parts" down there, the broker said.

Other pronouncements were equally hard to check, like that of the New York broker who said he was looking for just two new clients. One ex-client had died and another had retired, he explained.

THE GUILT TRIP: "This is supposed to be my dinner time," said one broker in a 30-minute talk on options. Another promised to be in his office till 10 p.m. should I want to call back.

THE 'ANTIDOTE': Then there was the lawyer whose advertisement told how a working couple lost their life savings "through constant turnover of contracts" (churning) by their broker. The ad went on with a pitch of its own for a free consultation on how to recover investment losses.

"My personal opinion," said the lawyer, "is that unless you're a floor broker on one of the commodity exchanges, you'd have to have loose marbles to trade in commodities."

general sense program trading refers to any large volume mechanical trading system. Such trading is generally based on some computerized model of theoretically appropriate price relationships. Normally a program will involve the simultaneous execution of trades in a number of stocks. The large capitalization stocks that are members of one of the major indexes such as the S&P 500 are particularly likely to be involved. Such trades also often involve the use of stock index futures or options on such index futures. Program trades for stocks listed on the New York Stock Exchange are facilitated by their DOT (designated order transfer) and SuperDOT systems. These two systems allow the near simultaneous execution of large trades of a number of stocks. The orders are submitted directly to the system and then transmitted electronically to the specific stock trading posts of each of the securities.

By far the most popular types of program trading are portfolio insurance and index arbitrage. Both involve the use of index contracts (futures or options on futures) and both are primarily instituted by large institutional investors and traders including some brokerage firms trading for their own accounts.

Portfolio Insurance.   The index futures example illustrates an increasingly popular strategy of portfolio managers. Portfolios, particularly large portfolios, can be managed to limit their exposure to market downturns. The process of limiting a portfolio's market exposure is called portfolio insurance. Such insurance can be structured to reduce greatly the possibility that losses will exceed some prespecified limit. At the same time the portfolio will still retain an opportunity to profit from a rising market. The portfolio insurer can employ various types of contracts including index futures, options on index futures, and options on individual stocks.[13]

Under one form of such downside protection the market is closely monitored by the insurer. When the stock market suffers a significant pullback, the client's portfolio is hedged. Usually the insurer sells an appropriate number (for the portfolio's size and beta) of index contracts. Alternatively, an equivalent number of stock index puts may be purchased. With either approach the impact of further down moves in the market is largely neutralized. For example, a short position in index contracts would appreciate as the value of the portfolio declined. Similarly, the index puts would place a floor on losses in the portfolio.

Both of these approaches to portfolio insurance (futures or options hedges) will generally protect the portfolio against a downturn. Such protection, however, has a cost. In addition to the relatively modest direct costs (insurer's fee, commission, and forgone interest of margin deposits), the investor sacrifices some potential gains. Purchasing puts incurs the premium paid for the option while selling index futures contracts shifts any profits from a stock market rise to the one purchasing the contracts. Moreover, the implementation of the strategy requires the availability of sufficient potential supply (at reasonable prices) of the hedging contracts. A major drop in stock prices may well create a major imbalance in the supply–demand relationships for such contracts. Everyone cannot abandon ship at once. The supply of available lifeboats is limited. As is almost always the case when money is involved, the investment market does not offer a free lunch. Portfolio insurance can provide some protection against market downturns. It is not, however, always possible to implement and when it is possible to apply, a portfolio insurance strategy may reduce potential profits from subsequent upturns.

Index Arbitrage.   The existence of stock index futures has facilitated and stimulated another relatively new type of trading. Index arbitrage is a strategy designed to take advantage of disparities between index futures prices and the cash market prices of the securities making up the index.

Suppose, for example, the futures contract on the S&P index is priced appreciably above the current value of the index itself. The final settlement price of an index futures contract is the closing value of the underlying index. Thus at the expiration of the index future, the index and the futures contract on the index must have the same value. Accordingly, a long position in the stocks making up the index coupled with a short position in futures on that index will produce a gain that is approximately equal to the difference between the cost of the two positions. Some adjustments must be made for the impacts of commissions, bid–ask spreads, and dividends on the underlying stocks. The precise amount of dividends and level of prices after deducting trading costs are not known at the outset. Moreover, the index programs must be put on quickly when price disparities open up. Still, when the futures price exceeds the corresponding index, something close to a guaranteed trading profit is possible. If such a profit is attractive compared with alternative risk-free returns, an index arbitrage trade is indicated.

Similar index arbitrage opportunities are available when the futures contract is priced somewhat below the index. Under this circumstance, the index arbitrager would sell the underlying stocks short while purchasing the futures contract. This type of program trade would only be profitable if the difference in the two prices were sufficient to offset the trading costs (commissions and bid–ask spreads) and dividends on the shorted stocks.

Program Trading and the Brady Commission, and the Crash of 1987.   Program trading and particularly index arbitrage has come in for a substantial amount of criticism in the wake of the stock market's 1987 crash. The exchanges' regulators and various others have studied the causes of the crash. The best-known of these studies is that sponsored by Congress and generally referred to as the Brady Commission. This commission was named after its chairman, Nicholas Brady, the former New Jersey senator. Other studies were sponsored by the NYSE, SEC, CFTC, CME (Chicago Mercantile Exchange), and GAO (General Accounting Office). Other prominent personalities testifying on the subject include Alan Greenspan, Federal Reserve Board chairman, and Donald Regan, formerly CEO at Merrill Lynch, Secretary of the Treasury, and Reagan Chief of Staff. Many financial commentators and some of the committee reports have blamed the crash, at least in part, on financial futures trading. Index arbitrage and portfolio insurance have come in for special attention. More generally trading in financial futures has been blamed for the apparent increase in stock market volatility. Indeed, the commissions, regulators, financial commentators, stock exchanges of New York, and the futures exchanges of Chicago have been arguing vigorously over this and related issues. No one would contend that financial futures have no impact on the markets for the underlying financial instruments. Whether the impact is relatively minor, short run, and perhaps stabilizing or is more serious, longer run, and destabilizing remains controversial.

One potential scenario involves the interaction of index arbitrage and portfolio insurers in a (crash) market downturn. As the stock market starts to drop, the portfolio insurers enter the market selling index futures to hedge their clients' portfolios. According to many observers, these sales tend to enter the market just as its decline is accelerating. The selling tends to push the futures index price below the spot market price of the index as reflected in the price of the underlying stocks. As futures prices fall below the prices in the stock market itself, index arbitragers enter the market. These traders buy index futures and simultaneously short the stocks making up that index. Their short selling pushes stock prices down further, perhaps bringing on more portfolio insurance selling of the index futures. The process may drive the market down substantially and even create a panic.

Such a scenario may well have been one of the factors that helped the 1987 crash happen or at least exacerbated the decline. Most critics of program trading would concede that fundamental factors (rising interest rates, concern about inflation and the dollar, etc.) were largely responsible for the 1987 stock market drop. Thus some sort of decline and perhaps a crash might well have happened anyway. On the other hand, these critics attribute the swiftness of the decline and panic of October 19, 1987, largely to the massive amount of program-induced selling pressure.

This analysis represents the allegations of those who blame the stock market crash (at least in part) on the financial futures market. Another principal concern relates to the limited amount of capital available to most specialists firms. To date these allegations remain just that, allegations. Not surprisingly the various constituencies have rather different perspectives.

The business of the futures markets depends heavily on financial futures trading and significantly on the futures trades that are involved with the programs. The participants in these markets seek to defend financial futures and oppose any severe restrictions on such trading. The brokerage community depends much more heavily on stock than futures market trading. Thus it has expressed considerable concern that program trading is scaring small investors out of the market. Several of these firms have announced that they will no longer engage in program trading for their own account.

Some steps have been taken and many others are under consideration. The New York Stock Exchange has sought to limit program trading during periods of very volatile market swings. When the Dow Jones Industrial Average moves more than 50 points in a single day, the exchange's computerized order routing (DOT and SuperDOT) system is not allowed to be used for executing programs. When the market moves more than 100 points in a day all program trading is supposed to stop. In the first test of these rules program trading continued after a 50-point move with hand-carried orders.

Most critics of the present system would like to restrict or even ban index arbitrage, program trading, or in some instances financial futures. One possibility would be to impose the same margin requirements on financial futures as are required on cash market instruments (e.g., stocks). Another proposal would seek to stop any panic by the installation of so-called circuit breakers. Both stock and financial futures trading would stop briefly if the market moved more than some predetermined amount. Others respond that any attempt to restrict or ban financial futures or cash market trading on U.S. exchanges will simply shift the markets overseas. No doubt this debate will long continue.

Commodity Mutual Funds

Commodity funds appeal to those who are tempted to trade commodities on their own but fear the tremendous volatility that is present with most commodities. While such funds have generally been no more successful than individual commodity traders, they do diversify risk, and a few have done very well.

COMMODITY-RELATED INVESTMENT AREAS

Puts, calls, convertibles, warrants, and mutual funds offer investment opportunities akin to but different from common stock. Similar investments are related to but distinct from commodity futures and options. For example, the commodities on which futures contracts are listed also have active spot markets. These spot markets provide an alternative of sorts to futures trading. Most such spot markets have relatively little speculative appeal, however. Greater leverage is possible and the inconvenience and direct costs of storage are avoided with a futures position in such physicals as corn, lumber, heating oil, and pork bellies. The spot markets for precious and semiprecious metals, in contrast, offer some advantages over the futures market. Storage costs are minimal and one can buy and trade them in small enough quantities to appeal to small investors. The relatively high minimum sizes of most futures contracts discourage many small investors from entering the arena. Thus many investors do purchase physical gold and other precious metals (silver, platinum, and palladium) as opposed to futures contracts on them. Moreover, some interesting physicals do not even have an active futures market. For example, the absence of a futures market in strategic metals forces interested speculators to trade the physical.

Gold

Bullion gold was (in a very real sense) an illegal substance for almost 40 years. That is, most U.S. citizens could not own bullion gold and no one could hold it as an investment. Individuals were only allowed to own nonbullion gold (jewelry, rare coins, dental gold, etc.). Fabricators and others who used gold in the ordinary course of their business could own limited quantities of bullion gold but only an amount reasonable for their day-to-day needs. On December 31, 1974, U.S. citizens were again allowed to own gold bullion without special permission. Gold again became a legal investment medium. A variety of outlets including department stores, jewelers, banks, and brokerage houses set themselves up to sell gold.

Citizens of other countries have long held gold as an inflation hedge. Some analysts also urge U.S. citizens to buy gold as a hedge against adverse economic fluctuations. While its appropriateness in investment portfolios is difficult to assess in the abstract, gold like most other investments does have some significant drawbacks.

First, the price of gold has exhibited considerable volatility. Soon after central banks stopped selling gold at $35 an ounce (the official price since the 1930s) the price rose to $200 per ounce (1974) only to fall back substantially once the U.S. market opened up. The metal's price had been speculated to too high a level in anticipation of the opening of the U.S. market. During the 1980 Afghan crisis gold reached a high of $850 per ounce and then fell to less than half that level. Clearly the gold price can fall as easily as it rises.

Second, gold yields no dividends, rents, interest, or other type of direct income payments. The only way to profit from gold ownership is from possible price appreciation. And the price can go down about as easily as up. Moreover insurance, storage, and financing costs will offset at least part of any price appreciation.

Third, the buying and selling prices of gold can differ appreciably. Depending on the quantity purchased, investors may pay as much as a 10% to 15% premium on a purchase and incur a similar discount when selling. Sales taxes may also be added to the price. Such transaction costs could easily absorb the gain from price appreciation. Moreover, investors may have to pay a fee to have their gold assayed when they try to sell.

Fourth, fraud, counterfeiting, and short weighing are potential problems for the unwary. In spite of its drawbacks, many investment advisors recommend that their clients hold some part of their portfolio in gold. Thus we shall explore the various direct and indirect types of gold investing.

Gold Bullion.   Buying gold bullion is one way to participate in the gold market. The bullion investor should seek to minimize the markup and avoid potentially counterfeited or short-weight gold. The offering price should be compared with the price reported in the financial press (*The Wall Street Journal*, for example). The markup will vary both with the quantity purchased and with the seller. Weight and fineness (percentage of gold) are measured and stamped on bullion by refiners.

Counterfeiting is less likely and buyers are more willing to purchase bullion with a well-known stamping.

Gold Futures and Options.   Gold futures are traded on the commodity exchanges. Like any futures contract gold futures allow investors to trade on margin, go short, or hedge—options not easily accomplished through bullion ownership. On the other hand, the large risks inherent in other types of commodity trading are also present with gold futures contracts. Options on gold contracts reduce the downside risk but are costly.

Gold Coins and Metals.   Gold coins and metals represent additional ways of buying and investing in gold. Some gold coins only command a small and relatively stable premium over their bullion value. Moreover, gold coins are more difficult to counterfeit and, in smaller quantities, may be marked up less than bullion.

The South African Krugerrand contains exactly one ounce of gold. It was designed to facilitate and stimulate gold speculation. Fractional Krugerrands are available in ½, ¼, and ¹⁄₁₀ ounce sizes. While their importation is now illegal, Krugerrands brought in before the ban continue to trade in the United States. The U.S., Canadian, Chinese, and various other public and private mints issue coins and metals that compete with the Krugerrand. The U.S. Eagle is the only legal way of investing pension funds in bullion gold. The Canadian Maple Leaf has displaced the Krugerrand as the primary bullion metal. The various issues of the Chinese Panda have been minted in somewhat limited quantities. Its relative rarity coupled with its esthetic appeal has led Pandas to be priced at a premium over their bullion values.

Gold Mining Company Stock.   Gold mining company stock prices are closely related to gold's price. Gold that is unattractive to mine at $35 per ounce may be quite profitably extracted at $350 per ounce. Moreover, relatively small price changes can substantially affect mining profits. Leverage works in both directions, however—a fall in gold prices can greatly reduce mining profits. Several mutual funds specialize in gold mining shares.

Gold mining stocks are, in fact, a rather effective way to invest in gold. Since they are stocks, trading costs are modest. Such stocks may be eligible for purchase on margin. Storage and assay costs are avoided. And yet the investor obtains much the same upside (and downside) potential as with bullion gold investments.

Gold Jewelry.   Jewelry prices always substantially exceed bullion values. Buying jewelry at bullion prices from a dealer who is in the business of trading scrap gold is one way of minimizing the markup. Such dealers may be willing to sell good jewelry at slightly higher prices than the refiners would pay them. The scrap price for gold is usually only a small fraction of retail.

To purchase gold in the form of jewelry the investor needs to be able to make the appropriate weight–price conversions. Jewelry is often priced relative to its weight in grams. This weight is usually stated relative to its gross weight rather than the weight of its gold content. Thus gross weight in grams must be converted to gold content weight in ounces. Most jewelry gold is 14 karats fine. Since pure gold is 24 karats fine, 14 karat gold is 14/24s (58⅓%) pure. An ounce contains about 31.1 grams. Thus the formula for converting price per gross gram to price per net ounce is:

$$Pno = Pgg/(K/24) \times 31.1$$

where:

$$Pno = \text{price per net ounce}$$
$$Pgg = \text{price per gross gram}$$
$$K = \text{karats of fineness}$$

For example a price of $10 per gram for 14 karat gold is equivalent to the following:

$$Pno = 10/(14/24) \times 31.1 = 10/.5833 \times 31.1 = \$533.17$$

Thus $10 per gram of 14 karat gold is equivalent to $533.17 per ounce for pure gold.

Gold Mutual Funds and Gold Depository Receipts.   Institutions similar to mutual funds manage portfolios of gold bullion. Their shares fluctuate with the price of gold. This concept offers small investors some of the advantages of large dealers. Fees and expenses are, however, borne by the fundholders. Finally the gold depository receipt is in essence a warehouse certificate for gold held in storage. Such receipts offer some convenience compared to holding physical gold. Having someone else hold gold is a safe procedure if the holder is well known and highly secure. Citibank, for example, will take phone orders and charge the bill to Visa or MasterCard.

On the other hand, a number of frauds have been based on the fiction of holding precious metal storage. For example, the International Gold Bullion Exchange (IGBE) sold gold at the spot price charging no fee for storage or trading. It advertised in such prestigious publications as *The Wall Street Journal* and maintained very visible memberships on the futures exchanges that listed gold contracts. It even paid interest to investors who left their gold on deposit. Customers eventually discovered that IGBE was running a Ponzi scheme when it ran out of money and gold.

Silver and Copper Bullion Value Coins

Just as gold coins provide an alternative to gold futures, silver and copper coins serve as alternatives to silver and copper futures. While bullion value coin investing is similar to precious metals trading, some important differences remain. Since coin values do not reflect bullion values precisely, an underlying move in the commodity price may lead to a greater or lesser move in coin prices. On the other hand, the coin's value cannot fall below its face value. Thus a $50 bag of pennies is worth $50 even if the copper value falls to $30 or $10.

Since coin trading is much less active and more diverse than the commodities market, the buy/sell price difference for coins is usually much greater. Markups of 20% to 50% on coins are typical. The markup on large quantities of bullion-related coins, while low relative to that on some other kinds of coins, is still above that of most other types of investment.

A number of coin-investment brokerage firms, however, permit margin purchases and storage—especially for bags of silver coins (often at substantial costs). Margin buyers who only receive a warehouse receipt cannot be sure that the coins actually exist. In some cases they did not. Such scams are a reminder of the "bucket shop" operations common in earlier days of the stock market.

Consider the following example of a silver coin transaction: On July 25, 1974, a New York coin dealer was selling $1,000 (face) bags of silver for $3,500 and buying for $3,400 (2.9% spread). Other dealers were quoting $3,350 bid and $3,550 asked (a 5.8% spread). New York residents would also incur a sales tax. Margin purchases required a 30% deposit and were charged an annual rate of 13½%, or $330 per year, on the $2,450 borrowed. This particular dealer would absorb the storage charge. The buy price would have to rise $430 (to $3,730) within a year for the investor to cover the $330 interest and $100 spread. This is equivalent to a percentage increase of 12.3% on the original price of $3,500. Thus, after investing $1,050, the price would have to rise by over 12% before a profit could be realized.

In comparison, on July 25, 1974, New York Mercantile Exchange contracts to receive $1,000 bags of silver in July 1975 (one year from date of purchase) traded for $3,710. This level was approximately the price that the coins needed to reach for one who bought them in the previous transaction to earn a profit ($3,730). The commodity trade had at least two advantages, however. First, the lower required margin on the futures contract meant that less interest was forgone on the amount invested. Second, the commodity contract commission would be much lower than the spread involved in an off-exchange transaction. Furthermore, as long as delivery is not taken, no sales tax is due on a commodity exchange transaction regardless of the buyer's residence.

While most bullion coin action is in gold and silver, copper could reach a level at which a cent's bullion value exceeded its face value. In early 1974 this looked like a possibility but by late 1974 the copper price had fallen enough to make pennies unattractive to copper speculators. Indeed, pennies continued to be made of copper through 1981 although a shift to zinc occurred quietly in 1982.

Strategic Metals

No futures markets yet exist in strategic metals such as titanium, antimony, beryllium, germanium, vandium, zirconium, cobalt, manganese, and molybdenum. Nonetheless some investors have shown considerable interest. As with many other investment fads, rapid price rises generate expectations of further rises. Unscrupulous promoters persuade investors to buy the metal for perhaps double the current wholesale price. Little is said about subsequent sales. No doubt strategic metals do offer some profitable opportunities, but unsophisticated investors are likely to learn of the problems the hard way. Indeed, most strategic metals seem quite unlikely to experience any serious shortages.

Deferred Delivery Foreign Exchange Contracts

Some foreign currencies are traded on futures exchanges. The bulk of the market, however, is in over-the-counter forward contracts. Futures and forward contracts differ primarily in two ways. First, almost all futures contracts are traded on a futures exchange while all forward contracts are traded over the counter. Second, futures contracts require margin deposits while no margin is required for futures. Otherwise the two types of contracts are quite similar. Both envision future delivery at a price negotiated at the time of the trade. Both offer international traders an opportunity to hedge their foreign exchange risks. Some spot speculation in foreign exchange also utilizes travelers checks, foreign bank accounts, and securities denominated in foreign currencies. Still others trade options.

Foreign exchange speculators bet on the relative movements in exchange rates. Thus one who expected the mark to appreciate relative to the dollar could buy marks or deferred delivery marks (either futures or forward contracts) with dollars. If the investor's analysis is correct, the position can subsequently be covered at a profit. If exchange rates move adversely, however, the position will produce a loss. This is another huge market but largely beyond the scope of this chapter.

SUMMARY AND CONCLUSIONS

A large dollar volume of futures trading takes place on the various futures exchanges. Standardized contracts in grade, size, location, and delivery date facilitate substantial hedge and speculative trading. The relatively low percentage margins required to trade futures allow investors to magnify greatly the profits and losses generated by a given price move in the underlying physical. Commodity trading has grown rapidly because of the poor performance in alternative markets and the introduction of a variety of new types of contracts. Commodity contracts exist in agricultural, mineral, and financial instruments. To succeed in the futures market a contract requires a physical with sufficient competition, standardization, storability, and price volatility to establish an active trading market.

Commodities differ from stocks in a number of ways including: term, trading limits, delivery possibility, margin percentages, absence of short restrictions, no interest on unpaid margin balances, no specialists, commission structure, and the need to open and close positions with the same broker. Because of their relatively independent (not related to the stock market) volatility, commodity contracts may be useful in diversification but their own volatility limits their appeal.

A variety of professional futures traders compete with the amateur speculator: scalpers trade on the floor of the exchange seeking very quick turns; day traders close their positions at the end of each day; position traders may hold for several days; arbitragers seek profits from disequilibrium price relations; firm representatives trade for the accounts of firms that deal in the underlying physical. A series of large disruptive trades have at times substantially altered price relationships.

Futures trades may be based on fundamental and technical analysis. Crop and weather forecasts play a large role in fundamental analysis of agriculture commodities. Combination trades involve offsetting positions in related contracts with the hope of profiting from relative price moves.

Specialized commodity instruments include interest and stock market futures, options on commodities, and commodity mutual funds. A number of commodity-related physicals also appeal to commodity speculators. Specifically, gold bullion, futures and option contracts on gold, gold coins, gold metals, stock in gold mining companies, gold jewelry, gold mutual funds, and warehouse receipts facilitate trading in the precious metal. Similar alternatives are available in silver and copper. Finally, strategic metals without a futures market and currency with an active forward market both appeal to futures-oriented investors.

REVIEW QUESTIONS

1. What characteristics are needed for a commodity contract to be traded actively on a futures exchange? In your discussion of this question mention some examples of recent contract attempts that succeeded and that failed.

2. What factors have led to the recent growth of commodity futures markets? What role have financial futures played in this growth?

3. Discuss the various types of professional commodity traders and the advantages possessed by each. What is the relevance of such traders to individual investors considering commodity trading?

4. What is the relevance to small investors of the various examples of disruptive large futures trades? Who has been involved in such trades?

5. Discuss the application of fundamental analysis to commodity trading. How do crop and weather forecasts fit in? How would one classify program trading?

6. What are combination commodity trades? Illustrate with some examples. What are the risks of such trades? How do these risks compare with those of individual trades?

7. Discuss commodity analysts. Who writes the commodity analysis column for *Forbes*? What kind of record has he had?

8. Compare commodity trading with stock market trading. How are the two markets similar and how are they different?

9. What are the pros and cons of commodity diversification? How has the introduction of financial futures expanded the risk reduction strategies?

10. How do interest rate futures work? What are some of the debt securities underlying such contracts?

11. How do stock index futures work? How can they be used to hedge a stock portfolio? What is such hedging called? What other methods are available for the implementation of such strategies?

12. Discuss the role of program trading in the stock crash of October 19, 1987. What has been done to limit such trading?

13. What is a commodity option? Discuss two major commodity option scams. What is a boiler room operation? How should one avoid being trapped in such scams?

14. What are the various ways of investing in gold? What are the pros and cons of each?

15. Discuss investing in silver and copper coins. What are the relative advantages of such investments compared with investing in the metals through bullion, coins, mining ventures, and futures contracts?

16. What are the drawbacks to investing in strategic metals? What about rare earths? Would similar concerns apply?

REVIEW PROBLEMS

1. Refer to Figure 19.1. Compute the dollar value of one contract for each of the different industrial futures contracts (March contract only). If margin is set at 15% of dollar value, what is the amount of margin required for five contracts of each of these futures? If 90% of the margin can be met with T-bills, what would be the total cash margin cost of purchasing five of each of these industrials?

2. You start with $5,000 that you invest in silver futures at $5 per ounce putting down margin equal to 10%. A month later silver rises to $6 per ounce. When your account is marked to market you use the excess in your margin account to buy more silver up to the maximum. A month later silver rises to $7 per ounce. You again buy the maximum amount of silver futures. When silver hits $8 per ounce you liquidate your position. How much have you made? Initially ignore the impact of commissions. Now recompute the results assuming trades in silver futures incur commissions of $60 per contract. Refer to the text to determine the size of a silver futures contract.

3. Suppose that in Problem 2 you had not liquidated your position and that you would receive a margin call when your account fell to 5% of the value of your positions. At what price of silver would you receive a margin call? Suppose you then sold enough contracts to bring your equity up to 10%. How much further must silver fall for you to get another margin call? What would your account be worth at that point?

4. Using the quotation in Figure 19.1, compute the carry for the soybean contract. Use the nearest to delivery as the spot price. Plot the constellation of prices. From this set of plots identify the primary harvest months. Using 8% as the cost of financing compute the implied cost of storage for each adjacent holding period.

5. Compute the carry for each adjacent holding period for gold (refer to Figure 19.1). The cost of storage and insurance for gold is small enough to ignore. Thus virtually all of the carry represents financing costs. Compute the implied financing costs for each holding period. If you could borrow at 7%, could a profit be made arbitraging against the implied financing cost of gold holding? If so, how?

6. A 60-pound bushel of soybeans is processed into 47 pounds of soybean meal and 11 pounds of soybean oil. The remaining two pounds are lost in processing. The processing costs about $.15 per bushel. For each of the delivery months of Figure 19.1, compute the profit or loss of a crush. Which would be appropriate for a crush and which for a reverse crush?

7. Refer to the lumber quotation of Figure 19.1. What kind of carry market is reflected in this quotation? Why would the futures market be priced in this manner? Explain.

8. Compute the break-even prices for each of the copper futures options of Figure 19.3. For the option quotation of Figure 19.3 the March, May, and July copper futures contracts closed at 103.59, 93.75, and 82.25, respectively. Which of the strikes are in the money and which ones are out of the money? How large a change is required in the futures prices for the option buyer to break even for each of the copper futures options of Figure 19.3?

9. Compute the number of contracts needed to neutralize a $50 million stock portfolio having a beta of 1.07. Assume the S&P contract is at 145.

10. Compute the gold bullion cost for purchasing 12 karat gold at $9 per gram.

REVIEW PROJECTS

1. Apply the Harlow and Teweles soybean trading rule to the past five years. Now apply it to five years that were covered by their study. Compare the two performances. Write a report.

2. Assemble a list of five commodity trade recommendations and track their performances. Write a report.

3. Select 10 futures contracts that are near expiration. Compute the basis on each. Now compute the basis monthly for these same contracts going back one year. Plot each set of bases over time. Do you see any pattern? Explain.

4. Compute the carry for price constellations of three agricultural and three metals contracts. Estimate the actual carrying cost for holding the physicals

from one delivery period to the next. Compare the two "carries." Repeat the computation for five prior periods.

5. Construct three combination trades and track their performances. Write a report.

6. Assume that a year ago you wished to hedge your $100 million portfolio of government bonds. Half were coming due in six months and the other half in a year. Your goal was to lock in a two-year return (one year beyond the current date). What interest futures contracts would you have bought? Compute the end-period value of your portfolio giving full effect to commissions, margin cost, and interest. Compare this result with what you would have achieved from an unhedged portfolio.

7. Assume that one year ago you wished to hedge your $50 million stock portfolio against an expected decline in the market. Assume that your portfolio's performance paralleled the S&P 500. How many S&P 500 contracts would you have traded to hedge your position? Would you have bought or sold? Compare the results of hedging and not hedging on your portfolio's current value.

8. Plot the various stock index futures relative to the performance of their underlying index for a year. How do the price constellations vary? Write a report.

9. Select five commodity options and compare the performance over the past year of long positions in the options versus the underlying futures contracts.

10. Track the history of five commodity funds for two years relative to a stock and a commodity index. Write a report.

11. Obtain gold quotes for bullion, futures, and Canadian Maple Leafs. Compare the prices and write a report.

12. Select five gold mining companies and plot their monthly performances relative to gold's price for two years. Compare the relative returns. Write a report.

13. Obtain current buy and sell quotes on five strategic metals. Compute the relative markups.

NOTES

1. B. Stewart, *An Analysis of Speculative Trading Grain Futures*, Technical Bulletin no. 10001 (Washington, D.C.: Department of Agriculture, Commodity Exchange Authority, October 1949).

2. K. Dusak, "Futures Trading and Investor Returns: An Investigation of Commodity Market Premiums," *Journal of Political Economy*, December 1973, 1387–1406.

3. C. Rockwell, "Normal Backwardation, Forecasting, and the Returns to Commodity Futures Traders," in *Food Research Institute Studies*, supplement to vol. VIII (Stanford, Calif.: Stanford University, 1967), 107–130.

4. E. Chang, "Returns to Speculators and the Theory of Normal Backwardation," *Journal of Finance*, March 1986, 193–208; E. Fama and K. French, "Commodity Futures Prices: Some Evidence on Forecast Power, Premiums, and the Theory of Storage," *Journal of Business*, January 1987, 55–73.

5. S. Alexander, "Price Movements in Speculative Markets: Trends or Random Walks," *Industrial Management Review*, May 1961, 7–26; R. Bear, "Martingale Movements in Commodity Futures," Ph.D. dissertation, University of Iowa, 1970; R. Gray, "Fundamental Price Behavior Characteristics in Commodity Futures," paper presented at the Futures Trading Seminar of the Chicago Board of Trade, Chicago, Ill., April 28–30, 1965; T. Martell and G. Philippatos, "An Option, Information and Dependence in Commodities Markets," *Journal of Finance*, May 1974, 493–498; G. Booth, F. Kaen, and P. Koveos, "Persistent Dependence in Gold Prices," *Journal of Financial Research*, Spring 1982, 85–94; S. Taylor, "Tests of the Random Walk Hypothesis Against Price-Trend Hypothesis," *Journal of Financial and Quantitative Analysis*, March 1982, 37–59.

6. C. Harlow and R. Teweles, "Commodities and Securities Compared," *Financial Analysts Journal*, September/October 1972, 64–70.

7. S. Angrist, "A Reverse Crush in Soybeans," *Forbes*, September 1, 1977, 78. S. Angrist, "A Relatively Riskless Trade," *Forbes*, December 1, 1976, 102–103.

8. S. Angrist, "Seattle Slew I'm Not," *Forbes*, July 1, 1977, 108.

9. S. Angrist, "Profits Top Losses Again!" *Forbes*, July 9, 1979, p. 148.

10. A. Robicheck, K. Cohn, and J. Pringle, "Returns on Alternate Investment Media and Implications for Portfolio Construction," *Journal of Business*, July 1972, 427–443; Z. Bodie, "An Innovation for Stable Real Retirement Income," *Journal of Portfolio Management*, Fall 1982, 5–13.

11. J. Hil and T. Schneeweis, "Reducing Volatility with Financial Futures," *Financial Analysts Journal*, November/December 1984, 34–40; H. Kaufold and M. Smirlock, "Managing Corporate Exchange and Interest Rate Exposure," *Financial Management*, Autumn 1986, 64–72; S. Hegde and K. Nunn, "A Multivariate Analysis of the Cross-Hedging Performance of T-Bond and GNMA Futures Markets," May 1985; M. Belongia and G. Santoni, "Interest Rate Risk, Market Value, and Hedging Financial Portfolios, *Journal of Financial Research*, Spring 1987, 47–55.

12. S. Benninga and M. Blume, "On the Optimality of Portfolio Insurance," *Journal of Finance*, December 1986, 1341–1352; R. Rendelman and R. McEnally, "Assessing the Costs of Portfolio Insurance," *Financial Analysts Journal*, May/June 1987, 27–37; M. Rubinstein, "Alternative Paths to Portfolio Insurance," *Financial Analysts Journal*, July/August 1985, 42–52.

13. R. Whaley, "Valuation of American Futures Options: Theory and Empirical Tests," *Journal of Finance*, March 1986, 127–150; J. Bodurtha and G. Courtadon, "Efficient Tests of the Foreign Currency Options Market," *Journal of Finance*, March 1986, 151–162; K. Ramaswamy and S. Sundaresan, "The Valuation of Options on Futures Contracts," *Journal of Finance*, December 1985, 1319–1340; M. Brenner, G. Courtadon, and M. Subrahmanyam, "Options on the Spot and Options on the Future," *Journal of Finance*, December 1985, 1303–1318.

Real Estate and Real Estate Stocks

Many investment courses do not cover investments in real estate. Such neglect of this important investment medium seems unfortunate. Even investors who prefer other media need some exposure to the subject to make an informed decision. This chapter provides the reader just such an exposure.

First real estate's role in the economy is explored. Then we examine its investment suitability and discuss specific guidelines and parameters. Next, 10 basic principles of real estate investing are considered followed by illustrations of three approaches to real estate valuation (market, cost, and income). In the process such topics as bargaining, loan negotiation, property management, and refinancing are discussed. Then various types of real estate investments are considered including: apartments, land, condominiums, recreational property, commercial property, franchises, and cemeteries. Finally, we examine the pros and cons of investing in different types of real estate companies and tax shelters.

THE ROLE OF REAL ESTATE IN THE ECONOMY

Real estate ownership is a large and profitable part of the economy. Because most real estate trades in relatively small localized markets, its size and importance are often underrated. In fact, the real estate market's size dwarfs the stock, bond, commodity, and option markets. Estimated U.S. real estate values are more than double those of corporate stocks and six times the value of all capital equipment.

In addition, two-thirds of all dwelling units are owner occupied. Thus a large percentage of the population is in one way or another involved in real estate investing. Real estate investing has proved quite profitable in the past. Indeed, average real estate returns have generally exceeded average stock returns by a wide margin.[1] The past is no guarantee of the future, however. That is, high average returns on real estate in the past do not ensure attractive returns on specific real estate investments in the future.

REAL ESTATE AS AN INVESTMENT

Who Should Invest in Real Estate?

In spite of the real estate market's importance, size, and profitable history, far more people are well positioned to invest in stocks or bonds than real estate (other than their own home). Anyone who is serious about becoming a real estate investor should be able to answer yes to each of the following five questions.

1. Can at least several thousand dollars be tied up for a minimum of several years? Most real estate investments cost at least several tens of thousands of dollars and typically require at least 25% down. Thus a small investor with only a few hundred to a few thousand dollars to invest is unlikely to find very many real estate investments in his or her price range. Furthermore, individual items of real estate are difficult to sell on short notice. Thus the investor should be prepared to hold properties for an appreciable period (perhaps a minimum of several years).

2. Is the investor likely to remain in the same geographic area for the foreseeable future? Real estate investments usually require frequent attention. Thus investors need to be near enough to their properties to supervise them properly.

3. Does the investor have the time and talent to manage property effectively? Rental property often requires a substantial amount of maintenance. New tenants must be found periodically. Rents must be collected. Records must be kept and bills must be paid. Even if others are contracted to do these tasks, someone still must hire the managers and monitor their work. Moreover, investors who do the tasks themselves enhance their returns relative to those who hire the work out.

4. Can the investor assume the substantial risk inherent in real estate investing? High leverage and low liquidity both add to real estate's risk. Only those positioned to absorb these risks should expose themselves to them.

5. Does the investor have the credit standing necessary to borrow on attractive terms? Most successful real estate investors use extensive leverage. The investor who is unable to make effective use of borrowed funds may find real estate relatively unprofitable. Since real estate loans are usually secured by the property values themselves, most people can answer yes to this question.

TABLE 20.1   Real Estate Investment Parameters

Type	Minimum Investment Period (Years)	Maximum Leverage	Minimum Capital Requirement	Potential Holding Period Return
Raw Land	3 to 4	50%	$5,000 to $10,000	300%
2-6 Unit Apartments	5 to 10	75 to 80%	$7,500 to $20,000	300%
Shopping Centers	5 to 7	75 to 80%	$50,000	500%
Garden Apartments	8 to 12	75 to 80%	$50,000	300%
Office Building	8 to 12	75 to 80%	$100,000	500%
Highrise Apartments	8 to 12	75 to 80%	$250,000	400%
Commercial Space	3 to 4	75 to 80%	$10,000 to $20,000	300%
Industrial Space	3 to 4	75 to 80%	$50,000	400%

Source: Adapted from *Successful Investing and Money Management* (USA: Hume Publishing, 1986), 4.9. Used with permission, all rights reserved.

Only investors who can answer each of these questions affirmatively are properly suited for real estate investing. No doubt one or more of these five criteria will rule out a large number of prospective investors. Many of these people should, however, still learn more about the topic. Some who are not now positioned to invest in real estate may eventually be better able to do so. Many of those not well situated for general real estate investing may still be prospective homeowners. Still others may prefer the stocks of real estate oriented companies. The following discussion is addressed to all such investors.

The Parameters of Different Types of Real Estate Investments

The minimum period that funds need to be invested, the amount of equity capital necessary, and the leverage percentage usually employed differ with the type of real estate. Table 20.1 represents one estimate of some of the typical parameters for several types of real estate investments.[2] The entries in Table 20.1 differ substantially in reliability. For example, the leverage numbers, derived from experience with banks and other lenders, are dependable estimates. Similarly, the estimates of minimum capital requirement reflect experience with current price levels. Thus they may seem relatively representative. Note, however, that they are minimum capital requirements and not average capital requirements. These minimums may be realistic for some areas of the country and totally unrealistic for others. The figures for potential return and minimum investment period are, in contrast, pure guesses.

These entries only represent one opinion, but they do provide some idea of the possible range of expectations. We see that expected minimum holding periods vary from 3 to 4 years in land to 8 to 12 years in various types of developed real estate. Minimum investment amounts range from $5,000 to $10,000 in land to $250,000 for high-rise apartments. Expected holding period returns range from 300% to 500% of the amount invested (the down payment).

REAL ESTATE INVESTING PRINCIPLES

The preceding discussion introduced real estate investing, considered its investor suitability, and briefly explored some relevant parameters. Now we turn to some specific aspects of real estate investing, beginning with 10 investment principles.

Principle 1.   Real estate values are determined by their highest and best (i.e., most profitable) uses. Potatoes could be grown in midtown Manhattan and a flea market operated on Miami beachfront property. Such locations will, however, almost certainly be put to much more profitable uses. The Manhattan land would earn more as a site for office buildings, apartments, hotels, department stores, or even parking lots. The Miami beachfront parcel should yield a much higher return as a hotel site.

Investors have a strong incentive to acquire and upgrade underutilized property. Bidding prices up to their most productive use values tends to maximize each property's productivity. Potential buyers and sellers should always evaluate real estate in terms of its most productive use. Poorly informed sellers may sometimes price their property below its highest use values. An efficient investment market should, however, make such bargains relatively rare. On the other hand, an investor never wants to sell real estate for less than its most productive use value. Thus determining realistic values is a key aspect of real estate investing.

Principle 2.   The supply of land is largely fixed while demand tends to increase over time. Heretofore worthless (for human usage) land may sometimes be made useful by draining, clearing, grading, or irrigating. In rare instances, air rights (the right to build over someone else's property) may substitute for high-priced land. Increasing the supply of usable land is relatively expensive and may encounter environmental (e.g., preserve the wetlands) objections, however.

Growing population and increasing affluence have tended to raise land values. Similarly, rising materials and labor prices have tended to increase construction costs. Since these trends seem likely to persist, real estate values should continue rising, at least in the long run.

Principle 3.   As with almost any investment, short-run individual price moves may differ substantially from the long-run aggregate trend. During the 1930s, real estate values plunged along with the price of almost every other investment asset. Much of the property bought in the 1920s remained below its purchase price until well into the 1940s. Some property bought in the Florida land boom of the 1920s is still worth less than the inflated sums paid at the peak of the hysteria. More recent boom–bust real estate cycles have involved such diverse areas as Hawaii, Hong Kong, Tucson, Miami Beach, and Anchorage.

Principle 4.   Careful comparison shopping is a useful first step in identifying real estate values. As with all investing, shopping around and bargaining is advisable. Paying more than is necessary or selling for less than top dollar reduces returns. Comparative fundamental analysis of an assortment of available properties is an important aspect of real estate investing. Similarly, obtaining properties at attractive prices usually requires information on alternative real estate opportunities. Few fortunes have been made with hasty, half-baked decisions.

Principle 5.   Effective real estate investing almost always involves a careful but extensive use of leverage. Few investors have the resources to buy very much real estate for cash. Moreover, property that earns more than the cost of financing it yields a positive differential. Thus investors should use the collateral value of their property to borrow heavily whenever the projected return safely exceeds the borrowing cost.

Banks, savings and loan associations, and other financial intermediaries are quite willing to lend a substantial percentage (usually up to 75% to 80%) of the purchase price of developed property. The interest expense is tax deductible while any unrealized price appreciation on the property is tax deferred. The lower the down payment of a particular purchase, the more of the buyer's funds remains available for investment in other properties. Borrowers must normally make a large enough down payment to protect the lenders in case they default.

Principle 6.   As with the purchase price, investors should shop around and bargain for the best financing terms. While the amount borrowed, length of repayment, and interest rate (or formula for a variable rate mortgage) are all important, other factors such as repayment flexibility should not be overlooked. Since an interest rate decline may make refinancing attractive, the absence of a prepayment penalty is especially desirable. Moreover, closing costs, insurance arrangements, and property tax escrow accounts should all be considered in negotiating a loan.

Closing costs include fees paid to the lender for granting the loan (points), lawyers' fees, title search expenses, and so on. A point is 1% of the loan principal. Lawyers charge fees for both drawing up the purchase and sales agreements and searching and guaranteeing the title. A number of loan provisions are designed to protect the lender from unexpected contingencies. For example, lenders will normally require fire and casualty insurance on any developed property and perhaps borrower life insurance equal to the outstanding loan principal. Any unpaid property taxes are assessed against the property. Thus the lender may require that the pro rata expected property taxes be added to the mortgage payment. Property taxes are due at specific times (once or twice) during the year. Thus borrowers who are not constrained with escrow payments have full use of the funds until the due date. Moreover, the escrow account may earn little or no interest.

At one time almost all real estate mortgages had fixed terms and interest rates. The initial payments of such loans (usually monthly) are primarily devoted to covering the interest charge. At first only a small portion of the monthly payment is available for principal repayment. Over time, however, the amount of the debt is reduced so that less of the fixed payment is required for interest and more is available for principal repayment. Economic uncertainty and increasingly volatile interest rates have more recently led most lenders to prefer making variable or adjustable rate mortgages (ARMs). Thus these are the types of mortgages that they try to write. Since ARMs' terms can differ substantially, the investor still needs to shop around and negotiate.

Many ARMs, for example, start with a set rate for the first year and limit how much the rate can vary per period and how high it can go (a cap on the rate).

Thus one lender might offer a 10% first-year rate and a rate in subsequent years that varies annually with a 13% maximum. Another might start at 11% and change the rate no more than 1% each year with no cap on the rate. In some mortgages the monthly payment is fixed with the variation in the rate affecting the number of payments. In most cases, however, the payment rate fluctuates with the interest rate.

Several new financing methods reduce what would otherwise be a substantial initial payment rate for the buyer. One of these is the appreciation mortgage. In exchange for a lower interest rate, the appreciation mortgage lender receives a portion of the gain that is realized when the property is sold. The lender in effect bets that the property will appreciate by more than enough to offset the difference in interest rates. Other types of mortgages include growing equity and graduated payment. Both types begin with relatively low mortgage payments that increase over time.

Knowledge of the available range of interest rates or rate formulae, minimum down payment percentages, point charges, escrow terms, available maturities, pre-payment penalties, and the like should help the investor to select the most attractive place to begin negotiations. Moreover, the terms of different lenders will be more attractive in some respects than in others (e.g., a lower interest rate but a higher down payment). Persistent negotiation with several lenders may afford the best of each world.

Principle 7.   Real estate investors should seek to limit all spending on improvements and maintenance to projects that are cost effective. For example, they should not automatically replace a deteriorating roof, repaint the exterior of a faded duplex, or remodel the interior of a now out-of-date office complex. The additional rents generated by the better maintained property may not be worth the higher costs. Any spending on maintenance and remodeling should be justified by the expected payback rather than the physical need. Rental rates that are depressed by rent control or a deteriorating neighborhood encourage the investor to realize what is possible with minimal maintenance and eventually to abandon the property. On the other hand, perfectly functional structures may at times be substantially altered or torn down if a different structure would earn enough to justify the conversion.

Principle 8.   Real estate should never be purchased without a careful on-site inspection and comparison with the relevant alternatives. Some companies use a free dinner and slide show to sell Sunbelt property to people living in other areas—especially the Snowbelt. An on-site inspection has no substitute, however. Such inspections may reveal a drainage problem; unpleasant odors from nearby factories, sewage treatment facilities, or garbage dumps; neighboring developments that limit land values; more attractively priced nearby property; and many other unexpected factors. Investors should only consider investing in property that is near enough to inspect. The following list contains some relevant characteristics to consider in any proposed property purchase.

1. Location: What changes are taking place? Will they work to the benefit of the property owner? Consider road access, utilities and services, and neighboring property development. If property is being bought for business purposes, do

surrounding businesses complement it? Are suppliers nearby? Is parking adequate? Would the owner be able to expand to adjacent property if need be?

2. Competition: What nearby properties have similar uses? Does this choice have any particular advantages or disadvantages? Will competitive moves in the area affect the owner?

3. Facilities and Maintenance: Does the physical quality of the buildings compare favorably with neighboring properties? Do the structures have multifaceted use? Are costly repairs likely to be required? If so, does the asking price reflect these projected costs? That is, would the combination of the cost of purchase and the cost of any needed repairs still make the property an attractive investment?

4. Financing: Can the property be financed by both the current buyer and a subsequent buyer? How committed is the original lender to financing the rest of the development? Would other area lenders consider financing the property? If not, why not?

5. Operating Expenses: How stable are the expenses for taxes, management, utilities, and insurance? Might they rise substantially? Would the new owner be adversely affected by rising energy costs? Are the figures provided consistent with the experience of owners of similar buildings? Do long-term leases provide sufficient additional revenues to cover these projected cost increases?

6. Income: If the property provides rental income, can rents be increased? How do the rents compare with those for similar property? Is the tenancy likely to be stable? Do government regulations allow the landlord to choose tenants selectively? What lease terms can the owner offer?

7. Price Asked: How does the price compare with that paid by other property buyers? Could the same dollar commitment buy attractively priced property in a more established area? If the property is income producing, does the price permit a positive cash flow after taxes and mortgage payments? How firm is the asking price?

Principle 9. Minimize the use of expensive professionals. Real estate investors often require the services of lawyers, realtors, appraisers, architects, accountants, contractors, property managers, and several other types of professionals. Such professionals are sometimes well worth their cost. At other times the owner may effectively perform the task and save the fee.

Realtor commissions are normally set at 6% to 7% on developed property and 10% or more for land. Thus the sale of a $150,000 house would generate a $9,000 to $10,500 fee. Suppose the owner were to sell the house directly. He or she might reduce the price $2,500 and spend $300 on classified advertising. If the effort was successful, the owner would save $6,000 to $7,500. Buyers should, where possible, also seek to purchase properties directly. Owners who avoid paying commissions can afford to sell for less.

Most owners can also handle such jobs as bookkeeping, appraising, and property managing. Some professional services are very nearly unavoidable, however. For example, few nonlawyers know how to do a title search and the lender is unlikely to accept the work of those who do. Similarly, few laypersons can design and contract major construction. Moreover, an independent appraisal of a very large parcel might be well worth its cost. Similarly, large property holdings may benefit from professional management and accounting. The issue really boils down to how highly the investor values his or her time and talent.

Principle 10.   Investors should continually keep abreast of relevant local, state, and federal agency policies and proposed policies. For example, moving quickly to secure property near new government projects, such as an interstate highway interchange or rapid transit terminal, may yield large profits. Other state or local government actions (e.g., rent control) can, in contrast, appreciably depress some real estate values. Accordingly, we shall now explore the impacts of such factors as major government and nongovernmental construction, legalized gambling, rent control, the environmental movement, national credit trends, and property tax levels.

Major Government and Nongovernmental Construction.   Developable property near successful shopping centers usually appreciates in the period immediately following the leasing up of the center. Since local zoning board approval is one key to shopping center development, real estate investors should keep abreast of the issues coming before such agencies. Federal installation constructions also offer profit opportunities.

Private enterprise is expected to provide support services for the new facility's employees. Since suppliers, restaurants, and shop owners will need space, nearby land will usually appreciate. Recreational land values near expanding government installations may also rise. For example, a planned dam that creates lakefront property or a new access road to some scenic or recreational attraction almost always increases nearby property values. To learn about proposed projects, investors should follow the activities of legislative agencies and their parks and public works committees. Many such proposals are easily approved. On the other hand, those that are likely to reduce nearby land values are generally hotly contested. For example, proposals for nuclear power plants, sewerage treatment facilities, prisons, and airports tend to be carefully scrutinized.

Legalized Gambling.   Legalizing casino gambling caused Atlantic City real estate values to soar. Property suitable for hotel casinos rose dramatically but even many residential property values quadrupled. The Atlantic City example illustrates the profit potential of anticipating and taking quick advantage of such an event. On the other hand, those who waited too long got hurt. Atlantic City was soon overbuilt, causing many property values to decline appreciably.

Rent Control.   Laws that constrain rent increases can appreciably reduce an investment's return. Accordingly, real estate investors should closely monitor rent control efforts. Local media generally report this issue thoroughly. Landlords may even take a leaf from the tenants' book and organize themselves.

The Environmental Movement.   While its relative importance may vary over time, the environment has clearly become one of the nation's major social concerns. Controlling real estate development constitutes an important aspect of the environmental movement. Downie has articulately presented the environmentalists' view of alleged real estate abuses.[3] He appears to be on firm ground in criticizing those who sell run-down inner-city houses to the poor at inflated prices. Usually the Federal Housing Administration (FHA) guarantees the loan. The FHA appraiser may be bribed to approve a loan at well above the property's market value. If, as often happens, the new owner is unable to keep up the payments, the FHA ends up with the overvalued property.

Downie also justifiably criticizes developers who use bribes to obtain favorable zoning or approval of clearly inadequate construction. Abuses of real estate sales companies are also effectively criticized. Not stopping here, however, Downie views with alarm the conversion of urban residential property to commercial use, the residential development of what had been agricultural land, the planned development of new towns, and even individual homeowner's preferences for dwellings with investment potential. His basic thesis seems to be that profit-oriented real estate development has led to the "rape" of America. He proposes that the government plan and control real estate development in ways that would greatly restrict profit opportunities. Downie's controversial views involve many debatable value judgments. In effect he questions the capitalistic approach to economic activity.

Regardless of one's own opinion, disregarding antidevelopment sentiment is hazardous. Views such as Downie's are popular, particularly with those who do not own rental and/or investment real estate. Land use and zoning regulation may require environmental impact findings, limit the owner's ability to subdivide property or convert apartments to condominiums, force expensive improvements such as buried telephone and transmission cables, and require that a major part of the land be left in its natural state. Vermont has even passed a special tax on land profits. These restrictions clearly limit the land's desirability and investment potential. Even if current legislation does not constrain development, restrictions may be imposed before the purchaser has time to realize a profit.

National Credit Trends.   National credit trends also affect real estate investors. When the high cost of mortgage loan money threatens real estate profits, investors should be particularly cautious. The opportunities and risks are correspondingly higher at such times. These investors should not, however, overlook the attractive opportunities that are created by high interest rates. No doubt such rates burden real estate buyers. On the other hand, burdensome carrying costs may force some property owners to sell at distress prices. Particularly well-positioned investors may find a tight credit–weak real estate market an excellent time to buy.

Property Taxes.   A shrinking tax base can adversely affect local real estate values. Similarly, an area that spends heavily on government services must finance that spending. High real estate taxes may reduce returns and thereby decrease potential price appreciation. Thus the investor should proceed cautiously when local tax rates are high. On the other hand, a high level of government services may enhance property values sufficiently to offset the taxes required to provide them.

DETERMINING REAL ESTATE VALUES

The 10 real estate investment principles summarized in Table 20.2 constitute a useful set of ad hoc advice for novice investors. They do not, however, come directly

TABLE 20.2 Principles of Real Estate Investing

1. Remember that the value of a property is determined by its most profitable uses.
2. Keep in mind that land supply is fixed while prices may rise with population and affluence.
3. Understand that real estate prices often fall in the short run.
4. Shop around and bargain for the best price on property.
5. Use leverage extensively where profitable.
6. Shop for attractive terms on interest, down payment, maturity, closing cost, insurance, points, escrow accounts, and so on.
7. Justify all expenses by expected incremental returns.
8. Never buy property sight unseen.
9. Minimize the use of professionals.
10. Be mindful of the impacts of government actions.

to grips with the basic issue of real estate valuation. Accordingly, we shall now explore three different ways of estimating real estate values.

The Market Approach

Most people would agree that an item is worth what it will sell for. The value of a particular property should not differ greatly from realistic asking prices and recent sale prices of similar real estate. Thus a check of the market and recent transactions should give some guide to what a particular property is worth. No two properties are precisely equivalent, however. Every property has a different location and other characteristics (size, condition, etc.) will usually vary, often substantially. Furthermore, a property's market value may differ appreciably from its worth to a particular investor. Thus the market approach should not be relied upon exclusively. On the other hand, a price that is above the comparable alternatives is surely too high while a price that is below the competition is at least worth further consideration.

The Cost Approach

Real estate values may also be based on the cost of equivalent land and construction. The construction cost should include the cost of funds tied up while the property is being built and allow for the differential values of new versus used structures. When replacement costs are below market prices, investors are encouraged to build rather than to buy. Developed property selling for less than its replacement cost may, depending on demand, be either a bargain or severely outdated or mislocated. Thus valuations based on replacement costs provide a much better ceiling than a floor on true values.

The Income Approach

Just as common stock values are related to expected future dividend payments, real estate values are strongly influenced by their expected future rental (or other) income. Suppose an apartment building yields annual rentals of $10,000; is to be purchased for cash (no mortgage); and has expected annual expenses (maintenance, property taxes, insurance, etc.) of $3,000. To simplify the computations assume that depreciation, income taxes, and resale value changes are offsetting. Thus the property is expected to generate a net annual cash inflow of $7,000.

The present value of a constant income stream is simply 1/r times the income stream (where r is the appropriate discount rate). Thus, discounted at 14%, the property's expected income stream is worth $50,000. An even simpler approach utilizes the multiples of gross rents. A property might be valued at five times its gross rents. This approach would also value the hypothetical property at $50,000. The appropriate multiple will, of course, vary with market interest rates. One might also take some account of other factors such as risk, leverage potential, net cash flow, and opportunities to upgrade the property.

These very rough-and-ready uses of the income approach can provide a cursory evaluation of a particular property. The potential investor simply estimates rental income and direct expenses (exclusive of mortgage payments and income taxes) to find the gross income of the real estate. Dividing this sum by the appropriate discount rate produces a "first pass" value estimate. Such an approach can help separate obviously unattractive opportunities from those deserving further study.

A much more detailed treatment is needed before a final decision is made, however. Specifically, the investor should consider the cash flows after loan payments and income taxes are paid, take account of the property's expected market price change, and relate the net return to the actual outlay (down payment) rather than the total cost.

Determining the Present Value of Real Estate.   Valuing real estate by the income approach is just another application of capital budgeting. In this instance the cash flows relate to real estate rather than, for example, a piece of equipment or a new product. The actual implementation of the income approach involves the following six steps:

1. Determine the appropriate discount rate r.
   a) Ascertain the current market cost of borrowing funds to finance the contemplated real estate purchase.
   b) Estimate the highest alternative low-risk return that might otherwise be earned on the funds required for the down payment.
   c) Determine the weighted average cost of funds: multiply the percentage to be borrowed by the borrowing rate; multiply the percentage of the down payment by its alternative rate; then sum the two values.
   d) Add a risk premium to this weighted average cost of funds. The size of the premium would depend on the project's risk. Thus a very low-risk project might warrant a 1% premium whereas a higher risk investment could deserve 4%.

2. Forecast future rental income. An established property's current rental rates are known. Rates on similar units provide a guide for newly constructed projects. Forecasting future rates is more difficult. In some cases the anticipated future rates may be built into the lease. Rental rates on comparable property,

vacancy rates, construction costs, and building activity are all relevant factors in rent determination. One should usually forecast rent increases conservatively.

3. Forecast the future expenses associated with maintaining the property including taxes, repairs, renovations, and management costs. A knowledge of the building's structural soundness should be helpful in estimating some of these costs. Current expenses might be projected to rise with inflation. Some adjustments may be required for anticipated needs (such as a new furnace). Note, however, that even experts have difficulty predicting future inflation rates. Since inflation's effects on rents and maintenance costs tend to be offsetting, one can at least assume consistent increases for both. Mortgage loan payments should be added to the other expense estimates to forecast the before-tax cost of maintaining the property. The property's taxable income must be determined before income taxes can be calculated.

4. Forecast the property's holding period and value at time of sale. Again, the investor should try to be consistent. The property's sale price should not normally be expected to rise faster than its ability to produce income.

5. Use these figures to estimate the real estate's value.
   a) Subtract expected costs for each year from anticipated revenues to obtain expected net cash flow.
   b) Use a present value table or financial calculator to compute the discounted value of each year's expected net income for the selected r.
   c) In like manner, find the present value of the property's expected sale price.
   d) Sum the present value of the expected net income and expected sale price to obtain the present value of the total.

6. Compare the present value of the expected income stream plus future sales price (the income approach valuation) with the price of the property. The higher the income approach valuation relative to the price, the more attractive is the potential investment.

The Income Approach: An Example.   Now consider a brief application of the income approach procedure:

1. Determine r.

> Borrowing cost: 17%
> Alternative yield on low-risk investment: 13%
> Percent down payment required: 25%
> Weighted average cost of capital: .25 × 13% + .75 × 17% = 16%
> Risk premium: 4%
> Total cost of capital (r): 16% + 4% = 20%

Note that in some market environments these rates may seem high (or perhaps low). They are not meant to be representative of a particular current situation.

2. Estimate current and future rental income.

    Current rental income: $2,000 per month, or $24,000 per year. To be conservative, use this amount for future years.

3. Estimate current and future property expenses.

Property Taxes	$4,000 per year
Repairs	400 per year
Miscellaneous	600 per year
Total	$5,000 per year

4. Forecast the expected holding period and selling price.

    Expected holding period: five years
    Expected selling price: $164,000 (a modest increase over the current asking price of $146,000)

5. Add figures.
    a. Net income per year: $24,000 − 5,000 = $19,000
    b. Discounted value of each year's expected net income:

	Net Yearly Income		Constant*		
Year 1	$19,000	×	.833	=	$15,827
Year 2	$19,000	×	.694	=	13,186
Year 3	$19,000	×	.597	=	11,001
Year 4	$19,000	×	.482	=	9,158
Year 5	$19,000	×	.402	=	7,638
Total					$56,810

    *From 20% column in present value table.

    c. Present value of expected sales price: $164,000 × .402 = $65,928.
    d. $56,810 + $65,928 = $122,738

6. The present value is appreciably less than the asking price ($122,738 versus $146,000), and thus the property seems relatively unattractive. If we could justify using a lower discount rate, however, the estimated value would increase. Similarly, a higher projected income stream would increase the value estimate. Finally, the seller might accept a lower price.

Note that while we used greater detail than in the earlier simplified example, this procedure still focuses on the whole project's return. The return on the investor's contribution, a more meaningful figure, will be taken up in greater detail later in the chapter.

Combining the Three Valuation Approaches

Attractive real estate opportunities are priced below their market, cost, and income valuations (Table 20.3). Real estate priced above any one of these three "values"

TABLE 20.3 Three Approaches to Valuing Real Estate

Market Approach	Base value on asking and sale prices of comparable properties
Cost Approach	Base value on cost of constructing equivalent property
Income Approach	Base value on present value of expected future net income stream

is probably an unwise investment. If, for example, the price is above either the market or replacement values, more attractively priced properties should be available elsewhere. A price that is high relative to the income approach valuation suggests that other investments (perhaps outside of real estate) offer higher returns. An investment's attractiveness varies inversely with its price, however. Moreover, real estate asking prices are often flexible.

Bargaining. Unlike most other investments, real estate transactions often involve some bargaining. Thus investors should bargain with the seller in an effort to purchase potentially attractive investment possibilities as cheaply as possible. Sellers generally expect to receive less than their asking price. Investors should seek to buy at the lower end of the realistic range.

The investor should begin the bargaining process with an offer high enough to be taken seriously but well below what is likely to be accepted. An offer of about 20% below the asking price (or 10% below a realistic market price) would normally be viewed as low but not ridiculously so. The appropriate level for an initial offer is difficult to prespecify in the abstract, however.

Some properties are so overpriced that an offer of two-thirds or even one-half of the asking price would be realistic. In other cases an offer 20% below the asking price might be insulting. The offer should be high enough to elicit a counteroffer while leaving the potential buyer maximum flexibility to continue the bargaining process. Unless the market is particularly strong, the seller will usually counter a noninsulting offer. The seller might, for example, drop 5% off the price. Then the investor can come back with a 5% to 10% increase. Once the investor's offer and the seller's asking price are close, one of the parties will usually suggest splitting the difference.

Uninformed sellers can pose both opportunities and difficulties. A seller who wants cash in a hurry or does not fully recognize the property's value may set too low a price. On the other hand, a seller who has an exaggerated vision of property values may try the buyer's patience. Examples of potential uninformed sellers include the following: an out-of-town heir who needs to pay estate taxes, a long-time owner who has not kept up with current prices, the owner of a run-down property who has not realized that much greater rents could be charged were it rehabilitated.

While some uninformed sellers may not know how much their property is worth, others may not know how little it should sell for. Some novice sellers may believe that the real estate market is so strong that eager buyers will meet almost any asking price. Perhaps having the property on the market for a few months will persuade such a seller to be more reasonable.

When an uninformed seller overestimates a property's value, the interested investor can look elsewhere or try out a reasonable offer. The investor might, for example, offer 5% to 10% below the property's full market value and then not budge unless and until the seller becomes reasonable. Alternatively, he or she might try out a very low price; for example, one-third below its market value. Who knows? The seller just might accept.

Seller Financing. Real estate investors may also use the seller to help finance the purchase. For example, a seller desiring a steady income might take back a below-market rate mortgage on the old property. Most people are unable to earn secure returns on their own investments as high as the rates paid to mortgage lenders. Thus the opportunity to earn a relatively low (compared to the market) mortgage rate may still seem attractive to them. The seller who receives partial payment in the form of a mortgage earns a steady monthly income and qualifies the transaction as an installment sale (reduced taxes).

A buyer who knows the seller's circumstances may be able to work out financing arrangements that are beneficial to both. For example, the buyer might make a 20% down payment, assume the seller's existing low-interest mortgage, and give the seller a five-year note for the remaining debt. The principal will, however, need to be refinanced or paid off well before a long-term mortgage would come due. Interest rates may or may not then be lower. Thus the buyer who relies on seller financing may only be postponing the inevitable.

Seller financing is helpful to buyers who need a few years to prepare for higher interest rates and mortgage payments but it should not be viewed as permanent financing. Indeed, borrowers frequently have difficulty paying off short-term seller financing. Moreover, even first mortgage default rates have increased in the past few years.

The seller should also understand the advantages and disadvantages of entering into a financing arrangement. On the plus side, providing seller financing helps market the property and may reduce the seller's tax liability (installment sale). On the minus side, the buyer's note almost always bears a below-market interest rate. As a "second" it should yield more than first mortgages. Thus if first mortgage rates are 10%, the market rate on a second mortgage should be 12% or more. A lower rate on a second mortgage is in effect a hidden price reduction. Moreover, a buyer who has difficulty paying off the note may pressure the seller into extending the loan. Clearly seller financing is no panacea for either party.

Negotiation Through Intermediaries. Third parties such as Realtors or lawyers are frequently brought into real estate negotiations. This approach helps avoid potential personality conflicts from direct buyer–seller contact. The seller may become defensive if the buyer directly notes the property's negative factors.

The agent only earns a commission if the buyer and seller come to terms. Accordingly, he or she has an incentive to convey the buyer's concerns in a tactful manner. Thus the agent should be able to comment effectively on the property's condition, location, and/or price relative to that of similar properties. While agents may pressure both the seller and the buyer to improve their offers, buyers are usually better able to resist. They almost always have alternative investment opportunities. Sellers, in contrast, often have only one sale to make.

Buyers should never tell an agent their maximum possible offer until they are ready to make that offer. An intermediary who knows the top figure may not be sufficiently vigorous in seeking a still better price from the seller. The negotiating agent should, however, be given some reasonable explanation for the size of the offer, particularly if it is low. Experienced sellers know not to expect top dollar for second-rate property. Once the buyer's position is clarified, the seller will often make significant concessions.

Closing the Deal.   If bargaining reaches an apparent impasse, the would-be buyer should consider low-cost concessions that might push a close negotiation to a conclusion. Thus offering to agree to an early closing date might elicit additional flexibility from a seller who is concerned about timing. An early closing means that the seller will promptly receive the proceeds from the sale. Similarly, relenting on some original demands such as ignoring certain small problems, offering to buy some of the seller's personal property, or working out a payment plan suitable to the seller could all clinch a deal at minimum expense to the buyer. If, however, negotiations proceed to differing figures that seem firm for both sides, the would-be buyer must decide whether to pay more or look elsewhere.

Negotiating the Loan.   Once a price that is satisfactory to both the buyer and seller has been established, the next step is obtaining financing. Finding financing is up to the investor. He or she might begin by making preliminary inquiries at a local bank and/or thrift institution. Suppose that the savings and loan is short of mortgage money. Since the buyer is a long-time depositor, the bank is willing to consider an application. The buyer then applies for a $100,000 loan (80% percent of the purchase price). The bank is willing to make a 20-year loan at 10%, plus two points. The bank had earlier quoted 9.5% but now notes that the rate was a month-old figure that applied to loans with 25% down payments. The bank then offers a $98,000 20-year loan at 10% with no points. The borrower asks for and receives an option to repay any time after three years without penalty as well as the right to handle property tax payments without an escrow account. The borrower is required to purchase a term life insurance policy equal to the face value of the mortgage loan, thereby providing effective low-cost family protection.

Completing the Transaction.   Once the financing has been arranged, the present owner's clear title must be established (a title search). The transaction also needs to be registered and taxes paid in the proper locality. At the closing, the buyer, the seller, and officer of the mortgage loan granting institution, and their attorneys meet and pass the final papers and funds.

AN EXTENDED EXAMPLE: OWNERSHIP OF A DUPLEX

We have discussed various aspects of real estate investing from a variety of viewpoints. An extended example is now in order.

Suppose a duplex priced at $140,000 can (after negotiations) be acquired for $133,800. A 12% loan of $100,350 (75% of $133,800) is assumable. Thus a down payment of $33,450 would be required. The monthly payments on a 25-year 12% loan of $100,350 would amount to $1,057 (a total annual mortgage payment of $12,684). The current monthly rental rates are set at $900 for one side and $840

Investments in Perspective

Applying technical analysis to the real estate market seems almost an impossibility. Nonetheless, that is exactly what the following article in *Barron's* discusses.

Real Estate

THE GROUND FLOOR
By MICHAEL A. SKLARZ

How a Technician Analyzes the Real-Estate Market

INVESTORS in bonds, stocks and commodities continually try to determine their markets' direction. Home buyers and other investors in real estate try to do that, too, but they face a big problem: accumulating sufficient and accurate price data.

Stocks, bonds and commodities are traded in highly visible national markets, where price fluctuations can be monitored. Real-estate markets, on the other hand, are less visible, less scrutinized and much more localized. Nationwide, there are literally thousands of individual real-estate markets, each behaving according to its own characteristics.

On the demand side, the basic forces determining real-estate values are essentially the same as those for other goods: demographics, income, employment, prices, rents, the cost and availability of credit, plus inflationary expectations, tax benefits, consumer tastes and preferences and the expectation of

capital gain. On the supply side, the basic forces are the availability and cost of land, labor and capital, anticipated demand, the competitive environment and planned supply.

As in the financial and commodity markets, fundamental forces of supply and demand are most useful in predicting longer term real-estate market trends. Short-term predictions, however, require different techniques. Locations Inc., the Honolulu-based company of which I'm research director, has developed a number of technical indicators to monitor the Hawaiian real-estate market. These factors, which we believe are widely applicable throughout the country, include the relationships between sales price and sales activity, the ratio of sold to listed price, the percent of listings sold, the time needed to sell property and the months of inventory remaining.

* * *

SALES activity, of course, shows whether demand is

increasing or decreasing. In this respect, real estate is no different from the other markets where volume precedes price. But volume generally is overlooked by most market participants. Human nature being what it is, people are more interested in sales prices, not sales activity. This is true even though volume is more likely a cause and price an effect. Chart A provides a good case study of this relationship by tracking sales and prices of one-bedroom condominiums in Waikiki. Notice how prices stayed relatively flat from 1977 until late 1978, while volume was increasing sharply. It wasn't until the very end of 1978 that prices exploded; they nearly doubled by the end of 1979. Then they remained on a plateau until late 1981 before falling sharply in 1982. Volume was a lead indicator. It peaked a good six to 12 months before prices and fell precipitously between late 1979 and late 1982. Notice how it has been on an upswing since early 1983, a trend that preceded a firming in prices.

* * *

THE NUMBER of homes that sell as a percentage of the total put on the market in a given year is another useful measure of supply and demand. In strong markets, a high percentage of those homes offered for sale will find a buyer. In soft markets, only the best-located and best-priced generally will find takers.

Look at charts B and C, which show the annual percentage of single-family listings sold in Oahu, along with the average single-family price appreciation rate. Notice how the two track one another very closely. The percent sold leads the real appreciation rate by about six to 12 months. There is a fundamental reason for this—prices generally won't rise as long as there's an excess of homes (indicated by a low percent sold) on the market.

* * *

THE NUMBER of days needed to sell properties is a good measure of demand. In an active market, properties turn over quickly as potential buyers feel an urgency to buy. Their biggest fear is that, by waiting, they're risking the possibility that someone else might purchase the home or investment property that appeals to them. In addition, the "buy now before prices move higher later" mentality may prevail.

Charts D and E show the average number of days needed to sell an Oahu condominium—along with the average condo price appreciation rate. Market times have been plotted on an inverse scale to be in sync with price peaks and valleys. As seen, this indicator acts much like overbought/oversold oscillators commonly used to technically forecast tops and bottoms in the stock and commodity markets.

* * *

SELLING a home also can be viewed within the framework of an auction, accentuated by problems such as spotty information, a non-homogeneous product and continuously shifting preferences. This causes a seller to generally "overprice" his property to some degree, to avoid the possibility of missing the highest bidder.

The percent of listing price received is an indicator somewhat like the stock market's bullish vs. bearish sentiment indexes. Both are indicative of general market psychology. In a "seller's" market, a property owner feels that, if his price is currently too high, it will be only a matter of time before the market catches up to it. Buyers sense this and must bid accordingly. A seller's market is also characterized by fast turnovers, which add pressure on buyers to act quickly and decisively. It is not uncommon in very strong markets to see properties selling for more than asking prices. This leads sellers to boost their prices far above what the market will bear. It's a sure sign that a market top isn't too far off.

A bearish, or "buyer's," market is exactly the opposite. Because real-estate information tends to move much slower than that of the financial markets, sellers take that much longer to catch on to a change in market direction. They tend to keep their asking prices high even though actual values have stabilized or declined.

* * *

THE ratio of available inventory to the current sales rate is another indicator of real-estate activity, analogous to the inventory-to-sales ratios used in manufacturing industries.

Months remaining is an excellent real-estate market indicator since it combines both supply (inventory for sale) and demand (sales rate) in one statistic. In simple terms, this indicator represents the numbers of months it would take to completely absorb all unsold homes in an area at the current sales rate.

Months remaining also is an inverse indicator. It's high in soft markets and low in strong ones. We have plotted the average annual values of inventory remaining, along with the percentage change in prices for new single-family homes throughout the country. The results are in Chart F.

* * *

REAL estate historically has been a good way to create and protect wealth. The indicators discussed in this article have helped us monitor and forecast Hawaii's real-estate market, and we think they should be equally applicable to any real-estate market. ■

for the other (a total annual rental income of $20,880). Current-year property taxes are $4,200; insurance, $1,200; repairs and upkeep, $1,500; and miscellaneous expenses, $600 ($7,500 total). Thus, gross annual income (ignoring interest, depreciation, and income taxes) amounts to $13,380 ($20,880 − $7,500). Gross annual income is a useful index of the cash generation potential of the property. It represents the amount of funds available for servicing debt and providing net income to the owner.

Income and expense forecasts may be based on previous experience. Since rent schedules are known and verifiable, income is usually easier to project than expenses.

Rents can generally be raised sufficiently to cover the impact of inflation on expenses. Moreover, proportional increases in rents and expenses should normally yield a positive incremental cash flow. A real estate broker or property manager may provide help in forecasting future rental rates. Assume the following set of projections is made:

Year	1	2	3	4	5
Rental Income	$21,780	$22,800	$23,220	$23,940	$24,660
Expense	7,800	8,100	8,400	8,700	9,000
Gross* Annual Income	$13,980	$14,700	$14,820	$15,240	$15,660

*Before deductions for mortgage payments, depreciation, and income taxes.

The property is available for $133,800. This sum is equal to about 10 times the property's current gross annual income (133,800/13,980 = 9.6). If this relation between gross income and market value is maintained, the property's market value will rise to about $152,000 in five years. The present values (using a 10% discount rate) of the gross income and sale price are:

$$PV = 13,980 \ (.909) + 14,700 \ (.825) + 14,820 \ (.751) + 15,240 \ (.683)$$
$$+ \ 15,660 \ (.621) + 152,000 \ (.621)$$
$$= \ 12,708 + 12,128 + 11,130 + 10,409 + 9,725 + 94,392$$
$$= \ \$150,492$$

If these expense and rent estimates are accurate, the property is a bargain at $133,800. Any price under $150,492 is expected to yield a 10% or greater return. Some additional factors should be considered, however.

First, are the revenue and expense estimates realistic? To be conservative one should recompute the present value reestimating revenues on the low side and expenses on the high side. While nothing may go wrong with the investment, a cushion would be helpful.

Second, can the required sum be borrowed at an attractive rate? In this case an existing mortgage loan is assumable. Such opportunities are relatively rare. In a more typical situation the buyer would need to obtain a new mortgage loan at the market rate. Any loan charges and fees should also be considered. These expenses are added to the property's purchase price at the closing. The loan should not, however, have a prepayment penalty. If such a clause is proposed, the borrower should resist or seek alternative lending. Also one should consider the investment's net cash flows. The investor would like to cover monthly payments out of net income. A high interest environment may, however, make this goal impossible. Even in a high interest environment rental income may eventually catch up with loan payments. One should, however, be prepared for several years of negative cash flows.

Third, can the owner sell the property at the expected price and do so without the aid of an agent? At least a modest amount of selling expenses should be anticipated.

Fourth, are better deals available elsewhere? Even though this property is attractively priced, other available properties may be still better bargains. Since every investor's funds are limited, some attractive properties may have to be passed up.

Fifth, will the owner accept a lower price? Sellers usually expect to bargain a bit over the price. How much can one reasonably expect to reduce the price through negotiation? Sixth, is the assumed 10% discount rate realistic in the current market? What would the property be worth at a 12% discount rate, for example?

Cash Flow

Now consider this investment's cash flow. Current expected monthly rental income and expenses are $1,740 and $624 respectively. The difference of $1,116 should cover the assumable mortgage loan payments of $1,057. Before continuing this examination of cash flow, however, some important questions need addressing.

Improvements

Real estate investors should look for ways to increase the values of their investments. For example, could additional revenue be generated without greatly increasing costs? Increasing the profitability of a real estate investment not only raises the owner's return while it is held but also increases its market value in a subsequent sale. In the present example the investor might seek a higher return by (1) turning the duplex into one large house, (2) dividing the duplex into a four-bedroom rooming house, or (3) remodeling the existing units and raising the rents.

Checking comparable rents shows that converting the duplex into a single residence would reduce the return. The second possibility is also ruled out. The four bedrooms with joint use of two kitchens and living rooms should each rent for $525 per month, or $2,100, compared with the current $1,840. Alteration costs would be minor, but the area is not zoned for such usage and the neighbors fear that a zoning change would reduce their property values. Rather than anger the neighbors, rezoning is not attempted. Finally, the existing neighborhood, while fine for current tenants, would not justify sufficiently higher rents to make a major remodeling worthwhile.

Some minor changes might produce additional profits, however. First, a large garage in the rear is rented for $45 a month. Second, a tenant offers to repaint his unit's interior for the cost of the paint. His choice of colors is approved and durable paint is purchased. A new paint job should make the duplex easier to rent if the tenant leaves. Moreover, the tenant is likely to take better care of the unit after spending time improving it.

Next, both tenants complain about their heating bills and ask for additional insulation. The insulation is added along with weather stripping, caulking, storm windows, and storm doors. The insulation reduces the tenants' heating bills by more than enough to cover a monthly rent increase of $30. The tenant who has just repainted is agreeable to the increase. The other tenant, who had been commuting a long distance to her new job, gives notice.

Having a vacancy creates an opportunity. Both units are currently unfurnished. A furnished unit might rent for $960 a month, however. Since the unit could be furnished for about $1,500, the extra $60 a month would cover the cost in less than two years. The furniture itself should last at least four years. A small advertisement is placed in the local paper offering the furnished duplex for $960 a month. Prospective tenants are told that the unit will be available in 30 days. Before the 30 days are up, a tenant is found. Some of the previous tenant's furnishings are bought and the rest is picked up at a used furniture shop and a garage sale for slightly below the $1,500 estimate.

The conversion to a furnished apartment proved so profitable that a similar move is planned for the other unit. The current tenant has a lease that cannot be broken without refunding one month's rent, however. Since he takes good care of his unit and has just repainted its interior, asking him to leave seems unfair. As luck would have it, when the lease expires he decides to move out. Furnishings costing $1,550 are moved in and a renter is quickly found at $1,050 per month. The rent on the other unit is increased to $975 a month.

The two units' monthly rents for the second, third, fourth, and fifth years are $1,080, $1,110, $1,140, $1,170 and $1,005, $1,035, $1,050, $1,095, respectively. The garage continues to rent for $45 a month. Expenses for the five years are: $7,800, $8,100, $8,400, $8,700, and $9,000. A cash flow analysis reveals the following:

Year	1	2	3	4	5
Rental Income	$24,840	$25,560	$26,280	$26,820	$27,720
Expenses	7,800	8,100	8,400	8,700	9,000
Difference	$17,040	$17,460	$17,880	$18,120	$18,720
Furnishing Cost	1,500	1,550	0	0	0
Net Income	$15,040	$15,910	$17,880	$18,120	$18,720
Loan Payments	12,864	12,864	12,864	12,864	12,864
Net Cash Flow*	$ 2,356	$ 3,046	$ 5,016	$ 5,256	$ 5,756
Cash Flow/Down Payment	7.1%	9.1%	15.0%	15.7%	17.2%

*Before taxes

In the third year net cash flow is coming in at a rate equal to 15% of the investor's original commitment, the down payment of $33,450. The actual return also needs to take account of the amortization of the mortgage loan, the appreciation of the property, and the impact of taxes. Let us now consider the return on the actual investment. More information is required to make the appropriate computations.

After-Tax Return

Since taxes are a critical part of the analysis, they should be incorporated into the assessment. This particular investment has earned much more than the original forecast. At the end of five years net annual rents exceed expenses by $18,720 compared with the earlier estimate of $15,660. A sale at about 10 times that amount ($182,000) would yield a substantial profit. Assume, however, that the duplex sells for only $170,000 (about nine times net income) and that the owner's marginal tax rate is 28%. What would the tax liability be for these assumptions? Answering this question requires a number of computations.

First, the property's taxable income is determined by subtracting all deductible expenses from rental income. The amortization portion of the loan payment cannot be subtracted, but depreciation, a noncash expense, is deductible. If, for example, the house has a 25-year life remaining and the land is worth $20,000, $4,552 can be deducted annually ($113,800 divided by 25). Land is not depreciated. The furniture is assumed to last five years. Thus, the first year's furniture depreciation is $300 and in subsequent years $630. These figures are put together with the bank's computation of the annual interest portion of the loan payments. The following sums are obtained:

Year	1	2	3	4	5
Rental Income	$24,840	$25,560	$26,280	$26,820	$27,720
Expenses	7,800	8,100	8,400	8,700	9,000
Gross Income	$17,040	$17,460	$17,880	$18,120	$18,720
Less: Depreciation	4,852	5,182	5,182	5,182	5,182
Operating Income	$12,188	$12,278	$12,698	$12,938	$13,538
Less: Interest	11,988	11,952	11,916	11,544	11,208
Taxable Income	$ 200	$ 326	$ 782	$ 1,394	$ 2,330
Tax (assuming a 28% rate)	56	91	219	390	652
After-Tax Income	$ 144	$ 235	$ 563	$ 1,004	$ 1,678

To obtain the net after-tax cash flows we must subtract tax liability from net cash flow before taxes.

Year	1	2	3	4	5
Net Cash Flow*	$2,356	$3,046	$5,016	$5,256	$5,756
Tax (assuming a 28% rate)	56	91	219	390	652
Net After-Tax Cash Flow	$2,300	$2,955	$4,797	$4,866	$5,104

*Before taxes

Next, the gain on the unit's sale is computed. The costs of closing ($3,000) and the furniture ($3,050) are added to the $133,800 purchase price and then depreciation ($25,580) is deducted to obtain a basis of $114,270. The basis is in turn subtracted from the expected net sale price of $160,000 (assuming commissions of 6% of the gross sales price of $170,000) to produce a taxable gain of

$55,730. Twenty-eight percent of this sum yields a tax of $15,604. Five years of amortization reduces the loan principal to $98,049. Subtracting the loan (assume no prepayment penalty) and taxes from the sale price yields the following:

Net Sale Price	$160,000
Loan Repayment	98,049
Difference	$ 61,951
Tax on Sale	15,604
Net Proceeds for Seller	$ 46,347

Thus expected net after-tax cash flow on the original investment of $33,450 is $2,300, $2,955, $4,797, $4,866, $5,104, and $46,347 for the first five years. These flows represent an anticipated after-tax annual return of over 25%. That is, the present value of this projected income stream discounted at 25% is greater than the $33,450 original investment.

Assessment

An investor could earn this much even in a high interest rate environment. The example does, however, make some rather optimistic assumptions. For instance, the occupancy rate in this example is assumed to be 100%. Such an occupancy rate over five years is possible but very unlikely. In addition, the duplex might require a new roof, a new furnace, an outside paint job, or some other major unexpected expense. Moreover, a tenant could leave owing back rent, taking some furniture, and/or seriously damaging the structure. Finally, the investor should realize that part of the return is compensation for managing the property. A fair amount of work is involved in collecting rents, making minor repairs, selling the property without a Realtor, and so on. The investor should expect to be well rewarded for these efforts.

EXAMPLE: THE APARTMENT BUILDING OWNER

Most real estate investors start small. They are likely to begin with duplexes and/or single-unit properties. After some years of investing in small-sized properties, a successful real estate investor who has been able to accumulate about $400,000 might next consider investing in an apartment building. Both the problems and the profit potential increase with the scale of investment.

The investor might look for an old but solidly built structure in an established neighborhood close to transportation routes. Suppose that a 10% minimum initial return is required. Note that the minimum acceptable return should vary with market interest rates. If government bonds are yielding 9%, for example, 10% would be too low.

Suppose that, after reviewing the various possibilities, the investor chooses an established section in his or her locality. Real estate brokers are then contacted and objectives explained. Market conditions, while not ideal, are considered acceptable.

TABLE 20.4 Financing and Cash Flow for 24-Unit Apartment Building

Financing		
First Mortgage, 13% due 2002		$1,000,000
Second Mortgage, 15% due 1992 (10-year amount)		600,000
Down Payment Required		400,000
Total Price (after negotiations)		$2,000,000
Annual Cash Flow		
Gross Income		$ 450,000
Operating Expenses:		
Fuel	$ 8,610	
Utilities	5,350	
Taxes	52,000	
Insurance	2,750	
Maintenance	17,500	
Superintendent (part-time)	12,580	
Management	64,500	
Vacancy (3%)	10,000	
Total Operating Expenses	$173,290	
Interest, First Mortgage	$129,345	
Interest, Second Mortgage	88,125	
Principal, First Mortgage	11,245	
Principal, Second Mortgage	28,035	
Total Loan Payments	$256,750	
Gross Cash Outflow		$ 430,040
Net Cash Flow		$ 19,960
Cash return on investment: 5.0%		
Return prior to principal repayment (+ $39,280): 14.8%		

Most available properties are either run-down or high priced. After three months, however, a new listing for a 24-unit apartment building looks promising. Since the property meets the desired physical objectives, its financial picture is carefully examined.

The seller's fact sheet shows gross income of $450,000, operating expenses of $350,000, and net cash flow of $100,000. A cash flow of 25% on the $400,000 down payment seems suspiciously high. In fact, it is too good. After careful examination, a more realistic picture emerges, as shown in Table 20.4.

The first year's cash return is 5% instead of the claimed 25%. Clearly, the potential investor should always seek to determine the true story. Assume the buyer has decided to use a small local company to manage the property. Their fee is based on the gross income of the apartment complex. Since the management company will look after the property's problems, why not get them into the act early? The buyer might well have the management company evaluate the building's price and general condition. Their fee for this service should be modest compared to the total amount of monies involved.

Suppose that a price of $2,000,000 is eventually agreed to. The investor is now an apartment owner. What about the risks? What safeguards does the investor have? Any risks involved with the neighborhood and its environment should be considered. If the management company selects responsible tenants and maintains the property well, the occupancy rate should be relatively high.

The building's superintendent is often given a rent-free apartment for keeping an eye on things and doing odd jobs. Thus such tasks as simple plumbing, carpentry, and electrical repairs will be up to the superintendent. Perhaps a share of profits would increase his or her interest. Beyond that, management problems belong to the management company. An occasional visit will reveal if its work is handled smoothly and show that the investor is more than just an absentee landowner.

If rents are reasonable for the area, turnover should be low and occupancy high. The tenants may be encouraged to fix up their apartments when they offer to do so. Their costs will be low (no charge for their own labor) and they will be happier with units that they can alter to suit themselves.

How can profits be increased? Perhaps buying quality furnishings for some of the apartments would allow a rent increase of $150 a month. In two or three years, the furniture would be paid for but it would probably last five or six years. Converting 12 of the apartments over several years could increase annual income by a few thousand dollars.

REFINANCING

Refinancing represents a useful option for many real estate investment situations. Assume that an apartment building was purchased five years ago for $900,000. The buyer borrowed $720,000 and made a $180,000 down payment. Now the property has appreciated and amortization has reduced the mortgage principal to $650,000. The owner could sell the property for a substantial gain but such a sale would have several significant drawbacks. A large part of the proceeds would have to be paid as taxes and subsequent appreciation would be forgone. Thus the owner may prefer to extract some funds by refinancing. Suppose that a reappraisal establishes $2,000,000 as a fair market value. The bank should now be willing to increase the loan by about $950,000 (to $1,600,000, or 80% of $2,000,000).

While refinancing may seem to be an attractive way to obtain additional funds, some potential pitfalls should be noted. An existing loan might have to be refinanced at a higher rate. Second, additional fees and penalties are associated with refinancing (e.g., a prepayment penalty, title search, and points). Third, the new loan will require an increase in the loan payments. Fourth, in extreme cases a refinancing will be viewed by the IRS as a quasi-sale and taxes will be assessed on the apparent gain.

Rather than a complete refinancing, the investor might take out a second mortgage loan. Thus the investor would retain the existing mortgage loan while paying the new (higher) rate only on the new loan. Depending on the relative loan size and rates involved, obtaining a second may be a less costly and more flexible way of extracting additional principal.

OTHER REAL ESTATE INVESTMENTS

Condominiums.   Apartments, duplexes, and single-unit houses are not the only types of residential real estate available to investors. Indeed, a substantial investment market has developed for condominiums. The rent on a unit will usually cover most of the investor's out-of-pocket costs. In addition to deducting interest and property taxes, the owner may also deduct depreciation (a noncash expense). Thus the investment may show a loss for tax purposes while producing a positive cash flow. Moreover, condominium investments require only limited management, and maintenance is covered by a monthly assessment to the owner's association. Some parents even purchase condominiums for their children to live in while attending college. Their goal is to provide their children with superior housing and eventually earn a profit on the investment.

Condominium investors have often earned high returns in the short period that the market has been active. Growth in the singles and older populations has helped boost condominium prices almost as rapidly as the prices of single-family homes have risen. Since the apartment shortage has added to the strength of the rental market, condominium investors have frequently received excellent rents while they wait to sell their units at attractive prices. As with all investments, however, condominiums are far from a sure thing.

While some financial institutions prefer borrowers who intend to live in their units, they will usually agree to lend to condominium investors when money is less tight. On the other hand, many communities have strictly limited the conversion of existing apartments to condominiums. Thus potential government restrictions are one major factor to consider before buying an apartment building for condominium conversion.

Land.   Land ownership appeals to many investors both because of its high profit potential and because, in a sense, land costs less than developed property. Relatively large land parcels are often available for less than $50,000 whereas most developed real estate sells for far more.

The attractiveness of undeveloped real estate is enhanced by a cash return. Such a return can cover at least part of the cost of carrying the property (taxes, insurance, financing, etc.). Some types of land are suitable for farming, grazing cattle, timber, hunting, or fishing. Thinning out woodlands allows the remaining trees to grow faster. Depending on the quality, the timber harvest might be sold for lumber, firewood, or Christmas trees.

Holding land for subsequent development is often quite profitable. The investor should, however, be prepared to wait years before the growth of a city, the construction of a highway or shopping center, or some other nearby activity makes development attractive. Once such an event takes place, the land's value might multiply many times.

Unlike loans for developed real estate, land loans are generally limited to 50% of the value of the undeveloped property. Moreover, the taxes and mortgage loan payments will at best only be partially covered by the land's modest return (if any). Land investors must be prepared to service the loan and pay the property taxes, largely from other sources.

Attractive land parcels are likely to have one or more of the following characteristics:

1. The property is the next step or the second step beyond the area's most recent development.

2. The property is already zoned for development and the local government might allow even higher density residential, commercial, or industrial use.

3. A nearby property owner might soon want to add the land to his or her own parcel.

4. Developers or other knowledgeable real estate entrepreneurs are buying or about to start buying in the area.

5. A public or private development has been announced for the area.

6. The land is producing an attractive yield from farming, grazing, or some other activity, helping offset holding costs.

Note, however, that even under the most attractive circumstances, raw land is a relatively risky investment. Moreover, as with other investments, largely overlooked land investment opportunities may be the most profitable.

Recreational Property.   At some times, sites that offer recreational opportunities, especially those near water, are hotly sought after. At other times, the high price and occasional scarcity of gasoline severely depresses the recreational real estate market. Thus investors should consider how potential owners would reach their property. On the other hand, many city dwellers still want to get away to fish, hunt, boat, hike, grow something, or just relax. Thus well-located recreational properties will always be marketable. Moreover, the transportation outlook can change or a population center might grow up near a heretofore isolated area. As with other types of real estate investing, predictions and generalizations are hazardous. Isolated out-of-the-way spots might suddenly seem much closer to civilization if an interstate highway is built or oil is discovered nearby.

Cemeteries.   Many states, particularly in the South and West, allow profit-making cemeteries. Such cemeteries are a potentially profitable form of land development. The economics are staggering. Depending on the configuration, between 1,000 and 1,500 graves may be obtained per acre. A successful cemetery will sell perhaps 500 to 800 graves per year and so 50 acres yield a 75-year supply. Grave sites may be priced for a few hundred up to several thousand dollars. While some of this fee must be put in a maintenance trust, even at a net of $100 per grave, an acre represents $100,000 of potential sales.

Commercial Property.   An investor could become a silent partner in a car wash, distributorship, or shopping center. That in effect is what commercial property investors are. Such investors do have the security of owning the property, however. If one tenant does poorly, perhaps another will be more successful. Since location

Investments in Perspective

People who own their own home are already real estate investors. Some of them may consider taking the next step and becoming rental property owners. One way of doing that on a small scale is to rent out a room. The following article taken from *The New York Times* discusses the trend toward bed and breakfast. Participants turn their houses into little businesses by renting out a spare room to guests.

PERSONAL FINANCE / Carole Gould

Turning a Spare Room Into a Business

Bed-and-breakfasts are popping up across America as homeowners earn extra cash — and have a good time, too.

EIGHT months ago, Peggy and Michael Ackerman decided they could not afford a home large enough for themselves and their two children in New York. Instead, they bought a house near Lake Wallenpaupack, a recreational area in northeast Pennsylvania, and opened a bed-and-breakfast. While Mr. Ackerman commutes to a new job in Scranton, his wife tends the guests. "They help pay the mortgage and besides, it's like being on vacation all the time," Mrs. Ackerman said.

Bed-and-breakfasts have traditionally been a European venture, but increasingly they are capturing the American imagination. Young couples like the Ackermans use the business to finance their first homes. Older couples can turn their children's empty rooms into cash. And, in at least one instance, two enterprising single women in New York City are renting their Upper East Side apartments to overnight guests: When either one expects a paying guest, she moves to her friend's apartment for the night.

To date there are about 10,000 bed-and-breakfasts across the United States, more than double the figure five years ago, and that number is growing about 20 percent a year. Mostly they are small ventures, typically with fewer than four rooms to rent. "You won't get wealthy by running a B-and-B, but it's a flexible business and you can have lots of fun," said Betty Rundback, co-author with Nancy Kramer of "Bed and Breakfast, U.S.A.," a guidebook published annually by E.P. Dutton Inc. ($9.95).

Before venturing in, consider these questions: Will the bed-and-breakfast be a sideline or a full-time business? Will the operation attract seasonal or year-round visitors? Are family members com-

fortable with the idea of sharing their home?

The next step is to investigate local zoning laws. Full-fledged inns are classified as commercial enterprises, but the smaller bed-and-breakfasts often fall into a gray area. Many communities have "customary home occupation" provisions, designed to permit only those businesses that will not violate the residential character of the area.

To find out the local rules, tell the zoning people "that you want to see the book because you want to put in a swimming pool, then flip through to find the relevant provisions," because businesses not specifically prohibited generally are permitted, advised Barbara Notarius, who is president of Bed and Breakfast, U.S.A., Ltd., a reservation service in Croton-on-Hudson, N.Y. That way, you may be able to avoid the tricky issue of obtaining permission directly from the zoning board, Ms. Notarius said.

In many cases, start-up expenses are minimal. Expect to spend about $500 for insurance, printing costs, smoke alarms or other equipment to make the house conform to local fire codes.

Rates should be about 40 percent lower than those of major hotels nearby. Add $10 for rooms with private baths, plus about $1.50 for continental breakfasts or $3 for full breakfasts. Check bed-and-breakfast guidebooks for comparable rates. The two New York City women charge $75 a night for either of their apartments, while the Ackermans charge $35 for a room in their Pennsylvania home.

Design a brochure that includes rates, a description of the home, the number of rooms and baths available, the type of breakfast served, minimum stay requirement, if any, and the cancellation policy. Include a reservation form.

Promote the business by distributing brochures to local universities and hospitals; the personnel office of nearby companies, for visiting and relocating executives; to caterers, who may send out-of-town wedding guests, Mrs. Rundback suggests.

Bed-and-breakfast owners may purchase professional management, including promotion, by joining a reservation service. For a $50 flat fee, annual dues of $25 to $100 and a 20 percent commission, these services will advertise, prescreen guests, mail confirmations and often collect the deposits. For information, contact Bed and Breakfast Reservation Services Worldwide, a trade group based in Baton Rouge, La.

Liability insurance, crucial for innkeepers, has become a problem in recent years. The $1 million group coverage policy offered to members of Bed and Breakfasts, U.S.A., Ltd., the service run by Ms. Notarius, jumped to $150 from $30 a few years ago; to buy a comparable policy privately, she said, would cost $1,000 or more.

Ask arriving guests to sign a ledger with their home and business addresses and telephone numbers, as well as information on whom to contact in the event of an emergency; a carbon copy can serve as a receipt. You might want to accept credit cards as payment, but first find out whether the charge for that service justifies the convenience.

To cut down on the number of no-shows, many bed-and-breakfast owners now require full payment in advance for overnight stays. For longer visits, ask for a 50 percent deposit; guests who cancel less than seven days in advance typically forfeit one night's charge, while those who give more than a week's notice receive their full deposit.

BED-AND-BREAKFASTS also offer the opportunity to convert some otherwise non-deductible personal expenses into business write-offs. Leslie and Arnold Gallo, two Manhattan psychiatrists, opted to turn their Victorian country home, situated on 60 acres in Lebanon Springs, N.Y., into a business venture. The Gallos estimate they spent several hundred thousand dollars renovating the property and building two tennis courts. After paying an innkeeper to handle the business and about $5,000 for annual maintenance, the couple earn approximately $8,000 a year for four rooms rented nightly at $85 each. While the profits are not impressive, "people are our business, and we have fun socializing with our guests," Mrs. Gallo said.

Source: C. Gould, "Turning a Spare Room into a Business," *The New York Times*, September 14, 1986, p. f11. © 1986 by The New York Times Company. Reprinted by permission.

---

is a very important aspect of profitable operations, potential investors should carefully evaluate main traffic arteries, exits, parking, and the proximity of competitors.

Investors in commercial property can normally borrow up to 75% of the property's price. Usually a five- or 10-year lease is signed obligating the tenant to pay all operating costs except for mortgage loan service, property insurance, and major renovations. The proposed tenant's credit rating should be carefully examined before executing a lease. The investor should expect to earn at least several percentage points above the current inflation rate.

Some owners charge a percentage of sales rather than a flat rental fee. Paying less in poor years provides renters with a bit of a cushion. They pay more in a good year when they can afford to. Assuming this added risk should generally increase the owner's return. Rents can also be structured as a flat amount plus a percentage of sales.

Franchises.   Rather than rent to a business, some investors may enter a business themselves. One seemingly attractive way of doing so is through a franchise. The franchiser supplies an identity, perhaps a product, and some expertise. Many franchises, however, do not succeed. Both poor locations and inferior products often cause franchise investors to fail. Their high mortality rate makes gas stations and fast food operations a poor place to invest retirement money.

Whether or not an investor should consider franchises depends on his or her risk orientation. Many well-known franchises such as Baskin Robbins and McDonald's earn attractive returns. Investors should ask the franchiser to cosign his or her lease. If the franchiser refuses, the investor should ask why. Don't they believe in their product? Such a question may put the franchiser's representative on the spot but better that than discover the problems after the contract is signed. Additionally, many franchisers will help secure the needed funds or offer a limited repayment guarantee for the borrowed capital. Prospective investors should determine if these options are available.

REAL ESTATE STOCKS AND TAX SHELTERS

Many investors are not well situated to own, manage, and assume the risks involved with direct real estate ownership. Yet, the returns that property has generated in the past will seem attractive to many investors. Such investors may want to consider other ways of participating in the real estate market. Commingled real estate funds, real estate investment trusts, real estate development companies, real estate tax shelters, real estate sales companies, and companies with substantial property holdings all represent indirect ways of investing in property. Each offers the opportunity to participate in the market without having a management involvement. Most of these investments are publicly traded companies that own, develop, manage, or sell real estate.

Commingled Real Estate Funds. Commingled real estate funds (CREFs) are in essence self-liquidating unit investment trusts that assemble and manage real estate portfolios. Most are managed by large life insurance companies or commercial banks for their pension fund clients. Others are available to trust department clients. Still others are sold directly to the public. While a relatively small industry, the funds have grown substantially since the mid-1970s. According to Miles and Esty, the larger and older funds have tended to produce the highest returns.[4] Moreover, the large funds are able to diversify more effectively. On the other hand, CREFs are rather costly to buy and sell. Secondary market trading in the units is very thin and initial sales to the public usually involve a substantial load.

Real Estate Investment Trusts. Beginning in 1961, Congress permitted the establishment of real estate investment trusts (REITs). They assemble and manage portfolios of real estate and real estate loans. REITs are organized like and their shares trade in the same markets as those of corporations. They are not, however, assessed corporate profits taxes if they pay out 95% or more of their income as dividends. Many such firms were formed in the early 1970s. Most initially offered relatively attractive dividend yields. By mid-1974, however, overbuilding had begun to take its toll. Many real estate developers defaulted on their loans. The REITs were forced to foreclose on unfinished property that frequently bore no income. The REITs' own debt continued to require servicing.

In 1976, many REIT stocks sold for 5% to 10% of their original issue prices. Some subsequently went bankrupt. Others only survived at the behest of their creditors. Eventually, however, most of the remaining REITs paid and/or swapped (for their own assets) their debts down to manageable levels. Many of the survivors now own substantial amounts of real estate that has appreciated dramatically. Some also have large tax-loss carryforwards. Moreover, Burns and Epley report that REITs provide excellent diversification for a stock and bond portfolio.[5]

Real Estate Development Companies. Real estate development companies own land, build on it, and then sell the developed properties. They may construct apartments, office buildings, shopping centers, townhouses, single units, or practically any other type of structure. Often these projects are undertaken as joint ventures with other firms. Obviously, the development company hopes to build and resell the property at a substantial profit. Developers need large sums of risk capital to finance their projects. If costs are higher or the market weaker than expected, the developer may incur a major loss. Thus these companies are frequently quite risky. Nonetheless, effectively managed companies often do well.

Real Estate Tax Shelters. Many companies make a business of selling investments structured primarily as tax shelters. These investments are designed to appeal to people in high (or at least above-average) tax brackets. Tax shelters are often built around wildcat oil wells, cattle farms, equipment leases, and real estate.

Real estate tax shelter syndicates were once very popular. They were generally formed to finance a construction project or the acquisition of existing properties. Subtracting depreciation, operating expenses, and interest from rental income produced a tax loss. Once rents rose sufficiently to generate a profit (in perhaps five years), the property was sold for a gain (so the tax was deferred until the sale). Thus, the shelter was designed to produce tax losses for a number of years. To be an attractive investment, the gain on the sale needed to exceed the operating loss total.

Under the Tax Reform Act of 1986 losses on such shelters are generally classified as passive. Passive losses can only be used to offset passive income.

Often an investment that seems attractive on paper does not produce the desired results. Promoters sometimes organize these shelters primarily to pay themselves unreasonably high sales and management fees. Such expenses come off the top of any returns the shelter may generate. In other instances, inefficient management and real estate sales reduce the return. Inflated prices are frequently paid to acquire the shelter's property, reducing any chance for a gain. Investments in most tax shelters are not very marketable. Moreover, the IRS will eventually disallow part or all of the tax-loss deduction on abusive tax shelters. Investors are charged interest and a penalty on the resulting tax underpayment. In other instances, tax laws may be changed to eliminate or substantially reduce the projected tax advantage of a particular type of deal. While tax shelters are ill suited to most small investors, the wealthy may still find the tax advantages worth the effort.

Real Estate Limited Partnerships. Real Estate Limited Partnerships, or RELPs, are specialized securities that provide investors with an interest in a portfolio of real estate properties. Organized as a limited partnership, such securities have much in common with corporations. Each investor's liabilities is limited to the amount that he or she initially invests. The management function rests with a group of hired managers. The securities may be freely bought and sold. The principal difference from a corporation is in the way the partnership's income is taxed.

A corporation is an entity that is subject to tax in its own right. The dividends that it pays are taxed a second time as income to the owners (assuming that they are subject to an income tax). A partnership is viewed as a conduit for transferring income to the owner. Thus the full amount of any partnership income is subject to the investor's income tax. No additional tax is assessed at the partnership level. Thus the partnership's income is only taxed once. Accordingly, the combination of limited liability and favorable tax treatment makes RELPs an ideal vehicle for individual participation in the real estate market.

A number of brokerage firms have sponsored the issuance of RELPs through public offerings. Others have been offered by the syndicator sponsor who is slated to manage the partnership once it is established. All limited partnerships must have a general partner who assumes general liability. Usually the sponsor takes on this role.

The principal drawbacks to RELPs are their relatively limited secondary markets and their relatively high overhead structure of fees and expenses. Such investments are generally difficult to sell prior to their scheduled liquidation. Moreover, the sponsoring syndicate usually structures the deal so that much of the profits go to them while most of the risks are borne by the investors. Average returns for RELPs have not thus far been particularly impressive.[6]

Real Estate Mutual Funds. At least five families of funds now offer real estate oriented funds. Fidelity, National Securities and Research, and Monarch Capital have funds that invest in the stocks of real estate companies. Vanguard, in contrast, manages a REIT whereas T. Rowe Price manages a group of real estate limited partnerships. The Fidelity and National Securities investments are mutual funds. Monarch's entry is organized as a variable annuity. All three of these funds have loads, are priced daily, and are redeemable upon demand. The Price funds trade in a relatively thin secondary market. The firm starts new funds periodically and each is set to be liquidated in seven to ten years. Similarly, the Vanguard REIT is a finite life entity. These various funds bring an element of diversification and liquidity to the real estate market. The organizers are, to be sure, extracting significant fees (loads, management fees, redemption fees, etc.) for their services.

Real Estate Sales Companies. Some companies sell retirement and investment homesites in Arizona, New Mexico, Florida, or even Australia. Marketing generally involves a professional sales demonstration coupled with a free dinner. The sales companies usually "promise" to install streets, recreation areas, and other improvements (swimming pools, tennis courts, golf courses, etc.) in their planned communities. The properties are offered for terms that provide for a minimum down payment. Principal is to be repaid over an extended period. Slides, movies, and glossy brochures are used to show the property to its maximum advantage. Rarely if ever are these promotion sales attractive to the buyer. Often the land is substantially overpriced and the promised improvements are frequently left undone.

The stocks of most real estate sales companies are also very risky. At one time, such companies were reporting rapidly increasing earnings by claiming the full profit on a real estate sale in the year that they received the down payment. Since subsequent defaults were very common, such profit figures were misleading, to say the least. Now the firms must report income as payments are received.

Companies with Real Estate Holdings. In addition to the real estate related investments, a number of other types of companies have substantial property holdings. In most instances their properties are related to their primary business, but in others they just happen to own the real estate. Among the real estate holders are the following:

Paper and Forest Products Companies: Such firms often have substantial land holdings from which they obtain timber and wood pulp. Some of this land may be worth far more as homesites, for example. Other property may be worth a good deal just as timberland.

Railroads: Many rails, particularly those located in the West, own substantial tracts of land, much of which goes back to 19th century government land grants. Other rails own valuable downtown property near their terminals. Rails with poor prospects as transport companies are often quite depressed. If their landholdings are ever liquidated, however, the profits to shareholders could be substantial.

Ranch and Farm Companies: Some agricultural operations with substantial landholdings are organized as corporations. Frequently this property is carried on the books at very low historical costs. The liquidation values of such firms are often well above the market prices of their stock.

Oil and Mining Companies: Generally their most valuable holdings are their mineral resources, but often these companies too own some real estate. As with the other types of firms, the stock price may not fully reflect the property's liquidation value.

Manufacturers: Most manufacturers only own the plants that they operate. Some own valuable office buildings and attractive landholdings that are often overlooked by the market.

Insurance Companies: Life insurance companies have huge sums to invest. While most of their funds go into bonds, mortgages, and other loans, some are invested in real estate. Moreover, in many instances the market seems to undervalue that property.

Movie Companies: While most moviemakers have sold off their real estate, some still have valuable studio property in Hollywood. Such property may or may not be recognized in the stock's price.

Retailers: Many large retailers have valuable real estate in the form of the store buildings in which they operate. Others have long-term leases at rental rates that are far below the current market levels.

The investment attractiveness of companies with substantial real estate holdings depends both on the extent to which their stock price reflects the holdings and on the likelihood that the property will be sold in the relatively near future.

SUMMARY AND CONCLUSIONS

This chapter considered a number of aspects of real estate investing. A prospective real estate investor should first determine his or her suitability for such investing. Can sufficient funds be tied up for several years? Is the investor likely to remain in the same geographic area for the foreseeable future? Are the talents needed to manage real estate present? Is the investor willing and able to accept the risks?

Next, certain principles of real estate investing were considered. These principles related to the determination of the price of a given parcel of land by its most valuable uses, the fixed supply of land, the possibility of adverse price moves, the importance of shopping around, the use of leverage, the control of expenses, the inspection of prospective real estate, the use of professionals, and the impact of government actions.

Then three approaches to real estate valuation (market, cost, and income) were considered, followed by a detailed application of the income approach. Bargaining, loan negotiation, property management, and refinancing were examined along the way.

Finally, various types of real estate investing and related investments were discussed (including duplexes, apartments, land, condominiums, recreational property, commercial property, franchises, cemeteries, and companies that own substantial amounts of real estate).

REVIEW QUESTIONS

1. What types of investors are and are not suited for real estate investing? How do these considerations apply to owner-occupied real estate?

2. Discuss 10 principles of real estate investment.

3. Compare the methods of valuing real estate and discuss the uses of each. Which is most like capital budgeting? What should the investor do when the three methods yield different valuations?

4. Examine the advantages and disadvantages of investing in real estate compared with common stock. What alternatives are available to the investor who likes the general prospects of real estate but is put off by some of the problems of direct real estate investing?

5. Consider indirect real estate investing via REITs, development companies, limited partnerships, operating companies with substantial real estate holdings, and tax shelters.

REVIEW PROBLEMS

1. Refer to Table 20.1. Assume that the estimates of the holding period return are correct for a holding period equal to the average of the range. What is the implied rate of return on each type of investment? Which of the various investment types offer the highest expected return? Recompute the answers for the minimum and maximum estimated holding periods. Discuss the results of this exercise.

2. You are considering the purchase of a home. Your first choice lists for $185,000 but you believe the seller will accept an offer of $179,000. Your

local banker will lend you 75% of the purchase price. You must, however, pay three points for the loan and a $500 loan application fee. A title search in your area costs 1.5% of the purchase price. Inspections for structural soundness cost $250. The real estate agent's fee is 7% of the sale price. Transferring the title will cost you ½% of the sale price. You must deposit in an escrow account six months' property taxes. Property taxes are set at 4% of assessed valuation. In the first year, assessed valuation will equal 85% of the sale price. You must also pay the first year's property (fire) insurance in advance. Insurance rates in your community are $4 per thousand dollars of protection. The bank requires that you insure your property for 90% of its assessed valuation or 100% of the mortgage balance outstanding, whichever is lower. To have a lawyer represent you at the closing will incur a fee of $200. Hooking up various utilities will require fees of $340 and deposits of another $500. How much must you pay in total for acquiring and occupying the house? How much of this amount will the seller receive? How much is the difference? If we consider the total difference to be the transaction costs, what percentage do these transactions costs represent of the total sale price?

3. You are considering the purchase of a parcel of land for $45,000. You can borrow up to 50% of the purchase price at a rate of 13%. Long-term government bonds are yielding 10%. What rate of return on the investment is required to make this offer attractive? Explain.

4. Using the same basic information as is supplied in the text presentation entitled "The Income Approach: An Example," recompute the net present value for the following rates: borrowing cost = 10%; alternative yield on low-risk investment = 8%; and risk premium = 2%.

5. You are offering a small apartment complex for sale. Your asking price is $850,000. A prospective buyer is able to obtain a first mortgage for 75% of the sale price. She asks you to take back a second mortgage for $150,000. She offers to pay 9% on the second with a partial amortization over five years and then a balloon payment of $100,000 (with an option to the buyer to convert the balloon to a 10-year amortized mortgage at 11%). She is willing to pay your offering price if you will accept her terms on the second. If the market rate on second mortgages such as the one she proposes would be 13.5%, how much of a price concession is she in effect seeking?

6. Continue with the facts of Problem 5. Suppose the bank views the second mortgage as a hidden price concession. How much would they then reduce the amount of the mortgage that they offer on the property? If the prospective buyer asks that you finance that difference on proportionally similar terms as the initial second, how much more of a price concession would be involved? Suppose the bank now views that additional amount as a concession. How much more would the bank reduce its mortgage? At what point would this process stop?

7. A duplex is offered for sale at $180,000. After expenses, it offers a net

rental income (after deducting all out-of-pocket expenses except financing costs and taxes) of $28,000 per year. The rents, expenses, and market value of the property are expected to remain constant for the foreseeable future. The buyer may borrow up to 90% of the purchase price at 11%. The seller agrees to deduct any closing costs from the purchase price. Should you buy it? Why or why not? Explain your answer.

8. Continue with the analysis begun in Problem 7. Assume that you do buy the duplex and borrow 90% on a 25-year loan and are in the 35% tax bracket. The apartment is depreciated over a 40-year period. Calculate after-tax cash flow for a 10-year period. Assume you sell for $180,000 at the end of the 10-year period. Interest on the loan is as follows:

Year	Interest	Principal	Principal Outstanding
1989	$22,631.97	$ 769.23	$161,230.77
1990	22,517.08	884.12	160,346.65
1991	22,385.06	1,016.14	159,370.51
1992	22,233.29	1,167.91	158,162.60
1993	22,058.89	1,342.31	156,820.29
1994	21,858.41	1,542.79	155,277.50
1995	21,628.02	1,773.18	153,504.32
1996	21,363.20	2,038.00	151,466.32
1997	21,058.85	2,342.35	148,123.97
1998	20,709.03	2,692.17	146,431.80

9. Refer to the information in the text presentation entitled "Example: The Apartment Building Owner." Assume that the building's rents, operating expenses, and market value increase at a 5% rate for the next five years. Compute the internal rate of return to the investor.

10. Suppose that you purchase 100 acres for a cemetery. You expect to obtain 1,000 graves per acre. You expect to sell 800 graves per year for $1,000 per sale. Of this amount $300 will go for preparation and selling expenses and $600 will go into a maintenance trust. The rest should be profit. Using a 12% discount rate, what is the present value of this business? How much would the value change if an 11% discount rate were used and the maintenance trust only required $550 per grave?

REVIEW PROJECTS

1. Ask three local bankers for their terms on rental property loans. Also determine closing costs. Compare the rates and write a report.

2. Ask a real estate agent to recommend three investments. Evaluate each investment's price using the income, market, and replacement cost approaches. Determine the highest price that should be paid for each property.

3. Evaluate the property where you now live. If you were the seller what would you ask for it? What is the least you would take for it? If you were a prospective buyer, how would you proceed? What is the most you would pay? What would you try to buy it for?

4. Assemble a list of companies with real estate holdings whose market values substantially exceed the values of their outstanding shares. Determine if a major shareholder group controls each company. Plot their performances over time. Write a report.

NOTES

1. H. Folger, M. Granito, and L. Smith, "A Theoretical Analysis of Real Estate Returns," *Journal of Finance*, July 1985, 711–721.

2. *Successful Investing and Money Management* (USA: Hume Publishing, 1986), 4.9.

3. L. Downie, *Mortgage on America* (New York: Praeger, 1974), 135–152.

4. M. Miles and A. Esty, "How Well Do Commingled Real Estate Funds Perform?" *Journal of Portfolio Management*, Winter 1982, 62–68.

5. W. Burns and D. Epley, "The Performance of Portfolios of REITs & Stocks," *Journal of Portfolio Management*, Spring 1982, 37–42.

6. S. Kapplin and A. Schwartz, "Investing in Real Estate Limited Partnerships," *American Association of Individual Investors Journal*, September 1986, 8–12.

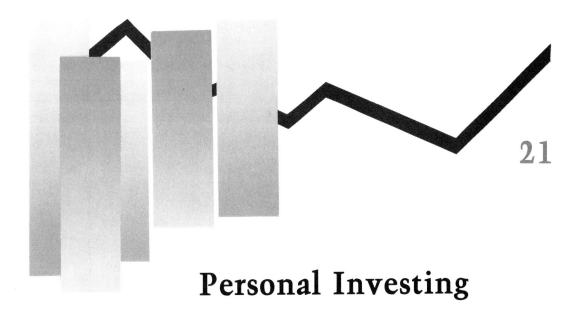

Personal Investing

Many people invest in stocks, bonds, and/or real estate, but many others do not or least have not yet begun to make such investments. Almost everyone, however, invests in some types of assets. For example, nearly every responsible adult has spent some money to acquire such assets as durable goods and an education. Defined broadly, an investment is any asset that is expected to confer benefits over time. Thus everyone who manages his or her own finances is an investor. Accordingly, a thorough treatment of investments should cover a variety of investment-related aspects of personal financial management. This chapter treats the following topics:

- Managing short-run finances
    Transaction balances
    Consumer credit
- Managing long-run finances
    Life insurance
    Pensions
    Savings
    Estate planning

Many books and entire courses are devoted to the topic of personal finance. Accordingly, this chapter can only scratch the surface of this important topic.

TABLE 21.1 Personal Balance Sheet Example before and after Debt Repayment

Assets	Before	After	Liabilities and Net Worth	Before	After
Short Term:			*Short Term:*		
Cash	35	35	Installment Credit	1,600	600
Checking Account	300	300			
S&L Account	4,700	400			
Intermediate Term:			*Intermediate Term:*		
Automobile	5,000	5,000	Auto Loan	3,300	0
Furniture and Personal					
Items	8,000	8,000			
Long Term:			*Long Term:*		
House	67,000	67,000	Loan on House	46,000	46,000
Life Insurance Cash			Total Liabilities	50,900	46,600
Value	5,000	5,000			
			Net Worth	39,135	39,135
Total Assets			Total Liabilities and Net		
	$90,035	$85,735	Worth	$90,035	$85,735

THE PERSONAL BALANCE SHEET

An important step in analyzing an individual's finances is assessing his or her current financial situation. A personal balance sheet is very helpful in making this assessment. Table 21.1 is a typical example of a personal balance sheet.

A personal balance sheet is also useful in developing a financial plan. The left side lists assets and their estimated values. Liabilities and net worth (assets minus liabilities) appear on the right. The *before* and *after* columns will be explained shortly.

Families typically have a variety of different types of assets. Its house is normally the family's most valuable tangible asset. An assortment of such consumer durables as motor vehicles, appliances, furniture, jewelry, silverware, and clothing are also listed. Most families also have such financial assets as cash, bank deposits, a life insurance policy (cash value), stocks, bonds, and limited partnership shares. Human capital (value of education and experience), often the household's most valuable asset, does not generally appear on the balance sheet.

Consumer and mortgage loans are the most common types of individual liabilities. Personal, credit card, and charge account debt are the principal types of consumer credit. Most home purchases are financed with long-term mortgages. Assets and liabilities are usually grouped by maturity. Short, intermediate, and long term refer to within a year, between one and five years, and more than five years, respectively.

Personal Debt Management

Most individuals incur debts in the course of managing their financial affairs. Debt can be an excellent financial tool when used effectively. One should always remember, however, that borrowing money is the easy job. Paying it back is the hard part. Debt payments can become a substantial burden on the family budget. Accordingly, a sound approach to debt management is one of the most important aspects of personal finance. The cost of financing one's debts is a function of both the amount borrowed and interest rate charged. Thus, effective debt management involves limiting both the amount borrowed and the rate charged without unduly sacrificing other needs.

Even modest-sized credit card and charge account balances deserve careful attention. Generally no interest charge is incurred if the balance is paid off within each billing period. Stores offering this "free credit" may, however, charge higher prices to cover their financing costs. Moreover, if any part of the balance remains unpaid at the end of the billing period, interest is assessed on the entire balance (including that month's payment). Such loans typically cost about 18% per year compounded monthly.

Borrowers should try to avoid (or minimize) the amounts borrowed at high interest rates. In particular, when a much lower rate is earned on investments, the borrower has an attractive alternative. For example, funds earning a low rate in a savings account could be used to pay down or pay off loans bearing a higher interest rate. Why pay 18% on a credit card balance when available funds are earning 5½% in a savings account?

Financial planners advise people to maintain a reserve for emergencies. Some experts recommend a reserve equal to six months' salary. Many people hold such a reserve in the form of a relatively low-yielding savings account. A line of credit offers an alternative way of obtaining equivalent protection. Switching to such a credit line reserve may well free up funds for more productive uses.

Credit lines are available from a variety of types of financial institutions. These lines may go under the name of a check/loan account, automatic overdraft privilege, margin account, home equity loan, and so on. The ability to borrow up to some previously agreed-upon sum offers an excellent short-term source of funds. Establishing these credit lines usually costs the individual nothing beyond the time and trouble of filling out the application form. Rates charged on any borrowed sums vary with the type of loan but are normally no higher than and may be below the rates on consumer credit loans.

Now reconsider the balance sheet in Table 21.1. The $4,700 in savings is probably designed to serve as an emergency reserve. If so, it might be replaced with a $5,000 line of credit. This action would free funds to pay off the $3,300 auto loan and $1,000 of installment credit and still leave a $400 balance for minor unexpected expenses. Savings earmarked for a vacation, addition to the house, or other soon-to-be-expected expense should not, however, be used to repay loans. Otherwise, one would soon have to take out a new loan to finance the anticipated expense.

Mortgage Debt.   Any additional available funds might be used to reduce an outstanding mortgage loan balance. Using reserves to pay down the balance on a mortgage loan may not offer the same kinds of attractions as repaying consumer loans. Consumer and mortgage loans differ in a number of important respects. Consumer loans are generally uncollateralized, written for relatively modest sums, and have relatively short time frames. A house's collateral value, in contrast, offers the lender much greater protection. Moreover, the cost of establishing and administering the mortgage loan is spread over a much larger sum and longer time. As a result market rates on new mortgage loans are generally appreciably below consumer loan rates. Thus the interest savings (difference between the investment return and the borrowing cost) from paying down a new mortgage loan may be relatively modest. Rates on mortgage loans established at an earlier time may, however, be very different from those available on new loans. One would normally want to retain low interest loans while reducing higher cost loan balances. When to reduce, refinance, or pay off a mortgage loan is, however, a complex issue. It has already been considered in the real estate chapter.

Shopping for a Loan.   Borrowers should devote at least as much effort to shopping for a major loan as they do shopping for a major purchase. The financing costs and terms of a loan can differ substantially from lender to lender. Indeed, the differences can easily be as great as the cost and quality differences for the items offered by the relevant retailers. Thus a careful examination of the loan alternatives may save a significant amount of money and trouble.

Consumers can seek to borrow funds in the form of a large variety of different loans. For example, they may undertake an auto, personal, home improvement, home equity, student, passbook, margin, life insurance cash value, or credit card loan. Commercial banks, savings banks, savings and loans, credit unions, finance companies, insurance companies, brokerage firms, and several government agencies all lend to consumers. This wide array of lenders and loan types illustrates the need for careful comparison shopping. A few points may, however, help to focus the search. First, government-subsidized loans (for example, loans to students, farmers, and homebuyers) are generally very attractive when available. Second, credit unions generally offer their members better rates than do other types of commercial lenders. Third, providing acceptable collateral usually reduces borrowing costs. Fourth, banks and savings and loans generally offer lower rates but require stronger credit records than do finance companies. Fifth, even within each loan category and lender type the costs and terms can vary.

Tax Impacts.   Most types of interest income are fully taxable (only municipal bond interest is tax free). Interest expense, in contrast, is not always deductible on the federal income tax return. Those who itemize may deduct the interest cost on loans used to finance investments (up to their investment income) and real estate holdings (on loans for amounts up to their original cost plus improvements). Those who do not itemize cannot deduct any of their interest payments. Those who itemize can deduct a small and declining percentage of consumer interest cost through 1990. The percentage of deductible consumer interest has been scheduled to decline from 20% in 1989 to 10% in 1990 and 0% in 1991.

Would-be investors should consider the tax implications when trying to decide whether to finance an investment with borrowed funds. Borrowing at 10% while earning 12% on an investment might seem attractive. If, however, the 12% return is fully taxable and the interest payments are not deductible (which would be the case for the taxpayer who does not itemize), such a transaction may not be profitable. Suppose the individual is in the 28% tax bracket. The after-tax cost of the loan is 10% as the loan does not affect the borrower's tax liability. The after-tax return of the investment is, in contrast, only 8.6% (.12 × .72). The funds used to finance the purchase would, in contrast, cost 10%. The net effect of the two transactions would be a negative 1.4% return.

Handling Liquid Assets

Cash and balances held in depository institutions (banks and similar institutions that hold and provide ready access to depositor funds) should provide convenient access to needed funds while earning an attractive yield. In general, the more accessible the funds, the lower is the return. Cash and the balances in some types of checking accounts earn no interest. Other types of accounts pay interest but require higher minimum balances and/or restrict access. Moreover, fees are charged for many of the services associated with maintaining a depository account. Thus choosing which types of accounts to have and how to distribute funds among them is an important aspect of money management.

Types of Bank Accounts. To manage money effectively individuals as investors need to know how various types of money-holding accounts differ. The first type of bank account that most people open is a savings account. Both the required minimum balance and the interest rate paid are relatively low. Furthermore, funds must be withdrawn at the bank or one of its automatic teller stations. The depositor cannot write checks on this type of (passbook savings) account. A variety of other types of accounts do permit checks to be written.

Regular and special checking accounts have relatively low minimum balances but do not earn interest. Of the two, the special accounts have a lower minimum balance but higher check clearing fees. NOW and superNOW accounts earn interest and permit check writing but require relatively high minimum balances. Of these two, NOW accounts have the lower minimum balances and pay a lower interest rate.

Actual minimum balance requirements vary from institution to institution and over time, but the following is representative: savings, $100; special, $100; regular, $250; NOW, $750; superNOW, $2,500. Fees and interest rates also vary. Typically the depositor would pay $.30 per check on special accounts and nothing on the other types as long as the minimum balance is maintained. A fee of a few dollars per month is typically charged on special accounts. Interest rates vary with credit conditions but superNOWs tend to yield somewhat more than NOW and savings accounts.

While superNOW rates tend to be a bit higher than any of the other types of unrestricted check writing accounts, still higher rates are available on other types of depository accounts. Money market accounts earn somewhat higher rates but allow the depositor only six withdrawals per month, only three of which may be by check. Each of these types of accounts is available at most depository institutions. In addition, mutual funds and brokerage firms offer some similar types of

TABLE 21.2   Types of Depository Accounts

	Non-interest-bearing
Special Checking Accounts	Low minimum balance
	Charge for each check
Regular Checking Accounts	Modest minimum balance
	No fees
	Low Interest Rates (5½% Typically)
NOW Accounts	Modest minimum balance
	No fees
Savings Accounts	Modest minimum balance
	No check writing privileges
	Money Market Based Interest Rates
SuperNOW Accounts	$1,000 minimum balance (or higher)
	Fees for some services
Cash Management Accounts	Extensive combination of financial accounts
Money Market Accounts	$1,000 minimum (or higher)
	Limited withdrawal rights
Money Market Mutual Funds	$1,000 minimum
	Not usually government insured

accounts. Table 21.2 summarizes the characteristics of the principal types of depository accounts.

LONG-TERM FINANCIAL PLANNING

Many otherwise talented people (especially busy professionals like doctors) mishandle their long-term finances. While the wealthy have long used financial consultants, their services are now available to the middle income group. Nonetheless, most people still prefer to do most of their own long-term planning. Even those who do seek expert help need at least a general knowledge of the subject.

A family's long-term financial security is affected by a number of different matters, including life insurance, private pension plans, Social Security, estate planning, accumulation of personal assets (car, appliances, furniture, etc.), home ownership, and long-term investing.

Life Insurance

Obtaining adequate life insurance protection at a reasonable cost is one important aspect of long-term financial planning. Most life insurance is purchased with the help of an agent. Indeed, agents say that life insurance policies are not bought, they are sold. The agents who do the selling are compensated in the form of commissions. Their commissions are based on the volume (size and number) of policies that they sell. Thus agents have a strong incentive to sell as much insurance as their customers can be convinced that they can afford. By no means do all agents seek to take unfair advantage of their clients. Still, potential buyers who understand the essentials of life insurance are far better able to tailor cost-effective plans to their own situation than those who rely solely on an insurance agent.

Who Needs Life Insurance?   Life insurance is designed to protect the beneficiary from the financial hardship that loss of the insured's income would otherwise cause. Thus sufficient life insurance should be purchased to provide financial security for one's dependents. Those who have no dependents or are sufficiently wealthy probably do not need life insurance. In the first instance no one needs protecting and in the second the estate already provides adequate financial security.

When to Purchase?   Agents frequently try to sell life insurance to people long before they have any dependents to protect. They may seek to sell a small initial policy and thus establish an agent–client relationship. They hope to sell additional insurance as needs and circumstances change. Several arguments are advanced for purchasing some amount of life insurance at a relatively young age. For example, the agent may warn the prospect that a physical examination could be more difficult to pass at an older age. However, only about 3% of those who take insurance physicals fail, while another 5% are put into a higher risk pool. Moreover, many whose health makes them uninsurable or puts them a high-risk class would have had similar problems at an earlier age. Thus the probability of now being insurable and becoming uninsurable later is relatively small.

Younger age groups do pay lower insurance rates. The lower premiums must, however, start sooner and be paid over a longer period. Thus the total cost of buying insurance at a young age may well be greater than it would be if the buyer waited until he or she was older. Moreover, most young people start out with relatively low initial incomes. Life insurance payments could unnecessarily strain their budgets. Finally, early initial purchase only reduces the rates for those who buy whole life insurance. Term insurance, in contrast, is often a better buy.

Term and Whole Life Insurance.   Life insurance rates are set in two basic ways. Both ways take account of the fact that younger people have longer life expectancies and thus insurance companies can afford to charge them lower rates. Term insurance rates rise with the age of the insured. Whole life premiums are based on the insured's age when the policy is purchased. Premiums on new whole life policies are initially set well above what is needed to satisfy claims. This rate is maintained over the life of the policy. The surplus and the earnings on it are initially held in a reserve. This reserve is eventually drawn down when the age group's mortality rate (likelihood of dying during that year) causes claims and other expenses to exceed premiums. Figure 21.1 illustrates this relationship.

Unlike whole life, term insurance policies do not provide for an accumulated surplus. As a result, term policy premiums are initially set at a much lower per year rate than an equivalent dollar amount of protection in the form of a whole life policy. Moreover, the agent's commission is based largely on the amount of the first year's premium. Accordingly, the agent will earn much less on term than on an equivalent amount of whole life insurance. This savings from a reduced amount of commissions tends to be passed on to the insured. This savings is one reason why term insurance tends to be a more attractive buy than whole life.

FIGURE 21.1   Whole Life Premium versus Risk of Dying at Various Ages

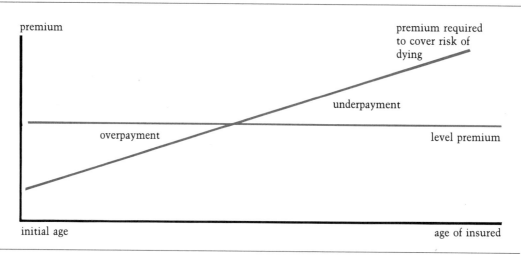

Young people's incomes tend to be relatively low while their expenses (setting up a household) may be relatively high.[1] Thus young people have very good reasons for wanting to economize on their insurance costs. On the other hand, they are in a stage of their life cycle where obtaining substantial protection relative to the cost is particularly attractive. In this regard term's lower initial cost is an important consideration.

Whether term or whole life is the better long-term value depends largely upon the implicit return on the higher initial premiums of the whole life policy. If the insured could invest the savings in insurance costs at a higher rate than that offered by the whole life policy, term is the better buy. In fact, most whole life policies are priced to offer no more than about a 6% return. Since many other investments offer higher returns, buying term and investing the difference in premiums is usually the superior strategy.

The accumulated surplus or cash value of a whole life policy does have two attractive features. First, the implicit return earned on life insurance policies is not taxed. Thus one should compare the return on insurance policies with the after-tax return on alternative investments. Note, however, that Congress has considered changing this tax advantage and sooner or later may do so. Second, the policyholder can usually borrow back up to the amount of the cash value (or perhaps 95% of the cash value) at a relatively low interest rate. Borrowing at such rates may seem attractive to the policyholder. The funds will, however, generally cost more to borrow back than their implicit return. That is, the cash balance may appreciate at a 6% rate while the loan costs 8%. Thus the net cost of the loan would be 2%. In contrast, one who bought term and invested the difference in premiums would have had access to this money for free.

Universal and Variable Life Insurance.   Difficult economic conditions (primarily higher market interest rates than those offered on the insurance companies' own products) began to reduce the insurance industry's sales in the late 1970s. Low yields on their investment portfolios (largely assembled when interest rates were lower) prevented insurance companies from offering higher returns on their existing policies. The insurance companies could offer more attractive terms on new products by segregating the resulting premium income from that of their existing policies.[2] Since any new funds are invested at current market yields, the newer policies can offer competitive returns. Variable life is similar to whole life except that its cash value growth rate will vary with the market return on the insurance company's investments.

Universal life is similar to variable life except that the policyholder can also vary the premium amount paid each year. In such a policy the cash value acts as a buffer. The higher the premium paid, the faster the cash value grows. As long, however, as the cash value remains above some predetermined minimum, the policyholder can choose to pay little or no premium. Thus within a rather wide range the policyholder can set the premium. A high premium payment will largely flow into cash value where it earns a tax-sheltered return. A low payment is offset by a drawdown in the existing cash value.

When interest rates are high, flowing through current market yields makes variable and universal more attractive than whole life. Nonetheless, *Consumer Reports* finds that even variable and universal life are relatively unattractive for most people. Their relatively high fees and selling costs make these types of policies generally less attractive than a strategy of buying term and investing the difference.[3]

Single Premium Deferred Annuities.   The Tax Reform Act of 1986 has increased interest in one type of life insurance: the single premium deferred annuity. This instrument calls for the insured to make a single initial payment. The purchaser thereby obtains immediate paid-up protection in the amount of the purchase. A surplus accumulates as the initial premium (less expenses) generates a return. Some policies guarantee a rate while others offer a variable return. The return on such policies is (under current, 1988, law) untaxed as long as the funds are not withdrawn. The insured can even borrow against the policy's cash value, usually at an attractive interest rate. The interest rate on such loans is typically set at a bit above the policy's own return. While technically a type of insurance, the cash value from such a policy can be withdrawn as retirement income any time after the insured reaches the age of 59½. Thus such policies provide some attractive tax benefits.

Several limitations of these types of policies also need to be noted. First, any withdrawals prior to age 59½ are subject to both the regular tax on the income and a penalty tax of 10% of the amount withdrawn. Second, many insurance companies also impose an additional penalty on early withdrawals. Third, some of the insurance companies that sold these types of policies subsequently went bankrupt. Policyholders usually got most of their initial investment back but they did not get the high returns that they had been promised. Fourth, the laws making these types of policies attractive may well be changed in the future. Congress is constantly looking for loopholes to close and thereby raise more tax money. This is one potential area for their attention. In fact, the 1986 act treated the insurance industry so well that many people expect it to be more of a target the next time the tax laws are revised.

Participating versus Nonparticipating Insurance.   The various types of life insurance can be purchased in either participating or nonparticipating forms. Premiums on nonparticipating policies are fixed. Any profits earned on the policies accrue to the issuing company's shareholders. Participating policies, in contrast, are issued by mutual (policyholder owned) insurance companies. Their premiums are set at higher levels than the companies expect to need to meet claims, expenses, and provide adequate reserves. The excess is returned to policyholders in the form of dividends. The net cost of participating policies may be a bit below that of equivalent nonparticipating policies. Poor investment experience can, however, reverse the relationship.

How Much Insurance Is Needed?   Buying the appropriate amount is at least as important as choosing the most suitable type of life insurance. The insured wants to protect his or her household's lifestyle without spending more on insurance than is necessary. Determining how much the family requires to live comfortably is an important first step. Bear in mind that the insured's death would also eliminate his or her support cost. Thus most families could maintain their lifestyle with less than their present income. Perhaps a typical family of four would require income in the range of 75% or 80% of its present level.

Once the family's income needs are determined, the next step is estimating the amount of income that it would otherwise have available. That is, how much income would be available before considering the income that might be provided by insurance? How much can the spouse net after child-care expense? What would Social Security pay the survivors? How much would be earned on investments? What kind of benefits would the insured's employer provide? Without life insurance, the family's income would be limited to these types of sources. How large is the gap that life insurance needs to fill? Determining the amount of life insurance needed requires answers to these types of questions. The following example illustrates how one might proceed to estimate one's life insurance needs.

John Q. Uninsured supports a family of four on an annual salary of $32,000. The other three members of the household could probably live about as comfortably on about $24,000 (75% of $32,000) as the family of four now lives on $32,000. Social Security survivorship payments would continue until the children reach 18 (and are presumably self-supporting). Benefits vary but in this case they might be about $600 per month ($7,200 of the needed $24,000). John's wife can net $4,000 (after child-care and job-related expenses) from a part-time job. John's pension plan would provide the family another $6,000 per year if he should die. Finally, the family's modest $5,000 in savings earns 8%, or $400, per year. These various income sources equal $17,600 of the needed $24,000. A gap of $6,400 is left for insurance.

Assuming the insurance proceeds could be invested at 8%, an $80,000 policy would be sufficient to generate $6,400 in annual income. The actual return would vary with market conditions. Depending upon the ages and life expectancies of the insured's dependents, a plan might be structured that would utilize part of the principal for support. This approach would require somewhat less insurance protection. On the other hand, more insurance might be purchased to provide an inflation reserve.

While this situation could be analyzed in greater detail, the end result would probably not greatly change. The essential steps are:

1. Determine how much income is required to maintain the family's lifestyle.

2. Ascertain the residual income that would be available without insurance.

3. Subtract the residual income from the amount needed.

4. Purchase sufficient life insurance to provide an income equal to the difference.

Should an Agent Be Used?   Once the questions of whether, what kind, and how much insurance to buy have been answered, the remaining question is, How should one go about purchasing the policy? Not surprisingly, the cost of a given type and amount of insurance will depend significantly on how and from whom it is purchased.

Life insurance is bought either through an agent or directly from the insurance company. As with load and no-load mutual funds, the two methods of purchasing life insurance each have advantages and disadvantages. Insurance agents are trained both to sell and to explain the nature of their products. Thus a well-trained insurance agent should be able to explain the available options and tailor a plan to the client's individual needs.

Careful readers of the relevant parts of this chapter should, however, be able to structure their own insurance programs. Doing so should allow them to purchase insurance protection without using an agent's services. Purchasers who avoid the agent's services also eliminate the insurance company's need to compensate a seller. This savings in commissions is passed on to the insured. As a result, one who purchases insurance directly from the company would save the equivalent of one year's premium.

Another problem with using an agent arises from the potential conflict of interest that agents face. They must advise their clients on the relative merits of the different policies that they offer. Inevitably some types of policies pay the agents proportionately greater commissions than do others. As a result, the agent may be faced with the problem of having to choose between recommending a policy that is more suitable to the client's needs or one that is more profitable for the agent to sell. How many agents have professional standards that are sufficiently high that they are prepared to make recommendations that cost them appreciable sums of money? Individuals who do not use agents to help them decide do not incur such conflicts.

Buying life insurance through an agent is easy. Agents are numerous and always looking for clients. Obtaining insurance protection without going through an agent may involve a bit more work. Group plans offered by an employer provide one excellent way of buying insurance directly from the issuer. Indeed, the employer may well retain benefit specialists to assist employees in such purchases. Group plans are also offered through many professional, alumni, and civic associations. Many mutual funds offer low-cost group rate insurance. The mutual savings banks in New York, Massachusetts, and Connecticut also sell low-cost policies. Finally, some insurance companies advertise direct sales in financial

Investments in Perspective

Unlike life insurance, disability insurance may well be advisable for almost everyone who depends upon a paycheck. Indeed, the person who has no one other than himself or herself to support still has one person to protect. The worker who dies no longer needs an income. The worker who becomes disabled, in contrast, still needs financial support. The following article from *The Wall Street Journal* discusses the need for disability coverage.

Planners Urge You to Assess the Adequacy Of Your Long-Term Disability Insurance

By WALT BOGDANICH
Staff Reporter of THE WALL STREET JOURNAL

NEW YORK—Just when you think your personal affairs are in order, financial planner Andrew E. Gross offers this thought: "You die only once, but you can be disabled many different times in your life."

Unpleasant as it is to contemplate, insurance industry statistics indicate that three of every 10 people will be disabled for more than 90 days between the ages of 30 and 65. If you are one of the three, would you lose your house? Your car? Your dignity?

Financial planners, such as Mr. Gross of Dennis M. Gurtz & Associates in Washington, D.C., say too many breadwinners avoid facing the prospect of disability. "Everyone seems to know they need life insurance" says Karen P. Schaeffer of American Financial Consultants Inc. in Silver Spring, Md. "It's something we have been brought up with. That's not the case with disability insurance."

Even consumer advocates say people ought to buy more disability insurance. "When a consumer group says a product is undersold, that says something," says J. Robert Hunter, president of National Insurance Consumers Organization in Alexandria, Va. Agents have traditionally played down

disability insurance because they earn bigger commissions selling life-insurance policies, Mr. Hunter says.

Some insurance industry officials acknowledge that disability coverage is more difficult to underwrite. "You don't have as clear a picture of your potential liabilities," says Richard Roth, manager of Provident Life & Casualty Insurance Co.'s New York office. "When you die, you die. When you are disabled, recovery can vary."

Don't think that just because you are covered under a group disability plan at work, your worries are over. Such plans frequently offer only short-term protection.

Social Security doesn't pay benefits unless your disability is expected to last at least one year or result in death. Even then, you must wait six months before receiving any help, and you must be unable to do any kind of work, not just your occupation, says John B. Trollinger, deputy press officer of the Social Security Administration. The average Social Security benefit paid to a wage earner with young children is $871 a month, Mr. Trollinger says.

Some additional disability protection is offered through state workers' compensation programs. But only five states—New York, New Jersey, Rhode Island, California and Hawaii—offer compensation for nonoccupational disabilities, and then only for a limited period.

If you already have disability insurance, you should review your policy periodically to see if benefits have kept pace with salary increases, says Charles L. Erickson, a vice president of Paul Revere Life Insurance Co. Review your coverage again when you switch jobs. "A significant number of small and medium firms don't have any coverage at all," cautions Mr. Roth of Provident.

Financial planners recommend buying a noncancelable policy offering protection to age 65. Under a good policy, "the company cannot change the premium and it cannot cancel the coverage," Mr. Erickson says.

You should also examine how your policy defines disability. Some policies pay benefits only if you are totally disabled. Others take into account partial disability. If you are 40% disabled, for example, Paul Revere offers an option that will pay 40% of what your regular policy would pay if you were totally disabled.

If you bought a policy more than five years ago, you might consider some new options. Some companies now regard pregnancy as a sickness disability. And for those who fear increases in inflation, there is an option that pays benefits based on the national Consumer Price Index.

You can deduct premiums for disability insurance from your income taxes, but if you do, any benefits you receive are taxed as ordinary income. Mr. Gross, the financial planner, recommends not deducting your premiums to keep your benefits tax free.

To determine how much disability coverage you need, the accompanying worksheet will help you estimate your annual living expenses. From this total, subtract all the income you will receive while disabled, including your spouse's earnings, if any, as well as dividends, interest and income from rental properties. The difference is the amount of coverage you need to reasonably maintain your standard of living while disabled.

Many financial planners recommend buying a policy whose benefits don't begin for 90 days or even a year after you are disabled, because premiums on these policies are cheaper. In estimating how long your family can live without policy benefits, consider your savings, accumulated sick days and the good will, if any, of your in-laws.

A sampling of rates at three companies specializing in disability insurance shows that a 40-year-old, mid-management employee would pay annual premiums of $879 to $1,210 for a noncancelable, long-term policy that begins paying benefits of $2,300 a month 90 days after disability.

While disability coverage isn't inexpensive, Mrs. Schaeffer of American Financial Consultants says such insurance can still be a bargain. "Disability means you can't go out and earn an income. It doesn't necessarily mean you will become a vegetable. Stop and think what six months of no income will mean to a family."

Estimating Your Disability Insurance Needs

	Family of four, income of $50,000	Your family
Living Expenses		
Housing (utilities, insurance, taxes, maintenance, rent or mortgage)	$11,000	_____
Food	9,000	_____
Clothing	2,500	_____
Transportation	4,000	_____
Entertainment, education	3,500	_____
Medical	2,000	_____
Personal care	1,000	_____
Life insurance, job-related expenses	2,500	_____
Total annual living expenses	$35,000	_____
Income during disability		
Spouse's after-tax income	$10,000	_____
Dividends, interest, capital gains	2,000	_____
Rents, annuities, pensions	1,000	_____
Total income during disability	$13,000	_____
Net annual disability income needs	$22,500	_____

TABLE 21.3 Types of Life Insurance

	Basic Types
Whole Life	Constant annual premiums are determined by the insured's age at purchase, providing insurance plus a savings feature.
Term	Premiums for this pure insurance rise with the insured's age.
	Variable-Value Types
Decreasing Term	Amount of coverage declines as the insured gets older.
Universal Life	Cash value varies with the policyholder's premium payments and return on the accumulated surplus.
Variable Life	Cash value varies with the return on the accumulated surplus.
	Type of Sellers
Participating	Sold by mutual insurance company, which flows through its "profits" to policyholders
Nonparticipating	Sold by stock company, which retains any profits for its shareholders
Individual	Sold separately by an agent who receives a substantial fee
Group	Sold without an agent, thereby saving what would have been the agent's fee

publications such as *The Wall Street Journal.* Table 21.3 lists the various types of life insurance and how they may be purchased.

Pensions

Providing life insurance protection for one's dependents is an important aspect of long-term financial planning. Providing a comfortable postretirement for oneself (and spouse) is an equally important aspect of the long-term plan. Continuing inflation and increasing life expectancies have heightened the need for effective pension planning. Determining the amount of income required for comfortable retirement is similar to the needed insurance computation. Some types of expenses generally decline with retirement (e.g., taxes, job-related expenses; see Table 21.4). Nonetheless, Social Security and employee pension plans are often inadequate. Many retirees face the unpleasant prospect of deciding how to cut back their standard of living to match their retirement income. Those who prepare adequately for their postretirement financial needs will not have such financial difficulties. The income gap could be filled with generalized savings and the returns on that savings. Most funds earmarked for retirement qualify for attractive tax treatment, however. The money saved in taxes can add to the amount set aside for retirement. Thus one can increase the value of the accumulated sum by utilizing one or more of the tax-sheltered retirement vehicles.

How much faster funds accumulate when taxes are deferred is illustrated in Table 21.5. In this case the investor is assumed to set aside $1,000 annually, earn 8% on savings, and fall in a tax bracket of 40% (combined federal, state, and local). The tax-deferred sum is subject to tax upon withdrawal, but a much larger amount has been saved because taxes were deferred. Moreover, retirees often fall in lower

TABLE 21.4 Equivalent Retirement Income

The last column of the table below shows the income required after retirement to maintain preretirement living standards. These figures were calculated by the President's Commission on Pension Policy in 1980 for people at various income levels.

Gross preretirement income	Taxes [1]	Work-related expenses [2]	Savings and investments [3]	Net pre-retirement income [4]	Post-retirement income taxes [5]	Equivalent retirement income [6]
			Single people			
$10,000	$ 2008	$ 480	$ 240 (3%)	$ 7272	—	$ 7272 (73%)
15,000	3703	678	678 (6%)	9941	—	9941 (66%)
20,000	5783	853	1280 (9%)	12,084	$ 198	12,282 (61%)
30,000	10,355	1179	2357 (12%)	16,109	1282	17,391 (58%)
50,000	22,249	1665	4163 (15%)	21,923	3752	25,675 (51%)
			Married couples			
$10,000	$ 1444	$ 513	$ 257 (3%)	$ 7786	—	$ 7786 (78%)
15,000	2860	728	728 (6%)	10,684	—	10,684 (71%)
20,000	4488	931	1396 (9%)	13,185	—	13,185 (66%)
30,000	8047	1317	2634 (12%)	17,999	$ 63	18,062 (60%)
50,000	17,824	1931	4826 (15%)	25,419	1965	27,384 (55%)

[1] Includes Federal income tax, Social Security taxes, state and local income taxes (calculated at 19% of Federal income taxes). Does not include property taxes.
[2] Estimated at 6% of income after taxes.
[3] Estimated at a percentage (shown) of income after taxes.
[4] Gross preretirement income less taxes, work-related expenses, and savings and investments.
[5] Post-retirement taxes are on income in excess of Social Security benefits, which are not taxable. Retirees without Social Security benefits would need higher retirement income.
[6] Equivalent retirement income as a percentage of preretirement gross income shown in parentheses.

Source: "Will You Ever Collect a Pension?" *Consumer Reports*, March 1982, 124–130. Copyright 1982 by Consumers Union of the United States, Inc., Mount Vernon, N.Y. 10550. Reprinted by permission from *Consumer Reports*, March 1982.

TABLE 21.5 Tax-Deferred versus Taxable Savings: $1,000 a Year Taxable at 40% (8% return)

Term	Tax-Deferred*	Taxable
1	$ 1,080	$ 648
5	6,335	3,461
10	15,645	7,835
15	29,323	13,366
20	49,421	20,356
25	78,951	29,195
30	113,080	40,369
35	186,097	54,494
40	279,774	72,351
45	417,417	94,925

*Taxable when withdrawn

tax brackets than they did before retirement. Tax-deferred retirement funds may be set aside in a number of ways.

Employer Pensions. Most employers provide retirement plans for qualifying employees. Benefits are largely determined by such predetermined factors as the employee's age, place of employment, length of service, and preretirement salary. Voluntary extra employee contributions may, however, increase the value of the pension. Such contributions and the returns they generate are not subject to tax until benefits begin. The timing of job changes can also affect pension rights. An employee must remain with the same employer for a minimum time (such as five years) to vest. Otherwise, all partially accrued retirement benefits are lost. Retirement benefits generally increase with the length of service, salary, and perhaps the retirement age. At special times, however, some employers may offer employees incentives to retire early. Thus employees should carefully evaluate the impact of a prospective employment action on both current and retirement income. Sometimes a higher current salary is offset by the adverse impact on retirement income.

IRA and Keogh Accounts. IRA and/or Keogh accounts can be used by many people to supplement other retirement plans. Provisions have frequently changed but, according to the 1986 Tax Reform Act, everyone with earned income may put up to $2,000 annually into an IRA account. Another $250 may be set aside in the name of a nonworking spouse. The contributed sums are deductible from taxable income for all employees who are not covered by private pension plans as well as all employees annually earning below $25,000 ($40,000 for a couple). A partial deduction is available for those earning up to $35,000 ($50,000 for a couple). Covered employees whose incomes exceed the maximums can still make nondeductible contributions.

Up to the lesser of $30,000 or 20% of self-employment income may be set aside in a Keogh plan. Everyone who earns self-employment income is eligible (whether or not he or she also earns salary income and/or participates in an IRA or company plan). Contributions are fully deductible from current taxable income (at the federal level). The income on both IRA and Keogh accounts is not subject to tax until it is withdrawn. Withdrawals from both types of accounts may begin by age $59\frac{1}{2}$ and must begin by age $70\frac{1}{2}$. Such withdrawals are taxable income to the recipient. Premature withdrawals incur an additional 15% penalty tax.

Allowable Investments. Retirement funds may be invested in most types of securities including stocks, bonds, mutual funds, and CDs. The funds may not, however, be invested in any type of asset that collateralizes a loan against it. Thus mortgaged real estate, futures contracts, and margined stock are not allowed in IRA or Keogh accounts. Tangible assets such as collectibles and gemstones are also off limits. The one exception to this restriction is that U.S. mint issue bullion coins (gold and silver Eagles) may be part of a retirement account portfolio.

Retirement Account Managers. Banks, thrifts, mutual funds, insurance companies, brokerage firms, and other types of financial institutions offer qualified IRA and Keogh plans. Most IRA and Keogh accounts are managed by the institution that set it up. Self-directed plans, in contrast, allow the owner to buy and sell specific securities much as he or she would with a personal investment portfolio. Fees for establishing and maintaining IRA and Keogh accounts are generally modest. As with life insurance, however, plans that are sold through agents can be relatively expensive.

Employee Stock Ownership Plans.   Employee stock ownership plans (ESOPs) allow a corporation to contribute up to an amount equal to 15% of its payroll into a profit-sharing plan on behalf of its employees. As a legitimate business expense these funds are tax deductible to the employer. Funds paid into an ESOP are viewed as part of the employees' total compensation package. As a result, an employer that establishes an ESOP reduces its need to pay other types of compensation. The ESOP funds are often invested in the firm's own newly issued stock. Thus the firm is able to confer this benefit on its employees by simply issuing additional shares of its stock. In effect, an ESOP allows the firm to raise equity capital from its employees while giving them a tax-sheltered benefit. Small, capital-poor companies may find ESOPs particularly attractive. Companies are permitted to offer their employees both ESOPs and pension plans.

Deferred Compensation Plans (401k).   Yet another tax-sheltering device is the 401k. Companies having such plans allow employees to place up to $7,000 per year into a tax-sheltered fund. No tax is due on the contributions or resulting income until the funds are withdrawn. Table 21.6 summarizes the various types of tax-sheltered retirement fund options.

TABLE 21.6   Types of Retirement Funds

IRAs	Allow any employee to set aside up to $2,000 per year into a tax-sheltered fund. The funds are sheltered from tax on their income for everyone; only certain people are eligible for a tax deduction on their contributions, however.
Keoghs	Allow the self-employed to set aside up to 20% of their self-employed income ($30,000 maximum) in a tax-sheltered fund.
ESOPs	Allow corporations to contribute up to 15% of employee payrolls into what is in effect a profit-sharing stock purchase plan.
Deferred Compensation	Allows employees to set aside up to 10% of their salaries in a tax-sheltered fund if the employer establishes such a plan.

The Role of Long-Term Investing

Three factors limit the attractiveness of tax-sheltered retirement plans. First, the amounts that each type of plan can shelter are limited. For example, no more than $2,000 per year can be put into an IRA. Moreover, many people are not eligible for a tax-deductible IRA. Second, sums placed in these funds are very costly to extract prior to retirement age. Typically early withdrawals incur both a regular and a penalty tax liability. Third, certain types of investments (particularly less traditional types of investments) are not permitted. Accordingly, most investors will want to maintain both tax-sheltered and taxable portfolios. Some funds can

TABLE 21.7   Value and Income from $1,000 Invested Annually for 30 Years at Various Interest Rates

Interest Rate	Value at End of 30 Years	Annual Income Starting after 30 Years
4%	$ 56,085	$ 2,243
6	79,060	4,744
8	113,280	9,062
10	164,490	16,490
12	241,330	28,960
14	356,786	49,950
16	530,311	84,849
18	790,948	142,371

be set aside in an unrestricted but taxable portfolio for such preretirement needs as a down payment on a house, an education fund for the children, a vacation home, buying a business to start a new career, and so on, as well as to supplement retirement income and to pass on to heirs.

Obviously investors seek a high return (taking due account of both risk and tax impacts) on funds invested in both tax-sheltered and taxable investments. We have already seen that investment management is a very complex topic. Nonetheless, three general points can be made here. First, only surplus funds should be committed to long-term investments. Liquidating investments prematurely to meet emergency needs can be quite costly. Second, a relatively modest sum set aside periodically will eventually grow to a substantial amount. Third, the accumulated total and income that can be earned on it will vary greatly with the yield. Table 21.7 illustrates the results of saving and investing $1,000 annually for 30 years. Clearly the yield has a major impact on the amount accumulated.

Estate Planning

Insurance protection, pension planning, and generalized savings have already been covered. A long-term financial plan should also deal with the disposition of one's estate. Effective estate planning seeks at least three objectives: (1) provide for a prompt distribution of assets according to the owner's wishes, (2) minimize the tax impact, and (3) do so at a reasonable cost to the estate.

No federal estate tax is assessed on bequests to one's spouse or the first $600,000 in bequests to other beneficiaries. The taxable basis on bequests is based on the value around the time that the estate is settled. No capital gains tax is assessed on any heretofore unrealized gains (at least up to 1988; this is another possible area for tax reform). On the other hand, large estates are subject to federal rates of as much as 50%. State inheritance taxes add to the total liability. Thus anyone who expects to have a sizable estate should consult an able lawyer specializing in estate planning.

Disposing of Assets.   An effective estate plan begins with a listing of assets, liabilities, and their values. Once the extent of the estate is known, the estate owner can begin to explore the two principal methods of asset disposal: gifts and bequests.

Giving assets away prior to one's death is designed to achieve several objectives. Such gifts may avoid the impact of estate taxes, allow the recipient earlier usage, avoid later misunderstandings, and permit the giver to make a personal presentation. Gifts to charities can yield substantial tax savings. Up to $10,000 ($20,000 per couple) may be given annually to each recipient without any gift or estate tax consequences.

Most people prefer to direct the disposition of their own estate regardless of how large or small it may be. Dealing with the assets of those who die intestate (without a valid will) requires a long, costly, and arbitrary proceeding. Most people will want a lawyer to prepare their will. Doing most of the preparatory work themselves, however, can reduce the cost and increase the plan's suitability. A simple will should not require more than a few hours of a lawyer's time nor cost more than a few hundred dollars to have prepared.

Trusts.   Trusts are legal arrangements for administering a portfolio of assets for the benefit of one or more individuals. They may be utilized with both gifts and bequests. Typically a bank trust department (or similar department in another type of financial institution) is paid a fee to administer the trust. Most trusts initially retain principal but distribute its income. The trust's principal must eventually also be distributed. Usually such distributions occur when the initial beneficiaries die or reach a prespecified age. One may establish a trust either as a part of the estate disposition plan or prior to one's death. As with wills most people need a lawyer to set up their trusts.

SUMMARY AND CONCLUSIONS

Sound personal financial management and planning should seek to accomplish a number of objectives. Specifically such planning should provide for the setting aside of the resources to: (1) deal with unexpected needs, (2) take advantage of unexpected opportunities, (3) protect one's dependents in the event of an untimely death, and (4) ensure one's own long-term financial security. Short-term assets and liabilities should be managed with several objectives in mind: (1) to minimize the financing costs on debts, (2) to maximize the return on short-term investments, (3) to maintain adequate flexibility, and (4) to keep risk to a manageable level. Savings, checking, NOW, superNOW, money market, and similar types of accounts should be selected to provide the optimum combination of flexibility, convenience, safety, and yield.

Longer term financial management includes consideration of life insurance needs, pension planning, long-term investing, and estate planning. Life insurance should protect the family's lifestyle. One should first determine the needed amount of protection and then shop for the most cost-effective way of obtaining it. Usually a term policy purchased through a group plan, perhaps from a mutually owned company, will offer the best policy terms.

IRAs, Keoghs, ESOPs, and 401ks allow qualifying individuals to set aside funds whose amounts and returns are tax deferred until withdrawn. Generalized savings may not be tax sheltered but may be spent and invested without restrictions. Finally, gifts, bequests, and trusts should be used to direct the disposition of an estate in a manner that carries out the owner's wishes and minimizes tax and probate costs.

REVIEW QUESTIONS

1. Discuss the primary goals of sound personal finance. How is personal finance like investing?

2. Under what circumstances should funds available for investment be used to reduce debts? In what sense is repaying a loan like making an investment?

3. How should one go about seeking a loan? What are some of the places one may go to seek out a loan?

4. Discuss the features of each type of depository account. What considerations are relevant to the choice of account type? What types of institutions provide such accounts? Are any of these institutions better than others?

5. Compare the ways of providing an emergency reserve. What are the advantages of a line of credit compared to a cash reserve?

6. What determines life insurance needs? List and respond to the arguments often given in favor of purchasing life insurance at a young age. Are any of the arguments for early purchase of life insurance valid? Explain why or why not.

7. Discuss the need for and advantage of tax-sheltered retirement plans. Would tax-sheltered municipal bonds be an appropriate investment for such plans? Explain why or why not.

8. Compare generalized savings with tax-sheltered retirement plans. What are the advantages and disadvantages of each approach to savings?

9. Why do most people not have to be concerned about estate taxes? What aspects of estate planning remain important? What types of investors still need to be concerned about estate taxes? What vehicles are available to lessen the blow of such taxes?

10. Discuss the role of gifts, bequests, and trusts in estate planning. What are the advantages and disadvantages of each?

REVIEW PROBLEMS

1. Analyze the following family balance sheet and recommend ways that the family might improve the structure of its finances.

Assets			Liabilities	
Short Term			*Short Term*	
Cash	$	150	Installment Credit	$ 450
Checking Account		300		
Savings Account		5,000		
Intermediate Term			*Intermediate Term*	
Auto		7,000	Auto Loan	5,000
Personal Items		12,000		
Long Term			*Long Term*	
House		90,000	Mortgage	65,000
Life Insurance Cash			Total Liabilities	70,450
Value		8,000		
Mutual Fund		10,000	Net Worth	62,000
			Total Liabilities and	
Total Assets		$132,450	Net Worth	$132,450

Savings account yields 5.5%
Money market mutual funds are yielding 7%
Life insurance cash value may be borrowed on at 6%
Mutual fund owns a diversified portfolio of low-risk stocks with a
    current dividend yield of 4%
Installment credit costs 18%
Auto loan costs 12%
Mortgage costs 11% and is being amortized over a 25-year period

2. How would your answer to Problem 1 change under each of the following circumstances?

    a. The family has an upcoming medical expense of $5,000.
    b. The family wins $5,000 in the state lottery.
    c. The father is offered an employee stock option whereby he can purchase stock with a market value of $5,000 for 60% of its market value.

3. You have just charged $1,800 worth of Christmas presents to your credit card. The bill will arrive in 10 days and be due in 15 days from receipt. At that point you may pay the balance off and not incur a finance charge. Alternatively, you may pay a minimum of 10% of the balance and a finance charge of 1½% per month. If you pay the minimum when due and the balance a month later, how much will you incur in finance charges? Relate this interest charge to the extra time that you took to pay the bill. What is the incremental annualized percentage interest cost of not paying off the initial balance within the grace period but paying it a month later?

4. Continue with the facts of Problem 3. Assume, however, that the outstanding balance is $3,000. By deferring your planned winter vacation until spring you can pay off the entire balance within the grace period. Alternatively, you can take the vacation now and pay off the credit card balance in three equal monthly installments. How much interest would you save by deferring the vacation? What is the annualized incremental interest cost to you for not deferring your vacation?

5. You now have $1,000 in a savings account earning 6½% and need to open a checking account. Your choices are as follows:

Type	Minimum Balance	Per Check Charge	Monthly Charge	Interest Rate on Average Balance
Special	$100	$.30	$5	none
Regular	$200	$.25	$3	none
NOW	$500	none	$5	5%

Your finances are so limited that you will be unable to maintain more than the required minimum balance. Moreover, that sum must come from your savings account. If you expect to write about five checks per month, what would each of these accounts cost? Suppose you were to write 20 checks per month. Then what would be the charges?

6. You now have a $100,000 mortgage at 11% for 25 years. You also have $10,000 in a money market account paying 6%. If you use the $10,000 to pay down the mortgage balance, the interest charges on the mortgage will be reduced to reflect the smaller balance. The mortgage itself will continue to require payments at the same monthly rate. The life of the mortgage will just be reduced by the prepayment. How much will the prepayment save in mortgage interest charges in the first year? How much will be lost in interest income on the money market account? What is the net interest effect of this maneuver in the first year? How much is the life of the mortgage shortened by this maneuver?

7. Determine the needed insurance protection for the following situation:

   Family: father, mother, and three children
   Family income: $36,000 per year
   Social Security survivor's benefits: $6,900 per year
   Survivor's pension: $3,000 per year
   Investment income: $2,000 per year
   Assumed interest rate for insurance principal: 8%

8. Continue with the basic facts of Problem 7. Suppose that the interest rate on the principal is 10% and that the need for income supplement would end in 10 years (when the last child is grown). Now how much insurance protection would be needed?

9. Assume that you are in the 28% tax bracket, can save $500 per year, and

earn 9% on your investments. Make a chart of the compound value of your savings after 5, 10, 20, 30, and 40 years for three circumstances:

1. Both the $500 and the return on it are taxed.
2. The $500 is taxed but the return is not.
3. Neither the $500 nor the return is taxed.

10. Using the results for Problem 9, assume that the sum accumulated at the end of 30 years is used to purchase an annuity that will pay 12% of the accumulation for the rest of your life. You remain in the 28% tax bracket. The part of your payment subject to tax equals the ratio of the accumulated sum that was not initially taxed to the total. Compute your after-tax payments for the three different tax circumstances.

REVIEW PROJECTS

1. Ask three local banks for rates on their various types of depository accounts. Do the same for three local thrifts including at least one credit union and one S&L. Prepare a table of the charges and yields. Now identify the most cost-effective account for each of the following:

Checks per Month	Average Balance
a. 10	$ 100
b. 25	$ 250
c. 35	$ 800
d. 40	$2,000
e. 30	$5,000

2. Write for rates on life insurance from several companies that do not use agents and make a table of the responses. Now ask several insurance agents for their rates and compare. Write a report.

NOTES

1. R. Ferber and L. Lee, "Asset Accumulation in Early Married Life," *Journal of Finance*, December 1980, 1173–1188.

2. D. Hertzberg, "Life Insurers Start Offering Policies That Look More Like Investments," *The Wall Street Journal*, February 23, 1983, p. 31.

3. Consumer's Union, "A Guide to Life Insurance: Parts 1, 2, and 3," *Consumer Reports*, January, February and March, 1981.

Glossary of Investment Terms

absolute priority of claims principle. The principle in bankruptcy law that each class of liability claims is repaid in full before the next highest priority category can receive even a partial payment.

accelerated depreciation. Writing assets off at a more rapid rate than proportional to their pro rata life expectancy.

acceptance. *See* banker's acceptance.

accrued interest. The pro rata interest obligation on a bond or other debt instrument that has accumulated since the last payment date. Most bonds trade at a price that reflects their net market price plus accrued interest. Defaulted and certain other bonds, however, trade "flat" (which see).

acid test. Cash and accounts receivable divided by current liabilities; used to measure short-term liquidity. Also called quick ratio.

actuarial tables. Tables reporting particular age groups' probabilities of death; based on past experience, with separate tables for men and women and certain hazardous occupations. An actuarial table might indicate that at age 25 a male would have 1 chance in 350 of dying within the next year and is expected to live 49 more years (to age 74). A 65-year-old male's chance of dying in the next year might be reported as 1 in 25 and his future life expectancy as 12 years (to age 77).

adjusted gross income (AGI). An interim figure that is reached on the way to computing tax liability; consists of total income less allowed adjustments, which include such items as moving expenses, IRA and Keogh contributions, and employee business expense. Taxable income then results from subtracting deductions and the allowance for exemptions from adjusted gross income.

ADR (American depository receipt). A U.S.-traded security representing stock in a foreign corporation.

after-tax cash flow. The difference in the actual cash income and outgo for an investment project after taking account of the tax impact.

after-tax return. The rate of return an investor receives after adjusting for inflation. Thus a 10% before-tax return corresponds to a 7.2% after-tax return for one in the 28% marginal tax bracket.

advisor's sentiment index. A technical market indicator based on a composite of investment advisor's forecasts; index users believe that bullish advisor's sentiment forecasts a market decline.

agency security. A debt security issued by federal agencies such as GNMA or Freddie Mac.

air rights. The right to build over someone else's property as, for example, an office complex above a downtown rail switching yard.

all-or-nothing order. An order that must be executed in its entirety or not at all.

alpha. The intercept term in the market model; provides an estimate of a security's return for a zero market return.

alternative minimum tax (AMT). Tax that may be applicable to those with large amounts of otherwise sheltered income (preferences) such as accelerated depreciation deductions; applies when the tax liability computed by disallowing these preferences exceeds the liability when the tax is computed the normal way.

amalgamation. Combining more than two firms into a single firm.

American Association of Individual Investors (AAII). Organization designed to help and promote the interests of small investors.

American Stock Exchange Index. A value-weighted index of AMEX stocks.

Americus Trust certificate. A type of security that divides the ownership of certain stocks into two categories of instruments: the primes receive dividends and are entitled to a liquidation value equal to the price of the stock at termination or a predetermined value, whichever is lower; the scores are entitled to the remaining termination values.

AMEX (American Stock Exchange). The second largest (in terms of primary security listings) U.S. stock exchange (after NYSE); occasionally abbreviated as ASE; listed firms tend to be of medium size compared with the larger NYSE issues and the typically smaller OTC issues.

amortization. The process of writing off the value of an asset or liability, particularly a paper asset or liability.

annual percentage rate (APR). The yield to maturity on a fixed income investment or the interest rate charged on a loan; computed using a compounding factor reflecting the balance still due.

annual report. A yearly report to shareholders containing financial statements (balance sheet, income statement, changes in financial position statement, and funds statement), auditor's statement, president's letter, and various other information.

annuity. An asset that usually promises to pay a fixed amount periodically for a predetermined period, although some pay a sum for an individual's lifetime; certain annuities' values are variable depending on the issuer's investment experience. Most are sold by insurance companies.

antidilution clause. A provision in a convertible bond or other security indenture restricting new share issues.

anxious trader effects. Short-run price distortions caused by sales or purchases of impatient large traders.

appreciation. Increase in the value of an investment over time.

appreciation mortgage. A mortgage in which the lender is given the rights to a percentage of any price appreciation derived when the property is sold. In exchange for giving up part of the profit potential, the borrower usually receives a more attractive rate than that charged on a standard loan.

arbitrage (pure). Simultaneously buying in one market and selling equivalent assets in another for a certain if modest profit. *See also* risk arbitrage.

arbitrage pricing theory (APT). A competitor to the capital asset pricing model that introduces more than one index in place of (or in addition to) CAPM's market index.

ARM (adjustable rate mortgage). A type of mortgage in which the interest rate is periodically adjusted as market rates change.

arrearage. An overdue payment, as in passed preferred dividends; if the dividends on the senior security are cumulative, arrearage must be made up before common dividends are resumed.

arithmetic mean return. The simple average return found by dividing the sum of the separate per period returns by the number of periods over which they were earned.

ask. The lowest price at which a security is currently offered for sale; may emanate from a specialist (exchange), market maker (OTC), or unexercised limit order.

asset. Any item of value; often income producing; appears on left of balance sheet.

asset allocation. A compromise approach to market timing. The asset allocator divides his or her portfolio among a number of categories such as low-risk stocks, high-risk stocks, short-term bonds, and long-term bonds. The percentage of the portfolio invested in each of these categories will be varied depending on whether the asset allocator's outlook is positive or negative.

asset play. A firm whose underlying assets are worth substantially more (after deducting the firm's liabilities) than the market value of its stock.

at-the-close order. An order that must be executed near or at that day's close.

at-the-opening order. An order that must be executed at that day's opening.

auditor's statement. A letter from the auditor to the company and its shareholders in which the accounting firm certifies the propriety of the methods used to produce the firm's financial statements.

Auto Ex. A division of Xerox that attempts to forecast large block trades for institutional clients.

back testing. Trying out a proposed investment strategy on prior period data to see if it would have been profitable to employ in the past. Successful back testing does not necessarily prove that the tested rule will work (be profitable) in the future; the past experience may not reflect the future market environment.

balanced fund. A mutual fund that invests in both stocks and bonds.

balance of payments. The difference between a country's international payments and its international receipts.

balance of trade. The difference between a country's expenditures on imports and its income from exports.

balance sheet. A financial statement providing an instant picture of a firm's or individual's financial position; lists assets, liabilities, and net worth.

balloon payment. A final large principal payment on a debt instrument whose interim payments either incompletely amortized or did not amortize the initial principal at all.

banker's acceptance. A money market instrument usually arising from international trade; made highly acceptable by a bank's guarantee or acceptance. Also called acceptance.

bankruptcy proceeding. A legal process for dealing formally with a defaulted obligation; may result in a liquidation or reorganization. *See also* Chapter X bankruptcy and Chapter XI bankruptcy.

bar chart. In technical analysis, a type of graph that plots the price over time; typically contains data on the high, low and volume.

Barron's. A major weekly investment periodical published by Dow Jones Inc.

Barron's Confidence Index. A technical indicator based on the yield differential between high-grade and average-grade corporate bonds, with a small differential signifying confidence in the future and a large differential signaling a lack of confidence.

basis (commodity). The difference between the spot price and the futures price.

basis (taxable). The acquisition cost of an asset less any capital distributions. The difference between the basis and the sale proceeds is the taxable gain.

basis point. One-hundredth of one percentage point; primarily used with interest rates.

basis risk. The risk that the basis of a commodity contract will move adversely.

bear. One who expects a declining market.

bearer bond. An unregistered bond whose ownership is determined by possession.

bear market. A declining market.

bear raid. An attempt to drive prices down by selling short.

benefactor. A person named to receive property or other resources as in a will or insurance policy.

Bernhard, (Arnold) and Company. The firm that owns Value Line and manages the Value Line mutual funds.

beta. A parameter that relates stock performance to market performance; for a z% change in the market, a stock will tend to change by z% (beta).

bid. The highest currently unexercised offer to buy a security; may emanate from a specialist (exchange), market maker (OTC), or limit order.

Big Board. A popular term for the New York Stock Exchange, the largest U.S. stock exchange.

bills. Government debt securities issued on a discount basis by the U.S. Treasury for periods of less than one year.

Billy Martin indicator. A whimsical indicator that hypothesizes that any time the New York Yankees name Billy Martin to be their manager, the stock market will decline.

black knight. A potential acquirer opposed by existing management and to which management would prefer to find an alternative (i.e., a white knight).

Black/Scholes formula. An option pricing formula based on the assumption that a riskless hedge between an option and its underlying stock should yield the riskless return; thus an option's value is a function of the stock price, striking price, stock return volatility, riskless interest rate, and length to expiration.

block trade. A trade involving 10,000 shares or more; usually handled by a block trader.

block trader. One who assembles the passive side of a block trade.

Bloody Monday. October 19, 1987, when the market experienced its worst one-day decline in its history; the Dow Jones Industrial Average dropped by 508 points, which was equivalent to a 23% decline.

blue chip stock. Shares of a large, mature company with a steady record of profits and dividends and a high probability of continued earnings.

blue sky laws. State laws designed to protect investors from security frauds.

Blume adjustment. A method of adjusting estimated betas toward unity to improve their general accuracy.

boiler room operations. High-pressure selling programs often associated with investment scams such as Ponzi schemes; characterized by aggressive sales forces utilizing banks of telephones to extract "investments" from unsophisticated individuals for risky and often worthless ventures.

bond. A debt obligation (usually long term) in which the borrower promises to pay a set coupon rate until the issue matures, at which time the principal is repaid; sometimes secured by a mortgage on a specific property, plant, or piece of equipment. *See also* debenture, collateral trust bond, and equipment trust certificate.

bond rating. An estimated index of the bond's investment quality and default risk.

bond swap. A technique for managing a bond portfolio by selling some bonds and buying others; may be designed to achieve benefits in the form of taxes, yields, maturity structure, or trading profits.

book value (of common shares). The total assets of an enterprise minus its liabilities, minority interests, and preferred stock par, divided by the number of outstanding common shares.

borrower life insurance. An insurance policy on the borrower's life equal to the outstanding loan principal and naming the lender as the beneficiary.

Boston Consulting Group (BCG). A strategic planning consulting firm famous for its growth–share matrix (BCG matrix).

box spread. A type of option spread in which the investor assembles a vertical spread with calls and a similar but offsetting spread with puts.

Brady Commission. One of a number of commissions that studied the causes for the stock market crash of October 19, 1987; set up by the U.S. Congress and named after Nicholas Brady, former New Jersey senator.

breakup value. The sum of the values of a company's individual assets if sold separately.

broker. An employee of a financial intermediary who acts as an agent in the buying and selling of securities. A broker, unlike a dealer, never owns the securities that he or she trades for his or her customers.

brokerage firm. A firm that offers various services such as access to the securities markets, account management, margin loans, investment advice, and underwriting.

broker call-loan rate. The interest rate charged by banks to brokers for loans that brokers use to support their margin loans to customers; usually scaled up for the margin loan rate.

bull. One who expects a rising market.

bullion. Gold, silver, or other precious metals in the form of bars, plates, or certain coins minted to contain a specific unit of weight (bullion coins).

bull market. A rising market.

business cycle. The pattern of fluctuations in the economy.

Business Week. A major business periodical published weekly by McGraw-Hill Inc.

butterfly spread. A type of spread in which two calls are sold at one striking price and one call each is purchased at striking prices above and below the sold calls.

buying power. The dollar value of additional marginable securities that can be purchased with the current equity in the account.

call. An option to buy stock or some other asset at a prespecified price over a prespecified period.

callable. The property of a security that allows the issuer to redeem it prior to maturity.

call feature on bond or preferred stock. An option of the issuing company to repurchase the securities at a set price over a prespecified period (prior to maturity).

call-loan rate. *see* broker call-loan rate.

call price. The price at which a bond, preferred, warrant, or other security may be redeemed prior to maturity; usually begins at a significant premium to the face value and then the premium declines as the instrument approaches its stated maturity. Also called the redemption price.

call protection. An indenture provision preventing a security (usually a bond or preferred stock) from being redeemed earlier than a certain time after its issue; for example, a 20-year bond might not be callable for the first five years.

call risk. The danger that a callable bond or preferred will be redeemed early (called) by the issuer.

capacity effect. The tendency of inflationary pressures to accelerate when the economy approaches the full employment level.

capital asset. Virtually any investment asset. To qualify as a capital asset (and thus be subject to the advantages, if any, of long-term capital gains treatment) an asset must be held as an investment rather than in inventory as an item of trade.

capital asset pricing model (CAPM). The theoretical relationship that seeks to explain returns as a function of the risk-free rate and market risk.

capital distribution. A dividend paid out of capital rather than from earnings. Such distributions are not taxed when received but do reduce the investment's basis.

capital gains (losses). The difference between the basis and sales price of an investment asset held for a period specified by the IRS; long-term gains received special tax treatment until 1988.

capitalizing of expenses. Placing current business expenses on the balance sheet and writing them off over time.

capital market line. The theoretical relation between an efficiently diversified portfolio's expected return and risk derived from the capital asset pricing model.

carry. The cost of holding a physical commodity until it is deliverable on a futures contract; primary components are storage and financing costs.

cash cow. A company or subsidiary of a company that in the normal course of its operations throws off a substantial cash surplus.

cash flow. Reported profits plus depreciation, depletion, and amortization.

cash management account. An individual financial account that combines checking, credit card, money fund, and margin accounts in order to maximize returns and minimize interest charges on transaction balances.

cash market. A market in which physical commodities (spot) are traded for cash.

cash surrender value. The accumulated savings element of a life insurance policy that can be recovered by canceling the policy or can be borrowed against at a specified interest rate.

CBOE (Chicago Board Options Exchange). The largest of the option exchanges; originator and promoter of organized options trading.

CBT (Chicago Board of Trade). The largest of the commodity exchanges; lists futures in a variety of physicals including wheat, corn, oats, soybeans, plywood, silver, stock indexes, GNMA, and long-term bonds.

CD (certificate of deposit). Special redeemable debt obligation issued by a bank and other depository institution.

CEA (Commodity Exchange Authority). A former government agency that had regulatory authority over agricultural futures markets; now regulated by the CFTC.

Central Certificate Service. An organization that allows clearing firms to effect security deliveries with computerized bookkeeping entries.

central market. A Congressionally mandated concept for a complete linkup of the various markets trading securities; the development was underway but incomplete as of 1988.

central unemployment rate. The unemployment rate for males in the 25 to 45 age group or some similar high-employment grouping.

CFTC (Commodity Futures Trading Commission). The federal regulator of the futures markets.

changes in financial position statement. An accounting statement that reports on a firm's cash inflows and outflows. Formerly called source and application of funds statement.

Chapter X bankruptcy. Formal, detailed, and usually time-consuming bankruptcy proceeding.

Chapter XI bankruptcy. Informal, less costly, and quicker procedure than Chapter X; only allowable when creditors agree.

characteristic line. The relationship between a security's expected return and the market return; defined by the security's α (intercept) and β (slope parameter).

chart reading. Attempting to forecast stock price changes from charts of past price and volume data.

Chicago Mercantile Exchange (the Merc). The second largest of the commodity exchanges; lists futures in a variety of physicals including cattle, hogs, pork bellies, fresh broilers, lumber stock indexes, currencies, and debt securities.

churning. Overactive trading of customer accounts designed to generate commissions for the manager/broker.

circuit breakers. A procedure for stopping trading when a market move reaches a prescribed threshold; for example, stock trading might be halted for 30 minutes whenever the market moved 150 points on the DJIA during a single day.

classified common stock. Different categories of stock, some of which may be nonvoting and others nondividend receiving.

clearing house. An organization that keeps track of and guarantees fulfillment of futures contracts or options contracts.

Clifford trust. A device for shifting tax liability on income, usually from parent to dependent child; trusts set up since the Tax Reform Act of 1986 do not achieve the desired goal.

CLOB (consolidated limit order book). A composite book of limit orders that could be executed in any market where a security is traded; a feature of the proposed central market.

closed-end fund. A type of investment company organized as a corporation with its stock traded in the same markets as other stocks; price may vary appreciably from fund's net asset value.

closing costs. Costs associated with obtaining a real estate loan and completing the purchase; may include title search, points, transfer taxes, and various other fees.

Coffee, Sugar and Cocoa Exchange. A commodity exchange located in New York City that lists futures contracts for coffee, sugar, and cocoa.

collateral. Asset pledged to assure repayment of debt; the lender may take ownership of the collateral if the loan is not repaid as promised.

collateral trust bond. A secured bond; for example, an equipment trust certificate secured by such collateral as railroad rolling stock or airplanes.

combination security. An asset combining characteristics of more than one type of security; includes convertible bonds, convertible preferred stocks, hybrid convertibles, equity notes, commodity-backed bonds, and stock-indexed bonds.

commercial paper. Short-term, usually low-risk debt issued by large corporations with very strong credit ratings.

commingled real estate fund (CREF). In effect a self-liquidating unit investment trust with a managed portfolio of real estate.

commissions. Fees charged by brokers for handling investment transactions such as security or real estate trades.

commodity. In general, any article of commerce; in investments, any of a select group of items traded on one of the commodity exchanges either spot (for immediate delivery) or in the futures market (for delivery at a prespecified future date).

commodity board. An electronic sign in the trading room of a commodity exchange that displays current market statistics.

commodity option. A put or call option to purchase or sell a futures contract.

common stock. Stock that represents proportional ownership of an incorporated enterprise; common stockholders are the residual claimants for earnings and assets after all holders of debt and preferred stock have received their contractual payments.

company analysis. Evaluating the strengths and weaknesses of a company and its investment appeal vis-à-vis its markets and competitors. Also called firm analysis.

compound interest. Interest earned on interest as a result of reinvesting one period's income to earn additional income the following period; compounding may take place as frequently as daily. For example, compounded annually, $100 earning 9% will yield $9 the first year. In the following year the 9% will be applied to $109 for a return of $9.81. In the third year the principal will have grown to $118.81 (100 + 9 + 9.81) and another 9% will add about $10.62. This process continues with the interest rate being applied to a larger and larger principal.

compound value. The end-period value of a sum earning a compounded return.

COMPUSTAT Data Tape. A data source containing balance sheet, income statement, and other information on a substantial number of companies for the most recent 20 years.

concentrated position. A margined portfolio having most of its value represented by one or a few securities; may have a higher margin maintenance percentage than that set by brokerage firms for more diversified accounts.

conditional forecast. A forecast based on some exogenous factor such as a stock performance forecast relative to market performance.

Conference Board. An organization that compiles quarterly capital appropriations statistics and reports them in *Manufacturing Industrial Statistics*.

conglomerate. A company with a diversified portfolio of business units; particularly one formed through a merger of a diverse array of formerly independent companies.

consol. A perpetual debt instrument that pays interest but never matures and thus never returns principal.

consumer credit. Personal debt as represented by credit card loans, finance company loans, or similar debts.

consumer durables. Long-life assets such as furniture or appliances.

Consumer Price Index (CPI). A monthly cost of living index prepared by the Bureau of Labor Statistics, U.S. Department of Labor.

Consumer Reports. A periodical that frequently contains articles oriented to personal finance.

consumption expenditures. Spending by individual consumers on final goods and services.

contingent liability. A potential claim against a company or other entity; for example, a lawsuit claiming damages would represent a contingent claim against the defendant.

contrary opinion. An investment approach that concentrates on out-of-favor securities; contrarians assert that what is not wanted today may be quite desirable in the future.

conversion. A complicated maneuver that involves purchasing options, shorting the underlying stock, and reinvesting the sale proceeds; a technique used by brokerage firms to earn substantial returns when option and stock prices are appropriately related.

conversion price. The face value of a convertible bond divided by the number of shares into which it is convertible.

conversion ratio. The number of common shares into which a convertible bond or preferred stock may be converted.

conversion value. The market price of a stock times the number of shares for which the convertible may be exchanged.

convertible. A bond or preferred stock that may be exchanged for a specific number of common shares.

convertible debenture. A debenture that may for the bond's life be exchanged for a specific number of shares of the issuing firm's common stock.

convertible preferred. A preferred stock that may be exchanged for a specific number of shares of the issuing company's common stock.

corner. The act of acquiring a large, often controlling, interest in a security issue or other specific type of asset that pushes the market price to a very high level and restricts supply; especially damaging to shorts, who may need to cover at very disadvantageous prices.

corporate bond fund. A mutual fund holding a diversified portfolio of corporate bonds.

corporates. Corporate bonds.

correlation coefficient. A measure of the comovement tendency of two variables, such as the returns on two securities.

country fund. A type of mutual fund that assembles and manages a portfolio of securities in a single country, such as the Japan Fund or the Mexico Fund.

coupon bond. A bond with attached coupons that must be clipped and sent in to receive interest payments.

coupon clipping. Claiming income on coupon bonds by detaching each physical coupon and presenting it for payment when due.

coupon-effect. The price impact of differential yield components derived from coupon versus price appreciation as a bond moves toward maturity. Thus a deep-discount, low-coupon bond will offer a yield to maturity that includes a substantial component of tax-deferred capital gains; such a bond's price will usually be affected favorably by the coupon effect.

coupon-equivalent yield. Yield on an investment computed to correspond with a bond that pays a semiannual coupon.

coupon rate. The stated dollar return of a fixed-income investment.

covariance. The covariance of variables x and y is: $Cov = E[x - E(x)][y - E(y)]$ where $E(z)$ is the expected value of z. If x and y tend to be above their means simultaneously and below their means simultaneously, the covariance is positive. If one is above, when the other tends to be below, the covariance is negative. If they are independent, the covariance is zero.

covered writing. Writing options against existing stock holdings.

covering. Repurchasing securities or other assets sold short.

crack. Combination commodity trade in which the trader buys crude oil futures and sells corresponding amounts of heating oil and gasoline futures.

cramdown. A procedure in a bankruptcy proceeding whereby, by a majority vote of the creditors (by both number and dollar value of claims), the plan is applied to all unsecured creditors.

Crash of 1987. The largest one-day decline in stock market history; on October 19, 1987, the Dow Jones Industrial Average dropped 508 points, which corresponded to 23% of its value the previous close.

credit balance. A positive balance, as in a brokerage account.

credit union. A cooperative association in which the members' pooled savings are available for loans to the membership.

Creditwatch. One of several short-term credit analysis services. A bond in danger of being downgraded would be likely to be placed on S&P's Creditwatch list once some degree of trouble is spotted.

CREF *See* commingled real estate fund.

CRISPE data tape. A data source containing daily stock price information.

crown jewel option. Antitakeover defense in which the most sought after subsidiary of a target firm is spun off.

crown loan. Interest-free loan, usually from parent to dependent child, designed to shift taxable income from a high- to low-bracket individual. The Tax Reform Act of 1986 ended the tax advantage of this maneuver.

crush. A combination trade, especially a commodity trade in which soybean futures are bought and corresponding amounts of soybean oil and meal futures are shorted.

cum-rights period. The time prior to the day of record that determines when shareholders receive a rights distribution; securities that sell cum-rights will reflect the imputed value of the rights to be distributed.

cumulative preferred. A preferred stock for which dividends in arrears must be paid before common dividends can be resumed.

cumulative voting. A method of voting for corporate directors that gives each shareholder votes equal to the product of the number of shares held times the number of director slots; allows a group of shareholders with a substantial but minority position to concentrate their votes on one or a few candidates and thereby elect at least their proportional share of directors.

Curb exchange. The American Stock Exchange, which until 1953 was called the New York Curb Exchange.

currency. Any form of money accepted by a country and in actual use within that country as a medium of exchange.

current assets. Assets that are expected to be used up or converted to cash within the next year or next operating period, whichever is longer; primarily cash, accounts receivable, and inventory.

current liabilities. Liabilities that will become due and payable in the next year or the next operating cycle, whichever is longer; includes accounts payable, short-term bank loans, the current portion of long-term debt, and taxes payable.

current ratio. The ratio of current assets to current liabilities; a measure of short-term liquidity.

current yield. A bond's coupon rate divided by its current market price or a stock's indicated dividend rate divided by its per share price.

day of record. The date on which ownership is determined for that quarter's dividends or for the issuance of some other distributions such as rights.

day order. An order that is canceled if it is not executed sometime during the day that it was entered.

day trader. A commodity trader who closes all of his or her positions by the end of the day, thus all transactions are opened and closed on the same day.

dealer. A security trader who acts as a principal rather than as an agent; thus, a specialist or a market maker but not a broker (brokers are agents).

debenture. A long-term debt obligation that unlike a collateralized bond only gives the lender a general claim against the borrower's assets. In a default the debentureholder has no claim against any specific assets.

debit balance. A negative balance in a margin account.

debt–equity ratio. The ratio of total debt to total equity.

debt securities. Bonds and similar securities that call for the payment of interest until maturity and principal at maturity. A firm that defaults on its interest or principal obligations may eventually be forced into bankruptcy.

decreasing term. A type of term insurance in which protection decreases with the insured's age.

deduction. In tax computation, an amount that may be subtracted from the adjusted gross income to determine taxable income; for example, if the taxpayer itemizes, state income taxes, charitable contributions, mortgage interest expenses, and certain other costs.

deep-discount bond. A bond selling for substantially less than its par value.

default. Failure to live up to any of the terms in a bond indenture or other credit agreement.

default risk. The risk that a debt security's contractual interest or principal will not be paid when due.

defeasance. The process whereby a debtor offsets the impact of a portion of its debt by purchasing high-quality debt instruments (usually governments) whose payments cover the payment obligations of the debt issue.

deferred compensation plan. A procedure whereby employees are permitted to set aside and defer the tax liability on a portion of their wages and salaries into approved deferred compensation plans.

deflation. An increase in the purchasing power of the dollar or some other currency unit; the opposite of inflation.

depletion. The writing off of assets, particularly mineral assets such as oil or natural gas, as they are exploited.

Depository Trust Company. A firm that facilitates exchange members' securities trading with one another by using bookkeeping entries rather than physically delivering the stock certificates.

depreciation. A deduction from income that allocates the cost of fixed assets over their useful lives.

depression. An economic collapse with high unemployment and negative growth.

dilution. Issuing additional shares and thereby reducing proportional ownership of existing shareholders.

disability insurance. Insurance protection designed to provide an offset to potential income loss from a health condition that reduces or ends the insured's ability to earn income.

discount brokers. Brokers who charge below-retail commission rates and usually offer a more limited set of investment services.

discount loan. A loan from the Federal Reserve System to a member bank to cure a temporary reserve deficiency.

discount rate (for Fed members). The interest rate charged by the Federal Reserve System on loans to member banks.

discount rate (for income stream). The interest rate applied to an income stream or expected income stream in estimating its present value.

discount yield. A yield computation in which the return is based on the final value of the asset; thus a bill that sells for $100 - x$ and matures in one year for 100 has a yield of x%.

disinflation. A slowing in the rate at which prices increase.

disintermediation. The tendency of high interest rates to draw funds out of thrift institutions and therefore away from the mortgage market.

diversifiable risk. Firm-specific or industry-specific risk; such risks tend to offset one another and thus average out in an efficiently diversified portfolio.

diversification. The technique of spreading an investment portfolio over different industries, companies, investment types, and risks; used to reduce risks by not having "all of your eggs in one basket."

dividend capture. A strategy in which an investor purchases securities in order to own them on the day of record and then quickly sells them; designed to capture the dividend but avoid the risk of a lengthy hold.

dividend discount model. An approach to stock valuation that evaluates stocks on the basis of the present value of their expected stream of dividends; the basic formula is $P = d/(r - g)$ where: P = stock price, d = initial year dividend, r = appropriate discount rate, and g = expected growth rate.

dividend exclusion. An amount of qualifying dividends that an individual may exclude from taxable income. Tax Reform Act of 1986 ended the exclusions.

dividend reinvestment plan. A company program that allows dividends to be reinvested in additional shares, which are often newly issued and may be sold at a discount from the current market price.

dividend restriction. The limitation placed on dividend payments in a bond indenture.

dividends. Payments made by companies to their stockholders; usually financed from profits.

divisor. The number divided into the sum of Dow Jones 30 stock prices to determine the average. The divisor is adjusted to preserve consistency when any of the components is split.

dollar averaging. A formula-investment-plan requiring periodic (such as monthly) fixed dollar amount investments. This practice tends to "average" the unit purchase cost of an investment made over time.

DOT (designated order transmission). A system on the New York Stock Exchange in which orders are routed electronically to the trading posts where the securities are traded; often used by program traders.

Dow. *see* Dow Jones Industrial Average.

Dow Jones Inc. The firm that publishes *The Wall Street Journal* and *Barron's* and also compiles Dow Jones stock indexes.

Dow Jones Industrial Average. The most commonly referred to index of stock prices; computed as the sum of the prices of 30 leading industrial firms divided by a divisor that is adjusted to reflect splits of its components. Dow Jones indexes are also computed for utilities and transportation companies. Also called simply Dow.

Dow Theory. A charting theory originated by Charles Dow (Dow Jones Inc.). According to Dow Theory a market uptrend is confirmed if the primary market index (such as the Dow Jones Industrial Average) hits a new high that is soon followed by a high in the secondary index (such as the Dow Jones Transportation Index). A downtrend is signaled in a similar fashion.

draft. A check-like instrument that calls for payment upon receipt.

dual fund. A type of closed-end investment company that divides its returns between dividend-receiving fundholders and capital gains holders.

dual listing. A security listed for trading on more than one exchange.

Dun & Bradstreet. A firm that rates the creditworthiness of many borrowers and generates financial ratios on many industry groups.

Dupont Equation. A profitability relationship that relates return on equity to several components; ROE = ROS $\times$ Sales/Assets $\times$ Assets/Equity.

duration. The weighted average rate of return of a bond's principal and interest; a superior index of the payback rate compared to length to maturity, which ignores returns prior to principal repayment.

earnings per common share (EPS). The net income of a company, minus any preferred dividend requirements, divided by the number of outstanding common shares; provides the investor or potential investor with information on the stability of dividends and capital gains potential; is considered one of the most important indications of the value of common stock.

econometric model. A model based on an analysis of economic data; particularly models of the economy.

econometrics. The statistical analysis of economic data.

economic analysis. An evaluation of a firm's investment potential within its economic setting.

efficient frontier. A set of risk–return trade-offs, each of which offers the highest expected return for a given risk.

efficient market hypothesis. The theory that the market correctly prices securities in light of the known relevant information. In its weak form the hypothesis implies that past price and volume data (technical analysis) cannot be profitably used in stock selection. The semistrong form implies that superior manipulation of public data is impossible; thus such data cannot be used to improve stock selection over what is possible through random selection. In the strong form of the hypothesis even inside (nonpublic) information is thought to be reflected accurately in prices.

efficient portfolio. Portfolio on the efficient frontier that offers the highest expected return for that risk level.

election-year cycle. The alleged tendency for the stock market to reach a peak about seven months after a presidential election and then fall to a low about 11 months later.

equipment trust certificate. A type of bond collateralized by equipment, particularly railroad rolling stock or airplanes.

equity. *See* net worth.

equity accounting. Partially consolidating income and equity of affiliates that are 20% or more owned by the parent firm.

equity kicker. A sweetener designed to make a debt issue more attractive by giving its owner an opportunity to benefit from the borrower's success.

equity notes. Debt securities that are automatically converted into stock on a prespecified date at a specific price or one based on a formula that is prespecified. Also called mandatory convertible notes.

ERISA (Employee Retirement Income Security Act). A 1974 federal law that protects workers' pension funds.

escrow account. In general, an account designed to hold a sum of money for a specific purpose; in real estate, the fund normally set up for monthly deposits of the expected pro rata real estate taxes.

ESOP (Employee Stock Ownership Plan). A program in which a corporation contributes newly issued company stock worth up to 15% of employee payrolls into what amounts to a tax-sheltered profit sharing plan.

estate. A person's total worth as determined by his or her vested interests in property and other assets, exclusive of any liabilities.

estate tax. A progressive tax on the assets left by deceased parties.

Eurobonds. Bonds that may be denominated in dollars or some other currency but must be traded internationally.

Eurodollars. Dollar-denominated deposits held in banks based outside the United States, mostly in Europe, but some in Asian and other area banks.

Euromarkets. Financial markets that operate outside any national jurisdiction and deal in securities that may pay unusually high interest rates. The securities are usually based on deposits of large, international corporations or governments of nations involved in extensive foreign trade.

ex ante. Before the fact; thus a procedure that consistently identifies attractive investments ex ante would generally facilitate a profitable trading strategy.

ex-dividend date. The day after the day of record. Purchases completed on or after the ex-dividend date do not receive that period's dividend even if the stock is held on the payment date.

executor. The person appointed to carry out the provisions of a will.

exemptions. A dollar sum per dependent that may be used to reduce an individual's taxable income.

exercise value (put). The striking price of a put less the price of the associated stock or zero if the difference is negative. Also called intrinsic value.

exercise value (warrant, call, or right). The price of the associated stock less the striking price of the option or zero if the difference is negative. Also called intrinsic value.

exordium clause. The introductory portion of a will or other legal document.

expected value. The sum of the probabilities multiplied by their associated outcomes; the mean or average value.

expense deferral. An accounting technique whereby expense recognitions are spread over time.

explanatory notes. Additional information in the form of notes; keyed to stock and bond quotations by letter symbols.

ex post. After the fact; thus a procedure that identifies attractive investments but relies on ex post data to do so would not by itself facilitate a profitable trading strategy.

ex-rights period. The time subsequent to the day of record for a rights distribution.

extraordinary gain (loss). An unusual nonrecurring gain (loss).

face value. The maturity value of a bond or other debt instrument; sometimes referred to as the bond's par value.

FASB (Financial Accounting Standards Board). An accounting organization that establishes rules for preparing financial statements.

FDIC (Federal Deposit Insurance Corporation). A federal agency that insures deposits at commercial banks up to $100,000 per depositor.

Fed. *See* Federal Reserve System.

Federal Funds Market. The market where banks and other financial institutions borrow and lend immediately deliverable reserve-free funds, usually on a one-day basis.

Federal Reserve Board of Governors. The governing body of the Federal Reserve System, comprised of seven members appointed by the President for long and staggered terms.

Federal Reserve System. The federal government agency that exercises monetary policy through its control over banking system reserves. Also called the Fed.

FHA (Federal Housing Administration). A federal government agency that insures home mortgages.

FIFO (first in, first out). An inventory valuation method whereby items taken out of inventory are assumed to have cost the amount paid for the earliest unused purchase.

fill-or-kill order. A type of security market order that must be canceled unless it can be filled immediately.

filter rules. Any mechanical trading rule, such as a rule to buy stocks when their PE ratio falls below some predetermined value or to trade whenever a particular price pattern is observed.

financial ratio. A ratio such as the debt/equity or times-interest-earned designed to reflect a firm's long-term financial strength.

firm analysis. *See* company analysis.

fiscalist. A type of economist who believes that fiscal (not monetary) policy is the primary economic tool.

fiscal policy. Government tax and spending policy that affects the economy.

Fitch Investors Service. A bond rating service that is considerably less well known than Moody's or Standard & Poor's.

fixed assets. Tangible assets with a relatively long expected life (greater than a year) that are not intended for resale and that are used in the operations of the business; includes plant and equipment but not inventories or accounts receivable.

fixed costs. Costs that do not vary with the firm's output in the short run.

fixed-income security. Any security that promises to pay a periodic nonvariable sum, such as a bond paying a fixed coupon amount per period.

fixed rate mortgage. A mortgage having a constant interest rate for the life of the debt.

flat. Term used to describe a type of trade; bonds trading for a net price that does not reflect any accrued interest are said to trade flat.

flipping. The act of quickly selling a recently acquired investment; thus an investor who subscribed to a new issue and then sold in the immediate aftermarket could be described as a flipper.

floating rate notes. A type of debt security whose coupon rate varies with market interest rates.

floating rate preferred. A type of preferred stock whose indicated dividend rate varies with market rates.

floor trader. One holding a seat on an exchange who trades for his or her own account. Also called RCMM.

Florida land boom. A 1920s speculative real estate boom followed by a crash in the price of Florida property.

flower bonds. Government bonds that may be used at their par value for estate tax payments.

flowthrough. A method of handling investment tax credits in which benefits are taken into income statements as they are incurred rather than spread over the acquired asset's life (normalization).

FNMA (Federal National Mortgage Association). A previously government-owned, but now privately owned corporation that operates a secondary market in mortgages. FNMA issues its own debt securities to finance its mortgage portfolio.

focal point. A round number value that is generally agreed upon or recognized.

footnotes (to a financial statement). Notes that explain or expand upon entries; an integral part of a financial statement.

Forbes. A twice-monthly popular investment periodical famous for its Forbes lists, such as the list of loaded laggers.

Form 10K. A detailed annual report that must be submitted to the SEC, to the listing exchange, and to any shareholders who request it.

Form 10Q. A detailed quarterly report that must be submitted to the SEC and the listing exchange and may be sent to shareholders who request it.

Form 13D. A required SEC filing of any individual or group owning 5% or more of any public corporation; form must disclose a number of matters including the actual ownership percentage, its cost, the intentions of the owner and any relevant agreements of owner with any other party.

four-nine position. A holding of approximately 4.9% of the outstanding shares of a company, which is about the limit for a quiet holding. At 5% the holder must file a Form 13d with the SEC revealing his or her position.

fourth market. Direct trading of listed securities between institutions.

Freddie Mac (The Federal Home Loan Mortgage Corporation). A government agency that assembles pools of conventional mortgages and sells participations in a secondary market.

front-end loading. Taking a large portion of the sales fee from the early payments of a long-term purchase contract.

front running. An illegal trading strategy in which the trader (usually an employee of a brokerage firm) learns that a large trade is about to take place (usually placed by a substantial customer) and runs ahead of that trade to place an order at the pretrade price. If the large trade causes a major price change, the position can be reversed at a nice profit. In effect the front runner is trading on inside information (knowledge of the forthcoming trade).

FSLIC (Federal Savings and Loan Insurance Corporation). A federal government agency that insures deposits at savings and loan associations up to $100,000 per depositor.

full employment. The unemployment rate that is thought to be the minimum level before inflationary pressures accelerate and the maximum level the public will view as reasonable. Opinions on this level have over time varied from around 4% to 6%.

full faith and credit. The promise backing a debenture or other type of uncollateralized debt instrument; the borrower promises to pay and pledges its full faith and credit.

fundamental analysis. The evaluation of firms and their investment-attractiveness based on their financial, competitive, earning, and managerial position or similar evaluation of other investments types.

futures. Deferred delivery commodities contracts.

GAAP (Generally Accepted Accounting Principles). A set of accounting principles that are supposed to be followed in preparing accounting statements.

gambler's ruin. The wiping out of an individual's original capital by a series of adverse events. Often used in the context of the risk of gambler's ruin.

gamma factor. The number of years of above-average growth at a rate equal to that of the recent past that is necessary to justify the current multiple on growth stocks.

general creditor. A creditor whose loan is not secured (uncollateralized) by any specific assets; debts are secured by the full faith and credit of the borrower.

general mortgage bond. A bond having a generalized claim against the issuing company's property.

general obligation. A municipal bond secured by the issuer's full faith and credit.

geometric mean return (GMR). The value obtained by taking the nth root of the product of n per period returns; the return that if earned over the entire set of periods produces the same ending compound value as the separate per period returns applied period by period.

GIC (Guaranteed Interest Contract). An investment sold by insurance companies that offers high yields plus the opportunity to earn similar returns on additions to plan.

gift tax. A progressive tax on gifts; now incorporated with estate taxes.

gilt-edge security. A very secure bond or other asset.

give up. A now-prohibited practice whereby brokers making trades for a mutual fund were directed to pay a portion of their commission fees to brokers who had sold the fund's shares.

Glass-Steagall Act. A 1933 federal act that required the separation of commercial and investment banking.

GNMA (Ginnie Mae) (Government National Mortgage Association). A government agency that provides special assistance on selected types of home mortgages; securities are backed both by GNMA mortgage portfolios and by the general credit of the government.

go-go fund. A type of mutual fund popular in the late 1960s that sought short-term trading profits. Also called a performance fund.

going private. The process of a company's buying back all of its publicly held stock so that ownership rests with a few owners and it becomes a privately held company.

going public. The process of a start-up or heretofore private firm selling its shares in a public offering.

golden handcuffs. An employment agreement that makes the departure prior to normal retirement age of upper level managers very costly to themselves; they may lose attractive stock options.

golden handshake. A provision in a preliminary merger agreement in which the target firm gives the acquiring firm an option to purchase its shares or assets at attractive prices or to receive a substantial bonus if the proposed takeover does not occur.

golden parachute. A very generous termination agreement for upper management that takes effect if control of their firm shifts.

good till canceled order (GTC). A type of order that remains in effect until executed or canceled.

goodwill. The amount by which a firm's going concern value exceeds its book value.

governments. U.S. Government bonds issued by the Treasury Department and backed by the full faith and credit of the federal government.

grace period. Time period in which offensive action is stayed until a defaulting debtor has an opportunity to cure the default.

Graham and Dodd approach. A type of securities analysis that stresses fundamentals. Its originator, Benjamin Graham, coauthored the investment text that dominated the market from the 1930s to 1950s. Also called Graham approach.

grantee. The individual receiving property under a deed.

grantor. The conveyor of property under a deed; the one who transfers property to another.

Gray approach. An investment timing device that seeks to identify over and undervalued market phases on the basis of interest rates relative to market PE ratios.

Great Crash. 1929 stock market decline.

greater-fool theory. The tongue-in-cheek view that a still "greater fool" will come along to bail out a foolish investment.

greenmail. The practice of acquiring a large percentage of a firm's stock and then being bought out at a premium after threatening to take over the firm.

gross income. Total income, either actual or estimated.

gross margin. The net sales of an enterprise minus its cost of goods sold.

Gross National Product (GNP). The sum of market values of all final goods and services produced annually in the country.

growth fund. A common stock mutual fund that seeks price appreciation by concentrating on growth stocks.

growth share matrix. A relationship popularized by the Boston Consulting Group that seeks to explain a large part of interfirm profit differences as due to the combined impacts of market share and growth.

growth stock. The shares of a company that is expected to achieve rapid growth; often carries above-average risks and PE ratios.

guarantee bond. A bond with a guarantee from a company other than the issuer.

guarantee preferred. A preferred stock with a guarantee from a company other than the issuer.

head and shoulders price formation. A technical pattern that looks like a head and shoulders and is said to forecast a price decline.

hedge fund. A type of mutual fund that seeks to offset some of its long positions with short positions.

hedging. Taking opposite positions in related securities in the hope of profiting from relative price movements (risk hedging) or of reducing an existing risk (pure hedging).

hemline indicator. A whimsical technical market indicator that forecasts stock market moves on the basis of women's hemlines.

histogram. A discrete probability distribution display.

holding company. A company set up to maintain voting control of other business enterprises.

holding period return (HPR). The rate of return over some specific time.

holding period return relative (HPRR). The end period compound value for a specific holding period.

horizontal spread. Short and long option positions on the same security with the same strike price but different expirations.

Hulbert Financial Digest. A publication containing ratings of investment advisory services.

hypothecation. The pledging of securities as loan collateral.

immunization. The process of buying bonds with durations equal to one's investment horizon or using interest futures to accomplish the same purpose.

inactive post. NYSE trading post for inactively traded securities.

in and out. The purchase and sale of the same security within a short period.

income anticipation. An accounting practice whereby a profit is reflected in the income statement before it is received.

income approach. Valuing real estate or some other asset as the discounted value of its expected income stream.

income bond. A bond on which interest is paid only if the issuer has sufficient earnings.

income fund. A common stock mutual fund that concentrates on stocks paying high dividends.

income statement. A financial statement of interim earnings; provides a financial accounting of revenues and expenses during a specified period, i.e., three months, one year, and so on.

income stock. A stock with a high indicated dividend rate.

incorporation. The forming into a legal body endowed with various rights and duties.

indenture (bond). The statement of promises the company makes to its bondholders, including a commitment to pay a stated coupon amount periodically and return the face value (usually $1,000) at the end of a certain period (such as 20 years after issue). A trustee, such as a bank, is charged with overseeing the issuing firm's commitments.

independence (statistical). The relationship between two variables if knowledge of one's value does not help explain the other's value. Thus, if IBM and AT&T stock returns are totally unrelated, knowing that AT&T stock returned x% over the most recent 12 months would not help explain IBM stock's return over the same period.

index arbitrage. A trading strategy involving offsetting positions in stock index futures contracts and the underlying cash market securities (stocks making up the index). If, for example, the index futures is priced above the stocks making up the index, the arbitrager would buy the stocks and sell the index. If, in contrast, the index was priced below its corresponding stocks, the arbitrager would short the stocks and buy the index.

index fund. A mutual fund that attempts to duplicate the performance of a market index such as the S&P 500.

industry analysis. The evaluation of an industry's position and prospects as they relate to its component firm's investment attractiveness.

inflation. The rate of rise in the price level; for example, if on the average $1.06 will buy what $1 would buy a year earlier, inflation has equaled 6%.

inflation hedge. An asset whose value varies directly with the price level.

informal workout. An approach to dealing with a troubled firm that seeks to avoid the problems of a bankruptcy proceeding by obtaining sufficient lender concessions to allow the company to continue.

in play. The status of being an actively pursued takeover candidate.

input–output model. A model that relates various industries' outputs to their derived demands from other industries.

insider trading. The buying or selling of traders with access to relevant nonpublic information relating to the company in question.

insolvency. Insufficient liquid assets to meet financial obligations that are currently due.

installment sale. In general, any sale that calls for payments to be made over time; in real estate transactions, an installment sale may reduce and postpone the tax liability if the payments are stretched out over a sufficiently long period.

Instinet. An automated communications network among block traders.

institutional investor. An organization that invests the pooled assets of others; includes pension funds, mutual funds, bank trust departments, insurance companies, and investment companies.

intercorporate dividend. Dividend payment from one corporation to another; 70% of such dividends are not subject to the corporate income tax.

interest. The amount a borrower pays for the use of a lender's funds; frequently expressed as an annual percentage of the principal balance outstanding and may be compounded on a monthly, quarterly, annually or on some other periodic basis.

interest futures. A commodity futures contract calling for delivery of a debt security such as a T-bill or long-term government bond.

interest rate risk. The risk that an interest rate rise will take place, thereby reducing the market value of fixed income securities.

international fund. A mutual fund that invests in securities of firms based outside the fund's home country.

International Monetary Market. A futures exchange associated with the Chicago Mercantile Exchange that trades futures contracts on gold, T-bills, Eurodollars, CDs, and several foreign currencies.

in-the-money option. An option whose striking price is more favorable to optionholders than the current market price of the underlying security.

intraday dependencies. Nonrandom price movements of transactions taking place over the course of a single day.

intrinsic value (option). *See* exercise value.

intrinsic value (stock). The underlying value that a careful evaluation would produce; generally takes into account both the going concern value and the liquidation or breakup value of the company. An efficient market would always price stocks at their intrinsic values, although an inefficient market would not necessarily do so.

inverted market. A futures market in which the futures price exceeds the spot.

investment banker. A firm that organizes a syndicate to underwrite or market a new issue of securities.

Investment Companies. Periodical that reports on mutual funds; published by Weisenberger.

investment company. A company that manages pooled portfolios for a group of owners; may be either a closed-end company, whose fixed number of shares outstanding are traded like other shares, or an open-end company (mutual fund), whose shares outstanding change by the amounts bought and sold.

Investment Company Institute. Organization of mutual funds and other institutional investors; publishes *Mutual Fund Forum.*

investment manager. One who manages an investment portfolio.

Investor's Daily. A national business newspaper that competes with *The Wall Street Journal.*

IRA (Individual Retirement Account). A retirement plan that allows employees to set aside up to $2,000 annually in a tax-sheltered instrument. Earnings are not taxed until they are withdrawn. The contributed sum is also deductible from taxable income if the individual is not covered by a company pension or has a relatively low income.

itemizing. One of two basic approaches to filing income taxes; involves taking deductions for specific allowed expenses. Taxpayers who do not itemize take a standard deduction.

January indicator. A technical timing device utilizing the assertion that as January goes so goes the year.

junk bonds. High-risk bonds usually promising a very high indicated return coupled with a substantial default risk.

Kansas City Board of Trade. A futures exchange listing wheat and Value Line stock index futures.

Keogh account. A retirement account that allows self-employed individuals to set aside (1987) up to $30,000 or 20% of their income in a tax-sheltered fund. Neither the contribution nor the earnings on it are subject to tax until they are withdrawn.

key person life insurance. Life insurance on key employees with their employer as the beneficiary; designed to assure creditors and suppliers and customers that the firm would survive the loss of the insured.

Krugerrand. A South African gold coin containing one ounce of gold that is often traded by gold speculators. Importation of these coins into the United States is now prohibited.

kurtosis. The degree to which a distribution departs from normal; see also platokurtosis and leptokurtosis.

lagging indicators. Government-compiled data series whose movements are identified as tending to follow turns in the overall economy.

law of one price. The principle that, whenever two assets offer equivalent payoff matrices, their prices must be identical.

leading indicators. Government-compiled data series whose movements are identified as tending to precede turns in the overall economy.

leakages. Funds that "leak" into savings, import purchases, or taxes during each round of stimulatory spending or tax-reduction, reduced each round by thus reducing the impact of fiscal policy.

learning curve. A relationship popularized by the Boston Consulting Group that hypothesizes that manufacturers are able to reduce costs substantially as they increase their cumulative volume; in one formulation, costs are said to decrease by 20% with each doubling of cumulative volume.

legal lists. Lists of stocks authorized by various states for fiduciary investing.

leg on. The process of assembling a spread or other combination position one side at a time.

leptokurtosis. The degree to which a distribution differs from the normal by having more probability in the peak and tails.

lettered stock. Newly issued stock sold at a discount to large investors prior to a public offering of the same issue; in accordance with SEC Rule 144, buyers agree not to sell their shares for a prespecified period.

leverage. Using borrowed funds or special types of securities (warrants, calls) to increase the potential return; usually increases both the risk and the expected return.

leveraged buy out (LBO). The takeover of a company financed largely by debt secured by the acquired firm's own assets.

liabilities. Debts; appear on right side of a balance sheet.

LIFO (last in, first out). An accounting method that for income reporting purposes values items taken out of inventory at the most recent unused invoice cost.

limited liability. Property that under most circumstances limits shareholders' liabilities for their corporation's debts to their initial investments.

limit order. An order to buy or sell at a prespecified price.

linear model. A method of estimating portfolio risks that requires only alpha and beta estimates of the components.

line of credit. Prearranged agreement from a lender to supply up to some maximum loan at prespecified terms.

liquidation. The process of selling all of a firm's assets and distributing the proceeds first to creditors and then any residual to shareholders.

liquidation value. The value of a going concern's assets if sold piecemeal.

liquidity. The ease with which an investment can be converted to cash for approximately its original cost plus its expected accrued interest.

liquidity preference hypothesis. The term structure of interest rates hypothesis that asserts that most borrowers prefer to borrow long and most lenders prefer to lend short; implies that long rates generally exceed short rates.

liquidity ratio. A ratio (e.g., current or quick) of a firm's short-run financial situation.

liquidity risk. The degree to which an asset's holding period return varies with interest rate moves.

listed stocks. Stocks approved for trading by one or more of the stock exchanges.

listing. The act of obtaining exchange approval for trading.

listing requirements. The qualifications that a company must meet in order to be listed on an exchange.

load. The selling fee applied to a load mutual fund purchase.

loaded lagger. A stock of a company whose assets, particularly its liquid assets, have high values relative to the stock's price.

load fund. A type of mutual fund sold through agents who receive fees that are typically 8.5% on small purchases and somewhat less on trades above $10,000.

lock-up agreement. An agreement between an acquirer and a target that makes the target unattractive to any other acquirer; similar to a golden handshake.

long interest. The number of futures or options contracts outstanding (owned and sold).

long position. The ownership of stocks or other securities as opposed to a short position, in which the investor has sold securities that are not owned.

long-term assets. *See* fixed assets.

long-term capital gain (loss). Gain (loss) on a capital asset held for at least six months.

long-term liabilities. Liabilities that are not due in the next year or next operating period, whichever is shorter; usually include outstanding bonds, debentures, mortgages, and term loans.

loss. Net revenues minus costs when costs exceed revenues.

low PE stocks. Stocks with low price–earnings ratios; sought out by value-oriented investors.

LYON. A complicated type of zero coupon convertible debt security that is both callable and redeemable at prices that escalate through time.

M1. The basic money supply; includes checking deposits and cash held by the public.

M2. A broader based money supply definition than M1; includes everything in M1 plus most savings and money market deposit accounts.

M3. A still broader based money supply definition than M2; includes everything in M2 plus large certificates of deposit and money market mutual funds sold to institutions.

management control. A situation in which no group owns enough of the firm's stock to exercise control and control is thus abdicated to the managers.

management-oriented company. A firm that is largely run in the interest of management as opposed to that of the shareholders.

mandatory convertible notes. *See* equity notes.

manufactured call. A call-like position generated by a combination put and long position in the underlying stock; position with a similar payoff matrix to a call.

manufactured put. A put-like position generated by a combination of a call and short position in the underlying stock; position with a similar payoff matrix to a put.

margin. Borrowing to finance a portion of a securities purchase; regulated by the Fed. For example, if a 60% margin rate is set,

$10,000 worth of stock may be purchased with up to $4,000 of borrowed money. Only securities of listed and some large OTC companies qualify for margin loans.

marginal tax rate. The percentage that must be paid in taxes on the next income increment.

margin call. A demand by a brokerage firm for more collateral or cash to support existing margin debt; a call is required when the borrower's equity position falls below a preset percentage (e.g., 35%) of the value of margined securities.

margin maintenance. The minimum percentage that an equity account must maintain to avoid a margin call.

margin rate. The percentage of the cost of a purchase of marginable securities that must be paid for with the investor's own money.

marketability. The ease with which an investment can be bought or sold without appreciably affecting its price; for example, blue chip stocks are usually highly marketable because they are actively traded.

market approach. Estimating the value of properties (particularly real estate) based on what similar properties are selling for.

market indexes. An average of security prices designed to reflect market performance. The Dow-Jones Industrial Average, the best known and most closely followed, is calculated by adding the market prices of 30 leading industrial companies and dividing by a divisor; the divisor is changed periodically to reflect stock splits. Dow Jones Inc. also compiles averages for utility and transportation stocks. Standard & Poor's investor service, the NYSE, NASD, and AMEX all compute their own indexes. Indexes are also compiled for bonds, commodities, options, and various other investment types.

market indicator. *See* technical indicator.

market maker. One who creates a market for a security by quoting a bid and asked price.

market model. Relating the price of individual security returns to market returns with a linear equation of the form: $R_{it} =$ $\alpha_{ai} + \beta_{ai}(R_{mt})$ where R_{it} = return of security i for period t; R_{mt} = market return for period t; and α_{ai} and β_{ai} are firm i parameters.

market on close order. An order that is to be held until just before the close and then executed.

market order. An order to buy or sell at the market price; requires immediate execution.

market portfolio. A hypothetical portfolio representing each investment asset in proportion to its relative weight in the universe of investment assets.

market price. The current price at which willing buyers and willing sellers will transact.

market risk. The return variability associated with general market movements; not diversifiable within the market. Also called systematic risk.

mark to market. Practice of recomputing equity position in a margin account (stock or futures) on a daily basis.

master limited partnership (MLP). A method of organizing a business that combines some of the advantages of a corporation with some of the advantages of a limited partnership. Shares of ownership trade much like corporate stock yet the MLP is taxed like a partnership; that is, profits are imputed to the owners and taxed only once.

matched and lost. Term applied to the outcome for the loser when two traders simultaneously arrive at the relevant trading post with equivalent orders, only one of which may be filled within the current market situation; they flip a coin to determine whose order is to be filled.

maturity. The length of time until a security must be redeemed by its issuer.

maturity date. The date at which a security's principal must be redeemed.

mean. The average or expected value of a sample or distribution.

me-first rules. Restrictions in a bond's indenture that limit a firm's ability to take on additional debt with similar standing to that of the bonds in question.

merger. The act of combining two firms into a single company.

MGIC (Mortgage Guarantee Insurance Corporation). One of a group of companies that for a fee guarantee the timely payment of a portion of certain mortgages' obligations.

middle-of-the-road fund. A mutual fund that invests in a balanced portfolio of stocks (some blue chips and some more speculative).

mode. The high point or most likely outcome of a distribution; for a symmetrical distribution the mode and mean (average value) are identical.

modern portfolio theory (MPT). The combination of the capital asset pricing model, efficient market hypothesis, and related theoretical models of security market pricing and performance.

Monday–Friday stock pattern. The observed tendency of stock prices to decline on Mondays and rise on Fridays.

monetarist. One who emphasizes the powerful economic role of monetary (as opposed to fiscal) policy.

monetary asset. An investment that is denominated in dollars.

monetary policy. Government policy that utilizes the money supply to affect the economy; implemented by the Fed through its control of bank reserves and required reserves.

money fund. *See* money market mutual fund.

money illusion. Failure to take account of inflation's impact; thus an individual who received a 10% raise and thought his or her financial situation had improved would suffer from money illusion if prices had risen by 20%.

Money Magazine. A monthly personal finance periodical published by Time Inc.

money market. The market for high-quality, short-term securities such as CDs, commercial paper, acceptances, Treasury bills, short-term tax-exempt notes, and Eurodollar loans.

money market account. A type of bank or thrift institution account that offers unregulated money market rates; requires a minimum deposit of $1,000 (many banks require $2,500); and limits withdrawals to six per month, only three of which may be by check.

money market mutual fund. A mutual fund that invests in short-term highly liquid securities. Also called money fund.

money multiplier. The ratio of a change in reserves to the change in the money supply; thus a money multiplier of five would imply that a $1 billion increase in reserves would result in a $5 billion increase in the money supply.

money supply. Generally defined as the sum of all coin, currency (outside bank holdings), and deposits on which check-like instruments may be written. *See* M1, M2, and M3.

mood indicators. Technical market indicators designed to reflect the market's pessimism or optimism.

Moody's Industrial Manual. An annual publication containing detailed historical information on most publicly traded firms.

Moody's Investor Service. A firm that publishes manuals containing extensive historical data on a large number of publicly traded firms. Moody's also rates bonds.

mortgage. A loan collateralized by property, particularly real estate; the lender is entitled to take possession of the property if the debt is not repaid in a timely manner.

mortgage-backed security. A debt instrument representing a share of ownership in a pool of mortgages (e.g., GNMA passthroughs) or backed by a pool of mortgages (e.g., FNMA bonds).

mortgage bond. Debt security for which specific property is pledged.

mortgagee. The lender under a mortgage loan.

mortgagor. The borrower under a mortgage loan.

multiplier. The ratio of the change in government spending to the resulting change in the GNP.

municipal bond fund. A mutual fund holding a portfolio of municipal bonds.

municipals. Tax-free bonds issued by state and local governments.

multi-index model. A method of estimating portfolio risk that utilizes a market index and indexes for various market subcategories.

mutual fund. A pooled investment in which managers buy and sell assets with the income and gains and losses accruing to the owners; may be either load (with sales fee) or no-load (no sales fee); stands ready to buy back its shares at their net asset value.

mutual fund cash position. A technical market indicator based on mutual fund liquidity; high fund liquidity is said to be associated with subsequent market rises.

naked option writing. Writing options without owning the underlying shares; the naked writer satisfies the contract with the optionholder, if it is exercised, by buying the required shares on the market.

NASD (National Association of Securities Dealers). The self-regulator of the OTC market.

NASDAQ (National Association of Securities Dealers Automated Quotations). An automated information system that provides brokers and dealers with price quotations on securities that are traded OTC.

NASDAQ Composite Index. A value-weighted index of OTC issues.

NASDAQ National List. The secondary list of OTC issues carried in many newspaper stock quotations. Stocks that are not sufficiently active for the NASDAQ list may appear on the National List.

NASDAQ National Market System List. The primary list of OTC issues carried in most newspaper stock quotations. Membership is determined by criteria similar to the AMEX listing.

NASDAQ Supplemental List. The tertiary list of OTC stocks carried in some newspaper stock quotations. Stocks not active enough to be on either of the two major NASDAQ lists may be included on the supplemental list.

National Association of Investment Clubs (NAIC). Organization that fosters and assists in the setting up of investment clubs.

NAV (Net Asset Value). The per share market value of a mutual fund's portfolio.

NBER (National Bureau of Economic Research). A private nonprofit research foundation that dates business cycles and sponsors economic research.

near money. Assets such as savings accounts and Treasury bills that can quickly and easily be converted into spendable form.

net-net. A stock whose market price is very low relative to the value of its liquid assets; more specifically, stock whose per share price is less than the pro rata amount of both short- and long-term debt subtracted from the company's per share liquid assets.

net worth. The dollar value of assets minus liabilities; the stockholders' residual ownership position. Also called equity.

new issue. An initial stock sale, usually of a company going public; also an initial sale of a bond issue.

new listing. A stock that has recently been listed on an exchange; may be the company's first listing on the particular exchange or first on any exchange.

New York Curb Exchange. The former name for what is now called the American Stock Exchange.

nifty fifty. A list of about 50 companies, with high multiples and rapid growth rates, that are preferred by many institutional investors.

no-load (mutual) fund. A fund whose shares are bought and sold directly at the fund's NAV. Unlike a load fund, no agent or sales fee is involved.

nonmarket risk. Individual risk not related to general market movements; the total risk of an investment may be decomposed into that associated with the market and that which is not. Also called unsystematic risk.

non-normal distribution. A distribution, such as a skewed distribution of returns, that differs from the normal shape. See leptokurtosis and platokurtosis.

nonparticipating insurance. A type of insurance sold by a stockholder-owned company as opposed to participating insurance, which is sold by an insurance company owned by its policyholders (mutual).

normal distribution. A distribution corresponding to the normal shape.

normalization. Spreading the benefits of investment tax or other types of credits across the life of an asset. *See also* flow-through.

notes. Intermediate-term debt securities issued with maturity dates of one to five years.

NOW (negotiable orders of withdrawal) accounts. A special type of deposit account that draws interest and allows check-like instruments to be written against it.

NYFE (New York Futures Exchange). A futures exchange associated with the NYSE; lists futures and option contracts on the NYSE Composite Index.

NYSE (New York Stock Exchange). The largest U.S. stock exchange.

NYSE Composite Index. A value-weighted index of all NYSE-listed securities.

odd-lot short ratio. A technical market indicator based on relative short trading by small investors; when such trading is heavy the market is said to be near a bottom.

odd-lotter. One who trades in odd lots.

odd lot trade. A transaction involving less than one round lot of stock; usually 100 shares, although a few stocks are traded in 10-share lots.

off-board trading. Trading that takes place off an exchange, particularly OTC trading in NYSE-listed securities. NYSE rule 390 restricts such trading by member firms.

one-decision stocks. A now largely discredited concept of the early 1970s that certain high-quality growth stocks should be bought and held; supposedly, the only decision necessary was to buy.

open-end investment company. A mutual fund or other pooled portfolio of investments that stands ready to buy or sell its shares at their NAV or NAV plus load if the fund has a load.

open interest. The number of option or commodity contracts outstanding; analogous to shares outstanding for stock.

open market committee. The Federal Reserve Board committee that decides on open market policy; consists of all seven of the Federal Reserve Board Governors plus five of the presidents of the regional Fed Banks including the president of the New York bank.

open market operations. Fed transactions in the government bond market that affect bank reserves and thereby influence the money supply, interest rates, and economic activity.

option. A put, call, warrant, right, or other security giving the holder the right but not the obligation to purchase or sell a security at a set price for a specific period.

ordinary least squares. A method of estimating regression parameters by choosing linear coefficients that minimize the square of the residuals.

organizational slack. Wasted firm resources due to managerial deadwood, lack of aggressiveness, carelessness, and so on.

OTC (Over the Counter). The market in unlisted securities and off-board trading in listed securities.

out-of-the-money option. An option whose striking price is less attractive than the current market price of its underlying stock.

overbought. An opinion that the market has risen too rapidly and is therefore poised for a downward correction.

oversold. An opinion that the market has fallen too rapidly and is therefore poised for an upward correction.

Pac Man defense. Tactic to avoid takeover by attempting to take over the attacking firm.

paper. *See* commercial paper.

paper loss. An unrealized loss.

paper profit. An unrealized gain.

par (bond). The face value at which the issue matures.

par (common stock). A stated amount below which per share equity (net worth) may not fall without barring dividend payments.

par (preferred stock). The value on which the security's dividend and liquidation value is based.

parking. The illegal practice of holding a security for another in an attempt to conceal the owner's true identity. Sometimes stock is parked during the period prior to launching a takeover attempt.

par ROI equation. An empirically estimated profitability equation of the Strategic Planning Institute.

participating bond. Bond that may pay extra coupon increment in years in which the issuing firm is especially profitable.

participating life insurance. Life insurance sold by a mutual company, which is owned by and shares its profits with its policyholders.

participating preferred. Preferred stock that may pay an extra dividend increment in years in which the issuing firm is especially profitable.

passed dividend. The omission of a regular dividend payment.

passthrough. A share of a mortgage pool whose interest and principal payments are flowed through to the holders.

payback period. The length of time until an original investment is recaptured.

payout ratio. Dividends per share as a percentage of earnings per share.

PE (price earnings ratio). The stock price relative to the most recent 12-month earnings per share.

penny stock market. A market for low-priced stocks (under $1 per share); especially active in Denver.

penny stocks. Low-priced stocks usually selling for under $1 per share; normally are issued by small speculative companies.

pension. A periodic or lump sum payment to a person following retirement from employment or to surviving dependents of a deceased former employee.

PE ratio model. A model designed to explain PE ratios.

percentage order. A market or limit order that is entered once a certain amount of stock has traded.

performance fund. *See* go-go fund.

per period return (PPR). The return earned for a particular period.

physical. The underlying physical delivery instrument for a particular futures contract.

PIKs (payment in kind securities). Securities whose yield is at the issuer's option payable in additional securities of like kind to the existing securities; thus a preferred

stock may choose to pay the dividend in additional preferred shares.

Pink Sheets. Quotation source for most publicly traded OTC issues.

Pink Sheet stocks. OTC stocks not traded on the NASDAQ system; issued by very small, obscure, and often speculative companies.

Pit. The name of the physical location where specific commodity contracts are traded.

planning horizon (portfolio management). The time frame in which a portfolio is managed.

platokurtosis. The degree to which a distribution differs from the normal by having less of the distribution concentrated at the peaks and tails.

point (stocks and bonds). Pricing units; for stocks, a point represents $1 per share; for bonds, a point is equivalent to $10.

point and figure chart. A technical chart that has no time dimension. An x is used to designate an up move of a certain magnitude while an o denotes a similar size down move. The xs are stacked on top of each other as long as the direction of movement remains up; a new column is begun when direction changes.

points (real estate). A fee charged for granting a loan, especially for a mortgage on real estate.

poison pill. Antitakeover defense in which a new diluting security is issued if control of the firm is about to shift.

Ponzi scheme. An investment scam promising high returns that are secretly paid out of investor capital; usually exposed when incoming funds are insufficient to cover promised outpayments. The scam depends upon fresh investor capital to pay its promised return.

pooling of interest accounting. A type of merger accounting in which an acquired firm's assets and liabilities are transferred to the acquiring firm's balance sheet without any valuation adjustment.

portfolio. A holding of one or more securities by a single owner (institution or individual).

portfolio insurance. A service in which the "insurer" endeavors to place a floor on the value of the "insured" portfolio. If the portfolio value falls to a prespecified level the insurer neutralizes it against a further fall by purchasing an appropriate number of index puts or selling an appropriate number of index options.

portfolio risk.   Risk that takes account of the diversifying impact of portfolio components.

position trader.   A commodity trader who takes and holds futures position for several days or more.

post.   One of eighteen horseshoe-shaped locations on the NYSE floor where securities are traded. Also called trading post.

postponable expenditures.   Purchases of long-term assets such as consumer durables.

preemptive rights.   Shareholder rights to maintain their proportional share of their firm by subscribing proportionally to any new stock issue.

preferred habitat.   One of four hypotheses for explaining the term structure of interest rates based on a tendency for borrowers and lenders to gravitate toward their preferred loan lengths.

preferred stock.   Shares whose indicated dividends and liquidation values must be paid before common shareholders receive any dividends or liquidation payments.

premium (bond).   The amount by which a bond's price exceeds its par.

premium (option).   The market price of an option; confusingly, the term is also sometimes used to refer to time value.

premium over conversion value.   The amount by which a convertible's price exceeds its conversion value.

premium over straight-debt value.   The amount by which a convertible's price exceeds its value as a nonconvertible debt security.

prepayment penalty.   The fee assessed for early liquidation of an outstanding debt.

present value.   The value of a future sum or sums discounted by the appropriate interest rate.

price dependencies.   Price movements that are related to past price movements.

price floor.   The support level of a convertible bond provided by its straight-debt value.

price stability.   The absence of inflation or deflation.

primary distribution.   The initial sale of a stock or bond (new issue).

primary market.   The market for initial sales of securities; later the securities are traded in the secondary market.

prime.   One of the two component securities created when appropriate shares are deposited into an Americus Trust. The prime receives the stock's dividends and up to some prespecified liquidation payment at the termination date; the score receives any value in excess of the amount assigned to the prime.

prime rate.   The rate that banks advertise as their best (although some very secure borrowers may receive a still lower super prime rate).

principal (in a trade).   The person or institution for whom the broker acts as an agent.

principal (of a bond).   The face value of a bond.

private placement.   A direct security sale to a small number of large buyers.

probability distribution.   A display of possible events along with their associated probabilities.

professional corporation pension plans.   Pension plans as a means to shelter income from taxes; set up by professionals such as doctors, lawyers, and architects after organizing their businesses as corporations. The 1982 tax act severely limited the amount of tax-sheltered contributions that may be put into such plans.

profit.   Net revenues minus costs when revenues exceed costs.

profitability models.   Models designed to explain company profit rates.

profitability ratio.   A ratio such as return on equity and return on sales designed to reflect the firm's profit rates.

profit and loss statement.   *See* income statement.

programs.   The actual trades instituted by a program trader. Market watchers might, for example, see a series of large trades in stocks making up the S&P 500 and conclude that programs are moving the market in a particular direction.

program trading. A type of mechanical trading in large blocks by institutional investors; usually involves both stock and index futures contracts as, for example, in index arbitrage or portfolio insurance. Also called programmed trading.

proprietorship. The condition of ownership of a business entity, usually referring to sole ownership.

prospectus. An official document that all companies offering new securities for public sale must file with the SEC; spells out in detail the financial position of the offering company, what the new funds will be used for, the qualifications of the corporate officers, and any other material information.

proxy. A shareholder ballot.

proxy fight. A contest for control of a company.

proxy material. A statement of relevant information that the firm must supply to shareholders when they solicit proxies.

public offering. A security sale made through dealers to the general public and registered with the SEC.

purchase accounting. A type of merger accounting in which the net assets of the merged firm are entered on the books of the acquiring firm at amounts that sum to the firm's acquisition price.

pure arbitrage. An arbitrage that involves no element of risk.

pure hedge. A hedge whose purpose is to reduce the risk on an existing position.

pure risk premium. The portion of the expected yield above the riskless rate that is due to pure risk aversion as opposed to the expected default loss.

put. An option to sell a stock at a specified price over a specified period.

put bond. A bond with an indenture provision allowing it to be sold back to the issuer at a prespecified price.

put–call parity. A theoretical relation between the value of a put and a call on the same underlying security with the same strike and expiration date.

quarterly earnings. Profits, usually per share profits, for a three-month period.

quarterly report. A report to shareholders containing three-month financial statements.

quick ratio. *See* acid test ratio.

raider. A hostile outside party that seeks to take over companies.

rally. A brisk general rise in security prices usually following a decline.

random walk. The random motion of stock prices, analogous to the movement of a drunk who at any time is as likely to move in one direction as another; implies that the next price change is as likely to be up as down regardless of past price behavior. This type of behavior is called Brownian motion in the physical sciences.

rate of return. A rate that takes into account both dividends and capital appreciation (increases in the price of the security); for example, a 9% rate of return implies that the owner of $100 worth of stock will earn a total of $9 in dividends and capital appreciation over the forthcoming year.

rating (bond). A quality or risk evaluation assigned by a rating agency such as Standard & Poor's or Moody's.

ratio analysis. Balance sheet and income statement analysis that utilizes ratios of financial aggregates.

RCMM (registered competitive market maker). *See* floor trader.

real estate limited partnership (RELP). A type of investment organized as a limited partnership that invests directly in real estate properties.

real estate sales company. A firm that sells property, especially at marketing events such as complimentary dinners; the property is often in a distant location and part of a projected retirement or vacation development.

real return. A return adjusted for changes in the price level; for example, if the nominal rate of return were 7, a 3% inflation rate would reduce the real return to 4%.

rebate. A return of a portion of a payment.

recession. An economic downturn categorized as a recession by the National Bureau of Economic Research (NBER); in the past, two successive quarters of decline in real (in noninflationary dollars) GNP have signaled the start.

record date. The shareholder registration date that determines the recipients for that period's dividends.

redemption fee. A charge sometimes assessed against those who cash in their mutual fund shares.

redemption price. *See* call price.

refinancing. The selling of new securities to finance the retirement of others that are maturing or being called.

registered bond. A bond whose ownership is determined by registration as opposed to possession (bearer bond).

Registered Competitive Market Maker (RCMM). *See* floor trader.

registered representative. A full-time employee of a NYSE member firm who is qualified to serve as an account executive for the firm's customers.

registered trader. An exchange member who trades stocks on the exchange floor for his or her own account (or account in which he or she is part owner).

registrar. A company such as a bank that maintains the shareholder records.

registration statement. A statement that must be filed with the SEC before a security is offered for sale; must contain all materially relevant information relating to the offering. A similar type of statement is required when a firm's shares are listed.

regional exchange. A U.S. stock exchange located outside New York City.

regression. An equation that is fitted to data by statistical techniques; computers often used to perform the calculations. In the simplest case a regression will have one variable to be explained (dependent variable) and one variable to explain it (independent variable) and would take the form: $x_t = a + by_t$ (where x_t = dependent variable; y_t = independent variable; and a and b are parameters selected by the computer that best fits the data). Graphically one can envision a scatter diagram relating x_t and y_t with a line drawn through the points close to line on the average) as the regression line. The "a" is the intercept and "b" the slope coefficient of this line. More complicated regression equations of the form $x_t = a + by_t + cz_t + dw_t + ev_t \ldots$ containing more than one explanatory variable may also be estimated. Again the computer can be used to select the best values of a, b, c, etc.

regression toward the mean. The tendency of many phenomena to migrate toward the average over time.

regulated investment company. A company such as a mutual fund or closed-end fund that qualifies for exemption from federal corporate income tax liability as a result of meeting the requirements set forth in Subchapter M of the Internal Revenue Code.

Regulation Q. A Fed rule that at one time limited interest rates that banks and thrifts could pay on certain types of deposits/investments; rendered ineffective by deregulation.

Regulation T. A Fed rule that governs credit to brokers and dealers for security purchases.

Regulation U. A Fed rule that governs margin credit limits.

reinvestment risk. The risk associated with reinvesting coupon payments at unknown future interest rates. The yield to maturity is generally computed for the assumption that coupons will be reinvested at the same rate as the bond's current yield to maturity; thus, if interest rates decline prior to the bond's maturity, the coupons will not generate the expected return.

REIT (real estate investment trust). Companies that buy and/or manage rental properties and/or real estate mortgages and pay out more than 95% of their income as dividends; no corporate profit taxes are due on their income.

relative strength. A technical analysis concept based on an assumption that stocks that have risen relative to the market exhibit relative strength, and this tends to carry them to still higher levels. Tests of the concept are largely negative.

REMIC (Real Estate Mortgage Investment Conduit). A type of mortgage-based debt security that restructures the payment streams into bond-like components. Thus the short-term REMICs receive most of the initial cash flows in a pattern similar to a short-term debt security. Similarly the longer term REMICs are promised a cash flow much like a long-term bond. The uncertain portion of the cash flow stream is left with a residual security called the resid.

reorganization.   Restructuring a firm's capital structure and operating facilities in the face of a default, near-default, or bankruptcy.

replacement cost approach.   The valuing of real estate or other asset on the basis of the cost of producing equivalent assets.

repo.   *See* repurchase agreement.

repurchase agreement.   A type of investment in which a security is sold with a prearranged purchase price and date designed to produce a particular yield.

reserve requirement.   The percentage of reserves the Fed requires each bank to have on deposit for each increment of demand or time deposits.

resid.   The residual security left as the various cash flows are assigned to the various term REMICs.

resistance level.   A price range that, according to technical analysis, tends to block further price rises.

retained earnings.   On the income statement, annual after-tax profits less dividends paid; on the balance sheet, the sum of annual retained earnings to date.

return on assets (ROA).   Profits before interest and taxes as a percentage of total assets. Also called return on investment.

return on equity (ROE).   Profits after taxes, interest, and preferred dividends as a percentage of common equity.

return on investment (ROI).   Profits before interest and taxes as a percentage of total assets. Also called return on assets.

return on sales (ROS).   Profits as a percentage of sales.

revenue bond.   A municipal bond backed by the revenues of the project that it finances.

reverse crush.   A commodity trade involving buying oil and meal and selling soybean futures.

reverse split.   A security exchange in which each shareholder receives a reduced number of shares but retains the same proportional ownership; thus a 10-for-1 reverse split would exchange 10 new shares for each 100 old shares.

riding the yield curve.   A bond portfolio management strategy of taking advantage of an upward sloping yield curve by purchasing intermediate term bonds and then selling them as they approach maturity.

right.   A security allowing shareholders to acquire new stock at a prespecified price over a prespecified period, generally issued proportional to the number of shares currently held; normally exercisable at a specified price that is usually below the current market price. Rights generally trade in a secondary market after they are issued.

risk.   The variance of the expected return, i.e., the degree of certainty associated with the expected return.

risk arbitrage.   The taking of offsetting positions in the securities of an acquisition candidate and the would-be acquirer when the combined position should show a profit if the merger takes place.

risk averse.   The property of preferring security and demonstrating a willingness to sacrifice return to achieve a more secure yield.

risk-free rate.   The interest rate on a riskless investment such as a Treasury bill.

risk hedge.   A hedge position undertaken from scratch that seeks to profit from relative price moves in the underlying positions; spreads are an example.

riskless investment.   An investment having an expected return that is certain; that is, if a riskless asset is expected to yield 6%, the chance of a 6% return is 100%.

risk neutral.   The property of preferring the highest return without regard to risk; indifference to risk.

risk premium.   The return in excess of the risk-free rate reflecting the investment's risk.

risk–return trade-off.   Tendency for more risky assets to be priced to yield higher expected returns.

risk–reward ratio.   A measure of the amount of risk assumed in seeking a specific level of profit.

Robert Morris Associates.   An organization of bankers that compiles averages of financial ratios for various industry groups.

rollover.   A change from one type of investment to another.

round lot. The basic unit in which securities are traded; usually 100 shares although some stocks trade in 10-unit lots.

Rule 144. An SEC rule restricting the sale of lettered stock.

Rule 390. A NYSE rule restricting members from off-board trading (not on an exchange).

Rule 415. An SEC rule allowing shelf registration of a security, which may then be sold periodically without separate registrations of each part.

Rule of 20. Market timing rule that asserts that the Dow Jones Industrial Average's PE plus the inflation rate generally tend toward a value of 20; thus departures in either direction tend to forecast a market move.

run. An uninterrupted series of price increases or of price decreases.

Sallie Mae (Student Loan Market Association). A federal government agency that sells notes backed by government-guaranteed student loans.

saturation effect. The impact on revenues and profits when a heretofore rapid growth firm or industry largely satisfies its market's demand.

savings bonds. Low-denomination Treasury issues designed to appeal to small investors.

scalper. A commodity trader who seeks to profit from very short-run price changes.

scorched-earth defense. An antitakeover tactic in which the defending company's management engages in practices designed to reduce the firm's value to such a degree that it is no longer attractive to the potential acquirer.

S Corporation. *See* Subchapter S corporation.

seasoning. The process of new issues acquiring market acceptance in after-issue trading.

seat. A membership on an exchange.

SEC (Securities and Exchange Commission). The government agency with direct regulatory authority over the securities industry.

secondary distribution. A large public securities offering made outside the usual exchange or OTC market; those making the offering wish to sell a larger quantity of the security than they believe can be easily absorbed by the market's usual channels. A secondary offering spreads out the period for absorption.

secondary market. The market for already-issued securities that may take place on the exchanges or OTC.

secondary stocks. Relatively obscure stocks not favored by institutional investors, thus individual investors are the primary market; may trade on the AMEX, NASD, regional exchanges or be among the smaller companies listed on the NYSE market.

second mortgage. A mortgage debt secured by a property's equity after the first mortgageholder's claim has been subtracted from the pledged asset's value.

sector fund. A type of mutual fund that specializes in a narrow segment of the market; for example, an industry (chemicals), region (Sunbelt), or category (small capitalization).

securities. Paper assets representing a claim on something of value, such as stocks, bonds, mortgages, warrants, rights, puts, calls, commodity contracts, or warehouse receipts.

Securities Amendment Act of 1970. An act restricting the front-end loading fees that mutual funds can charge.

securitization. The process of turning an asset with poor marketibility into a security with substantially greater acceptability; for example, a security that looks like a standard bond but is derived from real estate mortgage loans, auto loans, or credit card balances.

security market line. The theoretical relation between a security's market risk and its expected return.

segmented markets hypothesis. A theory that explains the term structure of interest rates as due to the supply and demand of each maturity class.

Self Tender. A firm tendering for its own shares; often used as an antitakeover defense.

seller financing. A procedure in which the real estate seller is used to finance part of purchase price.

selling short. The act of selling a security that belongs to someone else and is borrowed; the short seller covers by buying back equivalent securities and restoring them to the original owner.

semistrong form of the efficient market hypothesis. The view that market prices quickly and accurately reflect all public information; implies that fundamental analysis applied to public data is useless.

semiweak form of the efficient market hypothesis. The view that market prices cannot be successfully forecast with technical market indicators.

SEP (Simplified Employee Pension Plan). Pension plan in which both the employee and the employer contribute to an Individual Retirement Plan (IRA).

serial bond. A bond issue portions of which mature at stated intervals rather than all at once.

serial correlation. Correlation between adjacent time series data.

shark repellent. Antitakeover provisions such as a poison pill.

shelf registration. An SEC provision allowing preregistration of an amount of a security to be sold over time without specific registration of each sale; permitted by SEC Rule 415.

short against the box. The short selling of stock that is owned; usually employed as a tax device for extending the date of realizing a gain.

short covering. Buying an asset to offset an existing short position.

short interest (commodities and options). The number of futures or options contracts written and outstanding.

short interest (stocks). The number of shares sold short.

short position. To have sold an asset that is not owned in the hope of repurchasing it later at a lower price.

short squeeze. The result when powerful forces driving up the price of a stock have the effect of squeezing a substantial short interest.

short-swing profit. A gain made by an insider on stock held for less than six months; such gains must be paid back to the company.

short-swing rule. A tax rule that prevents a trader from realizing a tax loss on a sale and immediately repurchasing the issue in question; stock must be held at least 30 days before the sale and repurchase must be delayed at least 30 days after the sale.

short-term gains (losses). Gains (losses) on capital assets held less than six months.

short-term trading index. A technical market indicator based on the relative percent of advancing versus declining stocks.

short-term unit trust. A unit investment trust made up of an unmanaged portfolio of short-term securities; usually self-liquidating within six months of issue.

simple interest. Interest paid and computed only on the principal.

single-index model. A method of estimating portfolio risk that utilizes only the market index and market model as opposed to the full variance–covariance matrix.

single-premium deferred annuity contract. An annuity with a defined future value; sold by insurance companies.

sinking fund. An indenture provision requiring that a specific portion of a bond issue be redeemed periodically; required by many bond indentures so that all of the debt will not come due simultaneously.

SIPC (Securities Investors Protection Corporation). A federal government agency that guarantees the safety of brokerage accounts up to $500,000, no more than $100,000 of which may be in cash.

skewed distribution. A nonsymmetrical distribution that is spread out more on one side of its mode than the other.

skewness. The degree to which a distribution is skewed.

SMA (special miscellaneous account). A sum associated with a margin account; normally equal to the account's (margin) buying power. The account is increased when stock is sold and decreased when stock is purchased. At times the SMA of an account can become inflated (above the account's buying power) when the equity of the account is near or below the minimum for margin maintenance.

smokestack companies. Companies in basic industries whose profits and sales are cyclical with the economy.

social responsibility fund. A type of mutual fund that avoids investments in allegedly socially undesirable companies such as those involved with tobacco, alcohol, pollution, defense, South Africa, and so forth.

source and application of funds statement. An accounting statement reporting a firm's cash inflows and outflows. Now called changes in financial position statement.

S&P (Standard & Poor's Corporation). An important firm in the investment area that rates bonds, collects and reports data, and computes market indexes.

S&P 500 Index. A value-weighted stock index based on the share prices of 500 large firms.

specialist. An exchange member who makes a market in listed securities.

specialized dependencies. Predictable return patterns related to some specific type of event such as a new issue or tax-loss trading.

special offering. A large block of stock offered for sale on an exchange with special incentive fees paid to purchasing brokers. Also called spot secondary.

speculating. The act of committing funds for a short period at high risk in the hope of realizing a large gain.

SPI (Strategic Planning Institute). A strategic planning consulting firm that is best known for its par ROI equation.

split. An exchange of securities whereby each shareholder ends up with a larger number of shares representing the same percentage of the firm's ownership. In a two for one split a shareholder with 100 old shares would receive an additional 100 shares.

spot market. The market for immediate delivery of some commodity such as wheat or silver.

spot secondary. *See* special offering.

spread (bid–ask). The difference between the bid and the ask price.

spread (trade). A type of hedge trade such as a vertical or horizontal spread (options) or some comparable combination trade in the futures market; offsetting positions taken in similar securities in the hope of profiting from relative price moves.

standard deviation. A measure of the degree of compactness or spread of a distribution. About two times out of three the actual value will be within one standard deviation on either side of the mean value; about 19 out of 20 times it will be within two standard deviations. One standard deviation is the square root of the variance (which see).

Standard & Poor's Corporation Reports. An investment periodical containing quarterly analyses of most publicly traded firms.

Standard & Poor's Encyclopedia. A book containing analyses of S&P 500 stocks.

Standard & Poor's Investor Service. An important firm in the investment area that rates bonds; also computes market indexes, compiles investment information, and publishes various investment periodicals.

Standard & Poor's Stock Guide. A monthly publication with a compact line of data on most publicly traded corporations.

standstill agreement. A reciprocal understanding between a company's management and an outside party that owns a significant minority position in the company's stock, with each party giving up certain rights in exchange for corresponding concessions by the other party. For example, the outside group may agree to limit its ownership position to some pre-specified level. In exchange management may agree to minority board representation by the outside group.

Stein estimators. Statistical techniques for estimating a variable that assumes a regression toward the mean tendency.

Stock Clearing Corporation. A NYSE subsidiary that clears transactions for member firms.

stock dividend. A dividend paid in the form of additional stock; similar to a stock split although usually proportionately less new stock is distributed.

stock exchange. An organization for trading a specific list of securities over specific trading hours usually at a single location.

stockholder-oriented company. A company whose management is particularly responsive to the interest of its stockholders; a large ownership group may exercise effective control or management itself may own a large block of the stock.

stock split. The division of a company's existing stock into more shares (say, 2 for 1, or 3 for 1); usually done to reduce the price per share in the hope of improving the shares' marketability.

stop-limit order. An order to implement a limit order when the market price reaches a certain level.

stop-loss order. An order to sell or buy at market when a certain price is reached.

straddle (in commodities). Another name for a spread, where offsetting positions are taken in similar contracts such as adjacent expirations of the same physical.

straddle (in options). A combination put and call on the same stock at the same striking price.

straight-debt value. The value of a convertible bond as a straight-debt (nonconvertible) bond.

straight-line depreciation. A method of writing off assets at a constant dollar rate over their estimated lives.

strap. A combination of two calls and a put each having the same strike and expiration date.

street-name. Securities held in customer accounts at brokerage houses but registered in the firm's name.

strike. *See* striking price.

striking price. The amount an optionholder has to pay (or will receive) to exercise an option. Also called strike.

strip. A combination of two puts and a call each having the same strike and expiration date.

strip bond. A coupon bond with its coupons removed; returns only principal at maturity and thus is equivalent to a zero-coupon bond.

strong form of the efficient market hypothesis. The view that market prices quickly and accurately reflect all public and nonpublic information; implies that inside information is useless in security selection.

Subchapter M. The section of the Internal Revenue Code that sets forth the criteria for a regulated investment company (which see).

Subchapter S. The section of the Internal Revenue Code that sets forth the criteria for a Subchapter S corporation.

Subchapter S corporation. An arrangement whereby a corporation may be taxed as a partnership under the provisions of the Internal Revenue Code.

subordination provisions. Bond indenture provisions that give an issue a lower priority than other issues.

sum of the years' digits depreciation. A method of accelerated depreciation that assigns depreciation equal to the ratio of the number of years remaining to the sum of the years in the asset's estimated life.

Super Bowl indicator. A whimsical technical market indicator based on whether the Super Bowl is won by a former member of the old American Football League (AFL) or the National Football League (NFL). An NFL victory forecasts an up market for the coming year; an AFL victory forecasts a down market. No forecast is derived from an expansion team win.

Super Dot System. *See* DOT.

superNOW account. An interest-bearing checking account with no set maximum interest rate; most banks require a $2,500 minimum balance.

support level. A floor price that, according to technical analysis, tends to restrict downside price moves.

Survey Research Center. Research institute at the University of Michigan that surveys and publishes statistics on consumer sentiments.

swap fund. A type of mutual fund that allows purchases with shares of other companies at their market prices.

sweep account. A type of bank account that daily sweeps the portion of the balance exceeding some preassigned minimum into a money fund where rates are not limited by Fed restrictions.

syndicate. A group of investment bankers organized to underwrite a new issue or secondary offering.

systematic risk. *See* market risk.

takeover bid.   A tender offer designed to acquire a sufficient number of shares to achieve working control of the target firm.

tangible investments.   A broad group of commodities that includes precious metals, gemstones, artifacts, and some types of collectibles.

tangibles.   *See* tangible investments.

tax credit.   Amounts applied against computed taxes on a dollar-for-dollar basis, reducing the amount otherwise due.

tax-loss carryforward.   Unutilized prior-period losses that may be employed to offset subsequent income.

tax-loss trading.   Year-end selling of depressed securities designed to establish a tax loss.

tax-managed fund.   A type of investment company that sought to convert dividend income into capital gains; prior to IRS rulings disallowing the practice such funds organized themselves as corporations rather than as mutual funds and reinvested their portfolios' dividends.

tax shelter.   An investment that produces deductions from other income for the investor with a resulting savings in income taxes. The Tax Reform Act of 1986 severely restricted most types of tax shelters.

tax swap.   A type of bond swap in which an issue is sold to yield a tax loss and replaced with an equivalent issue.

T-bill.   *See* Treasury bill.

TEBF (Tax-Exempt Bond Fund).   A mutual fund that invests in municipal bonds, offering tax-free income to its holders.

technical analysis (broad form).   A method of forecasting general market movements with technical market indicators.

technical analysis (narrow form).   A method of evaluating securities based on past price and volume behavior; largely debunked by evidence favorable to the efficient market hypothesis.

technical indicator.   A data series or combination of data series said to be helpful in forecasting the market's future direction. Also called market indicator.

Templeton approach.   A fundamental approach to investment analysis named after renowned mutual fund manager John Marks Templeton; emphasizes a world view to finding undervalued issues.

tender offer.   An offer to purchase a large block of securities made outside the general market (exchanges, OTC) in which the securities are traded; often made as part of an effort to take over a company.

term insurance.   A type of life insurance, not having a savings feature for which rates rise with age to reflect the greater probability of death; *see also* whole life insurance.

term structure of interest rates.   A pattern of yields for differing maturities (risk controlled). *See also* segmented markets, unbiased expectations, and liquidity preference hypotheses.

term to maturity.   The length to maturity of a debt instrument.

tertiary stocks.   The most obscure group of stocks; much less popular than even the secondary stocks; trade on the Pink Sheets.

testator.   *See* testor.

testimonium.   The concluding portion of a will.

testor.   A person who leaves a will in force at his or her death. Also called testator.

thin market.   A market in which volume is low and transactions relatively infrequent.

third market.   The over-the-counter market in listed securities.

thrifts.   Institutions other than commercial banks that accept savings deposits, especially savings and loan associations, mutual savings banks, and credit unions.

tick.   The minimum size price change on a futures contract.

ticker symbols.   Symbols for identifying securities on the ticker tape and quotation machines; listed in *S&P Stock Guide* and several other publications.

ticker tape.   A device for displaying stock market trading.

Tigers (Treasury Investment Growth Receipts).   Zero-coupon securities assembled by Merrill Lynch and backed by a portfolio of Treasury issues.

tight money.   Restrictive monetary policy.

times-interest-earned ratio.   Before-tax, before-interest profit relative to a firm's interest obligation.

time value (option). The excess of an option's market price over its intrinsic value.

time value (present value). The value of a current as opposed to a future sum.

title search. A process whereby the validity of a title to a real estate parcel is evaluated.

TOLSR (Total Odd-Lot Short Ratio). A technical market indicator that relates odd-lot short sales to total odd-lot trading.

top-tier stocks. Established growth stocks preferred by many institutional investors.

total return. Dividend return plus capital gains return.

total risk. The sum of market and nonmarket risk.

trading post. *See* post.

transfer agent. The agent who keeps track of changes in shareholder ownership.

transfer tax. A New York State tax on the transfer of equity securities.

Treasury bill. Government debt security issued on a discount basis by the U.S. Treasury. Also called T-bill.

treasury stock. Previously issued stock reacquired by the issuing company.

trust. A property interest held by one person for the benefit of another.

trustee. A bank or other third party that administers the provisions of a bond indenture.

turnover. Trading volume in a security or the market.

Turov's Formula. A formula for computing the amount by which a stock price must change to produce equivalent returns on its options.

12b-1 fund. A type of mutual fund that does not charge a load but does take out a selling fee on an annual basis.

two-tier tender offer. Takeover tactic in which one offer is made for controlling interest of target (usually cash) and a second generally less attractive offer (usually securities) is made for the remainder.

unbiased expectations hypothesis. A theory explaining the term structure of interest rates as reflecting the market consensus of contiguous forthcoming short rates.

underwriter. An investment dealer who agrees to buy all or part of a new security issue and plans to sell the securities to the public at a slightly higher price.

underwriting fee. The difference between the price paid and the selling price on an underwritten issue.

unemployment rate. The percentage of those actively seeking employment who are out of work.

United Shareholders of America (USA). A shareholder rights organization sponsored by T. Boone Pickens, advocating such issues as equal voting rights for all classes of stock, secret proxy votes, and prohibition of poison pills.

unit investment trust. A self-liquidating unmanaged portfolio in which investors own shares.

universal life. A type of life insurance in which the cash value varies with the policyholder's payments and the company's investment returns.

Unlisted Market Guide. An investment publication that periodically covers small companies that are not found in larger periodicals such as Value Line and Standard and Poor's.

unlisted security. A security that trades only in the OTC market.

unsystematic risk. *See* nonmarket risk.

uptick. A transaction that takes place at a higher price than the immediately preceding price.

urgent selling index. A technical market indicator based on the relative volume in advancing and declining issues.

usable bond. A bond that may be used at face to exercise corresponding warrants.

VA (Veterans Administration). A federal government agency that guarantees mortgage loans of veterans.

Value Line. A firm that publishes quarterly analyses on about 1,700 firms and compiles the *Value Line Index;* owned by Arnold Bernhard and Company.

Value Line Index. An unweighted broadly based stock price index.

value oriented investor. Investor who seeks to assemble a portfolio of stocks that sell at low prices relative to their underlying values; that is, to their earnings, cash flows, book values, breakup values, and liquid assets.

variable annuity.   An investment vehicle similar to a mutual fund but sold by insurance companies.

variable life.   A type of life insurance in which the cash value varies with the return of the policyholder's portfolio.

variable rate mortgage.   A mortgage in which the interest rate is allowed to vary with market rates.

variance.   The expected (average) value of the square of the deviation from the mean; variance of $X = E(X - \bar{X})^2$ where $\bar{X}$ is the mean of X and E is the expected value.

variance–covariance model.   A method of estimating portfolio risk that utilizes the variances and covariances of all of the potential components.

Vasicek adjustment.   A method of adjusting estimated betas based on the uncertainty of the mean and specific beta estimates.

venture capital.   Risk capital extended to start-up or small going concerns.

versus purchase order.   Sale order that specifies purchase date of securities to be delivered for sale.

vertical spread.   Short and long option positions on the same security with the same expiration but different striking prices.

vested benefits.   Pension benefits that are retained even if the individual leaves his or her employer.

volume.   The number of shares traded in a particular period.

Wall Street Journal, The.   A business/investments newspaper published five days a week by Dow Jones Inc.

Wall Street Week (WSW).   A popular and long-running weekly business news television program.

warrants.   Certificates offering the right to purchase stock in a company at a specified price over a specified period.

wash sale.   A sale and repurchase made within 30 days, thereby failing to establish a taxable loss.

weak form of the efficient market hypothesis.   The view that market prices move randomly with respect to past price return patterns; implies that the broad form of technical analysis is useless.

Weisenberger.   A major publisher of mutual fund investment information, including *Investment Companies.*

when issued.   Trading in as yet unissued securities that have a projected future issue date.

white knight defense.   Finding an alternative and presumably more friendly acquirer than the immediate takeover threat.

white squire defense.   Finding an important ally to purchase a strong minority position of the firm now controlled by existing management but threatened by an outside group; presumably the white squire will oppose and hopefully block the efforts of the outsider to take control of the vulnerable company.

whole life insurance.   A type of policy that couples life insurance with a savings feature. Premiums are fixed with a surplus built up in the policy's early years to meet claims that exceed premiums when the policyholders are older.

will.   A legal statement of a person's wishes with regard to the disposition of his or her property or estate at the time of death.

Wilshire 5000 Index.   A value-weighted stock index based on a large number of NYSE, AMEX, and OTC stock.

wire house.   An exchange member electronically linked to an exchange.

withholding tax.   A portion of an employee's income withheld by the employer as partial payment of income tax.

working capital (gross).   The sum of the values of a firm's short-term assets.

working capital (net).   A firm's short-term assets minus its short-term liabilities.

working control.   The ownership of sufficient shares to elect a majority to the company's board of directors.

writer (of an option).   One who assumes the short side of a put or call contract and therefore stands ready to satisfy the potential exercise of the long side.

yield.   The return of an investment expressed as a percentage of its market value.

yield (current).   Current income (dividend, coupon, rent, etc.) divided by the price of the asset.

yield curve.   A relationship between yield to maturity and term to maturity (or duration) for equivalent risk debt securities.

yield curve notes.   Debt security whose coupon rate is structured to move inversely with market rates; thus when the market interest rates decline the coupon rate on the yield curve notes will rise, and vice versa.

yield to earliest call.   The holding-period return for the assumption that the issue is called as soon as the no-call provision expires.

yield to maturity.   The yield that takes account of both the coupon return and the principal repayment at maturity.

zero-coupon bond.   A bond issued at a discount to mature at its face value.

zero tick.   A transaction immediately preceded by a transaction at the same price.

Solutions to Selected End-of-Chapter Problems

Chapter 1

1. **a.** an investment in land purchased for $5,000 and sold for $7,000:

    $$\text{HPRR} = \$7,000/\$5,000 = 1.4$$
    $$\text{HPR} = 1.4 - 1.0 = .4$$

    b. a $3,000 land contract noninterest bearing note purchased for $1,800 and held until maturity at which time it is paid off at its face value:

    $$\text{HPRR} = \$3,000/\$1,800 = 1.667$$
    $$\text{HPR} = 1.667 - 1.000 = .667$$

    c. a building that is held for nine months during which time it generates $3,500 in rental income (in excess of costs) and is sold for a $30,000 profit. Its original purchase price was $195,000; sale price = $195,000 + $30,000 = $225,000; investment proceeds = $3,500 + $225,000 = $228,500:

    $$\text{HPRR} = \$228,500/\$195,000 = 1.17$$
    $$\text{HPR} = 1.17 - 1.00 = .17$$

2. **a.** an investment in 100 shares of stock costing $10 per share, sold one year later for $11 per share, during which time a 30 cent per share dividend is received. Ignore commissions.

    $$\text{Current investment value (per share)} = \$11.00 + \$.30 = \$11.30$$
    $$\text{HPRR} = 11.30/10 = 1.13$$
    $$\text{HPR} = .13, \text{ or } 13\%$$

    Since the holding period is one year, HPR is the same as the annual return for this and subsequent parts to this problem.

    b. A $1,000 one-year CD with a stated yield of 7% compounded quarterly. To compute its return determine what an equivalent one-year investment would have to earn if its returns were not compounded.

    $$.07/4 = .0175 \text{ (quarterly rate)}$$
    $$\text{HPRR} = 1.0175 \times 1.0175 \times 1.0175 \times 1.0175 = 1.07186$$
    $$\text{HPR} = .07186, \text{ or } 7.186\%$$

    c. Purchase a long-term bond for $890 and sell it a year later for $850. The bond pays a coupon of 8% of its face value ($1,000). The first coupon is payable in the middle of the one-year holding period. To be precise one should compute the interest earned on the coupon payments. Assume the interest on the coupon accrues at the same rate as the bond.

    First we need to compute the coupon income. Eight percent of $1,000 (the bond's face value) is $80. Half of this amount, or $40, would be received at midyear. At 10% (the approximate yield on the bond) that coupon payment would earn another $4. At year-end the bond would produce another $40 coupon payment. Thus the total coupon income would be approximately $84. The bond price fell by $50 so the net profit would be about $34 ($84 − $50).

The current value of the investment would be $934 ($850 + $84). Thus:

$$HPRR = \$934/\$890 = 1.0494$$
$$HPR = 0.494, \text{ or } 4.94\%$$

3. The appreciated value of an investment held for two years with a 10% return compounded annually, semiannually, quarterly, and monthly.

Annually: $1.1 \times 1.1 = 1.2100$
Semiannually: $(1.05)^4 = 1.2155$
Quarterly: $(1.025)^8 = 1.2184$
Monthly: $(1.008333)^{24} = 1.2203$

4. The arithmetic mean return for equal amounts invested in assets yielding returns of 7.8%, 9.3%, 4.5%, and 11.5% is:

$$(7.8\% + 9.3\% + 4.5\% + 11.5\%)/4 = 8.275\%$$

If the amounts invested were in the proportions of .2, .3, .4, and .1, the mean return would be:

$$.2(7.8) + .3(9.3) + .4(4.5) + .1(11.5) = 1.56 + 2.79 + 1.80 + 1.15$$
$$= 7.30\%$$

Chapter 2

1. The yield on U.S. Savings Bonds for a guaranteed minimum of 6%.
   a. five-year government bond rate of 7%:
      85% of 7% is 5.95% so 6% minimum applies.
   b. five-year government bond rate of 8%:
      85% of 8% is 6.80%, which exceeds the 6% minimum. Thus the rate would equal 6.80%.
   c. five-year government bond rate of 9%:
      85% of 9% is 7.65%, which exceeds the 6% minimum. Thus the rate would equal 7.65%.

2. The typical bond commission for:
   a. purchase seven bonds for a per bond price of 70:
      7 times $5 per bond is $35 so the $50 minimum applies.
   b. sell 15 bonds for a per bond price of 105:
      15 times $5 per bond is $75, which is above the minimum.
   c. purchase three bonds for a per bond price of 56:
      3 times $5 per bond is $15, which is below the $50 minimum. Thus the minimum commission of $50 would apply.

3. The percentage commissions for the dollar figures in Problem 2.
   a. 7 times $700 per bond is $4,900, which corresponds to percentage commission of 50/4900, or 1% of the dollar value.

    b. 15 times $1050 per bond is $15,750, which corresponds to percentage commission of 75/15750, or .5% of the dollar value.

    c. 3 times $560 per bond is $1,680, which corresponds to percentage commission of 50/1680, or 3% of the dollar value.

4.   The after-tax yield for a preferred stock with a before-tax return (all in the form of dividends) of 7.5% for an individual in the 28% bracket:

$$(1.00 - .28) \times 7.5 = .72 \times .75 = .54$$

and a corporation in the 36% bracket:

$$(1.00 - .20 \times .36) \times 7.5 = (1.00 - .072) \times 7.5 = .928 \times 7.5 = 6.96$$

Chapter 3

1.   Commissions using the schedule of Table 3.2:

    a. 300 shares selling at $21
      Principal value equals $21 \times 300 = $6,300.

      Commission = $30 + 1.25% of $6,300 + $8 per lot =
      $30 + $78.75 + $24 = $132.75

    b. 5,000 shares selling at $3¾
      Principal value equals 3.75 \times 5,000 = $18,750.

      Commission = $30 + 1.25% of $18,750 + $80 + $5.50 per lot over
      ten lots = $30 + $234.37 + $80 + $220 = $564.37

    c. 50 shares selling at $250
      Principal value equals 250 \times 50 = $12,500.

      Commission (by table) = $30 + 1.25% of $12,500 =
      $30 + $156.25 = $186.25

    This sum, however, amounts to $3.72 per share so $1 per share maximum obtains.

      Commission = $50

2.   Compute the total cost of the trade (commission plus bid–ask spread) for the following OTC trades. Assume that one buys at the bid and sells at the ask and pays commissions according to the schedule of Table 3.2:

    a. purchase 500 shares when the quote is 15–15½ and sell when the quote is 19–20.
      Purchase at ask of 15.50 \times 500
      Principal value of $7,750

      Commission = $30 + 1.25% \times $7,750 + $8 \times 5 =
      $30 + $96.87 + $40 = $168.87

      Total cost = $7,750 + $168.87 = $7,918.87
      Sale at bid of 19 \times 500
      Principal value of $9,500

      Commission = $30 + 1.25% of $9,500 + $8 \times 5 =
      $30 + $118.75 + $40 = $188.75

Net proceeds = $9,500 − $188.75 = $9,311.25

b. purchase 3,000 shares with a quote of 1–1⅜ and sell when the quote is 1¼–1⅝.

Purchase at ask of 1.375 × 3,000
Principal value of $4,125

Commission = $30 + 1.25% × $4,125 + $80 + $5.50 × 20 =
$30 + $51.56 + $80 + $110 = $271.50

Total cost = $4,125 + $271.50 = $4396.50
Sale at bid of 1.25 × 3,000
Principal value of $3,750

Commission = $30 + 1.25% × $3,750 + $80 + $5.50 × 20 =
$30 + $46.87 + $80 + $110 = $266.87

Net proceeds = $3,750 − $266.87 = $3,483.13

c. purchase 200 shares with a quote of 80–81 and sell when the quote is 105–106.

Purchase at ask of 81 × 200
Principal value of $1,620

Commission = $18 + 1.75% of $1,620 + $8 × 2 =
$18 + $28.35 + $16 = $62.35

Total cost $1,620 + $62.35 = $1,682.35
Sale at bid of 105 × 200
Principal value of $2,010

Commission = $18 + 1.75% of $2,010 + $8 × 2 =
$18 + $36.75 + $16 = $70.75

Net proceeds = $2,010 + $70.75 = $1,939.25

3. The spread, percentage spread, holding period return, and trading costs as a percentage of the initial costs for the quotes and transactions of Problem 2:

a. Spread for 15–15½: ½
Percentage spread: (½)/15 = 3.3%
Spread for 19–20: 1
Percentage spread: 1/19 = 5.26%
Holding period return:
Gain = $9,311.25 − $7,918.87 = $1,392.38 or 17.6% of initial cost of $7,918.87
Trading costs:
Purchase, spread = 1/2(500) = $250
Commission = $168.87; Total = $250 + $168.87 = $416.87
Sale, spread = 1(500) = $500
Commission = $188.75
Total = $500 + $188.75 = $688.75
Trading costs as a percentage of initial costs: ($416.87 + $688.75)/ $7,918.87 = $1,105.62/$7,918.87 = 13.96%

Parts **b** and **c** are to be done likewise.

4. From Table 3.2 compute the commission on a single trade of 1,500 shares at $7 per share.

TABLE 3.2 A Hypothetical Retail Commission Table

Stock Rights, and Warrants Selling for More Than $1.00

Principal Value	Commission
$0 – 300	11% of principal
$301 – 800	$9 + 2.75% of principal
$801 – 2,500	$18 + 1.75% of principal
$2,501 – 20,000	$30 + 1.25% of principal
$20,001 – 30,000	$125 + .90% of principal
$30,001 – 300,000	$210 + .60% of principal
$300,001 and over	$1,300 + .25% of principal

Lot Charges

Number of Shares	Charge
100 shares or less	No Charge
101 to 1,000 shares	8.00 per lot
1,001 or more	80.00 plus 5.50 per lot over 10

Maximum commission charge per share = $ 1.00
Minimum commission for principal value exceeding $300 = $35.00

Stocks, Rights, and Warrants Selling for Less Than $1.00

Principal Value	Commission
$0 – 1,000	11% of principal
$ 1,001 – 10,000	$ 50 + 7% of principal
10,001 and over	$200 + 5.5% of principal

Dollar value = 1,500 × 7 = $1,050
Commission = $18 + 1.75% × $1,050 + $80 + 5 × $5.50 =
$18 + $18.375 + $80 + $27.50 = $143.875

The commission on 15 separate 100-share trades at $7 per share:

Dollar value for one trade: 100 × 7 = $700
Commission = $9 + 2.75% × 700 = $9 + $19.25 = $28.25
Commission for 15 trades: 15 × $1.92 = $163.80

Clearly, of the two commissions, that for the single trade is the lower.

5. Assume you purchased XYZ stock in five 300-share blocks at prices of 15, 18, 31, 23, and 40 respectively. Then you sell 700 shares.
   Normally your basis would be based on the earliest trades. In this case the first 700 shares were bought 300 at 15; 300 at 18; and 100 at 31. Thus your total basis would be:

$$300 \times 15 + 300 \times 18 + 100 \times 31 = 4,500 + 5,400 + 3,100$$
$$= \$13,000$$

The maximum basis would result if the 700 shares were allocated to the trades at 40, 31, and 23:

$$300 \times 40 + 300 \times 31 + 100 \times 23 = 12,000 + 9,300 + 2,300$$
$$= \$24,400$$

One could achieve that basis by the use of appropriately specified versus purchase orders.

Chapter 4

1. The present value for income streams:
   a. $50 annually forever discounted at 10%

   $$\$50/.10 = \$500$$

   b. $200 annually for 20 years discounted at 20%
   Present value of $1 received annually for 20 years at 20% = $4.87; $4.87 × 200 = $974
   c. bond with $150 coupon for 12 years, maturing at $1,070 discounted at 16%
   Present value of $1 received annually for 12 years at 16% = $5.342; $1 to be received in 12 years at 16% = $0.168;
   Total present value = ($5.342 × 150) + ($0.168 × 1070) = $801.30 + $179.76 = $981.06
   d. payment stream of

   year 1: $200
   year 2: $300
   year 3: $400
   year 4: $500
   subsequent years: 0
   discount at 8%

   Present value of $1 received in 1, 2, 3 and 4 years at 8% = $0.926, $0.857, $0.794, $0.735:
   ($0.926 × 200) + ($0.857 × 300) + ($0.794 × 400) + ($0.735 × 500) = $185.20 + $257.10 + $317.60 + $367.50 = $1,127.40

2. The price of a 20-year bond with a 10% coupon when comparable market interest rates are:
   a. 7%
   This bond pays $100 per year for 20 years and then $1,000 at the end of 20 years. Thus one needs to find the present value of this income stream:

   $100 per year for 20 years at 7% = 10.595 × $100 = $1,059.50

   The present value of $1,000 to be received in 20 years = 0.258 × $1,000 = $258.
   Thus the total is $1,059.50 + $258 = $1,317.50.
   b. 9%

   9.129 × $100 = $912.90; 0
   .178 × $1,000 = $178
   Total = $912.90 + $178 = $1,090.90

   c. 10%

   8.514 × $100 = $851.40
   0.149 × $1,000 = $149
   Total = $851.40 + $149 = $1,000.40

   (Note the $0.40 difference is the result of rounding.)

d. 11%

$$7.063 \times \$100 = \$706.30$$
$$.124 \times \$1,000 = \$124$$
$$\text{Total} = \$706.30 + \$124 = \$830.30$$

e. 13%

$$7.025 \times \$100 = \$702.50$$
$$0.087 \times \$1,000 = \$87$$
$$\text{Total} = \$702.50 + \$87 = \$789.50$$

3. The American Pig Company (ticker symbol PORK) currently pays a dividend of $3.00 per share, which is expected to rise by $.25 per share for the next five years. The stock currently sells for $36 per share per year, a ratio of 12 times its current dividends. The same ratio of dividends to price is also expected at the end of five years. The present value of PORK's expected income stream for discount rates of 8%, 10%, 12%, 15%, 18%:

   Over the five-year period dividends will be paid out at the rate of $3.00, $3.25, $3.50, $3.75, and $4.00. At the end of 12 years the stock will sell for $12 \times \$4.00 = \$48$. Thus one needs to compute the present value of the income stream: $3.00, $3.25, $3.50, $3.75, and $4.00 + $48.00

   The present value factors at 8% are 0.926, 0.857, 0.794, 0.735 and 0.681 Thus the present value =

   ($3.00 × 0.926) + ($3.25 × 0.857) + ($3.50 × 0.794) + ($3.75 × 0.735) + ($52.00 × .681) = $2.78 + $2.78 + $2.78 + $2.76 + $38.22 = 49.32

   The computation for a stable dividend of $3.00:

   ($3.00 × 0.926) + ($3.00 × 0.857) + ($3.00 × 0.794) + ($3.00 × 0.735) + ($39.00 × 0.681) = $2.78 + $2.57 + $2.38 + $2.21 + $26.56 = $36.50

   The same basic approach should be applied for each of the other discount rates.

6. Using the dividend discount model, compute the market price for the following sets of information. Recall that $P = d/(r-g)$
   a. d = $1; g = 10%; r = 12%
   $P = 1/(.12 - .10) = 1/.02 = 50$
   b. d = $2; g = 11%; r = 12%
   $P = 2/(.12 - .11) = 2/.01 = 200$
   c. d = $1.50; g = 8%; r = 12%
   $P = 1.50/(.12 - .08) = 1.5/.04 = 37.50$

7. Assuming a payout of 55%, the PE ratios for Problem 6 would be computed as follows:
   First determine EPS as d/payout and then divide by price:
   a. EPS = $1/.55 = $1.82; PE = 50/1.82 = 27.5
   b. EPS = 2/.55 = $3.64; PE = 200/3.64 = 54.9
   c. EPS = 1.50/.55 = $2.72; PE = 37.5/2.74 = 13.7

8. The market implied expected long-term growth rate for the following information is computed as follows:
   $PE = p/(r - g)$
   Thus: $g = r - (p/PE)$

a. PE $= 8$; p $= 40\%$; r $= 12\%$
Thus: g $= .12 - (.4/8) = .12 - .05 = .07$
b. PE $= 10$; p $= 50\%$; r $= 12\%$
Thus: g $= .12 - (.5/10) = .12 - .05 = .07$
c. PE $= 15$; p $= 60\%$; r $= 12\%$
Thus: g $= .12 - (.6/15) = .12 - .04 = .08$

Chapter 5

1. The expected return and standard deviation for the following:
   a. Equally probable returns of: -5%, 0%, 5%, 10%
      Mean return $= (-5\% + 0\% + 5\% + 10\%)/4 = 10\%/4 = 2.5\%$
          To compute standard deviation, first form deviations from the mean (that is, subtract 2.5% from each possible return); then sum these deviations and divide by n, which in this case is 4; the result is the variance; the standard deviation is the square root of the variance.
   b. 10% chance of a 0% return
      15% chance of a 5% return
      25% chance of a 10% return
      25% chance of a 15% return
      15% chance of a 20% return
      10% chance of a 25% return
      Mean return $= (.10 \times 0\%) + (.15 \times 5\%) + (.25 \times 10\%) + (.25 \times 15\%)$
      $+ (.15 \times 20\%) + (.10 \times 25\%) = 0 + .75 + 2.50 + 3.75 + 3.00 + 2.50$
      $= 12.50\%$
          To compute the standard deviation follow the same procedure outlined above except that each deviation should be weighted by the probabilities of that outcome.
   c. 100% chance of a 10% return
      Mean return $= 10\%/1 = 10\%$
      Standard deviation $= 0\%$
          Now plot the risk and expected return for each investment (left as an exercise for the reader).

2. Compute the portfolio variance for the following:
   a. X $=$ Y $= .5$
      $\sigma_x^2 = \sigma_y^2 = .05$
      $C_{xy} = 0$

      Portfolio variance formula: $\sigma_p^2 = X^2\sigma_x^2 + 2XYC_{xy} + Y^2\sigma_y^2$
      $\sigma_p^2 = (.5)^2(.05) + (.5)^2(.05) = .25(.05) + .25(.05) = .5(.05) = .025$
   b. X $= .3$ Y $= .7$
      $\sigma_x^2 = .03$ $\sigma_y^2 = .05$
      $C_{xy} = .8$
   c. X $= .1$ Y $= .9$
      $\sigma_x^2 = .08$ $\sigma_y^2 = .06$
      $C_{xy} = -.05$

7. For three separate stocks having αs and βs of: .01, .7; .05, 1.1; and −.02, 1.5, respectively, their expected returns for market returns of .05, .10, .15, −.05 and −.10 would be computed as follows:

$$R_e = \alpha + \beta R_m$$

where:

$$R_e = \text{expected return}$$
$$R_m = \text{market return}$$

Thus for the first stock and first market return:

$$R_e = .01 + .7R_m = .01 + .7(.05) = .01 + .035 = .045$$

For the second market return the result is:

$$R_e = .01 + .7(.1) = .08.$$

The remaining computations are similar.

Chapter 6

6. Blume-adjusted βs for each of the following unadjusted βs: 1.34, .57, .78, 1.20, 1.47, 1.73, .45, 1.44, .89, .95, 1.80, 1.11, .69, .87, 1.15.
   Blume-adjusted β = .35 + .68 (average unadjusted β estimate based on last three years' data)
   Thus for the first entry:
   Blume-adjusted β = .35 + .68(1.34) = .35 + .91 = 1.25
   Similarly for the second entry:
   Blume-adjusted β = .35 + .68(.57) = .74
   The remaining computations are similar.

9. A diversified portfolio of stocks is expected to generate a return of 15% with a β of 1. A diversified portfolio of long-term bonds offers an expected return of 11% and has a β of .3. A diversified portfolio of short-term debt securities has an expected return of 8% and a β of .1. Combine investments in these choices to:
   a. maximize expected return
      The maximum expected return would be achieved by purchasing the diversified portfolio of stocks:
      The result would be an expected return of 15%.
   b. minimum risk
      The minimum risk portfolio would be achieved by purchasing the diversified portfolio of short-term debt securities:
      The result would be an expected return of 8% and a β of .1.
   c. provide a maximum β of .5 and a maximum return for that β level
      Since these portfolios are all well diversified, only market risk is present in each. The β of combinations equals the weighted average of the βs of the components. Similarly, the expected return of the combination is the weighted average of the separate expectations. The expected returns of these investments rise as risk (β) is increased. Accordingly the maximum return combination meeting the minimum risk criteria is sure to have an average β of exactly .5.

One possible combination would be to combine the stock and long-term bonds in proportions that have an average β of .5. Another possibility would be to combine the stock and short-term debt securities into a portfolio that has a β of .5.

The results of these two combinations are as follows:

First we must determine the weights that will yield a β of .5. We know that the weighted average β of the components is the β of the combined portfolio.

For the stock–bond combination the weights correspond to the following equation:

$$.5 = 1(w) + .3(1 - w) = .3 + .7w; .2 = .7w: w = .29$$

where:

$$w = \text{weight of stocks in combined portfolio} = .29$$
$$1 - w = \text{weight of bonds in combined portfolio} = .71$$

Similarly the expected return of the combination is the weighted average of the expected returns of the components.

Thus this combination's expected return is determined as follows:

$$R_e = w(.15) + (1 - w)(.11) = .29(.15) + .71(.11)$$
$$= .0435 + .0781 = .1216$$

We follow the same procedure for the stock/short-term debt securities combination.

Thus the weights would be:

$$.5 = 1(w) + .1(1 - w) = .1 + .9w; .4 = .9w; w = .44$$

Similarly this combination's expected return is determined as follows:

$$R_e = .44(.15) + .56(.8) = .066 + .0464 = .1124$$

Therefore the stock/bond combination offers a higher expected return. Other possible combinations that meet the maximum β criteria (such as one of all three portfolios) would offer lower returns than the stock/bond combination.

10. Suppose in Problem 9 that you also have the option of investing in a diversified international portfolio with an expected return of 14% and β of .3. The answers to Problem 9 would change as follows:

Parts **a** and **b** would remain as before.

For part **c** the new portfolio combination would allow a combination of domestic and foreign stocks.

The weights for this combination would be determined as follows:

$$.5 = 1(w) + .3(w - w); w = .29$$
$$R_e = w(.15) + (1 - w)(.11) = .29(.15) + .71(.14)$$
$$= .0435 + .0994 = .1429$$

Clearly this expected return is superior to that of the stock/bond combination.

Chapter 7

1. Assume that the market's dividend payout ratio is .50, the required rate of return is 13%, and the expected growth rate is 9%.
   a. The market PE.

$$PE = p/(r - g) \qquad (2)$$

where:

p = long-term payout ratio
d = anticipated dividend rate over forthcoming year
g = expected long-term growth rate for dividends
r = the appropriate discount rate for dividends

Thus: $PE = .50/(.13 - .09) = .50/.04 = 12.5$
   b. The market PE if the payout ratio fell to .45 and all else remained unchanged:

$$PE = .45/(.13 - .09) = .45/.04 = 11.25$$

   c. The market PE if the growth rate increased by 2% and everything else remained unchanged:

$$PE = .50/(.13 - .11) = .50/.02 = 25$$

Such a change represents a major revision in the market's outlook. Such a change is unlikely but not impossible.
   d. The market PE if the required rate of return declined to 10% and everything else remained unchanged:

$$PE = .50/(.10 - .09) = .50/.01 = 50$$

Such a change represents a major revision in the market's outlook. Such a change is unlikely but not impossible.

2. Assume that the market payout ratio is .55 and the required rate of return is .15. The expected growth rate to justify a market PE of 11:

$$g = r - p/PE = .15 - .55/11 = .15 - .05 = .10$$

Suppose the market PE rose to 20 while the payout and the required rate of return remained unchanged. Such a PE implies an expected growth rate:

$$g = r - p/PE = .15 - .55/20 = .15 - .0275 = .1225$$

The PE cannot reach a level that could not be explained by a growth rate expectation. No matter how high the PE reached, some level of expected growth rate could explain it.

9. The PE ratio equation for a firm with an expected payout, appropriate discount, and growth rate of .5, .1, and .05, respectively, would be computed as follows:

$$PE = p/(r - g) \qquad (2)$$

Thus: $PE = .5/(.1 - .05) = .5/.05 = 10$
If the payout ratio declined to half of its prior value while the expected growth rate increased to .07, the PE would become:

$$PE = .25/(.1 - .07) = .25/.03 = 8.3$$

10. The Go Go Corporation currently has a payout of .2 and is accorded a risk premium of 3% above the market required rate of return of 15%. It currently sells for 35 with EPS of $1.25. The implied growth rate would be determined as follows:

$$g = r - p/PE = .18 - .2/(35/1.25) = .18 - .2/28 = .18 - .007 = .173$$

Suppose EPS grows at a rate of 25% for five years and then declines to a rate of 10%, a rate that is expected to continue; the payout rises to .4; and the required return for Go Go declines 16%. To determine the stock's price one would first compute the new EPS:

$$EPS = 1.25(1 + .25)^5 = 1.25(3.052) = 3.82$$

Next one would compute the PE:

$$PE = p/(r - g) = .4/(.16 - .10) = .4/.06 = 6.67$$

Thus the stock price = EPS(PE) = 3.82 × 6.67 = 25.48

Chapter 8

1. The CDF Bank purchased at par $5 million in 20-year 9% Treasury bonds. A year later these bonds are selling in the market with a yield to maturity of 11%. It is the only marketable security held by CDF. It will show up on CDF's financial statements:

Nineteen-year government bonds with a 9% coupon and priced to yield 11% will sell for about 83. Five million dollars worth will have a market value of $4,150,000. Nonetheless, the bonds will show up on the books as having a value of $5,000,000, their historical cost. Thus the decline in market value will have no impact on the firm's stated net worth. The answer would, however, change if the bonds were to be sold. Indeed, their book value would be written down to their market value.

2. The ACF Corporation is a manufacturer of auto parts. It has annual revenues of $3,000,000, expenses of $2,500,000 (excluding depreciation and taxes), and 500,000 shares outstanding. Its depreciable assets (primarily plant and equipment) have a book value of $2,000,000 and an average useful life of 10 years. We wish to compute total and per share earnings assuming that either straight-line depreciation or depreciation equal to 20% of current book value is used. A 33% tax rate is applied to profits.

Its gross profit before depreciation and taxes is $3,000,000 − $2,500,000 = $500,000.

Straight-line depreciation = $2,000,000/10 = $200,000; 20% of $2,000,000 = $400,000.

Using straight line, taxable income is $500,000 − $200,000 = $300,000

Taxes would be .33 × $300,000 = $100,000

This leaves $300,000 − $100,000 = $200,000 as after-tax profits.

This sum corresponds to $200,000/500,000 or $.40 in per share earnings.

Using accelerated depreciation taxable income is $500,000 − $400,000 = $100,000

Taxes would be .33 × $100,000 = $33,000

This leaves $100,000 − $33,000 − $67,000 as after-tax profits.

This sum corresponds to $67,000/500,000, or $.134 in per share earnings.

3. One year later, sales have increased but ACF had sufficient excess capacity to cover the additional sales. Revenues and expenses (excluding depreciation and taxes) both increase by 10% and no additional depreciable assets are purchased. Accordingly revenues, operating expenses and gross profits would be:

    Revenues = 1.1 × $3,000,000 = $3,300,000
    Expenses = 1.1 × $2,500,000 = $2,750,000
    Gross profit = $3,300,000 − $2,750,000 = $550,000
    Using straight-line, depreciation would again be $200,000
    This would leave $550,000 − $200,000 = $350,000 as taxable income.
    Taxes would be .33 × $350,000 = $115,500.
    After-tax profits would therefore be $234,500.
    This sum corresponds to $234,000/500,000 = $.468 in per share earnings.
    Using accelerated depreciation, depreciation would be .2 × ($2,000,000 − $400,000) = .2 × $1,400,000 = $280,000.
    This would leave $550,000 − $280,000 = $270,000 as taxable income.
    Taxes would be .33 × $270,000 = $89,100.
    After-tax profits would therefore be $270,000 − $89,100 = $180,900.
    This sum corresponds to $180,900/500,000 = $.3618 in per share earnings.

6. The Acquirer Corporation takes over the Acquired Corporation utilizing pooling-of-interest accounting. Just prior to the merger Acquired reported assets of $150 million and debts of $50 million while Acquirer showed equity of $400 million and debts of $200 million. If the purchase of Acquired was accomplished with stock, the merged balance sheet would simply consolidate the two companies' balance sheets (figures in millions):

	Acquired	Acquirer	Consolidated
Assets	$150	$400	$550
Liabilities	$ 50	$200	$250
Equity	$100	$200	$300

7. Suppose Acquired Corporation was purchased by issuing bonds equal to the book value of its equity. The merged balance sheet would look similar except that the consolidated balance sheet would have an additional $100 in liabilities and that much less in equity (figures in millions):

	Acquired	Acquirer	Consolidated
Assets	$150	$400	$550
Liabilities	$ 50	$200	$350
Equity	$100	$200	$200

Chapter 9

1. The GRO Company has a PE of 25 and EPS of $1.00. Asset Play has a PE of 8 and EPS of $1.00. If in the next five years GRO's PE falls to 20 while its EPS increases at 10% per year, its stock will sell for:

    EPS after five years growth at 10% = $1.00 × (1.1)^5 = $1.00 × 1.61 = $1.61.
    At a PE of 20 GRO would sell for 32.2.

Similarly if in the next five years Asset Play's PE increases to 15 and its EPS grows at a 10% rate, its stock will sell for:

EPS after five years growth at 10% = $1.00 \times (1.1)^5$ = 1.00×1.61 = $1.61

At a PE of 15 Asset Play would sell for 24.15.

Ignoring the impacts of dividends, taxes, and commissions, the rates of return for investments in GRO and Asset Play are:

GRO's price increased from 25 to 32.2 in five years, a HPR of 34%.

This HPR for five years is equivalent to an annual growth rate of about 6%.

Asset Play's price increased from 8 to 24.15 in five years, a HPR of 102%. This is equivalent to an annual growth rate of about 25%.

2. Using the starting values given in Problem 1, assume that the EPS for both GRO and Asset Play has grown at a 5% rate (annual) for five years. If GRO's and Asset Play's PEs fall to 12 and 6, respectively, what will the stocks sell for?

EPS after five years growth at 5% = $1.00 \times (1.05)^5$ = 1.00×1.28 = $1.28.

At a PE of 12 GRO would sell for 15.36.

At a PE of 6 Asset Play would sell for 7.68.

3. Using the starting values given in Problem 1, assume that GRO's payout is .3 and its appropriate discount rate is 13%. Its expected growth rate would be:

$$g = r - p/PE = .13 - .3/25 = .13 - .012 = .118$$

Suppose Asset Play's payout is .5 and appropriate discount rate is 12%. Its implied expected growth rate is:

$$g = r - p/PE = .12 - .5/8 = .13 - .063 = .067$$

4. The Cash Cow Corporation currently generates a net cash flow after all expenses of $3 million. This cash flow is expected to grow at a rate of 5%; the appropriate discount rate is 12%. According to the cash flow takeover approach Cash Cow value would be determined as follows:

$$P = CF/(r - g) = \$3,000,000/(.12 - .05)$$
$$= \$3,000,000/.07 = \$42,857,140$$

5. Suppose the Cash Cow Corporation in Problem 4 has one million outstanding shares and the stock currently sells for 10. Thus Cash Cow is valued at $10,000,000 in the marketplace but worth over $40 million in a takeover. One who had the resources to finance such a takeover would want to proceed carefully.

The first step would probably be to acquire a 4.9% position quietly. Such purchases should not attract attention or run the price up. Then discreet feelers regarding the receptiveness of management to a takeover might be made.

At this point the next steps could go in one of several directions. With management's assistance a simple takeover could be negotiated. More likely management will not be thrilled at the prospect of having someone acquire their Cash Cow. They might be brought around by offering them a piece of a leveraged buyout.

Alternatively a hostile takeover might be necessary. If so, the next steps would be to acquire more stock in the open market and/or prepare a tender offer. Depending on management's response, one might next begin to prepare for a proxy contest.

Two objectives should be kept in mind: minimizing the costs and maximizing the likelihood of a successful acquisition. A secondary objective would be to position oneself to earn a profit on the minority position if the takeover effort fails.

Chapter 10

3. *The Wall Street Journal* quotation contains the following information for a NYSE listed stock:

1. The first two columns contain the stock's most recent 52-week high and low price.

2. Next comes an abbreviation of the company's name. If the abbreviation of the company name stands alone, the security in question is its common stock. If the abbreviation is followed by an additional symbol, a different security is involved. The possibilities include *pf* for preferred, *wt* for warrants, *rt* for rights, *un* for units, and *wi* for when-issued. Units are traded when two or more securities are traded as a single entity. A security will trade when issued if the trade is conditional. The security itself is authorized for issuance but has not actually been issued. The settlement of such when-issued trades occurs when and if the subject security is issued. If the security is not issued, the when-issued transactions are reversed.

3. After the name and any description of the security, its indicated dividend rate and the percentage yield are reported. For preferred shares the indicated rate is usually fixed by the terms stated in the prospectus when the stock was issued. For common stock the indicated rate may be raised or lowered by the firm's directors depending upon their assessment of business conditions. The percentage yield is obtained by dividing the indicated rate by the most recent stock price. Only cash dividends are used in computing the percentage yield.

4. The stock's PE appears next.

5. Then its most recent daily sales volume in units of 100 shares is reported.

6. The daily high, low, and closing prices appear next. Most securities without an entry in the PE column incurred recent losses. Warrants and preferred stocks also do not report a PE.

7. The last column reports the net change in price from the previous close.

The following additional information is available in a *Barron's* quote:

1. The yearly high and low, name of the company, dividend rate and yield, and PE ratio and sales. *Barron's* is published on a weekly basis. Thus it reports weekly sales, high, low, last, and net change figures.

2. *Barron's* quotations also include additional dividend and earnings information. The first entry of the earnings column contains the most recent earnings report. Depending upon the time that has elapsed since the end of the most recent fiscal year, earnings for three, six, nine, or 12 months may be reported.

3. This entry is followed by the previous year's comparable number.

4. The dividend columns begin with the amount of the latest quarterly declaration.

5. This is followed by the stock of record.

6. Finally payment dates are reported. Dividends are sent on the payment date to the owners as of the day of record.

4. Continuing with Problem 3, the OTC National List only contains:

1. Abbreviation for name of the company
2. Indicated dividend rate
3. Sales volume
4. Closing bid
5. Closing ask
6. Change in bid

Thus, compared to the NYSE quotation, the OTC National quote leaves out:

1. Yearly high and low
2. Current yield
3. PE
4. High, low, and last for day

The OTC Supplemental list contains even less:

1. Abbreviation for name
2. Closing bid
3. Closing ask

Thus, in addition to what is left out of the National List, the Supplemental List leaves out:

1. Indicated dividend rate
2. Sales volume
3. Change in bid

The Regional quotes contain the following:

1. Sales volume
2. Abbreviation for name of the company
3. High
4. Low
5. Close
6. Price change

Thus, compared to the NYSE quotation, the Regional quote leaves out:

1. Yearly high and low
2. Current yield
3. PE

6. The following table of the various broad-based stock market indexes contains: the number of stocks included, the method of weighting them, the nature of the stocks used, and the interpretation placed on the index.

Index	Number of Stocks	Weighting	Nature of Stocks	Interpretation
DJIA	30	equal	Industry Leaders	Blue Chips
DJTA	20	equal	Rails and Airlines	Transports
DJUA	15	equal	Electric Companies	Utilities
DJCA	65	equal	Combination	Composite
S&P 500	500	value	Diverse Group	Large Companies

S&P 400	400	value	Industrials	Large Industrials
S&P Utilities	40	value	Electric Companies	Utilities
S&P Finance	40	value	Banks, Thrifts, etc.	Finance
S&P Transports	20	value	Rails and Airlines	Transports
NYSE Composite	All NYSE	value	Diverse Group	Large and Medium
AMEX Composite	All AMEX	value	Diverse Group	Medium and Small
NASDAQ Composite	All NASD	value	Diverse Group	Medium and Small
Wilshire 5000	All three	value	Very Diverse Group	NYSE, AMEX, and NASD
Value Line	1700	equal	Diverse Group	Small Stocks

Chapter 11

1. The government decides to spend $1 billion on a space probe to Pluto. The impact of that decision on the economy would depend on how the spending is financed. The impact would be as follows for each of the stated assumptions:

   a. Spending on food stamps is reduced by $1 billion.

   The mix of government spending would change but the net economic impact (on aggregate demand, unemployment, and inflation) would be slight. A bit less would be spent on food and more on aerospace. Poor people would tend to have a somewhat lower standard of living.

   b. Spending on military aid to Third World countries is reduced by $1 billion.

   Again the mix of government spending would change but the net economic impact would be slight. Indeed, some of the same contractors who would otherwise be required to produce the military equipment may now be given an offsetting amount of NASA business.

   c. Taxes on beer are increased by $1 billion.

   Raising taxes on beer will take that amount of money directly out of middle income consumers' pockets and spend it on the space probe. These consumers will therefore spend less on consumer goods. Beer consumption might fall slightly. Some consumers might shift their spending toward other types of alcoholic beverages.

   d. Taxes on profits from corporate takeovers are increased by $1 billion.

   Taxing takeover profits will discourage takeover activity somewhat. Most raiders probably have a relatively low propensity to consume out of incremental income. Thus their lost income will have only a modest impact on consumption.

   e. One billion dollars is raised through the sale of savings bonds to U.S. citizens.

   This is an example of the government borrowing the money. The extra government spending would therefore be relatively stimulative to the economy. The impact would, however, depend upon the Fed's reaction. If the Fed maintained a tight money policy, the extra government borrowing would tend to squeeze out an equivalent amount of other borrowing.

   f. One billion dollars is raised through the sale of six-month Treasury bills to Japanese investors.

   This is another example of the government borrowing the money. The impact is potentially even more stimulative as foreigners are doing the lending. The Fed is much less likely to try to offset the increased borrowing through tightened monetary policy. Note, however, that with the Japanese buying only six-month T-bills, the debt will soon have to be refinanced.

6. In a stable price environment investments A, B, C, D, E, and F are expected to earn 3%, 5%, 2%, 6%, 10%, and 7%, respectively. If they are all perfect inflation hedges, their nominal and real expected returns for inflation rates of 2%, 4%, 6%, and 10% would be:

Investment	Real Return	Inflation Rate			
		2%	4%	6%	10%
A	3%	5%	7%	9%	13%
B	5	7	9	11	15
C	2	4	6	8	12
D	6	8	10	12	16
E	10	12	14	16	20
F	7	9	11	13	17

7. Compute after-tax real and nominal expected returns for the information supplied in Problem 6. Assume that the tax rate on nominal returns is 30%.

Investment	Real Return	Inflation Rate				After-Tax Return for Inflation Rate				Real After-Tax Return for Inflation Rate			
		2%	4%	6%	10%	2%	4%	6%	10%	2%	4%	6%	10%
A	3%	5%	7%	9%	13%	3.5%	4.9%	6.3%	9.1%	1.5%	.9%	.3%	−.9%
B	5	7	9	11	15	(The reader can fill in the rest of							
C	2	4	6	8	12	the entries in this table.)							
D	6	8	10	12	16								
E	10	12	14	16	20								
F	7	9	11	13	17								

9. The TUV Corporation is currently selling its product for $40 per unit. Its annual sales amount to 500,000 units. Last year it earned a profit of $2 million. Because of inflationary pressures, its variable costs will increase by $5 (from $20) per unit.

With this information we can determine its fixed costs. A profit of $2 million and sales of 500,000 at $40 per unit imply that its total revenues and total costs were $20 million and $18 million, respectively. Total variable costs are the product of sales and per unit variable costs: 500,000 × 20 = $10 million. Thus fixed costs must be $8 million.

If it absorbs the higher inputs costs (keeping per unit price unchanged), it can expand sales by 20% with existing capacity. Under these circumstances its profits will be determined as follows:

Sales Revenues = $40 × 500,000 × 1.2 = $40 × 600,000 = $24,000,000
Total Variable Costs = $25 × 600,000 = $15,000,000
Total Fixed Costs = $8,000,000
Total Costs = Total Variable Costs + Total Fixed Costs =
$15,000,000 + 8,000,000 = $23,000,000
Profits = Total Revenues − Total Costs = $24,000,000 − $23,000,000 =
$1,000,000

Alternatively, it can raise its price to cover the increased variable costs but will lose 20% of its unit sales. If it follows this strategy, its profit will be determined as follows:

Sales Revenues = $45 × 500,000 × .8 = $45 × 400,000 = $18,000,000
Total Variable Costs = $25 × 400,000 = $10,000,000

Total Fixed Costs = $8,000,000
Total Costs = Total Variable Costs + Total Fixed Costs =
$10,000,000 + 8,000,000 = $18,000,000
Profits = Total Revenues − Total Costs =
$18,000,000 − $18,000,000 = $0

Thus under these circumstances holding the line on prices and absorbing the cost increase would be the more profitable strategy. Note, however, that such a strategy depends on the existence of sufficient capacity to service the additional demand.

Chapter 12

6. The mathematical equivalence between Gray's equation and the PE equation is discussed in Chapters 4, 7, and 9.
    Gray's relationship is as follows:

$$r = [D/(E)]/[E/(P)] + g$$

where:

r = return on stock
D = dividend per share
E = earnings per share
P = price per share
g = long-term growth rate in price per share
(assumed to average 5%)
Note: D/E = payout ratio (assumed to average 55%)
E/P = earnings–price ratio

The PE ratio model is:

$$PE = p/(r - g)$$

where:

p = payout ratio

The other variables are as defined above.
Thus: $p = D/E$ and $E/(P) = 1/PE$
Making these substitutions into Gray's formula, we obtain:

$$r = [p/(1/PE)] + g \text{ or } r - g = p/PE$$

Solving for PE we obtain:

$$PE = p/(r - g)$$

which is the PE ratio form of the model.

7. To apply the Rule of 20, assume a sell signal is given when the sum of the inflation rate and market PE exceeds 20 by more than 1 whereas a buy signal occurs when the sum is below 20 by more than 1. Thus for inflation rates of 3%, 5%, 7%, 9%, and 12%, PEs above 18, 16, 14, 12, and 9, respectively, would generate sell signals. Similarly, PEs of below 16, 14, 13, 10, and 7 would generate buy signals.

For PEs of 6, 9, 12, 15, and 18, levels of inflation above 15%, 12%, 9%, 6%, and 3%, respectively, would lead to sell signals. Similarly inflation rates below 13%, 10%, 7%, 4%, and 1% would lead to buy signals.

8. If we repeat Problem 7, but this time use 18.5 as the average sum for the inflation rate and the market PE, all numbers are reduced by 1.5.

     If we use deviations from the average of 1.5 and 2 for the signals, buy signals require .5 and 1 lower for the sums while sell signals require .5 and 1 more for the sums.

11. Compute Barron's Confidence Index for the following values for high grade and average grade bond rates: 5.67%, 6.01%; 7.89%, 8.85%; 9.50%, 11.78%; and 10.34%, 13.89%.

     Confidence Index = High Grade Rates/Average Grade Rates

     Thus: 5.67%/6.01% = .943; 7.89%/8.85% = .892; 9.50%/11.78% = .806 and 10.34%/13.89% = .744. Note the Confidence Index is normally expressed as parts of 100. Thus the above results would generally be expressed as: 94.3; 89.2; 80.6; and 74.4.

Chapter 13

3. As treasurer of the Cash Rich Corporation you now manage a portfolio containing $50 million invested in short-term government bonds. A stockbroker approaches you with a dividend capture proposal.

     In a dividend capture program the corporate investor seeks to purchase and own stocks as they go ex-dividend. Then the shares are sold, typically for a loss. The corporation only pays taxes on 20% of the dividend (assuming the stock is held for at least 46 days). The loss, in contrast, is fully deductible.

     In deciding whether to use a dividend capture strategy the investor would consider the following parameters:

     1. Commissions on the trades
     2. The risks and any hedging strategy
     3. The expected return
     4. The tax consequences
     5. The possibility of a change in the relevant tax laws
     6. The firm's need for and ability to generate short-term funds

     Basically one wishes to determine the expected after-tax return and the risks associated with the proposed program.

4. A stockbroker friend approaches you with a proposal to invest in a new issue that he is peddling. The concept sounds attractive but the price seems high relative to the company's fundamentals. One should consider the following factors in deciding whether or not to participate:

     1. New issues with an exciting story often do well in the short run.
     2. During some periods new issues are particularly "hot."
     3. Firms that go public are often a disappointment to the market in the longer run.
     4. Popular new issues are often oversubscribed.

The following trading strategies are available should you decide to play:

1. Buy at issue and seek to sell in the immediate (hoped for) post-offer excitement.
2. Buy and hold for the long term.
3. Wait for the decline after the post-offer excitement subsides and then buy if the price becomes sufficiently attractive.

5. You see on the Dow Jones News ticker that the High Priced Stock Corporation is about to split its stock five for one. The stock currently sells for 150. Explain why you should or should not rush to buy this stock before the split occurs.

    Stock splits do not create any additional value for shareholders. After the split a larger number of shares represent ownership of the same corporation as before the split. If High Price splits five for one, its current per share price of 150 will probably fall to about 30 (150/5 = 30). Thus investors have no particular reason to purchase High Priced's stock before it splits.

6. You hear a rumor that the Asset Play Corporation is likely to be taken over. After a careful look you agree that it is vulnerable but by now its stock has risen 25% from the level a week before you heard the rumor (the market rose 3% over the same period). You would consider the following factors in deciding whether to act on your expectation of a takeover:

    1. The current stock price relative to the estimated breakup value. The higher the breakup value relative to the current stock price, the more attractive is the investment.
    2. The confidence you place in the estimates of the breakup value. Some estimates are very sensitive to future developments such as the price of oil or interest rates, etc.
    3. The ease or difficulty faced by a raider who would seek to take control. How much stock is in the hands of investors that are friendly to management? How much is in the hands of arbitragers and/or other investors looking for a quick profit? What kinds of antitakeover defenses are in place? What else is known about the ease or difficulty of executing a raid?
    4. How well does the corporation fit the profile of potential takeover candidates? What is its PE? How much free cash flow can it generate? Is the industry in play? Are large shareholders looking to sell?
    5. Do any other factors seem likely to discourage a takeover? For example, is antitrust a potential problem? Does the would-be acquirer appear to have sufficient financing? Do any state laws or poison pill provisions make takeover more difficult?
    6. If this particular takeover does not occur, what next? Would you be satisfied holding the stock as an investment? Is another takeover likely to come along?

Chapter 14

1. You have $10,000 to invest in a mutual fund. A friend who has just gone to work selling mutual funds offers to sell you shares from one of his funds at the standard load. The load amounts to:

    A commission of 8.5% on $10,000, or $850.

The amount left for investment would be:

$$\$10,000 - \$850 = \$9,150$$

A no-load, no-redemption-fee fund that you know about is expected to generate an average return of 8% per year for the next three years. To match the performance expected from the no-load fund, your friend's fund must earn:

$10,000 at 8% compounded annually for three years would grow to $12,597 $[(1.08)^3 \times \$10,000]$

The load fund would start with $9,150 and must grow to the same value ($12,597). This corresponds to a holding period return relative of 12,597/ 9,150 = 1.377. The required return will solve the following equation:

$$(1 + r)^3 = 1.377.$$

The value for r that solves this relation is 11.3%.

2. Compare the yearly performance of an investment of $3,000 per year for five years in each of the following:
   a. A no-load mutual fund
   b. A load mutual fund with standard fees assessed each year
   c. A front-end load plan assessing the maximum commission in the first year and the remainder in the second

If each fund generates a return on its net asset value of 11% per year, the following will be the yearly result:

Year	No-Load Fund	Load Fund	Front Load Purchase
1	$ 3,000	$ 2,550	$ 1,500
2	$ 6,330	$ 5,380	$ 3,915
3	$10,263	$ 8,522	$ 7,346
4	$14,392	$12,009	$11,154
5	$18,975	$15,760	$15,381

Clearly, the no-load fund offers the most attractive result. The annual purchase of the load fund outperforms the front-end load purchase plan, particularly in the early years.

4. The $$$ Mutual Fund has a portfolio valued at $650,000,000 and 30,000,000 shares outstanding. Its NAV is:

$$\$650,000,000/30,000,000 = \$21.67$$

Over the following 12 months the fund's portfolio value increases to $800,000,000 and shares outstanding increase by 2,000,000. The percentage increase in the NAV would be computed as follows:
   First the new NAV would equal (total portfolio value)/(total number of shares outstanding) or:

$$(650M + 800M)/(30M + 2M) = 1450M/32M = \$45.31$$

5. The $$$ Mutual Fund in Problem 4 is a load fund that charges the standard fee and paid a distribution of $.70 per share over the past year. The one-year return for an investor in the $$$ fund would be computed as follows:
   One share would have cost the NAV plus the standard load. The standard load of 8.5% would have amounted to NAV $\times [1/(1 - .085) - 1] = 21.60$

$\times$ (1.093 − 1) = 21.60 $\times$ .093 = $2.01. Thus the total cost of one share would have been $23.61 (21.60 + 2.01). After a year the investment would have grown to the new NAV plus the distribution. Thus $45.31 + $.70 = $46.01. The holding period return relative would be 46.01/23.61 = 1.949. Since the holding period is one year, this corresponds to an annual return of 94.9%

Chapter 15

1. The discount yield for a one-year T-bill priced at 95 is computed as follows:
   The formula for the discount-basis yield on a one-year security is:

   $$d = D/F \qquad (1)$$

   where:

   $$d = \text{discount-basis yield}$$
   $$F = \text{face value}$$
   $$D = \text{discount in face value}$$

   Thus a $1,000 face value one-year bond selling at 95 would cost $950; be priced at a $50 discount; and offer a discount yield of 5% ($50/$1,000).

2. The discount yield for a 180-day T-bill priced at 97.31 is computed as follows:
   The formula for maturities of less than one year is:

   $$d = (D/F)(360/M) \qquad (2)$$

   where:

   $$M = \text{number of days to maturity}$$

   Accordingly, a Treasury bill with 180 days until maturity would sell for 97.31 and be priced at $97^{31}/_{32}$, or $979.69 per $1,000 face. The bond would return the discount of $20.31 at maturity. Its discount yield is computed as follows:

   $$(\$20.31/\$1,000) \times (360/180) = .0203 \times 2 = 4.06\%$$

3. We can use the following formula to compute the simple-interest yield for the T-bill in Problem 2:

   $$i = (365\ d)/(360 - dM) \qquad (3)$$

   where:

   $$i = \text{simple-interest yield}$$

   Applying formula 3 to our previous example produces:

   $$i = 365\ (.0406)/[360 - (.0406)(180)] = 4.20\%$$

   We see that the simple interest yield (4.20%) is slightly higher than the discount yield (4.06%).

4. The coupon-equivalent yield for a 75-day T-bill priced at 98.4 is computed as follows:
   The simple-interest yield differs from the coupon-equivalent yield because the simple-interest formula assumes that the interest payments are received at

maturity while the coupon-equivalent yield takes account of semiannual interest payments. When a security has less than six months to run, the two rates are equivalent. Problem 4 deals with an instrument with less than six months, so the coupon-equivalent and simple interest yields are the same. The first step in computing the simple-interest yield is to compute the discount yield. The formula for maturities of less than one year is:

$$d = (D/F)(360/M) \tag{2}$$

where:

$$M = \text{number of days to maturity}$$

Accordingly, a Treasury bill with 75 days until maturity would sell for 98.4 and be priced at 98⁴⁄₃₂, or $981.25 per $1,000 face. The bond would return the discount of $18.75 at maturity. Its discount yield is computed as follows:

$$(\$18.75/\$1,000) \times (360/75) = 9.00\%$$

We can now compute the simple-interest yield from the discount-basis yield with the following formula:

$$i = (365\ d)/(360 - dM) \tag{3}$$

where:

$$i = \text{simple-interest yield}$$

Applying formula 3 to our previous example produces:

$$i = 365\ (.09)/[360 - (.09)(75)] = 9.30\%$$

Chapter 16

1. After all of its assets were sold, Bankrupt Corporation of America realized $453,000. Its legal liabilities were as follows:
   Secured creditors = $47,000 on assets having a value of $39,000
   Other unsecured creditors = $89,000
   Taxes = $29,000
   Back wages (no more than $600 per employee) incurred within the six-month period of the bankruptcy filing = $35,000
   Other back wages = $23,000
   Operating expenses incurred administering the bankrupt estate = $150,000
   Legal fees involved in the bankruptcy filing = $121,000
   Preferred shareholders par value = $150,000
   Number of common shares outstanding = 100,000
   To determine how much each class receives we need to consider the absolute-priority-of-claims principle. The priority of claims, amount of claims, and cumulative claims total is as follows:

   1. Expenses incurred in administering bankrupt estate (legal fees, operating expenses, debt obligations issued after bankruptcy): $150,000 (operating expenses) + $121,000 (legal fees); $271,000 (total to this point)
   2. Wages and salaries up to $600 per employee earned within six months of filing for bankruptcy: $35,000; $306,000 (cumulative total)

3. Federal, state, and local taxes: $29,000; $335,000
4. Secured creditors up to the value of pledged collateral with the remaining claims moved to the unsecured level: $39,000; $374,000
5. Unsecured creditors: $8,000 (uncovered claims of secured creditors) + $89,000 (other unsecured claims) = $97,000; $471,000
   5a. Subordinated unsecured creditors: none
6. Preferred stockholders: $150,000; $621,000
7. Common stockholders: no specified amount, residual claimants

With $453,000 available, 100% of the valid claims of classes 1 to 4 can be fully satisfied. Subtracting the total of $374,000 from the $453,000 available leaves $79,000 for the claims of class 5 (unsecured creditors). This class has claims totaling $97,000. Thus these claims would be settled on the basis of 81% of the amount of the claim. That is, each $1,000 in unsecured claims would receive $810.

2. To recompute the answer to Problem 1 if BCA's asset sale realized $351,000; $581,000 or $691,000, we would need to determine where the money would run out for each possibility.

   If $351,000 were available, the claims of classes 1 to 3 would be fully satisfied. Only $16,000 would be left for the secured creditors' claims of $39,000. Thus such claims would be settled on the basis of $.41 on the dollar of secured claims. Nothing would be left for the unsecured creditors, including the $8,000 uncovered by the collateral of the secured creditors.

   If $581,000 were available, the claims of classes 1 to 5 would be fully satisfied. An additional $110,000 would be left for preferred shareholders. Since their total claim amounts to $150,000, it would be satisfied on the basis of 73%. Nothing would be left for the common shareholders.

   If $691,000 were available, the claims of classes 1 to 6 would be fully satisfied. An additional $70,000 would be available for common shareholders. This sum would be distributed on a pro rata basis to the shareholders. With 100,000 shares outstanding, each share would receive a liquidating distribution of $.70.

6. One would compute the durations for the bonds as follows:

Bond	Price	Coupon	Length to Maturity
a	93	7.5%	10 years
b	96	8.5%	15 years
c	102	9.5%	20 years

Assume the next interest payment is due in six months.

The first task is to compute the yield to maturity for each bond. The results are: **a.** 8.06%; **b.** 9.05%; **c.** 9.35%

These yields can then be used to compute the present values of each bond's cash as follows. The results divided by the sum of the present values (the bond's market value) are the weights. These weights are multiplied by the length to maturity of each cash flow and the results summed to determine the duration of each bond.

The resulting durations are: **a.** 7.15; **b.** 8.60; **c.** 9.37.

7. Using the bond information in Problem 6 we can assemble an immunized bond portfolio for an eight-year time horizon as follows:

The duration of the bond portfolio equals the weighted average of the duration of the components. Bond a has a duration of less than eight years while the durations of b and c are greater than eight years. One could form a portfolio with bonds a and b; a and c; or a, b, and c. The weights must sum to one. Normally one would not allow short selling so the weights must be nonnegative. Accordingly, with a and b we must have:

$7.15(w) + 8.60(1 - w) = 8$ or $(7.15 - 8.60)w = 8 - 8.60$ or $1.45w = .6$

Thus $w = .6/1.45 = .41$ and $(1 - w) = .59$

The yield on this portfolio would be the weighted average of the two yields.

YTM for a and b $= .41(8.06) + .59(9.05) = 3.31 + 5.34 = 8.65\%$

Similarly for portfolio a and c we must have:

$7.15(w) + 9.37(1 - w) = 8$ or $(7.15 - 9.37)w$
$$= 8 - 9.37 \text{ or } 2.22w = 1.37$$

Thus $w = 1.37/2.22 = .62$ and $(1 - w) = .38$

YTM for a and c $= .62(8.06) + .38(9.35) = 5.00 + 3.55 = 8.55\%$

Clearly, the portfolio of a and b offers the higher YTM. An eight-year duration portfolio made up of all three bonds would offer a YTM intermediate between the two results stated above.

Chapter 17

1. IBM Call Quotation for January 20, 1988:

Strike	February	March	April (stock closed at 110⅞)
105	8⅛	9¾	11⅜
110	5⅞	7	8⅛
115	2⅞	4⅝	6
120	1⁷⁄₁₆	2¹⁵⁄₁₆	4
125	⅝	1¾	2¹³⁄₁₆

Intrinsic value 105s $= 110⅞ - 105 = 10⅞$
Intrinsic value 110s $= 110⅞ - 110 = ⅞$
Intrinsic value 115s $= 0$
Intrinsic value 120s $= 0$
Intrinsic value 125s $= 0$

Time Values for Calls:

Strike	February	March	April
105	3⅛	4¾	6⅜
110	⅞	2	3⅛
115	2⅞	4⅝	6
120	1⁷⁄₁₆	2¹⁵⁄₁₆	4
125	⅝	1¾	2¹³⁄₁₆

In the money: 105s and 110s; out of the money: 115s, 120s, and 125s

4. The QWE Corporation's stock now sells for 24. Its January 25 calls are priced at 1¾ while the January 30s sell for ⅞. The net cost (ignore commissions) of a vertical bull spread with these calls:

    Buy 25s for 1¾ and write 30s for ⅞; net cost = 1¾ − ⅞ = ⅞

    Its potential gain:

    Potential Gain = 5 − ⅞ = 4⅛

    The risk to reward ratio:

    Ratio = (4⅛)/(⅞) = 4.71

    If commissions equal 5% of the dollar value of each trade, these results would differ as follows:
    Cost of 25s = 1¾ + 5% = $1.84 (commission = $.09)
    Net proceeds from 30s = ⅞ − 5% = $.83 (commission = $.05)
    Cost of spread = $1.84 − $.83 = $1.01
    Cost of covering spread for stock at 30
    Net proceeds from sale of 25s = 5 − 5% = $4.75
    No cost to cover 30s; expire worthless (optimal result)
    Potential gain = $4.75 − $1.01 = $3.74
    Risk to reward ratio = $3.74/$1.01 = 3.7

8. Refer to the IBM quotation in Table 17.12.

Strike	February	March	April (stock closed at 110⅞)
105	8⅛	9¾	11⅜
110	5⅞	7	8⅛
115	2⅞	4⅝	6
120	1⁷⁄₁₆	2¹⁵⁄₁₆	4
125	⅝	1¾	2¹³⁄₁₆

    The payoff matrix for a ratio position involving a short of three April 125s for every one purchase of the 110s is as follows:
    First we compute the net cost (ignoring commissions) of the position.
    Long 110s costs 8.125
    Short three 125s proceeds 2 × (2¹³⁄₁₆) = 5.625
    Net cost = 2.5
    At prices below 110 the position is a total loss; the loss = 2.5.
    At prices above 110 but below 125 the position will have an intrinsic value equal to that of the 110. The maximum value is for the stock at 125 where the position's value equals 15 and profit = 15 − 2.5 = 12.5.
    At stock prices above 125 the position's intrinsic value declines by two points for each point the stock rises above 125.
    At 131¼ the position's value is zero.
    Above that point its value is negative.

    In contrast, a two-to-one ratio of the 110s and 120s has the following payoff matrix:
    Cost (ignoring commissions) = 8.125 − (2 × 4) = 8.125 − 8 = .125
    At prices below 110 the position is a total loss. The loss = .125.

At prices above 110 but below 120 the position will have an intrinsic value equal to that of the 110. The maximum value is at 120 where the position's value equals 10 and profit $= 10 - .125 = 9.875$.

At prices above 120 the position's intrinsic value declines by one point for each point the stock rises above 120.

At 129.875 the position's value is zero.

Above that point its value is negative.

9. XYZ stock is selling ex-rights at $50. The rights entitle the holder to 10 shares at $48. Thus their theoretical value assuming that XYZ stock remains at 50 is found by applying the following formula.

$$\frac{\text{Intrinsic Value of One Right}}{\text{During Cum-Rights Period}} = \frac{\text{(Market Price of Stock} - \text{Subscription Price)}}{\text{Number of Shares Needed to Subscribe to One Share} + \text{One Share}}$$

$$\frac{\text{Intrinsic Value of One Right}}{\text{During Cum-Rights Period}} = (50 - 48)/10 = 2/10 = .2$$

The theoretical value assuming that the stock price falls by the amount implied by the dilution is found with the following formula:

$$\frac{\text{Intrinsic Value of One Right}}{\text{During Ex-Rights Period}} = \frac{\text{(Market Value of Stock} - \text{Subscription Price)}}{\text{Number of Shares Needed to Subscribe to One Share}}$$

The key to solving for this equation is determining the price of the stock after it goes ex-rights. Presumably the stock will drop by the value of the rights distribution in the ex-rights period. Thus the ex-rights price of the rights should be 49.80 assuming nothing else changes. Thus

$$\frac{\text{Intrinsic Value of One Right}}{\text{During Ex-Rights Period}} = (49.20 - 48)/10 = 1.80/10 = .18$$

Chapter 18

1. A convertible preferred selling at $100 may be exchanged for two shares of common, trading at $40. What is the conversion premium?

$$\frac{\text{Conversion}}{\text{Value}} = \text{Number of Shares} \times \text{Market Price} = 2 \times \$40 \quad = \$80$$

$$\frac{\text{Conversion}}{\substack{\text{Premium} \\ \text{(in dollars)}}} = \text{Price} - \text{Conversion Value} \quad = \$100 - \$80 = \$20$$

$$\frac{\text{Conversion}}{\substack{\text{Premium} \\ \text{(in percents)}}} = \frac{\text{Price} - \text{Conversion Value}}{\text{Conversion Value}} \quad = \$20/\$80 \quad = 25\%$$

2. In the example in Problem 1, if the common goes to $60 the convertible preferred would sell for at least the conversion value:

    $$\text{Conversion Value} = 2 \times \$60 = \$120$$

    The preferred would sell for at least this amount and perhaps more to reflect a conversion premium.

3. The SOM Company convertible debentures sell for 105 while its common stock is priced at 4. The convertible's conversion ratio is 200 while its coupon rate is 10%. Its estimated straight-debt value is 90. The stock pays a dividend of $.20 per share per year. The bonds mature in 20 years and are callable at 107. Thus this convertible corresponds to the following:

    Conversion Price = 1,000/200 = 5
    Conversion Value = 200 × 4 = 800
    Premium Over Conversion Value = 1,050 − 800 = 250 (in dollars)
    Premium Over Straight-Debt Value = 105 −90 = 25
    Current Yield = 10/105 = 9.52%
    Yield to Maturity = 9.53%

Now suppose the bonds were purchased at par and the stock subsequently rose to 5½. The minimum profit per bond (ignoring the impact of commissions and coupon payments) would be determined as follows:

First determine the minimum value of the bonds: The conversion value is

200 × 5.5 = 1,100. The bond must sell for at least this amount or an arbitrage opportunity will open up.

This price corresponds to a profit per bond for one who purchased at par of 1,100 − 1,000 = 100 dollars.

Assume dividend payments are maintained at the current level and the bonds are called to force conversion in five years.

We would like to determine what price the stock must reach for an investment in the stock and the bonds to have produced equivalent percentage profits (ignoring the impact of commissions). For the moment we shall also ignore the impact of compounding.

One who invested in the stock would receive dividends of $.20 per share per year for five years and have the value of stock at that time.

One who invested in the bonds would receive coupon payments of $100 per bond and have the value of 200 shares at that time.

Assume one purchased the bonds at par and the stock was then trading at 4. An investor with $1,000 could purchase one bond or 250 shares. The dividends on the stock would amount to $50 per year compared with $100 per year in bond coupon. Thus the net difference in cash flow would amount to $50 per year, or $250 over the five years. The stock investor would have 250 shares compared with the right to 200 shares on the stock. Thus the bond investor receives $50 per year in income but has a claim on 50 fewer shares. If the stock traded at 5 at the end of five years the 50 fewer shares would be equivalent to the $250 in additional income.

Now we shall bring in the impact of compounding. The extra income would be paid over time and thus, at the end of five years, have a compound value in excess of the nominal sum. The compound value of $50 per year for five years at 10% (equivalent to the coupon rate on the bond) is $305. On that basis a price of $6.10 would make the 50 additional shares' value equivalent to the additional coupon income.

9. The American Pig Company (ticker symbol PORK) has issued $50,000,000 in bacon bonds. Each bond pays a 7% coupon and matures in 10 years from its date of issue. These bonds may be exchanged for 150 pounds of pork bellies that are certified for delivery in satisfaction of Chicago Mercantile Exchange pork belly contracts. For the bacon bonds to be worth at least par the bellies must sell for:

$$1000/150 = \$6.67 \text{ per pound}$$

For the bond to produce a yield to maturity of 10% the bacon must reach a price at maturity that will offset the amount below 10% that a coupon of 7% represents. Obviously, 7% is 3% below 10%. Thus the bacon must be worth enough at the bond's maturity to offset this amount of forgone coupon return. Looked at another way the bonds must at maturity produce a gain above par sufficient to offset the $30 per year in sub 10% coupon. Thus we first must find the compound value of a 10-year annuity of $30 per year at 10%. The result is 30 × 15.937 = 478.11. Accordingly, the bacon bond must be worth $1,478.11 at maturity. This implies a bacon price of ($1,478.11)/150 = $9.85 per pound.

Chapter 19

2. You start with $5,000 that you invest in silver futures at $5 per ounce putting down margin equal to 10%. Thus you purchase 10,000 ounces putting up $5,000 and incurring a margin obligation of $45,000. A month later silver rises to $6 per ounce.

    Your initial purchase of 10,000 ounces is now worth $60,000 and your equity is $15,000 ($60,000 − $45,000). The account only requires 10% of the value of the contracts or $6,000 in margin money. Excess margin equals $9,000 ($15,000 − $6,000).

    When your account is marked to market you use the excess in your margin account to buy more silver up to the maximum. The $9,000 in excess margin allows the purchase of another $90,000 of silver futures. This amount is equivalent to another 15,000 ounces.

    A month later silver rises to $7 per ounce. At this point you hold 25,000 ounces of silver with a total value of $175,000 ($7 × 25,000). Your margin account is obligated for the $45,000 on the initial purchase and $81,000 on the second purchase or a total of $126,000. Thus the equity in the account is $49,000 ($175,000 − $126,000). Only $17,500 is required. Thus excess equity amounts to $29,500 ($49,000 − $17,500).

    You again buy the maximum amount of silver futures. Excess equity of $29,500 can support the purchase of 42,000 ounces at $7 per ounce ($7 × 42,000 × 10%). The account will then contain 67,000 ounces of silver (here we ignore the fact that silver contracts are traded in 5,000-ounce units). The total value of the account is $469,000 ($7 × 67,000). Your equity is $49,000 so your margin obligation is $420,000.

    When silver hits $8 per ounce you liquidate your position. At that point the silver represented in the account is worth $536,000 ($8 × 67,000). Thus your equity is the difference or $116,000 ($536,000 − $420,000).

    Initially we have ignored the impact of commissions. Now we shall recompute the results assuming trades in silver futures incur commissions of

$60 per contract. Referring to the text we determine that the size of a silver futures contract is 5,000. Thus commissions on the purchase of 65,000 ounces (one could not have purchased 67,000 ounces) would have amounted to $780 (13 contracts) with a similar cost for the sale.

3. Suppose that in Problem 1 you had not liquidated your position and that you would receive a margin call when your account fell to 5% of the value of your positions. With silver at $8 the 67,000 ounces are worth $536,000 with a margin obligation of $420,000. The value of the silver must stay more than 5% above the margin obligation to avoid a margin call. At a value of $442,000 the account would have an equity of $22,000 ($442,000 − $420,000). Thus the account would require minimum margin of $22,100 (.05 × $442,000) and be just on the edge of receiving a margin call. At that value silver would be selling for $6.60 per ounce.

   Suppose you then sold enough contracts to bring your equity up to 10%. That would require the liquidation of half of your position. You would then have 33,500 ounces worth $221,000 ($6.60 × 33,500) and an equity of $22,000. Again we are ignoring the 5,000-ounce units in which silver futures are traded. Actually the seller would have to sell down to 30,000 to get the account's margin account above 10%.

   To get another margin call silver would have to fall to the point where your equity was only 5%. As we have seen, at $6.60 per ounce 33,500 ounces is worth $221,000 with a margin obligation of $199,000 ($221,000 − $22,000). If the account value fell to $209,500, the equity would equal $10,500 ($209,000 − $199,000). Similarly the required 5% in margin would imply an equity position of $10,450 (.05 × $209,000). At that point silver would be selling for $6.24 ($209,000/33,500).

9. To determine the number of contracts needed to neutralize a $50,000,000 stock portfolio having a beta of 1.07 and the S&P contract is priced at 145 would require solving the appropriate formula for hedging a stock portfolio:

$$\text{Number of Contracts Needed for Hedge} = \frac{\text{Portfolio Value}}{\text{Contract Value}} \times \text{Weight Average Beta of Portfolio}$$

The S&P contract value is 500 times the S&P index value which, in this example, is 145. Thus:

$$\text{One Contract's Value} = 145 \times 500 = \$72,500$$

Accordingly:

$$\text{Number of Contracts Needed for Hedge} = \frac{\$50,000,000}{\$72,500} \times 1.07 = 689.655 \times 1.07 = 737.93$$

Since contracts are only available in integral values, the hedge would require 738 contracts.

10. Compute the gold bullion cost for purchasing 12 karat gold at $9 per gram.
    The formula for converting price per gross gram to price per net ounce is:

$$\text{Pno} = \text{Pgg}/(K/24) \times 31.1$$

where:

$$\text{Pno} = \text{price per net ounce}$$
$$\text{Pgg} = \text{price per gross gram}$$
$$K = \text{karats of fineness}$$

Thus: Pno = $9/(12/24) × 31.1 = $9/.5 × 31.1 = $559.8

Chapter 20

2. You are considering the purchase of a home. Your first choice lists for $185,000 but you believe the seller will accept an offer of $179,000. Your local banker will lend you 75% of the purchase price. You must, however, pay three points for the loan and a $500 loan application fee. A title search in your area costs 1.5% of the purchase price. Inspections for structural soundness cost $250. The real estate agent's fee is 7% of the sale price. Transferring the title will cost you ½% of the sale price. You must deposit in an escrow account six months' property taxes. Property taxes are set at 4% of assessed valuation. In the first year assessed valuation will equal 85% of the sale price. You must also pay the first year's property (fire) insurance in advance. Insurance rates in your community are $4 per thousand dollars of protection. The bank requires that you insure your property for 90% of its assessed valuation or 100% of the mortgage balance outstanding, whichever is lower. To have a lawyer represent you at the closing will incur a fee of $200. Hooking up various utilities will require fees of $340 and deposits of another $500. How much must you pay in total for acquiring and occupying the house?

    Purchase price: $179,000

    Points: 3% of loan of 75% of $179,000; $.03 \times .75 \times \$179,000 = \$4,027$

    Loan application fee: $500

    Title search: 1.5% of $179,000 = $2,685

    Real estate agent's fee (paid by seller): 7% of $179,000 = $12,530

    Escrowed property taxes: ½ $\times$ 4% of 85% of $179,000 =

$.5 \times .04 \times .85 \times \$179,000 = \$3,043$

    Property insurance: You must first determine the required amount to insure:

    90% of assessed valuation = $.9 \times .85 \times \$179,000 = \$137,935$

    100% of mortgage = 75% of $179,000 = $134,250

    The lower number is $134,250 rounded up to $135,000;

    $4 per thousand is $4 $\times$ 134 = $540.

    Lawyer's fee: $200

    Utility fees: $340

    Utility deposits: $500

Total cost to buyer: $179,000 + $4,027 + $500 + $2,585 + $3,043 + $540 + $200 + $340 + $500 = $190,735

The seller will receive: sale price − commission = $179,000 − $12,530 = $166,470

The difference between the buyer's outlay and the proceeds to the seller: $190,735 − $166,470 = $24,265

    If we consider the total difference the transaction costs, these transactions costs represent the following percentage of the total sale price:

        Transactions cost/Sale price = $24,265/$179,000 = 13.56%

3. You are considering the purchase of a parcel of land for $45,000. You can borrow up to 50% of the purchase price at a rate of 13%. Long-term government bonds are yielding 10%. The rate of return on the investment required to make this offer attractive:

To Determine r

a. Borrowing cost: 13%

b. Alternative yield on low-risk investment: 10%

c. Percent down payment required: 50%

d. Weighted average cost of capital: $.50 \times 13\% + .50 \times 10\% = 11.5\%$

e. Risk premium: 4% (this is assumed)

f. Total cost of capital (r): $11.5\% + 4\% = 15.5\%$

One might use a somewhat higher or lower risk premium depending on an evaluation of the risk of this particular investment.

5. You are offering a small apartment complex for sale. Your asking price is $850,000. A prospective buyer is able to obtain a first mortgage for 75% of the sale price. She asks you to take back a second mortgage for $150,000. She offers to pay 9% on the second with a partial amortization over five years and then a balloon payment of $100,000 (with an option to the buyer to convert the balloon to a 10-year amortized mortgage at 11%). She is willing to pay your offering price if you will accept her terms on the second. Suppose the market rate on second mortgages such as the one she proposes would be 13.5%. For this market rate we would like to know how much of a price concession she is in effect seeking.

This question requires determination of the present value at 13.5% of the second mortgage. The mortgage itself consists of three parts: the 9% 50,000 five-year amortized mortgage; the $100,000 unamortized five-year debt; and the $100,000 11% amortized 10-year mortgage that is received in five years. The value of the second mortgage is the sum of the values of each of these.

The $50,000 amortized mortgage calls for payments of $12,853 per year. This value is obtained by determining the present value of a five-year annuity at 9% and then dividing that by the number of payments. Similarly the 9% payment of the unamortized $100,000 loan calls for payments of $9,000 per year. Thus the first five years' payments would amount to $21,853 per year. The present value of this income stream at 13.5% is determined as follows: a five-year annuity for $1 at 13.5% is worth $3.475. This value is found by interpolating between the 13% and 14% entries. Thus the first five years' payment stream is worth $75,939 (3.476 × $21,653).

The next step is to find the present value of a $100,000 11% mortgage discounted at 13.5%. Once that value is determined, the value can be discounted back five years. An 11% $100,000 fully amortized mortgage loan calls for payments of $16,981 per year. The present value of a $1 10-year annuity paid discounted at 13.5% is $5.321. Thus the payment stream, once it starts, has a present value of $90,356 (5.321 × $16,981). This amount, however, is the value of the mortgage loan once payments begin five years hence. Thus the sum must be discounted at 13.5% to its value when the entire second mortgage is given. The present value of $1 discounted at 13.5% to be received in five years is $.531. Thus the 10-year mortgage to be received in five years is now worth .531 × $90,356 = $47,979. The sum of the values of the first five years' cash flows and the next 10 is $75,939 + $47,979 = $123,918. Thus the second mortgage amounts to a price concession of about $26,000.

6. Continue with the facts of Problem 5. Suppose the bank views the second mortgage as a hidden price concession. It would then reduce the amount of the mortgage that it offers on the property. It wants to lend no more than 75% of the property's true market value. In effect, the property is being sold for a $26,000 discount from the amount asked. You had asked $850,000 but received cash and paper worth $824,000. Thus the bank would be likely to reduce the amount of its mortgage offer to 75% of $824,000, or $619,500

(from $637,500). That amounts to a reduction of $18,000 in the mortgage. Now suppose the prospective buyer asks that you finance that difference on proportionally similar terms as the initial second. The initial second mortgage amounted to a concession of $24,000 on $150,000, or 16%. A new second for $18,000 on proportionately similar terms would amount to a price concession of 16% of $18,000, or $2,880. Suppose the bank now views that additional amount as a concession. As a result the bank would reduce its mortgage by 75% of the $2,880 price reduction, or $2,160. To determine at what point this process would stop, we can carry the matter a bit further. Offering a second on $2,160 would amount to a price reduction of 16% of the amount, or $345.60. The bank would want to reduce its mortgage by 75% of this amount, or $257.20. A second for this amount would amount to a price reduction of 16%, or $41.47, and the bank would then reduce its mortgage by 75%, or $31.10. In a sense the process could go on forever but clearly the sums are already quite small and decreasing rapidly. The bank has reduced the mortgage by $18,000 + $2,160 + $257.20 + 31.10 + etc.

Up to the point that we stopped the total had reached $20,448.30. Each number is 12% of the preceding number. In fact, 12% is the product of 16% (the price reduction) and 75% (the loan percentage on the mortgage). In general we would like to know the sum of the following decreasing series:

$$\text{Sum} = k + k(.12) + k(.12)^2 + k(.12)^3 + \ldots + k(.12)^n + \ldots$$

We can solve this problem through the use of mathematical induction. That is, we would multiply the initial equation by .12 and subtract the resulting equation from the initial equation. We derive the formula as:

$$\text{Sum} = k/(1 - .12) = k/.88$$
$$\text{Our } k = \$18,000$$
$$\text{Thus: Sum} = \$18,000/.88 = \$20,454.45$$

We had already reached a partial total of $20,447.30 by brute force. Thus we were quite close to the precise answer.

7. A duplex is offered for sale at $180,000. After expenses, it offers a net rental income (after deducting all out-of-pocket expenses except financing costs and taxes) of $28,000 per year. The rents, expenses, and market value of the property are expected to remain constant for the foreseeable future. The buyer may borrow up to 90% of the purchase price at 11%. The seller agrees to deduct any closing costs from the purchase price.

The purchase would involve a mortgage of $162,000 (.90 × $180,000) and a down payment of $18,000 (.10 × $180,000 = $180,000 − $162,000). Nothing is said about closing costs so they are ignored. The mortgage calls for interest payments of $17,820 per year. The length of the mortgage is not stated so we cannot compute the amortization payments. Subtracting this amount of interest payment from the net rental income of $28,000 would leave $10,180 per year. Part of this remainder would go to amortize the mortgage and another part would be required to pay taxes on the income. On the other hand, the property might later be sold for a substantial gain. In any case a positive before-tax return of $10,180 per year on a down payment of $18,000 sounds quite attractive. One would, however, want to resolve the following questions:

1. Are all of the numbers relatively accurate? Do the expense estimates include everything?

2. Will the property hold or possibly increase its value over time?
3. Will the property remain rented at or above the present rental levels?
4. Is the property likely to require any major structural work?
5. What is the length of the mortgage? What would this imply for the amortization portion of the payments? What therefore would be the net before-tax cash flow on the investment?
6. What would be required for taxes? After tax payments what would the after-tax cash flow look like?
7. Carrying the matter further, what might eventually be possible in terms of refinancing?

On the face of it the investment looks so attractive that one wonders if something is missing in the description.

Chapter 21

3. You have just charged $1,800 worth of Christmas presents to your credit card. The bill will arrive in 10 days and be due in 15 days from receipt. At that point you may pay the balance off and not incur a finance charge. Alternatively, you may pay a minimum of 10% of the balance and then be responsible for a finance charge of 1½% per month. If you pay the minimum when due and the balance a month later, you will incur finance charges of:

Finance Charges = 1½% of the $1,800 (the first month) and 1½% of 90% of $1,800 (the second month)

$$= .015 \times (\$1,800 + \$1,620) = \$51.30$$

This interest charge is related to the extra time that you took to pay the bill as follows:

The $1,800 was available for 15 days and the $1,620 for another month; on the average $1,680 was available for a month and a half and cost $51.30; two-thirds of $51.30 is $34.20; dividing $34.20 by $1,680 yields a monthly interest cost of 2.04%. Actually, however, had the balance been paid off rather than the minimum, no interest would have been incurred. Thus the incremental available funds available by not paying off the balance were $1,620. From this perspective the entire interest charge of $51.30 is chargeable to that one month balance. Hence:

Finance Cost = $51.30/$1,620 = 3.17%

The incremental annualized percentage interest cost of not paying off the initial balance within the grace period is 3.17% × 12 = 38%.

5. You now have $1,000 in a savings account earning 6½% and need to open a checking account. Your choices are as follows:

Type	Minimum Balance	Per Check Charge	Monthly Charge	Interest Rate on Average Balance
Special	$100	$.30	$5	none
Regular	$200	$.25	$3	none
NOW	$500	none	$5	5%

Your finances are so limited that you will be unable to maintain more than the required minimum balance. We assume that the balance is always at the minimum. Thus the NOW account will earn no interest on any balance beyond the minimum. Moreover, that sum must come from your savings account, which is now earning 6.5%. You expect to write about five checks per month. You would like to know what each of these accounts would cost to maintain. The costs will come from several sources. Maintaining the minimum balance will involve an opportunity cost of 6.5% of the balance less any interest earned (none for the special and regular accounts and 5% for the NOW account). The per check (special and regular accounts) and monthly service charges (all three account types) also need to be factored in. Thus the annual costs of each account would be as follows:

Type	Minimum Balance	Per Check Charge	Monthly Charge	Interest Rate on Average Balance	Total
Special	$ 6.50	$18.00	$60	none	$84.50
Regular	$13.00	$15.00	$36	none	$64.00
NOW	$ 7.50	none	$60	5%	$67.50

If you were to write 20 checks per month, the relevant charges would be:

Type	Minimum Balance	Per Check Charge	Monthly Charge	Interest Rate on Average Balance	Total
Special	$ 6.50	$72.00	$60	none	$138.50
Regular	$13.00	$60.00	$36	none	$109.00
NOW	$ 7.50	none	$60	5%	$ 67.50

Thus if you write five checks a month the regular checking account would be cheapest while the NOW account would be best if you write 20 checks per month.

6. You now have a $100,000 25-year 11% mortgage. You also have $10,000 in a money market account paying 6%. If you use the $10,000 to pay down the mortgage balance, the interest charges on the mortgage will be reduced to reflect the smaller balance. The mortgage itself will continue to require payments at the same monthly rate. The life of the mortgage will just be reduced by the prepayment. Determining how much the $10,000 prepayment will save in mortgage interest charges in the first year is relatively straightforward:

    The prepayment would reduce the outstanding balance by $10,000. This reduction in the outstanding balance would reduce interest charges by 11% of that amount ($1,100) in the first year. The loss in interest income on the money market account would amount to 6% of the prepayment, or $600. Thus the net interest effect of this maneuver in the first year amounts to the difference, or a savings of $500 in interest.

    Determining how much the mortgage's life is shortened by this maneuver requires several steps. First we determine the annual payments on the mortgage. A 25-year 11% mortgage would require payments of $11,874 per year. We thus need to determine how many years of payments at this rate would be required to equal a present value of $90,000.

Dividing $90,000 by $11,874 yields a ratio of 7.60. That is, the ratio of principal to payment rate is 7.60. At 11% this ratio corresponds to an annuity of about 17.5 years. That is, a 17.5-year annuity discounted at 11% is worth about 7.60 times the payment amount. Subtracting 17.5 years from the 25-year initial term of the mortgage leaves 7.5 years. Thus the prepayment of $10,000 would save about 7.5 years of payments. At a rate of $11,874 per year this savings corresponds to 7.5 × $11,874, or $89,055.

7. We want to determine the needed insurance protection for the following situation:

Family consisting of father, mother, and three children
Family income: $36,000 per year
Social Security survivor's benefits: $6,900 per year
Survivor's pension: $3,000 per year
Investment income: $2,000 per year
Assumed interest rate for insurance principal: 8%

The family consists of five people. The death of the parent who is earning the $36,000 (we assume that income is earned by only one parent rather than as a joint income) would reduce the family size by 20%. To maintain its lifestyle the needed family income would also be expected to decline by about 20% to about .8 × $36,000 = $30,400.

The noninsurance sources of income are the sum of the following:

$$\$6,900 + \$3,000 + \$2,000 = \$11,900$$

The gap is thus $30,400 − $11,900 = $18,500.
At 8%, insurance of $231,250 would generate $18,500 in annual income. Other factors to consider would include the following:

1. The income the surviving parent might earn
2. The impact of the expected rate of inflation
3. The length of time until the children are grown and independent
4. Specific impacts of such matters as taxes, preparing for the children's education, education for the surviving parent, and other special major anticipated expenditures

Index

H